W9-BVK-895

Regulation of Lawyers: Statutes and Standards

Concise Edition 2012

EDITORIAL ADVISORS

Vicki Been
Elihu Root Professor of Law
New York University School of Law

Erwin Chemerinsky
Dean and Distinguished Professor of Law
University of California, Irvine, School of Law

Richard A. Epstein
Laurence A. Tisch Professor of Law
New York University School of Law
Peter and Kirsten Bedford Senior Fellow
The Hoover Institution
Senior Lecturer in Law
The University of Chicago

Ronald J. Gilson
Charles J. Meyers Professor of Law and Business
Stanford University
Marc and Eva Stern Professor of Law and Business
Columbia Law School

James E. Krier
Earl Warren DeLano Professor of Law
The University of Michigan Law School

Richard K. Neumann, Jr.
Professor of Law
Hofstra University School of Law

Robert H. Sitkoff
John L. Gray Professor of Law
Harvard Law School

David Alan Sklansky
Professor of Law
University of California at Berkeley School of Law

Kent D. Syverud
Dean and Ethan A. H. Shepley University Professor
Washington University School of Law

Elizabeth Warren
Leo Gottlieb Professor of Law
Harvard Law School

Regulation of Lawyers: Statutes and Standards

Concise Edition 2012

Stephen Gillers
Crystal Eastman Professor of Law
New York University

Roy D. Simon
Distinguished Professor of Legal Ethics Emeritus
Hofstra University

Andrew M. Perlman
Professor of Law
Suffolk University Law School

Wolters Kluwer
Law & Business

Copyright © 2012 Stephen Gillers, Roy D. Simon, and Andrew M. Perlman.

Published by Wolters Kluwer Law & Business in New York.

Wolters Kluwer Law & Business serves customers worldwide
with CCH, Aspen Publishers, and Kluwer Law International products.
(www.wolterskluwerlb.com)

No part of this publication may be reproduced or transmitted in any form or by any means, electronic or mechanical, including photocopy, recording, or utilized by any information storage or retrieval system, without written permission from the publisher. For information about permissions or to request permissions online, visit us at www.wolterskluwerlb.com, or a written request may be faxed to our permissions department at 212-771-0803.

To contact Customer Service, e-mail customer.service@wolterskluwer.com, call 1-800-234-1660, fax 1-800-901-9075, or mail correspondence to:

Wolters Kluwer Law & Business
Attn: Order Department
PO Box 990
Frederick, MD 21705

Printed in the United States of America.

1 2 3 4 5 6 7 8 9 0

ISBN 978-0-7355-0861-3
ISSN 1995-7995

About Wolters Kluwer Law & Business

Wolters Kluwer Law & Business is a leading global provider of intelligent information and digital solutions for legal and business professionals in key specialty areas, and respected educational resources for professors and law students. Wolters Kluwer Law & Business connects legal and business professionals as well as those in the education market with timely, specialized authoritative content and information-enabled solutions to support success through productivity, accuracy and mobility.

Serving customers worldwide, Wolters Kluwer Law & Business products include those under the Aspen Publishers, CCH, Kluwer Law International, Loislaw, Best Case, ftwilliam.com and MediRegs family of products.

CCH products have been a trusted resource since 1913, and are highly regarded resources for legal, securities, antitrust and trade regulation, government contracting, banking, pension, payroll, employment and labor, and healthcare reimbursement and compliance professionals.

Aspen Publishers products provide essential information to attorneys, business professionals and law students. Written by preeminent authorities, the product line offers analytical and practical information in a range of specialty practice areas from securities law and intellectual property to mergers and acquisitions and pension/benefits. Aspen's trusted legal education resources provide professors and students with high-quality, up-to-date and effective resources for successful instruction and study in all areas of the law.

Kluwer Law International products provide the global business community with reliable international legal information in English. Legal practitioners, corporate counsel and business executives around the world rely on Kluwer Law journals, looseleafs, books, and electronic products for comprehensive information in many areas of international legal practice.

Loislaw is a comprehensive online legal research product providing legal content to law firm practitioners of various specializations. Loislaw provides attorneys with the ability to quickly and efficiently find the necessary legal information they need, when and where they need it, by facilitating access to primary law as well as state-specific law, records, forms and treatises.

Best Case Solutions is the leading bankruptcy software product to the bankruptcy industry. It provides software and workflow tools to flawlessly streamline petition preparation and the electronic filing process, while timely incorporating ever-changing court requirements.

ftwilliam.com offers employee benefits professionals the highest quality plan documents (retirement, welfare and non-qualified) and government forms (5500/PBGC, 1099 and IRS) software at highly competitive prices.

MediRegs products provide integrated health care compliance content and software solutions for professionals in healthcare, higher education and life sciences, including professionals in accounting, law and consulting.

Wolters Kluwer Law & Business, a division of Wolters Kluwer, is headquartered in New York. Wolters Kluwer is a market-leading global information services company focused on professionals.

Summary of Contents

Dedications

Stephen Gillers dedicates this edition of the book to the memory of his mother Sylvia Gillers Wadler, who was born February 20, 1914, and died April 18, 2007, age 93. Sylvia didn't have much use for lawyers until her son became one and then an even greater appreciation when he married a lawyer. Nor did Sylvia need to think much about legal ethics. Like mothers everywhere, she intuitively knew right and wrong, good behavior and bad, so far as her children were concerned, which is what mostly mattered. And she had a powerful sanctioning system, usually implicit and summarized at the end of a description of a particular course of conduct that her children were expected to obey, or refrain from, with such words as "if you know what's good for you." We mostly did know. And it mostly was.

Roy Simon (Jr.) dedicates this edition of the book to the memory of his father, the original Roy Simon, who aspired to be a lawyer and studied pre-law subjects at the University of Illinois. But in 1929, when the Great Depression hit, he left college in the middle of his junior year to help his father at his clothing store in Chicago. A few years later, when the clothing store went bankrupt, my father began selling life insurance, and continued doing so for the next fifty years. My father taught me ethics by example throughout his life, and I continue to think about him every day, twenty-seven years after his untimely death in 1984 at age 73.

Andrew Perlman dedicates this edition of the book to the memory of his father, Murray Perlman, who died in 1986 at the age of 68. Murray became a father at an older age than most men, and I benefited enormously from his accumulated wisdom. He had a strong moral compass that was forged during the Great Depression and his time as a paratrooper in World War II. He taught me many lessons, but one of my lasting impressions of him was his strong sense of what was right. I like to think that he would have found some value in my work on legal ethics, so I dedicate this edition of the book to him.

Acknowledgments

The authors appreciate the time and effort of the dozens of people and organizations that have helped the authors keep this book accurate and up-to-date.

We begin by thanking the outstanding personnel of the ABA Center for Professional Responsibility and other ABA entities: Jeanne Gray, Director of the ABA Center for Professional Responsibility and Senior Director of Public Services; Art Garwin, Deputy Director of the ABA Center for Professional Responsibility; George Kuhlman, former Ethics Counsel, and Eileen Libby, Associate Ethics Counsel to the ABA Standing Committee on Ethics and Professional Responsibility; Ellyn Rosen, Lead Senior Counsel to the Center for Professional Responsibility and Counsel to the ABA Commission on Ethics 20/20; Will Hornsby, ABA Staff Counsel, Delivery of Legal Services; John Holtaway, Lead Senior Counsel, Client Protection and Policy Implementation; and Becky Stretch, who served as Special Counsel to the ABA Ethics 2000 Commission.

We also received assistance from lawyers in all parts of the country. We thank Randall Difuntorum of the California State Bar; William P. Smith III, General Counsel to the State Bar of Georgia; Dennis Rendleman, former General Counsel to the Illinois State Bar Association; Alice Neece Mine of the North Carolina State Bar; Cynthia Kuhn of the District of Columbia Bar; Robert Bloom, who works at the Supreme Judicial Court of Massachusetts; John Rabiej, Chief of the Rules Committee Support Office of the Administrative Office of the United States Courts; Kathleen Mulligan Baxter, Counsel to the New York State Bar Association; Jim McCauley, Ethics Counsel to the Virginia State Bar; Betsy Brandborg and Chris Manos of the State Bar of Montana; and many others who provided us with helpful information about changes in the standards and statutes governing lawyers.

The authors also thank the editors of the ABA/BNA Lawyer's Manual on Professional Conduct, whose biweekly Current Reports are indispensable to keeping up with state and national developments in the legal profession.

Stephen Gillers is as always grateful to Shirley Gray for her yearly help in bringing this book to press. He also expresses much thanks to Barbara S. Gillers for eliminating errors in his portion of the book.

Acknowledgments

Roy Simon thanks his secretary Nicole Jones, for her helpful work on this book, and he thanks the following students from Hofstra University School of Law for their invaluable assistance: Elise Dunton, Steve Henesy, and Nick Paslow. Their work was timely, thorough, and meticulous.

Andrew Perlman thanks Professors Kevin Mohr and Byron Stier as well as the ABA's Ellyn Rosen and Martin Whittaker for their helpful insights and suggestions.

We deeply appreciate the exceptional work done by our developmental editor, Darren Kelly of Aspen Publishers; and our editor, Troy Froebe of The Froebe Group.

The authors are enormously grateful to the American Bar Association for its permission to use numerous items, including all of the following:

- ABA Model Rules of Professional Conduct, 2011 Edition, available online at *http://www.americanbar.org/groups/professional_responsibility/publications/model_rules_of_professional_conduct/model_rules_of_professional_conduct_table_of_contents.html.* Copyright © 2011 by the American Bar Association. Reprinted with permission. Bound copies of ABA Model Rules of Professional Conduct, 2011 Edition are available from the American Bar Association's Service Center, 321 N. Clark Street, Chicago, IL 60654; 1-800-285-2221; *http://apps.americanbar.org/abastore/books/WebOrdFrm.pdf.*
- Excerpts from The Ethics 2000 Commission Report, published online at *http://www.americanbar.org/groups/professional_responsibility/policy/ethics_2000_commission.html.* Copyright © 2000 by the American Bar Association. Reprinted with permission.
- Reporter's Explanation of Changes, by The Ethics 2000 Commission, published online at *http://www.americanbar.org/content/dam/aba/migrated/cpr/e2k/10_85rem.authcheckdam.pdf.* Copyright © 2000 by the American Bar Association. *Reprinted with permission.*
- Excerpts from Client Representation in the 21st Century, a Report of the ABA Commission on Multijurisdictional Practice (August 2002), published online at *http://www.americanbar.org/content/dam/aba/migrated/final_mjp_rpt_121702_2.authcheckdam.pdf.* Copyright © 2002 by the American Bar Association. Reprinted with permission.
- Excerpts from ABA Model Code of Professional Responsibility (1981), available at *http://www.americanbar.org/content/dam/aba/migrated/cpr/mrpc/mcpr.authcheckdam.pdf.* Copyright © 1981 by the American Bar Association. Reprinted with permission. In 1983, the ABA Model Rules of Professional Conduct replaced the ABA Model Code of Professional Responsibility.
- Black Letter Standards were excerpted from the ABA Standards for Criminal Justice: Prosecution Function and Defense Function, 3rd Edition (1993), available online at *www.americanbar.org/groups/criminal_justice/policy/standards.html.* Copyright © 1993 by the American Bar Association. Reprinted with permission.
- Excerpts from the ABA Standards for Imposing Lawyer Sanctions (1992), by the ABA Joint Committee on Professional Sanctions, available online at *http://www.americanbar.org/content/dam/aba/migrated/cpr/regulation/standards_sanctions.authcheckdam.pdf.* Copyright © 2005 by the American Bar Association. Reprinted with permission.
- ABA Canons of Professional Ethics (1956), available online at *http://www.americanbar.org/content/dam/aba/migrated/cpr/mrpc/Canons_Ethics.authcheckdam.pdf.* Copyright © 1956 by the American Bar Association. Reprinted with permission.

- ABA Model Code of Judicial Conduct, 2008 Edition, available online at *http://www.americanbar.org/content/dam/aba/migrated/judicialethics/ABA_MCJC_approved.authcheckdam.pdf*. Copyright © 2008 by the American Bar Association. Reprinted with permission. Bound copies of ABA Model Code of Judicial Conduct, Second Edition 2011, are available for purchase from the American Bar Association's Service Center, 321 North Clark Street, Chicago, IL 60654; 1-800-285-2221; *http://apps.americanbar.org/abastore/books/WebOrdFrm.pdf*.
- Guideline C was excerpted from Guidelines for the Selection and Performance Standards of Retained Counsel, by the ABA Tort Trial & Insurance Practice Section's Special Task Force on Selection and Performance Standards of Retained Counsel. Copyright © 1992 by the American Bar Association. Reprinted with permission.
- Preface excerpted from the ABA Commission on Billable Hours Report, 2001-2002. Copyright © 2002 by the American Bar Association. Reprinted with permission.
- Model Court Rule on Insurance Disclosure, located online at *http://www.americanbar.org/content/dam/aba/migrated/cpr/clientpro/Model_Rule_InsuranceDisclosure.authcheckdam.pdf*. Copyright © 2005 by the American Bar Association. Reprinted with permission.
- Excerpts from the Preliminary Report of the American Bar Association Task Force on Corporate Responsibility (2002), located online at *http://www2.law.mercer.edu/lawreview/files/54310.pdf*. Copyright © 2002 by the American Bar Association. Reprinted with permission.

The authors also thank the following other copyright holders for their permission to reprint the materials in this book. The copyright holders reserve all rights to the following materials:

The American Law Institute, for permission to reprint the black letter sections from the Restatement (Third) of the Law Governing Lawyers, © 2000.

The American Trial Lawyer's Association, for permission to reprint its 1988 Code of Conduct and its 1986 Victim's Bill of Rights.

The Federal Bar Association, for permission to reprint excerpts from the Model Rules of Professional Conduct for Federal Lawyers © 1990.

The American Academy of Matrimonial Lawyers (AAML), for permission to reprint excerpts from the Bounds of Advocacy.

The Roscoe Pound Foundation (formerly the Roscoe Pound-American Trial Lawyers Foundation), for permission to reprint excerpts from the 1982 Revised Draft of the American Lawyer's Code of Conduct.

The National Association of Legal Assistants, Inc., 1516 S. Boston, Tulsa, OK 74119, for permission to reprint excerpts from the NALA's Model Standards and Guidelines for Utilization of Legal Assistants.

Finally, Roy Simon is grateful to his wife, Karen, and their four children, Daniel, Nicole, Joshua, and Rebecca, for their interest and support through all 23 editions of this book.

Introduction to the Regulation of Lawyers

This book contains rules regulating the behavior of lawyers and judges. These rules come from many sources: statutes, administrative regulations, rules of evidence and procedure, and, most prominently, ethical codes. These rules continue to grow and change, and this book tries to capture a sense of the breadth, pace, and direction of the changes.

What's New Since Our Last Edition?

This is the twenty-third edition of *Regulation of Lawyers: Statutes and Standards.* Like all of our previous editions, this edition has many new items and many updates to older materials. There are dozens of changes since last year. We provide here an overview of the major changes that have occurred since our last edition, as well as a summary of some possible future changes that were formally or informally under consideration when we went to press in September 2011.

NATIONAL DEVELOPMENTS

American Bar Association Developments

ABA Model Rules of Professional Conduct: The ABA has not amended any of the ABA Model Rules of Professional Conduct since our last edition. (The most recent amendments were in February and August of 2009, when the House of Delegates added and then revised the screening provision in Rule

1.10(a) and related Comments.) Nor were any proposed amendments to the Model Rules on the agenda at the ABA's Annual Meeting in August 2011. However, in August 2012, the House of Delegates may take up various amendments that will grow out of the work of the ABA Commission on Ethics 20/20.

ABA Commission on Ethics 20/20: The ABA Commission on Ethics 20/20, which was created in 2009, is reviewing and proposing changes to the ABA Model Rules of Professional Conduct and the American system of lawyer regulation in light of advances in technology and the increasingly global nature of law practice.

The 20/20 Commission created several working groups, and they gathered information and developed draft proposals concerning a number of topics, including outsourcing, alternative business structures (such as whether non-lawyers should be permitted to have an equity interest in law firms, as is the case in other parts of the world), confidentiality issues arising from lawyers' use of technology, ethics issues arising from online marketing, advertising and confidentiality issues created by companies that rank or rate lawyers and law firms, choice of law problems due to jurisdictional variations both domestically and internationally, third party litigation financing, and unauthorized practice issues for foreign attorneys who practice in the United States. Throughout 2011, the Commission released for comment numerous draft proposals in these areas, which can be found on the Ethics 20/20 Commission's website at *http://www.americanbar.org/groups/professional_responsibility/aba_commission_on_ethics_20_20.html.* The ABA House of Delegates is expected to vote on these proposals (or revised versions of them) at its August 2012 Annual Meeting.

ABA Model Rule on Admission by Motion: At its February 2011 Mid-Year Meeting, the ABA House of Delegates amended the ABA Model Rule on Admission by Motion to make it easier for in-house lawyers to obtain admission on motion. Section 1(c) of the Model Rule requires that an applicant "have been primarily engaged in the active practice of law . . . for five of the seven years immediately preceding the date upon which the application is filed." Before February of 2011, the Model Rule did not allow in-house lawyers to count the years they practiced as authorized in-house counsel in the jurisdiction where they sought admission on motion, but the amended Model Rule allows in-house lawyers to count their years of authorized practice. However, unauthorized in-house practice (*e.g.*, working as an unregistered in-house lawyer in a jurisdiction that permits registration) still will not count. For more on this issue (and for other coverage of the ABA Mid-Year Meeting) see *ABA Fine-Tunes Rule on Admission by Motion . . .*, 27 Law. Man. Prof. Conduct 134 (March 2, 2011). Finally, in September 2011 the ABA Commission on Ethics 20/20 circulated a proposed amendment to the Model Rule on Admission by Motion. The current Model Rule requires an applicant for admission by motion to have actively practiced in another jurisdiction for five out of the past seven years. The Commission's proposal would enable a lawyer to qualify for admission by motion after practicing in another jurisdiction for only three out of the past seven years.

ABA Resolution on Timely Disclosure by Prosecutors: At its August 2011 Annual Meeting, the ABA House of Delegates adopted a resolution urging federal, state, territorial and tribal governments to adopt disclosure rules requiring prosecutors to make timely disclosure to the defense before the commencement of trial, and before a guilty plea, of all information known to the prosecution that tends to "negate the guilt of the accused or mitigate the offense charged or sentence, except when relieved of this responsibility by a protective order." The resolution essentially parallels Rule 3.8(d) of the ABA Model Rules of Professional Conduct. We reprint the full resolution in the Related Materials following Rule 3.8.

Uniform Collaborative Law Act: The collaborative dispute resolution process (commonly known as "Collaborative Law") is a voluntary, non-adversarial dispute resolution process for parties represented by counsel. In a collaborative process, the parties and their attorneys all agree in advance that the attorneys are retained solely to negotiate a settlement, not to litigate. These terms are usually embodied in a "Participation Agreement" providing that if the parties are unable to reach a settlement, the lawyers will withdraw from the case and assist the clients in transitioning the case to trial attorneys.

In 2009, the Uniform Law Commission voted to approve a new Uniform Collaborative Law Act (UCLA) with the aim of increasing consistency from state to state regarding (i) the enforceability of collaborative law agreements, (ii) the confidentiality of communications during the collaborative process, (iii) the automatic stay of any pending court proceedings that are also the subject of the collaborative law process, and (iv) the privilege against disclosure if the collaborative process does not lead to settlement. In 2010, the Uniform Law Commission amended the UCLA to give states explicit options (a) to limit the UCLA to domestic relations matters, and (b) to adopt the UCLA in full or in part by court rule. The full text of the UCLA is available at *http://www.law.upenn.edu/bll/archives/ulc/ucla/2010_final_amends.htm.*

At the ABA's August 2011 Annual Meeting, the House of Delegates considered a resolution endorsing the UCLA . The ABA Section of Family Law, which has approved the UCLA, spoke out in support of the resolution but, after a contentious debate, the ABA House of Delegates voted 298-154 against the resolution.

Uniform Bar Exam: As noted last year, both the Council of the ABA Section of Legal Education and Admissions to the Bar and the Conference of Chief Justices adopted resolutions in 2010 encouraging states to consider adopting the Uniform Bar Examination (UBE). The UBE consists of the Multistate Bar Examination, six Multistate Essay Examination questions, and two Multistate Performance Test tasks. In 2010, Missouri and North Dakota became the first two states to approve the UBE, and in 2011 Alabama, Idaho, and Washington State announced that they will begin using the UBE in

2011, 2012, or 2013. For more information on the UBE, visit the website of the National Conference of Bar Examiners at *www.ncbex.org*.

Federal Statutes, Rules, and Regulations

Although the regulation of lawyers is primarily a matter of state law, Congress and federal rule makers and policy makers also sometimes regulate lawyers. This section of "What's New" reports on federal developments relevant to the regulation of lawyers.

Federal Rules of Civil Procedure: Significant amendments to Rule 26(a)(2) and Rule 26(b)(4) took effect as scheduled on December 1, 2010. The Advisory Committee Note says that the amendments "provide work-product protection against discovery regarding draft expert disclosures or reports and—with three specific exceptions—communications between expert witnesses and counsel." We reprint amended Rule 26(b)(4) in our chapter of Attorney-Client Privilege and Work Product Provisions.

Looking ahead, the March 2011 Report of the Judicial Conference Committee on Rules of Practice and Procedure notes that a subcommittee has been formed to implement and oversee further work on ideas resulting from the 2010 Conference on Civil Litigation held at Duke University School of Law. The ideas generated by the Duke Conference fall into four main categories: (1) ideas for fostering best practices through better education of lawyers and judges (without any rule changes); (2) ideas that provide a basis for pilot projects; (3) ideas that provide a starting point for further empirical research; and (4) ideas that may prompt revisions to the Civil Rules.

A second subcommittee of the Committee on Rules of Practice and Procedure is examining the recommendation, made by a panel at the same Duke Conference, that the Federal Rules of Civil Procedure be amended to provide better guidance to lawyers, litigants, and judges on preservation obligations and spoliation sanctions, particularly for electronically stored information. The issues include: (1) what triggers an obligation to preserve? (2) what is the scope and duration of the obligation to preserve? and (3) what are the appropriate sanctions for different types of failures to preserve?

For official updates, new proposals, and background information regarding federal rules, visit the official website of the U.S. Courts at *www.uscourts.gov* (click on "Federal Rulemaking") or contact John Rabiej, Chief of the Rules Committee Support Office, at (202) 502-2600.

Federal Rules of Criminal Procedure: The March 2011 Report of the Judicial Conference Committee on Rules of Practice and Procedure notes that the Advisory Committee on Practice and Procedure "is continuing to consider proposals to codify and expand the government's obligation to disclose exculpatory and impeaching information under *Brady v. Maryland*, 373 U.S. 83 (1963)." At its Fall 2010 meeting, the Advisory Committee continued deliberations on Rule 16 and considered new empirical data from the Federal Judicial Center. The empirical data includes preliminary results of a Federal Judicial Center survey on discovery concerns among defense attorneys, the Department of Justice, and judges. The preliminary results revealed that 51% of the judges surveyed and over 90% of the defense attorneys favor amending Rule 16, while the Department of Justice opposes any amendment. The Advisory Committee may also decide to recommend to the Federal Judicial Center changes to the Judges' Benchbook to improve supervision of prosecutors' compliance with disclosure obligations. The Benchbook changes might serve either as a supplement or an alternative to amending Rule 16. Finally, the Federal Judicial Center is considering publishing a guide to the "best practices" in criminal discovery. For more information, visit the official website of the U.S. Courts at *www.uscourts.gov.*

FTC "Red Flags Rule" Litigation and Legislation: In 2003, Congress enacted the Fair and Accurate Credit Transactions Act, which required businesses that act as "creditors" to establish a program to prevent identity theft. In 2007, to implement the Act, the Federal Trade Commission (FTC) and other federal agencies adopted a final rule—commonly called the "Red Flags Rule"—requiring creditors to develop policies for detecting and responding to various "red flags" concerning identity theft. Because lawyers typically are not paid for legal services until after work is completed, the FTC classified lawyers (and various other professionals) as "creditors" who must comply with the Red Flags Rule. The ABA tried and failed to persuade the FTC to change its mind, so in 2009 the ABA and over forty state and local bar associations sued to enjoin application of the Red Flags Rule to lawyers. The ABA won summary judgment and obtained declaratory and injunctive relief, see *American Bar Ass'n v. Federal Trade Comm'n,* 671 F. Supp. 2d 64 (D.D.C. 2009), but in February of 2010 the FTC appealed.

Congress then intervened. In December of 2010, while the appeal was pending, Congress passed and President Obama signed into law the Red Flag Program Clarification Act of 2010, which makes clear that lawyers (and most other professionals) are not "creditors" and are not subject to the Red Flags Rule. The legislation was not controversial—the House of Representatives passed the bill by voice vote after considering it under a procedure called "suspension of the rules," which limited debate to 40 minutes, barred any amendments, and required a two-thirds majority vote for passage. The Senate soon followed suit. *See House Clears Bill to Narrow Scope of FTC 'Red Flags' Rule,* 26 Law. Man. Prof. Conduct 758 (Dec. 22, 2010). As a consequence, in March of 2011, the D.C. Circuit vacated the district court's ruling in favor of the ABA and ordered the district court to dismiss the litigation as moot, noting that the new legislation was "clearly aimed at the precise matter in dispute."

Patent Law Reform: In the 1990s, some tax lawyers began patenting sophisticated tax strategies. Those patents faced other tax professionals with a Hobson's choice between paying royalties to the inventors or risking patent infringement actions for using those strategies without permission. Over the years, the USPTO granted 161 tax strategy patents. Now, there will be no more. On September 16, 2011, President Obama signed into law the Leahy-Smith America Invents Act, which "sets into motion the most comprehensive overhaul to our nation's patent system since 1836," according to the web site of the United States Patent and Trademark Office (USPTO). One small part of the law directly affects lawyers—the law prohibits the USPTO from approving any future tax strategy patents, including those for which applications are pending. Under the new law, tax strategies for "reducing, avoiding, or deferring tax liability" will be deemed "prior art" and will be not patentable. (An exclusion in the law allows the USPTO to continue granting patents for tax filing and preparation software.) The law does not invalidate tax strategy patents that have already been granted, but the USPTO is reviewing some of those patents and may determine that they were not properly issued.

Proposed Lawsuit Abuse Reduction Act (LARA): Before 1983, Rule 11 of the Federal Rules of Civil Procedure, which provides for sanctions in certain circumstances, was a toothless provision, and almost no one was ever sanctioned under it. In 1983, Rule 11 was amended to mandate sanctions for various types of litigation misconduct by lawyers and parties, but the courts were overwhelmed by sanctions motions. In 1993, the Judicial Conference of the United States sent the Supreme Court an amended version of Rule 11 that made sanctions discretionary rather than mandatory and created a "safe harbor" that allows a lawyer or party to escape sanctions by withdrawing an offending pleading or motion within 21 days after being served with a copy of a sanctions motion. If the offending pleading or motion is withdrawn, the sanctions motion is never filed. The Supreme Court voted 6-3 to send the amended version to Congress in 1993 (with Justices Scalia, Thomas, and Souter dissenting), and Congress went along with the amended rule.

In 2005 the House of Representatives passed a bill by a 228-184 vote that would have restored mandatory sanctions and deleted the safe harbor, thus resembling the 1983 version of Rule 11. The bill did not pass in the Senate, but a similar bill—the Lawsuit Abuse Reduction Act (H.R. 966, or LARA), whose chief sponsor is House Judiciary Committee chairman Rep. Lamar Smith (R-Tex.)—was the subject of a hearing before the House Constitution Subcommittee on March 11, 2011, The bill would make Rule 11 sanctions mandatory rather than discretionary (as was true from 1983 through 1993), and would make monetary sanctions the required penalty for a violation of the rule. On July 7, 2011, the House Judiciary Committee approved the bill by a vote of 20-13. Sen. Charles Grassley (R-Iowa) has introduced a companion bill (S. 533) in the Senate. For more information, see *House Panel Eyes Tougher Attorney Sanctions To Curb Frivolous Lawsuits Plaguing Business,* 27 Law. Man. Prof. Conduct 169 (March 16, 2011), and *House Judiciary Committee Approves Measure to Reduce Frivolous Lawsuits,* 27 Law. Man. Prof. Conduct 480 (July 20, 2011).

FDIC Insurance for IOLTA Funds: In October of 2008, to shore up confidence in banks, the Federal Deposit Insurance Corporation (FDIC) announced that it would provide unlimited deposit insurance coverage to client funds deposited into IOLTA accounts at FDIC-insured depository institutions. Congress has since amended the Federal Deposit Insurance Act to extend this unlimited coverage through December 31, 2012. For more information, see *http://www.fdic.gov/regulations/resources/TLGP.*

SEC Incentives for Whistleblowers: In 2010, Congress passed the Dodd-Frank Wall Street Reform and Consumer Protection Act. Section 922 of that Act authorized the SEC to award whistleblowers from 10% to 30% of any monetary penalties above $1 million imposed on securities law violators. In November of 2010, the SEC issued proposed rules for the new whistleblower program. After reviewing hundreds of comment letters, the SEC (by a 3-2 vote) adopted final rules effective August 12, 2011.

Under the final rules, whistleblowers are not eligible for awards based on information protected by the attorney-client privilege or an attorney's ethical duty of confidentiality unless (a) the applicable Rules of Professional Conduct or other law permit disclosure of the information to the SEC without the client's consent, or (b) the attorney-client privilege has been waived. The final rules also allow SEC staff members to respond directly to a communication from a potential whistleblower without giving notice to the corporation's attorneys. The SEC considers such ex parte contacts to be "authorized by law" under the no-contact rule (ABA Model Rule 4.2). However, the SEC decided not to adopt a rule governing the fees that may be charged by attorneys who represent whistleblowers. For extensive background on the proposed and final rules, see *SEC Proposes Whistleblower Program, Excludes Attorneys From Incentive Awards,* 26 Law. Man. Prof. Conduct 681 (Nov. 20, 2010), and *Final SEC Whistleblower Rules Restrict Lawyers' Eligibility for Awards,* 27 Law. Man. Prof. Conduct 367 (June 8, 2011).

Proposed Department of Labor "Persuader Agreement" Regulation: Section 203 of the Labor-Management Reporting and Disclosure Act, 29 U.S.C. § 433, generally requires the disclosure of agreements between employers and labor relations consultants to "persuade employees to exercise or not to exercise . . . the right to organize and bargain collectively"—but § 433(c) expressly exempts reporting of "persuader activities" by persons who merely give "advice" to an employer. Since 1989, the United States Department of Labor (DOL) has interpreted this statutory "advice" exemption to exclude lawyers from § 433 reporting requirements if the lawyers merely provide advice or other legal services directly to employer clients but have no direct contact with employees.

On June 21, 2011, however, the DOL published for public comment a proposed rule requiring reporting by a consultant (including a lawyer) who (a) engages in persuader activities that go beyond the plain meaning of "advice," even if the consultant has no direct contact with workers, or (b) engages in specified persuader actions or communications, such as planning a campaign to counter a union organizing or collective bargaining effort, even if the consultant also gives advice to the employer. The DOL received thousands of comments, including a detailed letter from the President of the ABA. The ABA opposes the proposed interpretation on grounds that the mandated reports would require lawyers to disclose "a substantial amount of confidential client information, including the existence of the client-lawyer relationship and the identity of the client, the general nature of the legal representation, and a description of the legal tasks performed," as well as detailed information regarding the legal fees paid by all of the lawyers' employer clients. When we went to press, the DOL was still considering the comments. For more information, including a link to the ABA letter, see *Proposed Persuader Rule Could Undermine Lawyer-Client Relationship, ABA Head Says*, 27 Law. Man. Prof. Conduct 614 (Sept. 28, 2011).

GAO Report on Aiding and Abetting Liability for Secondary Actors: Until 1994, courts interpreted § 10(b) of the Securities Exchange Act of 1934 and Securities and Exchange Commission Rule 10b-5 as authorizing investors to sue "secondary actors" such as accountants and lawyers for aiding and abetting securities law violations. In *Central Bank of Denver v. First Interstate Bank of Denver*, 511 U.S. 164 (1994), however, the Supreme Court held that there is no private cause of action for aiding and abetting a 10b-5 violation. The next year, in the Private Securities Litigation Reform Act of 1995, Congress restored the SEC's power to bring enforcement actions for aiding and abetting, but it did not restore that power to investors. In *Stoneridge Investment Partners v. Scientific-Atlanta*, 552 U.S. 148 (2008), the Supreme Court reinforced the distinction between the SEC and private investors by holding that §10(b) of the Securities Exchange Act of 1934 does not create a right of private action against aiders and abettors of securities law violations.

In 2009, Senator Arlen Specter (D-Pa.) introduced the Liability for Aiding and Abetting Securities Violations Act of 2009 (S. 1551), which was designed to override *Stoneridge* by authorizing private plaintiffs to bring civil suits against anyone who "knowingly or recklessly provides substantial assistance" to a person engaged in fraud. That bill did not became law, but a provision in the Dodd-Frank Wall Street Reform and Consumer Protection Act of 2010 ordered the Government Accountability Office (GAO) to report to Congress on the impact of creating a private right of action against secondary actors for aiding and abetting securities law violations. On July 21, 2011, the GAO sent Congress the mandated report, which is entitled "Securities Fraud Liability of Secondary Actors" (GAO-11-664). The report does not make any recommendations, but it summarizes the role of lawyers (and others) in securities transactions, reviews the potential liability of lawyers under current law, and examines the pros and cons of extending liability to aiders and abettors. For additional information, see *GAO Report Cites Pros, Cons of Expanding Aiding/Abetting Liability to Secondary Actors*, 27 Law. Man. Prof. Conduct 501 (Aug. 3, 2011).

Financial Accounting Standards Board (FASB): For years, investors have complained that corporate financial statements do not adequately disclose loss contingencies from litigation. In 2008, the Financial Accounting Standards Board (FASB), a private body whose standards are officially recognized by the Securities and Exchange Commission, circulated a proposed new rule requiring companies to disclose (among other things) management's estimate of the maximum exposure to loss from litigation. Opposition to the change was soon voiced by the ABA, the Association of Corporate Counsel, and many others, who argued that the new rule would erode the attorney-client privilege.

In July of 2010, the FASB proposed a less stringent standard, which required corporations to disclose the known facts and contentions of the parties in legal matters and to provide quantitative disclosures that enable readers of financial statements to make their own assessments about potential litigation losses. This new proposal, which was scheduled to take effect on January 1, 2011, generated 335 comment letters, many of them negative. At its November 10, 2010 meeting, the FASB directed its staff to work with the staffs of the SEC and the Public Company Auditing Oversight Board (PCAOB). (PCAOB is a nonprofit corporation established by Congress to oversee the audits of public companies in order to protect the interests of investors.) The FASB also decided that a final standard would not be effective for the 2010 calendar year-end reporting period. It will decide on an effective date at a future meeting, after it has substantially concluded its redeliberations. In October of 2010, the FASB announced that it was postponing the scheduled January 1, 2011 effective date and would not announce a new effective date until it finally decided on a new standard. For more background and a link to the hundreds of comment letters on the July 2010 proposal, see *FASB Votes to Delay Planned New Rules on Disclosures of Litigation Loss Risks,* 26 Law. Man. Prof. Conduct 683 (Nov. 10, 2010).

DEVELOPMENTS IN THE STATES

Broad Trends in the States

Before discussing developments in individual jurisdictions, we will discuss broad trends in the states. In discussing these issues, we rely heavily on data compiled by the ABA Center for Professional Responsibility (CPR), the national nerve center for professional responsibility issues. The CPR keeps track of professional responsibility developments at the federal level, in the states, and within the ABA. The CPR's website, which links to a wealth of contemporary, historical, and regulatory resources, is at *www.americanbar.org/groups/professional_responsibility.html.*

Of particular interest for our purposes is the CPR's Policy Implementation Committee, which promotes ABA policies to the bar and the public, assists jurisdictions in reviewing and implementing policies adopted by the ABA, and maintains a national clearinghouse of information on efforts to implement ABA policies. The website of the Policy Implementation Committee contains legislative history and up-to-date charts regarding state-by-state implementation of (a) the ABA Model Rules of Professional Conduct, (b) the policies of the ABA Multijurisdictional Practice Commission, (c) the August 2010 version of the ABA Model Code of Judicial Conduct, (d) the ABA Model Court Rule on Insurance Disclosure, (e) the ABA Model Court Rule on Provision of Legal Services Following Determination of Major Disaster (the "Katrina Rule" or "Major Disaster Rule"), and (f) the ABA Model Rule for Registration of In-House Counsel.

The Policy Implementation Committee's website, which contains links to many valuable charts and other materials, is located at *http://www.americanbar.org/groups/professional_responsibility/policy.html.*

"Ethics 2000" reviews: Nationally, since the ABA Ethics 2000 Commission released its final report in 2001, nearly all states have studied and reacted to the Ethics 2000 Commission's work. Specifically:

- forty-six (46) U.S. jurisdictions have significantly revised their Rules of Professional Conduct (AK, AL, AR, AZ, CO, CT, DC, DE, FL, IA, ID, IL, IN, KS, KY, LA, MA, MD, ME, MI, MN, MO, MS, MT, NC, ND, NE, NH, NJ, NM, NV, NY, OH, OK, OR, PA, RI, SC, SD, TN, UT, VA, VT, WA, WI, WY)
- three (3) states have circulated proposed rules that remain pending (CA, HI, WV)
- one (1) state has appointed a review committee that has not yet issued a report (GA)
- one (1) state has voted in a statewide referendum to reject revised rules (TX)

Since our last edition went to press in September 2010, significant amendments to the Rules of Professional Conduct have taken effect in the following jurisdictions:

- Arizona (effective February 10, 2011)
- Michigan (effective January 1, 2011)
- Mississippi (effective July 1, 2011)
- Montana (effective October 1, 2011)
- Tennessee (effective January 1, 2011)

Comments to the ABA Model Rules of Professional Conduct: With respect to the Comments to the ABA Model Rules, the state high courts fall into three basic categories. *Category No. 1:* About forty (40) jurisdictions have formally adopted the Comments as part of their Rules of Professional Conduct, but have added a proviso: "The Comments are intended as guides to interpretation, but the text of each rule is authoritative," or similar words. *Category No. 2:* Four (4) state high courts (ME, MI, MN, and NH) have authorized publication of the Comments as an "aid to understanding of the rules" or "as an aid to the reader" or "for convenience" but have not adopted the Comments. *Category No. 3:* Six (6) states (LA, MT, NV, NJ, NY, and OR) have adopted the Rules of Professional Conduct without any Comments (but in Louisiana the State Bar publishes the ABA Comments with the black letter Rules, and in New York the State Bar has adopted the Comments as "guides to interpretation").

Malpractice Insurance Disclosure Rules: In 2004, the ABA adopted a Model Court Rule on Insurance Disclosure. At that time, only a few states required lawyers to disclose their malpractice insurance coverage. Today, at least 24 states require some form of malpractice insurance disclosure. Eighteen (18) jurisdictions require disclosure on their bar registration statements (AZ, CO, DE, HI, ID, IL, KS, MA, MI, MN, ND, NE, NM, NV, RI, VA, WA, and WV), while seven (7) states require disclosure directly to clients (AK, CA, NH, NM, OH, PA, and SD). (NM is listed in both categories because it requires disclosure on the bar registration statement and directly to clients.) At least five additional states (ME, NY, SC, UT, and VT) are considering some form of legal malpractice disclosure rule. However, five states (AR, CT, FL, KY, TX) have rejected the ABA Model Court Rule on Insurance Disclosure, and one state (NC) formerly required insurance disclosure but dropped the requirement effective January 1, 2010. Only one state (OR) requires lawyers to carry legal malpractice insurance. For a state-by-state chart of insurance disclosure rules, visit the ABA Policy Implementation Committee's website at *http://www.americanbar.org/groups/professional_responsibility/policy.html.*

Multijurisdictional Practice Rules: Forty-four (44) U.S. jurisdictions have adopted a multijurisdictional practice rule identical, or substantially similar, to ABA Model Rule 5.5 (Unauthorized Practice of Law; Multijurisdictional Practice of Law). For a state-by-state chart, see *http://www.americanbar.org/groups/professional_responsibility/policy.html.*

In-house Counsel Registration Rules: Thirty-four (34) states have adopted some form of in-house registration rule. (An in-house registration rule authorizes in-house lawyers who are in good standing in at least one U.S. jurisdiction to engage in the practice of law without being fully admitted to the bar of the state where they work, subject to certain conditions.) Some other states have not adopted the ABA in-house registration rule but have adopted ABA Model Rule 5.5(d)(1) or other rules or policies that allow in-house lawyers to practice without being admitted. The ABA adopted the ABA Model Rule for Registration of In-House Counsel in August of 2008. (Some states adopted in-house registration rules before the ABA acted.) The most recent jurisdiction to adopt an in-house registration rule is New York, which adopted its own unique version effective April 20, 2011. For a state-by-state chart, see *http://www.americanbar.org/groups/professional_responsibility/policy.html.*

Major Disaster ("Katrina") Rule: In 2007, to respond to unauthorized practice problems caused by the dislocation of lawyers and clients after Hurricane Katrina, the ABA adopted the so-called "Katrina Rule" or "Major Disaster Rule" (formally known as the Model Court Rule on Provision of

Legal Services Following Determination of Major Disaster). Where adopted, the Katrina Rule authorizes out-of-state lawyers to provide pro bono services in a stricken state, and allows lawyers from the stricken state to carry on their home state practices in jurisdictions that have adopted the Katrina Rule. To date, thirteen (13) U.S. jurisdictions have adopted the rule (AZ, CO, DE, IA, LA, MN, MO, NH, NJ, NY, OR, TN, and WA), and many other jurisdictions are considering it, but six (6) jurisdictions have expressly decided not to adopt it (MI, NC, OH, PA, UT, and WY). In 2007, the Conference of Chief Justices adopted a resolution that "commends" the ABA Major Disaster Rule as the "foundation" upon which to create a rule regarding the provision of legal services following of major disaster,

Developments in Particular States

For detailed information about developments in particular jurisdictions, visit the websites given after each jurisdiction listed below, or click on a link to individual state resources at *http://www.americanbar.org/groups/professional_responsibility/resources/links_of_interest.html.* The following items describe some of the more interesting developments in particular states since our previous edition went to press in September of 2010.

Arkansas: On March 31, 2011, effective immediately, the Arkansas Supreme Court issued an administrative order allowing licensed out-of-state attorneys to provide needed pro bono legal services, but only if they work under the auspices of Arkansas legal services providers, complete any training required by the sponsoring legal service provider, agree to be subject to the Arkansas Rules of Professional Conduct, and meet certain other conditions. The court said that its order "will give in-house corporate counsel the opportunity to volunteer in the community and will make justice more accessible to low-income Arkansans." The full text is available at *https://courts.arkansas.gov.*

California (www.calbar.ca.gov, www.courtinfo.ca.gov, and ***www.leginfo.ca.gov):*** California is now the only state in the country that has not yet adopted some form of the ABA Model Rules, but that is expected to change before our next edition. Since 2002, California's Commission for the Revision of the Rules of Professional Conduct has been studying ways to revise and update California's rules. In 2010, the State Bar Board of Governors received final recommendations from the Commission and adopted 67 proposed new and amended rules.

On July 20, 2011, the State Bar submitted an initial group of six proposed Rules of Professional Conduct to the California Supreme Court for approval. Two or three additional groups of submissions will follow until the State Bar has submitted the full complement of recommended rules. The six proposed rules contained in the initial submission are:

- Rule 1.0 (Purpose and Scope of the Rules of Professional Conduct)
- Rule 7.1 (Communications Concerning the Availability of Legal Services)

- Rule 7.2 (Advertising)
- Rule 7.3 (Direct Contact with Prospective Clients)
- Rule 7.4 (Communication of Fields of Practice and Specialization)
- Rule 7.5 (Firm Names and Letterhead)

The State Bar also forwarded the remainder of the 67 proposed rules to provide context. The State Bar's request makes clear that the Supreme Court has the discretion either to approve any or all of the six initially submitted rules or to wait for the State Bar's later submissions. The Supreme Court also has the option to reject any of the proposed rules or to send them back to the bar for further work. For more information, including links to the complete set of 67 proposed rules, visit *ethics.calbar.ca.gov/Committees/RulesCommission/ProposedRulesofProfessionalConduct.aspx.*

Colorado (www.cobar.org): Effective February 10, 2011, the Colorado Supreme Court amended Rule 1.15 (Safekeeping Property), Rule 3.6 (Trial Publicity), and 3.8 (Special Responsibilities of a Prosecutor), and adopted a new Rule 1.16A (Client File Retention) that imposes detailed and stringent obligations on lawyers to retain client files unless certain conditions are met. For example, Rule 1.16A(c)(1) generally requires a lawyer to retain a criminal defendant's file "for the life of the client, if the matter resulted in a conviction and a sentence of death, life without parole, or an indeterminate sentence. . . ." In a separate development, the Colorado Supreme Court amended Rule 1.5 (Fees) effective July 1, 2011. The full text of the Colorado amendments is available at *http://www.courts.state.co.us/Courts/Supreme_Court/Rule_Changes/2011.cfm.*

Florida (www.flabar.org or ***www.floridasupremecourt.org):*** On July 5, 2011, the Florida Bar filed a petition with the Florida Supreme Court seeking approval for comprehensive changes to Florida's rules governing lawyer advertising. The rules are too lengthy and detailed to summarize here, but one notable feature is that the titles of the proposed rules are completely different from the titles of the ABA Model Rules governing lawyer advertising. Moreover, Florida would have thirteen separate rules on advertising, more than twice the number of advertising rules in the ABA Model Rules. Here are the numbers and titles of the proposed Florida rules:

- Rule 4-7.1 (Application of Rules)
- Rule 4-7.2 (Required Content)
- Rule 4-7.3 (Deceptive and Inherently Misleading Advertisements)
- Rule 4-7.4 (Potentially Misleading Advertisements)
- Rule 4-7.5 (Unduly Manipulative or Intrusive Advertisements)
- Rule 4-7.6 (Presumptively Valid Content)
- Rule 4-7.7 (Payment for Advertising and Promotion)
- Rule 4-7.8 (Direct Contact with Prospective Clients)
- Rule 4-7.9 (Evaluation of Advertisements)
- Rule 4-7.10 (Exemptions From the Filing and Review Requirement)

- Rule 4-7.11 (Firm Names and Letterhead)
- Rule 4-7.12 (Lawyer Referral Services)
- Rule 4-7.13 (Lawyer Directory)

Separately, in *In re Amendments to the Florida Rules of Civil Procedure*, 2010 WL 3488983 (Fla. 2010), the Florida Supreme Court adopted a new Rule 1.285 of the Florida Rules of Civil Procedure to address inadvertent disclosure of privileged materials. The new rule, which took effect on January 1, 2011, requires disclosing attorneys and parties to take specified steps (including notice to the recipients) to assert a claim of privilege after discovering the inadvertent disclosure of privileged materials. Reciprocally, the rule also specifies steps that recipients must take upon receiving a notice of inadvertent disclosure from the disclosing party or attorney.

In the courts, a First Amendment challenge by a law firm and Public Citizen, Inc. to various provisions of Florida's lawyer advertising rules remains pending. The latest decision is *Harrell v. The Florida Bar*, 608 F.3d 1241 (11th Cir. 2010), which reversed a summary judgment in favor of the Bar and remanded the case to the district court, where it is still pending. The suit turns largely on whether a law firm may include the phrase "Don't settle for less than you deserve" in the firm's advertisements.

Finally, on September 12, 2011, the Florida Supreme Court amended the oath sworn by newly admitted attorneys. The court added the following phrase: "To opposing parties and their counsel, I pledge fairness, integrity, and civility, not only in court, but also in all written and oral communications." The court said it adopted the new language to recognize "the necessity for civility in the inherently contentious setting of the adversary process."

Hawaii (www.hsba.org): The Hawaii Supreme Court's Disciplinary Board has proposed comprehensive amendments to the Hawaii Rules of Professional Conduct and has sent them to the Supreme Court for its review. The Supreme Court has not formally circulated the proposed revisions for public comment, but it has allowed them to be posted on the websites of the Disciplinary Board and the Hawaii State Bar Association for preliminary review. The proposals contain seventeen new or substantially revised rules. The deadline for commenting on the proposals was October 31, 2011. For the full set of proposed Hawaii rules and an executive summary of the proposed provisions, see *http://www.hsba.org/Hawaii_Rules_of_Professional_Conduct.aspx.*

Illinois (www.isba.org): Effective July 1, 2011, Rule 1.15 of the Illinois Rules of Professional Conduct, which governs lawyer trust accounts, was extensively amended. Among other things, the amendments expand the recordkeeping requirements for lawyer trust accounts and establish detailed regulations for dishonored instrument notification.

Indiana (www.inbar.org): Effective January 1, 2011, Indiana has extensively amended its rules governing advertising and solicitation by lawyers in that state. The amended rules have several key features: (1) they impose a 30-day ban on soliciting prospective clients after an accident or disaster;

(2) they prohibit targeted contact with clients in various additional situations; (3) they permit trade names for law firms—the trade names must include the name of a lawyer and may include terms that identify the field of law in which the firm concentrates, describe the geographic location of its offices, and indicate a language fluency; and (4) for the first time in Indiana, the black letter rules on advertising and solicitation are accompanied by Comments. The amendments also simplify the text of several rules by moving some provisions to the Comments. The full text of the amendments is available at *http://www.state.in.us/judiciary/orders/rule-amendments/2010/prof-conduct-1014.pdf.*

Louisiana (www.lsba.org): On October 1, 2009 Louisiana's new rules governing lawyer advertising finally took effect. On January 31, 2011, the Fifth Circuit handed down its decision in *Public Citizen Inc. v. Louisiana Attorney Disciplinary Bd.* 632 F.3d 212 (5th Cir. 2011), which upheld some rules but struck down others on First Amendment grounds.

Massachusetts: Effective March 15, 2011, Massachusetts has amended its version of Rule 1.5 (Fees). The amended rule includes two alternative forms for contingent fee agreements. The full text is available at *http://www.mass.gov/obcbbo/rpc1.htm#Rule1.5.*

Maine: Effective February 1, 2011, the Maine Supreme Court added a lengthy new Rule 9A to the Maine Bar Admission Rules. The new rule empowers the Court to grant "conditional admission" to bar applicants who have commenced but not completed rehabilitation from past conduct or behavior that indicated insufficient good moral character to qualify for admission to the bar but the misbehavior is unlikely to recur. According to a helpful Advisory Committee Note, the conditional admission rule "is designed to protect the public and the integrity of the profession in close cases for admission, while encouraging persons having a record of concerning conduct to seek professional assistance and rehabilitation." Conditional admission is not available to lawyers who are disbarred or suspended from practice, or who have resigned from practice in other jurisdictions. Rule 9A and the accompanying Advisory Committee Note are available at *http://www.maine.gov/tools/whatsnew/attach.php?id=193867&an=1.*

Michigan (www.michbar.org): Effective January 1, 2011, the Michigan Supreme Court amended seven existing Rules of Professional Conduct and added three new ones. The new rules are Rules 2.4 (Lawyer Serving as Third-Party Neutral), 5.7 (Responsibilities Regarding Law-Related Services), and 6.6 (Nonprofit and Court-Annexed Limited Legal Services Programs). The Supreme Court's action fell far short of what the State Bar of Michigan had recommended. The State Bar circulated comprehensive amendments to the Michigan Rules of Professional Conduct for public comment in July 2004. The Supreme Court took no action for years, waiting until 2009 to circulate selected proposed rules for public comment. In the end, the Supreme Court adopted only a fraction of what the State Bar had proposed. For details regarding the amended rules and their background, see *Updates to Michigan*

Rules Include MJP, But Not Most Other Model Rule Changes, 26 Law. Man. Prof. Conduct 679 (Nov. 10, 2010).

On May 19, 2011, the Michigan Supreme Court issued an order—with three of the seven justices dissenting—amending Rule 7.3 (Direct Contact with Prospective Clients) by prohibiting solicitation of accident victims or their families for 30 days after the injury, death, or accident occurred, and by requiring all solicitations to bear the label "Advertising Material." The rule was to take effect on September 1, 2011. But in a remarkable turn of events, the court issued another order on July 19, 2011 stating that "in light of concern expressed regarding the amendments adopted in this file by order of the Court dated May 19, 2011, the order that entered on that date is rescinded, effective immediately." The court also circulated the proposed language of Rule 7.3 for comment. The court's order is available online at *http://www.courts.michigan.gov/supremecourt/Resources/Administrative/2002-24-07-19-11-order.pdf.*

Finally, on March 22, 2011, the court solicited public comment on proposed further changes to the Michigan Rules of Professional Conduct. These changes would move language that protects clients from the Comments to the black letter text of the Rules. The court set a July 1, 2011 deadline for public comment. The language that would be moved to the black letter text does not appear in the text of the ABA Model Rules of Professional Conduct. A redline version of the proposed amendments is available at *http://op.bna.com/mopc.nsf/r?Open=kswn-8fdrak.*

Minnesota: Effective July 1, 2011, the Minnesota Supreme Court amended Rule 1.5(b) to set forth specific requirements for advance fees, flat fees, and "availability" fees. A companion amendment to Rule 1.15(c) adds a cross-reference to Rule 1.5(b). A redline version of the amended rules is available at *https://www.courts.state.mn.us/?page=511.*

Mississippi: Effective July 1, 2011, the Mississippi Supreme Court adopted a series of amendments that permit limited scope representation. The amendments are designed to encourage lawyers to provide legal services to clients with limited financial resources. The court also adopted a new Rule 6.5 (Nonprofit and Court-Annexed Limited Legal Services Programs) intended to encourage lawyers to provide volunteer services to legal hotlines and clinics without fear of creating conflicts of interest. For more information, see *http://www.mssc.state.ms.us/news/2011/01.27.11limitedrepresentationrule.pdf.*

Montana (courts.mt.gov): Effective October 1, 2011, the Montana Supreme Court amended various Rules of Professional Conduct and Rules of Civil Procedure to facilitate "ghostwriting" for clients who are nominally *pro se.* The Montana State Bar's ethics committee formally opposed the amendments, calling them "a troubling step in the direction of 'mass produced' or 'drive through' representation." A related change is an amendment to Rule 11 of the Montana Rules of Civil Procedure, which now provides as follows:

> (b) An attorney may help to draft a pleading, motion, or document filed by the otherwise self-represented person, and the attorney need not sign that

pleading, motion, or document. The attorney in providing such drafting assistance may rely on the otherwise self-represented person's representation of facts, unless the attorney has reason to believe that such representations are false or materially insufficient, in which instance the attorney shall make an independent reasonable inquiry into the facts.

This provision drew dissents from two Montana Supreme Court Justices who believe that a lawyer should be required to disclose assistance to seemingly unrepresented litigants. For more information, see *New Rules on Limited-Scope Representation Allow Montana Lawyers to Ghostwrite Filings,* 27 Law. Man. Prof. Conduct 264 (April 27, 2011). The orders adopting the amended rules are available at *http://courts.mt.gov/supreme/new_rules/default.mcpx.*

New Jersey (www.judiciary.state.nj.us/rules/apprpc.htm): On April 6, 2011, the New Jersey Supreme Court circulated a notice to the bar seeking comments on a proposal to add the following new sentence to Rule 7.5: "Use of a trade name shall be permissible so long as it describes the nature of the firm's legal practice in terms that are accurate, descriptive, and informative, but not misleading, comparative, unprofessional, or suggestive of the ability to obtain results. Such trade names should be accompanied by the name of the attorney who is responsible for the management of the organization." A proposed new paragraph in the Comment to Rule 7.5 would provide the bar with illustrative examples of acceptable and unacceptable trade names. Comments were due by May 6, 2011. A redlined version of the proposal is available at *http://www.judiciary.state.nj.us/notices/2011/n110408a.pdf.*

Apparently still pending is a proposed new Advertising Guideline that would prohibit an attorney or law firm from including, on a website or other advertisement, "a quotation from a judge or court opinion (oral or written) regarding the attorney's abilities or legal services." The New Jersey Supreme Court's Committee on Attorney Advertising proposed the new Guideline after reviewing an attorney's website that included two quotations from unpublished judicial opinions praising the attorney's legal abilities.

New York (www.nysba.org and ***www.courts.state.ny.us):*** Effective April 15, 2011, New York amended Rule 7.1 (Advertising) to respond to the holdings in *Alexander v. Cahill,* 634 F. Supp 239 (N.D.N.Y. 2007), *aff'd in part and rev'd in part,* 598 F.3d 79 (2d Cir. 2010) (Guido Calabresi, J.), *cert. denied,* 131 S. Ct. 820 (Dec. 13, 2010), which struck down various New York lawyer advertising provisions on First Amendment grounds.

The New York State Bar Association also amended dozens of Comments to the Rules during the past year. In November of 2010, the State Bar's Committee on Standards of Attorney Conduct (COSAC), with the approval of the State Bar's Executive Committee, made technical corrections to many of the Comments to the New York Rules of Professional Conduct to conform them more closely to the black letter text of the Rules. Some changes corrected inadvertent errors, while other changes addressed tension between the Comments and the text of the Rules. In January of 2011, COSAC proposed and the House of Delegates approved substantive changes to the Comments to Rule 1.8 (Current Clients: Specific Conflict of interest Rules), Rule 1.15 (Safekeeping Property), and 8.4 (Misconduct). In June of 2011, COSAC proposed and the House of Delegates approved a few substantive amendments to the Comments, plus many new Comments to explain provisions adopted by the courts in 2009 that were not proposed by COSAC and therefore were not accompanied by any Comments.

New York was also active in terms of court rules. Effective July 15, 2011, the Administrative Board of the Courts adopted a new rule, 22 NYCRR § 151.1 (Assignments in Cases Involving Contributors to Judicial Campaigns). The rule provides that (barring emergency, necessity, or the interests of justice): "No matter shall be assigned to a judge . . . if such assignment would give rise to a campaign contribution conflict." A campaign contribution conflict arises if an individual lawyer appearing before a judge has contributed $2,500 or more to the judge's campaign during a "window period" or if the "collective" contributions by the lawyer, her co-counsel, her clients, and the lawyer's law firm total $3,500 or more. According to the press release issued by the courts, the rule makes New York "the first in the country to systemically address the issue of money in judicial elections by administrative action."

Effective April 20, 2011, the New York Court of Appeals adopted a new 22 NYCRR Part 522 relating to the registration of in-house counsel in New York. The rule, which differs substantially from the ABA Model Rule for Registration of In-House Counsel, permits attorneys in good standing in U.S. jurisdictions with similar in-house registration rules to act as in-house counsel for a New York organization without taking the bar exam. For more information, see *New York Adopts Registration Rule for Out-of-State Corporate Counsel,* 27 Law. Man. Prof. Conduct 262 (April 27, 2011).

Effective February 9, 2011, New York adopted the ABA's Model Court Rule on Provision of Legal Services Following Determination of Major Disaster (commonly called the "Katrina Rule" or the "Major Disaster Rule"). The rule will allow out-of-state lawyers to carry on the practice of law in New York if their home states have been struck by a hurricane, flood, tornado, earthquake, or other disaster, and will allow out-of-state lawyers to perform pro bono work in New York if New York suffers a disaster.

In October of 2010, in response to widespread reports of "robosigning," false affidavits by bank employees, and other allegedly improper or fraudulent practices by lenders seeking to foreclose on residential mortgages, the New York courts began requiring lawyers for lenders in foreclosure actions to file a special affirmation. As amended on November 18, 2010, the affirmation requires a lender's lawyer to affirm, under penalty of perjury, that (a) the attorney has communicated with representatives of the lender who informed the lawyer that they have personally reviewed the underlying documents and confirmed their accuracy, and that (b) based on those communications and on the lawyer's "own inspection and other reasonable inquiry under the circumstances," the papers filed or submitted to the court contain no false statements of fact or law.

In a development relating to New York State statutes, a federal district court held that § 470 of the New York Judiciary Law, which requires New York lawyers who reside in other states to maintain a law office in New York, "infringes on nonresident attorneys' right to practice law in violation of the Privileges and Immunities Clause." *Schoenefeld v. New York*, 2011 WL 3957282 (N.D.N.Y. 2011).

Finally, in June of 2011, the New York State Bar Association House of Delegates approved a new Code of Judicial Conduct to replace New York's 1999 rules governing judges. The proposed new Code is the product of three years of work by the State Bar's Special Committee to Review the Code of Judicial Conduct, which included current and former judges as well as professors and practicing lawyers. The Reporter is Professor Pat Connors of Albany Law School. The Special Committee's recommendations are based in part on the 2007 version of the ABA Code of Judicial Conduct. The proposed new Code is currently in the hands of New York's courts, which may accept, reject, or modify the proposals.

Tennessee (www.tba.org): Effective January 1, 2011, the Tennessee Supreme Court adopted the first set of comprehensive amendments to the Tennessee Rules of Professional Conduct since the new rules took effect in March 2003. The amendments are the fruit of a six-year revision process initiated by the Tennessee Bar Association, followed by an extensive public comment period and an oral argument before the Supreme Court in June 2010. The amended Rules, plus helpful background materials, are available at *www.tba.org/ethics/index.html.*

Texas (www.texasbar.com): Early in 2011, Texas held a statewide referendum on a package of comprehensive revisions that had been jointly developed by a Texas Supreme Court Task Force and the State Bar's Committee on the Texas Disciplinary Rules of Professional Conduct. On February 17, 2011, the Texas State Bar announced that Texas lawyers had resoundingly rejected the proposed rule changes. The proposed rules were presented on the referendum ballot in six clusters. The most popular cluster was rejected by over 72% of Texas lawyers, and the rest were rejected by anywhere from 77% to 82% of the lawyers who voted. For background and details, see *Texas Lawyers Overwhelmingly Vote Down Proposed Renovation of Disciplinary Rules,* 27 Law. Man. Prof. Conduct 130 (March 2, 2011).

Virginia (www.vsb.org): Virginia has made many changes to its rules since our last edition. Effective June 23, 2011, the Supreme Court of Virginia amended Rule 1.15 (Safekeeping Property) by simplifying its language. There were no substantive changes to the rule.

Effective June 21, 2011, the Supreme Court of Virginia adopted a new Rule 1.18 (Duties to Prospective Client). The rule and its Comment are in many respects identical to ABA Model Rule 1.18, but subparagraphs (d)(2)(i) and (ii) of Virginia's version are more detailed than the ABA version and do not prohibit the screened lawyer from sharing in the fees from the screened matter.

Effective November 1, 2010, the Supreme Court of Virginia approved the Virginia State Bar's Rule 4.2 Task Force's proposed amendment to Comment 5 to Rule 4.2 to address the situation in which a defendant who is in custody, formally charged, and represented by counsel waives his rights under *Miranda v. Arizona* and wants to give a statement to a law enforcement officer without his counsel present. The question addressed by the Task Force was: "If the law enforcement officer seeks legal advice from a commonwealth's attorney regarding whether the officer may obtain a statement from the defendant under these circumstances, may the commonwealth's attorney advise the police officer without violating Rule 4.2?" The amended Comment 5 says:

> [5] In circumstances where applicable judicial precedent has approved investigative contacts prior to attachment of the right to counsel, and they are not prohibited by any provision of the United States Constitution or the Virginia Constitution, they should be considered to be authorized by law within the meaning of the Rule. Similarly, communications in civil matters may be considered authorized by law if they have been approved by judicial precedent. This Rule does not prohibit a lawyer from providing advice regarding the legality of an interrogation or the legality of other investigative conduct.

Amended Comment 5 does not, however, authorize a Commonwealth's Attorney to "script" or "mastermind" the police's interrogation of the defendant.

On December 9, 2010, the Virginia Bar's Standing Committee on Legal Ethics removed from consideration a proposed Rule 7.2(c)(4) and corresponding Comment 8 to Rule 7.2. The proposed language would have approved non-exclusive lead sharing arrangements between participating lawyers and other non-lawyer professionals. For example, the proposed provision would have permitted a lawyer to refer clients to a health care professional with an expectation that the healthcare professional might refer patients to the lawyer for legal representation. An opinion from Virginia's Attorney General said the proposed rule would (i) facilitate conduct by a "non-lawyer professional" that violates Virginia's "running and capping" statute, Va. Code Sec. 54.1-3939, and/or (ii) may entail a violation of the same provisions by the referring attorney.

The Virginia State Bar's Standing Committee on Legal Ethics sought public comment by September 14, 2011 on proposed amendments to Rules 7.1-7.5 of the Rules of Professional Conduct, which govern lawyer advertising and solicitation. Proposed changes to Rules 7.1, 7.3, and 7.5 were originally circulated in March of 2010 and were revised by the Standing Committee in response to comments. Especially noteworthy is that the Standing Committee's new proposal would eliminate Rules 7.2 and 7.4 as unnecessary.

Virginia has also amended a number of its court rules since our last edition. Effective February 17, 2011, Virginia amended its disciplinary procedures with respect to out-of-state and foreign lawyers (*e.g.*, *pro hac vice* lawyers and registered in-house counsel).

Effective April 15, 2011, the Virginia Supreme Court amended Supreme Court Rule 1A:5 (Corporate Counsel & Corporate Counsel Registrants) to allow Virginia corporate counsel admitted in States other than Virginia to do *pro bono* work in Virginia. The amended rule says that "a lawyer certified pursuant to Part I of this rule may, and is encouraged to, provide voluntary *pro bono publico* services in accordance with Rule 6.1 of the Virginia Rules of Professional Conduct." Effective June 13, 2011, the court further amended Rule1A:5 by adding an Appendix of Forms, which includes the "motion and oath" that must be submitted by an applicant for registration as in-house counsel.

Finally, the Virginia Supreme Court is also still considering whether to adopt the ABA Model Court Rule on Provision of Legal Services Following Determination of Major Disaster (often called the "Katrina Rule"), which the Bar recommended in July of 2008. The Virginia proposal generally follows the ABA model on this subject, with a few modifications.

Details and updates regarding changes and proposed changes in Virginia can be found at *http://www.vsb.org/pro-guidelines/index.php/rule_changes/,* which systematically lists the status of adopted, pending, and rejected rule amendments and provides links both to concise summaries and to primary sources.

Legal Ethics Websites

Much of the information discussed above was obtained by using some of the remarkable online research sources that are available regarding lawyer regulation. Among the most useful of these sites are the following:

www.americanbar.org/groups/professional_responsibility.html: This website, which is constantly updated by the staff of the ABA Center for Professional Responsibility, collects and posts vital information from the ABA Ethics 20/20 Commission, the ABA Ethics 2000 Commission, the ABA Commission on Multijurisdictional Practice, the ABA Commission on Multidisciplinary Practice, and other ABA sources. It also provides the full text of the ABA Model Rules of Professional Conduct, legislative history of the Model Rules, and links to dozens of other ethics resources, including all of the states and the District of Columbia. The site's breadth and depth reflects the fact that the ABA Center for Professional Responsibility is the central national source for information and action regarding ethics developments in the United States.

www.law.cornell.edu/ethics: This website, maintained by Cornell Law School, contains Cornell's American Legal Ethics Library, which links to ethics resources from every state. In addition, Cornell has commissioned lengthy narratives about the legal ethics rules in about eighteen states, including most of the largest states (though most are unfortunately not kept up to date).

www.legalethicsforum.com: This free site is a legal ethics blog at which many law professors and practitioners who work in the field of professional responsibility (including all three co-authors of this book) describe and comment on new developments and interesting news stories relevant to the regulation of lawyers.

www.legalethics.com: This website concentrates on the ethics of electronic communications and posts important new developments in that area on its home page. The site also links to resources from every state and to many other useful sources.

www.americanbar.org/groups/criminal_justice/policy/standards.html: This website, which is maintained by the ABA Criminal Justice Section, contains links to all of the ABA Standards for Criminal Justice, which we often cite and sometimes quote in our Related Materials following each ABA Model Rule of Professional Conduct.

www.lawprofessors.typepad.com/legal_profession: This blog, known as the Legal Profession Blog, covers various issues relating to the legal profession and legal ethics, and is a particularly good source of information for new developments in the area of lawyer discipline.

Areas of Regulation Deserving Special Attention

Several areas of variation among the ABA Model Rules of Professional Conduct and most state ethics rules deserve special attention. These areas include confidentiality, corporate representation, multijurisdictional practice, and lawyer advertising and solicitation. ABA Model Rules 1.6, 1.8(b), 1.9(c), 1.13(c), 3.3, and 4.1(b) prominently address confidentiality issues. Rule 1.13 addresses the responsibilities of a lawyer whose client is an organization. Rules 5.5 and 8.5 address multijurisdictional practice. Rules 7.1 through 7.6 concern advertising, solicitation, and other methods for marketing legal services.

Other areas in which we see significant variation among jurisdictions include conflicts of interest (Rules 1.7, 1.8, 1.9, 1.10, 1.11, 1.12, 1.13, and 1.18); fairness to opposing parties and counsel (Rule 3.4); relationships between lawyers and non-lawyers (Rule 5.4); and pro bono service (Rule 6.1).

Two dominant concerns underlie the provisions containing these variations. The first concern is the proper scope of the lawyer's loyalty to current and former clients, including the scope of the lawyer's duty to protect client confidential information. Competing demands on this loyalty come from the justice system, third persons, other clients, and the lawyer's personal or financial interests.

The second concern is competition, both from within and from outside the profession, in marketing and profiting from legal services. One question is whether nonlawyers should be permitted to invest in or share profits from organizations that sell legal services for a profit. This question brings up competition between lawyers and persons or entities outside the legal profession. Another question is what limits should be placed on the ways in which lawyers compete with other lawyers. This question addresses issues of lawyer advertising and solicitation.

Another issue, which was fiercely debated within the ABA in the early 1990s, was whether lawyers should be permitted to own "ancillary" non-law businesses (such as title insurance companies, investment advisors, and real estate developers) that serve both clients and non-clients. By a slim vote, the ABA said "no" when it originally adopted Rule 5.7 in 1991. But only a year later, again by a thin margin, the ABA repealed Rule 5.7. In 1994, the ABA adopted a redrafted version of Rule 5.7 that permits lawyers to own ancillary non-law businesses if the lawyers satisfy certain conditions. The 1994 rule remains in effect today.

Some Special Features of Our Book

The areas of special concern that we have just identified generated controversy within the legal profession prior to adoption of the Model Rules, and they have generated the most frequent and pronounced variations among the states. But other provisions of the ABA Model Rules have sparked serious debate during the drafting phase and have resulted in disagreements among the states. Every ABA Model Rule has its own history, and U.S. jurisdictions have put many twists on each ABA Model Rule. Moreover, the ABA continuously studies and monitors the rules to determine whether amendments or new rules are needed, and various committees, commissions, and task forces within and outside of the ABA frequently suggest amendments and new rules. In addition, many sources other than the ABA Model Rules directly or indirectly regulate or influence the conduct of lawyers.

To capture the history, complexity, context, and variety of the ABA Model Rules and their state counterparts, we have developed many special features for this book. Here are the most important of these special features:

- ***Editors' Introductions.*** At the beginning of each set of materials in this book, we have written an Editors' Introduction that provides an overview of the materials in the chapter and alerts readers to any significant changes since our last edition and to pending or anticipated proposals for significant change.
- ***Editors' Notes.*** To provide background or to highlight changes to particular items, we have written Editors' Notes throughout the book.
- ***Canon and Code Antecedents.*** The ABA has been drafting rules of ethics for the legal profession for more than 100 years. The earlier efforts (the 1908 Canons of Professional Ethics and the 1969 Code of Professional Responsibility) often differ sharply from the current ABA Model Rules, but they also often reveal common and enduring themes. After each

ABA Model Rule, therefore, we unlock this history by quoting the most closely related provisions from the ABA Canons of Professional Ethics and by citing the most closely related provisions of the old Model Code of Professional Responsibility. (The Disciplinary Rules of the Model Code are reprinted in full later in this volume.)

- ***Cross-References in Other Rules.*** The meaning and impact of a given ABA Model Rule are often illuminated by the number and content of cross-references to that rule elsewhere in the Model Rules. After each ABA Model Rule, therefore, we have compiled a complete list of "Cross-References in Other Rules." This list quotes every other place in the Rules and Comments where the rule at hand is mentioned.
- ***Legislative History.*** Alternative ways of phrasing the Model Rules are difficult to imagine in the abstract, but they become concrete when we examine earlier drafts of the same rule and read ABA committee reports supporting and explaining specific amendments since the Model Rules were originally adopted. We have therefore sifted through the four major drafts circulated by the Kutak Commission (which drafted the original ABA Model Rules between 1977 and 1983), as well as the comprehensive proposals by the ABA Ethics 2000 Commission (which reviewed the rules from 1997 to 2002), and we have assembled interesting variations showing what might have been. In our Legislative History following each Model Rule, we excerpt each Kutak Commission draft and each Ethics 2000 proposal that differs significantly from the rule now in force. Our Legislative History also frequently provides the text of a rule as originally adopted, or notes significant differences between the original version and the current version. Perhaps most important, our Legislative History describes *every* amendment and proposed amendment to each Model Rule since the Model Rules were originally adopted in 1983, and we often reprint excerpts from ABA committee reports submitted in support of proposed amendments.
- ***Selected State Variations.*** The ABA Model Rules are not binding on the states in any way, so each state is free to accept, reject, or modify the ABA Model Rules. The states have taken advantage of this freedom by adopting rules that reflect local conditions, politics, and values. Because the states differ sharply from the ABA and from each other, after each ABA Model Rule we gather Selected State Variations that differ in important ways from the equivalent ABA Model Rule. These variations are by no means comprehensive or exhaustive. Rather, they merely illustrate some possible alternative approaches to a particular issue. We have drawn these variations from dozens of jurisdictions, large and small, but we have systematically compared the ABA Model Rules to the ethics rules in the following 16 jurisdictions: Arizona, California, the District of Columbia, Florida, Georgia, Illinois, Massachusetts, Michigan, Missouri, New Jersey, New York, North Carolina, Ohio, Pennsylvania, Texas, and Virginia. If the Selected State Variations after

a particular ABA Model Rule do not point out any differences between the ABA Model Rule and the rules of one of these 16 jurisdictions, that generally means that the jurisdiction's rule is identical to or substantially similar to the equivalent ABA Model Rule. We also frequently describe variations in states that have amended their rules since our last edition went to press about a year ago, or in which amendments are scheduled to take effect before our next edition goes to press about a year from now. This wide variety of samples from different jurisdictions should dispel any notion that the ABA Model Rules of Professional Conduct are "the rules" of professional conduct. The ABA Model Rules have been and continue to be highly influential, but the ABA is only one voice among many on the subject of professional conduct rules for lawyers.

- ***Related Materials.*** Just as the ABA Model Rules of Professional Conduct are only one voice among many, so the rules of legal ethics adopted by the states are just one of many sources of regulation and guidance for the legal profession. Many other authorities and resources—some binding and some merely advisory—influence or mandate the conduct of lawyers. Among these other sources are state and federal statutes and court rules, common law doctrines, federal regulations, the United States Constitution, ethics opinions, ABA entities that regularly deal with particular types of issues (*e.g.*, the ABA Commission on Lawyer Assistance Programs or the ABA Commission on Multijurisdictional Practice), and United States Supreme Court cases. In addition, competing codes and guidelines have been drafted by other groups to guide lawyers in all areas of practice (*e.g.*, the Restatement of the Law Governing Lawyers), or to guide lawyers in particular fields of law (*e.g.*, the ABA Standards for Criminal Justice). Finally, our Related Materials always cite the most comparable provisions of the American Law Institute's Restatement of the Law Governing Lawyers and the most relevant ABA formal ethics opinions.
- ***Updated Index.*** At the end of the ABA Model Rules, we include an index updated to reflect all amendments through our press date. We have based this index on the index prepared by the ABA Center for Professional Responsibility, but we have added some of our own index terms as well.

Finally, judges are subject to special regulations beyond those that govern practicing lawyers. Some of these are in statutory law, while others are in state codes of judicial conduct. This book therefore includes a selection of judicial conduct materials, including the 2007 ABA Model Code of Judicial Conduct (which is the most recent version) and two federal statutes

(28 U.S.C. §§ 144 and 455) governing disqualification and discipline of federal judges.

We always appreciate news about developments and proposals in the field of legal ethics. If you have news about developments in the field of legal ethics, please contact us by e-mail at *stephen.gillers@nyu.edu, roy.simon@hofstra.edu,* and *aperlman@suffolk.edu.*

Stephen Gillers
Roy D. Simon
Andrew M. Perlman

November 2011

Model Codes and Standards

ABA Model Rules of Professional Conduct*
As amended through August 2011

Editors' Introduction. The rules that govern lawyer conduct in the United States are based primarily on the ABA Model Rules of Professional Conduct. Forty-nine states and the District of Columbia have adopted the Model Rules numbering system and most of the language suggested by the Model Rules. California is the lone holdout, having adopted its own system, but even California appears likely to adopt the Model Rules framework and much of its content within the next year.

Students need to understand three important points about the Model Rules. First, although nearly every state has adopted the format and much of the wording of the Model Rules, the Model Rules themselves are not binding on lawyers in any jurisdiction. They are merely suggested rules for each individual state to consider. The courts of each state adopt the jurisdiction's rules of professional conduct, and each state has the power to discipline its own lawyers. The American Bar Association—a voluntary, private organization with no government affiliation—has no power to discipline lawyers and no control over a state's rules of professional conduct beyond the power of persuasion.

Second, no state has adopted all of the ABA Model Rules verbatim. Many states still differ sharply from the ABA—and from each other—with respect to difficult issues, including confidentiality, conflicts of interest, advertising, trust accounts, pro bono service, and business relationships between lawyers and nonlawyers. Moreover, although the highest courts of nearly all jurisdictions have adopted the numbering system of the ABA Model Rules, in about ten jurisdictions the courts have not formally adopted the Comments. Because of all of these variations, no two states have adopted exactly the same ethics rules. Thus, the ABA Model Rules are merely a starting point for discussing

* Copyright ©1983, 1989-2011 by the American Bar Association. All rights reserved. Reprinted with permission of the American Bar Association. Copies of these rules are available from ABA Publishing, 321 North Clark Street, Chicago, IL 60654, or at *www.abanet.org/abastore/*.

the rules of legal ethics and represent only one of many possible approaches to the regulation of lawyers. For this reason, we have compiled "Selected State Variations" after each Model Rule to illustrate divergent approaches that states have taken to particular issues.

Third, although states have adopted different approaches to specific issues, the ABA Model Rules nevertheless reflect a broad consensus about lawyer conduct, including how the rules should be organized and formatted and what topics they should address. This consensus exists because the ABA's House of Delegates, which has the authority to adopt and amend the Model Rules, includes representatives from every state and from many different practice settings. Moreover, many jurisdictions defer to the organization and formatting of the Model Rules to ensure uniformity with other jurisdictions. Thus, although the wording of particular rules varies from state to state, few jurisdictions have added rules on subjects that the ABA Model Rules do not address, and few jurisdictions have declined to adopt more than a handful of the ABA Model Rules.

Historical background. The ABA Model Rules of Professional Conduct represent the third generation in the ABA's long tradition of drafting model ethics codes for the legal profession. In 1908, the ABA promulgated the ABA Canons of Professional Ethics, a broadly worded set of guidelines that most states adopted with few variations. These canons, with periodic amendments, governed the profession for more than 60 years and consisted primarily of general aspirational goals rather than specific legal obligations.

In 1969, after five years of study by a special committee (the Wright Committee), the ABA adopted the ABA Model Code of Professional Responsibility, which was far more specific than the Canons. The Code used a three-part structure: (1) nine "axiomatic" Canons that stated basic principles and themes, (2) numerous "aspirational" Ethical Considerations (ECs) for each Canon, and (3) "mandatory" Disciplinary Rules (DRs) organized by Canon. The Model Code quickly replaced the Canons of Professional Ethics in nearly every state, again with few variations.

The Code's shortcomings—including its confusing structure and its failure to address a number of common ethical problems—soon became apparent. In 1977, only eight years after adopting the Model Code, the ABA appointed another special commission (the Kutak Commission) to recommend revisions to the rules. The Kutak Commission's Chairperson was the late Robert Kutak of Omaha, and its Reporter was Professor Geoffrey Hazard, Jr., then of Yale Law School. The Kutak Commission soon decided that the Model Code should be completely rewritten and reorganized. Between 1979 and 1982, the Kutak Commission circulated four major drafts of its proposed Model Rules of Professional Conduct—the 1979 Unofficial Pre-Circulation Draft, the 1980 Discussion Draft, the 1981 Draft, and the 1982 Draft. After significantly revising some of the proposed rules, the ABA House of Delegates formally adopted the Model Rules in 1983. The rules abandoned the Model Code's confusing three-part formula in favor of a Restatement-style formula, with each black letter rule followed by its own explanatory Comment.

The ABA Ethics 2000 Commission. The ABA Model Rules of Professional Conduct have been amended many times since their original adoption in 1983. From 1987 through 2001, the ABA amended at least one or two Model Rules or Comments nearly every year. By the late 1990s, however, the ABA recognized that a more systematic approach to amending the Rules was required. Changes to the Rules were needed to account for the rapid development of technology, the globalization of the profession, and the extensive debate over the Restatement of the Law Governing Lawyers (which was written between 1986 and 2000). In 1997, therefore, the ABA appointed a new select body, the Ethics 2000 Commission, whose Mission Statement charged it with conducting "a comprehensive study and evaluation of the ethical and professionalism precepts of the legal profession" and "examining and evaluating the ABA Model Rules of Professional Conduct. . . ." The Chair of the Ethics 2000 Commission was the Honorable E. Norman Veasey, then Chief Justice of the State of Delaware. The Commission's Reporters were Professor Nancy Moore (who served as Chief Reporter), Professor Carl Pierce, and Professor Thomas Morgan.

From 1997 to 2001, the Ethics 2000 Commission held public hearings around the country and solicited public comments on various drafts of proposed amendments to the Model Rules. After debating the proposed changes in 2001 and 2002, the ABA House of Delegates adopted nearly all of the changes proposed by the Ethics 2000 Commission. The result was the most comprehensive revision of the Model Rules since their original adoption in 1983. The ABA added three new rules—Rule 1.18 (Duties to Prospective Clients), Rule 2.4 (Lawyer Serving as Third-Party Neutral), and Rule 6.5 (Nonprofit and Court-Annexed Limited Legal Services Programs)—and deleted one old rule, Rule 2.2 (Intermediary). The Ethics 2000 revisions also included scores of significant amendments to the existing Rules and Comments. (For a detailed chart of state-by-state responses and ongoing projects relating to the work of the Ethics 2000 Commission, visit *http://www.americanbar.org/groups/professional_responsibility/policy/ethics_2000_commission.html.*)

The ABA House of Delegates also rejected three of the Ethics 2000 Commission's most controversial proposals. With respect to Rule 1.5 (Fees), the ABA voted against a proposal to require lawyers to put all fee agreements in writing except when the lawyer is charging a "regularly represented client" on the same basis as before, or when the reasonably foreseeable costs and fees in a given matter are $500 or less. With respect to Rule 1.6 (Confidentiality of Information), the ABA voted against a proposal to permit a lawyer to reveal information "to prevent, mitigate or rectify substantial injury to the financial interests or property of another that is reasonably certain to result or has resulted from the client's commission of a crime or fraud in furtherance of which the client has used the lawyer's services." (After the ABA voted against that proposal, the Ethics 2000 Commission withdrew a related proposal that would have permitted lawyers to reveal information necessary to prevent, mitigate, or rectify injury from a client's past financial frauds or crimes in which the lawyer's services had been used.) With respect to Rule 1.10 (Imputation of Conflicts of Interest: General Rule), the ABA rejected a proposal to permit timely screening and written notice to avoid disqualification based on a conflict with a lateral attorney's former client. (As explained below, similar proposals regarding Rule 1.6 and Rule 1.10 were subsequently adopted by the House of Delegates in 2003 and 2009, respectively.)

The 2002 amendments to the Model Rules also included significant changes proposed by the ABA Commission on Multijurisdictional Practice (MJP Commission), which had been appointed in 2000 to study the practice of law by lawyers in jurisdictions where they are not admitted. Specifically, in 2002 the ABA House of Delegates amended both Rule 5.5 (Unauthorized Practice of Law; Multijurisdictional Practice of Law) and Rule 8.5 (Disciplinary Authority; Choice of Law).

Finally, based on a proposal by the ABA's Standing Committee on Ethics and Professional Responsibility, the ABA also amended Rule 7.2 (Advertising) in 2002 by adding a new subparagraph (b)(4), which permits lawyers to enter into nonexclusive reciprocal referral arrangements either with other lawyers or with nonlawyer professionals, provided the client is informed of the arrangement when a referral is made. The amendment was accompanied by a new Comment 8 to Rule 7.2 to explain the reciprocal referral provision, and by an amendment to Comment 1 to Rule 7.5 (Firm Names and Letterheads) branding it "misleading to use . . . the name of a nonlawyer" in a law firm's name.

Amendments since Ethics 2000. Significant changes to the Model Rules of Professional Conduct continued in 2003. In the wake of massive scandals at Enron, WorldCom, and other large corporations, and in the face of pressure from the Securities and Exchange Commission and from Congress's passage of the Sarbanes-Oxley Act of 2002, the ABA significantly amended Rule 1.6 (Confidentiality of Information) and Rule 1.13 (Organization as Client). Specifically, in 2003 the House of Delegates narrowly voted to amend Rule 1.6 by adopting the identical exceptions to confidentiality that the ABA had overwhelmingly rejected only two years earlier. The new paragraphs expanded the circumstances under which a lawyer may reveal client confidential information, especially to prevent, mitigate, or rectify injury from a client's crime or fraud in which the lawyer's services were used or are being used. At the same time, the House of Delegates amended Rule 1.13(b) to create a presumption that a lawyer must "report up" within an organization to expose wrongdoing by a corporate officer or employee, and the House amended Rule 1.13(c) to permit (but not require) a lawyer for an organization to "report out" by revealing client confidences outside the organization when the internal "reporting up" fails to stop certain serious wrongdoing.

Since 2003, there have been two other notable changes to the Model Rules. In 2008, the ABA House of Delegates amended Rule 3.8 and its Comment to impose significant post-conviction responsibilities on prosecutors. And in 2009, the ABA House of Delegates adopted and then fine-tuned significant amendments to Rule 1.10, which now permits law firms, in limited circumstances, to use "screens" to prevent a laterally hired lawyer's conflict of interest from being imputed to the rest of the firm, even without consent from the lateral's former client. This controversial rule change, which the ABA's House of Delegates had rejected during the Ethics 2000 process, will make it easier for law firms to hire attorneys from other private law firms in situations where amended Rule 1.10 applies.

The ABA Commission on Ethics 20/20. Many additional amendments are likely within the next few years. In 2009, ABA President Carolyn Lamm announced the creation of the "Commission on Ethics 20/20." The co-chairs of the Commission are Jamie Gorelick of Washington, D.C. (a former U.S. Deputy Attorney General) and Michael Traynor of California (the President-Emeritus and Chair of the Council of the American Law Institute). Professor Stephen Gillers (a co-author of this book) is a member of the Commission, and Professor Andrew Perlman (another co-author of this book) is the Commission's Chief Reporter. Professors Paul Paton, Anthony Sebok, and Bradley Wendel are also Commission Reporters.

The Commission is reviewing and proposing changes to the ABA Model Rules of Professional Conduct and the American system of lawyer regulation in light of advances in technology and the increasingly global nature of law practice. The Commission has created several working groups, and they have gathered information and developed draft proposals concerning a number of topics, including outsourcing, alternative business structures (such as whether nonlawyers should be permitted to have an equity interest in law firms, as is the case in other parts of the world), confidentiality issues arising from lawyers' use of technology, ethics issues arising from online marketing, choice of law problems due to jurisdictional variations both domestically and internationally, third-party litigation financing, and unauthorized practice issues for foreign attorneys who practice in the United States.

Throughout 2011, the Ethics 20/20 Commission released numerous draft proposals for public comment, as well as issues papers and informational reports, all of which can be found online at *www.americanbar.org/Ethics2020.* The ABA's House of Delegates is expected to vote on the Ethics 20/20 Commission's proposals at the ABA's August 2012 Annual Meeting.

How this book organizes the ABA Model Rules. The version of the ABA Model Rules of Professional Conduct reprinted below reflects all amendments through calendar year 2011. To capture the complexity, history, and variety of these Rules, to illustrate state approaches to the issues, and to put the Rules in context, we use a seven-part format to present each Rule:

(1) *Black letter rule.* The current version of the black letter ABA Model Rule of Professional Conduct;

(2) *Comment.* The official ABA Comment;

(3) *Canon and Code Antecedents,* compiled especially for this book so that readers can trace the ABA's historical treatment of related issues in the ABA Canons of Professional Ethics and the ABA Model Code of Professional Responsibility;

(4) *Cross-References in Other Rules,* compiled especially for this book to show each place in the Rules and Comments where a particular Rule is mentioned in the Model Rules;

(5) *Legislative History of the Model Rule,* compiled especially for this book to describe the four Kutak Commission drafts and the frequent amendments and proposed amendments to particular Rules since their original adoption;

(6) *Selected State Variations,* compiled especially for this book to show some of the ways in which states have diverged from the ABA Model Rules.

We have drawn these variations from many jurisdictions, but we have systematically noted significant differences, if any, between the ABA Model Rules of Professional Conduct and the ethics rules in the following 16 jurisdictions: Arizona, California, the District of Columbia, Florida, Georgia, Illinois, Massachusetts, Michigan, Missouri, New Jersey, New York, North Carolina, Ohio, Pennsylvania, Texas, and Virginia. (If the Selected State Variations after a particular ABA Model Rule do not point out any differences between the ABA Model Rule and the rules of one of these 16 jurisdictions, that generally means that the jurisdiction's rule is the same or substantially the same as the ABA Model Rule.); and

(7) *Related Materials,* compiled especially for this book to show such things as cross-references to equivalent sections of the Restatement of the Law Governing Lawyers (which is reprinted later in this volume), descriptions of ABA entities and national organizations that regularly deal with particular types of issues, and references to statutes, cases, ABA ethics opinions, and other items that may shed light on a particular Rule.

Finally, at the end of the ABA Model Rules, we include an index updated to reflect all amendments through 2011.

For extensive historical materials regarding the ABA Model Rules of Professional Conduct, including commission reports, summaries of House of Delegates actions, written testimony from public hearings, minutes of commission meetings, and other materials documenting the work of the Ethics 2000 Commission, the Commission on Multijurisdictional Practice, and other ABA commissions, committees, and task forces, and for updated information about the ABA Model Rules, including the ongoing work of the Ethics 20/20 Commission, visit the website of the ABA Center for Professional Responsibility at *http://www.americanbar.org/groups/professional_responsibility.html.*

Contents

PREAMBLE: A LAWYER'S RESPONSIBILITIES

[1] A lawyer, as a member of the legal profession, is a representative of clients, an officer of the legal system and a public citizen having special responsibility for the quality of justice.

[2] As a representative of clients, a lawyer performs various functions. As advisor, a lawyer provides a client with an informed understanding of the client's legal rights and obligations and explains their practical implications. As advocate, a lawyer zealously asserts the client's position under the rules of the adversary system. As negotiator, a lawyer seeks a result advantageous to the client but consistent with requirements of honest dealings with others. As an evaluator, a lawyer acts by examining a client's legal affairs and reporting about them to the client or to others.

[3] In addition to these representational functions, a lawyer may serve as a third-party neutral, a nonrepresentational role helping the parties to resolve a dispute or other matter. Some of these Rules apply directly to lawyers who are or have served as third-party neutrals. See, e.g., Rules 1.12 and 2.4. In addition, there are

Rules that apply to lawyers who are not active in the practice of law or to practicing lawyers even when they are acting in a nonprofessional capacity. For example, a lawyer who commits fraud in the conduct of a business is subject to discipline for engaging in conduct involving dishonesty, fraud, deceit or misrepresentation. See Rule 8.4.

[4] In all professional functions a lawyer should be competent, prompt and diligent. A lawyer should maintain communication with a client concerning the representation. A lawyer should keep in confidence information relating to representation of a client except so far as disclosure is required or permitted by the Rules of Professional Conduct or other law.

[5] A lawyer's conduct should conform to the requirements of the law, both in professional service to clients and in the lawyer's business and personal affairs. A lawyer should use the law's procedures only for legitimate purposes and not to harass or intimidate others. A lawyer should demonstrate respect for the legal system and for those who serve it, including judges, other lawyers and public officials. While it is a lawyer's duty, when necessary, to challenge the rectitude of official action, it is also a lawyer's duty to uphold legal process.

[6] As a public citizen, a lawyer should seek improvement of the law, access to the legal system, the administration of justice and the quality of service rendered by the legal profession. As a member of a learned profession, a lawyer should cultivate knowledge of the law beyond its use for clients, employ that knowledge in reform of the law and work to strengthen legal education. In addition, a lawyer should further the public's understanding of and confidence in the rule of law and the justice system because legal institutions in a constitutional democracy depend on popular participation and support to maintain their authority. A lawyer should be mindful of deficiencies in the administration of justice and of the fact that the poor, and sometimes persons who are not poor, cannot afford adequate legal assistance. Therefore, all lawyers should devote professional time and resources and use civic influence to ensure equal access to our system of justice for all those who because of economic or social barriers cannot afford or secure adequate legal counsel. A lawyer should aid the legal profession in pursuing these objectives and should help the bar regulate itself in the public interest.

[7] Many of a lawyer's professional responsibilities are prescribed in the Rules of Professional Conduct, as well as substantive and procedural law. However, a lawyer is also guided by personal conscience and the approbation of professional peers. A lawyer should strive to attain the highest level of skill, to improve the law and the legal profession and to exemplify the legal profession's ideals of public service.

[8] A lawyer's responsibilities as a representative of clients, an officer of the legal system and a public citizen are usually harmonious. Thus, when an opposing party is well represented, a lawyer can be a zealous advocate on behalf of a client and at the same time assume that justice is being done. So also, a lawyer can be sure that preserving client confidences ordinarily serves the public interest because people are more likely to seek legal advice, and thereby heed their legal obligations, when they know their communications will be private.

[9] In the nature of law practice, however, conflicting responsibilities are encountered. Virtually all difficult ethical problems arise from conflict between a lawyer's responsibilities to clients, to the legal system and to the lawyer's own interest in remaining an ethical person while earning a satisfactory living. The Rules of Professional Conduct often prescribe terms for resolving such conflicts. Within the

framework of these Rules, however, many difficult issues of professional discretion can arise. Such issues must be resolved through the exercise of sensitive professional and moral judgment guided by the basic principles underlying the Rules. These principles include the lawyer's obligation zealously to protect and pursue a client's legitimate interests, within the bounds of the law, while maintaining a professional, courteous and civil attitude toward all persons involved in the legal system.

[10] The legal profession is largely self-governing. Although other professions also have been granted powers of self-government, the legal profession is unique in this respect because of the close relationship between the profession and the processes of government and law enforcement. This connection is manifested in the fact that ultimate authority over the legal profession is vested largely in the courts.

[11] To the extent that lawyers meet the obligations of their professional calling, the occasion for government regulation is obviated. Self-regulation also helps maintain the legal profession's independence from government domination. An independent legal profession is an important force in preserving government under law, for abuse of legal authority is more readily challenged by a profession whose members are not dependent on government for the right to practice.

[12] The legal profession's relative autonomy carries with it special responsibilities of self-government. The profession has a responsibility to assure that its regulations are conceived in the public interest and not in furtherance of parochial or self-interested concerns of the bar. Every lawyer is responsible for observance of the Rules of Professional Conduct. A lawyer should also aid in securing their observance by other lawyers. Neglect of these responsibilities compromises the independence of the profession and the public interest which it serves.

[13] Lawyers play a vital role in the preservation of society. The fulfillment of this role requires an understanding by lawyers of their relationship to our legal system. The Rules of Professional Conduct, when properly applied, serve to define that relationship.

SCOPE

[14] The Rules of Professional Conduct are rules of reason. They should be interpreted with reference to the purposes of legal representation and of the law itself. Some of the Rules are imperatives, cast in the terms "shall" or "shall not." These define proper conduct for purposes of professional discipline. Others, generally cast in the term "may," are permissive and define areas under the Rules in which the lawyer has discretion to exercise professional judgment. No disciplinary action should be taken when the lawyer chooses not to act or acts within the bounds of such discretion. Other Rules define the nature of relationships between the lawyer and others. The Rules are thus partly obligatory and disciplinary and partly constitutive and descriptive in that they define a lawyer's professional role. Many of the Comments use the term "should." Comments do not add obligations to the Rules but provide guidance for practicing in compliance with the Rules.

[15] The Rules presuppose a larger legal context shaping the lawyer's role. That context includes court rules and statutes relating to matters of licensure, laws defining specific obligations of lawyers and substantive and procedural law in

general. The Comments are sometimes used to alert lawyers to their responsibilities under such other law.

[16] Compliance with the Rules, as with all law in an open society, depends primarily upon understanding and voluntary compliance, secondarily upon reinforcement by peer and public opinion and finally, when necessary, upon enforcement through disciplinary proceedings. The Rules do not, however, exhaust the moral and ethical considerations that should inform a lawyer, for no worthwhile human activity can be completely defined by legal rules. The Rules simply provide a framework for the ethical practice of law.

[17] Furthermore, for purposes of determining the lawyer's authority and responsibility, principles of substantive law external to these Rules determine whether a client-lawyer relationship exists. Most of the duties flowing from the client-lawyer relationship attach only after the client has requested the lawyer to render legal services and the lawyer has agreed to do so. But there are some duties, such as that of confidentiality under Rule 1.6, that attach when the lawyer agrees to consider whether a client-lawyer relationship shall be established. See Rule 1.18. Whether a client-lawyer relationship exists for any specific purpose can depend on the circumstances and may be a question of fact.

[18] Under various legal provisions, including constitutional, statutory and common law, the responsibilities of government lawyers may include authority concerning legal matters that ordinarily reposes in the client in private client-lawyer relationships. For example, a lawyer for a government agency may have authority on behalf of the government to decide upon settlement or whether to appeal from an adverse judgment. Such authority in various respects is generally vested in the attorney general and the state's attorney in state government, and their federal counterparts, and the same may be true of other government law officers. Also, lawyers under the supervision of these officers may be authorized to represent several government agencies in intragovernmental legal controversies in circumstances where a private lawyer could not represent multiple private clients. These Rules do not abrogate any such authority.

[19] Failure to comply with an obligation or prohibition imposed by a Rule is a basis for invoking the disciplinary process. The Rules presuppose that disciplinary assessment of a lawyer's conduct will be made on the basis of the facts and circumstances as they existed at the time of the conduct in question and in recognition of the fact that a lawyer often has to act upon uncertain or incomplete evidence of the situation. Moreover, the Rules presuppose that whether or not discipline should be imposed for a violation, and the severity of a sanction, depend on all the circumstances, such as the willfulness and seriousness of the violation, extenuating factors and whether there have been previous violations.

[20] Violation of a Rule should not itself give rise to a cause of action against a lawyer nor should it create any presumption in such a case that a legal duty has been breached. In addition, violation of a Rule does not necessarily warrant any other nondisciplinary remedy, such as disqualification of a lawyer in pending litigation. The Rules are designed to provide guidance to lawyers and to provide a structure for regulating conduct through disciplinary agencies. They are not designed to be a basis for civil liability. Furthermore, the purpose of the Rules can be subverted when they are invoked by opposing parties as procedural weapons. The fact that a Rule is a just basis for a lawyer's self-assessment, or for sanctioning a lawyer under

the administration of a disciplinary authority, does not imply that an antagonist in a collateral proceeding or transaction has standing to seek enforcement of the Rule. Nevertheless, since the Rules do establish standards of conduct by lawyers, a lawyer's violation of a Rule may be evidence of breach of the applicable standard of conduct.

[21] The Comment accompanying each Rule explains and illustrates the meaning and purpose of the Rule. The Preamble and this note on Scope provide general orientation. The Comments are intended as guides to interpretation, but the text of each Rule is authoritative.

Canon and Code Antecedents

ABA Canons of Professional Ethics*: The Preamble to the ABA Canons (which had no separate Scope section) provided as follows:

> In America, where the stability of Courts and of all departments of government rests upon the approval of the people, it is peculiarly essential that the system for establishing and dispensing Justice be developed to a high point of efficiency and so maintained that the public shall have absolute confidence in the integrity and impartiality of its administration. The future of the Republic, to a great extent, depends upon our maintenance of Justice pure and unsullied. It cannot be so maintained unless the conduct and the motives of the members of our profession are such as to merit the approval of all just men.
>
> No code or set of rules can be framed, which will particularize all the duties of the lawyer in the varying phases of litigation or in all the relations of professional life. The following canons of ethics are adopted by the American Bar Association as a general guide, yet the enumeration of particular duties should not be construed as a denial of the existence of others equally imperative, though not specifically mentioned.

ABA Model Code of Professional Responsibility: Compare Preamble and Preliminary Statement (reprinted later in this volume).

Cross-References in Other Rules

Scope ¶1; 21: "The Comment accompanying each Rule explains and illustrates the meaning and purpose of the Rule. The **Preamble** and this note on Scope provide general orientation. The Comments are intended as guides to interpretation, but the text of each Rule is authoritative."

Rule 1.6, Comment 3: "A lawyer may not disclose such information except as authorized or required by the Rules of Professional Conduct or other law. See also **Scope**."

Rule 1.7, Comment 3: "As to whether a client-lawyer relationship exists or, having once been established, is continuing, see Comment to Rule 1.3 and **Scope**."

* This and all other excerpts from the ABA Canons of Professional Ethics have been reprinted with permission of the American Bar Association. Copyright © 1956 by the American Bar Association. All rights reserved.

Rule 1.13, Comment 9: "Defining precisely the identity of the client and prescribing the resulting obligations of such lawyers may be more difficult in the government context and is a matter beyond the scope of these Rules. See **Scope** [18].... In addition, duties of lawyers employed by the government or lawyers in military service may be defined by statutes and regulation. This Rule does not limit that authority. See **Scope**."

Legislative History of Preamble and Scope

1980 Discussion Draft contained the following Preface:

> The decade past has witnessed an extraordinary concern with professional responsibility. Barely 10 years ago, the American Bar Association adopted its Model Code of Professional Responsibility, the product of a committee chaired by Edward L. Wright. . . . [I]n every sphere one finds searching inquiry into the meaning of professionally responsible conduct.
>
> That inquiry has led to reconsideration of the Model Code, the creation of the Commission on Evaluation of Professional Standards, and, finally, the development of this document—the Discussion Draft of the Model Rules of Professional Conduct.
>
> In reconsidering the concepts of professional standards, the Commission soon realized that more than a series of amendments or a general restatement of the Model Code of Professional Responsibility was in order. The Commission determined that a comprehensive reformulation was required. We have built on the Code's foundation, but we make no apology for having pushed beyond it.

1983 Rules: Most of the Preamble and Scope in the 1983 version were essentially the same as the 2002 version, but the 1983 version contained the following sentence regarding government lawyers near the end of what is now paragraph 18: "They also may have authority to represent the 'public interest' in circumstances where a private lawyer would not be authorized to do so." In addition, paragraph 20 (then paragraph 18) ended with the following sentence rather than the last sentence of the 2002 version: "Accordingly, nothing in the Rule should be deemed to augment any substantive legal duty of lawyers or the extra-disciplinary consequences of violating such a duty." Finally, the 1983 version contained the following two paragraphs that were entirely deleted in 2002:

> [19] Moreover, these Rules are not intended to govern or affect judicial application of either the attorney-client or work product privilege. Those privileges were developed to promote compliance with law and fairness in litigation. In reliance on the attorney-client privilege, clients are entitled to expect that communications within the scope of the privilege will be protected against compelled disclosure. The attorney-client privilege is that of the client and not of the lawyer. The fact that in exceptional situations the lawyer under the rules has a limited discretion to disclose a client confidence does not vitiate the proposition that, as a general matter, the client has a reasonable expectation that information relating to the client will not be voluntarily disclosed and that disclosure of such information may be judicially compelled only in accordance with recognized exceptions to the attorney-client and work product privileges.
>
> [20] The lawyer's exercise of discretion not to disclose information under Rule 1.6 should not be subject to reexamination. Permitting such reexamination would be incompatible with the general policy of promoting compliance with law through assurances that communications will be protected against disclosure.

2002 Amendments: At its February 2002 Mid-Year Meeting, the ABA House of Delegates adopted without change the ABA Ethics 2000 Commission proposal to amend the Preamble and Scope of the Model Rules of Professional Conduct. Most noteworthy were the addition of paragraph 3, the last sentence in paragraph 9, and the second and last sentences in paragraph 20, plus the deletion of paragraphs 19 and 20 of the former version of the Scope.

Selected State Variations

Arkansas adds the following paragraph to the Preamble:

> [13A] A lawyer owes a solemn duty to uphold the integrity and honor of the profession; to encourage respect for the law and for the courts; to act as a member of a learned profession; to conduct affairs so as to reflect credit on the legal profession; and to inspire the confidence, respect and trust of clients and the public. To accomplish those objectives, the lawyer must strive to avoid not only professional impropriety, but also the appearance of impropriety. The duty to avoid the appearance of impropriety is not a mere phrase. It is part of the foundation upon which are built the rules that guide lawyers in their moral and ethical conduct. This obligation should be considered in any instance where a violation of the rules of professional conduct are at issue. The principle pervades these Rules and embodies their spirit.

Colorado: Paragraph 20 of the Scope section provides that, since the Rules establish standards of conduct by lawyers, "in appropriate cases" a lawyer's violation of a Rule may be evidence of breach of the applicable standard of conduct.

Connecticut omits several sentences of paragraph 6 of the Preamble but restores all of paragraphs 19 and 20 from the 1983 version of the Scope section (see Legislative History above).

Delaware, Kansas, North Carolina, Oklahoma, and ***Virginia*** omit the last sentence of paragraph 20 ("since the Rules do establish standards of conduct by lawyers, a lawyer's violation of a Rule may be evidence of breach of the applicable standard of conduct").

District of Columbia deletes the Preamble entirely and compresses the Scope. The D.C. equivalent to paragraph 20 provides as follows:

> Nothing in these Rules, the Comments associated with them, or this Scope section is intended to enlarge or restrict existing law regarding the liability of lawyers to others or the requirements that the testimony of expert witnesses or other modes of proof must be employed in determining the scope of a lawyer's duty to others. Moreover, nothing in the Rules or associated Comments or this Scope section is intended to confer rights on an adversary of a lawyer to enforce the Rules in a proceeding other than a disciplinary proceeding. A tribunal presented with claims that the conduct of a lawyer appearing before that tribunal requires, for example, disqualification of the lawyer and/or the lawyer's firm may take such action as seems appropriate in the circumstances, which may or may not involve disqualification.

The next paragraph of the D.C. Scope section, which has no equivalent in the ABA Model Rules, states standards and principles for interpreting the Rules, including the following:

> In interpreting these Rules, the specific shall control the general in the sense that any rule that specifically addresses conduct shall control the disposition of matters

and the outcome of such matters shall not turn upon the application of a more general rule that arguably also applies. [C]ompliance with one rule does not generally excuse compliance with other rules. Accordingly, once a lawyer has analyzed the ethical considerations under a given rule, the lawyer must generally extend the analysis to ensure compliance with all other applicable rules.

Florida omits paragraph 18 of the ABA Scope section, and replaces paragraphs 12 and 13 of the ABA Preamble with the following:

> Lawyers are officers of the court and they are responsible to the judiciary for the propriety of their professional activities. Within that context, the legal profession has been granted powers of self-government. Self-regulation helps maintain the legal profession's independence from undue government domination. An independent legal profession is an important force in preserving government under law, for abuse of legal authority is more readily challenged by a profession whose members are not dependent on the executive and legislative branches of government for the right to practice. Supervision by an independent judiciary, and conformity with the rules the judiciary adopts for the profession, assures both independence and responsibility.
>
> Thus, every lawyer is responsible for observance of the Rules of Professional Conduct. A lawyer should also aid in securing their observance by other lawyers. Neglect of these responsibilities compromises the independence of the profession and the public interest that it serves.

Illinois deletes a portion of paragraph 6 and adds paragraphs 6A and 6B, which address a lawyer's responsibilities to perform pro bono work. Paragraph 6A specifically references Illinois Supreme Court Rule 756(f), which requires lawyers to disclose on their annual registration form the approximate amount of pro bono work that they performed in the past year. (See also the Illinois entry under Rule 6.1.)

Maryland replaces the last sentence of paragraph 20 by saying that "nothing in this Preamble and Scope is intended to detract from the holdings of the Court of Appeals in *Post v. Bregman*, 349 Md. 142 (1998), and *Son v. Margolius, Mallios, Davis, Rider & Tomar*, 349 Md. 441 (1998)."

Massachusetts: The Scope section, quoting case precedent, provides that "if a plaintiff can demonstrate that a disciplinary rule was intended to protect one in his position, a violation of that rule may be some evidence of the attorney's negligence."

Michigan: Rule 1.0(b), which is comparable to paragraph 20 of the Scope section in the ABA Model Rules, provides as follows:

> Failure to comply with an obligation or prohibition imposed by a rule is a basis for invoking the disciplinary process. The rules do not, however, give rise to a cause of action for enforcement of a rule or for damages caused by failure to comply with an obligation or prohibition imposed by a rule. In a civil or criminal action, the admissibility of the Rules of Professional Conduct is governed by the Michigan Rules of Evidence and other provisions of law.

Missouri: Missouri replaces the last sentence of ABA paragraph 20 with the following sentence taken verbatim from the pre-2002 version of the ABA Scope section: "Accordingly, nothing in the Rules should be deemed to augment any substantive legal duty of lawyers or the extra-disciplinary consequences of violating such a duty."

Nevada: Nevada omits the ABA Preamble but adds a new Rule 1.0A entitled "Guidelines for Interpreting the Nevada Rules of Professional Conduct," which begins by saying, "The preamble and comments to the ABA Model Rules of Professional Conduct are not enacted by this Rule but may be consulted for guidance in interpreting and applying the Nevada Rules of Professional Conduct, unless there is a conflict between the Nevada Rules and the preamble or comments." Rule 1.0A then incorporates language from paragraphs 14, 17, 19, and 20 of the Scope section of the ABA Model Rules as guides for interpreting the Nevada Rules.

New Hampshire replaces the entire ABA Preamble and Scope with a "Statement of Purpose" that includes parts of ABA paragraphs 14 and 20 but is otherwise unique to New Hampshire. A special New Hampshire Comment explains that New Hampshire has rejected the ABA Preamble and Scope because of the following perceived "defects" in the ABA language:

> Much of the Preamble and Scope consists of imprecise restatements or summaries of the Rules, which are generally unnecessary, potentially confusing, or both. . . .
>
> Portions of the Preamble and Scope are aspirational in nature, which runs the risk of converting goals into mandates. The Rules will succeed better if the distinction between worthy aspirations and basic mandates is kept clear.
>
> The length and lack of clarity in the wording of the Preamble and Scope materially diminish their utility to their readers.

New York: The Preamble and Scope contain only ten paragraphs, omitting many paragraphs that appear in the Model Rules. Of particular note is a change to paragraph 2. Rather than urging lawyers to "zealously" assert a client's position, the paragraph provides as follows:

> The touchstone of the client-lawyer relationship is the lawyer's obligation to assert the client's position under the rules of the adversary system, to maintain the client's confidential information except in limited circumstances, and to act with loyalty during the period of the representation.

Ohio: In its Preamble, Ohio eliminates paragraphs 7 and 8, most of paragraphs 9 and 10, and all of paragraphs 12 and 13 of the ABA version of the Preamble.

Oklahoma: At the end of paragraph 20, Oklahoma restores all of former paragraphs 19 and 20 from the 1983 version of the ABA Scope section—see Legislative History above.

Pennsylvania adds the following sentences to its Scope section: "The Rules omit some provisions that appear in the ABA Model Rules of Professional Conduct. The omissions should not be interpreted as condoning behavior proscribed by the omitted provision."

Related Materials

ABA Formal Ethics Opinions: See ABA Formal Ethics Ops. 90-358 (1990), 92-365 (1992), 92-366 (1992), 92-368 (1992) (withdrawn), 95-390 (1995), 96-400 (1996), 96-403 (1996), 97-407 (1997), 98-411 (1998), 00-417 (2000), 02-425 (2002), 04-433 (2004), 06-440 (2006), and 08-453 (2008).

IRS Regulations: The regulations governing practice before the IRS are found at 31 C.F.R. Part 10 (often called "Circular 230"). Section 10.0, entitled "Scope of Part," begins as follows: "This part contains rules governing the recognition of attorneys, certified public accountants, enrolled agents, and other persons representing taxpayers before the Internal Revenue Service." When the final regulations were published, see 69 Fed. Reg. 75839 (2004), the Federal Register included the following overall "Explanation of Provisions":

> Tax advisors play a critical role in the Federal tax system, which is founded on principles of compliance and voluntary self-assessment. The tax system is best served when the public has confidence in the honesty and integrity of the professionals providing tax advice. To restore, promote, and maintain the public's confidence in those individuals and firms, these final regulations set forth best practices applicable to all tax advisors. These regulations also provide mandatory requirements for practitioners who provide covered opinions. The scope of these regulations is limited to practice before the IRS. These regulations do not alter or supplant other ethical standards applicable to practitioners.

Restatement of the Law Governing Lawyers: The Restatement has no direct equivalent to the ABA Preamble or Scope, but it does contain a brief Introduction.

ARTICLE 1. CLIENT-LAWYER RELATIONSHIP

Rule 1.0 Terminology

(a) "Belief" or "believes" denotes that the person involved actually supposed the fact in question to be true. A person's belief may be inferred from circumstances.

(b) "Confirmed in writing," when used in reference to the informed consent of a person, denotes informed consent that is given in writing by the person or a writing that a lawyer promptly transmits to the person confirming an oral informed consent. See paragraph (e) for the definition of "informed consent." If it is not feasible to obtain or transmit the writing at the time the person gives informed consent, then the lawyer must obtain or transmit it within a reasonable time thereafter.

(c) "Firm" or "law firm" denotes a lawyer or lawyers in a law partnership, professional corporation, sole proprietorship or other association authorized to practice law; or lawyers employed in a legal services organization or the legal department of a corporation or other organization.

(d) "Fraud" or "fraudulent" denotes conduct that is fraudulent under the substantive or procedural law of the applicable jurisdiction and has a purpose to deceive.

(e) "Informed consent" denotes the agreement by a person to a proposed course of conduct after the lawyer has communicated adequate information and explanation about the material risks of and reasonably available alternatives to the proposed course of conduct.

(f) "Knowingly," "known," or "knows" denotes actual knowledge of the fact in question. A person's knowledge may be inferred from circumstances.

(g) "Partner" denotes a member of a partnership, a shareholder in a law firm organized as a professional corporation, or a member of an association authorized to practice law.

(h) "Reasonable" or "reasonably" when used in relation to conduct by a lawyer denotes the conduct of a reasonably prudent and competent lawyer.

(i) "Reasonable belief" or "reasonably believes" when used in reference to a lawyer denotes that the lawyer believes the matter in question and that the circumstances are such that the belief is reasonable.

(j) "Reasonably should know" when used in reference to a lawyer denotes that a lawyer of reasonable prudence and competence would ascertain the matter in question.

(k) "Screened" denotes the isolation of a lawyer from any participation in a matter through the timely imposition of procedures within a firm that are reasonably adequate under the circumstances to protect information that the isolated lawyer is obligated to protect under these Rules or other law.

(l) "Substantial" when used in reference to degree or extent denotes a material matter of clear and weighty importance.

(m) "Tribunal" denotes a court, an arbitrator in a binding arbitration proceeding or a legislative body, administrative agency or other body acting in an adjudicative capacity. A legislative body, administrative agency or other body acts in an adjudicative capacity when a neutral official, after the presentation of evidence or legal argument by a party or parties, will render a binding legal judgment directly affecting a party's interests in a particular matter.

(n) "Writing" or "written" denotes a tangible or electronic record of a communication or representation, including handwriting, typewriting, printing, photostating, photography, audio or video recording and e-mail. A "signed" writing includes an electronic sound, symbol or process attached to or logically associated with a writing and executed or adopted by a person with the intent to sign the writing.

COMMENT

Confirmed in Writing

[1] If it is not feasible to obtain or transmit a written confirmation at the time the client gives informed consent, then the lawyer must obtain or transmit it within a reasonable time thereafter. If a lawyer has obtained a client's informed consent, the lawyer may act in reliance on that consent so long as it is confirmed in writing within a reasonable time thereafter.

Firm

[2] Whether two or more lawyers constitute a firm within paragraph (c) can depend on the specific facts. For example, two practitioners who share office space and occasionally consult or assist each other ordinarily would not be regarded as constituting a firm. However, if they present themselves to the public in a way that suggests that they are a firm or conduct themselves as a firm, they should be regarded as a firm for purposes of the Rules. The terms of any formal agreement between associated lawyers are relevant in determining whether they are a firm, as

is the fact that they have mutual access to information concerning the clients they serve. Furthermore, it is relevant in doubtful cases to consider the underlying purpose of the Rule that is involved. A group of lawyers could be regarded as a firm for purposes of the Rule that the same lawyer should not represent opposing parties in litigation, while it might not be so regarded for purposes of the Rule that information acquired by one lawyer is attributed to another.

[3] With respect to the law department of an organization, including the government, there is ordinarily no question that the members of the department constitute a firm within the meaning of the Rules of Professional Conduct. There can be uncertainty, however, as to the identity of the client. For example, it may not be clear whether the law department of a corporation represents a subsidiary or an affiliated corporation, as well as the corporation by which the members of the department are directly employed. A similar question can arise concerning an unincorporated association and its local affiliates.

[4] Similar questions can also arise with respect to lawyers in legal aid and legal services organizations. Depending upon the structure of the organization, the entire organization or different components of it may constitute a firm or firms for purposes of these Rules.

Fraud

[5] When used in these Rules, the terms "fraud" or "fraudulent" refer to conduct that is characterized as such under the substantive or procedural law of the applicable jurisdiction and has a purpose to deceive. This does not include merely negligent misrepresentation or negligent failure to apprise another of relevant information. For purposes of these Rules, it is not necessary that anyone has suffered damages or relied on the misrepresentation or failure to inform.

Informed Consent

[6] Many of the Rules of Professional Conduct require the lawyer to obtain the informed consent of a client or other person (e.g., a former client or, under certain circumstances, a prospective client) before accepting or continuing representation or pursuing a course of conduct. See, e.g., Rules 1.2(c), 1.6(a) and 1.7(b). The communication necessary to obtain such consent will vary according to the Rule involved and the circumstances giving rise to the need to obtain informed consent. The lawyer must make reasonable efforts to ensure that the client or other person possesses information reasonably adequate to make an informed decision. Ordinarily, this will require communication that includes a disclosure of the facts and circumstances giving rise to the situation, any explanation reasonably necessary to inform the client or other person of the material advantages and disadvantages of the proposed course of conduct and a discussion of the client's or other person's options and alternatives. In some circumstances it may be appropriate for a lawyer to advise a client or other person to seek the advice of other counsel. A lawyer need not inform a client or other person of facts or implications already known to the client or other person; nevertheless, a lawyer who does not personally inform the client or other person assumes the risk that the client or other person is inadequately informed and the consent is invalid. In

determining whether the information and explanation provided are reasonably adequate, relevant factors include whether the client or other person is experienced in legal matters generally and in making decisions of the type involved, and whether the client or other person is independently represented by other counsel in giving the consent. Normally, such persons need less information and explanation than others, and generally a client or other person who is independently represented by other counsel in giving the consent should be assumed to have given informed consent.

[7] Obtaining informed consent will usually require an affirmative response by the client or other person. In general, a lawyer may not assume consent from a client's or other person's silence. Consent may be inferred, however, from the conduct of a client or other person who has reasonably adequate information about the matter. A number of Rules require that a person's consent be confirmed in writing. See Rules 1.7(b) and 1.9(a). For a definition of "writing" and "confirmed in writing," see paragraphs (n) and (b). Other Rules require that a client's consent be obtained in a writing signed by the client. See, e.g., Rules 1.8(a) and (g). For a definition of "signed," see paragraph (n).

Screened

[8] This definition applies to situations where screening of a personally disqualified lawyer is permitted to remove imputation of a conflict of interest under Rule 1.10, 1.11, 1.12 or 1.18.

[9] The purpose of screening is to assure the affected parties that confidential information known by the personally disqualified lawyer remains protected. The personally disqualified lawyer should acknowledge the obligation not to communicate with any of the other lawyers in the firm with respect to the matter. Similarly, other lawyers in the firm who are working on the matter should be informed that the screening is in place and that they may not communicate with the personally disqualified lawyer with respect to the matter. Additional screening measures that are appropriate for the particular matter will depend on the circumstances. To implement, reinforce and remind all affected lawyers of the presence of the screening, it may be appropriate for the firm to undertake such procedures as a written undertaking by the screened lawyer to avoid any communication with other firm personnel and any contact with any firm files or other materials relating to the matter, written notice and instructions to all other firm personnel forbidding any communication with the screened lawyer relating to the matter, denial of access by the screened lawyer to firm files or other materials relating to the matter and periodic reminders of the screen to the screened lawyer and all other firm personnel.

[10] In order to be effective, screening measures must be implemented as soon as practical after a lawyer or law firm knows or reasonably should know that there is a need for screening.

Canon and Code Antecedents

ABA Canons of Professional Ethics: The Canons did not contain any equivalent to the Terminology section.

ABA Model Code of Professional Responsibility: Compare the Definitions following DR 9-102.

Cross-References in Other Rules

Rule 1.4(a): "A lawyer shall promptly inform the client of any decision or circumstance with respect to which the client's informed consent, as defined in **Rule 1.0(e)**, is required by these Rules."

Rule 1.4, Comment 5: "In certain circumstances . . . the client must give informed consent, as defined in **Rule 1.0(e)**."

Rule 1.6, Comment 2: "See **Rule 1.0(e)** for the definition of informed consent."

Rule 1.6, Comment 7: "Paragraph (b)(2) is a limited exception to the rule of confidentiality that permits the lawyer to reveal information to the extent necessary to enable affected persons or appropriate authorities to prevent the client from committing a crime or fraud, as defined in **Rule 1.0(d)**. . . ."

Rule 1.7, Comment 1: "For definitions of 'informed consent' and 'confirmed in writing,' see **Rule 1.0(e) and (b)**."

Rule 1.7, Comment 17: "[M]ediation is not a proceeding before a 'tribunal' under **Rule 1.0(m)**."

Rule 1.7, Comment 18: "Informed consent requires that each affected client be aware of the relevant circumstances and of the material and reasonably foreseeable ways that the conflict could have adverse effects on the interests of that client. See **Rule 1.0(e)** (informed consent)."

Rule 1.7, Comment 20: "Paragraph (b) requires the lawyer to obtain the informed consent of the client, confirmed in writing. . . . See **Rule 1.0(b)**. See also **Rule 1.0(n)**. If it is not feasible to obtain or transmit the writing at the time the client gives informed consent, then the lawyer must obtain or transmit it within a reasonable time thereafter. See **Rule 1.0(b)**."

Rule 1.8, Comment 2: For a definition of informed consent, see **Rule 1.0(e)**.

Rule 1.8, Comment 13: See **Rule 1.0(e)** for a definition of informed consent.

Rule 1.9, Comment 9: "The provisions of this Rule are for the protection of former clients and can be waived if the client gives informed consent, which consent must be confirmed in writing under paragraphs (a) and (b). See **Rule 1.0(e)**."

Rule 1.10, Comment 1: "For purposes of the Rules of Professional Conduct, the term 'firm' denotes lawyers in a law partnership, professional corporation, sole proprietorship or other association authorized to practice law; or lawyers employed in a legal services organization or the legal department of a corporation or other organization. See **Rule 1.0(c)**. Whether two or more lawyers constitute a firm within this definition can depend on the specific facts. . . . See **Rule 1.0**, Comments [2]-[4]."

Rule 1.10, Comment 4: Paragraph (a) does not "prohibit representation if the lawyer is prohibited from acting because of events before the person became a lawyer . . . Such persons, however, ordinarily must be screened from any personal participation in the matter to avoid communication to others in the firm of confidential information that both the nonlawyers and the firm have a legal duty to protect. See **Rules 1.0(k)** and 5.3."

Rule 1.10, Comment 6: "For a definition of informed consent, see **Rule 1.0(e)**."

Rule 1.10, Comment 7: "A description of effective screening mechanisms appears in **Rule 1.0(k)**."

Rule 1.11, Comment 1: "See **Rule 1.0(e)** for the definition of informed consent."

Rule 1.11, Comment 6: "Paragraphs (b) and (c) contemplate a screening arrangement. See **Rule 1.0(k)** (requirements for screening procedures)."

Rule 1.12, Comment 2: "This Rule forbids such representation unless all of the parties to the proceedings give their informed consent, confirmed in writing. See **Rule 1.0(e) and (b)**."

Rule 1.12, Comment 4: "Requirements for screening procedures are stated in **Rule 1.0(k)**."

Rule 1.13, Comment 3: "As defined in **Rule 1.0(f)**, knowledge can be inferred from circumstances. . . ."

Rule 1.17, Comment 11: A lawyer selling a law practice has an "obligation to avoid disqualifying conflicts, and to secure the client's informed consent for those conflicts that can be agreed to (see Rule 1.7 regarding conflicts and **Rule 1.0(e)** for the definition of informed consent)."

Rule 1.18, Comment 5: "See **Rule 1.0(e)** for the definition of informed consent."

Rule 1.18, Comment 7: "[I]mputation may be avoided if the conditions of paragraph (d)(2) are met and all disqualified lawyers are timely screened and written notice is promptly given to the prospective client. See **Rule 1.0(k)** (requirements for screening procedures)."

Rule 2.3, Comment 5: "Where, however, it is reasonably likely that providing the evaluation will affect the client's interests materially and adversely, the lawyer must first obtain the client's consent after the client has been adequately informed concerning the important possible effects on the client's interests. See Rules 1.6(a) and **1.0(e)**."

Rule 2.4, Comment 5: "When the dispute-resolution process takes place before a tribunal, as in binding arbitration (see **Rule 1.0(m)**), the lawyer's duty of candor is governed by Rule 3.3."

Rule 3.3, Comment 1: "See **Rule 1.0(m)** for the definition of tribunal."

Rule 3.3, Comment 8: "A lawyer's knowledge that evidence is false, however, can be inferred from the circumstances. See **Rule 1.0(f)**."

Rule 3.5, Comment 5: "The duty to refrain from disruptive conduct applies to any proceeding of a tribunal, including a deposition. See **Rule 1.0(m)**."

Rule 3.7, Comment 6: "See **Rule 1.0(b)** for the definition of 'confirmed in writing' and **Rule 1.0(e)** for the definition of 'informed consent.' "

Rule 4.2, Comment 8: "The prohibition on communications with a represented person only applies in circumstances where the lawyer knows that the person is in fact represented in the matter to be discussed. This means that the lawyer has actual knowledge of the fact of the representation; but such actual knowledge may be inferred from the circumstances. See **Rule 1.0(f)**."

Rule 5.1, Comment 1: "Paragraph (a) applies to lawyers who have managerial authority over the professional work of a firm. See **Rule 1.0(c)**."

Legislative History of Terminology

1983 Terminology: As originally adopted in 1983, Rule 1.0 was called "Terminology" but was not given a rule number and did not include any Comment.

The only terms originally defined were: "Belief" or "believes"; "Consult" or "consultation"; "Firm" or "law firm"; "fraud" or "fraudulent"; "Knowingly," "known," or "knows"; "Partner"; "Reasonable" or "reasonably"; "reasonable belief" or "reasonably believes"; "Reasonably should know"; and "Substantial." As defined in 1983, the terms "Consult" or "consultation," "Firm" or "law firm," "Fraud," and "Partner" had the following meanings:

> (b) "Consult" or "consultation" denotes communication of information reasonably sufficient to permit the client to appreciate the significance of the matter in question.
>
> (c) "Firm" or "law firm" denotes a lawyer or lawyers in a private firm, lawyers employed in the legal department of a corporation or other organization and lawyers employed in a legal services organization. See Comment, Rule 1.10.
>
> (d) "Fraud" or "fraudulent" denotes conduct having a purpose to deceive and not merely negligent misrepresentation or failure to apprise another of relevant information.
>
> (g) "Partner" denotes a member of a partnership and a shareholder in a law firm organized as a professional corporation.

2002 Amendments: At its February 2002 Mid-Year Meeting, the ABA House of Delegates adopted, with only minor changes, the ABA Ethics 2000 Commission proposals to add, delete, or amend various definitions in the Terminology section, to add the entire Comment to the Terminology section, and to designate the Terminology section as "Rule 1.0." The ABA made no changes to the definitions of "Belief" or "believes"; "Knowingly," "known," or "knows"; "Reasonable" or "reasonably"; "Reasonable belief" or "reasonably believes"; "Reasonably should know"; and "Substantial." But the definitions of "Firm" or "law firm," "Fraud," and "Partner" were amended; the definitions of "Confirmed in writing," "Informed consent," "Screened," "Tribunal," and "Writing" were added; and the definition of "Consult" or "consultation" was deleted.

2009 Amendments: In February 2009, the ABA House of Delegates adopted a minor amendment to Comment 8 to include a reference to the new screening provision in Model Rule 1.10. (For related information, see "2009 Amendments to Model Rule 1.10" in the Legislative History following Rule 1.10.)

Selected State Variations

Alaska: Rule 9.1 (Alaska's terminology rule) adds an unusually detailed definition of "substantially related matters" to help guide lawyers in their assessment of conflicts of interest. The definition draws, in part, on Comment 3 to Model Rule 1.9.

Connecticut adds: " 'Client' or 'person' as used in these Rules includes an authorized representative unless otherwise stated."

District of Columbia defines "matter" as "any litigation, administrative proceeding, lobbying activity, application, claim, investigation, arrest, charge or accusation, the drafting of a contract, a negotiation, estate or family relationship practice issue, or any other representation, except as expressly limited in a particular Rule."

Massachusetts: Rule 9.1 retains the 1983 version of the ABA Terminology and adds a definition of "Qualified legal assistance organization." Amended Comment 3 to Rule 9.1 provides as follows: "The final category of qualified legal assistance organization requires that the organization 'receives no profit from the rendition of legal services.' That condition refers to the entire legal services operation of the organization; it does not prohibit the receipt of a court-awarded fee that would result in a 'profit' from that particular lawsuit."

New York adds definitions for the terms "advertisement," "computer-accessed communication," "differing interests," "domestic relations matters," "matter," "person," "reasonable lawyers," and "sexual relations." New York also includes a more detailed definition of "fraud," providing as follows:

> "Fraud" or "fraudulent" denotes conduct that is fraudulent under the substantive or procedural law of the applicable jurisdiction or has a purpose to deceive, provided that it does not include conduct that, although characterized as fraudulent by statute or administrative rule, lacks an element of scienter, deceit, intent to mislead, or knowing failure to correct misrepresentations that can be reasonably expected to induce detrimental reliance by another.

In addition, New York's definition of "confirmed in writing" includes "a statement by the person made on the record of any proceeding before a tribunal."

Ohio: Rule 1.0 defines "fraud" and "fraudulent" as denoting "conduct that has an intent to deceive and is either of the following:"

> (1) an actual or implied misrepresentation of a material fact that is made either with knowledge of its falsity or with such utter disregard and recklessness about its falsity that knowledge may be inferred; (2) a knowing concealment of a material fact where there is a duty to disclose the material fact.

Oregon adds or alters the meaning of a number of phrases, including "electronic communication," "informed consent," "law firm," "knowingly," and "matter."

Texas generally retains the 1983 version of the ABA Terminology, but modifies some of the 1983 definitions and adds others that are neither in the 1983 nor current versions of the ABA Terminology. Specifically, Texas includes the following definitions:

> "Adjudicatory Official" denotes a person who serves on a Tribunal.
>
> "Adjudicatory Proceeding" denotes the consideration of a matter by a Tribunal.
>
> "Competent" or "Competence" denotes possession or the ability to timely acquire the legal knowledge, skill, and training reasonably necessary for the representation of the client.
>
> "Firm" or "Law firm" denotes a lawyer or lawyers in a private firm; or a lawyer or lawyers employed in the legal department of a corporation, legal services organization, or other organization, or in a unit of government.
>
> "Fitness" denotes those qualities of physical, mental and psychological health that enable a person to discharge a lawyer's responsibilities to clients in conformity with the Texas Disciplinary Rules of Professional Conduct. Normally a lack of fitness is indicated most clearly by a persistent inability to discharge, or unreliability in carrying out, significant obligations.
>
> "Should know" when used in reference to a lawyer denotes that a reasonable lawyer under the same or similar circumstances would know the matter in question.
>
> "Substantial" when used in reference to degree or extent denotes a matter of meaningful significance or involvement.
>
> "Tribunal" denotes any governmental body or official or any other person engaged in a process of resolving a particular dispute or controversy. "Tribunal" includes such institutions as courts and administrative agencies when engaging in

adjudicatory or licensing activities as defined by applicable law or rules of practice or procedure, as well as judges, magistrates, special masters, referees, arbitrators, mediators, hearing officers and comparable persons empowered to resolve or to recommend a resolution of a particular matter; but it does not include jurors, prospective jurors, legislative bodies or their committees, members or staffs, nor does it include other governmental bodies when acting in a legislative or rule-making capacity.

Virginia retains the 1983 version of the Terminology section and adds: " 'Should' when used in reference to a lawyer's action denotes an aspirational rather than a mandatory standard."

Wisconsin: Wisconsin adds or alters the meaning of a number of phrases, including "consultation," "firm," "misrepresentation," and "prosecutor."

Related Materials

ABA Commission on Ethics 20/20: In 2009, the ABA created the ABA Commission on Ethics 20/20, which is comprehensively reviewing the ABA Model Rules of Professional Conduct in light of globalization and changes in information technology. On September 19, 2011, the Commission issued revised draft proposals on technology and confidentiality for public comment. One proposal relates to screening. The Commission did not propose any amendments to the black letter definition of "screened" in Rule 1.0(k), but did propose amending Comment 9 to Rule 1.0 to make clear that screening should prevent any contact with or access to any firm files or other information relating to the screened matter, "including information in electronic form." The Ethics 20/20 Commission may present this proposal to the ABA House of Delegates at the ABA's August 2012 Annual Meeting. For updates, see the Ethics 20/20 Commission's website at *http://www.americanbar.org/Ethics2020.*

ABA Formal Ethics Opinions: See, for example, ABA Formal Ethics Ops. 94-388 (1994), 95-390 (1995), 95-396 (1995), 98-411 (1998), 99-415 (1999), 04-433 (2004), 06-441 n.17 (2006), 11-460 (2011).

Model Rules of Professional Conduct for Federal Lawyers* add definitions of the terms "Federal Agency," "Federal lawyer," "Government lawyer," "Non-Government lawyer," and "Supervisory lawyer." The term "Government lawyer" is defined to mean "an individual who is a member of the bar . . . who represents persons before a Federal Agency," but the definition adds: "When a Government lawyer is engaged in the private practice of law or pro bono representation not related to the Government lawyer's official duties, the lawyer is considered a Non-Government lawyer."

Restatement of the Law Governing Lawyers: The Restatement does not have a separate Terminology section. Rather, the Restatement defines terms as needed within particular sections—see, for example, §87(1) (defining "work product") in our chapter on the Restatement later in this volume.

* This and all other excerpts from the Model Rules of Professional Conduct for Federal Lawyers, copyright © 1990 Federal Bar Association, 1815 H Street, NW, Washington, D.C. 20006-3697, have been directly quoted here with the permission of the Federal Bar Association.

Rule 1.1 Competence

Strickland v. Washington "effective"

A lawyer shall provide competent representation to a client. Competent representation requires the legal knowledge, skill, thoroughness and preparation reasonably necessary for the representation.

COMMENT

Legal Knowledge and Skill

[1] In determining whether a lawyer employs the requisite knowledge and skill in a particular matter, relevant factors include the relative complexity and specialized nature of the matter, the lawyer's general experience, the lawyer's training and experience in the field in question, the preparation and study the lawyer is able to give the matter and whether it is feasible to refer the matter to, or associate or consult with, a lawyer of established competence in the field in question. In many instances, the required proficiency is that of a general practitioner. Expertise in a particular field of law may be required in some circumstances.

[2] A lawyer need not necessarily have special training or prior experience to handle legal problems of a type with which the lawyer is unfamiliar. A newly admitted lawyer can be as competent as a practitioner with long experience. Some important legal skills, such as the analysis of precedent, the evaluation of evidence and legal drafting, are required in all legal problems. Perhaps the most fundamental legal skill consists of determining what kind of legal problems a situation may involve, a skill that necessarily transcends any particular specialized knowledge. A lawyer can provide adequate representation in a wholly novel field through necessary study. Competent representation can also be provided through the association of a lawyer of established competence in the field in question.

[3] In an emergency a lawyer may give advice or assistance in a matter in which the lawyer does not have the skill ordinarily required where referral to or consultation or association with another lawyer would be impractical. Even in an emergency, however, assistance should be limited to that reasonably necessary in the circumstances, for ill-considered action under emergency conditions can jeopardize the client's interest.

[4] A lawyer may accept representation where the requisite level of competence can be achieved by reasonable preparation. This applies as well to a lawyer who is appointed as counsel for an unrepresented person. See also Rule 6.2.

Thoroughness and Preparation

[5] Competent handling of a particular matter includes inquiry into and analysis of the factual and legal elements of the problem, and use of methods and procedures meeting the standards of competent practitioners. It also includes adequate preparation. The required attention and preparation are determined in part by what is at stake; major litigation and complex transactions ordinarily require more

extensive treatment than matters of lesser complexity and consequence. An agreement between the lawyer and the client regarding the scope of the representation may limit the matters for which the lawyer is responsible. See Rule 1.2 (c).

Maintaining Competence

[6] To maintain the requisite knowledge and skill, a lawyer should keep abreast of changes in the law and its practice, engage in continuing study and education and comply with all continuing legal education requirements to which the lawyer is subject.

Canon and Code Antecedents

ABA Canons of Professional Ethics: No comparable Canon.

ABA Model Code of Professional Responsibility: Compare DR 6-101 (reprinted later in this volume).

Cross-References in Other Rules

Rule 1.2, Comment 7: Limited representation "is a factor to be considered when determining the legal knowledge, skill, thoroughness and preparation reasonably necessary for the representation (see **Rule 1.1**)."

Rule 1.2, Comment 8: "All agreements concerning a lawyer's representation of a client must accord with the Rules of Professional Conduct and other law (see **Rules 1.1**, 1.8 and 5.6)."

Rule 1.5, Comment 7: "A lawyer should only refer a matter to a lawyer whom the referring lawyer reasonably believes is competent to handle the matter (see **Rule 1.1**)."

Rule 1.6, Comment 15: "A lawyer must act competently to safeguard information relating to the representation of a client against inadvertent or unauthorized disclosure by the lawyer or other persons who are participating in the representation of the client or who are subject to the lawyer's supervision (see **Rules 1.1**, 5.1 and 5.3)."

Rule 1.7, Comment 15: In the case of a conflict of interest, "representation is prohibited if in the circumstances the lawyer cannot reasonably conclude that the lawyer will be able to provide competent and diligent representation (see **Rules 1.1** and 1.3)."

Rule 1.17, Comment 11: A lawyer selling a law practice has an "obligation to exercise competence in identifying a purchaser qualified to assume the practice and the purchaser's obligation to undertake the representation competently (see **Rule 1.1**)."

Rule 1.18, Comment 9: "For the duty of competence of a lawyer who gives assistance on the merits of a matter to a prospective client, see **Rule 1.1**."

Rule 6.2, Comment 2: A lawyer has good cause to decline appointment by a court to represent a person "if the lawyer could not handle the matter competently, see **Rule 1.1**. . . ."

Legislative History of Model Rule 1.1

1979 Unofficial Pre-Circulation Draft:

> . . . (b) A lawyer acts incompetently in a particular matter, if:
>
> (i) He or she fails to use the knowledge, skill, preparation, and judgment that a reasonably competent lawyer would use in the circumstances; and
>
> (ii) The result of the lawyer's act or failure to act is substantial expense, delay, harm, or risk of harm to a client or other person for whose benefit the advice or assistance is provided.

1980 Discussion Draft: "A lawyer shall undertake representation only in matters in which the lawyer can act with adequate competence. . . ."

1981 Draft defined competence to include "efficiency."

1982 Draft was adopted.

2002 Amendments: At its February 2002 Mid-Year Meeting, the ABA House of Delegates adopted without change the ABA Ethics 2000 Commission proposal to amend Comment 6 to Rule 1.1 to say that lawyers should "keep abreast of changes in the law and its practice" and comply with CLE requirements. (The Ethics 2000 Commission did not propose any changes to the text of Rule 1.1.)

Selected State Variations

California: Rule 3-110 (Failing to Act Competently) provides as follows:

> (A) A member shall not intentionally, recklessly, or repeatedly fail to perform legal services with competence.
>
> (B) For purposes of this rule, "competence" in any legal service shall mean to apply the 1) diligence, 2) learning and skill, and 3) mental, emotional, and physical ability reasonably necessary for the performance of such service.
>
> (C) If a member does not have sufficient learning and skill when the legal service is undertaken, the member may nonetheless perform such services competently by 1) associating with or, where appropriate, professionally consulting another lawyer reasonably believed to be competent, or 2) by acquiring sufficient learning and skill before performance is required.

District of Columbia: Rule 1.1(a) is identical to ABA Model Rule 1.1, but D.C. adds Rule 1.1(b), which states: "A lawyer shall serve a client with skill and care commensurate with that generally afforded to clients by other lawyers in similar matters."

Michigan: Rule 1.1 retains some language from DR 6-101 of the ABA Model Code of Professional Responsibility.

New Hampshire: New Hampshire defines competence in detail, providing a long list of requirements that a lawyer must satisfy in order to achieve "legal competence."

New Jersey: Rule 1.1 provides that a lawyer shall not:

> (a) Handle or neglect a matter entrusted to the lawyer in such manner that the lawyer's conduct constitutes gross negligence.
>
> (b) Exhibit a pattern of negligence or neglect in the lawyer's handling of legal matters generally.

New York: New York substitutes the word "should" for "shall" and adds paragraphs (b) and (c), which are based on DR 6-101 and DR 7-101 of the old ABA Model Code.

Texas: Rule 1.01 provides as follows:

> (a) A lawyer shall not accept or continue employment in a legal matter which the lawyer knows or should know is beyond the lawyer's competence, unless:
>
> (1) another lawyer who is competent to handle the matter is, with the prior informed consent of the client, associated in the matter; or
>
> (2) the advice or assistance of the lawyer is reasonably required in an emergency and the lawyer limits the advice and assistance to that which is reasonably necessary in the circumstances.
>
> (b) In representing a client, a lawyer shall not:
>
> (1) neglect a legal matter entrusted to the lawyer; or
>
> (2) frequently fail to carry out completely the obligations that the lawyer owes to a client or clients.
>
> (c) As used in this Rule, "neglect" signifies inattentiveness involving a conscious disregard for the responsibilities owed to a client or clients.

Related Materials

ABA Commission on Ethics 20/20: In 2009, the ABA created the ABA Commission on Ethics 20/20, which is comprehensively reviewing the ABA Model Rules of Professional Conduct in light of globalization and changes in information technology. On September 19 2011, the Commission issued revised draft proposals on technology and confidentiality, as well as on outsourcing, for public comment. The Commission did not propose any changes to the text of Rule 1.1 but proposed to amend Comment 6 by adding the italicized words: "To maintain the requisite knowledge and skill, a lawyer should keep abreast of changes in the law and its practice, *including the benefits and risks associated with technology,* engage in continuing study and education and comply with all continuing legal education requirements to which the lawyer is subject." (Emphasis added.)

The revised draft of the Commission's proposals relating to outsourcing would also add a new Comment 6 providing, in part, as follows:

> [6] Before a lawyer retains or contracts with other lawyers outside the lawyer's own firm to provide or assist in the provision of legal services to a client, the lawyer should ordinarily obtain informed consent from the client and must reasonably believe that the other lawyers' services will contribute to the competent and ethical representation of the client. . . . When using the services of nonfirm lawyers in providing legal services to a client, a lawyer also must reasonably believe that such services meet the standard of competence under this Rule.

The remainder of the proposed new Comment lists factors for determining whether it is reasonable to retain or contract with lawyers outside the lawyer's own firm. The revised outsourcing proposals would also add a new Comment 7 to Rule 1.1, providing, in part, as follows:

> Where the client has chosen or suggested lawyers from other law firms to assist in the provision of legal services to the client on a particular matter, the law firms who will be assisting the client on that matter should consult with each other and the client about the allocation or scope of representation and responsibility, including the

allocation of responsibility for monitoring and supervision of any nonfirm nonlawyers who will be working on the client's matter. . . .

The 20/20 Commission may present these proposals (or revised versions of them) to the ABA House of Delegates at the ABA's August 2012 Annual Meeting. For updates, see the Ethics 20/20 Commission's website at *http://www.americanbar.org/Ethics2020.*

ABA Formal Ethics Opinions: See ABA Formal Ethics Ops. 87-354 (1987), 87-355 (1987), 93-379 (1993), 96-399 (1996), 98-411 n.2 (1998), 03-431 (2003), 06-441 (2006), 07-448 (2007), 07-449 (2007), 08-450 (2008), 08-451 (2008), 08-453 (2008), 09-455 (2009), 11-459 (2011).

ABA Guidelines for Appointment and Performance of Defense Counsel in Death Penalty Cases: Because capital cases are extraordinarily complex and demanding, defense counsel must possess a significantly greater degree of skill and experience than is required in most noncapital cases. To provide guidance for capital defense lawyers and capital defense programs, in 1989 the ABA House of Delegates adopted Guidelines for the Appointment and Performance of Defense Counsel in Death Penalty Cases. In 2003, the Guidelines were extensively amended. The Reporter for the amended Guidelines was Professor Eric Freedman of Hofstra University School of Law. Amended Guideline 1.1, entitled "Objective and Scope of Guidelines," provides as follows:

> A. The objective of these Guidelines is to set forth a national standard of practice for the defense of capital cases in order to ensure high quality legal representation for all persons facing the possible imposition or execution of a death sentence by any jurisdiction.
>
> B. These Guidelines apply from the moment the client is taken into custody and extend to all stages of every case in which the jurisdiction may be entitled to seek the death penalty, including initial and ongoing investigation, pretrial proceedings, trial, post-conviction review, clemency proceedings, and any connected litigation.

Guideline 2.1 urges each jurisdiction to "adopt and implement a plan formalizing the means by which high quality legal representation in death penalty cases is to be provided in accordance with these Guidelines." Remaining Guidelines establish (among other things) counsel's duties to be fully educated in the relevant fields of law, to conduct a complete investigation, to consider and thoroughly investigate all legal claims potentially available, to make full use of nonlawyer resources, and to cooperate with the legal strategies chosen by successor counsel, even if successor counsel seeks to prove that original counsel provided ineffective assistance.

Guidelines substantially similar to the ABA Guidelines have been adopted by the Alabama Circuit Court Judges Conference, the Georgia Public Defender Standards Council (except where the ABA Guidelines conflict with Georgia law), the State Bar of Texas (which adds two sections specific to Texas), the Nevada Supreme Court, and the Oregon Office of Public Defense Services. In Arizona, Rule 6.8(b)(1) of the Arizona Rules of Criminal Procedure provides that to be eligible for appointment as lead counsel in a capital case, an attorney must "be familiar with and guided by the performance standards in the 2003 American Bar Association Guidelines for the Appointment and Performance of Defense Counsel in Death Penalty Cases." The complete ABA Guidelines, together with extensive commentary and background, are available both in print at 31 Hofstra L. Rev. 913

(2003) and online at *www.probono.net/deathpenalty/*. A list showing which jurisdictions have implemented the Guidelines is available at *www.probono.net/deathpenalty/about/item.80-Guidelines_Implementation_Fact_Sheet.*

ABA Model Rule for Minimum Continuing Legal Education (MCLE): In 1986, the ABA House of Delegates approved a resolution declaring that the ABA supports mandatory continuing legal education for all active lawyers and urging states without mandatory MCLE to seriously consider its adoption. In 1987, the ABA House of Delegates approved a Model Rule for Minimum Continuing Legal Education.

Today, 44 states have adopted mandatory continuing legal education programs that require lawyers to take a minimum number of hours of CLE each year. (The most recent is New Jersey, where lawyers were first required to report CLE hours in 2011.) Nearly all of these states require that a portion of the MCLE hours be devoted to "ethics" or "professionalism." Many states adopted their MCLE programs after the ABA passed the 1986 resolution described above in support of MCLE. The only jurisdictions that have not adopted mandatory CLE are Connecticut, the District of Columbia, Hawaii, Maryland, Massachusetts, Michigan, and South Dakota. Michigan is the only state that has repealed an MCLE program; in 1994, after trying MCLE for a few years, the Michigan Supreme Court dropped the program as "ineffective."

Some states require mandatory CLE specifically regarding substance abuse and mental health. For example, California requires lawyers to take one hour of CLE every three years concerning the detection and prevention of substance abuse. Florida requires lawyers to take five hours of CLE every three years in ethics, professionalism, substance abuse, or mental health awareness. North Carolina requires one hour of CLE every three years relating to substance abuse or mental health. Ohio requires all law students to take a one-time, one-hour session on substance abuse in order to sit for the Ohio bar exam.

For a clickable map linking to each state's MCLE requirements, the full text of the ABA Model Rule for Minimum Continuing Legal Education, and other useful materials about CLE programs, see *http://www.americanbar.org/publications_cle/mandatory_cle.html.*

ABA Resolution on Legal Education: The ABA has expressed a strong interest in legal education for nearly a century. At its August 2011 Annual Meeting, for example, the House of Delegates adopted a resolution urging legal education providers to "implement curricular programs intended to develop practice ready lawyers including, but not limited to enhanced capstone and clinical courses that include client meetings and court appearances."

ABA Standards for Criminal Justice: The following Standard is related to ABA Model Rule 1.1:

Standard 4-6.1 Duty to Explore Disposition Without Trial

(a) Whenever the law, nature, and circumstances of the case permit, defense counsel should explore the possibility of an early diversion of the case from the criminal process through the use of other community agencies.

(b) Defense counsel may engage in plea discussions with the prosecutor. Under no circumstances should defense counsel recommend to a defendant acceptance of a plea unless appropriate investigation and study of the case has been completed, including an analysis of controlling law and the evidence likely to be introduced at trial.

ABA Standards for Imposing Lawyer Sanctions**: With respect to competence and lack of competence, the ABA Standards for Imposing Lawyer Sanctions provide as follows:

> 4.51. Disbarment is generally appropriate when a lawyer's course of conduct demonstrates that the lawyer does not understand the most fundamental legal doctrines or procedures, and the lawyer's conduct causes injury or potential injury to a client.
>
> 4.52. Suspension is generally appropriate when a lawyer engages in an area of practice in which the lawyer knows he or she is not competent, and causes injury or potential injury to a client.

ABA Standards for the Operation of a Telephone Hotline: In 2001, the ABA adopted Standards for the Operation of a Telephone Hotline Providing Legal Advice and Information. The Standards contain rules and extensive comments covering such topics as "Confidentiality and Expectations of Privacy," "Third Party Callers," "Prompt Service," "Managing Backlogs," "Referrals to Non-Legal Resources," "Identifying Callers," and "Emergency Matters."

IRS Regulations: In the regulations governing practice before the Internal Revenue Service, 31 C.F.R. §10.33(a) provides that tax advisors should adhere to a series of "best practices," including:

> (2) Establishing the facts, determining which facts are relevant, evaluating the reasonableness of any assumptions or representations, relating the applicable law (including potentially applicable judicial doctrines) to the relevant facts, and arriving at a conclusion supported by the law and the facts.

Law School Accreditation: The ABA Section of Legal Education and Admissions to the Bar was established in 1879 as one of the ABA's first committees. The Section promulgates Standards and Rules of Procedure for Approval of Law Schools. The Preface to the Standards states: "Concern for improving the competence of those entering the legal profession was a major reason for creating the American Bar Association in 1878. The Standards for Approval of Law Schools are promulgated to serve that objective."

The Standards are highly influential. In 1952, the United States Department of Education approved the Council of the ABA Section of Legal Education and Admissions to the Bar as the recognized national agency for accrediting law schools. Each state's bar admission authority decides whether to require graduation from an ABA-approved law school as a condition for taking the bar exam or gaining admission to the bar, but a majority of states rely upon ABA approval of a law school to determine whether a bar applicant has satisfied the state's legal education requirement.

In September 2008, the Council of the ABA Section of Legal Education and Admissions to the Bar began a comprehensive review of the ABA Standards that was expected to take at least two years. The Standards and related materials about law schools are available online at *http://www.americanbar.org/groups/legal_education/resources/standards.html.*

* This and all subsequent ABA Standards for Imposing Lawyer Sanctions are copyright © 1986 by the American Bar Association. All rights reserved. Reprinted with permission of the American Bar Association.

Malpractice: A lawyer who violates Rule 1.1 by failing to provide "competent representation" may be committing legal malpractice. According to §48 of the Restatement of the Law Governing Lawyers (reprinted later in this book), a lawyer is liable to a person for legal malpractice (also called "professional negligence") if (i) the lawyer "owes a duty of care" to the person, and (ii) the lawyer "fails to exercise care," and (iii) the failure to exercise care is "a legal cause of injury" to the person. Restatement §§51, 50, 52, and 53 elaborate on these elements. For a prominent treatise on legal malpractice, see Ronald E. Mallen & Jeffrey M. Smith, Legal Malpractice (Thomson West 2011 ed.).

Malpractice Insurance: In 2004, the ABA House of Delegates narrowly adopted an ABA Model Court Rule on Insurance Disclosure. Where adopted, the rule requires lawyers in private practice to notify the jurisdiction's highest court annually whether the lawyer "is currently covered by professional liability insurance [and] . . . intends to maintain insurance. . . ." For more information about the Model Court Rule, see the Related Materials following ABA Model Rule 1.8 later in this book.

Restatement of the Law Governing Lawyers: See Restatement §§16(2), 29(2), 48, 49, 50, 52, 53, and 54(1) in our chapter on the Restatement later in this volume.

Sixth Amendment: The Sixth Amendment to the United States Constitution guarantees criminal defendants "the assistance of counsel" for their defense. This phrase has consistently been interpreted to guarantee the "effective" assistance of counsel, which means that lawyers for criminal defendants must perform at a certain minimum level of competence to satisfy the Sixth Amendment guarantee of effective assistance. If a convicted defendant believes that a lawyer was ineffective, the defendant can challenge the conviction. In *Strickland v. Washington,* 466 U.S. 668 (1984), the Supreme Court said that whether a lawyer was "ineffective" depended on "whether, in light of all the circumstances, the identified acts or omissions were outside the wide range of professionally competent assistance." ABA Model Rule 1.1 may help to determine the range of professionally "competent" assistance.

Rule 1.2 Scope of Representation and Allocation of Authority Between Client and Lawyer

(a) Subject to paragraphs (c) and (d), a lawyer shall abide by a client's decisions concerning the objectives of representation and, as required by Rule 1.4, shall consult with the client as to the means by which they are to be pursued. A lawyer may take such action on behalf of the client as is impliedly authorized to carry out the representation. A lawyer shall abide by a client's decision whether to settle a matter. In a criminal case, the lawyer shall abide by the client's decision, after consultation with the lawyer, as to a plea to be entered, whether to waive jury trial and whether the client will testify.

(b) A lawyer's representation of a client, including representation by appointment, does not constitute an endorsement of the client's political, economic, social or moral views or activities.

(c) A lawyer may limit the scope of the representation if the limitation is reasonable under the circumstances and the client gives informed consent.

(d) A lawyer shall not counsel a client to engage, or assist a client, in conduct that the lawyer knows is criminal or fraudulent, but a lawyer

may discuss the legal consequences of any proposed course of conduct with a client and may counsel or assist a client to make a good faith effort to determine the validity, scope, meaning or application of the law.

COMMENT

Allocation of Authority Between Client and Lawyer

[1] Paragraph (a) confers upon the client the ultimate authority to determine the purposes to be served by legal representation, within the limits imposed by law and the lawyer's professional obligations. The decisions specified in paragraph (a), such as whether to settle a civil matter, must also be made by the client. See Rule 1.4(a)(1) for the lawyer's duty to communicate with the client about such decisions. With respect to the means by which the client's objectives are to be pursued, the lawyer shall consult with the client as required by Rule 1.4(a)(2) and may take such action as is impliedly authorized to carry out the representation.

[2] On occasion, however, a lawyer and a client may disagree about the means to be used to accomplish the client's objectives. Clients normally defer to the special knowledge and skill of their lawyer with respect to the means to be used to accomplish their objectives, particularly with respect to technical, legal and tactical matters. Conversely, lawyers usually defer to the client regarding such questions as the expense to be incurred and concern for third persons who might be adversely affected. Because of the varied nature of the matters about which a lawyer and client might disagree and because the actions in question may implicate the interests of a tribunal or other persons, this Rule does not prescribe how such disagreements are to be resolved. Other law, however, may be applicable and should be consulted by the lawyer. The lawyer should also consult with the client and seek a mutually acceptable resolution of the disagreement. If such efforts are unavailing and the lawyer has a fundamental disagreement with the client, the lawyer may withdraw from the representation. See Rule 1.16(b)(4). Conversely, the client may resolve the disagreement by discharging the lawyer. See Rule 1.16(a)(3).

[3] At the outset of a representation, the client may authorize the lawyer to take specific action on the client's behalf without further consultation. Absent a material change in circumstances and subject to Rule 1.4, a lawyer may rely on such an advance authorization. The client may, however, revoke such authority at any time.

[4] In a case in which the client appears to be suffering diminished capacity, the lawyer's duty to abide by the client's decisions is to be guided by reference to Rule 1.14.

Independence from Client's Views or Activities

[5] Legal representation should not be denied to people who are unable to afford legal services, or whose cause is controversial or the subject of popular disapproval. By the same token, representing a client does not constitute approval of the client's views or activities.

Agreements Limiting Scope of Representation

[6] The scope of services to be provided by a lawyer may be limited by agreement with the client or by the terms under which the lawyer's services are made available to the client. When a lawyer has been retained by an insurer to represent an insured, for example, the representation may be limited to matters related to the insurance coverage. A limited representation may be appropriate because the client has limited objectives for the representation. In addition, the terms upon which representation is undertaken may exclude specific means that might otherwise be used to accomplish the client's objectives. Such limitations may exclude actions that the client thinks are too costly or that the lawyer regards as repugnant or imprudent.

[7] Although this Rule affords the lawyer and client substantial latitude to limit the representation, the limitation must be reasonable under the circumstances. If, for example, a client's objective is limited to securing general information about the law the client needs in order to handle a common and typically uncomplicated legal problem, the lawyer and client may agree that the lawyer's services will be limited to a brief telephone consultation. Such a limitation, however, would not be reasonable if the time allotted was not sufficient to yield advice upon which the client could rely. Although an agreement for a limited representation does not exempt a lawyer from the duty to provide competent representation, the limitation is a factor to be considered when determining the legal knowledge, skill, thoroughness and preparation reasonably necessary for the representation. See Rule 1.1.

[8] All agreements concerning a lawyer's representation of a client must accord with the Rules of Professional Conduct and other law. See, e.g., Rules 1.1, 1.8, and 5.6.

Criminal, Fraudulent and Prohibited Transactions

[9] Paragraph (d) prohibits a lawyer from knowingly counseling or assisting a client to commit a crime or fraud. This prohibition, however, does not preclude the lawyer from giving an honest opinion about the actual consequences that appear likely to result from a client's conduct. Nor does the fact that a client uses advice in a course of action that is criminal or fraudulent of itself make a lawyer a party to the course of action. There is a critical distinction between presenting an analysis of legal aspects of questionable conduct and recommending the means by which a crime or fraud might be committed with impunity.

[10] When the client's course of action has already begun and is continuing, the lawyer's responsibility is especially delicate. The lawyer is required to avoid assisting the client, for example, by drafting or delivering documents that the lawyer knows are fraudulent or by suggesting how the wrongdoing might be concealed. A lawyer may not continue assisting a client in conduct that the lawyer originally supposed was legally proper but then discovers is criminal or fraudulent. The lawyer must, therefore, withdraw from the representation of the client in the matter. See Rule 1.16(a). In some cases, withdrawal alone might be insufficient. It may be necessary for the lawyer to give notice of the fact of withdrawal and to disaffirm any opinion, document, affirmation or the like. See Rule 4.1.

[11] Where the client is a fiduciary, the lawyer may be charged with special obligations in dealings with a beneficiary.

[12] Paragraph (d) applies whether or not the defrauded party is a party to the transaction. Hence, a lawyer must not participate in a transaction to effectuate criminal or fraudulent avoidance of tax liability. Paragraph (d) does not preclude undertaking a criminal defense incident to a general retainer for legal services to a lawful enterprise. The last clause of paragraph (d) recognizes that determining the validity or interpretation of a statute or regulation may require a course of action involving disobedience of the statute or regulation or of the interpretation placed upon it by governmental authorities.

[13] If a lawyer comes to know or reasonably should know that a client expects assistance not permitted by the Rules of Professional Conduct or other law or if the lawyer intends to act contrary to the client's instructions, the lawyer must consult with the client regarding the limitations on the lawyer's conduct. See Rule 1.4(a)(5).

Canon and Code Antecedents

ABA Canons of Professional Ethics: Canons 16, 24, and 32 provided as follows:

16. Restraining Clients from Improprieties

A lawyer should use his best efforts to restrain and to prevent his clients from doing those things which the lawyer himself ought not to do, particularly with reference to their conduct towards Courts, judicial officers, jurors, witnesses and suitors. If a client persists in such wrongdoing the lawyer should terminate their relation.

24. Right of Lawyer to Control the Incidents of the Trial

As to incidental matters pending the trial, not affecting the merits of the cause, or working substantial prejudice to the rights of the client, such as forcing the opposite lawyer to trial when he is under affliction or bereavement; forcing the trial on a particular day to the injury of the opposite lawyer when no harm will result from a trial at a different time; agreeing to an extension of time for signing a bill of exceptions, cross interrogatories and the like, the lawyer must be allowed to judge. In such matters no client has a right to demand that his counsel shall be illiberal, or that he do anything therein repugnant to his own sense of honor and propriety.

32. The Lawyer's Duty in Its Last Analysis

No client, corporate or individual, however powerful, nor any cause, civil or political, however important, is entitled to receive nor should any lawyer render any service or advice involving disloyalty to the law whose ministers we are, or disrespect of the judicial office, which we are bound to uphold, or corruption of any person or persons exercising a public office or private trust, or deception or betrayal of the public. When rendering any such improper service or advice, the lawyer invites and merits stern and just condemnation. Correspondingly, he advances the honor of his profession and the best interests of his client when he renders service or gives advice tending to impress upon the client and his undertaking exact compliance with the strictest principles of moral law. He must also observe and advise his client to observe the statute law, though until a statute shall have been construed and interpreted by competent adjudication, he is free and is entitled to advise as to its validity and as to what he conscientiously believes to be its just meaning and extent. But above all a lawyer will find his highest honor in a deserved reputation for fidelity to private trust and to public duty, as an honest man and as a patriotic and loyal citizen.

ABA Model Code of Professional Responsibility: Compare DR 2-110(C)(1)(c), DR 7-101(A)(1), DR 7-101(B)(1), DR 7-102(A)(6)-(7), DR 7-106, and DR 9-101(C) (reprinted later in this volume).

Cross-References in Other Rules

Rule 1.0, Comment 6: "Many of the Rules of Professional Conduct require the lawyer to obtain the informed consent of a client or other person before accepting or continuing representation or pursuing a course of conduct (see **Rules 1.2(c)**, 1.6(a) and 1.7(b))."

Rule 1.1, Comment 5: "An agreement between the lawyer and the client regarding the scope of the representation may limit the matters for which the lawyer is responsible. See **Rule 1.2(c)**."

Rule 1.3, Comment 1: "A lawyer may have authority to exercise professional discretion in determining the means by which a matter should be pursued. See **Rule 1.2**."

Rule 1.3, Comment 4: "Whether the lawyer is obligated to prosecute the appeal for the client depends on the scope of the representation the lawyer has agreed to provide to the client. See **Rule 1.2**."

Rule 1.4, Comment 2: "If these Rules require that a particular decision about the representation be made by the client, paragraph (a)(1) requires that the lawyer promptly consult with and secure the client's consent prior to taking action unless prior discussions with the client have resolved what action the client wants the lawyer to take. See **Rule 1.2(a)**."

Rule 1.6, Comment 7: "Although paragraph (b)(2) does not require the lawyer to reveal the client's misconduct, the lawyer may not counsel or assist the client in conduct the lawyer knows is criminal or fraudulent. See **Rule 1.2(d)**."

Rule 1.6, Comment 15: Some Rules require "disclosure of information relating to a client's representation to accomplish the purposes specified in paragraphs (b)(1) through (b)(6), only if such disclosure would be permitted by paragraph (b). See **Rules 1.2(d)**, 4.1(b), 8.1 and 8.3."

Rule 1.7, Comment 32: "Any limitations on the scope of the representation made necessary as a result of the common representation should be fully explained to the clients at the outset of the representation. See **Rule 1.2(c)**."

Rule 1.8, Comment 5: It is prohibited to partake in the "disadvantageous use of client information unless the client gives informed consent, except as permitted or required by these Rules. See **Rules 1.2(d)**, 1.6, 1.9(c), 3.3, 4.1(b), 8.1 and 8.3."

Rule 1.8, Comment 13: "**Rule 1.2(a)** protects each client's right to have the final say in deciding whether to accept or reject an offer of settlement and in deciding whether to enter a guilty or nolo contendere plea in a criminal case."

Rule 1.8, Comment 14: "An agreement in accordance with **Rule 1.2** that defines the scope of the representation" is not prohibited.

Rule 1.13, Comment 6: "If the lawyer's services are being used by an organization to further a crime or fraud by the organization. . . . **Rule 1.2(d)** may also be applicable," and withdrawal may be required.

Rule 1.14, Comment 4: "If the lawyer represents the guardian as distinct from the ward, and is aware that the guardian is acting adversely to the ward's interest, the lawyer may have an obligation to prevent or rectify the guardian's misconduct. See **Rule 1.2(d)**."

Rule 1.16, Comment 1: "Ordinarily, a representation in a matter is completed when the agreed-upon assistance has been concluded. See **Rules 1.2(c)** and 6.5."

Rule 2.3, Comment 1: "An evaluation may be performed at the client's direction or when impliedly authorized in order to carry out the representation. See **Rule 1.2.**"

Rule 3.3, Comment 3: "The obligation prescribed in **Rule 1.2(d)** not to counsel a client to commit or assist the client in committing a fraud applies in litigation. Regarding compliance with **Rule 1.2(d)**, see the Comment to that Rule."

Rule 3.3, Comment 11: The alternative to disclosing a client's deception to the court or to the other party "is that the lawyer cooperate in deceiving the court, thereby subverting the truth-finding process which the adversary system is designed to implement. See **Rule 1.2(d)**."

Rule 4.1, Comment 3: "Under **Rule 1.2(d)**, a lawyer is prohibited from counseling or assisting a client in conduct that the lawyer knows is criminal or fraudulent. Paragraph (b) states a specific application of the principle set forth in **Rule 1.2(d)**. . . . "

Rule 4.4, Comment 3: "Where a lawyer is not required by applicable law to do so, the decision to voluntarily return such a document is a matter of professional judgment ordinarily reserved to the lawyer. See **Rules 1.2** and 1.4."

Rule 6.4, Comment 1: "Lawyers involved in organizations seeking law reform generally do not have a client–lawyer relationship with the organization. . . . See also **Rule 1.2(b)**."

Rule 6.5, Comment 2: "A lawyer who provides short-term limited legal services pursuant to this Rule must secure the client's informed consent to the limited scope of the representation. See **Rule 1.2(c)**."

Rule 8.4, Comment 4: "The provisions of **Rule 1.2(d)** concerning a good faith challenge to the validity, scope, meaning or application of the law apply to challenges of legal regulation of the practice of law."

Legislative History of Model Rule 1.2

1980 Discussion Draft (then called Rule 1.3):

> (a) A lawyer shall accept a client's decisions concerning the objectives of the representation and the means by which they are to be pursued except as stated in paragraphs (b) and (c).
>
> (b) A lawyer shall not pursue a course of action on behalf of a client in violation of law or the rules of professional conduct.
>
> (c) The lawyer may decline to pursue a lawful course of action . . . and, if the client insists upon such course of action, the lawyer may withdraw from representation subject to the provisions of Rule 1.16.

The 1980 Draft also contained the following separate rules (then called Rules 2.3 and 2.4):

Advice Concerning Wrongful Conduct

(a) A lawyer shall not give advice which the lawyer can reasonably foresee will:

(1) Be used by the client to further an illegal course of conduct except as part of a good faith effort to determine the validity, scope, meaning, or application of the law; or

(2) Aid the client in contriving false testimony or making a legally wrongful misrepresentation.

(b) A lawyer may decline to give advice that might assist the client in any conduct that would violate the law or . . . that the lawyer considers repugnant.

Duty to Offer Advice

A lawyer who knows that a client contemplates a course of action which has a substantial likelihood of serious legal consequences shall warn the client of the legal implications of the conduct, unless a client has expressly or by implication asked not to receive such advice.

The 1980 Draft also contained the following rule (then called Rule 4.1) similar to the adopted version of Rule 1.2(a):

Disclosures to a Client

A lawyer conducting negotiations for a client shall:

(a) inform the client of facts relevant to the matter and of communications from another party that may significantly affect resolution of the matter;

(b) in connection with an offer, take reasonable steps to assure that the judgment of the client rather than that of the lawyer determines whether the offer will be accepted.

1981 Draft of Rule 1.2 (d) prohibited a lawyer from counseling or assisting a client "in the preparation of a written instrument containing terms the lawyer knows or reasonably should know are legally prohibited. . . ."

1982 Draft of Rule 1.2 was the same as adopted, except that Rule 1.2(d) also prohibited a lawyer from counseling or assisting "in the preparation of a written instrument containing terms the lawyer knows are expressly prohibited by law. . . ."

1983 Rule: From its original adoption in 1983 until its amendment in 2002, Rule 1.2 provided as follows:

Rule 1.2 Scope of Representation

(a) A lawyer shall abide by a client's decisions concerning the objectives of representation and shall consult with the client as to the means by which they are to be pursued. A lawyer shall abide by a client's decision whether to accept an offer of settlement of a matter. In a criminal case, the lawyer shall abide by the client's decision, after consultation with the lawyer, as to a plea to be entered, whether to waive jury trial and whether the client will testify.

(b) [Same as 2002 version of Rule 1.2(b).]

(c) A lawyer may limit the objectives of the representation if the client consents after consultation.

(d) [Same as 2002 version of Rule 1.2(d).]

(e) When a lawyer knows that a client expects assistance not permitted by the rules of professional conduct or other law, the lawyer shall consult with the client regarding the relevant limitations on the lawyer's conduct.

2002 Amendments: At its February 2002 Mid-Year Meeting, the ABA House of Delegates adopted with only minor changes the ABA Ethics 2000 Commission proposal to amend Rule 1.2 and its Comment. Before the amendment, Rule 1.2(a) did not contain the "impliedly authorized" sentence. The amendment also added "the limitation is reasonable under the circumstances and" to Rule 1.2(c). The amendment deleted paragraph (e) which provided: "When a lawyer knows that a client expects assistance not permitted by the rules of professional conduct or other law, the lawyer shall consult with the client regarding the relevant limitations on the lawyer's conduct." Comments 2, 3, and 7 were new.

Selected State Variations

Alaska: Rule 1.2(a) states as follows: "In a criminal case the lawyer shall abide by the client's decision . . . whether to take an appeal."

California: Rule 3-210 (Advising the Violation of Law) provides: "A member shall not advise the violation of any law, rule, or ruling of a tribunal unless the member believes in good faith that such law, rule, or ruling is invalid. A member may take appropriate steps in good faith to test the validity of any law, rule, or ruling of a tribunal." Business & Professions Code 6068(c) requires lawyers to "counsel or maintain those actions, proceedings, or defenses only as appear to him or her legal or just" except in defending a criminal case. In addition, §283 of the California Code of Civil Procedure gives a lawyer express statutory authority to bind a client in certain situations.

Colorado: Rule 1.2(a) and (c) and the Comment to Rule 1.2 encourage "limited representation" of pro se clients. Rule 1.2(c) provides that a lawyer may limit the scope or objectives, "or both," of the representation if the client consents after consultation, and a lawyer "may provide limited representation to pro se parties as permitted by C.R.C.P. 11(b) and C.R.C.P. 311(b)." The Comments to Colorado Rules 4.2 and 4.3 provide that a pro se party who is receiving "limited representation" is considered "unrepresented" for purposes of Rules 4.2 and 4.3.

Connecticut adds the following sentence to the end of Rule 1.2(a):

> Subject to revocation by the client and to the terms of the contract, a client's decision to settle a matter shall be implied where the lawyer is retained to represent the client by a third party obligated under the terms of a contract to provide the client with a defense and indemnity for the loss, and the third party elects to settle a matter without contribution by the client.

In addition, Connecticut adds to Rule 1.2(c) that a client's informed consent to limit the scope of a representation "shall not be required when a client cannot be located despite reasonable efforts where the lawyer is retained to represent a client by a third party which is obligated by contract to provide the client with a defense." An "Amendment Note" explains that these revisions "address the situation where an insured/client cannot be located despite diligent and good faith efforts by both the lawyer and the insurer."

District of Columbia: D.C. Rule 1.2 generally tracks the ABA Model Rule, but adds a paragraph (d) providing that a "government lawyer's authority and control over decisions concerning the representation may, by statute or regulation, be expanded beyond the limits imposed by paragraphs (a) and (c)." D.C. Rule 1.2(f)—formerly 1.2(e)—retains language that the ABA deleted in 2002.

Florida adds the words "or reasonably should know" in Rule 1.2(d). In addition, Florida's Statement of Client's Rights, which must be provided to every contingent fee client (see Florida Rule 4-1.5(f)), provides that "[y]ou, the client, have the right to make the final decision regarding settlement of a case. . . ."

Illinois: Illinois adds Rule 1.2(e), which provides that, "[a]fter accepting employment on behalf of a client, a lawyer shall not thereafter delegate to another lawyer not in the lawyer's firm the responsibility for performing or completing that employment, without the client's informed consent." Comment 14 offers the following explanation:

> The prohibition stated in paragraph (e) has existed in Illinois ethics rules and in the prior Code since 1980. It is intended to curtail abuses that occasionally occur when a lawyer attempts to transfer complete or substantial responsibility for a matter to an unaffiliated lawyer without the client's awareness or consent. . . . The Rule is not intended to prohibit lawyers from hiring lawyers outside of their firm to perform certain services on the client's or the law firm's behalf. Nor is it intended to prevent lawyers from engaging lawyers outside of their firm to stand in for discrete events in situations such as personal emergencies, illness or schedule conflicts.

Massachusetts: Rule 1.2(a) provides that a lawyer "does not violate this rule . . . by acceding to reasonable requests of opposing counsel which do not prejudice the rights of his or her client, by being punctual in fulfilling all professional commitments, by avoiding offensive tactics, or by treating with courtesy and consideration all persons involved in the legal process."

Michigan deletes Rule 1.2(b) and adds the following sentence to Rule 1.2(a): "In representing a client, a lawyer may, where permissible, exercise professional judgment to waive or fail to assert a right or position of the client." Where the official ABA Comment to Rule 1.2 refers to "criminal or fraudulent conduct," the Michigan Comment refers to "illegal or fraudulent conduct." Michigan places the substance of Rule 1.2(b) in the Comment to Rule 1.2.

Missouri: Rule 1.2(c) permits the unbundling of legal services, providing as follows:

> A lawyer may limit the scope of representation if the client gives informed consent in a writing signed by the client to the essential terms of the representation and the lawyer's limited role. Use of a written notice and consent form substantially similar to that contained in the comment to this Rule 4-1.2 creates the presumptions:
>
> (a) the representation is limited to the lawyer and the services described in the form, and (b) the lawyer does not represent the client generally or in any matters other than those identified in the form. . . ."

Missouri also retains Rule 1.2(e) from the 1983 version of ABA Model Rule 1.2 ("When a lawyer knows that a client expects assistance not permitted by the rules of professional conduct or other law, the lawyer shall consult with the client regarding the relevant limitations on the lawyer's conduct.").

New Hampshire: Rule 1.2(e) provides as follows:

> (e) It is not inconsistent with the lawyer's duty to seek the lawful objectives of a client through reasonably available means, for the lawyer to accede to reasonable requests of opposing counsel that do not prejudice the rights of the client, avoid the use of offensive or dilatory tactics, or treat opposing counsel or an opposing party with civility.

New Hampshire also adds Rule 1.2(f) to govern "limited representation to a client who is or may become involved in" litigation, and adds a detailed sample form for "Consent to Limited Representation" in a Rule 1.2(g).

New Mexico specifies in Rule 16-303(E) that a lawyer must disclose to a tribunal if the lawyer is representing the client in a "limited manner."

New York adds Rule 1.2(e)-(g), which are based on DR 7-101 of the old ABA Model Code. Comment 10 elaborates on what a lawyer must do when a client has undertaken an illegal or fraudulent course of action and "the representation will result in violation of the Rules of Professional Conduct or other law. . . ." Under these circumstances, "the lawyer must advise the client of any relevant limitation on the lawyer's conduct and remonstrate with the client. *See* Rules 1.4(a)(5) and 1.16(b)(1). Persuading a client to take necessary preventive or corrective action that will bring the client's conduct within the bounds of the law is a challenging but appropriate endeavor. If the client fails to take necessary corrective action and the lawyer's continued representation would assist client conduct that is illegal or fraudulent, the lawyer is required to withdraw."

North Carolina: Rule 1.2(a)(2) and (3) add language taken from DR 7-101(A)(1) and DR 7-101(B)(1) of the ABA Model Code of Professional Responsibility, and Rule 1.2(c) omits the ABA requirement that the client give informed consent.

Ohio: Rule 1.2(c) provides:

> A lawyer who undertakes representation of a client, other than by court appointment, shall confirm in writing, within a reasonable time, the nature and scope of the representation, unless the lawyer has regularly represented the client or the anticipated fee from the representation is $500.00 or less. A lawyer may limit the scope of a new or existing representation if the limitation is reasonable under the circumstances and communicated to the client in writing.

Texas omits ABA Model Rule 1.2(b). See also Texas Rule 1.05 and the annotations following Rule 1.6 below.

Virginia has moved the language of Rule 1.2(b) to Comment 3, and Virginia's Comment 1 requires lawyers to "advise the client about the advantages, disadvantages and availability of dispute resolution processes that might be appropriate in pursuing" the client's objectives. Virginia Rule 1.2(d) provides that a "lawyer may take such action on behalf of the client as is impliedly authorized to carry out the representation."

Wisconsin adds Rule 1.2(e) to clarify the obligations of counsel for an insurer.

Related Materials

ABA Formal Ethics Opinions: See ABA Formal Ethics Ops. 92-366 (1992), 93-371 (1993), 93-375 (1993), 94-380 (1994), 94-389 (1994), 96-399 (1996), 96-403 (1996), 97-405 (1997), 98-410 (1998), 01-421 (2001), 05-434 n.16 (2005), 06-438 (2006), 06-441 (2006), 07-446 (2007), 07-447 (2007), 07-448 (2007), and 08-452 (2008).

ABA Handbook on Limited Scope Representation: In 2003, the Modest Means Task Force of the ABA Section of Litigation published a lengthy report (149 pages) entitled Handbook on Limited Scope Legal Assistance. The report is available online at *http://apps.americanbar.org/litigation/taskforces/modest/report.pdf.*

ABA Standards for Criminal Justice: The following Standard is related to ABA Model Rule 1.2:

> *Standard 4-5.2 Control and Direction of the Case*
>
> (a) Certain decisions relating to the conduct of the case are ultimately for the accused and others are ultimately for defense counsel. The decisions which are to be made by the accused after full consultation with counsel include:
> what pleas to enter;
> whether to accept a plea agreement;
> whether to waive jury trial;
> whether to testify in his or her own behalf; and
> whether to appeal.
>
> (b) Strategic and tactical decisions should be made by defense counsel after consultation with the client where feasible and appropriate. Such decisions include what witnesses to call, whether and how to conduct cross-examination, what jurors to accept or strike, what trial motions should be made, and what evidence should be introduced.
>
> (c) If a disagreement on significant matters of tactics or strategy arises between defense counsel and the client, defense counsel should make a record of the circumstances, counsel's advice and reasons, and the conclusion reached. The record should be made in a manner which protects the confidentiality of the lawyer-client relationship.

Aiding and Abetting: In many jurisdictions, if a lawyer violates Rule 1.2(d) by counseling or assisting the client in criminal conduct, the lawyer would also be violating criminal laws prohibiting anyone from aiding or abetting the commission of a crime. For example, 18 U.S.C. §2(a) provides that "[w]hoever commits an offense against the United States or aids, abets, counsels, commands, induces or procures its commission, is punishable as a principal." Similarly, California Penal Code, Title 2 §31, provides:

> All persons concerned in the commission of a crime, whether it be felony or misdemeanor, and whether they directly commit the act constituting the offense, or aid and abet in its commission, or, not being present, have advised and encouraged its commission . . . are principals in any crime so committed.

In *Stoneridge Investment Partners v. Scientific-Atlanta,* 552 U.S. 148 (2008), the Supreme Court held that §10(b) of the Securities Exchange Act of 1934 does not create a private right of action against aiders and abettors of securities law violations. The decision meant that private plaintiffs could not bring class actions based on §10(b) against lawyers who allegedly aided and abetted their clients in committing securities fraud. Under *Stoneridge,* only the government may sue aiders and abettors. In 2009, Senator Arlen Specter introduced a bill known as the Liability for Aiding and Abetting Securities Violations Act of 2009 (S. 1551). The bill was intended to override *Stoneridge* by authorizing private plaintiffs to bring civil suits against anyone who "knowingly or recklessly provides substantial assistance" to a person engaged in fraud, but the bill did not become law and has not been reintroduced. However, on July 21, 2011, pursuant to a mandate in the Dodd-Frank Wall Street Reform and Consumer Protection Act, the Government Accountability Office (GAO) sent a report to Congress analyzing the impact of creating a private right of action against lawyers and other "secondary actors" for aiding and abetting securities law violations. The GAO report, entitled "Securities Fraud Liability of Secondary Actors," examined the pros and cons of extending liability to aiders and abettors but did not make any recommendations.

Collaborative Law: The collaborative dispute resolution process (commonly known as "collaborative law") is a form of limited-scope representation under Rule 1.2(c) in which the opposing parties agree to retain attorneys solely to negotiate a settlement, not to litigate. If either party ignores the agreement and goes to court, the attorneys must resign from the case. These terms are usually embodied in a "Participation Agreement" providing that if the parties are unable to reach a settlement, the lawyers will withdraw from the case and assist the clients in transitioning the case to trial attorneys. Practitioners of collaborative law generally believe that the agreement to collaborate and to withdraw if settlement cannot be achieved allows the parties and their lawyers to focus on problem-solving negotiations rather than tactical maneuvering. Collaborative law is most common in family law disputes, but its practice has spread to other areas of the law, including the settlement of contract and insurance disputes. For more information on collaborative law, visit *http://www.collaborativelaw.us.*

In 2009, the Uniform Law Commission (formerly the National Conference of Commissioners on Uniform State Laws) voted to approve a new Uniform Collaborative Law Act (UCLA) with the aim of increasing consistency from state to state regarding the enforceability of collaborative law agreements, the confidentiality of communications during the collaborative process, the automatic stay of any pending court proceedings that are also the subject of the collaborative law process, and the privilege against disclosure if the collaborative process does not lead to settlement. In 2010, the UCLA was amended to give states explicit options (a) to limit the act to domestic relations matters and (b) to adopt the UCLA in full or in part by court rule. The most recent version of the UCLA, as amended in 2010, is available at *http://www.law.upenn.edu/bll/archives/ulc/ucla/2010_final_amends.htm.* The UCLA has been enacted in three states (Utah, Nevada, and Texas), and has been introduced in the legislature in four jurisdictions (Alabama, Hawaii, Massachusetts, and the District of Columbia). The ABA Section of Family Law has approved the UCLA and favors its adoption in the states. But at the ABA's August 2011 Annual Meeting, after a contentious debate, the ABA House of Delegates voted 298-154 against a resolution endorsing the UCLA. For legislative updates and news of other developments regarding the UCLA, visit *http://www.nccusl.org/Act.aspx?title=Collaborative%20Law%20Act.*

Medicaid Fraud Legislation: As part of the Balanced Budget Act of 1997, Congress enacted the so-called "Granny's Lawyer Goes to Jail" law, 42 U.S.C. §1320a-7b(a)(6), which provides in part:

> Whoever . . . (6) for a fee knowingly and willfully counsels or assists an individual to dispose of assets (including by any transfer in trust) in order for the individual to become eligible for medical assistance . . . shall . . . (ii) . . . be guilty of a misdemeanor and upon conviction thereof fined not more than $10,000 or imprisoned for not more than one year, or both.

In *New York State Bar Ass'n v. Reno,* 999 F. Supp. 710 (N.D.N.Y. 1998), the court granted a preliminary injunction enjoining enforcement of the law. In *Magee v. United States,* 93 F. Supp. 2d 161 (D.R.I. 2000), however, a different court dismissed a suit challenging the law, even though the United States admitted that the law was "plainly unconstitutional," because in 1998

Attorney General Reno had informed Congress that the United States would not enforce the law, leaving no justiciable "case or controversy." For a history of the "Granny" statute, see *Rainey v. Guardianship of Mackey,* 773 So. 2d 118 (Fla. App. 4th Dist. 2000).

Restatement of the Law Governing Lawyers: See Restatement §§16, 21-23, 26, 51, 67, 82, 93, 94, and 120 in our chapter on the Restatement later in this volume. The Restatement has no provision comparable to ABA Model Rule 1.2(b).

Unbundled Legal Services: Some lawyers provide "unbundled" legal services, also called "discrete task representation," to clients otherwise acting pro se. Unbundled legal services are related to ABA Model Rule 1.2(c), which permits a lawyer to "limit the scope of the representation if the limitation is reasonable under the circumstances and the client gives informed consent." For example, if a person is conducting litigation pro se but wants some assistance from a lawyer, a lawyer who offers unbundled legal services might limit representation of the pro se litigant to drafting discovery requests, reviewing documents, or negotiating a settlement with the opposing lawyer. Some states, including California, Colorado, Florida, Maine, Missouri, Washington, Wisconsin, and Wyoming, have adopted rules expressly addressing unbundled legal services.

For extensive resources about unbundled legal services, including a 2005 white paper by the ABA Standing Committee on the Delivery of Legal Services entitled An Analysis of Rules that Enable Lawyers to Serve Pro Se Litigants, visit *http://apps.americanbar.org/legalservices/delivery/delunbund.html.* For a Handbook on Limited Scope Legal Assistance published by a task force of the ABA Section of Litigation, see *http://apps.americanbar.org/litigation/taskforces/modest/report.pdf.*

Rule 1.3 Diligence

A lawyer shall act with reasonable diligence and promptness in representing a client.

COMMENT

[1] A lawyer should pursue a matter on behalf of a client despite opposition, obstruction or personal inconvenience to the lawyer, and take whatever lawful and ethical measures are required to vindicate a client's cause or endeavor. A lawyer must also act with commitment and dedication to the interests of the client and with zeal in advocacy upon the client's behalf. A lawyer is not bound, however, to press for every advantage that might be realized for a client. For example, a lawyer may have authority to exercise professional discretion in determining the means by which a matter should be pursued. See Rule 1.2. The lawyer's duty to act with reasonable diligence does not require the use of offensive tactics or preclude the treating of all persons involved in the legal process with courtesy and respect.

[2] A lawyer's work load must be controlled so that each matter can be handled competently.

[3] Perhaps no professional shortcoming is more widely resented than procrastination. A client's interests often can be adversely affected by the passage of time or the change of conditions; in extreme instances, as when a lawyer overlooks a

statute of limitations, the client's legal position may be destroyed. Even when the client's interests are not affected in substance, however, unreasonable delay can cause a client needless anxiety and undermine confidence in the lawyer's trustworthiness. A lawyer's duty to act with reasonable promptness, however, does not preclude the lawyer from agreeing to a reasonable request for a postponement that will not prejudice the lawyer's client.

[4] Unless the relationship is terminated as provided in Rule 1.16, a lawyer should carry through to conclusion all matters undertaken for a client. If a lawyer's employment is limited to a specific matter, the relationship terminates when the matter has been resolved. If a lawyer has served a client over a substantial period in a variety of matters, the client sometimes may assume that the lawyer will continue to serve on a continuing basis unless the lawyer gives notice of withdrawal. Doubt about whether a client-lawyer relationship still exists should be clarified by the lawyer, preferably in writing, so that the client will not mistakenly suppose the lawyer is looking after the client's affairs when the lawyer has ceased to do so. For example, if a lawyer has handled a judicial or administrative proceeding that produced a result adverse to the client and the lawyer and the client have not agreed that the lawyer will handle the matter on appeal, the lawyer must consult with the client about the possibility of appeal before relinquishing responsibility for the matter. See Rule 1.4(a)(2). Whether the lawyer is obligated to prosecute the appeal for the client depends on the scope of the representation the lawyer has agreed to provide to the client. See Rule 1.2.

[5] To prevent neglect of client matters in the event of a sole practitioner's death or disability, the duty of diligence may require that each sole practitioner prepare a plan, in conformity with applicable rules, that designates another competent lawyer to review client files, notify each client of the lawyer's death or disability, and determine whether there is a need for immediate protective action. Cf. Rule 28 of the American Bar Association Model Rules for Lawyer Disciplinary Enforcement (providing for court appointment of a lawyer to inventory files and take other protective action in absence of a plan providing for another lawyer to protect the interests of the clients of a deceased or disabled lawyer).

Canon and Code Antecedents

ABA Canons of Professional Ethics: Canon 21 provided as follows:

21. Punctuality and Expedition

It is the duty of the lawyer not only to his client, but also to the Courts and to the public to be punctual in attendance, and to be concise and direct in the trial and disposition of causes.

ABA Model Code of Professional Responsibility: Compare DR 6-101, DR 7-101(A), and DR 7-101(A)(3) (reprinted later in this volume).

Cross-References in Other Rules

Rule 1.7, Comment 3: "As to whether a client-lawyer relationship exists or, having once been established, is continuing, see Comment to **Rule 1.3** and Scope."

Rule 1.7, Comment 15: In the case of a conflict of interest, "representation is prohibited if in the circumstances the lawyer cannot reasonably conclude that the lawyer will be able to provide competent and diligent representation (see Rules 1.1 and **1.3**)."

Rule 1.16, Comment 1: "Ordinarily, a representation in a matter is completed when the agreed-upon assistance has been concluded. See Rules 1.2(c) and 6.5. See also **Rule 1.3**, Comment [4]."

Legislative History of Model Rule 1.3

1980 Discussion Draft: "A lawyer shall attend promptly to matters undertaken for a client and give them adequate attention until completed or until the lawyer has properly withdrawn from representing the client."

1981 and ***1982 Drafts*** were the same as adopted.

1983 Rule: As originally adopted in 1983, Rule 1.3 was the same as the 2002 version.

2002 Amendments: At its February 2002 Mid-Year Meeting, the ABA House of Delegates adopted without change the ABA Ethics 2000 Commission proposal to amend the Comment to Rule 1.3 through additions and minor deletions. The amendments added Comments 2 and 5 and the final sentences in Comments 1, 3, and 4. The text of Rule 1.3 was not amended.

Selected State Variations

California: Rule 3-110(B) provides as follows:

> (A) A member shall not intentionally, recklessly, or repeatedly fail to perform legal services with competence.
>
> (B) For purposes of this rule, "competence" in any legal service shall mean to apply the 1) diligence, 2) learning and skill, and 3) mental, emotional, and physical ability reasonably necessary for the performance of such service.
>
> (C) If a member does not have sufficient learning and skill when the legal service is undertaken, the member may nonetheless perform such services competently by 1) associating with or, where appropriate, professionally consulting another lawyer reasonably believed to be competent, or 2) by acquiring sufficient learning and skill before performance is required.

District of Columbia: D.C Rule 1.3(a) and (b) provide as follows:

> (a) A lawyer shall represent a client zealously and diligently within the bounds of the law.
>
> (b) A lawyer shall not intentionally:
>
> (1) Fail to seek the lawful objectives of a client through reasonably available means permitted by law and the disciplinary rules. . . .

Georgia adds the following sentence to Rule 1.3: "Reasonable diligence as used in this Rule means that a lawyer shall not without just cause to the detriment of the client in effect willfully abandon or willfully disregard a legal matter entrusted to the lawyer."

Massachusetts: Rule 1.3 adds the following sentence: "The lawyer should represent a client zealously within the bounds of the law."

New York adds Rule 1.3(b)-(c), which is based on DR 6-101 of the old ABA Model Code. Moreover, rather than advising that reasonable diligence "does not require the use of offensive tactics," Comment 1 instructs lawyers that they "should not use offensive tactics."

Texas omits Rule 1.3.

Virginia adds the following subparagraphs (b) and (c) to Rule 1.3:

(b) A lawyer shall not intentionally fail to carry out a contract of employment entered into with a client for professional services, but may withdraw as permitted under Rule 1.16.

(c) A lawyer shall not intentionally prejudice or damage a client during the course of the professional relationship, except as required or permitted under Rule 1.6 and Rule 3.3.

Virginia also adds the following Comment to Rule 1.3:

[1a] Additionally, lawyers have long recognized that a more collaborative, problem-solving approach is often preferable to an adversarial strategy in pursuing the client's needs and interests. Consequently, diligence includes not only an adversarial strategy but also the vigorous pursuit of the client's interest in reaching a solution that satisfies the interests of all parties. The client can be represented zealously in either setting.

Related Materials

ABA Formal Ethics Opinions: See ABA Formal Ethics Ops. 92-369 (1992), 94-387 (1994), 96-399 (1996), and 06-441 (2006).

ABA Standards for Imposing Lawyer Discipline:

4.41. Disbarment is generally appropriate when:

(a) a lawyer abandons the practice and causes serious or potentially serious injury to a client; or

(b) a lawyer knowingly fails to perform services for a client and causes serious or potentially serious injury to a client; or

(c) a lawyer engages in a pattern of neglect with respect to client matters and causes serious or potentially serious injury to a client.

4.42. Suspension is generally appropriate when:

(a) a lawyer knowingly fails to perform services for a client and causes injury or potential injury to a client; or

(b) a lawyer engages in a pattern of neglect and causes injury or potential injury to a client.

"Diligence" is defined in Black's Law Dictionary (9th ed. 2009) as: "1. A continual effort to accomplish something. 2. Care; caution; the attention and care required from a person in a given situation."

IRS Regulations: In the regulations governing practice before the Internal Revenue Service, 31 C.F.R. §10.22(a) requires each attorney to "exercise due diligence" in preparing and filing tax returns, documents, affidavits, and other papers relating to Internal Revenue Service matters and in "determining the correctness of oral or written representations" to the Department of the Treasury or to clients in any matter administered by the Internal Revenue Service. Under §10.22(b), a practitioner will ordinarily be "presumed to have exercised due diligence . . . if the practitioner relies on the work product of another person and the practitioner used reasonable care in engaging, supervising, training, and evaluating the person, taking proper account of the nature of the relationship between the practitioner and the person."

Standards of Civility: In an effort to tamp down excessive zeal and "Rambo" litigation tactics, some bar associations have promulgated "standards of civility," and some tribunals have adopted these standards as guidelines. For example, on October 28, 2010, Chief Judge Carla Craig of the Bankruptcy Court for the Eastern District of New York issued an administrative order adopting guidelines for standards of civility for the legal profession. These guidelines were originally developed by the New York State Bar Association. Standards of civility vary from jurisdiction to jurisdiction and are invariably nonbinding.

Restatement of the Law Governing Lawyers: See Restatement §16(2) in our chapter on the Restatement later in this volume.

Rule 1.4 Communication 2.1

(a) A lawyer shall:

3.2 **(1) promptly inform the client of any decision or circumstance with respect to which the client's informed consent, as defined in Rule 1.0(e), is required by these Rules;**

(2) reasonably consult with the client about the means by which the client's objectives are to be accomplished;

(3) keep the client reasonably informed about the status of the matter;

(4) promptly comply with reasonable requests for information; and

(5) consult with the client about any relevant limitation on the lawyer's conduct when the lawyer knows that the client expects assistance not permitted by the Rules of Professional Conduct or other law.

(b) A lawyer shall explain a matter to the extent reasonably necessary to permit the client to make informed decisions regarding the representation.

1.2 CH13 lawyer's limits

COMMENT

[1] Reasonable communication between the lawyer and the client is necessary for the client effectively to participate in the representation.

Communicating with Client

[2] If these Rules require that a particular decision about the representation be made by the client, paragraph (a)(1) requires that the lawyer promptly consult with and secure the client's consent prior to taking action unless prior discussions with the client have resolved what action the client wants the lawyer to take. For example, a lawyer who receives from opposing counsel an offer of settlement in

a civil controversy or a proffered plea bargain in a criminal case must promptly inform the client of its substance unless the client has previously indicated that the proposal will be acceptable or unacceptable or has authorized the lawyer to accept or to reject the offer. See Rule 1.2(a).

[3] Paragraph (a)(2) requires the lawyer to reasonably consult with the client about the means to be used to accomplish the client's objectives. In some situations—depending on both the importance of the action under consideration and the feasibility of consulting with the client—this duty will require consultation prior to taking action. In other circumstances, such as during a trial when an immediate decision must be made, the exigency of the situation may require the lawyer to act without prior consultation. In such cases the lawyer must nonetheless act reasonably to inform the client of actions the lawyer has taken on the client's behalf. Additionally, paragraph (a)(3) requires that the lawyer keep the client reasonably informed about the status of the matter, such as significant developments affecting the timing or the substance of the representation.

[4] A lawyer's regular communication with clients will minimize the occasions on which a client will need to request information concerning the representation. When a client makes a reasonable request for information, however, paragraph (a)(4) requires prompt compliance with the request, or if a prompt response is not feasible, that the lawyer, or a member of the lawyer's staff, acknowledge receipt of the request and advise the client when a response may be expected. Client telephone calls should be promptly returned or acknowledged.

Explaining Matters

[5] The client should have sufficient information to participate intelligently in decisions concerning the objectives of the representation and the means by which they are to be pursued, to the extent the client is willing and able to do so. Adequacy of communication depends in part on the kind of advice or assistance that is involved. For example, when there is time to explain a proposal made in a negotiation, the lawyer should review all important provisions with the client before proceeding to an agreement. In litigation a lawyer should explain the general strategy and prospects of success and ordinarily should consult the client on tactics that are likely to result in significant expense or to injure or coerce others. On the other hand, a lawyer ordinarily will not be expected to describe trial or negotiation strategy in detail. The guiding principle is that the lawyer should fulfill reasonable client expectations for information consistent with the duty to act in the client's best interests, and the client's overall requirements as to the character of representation. In certain circumstances, such as when a lawyer asks a client to consent to a representation affected by a conflict of interest, the client must give informed consent, as defined in Rule 1.0(e).

[6] Ordinarily, the information to be provided is that appropriate for a client who is a comprehending and responsible adult. However, fully informing the client according to this standard may be impracticable, for example, where the client is a child or suffers from diminished capacity. See Rule 1.14. When the client is an organization or group, it is often impossible or inappropriate to inform every one of its members about its legal affairs; ordinarily, the lawyer should address communications to the appropriate officials of the organization. See Rule 1.13. Where many routine matters are involved, a system of limited or occasional reporting may be arranged with the client.

Withholding Information

[7] In some circumstances, a lawyer may be justified in delaying transmission of information when the client would be likely to react imprudently to an immediate communication. Thus, a lawyer might withhold a psychiatric diagnosis of a client when the examining psychiatrist indicates that disclosure would harm the client. A lawyer may not withhold information to serve the lawyer's own interest or convenience or the interests or convenience of another person. Rules or court orders governing litigation may provide that information supplied to a lawyer may not be disclosed to the client. Rule 3.4(c) directs compliance with such rules or orders.

Canon and Code Antecedents

ABA Canons of Professional Ethics: Canon 8 provided as follows:

8. Advising Upon the Merits of a Client's Cause

A lawyer should endeavor to obtain full knowledge of his client's cause before advising thereon, and he is bound to give a candid opinion of the merits and probable result of pending or contemplated litigation. The miscarriages to which justice is subject, by reason of surprises and disappointments in evidence and witnesses, and through mistakes of juries and errors of Courts, even though only occasional, admonish lawyers to beware of bold and confident assurances to clients, especially where the employment may depend upon such assurance. Whenever the controversy will admit of fair adjustment, the client should be advised to avoid or to end the litigation.

ABA Model Code of Professional Responsibility: Compare DR 6-101(A)(3) and DR 9-102(B)(1) (reprinted later in this volume).

Cross-References in Other Rules

Rule 1.2(a): "Subject to paragraphs (c) and (d), a lawyer shall abide by a client's decisions concerning the objectives of representation and, as required by **Rule 1.4**, shall consult with the client as to the means by which they are to be pursued."

Rule 1.2, Comment 1: "The decisions specified in paragraph (a) . . . must also be made by the client. See **Rule 1.4(a)(1)** for the lawyer's duty to communicate with the client about such decisions. With respect to the means by which the client's objectives are to be pursued, the lawyer shall consult with the client as required by **Rule 1.4 (a)(2)**. . . . "

Rule 1.2, Comment 3: "Absent a material change in circumstances and subject to **Rule 1.4**, a lawyer may rely on such an advance authorization."

Rule 1.2, Comment 13: "If a lawyer comes to know or reasonably should know that a client expects assistance not permitted by the Rules of Professional Conduct or other law or if the lawyer intends to act contrary to the client's instructions, the lawyer must consult with the client regarding the limitations on the lawyer's conduct. See **Rule 1.4(a)(5)**."

Rule 1.3, Comment 4: "Doubt about whether a client-lawyer relationship still exists should be clarified by the lawyer, preferably in writing, so that the client will not mistakenly suppose the lawyer is looking after the client's affairs when the lawyer has ceased to do so. See **Rule 1.4(a)(2)**."

Rule 1.6, Comment 12: "When disclosure of information relating to the representation appears to be required by other law, the lawyer must discuss the matter with the client to the extent required by **Rule 1.4**."

Rule 1.6, Comment 13: "In the event of an adverse ruling, the lawyer must consult with the client about the possibility of appeal to the extent required by **Rule 1.4**."

Rule 1.7, Comment 31: "As to the duty of confidentiality, continued common representation will almost certainly be inadequate if one client asks the lawyer not to disclose to the other client information relevant to the common representation. This is so because the lawyer has an equal duty of loyalty to each client, and each client has the right to be informed of anything bearing on the representation that might affect that client's interests and the right to expect that the lawyer will use that information to that client's benefit. See **Rule 1.4**."

Rule 2.1, Comment 5: "When a lawyer knows that a client proposes a course of action that is likely to result in substantial adverse legal consequences to the client, the lawyer's duty to the client under **Rule 1.4** may require that the lawyer offer advice if the client's course of action is related to the representation. Similarly, when a matter is likely to involve litigation, it may be necessary under **Rule 1.4** to inform the client of forms of dispute resolution that might constitute reasonable alternatives to litigation."

Rule 4.4, Comment 3: "Where a lawyer is not required by applicable law to do so, the decision to voluntarily return such a document is a matter of professional judgment ordinarily reserved to the lawyer. See Rules 1.2 and **1.4**."

Rule 5.5, Comment 20: "[A] lawyer who practices law in this jurisdiction pursuant to paragraphs (c) or (d) may have to inform the client that the lawyer is not licensed to practice law in this jurisdiction. For example, that may be required when the representation occurs primarily in this jurisdiction and requires knowledge of the law of this jurisdiction. See **Rule 1.4(b)**."

Legislative History of Model Rule 1.4

1979 Unofficial Pre-Circulation Draft (then Rule 1.3):

> (a) A lawyer shall keep a client informed about a matter in which the lawyer's services are being rendered. Informing the client includes:
>
> (1) Periodically advising the client of the status and progress of the matter;
>
> (2) Explaining the legal and practical aspects of the matter and foreseeable effects of alternative courses of action; and . . .
>
> (c) A lawyer may withhold information to which a client is otherwise entitled only when doing so is necessary to protect the client's interest or some superior interest.

1980 Discussion Draft prohibited a lawyer from withholding information to which a client was entitled "except when doing so is clearly necessary to protect the client's interest or to comply with the requirements of law or the rules of professional conduct."

1981 Draft provided:

> (b) A lawyer shall explain the legal and practical aspects of a matter and alternative courses of action to the extent reasonably necessary to permit the client to make informed decisions regarding the representation.

1982 Draft was adopted in 1983.

1983 Rule: As originally adopted in 1983, Rule 1.4(a) provided: "A lawyer shall keep a client reasonably informed about the status of a matter and promptly comply with reasonable requests for information." Rule 1.4(b) was the same as the 2002 version.

2002 Amendments: At its February 2002 Mid-Year Meeting, the ABA House of Delegates adopted without change the ABA Ethics 2000 Commission proposal to amend Rule 1.4 and its Comment. Subparagraphs (a)(1)-(5) of Rule 1.4 replaced the 1983 version of Rule 1.4(a). Rule 1.4(b) was unchanged. Comments 1-4 and the final sentence in Comment 5 were added.

Selected State Variations

Arizona adds Rule 1.4(c), which provides: "In a criminal case, a lawyer shall promptly inform a client of all proffered plea agreements."

Arkansas adds the following Rule 1.4(c), which describes a lawyer's obligation to "promptly notify a client in writing of the actual or constructive receipt by the attorney of a check or other payment . . . of a settlement, judgment, or other monies to which the client is entitled.":

> A lawyer shall promptly notify a client in writing of the actual or constructive receipt by the attorney of a check or other payment received from an insurance company, an opposing party, or from any other source which constitutes the payment of a settlement, judgment, or other monies to which the client is entitled.

California: Rule 3-500 provides:

> A member shall keep a client reasonably informed about significant developments relating to the employment or representation, including promptly complying with reasonable requests for information and copies of significant documents when necessary to keep the client so informed.

Rule 3-510 provides:

> (A) A member shall promptly communicate to the member's client:
>
> (1) All terms and conditions of any offer made to the client in a criminal matter; and
>
> (2) All amounts, terms, and conditions of any written offer of settlement made to the client in all other matters.
>
> (B) As used in this rule, "client" includes a person who possesses the authority to accept an offer of settlement or plea, or, in a class action, all the named representatives of the class.

California Business & Professions Code §6068(m) describes the same duties.

District of Columbia: D.C. adds Rule 1.4(c), which requires a lawyer "who receives an offer of settlement in a civil case or a proffered plea bargain in a criminal case" to "promptly" inform the client of its "substance."

Florida adds two rules relating to client communications that have no Model Rule counterpart. First, Rule 4-1.5(f)(4)(C) requires every lawyer who enters into a contingent fee agreement in a personal injury or property damage case to provide the client with a Statement of Client's Rights for Contingency Fees. The Statement must contain the following paragraph concerning the lawyer's obligation to communicate settlement offers:

> 10. . . . Your lawyer must notify you of all offers of settlement before and after the trial. Offers during the trial must be immediately communicated and you should consult with your lawyer regarding whether to accept a settlement. However, you must make the final decision to accept or reject a settlement.

Second, Rule 4-5.8 contains several provisions that restrict a lawyer's communications with clients when the lawyer decides to leave a law firm or when the law firm dissolves.

Louisiana: Rule 1.4(c) provides as follows:

> (c) A lawyer who provides any form of financial assistance to a client during the course of a representation shall, prior to providing such financial assistance, inform the client in writing of the terms and conditions under which such financial assistance is made, including but not limited to, repayment obligations, the imposition and rate of interest or other charges, and the scope and limitations imposed upon lawyers providing financial assistance as set forth in Rule 1.8(e).

Massachusetts: The Comment to Rule 1.4 states: "There will be circumstances in which a lawyer should advise a client concerning the advantages and disadvantages of available dispute resolution options. . . . "

Michigan adds to Rule 1.4(a): "A lawyer shall notify the client promptly of all settlement offers, mediation evaluations, and proposed plea bargains."

Missouri deletes subparagraphs (a)(1) and (a)(2) from ABA Model Rule 1.4.

Nevada has a Rule 1.4(c) entitled "Lawyer's Biographical Data Form." Among other details, it requires each lawyer or law firm to maintain a form containing "a factual statement detailing the background, training and experience of each lawyer or law firm." The form must list certain basic information and requires a lawyer or law firm to provide additional information upon request.

New York adds Rule 1.4(a)(1)(ii) and (iii), which provides that a lawyer should promptly inform a client of: "(ii) any information required by court rule or other law to be communicated to a client; and (iii) material developments in the matter including settlement or plea offers."

Ohio: Rule 1.4(c) provides:

> A lawyer shall inform a client at the time of the client's engagement of the lawyer or at any time subsequent to the engagement if the lawyer does not maintain professional liability insurance in the amounts of at least one hundred thousand dollars per occurrence and three hundred thousand dollars in the aggregate or if the lawyer's professional liability insurance is terminated. The notice shall be provided to the client on a separate form set forth following this rule and shall be signed by the client.

Rule 1.4(c) does not apply to government lawyers or to in-house counsel.

Virginia adds Rule 1.4(c), which requires a lawyer to "inform the client of facts pertinent to the matter and of communications from another party that may significantly affect settlement or resolution of the matter."

Related Materials

ABA Commission on Ethics 20/20: In 2009, the ABA created the ABA Commission on Ethics 20/20, which is comprehensively reviewing the ABA Model Rules of Professional Conduct in light of globalization and changes in information technology. On September 19, 2011, the Commission issued revised draft proposals on technology and confidentiality for public comment. These included a new proposal to delete the last sentence of Comment 4 to Rule 1.4, which currently says: "Client telephone calls should be promptly returned or acknowledged." The Commission proposes to replace that admonition with the following language: "Lawyers should promptly respond to or acknowledge client communications." The Commission believes that this language more accurately describes a lawyer's obligations in light of the increasing number of ways (*e.g.*, email, Twitter, instant messaging) in which clients use technology to communicate with lawyers. The 20/20 Commission may present these proposals (or revised versions of them) to the ABA House of Delegates at the ABA's August 2012 Annual Meeting. For updates, see the Ethics 20/20 Commission's website at *http://www.americanbar.org/Ethics2020.*

ABA Formal Ethics Opinions: See ABA Formal Ethics Ops. 92-362 (1992), 95-398 (1995), 96-399 (1996), 97-406 (1997), 99-414 (1999), 02-425 (2002), 02-426 (2002), 03-429 (2003), 06-441 (2006), 08-450 (2008), 08-453 n.14 (2008), 11-460 (2011).

ABA Standards for Imposing Lawyer Sanctions:

> 4.61. Disbarment is generally appropriate when a lawyer knowingly deceives a client with the intent to benefit the lawyer or another, and causes serious injury or potential serious injury to a client.
>
> 4.62. Suspension is generally appropriate when a lawyer knowingly deceives a client, and causes injury or potential injury to the client.

IRS Regulations: In the regulations governing practice before the Internal Revenue Service, 31 C.F.R. §10.33(a) provides that tax advisors should adhere to a series of "best practices," including:

> (1) Communicating clearly with the client regarding the terms of the engagement. For example, the advisor should determine the client's expected purpose for and use of the advice and should have a clear understanding with the client regarding the form and scope of the advice or assistance to be rendered. . . .
>
> (3) Advising the client regarding the import of the conclusions reached, including, for example, whether a taxpayer may avoid accuracy-related penalties under the Internal Revenue Code if a taxpayer acts in reliance on the advice. . . .

The explanatory material in 69 Fed. Reg. 75840 accompanying §10.33 says that these best practices are "aspirational" and that a practitioner who fails to comply with them "will not be subject to discipline under these regulations." Nevertheless, "tax professionals are expected to observe these practices to preserve public confidence in the tax system."

Restatement of the Law Governing Lawyers: See Restatement §20 in our chapter on the Restatement later in this volume.

Rule 1.5 Fees

(a) A lawyer shall not make an agreement for, charge, or collect an unreasonable fee or an unreasonable amount for expenses. The factors to be considered in determining the reasonableness of a fee include the following:

(1) the time and labor required, the novelty and difficulty of the questions involved, and the skill requisite to perform the legal service properly;

(2) the likelihood, if apparent to the client, that the acceptance of the particular employment will preclude other employment by the lawyer;

(3) the fee customarily charged in the locality for similar legal services;

(4) the amount involved and the results obtained;

(5) the time limitations imposed by the client or by the circumstances;

(6) the nature and length of the professional relationship with the client;

(7) the experience, reputation, and ability of the lawyer or lawyers performing the services; and

(8) whether the fee is fixed or contingent.

(b) The scope of the representation and the basis or rate of the fee and expenses for which the client will be responsible shall be communicated to the client, preferably in writing, before or within a reasonable time after commencing the representation, except when the lawyer will charge a regularly represented client on the same basis or rate. Any changes in the basis or rate of the fee or expenses shall also be communicated to the client.

(c) A fee may be contingent on the outcome of the matter for which the service is rendered, except in a matter in which a contingent fee is prohibited by paragraph (d) or other law. A contingent fee agreement shall be in a writing signed by the client and shall state the method by which the fee is to be determined, including the percentage or percentages that shall accrue to the lawyer in the event of settlement, trial or appeal; litigation and other expenses to be deducted from the recovery; and whether such expenses are to be deducted before or after the contingent fee is calculated. The agreement must clearly notify the client of any expenses for which the client will be liable whether or not the client is the prevailing party. Upon conclusion of a contingent fee matter, the lawyer shall provide the client with a written statement stating the outcome of the matter and, if there is a recovery, showing the remittance to the client and the method of its determination.

(d) A lawyer shall not enter into an arrangement for, charge, or collect:

(1) any fee in a domestic relations matter, the payment or amount of which is contingent upon the securing of a divorce or upon the amount of alimony or support, or property settlement in lieu thereof; or

(2) a contingent fee for representing a defendant in a criminal case.

(e) A division of a fee between lawyers who are not in the same firm may be made only if:

(1) the division is in proportion to the services performed by each lawyer or each lawyer assumes joint responsibility for the representation;

(2) the client agrees to the arrangement, including the share each lawyer will receive, and the agreement is confirmed in writing; and

(3) the total fee is reasonable.

COMMENT

Reasonableness of Fee and Expenses

[1] Paragraph (a) requires that lawyers charge fees that are reasonable under the circumstances. The factors specified in (1) through (8) are not exclusive. Nor will each factor be relevant in each instance. Paragraph (a) also requires that expenses for which the client will be charged must be reasonable. A lawyer may seek reimbursement for the cost of services performed in-house, such as copying, or for other expenses incurred in-house, such as telephone charges, either by charging a reasonable amount to which the client has agreed in advance or by charging an amount that reasonably reflects the cost incurred by the lawyer.

Basis or Rate of Fee

[2] When the lawyer has regularly represented a client, they ordinarily will have evolved an understanding concerning the basis or rate of the fee and the expenses for which the client will be responsible. In a new client-lawyer relationship, however, an understanding as to fees and expenses must be promptly established. Generally, it is desirable to furnish the client with at least a simple memorandum or copy of the lawyer's customary fee arrangements that states the general nature of the legal services to be provided, the basis, rate or total amount of the fee and whether and to what extent the client will be responsible for any costs, expenses or disbursements in the course of the representation. A written statement concerning the terms of the engagement reduces the possibility of misunderstanding.

[3] Contingent fees, like any other fees, are subject to the reasonableness standard of paragraph (a) of this Rule. In determining whether a particular contingent fee is reasonable, or whether it is reasonable to charge any form of contingent fee, a lawyer must consider the factors that are relevant under the circumstances. Applicable law may impose limitations on contingent fees, such as a ceiling on the percentage allowable, or may require a lawyer to offer clients an alternative basis for the fee. Applicable law also may apply to situations other than a contingent fee, for example, government regulations regarding fees in certain tax matters.

Terms of Payment

[4] A lawyer may require advance payment of a fee, but is obliged to return any unearned portion. See Rule 1.16(d). A lawyer may accept property in payment for services, such as an ownership interest in an enterprise, providing this does not involve acquisition of a proprietary interest in the cause of action or subject matter of the litigation contrary to Rule 1.8(i). However, a fee paid in property instead of money may be subject to the requirements of Rule 1.8(a) because such fees often have the essential qualities of a business transaction with the client.

[5] An agreement may not be made whose terms might induce the lawyer improperly to curtail services for the client or perform them in a way contrary to the client's interest. For example, a lawyer should not enter into an agreement whereby services are to be provided only up to a stated amount when it is foreseeable that

more extensive services probably will be required, unless the situation is adequately explained to the client. Otherwise, the client might have to bargain for further assistance in the midst of a proceeding or transaction. However, it is proper to define the extent of services in light of the client's ability to pay. A lawyer should not exploit a fee arrangement based primarily on hourly charges by using wasteful procedures.

Prohibited Contingent Fees

[6] Paragraph (d) prohibits a lawyer from charging a contingent fee in a domestic relations matter when payment is contingent upon the securing of a divorce or upon the amount of alimony or support or property settlement to be obtained. This provision does not preclude a contract for a contingent fee for legal representation in connection with the recovery of post-judgment balances due under support, alimony or other financial orders because such contracts do not implicate the same policy concerns.

Division of Fee

[7] A division of fee is a single billing to a client covering the fee of two or more lawyers who are not in the same firm. A division of fee facilitates association of more than one lawyer in a matter in which neither alone could serve the client as well, and most often is used when the fee is contingent and the division is between a referring lawyer and a trial specialist. Paragraph (e) permits the lawyers to divide a fee either on the basis of the proportion of services they render or if each lawyer assumes responsibility for the representation as a whole. In addition, the client must agree to the arrangement, including the share that each lawyer is to receive, and the agreement must be confirmed in writing. Contingent fee agreements must be in a writing signed by the client and must otherwise comply with paragraph (c) of this Rule. Joint responsibility for the representation entails financial and ethical responsibility for the representation as if the lawyers were associated in a partnership. A lawyer should only refer a matter to a lawyer whom the referring lawyer reasonably believes is competent to handle the matter. See Rule 1.1.

[8] Paragraph (e) does not prohibit or regulate division of fees to be received in the future for work done when lawyers were previously associated in a law firm.

Disputes over Fees

[9] If a procedure has been established for resolution of fee disputes, such as an arbitration or mediation procedure established by the bar, the lawyer must comply with the procedure when it is mandatory, and, even when it is voluntary, the lawyer should conscientiously consider submitting to it. Law may prescribe a procedure for determining a lawyer's fee, for example, in representation of an executor or administrator, a class or a person entitled to a reasonable fee as part of the measure of damages. The lawyer entitled to such a fee and a lawyer representing another party concerned with the fee should comply with the prescribed procedure.

Canon and Code Antecedents

ABA Canons of Professional Ethics: Canons 12, 13, 14, and 42 provided as follows:

12. Fixing the Amount of the Fee

In fixing fees, lawyers should avoid charges which overestimate their advice and services, as well as those which undervalue them. A client's ability to pay cannot justify a charge in excess of the value of the service, though his poverty may require a less charge, or even none at all. The reasonable requests of brother lawyers, and of their widows and orphans without ample means, should receive special and kindly consideration.

In determining the amount of the fee, it is proper to consider: (1) the time and labor required, the novelty and difficulty of the questions involved and the skill requisite properly to conduct the cause; (2) whether the acceptance of employment in the particular case will preclude the lawyer's appearance for others in cases likely to arise out of the transaction, and in which there is a reasonable expectation that otherwise he would be employed, or will involve the loss of other employment while employed in the particular case or antagonisms with other clients; (3) the customary charges of the Bar for similar services; (4) the amount involved in the controversy and the benefits resulting to the client from the services; (5) the contingency or the certainty of the compensation; and (6) the character of the employment, whether casual or for an established and constant client. No one of these considerations in itself is controlling. They are mere guides in ascertaining the real value of the service.

In determining the customary charges of the Bar for similar services, it is proper for a lawyer to consider a schedule of minimum fees adopted by a Bar Association, but no lawyer should permit himself to be controlled thereby or to follow it as his sole guide in determining the amount of his fee.

In fixing fees it should never be forgotten that the profession is a branch of the administration of justice and not a mere money-getting trade.

13. Contingent Fees

A contract for a contingent fee, where sanctioned by law, should be reasonable under all the circumstances of the case, including the risk and uncertainty of the compensation, but should always be subject to the supervision of a court, as to its reasonableness.

14. Suing a Client for a Fee

Controversies with clients concerning compensation are to be avoided by the lawyer so far as shall be compatible with his self-respect and with his right to receive reasonable recompense for his services; and lawsuits with clients should be resorted to only to prevent injustice, imposition or fraud.

42. Expenses of Litigation

A lawyer may not properly agree with a client that the lawyer shall pay or bear the expenses of litigation; he may in good faith advance expenses as a matter of convenience, but subject to reimbursement.

ABA Model Code of Professional Responsibility: Compare DR 2-106(A), DR 2-106(B), DR 2-106(C), and DR 2-107(A) (reprinted later in this volume).

Cross-References in Other Rules

Rule 1.8, Comment 1: Rule 1.8 "does not apply to ordinary fee arrangements between client and lawyer, which are governed by **Rule 1.5**."

Rule 1.8, Comment 9: Rule 1.8(d) "does not prohibit a lawyer representing a client in a transaction concerning literary property from agreeing that the lawyer's fee shall consist of a share in ownership in the property, if the arrangement conforms to **Rule 1.5**. . . ."

Rule 1.8, Comment 16: Rule 1.8(i) "states the traditional general rule that lawyers are prohibited from acquiring a proprietary interest in litigation. . . . The Rule is subject to specific exceptions. . . . Contracts for contingent fees in civil cases are governed by **Rule 1.5**."

Rule 1.17, Comment 5: "If an area of practice is sold and the lawyer remains in the active practice of law, the lawyer must cease accepting any matters in the area of practice that has been sold, either as counsel or co-counsel or by assuming joint responsibility for a matter in connection with the division of a fee with another lawyer as would otherwise be permitted by **Rule 1.5(e)**."

Rule 7.2, Comment 8: "Except as provided in **Rule 1.5(e)**, a lawyer who receives referrals from a lawyer or nonlawyer professional must not pay anything solely for the referral. . . ."

Legislative History of Model Rule 1.5

1979 Unofficial Pre-Circulation Draft (then Rule 1.4):

> (b) A fee agreement shall . . .
>
> (2) State with reasonable definiteness, expressly or by implication, the nature and extent of the services to be provided; and . . .
>
> (c) A fee agreement shall be expressed or confirmed in writing before the lawyer has rendered substantial services in the matter, except:
>
> (1) Where an agreement as to the fee is implied by the fact that the lawyer's services are of the same general kind as previously rendered to and paid for by the client;
>
> (2) For services rendered in an emergency where a written agreement or confirmation is impracticable. . . .

1980 Discussion Draft (then Rule 1.6):

> (b) The basis or rate of a lawyer's fee shall be put in writing before the lawyer has rendered substantial services in the matter, except when:
>
> (1) An agreement as to the fee is implied by the fact that the lawyer's services are of the same general kind as previously rendered to and paid for by the client; or
>
> (2) The services are rendered in an emergency where a writing is impracticable.
>
> (c) The form of a fee and the terms of a fee agreement shall involve no inducement for the lawyer to perform the services in a manner inconsistent with the best interests of the client. . . .
>
> (e) A division of fee between lawyers who are not in the same firm may be made only if:
>
> (1) The division is in proportion to the services performed by each lawyer, or both lawyers expressly assume responsibility as if they were partners;
>
> (2) The terms of the division are disclosed to the client. . . .

1981 Draft of Rule 1.5(b) continued to require that the "basis or rate of a lawyer's fee shall be communicated to the client in writing before the lawyer renders substantial services in a matter. . . ."

1982 Draft was substantially the same as adopted.

1983 Rule: From its original adoption in 1983 until its amendment in 2002, Rule 1.5 provided as follows:

Rule 1.5 Fees

(a) A lawyer's fee shall be reasonable. The factors to be considered in determining the reasonableness of a fee include the following:

(1)-(8) [Same as 2002 version of Rules 1.5(a)(1)-(8).]

(b) When the lawyer has not regularly represented the client, the basis or rate of the fee shall be communicated to the client, preferably in writing, before or within a reasonable time after commencing the representation.

(c) A fee may be contingent on the outcome of the matter for which the service is rendered, except in a matter in which a contingent fee is prohibited by paragraph (d) or other law. A contingent fee agreement shall be in a writing and shall state the method by which the fee is to be determined, including the percentage or percentages that shall accrue to the lawyer in the event of settlement, trial or appeal; litigation and other expenses to be deducted from the recovery; and whether such expenses are to be deducted before or after the contingent fee is calculated. Upon conclusion of a contingent fee matter, the lawyer shall provide the client with a written statement stating the outcome of the matter and, if there is a recovery, showing the remittance to the client and the method of its determination.

(d) [Same as 2002 version of Rule 1.5(d).]

(e) A division of a fee between lawyers who are not in the same firm may be made only if:

(1) the division is in proportion to the services performed by each lawyer or, by written agreement with the client, each lawyer assumes joint responsibility for the representation;

(2) the client is advised of and does not object to the participation of all lawyers involved; and

(3) the total fee is reasonable.

2002 Amendments: In 2001, the ABA House of Delegates adopted most of the ABA Ethics 2000 Commission's proposed amendments to Rule 1.5. Specifically, the ABA amended Rule 1.5(a) to forbid unreasonable expenses; amended Rule 1.5(c) to require that a contingent fee agreement be signed by the client and notify the client of expenses for which the client will be liable; and amended Rule 1.5(e)(2) to require that the client agree to "the share each lawyer will receive" and confirm the agreement "in writing." But regarding Rule 1.5(b), the House of Delegates rejected the Commission's proposal to delete the word "preferably" before the words "in writing" (which would have made written disclosure mandatory). In addition, the House substituted the words "to the client" for the words "in writing" at the end of Rule 1.5(b) (which requires lawyers to communicate any changes in the basis or rate of the fee or expenses). The amendments also added Comments 1, 3, 6, and 8 and amended various other Comments to reflect the changes in the text of the rule.

Selected State Variations

Alaska: Rule 1.5(b) requires all fee agreements to be in writing when the fee will exceed $1,000. Moreover, Rule 1.5(f) instructs lawyers that they "should seek to avoid controversies over fees with clients and should attempt to resolve amicably any differences on the subject."

Arizona: Rule 1.5(b) requires lawyers to enter written fee agreements "before or within a reasonable time after commencing the representation." Arizona adds Rule 1.5(d)(3), which provides that when a lawyer denominates a fee as "earned upon receipt" or "nonrefundable," the client must be informed "in writing that the client may nevertheless discharge the lawyer at any time and in that event may be entitled to a refund of all or part of the fee based upon the value of the representation pursuant to paragraph (a)." Finally, Comment 6 says that Rule 1.5(d) allows a contingent fee "for legal representation in connection with the recovery of post-judgment balances due under support, alimony or other financial orders because such contracts do not implicate the same policy concerns" as other domestic relations matters.

Arkansas: Rule 1.5(d)(1) adds that in a domestic relations matter, "after a final order or decree is entered a lawyer may enter into a contingent fee contract for collection of payments which are due pursuant to such decree or order."

California: Rule 4-200 forbids lawyers to "enter into an agreement for, charge, or collect an illegal or unconscionable fee." Unconscionability is determined based on facts "existing at the time the agreement is entered into except where the parties contemplate that the fee will be affected by later events." The rule contains 11 factors to weigh in determining conscionability, many of them derived from the Model Rules. In addition, see Business & Professions Code §§ 6147-6149 (governing contingency fee contracts and other fee arrangements), and Business & Professions Code §§ 6200-6206 (establishing a system and procedures for arbitrating fee disputes).

Colorado: Effective July 1, 2011, Rule 1.5(b) requires a lawyer who has not regularly represented a client to communicate the basis or rate of the fee and expenses "in writing." Moreover, Rule 1.5(b) provides that "[a]ny changes in the basis or rate of the fee or expenses shall also be promptly communicated to the client, in writing." Rule 1.5(c) requires more elaborate disclosures in contingency fee cases than the Model Rule.

Delaware: Rule 1.5(e) does not require that the client know how lawyers in different firms are dividing a fee. Delaware adds Rule 1.5(f), which allows the lawyer to require the client to pay fees in advance, provided that the lawyer gives the client "a written statement" explaining, among other things, that "the fee is refundable if not earned."

District of Columbia: D.C. Rule 1.5(b) requires a written fee agreement where the lawyer has not "regularly represented" the client. Rule 1.5(d) forbids contingent fees in criminal cases but not in matrimonial cases. Rule 1.5(e) does not require that the client be told how much each lawyer is to receive when fees are divided between lawyers not in the same firm, but the client must be told "the effect of the association of lawyers outside the firm on the fee to be charged."

Florida: Rule 4-1.5(a) prohibits any fee "generated by employment that was obtained through advertising or solicitation not in compliance with the Rules Regulating The Florida Bar" or that is "clearly excessive." A clearly excessive fee includes (1) a fee that exceeds a reasonable fee by so much that it constitutes "clear overreaching or an unconscionable demand," or (2) a fee sought or secured "by means of intentional misrepresentation or fraud upon the client, a nonclient party, or any court, as to either entitlement to, or amount of, the fee." Florida also caps the percentage amount of any contingent fee.

Rule 4-1.5(e) provides that "a fee for legal services that is nonrefundable in any part shall be confirmed in writing and shall explain the intent of the parties as to the nature and amount of the nonrefundable fee. The test of reasonableness found in subdivision (b), above, applies to all fees for legal services without regard to their characterization by the parties."

Regarding fee sharing between lawyers in different firms, Rule 4-1.5(f)(2) requires that each participating lawyer "shall sign the contract with the client and shall agree to assume joint legal responsibility to the client for the performance of the services in question as if each were partners of the other lawyer or law firm involved." Florida also tightly controls the terms on which lawyers in different firms may share fees. Rule 4-1.5(f)(4)(D) provides that "the lawyer assuming primary responsibility for the legal services" must receive "a minimum of 75% of the total fee," and "the lawyer assuming secondary responsibility" can receive "a maximum of 25% of the total fee. Any fee in excess of 25% shall be presumed to be clearly excessive." But if two or more lawyers expect to "accept substantially equal active participation in the providing of legal services," then they may seek court authorization to divide the fee however they propose "based upon a sworn petition signed by all counsel that shall disclose in detail those services to be performed."

Florida Rule 4-1.5(g) provides that if lawyers in different firms share fees on a basis not in proportion to the amount of work done, then each lawyer must not only agree to assume "joint legal responsibility for the representation" but must also agree "to be available for consultation with the client."

The Florida Supreme Court may also order any lawyer found guilty of violating the fee rules "to forfeit the fee or any part thereof," either by returning the excessive part of any fee to the client or by forfeiting all or part of an otherwise improper fee to the Florida Bar Clients' Security Fund. See Florida Supreme Court Rule 3-5.1(h).

Finally, Rule 4-1.5(i) provides that, if a retainer agreement includes a mandatory arbitration clause, the agreement must include a verbatim, bolded recitation of the notice that appears at the end of Rule 1.5(i).

Georgia adds to Rule 1.5(c) that a lawyer must include in the written statement at the conclusion of a contingent fee matter the amount of the attorney's fee and "(D) if the attorney's fee is divided with another lawyer who is not a partner in or an associate of the lawyer's firm or law office, the amount of fee received by each and the manner in which the division is determined." Georgia also adds to Rule 1.5(e)(2) that the client must be "advised of the share that each lawyer is to receive" when lawyers in different firms share a fee.

Illinois: Rule 1.5(e)(1) provides that a division of a fee with a lawyer in a different firm is permissible if it "is in proportion to the services performed by each lawyer, or if the primary service performed by one lawyer is the referral of the client to another lawyer and each lawyer assumes joint financial responsibility for the representation."

Maine includes two additional considerations in Rule 1.5(a): whether the client gave informed consent to the fee agreement and whether the fee agreement was in writing. In Rule 1.5(d)(3), Maine prohibits a lawyer from charging a fee based on "a percentage of the value of the estate" for administering an estate in probate.

Massachusetts: Effective March 15, 2011, Rule 1.5(c) does not require a contingent fee to be in writing if it concerns "the collection of commercial accounts" or "insurance company subrogation claims," but all other contingent fee agreements must be in writing and must contain greater detail than Model Rule 1.5(c) requires. Rule 1.5(e) permits a lawyer to pay a fee to a referring lawyer even when the referring lawyer does not perform any services or take joint responsibility for the matter. Although client consent to such a referral fee must be in writing, a comment indicates that the lawyer does not have to disclose the size of the referral fee unless the client asks. Finally, Massachusetts Rule 1.5 appends two model form contingency fee agreements, and Rule 1.5(f), which has no Model Rule equivalent, identifies explanations that a lawyer must provide to clients when using the model form contingency fee agreements.

Michigan: Rule 1.5(d) forbids contingent fees in "a domestic relations matter" without qualification. In personal injury and wrongful death claims, Michigan Court Rule 8.121 sets a maximum contingent fee of "one-third of the amount recovered" and provides that receiving, retaining, or sharing a larger contingent fee "shall be deemed to be the charging of a 'clearly excessive fee' in violation of" Rule 1.5(a). Michigan omits ABA Model Rule 1.5(e)(1).

New Hampshire: Rule 1.5(e) permits fee sharing between lawyers in different firms if the division is made "either: (a) in reasonable proportion to the services performed or responsibility or risks assumed by each, or (b) based on an agreement with the referring lawyer," provided that in either case the lawyers obtain the client's signed written agreement to the division of fees and the total fee charged by all lawyers "is not increased by the division of fees and is reasonable."

New Jersey: Rule 1.5(b) requires a fee agreement to be in writing if the lawyer has not regularly represented the client. In addition, New Jersey has adopted various court rules that tightly control contingent fees, especially in tort cases.

New York: Rule 1.5 contains numerous significant variations. For example, 1.5(a) relies on the definition of an excessive fee found in DR 2-106(B) of the old Model Code. Moreover, Rule 1.5(d) prohibits:

> (2) a fee prohibited by law or rule of court;
>
> (3) a fee based on fraudulent billing;
>
> (4) a nonrefundable retainer fee; provided that a lawyer may enter into a retainer agreement with a client containing a reasonable minimum fee clause if it defines in plain language and sets forth the circumstances under which such fee may be incurred and how it will be calculated. . . .

Comments 1A and 1B explain the purpose of Rule 1.5(d)(3) as follows:

> [1A] A billing is fraudulent if it is knowingly and intentionally based on false or inaccurate information. Thus, under an hourly billing arrangement, it would be fraudulent to knowingly and intentionally charge a client for more than the actual number of hours spent by the lawyer on the client's matter; similarly, where the client has agreed to pay the lawyer's cost of in-house services, such as for photocopying or telephone calls, it would be fraudulent knowingly and intentionally to charge a client more than the actual costs incurred. Fraudulent billing requires an element of scienter and does not include inaccurate billing due to an innocent mistake.
>
> [1B] A supervising lawyer who submits a fraudulent bill for fees or expenses to a client based on submissions by a subordinate lawyer has not automatically violated this Rule. In this situation, whether the lawyer is responsible for a violation must be determined by reference to Rules 5.1, 5.2, and 5.3. . . .

Comment 5A explains that "New York Court Rules require every lawyer with an office located in New York to post in that office, in a manner visible to clients of the lawyer, a 'Statement of Client's Rights.' " Rule 1.5(e) provides that a copy of this Statement must be provided to all domestic relations clients.

Finally, New York Court Rules supplement Rule 1.5(b) and provide that most fee agreements must be in writing. 22 N.Y.C.R.R. Part 1215 provides as follows:

Part 1215 Written Letter of Engagement

§1215.21 Requirements

(a) Effective March 4, 2002, an attorney who undertakes to represent a client and enters into an arrangement for, charges or collects any fee from a client shall provide to the client a written letter of engagement before commencing the representation, or within a reasonable time thereafter (i) if otherwise impracticable or (ii) if the scope of services to be provided cannot be determined at the time of the commencement of representation. For purposes of this rule, where an entity (such as an insurance carrier) engages an attorney to represent a third party, the term "client" shall mean the entity that engages the attorney. Where there is a significant change in the scope of services or the fee to be charged, an updated letter of engagement shall be provided to the client.

(b) The letter of engagement shall address the following matters:

(1) explanation of the scope of the legal services to be provided;

(2) explanation of attorney's fees to be charged, expenses and billing practices; and,

(3) where applicable, shall provide that the client may have a right to arbitrate fee disputes under Part 137 of this Title.

(c) Instead of providing the client with a written letter of engagement, an attorney may comply with the provisions of subdivision (a) of this section by entering into a signed written retainer agreement with the client, before or within a reasonable time after commencing the representation, provided that the agreement addresses the matters set forth in subdivision (b) of this section.

§1215.2 Exceptions

This section shall not apply to

(a) representation of a client where the fee to be charged is expected to be less than $3000;

(b) representation where the attorney's services are of the same general kind as previously rendered to and paid for by the client;

(c) representation in domestic relations matters subject to Part 1400 of this Title; or

(d) representation where the attorney is admitted to practice in another jurisdiction and maintains no office in the State of New York, or where no material portion of the services are to be rendered in New York.

North Carolina: Rule 1.5(a) forbids a "clearly excessive fee" but otherwise substantially tracks ABA Model Rule 1.5(a). North Carolina adds Rule 1.5(f), which provides as follows:

(f) Any lawyer having a dispute with a client regarding a fee for legal services must:

(1) make reasonable efforts to advise his or her client of the existence of the North Carolina State Bar's program of fee dispute resolution at least 30 days prior to initiating legal proceedings to collect the disputed fee; and

(2) participate in good faith in the fee dispute resolution process if the client submits a proper request.

Ohio: Rule 1.5(b) requires fee agreements to be in writing unless the lawyer has "regularly represented" the client and is charging on the same basis or the fee is $500 or less. Any change in the basis of a fee previously communicated must be "promptly communicated to the client in writing." Rule 1.5(e), in permitting division of fees, does not require that the client be informed of the amount each lawyer is receiving.

Oregon: Among other variations, Rule 1.5(d) permits a division of fees between lawyers in different firms if "(1) the client gives informed consent to the fact that there will be a division of fees, and (2) the total fee of the lawyers for all legal services they rendered the client is not clearly excessive."

Pennsylvania: Rule 1.5(a) prohibits an "illegal or clearly excessive fee" (rather than an "unreasonable" one) and makes no reference to expenses. Rule 1.5(b) requires a fee agreement to be "in writing" if a lawyer has not "regularly" represented a client. Pennsylvania Rule 1.5(e) requires only that "(1) the client is advised of and does not object to the participation of all the lawyers involved, and (2) the total fee of the lawyers is not illegal or clearly excessive. . . . "

Rhode Island: Rule 1.5(b) provides that if a lawyer has not regularly represented a client, the basis or rate of the fee "shall be communicated to the client in writing." The same rule requires lawyers to send quarterly bills unless the client agrees to a different billing schedule or the fee is fixed or contingent.

South Carolina: Rule 1.5(d)(1) expressly permits a lawyer to charge a contingency fee "in collection of past due alimony or child support."

Texas: Rule 1.04(a) forbids "illegal" or "unconscionable" fees and lists the same considerations as in ABA Model Rule 1.5. The Texas Rules do not forbid contingent fees in family law matters but the Comment says they are "rarely justified." Rule 1.04(f), which governs the division of fees between lawyers in different firms, generally parallels ABA Model Rule 1.5(e) but requires client consent "in writing to the terms of the arrangement prior to the time of the association or referral proposed. . . . "

Tennessee: In the rules effective January 1, 2011, Tennessee adds two additional factors to Rule 1.5(b): "(9) prior advertisements or statements by the lawyer with respect to the fees the lawyer charges; and (10) whether the fee agreement is in writing." Moreover, Tennessee adds Rule 1.5(f), which allows lawyers to collect nonrefundable fees and retainers as long as the fee agreement is in writing, is signed by the client, and "explains the intent of the parties as to the nature and amount of the nonrefundable fee."

Virginia: Rule 1.5(b) provides in part: "The lawyer's fee shall be adequately explained to the client." Rule 1.5(d)(1) forbids contingent fees in "a domestic relations matter, except in rare instances." Comment 3a says that those rare instances include situations where "the parties are divorced and reconciliation is not a realistic prospect." Rule 1.5(e) requires full disclosure to the client when lawyers are dividing a fee. The "terms of the division of the fee" must be "disclosed to the client," the client must consent, the total fee must be reasonable, and the fee division and client consent must be "obtained in advance of the rendering of legal services." However, while a writing is said to be preferable, none is required.

Wisconsin: Rule 1.5(e) permits lawyers in different firms to divide a fee only if the total fee is reasonable and the lawyers satisfy several other specific requirements.

Related Materials

ABA Commission on Billable Hours: In 2001, the ABA appointed the Commission on the Billable Hour. In 2002, the commission issued its report, which is available (together with a lengthy appendix and other useful materials on the billable hour). The Commission's purpose is eloquently explained in the preface to the report, which provides, in pertinent part, as follows:

> It has become increasingly clear that many of the legal profession's contemporary woes intersect at the billable hour. The 1960s marked the coming of age of the billable hour. . . .
>
> Today, unintended consequences of the billable hours model have permeated the profession. A recent study by the ABA shows that many young attorneys are leaving the profession due to a lack of balance in their lives. The unending drive for billable hours has had a negative effect not only on family and personal relationships, but on the public service role that lawyers traditionally have played in society. The elimination of discretionary time has taken a toll on pro bono work and our profession's ability to be involved in our communities. At the same time, professional development, workplace stimulation, mentoring and lawyer/client relationships have all suffered as a result of billable hour pressures.
>
> The profession is paying the price. Disaffection with the practice of law is illustrated by a feeling of frustration and isolation on the part of newer lawyers who, due to time-billing pressures, are not being as well mentored as in the past. Time pressures also result in less willingness on the part of lawyers to be collegial, which only exacerbates work load since it necessitates that everything be put in writing. Not coincidentally, public respect for lawyers has been waning since the 1970s. All this at a time when lawyers are less interested in climbing the corporate ladder and more interested in life balance. Many lawyers indicate that they would gladly take a substantial pay cut in exchange for a decrease in billable hours. . . .
>
> . . . The billable hour is fundamentally about quantity over quality, repetition over creativity. With no gauge for intangibles such as productivity, creativity, knowledge or technological advancements, the billable hours model is a counter-intuitive measure of value. Alternatives that encourage efficiency and improve processes not only increase profits and provide early resolution of legal matters, but are less likely to garner ethical concerns.
>
> That said, the outright elimination of time billing is not a likely proposition. In fact, time billing as one aspect of price-setting for legal services is an appropriate and necessary tool in certain situations. Our profession's goal, however, should be to adopt innovative billing methods that provide an accurate measure of value to the client and, at the same time, make the practice of law more fulfilling and enjoyable.

ABA Formal Ethics Opinions: See ABA Formal Ethics Ops. 87-354 (1987), 93-373 (1993), 93-379 (1993), 94-389 (1994), 00-418 (2000), 00-420 (2000), 02-426 (2002), and 08-451 (2008).

ABA Model Rules for Fee Arbitration: In 1992, the ABA Commission on Evaluation of Disciplinary Enforcement (the McKay Commission) recommended that each state establish mandatory arbitration for fee disputes. In 1995, the ABA adopted Model Rules for Fee Arbitration, which mandate fee arbitration if the client requests it. Some states go further than the ABA Model by making fee arbitration binding as well as mandatory. (A few states do not mandate fee arbitration, but make it binding if the lawyer and client agree to arbitrate the dispute.) No state gives lawyers the option to require fee arbitration. The Model Rules for Fee Arbitration are available online, together with links to other useful materials, at *http://www.americanbar.org/groups/professional_responsibility/resources/client_protection/contents.html.*

ABA TIPS Task Force on the Contingent Fee: In 2003, the Chair of the ABA Tort Trial & Insurance Practice Section (TIPS) appointed a Task Force on Contingent Fees. The Task Force is especially concerned about support by various state medical associations and other organizations for statutes and ethical rules severely limiting contingent fees. In 2004, the Task Force issued a lengthy Report on Contingent Fees in Medical Malpractice Litigation. The Report included the following conclusions:

> A. Limitations on fees by the formulae recently proposed in Florida and elsewhere risk compromising access to justice by medical malpractice victims. Without the prospect of reasonable fees, competent counsel would be unwilling to assume the high cost burden associated with typically complex medical malpractice actions.
>
> B. The right of people who have suffered injury as a result of medical malpractice to seek redress for their injuries in the courts must be ensured. A fair and reasonable contingent fee is essential to preserve that right.

However, to help keep contingent fee rates down, the Task Force proposed standardized disclosures such as (a) details about how medical malpractice cases are typically handled; (b) predicted costs of litigation (expert fees, investigation, discovery, etc.); (c) alternative fee arrangements, including how fees are calculated; (d) urging clients to seek out experienced, perhaps specialized, law firms; and (e) noting that interviewing several firms and requesting written bids can lower litigation costs. More information about the Task Force, and the full text of its Report, is available at *http://apps.americanbar.org/tips/contingent/home.html.*

Caps on Contingent Fees: Various state and federal laws place upper limits on contingent fees, especially in medical malpractice cases, tort cases, and government benefit cases. For example, at the federal level, 42 U.S.C. §406(b) provides that attorneys who successfully represent Social Security benefits claimants may not charge more than 25 percent of the past-due benefits recovered. Another federal law, 28 U.S.C. §2678, imposes a strict 25 percent maximum on fees in suits brought under the Federal Tort Claims Act, and a violation is subject to criminal penalties ("Any attorney who charges, demands, receives, or collects . . . in excess of that allowed under this section . . . shall be fined not more than $2,000 or imprisoned not more than one year, or both"). At the state level, California's Medical Injury Compensation Reform Act (MICRA) limits attorney fees in medical malpractice cases to 40 percent of the first $50,000 recovered, 33 percent of the second $50,000, 25 percent of a recovery between $100,000 and $600,000, and 15 percent of a recovery over $600,000. In New York, Judiciary Law §474-a establishes a similar sliding scale for medical malpractice cases. Outside the medical malpractice area, New York court rules such as 22 N.Y.C.R.R. §603.7(e) generally limit contingent fees to 33-1/3 percent in all personal injury and wrongful death cases.

In some states, ballot measures have limited contingent fees in medical malpractice cases. For example, in 2004, by a roughly 2-1 margin, Florida voters passed a constitutional amendment sponsored by Citizens for a Fair Share, a political action committee supported by the Florida Medical Association. The amendment, now codified as Article 1, §26 of the Florida Constitution, provides as follows:

> *Claimant's right to fair compensation.* In any medical liability claim involving a contingency fee, the claimant is entitled to receive no less than 70% of the first $250,000.00

> in all damages received by the claimant, exclusive of reasonable and customary costs, whether received by judgment, settlement, or otherwise, and regardless of the number of defendants. The claimant is entitled to 90% of all damages in excess of $250,000.00, exclusive of reasonable and customary costs and regardless of the number of defendants. This provision is self-executing and does not require implementing legislation.

Also in 2004, in a referendum that won by a 59 percent to 41 percent margin, Nevada voters passed a law entitled "Keep Our Doctors in Nevada" that limits attorney fees in medical malpractice cases to 40 percent of the first $50,000 recovered, 33-1/3 percent of the next $50,000, 25 percent of the next $500,000, and 15 percent of any amount over $600,000.

FTC Mortgage Assistance Relief Services Rule: During the mortgage foreclosure crisis that began in 2008, many lawyers and nonlawyers went into the business of obtaining modifications to home mortgages. According to the Federal Trade Commission (FTC), many nonlawyer mortgage relief firms pretend to be affiliated with the government or with government housing assistance programs and routinely charge up-front fees for services they often do not deliver. To combat these abuses, on November 19, 2010, the FTC issued a final Mortgage Assistance Relief Services Rule that prohibits mortgage relief companies from accepting any payment for their services until they obtain a documented offer from a mortgage lender or servicer that satisfies any promises made to a borrower seeking assistance. The rule also requires mortgage relief companies to tell consumers that consumers have the right to reject an offer without any charge, and requires companies to make certain other disclosures.

However, lawyers who provide mortgage assistance relief services as part of the practice of law (such as when giving bankruptcy advice) and who are licensed in the state where the borrower is located are generally exempt from all provisions of the final rule except the prohibition on advance fees—and lawyers are also exempt from that prohibition if they place any advance fees for loan mitigation services into a lawyer trust account and abide by state laws and regulations (including Rule 1.15) governing those accounts.

IRS Regulations: In the regulations governing practice before the Internal Revenue Service, 31 C.F.R. §10.27(a) prohibits an "unconscionable fee in connection with any matter before the Internal Revenue Service," and §10.27(b) ("Contingent fees") provides as follows:

> (1) Except as provided in paragraphs (b)(2), (3), and (4) of this section, a practitioner may not charge a contingent fee for services rendered in connection with any matter before the Internal Revenue Service.
>
> (2) A practitioner may charge a contingent fee for services rendered in connection with the Service's examination of, or challenge to —
>
> > (i) An original tax return; or
> >
> > (ii) An amended return or claim for refund or credit where the amended return or claim for refund or credit was filed within 120 days of the taxpayer receiving a written notice of the examination of, or a written challenge to the original tax return.
>
> (3) A practitioner may charge a contingent fee for services rendered in connection with a claim for credit or refund filed solely in connection with the determination of statutory interest or penalties assessed by the Internal Revenue Service.
>
> (4) A practitioner may charge a contingent fee for services rendered in connection with any judicial proceeding arising under the Internal Revenue Code.

Private Securities Litigation Reform Act: In 1995, over President Clinton's veto, Congress passed the Private Securities Litigation Reform Act, 15 U.S.C. §77z-1. Title I of the statute combats unreasonable fees by providing that total attorney fees and expenses awarded by a court "shall not exceed a reasonable percentage of the amount of any damages and prejudgment interest actually paid to the class." §77z-1(a)(6). According to the committee report, this provision is intended to replace the "lodestar" method of computing fees and to give courts flexibility to determine reasonable fees and expenses on a case-by-case basis.

Restatement of the Law Governing Lawyers: See Restatement §§17(1), 19(2), 34, 35, 37-43, and 47 in our chapter on the Restatement later in this volume.

Rule 1.6 Confidentiality of Information

(a) A lawyer shall not reveal information relating to the representation of a client unless the client gives informed consent, the disclosure is impliedly authorized in order to carry out the representation or the disclosure is permitted by paragraph (b).

(b) A lawyer may reveal information relating to the representation of a client to the extent the lawyer reasonably believes necessary:

(1) to prevent reasonably certain death or substantial bodily harm;

(2) to prevent the client from committing a crime or fraud that is reasonably certain to result in substantial injury to the financial interests or property of another and in furtherance of which the client has used or is using the lawyer's services;

(3) to prevent, mitigate or rectify substantial injury to the financial interests or property of another that is reasonably certain to result or has resulted from the client's commission of a crime or fraud in furtherance of which the client has used the lawyer's services;

(4) to secure legal advice about the lawyer's compliance with these Rules;

(5) to establish a claim or defense on behalf of the lawyer in a controversy between the lawyer and the client, to establish a defense to a criminal charge or civil claim against the lawyer based upon conduct in which the client was involved, or to respond to allegations in any proceeding concerning the lawyer's representation of the client; or

(6) to comply with other law or a court order.

COMMENT

[1] This Rule governs the disclosure by a lawyer of information relating to the representation of a client during the lawyer's representation of the client. See Rule 1.18 for the lawyer's duties with respect to information provided to the lawyer by a prospective client, Rule 1.9(c)(2) for the lawyer's duty not to reveal information relating to the lawyer's prior representation of a former client and Rules 1.8(b) and

1.9(c)(1) for the lawyer's duties with respect to the use of such information to the disadvantage of clients and former clients.

[2] A fundamental principle in the client-lawyer relationship is that, in the absence of the client's informed consent, the lawyer must not reveal information relating to the representation. See Rule 1.0(e) for the definition of informed consent. This contributes to the trust that is the hallmark of the client-lawyer relationship. The client is thereby encouraged to seek legal assistance and to communicate fully and frankly with the lawyer even as to embarrassing or legally damaging subject matter. The lawyer needs this information to represent the client effectively and, if necessary, to advise the client to refrain from wrongful conduct. Almost without exception, clients come to lawyers in order to determine their rights and what is, in the complex of laws and regulations, deemed to be legal and correct. Based upon experience, lawyers know that almost all clients follow the advice given, and the law is upheld.

[3] The principle of client-lawyer confidentiality is given effect by related bodies of law: the attorney-client privilege, the work-product doctrine and the rule of confidentiality established in professional ethics. The attorney-client privilege and work-product doctrine apply in judicial and other proceedings in which a lawyer may be called as a witness or otherwise required to produce evidence concerning a client. The rule of client-lawyer confidentiality applies in situations other than those where evidence is sought from the lawyer through compulsion of law. The confidentiality rule, for example, applies not only to matters communicated in confidence by the client but also to all information relating to the representation, whatever its source. A lawyer may not disclose such information except as authorized or required by the Rules of Professional Conduct or other law. See also Scope.

[4] Paragraph (a) prohibits a lawyer from revealing information relating to the representation of a client. This prohibition also applies to disclosures by a lawyer that do not in themselves reveal protected information but could reasonably lead to the discovery of such information by a third person. A lawyer's use of a hypothetical to discuss issues relating to the representation is permissible so long as there is no reasonable likelihood that the listener will be able to ascertain the identity of the client or the situation involved.

Authorized Disclosure

[5] Except to the extent that the client's instructions or special circumstances limit that authority, a lawyer is impliedly authorized to make disclosures about a client when appropriate in carrying out the representation. In some situations, for example, a lawyer may be impliedly authorized to admit a fact that cannot properly be disputed or to make a disclosure that facilitates a satisfactory conclusion to a matter. Lawyers in a firm may, in the course of the firm's practice, disclose to each other information relating to a client of the firm, unless the client has instructed that particular information be confined to specified lawyers.

Disclosure Adverse to Client

[6] Although the public interest is usually best served by a strict rule requiring lawyers to preserve the confidentiality of information relating to the representation

of their clients, the confidentiality rule is subject to limited exceptions. Paragraph (b)(1) recognizes the overriding value of life and physical integrity and permits disclosure reasonably necessary to prevent reasonably certain death or substantial bodily harm. Such harm is reasonably certain to occur if it will be suffered imminently or if there is a present and substantial threat that a person will suffer such harm at a later date if the lawyer fails to take action necessary to eliminate the threat. Thus, a lawyer who knows that a client has accidentally discharged toxic waste into a town's water supply may reveal this information to the authorities if there is a present and substantial risk that a person who drinks the water will contract a life-threatening or debilitating disease and the lawyer's disclosure is necessary to eliminate the threat or reduce the number of victims.

[7] Paragraph (b)(2) is a limited exception to the rule of confidentiality that permits the lawyer to reveal information to the extent necessary to enable affected persons or appropriate authorities to prevent the client from committing a crime or fraud, as defined in Rule 1.0(d), that is reasonably certain to result in substantial injury to the financial or property interests of another and in furtherance of which the client has used or is using the lawyer's services. Such a serious abuse of the client-lawyer relationship by the client forfeits the protection of this Rule. The client can, of course, prevent such disclosure by refraining from the wrongful conduct. Although paragraph (b)(2) does not require the lawyer to reveal the client's misconduct, the lawyer may not counsel or assist the client in conduct the lawyer knows is criminal or fraudulent. See Rule 1.2(d). See also Rule 1.16 with respect to the lawyer's obligation or right to withdraw from the representation of the client in such circumstances, and Rule 1.13(c) which permits the lawyer, where the client is an organization, to reveal information relating to the representation in limited circumstances.

[8] Paragraph (b)(3) addresses the situation in which the lawyer does not learn of the client's crime or fraud until after it has been consummated. Although the client no longer has the option of preventing disclosure by refraining from the wrongful conduct, there will be situations in which the loss suffered by the affected person can be prevented, rectified or mitigated. In such situations, the lawyer may disclose information relating to the representation to the extent necessary to enable the affected persons to prevent or mitigate reasonably certain losses or to attempt to recoup their losses. Paragraph (b)(3) does not apply when a person who has committed a crime or fraud thereafter employs a lawyer for representation concerning that offense.

[9] A lawyer's confidentiality obligations do not preclude a lawyer from securing confidential legal advice about the lawyer's personal responsibility to comply with these Rules. In most situations, disclosing information to secure such advice will be impliedly authorized for the lawyer to carry out the representation. Even when the disclosure is not impliedly authorized, paragraph (b)(4) permits such disclosure because of the importance of a lawyer's compliance with the Rules of Professional Conduct.

[10] Where a legal claim or disciplinary charge alleges complicity of the lawyer in a client's conduct or other misconduct of the lawyer involving representation of the client, the lawyer may respond to the extent the lawyer reasonably believes necessary to establish a defense. The same is true with respect to a claim involving the conduct or representation of a former client. Such a charge can arise in a civil, criminal, disciplinary or other proceeding and can be based on a wrong allegedly committed by the lawyer against the client or on a wrong alleged by a third person, for example, a person claiming to have been defrauded by the lawyer and client

acting together. The lawyer's right to respond arises when an assertion of such complicity has been made. Paragraph (b)(5) does not require the lawyer to await the commencement of an action or proceeding that charges such complicity, so that the defense may be established by responding directly to a third party who has made such an assertion. The right to defend also applies, of course, where a proceeding has been commenced.

[11] A lawyer entitled to a fee is permitted by paragraph (b)(5) to prove the services rendered in an action to collect it. This aspect of the rule expresses the principle that the beneficiary of a fiduciary relationship may not exploit it to the detriment of the fiduciary.

[12] Other law may require that a lawyer disclose information about a client. Whether such a law supersedes Rule 1.6 is a question of law beyond the scope of these Rules. When disclosure of information relating to the representation appears to be required by other law, the lawyer must discuss the matter with the client to the extent required by Rule 1.4. If, however, the other law supersedes this Rule and requires disclosure, paragraph (b)(6) permits the lawyer to make such disclosures as are necessary to comply with the law.

[13] A lawyer may be ordered to reveal information relating to the representation of a client by a court or by another tribunal or governmental entity claiming authority pursuant to other law to compel the disclosure. Absent informed consent of the client to do otherwise, the lawyer should assert on behalf of the client all non-frivolous claims that the order is not authorized by other law or that the information sought is protected against disclosure by the attorney-client privilege or other applicable law. In the event of an adverse ruling, the lawyer must consult with the client about the possibility of appeal to the extent required by Rule 1.4. Unless review is sought, however, paragraph (b)(6) permits the lawyer to comply with the court's order.

[14] Paragraph (b) permits disclosure only to the extent the lawyer reasonably believes the disclosure is necessary to accomplish one of the purposes specified. Where practicable, the lawyer should first seek to persuade the client to take suitable action to obviate the need for disclosure. In any case, a disclosure adverse to the client's interest should be no greater than the lawyer reasonably believes necessary to accomplish the purpose. If the disclosure will be made in connection with a judicial proceeding, the disclosure should be made in a manner that limits access to the information to the tribunal or other persons having a need to know it and appropriate protective orders or other arrangements should be sought by the lawyer to the fullest extent practicable.

[15] Paragraph (b) permits but does not require the disclosure of information relating to a client's representation to accomplish the purposes specified in paragraphs (b)(1) through (b)(6). In exercising the discretion conferred by this Rule, the lawyer may consider such factors as the nature of the lawyer's relationship with the client and with those who might be injured by the client, the lawyer's own involvement in the transaction and factors that may extenuate the conduct in question. A lawyer's decision not to disclose as permitted by paragraph (b) does not violate this Rule. Disclosure may be required, however, by other Rules. Some Rules require disclosure only if such disclosure would be permitted by paragraph (b). See Rules 1.2(d), 4.1(b), 8.1 and 8.3. Rule 3.3, on the other hand, requires disclosure in some circumstances regardless of whether such disclosure is permitted by this Rule. See Rule 3.3(c).

Acting Competently to Preserve Confidentiality

[16] A lawyer must act competently to safeguard information relating to the representation of a client against inadvertent or unauthorized disclosure by the lawyer or other persons who are participating in the representation of the client or who are subject to the lawyer's supervision. See Rules 1.1, 5.1 and 5.3.

[17] When transmitting a communication that includes information relating to the representation of a client, the lawyer must take reasonable precautions to prevent the information from coming into the hands of unintended recipients. This duty, however, does not require that the lawyer use special security measures if the method of communication affords a reasonable expectation of privacy. Special circumstances, however, may warrant special precautions. Factors to be considered in determining the reasonableness of the lawyer's expectation of confidentiality include the sensitivity of the information and the extent to which the privacy of the communication is protected by law or by a confidentiality agreement. A client may require the lawyer to implement special security measures not required by this Rule or may give informed consent to the use of a means of communication that would otherwise be prohibited by this Rule.

Former Client

[18] The duty of confidentiality continues after the client-lawyer relationship has terminated. See Rule 1.9(c)(2). See Rule 1.9(c)(1) for the prohibition against using such information to the disadvantage of the former client.

Canon and Code Antecedents

ABA Canons of Professional Ethics: Canon 37 provided as follows:

37. Confidences of a Client

It is the duty of a lawyer to preserve his client's confidences. This duty outlasts the lawyer's employment, and extends as well to his employees; and neither of them should accept employment which involves or may involve the disclosure or use of these confidences, either for the private advantage of the lawyer or his employees or to the disadvantage of the client, without his knowledge and consent, and even though there are other available sources of such information. A lawyer should not continue employment when he discovers that this obligation prevents the performance of his full duty to his former or to his new client.

If a lawyer is accused by his client, he is not precluded from disclosing the truth in respect to the accusation. The announced intention of a client to commit a crime is not included within the confidences which he is bound to respect. He may properly make such disclosures as may be necessary to prevent the act or protect those against whom it is threatened.

ABA Model Code of Professional Responsibility: Compare DR 4-101(A)-(C) (reprinted later in this volume).

Cross-References in Other Rules

Scope ¶17: "Most of the duties flowing from the client-lawyer relationship attach only after the client has requested the lawyer to render legal services and the lawyer has agreed to do so. But there are some duties, such as that of confidentiality under **Rule 1.6**, that attach when the lawyer agrees to consider whether a client-lawyer relationship shall be established."

Rule 1.0, Comment 6: "Many of the Rules of Professional Conduct require the lawyer to obtain the informed consent of a client or other person before accepting or continuing representation or pursuing a course of conduct (see Rules 1.2(c), **1.6(a)** and 1.7(b))."

Rule 1.8(f)(3): "A lawyer shall not accept compensation for representing a client from one other than the client unless information relating to representation of a client is protected as required by **Rule 1.6.**"

Rule 1.8, Comment 5: It is prohibited to partake in the "disadvantageous use of client information unless the client gives informed consent, except as permitted or required by these Rules. See Rules 1.2(d), **1.6**, 1.9(c), 3.3, 4.1(b), 8.1 and 8.3."

Rule 1.8, Comment 12: "If, however, the fee arrangement creates a conflict of interest for the lawyer. . . . The lawyer must conform to the requirements of **Rule 1.6** concerning confidentiality."

Rule 1.9(b): "A lawyer shall not knowingly represent a person in the same or a substantially related matter in which a firm with which the lawyer formerly was associated had previously represented a client whose interests are materially adverse to that person and about whom the lawyer had acquired information protected by **Rules 1.6** and 1.9(c) that is material to the matter. . . ."

Rule 1.9, Comment 5: "Paragraph (b) operates to disqualify the lawyer only when the lawyer involved has actual knowledge of information protected by **Rules 1.6** and 1.9(c)."

Rule 1.9, Comment 7: "Independent of the question of disqualification of a firm, a lawyer changing professional association has a continuing duty to preserve confidentiality of information about a client formerly represented. See **Rules 1.6** and 1.9(c)."

Rule 1.10(b)(2) restricts representation when "any lawyer remaining in the firm has information protected by **Rules 1.6** and 1.9(c) that is material to the matter."

Rule 1.10, Comment 5: When a lawyer who represents or formerly represented a client leaves a firm, the firm may not represent a person with interests adverse to that client where the matter is the same or substantially related and "any other lawyer currently in the firm has material information protected by **Rules 1.6** and 1.9 (c)."

Rule 1.12, Comment 3: "Although lawyers who serve as third-party neutrals do not have information concerning the parties that is protected under **Rule 1.6**, they typically owe the parties an obligation of confidentiality under law or codes of ethics governing third-party neutrals."

Rule 1.13, Comment 2: "When one of the constituents of an organizational client communicates with the organization's lawyer in that person's organizational capacity, the communication is protected by **Rule 1.6**. Thus, by way of example, if an organizational client requests its lawyer to investigate allegations of wrong-doing, interviews made in the course of that investigation between the lawyer and the client's employees or other constituents are covered by **Rule 1.6**. This does not mean, however, that constituents of an organizational client are the clients of the lawyer. The lawyer may not disclose to such constituents information relating to the representation except for disclosures explicitly or impliedly authorized by the organizational client in order to carry out the representation or as otherwise permitted by **Rule 1.6**."

Rule 1.13, Comment 6: Paragraph (c) of this Rule supplements **Rule 1.6(b)** by providing an additional basis upon which the lawyer may reveal information relating to the representation, but does not modify, restrict, or limit the provisions of **Rule 1.6(b)(1)-(6)**. . . . If the lawyer's services are being used by an organization to further a crime or fraud by the organization, **Rule 1.6(b)(2)** and **1.6(b)(3)** may permit the lawyer to disclose confidential information.

Rule 1.14(c): "Information relating to the representation of a client with diminished capacity is protected by **Rule 1.6**. When taking protective action pursuant to paragraph (b), the lawyer is impliedly authorized under **Rule 1.6(a)** to reveal information about the client, but only to the extent reasonably necessary to protect the client's interests."

Rule 1.14, Comment 8: "Disclosure of the client's diminished capacity could adversely affect the client's interests. . . . Information relating to the representation is protected by **Rule 1.6**. Therefore, unless authorized to do so, the lawyer may not disclose such information."

Rule 1.16, Comment 3: "Lawyers should be mindful of their obligations to both clients and the court under **Rules 1.6** and 3.3."

Rule 1.17, Comment 7: "Negotiations between seller and prospective purchaser prior to disclosure of information relating to a specific representation of an identifiable client no more violate the confidentiality provisions of Model **Rule 1.6** than do preliminary discussions concerning the possible association of another lawyer or mergers between firms, with respect to which client consent is not required. Providing the purchaser access to client-specific information relating to the representation and to the file, however, requires client consent."

Rule 1.17, Comment 11: A lawyer selling a law practice has "the obligation to protect information relating to the representation (see **Rules 1.6** and 1.9)."

Rule 2.3(c): "Except as disclosure is authorized in connection with a report of an evaluation, information relating to the evaluation is otherwise protected by **Rule 1.6**."

Rule 2.3, Comment 5: "Information relating to an evaluation is protected by **Rule 1.6**. In many situations, providing an evaluation to a third party poses no significant risk to the client; thus, the lawyer may be impliedly authorized to disclose information to carry out the representation. See **Rule 1.6(a)**. Where, however, it is reasonably likely that providing the evaluation will affect the client's interests materially and adversely, the lawyer must first obtain the client's consent after the client has been adequately informed concerning the important possible effects on the client's interests. See **Rules 1.6(a)** and 1.0(e)."

Rule 3.3(c): "The duties stated in paragraphs (a) and (b) continue to the conclusion of the proceeding, and apply even if compliance requires disclosure of information otherwise protected by **Rule 1.6**."

Rule 3.3, Comment 10: "If withdrawal from the representation is not permitted or will not undo the effect of the false evidence, the advocate must make such disclosure to the tribunal as is reasonably necessary to remedy the situation, even if doing so requires the lawyer to reveal information that otherwise would be protected by **Rule 1.6**."

Rule 3.3, Comment 15: "In connection with a request for permission to withdraw that is premised on a client's misconduct, a lawyer may reveal information relating to the representation only to the extent reasonably necessary to comply with this Rule or as otherwise permitted by **Rule 1.6**."

Rule 4.1(b): "In the course of representing a client a lawyer shall not knowingly fail to disclose a material fact when disclosure is necessary to avoid assisting a criminal or fraudulent act by a client, unless disclosure is prohibited by **Rule 1.6**."

Rule 4.1, Comment 3: "If the lawyer can avoid assisting a client's crime or fraud only by disclosing this information, then under paragraph (b) the lawyer is required to do so, unless the disclosure is prohibited by **Rule 1.6**."

Rule 5.7, Comment 10: "When a lawyer is obliged to accord the recipients of such services the protections of those Rules that apply to the client-lawyer relationship, the lawyer must . . . scrupulously adhere to the requirements of **Rule 1.6** relating to disclosure of confidential information."

Rule 6.5, Comment 2: Regarding "a lawyer who provides short-term limited legal services pursuant to this Rule . . . [e]xcept as provided in this Rule, the Rules of Professional Conduct, including **Rules 1.6** and 1.9(c), are applicable to the limited representation."

Rule 8.1(b): "[T]his rule does not require disclosure of information otherwise protected by **Rule 1.6**."

Rule 8.1, Comment 3: "A lawyer representing an applicant for admission to the bar, or representing a lawyer who is the subject of a disciplinary inquiry or proceeding, is governed by the rules applicable to the client-lawyer relationship, including **Rule 1.6** and, in some cases, Rule 3.3."

Rule 8.3(c): "This Rule does not require disclosure of information otherwise protected by **Rule 1.6** or information gained by a lawyer or judge while participating in an approved lawyers assistance program."

Rule 8.3, Comment 2: "A report about misconduct is not required where it would involve violation of **Rule 1.6**."

Legislative History of Model Rule 1.6

1979 Unofficial Pre-Circulation Draft:

(a) In giving testimony or providing evidence concerning a client's affairs, a lawyer shall not disclose matter concerning the client except as permitted under the applicable law of evidentiary privilege. In other circumstances, a lawyer shall not disclose information about a client acquired in serving the client in a professional capacity except as stated in paragraphs (b), (c) and (d).

(b) A lawyer shall disclose information about a client when directed to do so by the client and may do so when disclosure is necessary in the representation.

(c) A lawyer shall disclose information about a client

(1) to the extent necessary to prevent the client from committing an act that would seriously endanger the life or safety of a person, result in wrongful detention or incarceration of a person or wrongful destruction of substantial property, or corrupt judicial or governmental procedure;

(2) when disclosure by the lawyer is required by law or the rules of professional conduct.

(d) A lawyer may disclose information about a client

(1) to the extent necessary to prevent or rectify the consequences of a deliberately wrongful act by the client in which the lawyer's services are or were involved, except when the lawyer has been employed after the commission of such an act to represent the client concerning the act or its consequences. . . .

1980 Discussion Draft:

(b) A lawyer shall disclose information about a client to the extent it appears necessary to prevent the client from committing an act that would result in death or serious bodily harm to another person, and to the extent required by law or the rules of professional conduct.

(c) A lawyer may disclose information about a client only:

(1) For the purposes of serving the client's interest, unless it is information the client has specifically requested not to be disclosed;

(2) To the extent it appears necessary to prevent or rectify the consequences of a deliberately wrongful act by the client, except when the lawyer has been employed after the commission of such an act to represent the client concerning the act or its consequences. . . .

1981 Draft:

(b) A lawyer may reveal such information to the extent the lawyer believes necessary:

(1) to serve the client's interests, unless it is information the client has specifically requested not to be disclosed;

(2) to prevent the client from committing a criminal or fraudulent act that the lawyer believes is likely to result in death or substantial bodily harm, or substantial injury to the financial interest or property of another;

(3) to rectify the consequences of a client's criminal or fraudulent act in the commission of which the lawyer's services had been used. . . .

1982 Draft:

(b) A lawyer may reveal such information to the extent the lawyer reasonably believes necessary:

(1) to prevent the client from committing a criminal or fraudulent act that the lawyer reasonably believes is likely to result in death or substantial bodily harm, or in substantial injury to the financial interests or property of another;

(2) to rectify the consequences of a client's criminal or fraudulent act in the furtherance of which the lawyer's services had been used. . . .

1983 Rule: From its original adoption in 1983 until it was first amended in 2002, Rule 1.6 provided as follows:

Rule 1.6 Confidentiality of Information

(a) A lawyer shall not reveal information relating to the representation of a client unless the client consents after consultation, except for disclosures that are impliedly authorized in order to carry out the representation and except as stated in paragraph (b).

(b) A lawyer may reveal such information to the extent the lawyer reasonably believes necessary:

(1) to prevent the client from committing a criminal act that the lawyer believes is likely to result in imminent death or substantial bodily harm;

(2) [Same as self-defense exception in 2003 version of Rule 1.6(b)(5).]

1991 Proposal: In 1991, the Standing Committee on Ethics and Professional Responsibility proposed amending Rule 1.6(b) to permit a lawyer to reveal information that the lawyer reasonably believed necessary to "rectify the consequences of a client's criminal or fraudulent act in the commission of which the lawyer's services had been used." The House of Delegates defeated this proposal by a vote of 251 to 158. The rejected amendment would have been accompanied by several new Comments to Rule 1.6, including one that said: "To the extent a lawyer is prohibited from making disclosure, the interests of the potential victim are sacrificed in favor of preserving the client's confidences even though the client's purpose is wrongful."

2002 Amendments: In 2002, the ABA House of Delegates adopted without change most of the ABA Ethics 2000 Commission proposals to amend Rule 1.6 and its Comment. But in 2001, the House of Delegates had voted against a proposed new paragraph in Rule 1.6(b) that was identical to the proposal adopted two years later (in 2003) as Rule 1.6(b)(2). After the House of Delegates defeated proposed subparagraph (b)(2), the Ethics 2000 Commission withdrew a proposed paragraph (b)(3) before any vote was taken, but the withdrawn paragraph was also adopted in 2003, as Rule 1.6(b)(3). The two proposed paragraphs would have been accompanied by two new proposed Comments to Rule 1.6, which were likewise adopted in 2003 as Comments 7 and 8 to Rule 1.6.

The unsuccessful proposals were eventually adopted with the support of the ABA Task Force on Corporate Responsibility, chaired by attorney James H. Cheek, III, which recommended in April 2003 that the rejected paragraphs (b)(2) and (b)(3), and the accompanying Comments, be reconsidered and adopted. Until the 2002 amendments, ABA Model Rule 1.6 did not contain paragraphs (b)(4) and (b)(6) (relating to securing legal advice and complying with other laws or court orders). In addition, paragraph (b)(1) was originally much narrower, permitting revelation of client confidences only "to the extent the lawyer reasonably believes necessary . . . to prevent the *client* from committing a *criminal* act that the lawyer believes is likely to result in *imminent* death or substantial bodily harm." (Emphasis added.)

2003 Amendments: In 2003, by a vote of 218-201, the ABA House of Delegates added paragraphs (b)(2) and (b)(3) to Rule 1.6, added Comments 7 and 8, and deleted former Comment 14, which had provided, in relevant part, as follows:

> [14] If the lawyer's services will be used by the client in materially furthering a course of criminal or fraudulent conduct, the lawyer must withdraw. . . . Neither this Rule nor Rule 1.8(b) nor Rule 1.16(d) prevents the lawyer from giving notice of the fact of withdrawal, and the lawyer may also withdraw or disaffirm any opinion, document, affirmation, or the like. . . .

(Comment 14 was deleted because its substance was already separately addressed in the comments to Rules 1.2 and 4.1.) The ABA Ethics 2000 Commission had recommended the identical changes in 2001, but at that time the House had rejected (b)(2) by a significant margin, and (b)(3) was then withdrawn. The 2003 changes were part of a package of recommendations from the ABA Task Force on Corporate Responsibility. (For more information about the Task Force and for its full report, visit *http://www.americanbar.org/groups/business_law.html.*) In support of the 2003 amendments, the Task Force report states:*

> The Task Force believes that the interest of society, and the bar, in assuring that a lawyer's services are not used by a client in the furtherance of a crime or a fraud creates a demanding need for an exception to the important principle of confidentiality, as most states have recognized. The importance of protecting both society and the bar from the consequences of a client's misuse of the lawyer's services in the furtherance of a serious crime or fraud must be balanced against the importance to the client-lawyer relationship of the principle of confidentiality.
>
> The Model Rules leave no room for doubt as to whether a lawyer may permit his services to be used by a client for criminal or fraudulent activity. . . . But what if the client has misled the lawyer, leading the lawyer to believe that the client is pursuing a lawful and honest purpose while in fact using the lawyer's work product to perpetrate a crime or fraud? In such circumstances should the lawyer be prohibited from taking action to prevent or rectify such misuse of the lawyer's services?
>
> The Task Force believes, as did the Ethics 2000 Commission, that the use of the lawyer's services for such improper ends constitutes an abuse by the client of the client-lawyer relationship, forfeiting the client's absolute entitlement to the protection of Model Rule 1.6. In such circumstances, the Task Force believes that the lawyer must be permitted, where the crime or fraud has resulted or is reasonably certain to result in substantial injury to the financial interests or property of third parties, to reveal information relating to the representation as reasonably believed necessary to prevent the commission of, or to prevent or rectify the consequences of, the crime or fraud.
>
> [T]here is a long-standing exception to Model Rule 1.6 that permits a lawyer to reveal information relating to a representation "to establish a claim or defense on behalf of the lawyer in a controversy between the lawyer and the client." We believe that it is at least as important to society, and to the integrity of the profession, to permit disclosure in order to prevent the lawyer's services from being used in the commission of a crime or fraud as it is to permit disclosure in order to collect the lawyer's fee or to protect the lawyer from a client's unmeritorious civil claim.
>
> In opposition to the proposal to amend Model Rule 1.6, it has been suggested that the disclosure to third parties permitted under the laws of most states is "rarely if ever employed," and there is therefore no need to amend Rule 1.6. The Task Force is not persuaded by this suggestion. Even if the authorization to disclose afforded by most states' disciplinary rules is not often used, the existence of such authority gives lawyers the opportunity to use that power to encourage the client to remediate or refrain from unlawful conduct.

Selected State Variations

Editors' Note. American jurisdictions have adopted many variations on Rule 1.6 and its exceptions. Under DR 4-101(C)(3) of the old ABA Model Code of Professional Responsibility, a lawyer was authorized to reveal "the intention of his client to commit a crime and the information necessary to prevent the crime." Under the original version of Rule 1.6(b)(1), however, a

* Committee Reports do not represent official policy of the ABA. They are for information only, and the opinions are those of the authors of the report.

lawyer was authorized to reveal crimes by a client only if they were "likely to result in imminent death or substantial bodily harm." Among the questions addressed in state variations are the following:

- whether to continue the Code's authority to reveal any prospective crime, even if the crime will not cause death or substantial bodily harm;
- whether to extend the authority to reveal conduct other than criminal conduct, such as conduct that is reckless, fraudulent, or illegal, but not criminal;
- whether to keep the authority permissive or, instead, to mandate revelation of prospective criminal or harmful conduct;
- if revelation is mandatory, the prospective conduct that will be subject to the mandatory duty to reveal;
- whether to distinguish the right or obligation to disclose depending upon whether the lawyer's information is protected by the attorney-client privilege or only protected by the ethical duty of confidentiality.

Alaska, ***Arkansas***, ***Connecticut***, ***Illinois***, ***Maine***, ***Maryland***, ***New Hampshire***, ***New Mexico***, ***North Dakota***, ***Pennsylvania***, and ***Utah*** permit a lawyer to reveal information necessary to prevent the client from committing a criminal act "likely to result in substantial injury to the financial interest or property of another" (or words to that effect). Of these, Alaska, Arkansas, Connecticut, Illinois, Maine, Maryland, New Mexico, North Dakota, and Utah also permit revelation when the client's act is only fraudulent, but not criminal. New Jersey, Vermont, and Wisconsin go one step further, imposing a duty to reveal the information under these circumstances.

Arizona, ***Arkansas***, ***Colorado***, ***Idaho***, ***Illinois***, ***Kansas***, ***Michigan***, ***North Carolina***, ***Ohio***, ***Oregon***, ***South Carolina***, ***Washington***, and ***Wyoming*** essentially retain the formulation of DR 4-101(C)(3) of the ABA Model Code of Professional Responsibility—they all permit a lawyer to reveal "the intention of a client to commit a crime" (or words to that effect).

Arizona, ***Connecticut***, ***Florida***, ***Illinois***, ***Nevada***, ***New Jersey***, ***North Dakota***, ***Texas***, ***Tennessee***, ***Vermont***, and ***Wisconsin*** mandate disclosure of information to prevent the client from committing serious violent crimes. However, mandatory disclosure applies in North Dakota only if the harm is "imminent," and Florida's provision applies to all crimes, not just violent ones.

Alaska: Alaska adds Rule 1.6(b)(1)(C), which permits disclosures in order to "prevent the wrongful execution or incarceration of another." Alaska also adds Rule 1.6(c), which requires a lawyer to take reasonable precautions to guard against the inadvertent or unauthorized disclosure of a client's confidential information.

Arizona: Rule 1.6(d)(5) applies only to "other law or a final order of a court or tribunal of competent jurisdiction directing the lawyer to disclose such information." Arizona also has an unusual statute governing the attorney-client privilege for corporations and other entities—see the Arizona entry in the Selected State Variations following ABA Model Rule 1.13.

Arkansas: Rule 1.6(c) contains a noisy withdrawal provision, which states as follows: "Neither this Rule nor Rule 1.8(b) nor Rule 1.16(d) prevents the lawyer from giving notice of the fact of withdrawal, and the lawyer may also withdraw or disaffirm any opinion, document, affirmation or the like."

California: California Business & Professions Code §6068(e)(1) provides that it is the duty of an attorney "[t]o maintain inviolate the confidence, and at every peril to himself or herself to preserve the secrets, of his or her client." However, §6068(e)(2) provides that an attorney "may, but is not required to, reveal confidential information relating to the representation of a client to the extent that the attorney reasonably believes the disclosure is necessary to prevent a criminal act that the attorney reasonably believes is likely to result in death of, or substantial bodily harm to, an individual." In addition, Rule 3-100 of the California Rules of Professional Conduct provides as follows:

> (A) A member shall not reveal information protected from disclosure by Business and Professions Code section 6068, subdivision (e)(1) without the informed consent of the client, or as provided in paragraph (B) of this rule.
>
> (B) A member may, but is not required to, reveal confidential information relating to the representation of a client to the extent that the member reasonably believes the disclosure is necessary to prevent a criminal act that the member reasonably believes is likely to result in death of, or substantial bodily harm to, an individual.
>
> (C) Before revealing confidential information to prevent a criminal act as provided in paragraph (B), a member shall, if reasonable under the circumstances:
>
> (1) make a good faith effort to persuade the client: (i) not to commit or to continue the criminal act or (ii) to pursue a course of conduct that will prevent the threatened death or substantial bodily harm; or do both (i) and (ii); and
>
> (2) inform the client, at an appropriate time, of the member's ability or decision to reveal information as provided in paragraph (B).
>
> (D) In revealing confidential information as provided in paragraph (B), the member's disclosure must be no more than is necessary to prevent the criminal act, given the information known to the member at the time of the disclosure.
>
> (E) A member who does not reveal information permitted by paragraph (B) does not violate this rule.

District of Columbia: Rule 1.6 combines language from the ABA Model Code and the ABA Model Rules plus other language unique to D.C. Rule 1.6(c)(2) permits a lawyer to reveal client confidences "to prevent the bribery or intimidation of witnesses, jurors, court officials, or other persons who are involved in proceedings before a tribunal if the lawyer reasonably believes" such acts will likely occur without revelation. Rule 1.6(d) is substantially the same as Model Rule 1.6(b)(2) and (3), although differently phrased. Rule 1.6(h) applies the obligations of the Rule "to confidences and secrets learned prior to becoming a lawyer in the course of providing assistance to another lawyer."

Florida: Rule 1.6 provides that a lawyer "shall reveal" information the lawyer believes "necessary (1) to prevent a client from committing a crime or (2) to prevent a death or substantial bodily harm to another." In addition, Florida Rule 1.6(c) permits a lawyer to reveal information necessary "(1) to serve the client's interest unless it is information the client specifically requires not to be disclosed . . . or (5) to comply with the Rules of Professional Conduct." Florida also adds Rule 1.6(d): "When required by a tribunal to reveal such information, a lawyer may first exhaust all appellate remedies." Finally, Florida adds Rule 1.6(e), which provides that "[w]hen disclosure is mandated or permitted, the lawyer shall disclose no more information than is required to meet the requirements or accomplish the purposes of this rule."

Georgia: Rule 1.6(a) combines language from ABA Model Rule 1.6 and DR 4-101(A) of the ABA Model Code of Professional Responsibility, as follows:

> (a) A lawyer shall maintain in confidence all information gained in the professional relationship with a client, including information which the client has requested to be held inviolate or the disclosure of which would be embarrassing or would likely be detrimental to the client, unless the client consents after consultation, except for disclosures that are impliedly authorized in order to carry out the representation, or are required by these rules or other law, or by order of the Court.
>
> Georgia's Rule 1.6(b)(1) permits a lawyer to reveal protected information which the lawyer reasonably believes necessary "(i) to avoid or prevent harm or substantial financial loss to another as a result of client criminal conduct or third party criminal conduct clearly in violation of the law" or "(ii) to prevent serious injury or death not otherwise covered" by subparagraph (i). Georgia adds the following Rules 1.6(b)(2)-(3) and (c), (d), and (e):
>
> > (2) In a situation described in Subsection (1), if the client has acted at the time the lawyer learns of the threat of harm or loss to a victim, use or disclosure is permissible only if the harm or loss has not yet occurred.
> >
> > (3) Before using or disclosing information pursuant to Subsection (1), if feasible, the lawyer must make a good faith effort to persuade the client either not to act or, if the client has already acted, to warn the victim.
>
> (c) The lawyer may, where the law does not otherwise require, reveal information to which the duty of confidentiality does not apply under paragraph (b) without being subjected to disciplinary proceedings.
>
> (d) The lawyer shall reveal information under paragraph (b) as the applicable law requires.
>
> (e) The duty of confidentiality shall continue after the client-lawyer relationship has terminated.

Illinois adds Rule 1.6(c) and (d):

> (c) A lawyer shall reveal information relating to the representation of a client to the extent the lawyer reasonably believes necessary to prevent reasonably certain death or substantial bodily harm.
>
> (d) Information received by a lawyer participating in a meeting or proceeding with a trained intervener or panel of trained interveners of an approved lawyers' assistance program, or in an intermediary program approved by a circuit court in which nondisciplinary complaints against judges or lawyers can be referred, shall be considered information relating to the representation of a client for purposes of these Rules.

Maine: Before making a disclosure under Rule 1.6(b), lawyers must try to convince the client not to engage in the conduct that will produce the applicable harm. Moreover, Rule 1.6(d) and Comment 2 explain that the rule applies only to a client's confidences and secrets, not to the broader range of information (*i.e.*, "all information relating to the representation of the client") described in the Model Rule.

Massachusetts: Rule 1.6(b) provides as follows:

> A lawyer may reveal, and to the extent required by Rule 3.3, Rule 4.1(b), or Rule 8.3 must reveal, such information:
>
> (1) to prevent the commission of a criminal or fraudulent act that the lawyer reasonably believes is likely to result in death or substantial bodily harm, or in substantial injury to the financial interests or property of another, or to prevent the wrongful execution or incarceration of another; . . . or
>
> (3) to the extent the lawyer reasonably believes necessary to rectify client fraud in which the lawyer's services have been used, subject to Rule 3.3 (e). . . .

(Massachusetts was the first state to adopt an exception for preventing the wrongful execution or incarceration of another.)

Michigan essentially retains the language of DR 4-101 of the ABA Model Code of Professional Responsibility but deletes the self-defense exception in DR 4-101(C)(4). Michigan also adds Rule 1.6(c)(3), which allows a lawyer to reveal "confidences and secrets to the extent reasonably necessary to rectify the consequences of a client's illegal or fraudulent act in the furtherance of which the lawyer's services have been used."

Minnesota: Rule 1.6(b) provides, in relevant part, as follows:

> (b) A lawyer may reveal information relating to the representation of a client if:
>
> (1) the client gives informed consent;
>
> (2) the information is not protected by the attorney-client privilege under applicable law, the client has not requested that the information be held inviolate, and the lawyer reasonably believes the disclosure would not be embarrassing or likely detrimental to the client;
>
> (3) the lawyer reasonably believes the disclosure is impliedly authorized in order to carry out the representation; . . .
>
> (10) the lawyer reasonably believes the disclosure is necessary to inform the Office of Lawyers Professional Responsibility of knowledge of another lawyer's violation of the Rules of Professional Conduct that raises a substantial question as to that lawyer's honesty, trustworthiness, or fitness as a lawyer in other respects. See Rule 8.3.

Missouri: Missouri omits ABA Model Rules 1.6(b)(2) and (b)(3).

New Hampshire: Rule 1.6(b)(1) also permits disclosure to prevent the client from committing "a criminal act that the lawyer believes is likely to result in substantial injury to the financial interest or property of another," without any requirement that the client is using or has used the lawyer's services. New Hampshire omits ABA Model Rule 1.6(b)(3).

New Jersey: Rule 1.6(b) requires a lawyer to reveal confidential information "to the proper authorities . . . to prevent the client or another person (1) from committing a criminal, illegal or fraudulent act . . . likely to result in death or substantial bodily harm or substantial injury to the financial interest or property of another" or "(2) from committing a criminal, illegal or fraudulent act that the lawyer reasonably believes is likely to perpetrate a fraud upon a tribunal." Rule 1.6(c) permits a lawyer to reveal information as well "to the person threatened to the extent the lawyer reasonably believes is necessary to protect that person from death, substantial bodily harm, substantial financial injury, or substantial property loss."

New York: Rule 1.6 contains numerous variations as well as many new comments. For example, Rule 1.6(a) offers an elaborate definition of "confidential information," which provides as follows:

> "Confidential information" consists of information gained during or relating to the representation of a client, whatever its source, that is (a) protected by the attorney-client privilege, (b) likely to be embarrassing or detrimental to the client if disclosed, or (c) information that the client has requested be kept confidential. "Confidential information" does not ordinarily include (i) a lawyer's legal knowledge or legal research or (ii) information that is generally known in the local community or in the trade, field or profession to which the information relates.

Comment 4A, as amended in 2011, elaborates on this definition as follows:

> Information relates to the representation if it has any possible relevance to the representation or is received because of the representation. The accumulation of legal

> knowledge or legal research that a lawyer acquires through practice ordinarily is not client information protected by this Rule. However, in some circumstances, including where the client and the lawyer have so agreed, a client may have a proprietary interest in a particular product of the lawyer's research. Information that is generally known in the local community or in the trade, field or profession to which the information relates is also not protected, unless the client and the lawyer have otherwise agreed. Information is not "generally known" simply because it is in the public domain or available in a public file.

Drawing on DR 4-101(B) of the old Model Code, Rule 1.6(a) provides that a disclosure of confidential information violates the rule only when the disclosure occurs "knowingly."

Rule 1.6(b) does not permit disclosures to prevent or rectify financial injuries, but it adds to the Model Rule by permitting disclosures when the lawyer reasonably believes necessary:

> (3) to withdraw a written or oral opinion or representation previously given by the lawyer and reasonably believed by the lawyer still to be relied upon by a third person, where the lawyer has discovered that the opinion or representation was based on materially inaccurate information or is being used to further a crime or fraud; . . .

Comment 6A offers a list of factors for lawyers to consider when deciding whether to disclose information under Rule 1.6(b), including:

> (i) the seriousness of the potential injury to others if the prospective harm or crime occurs, (ii) the likelihood that it will occur and its imminence, (iii) the apparent absence of any other feasible way to prevent the potential injury, (iv) the extent to which the client may be using the lawyer's services in bringing about the harm or crime, (v) the circumstances under which the lawyer acquired the information of the client's intent or prospective course of action, and (vi) any other aggravating or extenuating circumstances. In any case, disclosure adverse to the client's interest should be no greater than the lawyer reasonably believes necessary to prevent the threatened harm or crime. When a lawyer learns that a client intends to pursue or is pursuing a course of conduct that would permit disclosure under paragraphs (b)(1), (b)(2) or (b)(3), the lawyer's initial duty, where practicable, is to remonstrate with the client. In the rare situation in which the client is reluctant to accept the lawyer's advice, the lawyer's threat of disclosure is a measure of last resort that may persuade the client. When the lawyer reasonably believes that the client will carry out the threatened harm or crime, the lawyer may disclose confidential information when permitted by paragraphs (b)(1), (b)(2) or (b)(3). A lawyer's permissible disclosure under paragraph (b) does not waive the client's attorney-client privilege; neither the lawyer nor the client may be forced to testify about communications protected by the privilege, unless a tribunal or body with authority to compel testimony makes a determination that the crime-fraud exception to the privilege, or some other exception, has been satisfied by a party to the proceeding. For a lawyer's duties when representing an organizational client engaged in wrongdoing, *see* Rule 1.13(b).

New York Rule 1.6(c) is nearly identical to DR 4-101(D) of the old Model Code.

North Carolina combines modified language from ABA Model Rule 1.6 with language from DR 4-101 of the old ABA Model Code of Professional Responsibility. For example, North Carolina's equivalent to ABA Model Rules 1.6(b)(2) and (b)(3) provides simply that a lawyer may reveal confidential information to the extent the lawyer reasonably believes necessary "to prevent, mitigate, or rectify the consequences of a client's criminal or fraudulent act in the commission of which the lawyer's services were used." North Carolina also adds a Rule 1.6(c), which provides that the duty of confidentiality "encompasses information received by a lawyer then acting as an agent of a lawyers' or judges' assistance program approved by the North Carolina State Bar or the North Carolina Supreme Court regarding another lawyer or judge seeking assistance or to whom assistance is being offered."

Ohio: Rule 1.6(b) permits a lawyer "to reveal the intention of the client or other person to commit a crime and the information necessary to prevent the crime," or to reveal confidential information "to mitigate substantial injury to the financial interests or property of another that has resulted from the client's commission of an illegal or fraudulent act, in furtherance of which the client has used the lawyer's services." Ohio omits ABA Model Rule 1.6(b)(2).

Oklahoma: Rule 1.6(b)(2) permits revelation only if "the lawyer has first made reasonable efforts to contact the client so that the client can rectify such criminal or fraudulent act, but the lawyer has been unable to do so, or the lawyer has contacted the client and called upon the client to rectify such criminal or fraudulent act and the client has refused or has been unable to do so."

Oregon: Rule 1.0(f) defines "information relating to the representation" as denoting "both information protected by the attorney-client privilege under applicable law, and other information gained in a current or former professional relationship that the client has requested be held inviolate or the disclosure of which would be embarrassing or would be likely to be detrimental to the client." In addition, Oregon permits a lawyer to disclose "the intention of the lawyer's client to commit a crime and the information necessary to prevent the crime." Also, Oregon Rule 1.6(b)(6) permits disclosure of specified information in discussions preliminary to the sale of a law practice under Rule 1.17, but states: "A potential purchasing lawyer shall have the same responsibilities as the selling lawyer to preserve confidences and secrets of such clients whether or not the sale of the practice closes or the client ultimately consents to representation by the purchasing lawyer."

Pennsylvania adds a Rule 1.6(d) that states: "The duty not to reveal information relating to representation of a client continues after the client-lawyer relationship has terminated." In addition, a lawyer may reveal information relating to the representation of a client that the lawyer reasonably believes necessary to "effectuate the sale of a law practice consistent with Rule 1.17."

Tennessee: In the rules effective January 1, 2011, Rule 1.6(c) provides that a lawyer "shall" reveal information relating to the representation of a client to the extent the lawyer reasonably believes disclosure is necessary:

> (1) to prevent reasonably certain death or substantial bodily harm;
> (2) to comply with an order of a tribunal requiring disclosure, but only if ordered to do so by the tribunal after the lawyer has asserted on behalf of the client all non-frivolous claims that the information sought by the tribunal is protected against disclosure by the attorney-client privilege or other applicable law; or
> (3) to comply with RPC 3.3, 4.1, or other law.

Tennessee's version of Rule 4.1, which requires disclosure of confidential information in certain circumstances, is described in the state variations for that Rule.

Texas: Rule 1.02(d)-(e) provides:

> (d) When a lawyer has confidential information clearly establishing that a client is likely to commit a criminal or fraudulent act that is likely to result in substantial

injury to the financial interests or property of another, the lawyer shall promptly make reasonable efforts under the circumstances to dissuade the client from committing the crime or fraud.

(e) When a lawyer has confidential information clearly establishing that the lawyer's client has committed a criminal or fraudulent act in the commission of which the lawyer's services have been used, the lawyer shall make reasonable efforts under the circumstances to persuade the client to take corrective action.

Texas Rule 1.05 divides "confidential information" into two categories—"privileged information," which means information protected by the attorney-client privilege, and "unprivileged client information," which "means all information relating to a client or furnished by the client, other than privileged information, acquired by the lawyer in the course of or by reason of the representation of the client." A lawyer "may reveal confidential information" in eight instances, including when "the lawyer has reason to believe it is necessary to do so in order to prevent the client from committing a criminal or fraudulent act," and to "the extent revelation reasonably appears necessary to rectify the consequences of a client's criminal or fraudulent act in the commission of which the lawyer's services had been used." Rules 1.05(c)(7) and (8).

Vermont: Rule 1.6 imposes a duty to disclose confidential information "(1) to prevent the client or another person from committing a criminal act that the lawyer reasonably believes is likely to result in the death of, or substantial bodily harm to, a person other than the person committing the act; or (2) to prevent the client from committing a crime or fraud that is reasonably certain to result in substantial injury to the financial interests or property of another and in furtherance of which the client has used or is using the lawyer's services; or (3) to prevent, mitigate or rectify substantial injury to the financial interests or property of another that is reasonably certain to result or has resulted from the client's commission of a crime or fraud in furtherance of which the client has used the lawyer's services."

Virginia: Rule 1.6(a) contains the Code's definitions of "confidence" and "secret" without using these terms. A lawyer may reveal a client confidence "which clearly establishes that the client has, in the course of the representation, perpetrated upon a third party a fraud related to the subject matter of the representation." Rule 1.6(b)(3). The lawyer must "promptly" reveal "the intention of a client, as stated by the client, to commit a crime and the information necessary to prevent the crime," but if feasible must first give the client the opportunity to desist and must advise the client of the lawyer's obligation. If "the crime involves perjury by the client," the lawyer must advise the client that he or she "shall seek to withdraw as counsel." Rule 1.6(c)(1). Rule 1.6(c)(2) also requires the lawyer to promptly reveal "information which clearly establishes that the client has, in the course of the representation, perpetrated a fraud related to the subject matter of the representation upon a tribunal." Information is clearly established when "the client acknowledges to the attorney that the client has perpetrated a fraud."

Related Materials

ABA Commission on Ethics 20/20: In 2009, the ABA created the ABA Commission on Ethics 20/20, which is comprehensively reviewing the ABA Model Rules of Professional Conduct in light of globalization and changes in information technology. On September 19, 2011, the Commission issued revised draft proposals on technology and confidentiality for public comment. Several proposals relate to confidential information. Regarding Rule 1.6, the Commission proposed adding a new subparagraph (b)(7) that would permit disclosure of confidential information to the extent a lawyer reasonably believes necessary:

> to determine if a conflict of interest would arise from the lawyer's association with a firm, but only when there is a reasonable possibility of such an association and the revealed information would not adversely affect the lawyer's client. Information revealed under this paragraph may not be used or revealed by the lawyers receiving the information for any purpose except the identification and resolution of potential conflicts of interest.

To explain Rule 1.6(b)(7), the Commission proposed to add a new Comment 14 to Rule 1.6 that would begin by stating: "Paragraph (b)(7) recognizes that, before a lawyer becomes associated with a firm, it may be necessary for the lawyer to reveal limited information about the lawyer's current and former clients to permit the lawyer and the firm to identify conflicts of interest that would arise from the lawyer's association with the firm." The rest of the new Comment discusses restrictions on such disclosures and restrictions on the hiring firm's use of the disclosed information.

The Commission also proposed adding a new paragraph (c) to Rule 1.6 that would provide: "A lawyer shall make reasonable efforts to prevent the inadvertent disclosure of, or unauthorized access to, information relating to the representation of a client." The Commission also proposed amending paragraphs 16 and 17 of the Comment to explain Rule 1.6(c).

The Ethics 20/20 Commission may place these proposals (or revised versions of them) before the ABA House of Delegates at the ABA's August 2012 Annual Meeting. For updates, see the Ethics 20/20 Commission's website at *http://www.americanbar.org/Ethics2020.*

In another development relating to confidentiality, the Ethics 20/20 Commission (pursuant to a February 2010 resolution by the ABA House of Delegates) explored confidentiality issues that might arise when lawyers provide information to entities such as Super Lawyers and Best Lawyers that rank and rate lawyers and law firms. In August 2011, the Commission finalized an Informational Report, which requested that the Standing Committee on Ethics and Professional Responsibility "consider whether a Formal Ethics Opinion on the application of Model Rule 1.6 to a lawyer's participation with entities that rate and rank lawyers and law firms is needed." The Commission noted that current Model Rule 1.6 "makes clear that a lawyer does not have the authority to provide to a third party information about the representation unless the lawyer obtains the client's informed consent to the disclosure." However, the Commission asked the ABA Standing Committee on Ethics and Professional Responsibility to "consider whether a Formal Ethics Opinion on the application of Model Rule 1.6 to a lawyer's participation with entities that rate and rank lawyers and law firms is needed."

ABA Formal Ethics Opinions: See ABA Formal Ethics Ops. 90-358 (1990), 92-365 (1992), 93-370 (1993), 94-380 (1994), 94-385 (1994), 95-393 (1995), 95-398 (1995), 98-411 (1998), 99-413 (1999), 03-431 (2003), 05-436 (2005), 06-440 (2006), 06-442

(2006), 07-449 (2007), 08-450 (2008), 08-451 (2008), 08-453 (2008), 09-455 (2009), 11-459 (2011), 11-460 (2011).

ABA Resolution on Inadvertent Disclosure: In 2006, the ABA House of Delegates approved a resolution regarding inadvertent disclosure of privileged materials. For details, see the Related Materials following ABA Model Rule 4.4.

ABA Standards for Imposing Lawyer Sanctions:

> 4.21. Disbarment is generally appropriate when a lawyer, with the intent to benefit the lawyer or another, knowingly reveals information relating to representation of a client not otherwise lawfully permitted to be disclosed, and this disclosure causes injury or potential injury to a client.
>
> 4.22. Suspension is generally appropriate when a lawyer knowingly reveals information relating to the representation of a client not otherwise lawfully permitted to be disclosed, and this disclosure causes injury or potential injury to a client.
>
> 4.23. Reprimand is generally appropriate when a lawyer negligently reveals information relating to representation of a client not otherwise lawfully permitted to be disclosed and this disclosure causes injury or potential injury to a client.
>
> 4.24. Admonition is generally appropriate when a lawyer negligently reveals information relating to representation of a client not otherwise lawfully permitted to be disclosed and this disclosure causes little or no actual or potential injury to a client.

ABA Task Force on the Attorney-Client Privilege: In 2004, the ABA appointed a Task Force on the Attorney-Client Privilege whose Chair is attorney William Ide, III, of Atlanta and whose Reporter is Professor Bruce Green of Fordham University School of Law. The mission of the Task Force is "to evaluate issues and recommend policy related to the attorney-client privilege and work product doctrine." The Task Force hopes to inform the public and the legal profession about the importance of the attorney-client privilege and the work product doctrine and to assist the ABA in developing policies that strike the right balance among competing demands. The Task Force home page, which contains the full text of Task Force documents, plus many other useful resources and links regarding the attorney-client privilege, is found at *http://www.abanow.org/issue/?attorney-client-privilege-client-confidentiality.*

In 2005, the Task Force issued an interim Report and (together with the ABA Section of Criminal Justice and the ABA Section of Tort Trial and Insurance Practice) recommended a resolution that the ABA House of Delegates adopted in 2005 with minor changes. As adopted, the Resolution reads:

> RESOLVED, that the American Bar Association strongly supports the preservation of the attorney-client privilege and work product doctrine as essential to maintaining the confidential relationship between client and attorney required to encourage clients to discuss their legal matters fully and candidly with their counsel so as to (1) promote compliance with law through effective counseling, (2) ensure effective advocacy for the client, (3) ensure access to justice and (4) promote the proper and efficient functioning of the American adversary system of justice; and
>
> FURTHER RESOLVED, that the American Bar Association opposes policies, practices and procedures of governmental bodies that have the effect of eroding the attorney-client privilege and work-product doctrine and favors policies, practices and procedures that recognize the value of those protections.
>
> FURTHER RESOLVED, that the American Bar Association opposes the routine practice by government officials of seeking to obtain a waiver of the attorney-client privilege or work product doctrine through the granting or denial of any benefit or advantage.

In 2006, the House of Delegates passed another resolution proposed by the Task Force, which provides as follows:

> RESOLVED, that the American Bar Association supports the preservation of the attorney-client privilege and work product doctrine in connection with audits of company financial statements.
>
> FURTHER RESOLVED, that the American Bar Association urges the Securities and Exchange Commission, the Public Company Accounting Oversight Board, the American Institute of Certified Public Accountants, the legal and accounting professions, and other relevant organizations to adopt standards, policies, practices and procedures and take other appropriate steps to ensure that attorney-client privilege and work product protections are preserved throughout the audit process.

Also in 2006, the House of Delegates passed a resolution proposed by the Task Force intended to protect employee rights that are tangentially related to the attorney-client privilege. The resolution provides as follows:

> RESOLVED, that the American Bar Association opposes government policies, practices and procedures that have the effect of eroding the constitutional and other legal rights of current or former employees, officers, directors or agents ("Employees") by requiring, encouraging or permitting prosecutors or other enforcement authorities to take into consideration any of the following factors in making a determination of whether an organization has been cooperative in the context of a government investigation:
>
> (1) that the organization provided counsel to, or advanced, reimbursed or indemnified the legal fees and expenses of, an Employee;
> (2) that the organization entered into or continues to operate under a joint defense, information sharing and common interest agreement with an Employee or other represented party with whom the organization believes it has a common interest in defending against the investigation;
> (3) that the organization shared its records or other historical information relating to the matter under investigation with an Employee; or
> (4) that the organization chose to retain or otherwise declined to sanction an Employee who exercised his or her Fifth Amendment right against self-incrimination in response to a government request for an interview, testimony, or other information.

ABA Task Force on Corporate Responsibility: In 2003, a Task Force of the American Bar Association, chaired by Tennessee lawyer James H. Cheek, III, issued a report in satisfaction of its charge to "examine systemic issues relating to corporate responsibility arising out of the unexpected and traumatic bankruptcy of Enron and other Enron-like situations." The report urged the ABA to adopt the exceptions to Rule 1.6 confidentiality that the ABA had rejected in 2002, and urged the ABA to modify Rule 1.13 to mandate "reporting up" and permit "reporting out" in specified circumstances. The ABA followed these recommendations. The Report and related events are discussed in the Special Section of the 2004 edition of this book.

Attorney-Client Privilege: Wigmore's famed treatise on the law of evidence defines the "attorney-client privilege" as follows:

> (1) Where legal advice of any kind is sought (2) from a professional legal advisor in his capacity as such, (3) the communications relating to that purpose, (4) made in confidence (5) by the client, (6) are at the client's instance permanently protected (7) from disclosure by himself or the legal advisor, (8) except the protection be waived.

Arthur Best, Wigmore on Evidence §2292 (4th ed., Aspen Publishers 1988). For primary sources on the attorney-client privilege, see our chapter on Attorney-Client Privilege and Work Product Provisions later in this volume.

Cell Phone Calls: In 1999, the ABA House of Delegates passed a resolution encouraging courts and bar disciplinary authorities to recognize explicitly that cell phone communications are protected by the attorney-client privilege.

E-mail Communications: Many ethics committees and commentators have considered whether communications by e-mail are protected by the attorney-client privilege. Some states have passed statutes protecting e-mail and other electronic communications. For example, in 1998, New York enacted a new statute, CPLR §4548, which provides as follows:

> No communication privileged under this article shall lose its privileged character for the sole reason that it is communicated by electronic means or because persons necessary for the delivery or facilitation of such electronic communication may have access to the content of the communication.

Federal Rules of Civil Procedure: Except in specified categories of proceedings or to the extent otherwise stipulated between the parties or ordered by the court, Rule 26(a) of the Federal Rules of Civil Procedure provides that each party to a civil suit "must, without awaiting a discovery request, provide to other parties" various categories of information, including: (A) the name, address, and telephone of each individual likely to have discoverable information (including the identity of any person who may be used at trial as an expert); (B) a copy or description of "all documents, electrically stored information, and tangible things" in the party's "possession, custody or control" that the disclosing party "may use to support its claims or defenses"; (C) "a computation of each category of damages claimed by the disclosing party"; and (D) any insurance agreement that may cover the judgment or a corresponding indemnification obligation. These provisions relate to ABA Model Rule 1.6 because clients who take part in litigation in federal court may be deemed to have "impliedly authorized" the disclosures mandated by Rule 26(a).

Moreover, a new Rule 26(b)(5)(B) took effect in 2006 to address the problem of inadvertently produced privileged information. The new rule provides that if a party receives notice that privileged information has been produced, together with notice of the basis for the claim of privilege, then "[a]fter being notified, a party must promptly return, sequester, or destroy the specified information and any copies it has [and] must not use or disclose the information until the claim is resolved. . . ." A companion 2006 amendment to Rule 16(b)(3)(B)(iv) provides that a district court's scheduling order may include "any agreements the parties reach for asserting claims of privilege or of protection as trial-preparation material after information is produced." For details, see the entry on the Federal Rules of Civil Procedure in the Related Materials following Rule 4.4.

Regarding expert witnesses, amendments to Rule 26(b)(4)(B) and (C) took effect on December 1, 2010. The amended provisions provide heightened protection against discovery of communications between experts and counsel. Specifically, amended Rule 26(b)(4)(B) protects "drafts of any report or disclosure required under Rule 26(a)(2), regardless of the form in which the draft is recorded." Amended Rule 26(b)(4)(C) protects "communications between the party's attorney and any witness required to provide a report under Rule 26(a)(2)(B)" unless the communications: (i) relate to "compensation for the expert's study or testimony";

or (ii) "identify facts or data that the party's attorney provided and that the expert considered in forming the opinions to be expressed"; or (iii) "identify assumptions that the party's attorney provided and that the expert relied on in forming the opinions to be expressed."

For updates, and for a wealth of information about recent and proposed amendments to the Federal Rules of Civil Procedure (and other federal court rules), check the official website of the United States Courts at *www.uscourts.gov* (look for "Federal Rulemaking").

Federal Rules of Evidence: In federal courts, Rule 501 of the Federal Rules of Evidence controls the application of privileges, including the attorney-client privilege. Rule 501 provides that, except as otherwise required by the Constitution, a federal statute, or a federal court rule, "the privilege of a witness, person, government, State, or political subdivision thereof shall be governed by the principles of the common law as they may be interpreted by the courts of the United States in the light of reason and experience."

In addition, in 2008, President George W. Bush signed a law enacting a new Rule 502 of the Federal Rules of Evidence. The new rule, which was based verbatim on a proposal by the Judicial Conference of the United States, clarifies and modifies common law rules relating to waiver of privilege and work product protection. For more information about the attorney-client privilege in federal courts, including the full text of Rule 502, see our chapter on Attorney-Client Privilege and Work Product Provisions later in this volume.

Model Rules of Professional Conduct for Federal Lawyers: Rule 1.6(b) provides: "A Federal lawyer shall reveal such information to the extent the Federal lawyer reasonably believes necessary to prevent the client from committing a criminal act that the Federal lawyer believes is likely to result in imminent death or substantial bodily harm, or imminent and significant impairment of national security or defense." The Comment also cautions that government lawyers have confidentiality obligations under many federal statutes and regulations, so "it is always advisable for Government lawyers to review the applicable Federal law . . . and to consult with their supervisors."

Restatement of the Law Governing Lawyers: See Restatement §§14, 15, 41, and 59-93 in our chapter on the Restatement later in this volume.

SEC Statement on Corporate Cooperation ("Seaboard Report"): In the SEC's Securities and Exchange Act Release No. 44969 (October 23, 2001), often referred to as the "Seaboard Report," the SEC set forth some of the criteria the SEC considers in determining "whether, and how much, to credit self-policing, self-reporting, remediation and cooperation—from the extraordinary step of taking no enforcement action to bringing reduced charges, seeking lighter sanctions, or including mitigating language in documents we use to announce and resolve enforcement actions." The following examples of these criteria are particularly relevant to Rule 1.6:

> 10. Did the company commit to learn the truth, fully and expeditiously? Did it do a thorough review of the nature, extent, origins and consequences of the conduct and related behavior? . . .
>
> 11. Did the company promptly make available to our staff the results of its review and provide sufficient documentation reflecting its response to the situation? Did the company identify possible violative conduct and evidence with sufficient precision to facilitate prompt enforcement actions against those who violated the law? Did the company produce a thorough and probing written report detailing the findings of its review?

Did the company voluntarily disclose information our staff did not directly request and otherwise might not have uncovered? Did the company ask its employees to cooperate with our staff and make all reasonable efforts to secure such cooperation?

12. . . . Did the company provide our staff with sufficient information for it to evaluate the company's measures to correct the situation and ensure that the conduct does not recur? . . .

United States Department of Justice Privilege Waiver Requests: Since 2003, the United States Department of Justice (DOJ) has adopted three different policies regarding DOJ requests that a corporation under federal investigation waive the attorney-client privilege or work product protection.

In 2003, the DOJ adopted Principles of Federal Prosecution of Business Organizations (the so-called Thompson Memorandum, written by then-Deputy Attorney General Larry D. Thompson). The Thompson Memorandum contained the following comment:

> One factor the prosecutor may weigh in assessing the adequacy of a corporation's cooperation is the completeness of its disclosure including, if necessary, *a waiver of the attorney-client and work product protections,* both with respect to its internal investigation and with respect to communications between specific officers, directors and employees and counsel. Such waivers permit the government to obtain statements of possible witnesses, subjects, and targets, without having to negotiate individual cooperation or immunity agreements. In addition, they are often critical in enabling the government to evaluate the completeness of a corporation's voluntary disclosure and cooperation. Prosecutors may, therefore, request a waiver in appropriate circumstances. The Department does not, however, consider waiver of a corporation's attorney-client and work product protection an absolute requirement, and prosecutors should consider the willingness of a corporation to waive such protection when necessary to provide timely and complete information as one factor in evaluating the corporation's cooperation. [Emphasis added.]

The Thompson Memorandum's waiver policy generated substantial objections from the ABA and the business community, and the DOJ responded to these criticisms. On December 12, 2006, the Thompson Memorandum was replaced by the so-called McNulty Memorandum (written by then-Deputy Attorney General Paul J. McNulty). The revised business prosecution principles included the following Principle VII:

> *VII. Charging a Corporation: The Value of Cooperation*
>
> *A. General Principle:* In determining whether to charge a corporation, that corporation's timely and voluntary disclosure of wrongdoing and its cooperation with the government's investigation may be relevant factors. In gauging the extent of the corporation's cooperation, the prosecutor may consider, among other things, whether the corporation made a voluntary and timely disclosure, and the corporation's willingness to provide relevant evidence and to identify the culprits within the corporation, including senior executives.

Comment 2 to Principle VII explained the Department of Justice's revised policy:

> . . . Prosecutors may only request waiver of attorney-client or work product protections when there is a legitimate need for the privileged information to fulfill their law enforcement obligations. A legitimate need for the information is not established by concluding it is merely desirable or convenient to obtain privileged information.

> The test requires a careful balancing of important policy considerations underlying the attorney-client privilege and work product doctrine and the law enforcement needs of the government's investigation.
>
> Whether there is a legitimate need depends upon: (1) the likelihood and degree to which the privileged information will benefit the government's investigation; (2) whether the information sought can be obtained in a timely and complete fashion by using alternative means that do not require waiver; (3) the completeness of the voluntary disclosure already provided; and (4) the collateral consequences to a corporation of a waiver.
>
> If a legitimate need exists, prosecutors should seek the least intrusive waiver necessary to conduct a complete and thorough investigation, and should follow a step-by-step approach to requesting information. . . .

The McNulty Memorandum then divided information into two categories. Prosecutors should first seek Category I information, which consists of "purely factual information, which may or may not be privileged, relating to the underlying misconduct." Before requesting that a corporation waive the attorney-client or work product protections for Category I information, prosecutors must obtain written authorization from the United States Attorney, and only if the purely factual information provides an incomplete basis to conduct a thorough investigation may prosecutors ask the corporation to provide Category II information, which consists of "attorney-client communications or non-factual attorney work product" (e.g., attorney notes, memoranda or reports containing counsel's mental impressions and conclusions, legal determinations reached as a result of an internal investigation, or legal advice given to the corporation). Prosecutors are cautioned to seek Category II information only in "rare circumstances," and must obtain written authorization from the Deputy Attorney General. But if a corporation declines to waive protection for Category II information, "prosecutors must not consider this declination against the corporation in making a charging decision."

Congressional critics of the McNulty Memorandum soon revived a bill called the Attorney-Client Privilege Protection Act. In August of 2008, the DOJ responded to this pressure by adopting revised Principles of Federal Prosecution of Business Organizations. Regarding waiver of the attorney-client privilege, the revised Principles, which are contained in the United States Attorney's Manual (USAM), provide, in pertinent part, as follows:

> USAM 9-28.710 *Attorney-Client and Work Product Protections*
>
> The attorney-client privilege and the attorney work product protection serve an extremely important function in the American legal system. The attorney-client privilege is one of the oldest and most sacrosanct privileges under the law. See Upjohn v. United States, 449 U.S. 383, 389 (1981). . . .
>
> For these reasons, waiving the attorney-client and work product protections has never been a prerequisite under the Department's prosecution guidelines for a corporation to be viewed as cooperative. Nonetheless, a wide range of commentators and members of the American legal community and criminal justice system have asserted that the Department's policies have been used, either wittingly or unwittingly, to coerce business entities into waiving attorney-client privilege and work-product protection. Everyone agrees that a corporation may freely waive its own privileges if it chooses to do so; indeed, such waivers occur routinely when corporations are victimized by their employees or others, conduct an internal investigation, and then disclose the details of the investigation to law enforcement officials in an effort to seek prosecution of the offenders. However, the contention, from a broad array of voices, is that the Department's position on attorney-client privilege and work product protection

waivers has promoted an environment in which those protections are being unfairly eroded to the detriment of all.

The Department understands that the attorney-client privilege and attorney work product protection are essential and long-recognized components of the American legal system. What the government seeks and needs to advance its legitimate (indeed, essential) law enforcement mission is not waiver of those protections, but rather the facts known to the corporation about the putative criminal misconduct under review. In addition, while a corporation remains free to convey non-factual or "core" attorney-client communications or work product—if and only if the corporation voluntarily chooses to do so—prosecutors should not ask for such waivers and are directed not to do so. The critical factor is whether the corporation has provided the facts about the events, as explained further herein.

USAM 9-28.720 *Cooperation: Disclosing the Relevant Facts*

Eligibility for cooperation credit is not predicated upon the waiver of attorney-client privilege or work product protection. Instead, the sort of cooperation that is most valuable to resolving allegations of misconduct by a corporation and its officers, directors, employees, or agents is disclosure of the relevant *facts* concerning such misconduct. In this regard, the analysis parallels that for a non-corporate defendant, where cooperation typically requires disclosure of relevant factual knowledge and not of discussions between an individual and his attorneys.

Thus, when the government investigates potential corporate wrongdoing, it seeks the relevant facts. . . . The party under investigation may choose to cooperate by disclosing the facts, and the government may give credit for the party's disclosures. If a corporation wishes to receive credit for such cooperation, which then can be considered with all other cooperative efforts and circumstances in evaluating how fairly to proceed, then the corporation, like any person, must disclose the relevant facts of which it has knowledge.

The complete August 2008 Department of Justice business prosecution principles are available at *www.usdoj.gov/usao/eousa/foia_reading_room/usam/title9//28mcrm.htm.*

Rule 1.7 Conflict of Interest: Current Clients

(a) Except as provided in paragraph (b), a lawyer shall not represent a client if the representation involves a concurrent conflict of interest. A concurrent conflict of interest exists if:

(1) the representation of one client will be directly adverse to another client; or

(2) there is a significant risk that the representation of one or more clients will be materially limited by the lawyer's responsibilities to another client, a former client or a third person or by a personal interest of the lawyer.

(b) Notwithstanding the existence of a concurrent conflict of interest under paragraph (a), a lawyer may represent a client if:

(1) the lawyer reasonably believes that the lawyer will be able to provide competent and diligent representation to each affected client;

(2) the representation is not prohibited by law;

(3) the representation does not involve the assertion of a claim by one client against another client represented by the lawyer in the same litigation or other proceeding before a tribunal; and

(4) each affected client gives informed consent, confirmed in writing.

COMMENT

General Principles

[1] Loyalty and independent judgment are essential elements in the lawyer's relationship to a client. Concurrent conflicts of interest can arise from the lawyer's responsibilities to another client, a former client or a third person or from the lawyer's own interests. For specific Rules regarding certain concurrent conflicts of interest, see Rule 1.8. For former client conflicts of interest, see Rule 1.9. For conflicts of interest involving prospective clients, see Rule 1.18. For definitions of "informed consent" and "confirmed in writing," see Rule 1.0(e) and (b).

[2] Resolution of a conflict of interest problem under this Rule requires the lawyer to: 1) clearly identify the client or clients; 2) determine whether a conflict of interest exists; 3) decide whether the representation may be undertaken despite the existence of a conflict, i.e., whether the conflict is consentable; and 4) if so, consult with the clients affected under paragraph (a) and obtain their informed consent, confirmed in writing. The clients affected under paragraph (a) include both of the clients referred to in paragraph (a)(1) and the one or more clients whose representation might be materially limited under paragraph (a)(2).

[3] A conflict of interest may exist before representation is undertaken, in which event the representation must be declined, unless the lawyer obtains the informed consent of each client under the conditions of paragraph (b). To determine whether a conflict of interest exists, a lawyer should adopt reasonable procedures, appropriate for the size and type of firm and practice, to determine in both litigation and non-litigation matters the persons and issues involved. See also Comment to Rule 5.1. Ignorance caused by a failure to institute such procedures will not excuse a lawyer's violation of this Rule. As to whether a client-lawyer relationship exists or, having once been established, is continuing, see Comment to Rule 1.3 and Scope.

[4] If a conflict arises after representation has been undertaken, the lawyer ordinarily must withdraw from the representation, unless the lawyer has obtained the informed consent of the client under the conditions of paragraph (b). See Rule 1.16. Where more than one client is involved, whether the lawyer may continue to represent any of the clients is determined both by the lawyer's ability to comply with duties owed to the former client and by the lawyer's ability to represent adequately the remaining client or clients, given the lawyer's duties to the former client. See Rule 1.9. See also Comments [5] and [29].

[5] Unforeseeable developments, such as changes in corporate and other organizational affiliations or the addition or realignment of parties in litigation, might create conflicts in the midst of a representation, as when a company sued by the lawyer on behalf of one client is bought by another client represented by the lawyer in an unrelated matter. Depending on the circumstances, the lawyer may

have the option to withdraw from one of the representations in order to avoid the conflict. The lawyer must seek court approval where necessary and take steps to minimize harm to the clients. See Rule 1.16. The lawyer must continue to protect the confidences of the client from whose representation the lawyer has withdrawn. See Rule 1.9(c).

Identifying Conflicts of Interest: Directly Adverse

[6] Loyalty to a current client prohibits undertaking representation directly adverse to that client without that client's informed consent. Thus, absent consent, a lawyer may not act as an advocate in one matter against a person the lawyer represents in some other matter, even when the matters are wholly unrelated. The client as to whom the representation is directly adverse is likely to feel betrayed, and the resulting damage to the client-lawyer relationship is likely to impair the lawyer's ability to represent the client effectively. In addition, the client on whose behalf the adverse representation is undertaken reasonably may fear that the lawyer will pursue that client's case less effectively out of deference to the other client, i.e., that the representation may be materially limited by the lawyer's interest in retaining the current client. Similarly, a directly adverse conflict may arise when a lawyer is required to cross-examine a client who appears as a witness in a lawsuit involving another client, as when the testimony will be damaging to the client who is represented in the lawsuit. On the other hand, simultaneous representation in unrelated matters of clients whose interests are only economically adverse, such as representation of competing economic enterprises in unrelated litigation, does not ordinarily constitute a conflict of interest and thus may not require consent of the respective clients.

[7] Directly adverse conflicts can also arise in transactional matters. For example, if a lawyer is asked to represent the seller of a business in negotiations with a buyer represented by the lawyer, not in the same transaction but in another, unrelated matter, the lawyer could not undertake the representation without the informed consent of each client.

Identifying Conflicts of Interest: Material Limitation

[8] Even where there is no direct adverseness, a conflict of interest exists if there is a significant risk that a lawyer's ability to consider, recommend or carry out an appropriate course of action for the client will be materially limited as a result of the lawyer's other responsibilities or interests. For example, a lawyer asked to represent several individuals seeking to form a joint venture is likely to be materially limited in the lawyer's ability to recommend or advocate all possible positions that each might take because of the lawyer's duty of loyalty to the others. The conflict in effect forecloses alternatives that would otherwise be available to the client. The mere possibility of subsequent harm does not itself require disclosure and consent. The critical questions are the likelihood that a difference in interests will eventuate and, if it does, whether it will materially interfere with the lawyer's independent professional judgment in considering alternatives or foreclose courses of action that reasonably should be pursued on behalf of the client.

Lawyer's Responsibilities to Former Clients and Other Third Persons

[9] In addition to conflicts with other current clients, a lawyer's duties of loyalty and independence may be materially limited by responsibilities to former clients under Rule 1.9 or by the lawyer's responsibilities to other persons, such as fiduciary duties arising from a lawyer's service as a trustee, executor or corporate director.

Personal Interest Conflicts

[10] The lawyer's own interests should not be permitted to have an adverse effect on representation of a client. For example, if the probity of a lawyer's own conduct in a transaction is in serious question, it may be difficult or impossible for the lawyer to give a client detached advice. Similarly, when a lawyer has discussions concerning possible employment with an opponent of the lawyer's client, or with a law firm representing the opponent, such discussions could materially limit the lawyer's representation of the client. In addition, a lawyer may not allow related business interests to affect representation, for example, by referring clients to an enterprise in which the lawyer has an undisclosed financial interest. See Rule 1.8 for specific Rules pertaining to a number of personal interest conflicts, including business transactions with clients. See also Rule 1.10 (personal interest conflicts under Rule 1.7 ordinarily are not imputed to other lawyers in a law firm).

[11] When lawyers representing different clients in the same matter or in substantially related matters are closely related by blood or marriage, there may be a significant risk that client confidences will be revealed and that the lawyer's family relationship will interfere with both loyalty and independent professional judgment. As a result, each client is entitled to know of the existence and implications of the relationship between the lawyers before the lawyer agrees to undertake the representation. Thus, a lawyer related to another lawyer, e.g., as parent, child, sibling or spouse, ordinarily may not represent a client in a matter where that lawyer is representing another party, unless each client gives informed consent. The disqualification arising from a close family relationship is personal and ordinarily is not imputed to members of firms with whom the lawyers are associated. See Rule 1.10.

[12] A lawyer is prohibited from engaging in sexual relationships with a client unless the sexual relationship predates the formation of the client-lawyer relationship. See Rule 1.8(j).

Interest of Person Paying for a Lawyer's Service

[13] A lawyer may be paid from a source other than the client, including a coclient, if the client is informed of that fact and consents and the arrangement does not compromise the lawyer's duty of loyalty or independent judgment to the client. See Rule 1.8(f). If acceptance of the payment from any other source presents a significant risk that the lawyer's representation of the client will be materially limited by the lawyer's own interest in accommodating the person paying the lawyer's fee or by the lawyer's responsibilities to a payer who is also a co-client, then

the lawyer must comply with the requirements of paragraph (b) before accepting the representation, including determining whether the conflict is consentable and, if so, that the client has adequate information about the material risks of the representation.

Prohibited Representations

[14] Ordinarily, clients may consent to representation notwithstanding a conflict. However, as indicated in paragraph (b), some conflicts are nonconsentable, meaning that the lawyer involved cannot properly ask for such agreement or provide representation on the basis of the clients consent. When the lawyer is representing more than one client, the question of consentability must be resolved as to each client.

[15] Consentability is typically determined by considering whether the interests of the clients will be adequately protected if the clients are permitted to give their informed consent to representation burdened by a conflict of interest. Thus, under paragraph (b)(1), representation is prohibited if in the circumstances the lawyer cannot reasonably conclude that the lawyer will be able to provide competent and diligent representation. See Rule 1.1 (competence) and Rule 1.3 (diligence).

[16] Paragraph (b)(2) describes conflicts that are nonconsentable because the representation is prohibited by applicable law. For example, in some states substantive law provides that the same lawyer may not represent more than one defendant in a capital case, even with the consent of the clients, and under federal criminal statutes certain representations by a former government lawyer are prohibited, despite the informed consent of the former client. In addition, decisional law in some states limits the ability of a governmental client, such as a municipality, to consent to a conflict of interest.

[17] Paragraph (b)(3) describes conflicts that are nonconsentable because of the institutional interest in vigorous development of each client's position when the clients are aligned directly against each other in the same litigation or other proceeding before a tribunal. Whether clients are aligned directly against each other within the meaning of this paragraph requires examination of the context of the proceeding. Although this paragraph does not preclude a lawyer's multiple representation of adverse parties to a mediation (because mediation is not a proceeding before a "tribunal" under Rule 1.0(m)), such representation may be precluded by paragraph (b)(1).

Informed Consent

[18] Informed consent requires that each affected client be aware of the relevant circumstances and of the material and reasonably foreseeable ways that the conflict could have adverse effects on the interests of that client. See Rule 1.0(e) (informed consent). The information required depends on the nature of the conflict and the nature of the risks involved. When representation of multiple clients in a single matter is undertaken, the information must include the implications of the common representation, including possible effects on loyalty, confidentiality and

the attorney-client privilege and the advantages and risks involved. See Comments [30] and [31] (effect of common representation on confidentiality).

[19] Under some circumstances it may be impossible to make the disclosure necessary to obtain consent. For example, when the lawyer represents different clients in related matters and one of the clients refuses to consent to the disclosure necessary to permit the other client to make an informed decision, the lawyer cannot properly ask the latter to consent. In some cases the alternative to common representation can be that each party may have to obtain separate representation with the possibility of incurring additional costs. These costs, along with the benefits of securing separate representation, are factors that may be considered by the affected client in determining whether common representation is in the client's interests.

Consent Confirmed in Writing

[20] Paragraph (b) requires the lawyer to obtain the informed consent of the client, confirmed in writing. Such a writing may consist of a document executed by the client or one that the lawyer promptly records and transmits to the client following an oral consent. See Rule 1.0(b). See also Rule 1.0(n) (writing includes electronic transmission). If it is not feasible to obtain or transmit the writing at the time the client gives informed consent, then the lawyer must obtain or transmit it within a reasonable time thereafter. See Rule 1.0(b). The requirement of a writing does not supplant the need in most cases for the lawyer to talk with the client, to explain the risks and advantages, if any, of representation burdened with a conflict of interest, as well as reasonably available alternatives, and to afford the client a reasonable opportunity to consider the risks and alternatives and to raise questions and concerns. Rather, the writing is required in order to impress upon clients the seriousness of the decision the client is being asked to make and to avoid disputes or ambiguities that might later occur in the absence of a writing.

Revoking Consent

[21] A client who has given consent to a conflict may revoke the consent and, like any other client, may terminate the lawyer's representation at any time. Whether revoking consent to the client's own representation precludes the lawyer from continuing to represent other clients depends on the circumstances, including the nature of the conflict, whether the client revoked consent because of a material change in circumstances, the reasonable expectations of the other client and whether material detriment to the other clients or the lawyer would result.

Consent to Future Conflict

[22] Whether a lawyer may properly request a client to waive conflicts that might arise in the future is subject to the test of paragraph (b). The effectiveness of such waivers is generally determined by the extent to which the client reasonably understands the material risks that the waiver entails. The more comprehensive the

explanation of the types of future representations that might arise and the actual and reasonably foreseeable adverse consequences of those representations, the greater the likelihood that the client will have the requisite understanding. Thus, if the client agrees to consent to a particular type of conflict with which the client is already familiar, then the consent ordinarily will be effective with regard to that type of conflict. If the consent is general and open-ended, then the consent ordinarily will be ineffective, because it is not reasonably likely that the client will have understood the material risks involved. On the other hand, if the client is an experienced user of the legal services involved and is reasonably informed regarding the risk that a conflict may arise, such consent is more likely to be effective, particularly if, e.g., the client is independently represented by other counsel in giving consent and the consent is limited to future conflicts unrelated to the subject of the representation. In any case, advance consent cannot be effective if the circumstances that materialize in the future are such as would make the conflict nonconsentable under paragraph (b).

Conflicts in Litigation

[23] Paragraph (b)(3) prohibits representation of opposing parties in the same litigation, regardless of the clients' consent. On the other hand, simultaneous representation of parties whose interests in litigation may conflict, such as coplaintiffs or codefendants, is governed by paragraph (a)(2). A conflict may exist by reason of substantial discrepancy in the parties' testimony, incompatibility in positions in relation to an opposing party or the fact that there are substantially different possibilities of settlement of the claims or liabilities in question. Such conflicts can arise in criminal cases as well as civil. The potential for conflict of interest in representing multiple defendants in a criminal case is so grave that ordinarily a lawyer should decline to represent more than one codefendant. On the other hand, common representation of persons having similar interests in civil litigation is proper if the requirements of paragraph (b) are met.

[24] Ordinarily a lawyer may take inconsistent legal positions in different tribunals at different times on behalf of different clients. The mere fact that advocating a legal position on behalf of one client might create precedent adverse to the interests of a client represented by the lawyer in an unrelated matter does not create a conflict of interest. A conflict of interest exists, however, if there is a significant risk that a lawyer's action on behalf of one client will materially limit the lawyer's effectiveness in representing another client in a different case; for example, when a decision favoring one client will create a precedent likely to seriously weaken the position taken on behalf of the other client. Factors relevant in determining whether the clients need to be advised of the risk include: where the cases are pending, whether the issue is substantive or procedural, the temporal relationship between the matters, the significance of the issue to the immediate and long-term interests of the clients involved and the clients' reasonable expectations in retaining the lawyer. If there is significant risk of material limitation, then absent informed consent of the affected clients, the lawyer must refuse one of the representations or withdraw from one or both matters.

[25] When a lawyer represents or seeks to represent a class of plaintiffs or defendants in a class-action lawsuit, unnamed members of the class are ordinarily

not considered to be clients of the lawyer for purposes of applying paragraph (a)(1) of this Rule. Thus, the lawyer does not typically need to get the consent of such a person before representing a client suing the person in an unrelated matter. Similarly, a lawyer seeking to represent an opponent in a class action does not typically need the consent of an unnamed member of the class whom the lawyer represents in an unrelated matter.

Nonlitigation Conflicts

[26] Conflicts of interest under paragraphs (a)(1) and (a)(2) arise in contexts other than litigation. For a discussion of directly adverse conflicts in transactional matters, see Comment [7]. Relevant factors in determining whether there is significant potential for material limitation include the duration and intimacy of the lawyer's relationship with the client or clients involved, the functions being performed by the lawyer, the likelihood that disagreements will arise and the likely prejudice to the client from the conflict. The question is often one of proximity and degree. See Comment [8].

[27] For example, conflict questions may arise in estate planning and estate administration. A lawyer may be called upon to prepare wills for several family members, such as husband and wife, and, depending upon the circumstances, a conflict of interest may be present. In estate administration the identity of the client may be unclear under the law of a particular jurisdiction. Under one view, the client is the fiduciary; under another view the client is the estate or trust, including its beneficiaries. In order to comply with conflict of interest rules, the lawyer should make clear the lawyer's relationship to the parties involved.

[28] Whether a conflict is consentable depends on the circumstances. For example, a lawyer may not represent multiple parties to a negotiation whose interests are fundamentally antagonistic to each other, but common representation is permissible where the clients are generally aligned in interest even though there is some difference in interest among them. Thus, a lawyer may seek to establish or adjust a relationship between clients on an amicable and mutually advantageous basis; for example, in helping to organize a business in which two or more clients are entrepreneurs, working out the financial reorganization of an enterprise in which two or more clients have an interest or arranging a property distribution in settlement of an estate. The lawyer seeks to resolve potentially adverse interests by developing the parties' mutual interests. Otherwise, each party might have to obtain separate representation, with the possibility of incurring additional cost, complication or even litigation. Given these and other relevant factors, the clients may prefer that the lawyer act for all of them.

Special Considerations in Common Representation

[29] In considering whether to represent multiple clients in the same matter, a lawyer should be mindful that if the common representation fails because the potentially adverse interests cannot be reconciled, the result can be additional cost,

embarrassment and recrimination. Ordinarily, the lawyer will be forced to withdraw from representing all of the clients if the common representation fails. In some situations, the risk of failure is so great that multiple representation is plainly impossible. For example, a lawyer cannot undertake common representation of clients where contentious litigation or negotiations between them are imminent or contemplated. Moreover, because the lawyer is required to be impartial between commonly represented clients, representation of multiple clients is improper when it is unlikely that impartiality can be maintained. Generally, if the relationship between the parties has already assumed antagonism, the possibility that the clients' interests can be adequately served by common representation is not very good. Other relevant factors are whether the lawyer subsequently will represent both parties on a continuing basis and whether the situation involves creating or terminating a relationship between the parties.

[30] A particularly important factor in determining the appropriateness of common representation is the effect on client-lawyer confidentiality and the attorney-client privilege. With regard to the attorney-client privilege, the prevailing rule is that, as between commonly represented clients, the privilege does not attach. Hence, it must be assumed that if litigation eventuates between the clients, the privilege will not protect any such communications, and the clients should be so advised.

[31] As to the duty of confidentiality, continued common representation will almost certainly be inadequate if one client asks the lawyer not to disclose to the other client information relevant to the common representation. This is so because the lawyer has an equal duty of loyalty to each client, and each client has the right to be informed of anything bearing on the representation that might affect that client's interests and the right to expect that the lawyer will use that information to that client's benefit. See Rule 1.4. The lawyer should, at the outset of the common representation and as part of the process of obtaining each client's informed consent, advise each client that information will be shared and that the lawyer will have to withdraw if one client decides that some matter material to the representation should be kept from the other. In limited circumstances, it may be appropriate for the lawyer to proceed with the representation when the clients have agreed, after being properly informed, that the lawyer will keep certain information confidential. For example, the lawyer may reasonably conclude that failure to disclose one client's trade secrets to another client will not adversely affect representation involving a joint venture between the clients and agree to keep that information confidential with the informed consent of both clients.

[32] When seeking to establish or adjust a relationship between clients, the lawyer should make clear that the lawyer's role is not that of partisanship normally expected in other circumstances and, thus, that the clients may be required to assume greater responsibility for decisions than when each client is separately represented. Any limitations on the scope of the representation made necessary as a result of the common representation should be fully explained to the clients at the outset of the representation. See Rule 1.2(c).

[33] Subject to the above limitations, each client in the common representation has the right to loyal and diligent representation and the protection of Rule 1.9 concerning the obligations to a former client. The client also has the right to discharge the lawyer as stated in Rule 1.16.

Organizational Clients

[34] A lawyer who represents a corporation or other organization does not, by virtue of that representation, necessarily represent any constituent or affiliated organization, such as a parent or subsidiary. See Rule 1.13(a). Thus, the lawyer for an organization is not barred from accepting representation adverse to an affiliate in an unrelated matter, unless the circumstances are such that the affiliate should also be considered a client of the lawyer, there is an understanding between the lawyer and the organizational client that the lawyer will avoid representation adverse to the client's affiliates, or the lawyer's obligations to either the organizational client or the new client are likely to limit materially the lawyer's representation of the other client.

[35] A lawyer for a corporation or other organization who is also a member of its board of directors should determine whether the responsibilities of the two roles may conflict. The lawyer may be called on to advise the corporation in matters involving actions of the directors. Consideration should be given to the frequency with which such situations may arise, the potential intensity of the conflict, the effect of the lawyer's resignation from the board and the possibility of the corporation's obtaining legal advice from another lawyer in such situations. If there is material risk that the dual role will compromise the lawyer's independence of professional judgment, the lawyer should not serve as a director or should cease to act as the corporation's lawyer when conflicts of interest arise. The lawyer should advise the other members of the board that in some circumstances matters discussed at board meetings while the lawyer is present in the capacity of director might not be protected by the attorney-client privilege and that conflict of interest considerations might require the lawyer's recusal as a director or might require the lawyer and the lawyer's firm to decline representation of the corporation in a matter.

Canon and Code Antecedents

ABA Canons of Professional Ethics: Canon 6 provided as follows:

6. Adverse Influences and Conflicting Interests

It is the duty of a lawyer at the time of retainer to disclose to the client all the circumstances of his relations to the parties, and any interest in or connection with the controversy, which might influence the client in the selection of counsel.

It is unprofessional to represent conflicting interests, except by express consent of all concerned given after a full disclosure of the facts. Within the meaning of this canon, a lawyer represents conflicting interests when, in behalf of one client, it is his duty to contend for that which duty to another client requires him to oppose.

The obligation to represent the client with undivided fidelity and not to divulge his secrets or confidences forbids also the subsequent acceptance of retainers or employment from others in matters adversely affecting any interest of the client with respect to which confidence has been reposed.

ABA Model Code of Professional Responsibility: Compare DR 5-101(A), DR 5-105(A), DR 5-105(C), and DR 5-107(B) (reprinted later in this volume).

Cross-References in Other Rules

Rule 1.0, Comment 6: "Many of the Rules of Professional Conduct require the lawyer to obtain the informed consent of a client or other person before accepting or continuing representation or pursuing a course of conduct (see **Rules** 1.2(c), 1.6(a) and **1.7(b)**)."

Rule 1.0, Comment 7: "A number of Rules require that a person's consent be confirmed in writing. See **Rules 1.7(b)** and 1.9(a)."

Rule 1.8, Comment 3: "The risk to a client is greatest when the client expects the lawyer to represent the client in the transaction itself or when the lawyer's financial interest otherwise poses a significant risk that the lawyer's representation of the client will be materially limited by the lawyer's financial interest in the transaction. Here the lawyer's role requires that the lawyer must comply, not only with the requirements of paragraph (a), but also with the requirements of **Rule 1.7**. Under that Rule, the lawyer must disclose the risks associated with the lawyer's dual role as both legal adviser and participant in the transaction, such as the risk that the lawyer will structure the transaction or give legal advice in a way that favors the lawyer's interests at the expense of the client. Moreover, the lawyer must obtain the client's informed consent. In some cases, the lawyer's interest may be such that **Rule 1.7** will preclude the lawyer from seeking the client's consent to the transaction."

Rule 1.8, Comment 8: "This Rule does not prohibit a lawyer from seeking to have the lawyer or a partner or associate of the lawyer named as executor of the client's estate or to another potentially lucrative fiduciary position. Nevertheless, such appointments will be subject to the general conflict of interest provision in **Rule 1.7** when there is a significant risk that the lawyer's interest in obtaining the appointment will materially limit the lawyer's independent professional judgment in advising the client concerning the choice of an executor or other fiduciary."

Rule 1.8, Comment 12: "Sometimes, it will be sufficient for the lawyer to obtain the client's informed consent regarding the fact of the payment and the identity of the third-party payer. If, however, the fee arrangement creates a conflict of interest for the lawyer, then the lawyer must comply with **Rule 1.7**. . . .

Under **Rule 1.7(a)**, a conflict of interest exists if there is significant risk that the lawyer's representation of the client will be materially limited by the lawyers own interest in the fee arrangement or by the lawyer's responsibilities to the third-party payer. . . . Under **Rule 1.7(b)**, the lawyer may accept or continue the representation with the informed consent of each affected client, unless the conflict is nonconsentable under that paragraph. Under **Rule 1.7(b)**, the informed consent must be confirmed in writing."

Rule 1.8, Comment 13: "Differences in willingness to make or accept an offer of settlement are among the risks of common representation of multiple clients by a single lawyer. Under **Rule 1.7**, this is one of the risks that should be discussed before undertaking the representation. . . ."

Rule 1.8, Comment 18: In the situation of client-lawyer sexual relationships, "before proceeding with the representation . . . , the lawyer should consider whether the lawyer's ability to represent the client will be materially limited by the relationship. See **Rule 1.7(a)(2)**."

Rule 1.9, Comment 9: "With regard to the effectiveness of an advance waiver, see Comment [22] to **Rule 1.7**."

Rule 1.10(a): "While lawyers are associated in a firm, none of them shall knowingly represent a client when any one of them practicing alone would be prohibited from doing so by **Rules 1.7** or 1.9, unless the prohibition is based on a personal interest of the prohibited lawyer and does not present a significant risk of materially limiting the representation of the client by the remaining lawyers in the firm."

Rule 1.10(c): "A disqualification prescribed by this rule may be waived by the affected client under the conditions stated in **Rule 1.7**."

Rule 1.10, Comment 5: Despite Rule 1.10(b), a law firm "may not represent a person with interests adverse to those of a present client of the firm, which would violate **Rule 1.7**."

Rule 1.10, Comment 6: "Rule 1.10(c) removes imputation with the informed consent of the affected client or former client under the conditions stated in **Rule 1.7**. The conditions stated in **Rule 1.7** require the lawyer to determine that the representation is not prohibited by **Rule 1.7** (b). . . . For a discussion of the effectiveness of client waivers of conflicts that might arise in the future, see **Rule 1.7**, Comment [22]."

Rule 1.11(d): "Except as law may otherwise expressly permit, a lawyer currently serving as a public officer or employee is subject to **Rules 1.7** and 1.9."

Rule 1.11, Comment 1: "A lawyer who has served or is currently serving as a public officer or employee is personally subject to the Rules of Professional Conduct, including the prohibition against concurrent conflicts of interest stated in **Rule 1.7**."

Rule 1.11, Comment 9: "Paragraphs (a) and (d) do not prohibit a lawyer from jointly representing a private party and a government agency when doing so is permitted by **Rule 1.7** and is not otherwise prohibited by law."

Rule 1.13(e): "A lawyer representing an organization may also represent any of its directors, officers, employees, members, shareholders or other constituents, subject to the provisions of **Rule 1.7**. If the organization's consent to the dual representation is required by **Rule 1.7**, the consent shall be given by an appropriate official of the organization other than the individual who is to be represented, or by the shareholders."

Rule 1.13, Comment 11: "[I]f the claim involves serious charges of wrongdoing by those in control of the organization, a conflict may arise between the lawyer's duty to the organization and the lawyer's relationship with the board. In those circumstances, **Rule 1.7** governs who should represent the directors and the organization."

Rule 1.17, Comment 11: A lawyer selling a law practice has an "obligation to avoid disqualifying conflicts, and to secure the client's informed consent for those conflicts that can be agreed to (see **Rule 1.7** regarding conflicts and Rule 1.0(e) for the definition of informed consent)."

Rule 1.18, Comment 4: "If the prospective client wishes to retain the lawyer, and if consent is possible under **Rule 1.7**, then consent from all affected present or former clients must be obtained before accepting the representation."

Rule 3.7(b): "A lawyer may act as advocate in a trial in which another lawyer in the lawyer's firm is likely to be called as a witness unless precluded from doing so by **Rule 1.7** or Rule 1.9."

Rule 3.7, Comment 4: In determining whether the lawyer should be disqualified, "[i]t is relevant that one or both parties could reasonably foresee that the lawyer would probably be a witness. The conflict of interest principles stated in **Rules 1.7**, 1.9 and 1.10 have no application to this aspect of the problem."

Rule 3.7, Comment 6: "In determining if it is permissible to act as advocate in a trial in which the lawyer will be a necessary witness, the lawyer must also consider that the dual role may give rise to a conflict of interest that will require compliance with **Rules 1.7** or 1.9. For example, if there is likely to be substantial conflict between the testimony of the client and that of the lawyer, the representation involves a conflict of interest that requires compliance with **Rule 1.7**. . . . If there is a conflict of interest, the lawyer must secure the client's informed consent, confirmed in writing. In some cases, the lawyer will be precluded from seeking the client's consent. See **Rule 1.7**."

Rule 3.7, Comment 7: "If, however, the testifying lawyer would also be disqualified by **Rule 1.7** or Rule 1.9 from representing the client in the matter, other lawyers in the firm will be precluded from representing the client by Rule 1.10 unless the client gives informed consent under the conditions stated in **Rule 1.7**."

Rule 5.2, Comment 2: "[I]f a question arises whether the interests of two clients conflict under **Rule 1.7**, the supervisor's reasonable resolution of the question should protect the subordinate professionally if the resolution is subsequently challenged."

Rule 5.7, Comment 10: "When a lawyer is obliged to accord the recipients of such services the protections of those Rules that apply to the client-lawyer relationship, the lawyer must take special care to heed the proscriptions of the Rules addressing conflict of interest (**Rules 1.7** through 1.11, especially **Rules 1.7** and 1.8(a), (b) and (f)). . . ."

Rule 6.3(a): "The lawyer shall not knowingly participate in a decision or action of the organization if participating in the decision or action would be incompatible with the lawyer's obligations to a client under **Rule 1.7**. . . ."

Rule 6.4, Comment 1: "In determining the nature and scope of participation in such activities, a lawyer should be mindful of obligations to clients under other Rules, particularly **Rule 1.7**."

Rule 6.5(a): "A lawyer who, under the auspices of a program sponsored by a nonprofit organization or court, provides short-term limited legal services to a client without expectation by either the lawyer or the client that the lawyer will provide continuing representation in the matter is subject to **Rules 1.7** and 1.9(a) only if the lawyer knows that the representation of the client involves a conflict of interest; and is subject to Rule 1.10 only if the lawyer knows that another lawyer associated with the lawyer in a law firm is disqualified by **Rule 1.7** or 1.9(a) with respect to the matter."

Rule 6.5, Comment 1: "Legal services organizations, courts and various nonprofit organizations have established programs through which lawyers provide short-term limited legal services. . . . Such programs are normally operated under circumstances in which it is not feasible for a lawyer to systematically screen for conflicts of interest as is generally required before undertaking a representation. See, e.g., **Rules 1.7**, 1.9 and 1.10."

Rule 6.5, Comment 3: "[P]aragraph (a) requires compliance with **Rules 1.7** or 1.9(a) only if the lawyer knows that the representation presents a conflict of interest for the lawyer, and with Rule 1.10 only if the lawyer knows that another lawyer in the lawyer's firm is disqualified by **Rules 1.7** or 1.9(a) in the matter."

Rule 6.5, Comment 4: "Paragraph (a)(2) requires the participating lawyer to comply with Rule 1.10 when the lawyer knows that the lawyer's firm is disqualified by **Rules 1.7** or 1.9(a)."

Rule 6.5, Comment 5: "If, after commencing a short-term limited representation in accordance with this Rule, a lawyer undertakes to represent the client in the matter on an ongoing basis, **Rules 1.7**, 1.9(a) and 1.10 become applicable."

Rule 7.2, Comment 8: "Conflicts of interest created by such [reciprocal referral] arrangements are governed by **Rule 1.7.**"

Legislative History of Model Rule 1.7

1980 Discussion Draft (then Rule 1.8) provided as follows:

> In circumstances in which a lawyer has interests, commitments, or responsibilities that may adversely affect the representation of a client, a lawyer shall not represent the client unless:
>
> (a) the services contemplated in the representation can otherwise be performed in accordance with the rules of professional conduct; and
>
> (b) the client consents after adequate disclosure of the circumstances.

1981 Draft:

> (a) A lawyer shall not represent a client if the lawyer's ability to consider, recommend or carry out a course of action on behalf of the client will be adversely affected by the lawyer's responsibilities to another client or to a third person, or by the lawyer's own interests.
>
> (b) When a lawyer's own interests or other responsibilities might adversely affect the representation of a client, the lawyer shall not represent the client unless:
>
> (1) the lawyer reasonably believes the other responsibilities or interests involved will not adversely affect the best interest of the client. . . .

1982 Draft was adopted.

1983 Rule: From its initial adoption in 1983 until the text was first amended in 2002, ABA Model Rule 1.7 provided as follows:

> *Rule 1.7 Conflict of Interest: General Rule*
>
> (a) A lawyer shall not represent a client if the representation of that client will be directly adverse to another client, unless:
>
> (1) the lawyer reasonably believes the representation will not adversely affect the relationship with the other client; and
>
> (2) each client consents after consultation.
>
> (b) A lawyer shall not represent a client if the representation of that client may be materially limited by the lawyer's responsibilities to another client or to a third person, or by the lawyer's own interests, unless:
>
> (1) the lawyer reasonably believes the representation will not be adversely affected; and
>
> (2) the client consents after consultation. When representation of multiple clients in a single matter is undertaken, the consultation shall include explanation of the implications of the common representation and the advantages and risks involved.

1987 Amendment: The ABA House of Delegates added the last sentence of what was then Comment 1 to Rule 1.7, and placed other parts of Comment 1 into a separate paragraph, which then became Comment 2.

2002 Amendments: At its February 2002 Mid-Year Meeting, the ABA House of Delegates adopted without change the ABA Ethics 2000 Commission's proposal to amend Rule 1.7 and its Comment extensively. This was the first time that the text of Rule 1.7 had been amended since the ABA originally adopted it in 1983.

Selected State Variations

California: Rule 3-310 (Avoiding the Representation of Adverse Interests) requires written informed consent to the conflicts it describes. This rule incorporates in one place principles spread across several rules in the ABA Model Rules, including current and former client conflicts and conflicts arising from the payment of a fee by a nonclient.

Section 2860 of the California Civil Code, adopted after the important decision in *San Diego Credit Union v. Cumis,* 208 Cal. Rptr. 494 (Ct. App. 1984), seeks to reconcile the multiple interests at stake when an insurance company has a duty to defend an insured whose interests might not be congruent with those of the insurer. The first paragraph of §2860 provides as follows:

> (a) If the provisions of a policy of insurance impose a duty to defend upon an insurer and a conflict of interest arises which creates a duty on the part of the insurer to provide independent counsel to the insured, the insurer shall provide independent counsel to represent the insured unless, at the time the insured is informed that a possible conflict may arise or does exist, the insured expressly waives, in writing, the right to independent counsel. An insurance contract may contain a provision which sets forth the method of selecting that counsel consistent with this section.

District of Columbia: Rule 1.7 differs significantly from the ABA Model Rule in its language but addresses the same current client conflicts. A unique provision is Rule 1.7(d), which in certain (but not all) instances allows a lawyer to continue with a conflicted representation when the conflict arises after the lawyer has begun work on a matter, but only if the conflict was "not reasonably foreseeable at the outset of a representation."

Florida adds Rule 1.7(d) (identical to the 1983 version of ABA Model Rule 1.8(i), now Comment 11 to ABA Model Rule 1.7), which provides:

> A lawyer related to another lawyer as parent, child, sibling, or spouse shall not represent a client in a representation directly adverse to a person who the lawyer knows is represented by the other lawyer except upon consent by the client after consultation regarding the relationship.

Florida also adds Rule 1.7(e), which requires a lawyer representing "an insured client at the expense of the insurer . . . to ascertain whether the lawyer will be representing both the insurer and the insured as clients, or only the insured, and to inform both the insured and the insurer regarding the scope of the representation."

Georgia has a unique version of Rule 1.7 that draws heavily on the Restatement of the Law Governing Lawyers. Georgia Rule 1.7 provides, in full, as follows:

(a) A lawyer shall not represent or continue to represent a client if there is a significant risk that the lawyer's own interests or the lawyer's duties to another client, a former client, or a third person will materially and adversely affect the representation of the client, except as permitted in (b).

(b) If client consent is permissible a lawyer may represent a client notwithstanding a significant risk of material and adverse effect if each affected or former client consents, preferably in writing, to the representation after:

(1) consultation with the lawyer,

(2) having received in writing reasonable and adequate information about the material risks of the representation, and

(3) having been given the opportunity to consult with independent counsel.

(c) Client consent is not permissible if the representation:

(1) is prohibited by law or these rules;

(2) includes the assertion of a claim by one client against another client represented by the lawyer in the same or substantially related proceeding; or

(3) involves circumstances rendering it reasonably unlikely that the lawyer will be able to provide adequate representation to one or more of the affected clients.

Illinois deletes the requirement that a client's consent to a conflict of interest be confirmed in writing.

Massachusetts retains the original 1983 version of ABA Model Rule 1.7, and the Comment to Massachusetts Rule 1.7 differs substantially from the Comment to ABA Model Rule 1.7. Among other things, the Massachusetts Comment addresses the situation of the lawyer who represents one member of a corporate family while opposing another member of the family, the issue of confidentiality and privilege in multiple representation, and the responsibilities of lawyers who represent classes. Comment 6 states that "a lawyer should not accept referrals from a referral source . . . if the lawyer's desire to continue to receive referrals from that source or the lawyer's relationship to that source would or would reasonably be viewed as discouraging the lawyer from representing the client zealously."

New Jersey: Rule 1.7(b)(1), the counterpart to ABA Model Rule 1.7(b)(4), contains a proviso to the effect "that a public entity cannot consent to any such representation." In addition, New Jersey adds a sentence from the original 1983 version of ABA Model Rule 1.7 requiring the lawyer, when representing multiple clients in a single matter, to explain "the advantages and risks involved" in common representation.

With respect to mortgage transactions, New Jersey has an unusual conflict of interest statute, N.J.S.A. §46:10A-6(b), which provides as follows:

> If a lender makes a written offer to a borrower to make a loan secured by real property located in this State, the lender shall disclose, in writing, prominently and in bold type, to the borrower before the acceptance of the offer by the borrower, that the interests of the borrower and lender are or may be different and may conflict, and that the lender's attorney represents only the lender and not the borrower and the borrower is, therefore, advised to employ an attorney of the borrower's choice licensed to practice law in this State to represent the interests of the borrower.

New York: Rule 1.7(a) draws, in part, on DR 5-101(A) and 5-105(A)-(B) of the old Model Code, providing as follows:

> (a) Except as provided in paragraph (b), a lawyer shall not represent a client if a reasonable lawyer would conclude that either:

> (1) the representation will involve the lawyer in representing differing interests; or
>
> (2) there is a significant risk that the lawyer's professional judgment on behalf of a client will be adversely affected by the lawyer's own financial, business, property or other personal interests.

The comments to the rule offer more detail than the Model Rule comments in several respects. For example, Comments 22 and 22A describe advance waivers of conflicts in detail, and Comments 34, 34A, and 34B all address conflicts involving a client's corporate affiliates.

Pennsylvania: Rule 1.7 tracks ABA Model Rule 1.7, except that Pennsylvania Rule 1.7(b)(4) does not require that client consent be "confirmed in writing."

Tennessee: In the rules effective January 1, 2011, Rule 1.7(c) expressly describes when a lawyer may represent two clients in the same criminal case.

Texas: Rule 1.06 provides as follows:

> (a) A lawyer shall not represent opposing parties to the same litigation.
>
> (b) In other situations and except to the extent permitted by paragraph (c), a lawyer shall not represent a person if the representation of that person:
>
> (1) involves a substantially related matter in which that person's interests are materially and directly adverse to the interests of another client of the lawyer or the lawyer's firm; or
>
> (2) reasonably appears to be or becomes adversely limited by the lawyer's or law firm's responsibilities to another client or to a third person or by the lawyer's or law firm's own interests.
>
> (c) A lawyer may represent a client in the circumstances described in (b) if:
>
> (1) the lawyer reasonably believes the representation of each client will not be materially affected; and
>
> (2) each affected or potentially affected client consents to such representation after full disclosure of the existence, nature, implications, and possible adverse consequences of the common representation and the advantages involved, if any.
>
> (d) A lawyer who has represented multiple parties in a matter shall not thereafter represent any of such parties in a dispute among the parties arising out of the matter, unless prior consent is obtained from all such parties to the dispute.
>
> (e) If a lawyer has accepted representation in violation of this Rule, or if multiple representation properly accepted becomes improper under this Rule, the lawyer shall promptly withdraw from one or more representations to the extent necessary for any remaining representation not to be in violation of these Rules.
>
> (f) If a lawyer would be prohibited by this Rule from engaging in particular conduct, no other lawyer while a member or associated with that lawyer's firm may engage in that conduct.

The Texas rule thus allows a lawyer to oppose a current client in a matter not "substantially related" to matters being handled for that client. However, in *In re Dresser Industries, Inc.*, 972 F.2d 540 (5th Cir. 1992), the Fifth Circuit refused to apply Texas Rule 1.06, stating that conflicts of interest in federal litigation are governed by "national standards," including ABA Model Rule 1.7 and the Restatement of the Law Governing Lawyers.

Washington: For consent to a conflict to be valid, Rule 1.7(b)(4) requires that each affected client gives informed consent, confirmed in writing "(following authorization from the other client to make any required disclosures)."

Related Materials

ABA Commission on Ethics 20/20: In 2009, the ABA created the ABA Commission on Ethics 20/20, which is comprehensively reviewing the ABA Model Rules of Professional Conduct in light of globalization and changes in information technology. On September 8, 2011, the Commission issued draft proposals for public comment regarding choice of law rules with respect to conflicts of interest. Specifically, the Commission proposed adding a new Comment 23 to Rule 1.7, under the heading "Choice of Rule Agreements," that would provide as follows:

> A matter may require a lawyer to perform work in multiple jurisdictions whose conflict rules differ. To ensure that a lawyer and client have the ability to reduce uncertainty and to predict which conflict rules will apply to a matter, the lawyer and client may agree that their relationship concerning the matter will be governed by the conflict rules of a specific United States or foreign jurisdiction, which may be other than the jurisdiction whose rules would apply under Rule 8.5(b) absent such agreement. Any such agreement, however, is subject to the following conditions: The client gives informed consent to the agreement, confirmed in writing; the lawyer advises the client in writing of the desirability of seeking independent counsel regarding the agreement; the client has a reasonable opportunity to consult with independent counsel regarding the agreement; the selected jurisdiction must be one in which the predominant effect of, or substantial work relating to, the matter is reasonably expected to occur; and the agreement may not result in the application of a conflict rule to which informed client consent is not permitted under the rules of the jurisdiction whose rules would otherwise govern the matter. See Rules 1.7(b) and 8.5(b). Client consent under this paragraph is more likely to be effective if the client is an experienced user of legal services.

The Ethics 20/20 Commission may place this proposal (or revised versions of it) before the ABA House of Delegates at the ABA's August 2012 Annual Meeting. For updates, see the Ethics 20/20 Commission's website at *http://www.americanbar.org/Ethics2020.*

ABA Formal Ethics Opinions: See ABA Formal Ethics Ops. 92-365 (1992), 93-372 (1993), 95-390 (1995), 97-406 (1997), 97-407 (1997), 02-426 (2002), 02-428 (2002), 04-432 (2004), 04-433 (2004), 05-434 (2005), 05-435 (2005), 05-436 (2005), 06-438 (2006), 07-447 (2007), 07-449 (2007), 08-450 (2008), 08-453 (2008), and 09-455 (2009).

ABA Report on Lawyers as Directors: In 1998, the ABA Section of Litigation's Task Force on the Independent Lawyer issued a lengthy report entitled "The Lawyer-Director: Implications for Independence." The report examines problems that may arise when a lawyer for a public or privately held corporation also serves as a director of the corporation. The report discourages lawyers from serving as both lawyer and director at the same time, but also suggests precautionary measures for lawyers who do serve in both capacities simultaneously. (The report is not available online.)

ABA Standards for Criminal Justice: The following Standard is relevant to ABA Model Rule 1.7:

Standard 4-3.5 Conflicts of Interest

> (a) Defense counsel should not permit his or her professional judgment or obligations to be affected by his or her own political, financial, business, property, or personal interests.

(b) Defense counsel should disclose to the defendant at the earliest feasible opportunity any interest in or connection with the case or any other matter that might be relevant to the defendant's selection of counsel to represent him or her or counsel's continuing representation. Such disclosure should include communication of information reasonably sufficient to permit the client to appreciate the significance of any conflict or potential conflict of interest.

(c) Except for preliminary matters such as initial hearings or applications for bail, defense counsel who are associated in practice should not undertake to defend more than one defendant in the same criminal case if the duty to one of the defendants may conflict with the duty to another. The potential for conflict of interest in representing multiple defendants is so grave that ordinarily defense counsel should decline to act for more than one of several codefendants except in unusual situations when, after careful investigation, it is clear either that no conflict is likely to develop at trial, sentencing, or at any other time in the proceeding or that common representation will be advantageous to each of the codefendants represented and, in either case, that:

(i) the several defendants give an informed consent to such multiple representation; and

(ii) the consent of the defendants is made a matter of judicial record. In determining the presence of consent by the defendants, the trial judge should make appropriate inquiries respecting actual or potential conflicts of interest of counsel and whether the defendants fully comprehend the difficulties that defense counsel sometimes encounters in defending multiple clients.

(d) Defense counsel who has formerly represented a defendant should not thereafter use information related to the former representation to the disadvantage of the former client unless the information has become generally known or the ethical obligation of confidentiality otherwise does not apply.

(e) In accepting payment of fees by one person for the defense of another, defense counsel should be careful to determine that he or she will not be confronted with a conflict of loyalty since defense counsel's entire loyalty is due the accused. Defense counsel should not accept such compensation unless:

(i) the accused consents after disclosure;

(ii) there is no interference with defense counsel's independence of professional judgment or with the client-lawyer relationship; and

(iii) information relating to the representation of the accused is protected from disclosure as required by defense counsel's ethical obligation of confidentiality.

Defense counsel should not permit a person who recommends, employs, or pays defense counsel to render legal services for another to direct or regulate counsel's professional judgment in rendering such legal services.

(f) Defense counsel should not defend a criminal case in which counsel's partner or other professional associate is or has been the prosecutor in the same case.

(g) Defense counsel should not represent a criminal defendant in a jurisdiction in which he or she is also a prosecutor.

(h) Defense counsel who formerly participated personally and substantially in the prosecution of a defendant should not thereafter represent any person in the same or a substantially related matter. Defense counsel who was formerly a prosecutor should not use confidential information about a person acquired when defense counsel was a prosecutor in the representation of a client whose interests are adverse to that person in a matter.

(i) Defense counsel who is related to a prosecutor as parent, child, sibling or spouse should not represent a client in a criminal matter where defense counsel knows the government is represented in the matter by such prosecutor. Nor should defense counsel who has a significant personal or financial relationship with a prosecutor represent a client in a criminal matter where defense counsel knows the government is represented in the matter by such prosecutor, except upon consent by the client after consultation regarding the relationship.

(j) Defense counsel should not act as surety on a bond either for the accused represented by counsel or for any other accused in the same or a related case.

(k) Except as law may otherwise expressly permit, defense counsel should not negotiate to employ any person who is significantly involved as an attorney or employee of the government in a matter in which defense counsel is participating personally and substantially.

ABA Standards for Imposing Lawyer Sanctions:

Failure to Avoid Conflicts of Interest

4.31. Disbarment is generally appropriate when a lawyer, without the informed consent of client(s):

(a) engages in representation of a client knowing that the lawyer's interests are adverse to the client's with the intent to benefit the lawyer or another, and causes serious or potentially serious injury to the client; or

(b) simultaneously represents clients that the lawyer knows have adverse interests with the intent to benefit the lawyer or another, and causes serious or potentially serious injury to a client; or

(c) represents a client in a matter substantially related to a matter in which the interests of a present or former client are materially adverse, and knowingly uses information relating to the representation of a client with the intent to benefit the lawyer or another, and causes serious or potentially serious injury to a client.

4.32. Suspension is generally appropriate when a lawyer knows of a conflict of interest and does not fully disclose to a client the possible effect of that conflict, and causes injury or potential injury to a client.

4.33. Reprimand is generally appropriate when a lawyer is negligent in determining whether the representation of a client may be materially affected by the lawyer's own interests, or whether the representation will adversely affect another client, and causes injury or potential injury to a client.

4.34. Admonition is generally appropriate when a lawyer engages in an isolated instance of negligence in determining whether the representation of a client may be materially affected by the lawyer's own interests, or whether the representation will adversely affect another client, and causes little or no actual or potential injury to a client.

Bankruptcy Law: Lawyers handling federal bankruptcy matters are subject to stringent statutes prohibiting conflicts of interest. One of the most prominent bankruptcy statutes is 11 U.S.C. §327, which provides, in part:

(a) Except as otherwise provided in this section, the trustee, with the court's approval, may employ one or more attorneys, accountants, appraisers, auctioneers, or other professional persons, that do not hold or represent an interest adverse to the estate, and that are disinterested persons, to represent or assist the trustee in carrying out the trustee's duties under this title. . . .

(c) In a case under chapter 7, 12, or 11 of this title, a person is not disqualified for employment under this section solely because of such person's employment by or representation of a creditor, unless there is objection by another creditor or the United States trustee, in which case the court shall disapprove such employment if there is an actual conflict of interest. . . .

(e) The trustee, with the court's approval, may employ . . . an attorney that has represented the debtor, if in the best interest of the estate, and if such attorney does not represent or hold any interest adverse to the debtor or to the estate with respect to the matter on which such attorney is to be employed.

IRS Regulations: In the regulations governing practice before the Internal Revenue Service, 31 C.F.R. §10.29, entitled "Conflicting Interests," essentially adopts

ABA Model Rule 1.7. In pertinent part, §10.29 provides that "a practitioner shall not represent a client in his or her practice before the Internal Revenue Service if the representation involves a conflict of interest" unless:

> (1) The practitioner reasonably believes that the practitioner will be able to provide competent and diligent representation to each affected client;
>
> (2) The representation is not prohibited by law;
>
> (3) Each affected client waives the conflict of interest and gives informed consent, confirmed in writing by each affected client, at the time the existence of the conflict of interest is known by the practitioner. . . .

Section 10.29(c) requires lawyers to keep copies of the written consents for at least 36 months after the representation of the affected clients concludes, and lawyers must provide the written consents to any officer or employee of the Internal Revenue Service on request.

Paralegal Conflicts: Courts and bar association ethics committees are devoting increasing attention to conflicts caused by paralegals and other members of a lawyer's staff. For example, Nebraska addresses "support person" conflicts in Rule 1.9(d), and Guideline 7 of the ABA Model Guidelines for the Utilization of Paralegal Services provides as follows: "A lawyer should take reasonable measures to prevent conflicts of interest resulting from a paralegal's other employment or interests."

Private Securities Litigation Reform Act: The Federal Private Securities Litigation Reform Act requires courts hearing securities lawsuits to determine whether ownership of securities in a defendant company creates a conflict of interest that disqualifies the plaintiffs' lawyer from representing the class. *See* 15 U.S.C. §77z-1(a)(8).

Restatement of the Law Governing Lawyers: See Restatement §§108, 121, 122, 125, 128–130, and 135 in our chapter on the Restatement later in this volume.

Sixth Amendment: The Sixth Amendment to the United States Constitution, which guarantees effective assistance of counsel, imposes certain obligations on courts regarding conflicts of interest. In *Holloway v. Arkansas,* 435 U.S. 475 (1978), the Court held that the Sixth Amendment requires automatic reversal when a trial court fails to conduct an inquiry either after a timely conflict objection, or after the court knows or reasonably should know that a particular conflict exists. In *Cuyler v. Sullivan,* 446 U.S. 335 (1980), the Court ruled that this "automatic reversal" rule does not apply when the trial court is not informed or is not on notice of a conflict. If a conflict is later alleged, the Sixth Amendment requires a defendant to establish that "an actual conflict of interest adversely affected his lawyer's performance." In *Mickens v. Taylor,* 535 U.S. 162 (2002), the Court held that, to demonstrate a Sixth Amendment violation due to the trial court's failure to inquire into a potential conflict of interest about which it knew or reasonably should have known, defendant must establish that this conflict of interest adversely affected counsel's performance.

Rule 1.8 Conflict of Interest: Current Clients: Specific Rules

(a) A lawyer shall not enter into a business transaction with a client or knowingly acquire an ownership, possessory, security or other pecuniary interest adverse to a client unless:

(1) the transaction and terms on which the lawyer acquires the interest are fair and reasonable to the client and are fully disclosed and transmitted in writing in a manner that can be reasonably understood by the client;

BEWARE 1.15

(2) the client is advised in writing of the desirability of seeking and is given a reasonable opportunity to seek the advice of independent legal counsel on the transaction; and

(3) the client gives informed consent, in a writing signed by the client, to the essential terms of the transaction and the lawyer's role in the transaction, including whether the lawyer is representing the client in the transaction.

(b) A lawyer shall not use information relating to representation of a client to the disadvantage of the client unless the client gives informed consent, except as permitted or required by these Rules.

(c) A lawyer shall not solicit any substantial gift from a client, including a testamentary gift, or prepare on behalf of a client an instrument giving the lawyer or a person related to the lawyer any substantial gift unless the lawyer or other recipient of the gift is related to the client. For purposes of this paragraph, related persons include a spouse, child, grandchild, parent, grandparent or other relative or individual with whom the lawyer or the client maintains a close, familial relationship.

(d) Prior to the conclusion of representation of a client, a lawyer shall not make or negotiate an agreement giving the lawyer literary or media rights to a portrayal or account based in substantial part on information relating to the representation.

(e) A lawyer shall not provide financial assistance to a client in connection with pending or contemplated litigation, except that:

(1) a lawyer may advance court costs and expenses of litigation, the repayment of which may be contingent on the outcome of the matter; and

(2) a lawyer representing an indigent client may pay court costs and expenses of litigation on behalf of the client.

(f) A lawyer shall not accept compensation for representing a client from one other than the client unless:

(1) the client gives informed consent;

(2) there is no interference with the lawyer's independence of professional judgment or with the client-lawyer relationship; and

(3) information relating to representation of a client is protected as required by Rule 1.6.

(g) A lawyer who represents two or more clients shall not participate in making an aggregate settlement of the claims of or against the clients, or in a criminal case an aggregated agreement as to guilty or nolo contendere pleas, unless each client gives informed consent, in a writing signed by the client. The lawyer's disclosure shall include the existence and nature of all the claims or pleas involved and of the participation of each person in the settlement.

(h) A lawyer shall not:

(1) make an agreement prospectively limiting the lawyer's liability to a client for malpractice unless the client is independently represented in making the agreement; or

(2) settle a claim or potential claim for such liability with an unrepresented client or former client unless that person is advised in writing of the desirability of seeking and is given a reasonable opportunity to seek the advice of independent legal counsel in connection therewith.

(i) A lawyer shall not acquire a proprietary interest in the cause of action or subject matter of litigation the lawyer is conducting for a client, except that the lawyer may:

(1) acquire a lien authorized by law to secure the lawyer's fee or expenses; and

(2) contract with a client for a reasonable contingent fee in a civil case.

(j) A lawyer shall not have sexual relations with a client unless a consensual sexual relationship existed between them when the client-lawyer relationship commenced.

(k) While lawyers are associated in a firm, a prohibition in the foregoing paragraphs (a) through (i) that applies to any one of them shall apply to all of them.

COMMENT

Business Transactions Between Client and Lawyer

[1] A lawyer's legal skill and training, together with the relationship of trust and confidence between lawyer and client, create the possibility of overreaching when the lawyer participates in a business, property or financial transaction with a client, for example, a loan or sales transaction or a lawyer investment on behalf of a client. The requirements of paragraph (a) must be met even when the transaction is not closely related to the subject matter of the representation, as when a lawyer drafting a will for a client learns that the client needs money for unrelated expenses and offers to make a loan to the client. The Rule applies to lawyers engaged in the sale of goods or services related to the practice of law, for example, the sale of title insurance or investment services to existing clients of the lawyer's legal practice. See Rule 5.7. It also applies to lawyers purchasing property from estates they represent. It does not apply to ordinary fee arrangements between client and lawyer, which are governed by Rule 1.5, although its requirements must be met when the lawyer accepts an interest in the client's business or other nonmonetary property as payment of all or part of a fee. In addition, the Rule does not apply to standard commercial transactions between the lawyer and the client for products or services that the client generally markets to others, for example, banking or brokerage services, medical services, products manufactured or distributed by the client, and utilities' services. In such transactions, the lawyer has no advantage in dealing with the client, and the restrictions in paragraph (a) are unnecessary and impracticable.

[2] Paragraph (a)(1) requires that the transaction itself be fair to the client and that its essential terms be communicated to the client, in writing, in a manner that can be reasonably understood. Paragraph (a)(2) requires that the client also be advised, in writing, of the desirability of seeking the advice of independent legal counsel. It also requires that the client be given a reasonable opportunity to

obtain such advice. Paragraph (a)(3) requires that the lawyer obtain the client's informed consent, in a writing signed by the client, both to the essential terms of the transaction and to the lawyer's role. When necessary, the lawyer should discuss both the material risks of the proposed transaction, including any risk presented by the lawyer's involvement, and the existence of reasonably available alternatives and should explain why the advice of independent legal counsel is desirable. See Rule 1.0(e) (definition of informed consent).

[3] The risk to a client is greatest when the client expects the lawyer to represent the client in the transaction itself or when the lawyer's financial interest otherwise poses a significant risk that the lawyer's representation of the client will be materially limited by the lawyer's financial interest in the transaction. Here the lawyer's role requires that the lawyer must comply, not only with the requirements of paragraph (a), but also with the requirements of Rule 1.7. Under that Rule, the lawyer must disclose the risks associated with the lawyer's dual role as both legal adviser and participant in the transaction, such as the risk that the lawyer will structure the transaction or give legal advice in a way that favors the lawyer's interests at the expense of the client. Moreover, the lawyer must obtain the client's informed consent. In some cases, the lawyer's interest may be such that Rule 1.7 will preclude the lawyer from seeking the client's consent to the transaction.

[4] If the client is independently represented in the transaction, paragraph (a)(2) of this Rule is inapplicable, and the paragraph (a)(1) requirement for full disclosure is satisfied either by a written disclosure by the lawyer involved in the transaction or by the client's independent counsel. The fact that the client was independently represented in the transaction is relevant in determining whether the agreement was fair and reasonable to the client as paragraph (a)(1) further requires.

Use of Information Related to Representation

[5] Use of information relating to the representation to the disadvantage of the client violates the lawyer's duty of loyalty. Paragraph (b) applies when the information is used to benefit either the lawyer or a third person, such as another client or business associate of the lawyer. For example, if a lawyer learns that a client intends to purchase and develop several parcels of land, the lawyer may not use that information to purchase one of the parcels in competition with the client or to recommend that another client make such a purchase. The Rule does not prohibit uses that do not disadvantage the client. For example, a lawyer who learns a government agency's interpretation of trade legislation during the representation of one client may properly use that information to benefit other clients. Paragraph (b) prohibits disadvantageous use of client information unless the client gives informed consent, except as permitted or required by these Rules. See Rules 1.2(d), 1.6, 1.9(c), 3.3, 4.1(b), 8.1 and 8.3.

Gifts to Lawyers

[6] A lawyer may accept a gift from a client, if the transaction meets general standards of fairness. For example, a simple gift such as a present given at a holiday or as a token of appreciation is permitted. If a client offers the lawyer a more substantial gift, paragraph (c) does not prohibit the lawyer from accepting it, although such a gift may be voidable by the client under the doctrine of undue influence,

which treats client gifts as presumptively fraudulent. In any event, due to concerns about overreaching and imposition on clients, a lawyer may not suggest that a substantial gift be made to the lawyer or for the lawyer's benefit, except where the lawyer is related to the client as set forth in paragraph (c).

[7] If effectuation of a substantial gift requires preparing a legal instrument such as a will or conveyance the client should have the detached advice that another lawyer can provide. The sole exception to this Rule is where the client is a relative of the donee.

[8] This Rule does not prohibit a lawyer from seeking to have the lawyer or a partner or associate of the lawyer named as executor of the client's estate or to another potentially lucrative fiduciary position. Nevertheless, such appointments will be subject to the general conflict of interest provision in Rule 1.7 when there is a significant risk that the lawyer's interest in obtaining the appointment will materially limit the lawyer's independent professional judgment in advising the client concerning the choice of an executor or other fiduciary. In obtaining the client's informed consent to the conflict, the lawyer should advise the client concerning the nature and extent of the lawyer's financial interest in the appointment, as well as the availability of alternative candidates for the position.

Literary Rights

[9] An agreement by which a lawyer acquires literary or media rights concerning the conduct of the representation creates a conflict between the interests of the client and the personal interests of the lawyer. Measures suitable in the representation of the client may detract from the publication value of an account of the representation. Paragraph (d) does not prohibit a lawyer representing a client in a transaction concerning literary property from agreeing that the lawyer's fee shall consist of a share in ownership in the property, if the arrangement conforms to Rule 1.5 and paragraphs (a) and (i).

Financial Assistance

[10] Lawyers may not subsidize lawsuits or administrative proceedings brought on behalf of their clients, including making or guaranteeing loans to their clients for living expenses, because to do so would encourage clients to pursue lawsuits that might not otherwise be brought and because such assistance gives lawyers too great a financial stake in the litigation. These dangers do not warrant a prohibition on a lawyer lending a client court costs and litigation expenses, including the expenses of medical examination and the costs of obtaining and presenting evidence, because these advances are virtually indistinguishable from contingent fees and help ensure access to the courts. Similarly, an exception allowing lawyers representing indigent clients to pay court costs and litigation expenses regardless of whether these funds will be repaid is warranted.

Person Paying for a Lawyer's Services

[11] Lawyers are frequently asked to represent a client under circumstances in which a third person will compensate the lawyer, in whole or in part. The third

person might be a relative or friend, an indemnitor (such as a liability insurance company) or a co-client (such as a corporation sued along with one or more of its employees). Because third-party payers frequently have interests that differ from those of the client, including interests in minimizing the amount spent on the representation and in learning how the representation is progressing, lawyers are prohibited from accepting or continuing such representations unless the lawyer determines that there will be no interference with the lawyer's independent professional judgment and there is informed consent from the client. See also Rule 5.4(c) (prohibiting interference with a lawyer's professional judgment by one who recommends, employs or pays the lawyer to render legal services for another).

[12] Sometimes, it will be sufficient for the lawyer to obtain the client's informed consent regarding the fact of the payment and the identity of the third-party payer. If, however, the fee arrangement creates a conflict of interest for the lawyer, then the lawyer must comply with Rule 1.7. The lawyer must also conform to the requirements of Rule 1.6 concerning confidentiality. Under Rule 1.7(a), a conflict of interest exists if there is significant risk that the lawyer's representation of the client will be materially limited by the lawyer's own interest in the fee arrangement or by the lawyer's responsibilities to the third-party payer (for example, when the third-party payer is a co-client). Under Rule 1.7(b), the lawyer may accept or continue the representation with the informed consent of each affected client, unless the conflict is nonconsentable under that paragraph. Under Rule 1.7(b), the informed consent must be confirmed in writing.

Aggregate Settlements

[13] Differences in willingness to make or accept an offer of settlement are among the risks of common representation of multiple clients by a single lawyer. Under Rule 1.7, this is one of the risks that should be discussed before undertaking the representation, as part of the process of obtaining the client's informed consent. In addition, Rule 1.2(a) protects each client's right to have the final say in deciding whether to accept or reject an offer of settlement and in deciding whether to enter a guilty or nolo contendere plea in a criminal case. The rule stated in this paragraph is a corollary of both these Rules and provides that, before any settlement offer or plea bargain is made or accepted on behalf of multiple clients, the lawyer must inform each of them about all the material terms of the settlement, including what the other clients will receive or pay if the settlement or plea offer is accepted. See also Rule 1.0(e) (definition of informed consent). Lawyers representing a class of plaintiffs or defendants, or those proceeding derivatively, may not have a full client-lawyer relationship with each member of the class; nevertheless, such lawyers must comply with applicable rules regulating notification of class members and other procedural requirements designed to ensure adequate protection of the entire class.

Limiting Liability and Settling Malpractice Claims

[14] Agreements prospectively limiting a lawyer's liability for malpractice are prohibited unless the client is independently represented in making the agreement

because they are likely to undermine competent and diligent representation. Also, many clients are unable to evaluate the desirability of making such an agreement before a dispute has arisen, particularly if they are then represented by the lawyer seeking the agreement. This paragraph does not, however, prohibit a lawyer from entering into an agreement with the client to arbitrate legal malpractice claims, provided such agreements are enforceable and the client is fully informed of the scope and effect of the agreement. Nor does this paragraph limit the ability of lawyers to practice in the form of a limited-liability entity, where permitted by law, provided that each lawyer remains personally liable to the client for his or her own conduct and the firm complies with any conditions required by law, such as provisions requiring client notification or maintenance of adequate liability insurance. Nor does it prohibit an agreement in accordance with Rule 1.2 that defines the scope of the representation, although a definition of scope that makes the obligations of representation illusory will amount to an attempt to limit liability.

[15] Agreements settling a claim or a potential claim for malpractice are not prohibited by this Rule. Nevertheless, in view of the danger that a lawyer will take unfair advantage of an unrepresented client or former client, the lawyer must first advise such a person in writing of the appropriateness of independent representation in connection with such a settlement. In addition, the lawyer must give the client or former client a reasonable opportunity to find and consult independent counsel.

Acquiring Proprietary Interest in Litigation

[16] Paragraph (i) states the traditional general rule that lawyers are prohibited from acquiring a proprietary interest in litigation. Like paragraph (e), the general rule has its basis in common law champerty and maintenance and is designed to avoid giving the lawyer too great an interest in the representation. In addition, when the lawyer acquires an ownership interest in the subject of the representation, it will be more difficult for a client to discharge the lawyer if the client so desires. The Rule is subject to specific exceptions developed in decisional law and continued in these Rules. The exception for certain advances of the costs of litigation is set forth in paragraph (e). In addition, paragraph (i) sets forth exceptions for liens authorized by law to secure the lawyer's fees or expenses and contracts for reasonable contingent fees. The law of each jurisdiction determines which liens are authorized by law. These may include liens granted by statute, liens originating in common law and liens acquired by contract with the client. When a lawyer acquires by contract a security interest in property other than that recovered through the lawyer's efforts in the litigation, such an acquisition is a business or financial transaction with a client and is governed by the requirements of paragraph (a). Contracts for contingent fees in civil cases are governed by Rule 1.5.

Client-Lawyer Sexual Relationships

[17] The relationship between lawyer and client is a fiduciary one in which the lawyer occupies the highest position of trust and confidence. The relationship is almost always unequal; thus, a sexual relationship between lawyer and client can

involve unfair exploitation of the lawyer's fiduciary role, in violation of the lawyer's basic ethical obligation not to use the trust of the client to the client's disadvantage. In addition, such a relationship presents a significant danger that, because of the lawyer's emotional involvement, the lawyer will be unable to represent the client without impairment of the exercise of independent professional judgment. Moreover, a blurred line between the professional and personal relationships may make it difficult to predict to what extent client confidences will be protected by the attorney-client evidentiary privilege, since client confidences are protected by privilege only when they are imparted in the context of the client-lawyer relationship. Because of the significant danger of harm to client interests and because the client's own emotional involvement renders it unlikely that the client could give adequate informed consent, this Rule prohibits the lawyer from having sexual relations with a client regardless of whether the relationship is consensual and regardless of the absence of prejudice to the client.

[18] Sexual relationships that predate the client-lawyer relationship are not prohibited. Issues relating to the exploitation of the fiduciary relationship and client dependency are diminished when the sexual relationship existed prior to the commencement of the client-lawyer relationship. However, before proceeding with the representation in these circumstances, the lawyer should consider whether the lawyer's ability to represent the client will be materially limited by the relationship. See Rule 1.7(a)(2).

[19] When the client is an organization, paragraph (j) of this Rule prohibits a lawyer for the organization (whether inside counsel or outside counsel) from having a sexual relationship with a constituent of the organization who supervises, directs or regularly consults with that lawyer concerning the organization's legal matters.

Imputation of Prohibitions

[20] Under paragraph (k), a prohibition on conduct by an individual lawyer in paragraphs (a) through (i) also applies to all lawyers associated in a firm with the personally prohibited lawyer. For example, one lawyer in a firm may not enter into a business transaction with a client of another member of the firm without complying with paragraph (a), even if the first lawyer is not personally involved in the representation of the client. The prohibition set forth in paragraph (j) is personal and is not applied to associated lawyers.

Canon and Code Antecedents

ABA Canons of Professional Ethics: Canons 10, 11, and 38 provided as follows:

10. Acquiring Interest in Litigation

The lawyer should not purchase any interest in the subject matter of the litigation which he is conducting.

11. Dealing with Trust Property

The lawyer should refrain from any action whereby for his personal benefit or gain he abuses or takes advantage of the confidence reposed in him by his client.

Money of the client or collected for the client or other trust property coming into the possession of the lawyer should be reported and accounted for promptly, and should not under any circumstances be commingled with his own or be used by him.

38. Compensation, Commissions and Rebates

A lawyer should accept no compensation, commissions, rebates or other advantages from others without the knowledge and consent of his client after full disclosure.

ABA Model Code of Professional Responsibility: Compare DR 4-101(B)(3), DR 5-103(A), DR 5-103(B), DR 5-104(A), DR 5-104(B), DR 5-106, DR 5-107(A)(1), and DR 6-102(A) (reprinted later in this volume).

Cross-References in Other Rules

Rule 1.0, Comment 7: Certain "Rules require that a client's consent be obtained in a writing signed by the client. See, e.g., **Rules 1.8(a)** and **(g)**."

Rule 1.2, Comment 8: "All agreements concerning a lawyer's representation of a client must accord with the Rules of Professional Conduct and other law. See, e.g., **Rules** 1.1, **1.8** and 5.6."

Rule 1.5, Comment 4: "A lawyer may accept property in payment for services, such as an ownership interest in an enterprise, providing this does not involve acquisition of a proprietary interest in the cause of action or subject matter of the litigation contrary to **Rule 1.8(i)**. However, a fee paid in property instead of money may be subject to the requirements of **Rule 1.8 (a)**. . . . "

Rule 1.6, Comment 1: See "**Rules 1.8(b)** and 1.9(c)(1) for the lawyer's duties with respect to the use of such information to the disadvantage of clients and former clients."

Rule 1.7, Comment 1: "For specific Rules regarding certain concurrent conflicts of interest, see **Rule 1.8**."

Rule 1.7, Comment 10: "See **Rule 1.8** for specific Rules pertaining to a number of personal interest conflicts, including business transactions with clients."

Rule 1.7, Comment 12: "A lawyer is prohibited from engaging in sexual relationships with a client unless the sexual relationship predates the formation of the client-lawyer relationship. See **Rule 1.8(j)**."

Rule 1.7, Comment 13: "A lawyer may be paid from a source other than the client, including a co-client, if the client is informed of that fact and consents and the arrangement does not compromise the lawyer's duty of loyalty or independent judgment to the client. See **Rule 1.8(f)**."

Rule 1.10, Comment 8: "Where a lawyer is prohibited from engaging in certain transactions under **Rule 1.8**, paragraph (**k**) of that Rule, and not this Rule, determines whether that prohibition also applies to other lawyers associated in a firm with the personally prohibited lawyer."

Rule 1.13, Comment 6: "[T]his Rule does not limit or expand the lawyer's responsibility under **Rule 1.8**, 1.16, 3.3 or 4.1."

Rule 5.4, Comment 2: Rule 5.4 "expresses traditional limitations on permitting a third party to direct or regulate the lawyer's professional judgment in rendering legal services to another. See also **Rule 1.8(f)**. . . ."

Rule 5.7, Comment 5: "When a client-lawyer relationship exists with a person who is referred by a lawyer to a separate law-related service entity controlled by the lawyer, individually or with others, the lawyer must comply with **Rule 1.8(a)**."

Rule 5.7, Comment 10: "When a lawyer is obliged to accord the recipients of such services the protections of those Rules that apply to the client-lawyer relationship, the lawyer must take special care to heed the proscriptions of the Rules addressing conflict of interest (Rules 1.7 through 1.11, especially Rules 1.7 and **1.8(a)**, **(b)**, and **(f)**). . . ."

Legislative History of Model Rule 1.8

1979 Unofficial Pre-Circulation Draft:

(e) A lawyer shall not provide financial assistance to a client in connection with pending or contemplated litigation, except that a lawyer may advance expenses, including:

Alternative (1): Court costs, expenses of investigation, medical and other experts, and obtaining and presenting evidence.

Alternative (2): Court costs, expenses of litigation, and living expenses.

1980 Discussion Draft (then called Rule 1.9):

(f) A lawyer may serve as general counsel to a corporation or other organization of which the lawyer is a director only if:

(1) There is adequate disclosure to and consent by all persons having an investment interest in the organization; or

(2) When doing so would not involve serious risk of conflict between the lawyer's responsibilities as general counsel and those as director.

1981 and ***1982 Drafts*** were substantially the same as adopted, except that Rule 1.8(f) contained no restrictions other than the client's consent "after consultation."

1983 Rule: From 1983 until its extensive amendment in 2002, Rule 1.8 provided:

(a) [Same as the 2002 version of Rule 1.8(a).]

(1) [Same as the 2002 version of Rule 1.8(a)(1).]

(2) the client is given a reasonable opportunity to seek the advice of independent counsel in the transaction; and

(3) the client consents in writing thereto.

(b) [Same as the 2002 version of Rule 1.8(b), but requiring that the client "consent after consultation" instead of "gives informed consent."]

(c) A lawyer shall not prepare an instrument giving the lawyer or a person related to the lawyer as parent, child, sibling, or spouse any substantial gift from a client, including a testamentary gift, except where the client is related to the donee.

(d) [Same as the 2002 version of Rule 1.8(d).]

(e) [Same as the 2002 version of Rule 1.8(e).]

(f) [Same as the 2002 version of Rule 1.8(f), but requiring that the client "consent after consultation" instead of "gives informed consent."]

(g) A lawyer who represents two or more clients shall not participate in making an aggregate settlement of the claims of or against the clients, or in a criminal case an aggregated agreement as to guilty or nolo contendere pleas, unless each client consents after consultation, including disclosure of the existence and nature of all the claims or pleas involved and of the participation of each person in the settlement.

(h) A lawyer shall not make an agreement prospectively limiting the lawyer's liability to a client for malpractice unless permitted by law and the client is independently represented in making the agreement, or settle a claim for such liability with an unrepresented client or former client without first advising that person in writing that independent representation is appropriate in connection therewith.

(i) A lawyer related to another lawyer as parent, child, sibling or spouse shall not represent a client in a representation directly adverse to a person whom the lawyer knows is represented by the other lawyer except upon consent by the client after consultation regarding the relationship.

(j) [Same as the 2002 version of Rule 1.8(i).]

2002 Amendments: At its February 2002 Mid-Year Meeting, the ABA House of Delegates adopted without change the ABA Ethics 2000 Commission's extensive proposal to amend Rule 1.8 and its Comment. Among other things, the amendment created the writing requirement in paragraph (a)(2) and added the description of the writing required in paragraph (a)(3). The amendment also added the writing requirement to paragraph (g). Paragraphs (j) and (k) were completely new. In addition, the Comment was extensively revised.

Also, former Rule 1.8(i) was deleted. Before 2002, Rule 1.8(i) prohibited lawyers in certain familial relationships (parent, child, sibling, or spouse) from representing adverse clients without consent after consultation. This provision was deleted in 2002 and replaced by a new Comment 11 to Rule 1.7. The Reporter explained that the deleted Rule 1.8(i) was both overinclusive and underinclusive. It was underinclusive "because it does not address personal-interest conflicts arising from close family or family-like relationships other than those enumerated in the Rules, such as couples who live together in a relationship approximating marriage." The rule was deemed overinclusive because it would permit client consent even of conflicts that would "be deemed nonconsentable under Rule 1.7." For these and other reasons, the Commission deleted the rule in favor of Rule 1.7 Comment 11.

Selected State Variations

Alabama: Alabama's Rule 1.8(e)(3) provides as follows:

> (3) a lawyer may advance or guarantee emergency financial assistance to the client, the repayment of which may not be contingent on the outcome of the matter, provided that no promise or assurance of financial assistance was made to the client by the lawyer, or on the lawyer's behalf, prior to the employment of the lawyer.

Alabama also adds Rule 1.8(k), which identifies when a lawyer can represent both parties to an uncontested divorce or domestic relations proceeding. Relating to Rule 1.8(h), the Alabama Legal Services Liability Act, Ala. Code §§6-5-570 et seq., provides as follows: "There shall be only one form and cause of action against legal service providers in courts in the State of Alabama and it shall be known as the legal service liability action." Finally, Rules 1.8(*l*) and (m) describe prohibitions on sexual relations between lawyers and clients. Notably, Rule 1.8(m) states that "except for a spousal relationship or a relationship that existed at the commencement of the lawyer-client relationship, sexual relations between the lawyer and the client shall be presumed to be exploitative [and thus violate Rule 1.8(*l*)]. This presumption is rebuttable."

Arizona: Rule 1.8(h)(2) adds a clause forbidding a lawyer to "make an agreement prospectively limiting the client's right to report the lawyer to appropriate professional authorities." Rule 1.8(*l*), which retains the 1983 version of ABA Model Rule 1.8(i), provides: "A lawyer related to another lawyer as parent, child, sibling, spouse or cohabitant shall not represent a client in a representation directly adverse to a person who the lawyer knows is represented by the other lawyer except upon consent by the client after consultation regarding the relationship."

California: California's rules are generally equivalent to Model Rule 1.8, but two exceptions deserve attention. Rule 3-320 provides as follows:

> A member shall not represent a client in a matter in which another party's lawyer is a spouse, parent, child, or sibling of the member, lives with the member, is a client of the member, or has an intimate personal relationship with the member, unless the member informs the client in writing of the relationship.

And Rule 4-210 provides in part as follows:

> (A) A member shall not directly or indirectly pay or agree to pay, guarantee, represent, or sanction a representation that the member or member's law firm will pay the personal or business expenses of a prospective or existing client, except that this rule shall not prohibit a member: . . . (2) After employment, from lending money to the client upon the client's promise in writing to repay such loan.

Connecticut adds the following language to Rule 1.8(a), providing that lawyers can enter into business transactions with clients under the following circumstances:

> (4) With regard to a business transaction, the lawyer advises the client or former client in writing either (A) that the lawyer will provide legal services to the client or former client concerning the transaction, or (B) that the lawyer will not provide legal services to the client or former client and that the lawyer is involved as a business person only and not as a lawyer representing the client or former client and that the lawyer is not one to whom the client or former client can turn for legal advice concerning the transaction.
>
> (5) With regard to the providing of investment services, the lawyer advises the client or former client in writing (A) whether such services are covered by legal liability insurance or other insurance, and [makes either disclosure set out in paragraph (a)(4)]. Investment services shall only apply where the lawyer has either a direct or indirect control over the invested funds and a direct or indirect interest in the underlying investment.
>
> For purposes of subsection (a)(1) through (a)(5), the phrase "former client" shall mean a client for whom the two year period starting from the conclusion of representation has not expired.

District of Columbia: D.C. Rule 1.8(d) permits lawyers to advance "financial assistance which is reasonably necessary to permit the client to institute or maintain the litigation or administrative proceeding." Rule 1.8(i) provides as follows:

> A lawyer may acquire and enforce a lien granted by law to secure the lawyer's fees or expenses, but a lawyer shall not impose a lien upon any part of a client's files, except upon the lawyer's own work product, and then only to the extent that the work product has not been paid for. This work product exception shall not apply when the client has become unable to pay, or when withholding the lawyer's work product would present a significant risk to the client of irreparable harm.

Florida: Rule 4-8.4(i) provides that a lawyer shall not engage in sexual conduct with a client "or a representative of a client that exploits or adversely affects the interests of the client or the lawyer-client relationship."

Georgia: Rule 1.8(a), drawing on DR 5-104 of the ABA Code of Professional Responsibility, applies "if the client expects the lawyer to exercise the lawyer's professional judgment therein for the protection of the client." Georgia retains the language of deleted ABA Model Rule 1.8(i) but adds that the disqualification of a lawyer due to a parent, child, sibling, or spousal relationship "is personal and is not imputed to members of firms with whom the lawyers are associated." Georgia adds that the maximum penalty for violating Rule 1.8(b) (which relates to confidentiality) is disbarment, but the maximum penalty for violating any other provision of Rule 1.8 is only a public reprimand.

Illinois: Rule 1.8(a)(2) omits the phrase "desirability of seeking."

Louisiana: Rule 1.8(g) permits an aggregate settlement if "a court approves the settlement in a certified class action." Rule 1.8(e) permits a lawyer to "provide financial assistance to a client who is in necessitous circumstances" subject to strict controls, including:

> (ii) The advance or loan guarantee, or the offer thereof, shall not be used as an inducement by the lawyer, or anyone acting on the lawyer's behalf, to secure employment.
>
> (iii) Neither the lawyer nor anyone acting on the lawyer's behalf may offer to make advances or loan guarantees prior to being hired by a client, and the lawyer shall not publicize nor advertise a willingness to make advances or loan guarantees to clients.

Massachusetts: Rule 1.8(b) forbids a lawyer to use confidential information "for the lawyer's advantage or the advantage of a third person" without consent.

Michigan: Rules 1.8(a)(2) and 1.8(h)(2) (regarding business transactions with clients and settlement of legal malpractice claims) both require that the client be given a reasonable opportunity to seek the advice of independent counsel but lack the ABA requirement that the client be "advised in writing of the desirability of seeking" independent counsel. Michigan Rule 1.8(g), regarding aggregate settlements, lacks the ABA requirement that the client's consent be "in a writing signed by the client." Michigan retains the language of deleted ABA Model Rule 1.8(i) verbatim.

Minnesota: Rule 1.8(e)(3) allows a lawyer to guarantee a loan necessary for a client to withstand litigation delay. Rule 1.8(k)'s provision on sexual relationships with clients prohibits a lawyer from having sexual relations with a client unless a consensual relationship existed between the lawyer and client when the client-lawyer relationship commenced. The rule also defines "sexual relations" and adds the following Rules 1.8(k)(2)-(3) to explain the meaning of sex with a "client" when a lawyer represents an organization:

> (2) if the client is an organization, any individual who oversees the representation and gives instructions to the lawyer on behalf of the organization shall be deemed to be the client. . . .
>
> (3) this paragraph does not prohibit a lawyer from engaging in sexual relations with a client of the lawyer's firm provided that the lawyer has no involvement in the performance of the legal work for the client. . . .

Mississippi: Rule 1.8(e)(2) permits a lawyer to advance medical and living expenses to a client under certain narrowly defined circumstances.

New Hampshire: The New Hampshire rules include a Rule 1.19 (Disclosure of Information to the Client), which requires a lawyer (other than a government or in-house lawyer) to inform a client at the time of engagement if "the lawyer does not maintain professional liability insurance" of at least $100,000 per occurrence and $300,000 in the aggregate "or if the lawyer's professional liability insurance ceases to be in effect."

New Jersey: Rule 1.8(e)(3) creates an exception allowing financial assistance by a "non-profit organization authorized under [other law]" if the organization is representing the indigent client without a fee. Rule 1.8(h)(1), while forbidding agreements prospectively limiting liability to a client, contains an exception if "the client fails to act in accordance with the lawyer's advice and the lawyer nevertheless continues to represent the client at the client's request." New Jersey Rule 1.8(k) and (*l*) provide as follows:

> (k) A lawyer employed by a public entity, either as a lawyer or in some other role, shall not undertake the representation of another client if the representation presents a substantial risk that the lawyer's responsibilities to the public entity would limit the lawyer's ability to provide independent advice or diligent and competent representation to either the public entity or the client.
>
> (*l*) A public entity cannot consent to a representation otherwise prohibited by this Rule.

New York: Rule 1.8(a) deletes the language "knowingly acquire an ownership, possessory, security or other pecuniary interest adverse to a client" and adds language from DR 5-104(A) of the old Model Code: "if they have differing interests therein and if the client expects the lawyer to exercise professional judgment therein for the protection of the client. . . . " Comments 3A and 4A-4F, which have no Model Rule equivalents, describe in detail the problem of business transactions with clients, including (in Comments 4D-4F) issues related to a lawyer's receipt of a client's securities. New York omits Comment 5.

Rule 1.8(d) draws, in part, on DR 5-104(B) of the old Model Code, and Comment 9 provides more guidance than the equivalent Model Rule provisions concerning a lawyer's acquisition of media or literary rights that relate to a client matter.

Finally, Rule 1.8(j) and (k) as well as Comments 17, 17A, 17B, and 18-20, all address sexual relationships with clients and provide significantly more guidance in this regard than the equivalent Model Rule provision. Comment 17B concludes that "[a] law firm's failure to educate lawyers about the restrictions on sexual relations—or a firm's failure to enforce those restrictions against lawyers who violate them—may constitute a violation of Rule 5.1, which obligates a law firm to make reasonable efforts to ensure that all lawyers in the firm conform to these Rules."

North Dakota: Rule 1.8(g), regarding aggregate settlements, applies "other than in class actions." North Dakota adds Rule 1.8(k), which restricts the practice of law by a part-time prosecutor or judge in certain circumstances.

Ohio: Rule 1.8(c) forbids a lawyer to solicit "any substantial gift from a client" and forbids a lawyer to "prepare on behalf of a client an instrument giving the lawyer, the lawyer's partner, associate, paralegal, law clerk or other employee of the lawyer's firm, a lawyer acting 'of counsel' in the lawyer's firm, or a person related to the lawyer any gift unless the lawyer or other recipient of the gift is related to the client." "Gift" is defined to include "a testamentary gift." Ohio Rule 1.8(f)(4) provides a detailed "statement of insured client's rights" that a lawyer "selected and paid by an insurer to represent an insured" must give to the client.

An Ohio statute (R.C. §1349.55) regulates companies that make cash advances to plaintiffs in pending civil cases in exchange for the right to receive part of the proceeds of any settlement, award, or judgment. Paragraph (C) of the statute provides that if a plaintiff gets into a dispute concerning the contract for the cash advance, "the responsibilities of the attorney representing the consumer [the plaintiff] in the civil action or claim shall be no greater than the attorney's responsibilities under the Ohio Rules of Professional Conduct."

Oregon: Rule 1.8(b) permits a lawyer to use confidential information to a client's disadvantage only if the client's consent is "confirmed in writing" (except as otherwise permitted or required by the Rules). Rule 1.8(e) permits a lawyer to advance litigation expenses only if "the client remains ultimately liable for such expenses to the extent of the client's ability to pay." Finally, Oregon's rule governing sexual relations with clients contains a detailed description of "sexual relations," providing that it includes "sexual intercourse or any touching of the sexual or other intimate parts of a person or causing such person to touch the sexual or other intimate parts of the lawyer for the purpose of arousing or gratifying the sexual desire of either party."

Pennsylvania: Rule 1.8(g) does not require that client consent be "confirmed in writing."

Texas: Rule 1.08(c) provides that prior to the conclusion of "all aspects of the matter giving rise to the lawyer's employment," a lawyer shall not make or negotiate an agreement "with a client, prospective client, or former client" giving the lawyer literary or media rights to a portrayal or account based in substantial part on information relating to the representation. Rule 1.08(d) provides as follows:

> (d) A lawyer shall not provide financial assistance to a client in connection with pending or contemplated litigation or administrative proceedings, except that:
>
> (1) a lawyer may advance or guarantee court costs, expenses of litigation or administrative proceedings, and reasonably necessary medical and living expenses, the repayment of which may be contingent on the outcome of the matter; and
>
> (2) a lawyer representing an indigent client may pay court costs and expenses of litigation on behalf of the client.

Virginia: Rule 1.8(b) forbids the use of information "for the advantage of the lawyer or of a third person or to the disadvantage of the client." Rule 1.8(e)(1) requires a client ultimately to be liable for court costs and expenses. Rule 1.8(h) contains an exception where the lawyer is "an employee" of the client "as long as the client is independently represented in making the agreement" prospectively limiting the lawyer's liability for malpractice.

Washington: Rule 1.8(e) permits a lawyer to (1) advance or guarantee the expenses of litigation "provided the client remains ultimately liable for such expenses; and (2) in matters maintained as class actions only, repayment of expenses of litigation may be contingent on the outcome of the matter." Washington deletes ABA Model Rule 1.8(e)(2) (permitting lawyers to pay litigation costs for indigent clients).

Wisconsin: Rule 1.8(c) creates an exception to testamentary gifts where:

> (1) the client is related to the donee, (2) the donee is a natural object of the bounty of the client, (3) there is no reasonable ground to anticipate a contest, or a claim of undue influence or for the public to lose confidence in the integrity of the bar, and (4) the amount of the gift or bequest is reasonable and natural under the circumstances.

Related Materials

ABA Formal Ethics Opinions: See ABA Formal Ethics Ops. 90-358 (1990), 92-364 (1992), 96-401 (1996), 00-416 (2000), 00-418 (2000), 01-421 (2001), 02-425 (2002), 02-426 (2002), 02-427 (2002), 02-428 (2002), 03-430 (2003), 04-432 (2004), 04-433 (2004), 05-435 (2005), 06-438 (2006), 08-448 (2008), and 08-450 (2008).

ABA Model Court Rule on Insurance Disclosure: The ABA has extensively explored problems relating to legal malpractice insurance and has developed a Model Court Rule on Insurance Disclosure. After considering public comments on several drafts (which are discussed in our 2007 edition at pp. 139-141), the ABA House of Delegates considered a final proposal at the ABA's August 2004 Annual Meeting. Both the ABA Tort Trial and Insurance Practice Section (TIPS) and the ABA Standing Committee on Professional Liability opposed the proposal on its merits and sought to postpone the vote until a later meeting. In the end, however, after the proposed rule was slightly amended, the House of Delegates approved the proposal by the slender vote of 213-203. As approved, the rule provides as follows:

ABA Model Court Rule on Insurance Disclosure

> A. Each lawyer admitted to the active practice of law shall certify to the [highest court of the jurisdiction] on or before [December 31 of each year]: 1) whether the lawyer is engaged in the private practice of law; 2) if engaged in the private practice of law, whether the lawyer is currently covered by professional liability insurance; 3) whether the lawyer intends to maintain insurance during the period of time the lawyer is engaged in the private practice of law; and 4) whether the lawyer is exempt from the provisions of this Rule because the lawyer is engaged in the practice of law as a full-time government lawyer or is counsel employed by an organizational client and does not represent clients outside that capacity. Each lawyer admitted to the active practice of law in this jurisdiction who reports being covered by professional liability insurance shall notify [the highest court in the jurisdiction] in writing within 30 days if the insurance policy providing coverage lapses, is no longer in effect or terminates for any reason.
>
> B. The foregoing shall be certified by each lawyer admitted to the active practice of law in this jurisdiction in such form as may be prescribed by the [highest court of the jurisdiction]. The information submitted pursuant to this Rule will be made available to the public by such means as may be designated by the [highest court of the jurisdiction].
>
> C. Any lawyer admitted to the active practice of law who fails to comply with this Rule in a timely fashion, as defined by the [highest court in the jurisdiction], may be suspended from the practice of law until such time as the lawyer complies. Supplying false information in response to this Rule shall subject the lawyer to appropriate disciplinary action.

The brackets throughout the rule indicate that each jurisdiction should adopt or modify the bracketed language to suit its own circumstances. The Report submitted in support of the ABA Model Court Rule on Insurance Disclosure is available online at *http://www.americanbar.org/content/dam/aba/migrated/cpr/clientpro/malprac_disc_report.authcheckdam.pdf.* For information on state malpractice insurance disclosure rules, see the entry below entitled "Malpractice Insurance Disclosure Requirements."

ABA Resolution on Fee Payment for Corporate Employees: In 2006, the ABA House of Delegates approved a resolution co-sponsored by the New York State Bar Association and the ABA Task Force on the Attorney-Client Privilege opposing various government "policies, practices and procedures that have the effect of eroding the constitutional and other legal rights of current or former employees, officers, directors, or agents." The ABA especially criticized the government's consideration of "whether an organization provided counsel to an employee or agreed to pay an employee's legal fees and expenses" in evaluating corporate cooperation with its investigations. For more information, see *http://apps.americanbar.org/buslaw/attorney-client/materials/hod/emprights_recommendation_adopted.pdf.*

ABA Tort Trial and Insurance Practice Section Guidelines: In 1991, the ABA's Section of Tort Trial and Insurance Practice (then called the Tort and Insurance Practice Section, or TIPS) approved Guidelines for the Selection and Performance of Retained Counsel. The following provisions relate to Rule 1.8(f):

c. Relationships Involving Three Parties—Attorney, Insured, and Insurer—Must Be Balanced with Legal and Contractual Obligations

> . . . When counsel is retained by an insurer to represent an insured, counsel's duty is owed to both clients to the extent that the interests of each party are aligned. When the interests of the insurer and the insured conflict, counsel's primary duty is to the insured.
>
> When counsel is retained by an insurer to represent an insured and a conflict exists between insured and insurer, counsel for the insured may not provide counsel to the insurer. All potential conflicts between insurer and insured must be identified and disclosed in detail to the insured by the insurer.
>
> If the insurer agrees to retain counsel to defend an insured (a) under a reservation of rights to deny coverage or (b) while contending that some of the allegations asserted against the insured are not covered by the insurance policy, counsel's primary duty is to the insured. In such a case, counsel should defend the action so as to avoid prejudice to, or impairment of, the rights of the insured.
>
> Where there are matters within the policy coverage and matters potentially outside the policy coverage, the insurer should advise the insured of the excess exposure and inform the insured of the right to retain personal counsel.

Litigation Finance Companies: Because Rule 1.8(e) generally prohibits lawyers from providing financial assistance to clients in connection with contemplated or pending litigation, nonlawyer companies have sprung up that give cash advances to plaintiffs in civil litigation in exchange for a share of the proceeds of any settlement or judgment. Litigation finance companies usually charge a plaintiff a high rate of interest (typically from 3 to 6 percent per month, but sometimes higher). However, such a cash advance is not usually considered a "loan" for purposes of usury laws because the advance is "nonrecourse," meaning that if the plaintiff loses the case, then the plaintiff does not have to repay the advance (*i.e.,* the litigation finance company has no recourse to the plaintiff's personal assets). Because some litigation finance companies have allegedly engaged in abusive practices, a number of court decisions, ethics opinions, and actions by state attorneys general have sought to regulate or reform the litigation finance industry. In addition, in 2009 an Ohio statute (R.C. §1349.55) imposed strict requirements on litigation finance companies. For a critique of the litigation finance industry, see Daniel Brook, Litigation by Loan Shark (Legal Affairs, Sept.-Oct. 2004). For an industry view, see the website of the American Litigation Finance Association (ALFA) at *www.americanlegalfin.com.*

Malpractice Insurance and Uninsured Lawyers: Although Model Rule 1.8(h) generally prohibits lawyers from prospectively limiting their liability to clients for legal malpractice, clients who successfully sue their lawyers for malpractice are not assured of any recovery. Only one jurisdiction (Oregon) requires its lawyers to maintain legal malpractice insurance, and a surprising number of lawyers in other states do not carry malpractice insurance. In Massachusetts, for example, a survey published in 1997 revealed that about 25 percent of the lawyers who responded said they did not carry professional liability insurance. The lawyers most likely to be insured were partners in private law firms (97.4 percent) and their associates (94.7 percent). Solo practitioners fell in the middle (75 percent). The lawyers least likely to be insured were lawyers employed by corporations (28.6 percent) and public service lawyers (17.4 percent). A 2002 survey by the Illinois Attorney Registration and Disciplinary Commission revealed that only 60 percent of the Illinois solo practitioners who responded had professional liability insurance, but 96 percent of lawyers in firms of two to ten lawyers were covered, and over 99 percent of lawyers in firms of 11 or more lawyers maintained professional liability insurance. For a detailed treatment of legal malpractice insurance, see Ronald Mallen, Legal Malpractice: The Law Office Guide to Purchasing Legal Malpractice Insurance (West 2011 ed.).

Malpractice Insurance Disclosure Requirements: Many lawyers do not carry legal malpractice insurance. States have responded to the problem of uninsured lawyers in various ways. In Illinois, for example, Supreme Court Rule 756(e) requires all lawyers to disclose on the annual attorney registration form whether they carry malpractice insurance. New Hampshire Rule 1.19(a) requires a lawyer to inform a client, both at the outset of an engagement and during an engagement, if the lawyer does not maintain professional liability insurance of at least $100,000 per occurrence and $300,000 in the aggregate or if the insurance ceases to be in effect. In Massachusetts, to qualify for the State Bar's Lawyer Referral Service, a lawyer must carry a policy of at least $250,000 per occurrence and $500,000 in the aggregate. In 2004, the ABA adopted an ABA Model Court Rule on Insurance Disclosure, set out above in these Related Materials.

At our press deadline in September of 2011, 24 states require some form of malpractice insurance disclosure. Of these, 17 states require disclosure in connection with bar registration, while only 7 states require disclosure directly to clients. (New Mexico requires both.) However, Oregon is the only state that requires lawyers to carry malpractice insurance. At least 5 states (Maine, New York, South Carolina, Utah, and Vermont) are still considering some form of legal malpractice insurance disclosure rule. But 5 states (Arkansas, Connecticut, Florida, Kentucky, and Texas) have formally rejected a proposed mandatory insurance disclosure rule, and North Carolina withdrew its insurance disclosure rule in 2010. For a state-by-state chart showing rules and proposed rules governing malpractice insurance disclosure, see *http://www.americanbar.org/content/dam/aba/migrated/2011_build/professional_responsibility/malprac_disc_chart.authcheckdam.pdf.*

Restatement of the Law Governing Lawyers: See Restatement §§18, 36, 43, 54, 62, 126, 127, and 134 in our chapter on the Restatement later in this volume.

Rule 1.9 Duties to Former Clients

(a) A lawyer who has formerly represented a client in a matter shall not thereafter represent another person in the same or a substantially related matter in which that person's interests are materially adverse to the interests of the former client unless the former client gives informed consent, confirmed in writing.

covered by 1.7

(b) A lawyer shall not knowingly represent a person in the same or a substantially related matter in which a firm with which the lawyer formerly was associated had previously represented a client

(1) whose interests are materially adverse to that person; and

(2) about whom the lawyer had acquired information protected by Rules 1.6 and 1.9(c) that is material to the matter;

unless the former client gives informed consent, confirmed in writing.

(c) A lawyer who has formerly represented a client in a matter or whose present or former firm has formerly represented a client in a matter shall not thereafter:

(1) use information relating to the representation to the disadvantage of the former client except as these Rules would permit or require with respect to a client, or when the information has become generally known; or

(2) reveal information relating to the representation except as these Rules would permit or require with respect to a client.

COMMENT

[1] After termination of a client-lawyer relationship, a lawyer has certain continuing duties with respect to confidentiality and conflicts of interest and thus may not represent another client except in conformity with this Rule. Under this Rule, for example, a lawyer could not properly seek to rescind on behalf of a new client a contract drafted on behalf of the former client. So also a lawyer who has prosecuted an accused person could not properly represent the accused in a subsequent civil action against the government concerning the same transaction. Nor could a lawyer who has represented multiple clients in a matter represent one of the clients against the others in the same or a substantially related matter after a dispute arose among the clients in that matter, unless all affected clients give informed consent. See Comment [9]. Current and former government lawyers must comply with this Rule to the extent required by Rule 1.11.

[2] The scope of a "matter" for purposes of this Rule depends on the facts of a particular situation or transaction. The lawyer's involvement in a matter can also be a question of degree. When a lawyer has been directly involved in a specific transaction, subsequent representation of other clients with materially adverse interests in that transaction clearly is prohibited. On the other hand, a lawyer who recurrently handled a type of problem for a former client is not precluded from later representing another client in a factually distinct problem of that type even though the subsequent representation involves a position adverse to the prior client. Similar considerations can apply to the reassignment of military lawyers between defense and prosecution functions within the same military jurisdictions. The underlying question is whether the lawyer was so involved in the matter that the subsequent representation can be justly regarded as a changing of sides in the matter in question.

[3] Matters are "substantially related" for purposes of this Rule if they involve the same transaction or legal dispute or if there otherwise is a substantial risk that confidential factual information as would normally have been obtained in the prior representation would materially advance the client's position in the subsequent matter.

For example, a lawyer who has represented a businessperson and learned extensive private financial information about that person may not then represent that person's spouse in seeking a divorce. Similarly, a lawyer who has previously represented a client in securing environmental permits to build a shopping center would be precluded from representing neighbors seeking to oppose rezoning of the property on the basis of environmental considerations; however, the lawyer would not be precluded, on the grounds of substantial relationship, from defending a tenant of the completed shopping center in resisting eviction for nonpayment of rent. Information that has been disclosed to the public or to other parties adverse to the former client ordinarily will not be disqualifying. Information acquired in a prior representation may have been rendered obsolete by the passage of time, a circumstance that may be relevant in determining whether two representations are substantially related. In the case of an organizational client, general knowledge of the client's policies and practices ordinarily will not preclude a subsequent representation; on the other hand, knowledge of specific facts gained in a prior representation that are relevant to the matter in question ordinarily will preclude such a representation. A former client is not required to reveal the confidential information learned by the lawyer in order to establish a substantial risk that the lawyer has confidential information to use in the subsequent matter. A conclusion about the possession of such information may be based on the nature of the services the lawyer provided the former client and information that would in ordinary practice be learned by a lawyer providing such services.

Lawyers Moving Between Firms

[4] When lawyers have been associated within a firm but then end their association, the question of whether a lawyer should undertake representation is more complicated. There are several competing considerations. First, the client previously represented by the former firm must be reasonably assured that the principle of loyalty to the client is not compromised. Second, the rule should not be so broadly cast as to preclude other persons from having reasonable choice of legal counsel. Third, the rule should not unreasonably hamper lawyers from forming new associations and taking on new clients after having left a previous association. In this connection, it should be recognized that today many lawyers practice in firms, that many lawyers to some degree limit their practice to one field or another, and that many move from one association to another several times in their careers. If the concept of imputation were applied with unqualified rigor, the result would be radical curtailment of the opportunity of lawyers to move from one practice setting to another and of the opportunity of clients to change counsel.

[5] Paragraph (b) operates to disqualify the lawyer only when the lawyer involved has actual knowledge of information protected by Rules 1.6 and 1.9(c). Thus, if a lawyer while with one firm acquired no knowledge or information relating to a particular client of the firm, and that lawyer later joined another firm, neither the lawyer individually nor the second firm is disqualified from representing another client in the same or a related matter even though the interests of the two clients conflict. See Rule 1.10(b) for the restrictions on a firm once a lawyer has terminated association with the firm.

[6] Application of paragraph (b) depends on a situation's particular facts, aided by inferences, deductions or working presumptions that reasonably may be

made about the way in which lawyers work together. A lawyer may have general access to files of all clients of a law firm and may regularly participate in discussions of their affairs; it should be inferred that such a lawyer in fact is privy to all information about all the firm's clients. In contrast, another lawyer may have access to the files of only a limited number of clients and participate in discussions of the affairs of no other clients; in the absence of information to the contrary, it should be inferred that such a lawyer in fact is privy to information about the clients actually served but not those of other clients. In such an inquiry, the burden of proof should rest upon the firm whose disqualification is sought.

[7] Independent of the question of disqualification of a firm, a lawyer changing professional association has a continuing duty to preserve confidentiality of information about a client formerly represented. See Rules 1.6 and 1.9(c).

[8] Paragraph (c) provides that information acquired by the lawyer in the course of representing a client may not subsequently be used or revealed by the lawyer to the disadvantage of the client. However, the fact that a lawyer has once served a client does not preclude the lawyer from using generally known information about that client when later representing another client.

[9] The provisions of this Rule are for the protection of former clients and can be waived if the client gives informed consent, which consent must be confirmed in writing under paragraphs (a) and (b). See Rule 1.0(e). With regard to the effectiveness of an advance waiver, see Comment [22] to Rule 1.7. With regard to disqualification of a firm with which a lawyer is or was formerly associated, see Rule 1.10.

Canon and Code Antecedents

ABA Canons of Professional Ethics: Canon 37 provided as follows:

37. Confidences of a Client

> It is the duty of a lawyer to preserve his client's confidences. This duty outlasts the lawyer's employment, and extends as well to his employees; and neither of them should accept employment which involves or may involve the disclosure or use of these confidences, either for the private advantage of the lawyer or his employees or to the disadvantage of the client, without his knowledge and consent, and even though there are other available sources of such information. A lawyer should not continue employment when he discovers that this obligation prevents the performance of his full duty to his former or to his new client.
>
> If a lawyer is accused by his client, he is not precluded from disclosing the truth in respect to the accusation. The announced intention of a client to commit a crime is not included within the confidences which he is bound to respect. He may properly make such disclosures as may be necessary to prevent the act or protect those against whom it is threatened.

ABA Model Code of Professional Responsibility: Compare DR 5-105(C) (reprinted later in this volume).

Cross-References in Other Rules

Rule 1.0, Comment 7: "A number of Rules require that a person's consent be confirmed in writing. See **Rules** 1.7(b) and **1.9(a)**."

Rule 1.6, Comment 1: See "**Rules** 1.8(b) and **1.9(c)(1)** for the lawyer's duties with respect to the use of such information to the disadvantage of clients and former clients."

Rule 1.6, Comment 18: "The duty of confidentiality continues after the client-lawyer relationship has terminated. See **Rule 1.9(c)(2)**. See **Rule 1.9(c)(1)** for the prohibition against using such information to the disadvantage of the former client."

Rule 1.7, Comment 1: "For former client conflicts of interest, see **Rule 1.9**."

Rule 1.7, Comment 4: "Where more than one client is involved, whether the lawyer may continue to represent any of the clients is determined both by the lawyer's ability to comply with duties owed to the former client and by the lawyer's ability to represent adequately the remaining client or clients, given the lawyer's duties to the former client. See **Rule 1.9**."

Rule 1.7, Comment 5: "The lawyer must continue to protect the confidences of the client from whose representation the lawyer has withdrawn. See **Rule 1.9(c)**."

Rule 1.7, Comment 9: "In addition to conflicts with other current clients, a lawyer's duties of loyalty and independence may be materially limited by responsibilities to former clients under **Rule 1.9**. . . ."

Rule 1.7, Comment 33: "Subject to the above limitations, each client in the common representation has the right to loyal and diligent representation and the protection of **Rule 1.9** concerning the obligations to a former client."

Rule 1.8, Comment 5: It is prohibited to partake in the "disadvantageous use of client information unless the client gives informed consent, except as permitted or required by these Rules. See **Rules** 1.2(d), 1.6, **1.9(c)**, 3.3, 4.1(b), 8.1 and 8.3."

Rule 1.10(a): "While lawyers are associated in a firm, none of them shall knowingly represent a client when any one of them practicing alone would be prohibited from doing so by **Rules** 1.7 or **1.9**, unless the prohibition is based on a personal interest of the prohibited lawyer and does not present a significant risk of materially limiting the representation of the client by the remaining lawyers in the firm."

Rule 1.10(b)(2) restricts representation when "any lawyer remaining in the firm has information protected by **Rules** 1.6 and **1.9(c)** that is material to the matter."

Rule 1.10, Comment 2: "When a lawyer moves from one firm to another, the situation is governed by **Rules 1.9(b)** and 1.10(b)."

Rule 1.10, Comment 5: When a lawyer who represents or formerly represented a client leaves a firm, the firm may not represent a person with interests adverse to that client where the matter is the same or substantially related and "any other lawyer currently in the firm has material information protected by **Rules** 1.6 and **1.9(c)**."

Rule 1.11(a): "Except as law may otherwise expressly permit, a lawyer who has formerly served as a public officer or employee of the government is subject to **Rule 1.9(c)**. . . ."

Rule 1.11(d): "Except as law may otherwise expressly permit, a lawyer currently serving as a public officer or employee is subject to **Rules** 1.7 and **1.9**."

Rule 1.17, Comment 11: A lawyer selling a law practice has an "obligation to protect information relating to the representation (see **Rules** 1.6 and **1.9**)."

Rule 1.18(b): "Even when no client-lawyer relationship ensues, a lawyer who has had discussions with a prospective client shall not use or reveal information learned in the consultation, except as **Rule 1.9** would permit with respect to information of a former client."

Rule 1.18, Comment 3: When a prospective client reveals information, "Paragraph (b) prohibits the lawyer from using or revealing that information, except as permitted by **Rule 1.9**, even if the client or lawyer decides not to proceed with the representation."

Rule 3.7(b): "A lawyer may act as advocate in a trial in which another lawyer in the lawyer's firm is likely to be called as a witness unless precluded from doing so by Rule 1.7 or **Rule 1.9**."

Rule 3.7, Comment 4: "It is relevant that one or both parties could reasonably foresee that the lawyer would probably be a witness. The conflict of interest principles stated in **Rules** 1.7, **1.9** and 1.10 have no application to this aspect of the problem."

Rule 3.7, Comment 6: "In determining if it is permissible to act as advocate in a trial in which the lawyer will be a necessary witness, the lawyer must also consider that the dual role may give rise to a conflict of interest that will require compliance with **Rules** 1.7 or **1.9**. . . . [A] lawyer who might be permitted to simultaneously serve as an advocate and a witness by paragraph (a)(3) might be precluded from doing so by **Rule 1.9**."

Rule 3.7, Comment 7: "If, however, the testifying lawyer would also be disqualified by Rule 1.7 or **Rule 1.9** from representing the client in the matter, other lawyers in the firm will be precluded from representing the client by Rule 1.10 unless the client gives informed consent under the conditions stated in Rule 1.7."

Rule 5.7, Comment 10: "When a lawyer is obliged to accord the recipients of such services the protections of those Rules that apply to the client-lawyer relationship, the lawyer must take special care to heed the proscriptions of the Rules addressing conflict of interest (**Rules 1.7 through 1.11**, especially Rules 1.7 and 1.8(a), (b) and (f)). . . . "

Rule 6.5(a): "A lawyer who, under the auspices of a program sponsored by a nonprofit organization or court, provides short-term limited legal services to a client without expectation by either the lawyer or the client that the lawyer will provide continuing representation in the matter is subject to **Rules** 1.7 and **1.9(a)** only if the lawyer knows that the representation of the client involves a conflict of interest; and is subject to Rule 1.10 only if the lawyer knows that another lawyer associated with the lawyer in a law firm is disqualified by **Rule** 1.7 or **1.9(a)** with respect to the matter."

Rule 6.5, Comment 1: "Legal services organizations, courts and various nonprofit organizations have established programs through which lawyers provide short-term limited legal services. . . . Such programs are normally operated under circumstances in which it is not feasible for a lawyer to systematically screen for conflicts of interest as is generally required before undertaking a representation. See, e.g., **Rules** 1.7, 1.9 and 1.10."

Rule 6.5, Comment 2: Regarding "a lawyer who provides short-term limited legal services pursuant to this Rule . . . [e]xcept as provided in this Rule, the Rules of Professional Conduct, including **Rules** 1.6 and **1.9(c)**, are applicable to the limited representation."

Rule 6.5, Comment 3: "[P]aragraph (a) requires compliance with **Rules** 1.7 or **1.9(a)** only if the lawyer knows that the representation presents a conflict of interest for the lawyer, and with Rule 1.10 only if the lawyer knows that another lawyer in the lawyer's firm is disqualified by **Rules** 1.7 or **1.9(a)** in the matter."

Rule 6.5, Comment 4: "Paragraph (a)(2) requires the participating lawyer to comply with Rule 1.10 when the lawyer knows that the lawyer's firm is disqualified by **Rules** 1.7 or **1.9(a)**."

Rule 6.5, Comment 5: "If, after commencing a short-term limited representation in accordance with this Rule, a lawyer undertakes to represent the client in the matter on an ongoing basis, **Rules** 1.7, **1.9(a)** and 1.10 become applicable."

Legislative History of Model Rule 1.9

1980 Discussion Draft: Rule 1.9(c) (then Rule 1.10(a)(2)) provided that a lawyer who has represented a client in a matter shall not thereafter "make use of information acquired in service to the client in a manner disadvantageous to the client . . . unless the information has become generally known or *accessible.*"

1981 Draft was substantially the same as adopted.

1982 Draft was adopted.

1983 Rule: From its original adoption in 1983 until its first amendment in 1989, Rule 1.9 provided as follows:

> A lawyer who has formerly represented a client in a matter shall not thereafter:
> (a) represent another person in the same or a substantially related matter in which that person's interests are materially adverse to the interests of the former client unless the former client consents after consultation; or
> (b) [Same as 2002 version of Rule 1.9(c)(2).]

1989 Amendments: In 1989, the ABA House of Delegates moved former Rule 1.10(b) to Rule 1.9(b), amended Rule 1.9(b) and redesignated it as Rule 1.9(c), amended the balance of Rule 1.9 in minor ways, and changed the Comments to Rules 1.9 and 1.10 to match the amendments. The most significant amendments were to add the phrase "or whose present or former firm has formerly represented a client in a matter" to the introductory language in Rule 1.9(c), which restricts a lawyer's use of confidential client information, and to add a new Rule 1.9(c)(2) providing that a lawyer shall not "reveal information relating to the representation except as these Rules would permit or require with respect to a client." The Committee Report to the House of Delegates explained the amendments to Rule 1.9(c) as follows:*

> The addition of explanatory language to . . . paragraph (c), is intended to eliminate another oversight in the drafting of Rule 1.9. The added language makes clear that a lawyer's duty of confidentiality with respect to former clients applies to clients who were personally represented by the lawyer and to clients who, although not personally represented by the lawyer, were represented by the lawyer's firm. In addition, a prohibition on the "revelation" of confidential information is added to Rule 1.9. As originally drafted, Rule 1.9 prohibited only the "use" of such information to the disadvantage of the former client. . . . The Comments to Rules 1.9 and 1.10 are amended in conformity with the amendments to the black letter Rules.

* Committee Reports do not represent official policy of the ABA. They are for information only, and the opinions are those of the authors of the report.

2002 Amendments: In 2002, the ABA House of Delegates adopted without change the ABA Ethics 2000 Commission proposal to amend Rule 1.9 and its Comment. The amendments added the requirement that the consent be "confirmed in writing" in Rules 1.9(a) and (b). In addition, Comments 1, 6, and 9 were significantly revised; Comment 3 was added; and former Comments 4, 5, 7, and 10 were deleted.

Selected State Variations

California: Rule 3-310(E) forbids representation adverse to a client or former client if a lawyer "by reason of the representation of the client or former client . . . has obtained confidential information material to the employment."

District of Columbia: Rule 1.9 contains only the language of ABA Model Rule 1.9(a), but does not require that consent be in writing or confirmed in writing. D.C.'s version of Rule 1.9(b), which appears in Rule 1.10(b), is substantially similar to 1.9(b) but provides an exception when "the lawyer participated in a previous representation or acquired information under the circumstances covered by Rule 1.6(h) or Rule 1.18."

Illinois deletes the requirement that a client's consent to a conflict of interest be confirmed in writing.

Massachusetts: Rule 1.9(c), which draws on DR 4-101(B)(3) of the ABA Model Code of Professional Responsibility, adds that a lawyer may not use confidential information "to the lawyer's advantage, or to the advantage of a third person" unless permitted or required by other rules, without the client's consent.

Nebraska adds Rules 1.9(d)-(f) to govern conflicts arising from the past work of law clerks, paralegals, secretaries, messengers, and any other "support person." Notably, Rule 1.9(d) parallels ABA Model Rule 1.9(b), but Nebraska Rule 1.9(e) does not impute support person conflicts to other lawyers at the firm if the former client consents or the conflicted support person is screened to protect the former client's confidential information.

New York: Rule 1.9 is substantially similar to the Model Rule, except that New York uses the term "confidential" information in Rule 1.9(c) instead of the phrase "information related to the representation." New York moves Comments 4-6 to the Comments following Rule 1.10.

Pennsylvania: Rule 1.9 tracks ABA Model Rule 1.9, except Pennsylvania Rule 1.9(a) and Rule 1.9(b)(2) do not require that client consent be "confirmed in writing."

Texas: Rule 1.09(a) provides that without prior consent, a lawyer who "personally" has formerly represented a client in a matter shall not thereafter represent another person in a matter adverse to the former client:

> (1) in which such other person questions the validity of the lawyer's services or work product for the former client;
>
> (2) if the representation in reasonable probability will involve a violation of Rule 1.05 [the Texas confidentiality rule]; or
>
> (3) if it is the same or a substantially related matter.

Virginia: Rule 1.9(b) requires the consent of both the present and former client.

Related Materials

ABA Formal Ethics Opinions: See ABA Formal Ethics Ops. 84-351 (1984), 88-356 (1988), 94-381 (1994), 95-395 (1995), 96-400 (1996), 96-403 (1996), 97-407 (1997), 97-409 (1997), 99-415 (1999), 00-417 (2000), 05-436 (2005), and 08-453 (2008).

ABA Standards for Imposing Lawyer Sanctions: See Standard 4.3 in the Related Materials following Model Rule 1.7.

Restatement of the Law Governing Lawyers: See Restatement §§33(2)(a), 77, and 132 in our chapter on the Restatement later in this volume.

Sixth Amendment: The Sixth Amendment to the United States Constitution, which guarantees effective assistance of counsel, imposes certain obligations on courts regarding conflicts of interest, but those obligations are less stringent for successive conflicts than for concurrent conflicts. In *Holloway v. Arkansas,* 435 U.S. 475 (1978), which involved a concurrent conflict, the Court held that the Sixth Amendment requires automatic reversal when a trial court fails to conduct an inquiry either after a timely conflict objection, or after the court knows or reasonably should know that a particular conflict exists. In *Cuyler v. Sullivan,* 446 U.S. 335 (1980), also a concurrent conflict case, the Court ruled that this "automatic reversal" rule did not apply when the trial court is not informed or is not on notice of a conflict. If a conflict is later alleged, the Sixth Amendment requires a defendant to establish that "an actual conflict of interest adversely affected his lawyer's performance."

Mickens v. Taylor, 535 U.S. 162 (2002), involved a successive conflict. A murder defendant was represented by a lawyer who, until a week before his appointment as defendant's counsel, had been representing the victim of the defendant's alleged homicide on an unrelated criminal matter. The same judge who dismissed the criminal charges against the now-deceased murder victim appointed the victim's lawyer to represent the alleged murderer a week later. The Court held that these facts did not require "automatic reversal" as in *Holloway.* "Since this was not a case in which (as in *Holloway*) counsel protested his inability simultaneously to represent multiple defendants . . . it was at least necessary, to void the conviction, for petitioner to establish that the conflict of interest adversely affected his counsel's performance." The Court left open the possibility that a defendant who alleged only a successive conflict might not even enjoy *Cuyler v. Sullivan*'s test for establishing ineffectiveness, but might instead be required to satisfy the stricter Sixth Amendment effectiveness test set out in *Strickland v. Washington,* 466 U.S. 668 (1984).

Rule 1.10 Imputation of Conflicts of Interest: General Rule

(a) While lawyers are associated in a firm, none of them shall knowingly represent a client when any one of them practicing alone would be prohibited from doing so by Rules 1.7 or 1.9, unless

(1) the prohibition is based upon a personal interest of the disqualified lawyer and does not present a significant risk of materially limiting the representation of the client by the remaining lawyers in the firm; or

(2) the prohibition is based upon Rule 1.9(a) or (b), and arises out of the disqualified lawyer's association with a prior firm, and

(i) the disqualified lawyer is timely screened from any participation in the matter and is apportioned no part of the fee therefrom;

(ii) written notice is promptly given to any affected former client to enable the former client to ascertain compliance with the provisions of this Rule, which shall include a description of the screening procedures employed; a statement of the firm's and of the screened lawyer's compliance with these Rules; a statement that review may be available before a tribunal; and an agreement by the firm to respond promptly to any written inquiries or objections by the former client about the screening procedures; and

(iii) certifications of compliance with these Rules and with the screening procedures are provided to the former client by the screened lawyer and by a partner of the firm, at reasonable intervals upon the former client's written request and upon termination of the screening procedures.

(b) When a lawyer has terminated an association with a firm, the firm is not prohibited from thereafter representing a person with interests materially adverse to those of a client represented by the formerly associated lawyer and not currently represented by the firm, unless

(1) the matter is the same or substantially related to that in which the formerly associated lawyer represented the client; and

(2) any lawyer remaining in the firm has information protected by Rules 1.6 and 1.9(c) that is material to the matter.

(c) A disqualification prescribed by this rule may be waived by the affected client under the conditions stated in Rule 1.7.

(d) The disqualification of lawyers associated in a firm with former or current government lawyers is governed by Rule 1.11.

3.6, 3.7(b), 3.7 cf 7

COMMENT

Definition of "Firm"

[1] For purposes of the Rules of Professional Conduct, the term "firm" denotes lawyers in a law partnership, professional corporation, sole proprietorship or other association authorized to practice law; or lawyers employed in a legal services organization or the legal department of a corporation or other organization. See Rule 1.0(c). Whether two or more lawyers constitute a firm within this definition can depend on the specific facts. See Rule 1.0, Comments [2]-[4].

Principles of Imputed Disqualification

[2] The rule of imputed disqualification stated in paragraph (a) gives effect to the principle of loyalty to the client as it applies to lawyers who practice in a law firm. Such situations can be considered from the premise that a firm of lawyers is essentially one lawyer for purposes of the rules governing loyalty to the client, or from the premise that each lawyer is vicariously bound by the obligation of loyalty owed by each lawyer with whom the lawyer is associated. Paragraph (a)(1) operates only among the

lawyers currently associated in a firm. When a lawyer moves from one firm to another, the situation is governed by Rules 1.9(b) and 1.10(a)(2) and (b).

[3] The rule in paragraph (a) does not prohibit representation where neither questions of client loyalty nor protection of confidential information are presented. Where one lawyer in a firm could not effectively represent a given client because of strong political beliefs, for example, but that lawyer will do no work on the case and the personal beliefs of the lawyer will not materially limit the representation by others in the firm, the firm should not be disqualified. On the other hand, if an opposing party in a case were owned by a lawyer in the law firm, and others in the firm would be materially limited in pursuing the matter because of loyalty to that lawyer, the personal disqualification of the lawyer would be imputed to all others in the firm.

[4] The rule in paragraph (a) also does not prohibit representation by others in the law firm where the person prohibited from involvement in a matter is a nonlawyer, such as a paralegal or legal secretary. Nor does paragraph (a) prohibit representation if the lawyer is prohibited from acting because of events before the person became a lawyer, for example, work that the person did while a law student. Such persons, however, ordinarily must be screened from any personal participation in the matter to avoid communication to others in the firm of confidential information that both the nonlawyers and the firm have a legal duty to protect. See Rules 1.0(k) and 5.3.

[5] Rule 1.10(b) operates to permit a law firm, under certain circumstances, to represent a person with interests directly adverse to those of a client represented by a lawyer who formerly was associated with the firm. The Rule applies regardless of when the formerly associated lawyer represented the client. However, the law firm may not represent a person with interests adverse to those of a present client of the firm, which would violate Rule 1.7. Moreover, the firm may not represent the person where the matter is the same or substantially related to that in which the formerly associated lawyer represented the client and any other lawyer currently in the firm has material information protected by Rules 1.6 and 1.9(c).

[6] Rule 1.10(c) removes imputation with the informed consent of the affected client or former client under the conditions stated in Rule 1.7. The conditions stated in Rule 1.7 require the lawyer to determine that the representation is not prohibited by Rule 1.7(b) and that each affected client or former client has given informed consent to the representation, confirmed in writing. In some cases, the risk may be so severe that the conflict may not be cured by client consent. For a discussion of the effectiveness of client waivers of conflicts that might arise in the future, see Rule 1.7, Comment [22]. For a definition of informed consent, see Rule 1.0(e).

[7] Rule 1.10(a)(2) similarly removes the imputation otherwise required by Rule 1.10(a), but unlike section (c), it does so without requiring that there be informed consent by the former client. Instead, it requires that the procedures laid out in sections (a)(2)(i)-(iii) be followed. A description of effective screening mechanisms appears in Rule 1.0(k). Lawyers should be aware, however, that, even where screening mechanisms have been adopted, tribunals may consider additional factors in ruling upon motions to disqualify a lawyer from pending litigation.

[8] Paragraph (a)(2)(i) does not prohibit the screened lawyer from receiving a salary or partnership share established by prior independent agreement, but that lawyer may not receive compensation directly related to the matter in which the lawyer is disqualified.

[9] The notice required by paragraph (a)(2)(ii) generally should include a description of the screened lawyer's prior representation and be given as soon as

practicable after the need for screening becomes apparent. It also should include a statement by the screened lawyer and the firm that the client's material confidential information has not been disclosed or used in violation of the Rules. The notice is intended to enable the former client to evaluate and comment upon the effectiveness of the screening procedures.

[10] The certifications required by paragraph (a)(2)(iii) give the former client assurance that the client's material confidential information has not been disclosed or used inappropriately, either prior to timely implementation of a screen or thereafter. If compliance cannot be certified, the certificate must describe the failure to comply.

[11] Where a lawyer has joined a private firm after having represented the government, imputation is governed by Rule 1.11(b) and (c), not this Rule. Under Rule 1.11(d), where a lawyer represents the government after having served clients in private practice, nongovernmental employment or in another government agency, former-client conflicts are not imputed to government lawyers associated with the individually disqualified lawyer.

[12] Where a lawyer is prohibited from engaging in certain transactions under Rule 1.8, paragraph (k) of that Rule, and not this Rule, determines whether that prohibition also applies to other lawyers associated in a firm with the personally prohibited lawyer.

Canon and Code Antecedents

ABA Canons of Professional Ethics: No comparable Canon.

ABA Model Code of Professional Responsibility: Compare DR 5-105(D) (reprinted later in this volume).

Cross-References in Other Rules

Rule 1.0, Comment 8: "This definition applies to situations where screening of a personally disqualified lawyer is permitted to remove imputation of a conflict of interest under **Rules 1.10**, 1.11, 1.12 or 1.18."

Rule 1.7, Comment 10: "See Rule 1.8 for specific Rules pertaining to a number of personal interest conflicts, including business transactions with clients. See also **Rule 1.10** (personal interest conflicts under Rule 1.7 ordinarily are not imputed to other lawyers in a law firm)."

Rule 1.7, Comment 11: "The disqualification arising from a close family relationship is personal and ordinarily is not imputed to members of firms with whom the lawyers are associated. See **Rule 1.10**."

Rule 1.9, Comment 5: "See **Rule 1.10(b)** for the restrictions on a firm once a lawyer has terminated association with the firm."

Rule 1.9, Comment 9: "With regard to disqualification of a firm with which a lawyer is or was formerly associated, see **Rule 1.10**."

Rule 1.11, Comment 2: "**Rule 1.10** is not applicable to the conflicts of interest addressed by this Rule."

Rule 1.11, Comment 3: "As with paragraphs (a)(1) and (d)(1), **Rule 1.10** is not applicable to the conflicts of interest addressed by these paragraphs."

Rule 1.18, Comment 7: "Under paragraph (c), the prohibition in this Rule is imputed to other lawyers as provided in **Rule 1.10**. . . ."

Rule 3.7, Comment 4: "It is relevant that one or both parties could reasonably foresee that the lawyer would probably be a witness. The conflict of interest principles stated in **Rules** 1.7, 1.9 and **1.10** have no application to this aspect of the problem."

Rule 3.7, Comment 7: "If, however, the testifying lawyer would also be disqualified by Rule 1.7 or Rule 1.9 from representing the client in the matter, other lawyers in the firm will be precluded from representing the client by **Rule 1.10** unless the client gives informed consent under the conditions stated in Rule 1.7."

Rule 5.7, Comment 10: "When a lawyer is obliged to accord the recipients of such services the protections of those Rules that apply to the client-lawyer relationship, the lawyer must take special care to heed the proscriptions of the Rules addressing conflict of interest (**Rules 1.7 through 1.11**, especially Rules 1.7 and 1.8(a), (b) and (f)). . . ."

Rule 6.5(a): "A lawyer who, under the auspices of a program sponsored by a non-profit organization or court, provides short-term limited legal services to a client without expectation by either the lawyer or the client that the lawyer will provide continuing representation in the matter is subject to Rules 1.7 and 1.9(a) only if the lawyer knows that the representation of the client involves a conflict of interest; and is subject to **Rule 1.10** only if the lawyer knows that another lawyer associated with the lawyer in a law firm is disqualified by Rule 1.7 or 1.9(a) with respect to the matter."

Rule 6.5(b): "Except as provided in paragraph (a)(2), **Rule 1.10** is inapplicable to a representation governed by this Rule."

Rule 6.5, Comment 1: "Legal services organizations, courts and various non-profit organizations have established programs through which lawyers provide short-term limited legal services. . . . Such programs are normally operated under circumstances in which it is not feasible for a lawyer to systematically screen for conflicts of interest as is generally required before undertaking a representation. See, e.g., **Rules** 1.7, 1.9 and **1.10.**"

Rule 6.5, Comment 3: "[P]aragraph (a) requires compliance with Rules 1.7 or 1.9(a) only if the lawyer knows that the representation presents a conflict of interest for the lawyer . . . and with **Rule 1.10** only if the lawyer knows that another lawyer in the lawyer's firm is disqualified by Rules 1.7 or 1.9(a) in the matter."

Rule 6.5, Comment 4: "[P]aragraph (b) provides that **Rule 1.10** is inapplicable to a representation governed by this Rule except as provided by paragraph (a)(2). Paragraph (a)(2) requires the participating lawyer to comply with Rule 1.10 when the lawyer knows that the lawyer's firm is disqualified by Rules 1.7 or 1.9(a)."

Rule 6.5, Comment 5: "If, after commencing a short-term limited representation in accordance with this Rule, a lawyer undertakes to represent the client in the matter on an ongoing basis, **Rules** 1.7, 1.9(a) and **1.10** become applicable."

Legislative History of Model Rule 1.10

1980 Discussion Draft had no comparable provision on imputed disqualification.

1981 Draft:

> (b) When lawyers terminate an association in a firm, none of them, nor any other lawyer with whom any of them subsequently become associated, shall undertake

or continue representation that involves a material risk of revealing information relating to representation of a client in violation of Rule 1.6, or of making use of information to the disadvantage of a former client in violation of Rule 1.9.

1982 Draft:

(b) When lawyers terminate an association in a firm, none of them, nor any other lawyer with whom any of them subsequently becomes associated, shall knowingly represent a client when doing so involves a material risk of violating Rule 1.6 or Rule 1.9.

1983 Rule: From its original adoption in 1983 until its amendment in 1989, Rule 1.10 provided as follows:

(a) While lawyers are associated in a firm, none of them shall knowingly represent a client when any one of them practicing alone would be prohibited from doing so by Rules 1.7, 1.8(c), 1.9 or 2.2.

(b) When a lawyer becomes associated with a firm, the firm may not knowingly represent a person in the same or a substantially related matter in which that lawyer, or a firm with which the lawyer was associated, had previously represented a client whose interests are materially adverse to that person and about whom the lawyer had acquired information protected by Rules 1.6 and 1.9(b) that is material to the matter.

(c) [Same as 2002 version of Rule 1.10(b) except that the 1983 version did not include the phrase "and not currently represented by the firm" at the end of the introductory clause.]

(d) [Same as 2002 version of Rule 1.10(c).]

1989 Amendments: At its 1989 Mid-Year Meeting, the House of Delegates amended Rule 1.10 by moving former Rule 1.10(b) to its current position as Rule 1.9(b), by moving the corresponding Comment paragraphs to Rule 1.9's Comment, by redesignating former Rule 1.10(c) as Rule 1.10(b), by adding the phrase "and not currently represented by the firm" at the end of the introductory phrase in new Rule 1.10(b), and by redesignating former Rule 1.10(d) as Rule 1.10(c). An excerpt from the Committee Report explaining the changes is reprinted in the Legislative History following Rule 1.9. The Committee's explanation regarding the amendment to former Rule 1.10(c) states:

Paragraph (c) (now paragraph (b)) of Rule 1.10 was never intended to permit the representation of a client whose interests are directly adverse to the interests of a present client of a firm. Such representation would violate Rule 1.7. In order to make it clear that when a lawyer leaves a law firm, this paragraph does not override the proscription in Rule 1.7, the limiting words "and not currently represented by the firm" are proposed to be added to Rule 1.10(b).

2002 Amendments: In 2001, the ABA House of Delegates adopted the ABA Ethics 2000 Commission proposal to amend Rules 1.10(a) and (d) without change, but rejected the Ethics 2000 Commission proposal to amend Rule 1.10(c). (The Ethics 2000 Commission did not propose any changes to Rule 1.10(b).) As amended, Rule 1.10 adds the language following "unless" in paragraph (a) (regarding conflicts based on a lawyer's personal interests) and adds paragraph (d) (regarding current or former government lawyers). In the Comment, new paragraphs 3, 4, 6, portions of 7, and 8 were added.

The rejected proposals would have permitted a law firm to use timely "screens" and related measures to overcome a former client's objections to an adverse representation. The rejected provisions of Rule 1.10(c) provided as follows:

(c) When a lawyer becomes associated with a firm, no lawyer associated in the firm shall knowingly represent a person in a matter in which that lawyer is disqualified under Rule 1.9 unless:

(1) the personally disqualified lawyer is timely screened from any participation in the matter and is apportioned no part of the fee therefrom; and

(2) written notice is promptly given to any affected former client to enable it to ascertain compliance with the provisions of this Rule.

By rejecting the proposed text of Rule 1.10(c), the ABA also rejected three proposed Comments that would have explained the proposed language. The three rejected Comments provided as follows:

[6] Where the conditions of paragraph (c) are met, imputation is removed, and consent to the new representation is not required. Lawyers should be aware, however, that courts may impose more stringent obligations in ruling upon motions to disqualify a lawyer from pending litigation.

[7] Requirements for screening procedures are stated in Rule 1.0(k). Paragraph (c)(2) does not prohibit the screened lawyer from receiving a salary or partnership share established by prior independent agreement, but that lawyer may not receive compensation directly related to the matter in which the lawyer is disqualified.

[8] Notice, including a description of the screened lawyer's prior representation and of the screening procedures employed, generally should be given as soon as practicable after the need for screening becomes apparent.

The Reporter's Explanation Memo regarding the rejected screening language provided, in relevant part, as follows:

*Model Rule 1.10-Reporter's Explanation of Changes**

A number of jurisdictions now provide that former-client conflicts of lawyers who have moved laterally are not imputed to the new law firm if the personally disqualified lawyer has been timely screened from participation in the matter and the former client is notified of the screen. The Commission is recommending that current Rule 1.10 be amended to permit nonconsensual screening of lawyers who have joined a law firm.

The Commission is persuaded that nonconsensual screening in these cases adequately balances the interests of the former client in confidentiality of information, the interests of current clients in hiring the counsel of their choice (including a law firm that may have represented the client in similar matters for many years) and the interests of lawyers in mobility, particularly when they are moving involuntarily because their former law firms have downsized, dissolved or drifted into bankruptcy. There are presently seven jurisdictions that permit screening of laterals by Rule. The testimony the Commission has heard indicates that there have not been any significant numbers of complaints regarding lawyers' conduct under these Rules.

In addition, in 2002, the ABA House of Delegates adopted with little change the Ethics 2000 Commission proposals to add two new rules to the Model Rules (Rules 1.18 and 6.5) to govern imputed conflicts of interest regarding two special categories of clients—prospective clients who ultimately did not retain a lawyer, and clients consulting a lawyer who (under the auspices of a program sponsored by a nonprofit organization or court) is providing "short-term limited legal services

* Committee Reports, and the Reporter's Explanation of Changes contained therein, do not represent official policy of the ABA. They are for information only, and the opinions are those of the authors of the report.

to a client without expectation by either the lawyer or the client that the lawyer will provide continuing representation in the matter." For more information about these rules, see the Legislative History following Rules 1.18 and 6.5 below.

2008 Proposed Amendment: At its August 2008 Annual Meeting, the ABA House of Delegates had been scheduled to debate a proposal by the ABA Standing Committee on Ethics and Professional Responsibility that would have permitted screening of laterally hired attorneys under certain circumstances. That proposal would have amended Rule 1.10(e) as follows:

> (e) notwithstanding paragraph (a), and in the absence of a waiver under paragraph (c), when a lawyer becomes associated with a firm, no lawyer associated in the firm shall knowingly represent a person in a matter in which that lawyer is disqualified under Rule 1.9 unless:
>
> (1) the personally disqualified lawyer is timely screened from any participation in the matter and is apportioned no part of the fee therefrom; and
>
> (2) written notice is promptly given to any affected former client to enable it to ascertain compliance with the provisions of this Rule.

The proposal also would have amended the Comment to Rule 1.10 as follows:

> [9] When the conditions of paragraph (e) are met, no imputation of a lawyer's disqualification occurs, and consent to the new representation is therefore not required. Lawyers should be aware, however, that courts may impose more stringent obligations in ruling upon motions to disqualify a lawyer from pending litigation.
>
> [10] Requirements for screening procedures are stated in Rule 1.0(k). Paragraph (e)(1) does not prohibit the screened lawyer from receiving a salary or partnership share established by prior independent agreement, but that lawyer may not receive compensation directly related to the matter in which the lawyer is disqualified.
>
> [11] Notice, including a description of the screened lawyer's prior representation and of the screening procedures employed, generally should be given as soon as practicable after the need for screening becomes apparent.

Before the House of Delegates voted on the Standing Committee's proposal, an opponent of screening moved to postpone "indefinitely" any further consideration of the topic. Reflecting how closely divided the profession is on this issue, the motion carried by a single vote, 192-191. (For a more detailed discussion of that debate, including the text of several amendments to the proposal that had been offered on the House floor, see the 2008 Proposed Amendments in the 2009 edition of this book.)

2009 Amendments: Undaunted by the August 2008 setback, the ABA Standing Committee on Ethics and Professional Responsibility submitted a revised screening proposal at the February 2009 House of Delegates meeting. This time it passed by a vote of 226-191. The House of Delegates also approved four new paragraphs in the Comment to Rule 1.10 (numbered 7 through 10) and renumbered former Comments 7 and 8 as Comments 11 and 12 (leaving the text of those comments unchanged). For the Report and Recommendation submitted to the ABA House of Delegates in support of the amendments, see *http://www.americanbar.org/groups/professional_responsibility/publications/model_rules_of_ professional_conduct/background_resources.html.*

The ABA's Section of Litigation had submitted a competing proposal, which would have permitted screening only when the lateral attorney had no substantial involvement in the matter and had not acquired any material confidential information about it. For details about that proposal, which the House of Delegates rejected by a vote of 182-267, see *http://www.americanbar.org/content/dam/aba/migrated/leadership/2009/midyear/recommendations/110.authcheckdam.pdf.*

The screening provision as adopted in February 2009 did not explicitly limit screening to laterally hired attorneys. As a result, the new Rule 1.10 appeared to allow a firm to sue its own former client in a substantially related matter, without obtaining client consent, as long as the firm screened off the lawyers who worked on the former client's matter. This was not intended. At the August 2009 House of Delegates meeting, therefore, the ABA Standing Committee on Ethics and Professional Responsibility proposed a modest amendment to clarify that the screening provision should apply only to laterally hired attorneys. Specifically, the proposal sought to amend Rule 1.10(a)(2) by adding the phrase "arises out of the disqualified lawyer's association with a prior firm." It also sought to replace the word "prohibited" with the word "disqualified" in Rule 1.10(a)(1). Both changes were uncontroversial and were adopted as part of the meeting's consent calendar.

Selected State Variations

Editors' Note. As of September 2011, approximately two dozen states provide that a timely and effective screen around a laterally hired attorney will prevent the imputation of certain types of conflicts. Some of these provisions differ from the Model Rule, often by permitting screening to avoid imputed conflicts only in more narrowly defined circumstances than Model Rule 1.10 allows.

Arizona: Rule 1.10(d) permits screening of a personally disqualified lateral lawyer if the "matter does not involve a proceeding before a tribunal in which the personally disqualified lawyer had a substantial role," the lawyer gets no part of the fee, and "written notice is promptly given to any affected former client to enable it to ascertain compliance with the provisions of this Rule."

California has no provision comparable to ABA Model Rule 1.10.

District of Columbia adds Rule 1.10(a)(2), which notes that imputation does not apply "if the representation is permitted by Rules 1.11, 1.12, or 1.18." The D.C. rule also contains a Rule 1.10(e) that creates a partial exception to imputation when a lawyer assists "the Office of the Attorney General of the District of Columbia in providing legal services to that agency."

Illinois: The screening provision in Rule 1.10 is substantially similar to the Model Rule, except that Illinois has not adopted the additional requirements contained in Model Rule 1.10(a)(2)(ii) and (iii).

Maine: Rule 1.10(e) provides that "[i]f a lawyer or law student affiliated both with a law school legal clinic and with one or more lawyers outside the clinic is required to decline representation of any client solely by virtue of this Rule 1.10, this rule imposes no disqualification on any other lawyer or law student who would otherwise be disqualified solely by reason of an affiliation with that individual, provided that the originally disqualified individual is screened from all participation in the matter at and outside the clinic."

Massachusetts: Rule 1.10(d) provides for screening a "personally disqualified lawyer" if he or she "had neither substantial involvement nor substantial material information relating to the matter . . . and is apportioned no part of the fee therefrom." Rule

1.10(e) describes an appropriate screening process, including a requirement in Rule 1.10(e)(4) that the former client receives an affidavit of the personally disqualified lawyer and the firm describing the screening procedures and attesting that:

> (i) the personally disqualified lawyer will not participate in the matter and will not discuss the matter or the representation with any other lawyer or employee of his or her current firm; (ii) no material information was transmitted by the personally disqualified lawyer before implementation of the screening procedures and notice to the former client; and (iii) during the period of the lawyer's personal disqualification those lawyers or employees who do participate in the matter will be apprised that the personally disqualified lawyer is screened from participating in or discussing the matter. . . .

In any matter not before a tribunal, "the firm, the personally disqualified lawyer, or the former client may seek judicial review in a court of general jurisdiction of the screening procedures used, or may seek court supervision to ensure that implementation of the screening procedures has occurred and that effective actual compliance has been achieved."

Michigan: The screening provision in Rule 1.10(b) is substantially similar to the Model Rule, except that Michigan has fewer disclosure requirements than Model Rule 1.10(a)(2)(ii) and omits all of the requirements contained in Model Rule 1.10(a)(2)(iii).

Minnesota includes the following screening provision in its version of Rule 1.10. It is based largely on §124 of the Restatement of the Law Governing Lawyers:

> (b) When a lawyer becomes associated with a firm, and the lawyer is prohibited from representing a client pursuant to Rule 1.9(b), other lawyers in the firm may represent that client if there is no reasonably apparent risk that confidential information of the previously represented client will be used with material adverse effect on that client because:
>
> (1) any confidential information communicated to the lawyer is unlikely to be significant in the subsequent matter;
>
> (2) the lawyer is subject to screening measures adequate to prevent disclosure of the confidential information and to prevent involvement by that lawyer in the representation; and
>
> (3) timely and adequate notice of the screening has been provided to all affected clients.

Nebraska adds Rules 1.9(d)-(f) to govern conflicts arising from the past work of law clerks, paralegals, secretaries, messengers, and any other "support person," but Rule 1.9(e) does not impute support person conflicts to other lawyers at the firm if the former client consents or if the conflicted support person is screened to protect the former client's confidential information.

New Jersey adds Rule 1.10(c), which permits screening of a conflicted lawyer who becomes associated with a firm unless that lawyer had "primary responsibility" for the matter. Rule 1.10(f) provides as follows:

> Any law firm that enters a screening arrangement, as provided by this Rule, shall establish appropriate written procedures to insure that: (1) all attorneys and other personnel in the law firm screen the personally disqualified attorney from any participation in the matter, (2) the screened attorney acknowledges the obligation to remain screened and takes action to insure the same, and (3) the screened attorney is apportioned no part of the fee therefrom.

Pursuant to Rule 1.7, public entities may not waive conflicts or agree to screening. And New Jersey Rule 1.9(c) reinforces Rule 1.10(c) by providing that "neither consent shall be sought from the client nor screening pursuant to RPC 1.10 permitted in any matter in which the attorney had sole or primary responsibility for the matter in the previous firm."

New York: Rule 1.10(c), which is simply the logical extension of Rule 1.9(b), specifies that a newly hired attorney does not create an imputed conflict of interest as long as that attorney had not acquired "any information protected by Rule 1.6 or Rule 1.9(c) that is material to the current matter." In effect, then, the New York rules do not permit non-consensual screening of lateral lawyers from private practice (*i.e.*, screening to avoid imputation without need for consent from the lateral lawyer's former client). The former New York Code did not do so either, but the New York Court of Appeals, in *Kassis v. TIAA,* 717 N.E.2d 674 (N.Y. 1999), ruled that screening would be allowed if the lateral lawyer's information with regard to the matter is "unlikely to be significant or material." It remains to be seen whether the new rules were intended to "overrule" *Kassis* and whether, if they were, they can.

New York adds Rule 1.10(e)-(g), which contains detailed recordkeeping requirements for new engagements. These additional requirements are described in more depth in Comments 9 and 9A-9G.

Finally, New York adds Rule 1.10(h), which provides as follows: "A lawyer related to another lawyer as parent, child, sibling or spouse shall not represent in any matter a client whose interests differ from those of another party to the matter who the lawyer knows is represented by the other lawyer unless the client consents to the representation after full disclosure and the lawyer concludes that the lawyer can adequately represent the interests of the client."

North Carolina: The screening provision in Rule 1.10(c) is substantially similar to the Model Rule, except that North Carolina omits the requirements contained in Model Rule 1.10(a)(2)(iii) and has fewer disclosure requirements than Model Rule 1.10(a)(2)(ii).

Ohio: Rule 1.10 permits screening of a lateral lawyer, but only if the lawyer did not have a "substantial role" in the matter.

Oregon has a screening procedure in Rule 1.10(c) that requires lawyers to submit affidavits confirming compliance with the screen.

Pennsylvania: The screening provision in Rule 1.10(b) is substantially similar to the Model Rule, except that Pennsylvania omits the requirements contained in Model Rule 1.10(a)(2)(iii) and has fewer disclosure requirements than Model Rule 1.10(a)(2)(ii).

South Carolina: Rule 1.10 tracks ABA Model Rule 1.10 verbatim but adds the following limited screening provision in Rule 1.10(e):

> (e) A lawyer representing a client of a public defender office, legal services association, or similar program serving indigent clients shall not be disqualified under this Rule because of the program's representation of another client in the same or a substantially related matter if:
>
> (1) the lawyer is screened in a timely manner from access to confidential information relating to and from any participation in the representation of the other client; and
>
> (2) the lawyer retains authority over the objectives of the representation pursuant to Rule 5.4(c).

Texas: Rule 1.09 provides:

(a) Without prior consent, a lawyer who personally has formerly represented a client in a matter shall not thereafter represent another person in a matter adverse to the former client:

(1) in which such other person questions the validity of the lawyer's services or work product for the former client;

(2) if the representation in reasonable probability will involve a violation of Rule 1.05; or

(3) if it is the same or a substantially related matter.

(b) Except to the extent authorized by Rule 1.10 [concerning government lawyers], when lawyers are or have become members of or associated with a firm, none of them shall knowingly represent a client if any one of them practicing alone would be prohibited from doing so by paragraph (a).

(c) When the association of a lawyer with a firm has terminated, the lawyers who were then associated with that lawyer shall not knowingly represent a client if the lawyer whose association with that firm has terminated would be prohibited from doing so by paragraph (a)(1) or if the representation in reasonable probability will involve a violation of Rule 1.05.

Wisconsin: Rule 1.10(a)(2) permits law firms to avoid imputation of a lateral lawyer's Rule 1.9 conflict if "(i) the personally disqualified lawyer performed no more than minor and isolated services in the disqualifying representation and did so only at a firm with which the lawyer is no longer associated"; (ii) the personally disqualified lawyer is timely screened and is apportioned no part of the fee from the matter; and (iii) written notice is promptly given to any affected former client to enable the former client to ascertain compliance with this rule.

Related Materials

ABA Commission on Ethics 20/20: In 2009, the ABA created the Commission on Ethics 20/20, which is comprehensively reviewing the ABA Model Rules of Professional Conduct and other regulations of the American legal profession in the context of globalization and changes in technology. With respect to Rule 1.10, the Commission is particularly interested in differing approaches to conflicts of interest, because a representation may create a conflict requiring client consent in one jurisdiction (in the U.S. or overseas) but not in another jurisdiction, thus affecting imputation under Rule 1.10. The Commission has preliminarily discussed possible amendments to Rule 1.10 (as well as to Rule 8.5) to provide better guidance on choice of law problems in light of domestic and international differences in the rules governing conflicts (and other areas), but when we went to press in September of 2011, the Commission had not released any proposals to amend Rules 1.10 or 8.5. However, the Commission has proposed adding a new Comment to Rule 1.7 that would, according to the accompanying report, "provide more predictability to clients and their lawyers by permitting them to agree in advance to be bound by the conflict rules of a particular jurisdiction." (See our entry on "ABA Commission on Ethics 20/20" in the Related Materials after Rule 1.7 for the text of that proposed Comment.) For updates, see the Ethics 20/20 Commission's website at *http://www.americanbar.org/Ethics2020.*

ABA Formal Ethics Opinions: See ABA Formal Ethics Ops. 84-351 (1984), 88-356 (1988), 90-357 (1990), 92-367 (1992), 96-400 (1996), 97-406 (1997), 97-407 (1997), 97-409 (1997), 98-410 (1998), 99-415 (1999), and 03-430 nn.38 & 39 (2003).

Model Rules of Professional Conduct for Federal Lawyers: Rule 1.10(a) provides that "Government lawyers working in the same Federal Agency are not automatically disqualified from representing a client because any of them practicing alone would be prohibited from doing so by Rules 1.7, 1.8(c), 1.9 or 2.2." The Comment states:

> The circumstances of Government service may require representation of opposing sides by Government lawyers working in the same Federal Agency. Such representation is permissible so long as conflicts of interest are avoided and independent judgment, zealous representation, and protection of client confidences are not compromised. Thus, the principle of imputed disqualification is not automatically controlling for Government lawyers. The knowledge, action, and conflicts of interest of one Government lawyer are not to be imputed to another simply because they operate from the same office. . . .

Restatement of the Law Governing Lawyers: See Restatement §§15(2), 123, 124, and 132 in our chapter on the Restatement later in this volume.

Rule 1.11 Special Conflicts of Interest for Former and Current Government Officers and Employees

(a) Except as law may otherwise expressly permit, a lawyer who has formerly served as a public officer or employee of the government:

(1) is subject to Rule 1.9(c); and

(2) shall not otherwise represent a client in connection with a matter in which the lawyer participated personally and substantially as a public officer or employee, unless the appropriate government agency gives its informed consent, confirmed in writing, to the representation.

(b) When a lawyer is disqualified from representation under paragraph (a), no lawyer in a firm with which that lawyer is associated may knowingly undertake or continue representation in such a matter unless:

(1) the disqualified lawyer is timely screened from any participation in the matter and is apportioned no part of the fee therefrom; and

(2) written notice is promptly given to the appropriate government agency to enable it to ascertain compliance with the provisions of this rule.

(c) Except as law may otherwise expressly permit, a lawyer having information that the lawyer knows is confidential government information about a person acquired when the lawyer was a public officer or employee, may not represent a private client whose interests are adverse to that person in a matter in which the information could be used to the material disadvantage of that person. As used in this Rule, the term

"confidential government information" means information that has been obtained under governmental authority and which, at the time this Rule is applied, the government is prohibited by law from disclosing to the public or has a legal privilege not to disclose and which is not otherwise available to the public. A firm with which that lawyer is associated may undertake or continue representation in the matter only if the disqualified lawyer is timely screened from any participation in the matter and is apportioned no part of the fee therefrom.

(d) Except as law may otherwise expressly permit, a lawyer currently serving as a public officer or employee:

(1) is subject to Rules 1.7 and 1.9; and

(2) shall not:

(i) participate in a matter in which the lawyer participated personally and substantially while in private practice or nongovernmental employment, unless the appropriate government agency gives its informed consent, confirmed in writing; or

(ii) negotiate for private employment with any person who is involved as a party or as lawyer for a party in a matter in which the lawyer is participating personally and substantially, except that a lawyer serving as a law clerk to a judge, other adjudicative officer or arbitrator may negotiate for private employment as permitted by Rule 1.12(b) and subject to the conditions stated in Rule 1.12(b).

(e) As used in this Rule, the term "matter" includes:

(1) any judicial or other proceeding, application, request for a ruling or other determination, contract, claim, controversy, investigation, charge, accusation, arrest or other particular matter involving a specific party or parties, and

(2) any other matter covered by the conflict of interest rules of the appropriate government agency.

COMMENT

[1] A lawyer who has served or is currently serving as a public officer or employee is personally subject to the Rules of Professional Conduct, including the prohibition against concurrent conflicts of interest stated in Rule 1.7. In addition, such a lawyer may be subject to statutes and government regulations regarding conflict of interest. Such statutes and regulations may circumscribe the extent to which the government agency may give consent under this Rule. See Rule 1.0(e) for the definition of informed consent.

[2] Paragraphs (a)(1), (a)(2) and (d)(1) restate the obligations of an individual lawyer who has served or is currently serving as an officer or employee of the government toward a former government or private client. Rule 1.10 is not applicable to the conflicts of interest addressed by this Rule. Rather, paragraph (b) sets forth a special imputation rule for former government lawyers that provides for screening and notice. Because of the special problems raised by imputation within

a government agency, paragraph (d) does not impute the conflicts of a lawyer currently serving as an officer or employee of the government to other associated government officers or employees, although ordinarily it will be prudent to screen such lawyers.

[3] Paragraphs (a)(2) and (d)(2) apply regardless of whether a lawyer is adverse to a former client and are thus designed not only to protect the former client, but also to prevent a lawyer from exploiting public office for the advantage of another client. For example, a lawyer who has pursued a claim on behalf of the government may not pursue the same claim on behalf of a later private client after the lawyer has left government service, except when authorized to do so by the government agency under paragraph (a). Similarly, a lawyer who has pursued a claim on behalf of a private client may not pursue the claim on behalf of the government, except when authorized to do so by paragraph (d). As with paragraphs (a)(1) and (d)(1), Rule 1.10 is not applicable to the conflicts of interest addressed by these paragraphs.

[4] This Rule represents a balancing of interests. On the one hand, where the successive clients are a government agency and another client, public or private, the risk exists that power or discretion vested in that agency might be used for the special benefit of the other client. A lawyer should not be in a position where benefit to the other client might affect performance of the lawyer's professional functions on behalf of the government. Also, unfair advantage could accrue to the other client by reason of access to confidential government information about the client's adversary obtainable only through the lawyer's government service. On the other hand, the rules governing lawyers presently or formerly employed by a government agency should not be so restrictive as to inhibit transfer of employment to and from the government. The government has a legitimate need to attract qualified lawyers as well as to maintain high ethical standards. Thus a former government lawyer is disqualified only from particular matters in which the lawyer participated personally and substantially. The provisions for screening and waiver in paragraph (b) are necessary to prevent the disqualification rule from imposing too severe a deterrent against entering public service. The limitation of disqualification in paragraphs (a)(2) and (d)(2) to matters involving a specific party or parties, rather than extending disqualification to all substantive issues on which the lawyer worked, serves a similar function.

[5] When a lawyer has been employed by one government agency and then moves to a second government agency, it may be appropriate to treat that second agency as another client for purposes of this Rule, as when a lawyer is employed by a city and subsequently is employed by a federal agency. However, because the conflict of interest is governed by paragraph (d), the latter agency is not required to screen the lawyer as paragraph (b) requires a law firm to do. The question of whether two government agencies should be regarded as the same or different clients for conflict of interest purposes is beyond the scope of these Rules. See Rule 1.13 Comment [9].

[6] Paragraphs (b) and (c) contemplate a screening arrangement. See Rule 1.0(k) (requirements for screening procedures). These paragraphs do not prohibit a lawyer from receiving a salary or partnership share established by prior independent agreement, but that lawyer may not receive compensation directly relating the lawyer's compensation to the fee in the matter in which the lawyer is disqualified.

[7] Notice, including a description of the screened lawyer's prior representation and of the screening procedures employed, generally should be given as soon as practicable after the need for screening becomes apparent.

[8] Paragraph (c) operates only when the lawyer in question has knowledge of the information, which means actual knowledge; it does not operate with respect to information that merely could be imputed to the lawyer.

[9] Paragraphs (a) and (d) do not prohibit a lawyer from jointly representing a private party and a government agency when doing so is permitted by Rule 1.7 and is not otherwise prohibited by law.

[10] For purposes of paragraph (e) of this Rule, a "matter" may continue in another form. In determining whether two particular matters are the same, the lawyer should consider the extent to which the matters involve the same basic facts, the same or related parties, and the time elapsed.

Canon and Code Antecedents

ABA Canons of Professional Ethics: No comparable Canon.

ABA Model Code of Professional Responsibility: Compare DR 9-101(B) (reprinted later in this volume).

Cross-References in Other Rules

Rule 1.0, Comment 8: "Screened" applies to "situations where screening of a personally disqualified lawyer is permitted to remove imputation of a conflict of interest under **Rules 1.11**, 1.12 or 1.18."

Rule 1.9, Comment 1: "Current and former government lawyers must comply with this Rule to the extent required by **Rule 1.11**."

Rule 1.10(d): "The disqualification of lawyers associated in a firm with former or current government lawyers is governed by **Rule 1.11**."

Rule 1.10, Comment 7: "Where a lawyer has joined a private firm after having represented the government, imputation is governed by **Rule 1.11(b)** and **(c)**. . . .

Under **Rule 1.11(d)**, where a lawyer represents the government after having served clients in private practice, nongovernmental employment, or in another government agency, former-client conflicts are not imputed to government lawyers associated with the individually disqualified lawyer."

Rule 1.12, Comment 1: "This Rule generally parallels **Rule 1.11**. . . . Compare the Comment to **Rule 1.11**."

Rule 5.7, Comment 10: "When a lawyer is obliged to accord the recipients of such services the protections of those Rules that apply to the client-lawyer relationship, the lawyer must take special care to heed the proscriptions of the Rules addressing conflict of interest (**Rules** 1.7 through **1.11**, especially Rules 1.7 and 1.8(a), (b) and (f)). . . ."

Legislative History of Model Rule 1.11

1980 Discussion Draft:

> . . . (e) If a lawyer is required by this rule to decline representation on account of personal and substantial participation in a matter, except where the participation was as a judicial law clerk, no lawyer in a firm with the disqualified lawyer may accept such employment. . . .

1981 and ***1982 Drafts*** were substantially the same as adopted.

1983 Rule: From its original adoption in 1983 until its amendment in 2002, Rule 1.11 provided as follows:

Rule 1.11 Successive Government and Private Employment

(a) Except as law may otherwise expressly permit, a lawyer shall not represent a private client in connection with a matter in which the lawyer participated personally and substantially as a public officer or employee, unless the appropriate government agency consents after consultation. No lawyer in a firm with which that lawyer is associated may knowingly undertake or continue representation in such a matter unless:

(1) [Same as 2002 version of Rule 1.11 except that the word "timely" did not modify "screened."]

(2) [Same as 2002 version of Rule 1.11(b)(2).]

(b) [Same as 2002 version of Rule 1.11 except that the word "timely" did not modify "screened" in the last sentence, and the definition of the term "confidential government information" was then in a separate Rule 1.11(e).]

(c) Except as law may otherwise expressly permit, a lawyer serving as a public officer or employee shall not:

(1) participate in a matter in which the lawyer participated personally and substantially while in private practice or nongovernmental employment, unless under applicable law no one is, or by lawful delegation may be, authorized to act in the lawyer's stead in the matter; or

(2) [Same as Rule 1.11(d)(ii) in 2002 version.]

(d) [Same definition of "matter" as in 2002 version of Rule 1.11(e).]

(e) [Same definition of "confidential government information" as in 2002 version of Rule 1.11(c).]

2002 Amendments: In its May 2001 report to the ABA House of Delegates, the Ethics 2000 Commission proposed several changes to Rule 1.11, including a proposed new subparagraph (a)(1) to make clear that a lawyer who has formerly served as a public officer or governmental employee "is subject to Rules 1.9(a) and (b), except that 'matter' is defined as in paragraph (e) of this Rule." Before the House of Delegates debated the proposal, however, the Commission revised its proposal by deleting the quoted paragraph.

In 2002, the House of Delegates adopted without change the revised ABA Ethics 2000 Commission proposal to amend Rule 1.11 and its Comment. As a result of the amendments to Rule 1.11, the successive conflicts of former government lawyers are determined solely by the terms of Rule 1.11. (In 1997, ABA Formal Ethics Op. 97-409 had reached the same conclusion.) Consequently, former government lawyers are exempt from the strictures of Rule 1.9(a) and (b), but are subject to the limitations in Rule 1.9(c) because that provision is incorporated by reference in Rule 1.11(a)(1).

Selected State Variations

Arizona, ***Connecticut***, and ***Florida*** omit the law clerk exception to ABA Model Rule 1.11(d)(2).

California has no provision comparable to ABA Model Rule 1.11.

Colorado: Rule 1.11(b)(2) requires the written notice to contain "a general description of the personally disqualified lawyer's prior participation in the matter and the screening procedures to be employed." Colorado also adds a subparagraph (b)(3) prohibiting other lawyers in the firm from undertaking or continuing representation unless the personally disqualified lawyer and the partners of the firm "reasonably believe that the steps taken to accomplish the screening of material information are likely to be effective in preventing material information from being disclosed to the firm and its client."

District of Columbia: Rule 1.11 tracks the basic provisions of ABA Model Rule 1.11, but D.C. requires a personally disqualified former government lawyer and another lawyer in the firm to file certain documents with the disqualified lawyer's former agency or department. As an alternative, the rule permits the former government lawyer to file those documents with bar counsel under seal if the firm's client requests it.

Georgia has adopted a Rule 9.5 that provides as follows:

> *Rule 9.5 Lawyer as a Public Official*
>
> (a) A lawyer who is a public official and represents the State, a municipal corporation in the State, the United States government, their agencies or officials, is bound by the provisions of these Rules.
>
> (b) No provision of these Rules shall be construed to prohibit such a lawyer from taking a legal position adverse to the State, a municipal corporation in the State, the United States government, their agencies or officials, when such action is authorized or required by the U.S. Constitution, the Georgia Constitution or statutes of the United States or Georgia.

Illinois: Rule 1.11(a) does not require consent to be confirmed in writing.

Iowa adds the following paragraph to Rule 1.11 relating to part-time prosecutors serving as criminal defense counsel:

> (f) Prosecutors for the state or county shall not engage in the defense of an accused in any criminal matter during the time they are engaged in such public responsibilities. However, this paragraph does not apply to a lawyer not regularly employed as a prosecutor for the state or county who serves as a special prosecutor for a specific criminal case, provided that the employment does not create a conflict of interest or the lawyer complies with the requirements of rule 32:1.7(b).

Massachusetts: The law clerk exception in Model Rule 1.11(d)(2)(ii) is extended to law clerks working for mediators.

Missouri: Rule 1.11(e) provides as follows:

> (1) A lawyer who also holds public office, whether full or part-time, shall not engage in activities in which his or her personal or professional interests are or foreseeably could be in conflict with his or her official duties or responsibilities. . . .
>
> (2) No lawyer in a firm in which a lawyer holding a public office is associated may undertake or continue representation in a matter in which the lawyer who holds public office would be disqualified, unless the lawyer holding public office is screened in the manner set forth in Rule 4-1.11(a).

New Hampshire adds a detailed provision regarding the responsibilities of "lawyer-officials," who are defined as lawyers who are "actively engaged in the practice of law" and who are members of a "governmental body."

New Jersey: Rules 1.11(a), (b), and (d) deviate from the Model Rules as follows:

> (a) Except as law may otherwise expressly permit, and subject to RPC 1.9, a lawyer who formerly has served as a government lawyer or public officer or employee of the government shall not represent a private client in connection with a matter:

(1) in which the lawyer participated personally and substantially as a public officer or employee; or

(2) for which the lawyer had substantial responsibility as a public officer or employee; or

(3) when the interests of the private party are materially adverse to the appropriate government agency, provided, however, that the application of this provision shall be limited to a period of six months immediately following the termination of the attorney's service as a government lawyer or public officer.

(b) Except as law may otherwise expressly permit, a lawyer who formerly has served as a government lawyer or public officer or employee of the government:

(1) shall be subject to RPC 1.9(c)(2) in respect of information relating to a private party or information that the lawyer knows is confidential government information about a person acquired by the lawyer while serving as a government lawyer or public officer or employee of the government, and

(2) shall not represent a private person whose interests are adverse to that private party in a matter in which the information could be used to the material disadvantage of that party. . . .

(d) Except as law may otherwise expressly permit, a lawyer serving as a government lawyer or public officer or employee of the government:

(1) shall be subject to RPC 1.9(c)(2) in respect of information relating to a private party acquired by the lawyer while in private practice or nongovernmental employment.

(2) shall not participate in a matter (i) in which the lawyer participated personally and substantially while in private practice or nongovernmental employment, or (ii) for which the lawyer had substantial responsibility while in private practice or nongovernmental employment, or (iii) with respect to which the interests of the appropriate government agency are materially adverse to the interests of a private party represented by the lawyer while in private practice or nongovernmental employment, unless under applicable law no one is, or by lawful delegation may be, authorized to act in the lawyer's stead in the matter or unless the private party gives its informed consent, confirmed in writing, and

(3) shall not negotiate for private employment with any person who is involved as a party or as attorney for a party in a matter in which the lawyer is participating personally and substantially or for which the lawyer has substantial responsibility, except that a lawyer serving as a law clerk shall be subject to RPC 1.12(c). . . .

New York: Rule 1.11(b) amplifies the procedures necessary to avoid the imputation of a conflict, including that a law firm must "notify, as appropriate, lawyers and nonlawyer personnel within the firm that the personally disqualified lawyer is prohibited from participating in the representation of the current client," and that "there are no other circumstances in the particular representation that create an appearance of impropriety." Several new comments offer further guidance regarding these procedures. Rule 1.11(e) specifies that the term "matter" does "not include or apply to agency rulemaking functions." Rule 1.11(f) is a nearly verbatim adoption of DR 8-101 of the old Model Code.

Oregon expands the "law clerk" exception to include a lawyer who is a "staff lawyer to or otherwise assisting in the official duties of" a judge, other adjudicative officer or arbitrator. Oregon Rule 1.11(d) adds language drawn partly from DR 8-101 of the ABA Model Code of Professional Responsibility providing that, except as law otherwise expressly permits, a lawyer shall not:

(i) use the lawyer's public position to obtain, or attempt to obtain, special advantage in legislative matters for the lawyer or for a client.

(ii) use the lawyer's public position to influence, or attempt to influence, a tribunal to act in favor of the lawyer or of a client.

(iii) accept anything of value from any person when the lawyer knows or it is obvious that the offer is for the purpose of influencing the lawyer's action as a public official.

(iv) either while in office or after leaving office use information the lawyer knows is confidential government information obtained while a public official to represent a private client.

Oregon also deletes ABA Model Rule 1.11(e) and adds these paragraphs to Rule 1.11:

(e) Notwithstanding any Rule of Professional Conduct, and consistent with the "debate" clause, Article IV, section 9, of the Oregon Constitution, or the "speech or debate" clause, Article I, section 6, of the United States Constitution, a lawyer-legislator shall not be subject to discipline for words uttered in debate in either house of the Oregon Legislative Assembly or for any speech or debate in either house of the United States Congress.

(f) A member of a lawyer-legislator's firm shall not be subject to discipline for representing a client in any claim against the State of Oregon provided:

(1) the lawyer-legislator is screened from participation or representation in the matter in accordance with the procedure set forth in Rule 1.10(c) (the required affidavits shall be served on the Attorney General); and

(2) the lawyer-legislator shall not directly or indirectly receive a fee for such representation.

Pennsylvania: Rule 1.11(a)(2) does not require that client consent be "confirmed in writing."

Texas: Rule 1.10(f) specifically excludes "regulation-making" and "rule-making" from the definition of "matter."

Virginia: Rule 1.11 is similar to the original 1983 version of ABA Model Rule 1.11, though Rule 1.11(b) requires consent from the private client in addition to consent from the appropriate government agency. Rule 1.11(e) adds that, when a lawyer who is serving as a public officer or employee is disqualified, the disqualification "does not disqualify other lawyers in the disqualified lawyer's agency." Rule 1.11(a) draws on the following language from DR 8-101 of the ABA Model Code of Professional Responsibility:

(a) A lawyer who holds public office shall not:

(1) use the public position to obtain, or attempt to obtain, a special advantage in legislative matters for the lawyer or for a client under circumstances where the lawyer knows or it is obvious that such action is not in the public interest;

(2) use the public position to influence, or attempt to influence, a tribunal to act in favor of the lawyer or of a client; or

(3) accept anything of value from any person when the lawyer knows or it is obvious that the offer is for the purpose of influencing the lawyer's action as a public official.

Related Materials

ABA Formal Ethics Opinions: See ABA Formal Ethics Ops. 97-409 (1997) and 99-415 n.8 (1999).

"Confidential Government Information": Model Rule 1.11(c) defines "confidential government information" to include information the government is "*prohibited* *by law* from disclosing to the public" or "has a *legal privilege* not to disclose," and (if the information satisfies one of those two criteria) is "not otherwise *available to the public*" (emphasis added).

As to disclosures "prohibited by law," prohibitions on public disclosure are contained in various federal statutes, including, for example, the Privacy Act of 1974, 5 U.S.C. §552a, and the Trade Secrets Act, 18 U.S.C. §1905.

As to "legal privilege not to disclose," the government has successfully claimed various privileges under Federal Rule of Evidence 501, including the executive privilege, the deliberative privilege, the national security privilege, and the attorney-client privilege.

As to whether information is "available to the public," the Freedom of Information Act (FOIA), 5 U.S.C. §552, makes a broad range of government information available to the public on demand but exempts specified categories of information from disclosure.

IRS Regulations: In the regulations governing practice before the Internal Revenue Service, 31 C.F.R. §10.25, entitled "Practice by Former Government Employees, Their Partners and Their Associates," sets forth elaborate restrictions on the practice of law by former government attorneys and their law firms.

Restatement of the Law Governing Lawyers: See Restatement §§74, 97, 124, and 133 in our chapter on the Restatement later in this volume.

Revolving Door Provisions: Rule 1.11(e)(2) refers to "the conflict of interest rules of the appropriate government agency." All former lawyers for the federal government are covered by the "revolving door" provision in 18 U.S.C. §207, which prohibits former government lawyers from opposing the government, either directly or in matters in which the government has "a direct and substantial interest," for two years after leaving government, if the lawyer was involved in the matter while in federal government service. For regulations generally implementing 18 U.S.C. §207, see 73 Fed. Reg. 36168 (June 25, 2008). In addition, several agencies of the federal government have their own "revolving door" provisions. *See, e.g.*, 45 C.F.R. Part 680 (National Science Foundation) and 22 C.F.R. Part 18 (Foreign Service). Many states have enacted parallel provisions.

Rule 1.12 Former Judge, Arbitrator, Mediator or Other Third-Party Neutral

2.4 & 3

2.4 **(a) Except as stated in paragraph (d), a lawyer shall not represent anyone in connection with a matter in which the lawyer participated personally and substantially as a judge or other adjudicative officer or law clerk to such a person or as an arbitrator, mediator or other third-party neutral, unless all parties to the proceeding give informed consent, confirmed in writing.**

(b) A lawyer shall not negotiate for employment with any person who is involved as a party or as lawyer for a party in a matter in which the lawyer is participating personally and substantially as a judge or other adjudicative officer or as an arbitrator, mediator or other third-party neutral. A lawyer serving as a law clerk to a judge or other adjudicative officer may negotiate for employment with a party or lawyer involved in a matter in which the clerk is participating personally and substantially, but only after the lawyer has notified the judge or other adjudicative officer.

(c) If a lawyer is disqualified by paragraph (a), no lawyer in a firm with which that lawyer is associated may knowingly undertake or continue representation in the matter unless:

(1) the disqualified lawyer is timely screened from any participation in the matter and is apportioned no part of the fee therefrom; and

(2) written notice is promptly given to the parties and any appropriate tribunal to enable them to ascertain compliance with the provisions of this rule.

(d) An arbitrator selected as a partisan of a party in a multimember arbitration panel is not prohibited from subsequently representing that party.

COMMENT

[1] This Rule generally parallels Rule 1.11. The term "personally and substantially" signifies that a judge who was a member of a multimember court, and thereafter left judicial office to practice law, is not prohibited from representing a client in a matter pending in the court, but in which the former judge did not participate. So also the fact that a former judge exercised administrative responsibility in a court does not prevent the former judge from acting as a lawyer in a matter where the judge had previously exercised remote or incidental administrative responsibility that did not affect the merits. Compare the Comment to Rule 1.11. The term "adjudicative officer" includes such officials as judges pro tempore, referees, special masters, hearing officers and other parajudicial officers, and also lawyers who serve as part-time judges. Compliance Canons A(2), B(2) and C of the Model Code of Judicial Conduct provide that a part-time judge, judge pro tempore or retired judge recalled to active service, may not "act as a lawyer in any proceeding in which he served as a judge or in any other proceeding related thereto." Although phrased differently from this Rule, those Rules correspond in meaning.

[2] Like former judges, lawyers who have served as arbitrators, mediators or other third-party neutrals may be asked to represent a client in a matter in which the lawyer participated personally and substantially. This Rule forbids such representation unless all of the parties to the proceedings give their informed consent, confirmed in writing. See Rule 1.0(e) and (b). Other law or codes of ethics governing third-party neutrals may impose more stringent standards of personal or imputed disqualification. See Rule 2.4.

[3] Although lawyers who serve as third-party neutrals do not have information concerning the parties that is protected under Rule 1.6, they typically owe the parties an obligation of confidentiality under law or codes of ethics governing third-party neutrals. Thus, paragraph (c) provides that conflicts of the personally disqualified lawyer will be imputed to other lawyers in a law firm unless the conditions of this paragraph are met.

[4] Requirements for screening procedures are stated in Rule 1.0(k). Paragraph (c)(1) does not prohibit the screened lawyer from receiving a salary or partnership share established by prior independent agreement, but that lawyer may not receive compensation directly related to the matter in which the lawyer is disqualified.

[5] Notice, including a description of the screened lawyer's prior representation and of the screening procedures employed, generally should be given as soon as practicable after the need for screening becomes apparent. 1.0(k)

Canon and Code Antecedents

ABA Canons of Professional Ethics: Canon 36 provided as follows:

36. Retirement from Judicial Position or Public Employment

A lawyer should not accept employment as an advocate in any matter upon the merits of which he has previously acted in a judicial capacity.

A lawyer, having once held public office or having been in the public employ, should not after his retirement accept employment in connection with any matter which he has investigated or passed upon while in such office or employ.

ABA Model Code of Professional Responsibility: Compare DR 5-105(C) and DR 9-101(A) (reprinted later in this volume).

Cross-References in Other Rules

Preamble, ¶3: "Some of these Rules apply directly to lawyers who are or have served as third-party neutrals. See, e.g., **Rules 1.12** and 2.4."

Rule 1.0, Comment 8: "Screened" "applies to situations where screening of a personally disqualified lawyer is permitted to remove imputation of a conflict of interest under **Rules** 1.11, **1.12** or 1.18."

Rule 1.11(d): "[A] lawyer serving as a law clerk to a judge, other adjudicative officer or arbitrator may negotiate for private employment as permitted by **Rule 1.12(b)** and subject to the conditions stated in **Rule 1.12(b)**."

Rule 2.4, Comment 4: "A lawyer who serves as a third-party neutral subsequently may be asked to serve as a lawyer representing a client in the same matter. The conflicts of interest that arise for both the individual lawyer and the lawyer's law firm are addressed in **Rule 1.12**."

Legislative History of Model Rule 1.12

1980 Discussion Draft (then Rules 1.11(d), 1.11(e), and 1.11(f)):

(d) A lawyer who has served as a judge in an adjudicatory proceeding shall not thereafter represent anyone in connection with the subject matter of the proceeding.

(e) If a lawyer is required by this rule to decline representation on account of personal and substantial participation in a matter, except where the participation was as a judicial law clerk, no lawyer in a firm with the disqualified lawyer may accept such employment.

(f) . . . The disqualification stated in paragraph (d) may be waived by the consent of all parties to the adjudication.

1981 and ***1982 Drafts:*** Substantially the same as adopted.

1983 Rule: From its original adoption in 1983 until its amendment in 2002, Rule 1.12 provided as follows:

Rule 1.12 Former Judge or Arbitrator

(a) Except as stated in paragraph (d), a lawyer shall not represent anyone in connection with a matter in which the lawyer participated personally and substantially as a judge or other adjudicative officer, arbitrator or law clerk to such a person, unless all parties to the proceeding consent after consultation.

(b) A lawyer shall not negotiate for employment with any person who is involved as a party or as attorney for a party in a matter in which the lawyer is participating personally and substantially as a judge or other adjudicative officer or arbitrator. A lawyer serving as a law clerk to a judge, other adjudicative officer or arbitrator may negotiate for employment with a party or lawyer involved in a matter in which the clerk is participating personally and substantially, but only after the lawyer has notified the judge, other adjudicative officer or arbitrator.

(c) [Same as 2002 version of Rule 1.12.]

(d) [Same as 2002 version of Rule 1.12.]

2002 Amendments: At its February 2002 Mid-Year Meeting, the ABA House of Delegates adopted with only minor changes the ABA Ethics 2000 Commission proposal to amend Rule 1.12 and its Comment. The amendments added Comments 2-5. The reference to "an arbitrator, mediator, or other third-party neutral" in Rule 1.12(a) and (b) is new, as is the requirement in Rule 1.12(a) that consent be informed and confirmed in writing.

Selected State Variations

California has no direct counterpart to Rule 1.12.

District of Columbia: Rule 1.12 does not include former judges.

Georgia: Rule 1.12(b) adds that a law clerk who accepts employment with a party or lawyer involved in a matter in which the clerk is participating personally and substantively "shall promptly provide written notice of acceptance of employment to all counsel of record in all such matters in which the prospective employee is involved."

Illinois: Rule 1.12(a) does not require consent to be confirmed in writing.

Massachusetts extends the law clerk exception in Rule 1.12(b) to law clerks working for mediators.

New York: Rule 1.12(a) is a nearly verbatim adoption of DR 9-101(A) of the old Model Code. Rule 1.12(d) describes in more detail the procedures necessary to avoid the imputation of a conflict, and several additional comments offer further guidance regarding these procedures.

Pennsylvania: Rule 1.12 tracks ABA Model Rule 1.12 except Pennsylvania Rule 1.12(a) does not require that client consent be "confirmed in writing."

Texas has no equivalent to Rule 1.12(d).

Related Materials

ABA Formal Ethics Opinions: No formal ethics opinions have construed Rule 1.12.

Code of Conduct for Law Clerks: In an article entitled *Some Ethical Considerations for Judicial Clerks,* 4 Geo. J. Legal Ethics 771, 786-790 (1991), Professor John Paul Jones of the University of Richmond School of Law proposes a Code of Conduct for Law Clerks. Proposed Canon 3(D) of this Code, which relates to Model Rule 1.12(b), provides:

> A law clerk should inform the appointing judge of any circumstance or activity of the law clerk that might serve as a basis for disqualification of the judge, *e.g.*, a prospective employment relation with a law firm, association of the law clerk's spouse with a law firm or litigant, etc.

Restatement of the Law Governing Lawyers: See Restatement §124 in our chapter on the Restatement later in this volume.

Rule 1.13 Organization as Client

(a) A lawyer employed or retained by an organization represents the organization acting through its duly authorized constituents.

(b) If a lawyer for an organization knows that an officer, employee or other person associated with the organization is engaged in action, intends to act or refuses to act in a matter related to the representation that is a violation of a legal obligation to the organization, or a violation of law that reasonably might be imputed to the organization, and that is likely to result in substantial injury to the organization, then the lawyer shall proceed as is reasonably necessary in the best interest of the organization. Unless the lawyer reasonably believes that it is not necessary in the best interest of the organization to do so, the lawyer shall refer the matter to higher authority in the organization, including, if warranted by the circumstances, to the highest authority that can act on behalf of the organization as determined by applicable law.

(c) Except as provided in Paragraph (d), if,

(1) despite the lawyer's efforts in accordance with paragraph (b), the highest authority that can act on behalf of the organization insists upon or fails to address in a timely and appropriate manner an action, or a refusal to act, that is clearly a violation of law, and

(2) the lawyer reasonably believes that the violation is reasonably certain to result in substantial injury to the organization, then the lawyer may reveal information relating to the representation whether or not Rule 1.6 permits such disclosure, but only if and to the extent the lawyer reasonably believes necessary to prevent substantial injury to the organization.

(d) Paragraph (c) shall not apply with respect to information relating to a lawyer's representation by an organization to investigate an alleged violation of law, or to defend the organization or an officer, employee or other constituent associated with the organization against a claim arising out of an alleged violation of law.

(e) A lawyer who reasonably believes that he or she has been discharged because of the lawyer's actions taken pursuant to Paragraphs (b) or (c), or who withdraws under circumstances that require or permit the lawyer to take action under either of those paragraphs, shall proceed as the lawyer reasonably believes necessary to assure that the organization's highest authority is informed of the lawyer's discharge or withdrawal.

(f) In dealing with an organization's directors, officers, employees, members, shareholders or other constituents, a lawyer shall explain the identity of the client when the lawyer knows or reasonably should know

that the organization's interests are adverse to those of the constituents with whom the lawyer is dealing.

(g) A lawyer representing an organization may also represent any of its directors, officers, employees, members, shareholders or other constituents, subject to the provisions of Rule 1.7. If the organization's consent to the dual representation is required by Rule 1.7, the consent shall be given by an appropriate official of the organization other than the individual who is to be represented, or by the shareholders.

1.7 cf 34 ; 35
§ 73 privilege
§ 73 - Privilege

COMMENT

The Entity as the Client

[1] An organizational client is a legal entity, but it cannot act except through its officers, directors, employees, shareholders and other constituents. Officers, directors, employees and shareholders are the constituents of the corporate organizational client. The duties defined in this Comment apply equally to unincorporated associations. "Other constituents" as used in this Comment means the positions equivalent to officers, directors, employees and shareholders held by persons acting for organizational clients that are not corporations.

[2] When one of the constituents of an organizational client communicates with the organization's lawyer in that person's organizational capacity, the communication is protected by Rule 1.6. Thus, by way of example, if an organizational client requests its lawyer to investigate allegations of wrongdoing, interviews made in the course of that investigation between the lawyer and the client's employees or other constituents are covered by Rule 1.6. This does not mean, however, that constituents of an organizational client are the clients of the lawyer. The lawyer may not disclose to such constituents information relating to the representation except for disclosures explicitly or impliedly authorized by the organizational client in order to carry out the representation or as otherwise permitted by Rule 1.6.

[3] When constituents of the organization make decisions for it, the decisions ordinarily must be accepted by the lawyer even if their utility or prudence is doubtful. Decisions concerning policy and operations, including ones entailing serious risk, are not as such in the lawyer's province. Paragraph (b) makes clear, however, that when the lawyer knows that the organization is likely to be substantially injured by action of an officer or other constituent that violates a legal obligation to the organization or is in violation of law that might be imputed to the organization, the lawyer must proceed as is reasonably necessary in the best interest of the organization. As defined in Rule 1.0(f), knowledge can be inferred from circumstances, and a lawyer cannot ignore the obvious.

[4] In determining how to proceed under Paragraph (b), the lawyer should give due consideration to the seriousness of the violation and its consequences, the responsibility in the organization and the apparent motivation of the person involved, the policies of the organization concerning such matters, and any other relevant considerations. Ordinarily, referral to a higher authority would be necessary.

In some circumstances, however, it may be appropriate for the lawyer to ask the constituent to reconsider the matter; for example, if the circumstances involve a constituent's innocent misunderstanding of law and subsequent acceptance of the lawyer's advice, the lawyer may reasonably conclude that the best interest of the organization does not require that the matter be referred to higher authority. If a constituent persists in conduct contrary to the lawyer's advice, it will be necessary for the lawyer to take steps to have the matter reviewed by a higher authority in the organization. If the matter is of sufficient seriousness and importance or urgency to the organization, referral to higher authority in the organization may be necessary even if the lawyer has not communicated with the constituent. Any measures taken should, to the extent practicable, minimize the risk of revealing information relating to the representation to persons outside the organization. Even in circumstances where a lawyer is not obligated by Rule 1.13 to proceed, a lawyer may bring to the attention of an organizational client, including its highest authority, matters that the lawyer reasonably believes to be of sufficient importance to warrant doing so in the best interest of the organization.

[5] Paragraph (b) also makes clear that when it is reasonably necessary to enable the organization to address the matter in a timely and appropriate manner, the lawyer must refer the matter to higher authority, including, if warranted by the circumstances, the highest authority that can act on behalf of the organization under applicable law. The organization's highest authority to whom a matter may be referred ordinarily will be the board of directors or similar governing body. However, applicable law may prescribe that under certain conditions the highest authority reposes elsewhere, for example, in the independent directors of a corporation.

Relation to Other Rules

[6] The authority and responsibility provided in this Rule are concurrent with the authority and responsibility provided in other Rules. In particular, this Rule does not limit or expand the lawyer's responsibility under Rule 1.8, 1.16, 3.3 or 4.1. Paragraph (c) of this Rule supplements Rule 1.6(b) by providing an additional basis upon which the lawyer may reveal information relating to the representation, but does not modify, restrict, or limit the provisions of Rule 1.6(b)(1)-(6). Under Paragraph (c) the lawyer may reveal such information only when the organization's highest authority insists upon or fails to address threatened or ongoing action that is clearly a violation of law, and then only to the extent the lawyer reasonably believes necessary to prevent reasonably certain substantial injury to the organization. It is not necessary that the lawyer's services be used in furtherance of the violation, but it is required that the matter be related to the lawyer's representation of the organization. If the lawyer's services are being used by an organization to further a crime or fraud by the organization, Rules 1.6(b)(2) and 1.6(b)(3) may permit the lawyer to disclose confidential information. In such circumstances Rule 1.2(d) may also be applicable, in which event, withdrawal from the representation under Rule 1.16(a)(1) may be required.

[7] Paragraph (d) makes clear that the authority of a lawyer to disclose information relating to a representation in circumstances described in paragraph (c) does not apply with respect to information relating to a lawyer's engagement by an

organization to investigate an alleged violation of law or to defend the organization or an officer, employee or other person associated with the organization against a claim arising out of an alleged violation of law. This is necessary in order to enable organizational clients to enjoy the full benefits of legal counsel in conducting an investigation or defending against a claim.

[8] A lawyer who reasonably believes that he or she has been discharged because of the lawyer's actions taken pursuant to paragraph (b) or (c), or who withdraws in circumstances that require or permit the lawyer to take action under either of these paragraphs, must proceed as the lawyer reasonably believes necessary to assure that the organization's highest authority is informed of the lawyer's discharge or withdrawal.

Government Agency

[9] The duty defined in this Rule applies to governmental organizations. Defining precisely the identity of the client and prescribing the resulting obligations of such lawyers may be more difficult in the government context and is a matter beyond the scope of these Rules. See Scope [18]. Although in some circumstances the client may be a specific agency, it may also be a branch of government, such as the executive branch, or the government as a whole. For example, if the action or failure to act involves the head of a bureau, either the department of which the bureau is a part or the relevant branch of government may be the client for purposes of this Rule. Moreover, in a matter involving the conduct of government officials, a government lawyer may have authority under applicable law to question such conduct more extensively than that of a lawyer for a private organization in similar circumstances. Thus, when the client is a governmental organization, a different balance may be appropriate between maintaining confidentiality and assuring that the wrongful act is prevented or rectified, for public business is involved. In addition, duties of lawyers employed by the government or lawyers in military service may be defined by statutes and regulation. This Rule does not limit that authority. See Scope.

Clarifying the Lawyer's Role

[10] There are times when the organization's interest may be or become adverse to those of one or more of its constituents. In such circumstances the lawyer should advise any constituent, whose interest the lawyer finds adverse to that of the organization of the conflict or potential conflict of interest, that the lawyer cannot represent such constituent, and that such person may wish to obtain independent representation. Care must be taken to assure that the individual understands that, when there is such adversity of interest, the lawyer for the organization cannot provide legal representation for that constituent individual, and that discussions between the lawyer for the organization and the individual may not be privileged. 4.2, 4.3

[11] Whether such a warning should be given by the lawyer for the organization to any constituent individual may turn on the facts of each case.

Dual Representation

[12] Paragraph (g) recognizes that a lawyer for an organization may also represent a principal officer or major shareholder.

Derivative Actions

[13] Under generally prevailing law, the shareholders or members of a corporation may bring suit to compel the directors to perform their legal obligations in the supervision of the organization. Members of unincorporated associations have essentially the same right. Such an action may be brought nominally by the organization, but usually is, in fact, a legal controversy over management of the organization.

[14] The question can arise whether counsel for the organization may defend such an action. The proposition that the organization is the lawyer's client does not alone resolve the issue. Most derivative actions are a normal incident of an organization's affairs, to be defended by the organization's lawyer like any other suit. However, if the claim involves serious charges of wrongdoing by those in control of the organization, a conflict may arise between the lawyer's duty to the organization and the lawyer's relationship with the board. In those circumstances, Rule 1.7 governs who should represent the directors and the organization.

Canon and Code Antecedents

ABA Canons of Professional Ethics: No comparable Canon.

ABA Model Code of Professional Responsibility: Compare DR 5-107(B) (reprinted later in this volume).

Cross-References in Other Rules

Rule 1.4, Comment 6: "When the client is an organization or group, it is often impossible or inappropriate to inform every one of its members about its legal affairs; ordinarily, the lawyer should address communications to the appropriate officials of the organization. See **Rule 1.13**."

Rule 1.6, Comment 7: "See . . . **Rule 1.13(c)**, which permits the lawyer, where the client is an organization, to reveal information relating to the representation in limited circumstances."

Rule 1.7, Comment 34: "A lawyer who represents a corporation or other organization does not, by virtue of that representation, necessarily represent any constituent or affiliated organization, such as a parent or subsidiary. See **Rule 1.13(a)**."

Rule 1.11, Comment 5: "The question of whether two government agencies should be regarded as the same or different clients for conflict of interest purposes is beyond the scope of these Rules. See **Rule 1.13** Comment [6]."

Rule 4.3, Comment 1: "For misunderstandings that sometimes arise when a lawyer for an organization deals with an unrepresented constituent, see **Rule 1.13(d)**."

Legislative History of Model Rule 1.13

1980 Discussion Draft:

An Organization as the Client

(a) A lawyer employed or retained by an organization represents the organization as distinct from its directors, officers, employees, members, shareholders, or other constituents.

(b) If a lawyer for an organization knows that an officer, employee, or other person associated with the organization is engaged in or intends action, or a refusal to act, that is a violation of law and is likely to result in significant harm to the organization, the lawyer shall use reasonable efforts to prevent the harm. [The rest of subparagraph (b) was substantially the same as adopted.]

(c) If, despite the lawyer's efforts in accordance with paragraph (b), the highest authority that can act on behalf of the organization insists upon action, or a refusal to act, that is clearly a violation of law and is likely to result in substantial injury to the organization, the lawyer may take further remedial action, including disclosure of client confidences to the extent necessary, if the lawyer reasonably believes such action to be in the best interest of the organization.

(d) A lawyer representing an organization may also represent any of its directors, officers, members, or shareholders subject to the provisions of Rule 1.7. A lawyer undertaking such dual representation shall disclose that fact to an appropriate official of the organization other than the person so represented.

(e) When a shareholder or member of an organization brings a derivative action, the lawyer for the organization may act as its advocate only as permitted by Rule 1.7.

(f) In dealing with an organization's officials and employees, a lawyer shall explain the identity of the client when necessary to avoid embarrassment or unfairness to them.

1981 Draft: Rule 1.13(a) was the same as 1980 Draft. In Rule 1.13(b), a lawyer discovering conduct likely to result in "material" injury (rather than "significant" injury) to the corporation was to "proceed as is reasonably necessary in the best interest of the organization." Rule 1.13(c), describing remedial action, provided:

Such action may include revealing information relating to the representation of the organization only if the lawyer reasonably believes that:

(1) the highest authority in the organization has acted to further the personal or financial interests of members of that authority which are in conflict with the interests of the organization; and

(2) revealing the information is necessary in the best interest of the organization.

1982 Draft: Substantially the same as 1981 Draft.

1983 Rule: From its original adoption in 1983 until its amendment in 2002, Rule 1.13 provided, in relevant part, as follows:

Rule 1.13 Organization as Client

(a) [Same as 2003 version of Rule 1.13(a).]

(b) If a lawyer for an organization knows that an officer, employee or other person associated with the organization is engaged in action, intends to act or refuses to act in a matter related to the representation that is a violation of a legal obligation to the organization, or a violation of law which reasonably might be imputed to the organization, and is likely to result in substantial injury to the organization, the lawyer shall proceed as is reasonably necessary in the best interest of the organization. In determining how to proceed, the lawyer shall give due consideration to the seriousness of the violation and its consequences, the scope and nature of the lawyer's representation, the responsibility in the organization and the apparent motivation of the person involved, the policies of the organization concerning such matters and any other relevant considerations. Any measures taken shall be designed to minimize disruption of the organization and the risk of revealing information relating to the representation to persons outside the organization. Such measures may include among others:

(1) asking for reconsideration of the matter;

(2) advising that a separate legal opinion on the matter be sought for presentation to appropriate authority in the organization; and

(3) referring the matter to higher authority in the organization, including, if warranted by the seriousness of the matter, referral to the highest authority that can act in behalf of the organization as determined by applicable law.

(c) If, despite the lawyer's efforts in accordance with paragraph (b), the highest authority that can act on behalf of the organization insists upon action, or a refusal to act, that is clearly a violation of law and is likely to result in substantial injury to the organization, the lawyer may resign in accordance with Rule 1.16.

(d) [Same as 2003 version of Rule 1.13(f).]

(e) [Same as 2003 version of Rule 1.13(g).]

2002 Amendments: At its February 2002 Mid-Year Meeting, the ABA House of Delegates adopted without change the ABA Ethics 2000 Commission proposal to amend Rule 1.13 and its Comment. The only substantive change in the Rule was to substitute "the lawyer knows or reasonably should know" for "it is apparent" in paragraph (d).

2003 Amendments: At its August 2003 Annual Meeting, by a margin of 239-147, the ABA House of Delegates voted to amend paragraphs (b) and (c) of Rule 1.13 significantly, and to add new paragraphs (d) and (e). (Former paragraphs (d) and (e) were redesignated paragraphs (f) and (g).) The amendment to Rule 1.13(b) had the effect of underscoring the lawyer's obligation to report the described misconduct to higher authority, including the highest authority of the organization. Lawyers must now do this unless they reasonably believe it is not necessary. The amendment to Rule 1.13(c) permits lawyers, when the preconditions are satisfied, to reveal the confidential information of the organizational client to outsiders, which in effect creates another exception to Rule 1.6. The ABA also added or substantially amended Comments 3-8. The changes were part of a package of recommendations from the ABA Presidential Task Force on Corporate Responsibility. (For more information about the Task Force and its work, including a copy of its full report, visit *http://www.americanbar.org/groups/business_law.html.*) In support of the changes, the Task Force report stated:*

> The key provision, in current Rule 1.13(b), is that the lawyer must take appropriate action in the best interest of the client, namely the organization. While this obligation is a mandate, the Rule cannot and does not prescribe precisely what action is appropriate; the lawyer is obligated to exercise informed professional judgment in determining what steps are "reasonably necessary in the best interest of the organization." That can

* Task Force Reports do not represent official policy of the ABA. They are for information only, and the opinions are those of the authors of the Report.

be determined, in specific detail, only in the context of the circumstances in which the problem arises. The current rule suggests, very generally, a few kinds of action open to the lawyer, but mandates none of them. The Task Force has concluded that these provisions confuse rather than clarify the mandatory nature of the lawyer's obligations under the rule, and accordingly recommends that they be deleted.

In lieu of those open-ended provisions, the Task Force recommends two substantive revisions to Rule 1.13(b). The first is a refinement of the definition of the circumstances that trigger the lawyer's duty to take action within the organization.

Editors' Note. The above recommendation was deleted through a friendly amendment during the debate in the ABA House of Delegates. The original Task Force recommendation would have added the words "facts from which a reasonable lawyer, under the circumstances, would conclude" after the word "knows" in the first sentence of Rule 1.13(b). The result of the friendly amendment deleting these proposed words was to leave the first sentence of Rule 1.13(b) unchanged from the 2002 version. The Task Force report continued as follows:

The second substantive change to Rule 1.13(b) recommended by the Task Force addresses the lawyer's obligation to report wrongdoing to higher authority in the organizational client. Currently, that rule identifies "reporting up" as a potential course of action when the lawyer has discerned an actual or threatened violation of law or violation of legal obligation to the organization, but the Rule imposes no clear obligation to pursue that course of action. The Task Force believes, however, that the Rule should more actively encourage such action, by requiring that the lawyer refer the matter to higher authority in the organization—including, if warranted, the organization's highest authority—unless the lawyer reasonably believes that it is not necessary to do so.

In its deliberations, the Task Force considered whether the lawyer's duties under the Rule should continue to be triggered only by matters that are "related to the representation." The Task Force's Preliminary Report recommended that the Rule require the lawyer to act with respect to any known violation, even if not related to the representation. Others pointed out, however, that it would be unfair to hold responsible a lawyer working in one field of the law to understand that facts of which he was aware should have led to a conclusion of law violation in a field with which he was unfamiliar. The Task Force is persuaded by this analysis and recommends that this qualification be retained in the Rule. . . .

The Task Force also recommends that Rule 1.13 be amended to include a new provision to assure that the organization's highest authority is made aware that a lawyer for the organization has withdrawn or is discharged in circumstances addressed by the Rule. In some instances, the actions of the lawyer within the organization, pursuant to Rule 1.13(b), may fail to prevent or avoid action that seriously threatens the interest of the organization. Current Rule 1.13(c) provides that a lawyer, in this circumstance, may choose to withdraw. In that event, or if the organizational client discharges the lawyer because of the lawyer's actions under Rule 1.13(b) in reporting to higher authority, the lawyer's professional obligations to act in the best interest of the organization should require the lawyer to take reasonable steps to assure that the organization's highest authority is aware of the withdrawal or discharge, and the lawyer's understanding of the circumstances that brought it about. . . .

In proposing amendments to Model Rule 1.6, the Task Force has reviewed confidentiality considerations that reflect a balance between the policy of preserving the confidentiality of client information and countervailing policy that a client may not abuse the client-lawyer relationship by using the lawyer's services to commit a crime or fraud. That balance of policy considerations applies to both individual and organizational clients. The Task Force has focused, however, on two additional aspects of the duty of confidentiality with respect to organizational clients. The first such aspect is the uncontroversial but perhaps not universally understood proposition that a lawyer does not violate Model Rule 1.6 by disclosing to an organizational constituent, acting as such, information relating to the representation that was imparted to the lawyer by another organizational constituent (e.g., by sharing with a corporation's general counsel or its board of directors facts learned from a corporate officer). Organizational constituents thus cannot legitimately expect that the lawyer will not reveal to others within the organization information they have imparted to the lawyer.

The second aspect on which the Task Force has focused arises because, just as with individual clients, full and frank communication with the organization's lawyer is encouraged if organizational constituents expect that information they communicate to the organization's lawyer will not be revealed outside the organization (except as the organization may decide). That expectation is undoubtedly valuable to an organizational client as a general proposition. The organization may have a countervailing interest, however, when a lawyer's actions within the organization, including advice to the organization's highest authority, are unavailing to protect the organization against substantial injury arising from a constituent's clear violation of law. In such a circumstance, the Task Force believes that [the] organization's interest in having the lawyer proceed "as is reasonably necessary in the best interest of the organization" outweighs the organization's general interest in preserving confidentiality.

The Task Force agrees with the Reporter to the ALI Restatement that Model Rule 1.6 ". . . should not be understood to preclude controlled disclosure beyond the organization in the limited circumstances where the wrongdoing is clear, the injury to the client organization is substantial, and disclosure would clearly be in the interest of the entity client." The Task Force considers this especially important in the circumstance in which the board of directors or other highest authority of the organizational client is disabled from acting in the best interest of the organization, e.g., because of self-interest or personal involvement in the violation.

Because such disclosure may reveal client information otherwise protected under Rule 1.6(a), the proposed addition to Rule 1.13 contains strict conditions that must exist before any "reporting out" is allowed. The lawyer must have a heightened level of certainty as to the violation of law, and the actual or threatened violation must be "clear." Moreover, there is no permission to "report out" when the organizational governance failure involves a violation of legal duty to the organization but is not otherwise a violation of law. As under Rule 1.6, communication of client information outside the organization must be limited to information reasonably believed to be necessary to prevent substantial injury to the organization that is reasonably certain to occur. In most circumstances, this limitation would permit communication only with persons outside the organization who have authority and responsibility to take appropriate preventive action.

Finally, although the following language was adopted at the ABA's 2003 Annual Meeting, it was subsequently deleted as an administrative matter (i.e., not by the House of Delegates) to ensure conformity with the friendly amendments described above:

The lawyer's obligation to proceed as is reasonably necessary in the best interest of the organization is determined by the conclusions that a reasonable lawyer would, under the circumstances, draw from the facts known. The terms "reasonable" and "reasonably" imply a range within which the lawyer's conduct will satisfy the requirements of Rule 1.13. In determining what is reasonable in the best interest of the organization the circumstances at the time of determination are relevant. Such circumstances may include, among others, the lawyer's area of expertise, the time constraints under which the lawyer is acting, and the lawyer's previous experience and familiarity with the client. For example, the facts suggesting a violation may be part of a large volume of information that the lawyer has insufficient time fully to comprehend. Or the facts known to the lawyer may be sufficient to signal the likely existence of a violation to an expert in a particular field of law but not to a lawyer who works in another specialty. Under such circumstances the lawyer would not have an obligation to proceed under Paragraph (b).

Selected State Variations

Arizona has adopted the 2003 version of ABA Model Rule 1.13 verbatim. Regarding entity clients, the Arizona Legislature has also enacted the following statute, A.R.S. §12-2234, to codify the attorney-client privilege for corporations and other entities in civil cases:

> (B) . . . [A]ny communication is privileged between an attorney for a corporation, governmental entity, partnership, business, association or other similar entity or an employer and any employee, agent or member of the entity or employer regarding acts or omissions of or information obtained from the employee, agent or member if the communication is either:
>
> 1. For the purpose of providing legal advice to the entity or employer or to the employee, agent or member.
>
> 2. For the purpose of obtaining information in order to provide legal advice to the entity or employer or to the employee, agent or member.
>
> (C) The privilege defined in this section shall not be construed to allow the employee to be relieved of a duty to disclose the facts solely because they have been communicated to an attorney.

The statute was passed in reaction to the Arizona Supreme Court's decision in *Samaritan Foundation v. Goodfarb,* 862 P.2d 870 (Ariz. 1993), which rejected the federal courts' broad view of the attorney-client privilege for corporations announced in *Upjohn Co. v. United States,* 449 U.S. 383 (1981). The *Samaritan* court instead adopted a "functional" test for the attorney-client privilege and required a defendant hospital to disclose information that the defendant contended was privileged. The following year, after intense lobbying by corporate interests, the Arizona Legislature enacted §12-2234, which effectively overruled the *Samaritan* opinion and adopted *Upjohn.* However, in *Roman Catholic Diocese of Phoenix v. Superior Court,* 62 P.3d 970 (Ariz. App. 2003), an intermediate appellate court held that §12-2334 applies only in civil proceedings and that *Samaritan* remains good law in criminal cases.

California: Rule 3-600 substantially follows the positions in Rule 1.13 as originally adopted. Among other things, it does not create an exception to confidentiality when conditions like those in Model Rule 1.13(c) are present but says only that the lawyer may, or must, resign.

District of Columbia omits paragraphs (c), (d), and (e) of ABA Model Rule 1.13.

Georgia: Rule 1.13 tracks the pre-2003 version of ABA Model Rule 1.13 verbatim, but Georgia adds the following paragraph (f): " 'Organization' as used herein includes governmental entities."

Maryland, Michigan, and ***New Jersey*** all retain verbatim the Kutak Commission's 1981 draft of Rule 1.13(c), which provides that "remedial action" may, if necessary, include "revealing information otherwise protected by Rule 1.6"—but "only if the lawyer reasonably believes that: (1) the highest authority in the organization has acted to further the personal or financial interests of members of the authority which are in conflict with the interests of the organization; and (2) revealing the information is necessary in the best interest of the organization."

Michigan: Rule 1.13(a) tracks the Kutak Commission's 1980 draft by providing that a lawyer for an organization represents the organization "as distinct from" its directors, officers, employees, members, shareholders, or other constituents. Moreover, Michigan Rule 1.13(f) provides as follows:

> For purposes of this rule "organization" includes any corporation, partnership, association, joint stock company, union, trust, pension fund, unincorporated association, proprietorship or other business entity, state or local government or political subdivision thereof, or non-profit organization.

Minnesota effectively deletes the requirement in ABA Rule 1.13(c)(2) that the lawyer "reasonably believes that the violation is reasonably certain to result in substantial injury to the organization." Minnesota also deletes ABA Model Rule 1.13(d).

Missouri: Missouri retains the 2002 version of ABA Model Rule 1.13 verbatim and thus has no equivalent to paragraphs (d) and (e) of the current version of ABA Model Rule 1.13.

New Jersey: Rule 1.13(a), which borrows from the Kutak Commission's 1980 draft, states that a lawyer employed or retained to represent an organization represents the organization "as distinct from" its directors, officers, employees, members, shareholders, or other constituents. In addition, New Jersey adds that for purposes of Rules 4.2 and 4.3 "the organization's lawyer shall be deemed to represent not only the organizational entity but also the members of its litigation control group," which is defined as follows:

> Members of the litigation control group shall be deemed to include current agents and employees responsible for, or significantly involved in, the determination of the organization's legal position in the matter whether or not in litigation, provided, however, that "significant involvement" requires involvement greater, and other than, the supplying of factual information or data respecting the matter. Former agents and employees who were members of the litigation control group shall presumptively be deemed to be represented in the matter by the organization's lawyer but may at any time disavow said representation.

New Jersey Rule 1.13(b) retains verbatim the 1983 version of ABA Model Rule 1.13(b). New Jersey Rule 1.13(c) retains verbatim the Kutak Commission's 1981 draft—see Maryland entry above. New Jersey has not adopted ABA Model Rules 1.13(d) and (e), and New Jersey's equivalent to ABA Model Rule 1.13(f) provides that in dealing with an organization's directors, officers, employees, members, shareholders or other constituents, a lawyer shall explain the identity of the client when the lawyer "believes that such explanation is necessary to avoid misunderstanding on their part." Finally, New Jersey also adds a subparagraph (f) that defines the term "organization" in Rule 1.13 to include "any corporation, partnership, association, joint stock company, union, trust, pension fund, unincorporated association, proprietorship or other business entity, state or local government or political subdivision thereof, or nonprofit organization."

New York: Rule 1.13 is substantially similar to the pre-2003 version of Model Rule 1.13.

Ohio: Rule 1.13(b) adds "or reasonably should know" after "knows" in the first sentence. Ohio omits ABA Model Rules 1.13(c), (d), and (e). Ohio Rule 1.13(c) provides: "The discretion or duty of the lawyer for an organization to reveal information relating to the representation outside the organization is governed by Rule 1.6(b) and (c)."

Pennsylvania retains the 1983 version of ABA Model Rule 1.13(b) essentially verbatim, and retains the 2002 version of ABA Model Rule 1.13(c).

Texas: Rule 1.12(a) says that a lawyer retained or employed by an organization "represents the entity." Texas Rule 1.12(d) relieves the lawyer of responsibilities to the entity when the lawyer properly withdraws from the representation. Texas Rule 1.12(e) (equivalent to ABA Model Rule 1.13(f)) requires a lawyer to explain the identity of the client "when explanation appears reasonably necessary to avoid misunderstanding. . . ."

Related Materials

ABA Formal Ethics Opinions: See ABA Formal Ethics Ops. 91-361 (1991), 92-364 (1992), 92-365 (1992), 92-366 (1992), 95-390 (1995), 99-415 (1999), 06-441 (2006), and 08-453 (2008).

ABA Task Force on Corporate Responsibility: In 2002, the President of the American Bar Association appointed a Task Force on Corporate Responsibility whose charge was to "examine systemic issues relating to corporate responsibility arising out of the unexpected and traumatic bankruptcy of Enron and other Enron-like situations." The Task Force Chair was Tennessee lawyer James H. Cheek, III, and its Reporter was Professor Lawrence Hamermesh of Widener University School of Law.

In April 2003, the Task Force issued a lengthy and influential final report recommending (among other things) that the ABA (1) adopt the exceptions to Rule 1.6 confidentiality that the ABA had rejected in 2002, and (2) modify Rule 1.13 to permit lawyers to reveal confidential information outside the organization in certain circumstances. At the ABA's August 2003 Annual Meeting, the ABA House of Delegates approved the substance of the Task Force's recommendations regarding Rules 1.6 and 1.13. (See "2003 Amendments" in the Legislative History following both Rule 1.6 and this Rule.) The Task Force's final report and related events are discussed in the Special Section at the end of the 2004 edition of this book. The final report and other useful related materials are available at *http://www.americanbar.org/groups/business_law.html.*

Model Rules of Professional Conduct for Federal Lawyers: Rule 1.13 provides (with emphasis added):

> (a) Except when representing another client pursuant to paragraphs (e), (f) and (g), a *Government lawyer represents the Federal Agency that employs the Government lawyer.* Government lawyers are often formally employed by a Federal Agency but assigned to an organizational element within the Federal Agency. Unless otherwise specifically provided, the Federal Agency, not the organizational element, is ordinarily considered the client. The Federal Agency acts through its authorized officials. These officials include

the heads of organizational elements within the Federal Agency. When a Government lawyer is assigned to an organizational element and designated to provide legal services and advice to the head of that organization, the client-lawyer relationship exists between the Government lawyer and the Federal Agency, as represented by the head of the organization. *The head of the organization may only invoke the attorney-client privilege or the rule of confidentiality for the benefit of the Federal Agency.* In so invoking either the attorney-client privilege or attorney-client confidentiality on behalf of the Federal Agency, the head of the organization is subject to being overruled by higher agency authority.

(b) . . . [The measures a Government lawyer may take] may include, among others: . . .

(3) Advising the person that the lawyer is ethically obligated to preserve the interests of the Federal agency and, as a result, must consider discussing the matter with supervisory lawyers within the Government lawyer's office or at a higher level within the Federal Agency.

(c) If, despite the Government lawyer's efforts in accordance with paragraph (b), the highest authority that can act concerning the matter insists upon action, or refusal to act, that is clearly a violation of law, the Government lawyer shall terminate representation with respect to the matter in question. In no event may the Government lawyer participate or assist in the illegal activity. . . .

(e) A Government lawyer shall not form a client-lawyer relationship or represent a client other than the Federal Agency unless specifically authorized or authorized by competent authority. . . .

(g) A Government lawyer who has been duly assigned or authorized to represent an individual who is subject to disciplinary action or administrative proceedings, or to provide civil legal assistance to an individual, has, for those purposes, a lawyer-client relationship with that individual.

The Comment to these Rules states, in part, as follows:

Except when a Government lawyer is assigned to represent the interest of another client, the Federal Agency that employs the Government lawyer is the client. This principle is critical to the application of these Rules, since the identity of the client affects significant confidentiality and conflict issues.

. . . Although arguments have been made that the Government lawyer's ultimate obligation is to serve the public interest or the "government as a whole," for practical purposes, these may be unworkable ethical guidelines, particularly with regard to client control and confidentiality.

A Federal Agency may, of course, establish different client-lawyer obligations by Executive or court order, regulation, or statute. See, e.g., 5 U.S.C. §2302 (defining "prohibited personnel practice" and assigning responsibility for preventing them).

Partnerships: Entities or Aggregates? A "partnership" is a form of business organization that exists whenever two or more people associate, without incorporating, for the purpose of doing business for profit. For purposes of identifying the client under Rule 1.13(a), does a lawyer for a partnership represent only the entity itself and not the partners (the "entity" theory), or does the lawyer for a partnership represent an aggregation of partners so that each partner is a client of the lawyer for the partnership (the "aggregate" theory)? In the original Uniform Partnership Act (UPA), which was approved by the National Conference of Commissioners on Uniform State Laws (NCCUSL) in 1914, a partnership was viewed not as a distinct entity but rather as an aggregation of individuals. The original UPA thus generally embraced the "aggregate" theory of partnerships. In contrast, §201 of the Revised Uniform Partnership Act (RUPA), provides: "A partnership is an entity distinct from its partners." The

RUPA thus embraces the "entity" theory of partnerships. (The UPA had no specific section comparable to §201 of the RUPA.) The RUPA was approved by NCCUSL in 1994 and has been adopted by 33 states and the District of Columbia.

Restatement of the Law Governing Lawyers: See Restatement §§67, 73, 82, 85, 96, 97, and 131 in our chapter on the Restatement later in this volume.

Sarbanes-Oxley Act and SEC Regulations: In 2002, in the wake of massive corporate scandals at Enron, WorldCom, and other corporations, Congress enacted the Sarbanes-Oxley Act of 2002. A provision of the Act especially important to attorneys is §307 (codified at 15 U.S.C. §7245), which provides as follows:

§7245. Rules of Professional Responsibility for Attorneys

> Not later than 180 days after July 30, 2002, the [Securities and Exchange] Commission shall issue rules, in the public interest and for the protection of investors, setting forth minimum standards of professional conduct for attorneys appearing and practicing before the Commission in any way in the representation of issuers, including a rule —
>
> (1) requiring an attorney to report evidence of a material violation of securities law or breach of fiduciary duty or similar violation by the company or any agent thereof, to the chief legal counsel or the chief executive officer of the company (or the equivalent thereof); and
>
> (2) if the counsel or officer does not appropriately respond to the evidence (adopting, as necessary, appropriate remedial measures or sanctions with respect to the violation), requiring the attorney to report the evidence to the audit committee of the board of directors of the issuer or to another committee of the board of directors comprised solely of directors not employed directly or indirectly by the issuer, or to the board of directors.

To carry out the mandate of the Act, in 2003 the SEC adopted detailed rules codified at 17 C.F.R. Part 205, which are reprinted below in our selection of Federal Statutes and Regulations. Additional context surrounding the Sarbanes-Oxley Act and the SEC regulations can be found in the Special Section at the end of the 2004 edition of this book.

SEC Statement on Corporate Cooperation ("Seaboard Report"): In the SEC's Securities and Exchange Act Release No. 44969 (October 23, 2001), often referred to as the "Seaboard Report," the SEC set forth some of the criteria the SEC considers in determining "whether, and how much, to credit self-policing, self-reporting, remediation and cooperation—from the extraordinary step of taking no enforcement action to bringing reduced charges, seeking lighter sanctions, or including mitigating language in documents we use to announce and resolve enforcement actions." The following examples of these criteria are particularly relevant to Rule 1.13:

> 1. What is the nature of the misconduct involved? Did it result from inadvertence, honest mistake, simple negligence, reckless or deliberate indifference to indicia of wrongful conduct, willful misconduct or unadorned venality? Were the company's auditors misled?
>
> 2. How did the misconduct arise? Is it the result of pressure placed on employees to achieve specific results, or a tone of lawlessness set by those in control of the company? What compliance procedures were in place to prevent the misconduct now uncovered? Why did those procedures fail to stop or inhibit the wrongful conduct?

5. How much harm has the misconduct inflicted upon investors and other corporate constituencies? Did the share price of the company's stock drop significantly upon its discovery and disclosure?

6. How was the misconduct detected and who uncovered it? . . .

8. What steps did the company take upon learning of the misconduct? Did the company immediately stop the misconduct? Are persons responsible for any misconduct still with the company? If so, are they still in the same positions? Did the company promptly, completely and effectively disclose the existence of the misconduct to the public, to regulators and to self-regulators? Did the company cooperate completely with appropriate regulatory and law enforcement bodies? Did the company identify what additional related misconduct is likely to have occurred? Did the company take steps to identify the extent of damage to investors and other corporate constituencies? Did the company appropriately recompense those adversely affected by the conduct?

9. What processes did the company follow to resolve many of these issues and ferret out necessary information? Were the Audit Committee and the Board of Directors fully informed? If so, when? . . .

In January 2010, the SEC announced a series of measures to strengthen its enforcement program by encouraging greater cooperation from individuals and companies in the agency's investigations and enforcement actions. Among other things, the SEC set out, for the first time, the way in which it will evaluate whether, how much, and in what manner to credit cooperation by individuals to ensure that potential cooperation arrangements maximize the SEC's law enforcement interests. The 2010 pronouncement, which is similar to the Seaboard Report, identifies four general considerations in assessing the value of cooperation: (1) "The assistance provided by the cooperating individual"; (2) "The importance of the underlying matter in which the individual cooperated"; (3) "The societal interest in ensuring the individual is held accountable for his or her misconduct"; and (4) "The appropriateness of cooperation credit based upon the risk profile of the cooperating individual." For more information, see *www.sec.gov/news/press/2010/2010-6.htm.*

Sentencing Guidelines: The U.S. Sentencing Guidelines set forth factors intended to guide courts in imposing criminal sentences. When a corporation is convicted of a crime, one factor militating toward a reduced sentence is cooperation. Following §8C2.5 of the Sentencing Guidelines, entitled "Culpability Score," the official Application Note explains "cooperation" as follows:

12. To qualify for a reduction . . . cooperation must be both timely and thorough. To be timely, the cooperation must begin essentially at the same time as the organization is officially notified of a criminal investigation. To be thorough, the cooperation should include the disclosure of all pertinent information known by the organization. A prime test of whether the organization has disclosed all pertinent information is whether the information is sufficient for law enforcement personnel to identify the nature and extent of the offense and the individual(s) responsible for the criminal conduct. However, the cooperation to be measured is the cooperation of the organization itself, not the cooperation of individuals within the organization. If, because of the lack of cooperation of particular individual(s), neither the organization nor law enforcement personnel are able to identify the culpable individual(s) within the organization despite the organization's efforts to cooperate fully, the organization may still be given credit for full cooperation.

Until 2006, the U.S. Sentencing Commission maintained a policy authorizing and encouraging prosecutors to require corporations and other business entities to waive the attorney-client privilege and constitutional protections in order to receive "credit" for "cooperating" in government investigations. In 2006, the Commission voted unanimously to rescind this policy and to delete the final sentence of the Application Note to §8C2.5, which had stated: "Waiver of attorney-client privilege and of work product protections is not a prerequisite to a reduction in culpability score . . . unless such waiver is necessary in order to provide timely and thorough disclosure of all pertinent information known to the organization."

Rule 1.14 Client with Diminished Capacity

(a) When a client's capacity to make adequately considered decisions in connection with a representation is diminished, whether because of minority, mental impairment or for some other reason, the lawyer shall, as far as reasonably possible, maintain a normal client-lawyer relationship with the client.

(b) When the lawyer reasonably believes that the client has diminished capacity, is at risk of substantial physical, financial or other harm unless action is taken and cannot adequately act in the client's own interest, the lawyer may take reasonably necessary protective action, including consulting with individuals or entities that have the ability to take action to protect the client and, in appropriate cases, seeking the appointment of a guardian ad litem, conservator or guardian.

(c) Information relating to the representation of a client with diminished capacity is protected by Rule 1.6. When taking protective action pursuant to paragraph (b), the lawyer is impliedly authorized under Rule 1.6(a) to reveal information about the client, but only to the extent reasonably necessary to protect the client's interests. § 24(2)

See 1.16 ct 6
See 1.4 ct 7

COMMENT

[1] The normal client-lawyer relationship is based on the assumption that the client, when properly advised and assisted, is capable of making decisions about important matters. When the client is a minor or suffers from a diminished mental capacity, however, maintaining the ordinary client-lawyer relationship may not be possible in all respects. In particular, a severely incapacitated person may have no power to make legally binding decisions. Nevertheless, a client with diminished capacity often has the ability to understand, deliberate upon, and reach conclusions about matters affecting the client's own well-being. For example, children as young as five or six years of age, and certainly those of ten or twelve, are regarded as having opinions that are entitled to weight in legal proceedings concerning their custody. So also, it is recognized that some persons of advanced age can be quite capable of handling routine financial matters while needing special legal protection concerning major transactions.

[2] The fact that a client suffers a disability does not diminish the lawyer's obligation to treat the client with attention and respect. Even if the person has a legal representative, the lawyer should as far as possible accord the represented person the status of client, particularly in maintaining communication.

[3] The client may wish to have family members or other persons participate in discussions with the lawyer. When necessary to assist in the representation, the presence of such persons generally does not affect the applicability of the attorney-client evidentiary privilege. Nevertheless, the lawyer must keep the client's interests foremost and, except for protective action authorized under paragraph (b), must look to the client, and not family members, to make decisions on the client's behalf.

[4] If a legal representative has already been appointed for the client, the lawyer should ordinarily look to the representative for decisions on behalf of the client. In matters involving a minor, whether the lawyer should look to the parents as natural guardians may depend on the type of proceeding or matter in which the lawyer is representing the minor. If the lawyer represents the guardian as distinct from the ward, and is aware that the guardian is acting adversely to the ward's interest, the lawyer may have an obligation to prevent or rectify the guardian's misconduct. See Rule 1.2(d).

Taking Protective Action

[5] If a lawyer reasonably believes that a client is at risk of substantial physical, financial or other harm unless action is taken, and that a normal client-lawyer relationship cannot be maintained as provided in paragraph (a) because the client lacks sufficient capacity to communicate or to make adequately considered decisions in connection with the representation, then paragraph (b) permits the lawyer to take protective measures deemed necessary. Such measures could include: consulting with family members, using a reconsideration period to permit clarification or improvement of circumstances, using voluntary surrogate decisionmaking tools such as durable powers of attorney or consulting with support groups, professional services, adult-protective agencies or other individuals or entities that have the ability to protect the client. In taking any protective action, the lawyer should be guided by such factors as the wishes and values of the client to the extent known, the client's best interests and the goals of intruding into the client's decisionmaking autonomy to the least extent feasible, maximizing client capacities and respecting the client's family and social connections.

[6] In determining the extent of the client's diminished capacity, the lawyer should consider and balance such factors as: the client's ability to articulate reasoning leading to a decision, variability of state of mind, and ability to appreciate consequences of a decision; the substantive fairness of a decision; and the consistency of a decision with the known long-term commitments and values of the client. In appropriate circumstances, the lawyer may seek guidance from an appropriate diagnostician.

[7] If a legal representative has not been appointed, the lawyer should consider whether appointment of a guardian ad litem, conservator or guardian is necessary to protect the client's interests. Thus, if a client with diminished capacity has substantial property that should be sold for the client's benefit, effective completion of the transaction may require appointment of a legal representative. In addition, rules of procedure in litigation sometimes provide that minors or persons with diminished capacity must be represented by a guardian or next friend if they do not have a general guardian. In many circumstances, however, appointment of a legal representative may be more expensive or traumatic for the client than circumstances in fact require. Evaluation of such circumstances is a matter entrusted to the professional judgment of the lawyer. In considering alternatives, however,

the lawyer should be aware of any law that requires the lawyer to advocate the least restrictive action on behalf of the client.

Disclosure of the Client's Condition

[8] Disclosure of the client's diminished capacity could adversely affect the client's interests. For example, raising the question of diminished capacity could, in some circumstances, lead to proceedings for involuntary commitment. Information relating to the representation is protected by Rule 1.6. Therefore, unless authorized to do so, the lawyer may not disclose such information. When taking protective action pursuant to paragraph (b), the lawyer is impliedly authorized to make the necessary disclosures, even when the client directs the lawyer to the contrary. Nevertheless, given the risks of disclosure, paragraph (c) limits what the lawyer may disclose in consulting with other individuals or entities or seeking the appointment of a legal representative. At the very least, the lawyer should determine whether it is likely that the person or entity consulted with will act adversely to the client's interests before discussing matters related to the client. The lawyer's position in such cases is an unavoidably difficult one.

Emergency Legal Assistance

[9] In an emergency where the health, safety or a financial interest of a person with seriously diminished capacity is threatened with imminent and irreparable harm, a lawyer may take legal action on behalf of such a person even though the person is unable to establish a client-lawyer relationship or to make or express considered judgments about the matter, when the person or another acting in good faith on that person's behalf has consulted with the lawyer. Even in such an emergency, however, the lawyer should not act unless the lawyer reasonably believes that the person has no other lawyer, agent or other representative available. The lawyer should take legal action on behalf of the person only to the extent reasonably necessary to maintain the status quo or otherwise avoid imminent and irreparable harm. A lawyer who undertakes to represent a person in such an exigent situation has the same duties under these Rules as the lawyer would with respect to a client.

[10] A lawyer who acts on behalf of a person with seriously diminished capacity in an emergency should keep the confidences of the person as if dealing with a client, disclosing them only to the extent necessary to accomplish the intended protective action. The lawyer should disclose to any tribunal involved and to any other counsel involved the nature of his or her relationship with the person. The lawyer should take steps to regularize the relationship or implement other protective solutions as soon as possible. Normally, a lawyer would not seek compensation for such emergency actions taken.

Canon and Code Antecedents

ABA Canons of Professional Ethics: No comparable Canon.

ABA Model Code of Professional Responsibility: No comparable Disciplinary Rule.

Cross-References in Other Rules

Rule 1.2, Comment 4: "In a case in which the client appears to be suffering diminished capacity, the lawyer's duty to abide by the client's decisions is to be guided by reference to **Rule 1.14**."

Rule 1.4, Comment 6: A client is to be provided with information appropriate for a "comprehending and responsible adult. However, . . . this standard may be impracticable, for example, where the client is a child or suffers from diminished capacity. See **Rule 1.14**."

Rule 1.16, Comment 6: "If the client has severely diminished capacity, the client may lack the legal capacity to discharge the lawyer, and in any event the discharge may be seriously adverse to the client's interests. The lawyer should make special effort to help the client consider the consequences and may take reasonably necessary protective action as provided in **Rule 1.14**."

Legislative History of Model Rule 1.14

1980 Discussion Draft:

> . . . (b) A lawyer shall secure the appointment of a guardian or other legal representative, or seek a protective order with respect to a client, when doing so is necessary in the client's best interests.

1981 Draft: Rule 1.14(a) was the same as the version finally adopted. Rule 1.14(b) required a lawyer to seek appointment of a guardian or a protective order "only when the lawyer reasonably believes that the client cannot adequately communicate or exercise judgment in the client-lawyer relationship."

1982 Draft was adopted.

1983 Rule: From its adoption in 1983 until its text was first amended in 2002, Rule 1.14 provided as follows:

> *Rule 1.14. Client Under a Disability*
>
> (a) When a client's ability to make adequately considered decisions in connection with the representation is impaired, whether because of minority, mental disability or for some other reason, the lawyer shall, as far as reasonably possible, maintain a normal client-lawyer relationship with the client.
>
> (b) A lawyer may seek the appointment of a guardian or take other protective action with respect to a client, only when the lawyer reasonably believes that the client cannot adequately act in the client's own interest.

1995 Proposal: In May 1995, the ABA Commission on Legal Problems of the Elderly filed a proposal to amend Rule 1.14. However, the proposal was withdrawn during the ABA's August 1995 Annual Meeting. The proposal would have revised Rule 1.14(b) and added new sections 1.14(c), (d), and (e) so that those sections would have provided as follows:

> (b) A lawyer may take protective action or seek the appointment of a guardian only when the lawyer reasonably believes the client cannot adequately act in the client's own interest.

(c) While it might be necessary to disclose information, the disclosure should be strictly limited to that which is necessary to accomplish the protective purpose.

(d) (1) A lawyer is an agent who acts upon the authority of a principal. In many cases, the lawyer will have a pre-existing relationship with a person or that person's family. In the absence of such a pre-existing relationship or a contractual agreement, express or implied, a lawyer generally may not act on behalf of a client.

(2) In certain circumstances, a lawyer may act as lawyer for a purported client even without express or limited agreement from the purported client, and may take those actions necessary to maintain the status quo or to avoid irreversible harm, if

(i) An emergency situation exists in which the purported client's substantial health, safety, financial, or liability interests would be irreparably damaged;

(ii) The purported client, in the lawyer's good faith judgment, lacks the ability to make or express considered judgments about action required to be taken because of an impairment of decision-making capacity;

(iii) Time is of the essence; and

(iv) The lawyer reasonably believes in good faith that no other lawyer who has an established relationship with the purported client is available or willing to act on behalf of the purported client.

(3) A "purported client" is a person who has contact with a lawyer and who would be a client but for the inability to enter into an express agreement.

(e) The lawyer should not be subject to professional discipline for invoking or failing to invoke the permissive conduct authorized by 1.14(b) if the lawyer has a reasonable basis for his or her action or inaction.

The proposal was accompanied by an 11-page report, which explained that the genesis of the proposal was a conference on Ethical Issues in Representing Older Clients held at Fordham University Law School in December 1993. Much of the report quoted or cited papers from that conference, which are published in 62 Fordham L. Rev. (March 1994).

1997 Amendment: In 1997, the ABA House of Delegates voted to add two new paragraphs to the Comment to Rule 1.14. (The amendment did not alter the text of Rule 1.14 or the existing Comment.) The new Comment paragraphs, co-sponsored by the ABA Standing Committee on Ethics and Professional Responsibility and the ABA Commission on Legal Problems of the Elderly, grew out of amendments to Rule 1.14 that the Commission proposed in 1995. The new Comment paragraphs explain what a lawyer should do when an "emergency" threatens the health, safety or financial interest of a disabled person who is not yet a client. The new paragraphs should be read in conjunction with ABA Ethics Op. 96-404 (1996), which addressed ethical issues that arise when existing clients are no longer mentally capable of handling their own affairs. The House of Delegates approved the new paragraphs exactly as proposed, by an overwhelming voice vote. We reprint here excerpts from the ABA Committee Report submitted in support of the 1997 amendment.

*ABA Report Explaining 1997 Amendment to Comment**

[A] lawyer may reasonably conclude that an elderly person who has not been judged incompetent is in need of emergency legal assistance, but is, or appears to be, unable to make decisions on his or her own behalf—including a decision to retain a lawyer. Such situations fall most naturally within the spirit of Model Rule 1.14 ("Client

* Committee Reports do not represent official policy of the ABA. They are for information only, and the opinions are those of the authors of the report.

Under a Disability"). The question is whether it is ethically permissible for a lawyer to take legal action on behalf of a disabled person who cannot, in the first instance, form a client-lawyer relationship.

The question whether and under what circumstances a lawyer may take emergency legal action on behalf of a disabled person who is not a client is not, of course, unique to the representation of the elderly. It may arise in a variety of practice settings where individuals appear to be in need of immediate legal assistance but are unable to make adequately considered decisions in connection with initiating legal representation.

Most of the duties arising under the Model Rules (the most notable exception being that of confidentiality) attach only after the formation of a client-lawyer relationship, and the Rules are silent with respect to any forms of representation that do not arise from such relationship. . . .

However, the Committee believes that such emergency action is permissible under the Model Rules, if properly limited. . . .

2002 Amendments: At its February 2002 Mid-Year Meeting, the ABA House of Delegates adopted without change the ABA Ethics 2000 Commission proposal to amend Rule 1.14 and its Comment. The amendments substantially revised paragraph (b) and added paragraph (c) and all or most of Comments 3, 5, 6, 7, and 8.

Selected State Variations

California has no rule comparable to ABA Model Rule 1.14.

Indiana adds Rule 1.14(d), which states: "This Rule is not violated if the lawyer acts in good faith to comply with the Rule."

Massachusetts: Rule 1.14(b) adds that a lawyer may take reasonably necessary measures to protect a client with diminished capacity, but only in "connection with the representation" and only when the client's diminished capacity "prevents the client from making an adequately considered decision regarding a specific issue that is part of the representation. . . . " Comment 7 explains that

> "[i]f a client is unable to make an adequately considered decision regarding an issue, and [when] achieving the client's expressed preferences would place the client at risk of a substantial harm, the attorney has four options. The attorney may: i. advocate the client's expressed preferences regarding the issue; ii. advocate the client's expressed preferences and request the appointment of a guardian ad litem or investigator to make an independent recommendation to the court; iii. request the appointment of a guardian ad litem or next friend to direct counsel in the representation; or iv. determine what the client's preferences would be if he or she were able to make an adequately considered decision regarding the issue and represent the client in accordance with that determination. . . . "

New York: Rule 1.14 is substantially similar to the Model Rule equivalent, but New York adds Comment 7A, which states as follows: "Prior to withdrawing from the representation of a client whose capacity is in question, the lawyer should consider taking reasonable protective action."

Texas: Rule 1.02(g) provides: "A lawyer shall take reasonable action to secure the appointment of a guardian or other legal representative for, or seek other protective orders with respect to, a client whenever the lawyer reasonably believes that the client lacks legal competence and that such action should be taken to protect the client."

Related Materials

ABA Formal Ethics Opinions: See ABA Formal Ethics Ops. 92-364 (1992), 96-404 (1996), and 07-448 (2007).

Americans with Disabilities Act: Lawyers in private practice should be mindful of Title III of the Americans with Disabilities Act, which took effect in 1992. Section 302(a) of Title III, 42 U.S.C. §12182(a), states the general rule:

> No individual shall be discriminated against on the basis of disability in the full and equal enjoyment of the goods, services, facilities, privileges, advantages, or accommodations of any place of public accommodation by any person who owns, leases (or leases to), or operates a place of public accommodation.

(The term "public accommodation" is defined in 42 U.S.C. §12181(7)(F) to include the "office of an accountant or lawyer" if the firm's operations affect commerce.)

Restatement of the Law Governing Lawyers: See Restatement §24 in our chapter on the Restatement later in this volume.

Rule 1.15 Safekeeping Property

(a) A lawyer shall hold property of clients or third persons that is in a lawyer's possession in connection with a representation separate from the lawyer's own property. Funds shall be kept in a separate account maintained in the state where the lawyer's office is situated, or elsewhere with the consent of the client or third person. Other property shall be identified as such and appropriately safeguarded. Complete records of such account funds and other property shall be kept by the lawyer and shall be preserved for a period of [five years] after termination of the representation. bank accounts

(b) A lawyer may deposit the lawyer's own funds in a client trust account for the sole purpose of paying bank service charges on that account, but only in an amount necessary for that purpose.

(c) A lawyer shall deposit into a client trust account legal fees and expenses that have been paid in advance, to be withdrawn by the lawyer only as fees are earned or expenses incurred. 1.5 ct 4

(d) Upon receiving funds or other property in which a client or third person has an interest, a lawyer shall promptly notify the client or third person. Except as stated in this rule or otherwise permitted by law or by agreement with the client, a lawyer shall promptly deliver to the client or third person any funds or other property that the client or third person is entitled to receive and, upon request by the client or third person, shall promptly render a full accounting regarding such property.

1.8(c) gifts
1.8(i) proprietary interest

(e) When in the course of representation a lawyer is in possession of property in which two or more persons (one of whom may be the lawyer) claim interests, the property shall be kept separate by the lawyer until the dispute is resolved. The lawyer shall promptly distribute all portions of the property as to which the interests are not in dispute.

COMMENT

[1] A lawyer should hold property of others with the care required of a professional fiduciary. Securities should be kept in a safe deposit box, except when some other form of safekeeping is warranted by special circumstances. All property that is the property of clients or third persons, including prospective clients, must be kept separate from the lawyer's business and personal property and, if monies, in one or more trust accounts. Separate trust accounts may be warranted when administering estate monies or acting in similar fiduciary capacities. A lawyer should maintain on a current basis books and records in accordance with generally accepted accounting practice and comply with any recordkeeping rules established by law or court order. See, e.g., ABA Model Financial Recordkeeping Rule.

[2] While normally it is impermissible to commingle the lawyer's own funds with client funds, paragraph (b) provides that it is permissible when necessary to pay bank service charges on that account. Accurate records must be kept regarding which part of the funds are the lawyer's.

[3] Lawyers often receive funds from which the lawyer's fee will be paid. The lawyer is not required to remit to the client funds that the lawyer reasonably believes represent fees owed. However, a lawyer may not hold funds to coerce a client into accepting the lawyer's contention. The disputed portion of the funds must be kept in a trust account and the lawyer should suggest means for prompt resolution of the dispute, such as arbitration. The undisputed portion of the funds shall be promptly distributed.

[4] Paragraph (e) also recognizes that third parties may have lawful claims against specific funds or other property in a lawyer's custody, such as a client's creditor who has a lien on funds recovered in a personal injury action. A lawyer may have a duty under applicable law to protect such third-party claims against wrongful interference by the client. In such cases, when the third-party claim is not frivolous under applicable law, the lawyer must refuse to surrender the property to the client until the claims are resolved. A lawyer should not unilaterally assume to arbitrate a dispute between the client and the third party, but, when there are substantial grounds for dispute as to the person entitled to the funds, the lawyer may file an action to have a court resolve the dispute.

[5] The obligations of a lawyer under this Rule are independent of those arising from activity other than rendering legal services. For example, a lawyer who serves only as an escrow agent is governed by the applicable law relating to fiduciaries even though the lawyer does not render legal services in the transaction and is not governed by this Rule.

[6] A lawyers' fund for client protection provides a means through the collective efforts of the bar to reimburse persons who have lost money or property as a result of dishonest conduct of a lawyer. Where such a fund has been established, a lawyer must participate where it is mandatory, and, even when it is voluntary, the lawyer should participate.

Canon and Code Antecedents

ABA Canons of Professional Ethics: Canon 11 provided as follows:

11. Dealing with Trust Property

> The lawyer should refrain from any action whereby for his personal benefit or gain he abuses or takes advantage of the confidence reposed in him by his client.
>
> Money of the client or collected for the client or other trust property coming into the possession of the lawyer should be reported and accounted for promptly, and should not under any circumstances be commingled with his own or be used by him.

ABA Model Code of Professional Responsibility: Compare DR 9-102(A) and DR 9-102(B) (reprinted later in this volume).

Cross-References in Other Rules

Rule 1.16, Comment 9: "Even if the lawyer has been unfairly discharged by the client, a lawyer must take all reasonable steps to mitigate the consequences to the client. The lawyer may retain papers as security for a fee only to the extent permitted by law. See **Rule 1.15**."

Rule 1.18, Comment 9: "For a lawyer's duties when a prospective client entrusts valuables or papers to the lawyer's care, see **Rule 1.15**."

Legislative History of Model Rule 1.15

1980 Discussion Draft (then Rule 1.12) provided in (a) that funds "shall be kept in a trust account." Subparagraph (d) provided:

> (d) When a lawyer and another person both have interests in property, the property shall be treated by the lawyer as trust property until an accounting and severance of their interests. If a dispute arises concerning their respective interests, the portion in dispute shall be treated as trust property until the dispute is resolved.

1981 and ***1982 Drafts*** were substantially the same as adopted.

1983 Rule: As originally adopted in 1983, Rule 1.15 consisted of only three paragraphs, which are today designated (a), (d), and (e). (Paragraphs (b) and (c) were not added until 2002.) Paragraphs (a) and (d) remain in their original form. The 1983 version of today's Rule 1.15(e) provided as follows:

> When in the course of representation a lawyer is in the possession of property in which both the lawyer and another person claim interests, the property shall be kept separate by the lawyer until there is an accounting and severance of their interests. If a dispute arises concerning their respective interest, the portion in dispute shall be kept separate by the lawyer until the dispute is resolved.

2002 Amendments: In 2002, the ABA House of Delegates adopted without change the ABA Ethics 2000 Commission proposal to amend Rule 1.15 and its Comment. The amendments added Rule 1.15(b) and (c), significantly revised Rule 1.15(e), added Comment 2, and amended the remaining Comments in relatively minor ways.

Selected State Variations

Editors' Note. Most state versions of Rule 1.15 diverge substantially from ABA Model Rule 1.15. The state variations tend to be lengthy (often several pages), highly detailed, and idiosyncratic. We reprint below only a small selection of the state variations on Rule 1.15.

Arizona permits lawyers to accept credit card payments to cover advance fees, costs, and expenses.

Colorado: Effective February 10, 2011, Rule 1.15(l) contains a special provision governing the handling of records and files when a lawyer departs from a firm. Rule 1.16(a) describes record retention obligations in elaborate detail.

District of Columbia: The language of D.C. Rule 1.15 differs significantly from the ABA Model Rule, though the basic requirements are the same.

Florida: Chapter 5 of Florida's Supreme Court Rules regulates lawyer trust accounts.

Georgia: Rule 1.15(I) generally tracks the 1983 version of ABA Model Rule 1.15, but Georgia adds Rule 1.15(II) to govern trust accounts and IOLTA accounts, and Rule 1.15(III) to govern trust account recordkeeping, overdraft notification, and auditing by disciplinary authorities. Rule 1.15(III) requires that lawyers deposit trust funds in a financial institution that agrees "to report to the State Disciplinary Board whenever any properly payable instrument is presented against a lawyer trust account containing insufficient funds, and the instrument is not honored." The Comment to Rule 1.15(III) explains the overdraft agreement as follows:

> [2] The overdraft agreement requires that all overdrafts be reported to the Office of General Counsel of the State Bar of Georgia whether or not the instrument is honored. It is improper for a lawyer to accept "overdraft privileges" or any other arrangement for a personal loan on a client trust account, particularly in exchange for the institution's promise to delay or not to report an overdraft. . . .
>
> [3] The overdraft notification provision is not intended to result in the discipline of every lawyer who overdraws a trust account. The lawyer or institution may explain occasional errors. The provision merely intends that the Office of General Counsel receive an early warning of improprieties so that corrective action, including audits for cause, may be taken.

Illinois: Effective September 1, 2011, Rule 1.15(c) provides that an "agreement for an advance payment retainer" must be in writing, signed by the client, and include a number of disclosures regarding how the lawyer intends to handle the advance payment. Comment 3B instructs lawyers to read the provision in conjunction with *Dowling v. Chicago Options Associates, Inc.*, 226 Ill. 2d 277 (2007), which distinguishes different types of retainers. According to the Comment, an "advance payment retainer" is "a present payment to the lawyer in exchange for the commitment to provide legal services in the future. Ownership of this retainer passes to the lawyer immediately upon payment."

Rule 1.15(j) contains a highly unusual provision, originally adopted in 1998 at the urging of the real estate bar, which under certain circumstances permits lawyers to hold funds that have been "deposited but not collected' in a separate Real Estate Funds Account (REFA).

Massachusetts: Rule 1.15 has extensive provisions for deposit of client funds in IOLTA accounts, and contains provisions to ensure that disciplinary authorities are notified in the event a lawyer's check is dishonored.

Michigan provides for IOLTA accounts in Rule 1.15(d) and for Trust Account Overdraft Notification in Rule 1.15(A).

Minnesota: Rule 1.15 differs significantly in structure and substance from ABA Model Rule 1.15.

New Jersey: Under Rule 1.15(a), funds must be deposited in New Jersey institutions, without exception. Rule 1.15(a) also incorporates the substance of ABA Model Rule 1.15(b), and requires lawyers to keep trust account records for seven years. New Jersey deletes ABA Model Rule 1.15(c), and New Jersey Rule 1.15(b) deletes the requirement in ABA Model Rule 1.15(d) that a lawyer promptly render a full accounting of property upon request. New Jersey adds 1.15(d), which refers lawyers to section 1:21-6 of the Court Rules on recordkeeping.

New York: Rule 1.15 addresses the same issues as the Model Rule, but in more detail. For example, New York imposes a seven-year recordkeeping requirement for eight specified categories of documents, such as "records of all deposits in and withdrawals from" trust accounts, and copies of "all retainer and compensation agreements with clients," "all bills rendered to clients," and "all records showing payments to lawyers, investigators or other persons, not in the lawyer's regular employ, for services rendered or performed."

Ohio: Rule 1.15 differs significantly from ABA Model Rule 1.15. Among other things, Rule 1.15(f) provides as follows: "Upon dissolution of any law firm, the former partners, managing partners, or supervisory lawyers shall promptly account for all client funds and shall make appropriate arrangements for one of them to maintain all records. . . . " Rule 1.15(h) imposes strict requirements on every lawyer or law firm that "owns an interest in a business that provides a law-related service. . . . "

Pennsylvania: The Pennsylvania rules include requirements and definitions that are far more detailed and nuanced than the Model Rule.

Vermont: Rule 1.15B requires lawyers to "maintain a pooled interest-bearing trust account for deposit of client funds that are not reasonably expected to earn a substantial amount of interest for the client, individually or in combination with other client funds held by the lawyer or law firm." The interest from the fund must be paid to the Vermont Bar Foundation, which uses most of the funds to support "legal services for the disadvantaged" and the remainder "for public education relating to the courts and legal matters."

Virginia: Effective June 23, 2011, Rule 1.15 differs significantly from the Model Rule and includes requirements that were carried forward from Virginia's former Code of Professional Responsibility.

Washington: Rule 1.15A(e) provides that a lawyer "must promptly provide a written accounting to a client or third person after distribution of property or upon request. A lawyer must provide at least annually a written accounting to a client or third person for whom the lawyer is holding funds."

Wisconsin: Rule 1.15 is so highly detailed and so long (about 16 pages) that it has its own table of contents. Rule 1.15(a) defines 10 separate terms (such as "Demand account," "Fiduciary property," and "Financial institution"). Rule 1.15(b)(4) provides: "Unearned fees and advanced payments of fees shall be held in trust until earned by the lawyer. . . . Funds advanced by a client or 3rd party for payment of costs shall be held in trust until the costs are incurred." Particularly interesting is Rule 1.15(e)(4), which elaborates on a series of "Prohibited transactions," including:

> a. **Cash.** No disbursement of cash shall be made from a trust account or from a deposit to a trust account, and no check shall be made payable to "Cash."

b. **Telephone transfers.** No deposits or disbursements shall be made to or from a pooled trust account by a telephone transfer of funds. This section does not prohibit any of the following: (1) wire transfers, and (2) telephone transfers between separate, non-pooled demand and separate, non-pooled, non-demand trust accounts that a lawyer maintains for a particular client.

c. **Internet transactions.** A lawyer shall not make deposits to or disbursements from a trust account by way of an Internet transaction.

d. **Electronic transfers by 3rd parties.** A lawyer shall not authorize a 3rd party to electronically withdraw funds from a trust account. A lawyer shall not authorize a 3rd party to deposit funds into the lawyer's trust account through a form of electronic deposit that allows the 3rd party making the deposit to withdraw the funds without the permission of the lawyer.

e. **Credit card transactions.** A lawyer shall not authorize transactions by way of credit card to or from a trust account. However, earned fees may be deposited by way of credit card to a lawyer's business account. . . .

Related Materials

ABA Commission on Interest on Lawyers' Trust Accounts: In 1986, to support the initiation and operation of IOLTA programs (see entry on "IOLTA Programs" below), the ABA created a nine-member ABA Commission on IOLTA, which (1) collects, maintains, analyzes, and disseminates information on programs involving the use of interest on lawyers' trust accounts for the support of law-related public service activities; (2) recommends ABA policies for creating and operating IOLTA programs; (3) maintains liaisons with state IOLTA programs; (4) oversees the IOLTA Clearing-house, which provides information, materials, and technical assistance on IOLTA program design and operation; and (5) monitors developments in areas that may affect IOLTA operations, such as banking law, grant-making law, tax law, and constitutional law. For additional information about IOLTA, visit *http://www.americanbar.org/groups/interest_lawyers_trust_accounts.html.*

ABA Financial Recordkeeping Rule: In 1993, to provide guidance for complying with Model Rule 1.15, the ABA approved a Model Financial Recordkeeping Rule. It required lawyers to maintain nine categories of records and to retain them for five years after a representation ended. The rule also provided guidelines for deposits, withdrawals, and bookkeeping, and for handling lawyer trust accounts upon dissolution of a law firm or sale of a law practice. In 2010, the ABA replaced the Financial Recordkeeping Rule with the ABA Model Rules for Client Trust Accounts (see entry below).

ABA Formal Ethics Opinions: See ABA Formal Ethics Ops. 92-369 (1992), 02-427 (2002), 11-460 n.9 (2011).

ABA Model Rules for Client Trust Account Records: At its August 2010 Annual Meeting, the ABA approved Model Rules for Client Trust Account Records (which replace the ABA Financial Recordkeeping Rule—see entry above). The new Model Rules, which expressly refer to ABA Model Rule 1.15, consist of five separate rules (with explanatory comments) entitled "Recordkeeping Generally," "Trust Account Safeguards," "Availability of Funds," "Dissolution of Law Firm," and "Sale of Law Practice." The Model Rules for Client Trust Account Records are available online at. *http://www.americanbar.org/content/dam/aba/migrated/2011_build/professional_responsibility/adopted_8_10_10.authcheckdam.pdf*.

ABA Model Rules for Lawyers' Funds for Client Protection: Some lawyers steal from their clients, and lawyers who steal from clients often lack sufficient financial resources to make restitution to their victims. The organized bar has responded by creating Client Protection Funds to provide necessary reimbursement. (For more information, see the entry below on "Client Protection Funds.") The ABA Model Rules for Lawyers' Funds for Client Protection seek to establish standards for effective financing and efficient administration of such funds to achieve meaningful, prompt, and cost-free reimbursement to clients who have been injured by a lawyer's dishonest conduct. The ABA originally adopted these rules in 1981 under the name Model Rules for Clients' Security Funds. In 1989, the ABA amended the rules and renamed them the Model Rules for Lawyers' Funds for Client Protection to avoid confusion about the word "security" (which could mean a stock or bond).

In 2006, the ABA House of Delegates amended Rules 1 and 10 of the Model Rules for Lawyers' Funds for Client Protection to respond to the 2002 amendments to ABA Model Rules 5.5 and 8.5 (both of which relate to multijurisdictional practice). The amended Model Rules for Lawyers' Funds for Client Protection are available online at *http://www.americanbar.org/groups/professional_responsibility/resources/client_protection/rule1.html.*

ABA Random Audit Rule: In 1993, by the narrow vote of 110 to 105, the ABA House of Delegates approved a Model Rule for the Random Audit of Lawyer Trust Accounts. The rule was opposed by the ABA Section on General Practice, which is composed mainly of sole practitioners and small firms. The Random Audit Rule and its Comment, available at *http://www.americanbar.org/groups/professional_responsibility/resources/client_protection/apreface.html,* provide in pertinent part as follows:

Random Audits of Lawyer Trust Accounts

[R]andom audits are a proven deterrent to the misuse of money and property in the practice of law. The examination of trust accounts by court-paid auditors also provides practitioners with expert and practical assistance in maintaining necessary records and supporting books of account.

1. The [highest court of the jurisdiction] shall approve procedures to randomly select lawyer or law firm trust accounts for audit.

2. An audit of a lawyer or law firm trust account conducted pursuant to this rule shall be commenced by the issuance of an investigative subpoena to compel the production of records relating to a lawyer's or law firm's trust accounts. . . .

5. In the event that the audit report asserts deficiencies in the audited lawyer's or law firm's records or procedures, the lawyer or law firm shall, within [10] business days after receipt of the report, provide evidence that the alleged deficiencies are incorrect, or that they have been corrected. . . .

6. All records produced for an audit conducted pursuant to this rule shall remain confidential, and their contents shall not be disclosed in violation of the attorney-client privilege.

7. Records produced for an audit conducted pursuant to this rule may be disclosed to:

(1) the lawyer disciplinary agency or to a court to the extent disclosure is necessary for the purposes of the particular audit;

(2) the lawyer disciplinary agency for the purposes of a disciplinary proceeding; and

(3) any other person, including a law enforcement agency, with the permission of the [highest court of the jurisdiction]. . . .

COMMENT

The Model Rule [for the Random Audit of Lawyer Trust Accounts] proposes a basic structure and system for a random audit program, including such procedural safeguards as adequate prior notice before the commencement of an audit; written audit reports; the opportunity for an audited lawyer or law firm to respond to an examiner's report; the preservation of confidentiality for law client records; and the frequency of audits conducted by random selection. . . .

ABA Standards for Imposing Lawyer Sanctions:

4.11. Disbarment is generally appropriate when a lawyer knowingly converts client property and causes injury or potential injury to a client.

4.12. Suspension is generally appropriate when a lawyer knows or should know that he is dealing improperly with client property and causes injury or potential injury to a client.

4.13. Reprimand is generally appropriate when a lawyer is negligent in dealing with client property and causes injury or potential injury to a client.

4.14. Admonition is generally appropriate when a lawyer is negligent in dealing with client property and causes little or no actual or potential injury to a client.

ABA Standing Committee on Client Protection: The ABA Standing Committee on Client Protection was established in 1984 by merging the ABA Standing Committee on Unauthorized Practice of Law with the ABA Standing Committee on Clients' Security Funds. The Committee's mission is to develop and strengthen mechanisms to protect clients from lawyers who misappropriate client funds. The Standing Committee has been influential in persuading states to establish lawyers' funds for client protection. (See "Client Protection Funds" entry below for more information.) The Standing Committee also promotes consumer and governmental interests in prohibiting or regulating nonlawyers who engage in law-related activities, which raises issues such as the interstate practice of law, the provision of legal services by nonlawyers, and the investment in law firms by nonlawyers. Finally, the Standing Committee on Client Protection sponsors educational programs, provides on-site consultations, develops model rules, and conducts surveys. For more information, see *http://www.americanbar.org/groups/professional_responsibility/committees_commissions/standing_committee_on_client_ protection.html.*.

Client Protection Funds: In keeping with Comment 6 to Rule 1.15, every jurisdiction has established a client protection fund (once called a "client security fund"). The purpose of these funds is to reimburse clients who have lost money or property as a result of dishonest conduct by lawyers. For example, Chapter 7 of Rules Regulating the Florida Bar authorizes establishment of a Clients' Security Fund "to provide monetary relief to persons who suffer reimbursable losses as a result of misappropriation, embezzlement, or other wrongful taking or conversion" by a Florida lawyer. For further information about client protection funds, see the website of the National Client Protection Organization at *www.ncpo.org.*

IOLTA Programs: ABA Model Rule 1.15(a) requires lawyers to hold funds belonging to clients or others in a special separate account, often referred to as a "lawyer trust account." (Common examples of such funds include a down payment on a house, an advance payment of attorney fees, or a settlement check.) Every state has a rule equivalent to Rule 1.15(a). However, since some client and third-party funds are too small or are held for too short a time to justify opening a separate bank account, lawyers usually pool these small or short-term funds in a single trust account. For many years, lawyers deposited these pooled funds into non-interest-bearing accounts because it was difficult to allocate small amounts of interest to individual clients or third parties.

In the late 1970s, however, states began requiring lawyers to deposit these small or short-term funds into interest-bearing accounts at banks that agreed to remit the interest directly to a special state-administered fund created for this purpose. (The first such program was created by Florida in 1978.) The programs establishing and administering these special state funds are typically referred to as "IOLTA" programs, which stands for "interest on lawyer trust accounts" (or in some states simply as "IOLA" programs). IOLTA funds are often governed by detailed statutes, court rules, and/or administrative regulations. For an example, see the IOLTA rules of the Ohio Legal Assistance Foundation (OLAF) at *www.olaf.org*, and see Ohio Stat. §§4705.09 and 4705.10. By 1995, every state had adopted some form of IOLTA program. About forty-three (43) of these IOLTA programs are mandatory (meaning every attorney must maintain an IOLTA account absent a specific exemption in the governing statute or rules); seven (7) are "opt-out" (meaning every lawyer must participate unless the lawyer affirmatively opts out); and one (1) is "opt-in" (meaning that no lawyer participates unless the lawyer voluntarily and affirmatively opts in). A chart showing the status of IOLTA programs in all U.S. jurisdictions is available online at *http://www.americanbar.org/groups/interest_lawyers_trust_accounts/resources/status_of_iolta_programs.html.*

Many state IOLTA programs generate millions of dollars per year, though the amounts have declined in recent years due to low interest rates. In Illinois, for example, the IOLTA program awarded $12.5 million in grants in fiscal 2009, but that amount dropped to $7.7 million in fiscal 2010, $7.5 million in fiscal 2011, and $7.2 million in fiscal 2012—see *www.ltf.org* (click on "Grant Information"). New Jersey's IOLTA Fund disbursed $14.3 million in grants in 2004 and $50.8 million in grants in 2007, but only $13.7 million in 2010 as interest rates plunged—see *www.ioltanj.org/grnt_home.html.* Since the inception of New Jersey's IOLTA Fund in 1988, it has distributed over $359 million in total grants. Nationwide, total IOLTA grants from all jurisdictions were $240 million in 2007 and $263.4 million in 2008, but fell to only $124.7 million in 2009 (the most recent year for which statistics are available). Funds are generally distributed to legal services offices, law school clinics, and other programs that provide legal services to the poor. For more information about IOLTA programs, see *http://www.iolta.org/.*

In the mid-1990s, the Washington Legal Foundation challenged mandatory IOLTA programs, arguing that such programs constituted an unconstitutional "taking" of client property (the interest) without compensation, thus violating the Fifth Amendment. Two cases reached the United States Supreme Court. In *Phillips v. Washington Legal Foundation,* 524 U.S. 156 (1998), the Court held (by a 5-4 decision) that the interest on lawyer trust accounts was "property" for purposes of the Takings Clause, but the Court remanded the case for a determination of whether there had been a "taking" (and, if so, what constituted just compensation). In *Brown v. Legal Foundation of Washington,* 538 U.S. 216 (2003) (also a 5-4 decision), the Court held that Washington's mandatory IOLTA plan constituted a "public use," was not a "taking," and did not entitle clients to any compensation for the interest earned on IOLTA accounts. Since that decision, which made clear that mandatory IOLTA programs did not violate the Takings Clause, nearly 40 states have converted their IOLTA programs from 'opt-out' or 'opt-in' programs to mandatory programs.

In 2008, the Federal Deposit Insurance Corporation (FDIC) extended unlimited deposit insurance coverage to client funds deposited in IOLTA accounts at participating financial institutions. The FDIC extended this unlimited coverage until December 31, 2010. Congress then amended the Federal Deposit Insurance Act, extending this unlimited coverage through December 31, 2012. Until then, all IOLTA accounts in all insured depository institutions are insured in full by the FDIC and are backed by the full faith and credit of the United States government. For more information about unlimited coverage and its history, see *www.fdic.gov/regulations/resources/TLGP.*

Model Rules of Professional Conduct for Federal Lawyers add a new subparagraph (d) that provides: "When property of a client or third party is admitted into evidence or otherwise included in the record of a proceeding, the Federal lawyer should take reasonable action to ensure its prompt return."

Money Laundering and Terrorist Financing: At its August 2010 Annual Meeting, the ABA House of Delegates approved a resolution adopting Voluntary Good Practices Guidance for Lawyers to Detect and Combat Money Laundering and Terrorist Financing, and encouraging state, local, and specialty bar associations "to embrace the Good Practices Guidance and to educate legal professionals and law students regarding the risks addressed by the Guidance." The Guidelines were accompanied by a lengthy report that explains the background of money laundering and terrorist financing and provides practice pointers to lawyers. Some of the Good Practices Guidelines concern lawyer trust accounts.

National Client Protection Organization (NCPO): The National Client Protection Organization, Inc. (NCPO) is a not-for-profit membership corporation that was organized in 1998. NCPO is primarily an educational resource facilitating the exchange of information among lawyers' funds for client protection throughout the United States and Canada. NCPO's purposes include providing help and support to client protection funds and developing and implementing programs to protect legal consumers from dishonest conduct by lawyers and their employees. In 2006, NCPO adopted Standards for Evaluating Lawyers' Funds for Client Protection. For more information, including the Standards and a map of client protection funds in the United States, visit NCPO's website at *www.ncpo.org.*

Restatement of the Law Governing Lawyers: See Restatement §§43-46 in our chapter on the Restatement later in this volume.

Rule 1.16 Declining or Terminating Representation

(a) Except as stated in paragraph (c), a lawyer shall not represent a client or, where representation has commenced, shall withdraw from the representation of a client if:

(1) the representation will result in violation of the rules of professional conduct or other law;

(2) the lawyer's physical or mental condition materially impairs the lawyer's ability to represent the client; or

(3) the lawyer is discharged.

(b) Except as stated in paragraph (c), a lawyer may withdraw from representing a client if:

(1) withdrawal can be accomplished without material adverse effect on the interests of the client;

(2) the client persists in a course of action involving the lawyer's services that the lawyer reasonably believes is criminal or fraudulent;

(3) the client has used the lawyer's services to perpetrate a crime or fraud;

(4) the client insists upon taking action that the lawyer considers repugnant or with which the lawyer has a fundamental disagreement;

(5) the client fails substantially to fulfill an obligation to the lawyer regarding the lawyer's services and has been given reasonable warning that the lawyer will withdraw unless the obligation is fulfilled;

(6) the representation will result in an unreasonable financial burden on the lawyer or has been rendered unreasonably difficult by the client; or

(7) other good cause for withdrawal exists. 3.1

(c) A lawyer must comply with applicable law requiring notice to or permission of a tribunal when terminating a representation. When ordered to do so by a tribunal, a lawyer shall continue representation notwithstanding good cause for terminating the representation.

(d) Upon termination of representation, a lawyer shall take steps to the extent reasonably practicable to protect a client's interests, such as giving reasonable notice to the client, allowing time for employment of other counsel, surrendering papers and property to which the client is entitled and refunding any advance payment of fee or expense that has not been earned or incurred. The lawyer may retain papers relating to the client to the extent permitted by other law.

1.2 ct 10- noisy withdraw

COMMENT

[1] A lawyer should not accept representation in a matter unless it can be performed competently, promptly, without improper conflict of interest and to completion. Ordinarily, a representation in a matter is completed when the agreed-upon assistance has been concluded. See Rules 1.2(c) and 6.5. See also Rule 1.3, Comment [4].

see 6.2

Mandatory Withdrawal

[2] A lawyer ordinarily must decline or withdraw from representation if the client demands that the lawyer engage in conduct that is illegal or violates the Rules of Professional Conduct or other law. The lawyer is not obliged to decline or withdraw simply because the client suggests such a course of conduct; a client may make such a suggestion in the hope that a lawyer will not be constrained by a professional obligation.

[3] When a lawyer has been appointed to represent a client, withdrawal ordinarily requires approval of the appointing authority. See also Rule 6.2. Similarly, court approval or notice to the court is often required by applicable law before a

lawyer withdraws from pending litigation. Difficulty may be encountered if withdrawal is based on the client's demand that the lawyer engage in unprofessional conduct. The court may request an explanation for the withdrawal, while the lawyer may be bound to keep confidential the facts that would constitute such an explanation. The lawyer's statement that professional considerations require termination of the representation ordinarily should be accepted as sufficient. Lawyers should be mindful of their obligations to both clients and the court under Rules 1.6 and 3.3.

Discharge

[4] A client has a right to discharge a lawyer at any time, with or without cause, subject to liability for payment for the lawyer's services. Where future dispute about the withdrawal may be anticipated, it may be advisable to prepare a written statement reciting the circumstances.

[5] Whether a client can discharge appointed counsel may depend on applicable law. A client seeking to do so should be given a full explanation of the consequences. These consequences may include a decision by the appointing authority that appointment of successor counsel is unjustified, thus requiring self-representation by the client.

[6] If the client has severely diminished capacity, the client may lack the legal capacity to discharge the lawyer, and in any event the discharge may be seriously adverse to the client's interests. The lawyer should make special effort to help the client consider the consequences and may take reasonably necessary protective action as provided in Rule 1.14.

Optional Withdrawal

[7] A lawyer may withdraw from representation in some circumstances. The lawyer has the option to withdraw if it can be accomplished without material adverse effect on the client's interests. Withdrawal is also justified if the client persists in a course of action that the lawyer reasonably believes is criminal or fraudulent, for a lawyer is not required to be associated with such conduct even if the lawyer does not further it. Withdrawal is also permitted if the lawyer's services were misused in the past even if that would materially prejudice the client. The lawyer may also withdraw where the client insists on taking action that the lawyer considers repugnant or with which the lawyer has a fundamental disagreement.

[8] A lawyer may withdraw if the client refuses to abide by the terms of an agreement relating to the representation, such as an agreement concerning fees or court costs or an agreement limiting the objectives of the representation.

Assisting the Client upon Withdrawal

[9] Even if the lawyer has been unfairly discharged by the client, a lawyer must take all reasonable steps to mitigate the consequences to the client. The lawyer may retain papers as security for a fee only to the extent permitted by law. See Rule 1.15.

Canon and Code Antecedents

ABA Canons of Professional Ethics: Canons 7 and 44 provided as follows:

7. Professional Colleagues and Conflicts of Opinion

A client's proffer of assistance of additional counsel should not be regarded as evidence of want of confidence, but the matter should be left to the determination of the client. A lawyer should decline association as colleague if it is objectionable to the original counsel, but if the lawyer first retained is relieved, another may come into the case.

When lawyers jointly associated in a cause cannot agree as to any matter vital to the interest of the client, the conflict of opinion should be frankly stated to him for his final determination. His decision should be accepted unless the nature of the difference makes it impracticable for the lawyer whose judgment has been overruled to co-operate effectively. In this event it is his duty to ask the client to relieve him.

Efforts, direct or indirect, in any way to encroach upon the professional employment of another lawyer, are unworthy of those who should be brethren at the Bar; but, nevertheless, it is the right of any lawyer, without fear or favor, to give proper advice to those seeking relief against unfaithful or neglectful counsel, generally after communication with the lawyer of whom the complaint is made.

44. Withdrawal from Employment as Attorney or Counsel

The right of an attorney or counsel to withdraw from employment, once assumed, arises only from good cause. Even the desire or consent of the client is not always sufficient. The lawyer should not throw up the unfinished task to the detriment of his client except for reasons of honor or self-respect. If the client insists upon an unjust or immoral course in the conduct of his case, or if he persists over the attorney's remonstrance in presenting frivolous defenses, or if he deliberately disregards an agreement or obligation as to fees or expenses, the lawyer may be warranted in withdrawing on due notice to the client, allowing him time to employ another lawyer. So also when a lawyer discovers that his client has no case and the client is determined to continue it; or even if the lawyer finds himself incapable of conducting the case effectively. Sundry other instances may arise in which withdrawal is to be justified. Upon withdrawing from a case after a retainer has been paid, the attorney should refund such part of the retainer as has not been clearly earned.

ABA Model Code of Professional Responsibility: Compare DR 2-109(A), DR 2-110(A), DR 2-110(B), and DR 2-110(C) (reprinted later in this volume).

Cross-References in Other Rules

Rule 1.2, Comment 2: When a lawyer and client disagree, the "lawyer should also consult with the client and seek a mutually acceptable resolution of the disagreement. If such efforts are unavailing and the lawyer has a fundamental disagreement with the client, the lawyer may withdraw from the representation. See **Rule 1.16(b)(4)**. Conversely, the client may resolve the disagreement by discharging the lawyer. See **Rule 1.16(a)(3)**."

Rule 1.2, Comment 10: "A lawyer may not continue assisting a client in conduct that the lawyer originally supposed was legally proper but then discovers is criminal or fraudulent. The lawyer must, therefore, withdraw from the representation of the client in the matter. See **Rule 1.16(a)**."

Rule 1.3, Comment 4: "Unless the relationship is terminated as provided in **Rule 1.16,** a lawyer should carry through to conclusion all matters undertaken for a client."

Rule 1.5, Comment 4: "A lawyer may require advance payment of a fee, but is obliged to return any unearned portion. See **Rule 1.16(d)**."

Rule 1.6, Comment 7: "See also **Rule 1.16** with respect to the lawyer's obligation or right to withdraw from the representation of the client in such circumstances. . . ."

Rule 1.7, Comment 4: "If a conflict arises after representation has been undertaken, the lawyer ordinarily must withdraw from the representation, unless the lawyer has obtained the informed consent of the client under the conditions of paragraph (b). See **Rule 1.16.**"

Rule 1.7, Comment 5: When unforeseeable circumstances create conflicts the "lawyer must seek court approval where necessary and take steps to minimize harm to the clients. See **Rule 1.16.**"

Rule 1.7, Comment 33: Each client in the common representation "has the right to discharge the lawyer as stated in **Rule 1.16.**"

Rule 1.13, Comment 6: When a lawyer's services are being used to further a crime or fraud, Rule 1.6 may permit the lawyer to reveal confidential information and Rule 1.2(d) may also be applicable, "in which event, withdrawal from the representation under **Rule 1.16(a)(1)** may be required."

Rule 1.13, Comment 6: "[T]his Rule does not limit or expand the lawyer's responsibility under Rule 1.8, **1.16**, 3.3 or 4.1."

Rule 1.17, Comment 12: "If approval of the substitution of the purchasing lawyer for the selling lawyer is required by the rules of any tribunal in which a matter is pending, such approval must be obtained before the matter can be included in the sale (see **Rule 1.16**)."

Rule 3.3, Comment 15: "The lawyer may . . . be required by **Rule 1.16(a)** to seek permission of the tribunal to withdraw if the lawyer's compliance with this Rule's duty of candor results in such an extreme deterioration of the client-lawyer relationship that the lawyer can no longer competently represent the client. Also see **Rule 1.16(b)** for the circumstances in which a lawyer will be permitted to seek a tribunal's permission to withdraw."

Legislative History of Model Rule 1.16

1980 Discussion Draft: Rule 1.16(b) provided:

> (b) Except as stated in paragraph (c), a lawyer may withdraw from representing a client if:
>
> (1) Withdrawal can be effected without material prejudice to the client;
>
> (2) The client persists in a course of conduct that is illegal or unjust; or
>
> (3) The client fails to fulfill an obligation to the lawyer regarding the lawyer's services.

1981 and *1982 Drafts* were substantially the same as adopted.

1983 Rule: From its original adoption in 1983 until its amendment in 2002, Rule 1.16 was nearly the same as the 2002 version. Only two provisions differed in any substantive way from the 2002 version. The 1983 counterpart to the 2002 version of Rule 1.16(b)(4) permitted withdrawal if "a client insists upon pursuing an objective that the lawyer considers repugnant or imprudent," and the 1983 version of Rule 1.16(c) provided simply: "When ordered to do so by a tribunal, a lawyer shall continue representation notwithstanding good cause for terminating the representation," which is identical to the second sentence of the 2002 version.

2002 Amendments: At its February 2002 Mid-Year Meeting, the ABA House of Delegates adopted without change the ABA Ethics 2000 Commission proposal to amend Rule 1.16 and its Comment. The most significant change was the deletion in Rule 1.16(b)(4) of the word "imprudent." A lawyer may no longer withdraw or seek permission to withdraw because the client wishes to pursue a course of action the lawyer considers merely "imprudent."

Selected State Variations

Arizona: Rule 1.16(d) adds that "upon the client's request, the lawyer shall provide the client with all of the client's documents, and all documents reflecting work performed for the client. The lawyer may retain documents reflecting work performed for the client to the extent permitted by other law only if retaining them would not prejudice the client's rights."

California: Rule 3-700 allows a lawyer to withdraw if a client "by other conduct renders it unreasonably difficult for the member to carry out the employment effectively" or if the client "breaches an agreement or obligation to the member as to expenses or fees." A lawyer may also withdraw if the "inability to work with co-counsel indicates that the best interests of the client likely will be served by withdrawal."

Connecticut: Connecticut adds the following sentence at the end of Rule 1.16(d): "If the representation of the client is terminated either by the lawyer withdrawing from representation or by the client discharging the lawyer, the lawyer shall confirm the termination in writing to the client before or within a reasonable time after the termination of the representation."

Florida: In Rule 1.16(a), Florida also requires withdrawal if:

> (4) the client persists in a course of action involving the lawyer's services that the lawyer reasonably believes is criminal or fraudulent, unless the client agrees to disclose and rectify the crime or fraud; or
>
> (5) the client has used the lawyer's services to perpetrate a crime or fraud, unless the client agrees to disclose and rectify the crime or fraud.

Florida Rule 1.16(b)(2) adds that a lawyer may withdraw if the client insists upon taking action that the lawyer considers "imprudent." Rule 1.16(d) provides that, upon termination, a lawyer may retain papers "and other property relating to or belonging to the client" to the extent permitted by law.

Florida also adds Rule 4-5.8, which has no Model Rule counterpart. The rule governs a lawyer's communications to clients when the lawyer ceases to represent a client as a result of the lawyer's departure from a law firm.

Louisiana: Rule 1.16(d) adds the following:

> Upon written request by the client, the lawyer shall promptly release to the client or the client's new lawyer the entire file relating to the matter. The lawyer may retain a copy of the file but shall not condition release over issues relating to the expense of

copying the file or for any other reason. The responsibility for the cost of copying shall be determined in an appropriate proceeding.

Maryland: Rule 1.16(b)(4) permits withdrawal if the client insists upon taking action "or inaction" that the lawyer considers repugnant.

Massachusetts: Rule 1.16(e) provides as follows:

> A lawyer must make available to a former client, within a reasonable time following the client's request for his or her file, the following:
>
> all papers, documents, and other materials the client supplied to the lawyer. The lawyer may at his or her own expense retain copies of any such materials.
>
> all pleadings and other papers filed with or by the court or served by or upon any party. The client may be required to pay any copying charge consistent with the lawyer's actual cost for these materials, unless the client has already paid for such materials.
>
> all investigatory or discovery documents for which the client has paid the lawyer's out-of-pocket costs, including but not limited to medical records, photographs, tapes, disks, investigative reports, expert reports, depositions, and demonstrative evidence. The lawyer may at his or her own expense retain copies of any such materials.
>
> if the lawyer and the client have not entered into a contingent fee agreement, the client is entitled only to that portion of the lawyer's work product (as defined in subparagraph (6) below) for which the client has paid.
>
> if the lawyer and the client have entered into a contingent fee agreement, the lawyer must provide copies of the lawyer's work product (as defined in subparagraph (6) below). The client may be required to pay any copying charge consistent with the lawyer's actual cost for the copying of these materials.
>
> for purposes of this paragraph (e), work product shall consist of documents and tangible things prepared in the course of the representation of the client by the lawyer or at the lawyer's direction by his or her employee, agent, or consultant, and not described in paragraphs (2) or (3) above. Examples of work product include without limitation legal research, records of witness interviews, reports of negotiations, and correspondence.
>
> notwithstanding anything in this paragraph (e) to the contrary, a lawyer may not refuse, on grounds of nonpayment, to make available materials in the client's file when retention would prejudice the client unfairly.

Minnesota deletes the last sentence of Rule 1.16(d) ("The lawyer may retain papers relating to the client to the extent permitted by other law") and adds a detailed set of rules regarding a client's right to documents.

Missouri: Rule 1.16(c) provides that, when a lawyer has filed a limited appearance pursuant to Missouri's version of Rule 1.2(c), the lawyer is not subject to the usual rule regarding termination of representation. Rule 1.16(c) provides as follows:

> A lawyer must comply with applicable law requiring notice to or permission of a tribunal when terminating a representation unless the lawyer has filed a notice of termination of limited appearance. Except when such notice is filed, a lawyer shall continue representation when ordered to do so by a tribunal notwithstanding good cause for terminating the representation.

New Hampshire: New Hampshire makes the protective steps in Rule 1.16(d) a "condition" to terminating a representation.

New York: Rule 1.16(a) and (b) is substantially similar to DR 2-109 and 2-110(B) of the old Model Code, respectively. Rule 1.16(c) adds numerous bases for discretionary withdrawals, which are drawn nearly verbatim from DR 2-110(C) of the old Model Code. Finally, Rule 1.16(d) specifies that, "if permission for withdrawal from employment is required by the rules of a tribunal, a lawyer shall not withdraw from employment in a matter before that tribunal without its permission."

North Carolina: Rule 1.16(b)(4) retains the word "imprudent" and permits withdrawal if the client insists upon taking action "contrary to the advice and judgment of the lawyer. . . . " North Carolina also adds Rule 1.16(b)(8), which permits withdrawal if "the client insists upon presenting a claim or defense that is not warranted under existing law and cannot be supported by good faith argument for an extension, modification, or reversal of existing law."

Texas: Rule 1.15(d) permits a lawyer to retain papers relating to the client to the extent permitted by other law "only if such retention will not prejudice the client in the subject matter of the representation."

Virginia: Rule 1.16(b)(1) replaces "criminal or fraudulent" with "illegal or unjust." Rule 1.16(e) specifies in detail the papers to which a client is entitled after a lawyer withdraws and whether the client or the lawyer must bear the cost of duplication. The client's entitlement does not depend upon "whether or not the client has paid the fees and costs owed a lawyer."

Related Materials

ABA Formal Ethics Opinions: See ABA Formal Ethics Ops. 92-366 (1992), 93-376 (1993), 94-380 (1994), 94-384 (1994), 96-399 (1996), 96-400 (1996), 96-404 (1996), 99-414 (1999), 00-418 n.33 (2000), 03-429 (2003), 03-431 (2003), 06-441 (2006), 07-448 (2007), and 08-450 (2008).

Collaborative Law: The collaborative dispute resolution process (commonly known as "collaborative law") is a voluntary, non-adversarial dispute resolution process for parties represented by counsel. In the collaborative law process, the parties and their attorneys agree in advance to retain attorneys solely to negotiate a settlement, not to litigate. If either party ignores the agreement and goes to court, the attorneys must resign from the case. These terms are usually embodied in a "Participation Agreement" providing that if the parties are unable to reach a settlement, the lawyers will withdraw from the case and assist the clients in transitioning the case to trial attorneys. For more information, see the website of the Global Collaborative Law Council at *http://www.collaborativelaw.us/process.html.*

Model Rules of Professional Conduct for Federal Lawyers: Rule 1.16(c) provides: "When properly ordered to do so by a tribunal or other competent authority, a Federal lawyer shall continue representation notwithstanding good cause for terminating the representation."

Restatement of the Law Governing Lawyers: See Restatement §§31-33, 40, and 46 in our chapter on the Restatement later in this volume.

Rule 1.17 Sale of Law Practice

A lawyer or a law firm may sell or purchase a law practice, or an area of law practice, including good will, if the following conditions are satisfied:

(a) The seller ceases to engage in the private practice of law, or in the area of practice that has been sold, [in the geographic area] [in the jurisdiction] (a jurisdiction may elect either version) in which the practice has been conducted;

(b) The entire practice, or the entire area of practice, is sold to one or more lawyers or law firms;

(c) The seller gives written notice to each of the seller's clients regarding:

(1) the proposed sale;

(2) the client's right to retain other counsel or to take possession of the file; and

(3) the fact that the client's consent to the transfer of the client's files will be presumed if the client does not take any action or does not otherwise object within ninety (90) days of receipt of the notice.

If a client cannot be given notice, the representation of that client may be transferred to the purchaser only upon entry of an order so authorizing by a court having jurisdiction. The seller may disclose to the court in camera information relating to the representation only to the extent necessary to obtain an order authorizing the transfer of a file.

(d) The fees charged clients shall not be increased by reason of the sale.

5.6(b)

COMMENT

[1] The practice of law is a profession, not merely a business. Clients are not commodities that can be purchased and sold at will. Pursuant to this Rule, when a lawyer or an entire firm ceases to practice, or ceases to practice in an area of law, and other lawyers or firms take over the representation, the selling lawyer or firm may obtain compensation for the reasonable value of the practice as may withdrawing partners of law firms. See Rules 5.4 and 5.6.

Termination of Practice by the Seller

[2] The requirement that all of the private practice, or all of an area of practice, be sold is satisfied if the seller in good faith makes the entire practice, or the area of practice, available for sale to the purchasers. The fact that a number of the seller's clients decide not to be represented by the purchasers but take their matters elsewhere, therefore, does not result in a violation. Return to private practice as a result of an unanticipated change in circumstances does not necessarily result in a violation. For example, a lawyer who has sold the practice to accept an appointment to judicial office does not violate the requirement that the sale be attendant to cessation of practice if the lawyer later resumes private practice upon being defeated in a contested or a retention election for the office or resigns from a judiciary position.

[3] The requirement that the seller cease to engage in the private practice of law does not prohibit employment as a lawyer on the staff of a public agency or a

legal services entity that provides legal services to the poor, or as in-house counsel to a business.

[4] The Rule permits a sale of an entire practice attendant upon retirement from the private practice of law within the jurisdiction. Its provisions, therefore, accommodate the lawyer who sells the practice on the occasion of moving to another state. Some states are so large that a move from one locale therein to another is tantamount to leaving the jurisdiction in which the lawyer has engaged in the practice of law. To also accommodate lawyers so situated, states may permit the sale of the practice when the lawyer leaves the geographical area rather than the jurisdiction. The alternative desired should be indicated by selecting one of the two provided for in Rule 1.17(a).

[5] This Rule also permits a lawyer or law firm to sell an area of practice. If an area of practice is sold and the lawyer remains in the active practice of law, the lawyer must cease accepting any matters in the area of practice that has been sold, either as counsel or co-counsel or by assuming joint responsibility for a matter in connection with the division of a fee with another lawyer as would otherwise be permitted by Rule 1.5(e). For example, a lawyer with a substantial number of estate planning matters and a substantial number of probate administration cases may sell the estate planning portion of the practice but remain in the practice of law by concentrating on probate administration; however, that practitioner may not thereafter accept any estate planning matters. Although a lawyer who leaves a jurisdiction or geographical area typically would sell the entire practice, this Rule permits the lawyer to limit the sale to one or more areas of the practice, thereby preserving the lawyer's right to continue practice in the areas of the practice that were not sold.

Sale of Entire Practice or Entire Area of Practice

[6] The Rule requires that the seller's entire practice, or an entire area of practice, be sold. The prohibition against sale of less than an entire practice area protects those clients whose matters are less lucrative and who might find it difficult to secure other counsel if a sale could be limited to substantial fee-generating matters. The purchasers are required to undertake all client matters in the practice or practice area, subject to client consent. This requirement is satisfied, however, even if a purchaser is unable to undertake a particular client matter because of a conflict of interest.

Client Confidences, Consent and Notice

[7] Negotiations between seller and prospective purchaser prior to disclosure of information relating to a specific representation of an identifiable client no more violate the confidentiality provisions of Model Rule 1.6 than do preliminary discussions concerning the possible association of another lawyer or mergers between firms, with respect to which client consent is not required. Providing the purchaser access to client-specific information relating to the representation and to the file, however, requires client consent. The Rule provides that before such information can be disclosed by the seller to the purchaser the client must be given actual written notice of the contemplated sale, including the identity of the purchaser, and

must be told that the decision to consent or make other arrangements must be made within 90 days. If nothing is heard from the client within that time, consent to the sale is presumed.

[8] A lawyer or law firm ceasing to practice cannot be required to remain in practice because some clients cannot be given actual notice of the proposed purchase. Since these clients cannot themselves consent to the purchase or direct any other disposition of their files, the Rule requires an order from a court having jurisdiction authorizing their transfer or other disposition. The Court can be expected to determine whether reasonable efforts to locate the client have been exhausted, and whether the absent client's legitimate interests will be served by authorizing the transfer of the file so that the purchaser may continue the representation. Preservation of client confidences requires that the petition for a court order be considered in camera. (A procedure by which such an order can be obtained needs to be established in jurisdictions in which it presently does not exist.)

[9] All the elements of client autonomy, including the client's absolute right to discharge a lawyer and transfer the representation to another, survive the sale of the practice or area of practice.

Fee Arrangements Between Client and Purchaser

[10] The sale may not be financed by increases in fees charged the clients of the practice. Existing arrangements between the seller and the client as to fees and the scope of the work must be honored by the purchaser.

Other Applicable Ethical Standards

[11] Lawyers participating in the sale of a law practice or a practice area are subject to the ethical standards applicable to involving another lawyer in the representation of a client. These include, for example, the seller's obligation to exercise competence in identifying a purchaser qualified to assume the practice and the purchaser's obligation to undertake the representation competently (see Rule 1.1); the obligation to avoid disqualifying conflicts, and to secure the client's informed consent for those conflicts that can be agreed to (see Rule 1.7 regarding conflicts and Rule 1.0(e) for the definition of informed consent); and the obligation to protect information relating to the representation (see Rules 1.6 and 1.9).

[12] If approval of the substitution of the purchasing lawyer for the selling lawyer is required by the rules of any tribunal in which a matter is pending, such approval must be obtained before the matter can be included in the sale (see Rule 1.16).

Applicability of the Rule

[13] This Rule applies to the sale of a law practice by a deceased, disabled or disappeared lawyer. Thus, the seller may be represented by a non-lawyer representative not subject to these Rules. Since, however, no lawyer may participate in a sale of a law practice which does not conform to the requirements of this Rule, the

representatives of the seller as well as the purchasing lawyer can be expected to see to it that they are met.

[14] Admission to or retirement from a law partnership or professional association, retirement plans and similar arrangements, and a sale of tangible assets of a law practice, do not constitute a sale or purchase governed by this Rule.

[15] This Rule does not apply to the transfers of legal representation between lawyers when such transfers are unrelated to the sale of a practice or an area of practice.

Canon and Code Antecedents

ABA Canons of Professional Ethics: No comparable Canon.

ABA Model Code of Professional Responsibility: No comparable Disciplinary Rule, but EC 4-6 provided that "a lawyer should not attempt to sell a law practice as a going business because . . . to do so would involve the disclosure of confidences and secrets."

Cross-References in Other Rules

Rule 5.4(a)(2) provides that "a lawyer who purchases the practice of a deceased, disabled, or disappeared lawyer may, pursuant to the provisions of **Rule 1.17,** pay to the estate or other representative of that lawyer the agreed-upon purchase price."

Rule 5.6, Comment 3: "This Rule does not apply to prohibit restrictions that may be included in the terms of the sale of a law practice pursuant to **Rule 1.17**."

Rule 7.2(b)(3) permits a lawyer to "pay for a law practice in accordance with **Rule 1.17**."

Legislative History of Model Rule 1.17

1990 Adoption: Rule 1.17 was adopted by the ABA House of Delegates in 1990. It was not proposed in any form in Kutak Commission drafts and was not part of the ABA Model Rules until 1990. As originally adopted, the unnumbered introductory language at the beginning of Rule 1.17 permitted the purchase or sale only of "a law practice," meaning that only an entire law practice could be bought or sold. In addition, Rule 1.17(d) as originally adopted provided that the purchaser may "refuse to undertake the representation unless the client consents to pay the purchaser fees at a rate not exceeding the fees charged by the purchaser for rendering substantially similar services prior to the initiation of the purchase negotiations."

The proposal to add Rule 1.17 to the Model Rules was initiated by the State Bar of California, based on California Rule 2-300, and was joined by the ABA Section of General Practice and the ABA Section of Law Practice Management. The Committee Report submitted to the House of Delegates in support of Rule 1.17 explained the Rule as follows:*

* Committee Reports do not represent official policy of the ABA. They are for information only, and the opinions are those of the authors of the report.

Impetus for Formulation of the Rule

Protection of Clients

[California] Rule of Professional Conduct 2-300 and proposed Model Rule 1.17 are consumer protection measures designed to address the disparity between the treatment of the clients of sole practitioners and the clients of law firms when the attorney handling the client matter leaves the practice, by ensuring that the client matters handled by sole practitioners are attended to when the sole practitioner leaves the practice.

If the attorney leaving the practice is or was part of a law firm, in most cases, the firm continues to handle the matter. In the majority of situations, the transition for the client is very smooth. However, if the attorney was in sole practice, the transition is not so smooth because there is no law firm standing ready to continue to handle the client matter. The clients of sole practitioners who leave the practice of law are relatively unprotected because there are no regulations in place to protect them during the transition.

Sole Practitioners in Unfair Financial Position

In addition to the issues of the client protection, sole practitioners are in an unfair financial position concerning the "good will" of their law practice. The "good will" of a business is "the expectation of continued public patronage." . . . Attorneys, like other business persons, may sell the physical assets of their law practice, such as equipment, the library or the furniture. However, case authority and ethics opinions held that the sale of "good will" of a law practice is unethical and against public policy. . . .

Treatment of "good will" in other contexts presents a mixed picture. For example, attorneys who are members of firms with two or more members may ethically enter into retirement agreements which may require lump sum payments that implicitly include sums for the attorney's share of the firm's "good will."

The estate of a deceased attorney may receive payments from the attorney who completes the unfinished client matters of the deceased attorney. However, in the absence of a rule like that which is being proposed, the payments are limited to the "proportion of the total compensation which fairly represents the services rendered by the deceased member" and thus do not permit an allowance for "good will." . . .

In marital dissolution proceedings, the "good will" of the attorney-spouse's share in his or her law practice may be valued for the purpose of determining the community or other divisible assets.

This inconsistent treatment of "good will" resulted in a series of awkward results: the estate of a sole practitioner could not receive payment for the "good will" of the law practice, while the estate of an attorney who was a member of a law firm could; upon retirement, an attorney who was a member of a law firm could receive compensation including "good will", while the compensation received by a sole practitioner could not include "good will"; the "good will" of a sole practice may be considered an asset of the marital community for purposes of a dissolution, but could not be sold.

2002 Amendments: In 2002, the ABA House of Delegates adopted with some changes the ABA Ethics 2000 Commission proposal to amend Rule 1.17 and its Comment. The proposal as drafted would have allowed the sale only of an "entire practice," but the House of Delegates voted also to allow the sale of "an area of practice." However, the House of Delegates approved the Ethics 2000 Commission proposal to delete language from subparagraph (d) that had permitted a purchaser to refuse to undertake a representation "unless the client consents to pay the purchaser fees at a rate not exceeding the fees charged by the purchaser for rendering substantially similar services prior to the initiation of the purchase negotiations." The amendments also added Comment 5 and amended Comments 1, 2, 4, 6, 9, and 15 to reflect the new right to sell "an area of practice," and deleted most of former Comment 9 and all of former Comment 10, which had provided as follows:

> [9] . . . The purchaser may, however, advise the client that the purchaser will not undertake the representation unless the client consents to pay the higher fees the purchaser usually charges. To prevent client financing of the sale, the higher fee the purchaser may charge must not exceed the fees charged by the purchaser for substantially similar service rendered prior to the initiation of the purchase negotiations.
>
> [10] The purchaser may not intentionally fragment the practice which is the subject of the sale by charging significantly different fees in substantially similar matters. Doing so would make it possible for the purchaser to avoid the obligation to take over the entire practice by charging arbitrarily higher fees for less lucrative matters, thereby increasing the likelihood that those clients would not consent to the new representation.

Selected State Variations

Arkansas adds Rule 1.17(e), which requires the seller to file a detailed and timely affidavit with the Committee on Professional Conduct showing that the seller has complied with the notice provisions of Rule 1.17.

California: Rule 2-300, using different language, addresses the same policy issues as Rule 1.17 and provides that "fees shall not be increased solely by reason of" the sale. "All or substantially all" of a practice may be sold.

Colorado: Rule 1.17(a) is satisfied only if the seller ceases to engage in the private practice of law "in Colorado," or in the area of practice "in Colorado" that has been sold.

Florida omits the requirement in ABA Model Rule 1.17(a) that the seller cease practicing law, and adds or modifies several provisions, including the following:

> (c) *Court Approval Required.* If a representation involves pending litigation, there shall be no substitution of counsel or termination of representation unless authorized by the court. . . .
>
> (d) *Client Objections.* If a client objects to the proposed substitution of counsel, the seller shall comply with the requirements of rule 4-1.16(d) [which governs withdrawal]. . . .
>
> (e) *Existing Fee Contracts Controlling.* The purchaser shall honor the fee agreements that were entered into between the seller and the seller's clients. The fees charged clients shall not be increased by reason of the sale.

Florida's Comment to subparagraph (f) provides as follows:

> The sale may not be financed by increases in fees charged the clients of the practice. Existing agreements between the seller and the client as to fees and the scope of the work must be honored by the purchaser. This obligation of the purchaser is a factor that can be taken into account by seller and purchaser when negotiating the sale price of the practice.

Georgia: Rule 1.17 tracks the 1990 version of ABA Model Rule 1.17 verbatim except that Georgia deletes paragraph (a) (requiring that the seller stop practicing law).

Illinois: Rule 1.17 also applies to "the estate of a deceased lawyer or the guardian or authorized representative of a disabled lawyer. . . ."

Kansas: Kansas omits ABA Model Rule 1.17 entirely.

Maryland: Rule 1.17 differs significantly from ABA Model Rule 1.17. Maryland Rule 1.17(a)(1) permits the sale of a law practice, upon appropriate notice, if "(1) Except in the case of death, disability, or appointment of the seller to judicial office, the entire practice that is the subject of the sale has been in existence at least five years prior to the date of sale" and "(2) The practice is sold as an entirety to another lawyer or law firm."

Michigan: Rule 1.17(a) provides that a "lawyer or a law firm may sell or purchase a private law practice, including good will, according to this rule." Michigan adds Rule 1.17(e), which permits the "sale of the good will of a law practice . . . conditioned upon the seller ceasing to engage in the private practice of law for a reasonable period of time within the geographical area in which the practice has been conducted."

Minnesota: Rule 1.17(b), which is based on the 1990 version of ABA Model Rule 1.17, provides as follows:

> (b) The buying lawyer or firm of lawyers shall not increase the fees charged to clients by reason of the sale for a period of at least one year from the date of the sale. The buying lawyer or firm of lawyers shall honor all existing fee agreements for at least one year from the date of the sale and shall continue to completion, on the same terms agreed to by the selling lawyer and the client, any matters that the selling lawyer has agreed to do on a pro bono publico basis or for a reduced fee.

Rule 1.17(d) provides that the notice to clients must include a "summary of the buying lawyer's or law firm's professional background, including education and experience and the length of time that the buyer lawyer or members of the buying law firm has been in practice." Minnesota also adds four paragraphs, including Rule 1.17(f), which permits the selling lawyer to promise that he or she "will not engage in the practice of law for a reasonable period of time within a reasonable geographic area and will not advertise for or solicit clients within that area for that time," and Rule 1.17(g), which provides that the selling lawyer "shall retain responsibility for the proper management and disposition of all inactive files that are not transferred as part of the sale of the law practice."

Missouri: Rule 1.17(d) adopts the ABA mandate that fees charged to clients shall not be increased by reason of the sale of the practice, but adds that the purchaser may "refuse to undertake the representation unless the client consents to pay the purchaser fees at a rate not exceeding the fees charged by the purchaser for rendering substantially similar services prior to the initiation of the purchase negotiations."

New Jersey: Rule 1.17 permits a lawyer or firm to sell or purchase a law practice, including goodwill, if the seller is ceasing to engage in private law practice in New Jersey, the practice is sold as an entirety and certain notices are given to the clients of the seller and by publication in the New Jersey Law Journal and the New Jersey Lawyer at least 30 days in advance of the sale.

New York: Rule 1.17 allows for the sale of a "law practice, including goodwill, to one or more lawyers or law firms." The parties may agree "on reasonable restrictions on the seller's private practice of law." Provisions are made for protecting confidential information and checking for conflicts.

North Carolina: Rule 1.17(d) provides that if a conflict of interest disqualifies the purchaser from representing a client, then "the seller's notice to the client shall advise the client to retain substitute counsel." In addition, Rule 1.17(g) permits the purchaser to pay the seller in installments—but the seller "shall have no say regarding the purchaser's conduct of the law practice."

Ohio: Rule 1.17 incorporates most of the substantive provisions of the Model Rule, but uses different language and adds many different provisions. For example, Ohio Rule 1.17(a) requires that a law practice must be sold "in its entirety, except where a conflict of interest is present that prevents the transfer of representation of a client or class of clients." In addition, Rule 1.17(a) prohibits the sale or purchase of a law practice "where the purchasing lawyer is buying the practice for the sole or primary purpose of reselling the practice to another lawyer or law firm," and Rule 1.17(d)(1) requires the sale agreement to include a statement that "the purchasing lawyer is purchasing the law practice in good faith and with the intention of delivering legal services to clients of the selling lawyer and others in need of legal services."

Ohio Rule 1.17(d)(2) requires the sale agreement to provide that "the purchasing lawyer will honor any fee agreements between the selling lawyer and the clients of the selling lawyer relative to legal representation that is ongoing at the time of the sale," but the purchasing lawyer "may negotiate fees with clients of the selling lawyer for legal representation that is commenced after the date of the sale." Rule 1.17(d)(3) generally permits the sale agreement to include terms that "reasonably limit the ability of the selling lawyer to reenter the practice of law," but prohibits such limitations "if the selling lawyer is selling his or her law practice to enter academic, government, or public service or to serve as in-house counsel to a business."

Ohio Rule 1.17(e) specifies in considerable detail what the notice to clients must contain, and a Rule 1.17(g) allows the selling lawyer and purchasing lawyer to give notice of the sale to a missing client by publishing notice of the sale in a newspaper. A Rule 1.17(i) provides as follows:

> (i) Neither the selling lawyer nor the purchasing lawyer shall attempt to exonerate the lawyer or law firm from or limit liability to the former or prospective client for any malpractice or other professional negligence. The provisions of Rule 1.8(h) shall be incorporated in all agreements for the sale or purchase of a law practice. The selling lawyer or the purchasing lawyer, or both, may agree to provide for the indemnification or other contribution arising from any claim or action in malpractice or other professional negligence.

Oklahoma: Rule 1.17(a) requires the selling lawyer to cease practice only "in the geographic area in Oklahoma in which the practice has been conducted," not in the entire state. Rule 1.17(b)(2) provides that matters shall not be transferred to a purchaser "unless the seller has reasonable basis to believe that the purchaser has the requisite knowledge and skill to handle such matters, or reasonable assurances are obtained that such purchaser will either acquire such knowledge and skill or associate with another lawyer having such competence." Rule 1.17(c) requires the "signed written consent of each client whose representation is proposed to be transferred" unless the client takes no action within 90 days of the notice. Rule 1.17(d) permits the purchaser to "refuse to undertake the representation unless the client consents to pay the purchaser fees at a rate not exceeding the fees charged by the purchaser for rendering substantially similar services prior to the initiation of the purchase negotiations."

Pennsylvania: Rule 1.17 differs significantly from ABA Model Rule 1.17. For example, Pennsylvania Rule 1.17(b) requires that the seller must sell the practice "as an entirety to a single lawyer," and explains that a practice is sold as an entirety "if the purchasing lawyer assumes responsibility for all of the active files" except those specified in Rule 1.17(g). Rule 1.17(d) adds the following: "Existing agreements between the seller and the client concerning fees and the scope of work must be honored by the purchaser, unless the client gives informed consent confirmed in writing." Pennsylvania also adds Rules 1.17(e) and (g), which provide as follows:

> (e) The agreement of sale shall include a clear statement of the respective responsibilities of the parties to maintain and preserve the records and files of the seller's practice, including client files.
>
> (g) The sale shall not be effective as to any client for whom the proposed sale would create a conflict of interest for the purchaser or who cannot be represented by the purchaser because of other requirements of the Pennsylvania Rules of Professional Conduct or rules of the Pennsylvania Supreme Court governing the practice of law in Pennsylvania, unless such conflict, requirement or rule can be waived by the client and the client gives informed consent.

Virginia requires the selling lawyer, when notifying clients about the proposed sale, to disclose "any proposed change in the terms of the future representation including the fee arrangement."

Related Materials

ABA Formal Ethics Opinions: No formal ethics opinions have construed Rule 1.17.

Restatement of the Law Governing Lawyers: The Restatement has no provision comparable to ABA Model Rule 1.17.

Rule 1.18 Duties to Prospective Client

(a) A person who discusses with a lawyer the possibility of forming a client-lawyer relationship with respect to a matter is a prospective client.

(b) Even when no client-lawyer relationship ensues, a lawyer who has had discussions with a prospective client shall not use or reveal information learned in the consultation, except as Rule 1.9 would permit with respect to information of a former client.

(c) A lawyer subject to paragraph (b) shall not represent a client with interests materially adverse to those of a prospective client in the same or a substantially related matter if the lawyer received information from the prospective client that could be significantly harmful to that person in the matter, except as provided in paragraph (d). If a lawyer is disqualified from representation under this paragraph, no lawyer in a

firm with which that lawyer is associated may knowingly undertake or continue representation in such a matter, except as provided in paragraph (d).

(d) When the lawyer has received disqualifying information as defined in paragraph (c), representation is permissible if:

(1) both the affected client and the prospective client have given informed consent, confirmed in writing, or:

(2) the lawyer who received the information took reasonable measures to avoid exposure to more disqualifying information than was reasonably necessary to determine whether to represent the prospective client; and

(i) the disqualified lawyer is timely screened from any participation in the matter and is apportioned no part of the fee therefrom; and

(ii) written notice is promptly given to the prospective client.

COMMENT

[1] Prospective clients, like clients, may disclose information to a lawyer, place documents or other property in the lawyer's custody, or rely on the lawyer's advice. A lawyer's discussions with a prospective client usually are limited in time and depth and leave both the prospective client and the lawyer free (and sometimes required) to proceed no further. Hence, prospective clients should receive some but not all of the protection afforded clients.

[2] Not all persons who communicate information to a lawyer are entitled to protection under this Rule. A person who communicates information unilaterally to a lawyer, without any reasonable expectation that the lawyer is willing to discuss the possibility of forming a client-lawyer relationship, is not a "prospective client" within the meaning of paragraph (a).

[3] It is often necessary for a prospective client to reveal information to the lawyer during an initial consultation prior to the decision about formation of a client-lawyer relationship. The lawyer often must learn such information to determine whether there is a conflict of interest with an existing client and whether the matter is one that the lawyer is willing to undertake. Paragraph (b) prohibits the lawyer from using or revealing that information, except as permitted by Rule 1.9, even if the client or lawyer decides not to proceed with the representation. The duty exists regardless of how brief the initial conference may be.

[4] In order to avoid acquiring disqualifying information from a prospective client, a lawyer considering whether or not to undertake a new matter should limit the initial interview to only such information as reasonably appears necessary for that purpose. Where the information indicates that a conflict of interest or other reason for non-representation exists, the lawyer should so inform the prospective client or decline the representation. If the prospective client wishes to retain the lawyer, and if consent is possible under Rule 1.7, then consent from all affected present or former clients must be obtained before accepting the representation.

[5] A lawyer may condition conversations with a prospective client on the person's informed consent that no information disclosed during the consultation will

prohibit the lawyer from representing a different client in the matter. See Rule 1.0(e) for the definition of informed consent. If the agreement expressly so provides, the prospective client may also consent to the lawyer's subsequent use of information received from the prospective client.

[6] Even in the absence of an agreement, under paragraph (c), the lawyer is not prohibited from representing a client with interests adverse to those of the prospective client in the same or a substantially related matter unless the lawyer has received from the prospective client information that could be significantly harmful if used in the matter.

[7] Under paragraph (c), the prohibition in this Rule is imputed to other lawyers as provided in Rule 1.10, but, under paragraph (d)(1), imputation may be avoided if the lawyer obtains the informed consent, confirmed in writing, of both the prospective and affected clients. In the alternative, imputation may be avoided if the conditions of paragraph (d)(2) are met and all disqualified lawyers are timely screened and written notice is promptly given to the prospective client. See Rule 1.0(k) (requirements for screening procedures). Paragraph (d)(2)(i) does not prohibit the screened lawyer from receiving a salary or partnership share established by prior independent agreement, but that lawyer may not receive compensation directly related to the matter in which the lawyer is disqualified.

[8] Notice, including a general description of the subject matter about which the lawyer was consulted, and of the screening procedures employed, generally should be given as soon as practicable after the need for screening becomes apparent.

[9] For the duty of competence of a lawyer who gives assistance on the merits of a matter to a prospective client, see Rule 1.1. For a lawyer's duties when a prospective client entrusts valuables or papers to the lawyer's care, see Rule 1.15.

Cross-References in Other Rules

Scope, ¶17: "Most of the duties flowing from the client-lawyer relationship attach only after the client has requested the lawyer to render legal services and the lawyer has agreed to do so. But there are some duties, such as that of confidentiality under Rule 1.6, that attach when the lawyer agrees to consider whether a client-lawyer relationship shall be established. See **Rule 1.18**."

Rule 1.0, Comment 8: The definition of "screened" "applies to situations where screening of a personally disqualified lawyer is permitted to remove imputation of a conflict of interest under Rules 1.11, 1.12 or **1.18**."

Rule 1.6, Comment 1: Regarding disclosure: "See **Rule 1.18** for the lawyer's duties with respect to information provided to the lawyer by a prospective client."

Rule 1.7, Comment 1: "For conflicts of interest involving prospective clients, see **Rule 1.18**."

Legislative History of Model Rule 1.18

2002 Adoption: Rule 1.18 was added to the Model Rules in February 2002. No equivalent rule was proposed in the Kutak Commission drafts or contained in the Model Rules before 2002. The new rule and its Comment were based on a proposal by the ABA Ethics 2000 Commission, which the ABA House of Delegates adopted without change. The Reporter's Explanation Memo that accompanied the Ethics 2000 Commission proposal provided, in relevant part, as follows:

*Model Rule 1.18—Reporter's Explanation of Changes**

Rule 1.18 is a proposed new Rule in response to the Commission's concern that important events occur in the period during which a lawyer and prospective client are considering whether to form a client-lawyer relationship. For the most part, the current Model Rules do not address that pre-retention period.

Paragraph (a) defines the limited circumstances to which this Rule applies by defining who qualifies as a "prospective client."

Paragraph (b) identifies the duty to treat all communications with a prospective client as confidential. This obligation is a well-settled matter under the law of attorney-client privilege, and the fact that Model Rule 1.9 does not now technically cover these communications is an omission that this proposal corrects.

Paragraph (c) extends the application of Rule 1.9 to prohibit representation adverse to the prospective client in the same or a substantially related matter. Unlike Rule 1.9, however, this Rule does so only if the lawyer received information from the prospective client that could be "significantly harmful" to that person in the later representation.

The prospective client situation justifies that different treatment because, prior to the representation decision, there is an inevitable period in which it is in the interest of the prospective client to share enough information with the lawyer to determine whether there is a conflict of interest or simple incompatibility. The lawyer may learn very early in the consultation, for example, that the party adverse to the prospective client is a client of the lawyer's firm. If the discussion stops before "significantly harmful" information is shared, it seems that the law firm's regular client should not be denied counsel of its choice if a substantially related matter arises. . . .

Paragraph (d) makes clear that the prohibition imposed by this Rule can be waived with the informed consent, confirmed in writing, of both the former prospective client and the client on whose behalf the lawyer later plans to take action adverse to the former prospective client. The expression of this requirement is parallel to that in Rules 1.7 and 1.9.

In the event that "significantly harmful" information is revealed, paragraph (d) provides that the lawyer who received the information may be screened from any involvement in the subsequent matter but others in the law firm may represent the adverse party.

Selected State Variations

Connecticut: Rule 1.18(a) defines a "prospective client" as a person who discusses "or communicates" with a lawyer concerning the possibility of forming a client-lawyer relationship with respect to a matter.

District of Columbia adopts the essence of Rule 1.18 except that it omits Model Rule 1.18(d)(2) and (2)(ii) while retaining the language in (2)(i).

Florida omits the words "significantly harmful" from paragraph (c), so a lawyer is personally disqualified if he or she received information "that could be used to the disadvantage" of the prospective client.

* Committee Reports, and the Reporter's Explanation of Changes contained therein, do not represent official policy of the ABA. They are for information only, and the opinions are those of the authors of the report.

Illinois: Rule 1.18(d) does not require that a prospective client receive notice when a firm employs a screen to avoid a conflict of interest.

Maryland deletes the introductory language in ABA Model Rule 1.18(d)(2) and all of Rule 1.18(d)(2)(ii). Thus, Maryland Rule 1.18(d) is a single sentence permitting representation if either "both the affected client and the prospective client have given informed consent, confirmed in writing, or the disqualified lawyer is timely screened from any participation in the matter and is apportioned no part of the fee therefrom."

Missouri: Rule 1.18(d)(2) deletes the ABA Model Rule requirements that the lawyer who received the disqualifying information be apportioned no part of the fee and that written notice be promptly given to the prospective client.

Nevada: Nevada adds the following new paragraphs to Rule 1.18:

> (e) A person who communicates information to a lawyer without any reasonable expectation that the lawyer is willing to discuss the possibility of forming a client-lawyer relationship, or for purposes which do not include a good faith intention to retain the lawyer in the subject matter of the consultation, is not a "prospective client" within the meaning of this Rule.
>
> (f) A lawyer may condition conversations with a prospective client on the person's informed consent that no information disclosed during the consultation will prohibit the lawyer from representing a different client in the matter. If the agreement expressly so provides, the prospective client may also consent to the lawyer's subsequent use of information received from the prospective client.
>
> (g) Whenever a prospective client shall request information regarding a lawyer or law firm for the purpose of making a decision regarding employment of the lawyer or law firm:
>
> > (1) The lawyer or law firm shall promptly furnish (by mail if requested) the written information described in Rule 1.4(c).
> >
> > (2) The lawyer or law firm may furnish such additional factual information regarding the lawyer or law firm deemed valuable to assist the client.
> >
> > (3) If the information furnished to the client includes a fee contract, the top of each page of the contract shall be marked "SAMPLE" in red ink in a type size one size larger than the largest type used in the contract and the words "DO NOT SIGN" shall appear on the client signature line.

New York: Rule 1.18(d) describes in more detail the procedures necessary to avoid a conflict as a result of consultations with prospective clients. Comments 7A-7C offer further guidance regarding these procedures. New York adds Rule 1.18(e), which provides (in language copied partly from Comment 2 to Model Rule 1.18) that a "prospective client" does not include a person who "(1) communicates information unilaterally to a lawyer, without any reasonable expectation that the lawyer is willing to discuss the possibility of forming a client-lawyer relationship" or "(2) communicates with a lawyer for the purpose of disqualifying the lawyer. . . ."

North Carolina omits the language in Rule 1.18(d)(2) requiring "reasonable measures to avoid exposure" to unnecessary confidential information. North Carolina does not require that a disqualified lawyer be denied part of the fee.

Oregon omits the language in Rule 1.18(d)(2) requiring "reasonable measures to avoid exposure" to unnecessary confidential information.

South Carolina: Rule 1.18(a) provides that a person with whom a lawyer discusses the possibility of forming a client-lawyer relationship with respect to a matter is a prospective client "only when there is a reasonable expectation that the lawyer is likely to form the relationship."

Vermont: Rule 1.18(a) extends prospective client status only to those people who are "in good faith" seeking to hire that attorney.

Virginia: Effective June 21, 2011, Virginia includes two additional requirements in Rule 1.18(d). First, the disqualified lawyer must reasonably believe "that the screen would be effective to sufficiently protect information that could be significantly harmful to the prospective client." And second, the written notice to the prospective client must include "a general description of the subject matter about which the lawyer was consulted and the screening procedures employed. . . ."

Related Materials

ABA Commission on Ethics 20/20: In 2009, the ABA created the Commission on Ethics 20/20, which is comprehensively reviewing the ABA Model Rules of Professional Conduct and other lawyer regulatory sources in light of globalization and changes in technology. In September 2011, the Commission circulated for public comment a proposal to amend Rule 1.18(a) and (b) to provide (in legislative style) as follows:

> (a) A person who ~~discusses~~ communicates with a lawyer about the possibility of forming a client-lawyer relationship and has a reasonable expectation that the lawyer is willing to consider forming a client-lawyer relationship with respect to a matter is a prospective client.
>
> (b) Even when no client-lawyer relationship ensues, a lawyer who has ~~had discussions with~~ learned information from a prospective client shall not use or reveal that information ~~learned in the consultation~~, except as Rule 1.9 would permit with respect to information of a former client.

The Commission also proposed to amend various paragraphs of the Comment to Rule 1.18 in minor ways, to add at the end of Comment 2 that "a person who communicates with a lawyer for the primary purpose of disqualifying the lawyer from handling a materially adverse representation on the same or a substantially related matter is not a "prospective client," and to add the following new Comment 3:

> [3] When a person initiates an electronic communication with a lawyer, such as through email or a website, the reasonableness of the person's expectations that the lawyer is willing to consider forming a client-lawyer relationship may depend on a number of factors, including whether the lawyer previously represented or declined to represent the person; whether the person, prior to communicating with the lawyer, encountered any warnings or cautionary statements that were intended to limit, condition, waive or disclaim the lawyer's obligations; whether those warnings or cautionary statements were clear, reasonably understandable, and conspicuously placed; and whether the lawyer acted or communicated in a manner that was contrary to the warnings or cautionary statements. For example, if a lawyer's website encourages a website visitor to submit a personal inquiry about a proposed representation and the website fails to include any cautionary language, the person submitting the information could become a prospective client. In contrast, if a website offers only information about the lawyer or the lawyer's firm, including the lawyer's contact information, this information alone is typically insufficient to create a reasonable expectation that the lawyer is willing to consider forming a client-lawyer relationship.

The Commission may present these proposals (or revised versions of them) to the ABA House of Delegates at its August 2012 Annual Meeting. For updates on the Ethics 20/20 Commission's work, visit *www.americanbar.org/Ethics2020.*

ABA Formal Ethics Opinions: See ABA Formal Ethics Op. 10-457 (2010).

Restatement of the Law Governing Lawyers: See Restatement §15 in our chapter on the Restatement later in this volume.

ARTICLE 2. COUNSELOR

Rule 2.1 Advisor

In representing a client, a lawyer shall exercise independent professional judgment and render candid advice. In rendering advice, a lawyer may refer not only to law but to other considerations such as moral, economic, social and political factors, that may be relevant to the client's situation.

COMMENT

Scope of Advice

[1] A client is entitled to straightforward advice expressing the lawyer's honest assessment. Legal advice often involves unpleasant facts and alternatives that a client may be disinclined to confront. In presenting advice, a lawyer endeavors to sustain the client's morale and may put advice in as acceptable a form as honesty permits. However, a lawyer should not be deterred from giving candid advice by the prospect that the advice will be unpalatable to the client.

[2] Advice couched in narrow legal terms may be of little value to a client, especially where practical considerations, such as cost or effects on other people, are predominant. Purely technical legal advice, therefore, can sometimes be inadequate. It is proper for a lawyer to refer to relevant moral and ethical considerations in giving advice. Although a lawyer is not a moral advisor as such, moral and ethical considerations impinge upon most legal questions and may decisively influence how the law will be applied.

[3] A client may expressly or impliedly ask the lawyer for purely technical advice. When such a request is made by a client experienced in legal matters, the lawyer may accept it at face value. When such a request is made by a client inexperienced in legal matters, however, the lawyer's responsibility as advisor may include indicating that more may be involved than strictly legal considerations.

[4] Matters that go beyond strictly legal questions may also be in the domain of another profession. Family matters can involve problems within the professional competence of psychiatry, clinical psychology or social work; business matters can involve problems within the competence of the accounting profession or of financial specialists. Where consultation with a professional in another field is itself something

a competent lawyer would recommend, the lawyer should make such a recommendation. At the same time, a lawyer's advice at its best often consists of recommending a course of action in the face of conflicting recommendations of experts.

Offering Advice

[5] In general, a lawyer is not expected to give advice until asked by the client. However, when a lawyer knows that a client proposes a course of action that is likely to result in substantial adverse legal consequences to the client, the lawyer's duty to the client under Rule 1.4 may require that the lawyer offer advice if the client's course of action is related to the representation. Similarly, when a matter is likely to involve litigation, it may be necessary under Rule 1.4 to inform the client of forms of dispute resolution that might constitute reasonable alternatives to litigation. A lawyer ordinarily has no duty to initiate investigation of a client's affairs or to give advice that the client has indicated is unwanted, but a lawyer may initiate advice to a client when doing so appears to be in the client's interest.

Canon and Code Antecedents

ABA Canons of Professional Ethics: No comparable Canon.

ABA Model Code of Professional Responsibility: Compare DR 5-107(B) (reprinted later in this volume).

Cross-References in Other Rules

Rule 7.2, Comment 8: "[R]eciprocal referral arrangements must not interfere with the lawyer's professional judgment as to making referrals or as to providing substantive legal services. See Rules 2.1 and 5.4(c)."

Legislative History of Model Rule 2.1

1980 Discussion Draft: The Introduction to the section entitled "Attorney as Advisor" contained the following paragraph:

> The lawyer's professional function historically originated as attorney and advocate, that is, appearing on behalf of a party to litigation. Giving legal advice evolved from giving advice about how to proceed in litigation. Today, serving as advisor is the lawyer's predominant role.

Rule 2.1 provided:

> *Independence and Candor*
>
> In advising a client a lawyer shall exercise independent and candid professional judgment, uncontrolled by the interests or wishes of a third person, or by the lawyer's own interests or wishes.

In addition, Rule 2.2 (now incorporated into Rule 2.1) provided:

Scope of Advice

In rendering advice a lawyer may refer to all relevant considerations unless in the circumstances it is evident that the client desires advice confined to strictly legal considerations.

1981 and ***1982 Drafts*** were the same as adopted.

1983 Rule: As originally adopted in 1983, Rule 2.1 was the same as the 2002 version.

2002 Amendments: At its February 2002 Mid-Year Meeting, the ABA House of Delegates adopted with only minor changes the ABA Ethics 2000 Commission proposal to amend the Comment to Rule 2.1. (The Ethics 2000 Commission did not propose any changes to the text of Rule 2.1.) The amendment added a sentence to Comment 5 to the effect that Rule 1.4 may require a lawyer representing a client in litigation to inform the client of other forms of dispute resolution.

Selected State Variations

California has no direct counterpart to Rule 2.1.

Colorado adds the following sentence at the end of Rule 2.1: "In a matter involving or expected to involve litigation, a lawyer should advise the client of alternative forms of dispute resolution that might reasonably be pursued to attempt to resolve the legal dispute or to reach the legal objective sought."

Georgia moves the second sentence of the ABA rule to a Comment, and adds the following sentence to the text of the rule in its place: "A lawyer should not be deterred from giving candid advice by the prospect that the advice will be unpalatable to the client."

New York: Rule 2.1 adds the word "psychological," after "moral, economic, social" but is otherwise the same as the Model Rule.

Texas: Rule 2.01 begins, "In advising or otherwise representing a client . . . ," and deletes the second sentence of ABA Model Rule 2.1.

Related Materials

ABA Formal Ethics Opinions: See ABA Formal Ethics Op. 92-364 (1992) and 00-418 (2000).

Restatement of the Law Governing Lawyers: See Restatement §94(3) in our chapter on the Restatement later in this volume.

Rule 2.2 Intermediary [deleted in 2002]

Editors' Note. Rule 2.2 is no longer part of the ABA Model Rules of Professional Conduct. At its February 2002 Mid-Year Meeting, based on a recommendation by the ABA Ethics 2000 Commission, the ABA House of Delegates deleted Rule 2.2 and its Comment from the Model Rules. At the same time, also based on a proposal by the Ethics 2000 Commission, the House of Delegates added a new Rule 2.4 (Lawyer Serving as Third-Party Neutral). For more information about the amendments, see the entry entitled "2002 Amendments" in the Legislative History following this rule and Rule 2.4. For the text of Rule 2.2, see the entry entitled "1983-2002 Rule" in the Legislative History below.

Canon and Code Antecedents

ABA Canons of Professional Ethics: No comparable Canon.

ABA Model Code of Professional Responsibility: Compare DR 5-105(B) and DR 5-105(C) (reprinted later in this volume).

Cross-References in Other Rules

None.

Legislative History of Model Rule 2.2

1980 Discussion Draft (then Rules 5.1 and 5.2) began with the following Introduction:

> A lawyer acts as intermediary in seeking to establish or adjust a relationship between clients on an amicable and mutually advantageous basis. . . .
>
> . . . In some nonlitigation situations, the stakes involved may be so modest that separate representation of the parties is financially impractical. Given these factors, all the clients may prefer that the lawyer act as intermediary. . . .
>
> This Rule does not deal with a lawyer acting as mediator or arbitrator between parties with whom the lawyer does not have a client-lawyer relationship, nor does it govern a situation where a lawyer represents a party in negotiation with a party who is unrepresented. A lawyer acts as intermediary under this Rule when the lawyer represents both parties. A key factor in defining the relationship is whether the parties share responsibility for paying the lawyer's fee, but the existence of a joint or common representation can be inferred from other circumstances. Because confusion can arise as to the lawyer's role and responsibility where each party is not separately represented, it is important that the lawyer make clear whom he represents in such situations.

Rules 5.1 and 5.2 of the 1980 Discussion Draft provided:

Conditions for Acting as an Intermediary

> (a) A lawyer may act as an intermediary between clients if:
>
> (1) the possibility of adjusting the clients' interests is strong; and
>
> (2) each client will be able to make adequately informed decisions in the matter, and there is little likelihood that any of the clients will be significantly prejudiced if the contemplated adjustment of interests is unsuccessful; and
>
> (3) the lawyer can act impartially and without improper effect on other services the lawyer is performing for any of the clients; and
>
> (4) the lawyer fully explains to each client the implications of the common representation, including the advantages and risks involved, and obtains each client's consent to the common representation.
>
> (b) Before serving as intermediary a lawyer shall explain fully to each client the decisions to be made and the considerations relevant to making them, so that each client can make adequately informed decisions.

Withdrawal as an Intermediary

> A lawyer shall withdraw as intermediary if any of the clients so requests, if the conditions stated in Rule 5.1 cannot be met, or if it becomes apparent that a mutually advantageous adjustment of interests cannot be made. Upon withdrawal, the lawyer may continue to represent any of the clients only to the extent compatible with the lawyer's responsibilities to the other client or clients.

1981 Draft: Rule 2.2(c) required a lawyer to withdraw if the conditions in (a) could not be met "or if in the light of subsequent events the lawyer reasonably should know that a mutually advantageous resolution cannot be achieved."

1982 Draft: Rule 2.2(a)(1) was substantially the same as adopted except that it did not require the lawyer to explain "the effect on the attorney-client privileges." Rule 2.2(c)'s second sentence provided: "Upon withdrawal, the lawyer shall not continue to represent any of the clients unless doing so is clearly compatible with the lawyer's responsibilities to the other client or clients." The remainder of Rule 2.2 was substantially the same as adopted.

1983 Rule: From the original adoption of the ABA Model Rules of Professional Conduct in 1983 until Rule 2.2 was deleted in 2002, Rule 2.2 provided as follows:

Rule 2.2 Intermediary

(a) A lawyer may act as an intermediary between clients if:

(1) the lawyer consults with each client concerning the implications of the common representation, including the advantages and risks involved, and the effect on the attorney-client privileges, and obtains each client's consent to the common representation;

(2) the lawyer reasonably believes that the matter can be resolved on terms compatible with the clients' best interests, that each client will be able to make adequately informed decisions in the matter and that there is little risk of material prejudice to the interests of any of the clients if the contemplated resolution is unsuccessful; and

(3) the lawyer reasonably believes that the common representation can be undertaken impartially and without improper effect on other responsibilities the lawyer has to any of the clients.

(b) While acting as intermediary, the lawyer shall consult with each client concerning the decisions to be made and the considerations relevant in making them, so that each client can make adequately informed decisions.

(c) A lawyer shall withdraw as intermediary if any of the clients so requests, or if any of the conditions stated in paragraph (a) is no longer satisfied. Upon withdrawal, the lawyer shall not continue to represent any of the clients in the matter that was the subject of the intermediation.

2002 Deletion: At its February 2002 Mid-Year Meeting, the ABA House of Delegates adopted without change the ABA Ethics 2000 Commission proposal to delete Rule 2.2 and its Comment and to move discussion of common representation to Rule 1.7's Comment. The Reporter's explanation for these changes stated:

[T]he Commission believes that the ideas expressed therein are better dealt with in the Comment to Rule 1.7. There is much in Rule 2.2 and its Comment that applies to all examples of common representation and ought to appear in Rule 1.7. Moreover, there is less resistance to common representation today than there was in 1983; thus, there is no longer any particular need to establish the propriety of common representation through a separate Rule.

Selected State Variations

California has no direct counterpart to ABA Model Rule 2.2.

Georgia: Rule 2.2 differs significantly from former ABA Model Rule 2.2. Essentially, Georgia has adopted only Rule 2.2(c), moving the substance of Rules 2.2(a)(2) and (3) to Comment 6 and deleting ABA Model Rules 2.2(a)(1) and 2.2(b) entirely.

Massachusetts has no equivalent to ABA Model Rule 2.2, but Comments 12 through 12F to Rule 1.7 provide guidance concerning joint representation.

New York omits Model Rule 2.2.

Related Materials

Restatement of the Law Governing Lawyers: The Restatement has no black letter provision directly comparable to former ABA Model Rule 2.2.

Rule 2.3 Evaluation for Use by Third Persons

(a) A lawyer may provide an evaluation of a matter affecting a client for the use of someone other than the client if the lawyer reasonably believes that making the evaluation is compatible with other aspects of the lawyer's relationship with the client.

(b) When the lawyer knows or reasonably should know that the evaluation is likely to affect the client's interests materially and adversely, the lawyer shall not provide the evaluation unless the client gives informed consent.

(c) Except as disclosure is authorized in connection with a report of an evaluation, information relating to the evaluation is otherwise protected by Rule 1.6.

COMMENT

Definition

[1] An evaluation may be performed at the client's direction or when impliedly authorized in order to carry out the representation. See Rule 1.2. Such an evaluation may be for the primary purpose of establishing information for the benefit of third parties; for example, an opinion concerning the title of property rendered at the behest of a vendor for the information of a prospective purchaser, or at the behest of a borrower for the information of a prospective lender. In some situations, the evaluation may be required by a government agency; for example, an opinion concerning the legality of the securities registered for sale under the securities laws. In other instances, the evaluation may be required by a third person, such as a purchaser of a business.

[2] A legal evaluation should be distinguished from an investigation of a person with whom the lawyer does not have a client-lawyer relationship. For example, a lawyer retained by a purchaser to analyze a vendor's title to property does not have a client-lawyer relationship with the vendor. So also, an investigation into a person's affairs by a government lawyer, or by special counsel by a government lawyer, or by special counsel employed by the government, is not an evaluation as that term is used in this Rule. The question is whether the lawyer is retained by the person whose affairs are being examined. When the lawyer is retained by that person, the general rules concerning loyalty to client and preservation of confidences apply, which is not the case if the lawyer is retained by someone else. For this reason, it is essential to identify the person by whom the lawyer is retained. This should be made clear not only to the person under examination, but also to others to whom the results are to be made available.

Duties Owed to Third Person and Client

[3] When the evaluation is intended for the information or use of a third person, a legal duty to that person may or may not arise. That legal question is beyond the scope of this Rule. However, since such an evaluation involves a departure from the normal client-lawyer relationship, careful analysis of the situation is required. The lawyer must be satisfied as a matter of professional judgment that making the evaluation is compatible with other functions undertaken in behalf of the client. For example, if the lawyer is acting as advocate in defending the client against charges of fraud, it would normally be incompatible with that responsibility for the lawyer to perform an evaluation for others concerning the same or a related transaction. Assuming no such impediment is apparent, however, the lawyer should advise the client of the implications of the evaluation, particularly the lawyer's responsibilities to third persons and the duty to disseminate the findings.

Access to and Disclosure of Information

[4] The quality of an evaluation depends on the freedom and extent of the investigation upon which it is based. Ordinarily a lawyer should have whatever latitude of investigation seems necessary as a matter of professional judgment. Under some circumstances, however, the terms of the evaluation may be limited. For example, certain issues or sources may be categorically excluded, or the scope of search may be limited by time constraints or the noncooperation of persons having relevant information. Any such limitations that are material to the evaluation should be described in the report. If after a lawyer has commenced an evaluation, the client refuses to comply with the terms upon which it was understood the evaluation was to have been made, the lawyer's obligations are determined by law, having reference to the terms of the client's agreement and the surrounding circumstances. In no circumstances is the lawyer permitted to knowingly make a false statement of material fact or law in providing an evaluation under this Rule. See Rule 4.1.

Obtaining Client's Informed Consent

[5] Information relating to an evaluation is protected by Rule 1.6. In many situations, providing an evaluation to a third party poses no significant risk to the client; thus, the lawyer may be impliedly authorized to disclose information to carry out the representation. See Rule 1.6(a). Where, however, it is reasonably likely that providing the evaluation will affect the client's interests materially and adversely, the lawyer must first obtain the client's consent after the client has been adequately informed concerning the important possible effects on the client's interests. See Rules 1.6(a) and 1.0(e).

Financial Auditors' Requests for Information

[6] When a question concerning the legal situation of a client arises at the instance of the client's financial auditor and the question is referred to the lawyer,

the lawyer's response may be made in accordance with procedures recognized in the legal profession. Such a procedure is set forth in the American Bar Association Statement of Policy Regarding Lawyers' Responses to Auditors' Requests for Information, adopted in 1975.

Canon and Code Antecedents

ABA Canons of Professional Ethics: No comparable Canon.
ABA Model Code of Professional Responsibility: No comparable Disciplinary Rule.

Cross-References in Other Rules

None.

Legislative History of Model Rule 2.3

1980 Discussion Draft (then Rules 6.1 through 6.3):

Confidential Evaluation (Rule 6.1)

A lawyer undertakes a confidential evaluation of a matter affecting a client when a report of the evaluation is to be given to the client alone and to be disclosed to others only at the direction of the client.

Independent Evaluation (Rule 6.2)

(a) A lawyer undertakes an independent evaluation of a matter affecting a client when a report of the evaluation is to be given to someone other than the client. A lawyer may make an independent evaluation if:

(1) Making the evaluation is compatible with other aspects of the lawyer's relationship with the client; and

(2) The terms upon which the evaluation is made are clearly described, particularly the lawyer's access to information and the persons to whom the report of the evaluation is to be made; and

(3) The client agrees that the lawyer may, within the terms upon which the evaluation is made, disclose information about the client, including matter otherwise confidential or privileged, that the lawyer determines ought to be disclosed in making a fair and accurate evaluation; and

(4) After adequate disclosure of the terms upon which the evaluation is to be made and their implications for the client, the client requests the lawyer to make the evaluation.

(b) In reporting the evaluation, the lawyer shall indicate any limitations on the scope of the inquiry that are reasonably necessary to a proper interpretation of the report.

(c) If, after a lawyer has commenced an independent evaluation, the client refuses to comply with the terms upon which it is to be made, the lawyer shall give to the person for whom the evaluation is intended the fullest report that can be made in the circumstances.

(d) Except as disclosure is required in connection with a report of the evaluation, information relating to an independent evaluation is confidential under Rule 1.7.

Financial Auditors' Requests for Information (Rule 6.3)

When a question concerning the legal situation of a client arises at the instance of the client's financial auditor and the question is referred to the lawyer, the lawyer's response shall be made in accordance with procedures recognized in the legal profession unless some other procedure is established after consent by the client upon adequate disclosure.

1981 Draft: Rule 2.3(a)(2) provided:

> the terms upon which the evaluation is to be made are stated in writing, particularly the terms relating to the lawyer's access to information, the contemplated disclosure of otherwise confidential information and the persons to whom report of the evaluation is to be made. . . .

Rule 2.3(b) provided: "In reporting the evaluation, the lawyer shall indicate any material limitations that were imposed on the scope of the inquiry or on the disclosure of information."

1982 Draft: Rule 2.3(a)(2) required that "the conditions of the evaluation [be] described to the client in writing, including contemplated disclosure of information otherwise protected by Rule 1.6. . . ."

1983 Rule: As originally adopted in 1983, Rule 2.3 provided as follows:

> (a) A lawyer may undertake an evaluation of a matter affecting a client for the use of someone other than the client if:
>
> (1) the lawyer reasonably believes that making the evaluation is compatible with other aspects of the lawyer's relationship with the client; and
>
> (2) the client consents after consultation.
>
> (b) Except as disclosure is required in connection with a report of an evaluation, information relating to the evaluation is otherwise protected by Rule 1.6.

2002 Amendments: At its February 2002 Mid-Year Meeting, the ABA House of Delegates adopted without change the ABA Ethics 2000 Commission proposal to amend Rule 2.3 and its Comment. The amendments added Rule 2.3(b), deleted former Comment 2, added Comment 5, and made minor changes elsewhere in the Rule and Comment.

Selected State Variations

California has no direct counterpart to ABA Model Rule 2.3.

Florida adds the following subparagraph: "*Limitation on Scope of Evaluation.* In reporting the evaluation, the lawyer shall indicate any material limitations that were imposed on the scope of the inquiry or on the disclosure of information."

Missouri: Missouri replaces ABA Model Rule 2.3(b) with Rule 2.3(a)(2), which permits a lawyer to undertake an evaluation "if the client consents after consultation."

New Jersey's version of Rule 2.3(b) and (d) provide as follows:

> (b) When the lawyer knows or reasonably should know that the evaluation is likely to affect the client's interests materially and adversely, the lawyer shall not provide the evaluation unless:
>
> (1) the lawyer describes the conditions of the evaluation to the client, in writing, including disclosure of information otherwise protected by RPC 1.6;
>
> (2) the lawyer consults with the client; and
>
> (3) the client gives informed consent. . . .
>
> (d) In reporting an evaluation, the lawyer shall indicate any material limitations that were imposed on the scope of the inquiry or on the disclosure of information.

Virginia: Rule 2.3(a) provides as follows: "(a) A lawyer acts as evaluator by examining a client's legal affairs and reporting about them to the client or to others." Rule 2.3(b) is substantially the same as ABA Model Rule 2.3(a) but requires client consent after consultation.

Related Materials

ABA Formal Ethics Opinions: No formal ABA ethics opinions have construed Rule 2.3.

IRS Regulations: A lawyer issuing an opinion evaluating a tax-shelter transaction must abide by strict IRS regulations, especially 31 C.F.R. §10.35. In that rule, §10.35(b) defines several types of tax opinions. For example, a lawyer's written advice constitutes a "reliance opinion" if the lawyer "concludes at a confidence level of at least more likely than not (a greater than 50 percent likelihood) that one or more significant Federal tax issues would be resolved in the taxpayer's favor." Written advice is not treated as a "reliance opinion," however, if the lawyer "prominently discloses in the written advice that it was not intended or written by the practitioner to be used, and that it cannot be used by the taxpayer, for the purpose of avoiding penalties that may be imposed on the taxpayer." A "marketed opinion" results if a practitioner "knows or has reason to know that the written advice will be used or referred to by a person other than the practitioner . . . in promoting, marketing or recommending a partnership or other entity, investment plan or arrangement to one or more taxpayer(s)." Section 10.35(d)(1) requires a lawyer who renders certain tax opinions and relies in any way upon the opinion of another lawyer to "identify the other opinion and set forth the conclusions reached."

Legal Opinion Letters: A major area governed by Rule 2.3 is the "legal opinion letter"—a letter issued by a lawyer to a third party (typically a buyer or lender) assuring that the lawyer believes the transaction is legal, the seller is authorized to sell, etc. Banks, opposing parties, and others often rely upon such legal opinion letters, and a satisfactory legal opinion letter from the seller's or borrower's lawyer is often a condition of completing a deal.

The ABA Section of Business Law has developed a Legal Opinion Accord that addresses numerous issues raised by legal opinion letters issued to third parties. The Legal Opinion Accord (sometimes called the "Silverado Accord") is reprinted with commentary in *Third-Party Legal Opinion Report, Including the Legal Opinion Accord, of the Section of Business Law, American Bar Association*, 47 Bus. Law. 167 (1991).

In addition, a group called the TriBar Opinion Committee was formed in 1977 to provide "guidelines and/or forms respecting lawyers' opinions in commercial transactions." (The TriBar Opinion Committee originally consisted of representatives from the New York City Bar, the New York County Lawyers' Association, and the New York State Bar Association. Today, the TriBar Opinion Committee has expanded to include lawyers from Boston, Delaware, Chicago, Ontario, and elsewhere.) TriBar reports have covered third-party "closing" opinions generally, as well as opinion letters in particular areas of practice, such as bankruptcy and real estate. Many TriBar and ABA reports on opinion letters are reprinted in Collected ABA and Tri-Bar Opinion Reports 2009 (ABA Section of Business Law 2009). For more information about opinion letters, see M. John Sterba, Jr., Editor, Legal Opinion Letters: A Comprehensive Guide to Opinion Letter Practice (3d ed., Aspen Publishers 2002), and Scott T. Fitzgibbon, Donald W. Glazer, & Steven O. Weise, Glazer and Fitzgibbon on Legal Opinions: Drafting, Interpreting, and Supporting Closing Opinions in Business Transactions (3d ed., Aspen Publishers 2008).

Restatement of the Law Governing Lawyers: See Restatement §§51, 79, 95, and 98 in our chapter on the Restatement later in this volume.

Rule 2.4 Lawyer Serving as Third-Party Neutral

(a) A lawyer serves as a third-party neutral when the lawyer assists two or more persons who are not clients of the lawyer to reach a resolution of a dispute or other matter that has arisen between them. Service as a third-party neutral may include service as an arbitrator, a mediator or in such other capacity as will enable the lawyer to assist the parties to resolve the matter.

(b) A lawyer serving as a third-party neutral shall inform unrepresented parties that the lawyer is not representing them. When the lawyer knows or reasonably should know that a party does not understand the lawyer's role in the matter, the lawyer shall explain the difference between the lawyer's role as a third-party neutral and a lawyer's role as one who represents a client.

COMMENT

[1] Alternative dispute resolution has become a substantial part of the civil justice system. Aside from representing clients in dispute-resolution processes, lawyers often serve as third-party neutrals. A third-party neutral is a person, such as a mediator, arbitrator, conciliator or evaluator, who assists the parties, represented or unrepresented, in the resolution of a dispute or in the arrangement of a transaction. Whether a third-party neutral serves primarily as a facilitator, evaluator or decisionmaker depends on the particular process that is either selected by the parties or mandated by a court.

[2] The role of a third-party neutral is not unique to lawyers, although, in some court-connected contexts, only lawyers are allowed to serve in this role or to handle certain types of cases. In performing this role, the lawyer may be subject to court rules or other law that apply either to third-party neutrals generally or to lawyers serving as third-party neutrals. Lawyer-neutrals may also be subject to various codes of ethics, such as the Code of Ethics for Arbitration in Commercial Disputes prepared by a joint committee of the American Bar Association and the American Arbitration Association or the Model Standards of Conduct for Mediators jointly prepared by the American Bar Association, the American Arbitration Association and the Society of Professionals in Dispute Resolution.

[3] Unlike nonlawyers who serve as third-party neutrals, lawyers serving in this role may experience unique problems as a result of differences between the role of a third-party neutral and a lawyer's service as a client representative. The potential for confusion is significant when the parties are unrepresented in the process. Thus, paragraph (b) requires a lawyer-neutral to inform unrepresented parties that the lawyer is not representing them. For some parties, particularly parties who frequently use dispute-resolution processes, this information will be sufficient. For others, particularly those who are using the process for the first time, more information will be required. Where appropriate, the lawyer should inform unrepresented parties of the important

differences between the lawyer's role as third-party neutral and a lawyer's role as a client representative, including the inapplicability of the attorney-client evidentiary privilege. The extent of disclosure required under this paragraph will depend on the particular parties involved and the subject matter of the proceeding, as well as the particular features of the dispute-resolution process selected.

[4] A lawyer who serves as a third-party neutral subsequently may be asked to serve as a lawyer representing a client in the same matter. The conflicts of interest that arise for both the individual lawyer and the lawyer's law firm are addressed in Rule 1.12.

[5] Lawyers who represent clients in alternative dispute-resolution processes are governed by the Rules of Professional Conduct. When the dispute-resolution process takes place before a tribunal, as in binding arbitration (see Rule 1.0(m)), the lawyer's duty of candor is governed by Rule 3.3. Otherwise, the lawyer's duty of candor toward both the third-party neutral and other parties is governed by Rule 4.1.

Canon and Code Antecedents

ABA Canons of Professional Ethics: No comparable Canon.

ABA Model Code of Professional Responsibility: No comparable Disciplinary Rule.

Cross-References in Other Rules

Preamble, ¶3: "Some of these Rules apply directly to lawyers who are or have served as third-party neutrals. See, e.g., **Rules** 1.12 and **2.4.**"

Rule 1.12, Comment 2: "Other law or codes of ethics governing third-party neutrals may impose more stringent standards of personal or imputed disqualification. See **Rule 2.4.**"

Legislative History of Model Rule 2.4

1983 Rule: As originally adopted in 1983, the ABA Model Rules did not contain Rule 2.4.

2002 Amendments: Rule 2.4 was added to the Model Rules in February 2002. The new rule and its Comment were based on a proposal by the ABA Ethics 2000 Commission, which the ABA House of Delegates adopted without change. The Reporter's Explanation Memo that accompanied the Ethics 2000 Commission proposal provided, in relevant part, as follows:

*Model Rule 2.4—Reporter's Explanation of Changes**

The role of third-party neutral is not unique to lawyers, but the Commission recognizes that lawyers are increasingly serving in these roles. Unlike nonlawyers who serve as neutrals, lawyers may experience unique ethical problems, for example, those arising from possible confusion about the nature of the lawyer's role. The Commission notes that there have been a number of attempts by various organizations to promulgate codes of ethics for neutrals (e.g., aspirational codes for arbitrators or mediators or court enacted rules governing court-sponsored mediators), but such codes do not typically address the special problems of lawyers. The Commission's proposed approach is designed to promote dispute resolution parties' understanding of the lawyer-neutral's role.

* Committee Reports, and the Reporter's Explanation of Changes contained therein, do not represent official policy of the ABA. They are for information only, and the opinions are those of the authors of the report.

Paragraph (a) defines the term "third-party neutral" and emphasizes assistance at the request of the parties who participate in the resolution of disputes and other matters.

Paragraph (b) requires the lawyer serving as a third-party neutral to inform unrepresented parties in all cases that the lawyer does not represent them. The potential for confusion is sufficiently great to mandate this requirement in all cases involving unrepresented parties. Consistent with the standard of Rule 4.3, paragraph (b) requires the lawyer to explain the differences in a lawyer's role as a third-party neutral and the role of a lawyer representing a party in situations where the lawyer knows or reasonably should know that the unrepresented party does not understand the lawyer's role as a third-party neutral.

Selected State Variations

Illinois: Rule 2.4(b) requires third-party neutrals to explain to unrepresented parties "the difference between the lawyer's role as a third-party neutral and a lawyer's role as one who represents a client" regardless of whether the lawyer believes the unrepresented parties misunderstand the lawyer's role.

New York: Rule 2.4 is substantially the same as Model Rule 2.4.

South Carolina: Rule 2.4 adds a new subparagraph (c) that permits a lawyer to serve as a neutral only if the lawyer or law firm does not represent (and has not previously represented) any party in the matter.

Tennessee: In the rules effective January 1, 2011, Rule 2.4 defines the circumstances under which a lawyer may act as a "dispute resolution neutral," the limitations on a lawyer who assumes that position, the circumstances under which the lawyer must withdraw from the position, and the lawyer's responsibilities following withdrawal. The rule and its comment are much more extensive than Model Rule 2.4.

Virginia: Long before the ABA adopted Model Rule 2.4 in 2002, Virginia adopted its own Rule 2.10 (Third Party Neutral) and Rule 2.11 (Mediator), which provide as follows:

Virginia Rule 2.10 Third Party Neutral

(a) A third party neutral assists parties in reaching a voluntary settlement of a dispute through a structured process known as a dispute resolution proceeding. The third party neutral does not represent any party.

(b) A lawyer who serves as a third party neutral

(1) shall inform the parties of the difference between the lawyer's role as third party neutral and the lawyer's role as one who represents a client;

(2) shall encourage unrepresented parties to seek legal counsel before an agreement is executed; and

(3) may encourage and assist the parties in reaching a resolution of their dispute; but

(4) may not compel or coerce the parties to make an agreement.

(c) A lawyer may serve as a third party neutral only if the lawyer has not previously represented and is not currently representing one of the parties in connection with the subject matter of the dispute resolution proceeding. . . .

(g) A lawyer who serves as a third party neutral shall not charge a fee contingent on the outcome of the resolution proceeding.

(h) This Rule does not apply to joint representation, which is covered by Rule 1.7.

Virginia Rule 2.11 Mediator

(a) A lawyer-mediator is a third party neutral (see Rule 2.10) who facilitates communication between the parties and, without deciding the issues or imposing a solution on the parties, enables them to understand and resolve their dispute.

(b) Prior to agreeing to mediate and throughout the mediation process a lawyer-mediator should reasonably determine that:

(1) mediation is an appropriate process for the parties;

(2) each party is able to participate effectively within the context of the mediation process; and

(3) each party is willing to enter and participate in the process in good faith.

(c) A lawyer-mediator may offer legal information if all parties are present or separately to the parties if they consent. The lawyer-mediator shall inform unrepresented parties or those parties who are not accompanied by legal counsel about the importance of reviewing the lawyer-mediator's legal information with legal counsel.

(d) A lawyer-mediator may offer evaluation of, for example, strengths and weaknesses of positions, assess the value and cost of alternatives to settlement or assess the barriers to settlement (collectively referred to as evaluation) only if such evaluation is incidental to the facilitative role and does not interfere with the lawyer-mediator's impartiality or the self-determination of the parties. . . .

Related Materials

Editors' Note. Comment 2 to Rule 2.4 notes that lawyer neutrals "may also be subject to various codes of ethics. . . ." The Related Materials below include some examples.

ABA Formal Ethics Opinions: See ABA Formal Ethics Op. 06-439 n.2 (2006).

Alternative Dispute Resolution (ADR) refers to a variety of techniques or procedures for resolving disputes without going to a court, or (if litigation has commenced) without holding a trial. Examples of ADR techniques include mediation, arbitration, conciliation, early neutral evaluation, summary jury trials, mini-trials, neutral fact finding, and nonjudicial settlement conferences.

American Arbitration Association (AAA): The American Arbitration Association, a nonprofit organization founded in 1926, is (according to its Mission Statement) "dedicated to the development and widespread use of prompt, effective and economical methods of dispute resolution." The AAA once concentrated on arbitration, but today it offers a broad range of alternative dispute resolution (ADR) services, including mediation, arbitration, fact finding, mini-trials, elections, and other out-of-court settlement procedures. The AAA typically administers well over 200,000 cases per year, using a roster of over 8,000 neutral experts to hear and resolve cases. Many of the neutral experts are lawyers, and are thus governed by Rule 2.4 in jurisdictions that have adopted it. The AAA also helps to develop legislation (such as the Uniform Arbitration Act, or UAA), and has helped develop arbitration procedures to govern many different specific types of disputes (*e.g.*, Construction Industry Arbitration Rules, Employment Dispute Arbitration Rules, Commercial Mediation Rules, and Securities Arbitration Rules). For more information about the AAA, visit *www.adr.org.*

Association for Conflict Resolution: The Association for Conflict Resolution (ACR) describes itself as "a professional organization dedicated to enhancing the practice and public understanding of conflict resolution." ACR serves an international audience that includes more than 6,000 mediators, arbitrators, facilitators, educators, and others involved in conflict resolution and collaborative decision-making. The organization was created through the merger of three other organizations active in the ADR field: the Academy of Family Mediators, the Conflict Resolution Education Network, and the Society of Professionals in Dispute Resolution (SPIDR). In 2010, ACR issued for comment a draft of Model Standards for Mediation Certification Programs. For more information, visit *www.acrnet.org.*

Code of Ethics for Arbitrators in Commercial Disputes: A Joint Committee of the ABA and the American Arbitration Association (AAA) has prepared a code of ethics for commercial arbitrators. It is expressly mentioned in Comment 2 to Rule 2.4. The Code seeks to provide ethical guidelines and standards of conduct for arbitrators and others involved in alternative dispute resolution. It was first promulgated in 1977, and was extensively amended in 2004 based on the work of another joint ABA-AAA working group. The 1977 Code is available online at *www.lectlaw.com/files/adr12.htm.* The 2004 Code is available online at *www.abanet.org/dispute/commercial_disputes.pdf.*

FINRA Codes for Arbitration and Mediation: The Financial Industry Regulatory Authority (FINRA) is the largest independent regulator for securities firms doing business in the United States. FINRA has developed a Code of Arbitration Procedure for Customer Disputes that applies to any dispute between a customer and a FINRA member (or a person associated with a FINRA member) if the dispute is submitted to arbitration under certain FINRA rules. FINRA has also developed a Code of Mediation Procedure that applies to any matter submitted to mediation at FINRA. For more information, see *http://www.finra.org/ArbitrationMediation/Rules/RuleGuidance/p009525.*

"Lawyer for the Situation": During the Senate hearings on the nomination of Louis Brandeis to the Supreme Court in 1916, Brandeis was criticized for alleged conflicts of interest in a complex bankruptcy where he said he was "counsel for the situation." The phrase "lawyer for the situation" has since mystified and intrigued legal scholars, but usually suggests that lawyers should facilitate common goals among multiple parties instead of adhering to the interests of any one client. A thorough recounting of the origin of the phrase is found in several sources, including Alden L. Todd, Justice on Trial: The Case of Louis D. Brandeis (1964); John Frank, *The Legal Ethics of Louis D. Brandeis,* 17 Stan. L. Rev. 683, 699-702 (1965); and John Dzienkowski, *Lawyers as Intermediaries: The Representation of Multiple Clients in the Modern Legal Profession,* 1992 U. Ill. L. Rev. 741 (1992).

Model Rules of Professional Conduct for Federal Lawyers: Federal lawyers are permitted to act as intermediaries only between two individuals. After withdrawal as an intermediary, a federal lawyer may continue to represent some of the clients in the same matter if each client consents.

Model Standards of Conduct for Mediators: In 1994, a joint task force of the ABA, the American Arbitration Association (AAA), and the Society of Professionals in Dispute Resolution (SPIDR) published Model Standards of Conduct for Mediators, which are expressly mentioned in Comment 2 to ABA Model Rule 2.4. The Model Standards are intended to govern all mediators, including lawyers serving as mediators. The Model Standards, as comprehensively amended in 2005, are available online at *www.abanet.org/dispute/documents/model_standards_conduct_april2007.pdf.*

Model Standards of Practice for Family and Divorce Mediation: In 2000, the Association of Family Conciliation Courts (AFCC) adopted the Model Standards of Practice for Family and Divorce Mediation. (The Model Standards replaced the 1984 ABA Standards of Practice for Lawyer Mediators in Family Disputes.) The 2000

Standards are, according to the Reporter's Foreword, "the latest milestone in a nearly twenty-year-old effort by the family mediation community to create standards of practice that will increase public confidence in an evolving profession and provide guidance for its practitioners." The Standards were spearheaded by the ABA Family Law Section and the ABA Mediation Committee, a broad-based committee whose members included several nonlawyer mediator groups, and were approved by the ABA in 2001. The Reporter for the ABA Mediation Committee was Professor Andrew Schepard of Hofstra University School of Law. The Model Standards, as approved by the ABA in 2001, are available at *www.abanet.org/family/reports/mediation.pdf.*

Restatement of the Law Governing Lawyers: See Restatement §§103 and 130 in our chapter on the Restatement later in this volume.

ARTICLE 3. ADVOCATE

Rule 3.1 Meritorious Claims and Contentions

A lawyer shall not bring or defend a proceeding, or assert or controvert an issue therein, unless there is a basis in law and fact for doing so that is not frivolous, which includes a good faith argument for an extension, modification or reversal of existing law. A lawyer for the defendant in a criminal proceeding, or the respondent in a proceeding that could result in incarceration, may nevertheless so defend the proceeding as to require that every element of the case be established.

COMMENT

[1] The advocate has a duty to use legal procedure for the fullest benefit of the client's cause, but also a duty not to abuse legal procedure. The law, both procedural and substantive, establishes the limits within which an advocate may proceed. However, the law is not always clear and never is static. Accordingly, in determining the proper scope of advocacy, account must be taken of the law's ambiguities and potential for change.

[2] The filing of an action or defense or similar action taken for a client is not frivolous merely because the facts have not first been fully substantiated or because the lawyer expects to develop vital evidence only by discovery. What is required of lawyers, however, is that they inform themselves about the facts of their clients' cases and the applicable law and determine that they can make good faith arguments in support of their clients' positions. Such action is not frivolous even though the lawyer believes that the client's position ultimately will not prevail. The action is frivolous, however, if the lawyer is unable either to make a good faith argument on the merits of the action taken or to support the action taken by a good faith argument for an extension, modification or reversal of existing law.

[3] The lawyer's obligations under this Rule are subordinate to federal or state constitutional law that entitles a defendant in a criminal matter to the assistance of counsel in presenting a claim or contention that otherwise would be prohibited by this Rule.

Canon and Code Antecedents

ABA Canons of Professional Ethics: Canons 5, 15, 30, and 31 provided as follows:

5. The Defense or Prosecution of Those Accused of Crime

It is the right of the lawyer to undertake the defense of a person accused of crime, regardless of his personal opinion as to the guilt of the accused; otherwise innocent persons, victims only of suspicious circumstances, might be denied proper defense. Having undertaken such defense, the lawyer is bound, by all fair and honorable means, to present every defense that the law of the land permits, to the end that no person may be deprived of life or liberty, but by due process of law.

The primary duty of a lawyer engaged in public prosecution is not to convict, but to see that justice is done. The suppression of facts or the secreting of witnesses capable of establishing the innocence of the accused is highly reprehensible.

15. How Far a Lawyer May Go in Supporting a Client's Cause

Nothing operates more certainly to create or to foster popular prejudice against lawyers as a class, and to deprive the profession of that full measure of public esteem and confidence which belongs to the proper discharge of its duties than does the false claim, often set up by the unscrupulous in defense of questionable transactions, that it is the duty of the lawyer to do whatever may enable him to succeed in winning his client's cause.

It is improper for a lawyer to assert in argument his personal belief in his client's innocence or in the justice of his cause.

The lawyer owes "entire devotion to the interest of the client, warm zeal in the maintenance and defense of his rights and the exertion of his utmost learning and ability," to the end that nothing be taken or be withheld from him, save by the rules of law, legally applied. No fear of judicial disfavor or public unpopularity should restrain him from the full discharge of his duty. In the judicial forum the client is entitled to the benefit of any and every remedy and defense that is authorized by the law of the land, and he may expect his lawyer to assert every such remedy or defense. But it is steadfastly to be borne in mind that the great trust of the lawyer is to be performed within and not without the bounds of the law. The office of attorney does not permit, much less does it demand of him for any client, violation of law or any manner of fraud or chicane. He must obey his own conscience and not that of his client.

30. Justifiable and Unjustifiable Litigations

The lawyer must decline to conduct a civil cause or to make a defense when convinced that it is intended merely to harass or to injure the opposite party or to work oppression or wrong. But otherwise it is his right, and, having accepted retainer, it becomes his duty to insist upon the judgment of the Court as to the legal merits of his client's claim. His appearance in Court should be deemed equivalent to an assertion on his honor that in his opinion his client's case is one proper for judicial determination.

31. Responsibility for Litigation

No lawyer is obliged to act either as adviser or advocate for every person who may wish to become his client. He has the right to decline employment. Every lawyer upon his own responsibility must decide what employment he will accept as counsel, what causes he will bring into Court for plaintiffs, what cases he will contest in Court for defendants. The responsibility for advising as to questionable transactions, for bringing questionable suits, for urging questionable defenses, is the lawyer's responsibility. He cannot escape it by urging as an excuse that he is only following his client's instructions.

ABA Model Code of Professional Responsibility: Compare DR 7-102(A)(1) and DR 7-102(A)(2) (reprinted later in this volume).

Cross-References in Other Rules

Rule 3.3, Comment 3: "An advocate is responsible for pleadings and other documents prepared for litigation, but is usually not required to have personal knowledge of matters asserted therein, for litigation documents ordinarily present assertions by the client, or by someone on the client's behalf, and not assertions by the lawyer. Compare **Rule 3.1**."

Legislative History of Model Rule 3.1

1980 Discussion Draft contained the following Introduction to Article 3:

> As advocate, a lawyer presents evidence and argument before a tribunal in behalf of a client. The advocate's duty in the adversary system is to present the client's case as persuasively as possible, leaving presentation of the opposing case to the other party. An advocate may not present a claim or defense lacking serious merit for the purpose of delay, although an advocate for the defendant in a criminal case may insist on proof of the offense charged. An advocate does not vouch for the justness of a client's cause but only its legal merit.

In addition, Rule 3.1 provided that

> (A) lawyer shall not:
>
> (1) file a complaint, motion, or pleading other than one that puts the prosecution to its proof in a criminal case, unless according to the lawyer's belief there is good ground to support it; . . .

1981 and ***1982 Drafts*** were substantially the same as adopted.

1983 Rule: As originally adopted in 1983, the first sentence of Rule 3.1 provided that a lawyer shall not bring or defend a proceeding, or assert or controvert an issue therein, unless there is "a basis for doing so" that is not frivolous, which includes a good faith argument for an extension, modification, or reversal of existing law. The second sentence of Rule 3.1 was the same as the 2002 version.

2002 Amendments: At its February 2002 Mid-Year Meeting, the ABA House of Delegates adopted without change the ABA Ethics 2000 Commission proposal to amend Rule 3.1 and its Comment. The amendment added the phrase "in law and fact" after the word "basis" in the first sentence, modified Comment 2, and added Comment 3. The second sentence of Rule 3.1 was not changed.

Selected State Variations

Arizona generally tracks ABA Model Rule 3.1, but the "unless" clause in the first sentence applies if there is a "good faith" basis in law and fact, which "may include" a good faith "and nonfrivolous" argument for an extension, modification, or reversal of existing law.

California: Rule 3-200 provides:

> A member shall not seek, accept, or continue employment if the member knows or should know that the objective of such employment is:
>
> (A) To bring an action, conduct a defense, assert a position in litigation, or take an appeal, without probable cause and for the purpose of harassing or maliciously injuring any person; or
>
> (B) To present a claim or defense in litigation that is not warranted under existing law, unless it can be supported by a good faith argument for an extension, modification, or reversal of such existing law.

Also, California Business & Professions Code §6068(c) states that an attorney has a duty to "counsel or maintain those actions, proceedings, or defenses only as appear to him or her legal or just, except the defense of a person charged with a public offense." In addition, California Civil Code §§128.5, 128.6, and 128.7 provide sanctions for bad faith lawsuits and for frivolous litigation tactics.

Colorado: Rule 1.2(c) permits a lawyer to "provide limited representation to pro se parties . . . ," but Rule 11(b) of the Colorado Rules of Civil Procedure provides as follows:

> *Limited Representation*
>
> . . . Pleadings or papers filed by the pro se party that were prepared with the drafting assistance of the attorney shall include the attorney's name, address, telephone number and registration number. . . . The attorney in providing such drafting assistance may rely on the pro se party's representation of facts, unless the attorney has reason to believe that such representations are false or materially insufficient, in which instance the attorney shall make an independent reasonable inquiry into the facts. . . .

Merely "helping to draft the pleading or paper filed by the pro se party" constitutes a certification by the attorney that the pro se client's document is "(1) well-grounded in fact based upon a reasonable inquiry of the pro se party by the attorney . . . and (3) is not interposed for any improper purpose, such as to harass or to cause unnecessary delay or needless increase in the cost of litigation."

District of Columbia: The second sentence of Rule 3.1 provides that a lawyer for the defendant in a criminal proceeding, or for the respondent in a proceeding that could result in "involuntary institutionalization, shall, if the client elects to go to trial or to a contested factfinding hearing, nevertheless so defend the proceeding as to require that the government carry its burden of proof."

Georgia rejects ABA Model Rule 3.1 and instead retains the language of DR 7-102(A)(1) and (A)(2) from the ABA Model Code of Professional Responsibility.

New Jersey adds the phrase "the lawyer knows or reasonably believes" after "unless" in the first sentence and adds "or the establishment of new law" at the end of the first sentence.

New Mexico creates a Rule 3.0 (Rule 16-300), which specifies as follows:

> In the course of any judicial or quasi-judicial proceeding before a tribunal, a lawyer shall refrain from intentionally manifesting, by words or conduct, bias or prejudice based on race, gender, religion, national origin, disability, age or sexual orientation against the judge, court personnel, parties, witnesses, counsel or others. This rule does not preclude legitimate advocacy when race, gender, religion, national origin, disability, age or sexual orientation is material to the issues in the proceeding.

New York adds Rule 3.1(b), which has no Model Rule equivalent. It defines conduct as "frivolous" if "(1) the lawyer knowingly advances a claim or defense that is unwarranted under existing law, except that the lawyer may advance such claim or defense if it can be supported by good faith argument for an extension, modification, or reversal of existing law; (2) the conduct has no reasonable purpose other than to delay or prolong the resolution of litigation, in violation of Rule 3.2, or serves merely to harass or maliciously injure another; or (3) the lawyer knowingly asserts material factual statements that are false."

Texas: Rule 3.01 ends after the word "frivolous" in the first sentence.

Related Materials

ABA Formal Ethics Opinions: See ABA Formal Ethics Ops. 92-363 (1992), 94-383 (1994), 94-387 (1994), and 08-452 (2008).

Asbestos and Silica Legislation: Since 2004, in response to allegedly frivolous product liability suits in which plaintiffs claim injuries arising from exposure to asbestos or silica (or both), at least seven states have enacted statutes making it more difficult to file such suits. (The seven states are Florida, Georgia, Kansas, Ohio, South Carolina, Tennessee, and Texas.) The statutes establish medical criteria and place other restrictions on plaintiffs. For example, the Silica and Asbestos Claims Act signed by Kansas Governor Kathleen Sebelius in May 2006 requires a plaintiff to (a) meet certain statutorily established medical standards before filing a lawsuit, (b) describe his or her work and medical history, (c) obtain a diagnosis by a qualified physician, (d) undergo recognized diagnostic tests, and (e) prove physical impairment as an essential element in any civil action asserting a silica or asbestos claim.

Congress has also considered bills relating to asbestos litigation. In 2005, the House of Representatives considered a bill that would have established a series of medical criteria for claimants seeking to prove that they suffer from eligible diseases or conditions caused by asbestos exposure. In 2006, the Senate considered the Fairness in Asbestos Injury Resolution (FAIR) Act of 2006. Neither the House bill nor the Senate bill became law. Each bill is related to ABA Model Rule 3.1 because the law is designed to combat allegedly frivolous lawsuits.

Federal Rules of Appellate Procedure: Rule 38, entitled "Frivolous Appeal—Damages and Costs," provides: "If a court of appeals determines that an appeal is frivolous, it may, after a separately filed motion or notice from the court and reasonable opportunity to respond, award just damages and single or double costs to the appellee."

Federal Rules of Civil Procedure: Rule 11(b)(1)-(2) provides that a lawyer's signature on a pleading, written motion, or other paper certifies, among other things, that to the best of the lawyer's "knowledge, information, and belief, formed after an inquiry reasonable under the circumstances":

> (1) it is not being presented for any improper purpose, such as to harass, cause unnecessary delay, or needlessly increase the cost of litigation;
>
> (2) the claims, defenses, and other legal contentions are warranted by existing law or by a nonfrivolous argument for extending, modifying, or reversing existing law or for establishing new law; . . .

Rule 11 also gives courts discretion to impose various monetary and other sanctions on those who violate the rule. When we went to press in September 2011, the House of Representatives was considering amendments to Rule 11—see our entry on "Law Suit Abuse Reduction Act" below in these Related Materials.

Fee Award Statutes: Dozens of state and federal statutes permit courts to award attorney fees to a prevailing party in litigation if the opposing party's position is frivolous or unjustified. In federal criminal prosecutions, for example, 18 U.S.C. §3006A provides that a court "may" award reasonable attorney fees and other litigation expenses to a federal criminal defendant (other than one represented by assigned counsel paid for by the public) "where the court finds that the position of the United States was vexatious, frivolous, or in bad faith, unless the court finds that special circumstances make such an award unjust." Similarly, in federal civil cases to which the United States is a party, the Equal Access to Justice Act, 28 U.S.C. §2412(d)(1), provides that a court "shall" award attorney fees to the prevailing party if the government's position in the litigation was not "substantially justified" unless "special circumstances make an award unjust."

IRS Regulations: In the regulations governing practice before the Internal Revenue Service, 31 C.F.R. §10.34(b) provides as follows:

> (b) Documents, affidavits, and other papers
>
> (1) A practitioner may not advise a client to take a position on a document, affidavit or other paper submitted to the Internal Revenue Service unless the position is not frivolous.
>
> (2) A practitioner may not advise a client to submit a document, affidavit or other paper to the Internal Revenue Service
>
> (i) The purpose of which is to delay or impede the administration of the Federal tax laws;
>
> (ii) That is frivolous; or
>
> (iii) That contains or omits information in a manner that demonstrates an intentional disregard of a rule or regulation unless the practitioner also advises the client to submit a document that evidences a good faith challenge to the rule or regulation.

Lawsuit Abuse Reduction Act: In March 2011, Rep. Lamar Smith (R-Texas) introduced and held hearings on a bill (H.R. 966) called the Lawsuit Abuse Reduction Act (LARA). Senator Charles Grassley (R-Iowa) introduced a companion bill (S. 533) in the Senate. The bill would (a) reinstate the pre-1993 requirement of mandatory sanctions for a violation of Rule 11 of the Federal Rules of Civil Procedure, (b) require that judges impose monetary sanctions, including the opposing party's costs and attorney's fees, against lawyers who file frivolous lawsuits, and (c) reverse the 1993 amendments to Rule 11 that allow parties and their attorneys to avoid sanctions for making frivolous claims by withdrawing the claims within 21 days after a motion for sanctions has been served.

Private Securities Litigation Reform Act: The Private Securities Litigation Reform Act (PSLRA), 15 U.S.C. §77z-1, Title I (entitled "Reduction of Abusive Litigation"), requires a court, upon "final adjudication" of a securities fraud action, to make "specific findings" as to whether each attorney in the action complied with Rule 11(b) of the Federal Rules of Civil Procedure with respect to any complaint, responsive pleading, or dispositive motion. The law also establishes a rebuttable presumption that a party who has violated Rule 11 should pay the opposing party's reasonable attorney fees and expenses as an appropriate sanction.

Restatement of the Law Governing Lawyers: See Restatement §§57(2) and 110(1) and (2) in our chapter on the Restatement later in this volume.

Rule 3.2 Expediting Litigation

A lawyer shall make reasonable efforts to expedite litigation consistent with the interests of the client.

COMMENT

[1] Dilatory practices bring the administration of justice into disrepute. Although there will be occasions when a lawyer may properly seek a postponement for personal reasons, it is not proper for a lawyer to routinely fail to expedite litigation solely for the convenience of the advocates. Nor will a failure to expedite be reasonable if done for the purpose of frustrating an opposing party's attempt to obtain rightful redress or repose. It is not a justification that similar conduct is often tolerated by the bench and bar. The question is whether a competent lawyer acting in good faith would regard the course of action as having some substantial purpose other than delay. Realizing financial or other benefit from otherwise improper delay in litigation is not a legitimate interest of the client.

Canon and Code Antecedents

ABA Canons of Professional Ethics: No comparable Canon.

ABA Model Code of Professional Responsibility: Compare DR 7-101(A)(1) and DR 7-102(A)(1) (reprinted later in this volume).

Cross-References in Other Rules

None.

Legislative History of Model Rule 3.2

1980 Discussion Draft (then Rule 3.3(a)) provided:

> A lawyer shall make every effort consistent with the legitimate interests of the client to expedite litigation. Realizing financial or other benefit from otherwise improper delay in litigation is not a legitimate interest of the client. A lawyer shall not engage in any procedure or tactic having no substantial purpose other than delay or increasing the cost of litigation to another party.

1981 Draft: "A lawyer shall make reasonable effort consistent with the *legitimate* interests of the client to expedite litigation."

1982 Draft was adopted.

1983 Rule: As originally adopted in 1983, Rule 3.2 was the same as the 2002 version.

2002 Amendments: At its February 2002 Mid-Year Meeting, the ABA House of Delegates adopted without change the ABA Ethics 2000 Commission proposal to amend the Comment to Rule 3.2. (The Ethics 2000 Commission did not propose any changes to the text of Rule 3.2.) The amendment to the Comment deleted the clause, "Delay should not be indulged merely for the convenience of the advocates," and replaced it with the entire second sentence and the beginning of the third sentence ("Although there will be occasions when a lawyer may properly seek a postponement for personal reasons, it is not proper for a lawyer to routinely fail to expedite litigation solely for the convenience of the advocates. Nor will a failure to expedite be reasonable if done . . . ").

Selected State Variations

California: The California Rules of Professional Conduct have no comparable provision. California Business & Professions Code §6128(b) provides that an attorney is "guilty of a misdemeanor," punishable by six months in jail and/or a $2,500 fine, if the attorney "[w]illfully delays his client's suit with a view to his own gain."

District of Columbia adds Rule 3.2(a), which provides: "In representing a client, a lawyer shall not delay a proceeding when the lawyer knows or when it is obvious that such action would serve solely to harass or maliciously injure another." Rule 3.2(b) is identical to ABA Model Rule 3.2.

Nevada: Rule 3.2(a) is identical to ABA Model Rule 3.2, but Nevada adds a new Rule 3.2(b) providing that paragraph (a) "does not preclude a lawyer from granting a reasonable request from opposing counsel for an accommodation, such as an extension of time, or from disagreeing with a client's wishes on administrative and tactical matters, such as scheduling depositions, the number of depositions to be taken, and the frequency and use of written discovery requests."

New Jersey adds "and shall treat with courtesy and consideration all persons involved in the legal process" at the end of Rule 3.2.

New York: Rule 3.2 provides that "a lawyer shall not use means that have no substantial purpose other than to delay or prolong the proceeding or to cause needless expense."

Ohio omits ABA Model Rule 3.2. A Note following the rule explains that the "substance" of ABA Model Rule 3.2 "is addressed by other provisions," including Rules 1.3, 3.1, and 4.4(a).

Texas: Rule 3.02 provides that during litigation a lawyer "shall not take a position that unreasonably increases the costs or other burdens of the case or that unreasonably delays resolution of the matter."

Virginia omits Rule 3.2.

Related Materials

ABA Formal Ethics Opinions: See ABA Formal Ethics Ops. 93-370 (1993), 93-379 (1993), and 96-400 (1996).

Abusive Litigation Tactics: 28 U.S.C. §1927 gives federal courts the authority to penalize litigants who engage in abusive litigation tactics. It provides as follows:

> Any attorney . . . who so multiplies the proceedings in any case unreasonably and vexatiously may be required by the court to satisfy personally the excess costs, expenses, and attorneys' fees reasonably incurred because of such conduct.

Alternative Dispute Resolution (ADR): Some lawyers believe that the obligation in Rule 3.2 to "expedite litigation" includes the obligation to inform a client about the availability of alternatives to litigation. For example, a Texas Bar Association Creed states: "I will advise my client regarding the availability of mediation [and] arbitration. . . . " Similarly, the Houston Bar Association has adopted guidelines stating: "When appropriate, I will counsel my client with respect to mediation, arbitration, and other alternative methods of dispute resolution." In the context of Rule 2.1, Colorado, Georgia, and Hawaii already require lawyers to advise clients about ADR, and numerous state and federal courts have adopted mandatory ADR to move litigation along more quickly and inexpensively.

Federal Rules of Civil Procedure: Fed. R. Civ. P. 1 provides that the Federal Rules of Civil Procedure shall be construed "to secure the just, speedy, and inexpensive determination of every action." Fed. R. Civ. P. 11, the broadest and most frequently invoked sanctions rule, requires attorneys to sign every pleading, motion, or other paper to certify that (among other things) the paper is not being presented for any improper purpose, such as to "cause unnecessary delay" in the litigation. Fed. R. Civ. P. 26(g)(1)(B)(ii) requires a similar certification for discovery requests, responses, and objections. Fed. R. Civ. P. 56(g) provides for sanctions whenever the court finds that any affidavit supporting or opposing a motion for summary judgment has been presented in bad faith "or solely for the purpose of delay."

Federal Rules of Evidence: Rule 102 of the Federal Rules of Evidence provides that the Rules shall be construed to secure "elimination of unjustifiable expense and delay. . . ."

Model Rules of Professional Conduct for Federal Lawyers: Rule 3.2 provides: "A Federal lawyer shall make reasonable efforts to expedite litigation and other proceedings consistent with the interests of the client and the lawyer's responsibilities to the tribunal to avoid unwarranted delay."

Restatement of the Law Governing Lawyers: The Restatement has no comparable provision.

Rule 3.3 Candor Toward the Tribunal

(a) A lawyer shall not knowingly:

(1) make a false statement of fact or law to a tribunal or fail to correct a false statement of material fact or law previously made to the tribunal by the lawyer;

(2) fail to disclose to the tribunal legal authority in the controlling jurisdiction known to the lawyer to be directly adverse to the position of the client and not disclosed by opposing counsel; or

(3) offer evidence that the lawyer knows to be false. If a lawyer, the lawyer's client, or a witness called by the lawyer, has offered material evidence and the lawyer comes to know of its falsity, the lawyer shall take reasonable remedial measures, including, if necessary, disclosure to the tribunal. A lawyer may refuse to offer evidence, other than the testimony of a defendant in a criminal matter, that the lawyer reasonably believes is false.

(b) A lawyer who represents a client in an adjudicative proceeding and who knows that a person intends to engage, is engaging or has

engaged in criminal or fraudulent conduct related to the proceeding shall take reasonable remedial measures, including, if necessary, disclosure to the tribunal.

(c) The duties stated in paragraphs (a) and (b) continue to the conclusion of the proceeding, and apply even if compliance requires disclosure of information otherwise protected by Rule 1.6.

(d) In an ex parte proceeding, a lawyer shall inform the tribunal of all material facts known to the lawyer that will enable the tribunal to make an informed decision, whether or not the facts are adverse.

COMMENT

[1] This Rule governs the conduct of a lawyer who is representing a client in the proceedings of a tribunal. See Rule 1.0(m) for the definition of "tribunal." It also applies when the lawyer is representing a client in an ancillary proceeding conducted pursuant to the tribunal's adjudicative authority, such as a deposition. Thus, for example, paragraph (a)(3) requires a lawyer to take reasonable remedial measures if the lawyer comes to know that a client who is testifying in a deposition has offered evidence that is false.

[2] This Rule sets forth the special duties of lawyers as officers of the court to avoid conduct that undermines the integrity of the adjudicative process. A lawyer acting as an advocate in an adjudicative proceeding has an obligation to present the client's case with persuasive force. Performance of that duty while maintaining confidences of the client, however, is qualified by the advocate's duty of candor to the tribunal. Consequently, although a lawyer in an adversary proceeding is not required to present an impartial exposition of the law or to vouch for the evidence submitted in a cause, the lawyer must not allow the tribunal to be misled by false statements of law or fact or evidence that the lawyer knows to be false.

Representations by a Lawyer

[3] An advocate is responsible for pleadings and other documents prepared for litigation, but is usually not required to have personal knowledge of matters asserted therein, for litigation documents ordinarily present assertions by the client, or by someone on the client's behalf, and not assertions by the lawyer. Compare Rule 3.1. However, an assertion purporting to be on the lawyer's own knowledge, as in an affidavit by the lawyer or in a statement in open court, may properly be made only when the lawyer knows the assertion is true or believes it to be true on the basis of a reasonably diligent inquiry. There are circumstances where failure to make a disclosure is the equivalent of an affirmative misrepresentation. The obligation prescribed in Rule 1.2(d) not to counsel a client to commit or assist the client in committing a fraud applies in litigation. Regarding compliance with Rule 1.2(d), see the Comment to that Rule. See also the Comment to Rule 8.4(b).

Legal Argument

[4] Legal argument based on a knowingly false representation of law constitutes dishonesty toward the tribunal. A lawyer is not required to make a disinterested exposition of the law, but must recognize the existence of pertinent legal authorities. Furthermore, as stated in paragraph (a)(2), an advocate has a duty to disclose directly adverse authority in the controlling jurisdiction that has not been disclosed by the opposing party. The underlying concept is that legal argument is a discussion seeking to determine the legal premises properly applicable to the case.

Offering Evidence

[5] Paragraph (a)(3) requires that the lawyer refuse to offer evidence that the lawyer knows to be false, regardless of the client's wishes. This duty is premised on the lawyer's obligation as an officer of the court to prevent the trier of fact from being misled by false evidence. A lawyer does not violate this Rule if the lawyer offers the evidence for the purpose of establishing its falsity.

[6] If a lawyer knows that the client intends to testify falsely or wants the lawyer to introduce false evidence, the lawyer should seek to persuade the client that the evidence should not be offered. If the persuasion is ineffective and the lawyer continues to represent the client, the lawyer must refuse to offer the false evidence. If only a portion of a witness's testimony will be false, the lawyer may call the witness to testify but may not elicit or otherwise permit the witness to present the testimony that the lawyer knows is false.

[7] The duties stated in paragraphs (a) and (b) apply to all lawyers, including defense counsel in criminal cases. In some jurisdictions, however, courts have required counsel to present the accused as a witness or to give a narrative statement if the accused so desires, even if counsel knows that the testimony or statement will be false. The obligation of the advocate under the Rules of Professional Conduct is subordinate to such requirements. See also Comment [9].

[8] The prohibition against offering false evidence only applies if the lawyer knows that the evidence is false. A lawyer's reasonable belief that evidence is false does not preclude its presentation to the trier of fact. A lawyer's knowledge that evidence is false, however, can be inferred from the circumstances. See Rule 1.0(f). Thus, although a lawyer should resolve doubts about the veracity of testimony or other evidence in favor of the client, the lawyer cannot ignore an obvious falsehood.

[9] Although paragraph (a)(3) only prohibits a lawyer from offering evidence the lawyer knows to be false, it permits the lawyer to refuse to offer testimony or other proof that the lawyer reasonably believes is false. Offering such proof may reflect adversely on the lawyer's ability to discriminate in the quality of evidence and thus impair the lawyer's effectiveness as an advocate. Because of the special protections historically provided criminal defendants, however, this Rule does not permit a lawyer to refuse to offer the testimony of such a client where the lawyer reasonably believes but does not know that the testimony will be false. Unless the lawyer knows the testimony will be false, the lawyer must honor the client's decision to testify. See also Comment [7].

Remedial Measures

[10] Having offered material evidence in the belief that it was true, a lawyer may subsequently come to know that the evidence is false. Or, a lawyer may be surprised when the lawyer's client, or another witness called by the lawyer, offers testimony the lawyer knows to be false, either during the lawyer's direct examination or in response to cross-examination by the opposing lawyer. In such situations or if the lawyer knows of the falsity of testimony elicited from the client during a deposition, the lawyer must take reasonable remedial measures. In such situations, the advocate's proper course is to remonstrate with the client confidentially, advise the client of the lawyer's duty of candor to the tribunal and seek the client's cooperation with respect to the withdrawal or correction of the false statements or evidence. If that fails, the advocate must take further remedial action. If withdrawal from the representation is not permitted or will not undo the effect of the false evidence, the advocate must make such disclosure to the tribunal as is reasonably necessary to remedy the situation, even if doing so requires the lawyer to reveal information that otherwise would be protected by Rule 1.6. It is for the tribunal then to determine what should be done-making a statement about the matter to the trier of fact, ordering a mistrial or perhaps nothing.

[11] The disclosure of a client's false testimony can result in grave consequences to the client, including not only a sense of betrayal but also loss of the case and perhaps a prosecution for perjury. But the alternative is that the lawyer cooperate in deceiving the court, thereby subverting the truth-finding process which the adversary system is designed to implement. See Rule 1.2(d). Furthermore, unless it is clearly understood that the lawyer will act upon the duty to disclose the existence of false evidence, the client can simply reject the lawyer's advice to reveal the false evidence and insist that the lawyer keep silent. Thus the client could in effect coerce the lawyer into being a party to fraud on the court.

Preserving Integrity of Adjudicative Process

[12] Lawyers have a special obligation to protect a tribunal against criminal or fraudulent conduct that undermines the integrity of the adjudicative process, such as bribing, intimidating or otherwise unlawfully communicating with a witness, juror, court official or other participant in the proceeding, unlawfully destroying or concealing documents or other evidence or failing to disclose information to the tribunal when required by law to do so. Thus, paragraph (b) requires a lawyer to take reasonable remedial measures, including disclosure if necessary, whenever the lawyer knows that a person, including the lawyer's client, intends to engage, is engaging or has engaged in criminal or fraudulent conduct related to the proceeding.

Duration of Obligation

[13] A practical time limit on the obligation to rectify false evidence or false statements of law and fact has to be established. The conclusion of the proceeding is a reasonably definite point for the termination of the obligation. A proceeding has

concluded within the meaning of this Rule when a final judgment in the proceeding has been affirmed on appeal or the time for review has passed.

Ex Parte Proceedings

[14] Ordinarily, an advocate has the limited responsibility of presenting one side of the matters that a tribunal should consider in reaching a decision; the conflicting position is expected to be presented by the opposing party. However, in any ex parte proceeding, such as an application for a temporary restraining order, there is no balance of presentation by opposing advocates. The object of an ex parte proceeding is nevertheless to yield a substantially just result. The judge has an affirmative responsibility to accord the absent party just consideration. The lawyer for the represented party has the correlative duty to make disclosures of material facts known to the lawyer and that the lawyer reasonably believes are necessary to an informed decision.

Withdrawal

[15] Normally, a lawyer's compliance with the duty of candor imposed by this Rule does not require that the lawyer withdraw from the representation of a client whose interests will be or have been adversely affected by the lawyer's disclosure. The lawyer may, however, be required by Rule 1.16(a) to seek permission of the tribunal to withdraw if the lawyer's compliance with this Rule's duty of candor results in such an extreme deterioration of the client-lawyer relationship that the lawyer can no longer competently represent the client. Also see Rule 1.16(b) for the circumstances in which a lawyer will be permitted to seek a tribunal's permission to withdraw. In connection with a request for permission to withdraw that is premised on a client's misconduct, a lawyer may reveal information relating to the representation only to the extent reasonably necessary to comply with this Rule or as otherwise permitted by Rule 1.6.

Canon and Code Antecedents

ABA Canons of Professional Ethics: Canons 5, 15, 22, and 41 provided, in pertinent part, as follows:

5. The Defense or Prosecution of Those Accused of Crime

It is the right of the lawyer to undertake the defense of a person accused of crime, regardless of his personal opinion as to the guilt of the accused; otherwise innocent persons, victims only of suspicious circumstances, might be denied proper defense. Having undertaken such defense, the lawyer is bound, by all fair and honorable means, to present every defense that the law of the land permits, to the end that no person may be deprived of life or liberty, but by due process of law.

15. How Far a Lawyer May Go in Supporting a Client's Cause

Nothing operates more certainly to create or to foster popular prejudice against lawyers as a class, and to deprive the profession of that full measure of public esteem and confidence which belongs to the proper discharge of its duties than does the false claim, often set up by the unscrupulous in defense of questionable transactions, that it is the duty of the lawyer to do whatever may enable him to succeed in winning his client's cause. . . .

The lawyer owes "entire devotion to the interest of the client, warm zeal in the maintenance and defense of his rights and the exertion of his utmost learning and ability," to the end that nothing be taken or be withheld from him, save by the rules of law, legally applied. No fear of judicial disfavor or public unpopularity should restrain him from the full discharge of his duty. In the judicial forum the client is entitled to the benefit of any and every remedy and defense that is authorized by the law of the land, and he may expect his lawyer to assert every such remedy or defense. But it is steadfastly to be borne in mind that the great trust of the lawyer is to be performed within and not without the bounds of the law. The office of attorney does not permit, much less does it demand of him for any client, violation of law or any manner of fraud or chicane. He must obey his own conscience and not that of his client.

22. *Candor and Fairness*

The conduct of the lawyer before the Court and with other lawyers should be characterized by candor and fairness.

It is not candid or fair for the lawyer knowingly to misquote the contents of a paper, the testimony of a witness, the language or the argument of opposing counsel, or the language of a decision or a textbook; or with knowledge of its invalidity, to cite as authority a decision that has been overruled, or a statute that has been repealed; or in argument to assert as a fact that which has not been proved, or in those jurisdictions where a side has the opening and closing arguments to mislead his opponent by concealing or withholding positions in his opening argument upon which his side then intends to rely.

It is unprofessional and dishonorable to deal other than candidly with the facts in taking the statements of witnesses, in drawing affidavits and other documents, and in the presentation of causes.

A lawyer should not offer evidence which he knows the Court should reject, in order to get the same before the jury by argument for its admissibility, nor should he address to the Judge arguments upon any point not properly calling for determination by him. Neither should he introduce into an argument, addressed to the court, remarks or statements intended to influence the jury or bystanders.

These and all kindred practices are unprofessional and unworthy of an officer of the law charged, as is the lawyer, with the duty of aiding in the administration of justice.

41. *Discovery of Imposition and Deception*

When a lawyer discovers that some fraud or deception has been practiced, which has unjustly imposed upon the court or a party, he should endeavor to rectify it; at first by advising his client, and if his client refuses to forego the advantage thus unjustly gained, he should promptly inform the injured person or his counsel, so that they may take appropriate steps.

ABA Model Code of Professional Responsibility: Compare DR 7-102(A)(3), DR 7-102(A)(4), DR 7-102(A)(5), DR 7-102(B)(1), and DR 7-106(B)(1) (reprinted later in this volume).

Cross-References in Other Rules

Rule 1.6, Comment 15: "***Rule 3.3*** . . . requires disclosure in some circumstances regardless of whether such disclosure is permitted by this Rule. See **Rule 3.3(c)**."

Rule 1.8, Comment 5: It is prohibited to partake in the "disadvantageous use of client information unless the client gives informed consent, except as permitted or required by these Rules. See Rules 1.2(d), 1.6, 1.9(c), **3.3**, 4.1(b), 8.1 and 8.3."

Rule 1.13, Comment 6: "[T]his Rule does not limit or expand the lawyer's responsibility under Rule 1.8, 1.16, **3.3** or 4.1."

Rule 1.16, Comment 3: "Lawyers should be mindful of their obligations to both clients and the court under Rules 1.6 and **3.3**."

Rule 2.4, Comment 5: "When the dispute-resolution process takes place before a tribunal, as in binding arbitration (see Rule 1.0(m)), the lawyer's duty of candor is governed by **Rule 3.3**."

Rule 3.9: "A lawyer representing a client before a legislative body or administrative agency in a nonadjudicative proceeding shall disclose that the appearance is in a representative capacity and shall conform to the provisions of **Rules 3.3(a)** through **(c)**, 3.4(a) through (c), and 3.5."

Rule 3.9, Comment 1: "In representation before bodies such as legislatures, municipal councils, and executive and administrative agencies acting in a rule-making or policy-making capacity" lawyers must deal "honestly and in conformity with applicable rules of procedure. See **Rules 3.3(a)** through **(c)**, 3.4(a) through (c) and 3.5."

Rule 8.1, Comment 3: "A lawyer representing an applicant for admission to the bar, or representing a lawyer who is the subject of a disciplinary inquiry or proceeding, is governed by the rules applicable to the client-lawyer relationship, including Rule 1.6 and, in some cases, **Rule 3.3**."

Legislative History of Model Rule 3.3

1980 Discussion Draft (then Rule 3.1) provided:

(a) A lawyer shall not: . . .

(3) except as provided in paragraph (f), offer evidence that the lawyer is convinced beyond a reasonable doubt is false, or offer without suitable explanation evidence that the lawyer knows is substantially misleading; or

(4) make a representation about existing legal authority that the lawyer knows to be inaccurate or so incomplete as to be substantially misleading.

(b) Except as provided in paragraph (f), if a lawyer discovers that evidence or testimony presented by the lawyer is false, the lawyer shall disclose that fact and take suitable measures to rectify the consequences, even if doing so requires disclosure of a confidence of the client or disclosure that the client is implicated in the falsification.

(c) If a lawyer discovers that the tribunal has not been apprised of legal authority known to the lawyer that would probably have a substantial effect on the determination of a material issue, the lawyer shall advise the tribunal of that authority.

(d) Except as provided in paragraph (f), a lawyer shall disclose a fact known to the lawyer, even if the fact is adverse, when disclosure:

(1) is required by law or the Rules of Professional Conduct; or

(2) is necessary to correct a manifest misapprehension resulting from a previous representation the lawyer has made to the tribunal.

(e) Except as provided in paragraph (f), a lawyer may apprise another party of evidence favorable to that party and may refuse to offer evidence that the lawyer believes with substantial reason to be false.

(f) A lawyer for a defendant in a criminal case:

(1) is not required to apprise the prosecutor or the tribunal of evidence adverse to the accused, except as law may otherwise provide;

(2) may not disclose facts as required by paragraph (d) if doing so is prohibited by applicable law;

(3) shall offer evidence regardless of belief as to whether it is false if the client so demands and applicable law requires that the lawyer comply with such a demand.

(g) A prosecutor has the further duty of disclosure stated in Rule 3.10.

1981 Draft was substantially the same as adopted in 1983 except that subparagraph (a) provided that a lawyer shall not knowingly:

(1) make a false statement of fact or law to a tribunal, or fail to disclose a fact in circumstances where the failure to make the disclosure is the equivalent of the lawyer's making a material misrepresentation;

(2) fail to make a disclosure of fact necessary to prevent a fraud on the tribunal. . . .

1982 Draft was adopted.

1983 Rule: As originally adopted in 1983, Rule 3.3 provided as follows:

(a) A lawyer shall not knowingly:

(1) make a false statement of material fact or law to a tribunal;

(2) fail to disclose a material fact to a tribunal when disclosure is necessary to avoid assisting a criminal or fraudulent act by the client;

(3) [Same as 2002 version of Rule 3.3(a)(2).]

(4) offer evidence that the lawyer knows to be false. If a lawyer has offered material evidence and comes to know of its falsity, the lawyer shall take reasonable remedial measures.

(b) The duties stated in paragraph (a) continue [remainder is same as in the 2002 version of Rule 3.3(c).]

(c) A lawyer may refuse to offer evidence that the lawyer reasonably believes is false.

(d) [Same as 2002 version of Rule 3.3(d).]

2002 Amendments: At its February 2002 Mid-Year Meeting, the ABA House of Delegates adopted without change the ABA Ethics 2000 Commission proposal to amend Rule 3.3 and its Comment. The amendments revised Rule 3.3(a)(1), deleted (a)(2), revised (a)(3), added (b), deleted (c) (moving its substance to (a)(3)), added Comments 1, 5-7, 12 and 15, and amended or deleted most other Comments. The pre-2002 version of Rule 3.3, which continues to influence the rules of many states, provided as follows:

(a) A lawyer shall not knowingly:

(1) make a false statement of material fact or law to a tribunal;

(2) fail to disclose a material fact to a tribunal when disclosure is necessary to avoid assisting a criminal or fraudulent act by the client;

(3) fail to disclose to the tribunal legal authority in the controlling jurisdiction known to the lawyer to be directly adverse to the position of the client and not disclosed by opposing counsel; or

(4) offer evidence that the lawyer knows to be false. If a lawyer has offered material evidence and comes to know of its falsity, the lawyer shall take reasonable remedial measures.

(b) The duties stated in paragraph (a) continue to the conclusion of the proceeding, and apply even if compliance requires disclosure of information otherwise protected by Rule 1.6.

(c) A lawyer may refuse to offer evidence that the lawyer reasonably believes is false.

(d) In an ex parte proceeding, a lawyer shall inform the tribunal of all material facts known to the lawyer that will enable the tribunal to make an informed decision, whether or not the facts are adverse.

Selected State Variations

California: Rule 5-200 provides as follows:

> In presenting a matter to a tribunal, a member:
>
> (A) Shall employ, for the purpose of maintaining the causes confided to the member such means only as are consistent with truth;
>
> (B) Shall not seek to mislead the judge, judicial officer, or jury by an artifice or false statement of fact or law;
>
> (C) Shall not intentionally misquote to a tribunal the language of a book, statute, or decision;
>
> (D) Shall not, knowing its invalidity, cite as authority a decision that has been overruled or a statute that has been repealed or declared unconstitutional; and
>
> (E) Shall not assert personal knowledge of the facts at issue, except when testifying as a witness.

In addition, California Business & Professions Code §6068(d) provides that it is the duty of an attorney to employ "those means only as are consistent with truth, and never to seek to mislead the judge or any judicial officer by an artifice or false statement of fact or law." And §6128(a) makes an attorney guilty of a misdemeanor if the attorney engages in "any deceit or collusion, or consents to any deceit or collusion, with intent to deceive the court or any party."

District of Columbia: Rule 3.3(a)(1) provides that a lawyer shall not knowingly make a false statement of fact or law to a tribunal or fail to correct a false statement of material fact or law previously made to the tribunal by the lawyer, "unless correction would require disclosure of information that is prohibited by Rule 1.6." Rule 3.3(a)(2) is nearly identical to ABA Model Rule 1.2(d). D.C.'s equivalent to ABA Model Rule 3.3(a)(2) applies to undisclosed, directly adverse legal authority in the controlling jurisdiction not disclosed by opposing counsel and known to be "dispositive of a question at issue."

D.C. Rule 3.3(a)(4) provides that a lawyer shall not knowingly offer evidence that the lawyer knows to be false, "except as provided in paragraph (b)." D.C. Rule 3.3(b) adopts the so-called "narrative method" for presenting false testimony by providing as follows:

> When the witness who intends to give evidence that the lawyer knows to be false is the lawyer's client and is the accused in a criminal case, the lawyer shall first make a good-faith effort to dissuade the client from presenting the false evidence; if the lawyer is unable to dissuade the client, the lawyer shall seek leave of the tribunal to withdraw.

> If the lawyer is unable to dissuade the client or to withdraw without seriously harming the client, the lawyer may put the client on the stand to testify in a narrative fashion, but the lawyer shall not examine the client in such manner as to elicit testimony which the lawyer knows to be false, and shall not argue the probative value of the client's testimony in closing argument.

Rule 3.3(c) provides simply: "The duties stated in paragraph (a) continue to the conclusion of the proceeding." D.C. omits both the second sentence of ABA Model Rule 3.3(a)(3) ("If a lawyer . . . has offered material evidence and the lawyer comes to know of its falsity . . . "), and all of ABA Model Rule 3.3(b) ("A lawyer . . . who knows that a person . . . has engaged in criminal or fraudulent conduct relating to the proceeding . . . ") but covers both situations by adding Rule 3.3(d), which provides as follows: "(d) A lawyer who receives information clearly establishing that a fraud has been perpetrated upon the tribunal shall promptly take reasonable remedial measures, including disclosure to the tribunal to the extent disclosure is permitted by Rule 1.6(d)." (The relevant part of D.C. Rule 1.6(d)(2) provides that when a client has used or is using a lawyer's services to further a crime or fraud, the lawyer may reveal client confidences and secrets to the extent reasonably necessary to "prevent, mitigate or rectify substantial injury to the financial interests or property of another that is reasonably certain to result or has resulted from the client's commission of the crime or fraud.") Finally, D.C. omits ABA Model Rule 3.3(d) (regarding ex parte proceedings).

Florida: Rule 3.3(d) provides that "the duties stated in Rule 3.3(a) continue beyond the conclusion of the proceeding. . . . "

Maryland adds the following Rule 3.3(e): "[A] lawyer for an accused in a criminal case need not disclose that the accused intends to testify falsely or has testified falsely if the lawyer reasonably believes that the disclosure would jeopardize any constitutional right of the accused."

Massachusetts: Rule 3.3(b) states that the conclusion of the proceedings includes "all appeals." Rule 3.3(e) permits a lawyer representing a criminal defendant to elicit false testimony in narrative fashion if withdrawal is not otherwise possible without prejudicing the defendant. However, "the lawyer shall not argue the probative value of the false testimony in closing argument or in any other proceedings, including appeals." A lawyer who is unable to withdraw when he or she knows that a criminal defendant will testify falsely "may not prevent the client from testifying" but must not "examine the client in such a manner as to elicit any testimony from the client the lawyer knows to be false."

Michigan: Effective January 1, 2011, Michigan omits the last sentence of Model Rule 3.3(a)(3) concerning a lawyer's ethical obligations when the lawyer reasonably believes, but does not know, that testimony the lawyer plans to offer will be false. Michigan also adds Rule 3.3(e), which describes in detail the procedures that a lawyer should follow upon discovering that testimony the lawyer previously offered is false.

New Jersey adheres closely to the pre-2002 version of ABA Model Rule 3.3 but adds, in a new Rule 3.3(a)(5), that a lawyer shall not fail to disclose to the tribunal a material fact "knowing that the omission is reasonably certain to mislead the tribunal." Also, New Jersey Rule 1.6(b)(2) requires a lawyer to reveal confidences to prevent a client from committing "a criminal, illegal or fraudulent act that the lawyer reasonably believes is likely to perpetrate a fraud upon a tribunal."

New Mexico specifies in Rule 16-303(E) that a lawyer must disclose to a tribunal whether the lawyer is representing the client in a "limited manner."

New York: Rule 3.3(c) omits the phrase "continue to the conclusion of the proceeding" (and thus has no express time limit). New York also adds Rule 3.3(e), which is substantially similar to 7-106(B)(2) of the old Model Code. Rule 3.3(f), which also has no Model Rule equivalent, is substantially similar to 7-106(C)(5)-(7) of the old Model Code, but it also prohibits "conduct intended to disrupt the tribunal." New York adds Comment 6A, which addresses the rule's application to prosecutors, and omits Comment 13 concerning the duration of the Rule 3.3 obligation.

North Dakota: Rule 3.3(a)(3) provides that if a lawyer, the lawyer's client, or a witness called by the lawyer has offered material evidence and the lawyer comes to know of its falsity, then:

> the lawyer shall take reasonable remedial measures, including, if necessary, disclosure to the tribunal unless the evidence was contained in testimony of the lawyer's client. If the evidence was contained in testimony of the lawyer's client, the lawyer shall make reasonable efforts to convince the client to consent to disclosure. If the client refuses to consent to disclosure, the lawyer shall seek to withdraw from the representation without disclosure. If withdrawal is not permitted, the lawyer may continue the representation and such continuation alone is not a violation of these rules. The lawyer may not use or argue the client's false testimony.

Ohio: Rule 3.3(c) provides that the duties stated in Rules 3.3(a) and (b) continue "until the issue to which the duty relates is determined by the highest tribunal that may consider the issue, or the time has expired for such determination. . . ."

Oregon provides that the duties in Rule 3.3(a) and (b) are suspended if "compliance requires disclosure of information otherwise protected by Rule 1.6."

Pennsylvania adds that it applies if a lawyer, the lawyer's client, or a witness called by the lawyer has offered material evidence "before a tribunal or in an ancillary proceeding conducted pursuant to a tribunal's adjudicative authority, such as a deposition. . . ."

Texas: Rule 3.03(b) and (c) provides:

> (b) If a lawyer has offered material evidence and comes to know of its falsity, the lawyer shall make a good faith effort to persuade the client to authorize the lawyer to correct or withdraw the false evidence. If such efforts are unsuccessful, the lawyer shall take reasonable remedial measures, including disclosure of the true facts.
>
> (c) The duties stated in paragraphs (a) and (b) continue until remedial legal measures are no longer reasonably possible.

Virginia: Rule 3.3(a)(2) provides that a lawyer shall not knowingly "fail to disclose a fact to a tribunal when disclosure is necessary to avoid assisting a criminal or fraudulent act by the client, subject to Rule 1.6." Virginia Rule 3.3(a)(3) requires disclosure only of "controlling" legal authority and omits the word "directly" before "adverse." (The Comment explains that "directly" was deleted because "the limiting effect of that term could seriously dilute the paragraph's meaning.") Virginia Rule 3.3(a)(4) and Rule 3.3(b) are identical to the pre-2002 version of ABA Model Rule 3.3(a)(4) and Rule 3.3(c). Virginia omits ABA Model Rules 3.3(b) and (c) and adds a new paragraph taken verbatim from DR 7-102(B)(2) of the ABA Model Code of Professional Responsibility that provides: "A lawyer who receives information clearly establishing that a person other than a client has perpetrated a fraud upon a tribunal shall promptly reveal the fraud to the tribunal."

Related Materials

ABA Formal Ethics Opinions: See ABA Formal Ethics Ops. 87-353 (1987), 93-376 (1993), 98-412 (1998), and 07-446 (2007).

ABA Standards for Criminal Justice: Defense Function Standard 4-7.5 (Presentation of Evidence) states: "(a) Defense counsel should not knowingly offer false evidence, whether by documents, tangible evidence, or the testimony of witnesses, or fail to take reasonable remedial measures upon discovery of its falsity."

The original draft of The Defense Function, which was drafted in the early 1970s, contained the following version of Standard 4-7.7, sometimes called the "narrative" method:

> If the defendant has admitted to defense counsel facts which establish guilt and counsel's independent investigation established that the admissions are true but the defendant insists on the right to trial, counsel must strongly discourage the defendant against taking the witness stand to testify perjuriously.
>
> If, in advance of trial, the defendant insists that he or she will take the stand to testify perjuriously, the lawyer may withdraw from the case, if that is feasible, seeking leave of the court if necessary, but the court should not be advised of the lawyer's reason for seeking to do so.
>
> If withdrawal from the case is not feasible or is not permitted by the court, or if the situation arises immediately preceding trial or during the trial and the defendant insists upon testifying perjuriously in his or her own behalf, it is unprofessional conduct for the lawyer to lend aid to the perjury or use the perjured testimony. Before the defendant takes the stand in these circumstances, the lawyer should make a record of the fact that the defendant is taking the stand against the advice of counsel in some appropriate manner without revealing the fact to the court. The lawyer may identify the witness as the defendant and may ask appropriate questions of the defendant when it is believed that the defendant's answers will not be perjurious. As to matters for which it is believed the defendant will offer perjurious testimony, the lawyer should seek to avoid direct examination of the defendant in the conventional manner; instead, the lawyer should ask the defendant if he or she wishes to make any additional statement concerning the case to the trier or triers of the facts. A lawyer may not later argue the defendant's known false version of facts to the jury as worthy of belief, and may not recite or rely upon the false testimony in his or her closing argument.

When Standard 4-7.7 was published, it was accompanied by the following official Editorial Note written by the ABA:

> This proposed standard was approved by the ABA Standing Committee on Association Standards for Criminal Justice but was withdrawn prior to submission of this chapter to the ABA House of Delegates. Instead, the question of what should be done in situations dealt with by the standard has been deferred until the ABA Special Commission on Evaluation of Professional Standards [the Kutak Commission] reports its final recommendations.

The final recommendation of the Kutak Commission is found in the original version of ABA Model Rule 3.3 and its Comment. In particular, the original Comment 9 to Rule 3.3 (deleted in 2002) expressly referred to the "narrative" approach suggested in Standard 4-7.7, but both Rule 3.3 and its Comment appeared to reject the narrative method. ABA Formal Ethics Op. 87-353 (1987) rejected the narrative method explicitly. *See also Nix v. Whiteside,* 475 U.S. 157 (1986). Nevertheless, some courts continue to approve the narrative method, and at least three jurisdictions (D.C., Florida, and Massachusetts) expressly permit a narrative in certain circumstances.

ABA Standards for Imposing Lawyer Sanctions:

> 6.11. Disbarment is generally appropriate when a lawyer, with the intent to deceive the court, makes a false statement, submits a false document, or improperly withholds material information, and causes serious or potentially serious injury to a party, or causes a significant or potentially significant adverse effect on the legal proceeding.
>
> 6.12. Suspension is generally appropriate when a lawyer knows that false statements or documents are being submitted to the court or that material information is improperly being withheld, and takes no remedial action, and causes injury or potential injury to a party to the legal proceeding, or causes an adverse or potentially adverse effect on the legal proceeding.
>
> 6.13. Reprimand is generally appropriate when a lawyer is negligent either in determining whether statements or documents are false or in taking remedial action when material information is being withheld, and causes injury or potential injury to a party to the legal proceeding, or causes an adverse or potentially adverse effect on the legal proceeding.
>
> 6.14. Admonition is generally appropriate when a lawyer engages in an isolated instance of neglect in determining whether submitted statements or documents are false or in failing to disclose material information upon learning of its falsity, and causes little or no actual or potential injury to a party, or causes little or no adverse or potentially adverse effect on the legal proceeding. . . .
>
> 6.31. Disbarment is generally appropriate when a lawyer:
>
> . . . (b) makes an ex parte communication with a judge or juror with intent to affect the outcome of the proceeding, and causes serious or potentially serious injury to a party, or causes significant or potentially significant interference with the outcome of the legal proceeding. . . .

Federal Rules of Civil Procedure: Under Fed. R. Civ. P. 26(e)(1)(A), parties have a duty to supplement or correct all discovery information given to the other side (whether the information was given under the automatic initial disclosure provisions of Rule 26(a)(1) or in response to a party's specific request). The duty arises if additional disclosure is ordered by a court, or if the disclosing party "learns that in some material respect the information disclosed is incomplete or incorrect" and "the additional or corrective information has not otherwise been made known to the other parties during the discovery process or in writing."

IRS Regulations: In the regulations governing practice before the Internal Revenue Service, 31 C.F.R. §10.21 provides as follows:

> *§10.21. Knowledge of Client's Omission*
>
> A practitioner who, having been retained by a client with respect to a matter administered by the Internal Revenue Service, knows that the client has not complied with the revenue laws of the United States or has made an error in or omission from any return, document, affidavit, or other paper which the client submitted or executed under the revenue laws of the United States, must advise the client promptly of the fact of such noncompliance, error, or omission. The practitioner must advise the client of the consequences as provided under the Code and regulations of such noncompliance, error, or omission.

Restatement of the Law Governing Lawyers: See Restatement §§111, 112, 118(1), and 120 in our chapter on the Restatement later in this volume.

Rule 3.4 Fairness to Opposing Party and Counsel

A lawyer shall not:

(a) unlawfully obstruct another party's access to evidence or unlawfully alter, destroy or conceal a document or other material having potential evidentiary value. A lawyer shall not counsel or assist another person to do any such act;

(b) falsify evidence, counsel or assist a witness to testify falsely, or offer an inducement to a witness that is prohibited by law;

(c) knowingly disobey an obligation under the rules of a tribunal, except for an open refusal based on an assertion that no valid obligation exists;

(d) in pretrial procedure, make a frivolous discovery request or fail to make reasonably diligent effort to comply with a legally proper discovery request by an opposing party;

(e) in trial, allude to any matter that the lawyer does not reasonably believe is relevant or that will not be supported by admissible evidence, assert personal knowledge of facts in issue except when testifying as a witness, or state a personal opinion as to the justness of a cause, the credibility of a witness, the culpability of a civil litigant or the guilt or innocence of an accused; or

(f) request a person other than a client to refrain from voluntarily giving relevant information to another party unless:

(1) the person is a relative or an employee or other agent of a client; and

(2) the lawyer reasonably believes that the person's interests will not be adversely affected by refraining from giving such information.

COMMENT

[1] The procedure of the adversary system contemplates that the evidence in a case is to be marshalled competitively by the contending parties. Fair competition in the adversary system is secured by prohibitions against destruction or concealment of evidence, improperly influencing witnesses, obstructive tactics in discovery procedure, and the like.

[2] Documents and other items of evidence are often essential to establish a claim or defense. Subject to evidentiary privileges, the right of an opposing party, including the government, to obtain evidence through discovery or subpoena is an important procedural right. The exercise of that right can be frustrated if relevant material is altered, concealed or destroyed. Applicable law in many jurisdictions makes it an offense to destroy material for the purpose of impairing its availability in a pending proceeding or one whose commencement can be foreseen. Falsifying evidence is also generally a criminal offense. Paragraph (a) applies to evidentiary material generally, including computerized information. Applicable law may permit a lawyer to take temporary possession of physical evidence of client crimes for the

purpose of conducting a limited examination that will not alter or destroy material characteristics of the evidence. In such a case, applicable law may require the lawyer to turn the evidence over to the police or other prosecuting authority, depending on the circumstances.

[3] With regard to paragraph (b), it is not improper to pay a witness's expenses or to compensate an expert witness on terms permitted by law. The common law rule in most jurisdictions is that it is improper to pay an occurrence witness any fee for testifying and that it is improper to pay an expert witness a contingent fee.

[4] Paragraph (f) permits a lawyer to advise employees of a client to refrain from giving information to another party, for the employees may identify their interests with those of the client. See also Rule 4.2.

Canon and Code Antecedents

ABA Canons of Professional Ethics: Canons 15, 17, 25, and 39 provided, in pertinent part, as follows:

15. How Far a Lawyer May Go in Supporting a Client's Cause

Nothing operates more certainly to create or to foster popular prejudice against lawyers as a class, and to deprive the profession of that full measure of public esteem and confidence which belongs to the proper discharge of its duties than does the false claim, often set up by the unscrupulous in defense of questionable transactions, that it is the duty of the lawyer to do whatever may enable him to succeed in winning his client's cause.

It is improper for a lawyer to assert in argument his personal belief in his client's innocence or in the justice of his cause. . . .

17. Ill-Feeling and Personalities Between Advocates

Clients, not lawyers, are the litigants. Whatever may be the ill-feeling existing between clients, it should not be allowed to influence counsel in their conduct and demeanor toward each other or toward suitors in the case. All personalities between counsel should be scrupulously avoided. In the trial of a cause it is indecent to allude to the personal history or the personal peculiarities and idiosyncrasies of counsel on the other side. Personal colloquies between counsel which cause delay and promote unseemly wrangling should also be carefully avoided.

25. Taking Technical Advantage of Opposite Counsel; Agreements with Him

A lawyer should not ignore known customs or practice of the Bar or of a particular Court, even when the law permits, without giving timely notice to the opposing counsel. As far as possible, important agreements, affecting the rights of clients, should be reduced to writing; but it is dishonorable to avoid performance of an agreement fairly made because it is not reduced to writing, as required by rules of Court.

39. Witnesses

A lawyer may properly interview any witness or prospective witness for the opposing side in any civil or criminal action without the consent of opposing counsel or party. In doing so, however, he should scrupulously avoid any suggestion calculated to induce the witness to suppress or deviate from the truth, or in any degree to affect his free and untrammeled conduct when appearing at the trial or on the witness stand.

ABA Model Code of Professional Responsibility: Compare DR 7-102(A)(6), DR 7-104(A)(2), DR 7-106(A), DR 7-106(C)(1), DR 7-106(C)(2), DR 7-106(C)(3), DR 7-106(C)(4), DR 7-106(C)(5), DR 7-106(C)(7), DR 7-109(A), and DR 7-109(C) (reprinted later in this volume).

Cross-References in Other Rules

Rule 1.4, Comment 7: "Rules or court orders governing litigation may provide that information supplied to a lawyer may not be disclosed to the client. **Rule 3.4(c)** directs compliance with such rules or orders."

Rule 3.6, Comment 2: "Special rules of confidentiality may validly govern proceedings in juvenile, domestic relations and mental disability proceedings, and perhaps other types of litigation. **Rule 3.4(c)** requires compliance with such rules."

Rule 3.9: "A lawyer representing a client before a legislative body or administrative agency in a nonadjudicative proceeding shall disclose that the appearance is in a representative capacity and shall conform to the provisions of **Rules** 3.3(a) through (c), **3.4(a)** through **(c)**, and 3.5."

Rule 3.9, Comment 1: "In representation before bodies such as legislatures, municipal councils, and executive and administrative agencies acting in a rule-making or policy-making capacity" lawyers must deal "honestly and in conformity with applicable rules of procedure. See **Rules** 3.3(a) through (c), **3.4(a)** through **(c)** and 3.5."

Rule 4.2, Comment 7: "If a constituent of the organization is represented in the matter by his or her own counsel, the consent by that counsel to a communication will be sufficient for purposes of this Rule. Compare **Rule 3.4(f)**."

Legislative History of Model Rule 3.4

1980 Discussion Draft (then Rule 3.2):

(a) A lawyer shall be fair to other parties and their counsel, accord them their procedural rights, and fulfill obligations under the procedural law and established practices of the tribunal.

(b) A lawyer shall not:

(1) improperly obstruct another party's access to evidence, destroy, falsify or conceal evidence, or use illegal methods of obtaining evidence;

(2) disobey an obligation under procedural law, except for an open refusal based on a good faith belief that no valid obligation exists;

(3) refer in a proceeding to a matter that the lawyer has no reasonable basis to believe is relevant thereto, or does not reasonably expect will be supported by admissible evidence;

(4) make a knowing misrepresentation of fact or law to an opposing party or counsel;

(5) interview or otherwise communicate with a party who the lawyer knows is represented by other counsel concerning the subject matter of the representation, except with the consent of that party's counsel or as authorized by law.

In addition, the 1980 Discussion Draft contained the following Rule 2.5:

Alteration or Destruction of Evidence

A lawyer shall not advise a client to alter or destroy a document or other material when the lawyer reasonably should know that the material is relevant to a pending proceeding or one that is clearly foreseeable.

1981 Draft: Substantially the same as finally adopted, except subparagraph (a), which provided:

> A lawyer shall not:
>
> (a) unlawfully obstruct another party's access to evidence or alter, destroy or conceal a document or other material that the lawyer knows or reasonably should know is relevant to a pending proceeding or one that is reasonably foreseeable. A lawyer shall not counsel or assist another person to do any such act.

1982 Draft was adopted.

1983 Rule: As originally adopted in 1983, Rule 3.4 was the same as the 2002 version.

2002 Amendments: At its February 2002 Mid-Year Meeting, the ABA House of Delegates adopted with only minor changes the ABA Ethics 2000 Commission proposal to amend Comment 2 to Rule 3.4 by adding the last two sentences. (The Ethics 2000 Commission did not propose any changes to the text of Rule 3.4 or to the remaining Comments.)

Selected State Variations

Alabama adds two exceptions that allow a lawyer to ask a non-client not to give information to another party if: "(2) the person may be required by law to refrain from disclosing the information; or (3) the information pertains to covert law enforcement investigations in process, such as the use of undercover law enforcement agents."

California: Compare Rule 5-200 (reprinted in the Selected State Variations following ABA Model Rule 3.3 above) and Rule 5-220, which provides that a lawyer "shall not suppress any evidence that the member or the member's client has a legal obligation to reveal or to produce." Also, Rule 5-310 provides that a member shall not:

> (A) Advise or directly or indirectly cause a person to secrete himself or herself or to leave the jurisdiction of a tribunal for the purpose of making that person unavailable as a witness therein.
>
> (B) Directly or indirectly pay, offer to pay, or acquiesce in the payment of compensation to a witness contingent upon the content of the witness's testimony or the outcome of the case. Except where prohibited by law, a member may advance, guarantee, or acquiesce in the payment of:
>
> (1) Expenses reasonably incurred by a witness in attending or testifying.
>
> (2) Reasonable compensation to a witness for loss of time in attending or testifying.
>
> (3) A reasonable fee for the professional services of an expert witness.

In addition, California Penal Code §135, which was enacted in 1872, provides as follows:

> *Destroying evidence.* Every person who, knowing that any book, paper, record, instrument in writing, or other matter or thing, is about to be produced in evidence upon any trial, inquiry, or investigation whatever, authorized by law, willfully destroys or conceals the same, with intent thereby to prevent it from being produced, is guilty of a misdemeanor.

District of Columbia: Rule 3.4 provides that a lawyer shall not:

> (a) Obstruct another party's access to evidence or alter, destroy, or conceal evidence, or counsel or assist another person to do so, if the lawyer reasonably should know that the evidence is or may be the subject of discovery or subpoena in any pending or imminent proceeding. Unless prohibited by law, a lawyer may receive physical evidence of any kind from the client or from another person. If the evidence received by the lawyer belongs to anyone other than the client, the lawyer shall make a good-faith effort to preserve it and to return it to the owner, subject to Rule 1.6; . . .
>
> (g) Peremptorily strike jurors for any reason prohibited by law.

Florida: Rule 3.4(a) replaces the ABA phrase "having potential evidentiary value" with the phrase "that the lawyer knows or reasonably should know is relevant to a pending or a reasonably foreseeable proceeding. . . ." Rule 3.4(b) provides that a lawyer shall not "fabricate" evidence, and provides that a lawyer shall not

> offer an inducement to a witness, except a lawyer may pay a witness reasonable expenses incurred by the witness in attending or testifying at proceedings; a reasonable, noncontingent fee for professional services of an expert witness; and reasonable compensation to reimburse a witness for the loss of compensation incurred by reason of preparing for, attending, or testifying at proceedings.

Florida Rule 3.4(d) deletes the phrase "to make a reasonably diligent effort," instead providing that a lawyer shall not "intentionally" fail to comply with a legally proper discovery request by an opposing party. Florida Rules 3.4(g) and (h) expand upon DR 7-105 of the ABA Model Code of Professional Responsibility by providing that a lawyer must not present, participate in presenting, or threaten to present either criminal charges or "disciplinary charges under these rules" solely to obtain an advantage in a civil matter.

Georgia: Rule 3.4(b) borrows language from DR 7-109(C) of the ABA Model Code of Professional Responsibility. Georgia omits ABA Model Rules 3.4(c), (d), and (e) entirely. Georgia Rule 3.4(f) adds that a lawyer may request a person not to volunteer information to another party "if the information is subject to the assertion of a privilege by the client."

Georgia also adds a new Rule 3.4(g), based on ABA Model Rule 4.4, which provides that a lawyer shall not "use methods of obtaining evidence that violate the legal rights of the opposing party or counsel," and a new Rule 3.4(h), taken verbatim from DR 7-105 of the ABA Model Code, which provides that a lawyer shall not "present, participate in presenting or threaten to present criminal charges solely to obtain an advantage in a civil matter."

Illinois expands on ABA Model Rule 3.4(b)'s command not to "offer an inducement to a witness that is prohibited by law." Comment 3 elaborates on this restriction in even more detail.

Massachusetts: Rule 3.4(g) tracks DR 7-109(C) of the ABA Model Code of Professional Responsibility. Rule 3.4(h) retains the language of DR 7-105. Rule 3.4(i) says that a lawyer shall not, "in appearing in a professional capacity before a tribunal, engage in conduct manifesting bias or prejudice based on race, sex, religion, national origin, disability, age, or sexual orientation against a party, witness, counsel, or other person," but the paragraph expressly does not preclude "legitimate advocacy" when the same factors or similar ones are "an issue in the proceeding."

New Jersey adds Rule 3.4(g), which provides, based on DR 7-105 of the ABA Model Code of Professional Responsibility, that a lawyer shall not "present, participate in presenting, or threaten to present criminal charges to obtain an improper advantage in a civil matter."

New York: Rule 3.4 draws almost exclusively on the old Model Code. Rule 3.4(a)(1)-(2) is substantially the same as DR 7-109(A)-(B). Rule 3.4(a)(3)-(6) is substantially the same as DR 7-102(A)(3), (4), (6), and (8). Rule 3.4(b) is substantially similar to DR 7-109(C). Rule 3.4(c) is substantially the same as DR 7-106(A), and Rule 3.4(d) is substantially the same as DR 7-106(C)(1)-(4). New York adds several comments, including Comment 5, which describes the use of threats:

> The use of threats in negotiation may constitute the crime of extortion. However, not all threats are improper. For example, if a lawyer represents a client who has been criminally harmed by a third person (for example, a theft of property), the lawyer's threat to report the crime does not constitute extortion when honestly claimed in an effort to obtain restitution or indemnification for the harm done. But extortion is committed if the threat involves conduct of the third person unrelated to the criminal harm (for example, a threat to report tax evasion by the third person that is unrelated to the civil dispute).

North Carolina: Rule 3.4(b) adds that a lawyer shall not "counsel or assist a witness to hide or leave the jurisdiction for the purpose of being unavailable as a witness." Rule 3.4(c) provides that a lawyer shall not "advise a client to disobey" an obligation under the rules of a tribunal, except that "a lawyer acting in good faith may take appropriate steps to test the validity of such an obligation." Rule 3.4(f)(1) limits the "employee" exception to a "managerial employee."

Ohio: The exception clause in Ohio Rule 3.4(c) applies to an open refusal based on a "good faith" assertion that no valid obligation exists. Rule 3.4(d) provides that a lawyer engaged in pretrial procedure shall not "intentionally or habitually" make a frivolous "motion or" discovery request. Ohio omits Rule 3.4(f) because it is inconsistent with a lawyer's obligations under Ohio law, and Ohio adds a new Rule 3.4(g) that provides that a lawyer shall not "advise or cause a person to hide or to leave the jurisdiction of a tribunal for the purpose of becoming unavailable as a witness."

Oklahoma omits the clause "other than the testimony of a defendant in a criminal matter" in the last sentence of Rule 3.4(a)(3). In addition, Okalahoma adds a new Rule 3.4(a)(4), which provides that a lawyer "shall not knowingly . . . fail to disclose a fact to a tribunal when disclosure is necessary to avoid assisting a criminal or fraudulent act by the client."

Oregon: Rules 3.4(b) and (g) provide that a lawyer shall not:

> (b) falsify evidence; counsel or assist a witness to testify falsely; offer an inducement to a witness that is prohibited by law; or pay, offer to pay, or acquiesce in payment of compensation to a witness contingent upon the content of the witness's testimony or the outcome of the case; except that a lawyer may advance, guarantee or acquiesce in the payment of: (1) expenses reasonably incurred by a witness in attending or testifying; (2) reasonable compensation to a witness for the witness's loss of time in attending or testifying; or (3) a reasonable fee for the professional services of an expert witness. . . .
>
> (g) threaten to present criminal charges to obtain an advantage in a civil matter unless the lawyer reasonably believes the charge to be true and if the purpose of the lawyer is to compel or induce the person threatened to take reasonable action to make good the wrong which is the subject of the charge.

Pennsylvania: Rule 3.4(b) deletes the ABA phrase "or offer an inducement to a witness that is prohibited by law" and substitutes language nearly identical to DR 7-109(C) of the ABA Model Code of Professional Responsibility. Pennsylvania deletes ABA Model Rule 3.4(c) and substitutes the language of DR 7-106(C)(4). Pennsylvania deletes subparagraphs (d) and (e) of ABA Model Rule 3.4, and adds "and such conduct is not prohibited by Rule 4.2" at the end of Pennsylvania Rule 3.4(d), which is equivalent to ABA Model Rule 3.4(f).

Texas: Rule 3.04(a)'s prohibition on unlawfully altering, destroying, or concealing evidence applies "in anticipation of a dispute." (Regarding "unlawfully," Texas Penal Law §37.09 makes it a felony if a person "knowing that an investigation or official proceeding is pending or in progress . . . alters, destroys, or conceals any record, document, or thing with intent to impair its verity, legibility, or availability as evidence," but §37.09 does not apply to items that are "privileged" or "work product.") Texas Rule 3.04(b) retains the substance of DR 7-109(C) of the ABA Model Code of Professional Responsibility. Rule 3.04(c) retains language from DR 7-106(C), and Rule 3.04(c)(5) provides that a lawyer shall not "engage in conduct intended to disrupt the proceedings." Rule 3.04(d) provides that a lawyer shall not knowingly disobey "or advise the client to disobey" an obligation under the tribunal's "standing rules" or under a "ruling" by the tribunal, except for an open refusal based *either* on an assertion that no valid obligation exists "or on the client's willingness to accept any sanctions arising from such disobedience."

Virginia eliminates the word "unlawfully" from Rule 3.4(a), and provides that a lawyer shall not alter, destroy or conceal material having potential evidentiary value "for the purpose of obstructing a party's access to evidence." Rule 3.4 (b) and (c) incorporates language from DR 7-109(B) and (C) of the ABA Model Code of Professional Responsibility. Rule 3.4(i), which expands on DR 7-105 of the Model Code, provides that a lawyer shall not present or threaten to present criminal "or disciplinary" charges solely to obtain an advantage in a civil matter, and Rule 3.4(j) is taken verbatim from DR 7-102(A)(1) of the Model Code but adds "or initiate criminal charges" to the list of forbidden conduct.

Related Materials

ABA Civil Discovery Standards: In 1999, the ABA approved Civil Discovery Standards to help courts and lawyers deal with discovery issues that frequently occur in civil litigation but that often fall outside the scope of the statutes and court rules governing civil discovery. The Standards, which were developed by the ABA Section of Litigation, relate to ABA Model Rule 3.4(d). The Standards, as updated in 2004, are available at *www.maestro.abanet.org/leadership/2004/annual/dailyjournal/103B.doc.*

ABA Formal Ethics Opinions: See ABA Formal Ethics Ops. 93-378 (1993), 96-402 (1996), and 09-454 (2009).

ABA Standards for Criminal Justice: See Prosecution Function Standards 3-5.2 (Courtroom Professionalism) and 3-5.6 (Presentation of Evidence) and Defense Function Standards 4-1.2 (The Function of Defense Counsel), 4-4.3 (Relations with Prospective Witnesses), 4-4.5 (Compliance with Discovery Procedure), 4-4.6 (Physical Evidence), and 4-7.1 (Courtroom Professionalism). Standard 4-4.6 is especially important because it concerns a criminal defense lawyer's obligations upon the receipt of physical evidence. It provides:

> *Standard 4-4.6. Physical Evidence*
>
> (a) Defense counsel who receives a physical item under circumstances implicating a client in criminal conduct should disclose the location of or should deliver that item to law enforcement authorities only: (1) if required by law or court order, or (2) as provided in paragraph (d).
>
> (b) Unless required to disclose, defense counsel should return the item to the source from whom defense counsel received it, except as provided in paragraphs (c) and (d). In returning the item to the source, defense counsel should advise the source of the legal consequences pertaining to possession or destruction of the item. Defense counsel should also prepare a written record of these events for his or her file, but should not give the source a copy of such record.
>
> (c) Defense counsel may receive the item for a reasonable period of time during which defense counsel: (1) intends to return it to the owner; (2) reasonably fears that return of the item to the source will result in destruction of the item; (3) reasonably fears that return of the item to the source will result in physical harm to anyone; (4) intends to test, examine, inspect, or use the item in any way as part of defense counsel's representation of the client; or (5) cannot return it to the source. If defense counsel tests or examines the item, he or she should thereafter return it to the source unless there is reason to believe that the evidence might be altered or destroyed or used to harm another or return is otherwise impossible. If defense counsel retains the item, he or she should retain it in his or her law office in a manner that does not impede the lawful ability of law enforcement authorities to obtain the item.
>
> (d) If the item received is contraband, i.e. an item, possession of which is in and of itself a crime, such as narcotics, defense counsel may suggest that the client destroy it where there is no pending case or investigation relating to this evidence and where such destruction is clearly not in violation of any criminal statute. If such destruction is not permitted by law or if in defense counsel's judgment he or she cannot retain the item, whether or not it is contraband, in a way that does not pose an unreasonable risk of physical harm to anyone, defense counsel should disclose the location of or should deliver the item to law enforcement authorities.
>
> (e) If defense counsel discloses the location of or delivers the item to law enforcement authorities under paragraphs (a) or (d), or to a third party under paragraph (c)(1), he or she should do so in the way best designed to protect the client's interests.

In the chapter of the ABA Standards for Criminal Justice entitled "Discovery," Standard 11-3.2 (Preservation of Evidence and Testing or Evaluation by Experts) provides: "(a) If either party intends to destroy or transfer out of its possession any objects or information otherwise discoverable under the standards, the party should give notice to the other party sufficiently in advance to afford that party an opportunity to object or take other appropriate action." In addition, Standard 11-6.3 (Investigations Not to Be Impeded) provides:

> Neither the counsel for the parties nor other prosecution or defense personnel should advise persons (other than the defendant) who have relevant material or information to refrain from discussing the case with opposing counsel or showing opposing counsel any relevant material, nor should they otherwise impede opposing counsel's investigation of the case.

ABA Standards for Imposing Lawyer Sanctions:

6.2. Abuse of the Legal Process

6.21. Disbarment is generally appropriate when a lawyer knowingly violates a court order or rule with the intent to obtain a benefit for the lawyer or another, and causes serious injury or potentially serious injury to a party or causes serious or potentially serious interference with a legal proceeding.

6.22. Suspension is generally appropriate when a lawyer knows that he or she is violating a court order or rule, and causes injury or potential injury to a client or a party, or causes interference or potential interference with a legal proceeding.

See also Standard 6.3, reprinted in the Related Materials following Model Rule 4.2.

Contempt of Court: Various statutes and court rules make it a civil or criminal offense to disobey the rules of a tribunal, and give judges power to punish such contempt of court with fines or imprisonment. For example, 18 U.S.C. §401 (Power of Court) gives a federal court the power to punish, by fine, imprisonment, or both, "(1) Misbehavior of any person in its presence or so near thereto as to obstruct the administration of justice; (2) Misbehavior of any of its officers in their official transactions; [and] (3) Disobedience or resistance to its lawful writ, process, order, rule, decree, or command." Similarly, Rule 42(b) of the Federal Rules of Criminal Procedure provides that a federal judge "may summarily punish a person who commits criminal contempt in its presence if the judge saw or heard the contemptuous conduct and so certifies." For a state statute defining contempt of court, see §1209 of the California Code of Civil Procedure.

Cooperation Proclamation: In 2008, The Sedona Conference—a nonprofit group that includes judges, lawyers, and experts—issued The Sedona Conference Cooperation Proclamation to "promote open and forthright information sharing, dialogue (internal and external), training, and the development of practical tools to facilitate cooperative, collaborative, transparent discovery." The Cooperation Proclamation "calls on trial lawyers, in-house counsel, and judges to rethink the contentious practices that have grown up around civil discovery and refocus litigation toward the substantive resolution of legal disputes." It has been endorsed by more than 100 federal and state judges and has been cited in dozens of court opinions addressing discovery disputes. The Cooperation Proclamation, which relates to ABA Model Rule 3.4(d), is available online at *www.thesedonaconference.org.*

Electronic Evidence: The exponential growth in the use of e-mail and other electronic methods to create and preserve documents has raised many new issues in discovery, and the intentional or negligent failure to preserve electronic evidence has sometimes led to civil sanctions or criminal prosecution. For an extended treatment of these issues, see Paul Rice, Electronic Evidence: Law and Practice (ABA 2d ed., 2008).

Federal Rules of Appellate Procedure: Fed. R. App. P. 46(c) provides that a federal court of appeals, after reasonable notice and a hearing if requested, may discipline an attorney who practices before it for "conduct unbecoming a member of the bar or for failure to comply with any court rule."

Federal Rules of Civil Procedure: Various provisions of the Federal Rules of Civil Procedure penalize the kinds of behavior condemned in Rule 3.4. With respect to Rule 3.4(c), Fed. R. Civ. P. 41(b) provides: "If the plaintiff fails to prosecute or to comply with these rules or a court order, a defendant may move to dismiss the action or any claim against it," and such a dismissal ordinarily "operates as an adjudication on the merits." Fed. R. Civ. P. 45(e) provides that the court many hold any person in contempt who "fails without adequate excuse to obey a subpoena." With respect to Rule 3.4(d), Fed. R. Civ. P. 26(g) provides sanctions for improper or bad faith conduct in discovery, and Fed. R. Civ. P. 37 authorizes courts to compel a party to respond to discovery requests and to sanction an unjustified failure to respond to discovery.

Model Rules of Professional Conduct for Federal Lawyers clarify that Rule 3.4 applies to an obligation "to an opposing party and counsel." The Rules for Federal Lawyers address obligations to a tribunal in a new Rule 3.3(a)(5), quoted after Rule 3.3 above.

Restatement of the Law Governing Lawyers: See Restatement §§105, 107, 110(3), and 116-119 in our chapter on the Restatement later in this volume.

Spoliation of Evidence: "Spoliation" is a term often used by courts to describe the intentional or negligent loss or destruction of evidence. Spoliation is thus related to ABA Model Rule 3.4(a), which provides that a lawyer shall not unlawfully "destroy" material evidence. In some jurisdictions, spoliation of evidence is an independent tort, and a party who has been damaged by spoliation may sue the spoliator for damages. In virtually all jurisdictions, courts have authority to punish spoliation with sanctions, such as adverse inferences, preclusion of testimony about the destroyed item, or even dismissal of claims or defenses. For an extended treatment of spoliation, see Margaret M. Koesel, Tracey L. Turnbull, & Daniel F. Gourash, Spoliation of Evidence: Sanctions and Remedies for Destruction of Evidence in Civil Litigation (2d ed., ABA 2006).

Witness Tampering: Federal law makes it a crime to kill, intimidate, or harass a witness, victim, or informant in an official proceeding, and many states have parallel laws. The main federal statute on witness tampering is 18 U.S.C. §1512. A typical example of a parallel state statute is Missouri Revised Statutes §575.270, which provides that "a person commits the crime of tampering with a witness if, with purpose to induce a witness or a prospective witness to disobey a subpoena or other legal process, or to absent himself or avoid subpoena or other legal process, or to withhold evidence, information or documents, or to testify falsely, he: (1) Threatens or causes harm to any person or property; or (2) Uses force, threats or deception; or (3) Offers, confers or agrees to confer any benefit, direct or indirect, upon such witness; or (4) Conveys any of the foregoing to another in furtherance of a conspiracy."

18 U.S.C. §201: Paragraph (c)(2) provides that whoever "directly or indirectly, gives, offers, or promises anything of value to any person, for or because of the testimony . . . given or to be given by such person as a witness upon a trial, hearing, or other proceeding," shall be imprisoned for up to two years, or fined, or both. However, 18 U.S.C. §201(d) makes clear that the statute does not prohibit paying an ordinary witness "the reasonable cost of travel and subsistence incurred and the reasonable value of time lost in attendance at any such trial, hearing, or proceeding" or paying an expert witness "a reasonable fee for time spent" in preparing an expert opinion and in "appearing and testifying."

Rule 3.5 Impartiality and Decorum of the Tribunal

A lawyer shall not:

(a) seek to influence a judge, juror, prospective juror or other official by means prohibited by law;

(b) communicate ex parte with such a person during the proceeding unless authorized to do so by law or court order;

(c) communicate with a juror or prospective juror after discharge of the jury if:

(1) the communication is prohibited by law or court order; or

(2) the juror has made known to the lawyer a desire not to communicate; or

(3) the communication involves misrepresentation, coercion, duress or harassment; or 4.1, 4.4(a)

(d) engage in conduct intended to disrupt a tribunal. 3.2

COMMENT

[1] Many forms of improper influence upon a tribunal are proscribed by criminal law. Others are specified in the ABA Model Code of Judicial Conduct, with which an advocate should be familiar. A lawyer is required to avoid contributing to a violation of such provisions.

[2] During a proceeding a lawyer may not communicate ex parte with persons serving in an official capacity in the proceeding, such as judges, masters or jurors, unless authorized to do so by law or court order.

[3] A lawyer may on occasion want to communicate with a juror or prospective juror after the jury has been discharged. The lawyer may do so unless the communication is prohibited by law or a court order but must respect the desire of the juror not to talk with the lawyer. The lawyer may not engage in improper conduct during the communication.

conflicts 1.1 1.3 cl 1

[4] The advocate's function is to present evidence and argument so that the cause may be decided according to law. Refraining from abusive or obstreperous conduct is a corollary of the advocate's right to speak on behalf of litigants. A lawyer may stand firm against abuse by a judge but should avoid reciprocation; the judge's default is no justification for similar dereliction by an advocate. An advocate can present the cause, protect the record for subsequent review and preserve professional integrity by patient firmness no less effectively than by belligerence or theatrics.

[5] The duty to refrain from disruptive conduct applies to any proceeding of a tribunal, including a deposition. See Rule 1.0(m).

Canon and Code Antecedents

ABA Canons of Professional Ethics: Canons 3 and 23 provided as follows:

3. Attempts to Exert Personal Influence on the Court

Marked attention and unusual hospitality on the part of a lawyer to a Judge, uncalled for by the personal relations of the parties, subject both the Judge and the lawyer to misconstructions of motive and should be avoided. A lawyer should not communicate or argue privately with the Judge as to the merits of a pending cause, and he deserves rebuke and denunciation for any device or attempt to gain from a Judge special personal consideration or favor. A self-respecting independence in the discharge of professional duty, without denial or diminution of the courtesy and respect due the Judge's station, is the only proper foundation for cordial personal and official relations between Bench and Bar.

23. Attitude Toward Jury

All attempts to curry favor with juries by fawning, flattery or pretended solicitude for their personal comfort are unprofessional. Suggestions of counsel, looking to the comfort or convenience of jurors, and propositions to dispense with argument, should be made to the Court out of the jury's hearing. A lawyer must never converse privately with jurors about the case; and both before and during the trial he should avoid communicating with them, even as to matters foreign to the cause.

ABA Model Code of Professional Responsibility: Compare DR 7-106(C)(6), DR 7-108(A), DR 7-108(B), and DR 7-110(B) (reprinted later in this volume).

Cross-References in Other Rules

Rule 3.9: "A lawyer representing a client before a legislative body or administrative agency in a nonadjudicative proceeding shall disclose that the appearance is in a representative capacity and shall conform to the provisions of **Rules** 3.3(a) through (c), 3.4(a) through (c), and **3.5.**"

Rule 3.9, Comment 1: "In representation before bodies such as legislatures, municipal councils, and executive and administrative agencies acting in a rule-making or policy-making capacity" lawyers must deal "honestly and in conformity with applicable rules of procedure. See **Rules** 3.3(a) through (c), 3.4(a) through (c) and **3.5.**"

Legislative History of Model Rule 3.5

1980 Discussion Draft (then called **Rule 3.7**) provided as follows:

(a) A lawyer shall assist a tribunal in maintaining impartiality and conducting the proceedings with decorum.

(b) A lawyer shall not:

(1) seek improperly to influence a judge, juror, or other decision-maker, or, except as permitted by law, communicate ex parte with such a person;

(2) seek improperly to influence a witness;

(3) be abusive or obstreperous;

(4) refuse to comply with an obligation of procedural law or an order of the tribunal, except for an open refusal based on a good faith belief that compliance is not legally required.

1981 Draft was substantially the same as adopted, except that subparagraph (a) used the phrase "other decision-maker" instead of "other official."

1982 Draft was adopted.

1983 Rule: As originally adopted in 1983, Rule 3.5 had only three paragraphs. It provided that a lawyer shall not:

(a) [Same as 2002 version of Rule 3.5(a).]
(b) communicate ex parte with such a person except as permitted by law; or
(c) [Same as 2002 version of Rule 3.5(d).]

2002 Amendments: At its February 2002 Mid-Year Meeting, the ABA House of Delegates adopted without change the ABA Ethics 2000 Commission proposal to amend Rule 3.5 and its Comment. The amendments slightly changed Rule 3.5(a), added all of Rule 3.5(c), re-lettered the old paragraph (c) as paragraph (d), and added Comments 2, 3, and 5.

Selected State Variations

Arizona clarifies that Rule 3.5(a) applies only to an official "of a tribunal," and substitutes "likely" for "intended" in Rule 3.5(d).

California: Rule 5-300 provides as follows:

> (A) A member shall not directly or indirectly give or lend anything of value to a judge, official, or employee of a tribunal unless the personal or family relationship between the member and the judge, official, or employee is such that gifts are customarily given and exchanged. Nothing contained in this rule shall prohibit a member from contributing to the campaign fund of a judge running for election or confirmation pursuant to applicable law pertaining to such contributions.
>
> (B) A member shall not directly or indirectly communicate with or argue to a judge or judicial officer upon the merits of a contested matter pending before such judge or judicial officer, except:
>
> (1) In open court; or
> (2) With the consent of all other counsel in such matter; or
> (3) In the presence of all other counsel in such matter; or
> (4) In writing with a copy thereof furnished to such other counsel; or
> (5) In ex parte matters.
>
> (C) As used in this rule, "judge" and "judicial officer" shall include law clerks, research attorneys, or other court personnel who participate in the decision-making process.

Florida: Rule 3.5(a) provides that a lawyer shall not seek to influence a judge, juror, prospective juror, or other decision maker "except as permitted by law or the rules of court." Rule 3.5(d), governing communications with jurors, former jurors, and prospective jurors, generally tracks DR 7-108 of the ABA Model Code of Professional Responsibility, but adds that a lawyer shall not:

> (4) after dismissal of the jury in a case with which the lawyer is connected, initiate communication with or cause another to initiate communication with any juror regarding the trial except to determine whether the verdict may be subject to legal challenge; provided, a lawyer may not interview jurors for this purpose unless the lawyer has reason to believe that grounds for such challenge may exist; and provided further, before conducting any such interview the lawyer must file in the cause a notice of intention to interview setting forth the name of the juror or jurors to be interviewed. A copy of the notice must be delivered to the trial judge and opposing counsel a reasonable time before such interview. . . .

Georgia: Rule 3.5 adopts most of the pre-2002 version of ABA Model Rule 3.5 verbatim, but alters the introductory phrase to make clear that the prohibitions apply "without regard to whether the lawyer represents a client in the matter."

Maryland: Rule 3.5 includes several sui generis provisions, including a prohibition against discussing employment of a judge before whom the lawyer's firm has a matter, a limitation on contacts with discharged jurors, and a requirement to report knowledge of improper contacts with jurors or prospective jurors.

Massachusetts: Rule 3.5(d) restricts the ability of lawyers connected to a case to initiate a communication with a member of the jury after discharge without leave of the court.

Nevada adds Rule 3.5(e):

> (e) Before the jury is sworn to try the cause, a lawyer may investigate the prospective jurors to ascertain any basis for challenge, provided that a lawyer or the lawyer's employees or independent contractors may not, at any time before the commencement of the trial, conduct or authorize any investigation of the prospective jurors, through any means which are calculated or likely to lead to communication with prospective jurors of any allegations or factual circumstances relating to the case at issue. Conduct prohibited by this Rule includes, but is not limited to, any direct or indirect communication with a prospective juror, a member of the juror's family, any employer, or any other person that may lead to direct or indirect communication with a prospective juror.

New Jersey: Rule 3.5(b) provides only that a lawyer shall not communicate ex parte with anyone specified in subparagraph (a) "except as permitted by law," and New Jersey Rule 3.5(c) says only that a lawyer shall not "engage in conduct intended to disrupt a tribunal." New Jersey deletes ABA Model Rules 3.5(c)(1)-(3) and Rule 3.5(d).

New York: Rule 3.5 draws heavily on the old Model Code. Rule 3.5(a)(1)-(2) is similar to 7-110(A) and (B), respectively. Rule 3.5(a)(4) is similar to DR 7-108(A) and (B)(1), and Rule 3.5(a)(6) is similar to DR 7-108(E). Rule 3.5(b)-(d) is nearly identical to DR 7-108(B)(2), 7-108(F), and 7-108(G), respectively.

North Carolina: Rule 3.5 adds language from DR 7-106(C)(5)-(7), DR 7-108(D),(F), and (G), and DR 7-110(B) of the ABA Model Code of Professional Responsibility.

Ohio replaces the term "judge" with the term "judicial officer" throughout Rule 3.5. Ohio adds Rule 3.5(a)(2), which provides that a lawyer shall not "lend anything of value or give anything of more than *de minimis* value to a judicial officer, official, or employee of a tribunal." Ohio Rule 3.5(a)(3) provides that a lawyer shall not communicate ex parte with "(i) a judicial officer or other official as to the merits of the case during the proceeding unless authorized to do so by law or court order" or "(ii) a juror or prospective juror during the proceeding unless otherwise authorized to do so by law or court order." Ohio also adds a new Rule 3.5(b), which provides that a lawyer "shall reveal promptly to the tribunal improper conduct by a juror or prospective juror, or by another toward a juror, prospective juror, or family member of a juror or prospective juror, of which the lawyer has knowledge."

Texas: Rule 3.05 is substantially the same as DR 7-110(B) of the ABA Model Code of Professional Responsibility. Rule 3.06 borrows heavily from DR 7-108, but rearranges the order somewhat, adds references to an "alternate juror," and provides in Rule 3.06(A)(2) that a lawyer shall not "seek to influence a venireman or juror concerning the merits of a pending matter by means prohibited by law or applicable rules of practice or procedure."

Virginia: Rule 3.5(a)(2) generally tracks DR 7-108(D) of the ABA Model Code of Professional Responsibility but adds that a lawyer shall not "after discharge of the jury from further consideration of a case: (i) ask questions of or make comments to a member of that jury that are calculated merely to harass or embarrass the juror or to influence the juror's actions in future jury service." A new Rule 3.5(e) adds exceptions to the rule against ex parte communications with a judge.

Related Materials

ABA Formal Ethics Opinions: See ABA Formal Ethics Op. 07-449 (2007).

ABA Model Code of Judicial Conduct: The ABA Model Code of Judicial Conduct, which is cited in Rule 3.5, Comment 1, is reprinted in full later in this volume.

ABA Standards for Criminal Justice: See Prosecution Function Standard 3-2.8 (Relations with the Courts and Bar), Standard 3-5.2 (Courtroom Professionalism), Standard 3-5.4 (Relations with Jury), and Defense Function Standard 4-7.1 (Courtroom Professionalism) and Standard 4-7.3 (Relations with Jury). See also ABA Standards for Special Functions of the Trial Judge.

ABA Standards for Imposing Lawyer Sanctions: See Standard 6.3, which is reprinted in the Related Materials following ABA Model Rule 4.2.

Federal Rules of Civil Procedure: Rule 65(b)(1) permits ex parte communications by attorneys for parties seeking temporary restraining orders under the following circumstances:

> *Issuing Without Notice.* The court may issue a temporary restraining order without written or oral notice to the adverse party or its attorney only if:
>
> (A) specific facts in an affidavit or a verified complaint clearly show that immediate and irreparable injury, loss, or damage will result to the movant before the adverse party can be heard in opposition; and
>
> (B) the movant's attorney certifies in writing any efforts made to give notice and the reasons why it should not be required.

Model Rules of Professional Conduct for Federal Lawyers: Rule 3.5(a) prohibits a federal lawyer from seeking to influence "a tribunal, a member of a tribunal, a prospective member of a tribunal, or other official by means prohibited by law."

Obstruction of Justice: Various federal and state statutes make it a crime to obstruct justice. For example, 18 U.S.C. §1503, entitled "Influencing or Injuring Officer or Juror Generally," makes it illegal to use "threats or force . . . to influence, intimidate, or impede any grand or petit juror, or officer in or of any court of the United States . . . in the discharge of his duty"; and 18 U.S.C. §1512, entitled "Tampering with a Witness, Victim or an Informant," makes it a crime to kill, intimidate, harass, or threaten a witness, victim, or informant in connection with an official proceeding. (We reprint §§1503 and 1512 below in our chapter of Federal Provisions on Conflicts, Confidentiality, and Crimes.)

Restatement of the Law Governing Lawyers: See Restatement §§112, 113, and 115 in our chapter on the Restatement later in this volume.

Rule 3.6 Trial Publicity

(a) A lawyer who is participating or has participated in the investigation or litigation of a matter shall not make an extrajudicial statement

that the lawyer knows or reasonably should know will be disseminated by means of public communication and will have a substantial likelihood of materially prejudicing an adjudicative proceeding in the matter.

(b) Notwithstanding paragraph (a), a lawyer may state:

(1) the claim, offense or defense involved and, except when prohibited by law, the identity of the persons involved;

(2) information contained in a public record;

(3) that an investigation of a matter is in progress;

(4) the scheduling or result of any step in litigation;

(5) a request for assistance in obtaining evidence and information necessary thereto;

(6) a warning of danger concerning the behavior of a person involved, when there is reason to believe that there exists the likelihood of substantial harm to an individual or to the public interest; and

(7) in a criminal case, in addition to subparagraphs (1) through (6):

(i) the identity, residence, occupation and family status of the accused;

(ii) if the accused has not been apprehended, information necessary to aid in apprehension of that person;

(iii) the fact, time and place of arrest; and

(iv) the identity of investigating and arresting officers or agencies and the length of the investigation.

(c) Notwithstanding paragraph (a), a lawyer may make a statement that a reasonable lawyer would believe is required to protect a client from the substantial undue prejudicial effect of recent publicity not initiated by the lawyer or the lawyer's client. A statement made pursuant to this paragraph shall be limited to such information as is necessary to mitigate the recent adverse publicity.

(d) No lawyer associated in a firm or government agency with a lawyer subject to paragraph (a) shall make a statement prohibited by paragraph (a).

COMMENT

[1] It is difficult to strike a balance between protecting the right to a fair trial and safeguarding the right of free expression. Preserving the right to a fair trial necessarily entails some curtailment of the information that may be disseminated about a party prior to trial, particularly where trial by jury is involved. If there were no such limits, the result would be the practical nullification of the protective effect of the rules of forensic decorum and the exclusionary rules of evidence. On the other hand, there are vital social interests served by the free dissemination of information about events having legal consequences and about legal proceedings themselves. The public has a right to know about threats to its safety and measures

aimed at assuring its security. It also has a legitimate interest in the conduct of judicial proceedings, particularly in matters of general public concern. Furthermore, the subject matter of legal proceedings is often of direct significance in debate and deliberation over questions of public policy.

[2] Special rules of confidentiality may validly govern proceedings in juvenile, domestic relations and mental disability proceedings, and perhaps other types of litigation. Rule 3.4(c) requires compliance with such rules.

[3] The Rule sets forth a basic general prohibition against a lawyer's making statements that the lawyer knows or should know will have a substantial likelihood of materially prejudicing an adjudicative proceeding. Recognizing that the public value of informed commentary is great and the likelihood of prejudice to a proceeding by the commentary of a lawyer who is not involved in the proceeding is small, the rule applies only to lawyers who are, or who have been involved in the investigation or litigation of a case, and their associates.

[4] Paragraph (b) identifies specific matters about which a lawyer's statements would not ordinarily be considered to present a substantial likelihood of material prejudice, and should not in any event be considered prohibited by the general prohibition of paragraph (a). Paragraph (b) is not intended to be an exhaustive listing of the subjects upon which a lawyer may make a statement, but statements on other matters may be subject to paragraph (a).

[5] There are, on the other hand, certain subjects that are more likely than not to have a material prejudicial effect on a proceeding, particularly when they refer to a civil matter triable to a jury, a criminal matter, or any other proceeding that could result in incarceration. These subjects relate to:

(1) the character, credibility, reputation or criminal record of a party, suspect in a criminal investigation or witness, or the identity of a witness, or the expected testimony of a party or witness;

(2) in a criminal case or proceeding that could result in incarceration, the possibility of a plea of guilty to the offense or the existence or contents of any confession, admission, or statement given by a defendant or suspect or that person's refusal or failure to make a statement;

(3) the performance or results of any examination or test or the refusal or failure of a person to submit to an examination or test, or the identity or nature of physical evidence expected to be presented;

(4) any opinion as to the guilt or innocence of a defendant or suspect in a criminal case or proceeding that could result in incarceration;

(5) information that the lawyer knows or reasonably should know is likely to be inadmissible as evidence in a trial and that would, if disclosed, create a substantial risk of prejudicing an impartial trial; or

(6) the fact that a defendant has been charged with a crime, unless there is included therein a statement explaining that the charge is merely an accusation and that the defendant is presumed innocent until and unless proven guilty.

[6] Another relevant factor in determining prejudice is the nature of the proceeding involved. Criminal jury trials will be most sensitive to extrajudicial speech. Civil trials may be less sensitive. Non-jury hearings and arbitration proceedings may be even less affected. The Rule will still place limitations on prejudicial comments in these cases, but the likelihood of prejudice may be different depending on the type of proceeding.

[7] Finally, extrajudicial statements that might otherwise raise a question under this Rule may be permissible when they are made in response to statements made publicly by another party, another party's lawyer, or third persons, where a reasonable lawyer would believe a public response is required in order to avoid prejudice to the lawyer's client. When prejudicial statements have been publicly made by others, responsive statements may have the salutary effect of lessening any resulting adverse impact on the adjudicative proceeding. Such responsive statements should be limited to contain only such information as is necessary to mitigate undue prejudice created by the statements made by others.

[8] See Rule 3.8(f) for additional duties of prosecutors in connection with extrajudicial statements about criminal proceedings.

Canon and Code Antecedents

ABA Canons of Professional Ethics: Canon 20 provided as follows:

20. Newspaper Discussion of Pending Litigation

> Newspaper publications by a lawyer as to pending or anticipated litigation may interfere with a fair trial in the Courts and otherwise prejudice the due administration of justice. Generally they are to be condemned. If the extreme circumstances of a particular case justify a statement to the public, it is unprofessional to make it anonymously. An *ex parte* reference to the facts should not go beyond quotation from the records and papers on file in the court; but even in extreme cases it is better to avoid any *ex parte* statement.

ABA Model Code of Professional Responsibility: Compare DR 7-107 (reprinted later in this volume).

Cross-References in Other Rules

Rule 3.8(f) provides that the prosecutor of a criminal case shall "exercise reasonable care to prevent investigators . . . or other persons . . . from making an extrajudicial statement that the prosecutor would be prohibited from making under **Rule 3.6** or this Rule."

Rule 3.8, Comment 5: "Paragraph (f) supplements **Rule 3.6,** which prohibits extrajudicial statements that have a substantial likelihood of prejudicing an adjudicatory proceeding. . . . Nothing in this Comment is intended to restrict the statements which a prosecutor may make which comply with **Rule 3.6(b)** or **3.6(c)**."

Legislative History of Model Rule 3.6

1980 Discussion Draft (then Rule 3.8) was essentially an amalgam and reorganization of DR 7-107, except that paragraphs (F), (I), and (J) of DR 7-107 were deleted, and the following new provisions were added:

(a) To ensure a fair trial, a lawyer involved in the investigation of a criminal matter or in criminal or civil litigation shall not, except as provided in paragraph (b), make an extrajudicial statement: . . .

(2) when the matter under investigation or in litigation is a criminal case or a civil case triable to a jury and the statement relates to: . . .

(v) information the lawyer knows or reasonably should know would be inadmissible as evidence in a trial;

(vi) any other matter that similarly creates a serious and imminent risk of prejudicing an impartial trial.

(b) A lawyer involved in the investigation or litigation of a matter may state without elaboration . . .

(6) in a criminal case: . . .

(vi) that the accused denies the charges.

(c) When evidence or information received in or relating to a proceeding is by law or order of a tribunal to be kept confidential, the lawyer shall not unlawfully disclose the evidence or information.

1981 Draft was the same as adopted, except (b)(7)(iii), which provided: "the fact, time, and place of arrest, resistance, pursuit and use of weapons."

1982 Draft was adopted.

1983 Rule: From its original adoption in 1983 until its amendment in 1994, Rule 3.6 provided as follows:

(a) A lawyer shall not make an extrajudicial statement that a reasonable person would expect to be disseminated by means of public communication if the lawyer knows or reasonably should know that it will have a substantial likelihood of materially prejudicing an adjudicative proceeding.

(b) A statement referred to in paragraph (a) ordinarily is likely to have such an effect when it refers to a civil matter triable to a jury, a criminal matter, or any other proceeding that could result in incarceration, and the proceeding relates to:

(1)-(6) [Same as items (1) through (6) in Comment 5 to 2002 version of Rule 3.6.]

(c) Notwithstanding paragraph (a) and (b)(1-5), a lawyer involved in the investigation or litigation of a matter may state without elaboration:

(1) the general nature of the claim or defense;

(2) [Same as (b)(2) in 2002 version of Rule 3.6.]

(3) that an investigation of the matter is in progress, including the general scope of the investigation, the offense or claim or defense involved and, except when prohibited by law, the identity of the persons involved;

(4)-(6) [Same as (b)(4)-(6) in 2002 version of Rule 3.6.]

(7) In a criminal case:

(i)-(iv) [Same as (b)(7)(i)-(iv) in 2002 version of Rule 3.6.]

1994 Amendment: At its August 1994 Annual Meeting, by a voice vote, the ABA House of Delegates significantly amended Rule 3.6. The amendment was spurred by the Supreme Court's decision in *Gentile v. Nevada State Bar,* 501 U.S. 1030 (1991), which cast doubt on the constitutionality of some parts of Rule 3.6. (Companion amendments to Rule 3.8 were approved at the same time, also in response to *Gentile.*)

The 1994 amendment to Rule 3.6 had three purposes: (1) to list various types of information that a lawyer may disclose in out-of-court statements despite the general ban on extrajudicial statements substantially likely to prejudice a court proceeding; (2) to create a "safe harbor" that allows a lawyer to protect clients against undue prejudice resulting from recent publicity not initiated by the lawyer or client; and (3) to make clear that all lawyers in a firm or government agency are governed by Rule 3.6. For a legislative-style version of the Rule showing what was added and deleted by the 1994 amendment, see our 1995 edition.

The 1994 amendment also substantially rewrote the Comment and Code Comparison, deleting former paragraph 2 of the Comment and adding paragraphs 3 through 7. The deleted paragraph of the Comment had stated as follows:

> [2] No body of rules can simultaneously satisfy all interests of fair trial and all those of free expression. The formula in this Rule is based upon the ABA Model Code of Professional Responsibility and the ABA Standards Relating to Fair Trial and Free Press, as amended in 1978.

The amendment was co-sponsored by the ABA Standing Committee on Ethics and Professional Responsibility and the ABA Criminal Justice Section. Below are excerpts from the joint ABA report explaining the amendments.

*Excerpts from ABA Report Explaining 1994 Amendments**

> In *Gentile,* a criminal defense lawyer challenged disciplinary action taken against him by the State Bar of Nevada under its version of Rule 3.6, because of certain remarks made by him at a press conference relating to his client's anticipated defense. The lawyer challenged the state's action on grounds that his extrajudicial statements were protected by the First Amendment, and that in any event his remarks were within the Rule's "safe harbor" provision.
>
> The Supreme Court unanimously upheld the Rule's "substantial likelihood of material prejudice" test. However, a majority of five Justices held the Rule void for vagueness as interpreted and applied by the Nevada State Bar in the circumstances of the case. . . . The five members of the Court who reversed the state's disciplin ary action noted that the safe harbor provision of Rule 3.6 allows a criminal lawyer to explain the "general" nature of his client's defense "without elaboration," and pointed out that the terms "general" and "elaboration" have "no settled usage or tradition of interpretation in law." As worded, they said, the provision gives a lawyer "no principle for determining when his remarks pass from the safe harbor of the general to the forbidden sea of the elaborated," and creates "a trap for the wary as well as the unwary."
>
> The Standing Committee on Ethics and Professional Responsibility . . . proposes to revise the Rule's safe harbor provision by deleting the qualifying terms which the Supreme Court held unconstitutionally vague. . . .
>
> The Committee adopted . . . a provision entitling a lawyer to respond where adverse publicity has been initiated by an opposing party or third persons, in order to avoid substantial undue prejudice to the lawyer's client. The Committee felt that in this situation, the danger of the second statement prejudicing the proceeding is minimized, and the rights of the client can be protected.
>
> [F]or completeness, the Rule must also extend to lawyers associated with those participating in a matter, and those who formerly participated in a matter. The need for lawyers outside a proceeding to interpret those proceedings to the public is so great, and the right of comment on government process so fundamental that the Committee felt that the lawyers affected by speech restrictions of Rule 3.6 should be clearly and narrowly defined.

* Committee Reports do not represent official policy of the ABA. They are for information only, and the opinions are those of the authors of the report.

> The Committee also considered whether Rule 3.6 should be limited to criminal cases, or to cases involving jury trials. While . . . there is less chance of prejudice from statements made in the course of a civil proceeding than in the context of a criminal matter, and in a bench trial than in a jury trial, it is the Committee's view that the nature of the proceeding and the identity of the trier of fact are relevant to but not dispositive of the issue of likelihood of prejudice. . . .

2002 Amendments: At its February 2002 Mid-Year Meeting, the ABA House of Delegates adopted without change the ABA Ethics 2000 Commission proposal to amend Rule 3.6(a) and to add Comment 8. The rest of Rule 3.6 and its Comment were unchanged. The former version of Rule 3.6(a) applied to an extrajudicial statement that "a reasonable person would expect" to be disseminated by means of public communication, instead of "if the lawyer knows or reasonably should know" as provided in the current rule.

Selected State Variations

Alabama: Rule 3.8(a) provides as follows:

> (a) A lawyer shall not make an extrajudicial statement that a reasonable person would expect to be disseminated by means of public communication if the lawyer knows or reasonably should know that it will have a substantial likelihood of materially prejudicing an adjudicative proceeding in the matter.

Alabama Rule 3.8(b) provides that a statement referred to in Rule 3.8(a) ordinarily is likely to have a materially prejudicial effect if it refers to "a civil matter triable to a jury, a criminal matter, or any other proceeding that could result in incarceration" and the statement relates to one of the subjects listed in Comment 5 to ABA Model Rule 3.6 (which Alabama moves to the text of the rule). Alabama omits Rule 3.6(d).

California: Rule 5-120 tracks the pre-2002 version of ABA Model Rule 3.6 nearly verbatim, except that California omits subparagraph (d).

District of Columbia: Rule 3.6 consists of only one sentence: "A lawyer engaged in a case being tried to a judge or jury shall not make an extrajudicial statement that the lawyer knows or reasonably should know will be disseminated by means of mass public communication and will create a serious and imminent threat of material prejudice to the proceeding."

Florida: Rule 3.6(a) omits the ABA phrase "who is participating or has participated in the investigation or litigation of a matter" and provides that a lawyer shall not make an extrajudicial statement that a "reasonable person" would expect to be disseminated by means of public communication if the lawyer knows or reasonably should know that it will have a substantial likelihood of materially prejudicing an adjudicative proceeding "due to its creation of an imminent and substantial detrimental effect on that proceeding." Florida deletes ABA Model Rule 3.6(b), (c), and (d), and substitutes the following Rule 3.6(b):

> *Statements of Third Parties.* A lawyer shall not counsel or assist another person to make such a statement. Counsel shall exercise reasonable care to prevent investigators, employees, or other persons assisting in or associated with a case from making extrajudicial statements that are prohibited under this rule.

Georgia: Rule 3.6(a), (c), and (d) tracks the pre-2002 version of ABA Model Rule 3.6 verbatim, but Georgia has relegated Rule 3.6(b) to a new paragraph 5B of the Comment, which notes that there are "certain subjects which are more likely than not to have no material prejudicial effect on a proceeding." The Comment then lists all of the items in ABA Model Rule 3.6(b) as examples of things that a lawyer may "usually" state.

Illinois: Rule 3.6(a) prohibits an extrajudicial statement if the lawyer "knows or reasonably should know" that the statement would "pose a serious and imminent threat to the fairness of an adjudicative proceeding in the matter."

Iowa: In Rule 3.6, Iowa adds a paragraph (e) that provides: "Any communication made under paragraph (b) that includes information that a defendant will be or has been charged with a crime must also include a statement explaining that a criminal charge is merely an accusation and the defendant is presumed innocent until and unless proven guilty."

Michigan: Effective January 1, 2011, Rule 3.6(a) includes a lengthy explanation of when "a statement is likely to have a substantial likelihood of materially prejudicing an adjudicative proceeding," drawing nearly verbatim from a description of such statements contained in Comment 5 to Model Rule 3.6.

New Jersey deletes ABA Model Rule 3.6(d).

New York moves Rule 3.6(b)-(d) to Rule 3.6(c)-(e) and uses 3.6(b) for a list of subjects that are likely to "prejudice materially an adjudicative proceeding." The list is drawn nearly verbatim from Comment 5 of the Model Rules.

North Carolina adds Rule 3.6(e), which provides that Rule 3.6 does not "preclude a lawyer from replying to charges of misconduct publicly made against the lawyer or from participating in the proceedings of legislative, administrative, or other investigative bodies."

Ohio: Rule 3.6(b) makes clear that a lawyer may not engage in trial publicity if doing so would violate a duty of confidentiality under Rule 1.6.

Texas: Rule 3.07(a) begins "[i]n the course of representing a client" in place of the ABA phrase "[a] lawyer who is participating or has participated in the investigation or litigation of a matter," then tracks ABA Model Rule 3.6(a) verbatim, but Texas, at the end of Rule 3.07(a), adds that a lawyer "shall not counsel or assist another person to make such a statement."

Texas Rule 3.07(b) provides that a lawyer "ordinarily will violate paragraph (a), and the likelihood of a violation increases if the adjudication is ongoing or imminent," by making an extrajudicial statement described in Rule 3.07(a) if the statement refers to five specified categories of information, which track verbatim the items listed in Comment 5 to ABA Model Rule 3.6—except that Texas omits from this list "(6) the fact that a defendant has been charged with a crime, unless there is included therein a statement explaining that the charge is merely an accusation and that the defendant is presumed innocent until and unless proven guilty."

Texas Rule 3.07(c) generally tracks ABA Model Rule 3.6(b), with slight variations. Texas omits ABA Model Rule 3.6(c) and (d).

Virginia: Rule 3.6 provides as follows:

> (a) A lawyer participating in or associated with the investigation or the prosecution or the defense of a criminal matter that may be tried by a jury shall not make or participate in making an extrajudicial statement that a reasonable person would expect to be disseminated by means of public communication that the lawyer knows,

or should know, will have a substantial likelihood of interfering with the fairness of the trial by a jury.

(b) A lawyer shall exercise reasonable care to prevent employees and associates from making an extrajudicial statement that the lawyer would be prohibited from making under this Rule.

Related Materials

ABA Formal Ethics Opinions: No ABA formal ethics opinion has discussed ABA Model Rule 3.6.

ABA Standards of Criminal Justice: See Prosecution Function Standard 3-1.4 (Public Statements). Also, in 1991 the ABA House of Delegates approved a section of the ABA Standards for Criminal Justice entitled "Fair Trial and Free Press." Standard 8-1.1 (Extrajudicial Statements by Attorneys) parallels an earlier version of ABA Model Rule 3.6. The Standards governing Fair Trial and Free Press are available online at *http://www.americanbar.org/publications/criminal_justice_section_archive/crimjust_standards_fairtrial_blk.html.*

Department of Justice Guidelines: To help "ensure uniformity of practice" and to help strike "a fair balance between the protection of individuals accused of crime or involved in civil proceedings with the Government," on the one hand, and "public understandings of the problems of controlling crime and administering government," on the other hand, the United States Department of Justice has adopted 28 C.F.R. §50.2 (Release of Information by Personnel of the Department of Justice Relating to Criminal and Civil Proceedings), which we reprint in our chapter on Federal Provisions on Conflicts, Confidentiality, and Crimes.

Model Rules of Professional Conduct for Federal Lawyers: Rule 3.6(a) prohibits extrajudicial statements likely to prejudice an adjudicative proceeding "or an official review process thereof." Rule 3.6(b)(4) states that Rule 3.6 applies to any proceeding that could result in incarceration "or other adverse action." The Rules for Federal Lawyers also add Rule 3.6(d), which provides: "The protection and release of information in matters pertaining to the Government shall be consistent with law."

Restatement of the Law Governing Lawyers: See Restatement §109 in our chapter on the Restatement later in this volume.

United States Attorney's Manual: The United States Attorney's Manual, which is designed to be "a quick and ready reference" for U.S. Attorneys, Assistant U.S. Attorneys, and Department of Justice attorneys responsible for prosecuting violations of federal law, contains a series of rules at §§1-7.000 *et seq.* entitled "Media Relations." Section 1-7.112 (Need for Free Press and Public Trial) states:

> [C]areful weight must be given in each case to the constitutional requirements of a free press and public trials as well as the right of the people in a constitutional democracy to have access to information about the conduct of law enforcement officers, prosecutors and courts, consistent with the individual rights of the accused. Further, recognition should be given to the needs of public safety, the apprehension of fugitives, and the rights of the public to be informed on matters that can affect enactment or enforcement of public laws or the development or change of public policy.

These principles must be evaluated in each case and must involve a fair degree of discretion and the exercise of sound judgment, as every possibility cannot be predicted and covered by written policy statement.

Section 1-7.210 vests final responsibility for "all matters involving the news media and the Department of Justice" in the Director of the DOJ's Office of Public Affairs (OPA). Other sections require prosecutors to consult with the Director of OPA before commenting in the public media about a criminal case. To read United States Attorney's Manual sections on media relations, see *www.usdoj.gov/usao/eousa/foia_reading_room/usam/title1/7mdoj.htm.*

Rule 3.7 Lawyer as Witness

(a) A lawyer shall not act as advocate at a trial in which the lawyer is likely to be a necessary witness unless:

(1) the testimony relates to an uncontested issue;

(2) the testimony relates to the nature and value of legal services rendered in the case; or

(3) disqualification of the lawyer would work substantial hardship on the client.

(b) A lawyer may act as advocate in a trial in which another lawyer in the lawyer's firm is likely to be called as a witness unless precluded from doing so by Rule 1.7 or Rule 1.9.

COMMENT

[1] Combining the roles of advocate and witness can prejudice the tribunal and the opposing party and can also involve a conflict of interest between the lawyer and client.

Advocate-Witness Rule

[2] The tribunal has proper objection when the trier of fact may be confused or misled by a lawyer serving as both advocate and witness. The opposing party has proper objection where the combination of roles may prejudice that party's rights in the litigation. A witness is required to testify on the basis of personal knowledge, while an advocate is expected to explain and comment on evidence given by others. It may not be clear whether a statement by an advocate-witness should be taken as proof or as an analysis of the proof.

[3] To protect the tribunal, paragraph (a) prohibits a lawyer from simultaneously serving as advocate and necessary witness except in those circumstances specified in paragraphs (a)(1) through (a)(3). Paragraph (a)(1) recognizes that if the testimony will be uncontested, the ambiguities in the dual role are purely theoretical. Paragraph (a)(2) recognizes that where the testimony concerns the extent and

value of legal services rendered in the action in which the testimony is offered, permitting the lawyers to testify avoids the need for a second trial with new counsel to resolve that issue. Moreover, in such a situation the judge has firsthand knowledge of the matter in issue; hence, there is less dependence on the adversary process to test the credibility of the testimony.

[4] Apart from these two exceptions, paragraph (a)(3) recognizes that a balancing is required between the interests of the client and those of the tribunal and the opposing party. Whether the tribunal is likely to be misled or the opposing party is likely to suffer prejudice depends on the nature of the case, the importance and probable tenor of the lawyer's testimony, and the probability that the lawyer's testimony will conflict with that of other witnesses. Even if there is risk of such prejudice, in determining whether the lawyer should be disqualified, due regard must be given to the effect of disqualification on the lawyer's client. It is relevant that one or both parties could reasonably foresee that the lawyer would probably be a witness. The conflict of interest principles stated in Rules 1.7, 1.9 and 1.10 have no application to this aspect of the problem.

[5] Because the tribunal is not likely to be misled when a lawyer acts as advocate in a trial in which another lawyer in the lawyer's firm will testify as a necessary witness, paragraph (b) permits the lawyer to do so except in situations involving a conflict of interest.

Conflict of Interest

[6] In determining if it is permissible to act as advocate in a trial in which the lawyer will be a necessary witness, the lawyer must also consider that the dual role may give rise to a conflict of interest that will require compliance with Rules 1.7 or 1.9. For example, if there is likely to be substantial conflict between the testimony of the client and that of the lawyer, the representation involves a conflict of interest that requires compliance with Rule 1.7. This would be true even though the lawyer might not be prohibited by paragraph (a) from simultaneously serving as advocate and witness because the lawyer's disqualification would work a substantial hardship on the client. Similarly, a lawyer who might be permitted to simultaneously serve as an advocate and a witness by paragraph (a)(3) might be precluded from doing so by Rule 1.9. The problem can arise whether the lawyer is called as a witness on behalf of the client or is called by the opposing party. Determining whether or not such a conflict exists is primarily the responsibility of the lawyer involved. If there is a conflict of interest, the lawyer must secure the client's informed consent, confirmed in writing. In some cases, the lawyer will be precluded from seeking the client's consent. See Rule 1.7. See Rule 1.0(b) for the definition of "confirmed in writing" and Rule 1.0(e) for the definition of "informed consent."

1.10 [7] Paragraph (b) provides that a lawyer is not disqualified from serving as an advocate because a lawyer with whom the lawyer is associated in a firm is precluded from doing so by paragraph (a). If, however, the testifying lawyer would also be disqualified by Rule 1.7 or Rule 1.9 from representing the client in the matter, other lawyers in the firm will be precluded from representing the client by Rule 1.10 unless the client gives informed consent under the conditions stated in Rule 1.7.

Canon and Code Antecedents

ABA Canons of Professional Ethics: Canons 18 and 19 provided as follows:

18. Treatment of Witnesses and Litigants

A lawyer should always treat adverse witnesses and suitors with fairness and due consideration, and he should never minister to the malevolence or prejudices of a client in the trial or conduct of a cause. The client cannot be made the keeper of the lawyer's conscience in professional matters. He has no right to demand that his counsel shall abuse the opposite party or indulge in offensive personalities. Improper speech is not excusable on the ground that it is what the client would say if speaking in his own behalf.

19. Appearance of Lawyer as Witness for His Client

When a lawyer is a witness for his client, except as to merely formal matters, such as the attestation or custody of an instrument and the like, he should leave the trial of the case to other counsel. Except when essential to the ends of justice, a lawyer should avoid testifying in court in behalf of his client.

ABA Model Code of Professional Responsibility: Compare DR 5-101(B), DR 5-102(A), and DR 5-102(B) (reprinted later in this volume).

Cross-References in Other Rules

None.

Legislative History of Model Rule 3.7

1980 Discussion Draft (then Rule 3.9) prohibited a lawyer from acting as an advocate, "except on the lawyer's own behalf, in litigation in which the lawyer's own conduct is a material issue or in which the lawyer is likely to be a witness," unless the lawyer satisfied exceptions that were substantially the same as finally adopted.

1981 Draft was substantially the same as adopted.

1982 Draft was adopted.

1983 Rule: As originally adopted in 1983, Rule 3.7 was essentially the same as the 2002 version.

2002 Amendments: At its February 2002 Mid-Year Meeting, the ABA House of Delegates adopted without change the ABA Ethics 2000 Commission proposal to amend Rule 3.7 and its Comment. The amendments changed "except where" to "unless" in the text of Rule 3.7(a), made minor changes to Comments 1 through 4, added Comment 5, significantly amended Comment 6, and added Comment 7.

Selected State Variations

California: Rule 5-210 provides as follows:

A member shall not act as an advocate before a jury which will hear testimony from the member unless:

(A) The testimony relates to an uncontested matter; or

(B) The testimony relates to the nature and value of legal services rendered in the case; or

(C) The member has the informed written consent of the client. If the member represents the People or a governmental entity, the consent shall be obtained from the head of the office or a designee of the head of the office by which the member is employed and shall be consistent with principles of recusal.

District of Columbia: Rule 3.7(b) provides that a lawyer may not act as advocate in a trial in which another lawyer in the lawyer's firm is likely to be called as a witness "if the other lawyer would be precluded from acting as advocate in the trial by Rule 1.7 or Rule 1.9." D.C. also adds that the provisions of Rule 3.7(b) "do not apply if the lawyer who is appearing as an advocate is employed by, and appears on behalf of, a government agency."

Florida: Rule 3.7(a) applies when a lawyer is likely to be a necessary witness "on behalf of the client," and creates an exception when "the testimony will relate solely to a matter of formality and there is no reason to believe that substantial evidence will be offered in opposition to the testimony." Florida adopts ABA Model Rule 3.7(b) verbatim.

New York: Rule 3.7(a) applies only when a lawyer is likely to be a necessary witness "on a significant issue of fact." Rule 3.7(a) also adds two additional exceptions: "(4) the testimony will relate solely to a matter of formality, and there is no reason to believe that substantial evidence will be offered in opposition to the testimony; or (5) the testimony is authorized by the tribunal."

Ohio adds a new Rule 3.7(c), which provides as follows: "A government lawyer participating in a case shall not testify or offer the testimony of another lawyer in the same government agency, except where division (a) applies or where permitted by law."

Texas: Rule 3.08(a) disqualifies a lawyer if the lawyer knows or believes that the lawyer is or may be a witness "necessary to establish an essential fact on behalf of the lawyer's client," unless specified exceptions apply. The exceptions are substantially identical to DR 5-101(B)(1)-(3) of the ABA Model Code of Professional Responsibility, but Texas adds an exception if "(4) the lawyer is a party to the action and is appearing pro se," and Texas applies the "substantial hardship" exception only if "the lawyer has promptly notified opposing counsel that the lawyer expects to testify in the matter. . . ." Texas Rules 3.08(b) and (c) provide as follows:

> (b) A lawyer shall not continue as an advocate in a pending adjudicatory proceeding if the lawyer believes that the lawyer will be compelled to furnish testimony that will be substantially adverse to the lawyer's client, unless the client consents after full disclosure.
>
> (c) Without the client's informed consent, a lawyer may not act as advocate in an adjudicatory proceeding in which another lawyer in the lawyer's firm is prohibited by paragraphs (a) or (b) from serving as advocate. If the lawyer to be called as a witness could not also serve as an advocate under this Rule, that lawyer shall not take an active role before the tribunal in the presentation of the matter.

Virginia: In Rule 3.7(a), Virginia substitutes "adversarial proceeding" for "trial." In Rule 3.7(b), Virginia incorporates language from DR 5-102(B) of the ABA Model Code of Professional Responsibility to deal with situations in which a lawyer learns that he or she may be called as a witness "other than on behalf of the client" after accepting the representation.

Related Materials

ABA Formal Ethics Opinions: See ABA Formal Ethics Ops. 90-357 (1990), 97-407 (1997), 98-410 n.26 (1998), and 08-452 (2008).

Model Rules of Professional Conduct for Federal Lawyers: Rule 3.7(a)(2) permits a lawyer to testify to the nature, value, "and quality" of legal services rendered in the case.

Restatement of the Law Governing Lawyers: See Restatement §108 in our chapter on the Restatement later in this volume.

Rule 3.8 Special Responsibilities of a Prosecutor

The prosecutor in a criminal case shall:

(a) refrain from prosecuting a charge that the prosecutor knows is not supported by probable cause; 3.1 – Δ lawyer

(b) make reasonable efforts to assure that the accused has been advised of the right to, and the procedure for obtaining, counsel and has been given reasonable opportunity to obtain counsel;

(c) not seek to obtain from an unrepresented accused a waiver of important pretrial rights, such as the right to a preliminary hearing;

(d) make timely disclosure to the defense of all evidence or information known to the prosecutor that tends to negate the guilt of the accused or mitigates the offense, and, in connection with sentencing, disclose to the defense and to the tribunal all unprivileged mitigating information known to the prosecutor, except when the prosecutor is relieved of this responsibility by a protective order of the tribunal;

(e) not subpoena a lawyer in a grand jury or other criminal proceeding to present evidence about a past or present client unless the prosecutor reasonably believes:

(1) the information sought is not protected from disclosure by any applicable privilege;

(2) the evidence sought is essential to the successful completion of an ongoing investigation or prosecution; and

(3) there is no other feasible alternative to obtain the information;

(f) except for statements that are necessary to inform the public of the nature and extent of the prosecutor's action and that serve a legitimate law enforcement purpose, refrain from making extrajudicial comments that have a substantial likelihood of heightening public condemnation of the accused and exercise reasonable care to prevent investigators, law enforcement personnel, employees or other persons assisting or associated with the prosecutor in a criminal case from making an extrajudicial statement that the prosecutor would be prohibited from making under Rule 3.6 or this Rule. 3.6(b)(7) ; 3.6 cmt 5

(g) When a prosecutor knows of new, credible and material evidence creating a reasonable likelihood that a convicted defendant did not commit an offense of which the defendant was convicted, the prosecutor shall:

(1) promptly disclose that evidence to an appropriate court or authority, and

(2) if the conviction was obtained in the prosecutor's jurisdiction,

(A) promptly disclose that evidence to the defendant unless a court authorizes delay, and

(B) undertake further investigation, or make reasonable efforts to cause an investigation, to determine whether the defendant was convicted of an offense that the defendant did not commit.

(h) When a prosecutor knows of clear and convincing evidence establishing that a defendant in the prosecutor's jurisdiction was convicted of an offense that the defendant did not commit, the prosecutor shall seek to remedy the conviction.

COMMENT

[1] A prosecutor has the responsibility of a minister of justice and not simply that of an advocate. This responsibility carries with it specific obligations to see that the defendant is accorded procedural justice and that guilt is decided upon the basis of sufficient evidence, and that special precautions are taken to prevent and to rectify the conviction of innocent persons. The extent of mandated remedial action is a matter of debate and varies in different jurisdictions. Many jurisdictions have adopted the ABA Standards of Criminal Justice Relating to the Prosecution Function, which are the product of prolonged and careful deliberation by lawyers experienced in both criminal prosecution and defense. Competent representation of the sovereignty may require a prosecutor to undertake some procedural and remedial measures as a matter of obligation. Applicable law may require other measures by the prosecutor and knowing disregard of those obligations or a systematic abuse of prosecutorial discretion could constitute a violation of Rule 8.4.

[2] In some jurisdictions, a defendant may waive a preliminary hearing and thereby lose a valuable opportunity to challenge probable cause. Accordingly, prosecutors should not seek to obtain waivers of preliminary hearings or other important pretrial rights from unrepresented accused persons. Paragraph (c) does not apply, however, to an accused appearing pro se with the approval of the tribunal. Nor does it forbid the lawful questioning of an uncharged suspect who has knowingly waived the rights to counsel and silence.

[3] The exception in paragraph (d) recognizes that a prosecutor may seek an appropriate protective order from the tribunal if disclosure of information to the defense could result in substantial harm to an individual or to the public interest.

[4] Paragraph (e) is intended to limit the issuance of lawyer subpoenas in grand jury and other criminal proceedings to those situations in which there is a genuine need to intrude into the client-lawyer relationship.

[5] Paragraph (f) supplements Rule 3.6, which prohibits extrajudicial statements that have a substantial likelihood of prejudicing an adjudicatory proceeding. In the context of a criminal prosecution, a prosecutor's extrajudicial statement can create the additional problem of increasing public condemnation of the accused. Although the announcement of an indictment, for example, will necessarily have severe consequences for the accused, a prosecutor can, and should, avoid comments which have no legitimate law enforcement purpose and have a substantial likelihood of increasing public opprobrium of the accused. Nothing in this Comment is intended to restrict the statements which a prosecutor may make which comply with Rule 3.6(b) or 3.6(c).

[6] Like other lawyers, prosecutors are subject to Rules 5.1 and 5.3, which relate to responsibilities regarding lawyers and nonlawyers who work for or are associated with the lawyer's office. Paragraph (f) reminds the prosecutor of the importance of these obligations in connection with the unique dangers of improper extrajudicial statements in a criminal case. In addition, paragraph (f) requires a prosecutor to exercise reasonable care to prevent persons assisting or associated with the prosecutor from making improper extrajudicial statements, even when such persons are not under the direct supervision of the prosecutor. Ordinarily, the reasonable care standard will be satisfied if the prosecutor issues the appropriate cautions to law-enforcement personnel and other relevant individuals.

[7] When a prosecutor knows of new, credible and material evidence creating a reasonable likelihood that a person outside the prosecutor's jurisdiction was convicted of a crime that the person did not commit, paragraph (g) requires prompt disclosure to the court or other appropriate authority, such as the chief prosecutor of the jurisdiction where the conviction occurred. If the conviction was obtained in the prosecutor's jurisdiction, paragraph (g) requires the prosecutor to examine the evidence and undertake further investigation to determine whether the defendant is in fact innocent or make reasonable efforts to cause another appropriate authority to undertake the necessary investigation, and to promptly disclose the evidence to the court and, absent court-authorized delay, to the defendant. Consistent with the objectives of Rules 4.2 and 4.3, disclosure to a represented defendant must be made through the defendant's counsel, and, in the case of an unrepresented defendant, would ordinarily be accompanied by a request to a court for the appointment of counsel to assist the defendant in taking such legal measures as may be appropriate.

[8] Under paragraph (h), once the prosecutor knows of clear and convincing evidence that the defendant was convicted of an offense that the defendant did not commit, the prosecutor must seek to remedy the conviction. Necessary steps may include disclosure of the evidence to the defendant, requesting that the court appoint counsel for an unrepresented indigent defendant and, where appropriate, notifying the court that the prosecutor has knowledge that the defendant did not commit the offense of which the defendant was convicted.

[9] A prosecutor's independent judgment, made in good faith, that the new evidence is not of such nature as to trigger the obligations of sections (g) and (h), though subsequently determined to have been erroneous, does not constitute a violation of this Rule.

Canon and Code Antecedents

ABA Canons of Professional Ethics: Canon 5 provided, in relevant part, as follows:

5. *The Defense or Prosecution of Those Accused of Crime*

> . . . The primary duty of a lawyer engaged in public prosecution is not to convict, but to see that justice is done. The suppression of facts or the secreting of witnesses capable of establishing the innocence of the accused is highly reprehensible.

ABA Model Code of Professional Responsibility: Compare DR 7-103(A) and DR 7-103(B) (reprinted later in this volume).

Cross-References in Other Rules

Rule 3.6, Comment 8: "See **Rule 3.8(f)** for additional duties of prosecutors in connection with extrajudicial statements about criminal proceedings."

Legislative History of Model Rule 3.8

1980 Discussion Draft (then Rule 3.10) provided that the prosecutor in a criminal case shall:

> (a) refrain from prosecuting a charge that the prosecutor knows is not supported by probable cause;
>
> (b) advise the defendant of the right to counsel and provide assistance in obtaining counsel;
>
> (c) not induce an unrepresented defendant to surrender important procedural rights, such as the right to a preliminary hearing;
>
> (d) seek all evidence, whether or not favorable to the accused, and make timely disclosure to the defense of all evidence supporting innocence or mitigating the offense;
>
> (e) not discourage a person from giving relevant information to the defense;
>
> (f) in connection with sentencing, disclose to the defendant and to the court all unprivileged information known to the prosecution that is relevant thereto.

The 1980 Discussion Draft also contained a separate rule, with no direct counterpart in the Rules as adopted, that read as follows:

Special Responsibilities of Defense Counsel in a Criminal Case

> A lawyer for the accused in a criminal case, shall not:
>
> (a) agree to represent a person proposing to commit a crime, except as part of a good faith effort to determine the validity, scope, meaning, or application of the law;
>
> (b) act in a case in which the lawyer's partner or other professional associate is or has been the prosecutor;
>
> (c) accept payment of fees by one person for the defense of another except with the consent of the accused after adequate disclosure; or
>
> (d) charge a contingent fee.

1981 Draft: Substantially the same as adopted, except subparagraph (d), which included an obligation to "make reasonable efforts to seek all evidence, whether or not favorable to the defendant," but did not refer to protective orders. Also, the 1981 Draft did not include subparagraph (e) of the rule as adopted.

1982 Draft: Same as adopted, except that the 1982 Draft did not include subparagraph (e) of the rule as adopted.

1983 Rule: As originally adopted in 1983, Rule 3.8(a)-(d) was the same as the 2002 version of ABA Model Rule 3.8, but the original version did not contain any equivalent to the 2002 version of Rule 3.8(e). In addition, Rule 3.8(e) of the original rule provided that a prosecutor shall:

> (e) exercise reasonable care to prevent investigators, law enforcement personnel, employees or other persons assisting or associated with the prosecutor in a criminal case from making an extrajudicial statement that the prosecutor would be prohibited from making under Rule 3.6.

1990 Amendment: At its 1990 Mid-Year Meeting, the ABA House of Delegates added paragraph (f) (now (e)) to Rule 3.8 to govern subpoenas to lawyers, and added paragraph 4 to the Comment. The ABA's Standing Committee on Ethics and Professional Responsibility explained the amendment as follows:

*Excerpt from ABA Report Explaining 1990 Amendment**

> Any rule regulating subpoenas to lawyers must, at a minimum, provide for full protection of the privilege.
>
> A subpoena rule which does no more than recognize the attorney-client privilege, however, will ignore other important aspects of the relationship between a client and his attorney. . . . Because information protected by the attorney-client privilege is not coterminous with information which an ethical attorney is supposed to hold confidential, there is much information in the hands of an attorney which remains exposed to the subpoena power, even if that power is limited by the privilege. For example, the prevailing judicial position is that, absent special circumstances, an attorney may be compelled by subpoena to reveal information about the identity of the client and the size and source of the fee-information frequently sought by government attorneys. Similarly, an attorney in possession of documents received from a client in the course of a case may be compelled by subpoena to produce those documents, assuming that the client personally could be compelled to produce the documents were they in the client's hands.
>
> Since a subpoena may compel production of information which, though unprivileged, is certainly confidential under Rule 1.6 and DR 4-101, the mere issuance of the subpoena undermines the client's confidence and trust. . . .
>
> . . . Confronted by a powerful adversary and by a seemingly bewildering array of procedures, with their liberty at stake, clients rightfully expect that their lawyer will, within the constraints of the law and the profession's code of ethics, zealously argue their case at every turn. There could be few things more destructive of this expectation than the spectacle of their own attorney forced by their adversary to supply information detrimental to their interest.

1994 Amendment: At its August 1994 Annual Meeting, by a voice vote, the ABA House of Delegates amended Rule 3.8 by adding a new paragraph (g) (now (f)) that permits prosecutors to make statements "necessary to inform the public of the nature and extent of the prosecutor's action and that serve a legitimate law enforcement purpose," even if these statements may heighten "public condemnation of the accused." The amendment added a corresponding paragraph to the Comment. The amendment supplements the 1994 amendment to Rule 3.6, which generally governs extrajudicial statements by lawyers.

* Committee Reports do not represent official policy of the ABA. They are for information only, and the opinions are those of the authors of the report.

The amendment was co-sponsored by the ABA Standing Committee on Ethics and Professional Responsibility and the ABA Criminal Justice Section, which submitted a joint report in support of the 1994 amendment to Rule 3.6 and Rule 3.8. We reprint below the small portion of the joint ABA report explaining the amendment to Rule 3.8. (Excerpts from the remainder of the report, which provides further background and context for the amendment, are found in the Legislative History section following Rule 3.6.)

*Excerpts from ABA Report Explaining 1994 Amendment**

In connection with its proposed revision of Rule 3.6, the Committee also proposes to add a new section (g) to Rule 3.8, prohibiting gratuitous comments by a prosecutor which have a substantial likelihood of increasing public opprobrium toward the accused. Not only can pretrial publicity taint the fairness of a trial, but it can also subject the accused to unfair and unnecessary condemnation before the trial takes place. Because of a prosecutor's special power and visibility, a prosecutor should use special care to avoid such publicity.

1995 Amendment: At its August 1995 Annual Meeting, the ABA House of Delegates voted 187-113 to amend Rule 3.8 by deleting subparagraph (f)(2), which had required prosecutors to obtain "prior judicial approval after an opportunity for an adversarial hearing" before serving a subpoena on a lawyer in a grand jury or other criminal proceeding to seek evidence about the lawyer's past or present clients. The ABA also removed the last sentence of Comment 4, which had explained the need for judicial approval. The amendment was jointly sponsored by the ABA's Standing Committee on Ethics and Professional Responsibility and the ABA Criminal Justice Section. Below are excerpts from the joint Committee Report explaining the amendment.

Excerpts from ABA Report Explaining 1995 Amendment

Subparagraph (2) of Rule 3.8(f) is an anomaly in the Model Rules. Rather than stating a substantive ethical precept, it sets out a type of implementing requirement that is properly established by rules of criminal procedure rather than established as an ethical norm. Moreover, while nominally addressed to the conduct of prosecutors, subparagraph (2) affects the operation of courts and grand juries by "requir[ing] the erection of novel court procedures and interject[ing] an additional layer of judicial supervision over the grand jury subpoena process." Baylson v. Disciplinary Board, 764 F. Supp. 328, 337 (E.D. Pa. 1991). The procedural obligations it seeks to impose as a matter of professional ethics have no parallel in any other enforceable provision of the Model Rules.

We therefore recommend deletion of subparagraph (2) of Rule 3.8(f). . . . The limiting description of the circumstances in which a prosecutor could ethically issue such a subpoena, set forth in subparagraph (1), would remain unchanged. The proposed amendment would remove the feature of the rule that courts have found objectionable. . . .

2002 Amendments: At its February 2002 Mid-Year Meeting, the ABA House of Delegates adopted without change the ABA Ethics 2000 Commission proposal to amend Rule 3.8 and its Comment. The amendment to the text redesignated former Rule 3.8(f) as Rule 3.8(e), redesignated former Rule 3.8(g) as Rule 3.8(f) and moved all of the language in former Rule 3.8(e) to its current position at the end of Rule

* Committee Reports do not represent official policy of the ABA. They are for information only, and the opinions are those of the authors of the report.

3.8(f) (beginning with "exercise reasonable care"). The amendment to the Comment moderately changed Comments 1, 2, 4, and 5, and added all of Comment 6.

2008 Amendments: At its February 2008 Mid-Year Meeting, by voice vote (signifying overwhelming approval), the ABA House of Delegates amended Rule 3.8 by adding new paragraphs (g) and (h), which impose certain post-conviction responsibilities on prosecutors. At the same time, the ABA amended Comment 1 to Rule 3.8 to reflect the new obligations and added new Comments 7, 8, and 9 to explain the new paragraphs.

The amendments were spearheaded by the ABA Criminal Justice Section (chaired by Professor Stephen J. Saltzburg of The George Washington University Law School) and were co-sponsored by the ABA Standing Committee on Ethics and Professional Responsibility, the ABA Death Penalty Representation Project, the ABA Section of Individual Rights and Responsibilities, the ABA Section of Litigation, the ABA Section of State and Local Government Law, the ABA Government and Public Sector Lawyers Division, the ABA Commission on Domestic Violence, the New York State Bar Association, the Association of the Bar of the City of New York, and the National Organization of Bar Counsel. The full Report submitted by the ABA Section of Criminal Justice to explain the history and purpose of the amendments is available online at *www.abanet.org/cpr/mrpc/ model_rules.html.* Here are extensive excerpts from that Report (with most footnotes omitted):

*Excerpts from ABA Report Explaining 2008 Amendments**

In Achieving Justice: Freeing the Innocent, Convicting the Guilty, the ABA's Section of Criminal Justice explored the systemic causes for wrongful convictions in our criminal justice system. Its report made numerous recommendations for systemic remedies to better ensure that individuals will not be convicted of crimes that they did not commit and that the innocent will be exonerated. That report did not address the well established ethical obligations of a prosecutor toward innocent persons.

The United States Supreme Court recognized in *Imbler v. Pachtman,* 424 U.S. 409, 427 n. 25 (1976), that prosecutors are "bound by the ethics of [their] office to inform the appropriate authority of after-acquired or other information that casts doubt upon the correctness of the conviction." Further, when a prosecutor concludes upon investigation of such evidence that an innocent person was convicted, it is well recognized that the prosecutor has an obligation to endeavor to rectify the injustice. These obligations have not, however, been codified in Rule 3.8 of the ABA Model Rules of Professional Conduct, which identifies the "Special Responsibilities of a Prosecutor." Proposed Rules 3.8(g) and (h), and the accompanying Comments would rectify this omission.

Proposed Rules 3.8(g) and (h) and the accompanying Comments are based on provisions adopted by the House of Delegates of the New York State Bar Association on November 4, 2006 in the course of its comprehensive review of the state's disciplinary code. The rules had their genesis in a 2006 Report of the Association of the Bar of the City of New York ("ABCNY"), which considered various aspects of prosecutors' duties. Among other provisions, against the background of recent knowledge about the fallibility of the criminal justice process, the Report proposed a rule regarding the prosecutor's obligation when a convicted defendant may be innocent. The report stated: "In light of the large number of cases in which defendants have been exonerated . . . it is appropriate to obligate prosecutors' offices to" . . . consider "credible post-conviction claims of innocence." The premise of the proposal was that prosecutors have ethical

* Committee Reports do not represent official policy of the ABA. They are for information only, and represent only the opinions of the authors.

responsibilities upon learning of new and material evidence that shows that it is likely that a convicted person was innocent. These responsibilities include a duty to disclose the evidence, to conduct an appropriate investigation, and, upon becoming convinced that a miscarriage of justice occurred, to take steps to remedy it.

The ABCNY proposal was presented to the state bar's Committee on Standards of Attorney Conduct ("COSAC"), which agreed with the premise of the ABCNY proposal and drafted provisions that captured the substance of the proposal, and circulated them for a lengthy period of public comment. COSAC's original proposed Rules 3.8(g) and (h) received comment from a wide range of state and federal prosecutors and district attorneys' organizations, defense organizations and bar associations, and revised its proposals in light of suggestions received from around the state.

The version adopted by the New York State Bar Association was closely examined and refined by the ABA Section of Criminal Justice, which drew on the experience and expertise of prosecutors, criminal defense lawyers and legal academics in its leadership, including those who serve as representatives of other national organizations such as the National District Attorneys Association. It was then further refined in collaboration with the ABA Standing Committee on Ethics and Professional Responsibility, to ensure its general consistency with the philosophy, purposes, structure and style of the ABA Model Rules of Professional Conduct.

As the proposed provisions reflect, it is important to codify prosecutorial duties upon learning of possible false convictions. The obligations in the proposed rule are triggered when a prosecutor either "knows" of new, credible and material evidence creating a reasonable likelihood of a convicted defendant's innocence or "knows" of clear and convincing evidence establishing the convicted defendant's innocence. The ABA Model Rules define "knows" to "denote[] actual knowledge of the fact in question"; therefore, indirect or imputed knowledge will not suffice.

The obligation to avoid and rectify convictions of innocent people, to which the proposed provisions give expression, is the most fundamental professional obligation of criminal prosecutors. The inclusion of these provisions in the rules of professional conduct, rather than only in the provisions of the ABA Standards Relating to the Administration of Justice, which are not intended to be enforced, will express the vital importance that the profession places on this obligation. Further, it is important not simply to educate prosecutors but to hold out the possibility of professional discipline for lawyers who intentionally ignore persuasive evidence of an unjust conviction. Prosecutors' offices have institutional disincentives to comport with these obligations and, as courts have recognized, their failures are not self-correcting by the criminal justice process. Codification of these obligations, which are meant to express prosecutors' minimum responsibilities, will help counter these institutional disincentives. . . .

The Rule and Comments are designed to provide clear guidance to prosecutors concerning their minimum disciplinary responsibilities,[1] with the expectation that, as

1. Prosecutors and their representative organizations involved in the drafting process generally agreed on the need to identify specific measures to be taken upon learning of new evidence of a convicted defendant's innocence. Accordingly, the proposed provisions specifically identify when a prosecutor's disciplinary obligations are implicated regarding disclosure, investigation, and remedial measures. Recognizing, however, that individual cases and jurisdictions differ, the rule does not prescribe particular investigative steps and remedial measures that must be pursued. Although the proposed Comments identify steps that might be taken when necessary to remedy a wrongful conviction, the list is not exclusive. Sometimes disclosure to the defendant or the court, or making or joining in an application to the court, will suffice, whereas in jurisdictions where courts lack jurisdiction to release an innocent individual, the appropriate step may be to make, or join in, an application for executive clemency. [*Footnote by the ABA Committee—Eds.*]

ministers of justice, prosecutors routinely will and should go beyond the disciplinary minimum. In many instances, a prosecutor will receive information about a defendant that does not trigger the rule's disclosure obligation and will be called upon to decide whether that information is nevertheless sufficient to require some investigation. The quality and specificity of the information received by a prosecutor often will vary dramatically, and it is expected that a prosecutor will decide whether and how to investigate based upon a good faith assessment of the information received. In some cases, the prosecutor may recognize the need to reinvestigate the underlying case; in others, it may be appropriate to await development of the record in collateral proceedings initiated by the defendant.

With the understanding that prosecutors should be presumed to take their ethical and professional obligations seriously, the Comment specifically notes that good faith exercises of judgment are not disciplinary violations under the proposed provisions. A convicted defendant might easily complain that a prosecutor "knows" that the defendant is innocent. Indeed, the defendant may support a complaint by relying on much the same evidence that might have been presented at trial. We are confident, however, that disciplinary authorities will not assume that prosecutors ignore substantial evidence of innocence and will not burden prosecutors with the need to respond to and defend ethics charges that are not supported by specific and particular credible evidence that the prosecutor violated his or her disciplinary responsibilities.

The provisions build upon the ABA's historic commitment to developing policies and standards designed to give concrete meaning to the "duty of prosecutors to seek justice, not merely to convict," and, in particular, to prevent and rectify the conviction of innocent defendants. For example, the ABA has endorsed draft legislation that would generally ensure the preservation of material evidence for post-conviction review, and that would require the preservation of DNA evidence in particular until the convicted defendant has completed his sentence. These prior resolutions implicitly recognized the need to reexamine convictions in light of newly discovered, material exculpatory evidence. The proposed additions to the ABA Model Rules will codify public prosecutors' obligations to conduct such reexaminations.

Selected State Variations

Editors' Note. When this book went to press in September 2011, only five states—Colorado, Delaware, Idaho, Tennessee, and Wisconsin—had adopted the 2008 amendments to ABA Model Rule 3.8 in substantially equivalent form. For up-to-date state-by-state information on adoptions of the 2008 amendments to Model Rule 3.8, see *http://www.americanbar.org/content/dam/aba/migrated/cpr/pic/3_8_g_h.authcheckdam.pdf*.

California: Rule 5-110 provides as follows:

> A member in government service shall not institute or cause to be instituted criminal charges when the member knows or should know that the charges are not supported by probable cause. If, after the institution of criminal charges, the member in government service having responsibility for prosecuting the charges becomes aware that those charges are not supported by probable cause, the member shall promptly so advise the court in which the criminal matter is pending.

In addition, Rule 5-220 provides that a lawyer "shall not suppress any evidence that the member or the member's client has a legal obligation to reveal or to produce."

Connecticut omits paragraphs (e) and (f).

District of Columbia: Every paragraph of Rule 3.8 differs from the Model Rule. The D.C. version of Rule 3.8 provides that the prosecutor in a criminal case shall not:

> (a) In exercising discretion to investigate or to prosecute, improperly favor or invidiously discriminate against any person;
>
> (b) File in court or maintain a charge that the prosecutor knows is not supported by probable cause;
>
> (c) Prosecute to trial a charge that the prosecutor knows is not supported by evidence sufficient to establish a *prima facie* showing of guilt;
>
> (d) Intentionally avoid pursuit of evidence or information because it may damage the prosecution's case or aid the defense;
>
> (e) Intentionally fail to disclose to the defense, upon request and at a time when use by the defense is reasonably feasible, any evidence or information that the prosecutor knows or reasonably should know tends to negate the guilt of the accused or to mitigate the offense, or in connection with sentencing, intentionally fail to disclose to the defense upon request any unprivileged mitigating information known to the prosecutor and not reasonably available to the defense, except when the prosecutor is relieved of this responsibility by a protective order of the tribunal;
>
> (f) Except for statements which are necessary to inform the public of the nature and extent of the prosecutor's action and which serve a legitimate law enforcement purpose, make extrajudicial comments which serve to heighten condemnation of the accused; or
>
> (g) In presenting a case to a grand jury, intentionally interfere with the independence of the grand jury, preempt a function of the grand jury, abuse the processes of the grand jury, or fail to bring to the attention of the grand jury material facts tending substantially to negate the existence of probable cause.

Florida omits paragraphs (b), (e), and (f) of ABA Model Rule 3.8.

Georgia: In place of Rule 3.8(b) and (c), Georgia substitutes the simple caution that a prosecutor shall "refrain from making any effort to prevent the accused from exercising a reasonable effort to obtain counsel." Georgia also shortens Rule 3.8(d) by eliminating the part that begins "in connection with sentencing." Georgia also limits the application of Rule 3.8(e) to statements the prosecutor would be prohibited from making only under Rule 3.6(g) (as opposed to the entire rule).

Illinois: Rule 3.8 adds the following sentence: "The duty of a public prosecutor or other government lawyer is to seek justice, not merely to convict." Comment 1A elaborates on this sentence, quoting cases concerning a prosecutor's duties.

Massachusetts: Rule 3.8(c) prohibits prosecutors from seeking waivers of important pretrial rights from unrepresented defendants unless "a court has first obtained from the accused a knowing and intelligent written waiver of counsel." Massachusetts Rule 3.8(f) tracks ABA Model Rule 3.8(e), but adds that the prosecutor must obtain "prior judicial approval after an opportunity for an adversarial proceeding."

Massachusetts also adds paragraphs (h) and (i), which track DR 7-106(C)(3) and (4), and adds a new paragraph (j) providing that a prosecutor in a criminal case shall "not intentionally avoid pursuit of evidence because the prosecutor believes it will damage the prosecution's case or aid the accused."

The Massachusetts federal court version of Rule 3.8(e)—Local Rule 3.8(f)—was declared invalid in *Stern v. United States District Court for the District of Massachusetts,* 16 F. Supp. 2d 88 (1st Cir.), *reh'g and reh'g en banc denied,* 214 F.3d 4

(1st Cir. 2000) (concluding that "the adoption of Local Rule 3.8(f) exceeded the district court's lawful authority to regulate both grand jury and trial subpoenas" in federal courts).

Michigan omits paragraphs (e) and (f).

New Jersey: Rule 3.8(c) prohibits a prosecutor from seeking to obtain from an unrepresented accused a waiver only of important "post-indictment" pretrial rights, and New Jersey Rule 3.8(d) requires timely disclosure to the defense only of all "evidence," not "information."

New York: Rule 3.8 is substantially similar to DR 7-103(A) of the old Model Code. Rather than adopting Model Rule 3.8(g) and (h), New York endorses similar, but less strict, procedures in Comments 6A-6E (which were amended in November 2010).

North Carolina: Rule 3.8(e) adds that the prosecutor shall not "participate in the application for the issuance of a search warrant to a lawyer for the seizure of information of a past or present client in connection with an investigation of someone other than the lawyer," unless the conditions stated in ABA Model Rule 3.8(e) are satisfied.

Ohio: Rule 3.8(a) provides that a prosecutor shall not "pursue or" prosecute a charge that the prosecutor knows is not supported by probable cause. (A note by the drafters says the rule is thus expanded to prohibit either the pursuit or prosecution of unsupported charges and thus is broad enough to include grand jury proceedings.) Ohio omits Rule 3.8(b) because (according to a Model Rules Comparison) ensuring that the defendant is advised about the right to counsel is a police and judicial function, and because Rule 4.3 already sets forth duties applicable to all lawyers in dealing with unrepresented persons. Ohio also omits Rule 3.8(c) because that rule has a potential adverse impact on defendants who seek continuances or seek to participate in diversion programs. Rule 3.8(d) deletes the words "and to the tribunal" in connection with sentencing disclosures. Ohio omits Rule 3.8(f) because prosecutors, like all lawyers, are already subject to Rule 3.6.

Pennsylvania deletes Rule 3.8(e) (governing subpoenas to lawyers) and instead adopts a separate rule, Pennsylvania Rule 3.10, which forbids a prosecutor or other governmental lawyer, absent judicial approval, to subpoena a lawyer before a grand jury or other tribunal investigating criminal conduct if the prosecutor seeks to compel evidence concerning a current or former client of the lawyer.

Texas: Rule 3.09(a) provides that a prosecutor shall refrain from prosecuting "or threatening to prosecute" a charge that the prosecutor knows is not supported by probable cause. Texas Rule 3.09(b) and (c) provides that a prosecutor shall:

> (b) refrain from conducting or assisting in a custodial interrogation of an accused unless the prosecutor has made reasonable efforts to be assured that the accused has been advised of any right to, and the procedure for obtaining, counsel and has been given reasonable opportunity to obtain counsel;
>
> (c) not initiate or encourage efforts to obtain from an unrepresented accused a waiver of important pre-trial, trial or post-trial rights.

Texas omits paragraph (e) and the first half of ABA Model Rule 3.8(f) but retains in Rule 3.07 the obligation to exercise reasonable care to prevent "persons employed or controlled by the prosecutor" in a criminal case from making an extrajudicial statement that the prosecutor would be prohibited from making.

Utah: Rule 3.8(d) eliminates the obligation to disclose unprivileged mitigating information "to the tribunal" in connection with sentencing; Utah omits ABA

Model Rule 3.8(e) (regarding subpoenas to lawyers); and Utah's equivalent to ABA Model Rule 3.8(f) deletes everything up to the phrase "exercise reasonable care."

Virginia: Rule 3.8, which Virginia calls "Additional Responsibilities of a Prosecutor," states that a prosecutor shall:

> (b) not knowingly take advantage of an unrepresented defendant.
>
> (c) not instruct or encourage a person to withhold information from the defense after a party has been charged with an offense.
>
> (d) make timely disclosure to counsel for the defendant, or to the defendant if he has no counsel, of the existence of evidence which the prosecutor knows tends to negate the guilt of the accused, mitigate the degree of the offense, or reduce the punishment, except when disclosure is precluded or modified by order of a court; . . .

Virginia omits paragraph (e) and the first half of paragraph (f) of ABA Model Rule 3.8 and replaces the duty to "exercise reasonable care to prevent" in the second half of Rule 3.8(f) with a mandate that a prosecutor not "direct or encourage" others to make statements that Rule 3.6 would prohibit the prosecutor from making.

Wisconsin: Rule 3.8(b) requires a prosecutor who is "communicating with an unrepresented person in the context of an investigation or proceeding" to "inform the person of the prosecutor's role and interest in the matter."

Related Materials

ABA Formal Ethics Opinions: See ABA Formal Ethics Ops. 92-363 n.5 (1992) and 09-454 (2009).

ABA Resolution on Timely Disclosure by Prosecutors: At its August 2011 Annual Meeting, the ABA House of Delegates adopted the following resolution related to Rule 3.8(d):

> RESOLVED, That the American Bar Association urges federal, state, territorial and tribal governments to adopt disclosure rules requiring the prosecution to seek from its agents and to timely disclose to the defense before the commencement of trial all information known to the prosecution that tends to negate the guilt of the accused, mitigate the offense charged or sentence, or impeach the prosecution's witnesses or evidence, except when relieved of this responsibility by a protective order.
>
> FURTHER RESOLVED, That the American Bar Association urges federal, state, territorial and tribal governments to adopt disclosure rules requiring the prosecution to make timely disclosure to the defense before a guilty plea of all information, which may include impeachment evidence, known to the prosecution that tends to negate the guilt of the accused or mitigate the offense charged or sentence, except when relieved of this responsibility by a protective order.

ABA Standards for Criminal Justice: The following ABA Standards for Criminal Justice are related to ABA Model Rule 3.8:

Standard 3-2.5 Prosecutor's Handbook; Policy Guidelines and Procedures

> (a) Each prosecutor's office should develop a statement of (i) general policies to guide the exercise of prosecutorial discretion and (ii) procedures of the office. The objectives of these policies as to discretion and procedures should be to achieve a fair, efficient, and effective enforcement of the criminal law.
>
> (b) In the interest of continuity and clarity, such statement of policies and procedures should be maintained in an office handbook. This handbook should be available

to the public, except for subject matters declared "confidential," when it is reasonably believed that public access to their contents would adversely affect the prosecution function.

Standard 3-3.9 Discretion in the Charging Decision

(a) A prosecutor should not institute, or cause to be instituted, or permit the continued pendency of criminal charges when the prosecutor knows that the charges are not supported by probable cause. A prosecutor should not institute, cause to be instituted, or permit the continued pendency of criminal charges in the absence of sufficient admissible evidence to support a conviction.

(b) The prosecutor is not obliged to present all charges which the evidence might support. The prosecutor may in some circumstances and for good cause consistent with the public interest decline to prosecute, notwithstanding that sufficient evidence may exist which would support a conviction. Illustrative of the factors which the prosecutor may properly consider in exercising his or her discretion are:

(i) the prosecutor's reasonable doubt that the accused is in fact guilty;

(ii) the extent of the harm caused by the offense;

(iii) the disproportion of the authorized punishment in relation to the particular offense or the offender;

(iv) possible improper motives of a complainant;

(v) reluctance of the victim to testify;

(vi) cooperation of the accused in the apprehension or conviction of others; and

(vii) availability and likelihood of prosecution by another jurisdiction.

(c) A prosecutor should not be compelled by his or her supervisor to prosecute a case in which he or she has a reasonable doubt about the guilt of the accused.

(d) In making the decision to prosecute, the prosecutor should give no weight to the personal or political advantages or disadvantages which might be involved or to a desire to enhance his or her record of convictions.

(e) In cases which involve a serious threat to the community, the prosecutor should not be deterred from prosecution by the fact that in the jurisdiction juries have tended to acquit persons accused of the particular kind of criminal act in question.

(f) The prosecutor should not bring or seek charges greater in number or degree than can reasonably be supported with evidence at trial or than are necessary to fairly reflect the gravity of the offense.

(g) The prosecutor should not condition a dismissal of charges, nolle prosequi, or similar action on the accused's relinquishment of the right to seek civil redress unless the accused has agreed to the action knowingly and intelligently, freely and voluntarily, and where such waiver is approved by the court.

Standard 3-3.11 Disclosure of Evidence by the Prosecutor

(a) A prosecutor should not intentionally fail to make timely disclosure to the defense, at the earliest feasible opportunity, of the existence of all evidence or information which tends to negate the guilt of the accused or mitigate the offense charged or which would tend to reduce the punishment of the accused.

(b) A prosecutor should not fail to make a reasonably diligent effort to comply with a legally proper discovery request.

(c) A prosecutor should not intentionally avoid pursuit of evidence because he or she believes it will damage the prosecution's case or aid the accused.

Standard 3-4.1 Availability for Plea Discussions

(a) The prosecutor should have and make known a general policy or willingness to consult with defense counsel concerning disposition of charges by plea.

> (b) A prosecutor should not engage in plea discussions directly with an accused who is represented by defense counsel, except with defense counsel's approval. Where the defendant has properly waived counsel, the prosecuting attorney may engage in plea discussions with the defendant, although, where feasible, a record of such discussions should be made and preserved.
>
> (c) A prosecutor should not knowingly make false statements or representations as to fact or law in the course of plea discussions with defense counsel or the accused.

ABA Standards for Imposing Lawyer Sanctions: See Standard 5.2, which is reprinted in the Related Materials following Model Rule 8.4.

American Lawyer's Code of Conduct: Chapter 9 of the American Lawyer's Code of Conduct, entitled "Responsibilities of Government Lawyers," contains the following provisions:

> 9.3. A lawyer serving as public prosecutor shall not seek or sign formal charges, or proceed to trial, unless a fair-minded juror could conclude beyond a reasonable doubt that the accused is guilty, on the basis of all of the facts that are known to the prosecutor and likely to be admissible into evidence. . . .
>
> 9.5. A lawyer serving as public prosecutor shall not use unconscionable pressures in plea bargaining, such as charging the accused in several counts for what is essentially a single offense, or charging the accused with a more serious offense than is warranted under Rule 9.3. . . .
>
> 9.7. A lawyer serving as public prosecutor shall promptly make available to defense counsel, without request for it, any information that the prosecutor knows is likely to be useful to the defense. . . .
>
> 9.9. A lawyer serving as public prosecutor, who knows that a defendant is not receiving or has not received effective assistance of counsel, shall promptly advise the court, on the record when possible.

Attorney Fee Forfeiture: A topic often intertwined with subpoenas to defense attorneys is attorney fee forfeiture—seizing an attorney's fees when the government can prove that the money used to pay the fees is the fruit of federal drug crimes or RICO violations. In 1989, the Supreme Court decided two cases on fee forfeiture, *Caplin & Drysdale v. United States,* 491 U.S. 617 (1989), and *United States v. Monsanto,* 491 U.S. 600 (1989).

Brady Material: The constitutional basis for the disclosure obligations in Rule 3.8(d) is found in *Brady v. Maryland,* 373 U.S. 83, 87 (1963), which held that "the suppression by the prosecution of evidence favorable to an accused upon request violates due process where the evidence is material. . . ."

Federal Rules of Criminal Procedure: Rules 16 and 26.2 of the Federal Rules of Criminal Procedure impose disclosure obligations on both sides in criminal cases. Before trial, Rule 16(a)(1) provides that federal prosecutors must allow a criminal defendant to inspect seven categories of information, including: (A) defendant's oral statement; (B) defendant's written or recorded statement; (C) in the case of an organizational defendant, any oral, written, or recorded statement by a person who "(i) was legally able to bind the defendant regarding the subject of the statement because of that person's position as the defendant's director, officer, employee, or agent; or (ii) was personally involved in the alleged conduct constituting the offense and was legally able to bind the defendant regarding that conduct because of that person's position as the defendant's director, officer, employee, or agent"; (D) the defendant's prior criminal record; (E) books, papers, documents, photographs, tangible objects, buildings or places that are material to the preparation of the defense, or are intended for use by the government as evidence in chief at trial, or were obtained from or belong to the defendant; (F) results or reports of physical or mental examinations, and scientific tests or experiments, which are material to the preparation of the defense or which the government intends to use as evidence in chief at trial; and (G) a written summary of any expert testimony that the government intends to use during its case-in-chief at trial. However, Rules 16(a)(2) and (3) provide that the government's duty to disclose does not apply to the prosecutor's work product ("reports, memoranda, or other internal government documents made by the attorney for the government or other government agents in connection with the investigation or prosecution of the case"), or to statements made by the government's prospective witnesses "except as provided by 18 U.S.C. §3500," or to most grand jury transcripts.

Conversely, Rule 16(b)(1) provides that if the government complies with a defendant's request for documents and tangible objects, or scientific tests and reports, then the defendant must permit the government to inspect and copy the same categories of materials in the control of the defendant. However, Rule 16(b)(2) protects the defense attorney's work product. Rule 16(c) imposes a continuing duty to disclose on both sides, and Rule 16(d)(2)(C) provides for protective orders or sanctions, including an order to "prohibit a party from introducing the undisclosed evidence."

At trial, Rule 26.2(a) provides that after any witness other than the defendant has testified on direct examination, the court, on motion of a party who did not call the witness, shall order whichever side called the witness to produce "any statement of the witness that is in their possession and that relates to the subject matter of the witness's testimony."

Model Rules of Professional Conduct for Federal Lawyers: Rule 3.8(a) mandates that a prosecutor shall "[r]efrain from prosecuting a charge that the prosecutor knows is not supported by probable cause, or if not authorized to decline the prosecution of a charge to recommend to the appropriate authority that any charge not warranted by the evidence be withdrawn." Rule 3.8(d) requires timely disclosure only to the defense, not to the tribunal. Rule 3.8(f) obligates a prosecutor to "[r]espect the attorney-client privilege of defendants and not diminish the privilege through investigative or judicial processes."

Restatement of the Law Governing Lawyers: See Restatement §§97 and 109(2) in our chapter on the Restatement later in this volume.

United States Attorney's Manual: The United States Attorney's Manual (USAM) is a set of guidelines designed to be "a quick and ready reference" for U.S. Attorneys, Assistant U.S. Attorneys, and Department of Justice attorneys responsible for prosecuting violations of federal law. Title 9 of the USAM, entitled "Criminal Division," sets forth Department of Justice policies on a wide range of subjects related to criminal prosecution. The entire USAM is available at *www.usdoj.gov/usao/eousa/foia_reading_room/usam/index.html.*

Witness Statements (Jencks Act): In federal criminal trials, a prosecutor's "timely disclosure" of witness statements is governed by 18 U.S.C. §3500 (often called the Jencks Act), which provides, in pertinent part:

§3500. Demands for Production of Statements and Reports of Witnesses

(b) After a witness called by the United States has testified on direct examination, the court shall, on motion of the defendant, order the United States to produce any statement (as hereinafter defined) of the witness in the possession of the United States which relates to the subject matter as to which the witness has testified. If the entire contents of any such statement relate to the subject matter of the testimony of the witness, the court shall order it to be delivered directly to the defendant for his examination and use.

Rule 3.9 Advocate in Nonadjudicative Proceedings

A lawyer representing a client before a legislative body or administrative agency in a nonadjudicative proceeding shall disclose that the appearance is in a representative capacity and shall conform to the provisions of Rules 3.3(a) through (c), 3.4(a) through (c), and 3.5.

COMMENT

[1] In representation before bodies such as legislatures, municipal councils, and executive and administrative agencies acting in a rule-making or policy-making capacity, lawyers present facts, formulate issues and advance argument in the matters under consideration. The decision-making body, like a court, should be able to rely on the integrity of the submissions made to it. A lawyer appearing before such a body must deal with it honestly and in conformity with applicable rules of procedure. See Rules 3.3(a) through (c), 3.4(a) through (c) and 3.5.

[2] Lawyers have no exclusive right to appear before nonadjudicative bodies, as they do before a court. The requirements of this Rule therefore may subject lawyers to regulations inapplicable to advocates who are not lawyers. However, legislatures and administrative agencies have a right to expect lawyers to deal with them as they deal with courts.

[3] This Rule only applies when a lawyer represents a client in connection with an official hearing or meeting of a governmental agency or a legislative body to which the lawyer or the lawyer's client is presenting evidence or argument. It does not apply to representation of a client in a negotiation or other bilateral transaction with a governmental agency or in connection with an application for a license or other privilege or the client's compliance with generally applicable reporting requirements, such as the filing of income-tax returns. Nor does it apply to the representation of a client in connection with an investigation or examination of the client's affairs conducted by government investigators or examiners. Representation in such matters is governed by Rules 4.1 through 4.4.

Canon and Code Antecedents

ABA Canons of Professional Ethics: Canon 26 provided as follows:

26. Professional Advocacy Other Than Before Courts

A lawyer openly, and in his true character may render professional services before legislative or other bodies, regarding proposed legislation and in advocacy of claims before departments of government, upon the same principles of ethics which justify his appearance before the Courts; but it is unprofessional for a lawyer so engaged to conceal his attorneyship, or to employ secret personal solicitations, or to use means other than those addressed to the reason and understanding, to influence action.

ABA Model Code of Professional Responsibility: Compare DR 7-106(B)(1) (reprinted later in this volume).

Cross-References in Other Rules

None.

Legislative History of Model Rule 3.9

1980 Draft (then Rule 3.12) provided as follows:

(a) A lawyer representing a client before a legislative or administrative tribunal in a nonadjudicative proceeding shall deal fairly with the body conducting the proceeding and with other persons making presentations therein and their counsel.

(b) A lawyer in such a proceeding shall:

(1) identify the client on whose behalf the lawyer appears, unless the identity of the client is privileged;

(2) conform to the provisions of Rules 3.1 and 3.4.

1981 and ***1982 Drafts*** were the same as adopted.

1983 Rule: As originally adopted in 1983, Rule 3.9 provided:

A lawyer representing a client before a legislature or administrative tribunal in a nonadjudicative proceeding shall disclose that the appearance is in a representative capacity and shall conform to the provisions of Rules 3.3(a) through (c), 3.4(a) through (c), and 3.5.

2002 Amendments: At its February 2002 Mid-Year Meeting, the ABA House of Delegates adopted without change the ABA Ethics 2000 Commission proposal to amend Rule 3.9 and its Comment. The amendments substituted the current phrase "legislative body or administrative agency" for the former phrase "legislative body or tribunal" in the text of the rule, added the cross-references at the end of Comment 1, and expanded Comment 3, which previously said only, "This Rule does not apply to representation of a client in a negotiation or other bilateral transaction with a government agency; such a transaction is governed by Rules 4.1 through 4.4."

Selected State Variations

California has no direct counterpart to ABA Model Rule 3.9.

Colorado adds the following in lieu of the second sentence of ABA Model Rule 3.9:

Further, in such a representation, the lawyer:

(a) shall conform to the provisions of Rules 3.3(a)(1), 3.3(a)(3), 3.3(b), 3.3(c), and 3.4(a) and (b);

(b) shall not engage in conduct intended to disrupt such proceeding unless such conduct is protected by law; and

(c) may engage in ex parte communications, except as prohibited by law.

District of Columbia: Rule 3.9 applies to a lawyer representing a client before a "legislative or administrative body" (rather than "legislative body or administrative agency").

Florida omits the reference to Rule 3.5.

New Jersey: Rule 3.9 tracks ABA Model Rule 3.9 essentially verbatim, but New Jersey's cross-references to Rules 3.3, 3.4, and 3.5 differ slightly due to differences in New Jersey's versions of those rules.

New York: Rule 3.9 is reworded as follows: "A lawyer communicating in a representative capacity with a legislative body or administrative agency in connection with a pending non-adjudicative matter or proceeding shall disclose that the appearance is in a representative capacity, except when the lawyer seeks information from an agency that is available to the public." Comment 1A emphasizes that "Rule 3.9 does not apply to adjudicative proceedings before a tribunal."

North Carolina omits Rule 3.9.

Virginia omits Rule 3.9.

Related Materials

ABA Formal Ethics Opinions: No ABA formal ethics opinion has discussed ABA Model Rule 3.9.

Lobbying Laws: The federal government and all states have laws regulating lobbyists, including lobbyists who are lawyers. On the federal level, the most prominent statute is the Lobbying Disclosure Act of 1995, 2 U.S.C. §§1601-1612, which requires registration of federal lobbyists and regulates their conduct. Lawyer-lobbyists are also regulated by a host of other federal statutes and regulations, such as the Foreign Agents Registration Act (22 U.S.C. §§611 *et seq.* and 28 C.F.R. Part 5), the HUD Reform Act of 1989 (42 U.S.C. §3545), Federal Acquisition Regulations, and Office of Management and Budget Regulations. These statutes and regulations are thoroughly explained in William V. Luneburg, Thomas M. Susman, & Rebecca H. Gordon eds., The Lobbying Manual: A Complete Guide to Federal Law Governing Lawyers and Lobbyists (4th ed., ABA 2009), published by the ABA Section of Administrative Law and Regulatory Practice.

On the state level, an example of a lobbying law is 25 Illinois Compiled Statutes 170/1 through 170/12 (the Lobbyist Registration Act), which requires registration of any person who "undertakes to influence executive, legislative or administrative action" (or employs another for that purpose). State and federal lobbying laws and regulations are discussed in detail in Abner Mikva & Eric Lane, The Legislative Process (3d ed., Aspen 2009).

Restatement of the Law Governing Lawyers: See Restatement §104 in our chapter on the Restatement later in this volume.

ARTICLE 4. TRANSACTIONS WITH PERSONS OTHER THAN CLIENTS

Rule 4.1 Truthfulness in Statements to Others

In the course of representing a client a lawyer shall not knowingly:
 (a) make a false statement of material fact or law to a third person;
or 3.3, 8.2(a)
 (b) fail to disclose a material fact to a third person when disclosure is necessary to avoid assisting a criminal or fraudulent act by a client, unless disclosure is prohibited by Rule 1.6.

1.2(d), 3.3(b), 1.6(b)(2)&(3)

COMMENT

5.7 - Non-Law
Services (ct9)

Misrepresentation

[1] A lawyer is required to be truthful when dealing with others on a client's behalf, but generally has no affirmative duty to inform an opposing party of relevant facts. A misrepresentation can occur if the lawyer incorporates or affirms a statement of another person that the lawyer knows is false. Misrepresentations can also occur by partially true but misleading statements or omissions that are the equivalent of affirmative false statements. For dishonest conduct that does not amount to a false statement or for misrepresentations by a lawyer other than in the course of representing a client, see Rule 8.4.

Statements of Fact

[2] This Rule refers to statements of fact. Whether a particular statement should be regarded as one of fact can depend on the circumstances. Under generally accepted conventions in negotiation, certain types of statements ordinarily are not taken as statements of material fact. Estimates of price or value placed on the subject of a transaction and a party's intentions as to an acceptable settlement of a claim are ordinarily in this category, and so is the existence of an undisclosed principal except where nondisclosure of the principal would constitute fraud. Lawyers should be mindful of their obligations under applicable law to avoid criminal and tortious misrepresentation.

see 4.3 ct 2

Crime or Fraud by Client

[3] Under Rule 1.2(d), a lawyer is prohibited from counseling or assisting a client in conduct that the lawyer knows is criminal or fraudulent. Paragraph (b) states a specific application of the principle set forth in Rule 1.2(d) and addresses the situation where a client's crime or fraud takes the form of a lie

1.2(d), 3.3(b), 1.6(b)(2)&(3)

or misrepresentation. Ordinarily, a lawyer can avoid assisting a client's crime or fraud by withdrawing from the representation. Sometimes it may be necessary for the lawyer to give notice of the fact of withdrawal and to disaffirm an opinion, document, affirmation or the like. In extreme cases, substantive law may require a lawyer to disclose information relating to the representation to avoid being deemed to have assisted the client's crime or fraud. If the lawyer can avoid assisting a client's crime or fraud only by disclosing this information, then under paragraph (b) the lawyer is required to do so, unless the disclosure is prohibited by Rule 1.6.

Canon and Code Antecedents

ABA Canons of Professional Ethics: No comparable Canon.

ABA Model Code of Professional Responsibility: Compare DR 7-102(A)(3) and DR 7-102(A)(5) (reprinted later in this volume).

Cross-References in Other Rules

Rule 1.2, Comment 10: "A lawyer may not continue assisting a client in conduct that the lawyer originally supposed was legally proper but then discovers is criminal or fraudulent. The lawyer must, therefore, withdraw from the representation. . . . In some cases, withdrawal alone might be insufficient. It may be necessary for the lawyer to give notice of the fact of withdrawal and to disaffirm any opinion, document, affirmation or the like. See **Rule 4.1**."

Rule 1.6, Comment 15: Some Rules require "disclosure of information relating to a client's representation to accomplish the purposes specified in paragraphs (b)(1) through (b)(6)," only if such disclosure would be permitted by paragraph (b). See **Rules** 1.2(d), **4.1(b)**, 8.1 and 8.3.

Rule 1.8, Comment 5: It is prohibited to partake in the "disadvantageous use of client information unless the client gives informed consent, except as permitted or required by these Rules. See **Rules** 1.2(d), 1.6, 1.9(c), 3.3, **4.1(b)**, 8.1 and 8.3."

Rule 1.13, Comment 6: "[T]his Rule does not limit or expand the lawyer's responsibility under **Rule** 1.8, 1.16, 3.3 or **4.1**."

Rule 2.3, Comment 4: "In no circumstances is the lawyer permitted to knowingly make a false statement of material fact or law in providing an evaluation under this Rule. See **Rule 4.1**."

Rule 2.4, Comment 5: "When the dispute-resolution process takes place before a tribunal, as in binding arbitration (see Rule 1.0(m)), the lawyer's duty of candor is governed by Rule 3.3. Otherwise, the lawyer's duty of candor toward both the third-party neutral and other parties is governed by **Rule 4.1**."

Rule 3.9, Comment 3: This Rule "does not apply to representation of a client in a negotiation or other bilateral transaction with a governmental agency. . . . Representation in such matters is governed by **Rules 4.1** through 4.4."

Legislative History of Model Rule 4.1

1980 Discussion Draft contained the following Introduction:

Negotiator

. . . A negotiator should seek the most advantageous result for the client that is consistent with the requirements of law and the lawyer's responsibilities under the Rules of Professional Conduct. As negotiator, a lawyer should consider not only the client's short-run advantage but also his or her long-run interests, such as the state of future relations between the parties. The lawyer should help the client appreciate the interests and position of the other party and should encourage concessions that will effectuate the client's larger objectives. A lawyer should not transform a bargaining situation into a demonstration of toughness or hypertechnicality or forget that the purely legal aspects of an agreement are often subordinate to its practical aspects. When the alternative to reaching agreement is likely to be litigation, the lawyer should be aware that, although litigation is wholly legitimate as a means of resolving controversy, a fairly negotiated settlement generally yields a better conclusion. A lawyer should also recognize that the lawyer's own interest in resorting to litigation may be different from a client's interest in doing so.

. . . [I]n negotiations a lawyer is the agent for the client and not an arbitrator or mediator. Negotiation is in part a competition for advantage between parties who have the legal competence to settle their own affairs. A lawyer as negotiator should not impose an agreement on the client, even if the lawyer believes the agreement is in the client's best interests. By the same token, a lawyer does not necessarily endorse the substance of an agreement arrived at through his or her efforts.

The 1980 Discussion Draft of Rule 4.1 (then called Rule 4.2) provided as follows:

Fairness to Other Participants

(a) In conducting negotiations a lawyer shall be fair in dealing with other participants.

(b) A lawyer shall not make a knowing misrepresentation of fact or law, or fail to disclose a material fact known to the lawyer, even if adverse, when disclosure is:

(1) required by law or the Rules of Professional Conduct; or

(2) necessary to correct a manifest misapprehension of fact or law resulting from a previous representation made by the lawyer or known by the lawyer to have been made by the client. . . .

1980 Discussion Draft also contained the following provision (then called Rule 4.3) that has no equivalent in the Rules as adopted:

Illegal, Fraudulent, or Unconscionable Transactions

A lawyer shall not conclude an agreement, or assist a client in concluding an agreement, that the lawyer knows or reasonably should know is illegal, contains legally prohibited terms, would work a fraud, or would be held to be unconscionable as a matter of law.

1981 Draft: Subparagraph (a) was substantially the same as adopted. Subparagraph (b) provided that a lawyer must not:

> (b) knowingly fail to disclose a fact to a third person when:
> (1) in the circumstances failure to make the disclosure is equivalent to making a material misrepresentation;
> (2) disclosure is necessary to prevent assisting a criminal or fraudulent act, as required by Rule 1.2(d); or
> (3) disclosure is necessary to comply with other law.

1982 Draft: Substantially the same as adopted, except that Rule 4.1(b) provided: "The duties stated in this Rule apply even if compliance requires disclosure of information otherwise protected by Rule 1.6."

1983 Rule: As originally adopted in 1983, Rule 4.1 was the same as the 2002 version.

2002 Amendments: At its February 2002 Mid-Year Meeting, the ABA House of Delegates adopted without change the ABA Ethics 2000 Commission proposal to amend Comments 1, 2, and 3 to Rule 4.1. (The Ethics 2000 Commission did not propose any changes to the text of Rule 4.1.) The amendments added the language of Comment 1 beginning with "partially true but misleading" in place of the former phrase "failure to act," added the last sentence of Comment 2, and significantly expanded Comment 3, which formerly consisted of only the following two sentences: "Paragraph (b) recognizes that substantive law may require a lawyer to disclose certain information to avoid being deemed to have assisted the client's crime or fraud. The requirement of disclosure created by this paragraph is, however, subject to the obligations created by Rule 1.6."

Selected State Variations

California: Business & Professions Code §6128(a) provides that an attorney commits a misdemeanor if the attorney is "guilty of any deceit or collusion, or consents to any deceit or collusion, with intent to deceive the court or any party."

District of Columbia: Rule 4.1 is identical to ABA Model Rule 4.1.

Illinois: Rule 4.1 is the same as the ABA rule.

Kansas: The disclosure obligation under Rule 4.1(b) applies unless disclosure is prohibited by "or made discretionary under" Rule 1.6.

Maryland adds a separate paragraph (b) providing: "The duties stated in this Rule apply even if compliance requires disclosure of information otherwise protected by Rule 1.6."

Massachusetts: Comment 3 to Massachusetts Rule 4.1 defines "assisting" to refer "to that level of assistance which would render a third party liable for another's crime or fraud, i.e., assistance sufficient to render one liable as an aider or abettor under criminal law or as a joint tortfeasor under principles of tort and agency law." The comment also cross-references "the special meaning of 'assistance' in the context of a lawyer's appearance before a tribunal in Comment 2A to Rule 3.3."

Michigan: Rule 4.1 says only: "In the course of representing a client, a lawyer shall not knowingly make a false statement of material fact or law to a third person."

Mississippi: Rule 4.1(b) omits the phrase "unless disclosure is prohibited by Rule 1.6."

New Jersey adds a separate paragraph (b) stating: "The duties stated in this Rule apply even if compliance requires disclosure of information otherwise protected by RPC 1.6."

New York omits Model Rule 4.1(b).

North Carolina omits Rule 4.1(b).

North Dakota: Rule 4.1 provides only that "[i]n the course of representing a client a lawyer shall not make a statement to a third person of fact or law that the lawyer knows to be false."

Ohio: Rule 4.1(b) prohibits lawyers from assisting "illegal" and fraudulent acts of clients, (rather than "criminal" and fraudulent acts), and omits the phrase "unless disclosure is prohibited by Rule 1.6."

Pennsylvania: Rule 4.1(b) replaces the ABA word "assisting" with the phrase "aiding and abetting."

Tennessee adopts Rule 4.1(a). Effective January 1, 2011, Rule 4.1(b) provides:

> (b) If, in the course of representing a client in a nonadjudicative matter, a lawyer knows that the client intends to perpetrate a crime or fraud, the lawyer shall promptly advise the client to refrain from doing so and shall discuss with the client the consequences of the client's conduct. If after such discussion, the lawyer knows that the client still intends to engage in the wrongful conduct, the lawyer shall:
>
> (1) withdraw from the representation of the client in the matter; and
>
> (2) give notice of the withdrawal to any person who the lawyer knows is aware of the lawyer's representation of the client in the matter and whose financial or property interests are likely to be injured by the client's criminal or fraudulent conduct. The lawyer shall also give notice to any such person of the lawyer's disaffirmance of any written statements, opinions, or other material prepared by the lawyer on behalf of the client and which the lawyer reasonably believes may be used by the client in furtherance of the crime or fraud.
>
> (c) If a lawyer who is representing or has represented a client in a nonadjudicative matter comes to know, prior to the conclusion of the matter, that the client has, during the course of the lawyer's representation of the client, perpetrated a crime or fraud, the lawyer shall promptly advise the client to rectify the crime or fraud and discuss with the client the consequences of the client's failure to do so. If the client refuses or is unable to rectify the crime or fraud, the lawyer shall:
>
> (1) if currently representing the client in the matter, withdraw from the representation and give notice of the withdrawal to any person whom the lawyer knows is aware of the lawyer's representation of the client in the matter and whose financial or property interests are likely to be injured by the client's criminal or fraudulent conduct; and
>
> (2) give notice to any such person of the lawyer's disaffirmance of any written statements, opinions, or other material prepared by the lawyer on behalf of the client and that the lawyer reasonably believes may be used by the client in furtherance of the crime or fraud.

Texas: Rule 4.01(b) provides that a lawyer shall not fail to disclose a material fact to a third person when disclosure is necessary to "avoid making the lawyer a party to a criminal act or knowingly assisting a fraudulent act perpetrated by a client."

Virginia: In both subparagraphs of Rule 4.1, Virginia deletes the words "material" and "to a third person." At the end of Rule 4.1(b), Virginia deletes the phrase "unless disclosure is prohibited by Rule 1.6."

Wisconsin: Rule 4.1(c) states that notwithstanding Wisconsin Rules 5.3(c)(1) and 8.4, which address supervision of non-legal personnel and the duty not to violate a rule through another respectively, "a lawyer may advise or supervise others with respect to lawful investigative activities."

Related Materials

ABA Formal Ethics Opinions: See ABA Formal Ethics Ops. 92-363 (1992), 93-370 (1993), 93-375 (1993), 93-378 (1993), 94-383 (1994), 94-387 (1994), 95-397 (1995), 01-422 (2001), 06-439 (2006), 07-446 (2007), and 10-457 (2010).

Ethical Guidelines for Settlement Negotiations: In 2002, the ABA Section of Litigation issued Ethical Guidelines for Settlement Negotiations. They are organized into three sections: "Settlement Negotiations Generally," "Issues Relating to Lawyers and Their Clients," and "Issues Relating to a Lawyer's Negotiations with Opposing Parties." They are available online at *http://www.aspenlawschool.com/books/folberg_resolvingdisputes/egsn.pdf*.

Restatement of the Law Governing Lawyers: See Restatement §§51, 56 and 98 in our chapter on the Restatement later in this volume.

Rule 4.2 Communication with Person Represented by Counsel

In representing a client, a lawyer shall not communicate about the subject of the representation with a person the lawyer knows to be represented by another lawyer in the matter, unless the lawyer has the consent of the other lawyer or is authorized to do so by law or a court order.

COMMENT

[1] This Rule contributes to the proper functioning of the legal system by protecting a person who has chosen to be represented by a lawyer in a matter against possible overreaching by other lawyers who are participating in the matter, interference by those lawyers with the client-lawyer relationship and the uncounseled disclosure of information relating to the representation.

[2] This Rule applies to communications with any person who is represented by counsel concerning the matter to which the communication relates.

[3] The Rule applies even though the represented person initiates or consents to the communication. A lawyer must immediately terminate communication with a person if, after commencing communication, the lawyer learns that the person is one with whom communication is not permitted by this Rule.

[4] This Rule does not prohibit communication with a represented person, or an employee or agent of such a person, concerning matters outside the representation. For example, the existence of a controversy between a government agency and a private party, or between two organizations, does not prohibit a lawyer for either from communicating with nonlawyer representatives of the other regarding a separate matter. Nor does this Rule preclude communication with a represented person who is seeking advice from a lawyer who is not otherwise representing a client in the matter. A lawyer may not make a communication prohibited by this Rule through

the acts of another. See Rule 8.4(a). Parties to a matter may communicate directly with each other, and a lawyer is not prohibited from advising a client concerning a communication that the client is legally entitled to make. Also, a lawyer having independent justification or legal authorization for communicating with a represented person is permitted to do so.

[5] Communications authorized by law may include communications by a lawyer on behalf of a client who is exercising a constitutional or other legal right to communicate with the government. Communications authorized by law may also include investigative activities of lawyers representing governmental entities, directly or through investigative agents, prior to the commencement of criminal or civil enforcement proceedings. When communicating with the accused in a criminal matter, a government lawyer must comply with this Rule in addition to honoring the constitutional rights of the accused. The fact that a communication does not violate a state or federal constitutional right is insufficient to establish that the communication is permissible under this Rule.

[6] A lawyer who is uncertain whether a communication with a represented person is permissible may seek a court order. A lawyer may also seek a court order in exceptional circumstances to authorize a communication that would otherwise be prohibited by this Rule, for example, where communication with a person represented by counsel is necessary to avoid reasonably certain injury.

[7] In the case of a represented organization, this Rule prohibits communications with a constituent of the organization who supervises, directs or regularly consults with the organization's lawyer concerning the matter or has authority to obligate the organization with respect to the matter or whose act or omission in connection with the matter may be imputed to the organization for purposes of civil or criminal liability. Consent of the organization's lawyer is not required for communication with a former constituent. If a constituent of the organization is represented in the matter by his or her own counsel, the consent by that counsel to a communication will be sufficient for purposes of this Rule. Compare Rule 3.4(f). In communicating with a current or former constituent of an organization, a lawyer must not use methods of obtaining evidence that violate the legal rights of the organization. See Rule 4.4.

[8] The prohibition on communications with a represented person only applies in circumstances where the lawyer knows that the person is in fact represented in the matter to be discussed. This means that the lawyer has actual knowledge of the fact of the representation; but such actual knowledge may be inferred from the circumstances. See Rule 1.0(f). Thus, the lawyer cannot evade the requirement of obtaining the consent of counsel by closing eyes to the obvious.

[9] In the event the person with whom the lawyer communicates is not known to be represented by counsel in the matter, the lawyer's communications are subject to Rule 4.3.

Canon and Code Antecedents

ABA Canons of Professional Ethics: Canon 9 provided as follows:

9. Negotiations with Opposite Party

A lawyer should not in any way communicate upon the subject of controversy with a party represented by counsel; much less should he undertake to negotiate or compromise the matter with him, but should deal only with his counsel. It is incumbent upon the lawyer most particularly to avoid everything that may tend to mislead a party not represented by counsel, and he should not undertake to advise him as to the law.

ABA Model Code of Professional Responsibility: Compare DR 7-104(A)(1) (reprinted later in this volume).

Cross-References in Other Rules

Rule 3.4, Comment 4: "Paragraph (f) permits a lawyer to advise employees of a client to refrain from giving information to another party, for the employees may identify their interests with those of the client. See also **Rule 4.2**."

Rule 3.9, Comment 3: This Rule "does not apply to representation of a client in a negotiation or other bilateral transaction with a governmental agency. . . . Representation in such matters is governed by **Rules 4.1** through **4.4**."

Legislative History of Model Rule 4.2

1980 Discussion Draft (then Rule 3.2(b)(5)) provided that a lawyer shall not "interview or otherwise communicate with a party who the lawyer knows is represented by other counsel concerning the subject matter of the representation, except with the consent of that party's counsel or as authorized by law."

1981 Draft was substantially the same as adopted.

1982 Draft was adopted.

1983 Rule: As originally adopted in 1983, Rule 4.2 provided: "In representing a client, a lawyer shall not communicate about the subject of the representation with a *party* the lawyer knows to be represented by another lawyer in the matter, unless the lawyer has the consent of the other lawyer or is authorized by law to do so." (Emphasis added.)

1994 Proposal: In May of 1994, the ABA's Standing Committee on Ethics and Professional Responsibility submitted a proposed amendment to Rule 4.2. In June of 1994, however, after receiving criticism of the proposal, the Standing Committee withdrew the proposal to circulate it for public comment. The withdrawn proposal would have substituted the word "person" for "party" and added the phrase "or reasonably should know" to the text of the rule. Had the proposed amendments been adopted, Rule 4.2 would have provided:

> In representing a client, a lawyer shall not communicate about the subject of the representation with a *person* the lawyer knows *or reasonably should know* to be represented by another lawyer in the matter, unless the lawyer has the consent of the other lawyer or is authorized by law to do so. (Emphasis added.)

A proposed addition to the Comment stated:

> Because of the interest in ensuring that persons have the assistance of counsel who represent them in a matter, a lawyer has an affirmative obligation to act as would a lawyer of reasonable prudence and competence to ascertain whether a person is represented in a matter before undertaking further communication on that matter with that person; and if the person is so represented, to communicate only as the Rule allows.

The Standing Committee's report in support of the proposed amendment explained:*

> The situation presented by the current language of the Rule permits a lawyer who believes or suspects that a person is represented in the matter by another lawyer to subvert the purpose and spirit of the Rule by avoiding learning whether that belief or suspicion is correct. The protection of represented persons the Rule is designed to foster . . . would be enhanced by an amendment to Model Rule 4.2 requiring a lawyer contemplating communicating with other persons . . . to *ascertain* whether the person with whom communication is sought is represented in the matter by another lawyer.
>
> The Standing Committee has also taken the occasion presented by this amendment to clarify the fact that the Rule protects represented *persons* whether or not they are, in a formal sense, actual or prospective "*parties*" to a proceeding or transaction. . . . (Emphasis added.)

1995 Amendment: At the ABA's 1995 Annual Meeting, the House of Delegates voted to amend Rule 4.2 by changing the word "party" to "person" in Rule 4.2. (Unlike the withdrawn 1994 proposal, the 1995 proposal omitted the phrase "or reasonably should know.") The House of Delegates also added three new paragraphs to the Comment and revised the three original paragraphs. The amendment was overwhelmingly approved on a voice vote. For a legislative-style version of the Rule and Comment, see our 1996 edition.

The sole sponsor of the 1995 amendment was the ABA Standing Committee on Ethics and Professional Responsibility. The United States Department of Justice, which followed its own rules on communications with represented parties and persons (reprinted in the Special Section at the end of our 1996 edition), officially opposed the amendment and spoke against it during the House of Delegates debate. The ABA Section on Criminal Justice also voted against the amendment. The Standing Committee's report in support of the amendment provided, in part, as follows (with all citations omitted).

*Excerpt from ABA Report Explaining 1995 Amendment***

[II] C. SUBSTITUTION OF THE WORD "PERSON" FOR "PARTY"

> In choosing whether "party" or "person" better describes the proper scope of the Rule, the Standing Committee . . . has addressed the question of what the meaning of the Rule *should* be, in light of the purposes the Rule is designed to serve.
>
> . . . [T]he appropriate operative term is "person," and not "party," for neither the need to protect uncounselled persons against being taken advantage of by opposing counsel nor the importance of preserving the client-attorney relationship is limited to those circumstances where the represented person is a party to an adjudicative or other formal proceeding. The interests sought to be protected by the Rule may equally well be involved when litigation is merely under consideration, even though it has not actually been instituted, and the persons who are potentially parties to the litigation have retained counsel with respect to the matter in dispute.

* Committee Reports do not represent official policy of the ABA. They are for information only, and represent only the opinions of the authors.

** Committee Reports do not represent official policy of the ABA. They are for information only, and the opinions are those of the authors of the report.

Concerns regarding the need to protect uncounselled persons against the wiles of opposing counsel and preserving the attorney-client relationship may also be involved where a person is a target of a criminal investigation, knows this, and has retained counsel to advise him with respect to the investigation. The same concerns may be involved where a "third-party" witness furnishes testimony in an investigation or proceeding and, even though not a formal party, has seen fit to retain counsel to advise him with respect thereto. Such concerns are equally applicable in a non-adjudicatory context, such as a commercial transaction involving a sale, a lease or some other form of contract.

E. OBJECTIONS TO THE PROPOSED CHANGE IN THE RULE

. . . The Rule now applies, and as amended would continue to apply, only where the person to be contacted is known to be represented with respect to the particular matter that is the subject of the prospective communication. The fact that a particular entity or person has retained a lawyer for one matter does not mean that the representation extends to any other matter; and even a general representation for all purposes, such as might be asserted by inside counsel for a corporation, does not, for purposes of the Rule, necessarily imply a representation with respect to a matter that has not in fact been brought to the attention of such counsel. . . .

III. The Proposed Change to Clarify That an Attorney's Knowledge Regarding Representation May Be Inferred from the Circumstances

C. REASONS FOR THE PROPOSED CHANGE

It would not . . . be reasonable to require a lawyer in all circumstances where the lawyer wishes to speak to a third person in the course of his representation of a client first to inquire whether the person is represented by counsel: among other things, such a routine inquiry would unnecessarily complicate perfectly routine fact-finding, and might well unnecessarily obstruct such fact-finding by conveying a suggestion that there was a need for counsel in circumstances where there was none, and thus discouraging witnesses from talking. In consequence, the Rule's requirement of securing permission of counsel is reasonably limited to those circumstances where the inquiring lawyer *knows* that the person to whom he wants to speak is represented by counsel with respect to the subject of the communication.

However, a lawyer should not be able to ignore the obvious and then claim lack of certain knowledge, thus excusing a failure to secure consent of counsel whose likely involvement should have been obvious. . . . [A] lawyer may not avoid Rule 4.2 by closing eyes to what is plainly to be seen.

1999 Proposal (withdrawn): In 1999, in an effort to resolve years of stalemated negotiations between the United States Department of Justice (representing all federal government lawyers) and the Conference of Chief Justices (representing the high courts of the fifty states and the District of Columbia), the ABA's Standing Committee on Ethics and Professional Responsibility proposed to add the following new paragraphs (b) and (c) to Rule 4.2:

(b) A government lawyer supervising a criminal or civil law enforcement investigation may authorize an investigative agent to communicate with a person represented in the matter prior to the arrest of or the filing of a formal criminal charge or civil complaint against that person in the matter, if the lawyer makes reasonable efforts to ensure that the agent's conduct is compatible with paragraph (c).

(c) Unless permitted to do otherwise by the consent of the represented person's lawyer, a lawyer communicating with a represented person pursuant to this Rule shall not

(1) seek information protected by the attorney-client privilege or as attorney work product;

(2) attempt to induce the represented person to forego representation by or disregard the advice of his or her lawyer; or

(3) initiate or engage in negotiation of an agreement, settlement or plea with respect to the matter in which the person is represented by a lawyer, except as authorized by law or court order.

The Standing Committee also proposed extensively amending the Comment to Rule 4.2. One of the proposed new paragraphs provided as follows:

> Ordinarily a lawyer may not direct an investigative agent to communicate with a represented person in circumstances where the lawyer would be prohibited from doing so by this Rule. . . . This prohibition is qualified by paragraph (b) of this Rule to permit government lawyers to supervise criminal and civil law enforcement investigations. The lawyer representing the government in the matter must not directly and personally communicate with the represented person unless otherwise permitted to do so by paragraph (a) of this Rule. In addition, the lawyer must make reasonable efforts to ensure that investigative agents comply with paragraph (c). . . .

The Committee Report explaining the proposed changes noted that Department of Justice lawyers have for years "expressed concerns that Rule 4.2 imposes undue restrictions on law enforcement investigations directly or by creating ambiguities as to the allowable parameters of investigative methods." The ABA negotiated with the Department of Justice in an effort to address those concerns, but the Department of Justice did not endorse the proposal, so the ABA withdrew it from consideration shortly before the ABA's 1999 Annual Meeting. Discussions between the ABA and the Department of Justice continued, however, and the ABA Ethics 2000 Commission proposals reflected some of the Department of Justice's concerns. For information about other historical developments pertaining to Rule 4.2, see the Related Materials following Rule 4.2.

2002 Amendments: At its February 2002 Mid-Year Meeting, the ABA House of Delegates adopted with only minor changes the ABA Ethics 2000 Commission proposal to amend Rule 4.2 and its Comment. The amendments added "or a court order" to the text, added Comments 1, 3, and 6, and extensively amended Comments 2, 4, 5, 7, and 8.

Selected State Variations

Arizona: Rule 4.2 restricts communication with a "party" rather than a "person" and omits the phrase "or a court order."

California: Rule 2-100 (Communication with a Represented Party), provides as follows:

> (A) While representing a client, a member shall not communicate directly or indirectly about the subject of the representation with a party the member knows to

be represented by another lawyer in the matter, unless the member has the consent of the other lawyer.

(B) For purposes of this rule, a "party" includes:

(1) An officer, director, or managing agent of a corporation or association, and a partner or managing agent of a partnership; or

(2) An association member or an employee of an association, corporation, or partnership, if the subject of the communication is any act or omission of such person in connection with the matter which may be binding upon or imputed to the organization for purposes of civil or criminal liability or whose statement may constitute an admission on the part of the organization.

(C) This rule shall not prohibit:

(1) Communications with a public officer, board, committee, or body; or

(2) Communications initiated by a party seeking advice or representation from an independent lawyer of the party's choice; or

(3) Communications otherwise authorized by law.

District of Columbia adds the following three paragraphs to Rule 4.2:

(b) During the course of representing a client, a lawyer may communicate about the subject of the representation with a nonparty employee of an organization without obtaining the consent of that organization's lawyer. If the organization is an adverse party, however, prior to communicating with any such nonparty employee, a lawyer must disclose to such employee both the lawyer's identity and the fact that the lawyer represents a party that is adverse to the employee's employer.

(c) For purposes of this rule, the term "party" or "person" includes any person or organization, including an employee of an organization, who has the authority to bind an organization as to the representation to which the communication relates.

(d) This rule does not prohibit communication by a lawyer with government officials who have the authority to redress the grievances of the lawyer's client, whether or not those grievances or the lawyer's communications relate to matters that are the subject of the representation, provided that in the event of such communications the disclosures specified in (b) are made to the government official to whom the communication is made.

Florida: Rule 4.2 deletes the phrase "or is authorized to do so by law or a court order" and substitutes the following new language:

[A]n attorney may, without such prior consent, communicate with another's client in order to meet the requirements of any statute, court rule, or contract requiring notice or service of process directly on an adverse party, in which event the communication shall be strictly restricted to that required by the court rule, statute or contract, and a copy shall be provided to the adverse party's attorney.

In addition, Florida adds a new paragraph (b) stating as follows:

(b) An otherwise unrepresented person to whom limited representation is being provided or has been provided in accordance with Rule Regulating the Florida Bar 4-1.2 is considered to be unrepresented for purposes of this rule unless the opposing lawyer knows of, or has been provided with, a written notice of appearance under which, or a written notice of time period during which, the opposing lawyer is to communicate with the limited representation lawyer as to the subject matter within the limited scope of the representation.

Georgia replaces the phrase "authorized to do so by law" with the phrase "authorized to do so by constitutional law or statute." Georgia also adds a new paragraph (b) that provides: "Attorneys for the State and Federal Government shall be subject to this Rule in the same manner as other attorneys in this State."

Illinois adopts ABA Model Rule 4.2 in substance.

Louisiana adds a new paragraph (b) that prohibits communication with:

> a person the lawyer knows is presently a director, officer, employee, member, shareholder, or other constituent of a represented organization and
>
> (1) Who supervises, directs or regularly consults with the organization's lawyer concerning the matter;
>
> (2) Who has the authority to obligate the organization with respect to the matter; or
>
> (3) Whose act or omission in connection with the matter may be imputed to the organization for purpose of civil or criminal liability.

Maryland adds the following paragraphs to Rule 4.2 and limits the reach of paragraph (a), which is the same as ABA Model Rule 4.2, by reference to paragraph (c):

> (b) If the person represented by another lawyer is an organization, the prohibition extends to each of the organization's (1) current officers, directors, and managing agents and (2) current agents or employees who supervise, direct, or regularly communicate with the organization's lawyers concerning the matter or whose acts or omissions in the matter may bind the organization for civil or criminal liability. The lawyer may not communicate with a current agent or employee of the organization unless the lawyer first has made inquiry to ensure that the agent or employee is not an individual with whom communication is prohibited by this paragraph and has disclosed to the individual the lawyer's identity and the fact that the lawyer represents a client who has an interest adverse to the organization.
>
> (c) A lawyer may communicate with a government official about matters that are the subject of the representation if the government official has the authority to redress the grievances of the lawyer's client and the lawyer first makes the disclosures specified in paragraph (b).

Michigan currently retains the pre-2002 version of ABA Model Rule 4.2 (which lacks an express "court order" exception).

New Jersey: Rule 4.2 provides as follows:

> In representing a client, a lawyer shall not communicate about the subject of the representation with a person the lawyer knows, or by the exercise of reasonable diligence should know, to be represented by another lawyer in the matter, including members of an organization's litigation control group as defined by RPC 1.13, unless the lawyer has the consent of the other lawyer, or is authorized by law or court order to do so, or unless the sole purpose of the communication is to ascertain whether the person is in fact represented. Reasonable diligence shall include, but not be limited to, a specific inquiry of the person as to whether that person is represented by counsel. Nothing in this rule shall, however, preclude a lawyer from counseling or representing a member or former member of an organization's litigation control group who seeks independent legal advice.

Rule 4.2 must be read in conjunction with New Jersey's Rule 1.13, which defines the phrase "litigation control group" as follows:

> For the purposes of RPC 4.2 and 4.3 . . . the organization's lawyer shall be deemed to represent not only the organizational entity but also the members of its litigation control group. Members of the litigation control group shall be deemed to include

> current agents and employees responsible for, or significantly involved in, the determination of the organization's legal position in the matter whether or not in litigation, provided, however, that "significant involvement" requires involvement greater, and other than, the supplying of factual information or data respecting the matter. Former agents and employees who were members of the litigation control group shall presumptively be deemed to be represented in the matter by the organization's lawyer but may at any time disavow said representation.

New Mexico adds the following sentence to Rule 4.2: "Except for persons having a managerial responsibility on behalf of the organization, an attorney is not prohibited from communicating directly with employees of a corporation, partnership or other entity about the subject matter of the representation even though the corporation, partnership or entity itself is represented by counsel."

New York: New York Rule 4.2(a) is the same as Model Rule 4.2 except that New York substitutes "party" for "person," adds "or cause another to communicate" before "about," and deletes "or a court order." New York adds Rule 4.2(b), which uses "person," not "party," as follows:

> Notwithstanding the prohibitions of paragraph (a), and unless otherwise prohibited by law, a lawyer may cause a client to communicate with a represented person unless the represented person is not legally competent, and may counsel the client with respect to those communications, provided the lawyer gives reasonable advance notice to the represented person's counsel that such communications will be taking place.

North Carolina: Rule 4.2(a) adds: "It is not a violation of this rule for a lawyer to encourage his or her client to discuss the subject of the representation with the opposing party in a good-faith attempt to resolve the controversy." North Carolina also adds a new Rule 4.2(b) that provides as follows:

> (b) Notwithstanding section (a) above, in representing a client who has a dispute with a government agency or body, a lawyer may communicate about the subject of the representation with the elected officials who have authority over such government agency or body, even if the lawyer knows that the government agency or body is represented by another lawyer in the matter, but such communications may only occur under the following circumstances:
>
> (1) in writing, if a copy of the writing is promptly delivered to opposing counsel;
>
> (2) orally, upon adequate notice to opposing counsel; or
>
> (3) in the course of official proceedings.

Oregon: Rule 4.2 provides as follows:

> In representing a client or the lawyer's own interests, a lawyer shall not communicate or cause another to communicate on the subject of the representation with a person the lawyer knows to be represented by a lawyer on that subject unless:
>
> (a) the lawyer has the prior consent of a lawyer representing such other person;
>
> (b) the lawyer is authorized by law or by court order to do so; or
>
> (c) a written agreement requires a written notice or demand to be sent to such other person, in which case a copy of such notice or demand shall also be sent to such other person's lawyer.

Texas: Rule 4.02 provides:

(a) In representing a client, a lawyer shall not communicate or cause or encourage another to communicate about the subject of the representation with a person, organization or entity of government the lawyer knows to be represented by another lawyer regarding that subject, unless the lawyer has the consent of the other lawyer or is authorized by law to do so.

(b) In representing a client a lawyer shall not communicate or cause another to communicate about the subject of representation with a person or organization a lawyer knows to be employed or retained for the purpose of conferring with or advising another lawyer about the subject of the representation, unless the lawyer has the consent of the other lawyer or is authorized by law to do so.

(c) For the purpose of this rule, "organization or entity of government" includes: (1) those persons presently having a managerial responsibility with an organization or entity of government that relates to the subject of the representation, or (2) those persons presently employed by such organization or entity and whose act or omission in connection with the subject of representation may make the organization or entity of government vicariously liable for such act or omission.

(d) When a person, organization, or entity of government that is represented by a lawyer in a matter seeks advice regarding that matter from another lawyer, the second lawyer is not prohibited by paragraph (a) from giving such advice without notifying or seeking consent of the first lawyer.

Utah: Rule 4.2 contains 17 separate paragraphs and subparagraphs. Rule 4.2(a) begins by tracking ABA Model Rule 4.2, but omits "or is authorized to do so by law or court order" and adds that an attorney may, without prior consent, communicate with another lawyer's client "if authorized to do so by any law, rule, or court order . . . or as authorized by paragraph (b), (c), (d) or (e) of this Rule." Paragraphs (b) and (d) cover "Rules Relating to Unbundling of Legal Services" and "Organizations as Represented Persons." Paragraph (c), which is highly unusual, provides as follows:

(c) *Rules Relating to Government Lawyers Engaged in Civil or Criminal Law Enforcement.* A government lawyer engaged in a criminal or civil law enforcement matter, or a person acting under the lawyer's direction in the matter, may communicate with a person known to be represented by a lawyer if:

(1) the communication is in the course of, and limited to, an investigation of a different matter unrelated to the representation or any ongoing, unlawful conduct; or

(2) the communication is made to protect against an imminent risk of death or serious bodily harm or substantial property damage that the government lawyer reasonably believes may occur and the communication is limited to those matters necessary to protect against the imminent risk; or

(3) the communication is made at the time of the arrest of the represented person and after that person is advised of the right to remain silent and the right to counsel and voluntarily and knowingly waives these rights; or

(4) the communication is initiated by the represented person, directly or through an intermediary, if prior to the communication the represented person has given a written or recorded voluntary and informed waiver of counsel, including the right to have substitute counsel, for that communication.

Paragraph (e), which covers "Limitations on Communications," provides that when communicating with a represented person pursuant to this Rule, no lawyer may:

> (e) (1) inquire about privileged communications between the person and counsel or about information regarding litigation strategy or legal arguments of counsel or seek to induce the person to forgo representation or disregard the advice of the person's counsel; or
>
> (2) engage in negotiations of a plea agreement, settlement, statutory or non-statutory immunity agreement or other disposition of actual or potential criminal charges or civil enforcement claims or sentences or penalties with respect to the matter in which the person is represented by counsel unless such negotiations are permitted by law, rule or court order.

Wyoming makes clear that Rule 4.2 applies to communications with a person "or entity" represented by another lawyer.

Related Materials

ABA Formal Ethics Opinions: See ABA Formal Ethics Ops. 91-359 (1991), 93-378 (1993), 95-396 (1995), and 07-445 (2007).

ABA Standards for Criminal Justice: See Prosecution Function Standard 3-4.1(b) (Availability for Plea Discussions).

ABA Standards for Imposing Lawyer Sanctions:

> *6.3. Improper Communications with Individuals in the Legal System*
>
> 6.31. Disbarment is generally appropriate when a lawyer:
>
> (a) intentionally tampers with a witness and causes serious or potentially serious injury to a party, or causes significant or potentially significant interference with the outcome of the legal proceeding; or
>
> (b) makes an ex parte communication with a judge or juror with intent to affect the outcome of the proceeding, and causes serious or potentially serious injury to a party, or causes significant or potentially significant interference with the outcome of the legal proceeding; or
>
> (c) improperly communicates with someone in the legal system other than a witness, judge, or juror with the intent to influence or affect the outcome of the proceeding, and causes significant or potentially significant interference with the outcome of the legal proceeding.
>
> 6.32. Suspension is generally appropriate when a lawyer engages in communication with an individual in the legal system when the lawyer knows that such communication is improper, and causes injury or potential injury to a party or causes interference or potential interference with the outcome of the legal proceeding.
>
> 6.33. Reprimand is generally appropriate when a lawyer is negligent in determining whether it is proper to engage in communication with an individual in the legal system, and causes injury or potential injury to a party or interference or potential interference with the outcome of the legal proceeding.

American Lawyer's Code of Conduct: Rule 3.9 provides: "[A] lawyer may send a written offer of settlement directly to an adverse party, seven days or more after that party's attorney has received the same offer of settlement in writing."

Department of Justice Rules: In 1989, U.S. Attorney General Richard Thornburgh issued a memorandum, widely known as the "Thornburgh Memorandum," arguing that Rule 4.2 did not prohibit Department of Justice employees and their agents and investigators from communicating with a represented person before indictment.

Thornburgh also argued that (1) the Supremacy Clause prohibited state ethics rules from controlling federal employees, and (2) federal undercover investigations, including undercover contacts with suspects or unindicted grand jury targets known to be represented by counsel, were "authorized by law" within the meaning of Rule 4.2. In 1991, however, a federal court held that the Thornburgh Memorandum did not have the force of law, and the court dismissed an indictment on grounds that a prosecutor had contacted a defendant represented by counsel without being "authorized by law." *United States v. Lopez,* 765 F. Supp. 1433 (N.D. Cal. 1991), *vacated on other grounds,* 989 F.2d 1032 (9th Cir. 1993).

President George H. W. Bush sought to remedy this problem by publishing proposed regulations resembling the Thornburgh Memorandum in the Federal Register for public comment in late 1992. (*See* 57 Fed. Reg. 54737.) Criminal defense lawyers harshly criticized these proposed regulations, but the proposals would have become law automatically if the Clinton administration had not withdrawn the proposals two days after taking office. Later in 1993, under Attorney General Janet Reno, the Department of Justice republished the original proposed regulations with only minor changes for 30 days of public comment. (*See* 58 Fed. Reg. 39976.) Criticism was again harsh.

In 1994, the Department of Justice circulated a third set of proposed regulations for public comment. (*See* 59 Fed. Reg. 10086.) Finally, effective September 6, 1994, the Department of Justice issued a "final rule" on the subject, sometimes called the "Reno Rules." (*See* 59 Fed. Reg. 39910, formally codified at 28 C.F.R. Part 77.) The final rule was expressly intended "to preempt the entire field of rules concerning" contacts by government attorneys with represented parties. (We reprinted the full text of the Reno Rules in our Special Section at the end of our 1996 edition.)

In *O'Keefe v. McDonnell Douglas Corp.,* 132 F.3d 1252 (8th Cir. 1998), however, the court held that the Department of Justice had lacked authority to promulgate the Reno Rules. Congress then enacted 28 U.S.C. §530B, entitled "Ethical Standards for Attorneys for the Government," which provides that federal government attorneys are subject to the same ethical standards as other attorneys practicing in the same state. Section 530B also commanded the Attorney General to amend the Department of Justice's rules "to assure compliance with this section." (The full text of §530B is reprinted below in these Related Materials under the heading "Ethical Standards for Attorneys for the Government.") Pursuant to the statutory directive, the Attorney General then amended 28 C.F.R. Part 77.

Ethical Standards for Attorneys for the Government: In 1998, Congress enacted a new statute, 28 U.S.C. §530B (often called the "McDade Amendment," after its main sponsor in the House of Representatives), which provides as follows:

§530B. Ethical Standards for Attorneys for the Government

(a) An attorney for the Government shall be subject to State laws and rules, and local Federal court rules, governing attorneys in each State where such attorney engages in that attorney's duties, to the same extent and in the same manner as other attorneys in that State.

(b) The Attorney General shall make and amend rules of the Department of Justice to assure compliance with this section.

(c) As used in this section, the term "attorney for the Government" includes any attorney described in section 77.2(a) of part 77 of title 28 of the Code of Federal

Regulations and also includes any independent counsel, or employee of such a counsel, appointed under chapter 40.

Federal Rules of Civil Procedure: Rule 5(b)(1) provides: "If a party is represented by an attorney, service under this rule must be made on the attorney unless the court orders service on the party."

Federal Rules of Evidence: Rule 801(d)(2)(D), often cited in opinions regarding Rule 4.2, provides:

> (d) *Statements which are not hearsay.* A statement is not hearsay if—
>
> (2) *Admission by party-opponent.* The statement is offered against a party and is . . .
>
> (D) a statement by the party's agent or servant concerning a matter within the scope of the agency or employment, made during the existence of the relationship. . . .

Joint Proposal by U.S. Department of Justice and Conference of Chief Justices: In 1997, the Conference of Chief Justices (the Conference), representing all state courts,, and the United States Department of Justice (the DOJ), representing all federal government lawyers, circulated a joint proposal to amend ABA Model Rule 4.2. The proposal, which took more than two years to negotiate, represented a compromise between the DOJ's position that the so-called "Reno Rules" (28 C.F.R. Part 77) govern all federal lawyers, on the one hand, and the Conference's position that state ethics rules govern all federal lawyers, on the other. The tentative plan was that the DOJ would withdraw the Reno Rules in states that adopted the proposed amendment to Rule 4.2.

After soliciting public comments on the joint proposal, the Conference of Chief Justices determined that there was "a decided lack of consensus in the national legal community as to both the principles underlying the draft and the specific language of the proposal." The Conference also noted that the ABA and various other groups were then "actively considering" proposals to amend Rule 4.2. Therefore, in 1998 the Conference passed a resolution stating that it was "premature for the Conference to take action on the draft at this time." The Conference never acted on the draft proposal. The full text of the joint proposal to amend Rule 4.2 and the Conference's 1998 resolution regarding the joint proposal are reprinted in the Special Section at the end of our 1999 edition.

Model Rules of Professional Conduct for Federal Lawyers: In a criminal matter, Rule 4.2(a) creates an exception to the no-contact rule "if the individual initiates the communication with the Government lawyer and voluntarily and knowingly waives the right to counsel for the purposes of that communication. . . ." The Comment explains:

> In a criminal case there may be times when communications between a defendant and a Federal Agency without notice to defense counsel are in the interest of the defendant. Some communications will serve to protect the defendant and to identify sham representations. For example, in certain criminal enterprises, such as organized crime or drug rings, a defendant may wish to cooperate with a Federal Agency, but the counsel may also be the counsel of others involved in the enterprise. To insure that in such instances there is no abuse, this rule would permit communications by the defendant with the Government lawyer, as long as the defendant voluntarily and knowingly waives the right to counsel.

In addition, Rule 4.2(b) of the Model Rules of Professional Conduct for Federal Lawyers provides:

> (b) This Rule does not prohibit communications by a Non-Government lawyer with Federal Agency officials who have the authority to resolve a matter affecting the lawyer's client, whether or not the lawyer's communications relate to matters that are the subject of the representation, provided that the lawyer discloses the lawyer's identity; the fact that the lawyer represents a client in a matter involving the official's Federal Agency; and that the matter is being handled for the Federal Agency by a Government lawyer.

Restatement of the Law Governing Lawyers: See Restatement §§99-102 in our chapter on the Restatement later in this volume.

Rule 4.3 Dealing with Unrepresented Person

In dealing on behalf of a client with a person who is not represented by counsel, a lawyer shall not state or imply that the lawyer is disinterested. When the lawyer knows or reasonably should know that the unrepresented person misunderstands the lawyer's role in the matter, the lawyer shall make reasonable efforts to correct the misunderstanding. The lawyer shall not give legal advice to an unrepresented person, other than the advice to secure counsel, if the lawyer knows or reasonably should know that the interests of such a person are or have a reasonable possibility of being in conflict with the interests of the client.

COMMENT

[1] An unrepresented person, particularly one not experienced in dealing with legal matters, might assume that a lawyer is disinterested in loyalties or is a disinterested authority on the law even when the lawyer represents a client. In order to avoid a misunderstanding, a lawyer will typically need to identify the lawyer's client and, where necessary, explain that the client has interests opposed to those of the unrepresented person. For misunderstandings that sometimes arise when a lawyer for an organization deals with an unrepresented constituent, see Rule 1.13(f).

[2] The Rule distinguishes between situations involving unrepresented persons whose interests may be adverse to those of the lawyer's client and those in which the person's interests are not in conflict with the client's. In the former situation, the possibility that the lawyer will compromise the unrepresented person's interests is so great that the Rule prohibits the giving of any advice, apart from the advice to obtain counsel. Whether a lawyer is giving impermissible advice may depend on the experience and sophistication of the unrepresented person, as well as the setting in which the behavior and comments occur. This Rule does not prohibit a lawyer from negotiating the terms of a transaction or settling a dispute with an unrepresented person. So long as the lawyer has explained that the lawyer represents an adverse party and is not representing the person, the lawyer may inform the person of the terms on which the lawyer's client will enter into an agreement or

settle a matter, prepare documents that require the person's signature and explain the lawyer's own view of the meaning of the document or the lawyer's view of the underlying legal obligations.

Canon and Code Antecedents

ABA Canons of Professional Ethics: Canon 9 provided as follows:

9. Negotiations with Opposite Party

A lawyer should not in any way communicate upon the subject of controversy with a party represented by counsel; much less should he undertake to negotiate or compromise the matter with him, but should deal only with his counsel. It is incumbent upon the lawyer most particularly to avoid everything that may tend to mislead a party not represented by counsel, and he should not undertake to advise him as to the law.

ABA Model Code of Professional Responsibility: Compare DR 7-104(A)(2) (reprinted later in this volume).

Cross-References in Other Rules

Rule 3.9, Comment 3: This Rule "does not apply to representation of a client in a negotiation or other bilateral transaction with a governmental agency. . . . Representation in such matters is governed by **Rules 4.1** through **4.4.**"

Rule 4.2, Comment 9: "In the event the person with whom the lawyer communicates is not known to be represented by counsel in the matter, the lawyer's communications are subject to **Rule 4.3.**"

Legislative History of Model Rule 4.3

1980 Discussion Draft (then Rule 3.6) provided as follows:

Appearing Against an Unrepresented Party

When an opposing party is unrepresented, a lawyer shall refrain from unfairly exploiting that party's ignorance of the law or the practices of the tribunal.

1981 Draft was substantially the same as adopted.

1982 Draft was adopted.

1983 Rule: As originally adopted in 1983, Rule 4.3 was the same as the first two sentences of the 2002 version of Rule 4.3, but did not contain the third sentence.

2002 Amendments: At its February 2002 Mid-Year Meeting, the ABA House of Delegates adopted without change the ABA Ethics 2000 Commission proposal to amend Rule 4.3 and its Comment. The amendments changed the text of Rule 4.3 by adding the last sentence (the substance of which had previously been in Comment 1) and amended the Comment by adding the last two sentences of Comment 1 and all of Comment 2.

Selected State Variations

California has no comparable provision.

District of Columbia: Rule 4.3 contains the same words as ABA Model Rule 4.3, but D.C. divides the rule into paragraphs and subparagraphs.

Florida: The last sentence of Rule 4.3 provides only that a lawyer "shall not give legal advice to an unrepresented person, other than the advice to secure counsel." Florida also adds a new Rule 4.3(b) that provides as follows:

> (b) An otherwise unrepresented person to whom limited representation is being provided or has been provided in accordance with Rule Regulating the Florida Bar 4-1.2 is considered to be unrepresented for purposes of this rule unless the opposing lawyer knows of, or has been provided with, a written notice of appearance under which, or a written notice of time period during which, the opposing lawyer is to communicate with the limited representation lawyer as to the subject matter within the limited scope of the representation.

(Florida's version of Rule 1.2(c) provides, in part, that "a lawyer and client may agree to limit the objectives or scope of the representation if the limitation is reasonable under the circumstances and the client consents in writing after consultation.")

Georgia adds that a lawyer shall not:

> (c) initiate any contact with a potentially adverse party in a matter concerning personal injury or wrongful death or otherwise related to an accident or disaster involving the person to whom the contact is addressed or a relative of that person, unless the accident or disaster occurred more than 30 days prior to the contact.

Kansas, Maryland, and ***Michigan*** retain the pre-2002 version of Rule 4.3.

New Jersey: Rule 4.3 deletes the last sentence of ABA Model Rule 4.3 and adds the following new sentence:

> If the person is a director, officer, employee, member, shareholder or other constituent of an organization concerned with the subject of the lawyer's representation but not a person defined by RPC 1.13(a), the lawyer shall also ascertain by reasonable diligence whether the person is actually represented by the organization's attorney pursuant to RPC 1.13(e) or who has a right to such representation on request, and, if the person is not so represented or entitled to representation, the lawyer shall make known to the person that insofar as the lawyer understands, the person is not being represented by the organization's attorney.

New Jersey Rule 4.3 must be read in conjunction with New Jersey Rule 1.13(a). See Selected State Variations under Rule 4.2.

New York: Rule 4.3 tracks the ABA Model Rule except that it substitutes "communicating" for "dealing" as the second word of the rule.

North Carolina and ***Pennsylvania:*** Rule 4.3 tracks the substance of ABA Model Rule 4.3, but reorders the language and divides the rule into subparagraphs.

Utah adds Rule 4.3(b), which provides that if a person's counsel does not represent the person in all aspects of a particular matter, a lawyer may consider the person to be entirely "unrepresented" for purposes of this Rule and Rule 4.2, "unless that person's counsel has provided written notice to the lawyer of those aspects of the matter or the time limitation for which the person is represented. Only as to such aspects and time is the person considered to be represented by counsel."

Washington: Washington adds the following Comments to Rule 4.3:

"An otherwise unrepresented person to whom limited representation is being provided or has been provided in accordance with Rule 1.2(c) is considered to be unrepresented for purposes of this Rule unless the opposing lawyer knows of, or has been provided with, a written notice of appearance under which, or a written notice of time period during which, he or she is to communicate only with the limited representation lawyer as to the subject matter within the limited scope of the representation."

"Government lawyers are frequently called upon by unrepresented persons, and in some instances by the courts, to provide general information on laws and procedures relating to claims against the government. The provision of such general information by government lawyers is not a violation of this Rule."

Wisconsin: The first sentence of Rule 4.3 provides that in dealings on behalf of a client with a person who is not represented by counsel, "a lawyer shall inform such person of the lawyer's role in the matter."

Related Materials

ABA Formal Ethics Opinions: See ABA Formal Ethics Ops. 91-359 (1991), 92-362 (1992), 93-378 (1993), 95-396 (1995), 97-408 (1997), 06-443 (2006), and 07-445 (2007).

ABA Standards for Criminal Justice: See Prosecution Function Standards 3-3.2(b) (Relations with Victims and Prospective Witnesses) and 3-3.10(c) (Role in First Appearance and Preliminary Hearing).

American Academy of Matrimonial Lawyers: In the Bounds of Advocacy, Rule 3.2 provides that an attorney "should not advise an unrepresented party," and the Comment to Rule 3.2 provides as follows:

> Once it becomes apparent that another party intends to proceed without a lawyer, the attorney should, at the earliest opportunity, inform the opposing party in writing as follows:
>
> 1. I am your spouse's lawyer.
> 2. I do not and will not represent you.
> 3. I will at all times look out for your spouse's interests, not yours.
> 4. Any statements I make to you about this case should be taken by you as negotiation or argument on behalf of your spouse and not as advice to you as to your best interest.
> 5. I urge you to obtain your own lawyer.

Restatement of the Law Governing Lawyers: See Restatement §103 in our chapter on the Restatement later in this volume.

Rule 4.4 Respect for Rights of Third Persons

conflict 1.1

(a) In representing a client, a lawyer shall not use means that have no substantial purpose other than to embarrass, delay, or burden a third person, or use methods of obtaining evidence that violate the legal rights of such a person.

3.1 3.2

(b) A lawyer who receives a document relating to the representation of the lawyer's client and knows or reasonably should know that the document was inadvertently sent shall promptly notify the sender.

COMMENT

[1] Responsibility to a client requires a lawyer to subordinate the interests of others to those of the client, but that responsibility does not imply that a lawyer may disregard the rights of third persons. It is impractical to catalogue all such rights, but they include legal restrictions on methods of obtaining evidence from third persons and unwarranted intrusions into privileged relationships, such as the client-lawyer relationship.

[2] Paragraph (b) recognizes that lawyers sometimes receive documents that were mistakenly sent or produced by opposing parties or their lawyers. If a lawyer knows or reasonably should know that such a document was sent inadvertently, then this Rule requires the lawyer to promptly notify the sender in order to permit that person to take protective measures. Whether the lawyer is required to take additional steps, such as returning the original document, is a matter of law beyond the scope of these Rules, as is the question of whether the privileged status of a document has been waived. Similarly, this Rule does not address the legal duties of a lawyer who receives a document that the lawyer knows or reasonably should know may have been wrongfully obtained by the sending person. For purposes of this Rule, "document" includes e-mail or other electronic modes of transmission subject to being read or put into readable form.

[3] Some lawyers may choose to return a document unread, for example, when the lawyer learns before receiving the document that it was inadvertently sent to the wrong address. Where a lawyer is not required by applicable law to do so, the decision to voluntarily return such a document is a matter of professional judgment ordinarily reserved to the lawyer. See Rules 1.2 and 1.4.

Canon and Code Antecedents

ABA Canons of Professional Ethics: Canon 18 provided as follows:

18. Treatment of Witnesses and Litigants

A lawyer should always treat adverse witnesses and suitors with fairness and due consideration, and he should never minister to the malevolence or prejudices of a client in the trial or conduct of a cause. The client cannot be made the keeper of the lawyer's conscience in professional matters. He has no right to demand that his counsel shall abuse the opposite party or indulge in offensive personalities. Improper speech is not excusable on the ground that it is what the client would say if speaking in his own behalf.

ABA Model Code of Professional Responsibility: Compare DR 7-102(A)(1), DR 7-106(C)(2), DR 7-108(D), and DR 7-108(E) (reprinted later in this volume).

Cross-References in Other Rules

Rule 3.9, Comment 3: This transaction "does not apply to representation of a client in a negotiation or other bilateral transaction with a governmental agency. . . . Representation in such matters is governed by **Rules** 4.1 through **4.4.**"

Rule 4.2, Comment 7: "In communicating with a current or former constituent of an organization, a lawyer must not use methods of obtaining evidence that violate the legal rights of the organization. See **Rule 4.4.**"

Legislative History of Model Rule 4.4

1980 Discussion Draft (then Rule 3.4) provided as follows:

> (a) In preparing and presenting a cause, a lawyer shall respect the interests of third persons, including witnesses, jurors, and persons incidentally concerned with the proceeding. . . .

1981 and ***1982 Drafts*** were the same as adopted.

1983 Rule: As originally adopted in 1983, Rule 4.4 contained only one sentence, which was identical to the 2002 version of Rule 4.4(a). There was no Rule 4.4(b) in the 1983 rule.

2002 Amendments: Before the ABA's February 2002 Mid-Year Meeting the ABA Ethics 2000 Commission revised its May 2001 proposal to amend Rule 4.4 by adding "relating to the representation of the lawyer's client" to Rule 4.4(b) and revising the Comment to Rule 4.4 accordingly. At its February 2002 Mid-Year Meeting, the ABA House of Delegates adopted without change the ABA Ethics 2000 Commission's revised proposal to amend Rule 4.4 and its Comment. The amendments added Rule 4.4(b), added the last clause of Comment 1 ("and unwarranted intrusions . . ."), and added all of Comments 2 and 3.

Selected State Variations

Alabama: Alabama Rule 4.4(b) provides:

> (b) A lawyer who receives a document that on its face appears to be subject to the attorney-client privilege or otherwise confidential, and who knows or reasonably should know that the document was inadvertently sent, should promptly notify the sender and
>
> (1) abide by the reasonable instructions of the sender regarding the disposition of the document; or
>
> (2) submit the issue to an appropriate tribunal for a determination of the disposition of the document.

Arizona has adopted ABA Model Rule 4.4(b) but, in addition to requiring the lawyer who receives an inadvertently transmitted document to notify the sender, Arizona Rule 4.4(b) requires the lawyer to "preserve the status quo for a reasonable period of time in order to permit the sender to take protective measures."

California: Rule 3-200(A) provides that a member "shall not seek, accept, or continue employment if the member knows or should know that the objective of such employment is: (A) To bring an action, conduct a defense, assert a position in litigation, or take an appeal, without probable cause and for the purpose of harassing or maliciously injuring any person." Rule 5-100 provides:

(A) A member shall not threaten to present criminal, administrative, or disciplinary charges to obtain an advantage in a civil dispute.

(B) As used in paragraph (A) of this rule, the term "administrative charges" means the filing or lodging of a complaint with a federal, state, or local governmental entity which may order or recommend the loss or suspension of a license, or may impose or recommend the imposition of a fine, pecuniary sanction, or other sanction of a quasi-criminal nature but does not include filing charges with an administrative entity required by law as a condition precedent to maintaining a civil action.

(C) As used in paragraph (A) of this rule, the term "civil dispute" means a controversy or potential controversy over the rights and duties of two or more parties under civil law, whether or not an action has been commenced, and includes an administrative proceeding of a quasi-civil nature pending before a federal, state, or local governmental entity.

California Business & Professions Code §§6068(c), 6068(f), and 6068(g) provide that it is the "duty" of an attorney to do all of the following:

(c) To counsel or maintain those actions, proceedings, or defenses only as appear to him or her legal or just, except the defense of a person charged with a public offense. . . .

(f) To advance no fact prejudicial to the honor or reputation of a party or witness, unless required by the justice of the cause with which he or she is charged.

(g) Not to encourage either the commencement or the continuance of an action or proceeding from any corrupt motive of passion or interest.

Section 6128(b) provides that an attorney is guilty of a misdemeanor who "[w]illfully delays his client's suit with a view to his own gain."

Colorado adds the following additional paragraph to Rule 4.4:

(c) Unless otherwise permitted by court order, a lawyer who receives a document relating to the representation of the lawyer's client and who, before reviewing the document, receives notice from the sender that the document was inadvertently sent, shall not examine the document and shall abide by the sender's instructions as to its disposition.

Colorado has also adopted the following Rule 4.5:

(a) A lawyer shall not threaten criminal, administrative or disciplinary charges to obtain an advantage in a civil matter nor shall a lawyer present or participate in presenting criminal, administrative or disciplinary charges solely to obtain an advantage in a civil matter.

(b) It shall not be a violation of Rule 4.5 for a lawyer to notify another person in a civil matter that the lawyer reasonably believes that the other's conduct may violate criminal, administrative or disciplinary rules or statutes.

(A version of Rule 4.5(a) is in the ABA Code of Professional Responsibility as DR 7-105 but is limited to criminal conduct.)

District of Columbia: Rule 4.4(b) provides that a lawyer who receives a "writing" relating to the representation of a client and "knows, before examining the writing, that it has been inadvertently sent, shall not examine the writing, but shall notify the sending party and abide by the instructions of the sending party regarding the return or destruction of the writing."

Florida: Rule 4.4(a) provides that a lawyer shall not "knowingly" use methods of obtaining evidence that violate the legal rights of a third person. Florida has adopted ABA Model Rule 4.4(b) verbatim.

Idaho: Rule 4.4 provides that a lawyer, in representing a client, shall not use means that have no substantial purpose other than to embarrass, delay, or burden a third person, "including conduct intended to appeal to or engender bias against a person on account of that person's gender, race, religion, national origin, or sexual preference, whether that bias is directed to other counsel, court personnel, witnesses, parties, jurors, judges, judicial officers, or any other participants." In subparagraphs (a)(3) and (a)(4), Idaho retains the substance of DR 7-105 of the ABA Model Code of Professional Responsibility. Idaho Rule 4.4(b) deletes the phrase "relating to the representation of the lawyer's client."

Kentucky: Kentucky Rule 4.4(b) provides as follows:

> (b) A lawyer who receives a document relating to the representation of the lawyer's client and knows or reasonably should know that the document was inadvertently sent shall:
>
> (1) refrain from reading the document,
> (2) promptly notify the sender, and
> (3) abide by the instructions of the sender regarding its disposition.

Louisiana adopts ABA Model Rule 4.4(a) verbatim but modifies Rule 4.4(b) to provide as follows:

> (b) A lawyer who receives a writing that, on its face, appears to be subject to the attorney-client privilege or otherwise confidential, under circumstances where it is clear that the writing was not intended for the receiving lawyer, shall refrain from examining the writing, promptly notify the sending lawyer, and return the writing.

Maryland adds the following paragraph (b) to Rule 4.4:

> (b) In communicating with third persons, a lawyer representing a client in a matter shall not seek information relating to the matter that the lawyer knows or reasonably should know is protected from disclosure by statute or by an established evidentiary privilege, unless the protection has been waived. The lawyer who receives information that is protected from disclosure shall (1) terminate the communication immediately and (2) give notice of the disclosure to any tribunal in which the matter is pending and to the person entitled to enforce the protection against disclosure.

Michigan omits Rule 4.4(b).

New Jersey adopts ABA Model Rule 4.4(a) verbatim but modifies Rule 4.4(b) to provide as follows:

> (b) A lawyer who receives a document and has reasonable cause to believe that the document was inadvertently sent shall not read the document or, if he or she has begun to do so, shall stop reading the document, promptly notify the sender, and return the document to the sender.

New York: Rule 4.4(a) substitutes "embarrass or harm" for "embarrass, delay, or burden" a third person. Rule 4.4(b) is the same as the Model Rule.

North Carolina: Rule 4.4(b) replaces the ABA word "document" with "writing."

North Dakota adds a new Rule 4.5(a) that is identical to ABA Model Rule 4.4(b), and adds a new Rule 4.5(b) providing that a lawyer who receives a document under the circumstances specified in Rule 4.5(a) "does not violate Rule 1.2 or Rule 1.4 by not communicating to or consulting with the client regarding the receipt or the return of the document."

Ohio: Rule 4.4(a) adds the word "harass" to the list of forbidden purposes.

South Carolina adds a new Rule 4.5, which says a lawyer "shall not present, participate in presenting, or threaten to present criminal or professional disciplinary charges solely to obtain an advantage in a civil matter."

Tennessee: Effective January 1, 2011, Rule 4.4(b) forbids a lawyer to threaten to present a criminal charge or lawyer disciplinary charge, or to offer or to agree to refrain from filing such a charge, for the purpose of obtaining an advantage in a civil matter. Rule 4.4(b) provides:

> (b) A lawyer who receives information relating to the representation of the lawyer's client that the lawyer knows or reasonably should know is protected by RPC 1.6 (including information protected by the attorney-client privilege or the work-product rule) and has been disclosed to the lawyer inadvertently or by a person not authorized to disclose such information to the lawyer, shall:
>
> (1) immediately terminate review or use of the information;
>
> (2) notify the person, or the person's lawyer if communication with the person is prohibited by RPC 4.2, of the inadvertent or unauthorized disclosure; and
>
> (3) abide by that person's or lawyer's instructions with respect to disposition of written information or refrain from using the written information until obtaining a definitive ruling on the proper disposition from a court with appropriate jurisdiction.

Texas: Rule 4.04(b) forbids lawyers to present or threaten disciplinary or criminal charges "solely to gain an advantage in a civil matter" or civil, criminal, or disciplinary charges "solely" to prevent participation by a complainant or witness in a disciplinary matter.

Virginia: Rule 4.4(a) deletes the word "substantial" before the word "purpose." Virginia has not adopted Rule 4.4(b).

Wyoming adds Rule 4.4(c), which provides that a lawyer "shall not present, participate in presenting, or threaten to present criminal charges solely to obtain an advantage in a civil matter."

Related Materials

ABA Commission on Ethics 20/20: In 2009, the ABA created the ABA Commission on Ethics 20/20, which is comprehensively reviewing the ABA Model Rules of Professional Conduct in light of globalization and changes in information technology. On September 19, 2011, the Commission issued revised draft proposals on technology and confidentiality for public comment, including a proposal to amend Rule 4.4(b) to provide (in legislative style) as follows:

> (b) A lawyer who receives a document or electronically stored information relating to the representation of the lawyer's client and knows or reasonably should know that the document or electronically stored information was not intended to be disclosed to the lawyer ~~inadvertently sent~~ shall promptly notify the sender.

The Commission also proposed amendments to Comments 2 and 3 to Rule 4.4 to explain the changes. One proposed sentence in Comment 2 would provide, in part, as follows:

> For purposes of this Rule, "document or electronically stored information" includes paper documents, email, and other forms of electronically stored information,

including electronic documents and the hidden data about the information contained in those documents (commonly referred to as "metadata"). . . .

The Commission may present these proposals (or revised versions of them) to the ABA House of Delegates at the ABA's August 2012 Annual Meeting. For updates, see the Ethics 20/20 Commission's website at *http://www.americanbar.org/Ethics2020.*

ABA Formal Ethics Opinions: See ABA Formal Ethics Ops. 92-363 (1992), 92-368 (1992) (withdrawn), 94-382 (1994) (withdrawn), 01-422 (2001), 05-437 (2005), 06-440 (2006), 06-442 (2006), 11-460 (2011).

ABA Standards for Criminal Justice: See Prosecution Function Standards 3-2.9(b) (Prompt Disposition of Criminal Charges), 3-3.1(c) (Investigative Function of Prosecutor), and 3-5.7(a) (Examination of Witnesses); and Defense Function Standards 4-4.2 (Illegal Investigation), 4-7.1(a) (Courtroom Professionalism), and 4-7.6(a) (Examination of Witnesses).

Federal Rules of Civil Procedure: In 2006, the Federal Rules of Civil Procedure were amended to address inadvertent production of documents and waiver of attorney-client privilege during discovery. The amendment added a new Rule 26(b)(5)(B)—which is much more demanding than ABA Model Rule 4.4(b)—that provides as follows:

> *(B) Information Produced.* If information produced in discovery is subject to a claim of privilege or of protection as trial-preparation material, the party making the claim may notify any party that received the information of the claim and the basis for it. After being notified, a party must promptly return, sequester, or destroy the specified information and any copies it has; must not use or disclose the information until the claim is resolved; must take reasonable steps to retrieve the information if the party disclosed it before being notified; and may promptly present the information to the court under seal for a determination of the claim. The producing party must preserve the information until the claim is resolved.

The Advisory Committee Note to Subdivision 26(b)(5) explains the quoted provision as follows:

> The Committee has repeatedly been advised that the risk of privilege waiver, and the work necessary to avoid it, add to the costs and delay of discovery. When the review is of electronically stored information, the risk of waiver, and the time and effort required to avoid it, can increase substantially because of the volume of electronically stored information and the difficulty in ensuring that all information to be produced has in fact been reviewed. Rule 26(b)(5)(A) provides a procedure for a party that has withheld information on the basis of privilege or protection as trial-preparation material to make the claim so that the requesting party can decide whether to contest the claim and the court can resolve the dispute. Rule 26(b)(5)(B) is added to provide a procedure for a party to assert a claim of privilege or trial-preparation material protection after information is produced in discovery in the action and, if the claim is contested, permit any party that received the information to present the matter to the court for resolution.
>
> Rule 26(b)(5)(B) does not address whether the privilege or protection that is asserted after production was waived by the production. The courts have developed principles to determine whether, and under what circumstances, waiver results from inadvertent production of privileged or protected information. Rule 26(b)(5)(B) provides a procedure for presenting and addressing these issues. . . .
>
> A party asserting a claim of privilege or protection after production must give notice to the receiving party. That notice should be in writing unless the circumstances

preclude it. Such circumstances could include the assertion of the claim during a deposition. The notice should be as specific as possible in identifying the information and stating the basis for the claim. . . . Courts will continue to examine whether a claim of privilege or protection was made at a reasonable time when delay is part of the waiver determination under the governing law.

After receiving notice, each party that received the information must promptly return, sequester, or destroy the information and any copies it has. . . . No receiving party may use or disclose the information pending resolution of the privilege claim. The receiving party may present to the court the questions whether the information is privileged or protected as trial-preparation material, and whether the privilege or protection has been waived. . . . In presenting the question, the party may use the content of the information only to the extent permitted by the applicable law of privilege, protection for trial-preparation material, and professional responsibility.

If a party disclosed the information to nonparties before receiving notice of a claim of privilege or protection as trial-preparation material, it must take reasonable steps to retrieve the information and to return it, sequester it until the claim is resolved, or destroy it.

Whether the information is returned or not, the producing party must preserve the information pending the court's ruling on whether the claim of privilege or of protection is properly asserted and whether it was waived. As with claims made under Rule 26(b)(5)(A), there may be no ruling if the other parties do not contest the claim.

A companion 2006 amendment to Rule 26(f) provides that in most cases, before a scheduling conference is held or a scheduling order is due, the parties must confer to develop a proposed discovery plan that indicates the parties' views and proposals concerning "(4) any issues relating to claims of privilege or of protection as trial-preparation material, including—if the parties agree on a procedure to assert such claims after production—whether to ask the court to include their agreement in an order." The Advisory Committee Note explaining the amendment to Rule 26(f)(4) says:

Rule 26(f) is also amended to provide that the parties should discuss any issues relating to assertions of privilege or of protection as trial-preparation materials, including whether the parties can facilitate discovery by agreeing on procedures for asserting claims of privilege or protection after production and whether to ask the court to enter an order that includes any agreement the parties reach. The Committee has repeatedly been advised about the discovery difficulties that can result from efforts to guard against waiver of privilege and work-product protection. Frequently parties find it necessary to spend large amounts of time reviewing materials requested through discovery to avoid waiving privilege. These efforts are necessary because materials subject to a claim of privilege or protection are often difficult to identify. A failure to withhold even one such item may result in an argument that there has been a waiver of privilege as to all other privileged materials on that subject matter. Efforts to avoid the risk of waiver can impose substantial costs on the party producing the material and the time required for the privilege review can substantially delay access for the party seeking discovery. . . .

Parties may attempt to minimize these costs and delays by agreeing to protocols that minimize the risk of waiver. They may agree that the responding party will provide certain requested materials for initial examination without waiving any privilege or protection—sometimes known as a "quick peek." The requesting party then designates the documents it wishes to have actually produced. This designation is the Rule 34 request. The responding party then responds in the usual course, screening only those documents actually requested for formal production and asserting privilege claims as provided in Rule 26(b)(5)(A). On other occasions, parties enter agreements—sometimes called "clawback agreements"—that production without intent to waive privilege or protection should not be a waiver so long as the responding party identifies the documents mistakenly produced, and that the documents should be returned under those circumstances. Other voluntary arrangements may be appropriate depending on the circumstances of each litigation. In most circumstances, a party who receives information under such an arrangement cannot assert that production of the information waived a claim of privilege or of protection as trial-preparation material. . . .

Rule 26(b)(5)(B) is added to establish a parallel procedure to assert privilege or protection as trial-preparation material after production, leaving the question of waiver to later determination by the court.

A related 2006 amendment to Rule 16(b)(3)(B)(iv) provides that a district court's scheduling order may include "any agreements the parties reach for asserting claims of privilege or of protection as trial preparation material after information is produced." The Advisory Committee Note explains that this amendment "recognizes the propriety of including such agreements in the court's order. The rule does not provide the court with authority to enter such a case-management or other order without party agreement, or limit the court's authority to act on motion."

For updates on the Federal Rules of Civil Procedure, visit the official website of the United States Courts at *www.uscourts.gov.* For more information about the attorney-client privilege and work product generally, see our chapter on Attorney-Client Privilege and Work Product Provisions in the Federal Materials below.

Federal Rules of Evidence: In 2008, President George W. Bush signed into law a new Rule 502 of the Federal Rules of Evidence. The new rule, based on a proposal by the Judicial Conference of the United States, was enacted as a statute by Congress because it concerns privilege. Rule 502 includes the following section on inadvertent disclosure, and is thus related to Rule 4.4(b):

(b) *Inadvertent disclosure.* When made in a federal proceeding or to a federal office or agency, the disclosure [of a communication or information covered by the attorney-client privilege or work product protection] does not operate as a waiver in a federal or state proceeding if:

(1) the disclosure is inadvertent;

(2) the holder of the privilege or protection took reasonable precautions to prevent disclosure; and

(3) the holder promptly took reasonable steps to rectify the error, including (if applicable) following in Fed. R. Civ. P. 26(b)(5)(B).

For further background and for the full text Rule 502, see our chapter on Attorney-Client Privilege and Work Product Provisions below.

Restatement of the Law Governing Lawyers: See Restatement §§30, 51, 56, 102, and 106 in our chapter on the Restatement later in this volume.

ARTICLE 5. LAW FIRMS AND ASSOCIATIONS

Rule 5.1 Responsibilities of Partners, Managers, and Supervisory Lawyers

(a) A partner in a law firm, and a lawyer who individually or together with other lawyers possesses comparable managerial authority in a law

firm, **shall make reasonable efforts to ensure that the firm has in effect** _8.3_ **measures giving reasonable assurance that all lawyers in the firm conform to the Rules of Professional Conduct.**

(b) A lawyer having direct supervisory authority over another lawyer shall make reasonable efforts to ensure that the other lawyer conforms to the Rules of Professional Conduct. _5.2 for subordinate_

(c) A lawyer shall be responsible for another lawyer's violation of the Rules of Professional Conduct if:

> **(1) the lawyer orders or, with knowledge of the specific conduct, ratifies the conduct involved; or** _8.4(a)_
>
> **(2) the lawyer is a partner or has comparable managerial authority in the law firm in which the other lawyer practices, or has direct supervisory authority over the other lawyer, and knows of the conduct at a time when its consequences can be avoided or mitigated but fails to take reasonable remedial action.** _Cf. 5_ _5.3(c) for non-lawyers_

COMMENT

[1] Paragraph (a) applies to lawyers who have managerial authority over the professional work of a firm. See Rule 1.0(c). This includes members of a partnership, the shareholders in a law firm organized as a professional corporation, and members of other associations authorized to practice law; lawyers having comparable managerial authority in a legal services organization or a law department of an enterprise or government agency; and lawyers who have intermediate managerial responsibilities in a firm. Paragraph (b) applies to lawyers who have supervisory authority over the work of other lawyers in a firm.

[2] Paragraph (a) requires lawyers with managerial authority within a firm to make reasonable efforts to establish internal policies and procedures designed to provide reasonable assurance that all lawyers in the firm will conform to the Rules of Professional Conduct. Such policies and procedures include those designed to detect and resolve conflicts of interest, identify dates by which actions must be taken in pending matters, account for client funds and property and ensure that inexperienced lawyers are properly supervised.

[3] Other measures that may be required to fulfill the responsibility prescribed in paragraph (a) can depend on the firm's structure and the nature of its practice. In a small firm of experienced lawyers, informal supervision and periodic review of compliance with the required systems ordinarily will suffice. In a large firm, or in practice situations in which difficult ethical problems frequently arise, more elaborate measures may be necessary. Some firms, for example, have a procedure whereby junior lawyers can make confidential referral of ethical problems directly to a designated senior partner or special committee. See Rule 5.2. Firms, whether large or small, may also rely on continuing legal education in professional ethics. In any event, the ethical atmosphere of a firm can influence the conduct of all its members and the partners may not assume that all lawyers associated with the firm will inevitably conform to the Rules.

[4] Paragraph (c) expresses a general principle of personal responsibility for acts of another. See also Rule 8.4(a).

[5] Paragraph (c)(2) defines the duty of a partner or other lawyer having comparable managerial authority in a law firm, as well as a lawyer who has direct supervisory authority over performance of specific legal work by another lawyer. Whether a lawyer has supervisory authority in particular circumstances is a question of fact. Partners and lawyers with comparable authority have at least indirect responsibility for all work being done by the firm, while a partner or manager in charge of a particular matter ordinarily also has supervisory responsibility for the work of other firm lawyers engaged in the matter. Appropriate remedial action by a partner or managing lawyer would depend on the immediacy of that lawyer's involvement and the seriousness of the misconduct. A supervisor is required to intervene to prevent avoidable consequences of misconduct if the supervisor knows that the misconduct occurred. Thus, if a supervising lawyer knows that a subordinate misrepresented a matter to an opposing party in negotiation, the supervisor as well as the subordinate has a duty to correct the resulting misapprehension.

[6] Professional misconduct by a lawyer under supervision could reveal a violation of paragraph (b) on the part of the supervisory lawyer even though it does not entail a violation of paragraph (c) because there was no direction, ratification or knowledge of the violation.

[7] Apart from this Rule and Rule 8.4(a), a lawyer does not have disciplinary liability for the conduct of a partner, associate or subordinate. Whether a lawyer may be liable civilly or criminally for another lawyer's conduct is a question of law beyond the scope of these Rules.

[8] The duties imposed by this Rule on managing and supervising lawyers do not alter the personal duty of each lawyer in a firm to abide by the Rules of Professional Conduct. See Rule 5.2(a).

Canon and Code Antecedents

ABA Canons of Professional Ethics: No comparable Canon.

ABA Model Code of Professional Responsibility: Compare DR 1-102 and DR 1-103(A) (reprinted later in this volume).

Cross-References in Other Rules

Rule 1.6, Comment 16: "A lawyer must act competently to safeguard information relating to the representation of a client against inadvertent or unauthorized disclosure by the lawyer or other persons who are participating in the representation of the client or who are subject to the lawyer's supervision. See **Rules** 1.1, **5.1** and 5.3."

Rule 1.7, Comment 3: "To determine whether a conflict of interest exists, a lawyer should adopt reasonable procedures, appropriate for the size and type of firm and practice, to determine in both litigation and non-litigation matters the persons and issues involved. See also Comment to **Rule 5.1**."

Rule 3.8, Comment 6: "Like other lawyers, prosecutors are subject to **Rules 5.1** and 5.3, which relate to responsibilities regarding lawyers and nonlawyers who work for or are associated with the lawyer's office."

Rule 5.3, Comment 2: "Paragraph (a) requires lawyers with managerial authority within a law firm to make reasonable efforts to establish internal policies and procedures designed to provide reasonable assurance that nonlawyers in the firm will act in a way compatible with the Rules of Professional Conduct. See Comment [1] to **Rule 5.1**."

Legislative History of Model Rule 5.1

1980 Discussion Draft of Rule 5.1 (then Rule 7.2) provided as follows:

Responsibilities of a Supervisory Lawyer

(a) A lawyer having supervisory authority over another lawyer shall make a reasonable effort to see that the conduct of the lawyer under supervision conforms to the Rules of Professional Conduct.

(b) A lawyer is chargeable with another lawyer's violation of the Rules of Professional Conduct if:

(1) the lawyer orders or ratifies the conduct involved; or

(2) the lawyer has supervisory responsibility over the other lawyer and has knowledge of the conduct at a time when its consequences can be avoided or mitigated but fails to take appropriate remedial action.

1981 Draft was substantially the same as adopted, except that Rule 5.2(a) applied to "all lawyers in the firm, including other partners. . . ."

1982 Draft was adopted.

1983 Rule: As originally adopted in 1983, Rule 5.1 provided as follows:

(a) A partner in a law firm shall make reasonable efforts to ensure that the firm has in effect measures giving reasonable assurance that all lawyers in the firm conform to the Rules of Professional Conduct.

(b) [Same as 2002 version of Rule 5.1(b).]

(c) [Same as 2002 version of Rule 5.1(c).]

(1) [Same as 2002 version of Rule 5.1(c)(1).]

(2) [Same as 2002 version of Rule 5.1(c)(2), except that the 1983 rule did not include the phrase "or comparable managerial authority" after "partner" in the first line.]

2002 Amendments: In 2002, the ABA House of Delegates adopted without change the ABA Ethics 2000 Commission proposal to amend Rule 5.1 and its Comment. The amendments added the clause following the first six words of paragraph (a) (beginning "and a lawyer who"), added the reference to "comparable managerial authority" in paragraph (c)(2), added Comments 2 and 8, and made other minor changes.

Selected State Variations

California has no counterpart to Rule 5.1.

District of Columbia: Rule 5.1 substantially tracks the Model Rule.

Illinois adopts the ABA Model Rule.

New Hampshire Rules 5.1(a) and (b) impose duties on "each" partner in a firm, "each" lawyer with comparable managerial authority, and "each" lawyer with direct supervisory authority. A New Hampshire Comment explains that the change "is intended to emphasize that the obligations created by the rule are shared by all of the managers of a law firm and cannot be delegated to one manager by the others."

New Jersey begins Rule 5.1(a) with: "Every law firm and organization authorized by the Court Rules to practice law in this jurisdiction . . ." instead of "A partner in a law firm." Rule 5.1(c)(2) applies only to lawyers having "direct supervisory authority"; it deletes "is a partner or has comparable managerial authority in the law firm in which the other lawyer practices."

New York: Rule 5.1 provides:

> (a) A law firm shall make reasonable efforts to ensure that all lawyers in the firm conform to these Rules.
>
> (b)(1) A lawyer with management responsibility in a law firm shall make reasonable efforts to ensure that other lawyers in the law firm conform to these Rules.
>
> (2) A lawyer with direct supervisory authority over another lawyer shall make reasonable efforts to ensure that the supervised lawyer conforms to these Rules.
>
> (c) A law firm shall ensure that the work of partners and associates is adequately supervised, as appropriate. A lawyer with direct supervisory authority over another lawyer shall adequately supervise the work of the other lawyer, as appropriate. In either case, the degree of supervision required is that which is reasonable under the circumstances, taking into account factors such as the experience of the person whose work is being supervised, the amount of work involved in a particular matter, and the likelihood that ethical problems might arise in the course of working on the matter.
>
> (d) A lawyer shall be responsible for a violation of these Rules by another lawyer if:
>
> (1) the lawyer orders or directs the specific conduct or, with knowledge of the specific conduct, ratifies it; or
>
> (2) the lawyer is a partner in a law firm or is a lawyer who individually or together with other lawyers possesses comparable managerial responsibility in a law firm in which the other lawyer practices or is a lawyer who has supervisory authority over the other lawyer; and
>
> (i) knows of such conduct at a time when it could be prevented or its consequences avoided or mitigated but fails to take reasonable remedial action; or
>
> (ii) in the exercise of reasonable management or supervisory authority should have known of the conduct so that reasonable remedial action could have been taken at a time when the consequences of the conduct could have been avoided or mitigated.

Oregon: Rule 5.1 deletes the language of ABA Model Rules 5.1(a) and (b), but adopts ABA Model Rule 5.1(c) verbatim.

Texas: The text of Texas Rule 5.01 has no equivalent to ABA Model Rules 5.1(a) and (b), but Comment 6 to Texas Rule 5.01 provides:

> Wholly aside from the dictates of these rules for discipline, a lawyer in a position of authority in a firm or government agency or over another lawyer should feel a moral compunction to make reasonable efforts to ensure that the office, firm, or agency has in effect appropriate procedural measures giving reasonable assurance that all lawyers in the office conform to these rules. This moral obligation, although not required by these rules, should fall also upon lawyers who have intermediate managerial responsibilities in the law department of an organization or government agency.

Texas Rule 5.01(b), which is similar to ABA Model Rule 5.1(c)(2), also applies to "the general counsel of a government agency's legal department."

Related Materials

ABA Formal Ethics Opinions: See ABA Formal Ethics Ops. 94-388 (1994), 96-401 (1996), 01-423 (2001), 03-429 (2003), 06-441 (2006), 08-449 (2008), 08-451 (2008), 09-453 (2009), and 09-455 (2009).

IRS Regulations: In the regulations governing practice before the Internal Revenue Service, 31 C.F.R. §10.33(b) provides:

> *(b) Procedures to ensure best practices for tax advisors.* Tax advisors with responsibility for overseeing a firm's practice of providing advice concerning Federal tax issues or of preparing or assisting in the preparation of submissions to the Internal Revenue Service should take reasonable steps to ensure that the firm's procedures for all members, associates, and employees are consistent with the best practices set forth in paragraph (a) of this section.

The best practices set forth in §10.33(a) are excerpted in the entry entitled "IRS Regulations" in the Related Materials following ABA Model Rule 1.4 above.

Model Rules of Professional Conduct for Federal Lawyers add the following new subparagraphs to Rule 5.1:

> (c) A Federal lawyer, who is a supervisory lawyer, is responsible for ensuring that the subordinate lawyer is properly trained and is competent to perform the duties to which the subordinate lawyer is assigned.
>
> (d) A Government lawyer, who is a supervisory lawyer, should encourage subordinate lawyers to participate in pro bono publico service activities and the activities of bar associations and law reform organizations.

Partnership Law: Model Rule 5.1 roughly parallels partnership law provisions concerning the financial liability and tort liability of general partners for the wrongful acts or omissions of other partners in the ordinary course of business. Section 305 of the Revised Uniform Partnership Act (RUPA), which has been adopted in more than 30 states, provides:

> *§305. Partnership Liable for Partner's Actionable Conduct.*
>
> (a) A partnership is liable for loss or injury caused to a person, or for a penalty incurred, as a result of a wrongful act or omission, or other actionable conduct, of a partner acting in the ordinary course of business of the partnership or with authority of the partnership.
>
> (b) If, in the course of the partnership's business or while acting with authority of the partnership, a partner receives or causes the partnership to receive money or property of a person not a partner, and the money or property is misapplied by a partner, the partnership is liable for the loss.

Restatement of the Law Governing Lawyers: See Restatement §§11(1)-(3) and 58 in our chapter on the Restatement later in this volume.

Rule 5.2 Responsibilities of a Subordinate Lawyer

(a) A lawyer is bound by the Rules of Professional Conduct notwithstanding that the lawyer acted at the direction of another person.

(b) A subordinate lawyer does not violate the Rules of Professional Conduct if that lawyer acts in accordance with a supervisory lawyer's reasonable resolution of an arguable question of professional duty.

COMMENT

[1] Although a lawyer is not relieved of responsibility for a violation by the fact that the lawyer acted at the direction of a supervisor, that fact may be relevant in determining whether a lawyer had the knowledge required to render conduct a violation of the Rules. For example, if a subordinate filed a frivolous pleading at the direction of a supervisor, the subordinate would not be guilty of a professional violation unless the subordinate knew of the document's frivolous character.

[2] When lawyers in a supervisor-subordinate relationship encounter a matter involving professional judgment as to ethical duty, the supervisor may assume responsibility for making the judgment. Otherwise a consistent course of action or position could not be taken. If the question can reasonably be answered only one way, the duty of both lawyers is clear and they are equally responsible for fulfilling it. However, if the question is reasonably arguable, someone has to decide upon the course of action. That authority ordinarily reposes in the supervisor, and a subordinate may be guided accordingly. For example, if a question arises whether the interests of two clients conflict under Rule 1.7, the supervisor's reasonable resolution of the question should protect the subordinate professionally if the resolution is subsequently challenged.

Canon and Code Antecedents

ABA Canons of Professional Ethics: No comparable Canon.

ABA Model Code of Professional Responsibility: No comparable Disciplinary Rule.

Cross-References in Other Rules

Rule 5.1, Comment 3: "Some firms . . . have a procedure whereby junior lawyers can make confidential referral of ethical problems directly to a designated senior partner or special committee. See **Rule 5.2**."

Rule 5.1, Comment 8: "The duties imposed by this Rule on managing and supervising lawyers do not alter the personal duty of each lawyer in a firm to abide by the Rules of Professional Conduct. See **Rule 5.2(a)**."

Legislative History of Model Rule 5.2

1980 Discussion Draft (then Rule 7.3) provided as follows:

> (a) A lawyer acting under the supervisory authority of another person is bound by the Rules of Professional Conduct notwithstanding the fact that the lawyer's conduct was ordered by the supervisor.

1981 Draft was substantially the same as adopted.

1982 Draft was adopted.

1983 Rule: As originally adopted in 1983, Rule 5.2 was the same as the 2002 version.

2002 Amendments: The ABA Ethics 2000 Commission did not propose any changes to the text or Comment of Rule 5.2.

Selected State Variations

California has no provision comparable to ABA Model Rule 5.2.

Connecticut deletes ABA Model Rule 5.2(b).

District of Columbia has adopted ABA Model Rule 5.2.

Illinois adopts the ABA Model Rule.

New York: Rule 5.2 is the same as the ABA Model Rule.

Ohio: Rule 5.2(b) omits the word "arguable" before "question of professional duty."

Virginia omits Rule 5.2.

Related Materials

ABA Formal Ethics Opinions: See ABA Formal Ethics Ops. 88-356 n.9 (1988) and 06-441 (2006).

Restatement of the Law Governing Lawyers: See Restatement §12 in our chapter on the Restatement later in this volume.

1.10 ct 4
5.1

Rule 5.3 Responsibilities Regarding Nonlawyer Assistants

With respect to a nonlawyer employed or retained by or associated with a lawyer:

(a) a partner, and a lawyer who individually or together with other lawyers possesses comparable managerial authority in a law firm shall make reasonable efforts to ensure that the firm has in effect measures giving reasonable assurance that the person's conduct is compatible with the professional obligations of the lawyer;

(b) a lawyer having direct supervisory authority over the nonlawyer shall make reasonable efforts to ensure that the person's conduct is compatible with the professional obligations of the lawyer; and

(c) a lawyer shall be responsible for conduct of such a person that would be a violation of the Rules of Professional Conduct if engaged in by a lawyer if:

(1) the lawyer orders or, with the knowledge of the specific conduct, ratifies the conduct involved; or

(2) the lawyer is a partner or has comparable managerial authority in the law firm in which the person is employed, or has direct supervisory authority over the person, and knows of the conduct at

Widener Rule - extends to law students

a time when its consequences can be avoided or mitigated but fails to take reasonable remedial action.

COMMENT

[1] Lawyers generally employ assistants in their practice, including secretaries, investigators, law student interns, and paraprofessionals. Such assistants, whether employees or independent contractors, act for the lawyer in rendition of the lawyer's professional services. A lawyer must give such assistants appropriate instruction and supervision concerning the ethical aspects of their employment, particularly regarding the obligation not to disclose information relating to representation of the client, and should be responsible for their work product. The measures employed in supervising nonlawyers should take account of the fact that they do not have legal training and are not subject to professional discipline.

[2] Paragraph (a) requires lawyers with managerial authority within a law firm to make reasonable efforts to establish internal policies and procedures designed to provide reasonable assurance that nonlawyers in the firm will act in a way compatible with the Rules of Professional Conduct. See Comment [1] to Rule 5.1. Paragraph (b) applies to lawyers who have supervisory authority over the work of a nonlawyer. Paragraph (c) specifies the circumstances in which a lawyer is responsible for conduct of a nonlawyer that would be a violation of the Rules of Professional Conduct if engaged in by a lawyer.

Canon and Code Antecedents

ABA Canons of Professional Ethics: No comparable Canon.

ABA Model Code of Professional Responsibility: Compare DR 4-101(D) (reprinted later in this volume).

Cross-References in Other Rules

Rule 1.6, Comment 16: "A lawyer must act competently to safeguard information relating to the representation of a client against inadvertent or unauthorized disclosure by the lawyer or other persons who are participating in the representation of the client or who are subject to the lawyer's supervision (see **Rules** 1.1, 5.1 and **5.3**)."

Rule 1.10, Comment 4: Paragraph (a) does not "prohibit representation if the lawyer is prohibited from acting because of events before the person became a lawyer. . . . Such persons, however, ordinarily must be screened from any personal participation in the matter to avoid communication to others in the firm of confidential information that both the nonlawyers and the firm have a legal duty to protect. See **Rules** 1.0(k) and **5.3**."

Rule 3.8, Comment 6: "Like other lawyers, prosecutors are subject to **Rules** 5.1 and **5.3,** which relate to responsibilities regarding lawyers and nonlawyers who work for or are associated with the lawyer's office."

Rule 5.5, Comment 2: "This Rule does not prohibit a lawyer from employing the services of paraprofessionals and delegating functions to them, so long as the lawyer supervises the delegated work and retains responsibility for their work. See **Rule 5.3.**"

Rule 5.7, Comment 8: When rendering both legal and law-related services in the same matter, "a lawyer will be responsible for assuring that both the lawyer's conduct and, to the extent required by **Rule 5.3,** that of nonlawyer employees in the distinct entity that the lawyer controls complies in all respects with the Rules of Professional Conduct."

Rule 7.2, Comment 5: "See **Rule 5.3** for the duties of lawyers and law firms with respect to the conduct of nonlawyers who prepare marketing materials for them."

Rule 7.2, Comment 7: "A lawyer who accepts assignments or referrals from a legal service plan or referrals from a lawyer referral service must act reasonably to assure that the activities of the plan or service are compatible with the lawyer's professional obligations. See **Rule 5.3.**"

Legislative History of Model Rule 5.3

1980 Discussion Draft (then Rule 7.4) provided:

Supervision of Nonlawyer Assistants

A lawyer shall use reasonable effort to ensure that nonlawyers employed or retained by the lawyer conduct themselves in a manner compatible with the professional obligations of the lawyer.

1981 Draft was substantially the same as adopted.

1982 Draft was adopted.

1983 Rule: As originally adopted in 1983, Rule 5.3 was the same as the 2002 version of Rule 5.3, except that the 1983 version of Rule 5.3(a) did not include the phrase "and a lawyer who individually or together with other lawyers possesses comparable managerial authority," and Rule 5.3(c)(2) did not contain the phrase "or has comparable managerial authority."

2002 Amendments: In 2002, the ABA House of Delegates adopted without change the ABA Ethics 2000 Commission proposal to amend Rule 5.3 and its Comment. The amendments insert the same references to "managerial authority" in the text of paragraphs (a) and (c)(2) as were inserted by the amendments to Rule 5.1. Comment 2 was added.

Selected State Variations

California has no provision comparable to ABA Model Rule 5.3.

Georgia adds a new Rule 5.3(d) that indirectly restricts the activities of suspended or disbarred lawyers who work in a law office.

Illinois: The Illinois rule is the same as the ABA Model Rule.

New Hampshire: Rules 5.3(a) and (b) impose duties on "each" partner in a firm, "each" lawyer with comparable managerial authority, and "each" lawyer with direct supervisory authority. Separately, New Hampshire Supreme Court Rule 35

(Guidelines for the Utilization by Lawyers of the Services of Legal Assistants under the New Hampshire Rules of Professional Conduct) contains nine rules for using the services of legal assistants in compliance with Rule 5.3. For example, Rule 1 provides:

> It is the responsibility of the lawyer to take all steps reasonably necessary to ensure that a legal assistant for whose work the lawyer is responsible does not provide legal advice or otherwise engage in the unauthorized practice of law; provided, however, that with adequate lawyer supervision the legal assistant may provide information concerning legal matters and otherwise act as permitted under these rules.

New Jersey: Rule 5.3(a) provides that "every lawyer or organization authorized by the Court Rules to practice law in this jurisdiction shall adopt and maintain reasonable efforts to ensure that the conduct of nonlawyers retained or employed by the lawyer, law firm or organization is compatible with the professional obligations of the lawyer." In addition, New Jersey has added Rule 5.3(c)(3), which provides that a lawyer is responsible for the conduct of a nonlawyer employee if "the lawyer has failed to make reasonable investigation of circumstances that would disclose past instances of conduct by the nonlawyer incompatible with the professional obligations of a lawyer, which evidence a propensity for such conduct."

New York: Rule 5.3 provides:

> (a) A law firm shall ensure that the work of nonlawyers who work for the firm is adequately supervised, as appropriate. A lawyer with direct supervisory authority over a nonlawyer shall adequately supervise the work of the nonlawyer, as appropriate. In either case, the degree of supervision required is that which is reasonable under the circumstances, taking into account factors such as the experience of the person whose work is being supervised, the amount of work involved in a particular matter and the likelihood that ethical problems might arise in the course of working on the matter.
>
> (b) A lawyer shall be responsible for conduct of a nonlawyer employed or retained by or associated with the lawyer that would be a violation of these Rules if engaged in by a lawyer, if:
>
> (1) the lawyer orders or directs the specific conduct or, with knowledge of the specific conduct, ratifies it; or
>
> (2) the lawyer is a partner in a law firm or is a lawyer who individually or together with other lawyers possesses comparable managerial responsibility in a law firm in which the nonlawyer is employed or is a lawyer who has supervisory authority over the nonlawyer; and
>
> (i) knows of such conduct at a time when it could be prevented or its consequences avoided or mitigated but fails to take reasonable remedial action; or
>
> (ii) in the exercise of reasonable management or supervisory authority should have known of the conduct so that reasonable remedial action could have been taken at a time when the consequences of the conduct could have been avoided or mitigated.

Oregon: Rule 5.3(b) begins: "except as provided by Rule 8.4(b). . . ." Under Oregon Rule 8.4(b), it is generally not professional misconduct for a lawyer to give advice about or to supervise "lawful covert activity in the investigation of violations of civil or criminal law or constitutional rights" provided the lawyer otherwise abides by the Rules of Professional Conduct. Rule 8.4(b) continues:

> "Covert activity," as used in this rule, means an effort to obtain information on unlawful activity through the use of misrepresentations or other subterfuge. "Covert

activity" may be commenced by a lawyer or involve a lawyer as an advisor or supervisor only when the lawyer in good faith believes there is a reasonable possibility that unlawful activity has taken place, is taking place or will take place in the foreseeable future.

Rhode Island: Immediately after the Comment to Rule 5.3, Rhode Island includes a lengthy set of "Guidelines" for the use of legal assistants. These Guidelines are a heavily modified version of the ABA Model Guidelines for the Utilization of Paralegal Services (see Related Materials below). For example, Rhode Island's Guideline 3, which is closely related to Rule 5.3, provides as follows:

> 3. A lawyer shall direct a legal assistant to avoid any conduct which if engaged in by a lawyer would violate the Rules of Professional Conduct. In particular, the lawyer shall instruct the legal assistant regarding the confidential nature of the attorney/client relationship, and shall direct the legal assistant to refrain from disclosing any confidential information obtained from a client or in connection with representation of a client.

Texas relegates ABA Model Rule 5.3(a) to Comment 2 after Texas Rule 5.03. The Comment applies to "[e]ach lawyer in a position of authority in a law firm or in a government agency," including lawyers having supervisory authority or "intermediate managerial responsibilities in the law department of any enterprise or government agency." Texas Rule 5.03(b), which is equivalent to ABA Model Rule 5.3(c), subjects a lawyer to discipline for a nonlawyer's misconduct if (1) the lawyer orders, "encourages, or permits" the conduct involved; or (2) the lawyer:

> (i) is a partner in the law firm in which the person is employed, retained by, or associated with; or is the general counsel of a government agency's legal department in which the person is employed, retained by or associated with; or has direct supervisory authority over such person; and
>
> (ii) with knowledge of such misconduct by the nonlawyer knowingly fails to take reasonable remedial action to avoid or mitigate the consequences of that person's misconduct.

Virginia: Rule 5.3(c)(2) applies if a lawyer knows "or should have known" of the conduct in question.

Related Materials

ABA Commission on Ethics 20/20: In 2009, the ABA created the Commission on Ethics 20/20, which is comprehensively reviewing the ABA Model Rules of Professional Conduct and other lawyer regulatory sources in light of globalization and changes in technology. The Commission has not proposed any changes to the black letter text of Rule 5.3, but in September 2011, in revised proposals on outsourcing, the Commission circulated for public comment a proposal to amend Comment 2 in relatively minor ways and to add the following new paragraphs to the Comment to Rule 5.3 under the heading "Nonlawyers Outside the Firm":

> [3] A lawyer may use nonlawyers outside the firm to assist the lawyer in rendering legal services to the client. Examples include the retention of an investigative or paraprofessional service, hiring a document management company to create and maintain a database for complex litigation, sending client documents to a third party for printing or scanning, and using an Internet-based service to

store client information. When using such services outside the firm, a lawyer must make reasonable efforts to ensure that the services are provided in a manner that is compatible with the lawyer's professional obligations. The extent of this obligation will depend upon the circumstances, including the education, experience and reputation of the nonlawyer; the nature of the services involved; the terms of any arrangements concerning the protection of client information; and the legal and ethical environments of the jurisdictions in which the services will be performed, particularly with regard to confidentiality. See also Rules 1.1 (competence), 1.2 (allocation of authority), 1.4 (communication with client), 1.6 (confidentiality), 5.4(a) (professional independence of the lawyer), and 5.5(a) (unauthorized practice of law). When retaining or directing a nonlawyer outside the firm, a lawyer should communicate directions appropriate under the circumstances to give reasonable assurance that the nonlawyer's conduct is compatible with the professional obligations of the lawyer.

[4] Where the client has chosen or suggested a particular nonlawyer service provider outside the firm, the lawyer or law firm ordinarily should consult with the client concerning the allocation of responsibility for monitoring as between the client and the lawyer or law firm. See Rule 1.2. When making such an allocation in a matter pending before a tribunal, lawyers and parties may have additional obligations that are a matter of law beyond the scope of these Rules.

The Commission may present these proposals (or revised versions of them) to the ABA House of Delegates at its August 2012 Annual Meeting. For updates on the Ethics 20/20 Commission's work, visit *www.americanbar.org/Ethics2020.*

ABA Definition of "Legal Assistant": In 1997, the ABA Board of Governors adopted the following definition of the phrase "legal assistant," a phrase used interchangeably with the term "paralegal":

> A legal assistant or paralegal is a person qualified by education, training or work experience who is employed or retained by a lawyer, law office, corporation, governmental agency or other entity who performs specifically delegated substantive legal work for which a lawyer is responsible.

In 2001, the National Association of Legal Assistants adopted the ABA definition. To see how this definition has evolved over the years, visit *www.nala.org/terms.aspx.*

ABA Formal Ethics Opinions: See ABA Formal Ethics Ops. 94-388 (1994), 95-396 (1995), 95-398 (1995), 08-451 (2008), and 08-453 (2008).

ABA Guidelines for Approval of Paralegal Education Programs: In 1973, the ABA adopted Guidelines for the Approval of Paralegal Education Programs. These Guidelines, which were amended in 2006, 2007, and 2008, are enforced by an ABA Approval Commission that examines and approves paralegal education programs. Like the accreditation process for law schools, the approval process for paralegal programs consists of several stages, including (a) the preparation of a self-evaluation report and supporting documents, (b) review by educational consultants, (c) an onsite evaluation of all program operations to verify that they operate in compliance with ABA guidelines, and (d) consideration by the Standing Committee on Paralegals & Approval Commission. The United States has an estimated 600 paralegal education programs, of which 258 were approved by the ABA as of June 2004 (the most recent available data). The ABA works closely with the American Association for Paralegal Education (see entry below). The Guidelines for Approval of Paralegal Education Programs and other materials on paralegal education are available at *http://www.americanbar.org/groups/paralegals.html.*

ABA Model Guidelines for the Utilization of Paralegal Services: In 1991, the ABA Standing Committee on Paralegals drafted the ABA Model Guidelines for the Utilization of Legal Assistant Services and the ABA House of Delegates adopted them. In 2004, the ABA amended the Guidelines, substituting the term "paralegal" for the old term "legal assistant." The Guidelines are aimed at lawyers rather than paralegals, and are intended to encourage lawyers to use paralegal services effectively. The following two Guidelines are closely related to ABA Model Rule 5.3:

> *Guideline 1.* A lawyer is responsible for all of the professional actions of a paralegal performing services at the lawyer's direction and should take reasonable measures to ensure that the paralegal's conduct is consistent with the lawyer's obligations under the rules of professional conduct of the jurisdiction in which the lawyer practices.
>
> *Guideline 6.* A lawyer is responsible for taking reasonable measures to ensure that all client confidences are preserved by a paralegal.

Some states have adopted paralegal guidelines based on the ABA Guidelines. The complete ABA Guidelines for the Utilization of Paralegal Services are available online at *http://apps.americanbar.org/legalservices/paralegals/downloads/modelguidelines.pdf.*

ABA Standards for Criminal Justice: See Prosecution Function Standards 3-3.1(a) and (c) (Investigative Function of the Prosecutor) and Defense Function Standard 4-4.2 (Illegal Investigations).

ABA Standing Committee on Paralegals: The ABA Standing Committee on Paralegals has jurisdiction over matters relating to the education, employment, training, and effective use of paralegals, and it monitors trends in the field and advises and acts on behalf of the ABA on all matters relating to the roles of paralegals. Through its Approval Commission, the Standing Committee sets standards for quality paralegal education and recommends that the ABA House of Delegates approve (or reapprove) paralegal training programs that meet those standards. The Standing Committee also provides information in response to more than 6,000 requests a year from people interested in becoming paralegals. For more information, visit *http://www.americanbar.org/groups/paralegals.html.*

American Association for Paralegal Education: The American Association for Paralegal Education (AAfPE) is an organization for those who educate paralegals. According to its mission statement, the AAfPE "promotes quality paralegal education, develops educational standards and encourages professional growth, in order to prepare graduates to perform a significant role in the delivery of legal services." A central focus of the AAfPE has been establishing standards by which to measure paralegal education. The AAfPE works closely with the ABA Approval Commission to ensure that paralegal programs are providing quality education. For more information, see *www.aafpe.org.*

Independent Paralegals: Some states allow "independent paralegals" (also called "freelance paralegals") who are retained by lawyers on an "as needed" basis but are not employees of any lawyer or law firm. Because Rule 5.3 covers nonlawyers who are "retained by or associated with" a lawyer, the rule apparently reaches independent paralegals.

International Paralegal Management Association: The International Paralegal Management Association promotes the development, professional standing and visibility of paralegal management professionals. For more information about IPMA, including a fascinating "Utilization Survey" showing how law firms, corporations, and government agencies use paralegals, visit *www.paralegalmanagement.org.*

National Association of Legal Assistants: The National Association of Legal Assistants, Inc. (NALA), an organization of more than 18,000 legal assistants, publishes Model Standards and Guidelines for Utilization of Legal Assistants Annotated. The NALA Guidelines, most recently amended in 2007, may help lawyers understand their supervisory responsibilities under Model Rule 5.3. Excerpts from the Guidelines are reprinted in the Related Materials following Rule 5.5 (Unauthorized Practice of Law) and are available with Comments at *www.nala.org/model.aspx.*

NALA has also adopted a very brief Code of Ethics and Professional Responsibility for legal assistants. Canon 9 of this Code, which is the reciprocal of ABA Model Rule 5.3, provides: "A legal assistant must do all other things incidental, necessary, or expedient for the attainment of the ethics and responsibilities as defined by statute or rule of court." The code is available at *www.nala.org/code.aspx.*

Respondeat Superior: The doctrine of "respondeat superior" (a Latin phrase meaning "let the master answer") provides, in essence, that employers (principals) are responsible for the wrongful acts or omissions of their employees (agents) during the course of employment.

Restatement of the Law Governing Lawyers: See Restatement §§11(4) and 58 in our chapter on the Restatement later in this volume.

Student Practice Rules: All states have student practice rules that permit law students to represent clients under certain conditions. These provisions, which are codified in state statutes, court rules, and state bar rules, typically require lawyers to supervise the law students. For example, Florida Rule 11-1.2(b) provides as follows:

> An eligible law student may appear in any court or before any administrative tribunal in this state on behalf of any indigent person if the person on whose behalf the student is appearing has indicated in writing consent to that appearance and the supervising lawyer has also indicated in writing approval of that appearance. In those cases in which an indigent has a right to appointed counsel, the supervising attorney shall be personally present at all critical stages of the proceeding. In all cases, the supervising attorney shall be personally present when required by the court or administrative tribunal who shall determine the extent of the eligible law student's participation in the proceeding.

To view student practice rules and forms adopted by both federal and state courts, visit *www.ll.georgetown.edu/guides/StudentPractice.cfm.*

Unauthorized Practice of Law: A lawyer who authorizes or permits a paralegal to perform law-related tasks but fails to supervise the paralegal adequately may be assisting the paralegal in the unauthorized practice of law, in violation of Rule 5.5. (For examples of statutes governing the unauthorized practice of law, see the Related Materials following ABA Model Rule 5.5 below.)

Rule 5.4 Professional Independence of a Lawyer

(a) A lawyer or law firm shall not share legal fees with a nonlawyer, except that:

(1) an agreement by a lawyer with the lawyer's firm, partner, or associate may provide for the payment of money, over a reasonable period of time after the lawyer's death, to the lawyer's estate or to one or more specified persons;

(2) a lawyer who purchases the practice of a deceased, disabled, or disappeared lawyer may, pursuant to the provisions of Rule 1.17, pay to the estate or other representative of that lawyer the agreed-upon purchase price;

(3) a lawyer or law firm may include nonlawyer employees in a compensation or retirement plan, even though the plan is based in whole or in part on a profit-sharing arrangement; and

(4) a lawyer may share court-awarded legal fees with a nonprofit organization that employed, retained or recommended employment of the lawyer in the matter.

(b) A lawyer shall not form a partnership with a nonlawyer if any of the activities of the partnership consist of the practice of law.

(c) A lawyer shall not permit a person who recommends, employs, or pays the lawyer to render legal services for another to direct or regulate the lawyer's professional judgment in rendering such legal services.

(d) A lawyer shall not practice with or in the form of a professional corporation or association authorized to practice law for a profit, if:

(1) a nonlawyer owns any interest therein, except that a fiduciary representative of the estate of a lawyer may hold the stock or interest of the lawyer for a reasonable time during administration;

(2) a nonlawyer is a corporate director or officer thereof or occupies the position of similar responsibility in any form of association other than a corporation; or

(3) a nonlawyer has the right to direct or control the professional judgment of a lawyer.

COMMENT

[1] The provisions of this Rule express traditional limitations on sharing fees. These limitations are to protect the lawyer's professional independence of judgment. Where someone other than the client pays the lawyer's fee or salary, or recommends employment of the lawyer, that arrangement does not modify the lawyer's obligation to the client. As stated in paragraph (c), such arrangements should not interfere with the lawyer's professional judgment.

[2] This Rule also expresses traditional limitations on permitting a third party to direct or regulate the lawyer's professional judgment in rendering legal services to another. See also Rule 1.8(f) (lawyer may accept compensation from a third party as long as there is no interference with the lawyer's independent professional judgment and the client gives informed consent).

Canon and Code Antecedents

ABA Canons of Professional Ethics: Canons 33, 34, and 35 provided as follows:

33. Partnerships—Names

Partnerships among lawyers for the practice of their profession are very common and are not to be condemned. In the formation of partnerships and the use of partnership names care should be taken not to violate any law, custom, or rule of court locally applicable. Where partnerships are formed between lawyers who are not all admitted to practice in the courts of the state, care should be taken to avoid any misleading name or representation which would create a false impression as to the professional position or privileges of the member not locally admitted. In the formation of partnerships for the practice of law, no person should be admitted or held out as a practitioner or member who is not a member of the legal profession duly authorized to practice, and amenable to professional discipline. In the selection and use of a firm name, no false, misleading, assumed or trade name should be used. The continued use of the name of a deceased or former partner, when permissible by local custom, is not unethical, but care should be taken that no imposition or deception is practiced through this use. When a member of the firm, on becoming a judge, is precluded from practicing law, his name should not be continued in the firm name.

Partnerships between lawyers and members of other professions or nonprofessional persons should not be formed or permitted where any part of the partnership's employment consists of the practice of law.

34. Division of Fees

No division of fees for legal services is proper, except with another lawyer, based upon a division of service or responsibility.

35. Intermediaries

The professional services of a lawyer should not be controlled or exploited by any lay agency, personal or corporate, which intervenes between client and lawyer. A lawyer's responsibilities and qualifications are individual. He should avoid all relations which direct the performance of his duties by or in the interest of such intermediary. A lawyer's relation to his client should be personal, and the responsibility should be direct to the client. Charitable societies rendering aid to the indigents are not deemed such intermediaries.

A lawyer may accept employment from any organization, such as an association, club or trade organization, to render legal services in any matter in which the organization, as an entity, is interested, but this employment should not include the rendering of legal services to the members of such an organization in respect to their individual affairs.

ABA Model Code of Professional Responsibility: Compare DR 3-102(A), DR 3-103(B), DR 5-107(B), and DR 5-107(C) (reprinted later in this volume).

Cross-References in Other Rules

Rule 1.8, Comment 11: "See also **Rule 5.4(c)** (prohibiting interference with a lawyer's professional judgment by one who recommends, employs or pays the lawyer to render legal services for another)."

Rule 1.17, Comment 1: "[W]hen a lawyer or an entire firm ceases to practice, or ceases to practice in an area of law, and other lawyers or firms take over the representation, the selling lawyer or firm may obtain compensation for the reasonable value of the practice as may withdrawing partners of law firms. See **Rules 5.4** and 5.6."

Rule 7.2, Comment 8: "[R]eciprocal referral arrangements must not interfere with the lawyer's professional judgment as to making referrals or as to providing substantive legal services. See **Rules** 2.1 and **5.4(c)**."

Legislative History of Model Rule 5.4

1980 Discussion Draft (then Rule 7.5) provided as follows:

Professional Independence of a Firm

A lawyer shall not practice with a firm in which an interest is owned or managerial authority is exercised by a nonlawyer, unless services can be rendered in conformity with the Rules of Professional Conduct. The terms of the relationship shall expressly provide that:

(a) there is no interference with the lawyer's independence of professional judgment or with the client-lawyer relationship; and

(b) the confidences of clients are protected as required by Rule 1.7; and

(c) the arrangement does not involve advertising or solicitation prohibited by Rules 9.2 and 9.3; and

(d) the arrangement does not result in charging a client a fee which violates Rule 1.6.

1981 Draft:

Professional Independence of a Firm

A lawyer may be employed by an organization in which a financial interest is held or managerial authority is exercised by a non-lawyer, or by a lawyer acting in a capacity other than that of representing clients, such as a business corporation, insurance company, legal services organization or government agency, but only if the terms of the relationship provide in writing that:

(a) there is no interference with the lawyer's independence of professional judgment or with the client-lawyer relationship;

(b) information relating to representation of a client is protected as required by Rule 1.6;

(c) the arrangement does not involve advertising or personal contract with prospective clients prohibited by Rules 7.2 and 7.3; and

(d) the arrangement does not result in charging a fee that violates Rule 1.5.

1982 Draft was substantially the same as the 1981 Draft.

1983 Rule: The version of Rule 5.4 finally adopted in 1983 was proposed by the ABA's General Practice Section as a substitute for the Kutak Commission's draft. (Rule 5.4 was the only rule from the 1982 Draft that was completely rejected and rewritten by the House of Delegates in 1983.) As adopted in 1983, Rule 5.4 was the same as the 2002 version of Rule 5.4, except that Rule 5.4(a)(4) was not yet in the rule, and Rules 5.4(a)(2) and (d)(2) provided:

(a)(2) a lawyer who undertakes to complete unfinished legal business of a deceased lawyer may pay to the estate of the deceased lawyer that proportion of the total compensation which fairly represents the services rendered by the deceased lawyer.

(d)(2) a nonlawyer is a corporate director or officer thereof.

1990 Amendment: In 1990, the ABA House of Delegates amended Rule 5.4(a)(2) to conform to Rule 1.17 (permitting the sale of a law practice), which was added to the Rules at the same meeting. (There was no Committee Report to explain the change, but the reason for the change is obvious.) Before the amendment, Rule 5.4(a)(2) had provided that "a lawyer who undertakes to complete unfinished legal business of a deceased lawyer may pay to the estate of the deceased lawyer that proportion of the total compensation which fairly represents the services rendered by the deceased lawyer."

2002 Amendments: In 2002, the ABA House of Delegates adopted without change the ABA Ethics 2000 Commission proposal to amend Rule 5.4 and its Comment. The amendments added (a)(4) to the text of the rule, added the language following "thereof" in paragraph (d)(2) of the text, and added all of Comment 2.

Selected State Variations

California: Rule 1-310 forbids lawyers to form partnerships with nonlawyers if "any of the activities of that partnership consist of the practice of law." Rule 1-320 forbids sharing legal fees with nonlawyers with exceptions, including those described in Rules 5.4(1) and (3).

Connecticut: Connecticut omits ABA Model Rule 5.4(a)(4) (relating to fee sharing with nonprofit organizations).

District of Columbia: D.C. Rules 5.4(a)(4) and (b), which are unique in the United States, permit fee sharing between lawyers and nonlawyers "in a partnership or other form of organization which meets the requirements of paragraph (b)." Paragraph (b) provides:

> (b) A lawyer may practice law in a partnership or other form of organization in which a financial interest is held or managerial authority is exercised by an individual nonlawyer who performs professional services which assist the organization in providing legal services to clients, but only if:
>
> (1) The partnership or organization has as its sole purpose providing legal services to clients;
>
> (2) All persons having such managerial authority or holding a financial interest undertake to abide by these Rules of Professional Conduct;
>
> (3) The lawyers who have a financial interest or managerial authority in the partnership or organization undertake to be responsible for the nonlawyer participants to the same extent as if nonlawyer participants were lawyers under Rule 5.1;
>
> (4) The foregoing conditions are set forth in writing.

In addition, D.C. Rule 5.4(a)(5) permits a lawyer to "share legal fees, whether awarded by a tribunal or received in settlement of a matter, with a nonprofit organization that employed, retained, or recommended employment of the lawyer in the matter and that qualifies under Section 501(c)(3) of the Internal Revenue Code."

Florida: In place of ABA Model Rule 5.4(a)(2), Florida retains the language from the 1983 Model Rule providing that "a lawyer who undertakes to complete unfinished legal business of a deceased lawyer may pay to the estate of the deceased lawyer that proportion of the total compensation which fairly represents the services rendered by the deceased lawyer."

Florida Rule 4-8.6 describes the business entities through which lawyers may practice law and forbids practice other than through "officers, directors, partners, agents, or employees who are qualified to render legal services in this state." Further, only persons who are so qualified may serve as "a partner, manager, director, or executive officer" of such an entity. Florida has substantially adopted Rule 5.4(a)(4).

Illinois tracks the Model Rule. Illinois Rule 5.4(d)(2) permits a nonlawyer to serve as secretary for a professional corporation or for-profit association authorized to practice law "if such secretary performs only ministerial duties."

Indiana deletes ABA Model Rule 5.4(a)(4).

Iowa deletes ABA Model Rule 5.4(a)(4).

Kansas: Kansas replaces ABA Model Rule 5.4(a)(2) with language from the 1983 version of ABA Model Rule 5.4 providing that "a lawyer who undertakes to complete unfinished legal business of a deceased lawyer may pay to the estate of the deceased lawyer that proportion of the total compensation which fairly represents the services rendered by the deceased lawyer." Kansas makes no reference to the purchase of a law practice or to Rule 1.17, which Kansas has not adopted.

Maryland restores language from the 1983 version of ABA Model Rule 5.4 providing that "a lawyer who undertakes to complete unfinished legal business of a deceased, retired, disabled, or suspended lawyer may pay to that lawyer or that lawyer's estate the proportion of the total compensation which fairly represents the services rendered by the former lawyer."

Massachusetts: Rule 5.4(a) allows a lawyer or law firm to share "a statutory or tribunal-approved" legal fee with "a qualified legal assistance organization that referred the matter to the lawyer or law firm" if the organization is not for profit and tax-exempt, the fee is made in connection with a proceeding to advance the organization's purposes, and the client consents. The Comment to this rule explains that the "financial needs of these organizations, which serve important public ends, justify a limited exception to the prohibition against fee-sharing with nonlawyers." The Comment also explains that the exception does not extend to fees generated in connection with proceedings unrelated to the organization's tax-exempt purpose, "such as generating business income for the organization." Massachusetts Rule 5.4(b) prohibits a lawyer from forming a partnership "or other business entity" with a nonlawyer if any of the activities of the "entity" consist of the practice of law.

Minnesota: Rule 5.4(a)(4) permits a lawyer to share court-awarded fees with a nonprofit organization only "subject to full disclosure and court approval," and Rule 5.4(a)(5) restores language from the 1983 version of ABA Model Rule 5.4 providing that "a lawyer who undertakes to complete unfinished legal business of a deceased lawyer may pay to the estate of the deceased lawyer the proportion of the total compensation that fairly represents the services rendered by the deceased lawyer."

Missouri restores language from the 1983 version of ABA Model Rule 5.4(a) permitting a lawyer who completes unfinished legal business of a deceased lawyer to pay the deceased lawyer's estate "that proportion of the total compensation that fairly represents the services rendered by the deceased lawyer."

New Hampshire: Rule 5.4(a)(4) permits a lawyer to "share legal fees with a non-profit organization that employed, retained or recommended employment of the lawyer in the matter," whether or not the fees are "court-awarded."

New Jersey Rule 5.4(a)(5) provides that "a lawyer may share court-awarded legal fees with a nonprofit organization that employed, retained, or recommended employment of the lawyer in the matter."

New York: Rule 5.4 is substantially the same as the Model Rule except New York omits Rule 5.4(a)(4).

North Carolina omits ABA Model Rule 5.4(d)(2) and adds Rule 5.4(a)(3), which permits a lawyer who undertakes to complete unfinished legal business of a deceased lawyer "or a disbarred lawyer" may pay to the estate of the deceased lawyer "or to the disbarred lawyer" that proportion of the total compensation which fairly represents the services rendered by the deceased lawyer "or the disbarred lawyer."

Ohio: Rule 5.4(a)(4) omits the words "or recommended employment of" and inserts "or" between "employed" and "retained." Rule 5.4(a)(5) permits a lawyer to "share legal fees with a non-profit organization that recommended employment of the lawyer in the matter," whether or not the fees are court-awarded, provided that the nonprofit organization complies with Ohio's Supreme Court Rules governing lawyer referral and information services.

Oklahoma: Rule 5.4(2A) adds language from the 1983 version of ABA Model Rule 5.4 providing that "a lawyer who undertakes to complete unfinished legal business of a deceased lawyer may pay to the estate of the deceased lawyer that proportion of the total compensation which fairly represents the services rendered by the deceased lawyer." Oklahoma Rule 5.4(a)(4) says, in brackets: "The concept of this subsection of the ABA Model Rule is addressed in the Comment." Oklahoma's Comment says that Rule 5.4(a) "does not prohibit a lawyer from *voluntarily* sharing court-awarded legal fees with a nonprofit organization that employed, retained or recommended employment of the lawyer in the matter. This shall not be deemed a sharing of attorneys fees." (Emphasis added.)

Oregon adds a new Rule 5.4(e) providing that a lawyer "shall not refer a client to a nonlawyer with the understanding that the lawyer will receive a fee, commission or anything of value in exchange for the referral, but a lawyer may accept gifts in the ordinary course of social or business hospitality."

Pennsylvania adds Rule 5.4(d)(4), which provides that "in the case of any form of association other than a professional corporation, the organic law governing the internal affairs of the association provides the equity owners of the association with greater liability protection than is available to the shareholders of a professional corporation." Rule 5.4(d) concludes by stating that subparagraphs (d)(1), (2), and (4) "shall not apply to a lawyer employed in the legal department of a corporation or other organization." The provision that does apply, Rule 5.4(d)(3), is the same as Model Rule 5.4(d)(3).

Rhode Island: After some uncertainty over whether Rhode Island would subscribe to the position in Rule 5.4(a)(4), as described in Selected State Variations for our 2008 edition, Rhode Island has adopted the following version of ABA Model Rule 5.4(a)(4):

> (4) a lawyer or law firm may agree to share a statutory or tribunal-approved fee award, or a settlement in a matter eligible for such an award, with an organization that referred the matter to the lawyer or law firm if: (i) the organization is one that is not for profit; (ii) the organization is tax-exempt under federal law; (iii) the fee award or

settlement is made in connection with a proceeding to advance one or more of the purposes by virtue of which the organization is tax-exempt; and (iv) the tribunal approves the fee-sharing arrangement.

Tennessee: Effective January 1, 2011, Rule 5.4(a) provides, in pertinent part:

> (4) a lawyer may share a court-awarded fee with a client represented in the matter or with a non-profit organization that employed, retained, or recommended employment of the lawyer in the matter;
>
> (5) a lawyer who is a full-time employee of a client may share a legal fee with the client to the extent necessary to reimburse the client for the actual cost to the client of permitting the lawyer to represent another client while continuing in the full-time employ of the client with whom the fee will be shared; and
>
> (6) a lawyer may pay to a registered non-profit intermediary organization a referral fee calculated by reference to a reasonable percentage of the fee paid to the lawyer by the client referred to the lawyer by the intermediary organization.

Texas: Under Texas Rule 5.04(a)(1), either a lawyer's agreement or a lawful court order may provide for the payment of money over time to the lawyer's estate "to or for the benefit of the lawyer's heirs or personal representatives, beneficiaries, or former spouse, after the lawyer's death or as otherwise provided by law or court order."

Virginia omits Rule 5.4(a)(4) and substitutes "a lawyer may accept discounted payment of his fee from a credit card company on behalf of a client."

Related Materials

ABA Commission on Ethics 20/20: In 2009, the ABA created the Commission on Ethics 20/20, which is comprehensively reviewing the ABA Model Rules of Professional Conduct and other lawyer regulatory sources in light of globalization and changes in technology. In the fall of 2011, the Commission circulated for public comment possible revisions to Model Rule 5.4 that would allow nonlawyers, under limited circumstances, to have an ownership interest in law firms (as is increasingly permitted abroad). If these revisions were to be adopted, Model Rule 5.4 would be similar in many respects—but with several additional restrictions—to the District of Columbia's version of Rule 5.4 (see the Selected State Variations following Rule 5.4 above). For updates on the Commission's work, visit *www.americanbar.org/Ethics2020.*

ABA Commission on Multidisciplinary Practice: In 1998, the ABA appointed a Commission on Multidisciplinary Practice (MDP Commission) to study and report on efforts by accounting firms and other nonlawyer professional service firms to provide legal services to the public. (Unauthorized practice of law statutes and ethics rules like Rule 5.4 prohibited lawyers from offering legal services to the public through nonlegal entities such as accounting firms, but lawyers in some professional service firms owned by nonlawyers allegedly did so anyway.) The MDP Commission's Reporter was the late Mary Daly, who was then a professor at Fordham University School of Law.

During 1998 and 1999, the MDP Commission held public hearings, received written comments, and issued a "Background Paper" and some "Hypotheticals and Models" to focus public discussion. The MDP Commission's first report, issued in

June 1999, recommended amendments to the ABA Model Rules of Professional Conduct that would have permitted nonlawyers to become partners with lawyers if the nonlawyers agreed to be bound by the ethics rules that govern lawyers. Specifically, the MDP Commission recommended that the ABA amend Model Rule 5.4 to permit fee sharing between lawyers and nonlawyers within a new type of multidisciplinary practice entity called an "MDP," which was defined as:

> a partnership, professional corporation, or other association or entity that includes lawyers and nonlawyers and has as one, but not all, of its purposes the delivery of legal services to a client(s) other than the MDP itself or that holds itself out to the public as providing nonlegal, as well as legal, services. It includes an arrangement by which a law firm joins with one or more other professional firms to provide services, and there is a direct or indirect sharing of profits as part of the arrangement.

At the ABA's August 1999 Annual Meeting, however, the House of Delegates voted overwhelmingly (304 to 98) to reject the MDP Commission's recommendations. Instead, the ABA adopted a resolution not to change the ABA Model Rules to permit multidisciplinary practice "unless and until additional study demonstrates that such changes will further the public interest without sacrificing or compromising lawyer independence and the legal profession's tradition of loyalty to clients."

In July 2000, after holding additional public hearings, the MDP Commission issued a new report to the House of Delegates with more modest proposals, but the House of Delegates voted 314-106 to reject the MDP Commission's report. Instead, the House adopted a recommendation that the ABA continue to prohibit partnerships with nonlawyers and continue to prohibit nonlawyer equity interests in law firms. In the Special Section at the end of our 2001 edition, we reprinted the MDP Commission's July 2000 report and the ABA's July 2000 recommendation. For additional information, including copies of public comments and all of the MDP Commission's reports, visit the MDP Commission's website at *http://www.americanbar.org/groups/professional_responsibility/commission_multidisciplinary_practice.html.*

ABA Formal Ethics Opinions: See ABA Formal Ethics Ops. 87-355 (1987), 88-356 (1988), 91-360 (1991), 93-374 (1993), 95-392 (1995), 96-401 (1996), 01-423 (2001), 02-428 (2002), and 03-430 (2003).

ABA Model Guidelines for the Utilization of Paralegal Services: Guideline 9 of the ABA Model Guidelines for the Utilization of Paralegal Services parallels ABA Model Rule 5.4(a) by providing as follows:

> A lawyer may not split legal fees with a paralegal nor pay a paralegal for the referral of legal business. A lawyer may compensate a paralegal based on the quantity and quality of the paralegal's work and the value of that work to a law practice, but the paralegal's compensation may not be contingent, by advance agreement, upon the outcome of a particular case or class of cases.

The complete ABA Guidelines for the Utilization of Paralegal Services are online at *http://apps.americanbar.org/legalservices/paralegals/downloads/modelguidelines.pdf.*

American Lawyer's Code of Conduct: Rule 4.7 provides:

> If a lawyer forms a partnership with a nonlawyer for the purpose of more effectively serving clients' interests, the terms of the partnership shall be consistent with the lawyer's obligations under this Code, with particular reference to Rule 2.1, requiring undivided fidelity to the client.

Limited Liability Companies: Rule 5.4(d) governs lawyers who practice with or in the form of "a professional corporation or association authorized to practice law for a profit" if certain circumstances apply. Some states expressly extend coverage of Rule 5.4(d) to limited liability companies (LLCs), which combine the benefits of partnership taxation rules with the benefits of limited liability for corporations. Since Wyoming passed the first Limited Liability Company Act in the United States in 1977, all states have enacted statutes permitting LLCs, or their close cousins limited liability partnerships (LLPs), or both.

Model Rules of Professional Conduct for Federal Lawyers insert a substantially different version of Rule 5.4, the most interesting parts of which provide as follows:

> (d) A Government lawyer shall obey the lawful orders of superiors when representing the United States and individual clients, but a Government lawyer shall not permit a nonlawyer to direct or regulate the Government lawyer's professional judgment in rendering legal services.
>
> (e) A Non-Government lawyer shall not permit a nonlawyer who recommends, employs, or pays the Non-Government lawyer to render legal services for another to direct or regulate the Non-Government lawyer's professional judgment in rendering legal services.
>
> (f) A Non-Government lawyer shall comply with the Rules of Professional Conduct or other applicable laws of the jurisdiction in which the Non-Government lawyer is licensed or is practicing law concerning the limitations on sharing fees and the organizational form of their practice.

Restatement of the Law Governing Lawyers: See Restatement §§10 and 134 in our chapter on the Restatement later in this volume.

Strategic Alliances: Since Rule 5.4 prohibits law firms from forming partnerships with nonlawyers, some law firms have instead formed "strategic alliances" with nonlegal entities. A strategic alliance typically provides for non-exclusive reciprocal referrals between the law firm and the nonlegal entity, and sometimes provides for shared offices, shared overhead expenses, and joint marketing.

Rule 5.5 Unauthorized Practice of Law; Multijurisdictional Practice of Law

(a) A lawyer shall not practice law in a jurisdiction in violation of the regulation of the legal profession in that jurisdiction, or assist another in doing so.

(b) A lawyer who is not admitted to practice in this jurisdiction shall not:

(1) except as authorized by these Rules or other law, establish an office or other systematic and continuous presence in this jurisdiction for the practice of law; or

(2) hold out to the public or otherwise represent that the lawyer is admitted to practice law in this jurisdiction.

(c) A lawyer admitted in another United States jurisdiction, and not disbarred or suspended from practice in any jurisdiction, may provide legal services on a temporary basis in this jurisdiction that:

(1) are undertaken in association with a lawyer who is admitted to practice in this jurisdiction and who actively participates in the matter;

(2) are in or reasonably related to a pending or potential proceeding before a tribunal in this or another jurisdiction, if the lawyer, or a person the lawyer is assisting, is authorized by law or order to appear in such proceeding or reasonably expects to be so authorized;

(3) are in or reasonably related to a pending or potential arbitration, mediation, or other alternative dispute resolution proceeding in this or another jurisdiction, if the services arise out of or are reasonably related to the lawyer's practice in a jurisdiction in which the lawyer is admitted to practice and are not services for which the forum requires pro hac vice admission; or

(4) are not within paragraphs (c)(2) or (c)(3) and arise out of or are reasonably related to the lawyer's practice in a jurisdiction in which the lawyer is admitted to practice.

(d) A lawyer admitted in another United States jurisdiction, and not disbarred or suspended from practice in any jurisdiction, may provide legal services in this jurisdiction that:

(1) are provided to the lawyer's employer or its organizational affiliates and are not services for which the forum requires pro hac vice admission; or

(2) are services that the lawyer is authorized by federal or other law to provide in this jurisdiction.

COMMENT

[1] A lawyer may practice law only in a jurisdiction in which the lawyer is authorized to practice. A lawyer may be admitted to practice law in a jurisdiction on a regular basis or may be authorized by court rule or order or by law to practice for a limited purpose or on a restricted basis. Paragraph (a) applies to unauthorized practice of law by a lawyer, whether through the lawyer's direct action or by the lawyer assisting another person.

[2] The definition of the practice of law is established by law and varies from one jurisdiction to another. Whatever the definition, limiting the practice of law to members of the bar protects the public against rendition of legal services by unqualified persons. This Rule does not prohibit a lawyer from employing the services of paraprofessionals and delegating functions to them, so long as the lawyer supervises the delegated work and retains responsibility for their work. See Rule 5.3.

[3] A lawyer may provide professional advice and instruction to nonlawyers whose employment requires knowledge of the law; for example, claims adjusters, employees of financial or commercial institutions, social workers, accountants and persons employed in government agencies. Lawyers also may assist independent nonlawyers, such as paraprofessionals, who are authorized by the law of a jurisdiction

to provide particular law-related services. In addition, a lawyer may counsel nonlawyers who wish to proceed pro se.

[4] Other than as authorized by law or this Rule, a lawyer who is not admitted to practice generally in this jurisdiction violates paragraph (b) if the lawyer establishes an office or other systematic and continuous presence in this jurisdiction for the practice of law. Presence may be systematic and continuous even if the lawyer is not physically present here. Such a lawyer must not hold out to the public or otherwise represent that the lawyer is admitted to practice law in this jurisdiction. See also Rules 7.1(a) and 7.5(b).

[5] There are occasions in which a lawyer admitted to practice in another United States jurisdiction, and not disbarred or suspended from practice in any jurisdiction, may provide legal services on a temporary basis in this jurisdiction under circumstances that do not create an unreasonable risk to the interests of their clients, the public or the courts. Paragraph (c) identifies four such circumstances. The fact that conduct is not so identified does not imply that the conduct is or is not authorized. With the exception of paragraphs (d)(1) and (d)(2), this Rule does not authorize a lawyer to establish an office or other systematic and continuous presence in this jurisdiction without being admitted to practice generally here.

[6] There is no single test to determine whether a lawyer's services are provided on a "temporary basis" in this jurisdiction, and may therefore be permissible under paragraph (c). Services may be "temporary" even though the lawyer provides services in this jurisdiction on a recurring basis, or for an extended period of time, as when the lawyer is representing a client in a single lengthy negotiation or litigation.

[7] Paragraphs (c) and (d) apply to lawyers who are admitted to practice law in any United States jurisdiction, which includes the District of Columbia and any state, territory or commonwealth of the United States. The word "admitted" in paragraph (c) contemplates that the lawyer is authorized to practice in the jurisdiction in which the lawyer is admitted and excludes a lawyer who while technically admitted is not authorized to practice, because, for example, the lawyer is on inactive status.

[8] Paragraph (c)(1) recognizes that the interests of clients and the public are protected if a lawyer admitted only in another jurisdiction associates with a lawyer licensed to practice in this jurisdiction. For this paragraph to apply, however, the lawyer admitted to practice in this jurisdiction must actively participate in and share responsibility for the representation of the client.

[9] Lawyers not admitted to practice generally in a jurisdiction may be authorized by law or order of a tribunal or an administrative agency to appear before the tribunal or agency. This authority may be granted pursuant to formal rules governing admission pro hac vice or pursuant to informal practice of the tribunal or agency. Under paragraph (c)(2), a lawyer does not violate this Rule when the lawyer appears before a tribunal or agency pursuant to such authority. To the extent that a court rule or other law of this jurisdiction requires a lawyer who is not admitted to practice in this jurisdiction to obtain admission pro hac vice before appearing before a tribunal or administrative agency, this Rule requires the lawyer to obtain that authority.

[10] Paragraph (c)(2) also provides that a lawyer rendering services in this jurisdiction on a temporary basis does not violate this Rule when the lawyer engages

in conduct in anticipation of a proceeding or hearing in a jurisdiction in which the lawyer is authorized to practice law or in which the lawyer reasonably expects to be admitted pro hac vice. Examples of such conduct include meetings with the client, interviews of potential witnesses, and the review of documents. Similarly, a lawyer admitted only in another jurisdiction may engage in conduct temporarily in this jurisdiction in connection with pending litigation in another jurisdiction in which the lawyer is or reasonably expects to be authorized to appear, including taking depositions in this jurisdiction.

[11] When a lawyer has been or reasonably expects to be admitted to appear before a court or administrative agency, paragraph (c)(2) also permits conduct by lawyers who are associated with that lawyer in the matter, but who do not expect to appear before the court or administrative agency. For example, subordinate lawyers may conduct research, review documents, and attend meetings with witnesses in support of the lawyer responsible for the litigation.

[12] Paragraph (c)(3) permits a lawyer admitted to practice law in another jurisdiction to perform services on a temporary basis in this jurisdiction if those services are in or reasonably related to a pending or potential arbitration, mediation, or other alternative dispute resolution proceeding in this or another jurisdiction, if the services arise out of or are reasonably related to the lawyer's practice in a jurisdiction in which the lawyer is admitted to practice. The lawyer, however, must obtain admission pro hac vice in the case of a court-annexed arbitration or mediation or otherwise if court rules or law so require.

[13] Paragraph (c)(4) permits a lawyer admitted in another jurisdiction to provide certain legal services on a temporary basis in this jurisdiction that arise out of or are reasonably related to the lawyer's practice in a jurisdiction in which the lawyer is admitted but are not within paragraphs (c)(2) or (c)(3). These services include both legal services and services that nonlawyers may perform but that are considered the practice of law when performed by lawyers.

[14] Paragraphs (c)(3) and (c)(4) require that the services arise out of or be reasonably related to the lawyer's practice in a jurisdiction in which the lawyer is admitted. A variety of factors evidence such a relationship. The lawyer's client may have been previously represented by the lawyer, or may be resident in or have substantial contacts with the jurisdiction in which the lawyer is admitted. The matter, although involving other jurisdictions, may have a significant connection with that jurisdiction. In other cases, significant aspects of the lawyer's work might be conducted in that jurisdiction or a significant aspect of the matter may involve the law of that jurisdiction. The necessary relationship might arise when the client's activities or the legal issues involve multiple jurisdictions, such as when the officers of a multinational corporation survey potential business sites and seek the services of their lawyer in assessing the relative merits of each. In addition, the services may draw on the lawyer's recognized expertise developed through the regular practice of law on behalf of clients in matters involving a particular body of federal, nationally-uniform, foreign, or international law. Lawyers desiring to provide pro bono legal services on a temporary basis in a jurisdiction that has been affected by a major disaster, but in which they are not otherwise authorized to practice law, as well as lawyers from the affected jurisdiction who seek to practice law temporarily in another jurisdiction, but in which they are not otherwise authorized to practice

law, should consult the Model Court Rule on Provision of Legal Services Following Determination of Major Disaster.

> **Editors' Note.** The ABA Model Court Rule on Provision of Legal Services Following Determination of Major Disaster referenced in Comment 14 is reprinted below in the Related Materials following Rule 5.5.

[15] Paragraph (d) identifies two circumstances in which a lawyer who is admitted to practice in another United States jurisdiction, and is not disbarred or suspended from practice in any jurisdiction, may establish an office or other systematic and continuous presence in this jurisdiction for the practice of law as well as provide legal services on a temporary basis. Except as provided in paragraphs (d)(1) and (d)(2), a lawyer who is admitted to practice law in another jurisdiction and who establishes an office or other systematic or continuous presence in this jurisdiction must become admitted to practice law generally in this jurisdiction.

[16] Paragraph (d)(1) applies to a lawyer who is employed by a client to provide legal services to the client or its organizational affiliates, i.e., entities that control, are controlled by, or are under common control with the employer. This paragraph does not authorize the provision of personal legal services to the employer's officers or employees. The paragraph applies to in-house corporate lawyers, government lawyers and others who are employed to render legal services to the employer. The lawyer's ability to represent the employer outside the jurisdiction in which the lawyer is licensed generally serves the interests of the employer and does not create an unreasonable risk to the client and others because the employer is well situated to assess the lawyer's qualifications and the quality of the lawyer's work.

[17] If an employed lawyer establishes an office or other systematic presence in this jurisdiction for the purpose of rendering legal services to the employer, the lawyer may be subject to registration or other requirements, including assessments for client protection funds and mandatory continuing legal education.

[18] Paragraph (d)(2) recognizes that a lawyer may provide legal services in a jurisdiction in which the lawyer is not licensed when authorized to do so by federal or other law, which includes statute, court rule, executive regulation or judicial precedent.

[19] A lawyer who practices law in this jurisdiction pursuant to paragraph (c) or (d) or otherwise is subject to the disciplinary authority of this jurisdiction. See Rule 8.5(a).

[20] In some circumstances, a lawyer who practices law in this jurisdiction pursuant to paragraph (c) or (d) may have to inform the client that the lawyer is not licensed to practice law in this jurisdiction. For example, that may be required when the representation occurs primarily in this jurisdiction and requires knowledge of the law of this jurisdiction. See Rule 1.4(b).

[21] Paragraphs (c) and (d) do not authorize communications advertising legal services to prospective clients in this jurisdiction by lawyers who are admitted to practice in other jurisdictions. Whether and how lawyers may communicate the availability of their services to prospective clients in this jurisdiction is governed by Rules 7.1 to 7.5.

Canon and Code Antecedents

ABA Canons of Professional Ethics: Canon 47 provided as follows:

> *47. Aiding the Unauthorized Practice of Law*
>
> No lawyer shall permit his professional services, or his name, to be used in aid of, or to make possible, the unauthorized practice of law by any lay agency, personal or corporate.

ABA Model Code of Professional Responsibility: Compare DR 3-101(A) and DR 3-101(B) (reprinted later in this volume).

Cross-References in Other Rules

None.

Legislative History of Model Rule 5.5

1980 Discussion Draft (then Rule 10.4(d) and (e)) provided that it was "professional misconduct" for a lawyer to "(d) practice law in a jurisdiction in violation of the regulation of the legal profession in that jurisdiction; or (e) aid a person who is not a member of the bar in the performance of activity that constitutes the practice of law."

1981 and ***1982 Drafts*** (then Rule 8.4(d) and (e)) were the same as adopted.

1983 Rule: From 1983 to 2002, Rule 5.5 provided, in full, as follows:

> *Rule 5.5 Unauthorized Practice of Law*
>
> A lawyer shall not:
>
> (a) practice law in a jurisdiction where doing so violates the regulation of the legal profession in that jurisdiction; or
>
> (b) assist a person who is not a member of the bar in the performance of activity that constitutes the unauthorized practice of law.

2002 Amendments: In 2002, by voice vote (meaning the vote was overwhelming), the ABA House of Delegates approved significant amendments to ABA Model Rule 5.5. These amendments were proposed by the ABA Commission on Multijurisdictional Practice, which was formed in 2000 to consider a host of issues pertaining to the practice of law by lawyers in jurisdictions where they are not admitted to practice, either permanently or pro hac vice. The amendments substantially changed the Rule. Paragraph (b) was entirely rewritten and paragraphs (c) and (d) were new. All comments were new except for portions of Comments 2 and 3. (The ABA Ethics 2000 Commission had also considered amendments to Rule 5.5 but eventually deferred to the Commission on Multijurisdictional Practice, which was studying the issues more comprehensively.)

The full report of the ABA Commission on Multijurisdictional Practice regarding Rule 5.5 and related multijurisdictional practice issues may be found at *http://www.americanbar.org/groups/professional_responsibility/committees_commissions/*

commission_on_multijurisditional_practice.html (scroll down to "Final Reports, as adopted August 12, 2002").

2007 Amendment: At its February 2007 Mid-Year Meeting, the ABA House of Delegates adopted the ABA Model Court Rule on Provision of Legal Services Following Determination of Major Disaster (often called the "Katrina Rule"). At the same time, the House of Delegates added the last sentence of Comment 14 to Rule 5.5 to reflect the adoption of the Model Court Rule. (The text of the ABA Model Court Rule is reprinted below in the Related Materials following Rule 5.5.)

Selected State Variations

Editors' Note. At least 44 jurisdictions have adopted multijurisdictional practice rules similar or identical to ABA Model Rule 5.5 as amended in 2002. Three states are still studying those amendments, and one state has recommended adoption of a rule similar to Rule 5.5. New York and Kansas have amended their rules since the ABA's adoption of Rule 5.5 in its current form but did not include the 2002 amendments to Rule 5.5. For up-to-date charts showing how all American jurisdictions have responded to the recommendations of the ABA Commission on Multijurisdictional Practice, go to *http://www.americanbar.org/groups/professional_responsibility/committees_commissions/commission_on_multijurisditional_practice.html.*

Alabama: Alabama Rule 5.5(b) is similar to ABA Model Rule 5.5(c), but Alabama limits the activities of out-of-state lawyers to services that

> (1) are performed on a temporary basis by a lawyer admitted and in good standing in another United States jurisdiction, including transactional, counseling, or other nonlitigation services that arise out of or are reasonably related to the lawyer's practice in a jurisdiction in which the lawyer is admitted to practice;
>
> (2) are in or reasonably related to a pending or potential arbitration, mediation, or other alternative dispute resolution proceeding held or to be held in this or in another jurisdiction; or
>
> (3) are performed by an attorney admitted as an authorized house counsel under Rule IX of the Rules Governing Admission to the Alabama State Bar and who is performing only those services defined in that rule.

Arizona augments ABA Model Rule 5.5 by adding these paragraphs:

> (e) Any attorney who engages in the authorized multijurisdictional practice of law in the State of Arizona under this rule must advise the lawyer's client that the lawyer is not admitted to practice in Arizona, and must obtain the client's informed consent to such representation.
>
> (f) Attorneys not admitted to practice in the State of Arizona, who are admitted to practice law in any other jurisdiction in the United States and who appear in any court of record or before any administrative hearing officer in the State of Arizona, must also comply with Rules of the Supreme Court of Arizona governing pro hac vice admission.
>
> (g) Any attorney who engages in the multijurisdictional practice of law in the State of Arizona, whether authorized in accordance with these Rules or not, shall be subject to the Rules of Professional Conduct and the Rules of the Supreme Court regarding attorney discipline in the State of Arizona.

In addition, Arizona's lead-in language to Rule 5.5(d) requires the lawyer who relies on that paragraph to have "registered pursuant to Rule 38(i) of these rules." That rule recognizes limited admission status for "an attorney who is employed within the State of Arizona as in-house counsel or a related position for a for-profit or a non-profit corporation, association, or other organizational entity, which can include its parents, subsidiaries and/or affiliates, the business of which is lawful and is other than the practice of law or the provision of legal services."

California: California Supreme Court Rules 9.45, 9.46, 9.47, and 9.48 give lawyers admitted in other American jurisdictions limited authority to provide legal services in California. The four rules deal with in-house counsel, legal services lawyers, lawyers involved in dispute resolution, and lawyers providing other legal services in California. The California rules are less expansive than ABA Model Rule 5.5(c). In addition, two other rules—9.43 and 9.44—provide authority for lawyers who enter California to participate in arbitrations and for lawyers admitted in foreign countries to register as foreign legal consultants.

Colorado: Rule 5.5(a)(1) provides that a lawyer shall not "practice law in this jurisdiction without a license to practice law issued by the Colorado Supreme Court unless specifically authorized by C.R.C.P. 220, C.R.C.P. 221, C.R.C.P. 221.1, C.R.C.P. 222 or federal or tribal law. . . ."

Colorado Rule of Civil Procedure 220, entitled "Out-of-State Attorney-Conditions of Practice," permits an out-of-state attorney who is not domiciled in Colorado and has not established a place for the regular practice of law in Colorado to "practice law in the state of Colorado except that an out-of-state attorney who wishes to appear in any state court of record must comply with [rules] concerning pro hac vice admission." Unlike ABA Model Rule 5.5, Colorado's Rule 220 does not restrict out-of-state lawyers to "temporary" law practice. However, Rule 220 permits an out-of-state lawyer to practice in Colorado only if the lawyer "has not established domicile in Colorado" and "has not established a place for the regular practice of law in Colorado from which such attorney holds himself or herself out to the public as practicing Colorado law or solicits or accepts Colorado clients." Rule 222 provides for admission of single-client lawyers (effectively a house counsel rule): "An attorney who is not licensed to practice law in the state of Colorado may be certified to act as counsel for a single-client upon application to and approval by the Colorado Supreme Court" under conditions and with limitations specified.

Connecticut adopts most of ABA Model Rule 5.5 verbatim, with some additions and modifications. Rule 5.5(a) adds that the "practice of law" in Connecticut "is defined in Practice Book Section 2-44A," a lengthy and detailed court rule. Rule 5.5(a) also adds that conduct described in Rules 5.5(c) and (d) in another jurisdiction "shall not be deemed the unauthorized practice of law for purposes of this paragraph (a)."

Most significantly, Connecticut Rule 5.5(c) extends temporary practice privileges only to a lawyer admitted in another United States jurisdiction "which accords similar privileges to Connecticut lawyers in its jurisdiction." Connecticut Rule 5.5(d)(1) applies only if the lawyer "is an authorized house counsel as provided in Practice Book Section 2-15A." Section 2-15A(c)(1) authorizes an in-house lawyer to engage in the following activities in Connecticut:

> (A) the giving of legal advice to the directors, officers, employees, and agents of the organization with respect to its business and affairs;

> (B) negotiating and documenting all matters for the organization; and
>
> (C) representation of the organization in its dealings with any administrative agency, tribunal or commission having jurisdiction; provided, however, authorized house counsel shall not be permitted to make appearances as counsel before any state or municipal administrative tribunal, agency, or commission, and shall not be permitted to make appearances in any court of this state, unless the attorney is specially admitted to appear in a case before such tribunal, agency, commission or court.

However, §2-15(A)(c)(4) provides that an authorized house counsel "shall not express or render a legal judgment or opinion to be relied upon by any third person or party other than legal opinions rendered in connection with commercial, financial or other business transactions to which the authorized house counsel's employer organization is a party and in which the legal opinions have been requested from the authorized house counsel by another party to the transaction."

A lawyer licensed in a "foreign jurisdiction" may qualify as an authorized house counsel.

Drawing on ABA Model Rule 8.5(a), Connecticut adds a new Rule 5.5(e), which provides: "A lawyer not admitted to practice in this jurisdiction and authorized by the provisions of this Rule to engage in providing legal services on a temporary basis in this jurisdiction is thereby subject to the disciplinary rules of this jurisdiction with respect to the activities in this jurisdiction." Finally, Connecticut adds an unusual new Rule 5.5(f), which provides:

> A lawyer desirous of obtaining the privileges set forth in subparagraphs (c)(3) or (4), (1) shall notify the Statewide Bar Counsel as to each separate matter prior to any such representation in Connecticut, (2) shall notify the Statewide Bar Counsel upon termination of each such representation in Connecticut, and (3) shall pay such fees as may be prescribed by the Judicial Branch.

Delaware has adopted Rule 5.5 and adds lawyers "admitted . . . in a foreign jurisdiction" to the authority granted in Rule 5.5(c) and 5.5(d). Delaware Supreme Court Rule 55.1 implements the authority of Rule 5.5(d)(1).

District of Columbia retains the pre-2002 version of ABA Model Rule 5.5. In addition, D.C. has developed one of the most detailed unauthorized practice rules in the country (D.C. Rule 49). The rule contains many exceptions to the general prohibition against unauthorized practice. These include exceptions for lawyers providing legal services to the United States while employed by the United States; lawyers appearing before a "special court, department or agency of the United States" where authorized by statute; employees of the District of Columbia and lawyers practicing before "a department or agency of the District of Columbia" pursuant to statutory authorization; employed lawyers where the employer "does not reasonably expect that it is receiving advice from a person" admitted in the District; lawyers who have moved to the District for a period of 360 days while applying for admission in the District and so long as they are under "the direct supervision of an enrolled, active member" of the D.C. Bar; up to five appearances per year for lawyers coming into the district for an ADR proceeding; up to five pro hac vice applications per year; and lawyers providing pro bono services under limited circumstances. Foreign lawyers are also exempt from the UPL prohibition for "incidental and temporary" work in the District.

Florida: Rule 5.5 is based on ABA Model Rule 5.5 but has many significant differences. For example, Florida Rule 5.5(c) permits temporary practice only by lawyers who have neither been disbarred from practice in any jurisdiction "nor disciplined or held in contempt in Florida by reason of misconduct committed while engaged in the practice of law permitted pursuant to this rule." Rule 5.5(b) adds a provision forbidding an outside lawyer to "(3) appear in court, before an administrative agency, or before any other tribunal unless authorized to do so by the court, administrative agency, or tribunal pursuant to the applicable rules of the court, administrative agency, or tribunal." Florida Rule 5.5(c)(3) adds that a lawyer may provide temporary legal services related to an alternative dispute resolution proceeding or non-litigation services "if the services are performed for a client who resides in or has an office in the lawyer's home state" or the services arise out of or are reasonably related to the lawyer's [home state] practice." The same language describes the scope of other (transactional) services. Florida also adds a subparagraph entitled "Authorized Temporary Practice by Lawyer Admitted in a Non-United States Jurisdiction," which largely parallels the portions of Rule 5.5 governing temporary practice by lawyers admitted in other U.S. jurisdictions.

Georgia: Rule 5.5 generally tracks ABA Model Rule 5.5, but Georgia distinguishes between a "Domestic Lawyer" (defined in Georgia's Terminology section as, essentially, a lawyer admitted elsewhere in the United States or its territories but not in Georgia) and a "Foreign Lawyer" (defined as "a person authorized to practice law by the duly constituted and authorized governmental body of any foreign nation" but not by Georgia). Georgia adds Rule 5.5(e) to permit temporary practice in Georgia by Foreign Lawyers on terms roughly equivalent to those that govern Domestic Lawyers, provided the foreign lawyer is "a member in good standing of a recognized legal profession in a foreign jurisdiction, the members of which are admitted to practice as lawyers or counselors at law or the equivalent and subject to effective regulation and discipline by a duly constituted professional body or a public authority."

Illinois: Illinois Rule 5.5 tracks ABA Model Rule 5.5. In addition, Supreme Court Rule 716, entitled "Limited Admission of House Counsel," permits an out-of-state lawyer to receive a limited license to perform legal services in Illinois when the lawyer is "employed in Illinois as house counsel exclusively for a single . . . legal entity (as well as any parent, subsidiary or affiliate thereof). . . ." The legal services must be limited to (a) advising the directors, officers, employees and agents of the employer regarding its business and affairs, and (b) negotiating, documenting and consummating transactions to which the employer is a party. An in-house lawyer may not appear as counsel before any court, administrative tribunal, agency or commission in Illinois unless (a) that body's rules authorize the appearance or (b) the body specially admits the lawyer for the particular matter. Lawyers licensed under the house counsel rule "shall not offer legal services or advice to the public or in any manner hold themselves out to be so engaged or authorized."

Illinois Supreme Court Rule 717, entitled "Limited Admission of Legal Service Program Lawyers," permits an out-of-state lawyer to receive a limited license to practice law in Illinois, for a maximum of 18 months, when the lawyer is "employed in Illinois for an organized legal service, public defender or law school clinical program providing legal assistance to indigent persons." A lawyer holding this limited license may perform legal services "solely on behalf of such employer and the indigent clients represented by such employer," and in felony cases the lawyer may participate in the proceedings only as "an assistant of a supervising member of the bar who shall be present and responsible for the conduct of the proceedings."

Kansas: Kansas retains the original 1983 version of ABA Model Rule 5.5 verbatim.

Louisiana adopts Model Rule 5.5(a)-(d) with minor modifications.

Maine: Maine adopts Model Rule 5.5.

Michigan: Effective January 1, 2011, Michigan adopts ABA Model Rule 5.5.

Minnesota: Rule 5.5(a) adds an "immunity clause" for Minnesota lawyers by providing that a Minnesota lawyer "does not violate this rule by conduct in another jurisdiction" that an out-of-state lawyer may do in Minnesota pursuant to Rules 5.5(c) and (d). Minnesota also deletes Rule 5.5(d)(1) (which governs legal services provided to a lawyer's employer).

Missouri renumbers paragraph (c)(4) as (c)(5) and adds as Rule 5.5(c)(4) permission for temporary legal services that "are provided to the lawyer's employer or its organizational affiliates and are not services for which the forum requires pro hac vice admission." In addition, Missouri Rule 5.5(d) omits paragraph (d)(2) and substantially adopts paragraph (d)(1) but requires that the lawyer have "obtained a limited license pursuant to Rule 8.105" (quoted below). Finally, Missouri adds a new Rule 5.5(e), which prohibits the practice of law by a lawyer who has been reported to the authorities for failure to comply with Missouri's Continuing Legal Education requirements.

Missouri Supreme Court Rule 8.105 provides:

> A lawyer admitted to the practice of law in another state or territory of the United States may receive a limited license to practice law in this state if the lawyer:
>
> (1) Is employed in Missouri as a lawyer exclusively for: a corporation, its subsidiaries or affiliates; an association; a business; or a governmental entity and the employer's lawful business consists of activities other than the practice of law or the provision of legal services;
>
> (2) Was conferred a professional degree in law (J.D. or L.L.B) by a law school that at the time of the lawyer's graduation was approved by the American Bar Association;
>
> (3) Has filed such application forms as prescribed by the board and paid the prescribed fee, which is non-refundable; and
>
> (4) Receives the approval of the board.

New Jersey: Effective, September 1, 2010, Rule 5.5(b) provides:

> A lawyer not admitted to the Bar of this State who is admitted to practice law before the highest court of any other state, territory of the United States, Puerto Rico, or the District of Columbia (hereinafter a United States jurisdiction) may engage in the lawful practice of law in New Jersey only if:
>
> (1) the lawyer is admitted to practice *pro hac vice* pursuant to R. 1:21-2 or is preparing for a proceeding in which the lawyer reasonably expects to be so admitted and is associated in that preparation with a lawyer admitted to practice in this jurisdiction; or
>
> (2) the lawyer is an in-house counsel and complies with R. 1:27-2; or
>
> (3) under any of the following circumstances:
>
> (i) the lawyer engages in the negotiation of the terms of a transaction in furtherance of the lawyer's representation on behalf of an existing client in a jurisdiction in which the lawyer is admitted to practice and the transac-

tion originates in or is otherwise related to a jurisdiction in which the lawyer is admitted to practice;

(ii) the lawyer engages in representation of a party to a dispute by participating in arbitration, mediation or other alternate or complementary dispute resolution program and the services arise out of or are reasonably related to the lawyer's practice in a jurisdiction in which the lawyer is admitted to practice and are not services for which pro hac vice admission pursuant to R. 1:21-2 is required;

(iii) the lawyer investigates, engages in discovery, interviews witnesses or deposes witnesses in this jurisdiction for a proceeding pending or anticipated to be instituted in a jurisdiction in which the lawyer is admitted to practice;

(iv) the lawyer associates in a matter with a lawyer admitted to the Bar of this State who shall be held responsible for the conduct of the out-of-State lawyer in the matter; or

(v) the lawyer practices under circumstances other than (i) through (iii) above, with respect to a matter where the practice activity arises directly out of the lawyer's representation on behalf of an existing client in a jurisdiction in which the lawyer is admitted to practice, provided that such practice in this jurisdiction is occasional and is undertaken only when the lawyer's disengagement would result in substantial inefficiency, impracticality or detriment to the client.

(c) A lawyer admitted to practice in another jurisdiction who acts in this jurisdiction pursuant to paragraph (b) above shall:

(1) be licensed and in good standing in all jurisdictions of admission and not be the subject of any pending disciplinary proceedings, nor a current or pending license suspension or disbarment;

(2) be subject to the Rules of Professional Conduct and the disciplinary authority of the Supreme Court of this jurisdiction;

(3) consent in writing on a form approved by the Supreme Court to the appointment of the Clerk of the Supreme Court as agent upon whom service of process may be made for all actions against the lawyer or the lawyer's firm that may arise out of the lawyer's participation in legal matters in this jurisdiction, except that a lawyer who acts in this jurisdiction pursuant to subparagraph (b)(3)(ii) or (b)(3)(iii) above shall be deemed to have consented to such appointment without completing the form;

(4) not hold himself or herself out as being admitted to practice in this jurisdiction;

(5) maintain a bona fide office in conformance with R. 1:21-1(a), except that, when admitted pro hac vice, the lawyer may maintain the bona fide office within the bona fide law office of the associated New Jersey attorney pursuant to R. 1:21-2(a)(1)(B); and

(6) except for a lawyer who acts in this jurisdiction pursuant to subparagraph (b)(3)(ii) or (b)(3)(iii) above, annually register with the New Jersey Lawyers' Fund for Client Protection and comply with R. 1:20-1(b) and (c), R. 1:28-2, and R. 1:28B-1(e) during the period of practice.

New Jersey Rule 1:27-2(a) defines in-house counsel for purposes of its Rule 5.5(b)(2) as follows:

> In-House Counsel is a lawyer who is employed in New Jersey for a corporation, a partnership, association, or other legal entity (taken together with its respective parents, subsidiaries, and affiliates) authorized to transact business in this State that is not itself engaged in the practice of law or the rendering of legal services outside such organization, whether for a fee or otherwise, and does not charge or

collect a fee for the representation or advice other than to entities comprising such organization.

New Jersey Rule 1:27-2(b)(iii) permits the in-house lawyer to provide legal services "solely for the identified employer and its constituents (employees, directors, officers, members, partners, shareholders) in respect of the same proceeding or claim as the employer, provided that the performance of such services is consistent with RPC 1.13 and RPC 1.7."

New Jersey Rule 1:21-1(e) provides:

> (e) *Legal Services Organizations.* Nonprofit organizations incorporated in this or any other state for the purpose of providing legal services to the poor or functioning as a public interest law firm, and other federally tax exempt legal services organizations or trusts . . . which provide legal services to a defined and limited class of clients, may practice law in their own names through staff attorneys who are members of the bar of the State of New Jersey, provided that: (1) the legal work serves the intended beneficiaries of the organizational purpose, (2) the staff attorney responsible for the matter signs all papers prepared by the organization, and (3) the relationship between staff attorney and client meets the attorney's professional responsibilities to the client and is not subject to interference, control, or direction by the organization's board or employees except for a supervising attorney who is a member of the New Jersey bar.

New Jersey Rule 1:21-1(a) requires that every attorney practicing law in New Jersey maintain "a bona fide office for the practice of law" in any United States jurisdiction, not necessarily New Jersey. The rule continues as follows:

> For the purpose of this section, a bona fide office is a place where clients are met, files are kept, the telephone is answered, mail is received and the attorney or a responsible person acting on the attorney's behalf can be reached in person and by telephone during normal business hours to answer questions posed by the courts, clients or adversaries and to ensure that competent advice from the attorney can be obtained within a reasonable period of time.

New Jersey Rule 1-21-10 substantially adopts the ABA's rule permitting temporary practice of out-of-state lawyers in the event of a "major disaster" ("the Katrina Rule").

New York: New York Rule 5.5 adopts the language of former DR 3-101 with minor variations. In 2011, New York adopted a heavily modified version of the ABA Model Rule on Registration of In-House Counsel, See 22 NYCRR Part 522.

North Carolina: Rule 5.5 does not use the word "temporary" as it appears in ABA Model Rule 5.5(c), but Rule 5.5(b)(1) forbids a "systematic and continuous presence" in the jurisdiction for the practice of law. North Carolina Rule 5.5(c)(2)(E) adds an additional category that permits a lawyer admitted in another jurisdiction to practice in North Carolina if "the lawyer is providing services limited to federal law, international law, the law of a foreign jurisdiction, or the law of the jurisdiction in which the lawyer is admitted to practice."

Ohio: Rule 5.5(c)(4) permits a lawyer to "provide legal services on a temporary basis" in Ohio if "the lawyer engages in negotiations, investigations, or other nonlitigation activities that arise out of or are reasonably related to the lawyer's practice in a jurisdiction in which the lawyer is admitted to practice." Otherwise, the Ohio rule is substantially the same as the Model Rule.

Oregon moves Rule 5.5(d)(1) (which permits temporary legal services that are provided to the lawyer's employer or its affiliates) to Rule 5.5(c)(5), meaning that these services may be performed only on a "temporary" basis.

Pennsylvania changes the lead-in language to Rule 5.5(c) to apply to a lawyer admitted in another United States jurisdiction "or in a foreign jurisdiction."

Tennessee: Effective January 1, 2011, Tennessee adopted the 2003 amendments to ABA Model Rule 5.5, except that Tennessee Rule 5.5(c)(3) and (c)(4) require that the work "arise out of or [be] reasonably related to the lawyer's representation of an existing client in a jurisdiction in which the lawyer is admitted to practice." In addition, Tennessee adds the following paragraphs:

> (e) A lawyer authorized to provide legal services in this jurisdiction pursuant to paragraph (d)(1) of this Rule may also provide pro bono legal services in this jurisdiction, provided that these services are offered through an established not-for-profit bar association, pro bono program or legal services program or through such organization(s) specifically authorized in this jurisdiction and provided that these are services for which the forum does not require pro hac vice admission.
>
> (f) A lawyer providing legal services in Tennessee pursuant to paragraph (c) or (d) shall advise the lawyer's client that the lawyer is not admitted to practice in Tennessee and shall obtain the client's informed consent to such representation.
>
> (g) A lawyer providing legal services in Tennessee pursuant to paragraph (c) or (d) shall be deemed to have submitted himself or herself to personal jurisdiction in Tennessee for claims arising out of the lawyer's actions in providing such services in this state.

Virginia Rule 5.5(d)(4) substantially tracks the temporary practice authority granted in ABA Rule 5.5(c) and extends that authority to "foreign lawyers," defined to include a "person authorized to practice law by the duly constituted and authorized governmental body of any State or Territory of the United States or the District of Columbia, or a foreign nation, but is neither licensed by the Supreme Court of Virginia or authorized under its rules to practice law generally in the Commonwealth of Virginia, nor disbarred or suspended from practice in any jurisdiction."

Washington: Rule 5.5(e) permits lawyers practicing in the state under the equivalent to Rule 5.5(d)(1) also to provide pro bono services to clients through a "qualified legal services provider."

Wisconsin: Wisconsin adopts ABA Rule 5.5 but adds a clause to the effect that the Clerk of the Wisconsin Supreme Court may accept service of process "for all actions against the lawyer or the lawyer's firm that may arise out of the lawyer's participation in legal matters in this jurisdiction."

Related Materials

ABA Commission on Ethics 20/20: In 2009, then–ABA President Carolyn Lamm announced the creation of the ABA Commission on Ethics 20/20, which is comprehensively reviewing the ABA Model Rules of Professional Conduct and other professional regulations in light of globalization and changes in technology. The Commission is examining a number of issues relating to multijurisdictional practice.

In June of 2010, the 20/20 Commission issued for public comment (i) a draft proposal to amend Rule 5.5 to make it possible for lawyers from a "foreign jurisdiction" (a defined term) to appear in court in the United States, and (ii) a draft proposal to add foreign lawyers to the ABA Model Rule for Registration of In-House Counsel and the ABA Model Rule for Pro Hac Vice Admission.

In May of 2011, the 20/20 Commission issued (i) a draft proposal concerning outsourcing, with the objective of offering lawyers clearer guidance on their ethical obligations when using U.S. or foreign lawyers and nonlawyers from outside the firm, and (ii) a revised draft proposal on limited practice authorization for inbound foreign lawyers that takes into account the comments received on the June 2010 draft proposal on that topic. The draft proposals relating to inbound foreign lawyers "recognize the reality that clients need and want lawyers from other countries to be able to represent them in the U.S. for limited purposes." Proposed changes to the ABA Model Rule for Registration of In-House Counsel and the ABA Model Rule for Pro Hac Vice Admission "are crafted to recognize this reality by providing opportunity for such limited practice authority with appropriate regulatory safeguards." The proposed amendments to Rule 5.5 account for these changes and merge the ABA Model Rule for Temporary Practice by Foreign Lawyers into Rule 5.5.

In September of 2011, the Commission proposed adding a new subparagraph (d)(3) to Rule 5.5, which would provide as follows:

> (d) A lawyer admitted in another United States jurisdiction, and not disbarred or suspended from practice in any jurisdiction, may provide legal services through an office or other systematic and continuous presence in this jurisdiction that . . .
>
> (3) are provided for no more than [365] days, but only if the lawyer submits an application for admission by motion, by examination, or as a foreign legal consultant within [60] days of first providing legal services in this jurisdiction, reasonably expects to fulfill all of this jurisdiction's requirements for that form of admission, notifies [disciplinary counsel and the licensing authority] in writing prior to initiating practice pursuant to this Rule that the lawyer is practicing pursuant to the authority in this paragraph, is associated with a lawyer who is admitted to practice in this jurisdiction, and has not previously been denied admission to practice in this jurisdiction or failed this jurisdiction's bar examination. If the lawyer seeks admission as a foreign legal consultant, the lawyer's services must be limited to those that may be provided in this jurisdiction by foreign legal consultants. Prior to admission by motion or examination, the lawyer may not appear before a tribunal in this jurisdiction that requires pro hac vice admission unless the lawyer is granted such admission. The authority in this paragraph shall terminate immediately if the lawyer's application for admission is denied prior to [365] days or if the lawyer fails to file the application for admission within [60] days of first providing legal services in this jurisdiction.

In addition, the Commission proposed to add a new Comment 19 to Rule 5.5 to explain Rule 5.5(d)(3). The Commission may present these proposals (or revised versions of them) to the ABA House of Delegates at its August 2012 Annual Meeting. For updates on the work of the ABA Ethics 20/20 Commission, visit *www.americanbar.org/Ethics2020.*

ABA Commission on Multidisciplinary Practice: Lawyers who provide legal services to the public through accounting firms or other professional service firms controlled by nonlawyers are violating Rule 5.5(a) (among other rules) by assisting nonlawyers in the unauthorized practice of law. In 1998, the ABA appointed a Commission on Multidisciplinary Practice (MDP Commission) to study and report on efforts by accounting firms and other nonlawyer professional service firms to provide legal services to the public. The MDP Commission sought to persuade the

ABA to liberalize the rules governing relationships between lawyers and nonlawyers, but the ABA House of Delegates overwhelmingly defeated the MDP Commission's proposals to amend the rules. For further information, see the entry on "ABA Commission on Multidisciplinary Practice" in the Related Materials after Rule 5.4 or visit the website of the ABA Commission on Multidisciplinary Practice at *http://www.americanbar.org/groups/professional_responsibility/commission_multidisciplinary_practice.html.*

ABA Commission on Multijurisdictional Practice: In 2000, the ABA created a Commission on Multijurisdictional Practice (the MJP Commission—not to be confused with the MDP Commission). Its mission was to research, study, and report on how ethics and bar admission rules applied to lawyers who practiced law both in jurisdictions where they were admitted and in jurisdictions where they were not admitted. Professor Bruce Green of Fordham was the MJP Commission's Reporter, and Professor Stephen Gillers (a co-author of this book) was a member of the Commission.

The MJP Commission held public hearings and solicited public comments to enable it to analyze the impact of ethics and bar admission rules on in-house counsel, transactional lawyers, litigators, and arbitrators, and on lawyers and law firms that maintain offices and practice in multiple state and federal jurisdictions. In June 2002, the MJP Commission submitted its Final Report to the ABA House of Delegates recommending that ABA Model Rules 5.5 and 8.5 be amended to their present form and that seven other measures be taken to facilitate and regulate the multijurisdictional practice of law. In 2002, the House of Delegates adopted all nine of the MJP Commission's recommendations. The MJP Commission's Final Report and other useful materials are available on the MJP Commission's website at *http://www.americanbar.org/groups/professional_responsibility/committees_commissions/commission_on_multijurisditional_practice.html.*

ABA Commission on Nonlawyer Practice: In 1992, the ABA appointed a 17-member Commission on Nonlawyer Practice, composed of both lawyers and nonlawyers, to examine all aspects of work done by nonlawyers. The Commission held hearings in nine cities, heard 337 witnesses, and reviewed more than 12,000 pages of statements, studies, statutes, reports, and scholarly articles. In 1995, the Commission issued a final report entitled "NonLawyer Activity in Law-Related Situations, which concluded that "[w]hen adequate protections for the public are in place, nonlawyers have important roles to perform in providing the public with access to justice." The Commission reported that as many as 70 percent of people with low and moderate incomes do not hire lawyers to meet their law-related needs, but instead go without any help, represent themselves, or turn to nonprofit agencies or nonlawyers. However, the ABA Board of Governors did not reappoint the Commission on Nonlawyer Practice, which therefore automatically ceased to exist on August 31, 1995. Moreover, the Commission's report was never transmitted to the ABA House of Delegates for approval. But the report is available online at *http://www.americanbar.org/content/dam/aba/migrated/2011_build/professional_responsibility/non_lawyer_activity.authcheckdam.pdf.*

ABA Formal Ethics Opinions: See ABA Formal Ethics Ops. 87-355 (1987), 01-423 (2001), and 08-451 (2008).

ABA Model Court Rule on Provision of Legal Services Following Determination of Major Disaster: In 2007, the ABA House of Delegates adopted a Model Court Rule on the Provision of Legal Services Following Determination of Major Disaster, commonly called the "Katrina Rule" (after Hurricane Katrina) or the "Major Disaster Rule" (to reflect that it applies after all types of disasters). Under the Major Disaster Rule lawyers from states that have suffered a major disaster may carry on their practices temporarily in other states if they have adopted the Major Disaster Rule, and lawyers in other states may perform pro bono work both in states that have suffered the disaster and in states to which persons displaced by the disaster have temporarily relocated. The Major Disaster Rule provides, in full, as follows:

(a) *Determination of existence of major disaster.* Solely for purposes of this Rule, this Court shall determine when an emergency affecting the justice system, as a result of a natural or other major disaster has occurred in:

(1) this jurisdiction and whether the emergency caused by the major disaster affects the entirety or only a part of this jurisdiction, or

(2) another jurisdiction but only after such a determination and its geographical scope have been made by the highest court of that jurisdiction. The authority to engage in the temporary practice of law in this jurisdiction pursuant to paragraph (c) shall extend only to lawyers who principally practice in the area of such other jurisdiction determined to have suffered a major disaster causing an emergency affecting the justice system and the provision of legal services.

(b) *Temporary practice in this jurisdiction following major disaster.* Following the determination of an emergency affecting the justice system in this jurisdiction pursuant to paragraph (a) of this Rule, or a determination that persons displaced by a major disaster in another jurisdiction and residing in this jurisdiction are in need of pro bono services and the assistance of lawyers from outside of this jurisdiction is required to help provide such assistance, a lawyer authorized to practice law in another United States jurisdiction, and not disbarred, suspended from practice or otherwise restricted from practice in any jurisdiction, may provide legal services in this jurisdiction on a temporary basis. Such legal services must be provided on a pro bono basis without compensation, expectation of compensation or other direct or indirect pecuniary gain to the lawyer. Such legal services shall be assigned and supervised through an established not-for-profit bar association, pro bono program or legal services program or through such organization(s) specifically designated by this Court.

(c) *Temporary practice in this jurisdiction following major disaster in another jurisdiction.* Following the determination of a major disaster in another United States jurisdiction, a lawyer who is authorized to practice law and who principally practices in that affected jurisdiction, and who is not disbarred, suspended from practice or otherwise restricted from practice in any jurisdiction, may provide legal services in this jurisdiction on a temporary basis. Those legal services must arise out of and be reasonably related to that lawyer's practice of law in the jurisdiction, or area of such other jurisdiction, where the major disaster occurred.

(d) *Duration of authority for temporary practice.* The authority to practice law in this jurisdiction granted by paragraph (b) of this Rule shall end when this Court determines that the conditions caused by the major disaster in this jurisdiction have ended except that a lawyer then representing clients in this jurisdiction pursuant to paragraph (b) is authorized to continue the provision of legal services for such time as is reasonably necessary to complete the representation, but the lawyer shall not thereafter accept new clients. The authority to practice law in this jurisdiction granted by paragraph (c) of this Rule shall end [60] days after this Court declares that the conditions caused by the major disaster in the affected jurisdiction have ended.

(e) *Court appearances.* The authority granted by this Rule does not include appearances in court except:

(1) pursuant to that court's pro hac vice admission rule and, if such authority is granted, any fees for such admission shall be waived; or

(2) if this Court, in any determination made under paragraph (a), grants blanket permission to appear in all or designated courts of this jurisdiction to lawyers providing legal services pursuant to paragraph (b). If such an authorization is included, any pro hac vice admission fees shall be waived.

(f) *Disciplinary authority and registration requirement.* Lawyers providing legal services in this jurisdiction pursuant to paragraphs (b) or (c) are subject to this Court's disciplinary authority and the Rules of Professional Conduct of this jurisdiction as provided in Rule 8.5 of the Rules of Professional Conduct. Lawyers providing legal services in this jurisdiction under paragraphs (b) or (c) shall, within 30 days from the commencement of the provision of legal services, file a registration statement with the Clerk of this Court. The registration statement shall be in a form prescribed by this Court. Any lawyer who provides legal services pursuant to this Rule shall not be considered to be engaged in the unlawful practice of law in this jurisdiction.

(g) *Notification to clients.* Lawyers authorized to practice law in another United States jurisdiction who provide legal services pursuant to this Rule shall inform clients in this jurisdiction of the jurisdiction in which they are authorized to practice law, any limits of that authorization, and that they are not authorized to practice law in this jurisdiction except as permitted by this Rule. They shall not state or imply to any person that they are otherwise authorized to practice law in this jurisdiction.

Professor Stephen Gillers (a co-author of this book) was instrumental in drafting the Major Disaster Rule. The revised report submitted to the ABA in support of the Model Court Rule on Provision of Legal Services Following Determination of Major Disaster is at *http://www.americanbar.org/content/dam/aba/migrated/cpr/Katrina.authcheckdam.pdf.* For more information about the ABA's pro bono projects and policies, visit *http://www.americanbar.org/groups/probono_public_service/policy.html.* A chart tracking state-by-state implementation of the Major Disaster Rule is available at *http://www.americanbar.org/content/dam/aba/migrated/cpr/clientpro/katrina_chart.authcheckdam.pdf.*

ABA Model Guidelines for the Utilization of Paralegal Services: Guidelines 2, 3, and 4 of the ABA Model Guidelines for the Utilization of Paralegal Services, which relate closely to Rule 5.5(a), provide as follows:

Guideline 2: Provided the lawyer maintains responsibility for the work product, a lawyer may delegate to a paralegal any task normally performed by the lawyer except those tasks proscribed to a nonlawyer by statute, court rule, [etc.].

Guideline 3: A lawyer may not delegate to a paralegal:

(a) Responsibility for establishing an attorney-client relationship.

(b) Responsibility for establishing the amount of a fee to be charged for a legal service.

(c) Responsibility for a legal opinion rendered to a client.

Guideline 4: A lawyer is responsible for taking reasonable measures to ensure that clients, courts, and other lawyers are aware that a paralegal, whose services are utilized by the lawyer in performing legal services, is not licensed to practice law.

The ABA Model Guidelines for the Utilization of Paralegal Services are available online at *http://apps.americanbar.org/legalservices/paralegals/downloads/modelguidelines.pdf.*

ABA Model Rule for the Licensing and Practice of Foreign Legal Consultants: In 1993, the ABA House of Delegates approved a Model Rule for the Licensing of

Foreign Legal Consultants. A registered Foreign Legal Consultant is an attorney or counselor at law (or equivalent) who is licensed in another country and has received a Certificate of Registration from a U.S. State as a Foreign Legal Consultant. The rule allowing Foreign Legal Consultants to practice was motivated by concern that foreign countries might not allow American lawyers to practice abroad if the United States does not allow foreign lawyers to practice in America. Section 1 of the Model Rule allows a state to license a "legal consultant" without requiring an examination if the applicant:

> (a) is, and for at least five years has been, a member in good standing of a recognized legal profession in a foreign country, the members of which are admitted to practice as lawyers or counselors at law or the equivalent and are subject to effective regulation and discipline by a duly constituted professional body or a public authority;
>
> (b) for at least five years preceding his or her application, has been a member in good standing of such legal profession and has been lawfully engaged in the practice of law in the foreign country or elsewhere substantially involving or relating to the rendering of advice or the provision of legal services concerning the law of the foreign country;
>
> (c) possesses the good moral character and general fitness requisite for a member of the bar of this jurisdiction; and
>
> (d) intends to practice as a foreign legal consultant in this jurisdiction and to maintain an office in this jurisdiction for that purpose.

Other sections of the Model Rule for the Licensing of Foreign Legal Consultants set forth application procedures, limit the scope of the practice by foreign legal consultants, and govern discipline, bar admission, and other subjects. Foreign legal consultants are not "admitted to the bar" in the U.S. licensing state but are "subject to professional discipline in the same manner and to the same extent as members of the bar" of the U.S. licensing jurisdiction. When we went to press in September 2011, about 31 states had adopted a foreign legal consultant rule, and various other states were actively considering a foreign legal consultant rule or were reviewing their existing temporary practice rules. To view the full text of the ABA Model Rule for the Licensing of Foreign Legal Consultants, visit *http://www.americanbar.org/content/dam/aba/migrated/cpr/mjp/FLC.authcheckdam.pdf.*

For a list of states that have adopted foreign legal consultant rules, visit *http://www.americanbar.org/groups/professional_responsibility/committees_commissions/commission_on_multijurisditional_practice.html* and click on "Quick Guide Chart on State Adoption of MJP Recommendations 8 and 9." For state-by-state citations and links to licensing rules for foreign legal consultants, visit the same website and scroll down to "Foreign Legal Consultants." For a state-by-state chart showing the number of foreign legal consultants admitted to practice each year in recent years, visit *www.ncbex.org/bar-admissions/stats,* click on a year, and search the downloaded PDF for "Foreign Legal Consultants."

ABA Model Rule on Admission by Motion: In 2002, by a vote of 257-150, the ABA adopted a Model Rule on Admission by Motion, which was part of the package proposed by the ABA Commission on Multijurisdictional Practice. This Model Rule describes the procedures by which lawyers admitted in one jurisdiction may gain admission in another jurisdiction without taking the other jurisdiction's bar examination. Currently, more than 40 jurisdictions have an admission by motion procedure, but many of those jurisdictions impose requirements that do not exist in the

Model Rule. At its February 2011 Mid-Year Meeting, pursuant to a proposal by the ABA Section on Legal Education and Admission to the Bar an the ABA Standing Committee on Client Protection, the ABA amended the Model Rule on Admission by Motion. As amended, it provides as follows (with February 2011 amendments indicated in legislative style):

ABA Model Rule on Admission by Motion

1. An applicant who meets the requirements of (a) through (g) of this Rule may, upon motion, be admitted to the practice of law in this jurisdiction.

The applicant shall:

(a) have been admitted to practice law in another state, territory, or the District of Columbia;

(b) hold a ~~first professional degree in law (~~J.D. or LL.B.~~)~~ degree from a law school approved by the Council of the Section of Legal Education and Admission to the Bar of the American Bar Association at the time the ~~graduate~~ applicant matriculated or graduated;

(c) have been primarily engaged in the active practice of law in one or more states, territories or the District of Columbia for five of the seven years immediately preceding the date upon which the application is filed;

(d) establish that the applicant is currently a member in good standing in all jurisdictions where admitted;

(e) establish that the applicant is not currently subject to lawyer discipline or the subject of a pending disciplinary matter in any ~~other~~ jurisdiction;

(f) establish that the applicant possesses the character and fitness to practice law in this jurisdiction; and

(g) designate the Clerk of the jurisdiction's highest court for service of process.

2. For the purposes of this rule, the "active practice of law" shall include the following activities, if performed in a jurisdiction in which the applicant is admitted and authorized to practice, or if performed in a jurisdiction that affirmatively permits such activity by a lawyer not admitted to practice in that jurisdiction; however, in no event shall any activities ~~listed under (2)(e) and (f)~~ that were performed in advance of bar admission in ~~the jurisdiction to which application is being made~~ some state, territory, or the District of Columbia be accepted toward the durational requirement:

(a) Representation of one or more clients in the practice of law;

(b) Service as a lawyer with a local, state, territorial or federal agency, including military service;

(c) Teaching law at a law school approved by the Council of the Section of Legal Education and Admissions to the Bar of the American Bar Association;

(d) Service as a judge in a federal, state, territorial or local court of record;

(e) Service as a judicial law clerk; or

(f) Service as ~~corporate counsel~~ provided to the lawyer's employer or its organizational affiliates.

3. For the purposes of this Rule, the active practice of law shall not include work that, as undertaken, constituted the unauthorized practice of law in the jurisdiction in which it was performed or in the jurisdiction in which the clients receiving the unauthorized services were located.

4. An applicant who has failed a bar examination administered in this jurisdiction within five years of the date of filing an application under this rule shall not be eligible for admission on motion.

In September 2011, the ABA Commission on Ethics 20/20 proposed further amendments to the Model Rule on Admission by Motion that would enable lawyers to qualify for admission by motion earlier in their careers (after three years of law practice instead of five). The current version of the Model Rule (as amended in February 2011) is online at *http://qa.americanbar.org/content/dam/aba/administrative/legal_education_and_admissions_to_the_bar/council_reports_and_resolutions/20110201_legaled_model_rule_on_aom.authcheckdam.pdf.*

ABA Model Rule on Pro Hac Vice Admission: Litigators who are not licensed to practice permanently in a certain jurisdiction may nevertheless seek admission "pro hac vice" to allow them to participate in a particular case in that jurisdiction. In 2002, to foster greater national uniformity, the ABA adopted a lengthy and detailed Model Rule on Pro Hac Vice Admission. The Model Rule on Pro Hac Vice Admission can be found at *http://www.americanbar.org/groups/professional_responsibility/committees_commissions/commission_on_multijurisdictional_practice.html.* For more information, see the entry below entitled "Pro Hac Vice Admission" in these Related Materials.

ABA Model Rule on Registration of In-House Counsel: In 2008, the ABA House of Delegates overwhelmingly approved, by voice vote, a Model Rule on Registration of In-House Counsel. The Model Rule provides as follows:

GENERAL PROVISIONS:

A. A lawyer admitted to the practice of law in another United States jurisdiction who has a continuous presence in this jurisdiction and is employed as a lawyer by an organization as permitted pursuant to Rule 5.5(d)(1) of the Model Rules of Professional Conduct, the business of which is lawful and consists of activities other than the practice of law or the provision of legal services, shall register as in-house counsel within [180] days of the commencement of employment as a lawyer or if currently so employed then within [180] days of the effective date of this rule, by submitting to the [registration authority] the following:

1. A completed application in the form prescribed by the [registration authority];
2. A fee in the amount determined by the [registration authority];
3. Documents proving admission to practice law and current good standing in all jurisdictions in which the lawyer is admitted to practice law; and
4. An affidavit from an officer, director, or general counsel of the employing entity attesting to the lawyer's employment by the entity and the capacity in which the lawyer is so employed, and stating that the employment conforms to the requirements of this rule.

SCOPE OF AUTHORITY OF REGISTERED LAWYER:

B. A lawyer registered under this section shall have the rights and privileges otherwise applicable to members of the bar of this jurisdiction with the following restrictions:

1. The registered lawyer is authorized to provide legal services to the entity client or its organizational affiliates, including entities that control, are controlled by, or are under common control with the employer, and for employees, officers and directors of such entities, but only on matters directly related to their work for the entity and only to the extent consistent with Rule 1.7 of the Model Rules of Professional Conduct [or equivalent provision in the jurisdiction]; and

2. The registered lawyer shall not:

a. Except as otherwise permitted by the rules of this jurisdiction, appear before a court or any other tribunal as defined in Rule 1.0(m) of the Model Rules of Professional Conduct [or jurisdictional equivalent], or

b. Offer or provide legal services or advice to any person other than as described in paragraph B.1., or hold himself or herself out as being authorized to practice law in this jurisdiction other than as described in paragraph B.1.

PRO BONO PRACTICE:

C. Notwithstanding the provisions of paragraph B above, a lawyer registered under this section is authorized to provide pro bono legal services through an established not-for-profit bar association, pro bono program or legal services program or through such organization(s) specifically authorized in this jurisdiction.

OBLIGATIONS:

D. A lawyer registered under this section shall:

1. Pay an annual fee in the amount of $________;

2. Fulfill the continuing legal education requirements that are required of active members of the bar in this jurisdiction;

3. Report within [_____] days to the jurisdiction the following:

a. Termination of the lawyer's employment as described in paragraph A.4.;

b. Whether or not public, any change in the lawyer's license status in another jurisdiction, including by the lawyer's resignation;

c. Whether or not public, any disciplinary charge, finding, or sanction concerning the lawyer by any disciplinary authority, court, or other tribunal in any jurisdiction.

LOCAL DISCIPLINE:

E. A registered lawyer under this section shall be subject to the [jurisdiction's Rules of Professional Conduct] and all other laws and rules governing lawyers admitted to the active practice of law in this jurisdiction. The [jurisdiction's disciplinary counsel] has and shall retain jurisdiction over the registered lawyer with respect to the conduct of the lawyer in this or another jurisdiction to the same extent as it has over lawyers generally admitted in this jurisdiction.

AUTOMATIC TERMINATION:

F. A registered lawyer's rights and privileges under this section automatically terminate when:

1. The lawyer's employment terminates;

2. The lawyer is suspended or disbarred from practice in any jurisdiction or any court or agency before which the lawyer is admitted; or

3. The lawyer fails to maintain active status in at least one jurisdiction

REINSTATEMENT:

G. A registered lawyer whose registration is terminated under paragraph F.1. above, may be reinstated within [xx] months of termination upon submission to the [registration authority] of the following:

1. An application for reinstatement in a form prescribed by the [registration authority];

2. A reinstatement fee in the amount of $_____;

3. An affidavit from the current employing entity as prescribed in paragraph A.4.

SANCTIONS:

H. A lawyer under this rule who fails to register shall be:

1. Subject to professional discipline in this jurisdiction;

2. Ineligible for admission on motion in this jurisdiction;

3. Referred by the [registration authority] to the [jurisdiction's bar admission authority]; and

4. Referred by the [registration authority] to the disciplinary authority of the jurisdictions of licensure.

The report submitted in 2006 in support of the Model Rule on Registration of In-House Counsel provided, in part, as follows:*

The Council of the Section of Legal Education and Admissions to the Bar . . . approved the Model Rule for Registration of House Counsel (Rule) for use by jurisdictions adopting or intending to adopt amended Model Rule 5.5(d) of the Model Rules of Professional Conduct. Rule 5.5(d) now excludes from the definition of unauthorized practice of law the provision of legal services by in-house counsel admitted in one jurisdiction and practicing in another jurisdiction, when the lawyer is providing legal services solely to the lawyer's employer. Rule 5.5(d) states:

A lawyer admitted in another United States jurisdiction, and not disbarred or suspended from practice in any jurisdiction, may provide legal services in this jurisdiction that:

(1) are provided to the lawyer's employer or its organizational affiliates and are not services for which the forum requires pro hac vice admission.

Rule 5.5(d) applies to lawyers who are in-house corporate lawyers, government lawyers, and others who are employed to render legal services to the employer. The provision assumes that the in-house lawyer can establish an office or other "systematic presence" in the jurisdiction and forgo local licensure without unreasonable risk to the client or others because the employer is able to assess the lawyer's qualifications and the quality of the lawyer's work.

Model Rule 5.5, Comment [17], states that lawyers who establish an office or continuous presence in the state "may be subject to registration or other requirements, including assessments for client protection funds and mandatory continuing legal education." In an effort to create a regulatory model useful to states that might wish to follow the registration approach, the Bar Admission Committee drafted, and the Council of the Section has approved for submission to the House, this Rule.

* Committee Reports do not represent official policy of the ABA. They are for information only, and the opinions are those of the authors of the report.

PURPOSE OF REGISTRATION RULE

The Council recognizes that in addition to client security fund assessments and continuing legal education requirements, registration would make an in-house counsel's status known to the public. . . . Furthermore, a lawyer who practices pursuant to this rule is subject to the disciplinary authority of the local jurisdiction. (*See* Rules 5.5 and 8.5, ABA *Model Rules of Professional Conduct.*)

The Registration Rule would provide a mechanism for jurisdictions to identify and monitor in-house counsel who are practicing in the jurisdiction. The Rule also provides sanctions for those who fail to register. . . .

During the floor debate in the House of Delegates, the House amended the proposed rule to add the phrase "a continuous presence" in Paragraph A to define the limits of the rule. The House also rejected a proposed amendment to prohibit in-house lawyers working outside their home states from handling pro bono cases unless they were supervised by a volunteer lawyer program. The Model Rule for Registration of In-House Counsel is at *http://www.americanbar.org/content/dam/aba/migrated/cpr/mjp/in_house_registration.authcheckdam.pdf.* A chart describing each state's in-house counsel regulations is available at *http://www.americanbar.org/content/dam/aba/migrated/cpr/mjp/in_house_comp.authcheckdam.pdf.*

ABA Model Rule for Temporary Practice by Foreign Lawyers: In 2002, the ABA adopted a Model Rule for Temporary Practice by Foreign Lawyers, which was part of the package proposed by the ABA Commission on Multijurisdictional Practice. As of our press deadline in September 2011, six U.S. jurisdictions (Delaware, Florida, Georgia, New Hampshire, Pennsylvania, and Virginia) had adopted a rule explicitly referring to foreign lawyer temporary practice, and three other jurisdictions (D.C. Illinois, and North Carolina) appeared to permit foreign lawyer temporary practice through other rules.

The ABA Model Rule for Temporary Practice by Foreign Lawyers and the report explaining the rule and recommending its adoption are available online at *http://www.americanbar.org/groups/professional_responsibility/committees_commissions/commission_on_multijurisditional_practice.html* (scroll down to "Final Reports, as adopted August 12, 2002," and click on "Report 201J (Temporary Practice by Foreign Lawyers)"). The Model Rule for Temporary Practice by Foreign Lawyers provides as follows:

(a) A lawyer who is admitted only in a non-United States jurisdiction shall not, except as authorized by this Rule or other law, establish an office or other systematic and continuous presence in this jurisdiction for the practice of law, or hold out to the public or otherwise represent that the lawyer is admitted to practice law in this jurisdiction. Such a lawyer does not engage in the unauthorized practice of law in this jurisdiction when on a temporary basis the lawyer performs services in this jurisdiction that:

(1) are undertaken in association with a lawyer who is admitted to practice in this jurisdiction and who actively participates in the matter;

(2) are in or reasonably related to a pending or potential proceeding before a tribunal held or to be held in a jurisdiction outside the United States if the lawyer, or a person the lawyer is assisting, is authorized by law or by order of the tribunal to appear in such proceeding or reasonably expects to be so authorized;

(3) are in or reasonably related to a pending or potential arbitration, mediation or other alternative dispute resolution proceeding held or to be held in this or another jurisdiction, if the services arise out of or are reasonably related to the lawyer's practice in a jurisdiction in which the lawyer is admitted to practice;

(4) are not within paragraphs (2) or (3) and

(i) are performed for a client who resides or has an office in a jurisdiction in which the lawyer is authorized to practice to the extent of that authorization; or

(ii) arise out of or are reasonably related to a matter that has a substantial connection to a jurisdiction in which the lawyer is authorized to practice to the extent of that authorization; or

(5) are governed primarily by international law or the law of a non-United States jurisdiction.

(b) For purposes of this grant of authority, the lawyer must be a member in good standing of a recognized legal profession in a foreign jurisdiction, the members of which are admitted to practice as lawyers or counselors at law or the equivalent and subject to effective regulation and discipline by a duly constituted professional body or a public authority.

ABA Model Rules for Advisory Opinions on Unauthorized Practice of Law: In 1984, the ABA House of Delegates adopted Model Rules for Advisory Opinions on Unauthorized Practice of Law, which set forth model procedures for committees and courts to follow in issuing opinions on unauthorized practice. These rules, according to their Preamble, recognize "the need to prevent harm to the public from the unauthorized practice of law and to make public a clear and timely understanding of what is the unauthorized practice of law." The Model Rules for Advisory Opinions on Unauthorized Practice of Law are available at *http://www.americanbar.org/content/dam/aba/migrated/cpr/clientpro/upl_op_rules.authcheckdam.pdf.*

ABA Resolution on Unauthorized Practice: In 1999, by a vote of 305-118, the ABA House of Delegates passed a resolution urging every jurisdiction to "establish and implement effective procedures for the discovery and investigation of any apparent violation of its laws prohibiting the unauthorized practice of law and to pursue active enforcement of those laws." The resolution also required the ABA to "establish and support a mechanism for identifying and reporting to state, local, and territorial bar associations and designated authorities instances of persons or organizations engaging in the unauthorized practice of law in more than one jurisdiction." The report submitted in support of the resolution noted that statutes prohibiting the unauthorized practice of law (which are in force in virtually every state) have not been enforced aggressively or effectively. The report added: "It is becoming more apparent that unlicensed and unsupervised persons are peddling legal services to the public and that adequate protection to the public is not being provided."

ABA Task Force on the Model Definition of the Practice of Law: In August 2002, the ABA House of Delegates created a seven-member Task Force on the Model Definition of the Practice of Law. The Task Force worked with the ABA Standing Committee on Client Protection to develop a model definition of the practice of law. In September 2002, the task force sought public comments on the following preliminary draft definition:

Definition of the Practice of Law

(a) The practice of law shall be performed only by those authorized by the highest court of this jurisdiction.

(b) Definitions:

(1) The "practice of law" is the application of legal principles and judgment with regard to the circumstances or objectives of a person that require the knowledge and skill of a person trained in the law.

(2) "Person" includes the plural as well as the singular and denotes an individual or any legal or commercial entity.

(3) "Adjudicative body" includes a court, a mediator, an arbitrator or a legislative body, administrative agency or other body acting in an adjudicative capacity. A legislative body, administrative agency or other body acts in an adjudicative capacity when a neutral official, after the presentation of evidence or legal argument by a party or parties, will render a binding legal judgment directly affecting a party's interests in a particular matter.

(c) A person is presumed to be practicing law when engaging in any of the following conduct on behalf of another:

(1) Giving advice or counsel to persons as to their legal rights or responsibilities or to those of others;

(2) Selecting, drafting, or completing legal documents or agreements that affect the legal rights of a person;

(3) Representing a person before an adjudicative body, including, but not limited to, preparing or filing documents or conducting discovery; or

(4) Negotiating legal rights or responsibilities on behalf of a person.

(d) Exceptions and exclusions: Whether or not they constitute the practice of law, the following are permitted:

(1) Practicing law authorized by a limited license to practice;

(2) Pro se representation;

(3) Serving as a mediator, arbitrator, conciliator or facilitator; and

(4) Providing services under the supervision of a lawyer in compliance with the Rules of Professional Conduct.

(e) Any person engaged in the practice of law shall be held to the same standard of care and duty of loyalty to the client independent of whether the person is authorized to practice law in this jurisdiction. With regard to the exceptions and exclusions listed in paragraph (d), if the person providing the services is a nonlawyer, the person shall disclose that fact in writing. In the case of an entity engaged in the practice of law, the liability of the entity is unlimited and the liability of its constituent members is limited to those persons participating in such conduct and those persons who had knowledge of the conduct and failed to take remedial action immediately upon discovery of same.

(f) If a person who is not authorized to practice law is engaged in the practice of law, that person shall be subject to the civil and criminal penalties of this jurisdiction.

The Task Force received many comments on the proposed definition. Of particular interest was a letter dated December 20, 2002, jointly sent by the Federal Trade Commission (FTC) and the U.S. Department of Justice's Antitrust Division. The joint letter harshly criticized the draft proposal, saying it was so broad that it could prevent nonlawyers from offering many services they already offer, leading to higher prices for legal services and fewer choices for consumers. For example, the joint letter said, the proposed definition could be interpreted to prohibit real estate agents from explaining smoke detector ordinances and termite inspection laws, to prohibit tax preparers from interpreting tax code provisions, and to prohibit software makers from selling software to write wills and other legal documents.

In April 2003, after holding a hearing on the proposed definition, the Task Force decided not to attempt a single uniform nationwide definition of the practice of law, but instead recommended that every jurisdiction adopt its own definition of the practice of law. The ABA acted on this recommendation by adopting the following resolution in August 2003:

RESOLVED, That the American Bar Association recommends that every state and territory adopt a definition of the practice of law.

FURTHER RESOLVED, That each state's and territory's definition should include the basic premise that the practice of law is the application of legal principles and judgment to the circumstances or objectives of another person or entity.

FURTHER RESOLVED, That each state and territory should determine who may provide services that are included within the state's or territory's definition of the practice of law and under what circumstances, based upon the potential harm and benefit to the public. The determination should include consideration of minimum qualifications, competence and accountability.

Admission to the Bar by Motion: Nearly every U.S. jurisdiction allows some form of admission to the bar "by motion" or "on motion," meaning admission without taking and passing the state's bar examination. However, a majority of jurisdictions allow admission by motion only to lawyers admitted in states that would allow reciprocal rights of admission on motion to lawyers admitted in the first jurisdiction. Oregon's Supreme Court Rule 15.05, entitled 15.05, "Admission of Attorneys Licensed to Practice Law in other Jurisdictions," is a good example of admission by motion restricted to applicants from states that grant reciprocity. As amended effective January 1, 2010, that rule provides as follows:

(1) Attorneys who have taken and passed the bar examination in another qualifying jurisdiction, who are active members of the bar in that qualifying jurisdiction, and who have lawfully engaged in the active, substantial and continuous practice of law for no less than five of the seven years immediately preceding their application for admission under this rule may be admitted to the practice of law in Oregon without having to take and pass the Oregon bar examination, subject to the requirements of this rule.

(2) For purposes of this rule, a "qualifying jurisdiction" means any other United States jurisdiction which allows attorneys licensed in Oregon to become regular members of the bar in that jurisdiction without passage of that jurisdiction's bar examination. . . .

Admission by motion rules typically require applicants to demonstrate good moral character, pay substantial fees, and meet various other requirements. For a chart summarizing the rules and policies for admission on motion in every U.S. jurisdiction, visit *http://www.americanbar.org/content/dam/aba/migrated/cpr/mjp/admission_motion_comp.authcheckdam.pdf.*

European Community Law on Multijurisdictional Practice: The member states of the European Community (EC) are much more permissive of cross-border practice than are American jurisdictions, even though the members of the EC are different nations, not just different states within a single nation. The EC's approach to multijurisdictional practice is explained in depth in an online interview with Professor Laurel Terry of Penn State Dickinson School of Law, which we reprinted in the Special Section of our 2002 edition (see pp. 1052-1056). For more background information about the EC, see Laurel S. Terry, *A Case Study of the Hybrid Model for Facilitating Cross-Border Legal Practice: The Agreement Between the American Bar Association and the Brussels Bars,* 21 Fordham Intl. L.J. 1382 (1998); Florence R. Liu, *The Establishment of a Cross-Border Legal Practice in the European Union,* 20 B.C. Intl. & Comp. L. Rev. 369 (1997); and Diane M. Venezia, *EU Lawyer's Right to Practice Throughout the European Union,* 3 Cardozo J. Intl. & Comp. L. 427 (1995).

Foreign Countries and U.S. Lawyers: As would be expected, foreign countries have widely varying policies regarding the activities of U.S. lawyers. For example, the Bombay High Court in India ruled in December of 2009, in *Lawyers Collective v. Bar Council of India,* that "practising non-litigious matters amounts to 'practising the profession of law' under section 29 of the Advocates Act, 1961," India's unauthorized practice of law statute. The effect was to prohibit all U.S. lawyers (and other foreign lawyers) from practicing law in India. In Israel, however, U.S. lawyers are permitted to establish an office to advise Israeli clients about U.S. law (but not Israeli law). For materials summarizing the policies of various countries regarding law practice by U.S. lawyers, visit *www.personal.psu.edu/faculty/l/s/lst3/publications%20by%20topic.htm#1.*

Foreign-Educated Bar Applicants: Lawyers who received their legal education outside the United States are sometimes eligible to take the bar exam without attending law school in the United States. The rules on the eligibility of foreign-educated lawyers to sit for the bar exam vary from state to state. From 2000 through 2005, the number of foreign-educated lawyers sitting for a bar exam somewhere in the United States increased by 28 percent, to 3,571. In 2005, all but 234 of the foreign-educated lawyers who took a U.S. bar exam sat for the bar exam in New York, which has relatively liberal policies on eligibility to take the bar exam. In contrast, none of the foreign-educated lawyers took the bar exam in 2005 in Florida, which requires a foreign-educated lawyer to have 10 years of experience in a U.S. jurisdiction before sitting for Florida's bar exam.

General Agreement on Trade in Services (GATS): In 1993, the so-called Uruguay Round of international trade negotiations produced a revised multilateral trade system based upon the 1994 document known as the Agreement Establishing the World Trade Organization (WTO). The General Agreement on Trade in Services, referred to as "GATS," is an "Annex" to the Agreement Establishing the World Trade Organization and is thus binding on countries that belong to the WTO, including the United States. The GATS is the first multilateral trade agreement that applies to services, including legal services.

The current round of GATS negotiations is commonly called the "Doha Round." WTO member countries are negotiating more liberal access to the service markets covered by the GATS. The Office of the United States Trade Representative (USTR), a Cabinet-level position, conducts the GATS negotiations on behalf of all service sectors in the United States, including legal services. The USTR is seeking to make it easier for U.S. lawyers to practice law in foreign countries. But any agreement regarding the ability of American lawyers to offer legal services abroad will also make it easier for foreign (non-U.S.) lawyers to offer legal services in the United States. The GATS agreements could also affect American legal education standards, bar admissions criteria, licensing requirements, rules of professional conduct, disciplinary enforcement rules, and other regulations of the legal profession that have historically been adopted and enforced in the United States by states in U.S. jurisdictions.

In December 2005, WTO members agreed that they would try to conclude the GATS negotiations by the end of 2006. That did not happen, however, and when we went to press in September 2011 the Doha Round was stalled and perhaps near collapse. On July 26, 2011, WTO members acknowledged that a package of issues selected from the Doha Round agenda for the December 2011 Ministerial

Conference "is not taking shape." The members accepted Director-General Pascal Lamy's call to focus on how to proceed afterwards in order to end the "paralysis" in the organization's ability to negotiate. For a wealth of material on GATS and its potential impact on the U.S. legal profession, see the website about GATS maintained by Professor Laurel Terry of Penn State Dickinson School of Law at *www.personal.psu.edu/faculty/l/s/lst3/gats3.htm.*

In-House Lawyers: A lawyer who regularly practices law in a jurisdiction in which the lawyer is not licensed to practice is generally engaged in the unauthorized practice of law. However, the majority of U.S. jurisdictions have statutes or court rules that permit an in-house lawyer who is licensed and in good standing in at least one U.S. jurisdiction to provide legal services to an employer (such as a corporation) even though the lawyer is not licensed to practice law in the jurisdiction where the services are performed, provided the in-house lawyer registers with the appropriate authority in that jurisdiction. Other states have issued court decisions, policy statements, or ethics opinions stating that in-house lawyers who serve only their employer are not engaged in unauthorized practice despite lack of admission to the bar in the state where the services are performed. In 2008, the ABA responded to the proliferation of state in-house registration rules by approving the ABA Model Rule on Registration of In-House Counsel (see entry above in this section). A chart describing each state's rules and regulations regarding in-house counsel is available at *http://www.americanbar.org/content/dam/aba/migrated/cpr/mjp/in_house_comp.authcheckdam.pdf.*

IRS Regulations: In the regulations governing practice before the Internal Revenue Service, 31 C.F.R. §10.3(c) is in essence the opposite of an unauthorized practice law statute—it expressly authorizes certain categories of nonlawyers to appear before the IRS as "enrolled agents" on the same terms (or nearly the same terms) as attorneys. According to §10.4(a), the IRS may grant "enrolled agent" status to an applicant "who demonstrates special competence in tax matters by written examination . . . and who has not engaged in any conduct that would justify the censure, suspension, or disbarment. . . ." Under §10.4(c), former IRS employees may become enrolled agents without examination. However, §10.24(a) provides that a practitioner may not knowingly, directly or indirectly, "[a]ccept assistance from or assist any person who is under disbarment or suspension from practice before the Internal Revenue Service if the assistance relates to a matter or matters constituting practice before the Internal Revenue Service." Moreover, §10.32 provides that "[n]othing in the regulations in this part shall be construed as authorizing persons not members of the bar to practice law."

Model Rules of Professional Conduct for Federal Lawyers: Rule 5.5(a) provides that "[e]xcept as authorized by law," a federal lawyer shall not practice in a jurisdiction where doing so violates the regulation of the legal profession in that jurisdiction.

National Association of Legal Assistants: The National Association of Legal Assistants, an organization comprised of more than 18,000 paralegals, publishes the NALA Code of Ethics and Professional Responsibility. Canon 3 of the NALA Code, which complements Rule 5.5(a) of the ABA Model Rules of Professional Conduct, provides:

> A legal assistant must not: (a) engage in, encourage, or contribute to any act which could constitute the unauthorized practice of law; and (b) establish attorney-client relationships, set fees, give legal opinions or advice or represent a client before

a court or agency unless so authorized by that court or agency; and (c) engage in conduct or take any action which would assist or involve the attorney in a violation of professional ethics or give the appearance of professional impropriety.

NALA also publishes the NALA Model Standards and Guidelines for Utilization of Paralegals, which is more detailed than the NALA Code of Ethics. Guideline 3 provides that legal assistants may "perform services for an attorney in the representation of a client" if the following conditions are met:

1. The services performed by the legal assistant do not require the exercise of independent professional legal judgment;
2. The attorney maintains a direct relationship with the client and maintains control of all client matters;
3. The attorney supervises the legal assistant;
4. The attorney remains professionally responsible for all work on behalf of the client, including any actions taken or not taken by the legal assistant in connection therewith; and
5. The services performed supplement, merge with and become the attorney's work product.

Guideline 5 generally permits a legal assistant to perform "any function delegated by an attorney, including but not limited to the following":

1. Conduct client interviews and maintain general contact with the client after the establishment of the attorney-client relationship, so long as the client is aware of the status and function of the legal assistant, and the client contact is under the supervision of the attorney.
2. Locate and interview witnesses, so long as the witnesses are aware of the status and function of the legal assistant.
3. Conduct investigations and statistical and documentary research for review by the attorney.
4. Conduct legal research for review by the attorney.
5. Draft legal documents for review by the attorney.
6. Draft correspondence and pleadings for review by and signature of the attorney.
7. Summarize depositions, interrogatories, and testimony for review by the attorney.
8. Attend executions of wills, real estate closings, depositions, court or administrative hearings and trials with the attorney.
9. Author and sign letters provided the legal assistant's status is clearly indicated and the correspondence does not contain independent legal opinions or legal advice.

The Guidelines are available with Comments at *www.nala.org* (hover over "About Paralegals," then scroll down to "Model Standards and Guidelines for Utilization of Legal Assistants").

National Federation of Paralegal Associations: The National Federation of Paralegal Associations, Inc. (NFPA), founded in 1974, is a nonprofit federation comprised of more than 50 member associations representing over 11,000 individual members. The NFPA's "core purpose" is to "advance the paralegal profession." In 1993, the NFPA adopted a Model Code of Ethics and Professional Responsibility. Section 1 of the Code contains Rules and Ethical Considerations governing topics such as competence, confidentiality, and conflicts. Section 2 establishes a Disciplinary Committee and disciplinary procedures for paralegals who violate the Code. The Code is available at *www.paralegals.org* (click on the top menu on

"Positions & Issues," then on the drop-down menu click on either "Model Code of Ethics" or "Ethics").

Patent "Agents" and Patent "Attorneys": The United States Patent and Trademark Office (USPTO) registers people who are attorneys at law (referred to as "patent attorneys") and people who are not attorneys at law (referred to as "patent agents") to practice before the USPTO. Under USPTO rules, both patent attorneys and patent agents may prepare patent applications and prosecute patents in the USPTO. Patent agents, however, cannot conduct patent litigation in the courts or perform services that a state considers to be the practice of law (other than preparing patent applications and prosecuting patents). For example, a patent agent could not draw up a contract relating to a patent, such as an assignment or a license, if the state in which the patent agent resides considers drafting contracts to be the practice of law. For more information, see *www.uspto.gov.*

Pro Hac Vice Admission: In all states, courts have authority to admit out-of-state lawyers to practice before the court "pro hac vice," meaning for a particular matter. Most states allow pro hac vice admission only to lawyers from other U.S. jurisdictions, but at least 13 states also extend pro hac vice admission to foreign (non-U.S.) lawyers. A typical example of a pro hac vice admission provision is Michigan Court Rule 8.126 (Temporary Admission to the Bar), which begins as follows:

> (A) *Temporary Admission.* Any person who is licensed to practice law in another state . . . or in any foreign country, and who is not disbarred or suspended in any jurisdiction, and who is eligible to practice in at least one jurisdiction, may be permitted to appear and practice in a specific case in a court or before an administrative tribunal or agency in this state when associated with and on motion of an active member of the State Bar of Michigan who appears of record in the case. An out-of-state attorney may appear and practice under this rule in no more than five cases in a 365-day period. Permission to appear and practice is within the discretion of the court or administrative tribunal or agency, and may be revoked at any time for misconduct. . . .

A more detailed and complex pro hac vice rule is District of Columbia Rule 49(c)(7)(ii). In addition to prohibiting a lawyer from applying for admission pro hac vice in more than five cases pending in D.C. courts per calendar year absent "exceptional cause," the D.C. rule requires each applicant for admission pro hac vice to file a sworn statement meeting the following criteria:

> . . . (3) certifying that there are no disciplinary complaints pending against the applicant for violation of the rules of any jurisdiction or court, or describing all pending complaints, (4) certifying that the applicant has not been suspended or disbarred for disciplinary reasons or resigned with charges pending in any jurisdiction or court, or describing the circumstances of all suspensions, disbarments, or resignations, (5) certifying that the person has not had an application for admission to the D.C. Bar denied, or describing the circumstances of all such denials, (6) agreeing promptly to notify the Court if, during the course of the proceeding, the person is suspended or disbarred for disciplinary reasons or resigns with charges pending in any jurisdiction or court, . . . (8) certifying that the applicant does not practice or hold out to practice law in the District of Columbia or that the applicant qualifies under an identified exception in Rule 49(c), . . . (10) explaining the reasons for the application, (11) acknowledging the power and jurisdiction of the courts of the District of Columbia over the applicant's professional conduct in or related to the proceeding, and (12) agreeing to be bound by the District of Columbia Court of Appeals Rules of Professional Conduct in the matter, if the applicant is admitted pro hac vice.

In California, Utah, and perhaps in other jurisdictions, a lawyer may also be admitted pro hac vice in arbitration proceedings—see California Code of Civil Procedure §1282.4.

More than 25 states charge a fee to out-of-state attorneys who appear pro hac vice in state courts. (Federal courts do not charge any similar fee.) In Texas, for example, Government Code §82.0361 (entitled "Nonresident Attorney Fee") requires an out-of-state lawyer to pay the Texas Board of Law Examiners a $250 fee for each case in which the attorney is asking to participate pro hac vice. In Arizona, Supreme Court Rule 38(a) requires applicants for admission pro hac vice to pay a non-refundable application fee equal to the current annual dues paid by active members of the State Bar of Arizona (currently $460). For a state-by-state chart of pro hac vice admission rules in every U.S. jurisdiction, see *http://www.americanbar.org/content/dam/aba/migrated/cpr/mjp/prohac_admin_rules.authcheckdam.pdf.*

Restatement of the Law Governing Lawyers: See Restatement §§2-4 in our chapter on the Restatement later in this volume.

Retired Attorneys: Some jurisdictions permit retired attorneys to represent pro bono clients or legal services clients under certain circumstances. For example, in 2009, New Mexico adopted Supreme Court Rule 15-301.2 (Legal Services Provider Limited Law License for Emeritus and Non-Admitted Attorneys). The rule permits retired attorneys in good standing who have at least 20 years of practice experience to apply for a limited law license that will authorize them to "represent legal services clients through a qualified legal services provider."

Tax Consequences of Multijurisdictional Practice: Lawyers who take advantage of temporary practice rules similar to ABA Model Rule 5.5(b) may be required to comply with tax laws and pay income taxes based on their work in states where they are not licensed. For example, West Virginia State Tax Department Publication TSD-423 (revised August 2007), entitled "Nonresident Lawyers—Tax Reporting and Filing Requirements," advises out-of-state lawyers about many tax obligations arising out of law practice in West Virginia. To learn more, visit *www.state.wv.us/taxrev/taxdoc/tsd423.pdf.*

Tax Court Rules of Practice: The Tax Court Rules of Practice (which are completely separate from IRS regulations) permit qualified nonlawyers to practice before the Tax Court. For example, Tax Court Rule 200(a)(3) allows nonlawyers to practice before the Tax Court if they pay a fee and pass a written examination (and, in the court's discretion, an oral examination as well).

Unauthorized Practice Laws: Most states have enacted statutes making it a crime to engage in the unauthorized practice of law. California Business and Professions Code §6126 (Unauthorized Practice or Advertising as Misdemeanor) is typical:

> Any person advertising or holding himself or herself out as practicing or entitled to practice law or otherwise practicing law who is not an active member of the State Bar, or otherwise authorized pursuant to statute or court rule to practice law in this state at the time of doing so, is guilty of a misdemeanor punishable by up to one year in a county jail or by a fine of up to one thousand dollars ($1,000) or by both. . . .

A similar but harsher statute is found in Florida, where the legislature amended Florida's unauthorized practice statute in 2004 to make the unauthorized practice of law a felony. The amended statute, F.S.A. §454.23 (entitled "Penalties"), provides as follows:

> Any person not licensed or otherwise authorized to practice law in this state who practices law in this state or holds himself or herself out to the public as qualified to practice law in this state, or who willfully pretends to be, or willfully takes or uses any name, title, addition, or description implying that he or she is qualified, or recognized by law as qualified, to practice law in this state, commits a felony of the third degree. . . .

(A felony in the third degree in Florida is punishable by a term of imprisonment not exceeding five years and a fine not exceeding $5,000.)

A more detailed definition of the unauthorized practice of law is contained in Georgia Statutes Annotated §15-19-50 (Practice of Law Defined), which provides:

> The practice of law in this state is defined as: (1) Representing litigants in court and preparing pleadings and other papers incident to any action or special proceedings in any court or other judicial body; (2) Conveyancing; (3) The preparation of legal instruments of all kinds whereby a legal right is secured; (4) The rendering of opinions as to the validity or invalidity of titles to real or personal property; (5) The giving of any legal advice; and (6) Any action taken for others in any matter connected with the law.

Regarding electronic media, some have claimed that providing legal advice through computer programs, disks, and the Internet constitutes the unauthorized practice of law. In 1999, the Texas Legislature responded to these claims by enacting Texas Government Code §81.101(c) to govern websites, CD-ROMs, and other electronic media. The statute provides:

> In this chapter, the "practice of law" does not include the design, creation, publication, distribution, display or sale, including publication, distribution, display, or sale by means of an Internet web site, of written materials, books, forms, computer software, or similar products if the products clearly and conspicuously state that the products are not a substitute for the advice of an attorney. . . .

For a highly detailed court rule governing unauthorized practice, see D.C. Court of Appeals Rule 49, available at *www.dcappeals.gov/dccourts/docs/DCCA_Rules.pdf.*

In many states, the state bar has authority to enforce unauthorized practice laws. In Florida, for example, Rule 1-8.2 of the Rules Regulating the Florida Bar provides: "The board of governors shall act as an arm of the Supreme Court of Florida for the purpose of seeking to prohibit the unlicensed practice of law by investigating, prosecuting, and reporting to this court and to appropriate authorities incidents involving the unlicensed practice of law in accordance with chapter 10." (Chapter 10 of the Rules Regulating the Florida Bar sets forth detailed procedures for investigating and prosecuting unauthorized practice cases.)

Some jurisdictions issue advisory opinions as to whether a specific activity constitutes the unauthorized practice of law. For example, in 2010 the Virginia Supreme Court approved the State Bar's petition to amend Virginia's Rules of Court (Part Six, ¶10) to establish detailed procedures for lawyers to request unauthorized practice of law opinions. However, mindful of the possible antitrust implications of enforcing unauthorized practice laws, §10-2(E) of the amended rule provides that whenever a bar committee concludes that the conduct in question constitutes or would constitute the unauthorized practice of law, "the Bar shall seek comment from the Attorney General's office analyzing any restraint on competition that might result from the promulgation and implementation of the opinion."

Rule 5.6 Restrictions on Right to Practice

5.4(a)(1) **A lawyer shall not participate in offering or making:**

(a) a partnership, shareholders, operating, employment, or other similar type of agreement that restricts the right of a lawyer to practice after termination of the relationship, except an agreement concerning benefits upon retirement; or

1.17 **(b) an agreement in which a restriction on the lawyer's right to practice is part of the settlement of a client controversy.**

COMMENT

[1] An agreement restricting the right of lawyers to practice after leaving a firm not only limits their professional autonomy but also limits the freedom of clients to choose a lawyer. Paragraph (a) prohibits such agreements except for restrictions incident to provisions concerning retirement benefits for service with the firm.

[2] Paragraph (b) prohibits a lawyer from agreeing not to represent other persons in connection with settling a claim on behalf of a client.

[3] This Rule does not apply to prohibit restrictions that may be included in the terms of the sale of a law practice pursuant to Rule 1.17.

Canon and Code Antecedents

ABA Canons of Professional Ethics: No comparable Canon.

ABA Model Code of Professional Responsibility: Compare DR 2-108 (reprinted later in this volume).

Cross-References in Other Rules

Rule 1.2, Comment 8: "All agreements concerning a lawyer's representation of a client must accord with the Rules of Professional Conduct and other law. See, e.g., **Rules** 1.1, 1.8 and **5.6.**"

Rule 1.17, Comment 1 provides that "when a lawyer or an entire firm ceases to practice, or ceases to practice in an area of law, and other lawyers or firms take over the representation, the selling lawyer or firm may obtain compensation for the reasonable value of the practice as may withdrawing partners of law firms. See **Rules** 5.4 and **5.6.**"

Legislative History of Model Rule 5.6

1980 and ***1981 Drafts*** had no equivalent to Rule 5.6.

1982 Draft was adopted.

1983 Rule: As originally adopted in 1983, ABA Model Rule 5.6 provided:

A lawyer shall not participate in offering or making:

(a) a partnership or employment agreement that restricts the rights of a lawyer to practice after termination of the relationship, except an agreement concerning benefits upon retirement; or

(b) [Same as 2002 version of Rule 5.6(b).]

2002 Amendments: The ABA Ethics 2000 Commission recommended replacing the phrase "controversy between private parties" with the phrase "client controversy" at the end of Rule 5.6(b), thus making clear that the Rule applies to settlements between private parties and the government, not just to settlements between private parties. The proposal also expanded the phrase "partnership or employment agreement" in Rule 5.6(a) to include a "partnership, shareholders, operating, employment, or other similar type of agreement." In 2002, the ABA House of Delegates adopted without change the Ethics 2000 proposal to amend Rule 5.6 and its Comment. The changes to the Comment were minor (replacing "partners or associates" with "lawyers" in Comment 1).

Selected State Variations

Arkansas: Rule 5.6(a) deletes references to a shareholder, operating, or other similar type of agreement, but adds a reference to "an agreement pursuant to the provisions of Rule 1.17" (which governs the sale of a law practice).

California: Rule 1-500 is essentially the same as Rule 5.6, but adds references to certain statutory exceptions.

Florida: Without amending the text of Rule 5.6, Florida added the following new paragraph to the Comment to its version of Rule 5.6:

> This rule is not a per se prohibition against severance agreements between lawyers and law firms. Severance agreements containing reasonable and fair compensation provisions designed to avoid disputes required by time-consuming quantum meruit analysis are not prohibited by this rule. Severance agreements, on the other hand, that contain punitive clauses, the effect of which are to restrict competition or encroach upon a client's inherent right to select counsel, are prohibited. . . .

In addition, a new Florida Rule 4-5.8 prohibits a lawyer who is leaving a law firm from unilaterally notifying clients of the anticipated departure, or soliciting representation of the firm's clients, unless bona fide negotiations between the lawyer and the law firm to draft a joint communication have failed. Similarly, a lawyer in a law firm undergoing dissolution must not unilaterally contact the firm's clients unless bona fide negotiations among authorized members of the firm have failed to produce an agreement on a method for notifying clients of the dissolution. If there is no agreement on notice to client, the rule provides: "When a joint response has not been successfully negotiated, unilateral contact by individual members or the law firm shall give notice to clients that the lawyer is leaving the law firm and provide options to the clients to choose to remain a client of the law firm, to choose representation by the departing lawyer, or to choose representation by other lawyers or law firms."

Georgia has adopted the pre-2002 version of ABA Model Rule 5.6 and its Comment essentially verbatim. (Georgia's previous DR 2-108(B) permitted a lawyer to agree in a settlement not to "accept any other representation arising out of a transaction or event embraced in the subject matter of the controversy or suit thus settled.")

Illinois adopts the ABA Model Rule.

New York: New York follows Model Rule 5.6 except New York adds that the rule "does not prohibit restrictions that may be included in the terms of the sale of a law practice pursuant to Rule 1.17."

Oregon: Rule 5.6(b) applies to a "direct or indirect" restriction on a lawyer's right to practice.

Pennsylvania: Rule 5.6(a) permits an agreement that restricts the rights of a lawyer to practice as part of "an agreement for the sale of a law practice consistent with Rule 1.17."

Texas: Rule 5.06(b) adds that "as part of the settlement of a disciplinary proceeding against a lawyer an agreement may be made placing restrictions on the right of that lawyer to practice."

Virginia: Rule 5.6(b) forbids an agreement in which a restriction of the lawyer's right to practice is part of the settlement of a controversy, "except where such a restriction is approved by a tribunal or a governmental entity."

Related Materials

ABA Formal Ethics Opinions: See ABA Formal Ethics Ops. 93-371 (1993), 94-381 (1994), 95-394 (1995), 00-417 (2000), and 06-444 (2006).

Arbitration Provisions: To reduce the expense of litigating disputes that often arise when partners leave their law firms, many partnership agreements contain arbitration agreements. These arbitration provisions are encouraged by legal malpractice insurers. In Pennsylvania, for example, Bertholon-Rowland Agencies has sometimes given a 5 percent "quality of management credit" on professional liability policies that contain the following paragraph:

> Any controversy or claim arising out of or relating to the dissolution of the partnership, or relating to a partner's withdrawal from the partnership, shall be settled through mediation conducted in accordance with the then-existing rules of the Pennsylvania Bar Association Lawyer Dispute Resolution Program (the "PBA Program"). Any issues that are not resolved through such mediation shall be submitted for arbitration conducted in accordance with the then-existing rules of the PBA Program. . . .

Non-Compete Provisions: A non-compete clause is a restrictive covenant that bars an ex-employee from going to work for a competitor. Outside of the legal profession, non-compete clauses in employment and partnership agreements are common, and are generally valid if they are reasonable in temporal duration, geographic scope, and the nature of the restricted activities. In the legal profession, however, non-compete clauses for lawyers (whether partners, associates, or of counsel) are barred in most jurisdictions by Rule 5.6(a).

Nevertheless, some law firm partnership agreements provide greater benefits or pay greater severance payments to departing lawyers who do not compete with the firm than to those who do compete. In a variation, severance payments to departing partners may be based on a sliding scale so that partners who earn more than a specified amount after they leave (such as those who join competing law firms) will receive less than partners who earn less than the specified amount (such as partners who leave to enter government service or to take a public interest job). Such provisions have met with mixed results when challenged.

No-Sue Promises: For an argument that Rule 5.6(b) should be amended, see Stephen Gillers & Richard W. Painter, *Free the Lawyers: A Proposal to Permit No-Sue Promises in Settlement Agreements,* 18 Geo. J. Legal Ethics 291 (2005).

Restatement of the Law Governing Lawyers: See Restatement §§9 and 13 in our chapter on the Restatement later in this volume.

Rule 5.7 Responsibilities Regarding Law-Related Services

(a) A lawyer shall be subject to the Rules of Professional Conduct with respect to the provision of law-related services, as defined in paragraph (b), if the law-related services are provided:

(1) by the lawyer in circumstances that are not distinct from the lawyer's provision of legal services to clients; or

(2) in other circumstances by an entity controlled by the lawyer individually or with others if the lawyer fails to take reasonable measures to assure that a person obtaining the law-related services knows that the services are not legal services and that the protections of the client-lawyer relationship do not exist.

(b) The term "law-related services" denotes services that might reasonably be performed in conjunction with and in substance are related to the provision of legal services, and that are not prohibited as unauthorized practice of law when provided by a nonlawyer.

COMMENT

[1] When a lawyer performs law-related services or controls an organization that does so, there exists the potential for ethical problems. Principal among these is the possibility that the person for whom the law-related services are performed fails to understand that the services may not carry with them the protections normally afforded as part of the client-lawyer relationship. The recipient of the law-related services may expect, for example, that the protection of client confidences, prohibitions against representation of persons with conflicting interests, and obligations of a lawyer to maintain professional independence apply to the provision of law-related services when that may not be the case.

[2] Rule 5.7 applies to the provision of law-related services by a lawyer even when the lawyer does not provide any legal services to the person for whom the law-related services are performed and whether the law-related services are performed through a law firm or a separate entity. The Rule identifies the circumstances in which all of the Rules of Professional Conduct apply to the provision of law-related services. Even when those circumstances do not exist, however, the conduct of a lawyer involved in the provision of law-related services is subject to those Rules that apply generally to lawyer conduct, regardless of whether the conduct involves the provision of legal services. See, e.g., Rule 8.4.

[3] When law-related services are provided by a lawyer under circumstances that are not distinct from the lawyer's provision of legal services to clients, the lawyer in providing the law-related services must adhere to the requirements of the Rules of Professional Conduct as provided in paragraph (a)(1). Even when the law-related and legal services are provided in circumstances that are distinct from each other, for example through separate entities or different support staff within the law firm, the Rules of Professional Conduct apply to the lawyer as provided in paragraph (a)(2) unless the lawyer takes reasonable measures to assure that the recipient of the law-related services knows that the services are not legal services and that the protections of the client-lawyer relationship do not apply.

[4] Law-related services also may be provided through an entity that is distinct from that through which the lawyer provides legal services. If the lawyer individually or with others has control of such an entity's operations, the Rule requires the lawyer to take reasonable measures to assure that each person using the services of the entity knows that the services provided by the entity are not legal services and that the Rules of Professional Conduct that relate to the client-lawyer relationship do not apply. A lawyer's control of an entity extends to the ability to direct its operation. Whether a lawyer has such control will depend upon the circumstances of the particular case.

[5] When a client-lawyer relationship exists with a person who is referred by a lawyer to a separate law-related service entity controlled by the lawyer, individually or with others, the lawyer must comply with Rule 1.8(a).

[6] In taking the reasonable measures referred to in paragraph (a)(2) to assure that a person using law-related services understands the practical effect or significance of the inapplicability of the Rules of Professional Conduct, the lawyer should communicate to the person receiving the law-related services, in a manner sufficient to assure that the person understands the significance of the fact, that the relationship of the person to the business entity will not be a client-lawyer relationship. The communication should be made before entering into an agreement for provision of or providing law-related services, and preferably should be in writing.

[7] The burden is upon the lawyer to show that the lawyer has taken reasonable measures under the circumstances to communicate the desired understanding. For instance, a sophisticated user of law-related services, such as a publicly held corporation, may require a lesser explanation than someone unaccustomed to making distinctions between legal services and law-related services, such as an individual seeking tax advice from a lawyer-accountant or investigative services in connection with a lawsuit.

[8] Regardless of the sophistication of potential recipients of law-related services, a lawyer should take special care to keep separate the provision of law-related and legal services in order to minimize the risk that the recipient will assume that the law-related services are legal services. The risk of such confusion is especially acute when the lawyer renders both types of services with respect to the same matter. Under some circumstances the legal and law-related services may be so closely entwined that they cannot be distinguished from each other, and the requirement of disclosure and consultation imposed by paragraph (a)(2) of the Rule cannot be met. In such a case a lawyer will be responsible for assuring that both the lawyer's conduct and, to the extent required by Rule 5.3, that of nonlawyer employees in the distinct entity that the lawyer controls complies in all respects with the Rules of Professional Conduct.

A.\

[9] A broad range of economic and other interests of clients may be served by lawyers' engaging in the delivery of law-related services. Examples of law-related services include providing title insurance, financial planning, accounting, trust services, real estate counseling, legislative lobbying, economic analysis, social work, psychological counseling, tax preparation, and patent, medical or environmental consulting.

[10] When a lawyer is obliged to accord the recipients of such services the protections of those Rules that apply to the client-lawyer relationship, the lawyer must take special care to heed the proscriptions of the Rules addressing conflict of interest (Rules 1.7 through 1.11, especially Rules 1.7(a)(2) and 1.8(a), (b) and (f)), and to scrupulously adhere to the requirements of Rule 1.6 relating to disclosure of confidential information. The promotion of the law-related services must also in all respects comply with Rules 7.1 through 7.3, dealing with advertising and solicitation. In that regard, lawyers should take special care to identify the obligations that may be imposed as a result of a jurisdiction's decisional law.

[11] When the full protections of all of the Rules of Professional Conduct do not apply to the provision of law-related services, principles of law external to the Rules, for example, the law of principal and agent, govern the legal duties owed to those receiving the services. Those other legal principles may establish a different degree of protection for the recipient with respect to confidentiality of information, conflicts of interest and permissible business relationships with clients. See also Rule 8.4 (Misconduct).

Canon and Code Antecedents

ABA Canons of Professional Ethics: No comparable Canon.

ABA Model Code of Professional Responsibility: No comparable Disciplinary Rule.

Cross-References in Other Rules

Rule 1.8, Comment 1: "The Rule applies to lawyers engaged in the sale of goods or services related to the practice of law. . . . See **Rule 5.7**."

Legislative History of Model Rule 5.7

1980, 1981, and ***1982 Drafts:*** None of the Kutak Commission drafts had any provision equivalent to Rule 5.7.

1983 Rule: As originally adopted in 1983, the ABA Model Rules had no equivalent to Rule 5.7.

1991 Adoption: Rule 5.7 was originally added to the Model Rules in 1991. The rule adopted in 1991 was proposed by the ABA's Litigation Section, which had been studying ancillary businesses for several years. Before the House of Delegates voted on the Litigation Section's proposal, it rejected by voice vote an alternative version of Rule 5.7 proposed by the ABA's Standing Committee on Ethics and Professional

Responsibility. After rejecting the Standing Committee's proposal, the House of Delegates voted 197-186 to adopt the Litigation Section's version of Rule 5.7. The original version of Rule 5.7 provided as follows:

Provision of Ancillary Services

(a) A lawyer shall not practice law in a law firm which owns a controlling interest in, or operates, an entity which provides non-legal services which are ancillary to the practice of law, or otherwise provides such ancillary non-legal services, except as provided in paragraph (b).

(b) A lawyer may practice law in a law firm which provides non-legal services which are ancillary to the practice of law if:

(1) The ancillary services are provided solely to clients of the law firm and are incidental to, in connection with and concurrent to, the provision of legal services by the law firm to such clients;

(2) Such ancillary services are provided solely by employees of the law firm itself and not by a subsidiary or other affiliate of the law firm;

(3) The law firm makes appropriate disclosure in writing to its clients; and

(4) The law firm does not hold itself out as engaging in any non-legal activities except in conjunction with the provision of legal services, as provided in this rule.

(c) One or more lawyers who engage in the practice of law in a law firm shall neither own a controlling interest in, nor operate, an entity which provides non-legal services which are ancillary to the practice of law, nor otherwise provide such ancillary non-legal services, except that their firms may provide such services as provided in paragraph (b).

(d) Two or more lawyers who engage in the practice of law in separate law firms shall neither own a controlling interest in, nor operate, an entity which provides non-legal services which are ancillary to the practice of law, nor otherwise provide such ancillary non-legal services.

The Comment to the 1991 version of Rule 5.7 was nineteen paragraphs, making it one of the longest comments in the Model Rules. The following excerpt from the original Comment explains the origin and purpose of the 1991 version of Rule 5.7:

Excerpt from Comment to 1991 Version of Rule 5.7

[1] For many years, lawyers have provided to their clients non-legal services which are ancillary to the practice of law. Such services included title insurance, trust services and patent consulting. In most instances, these ancillary non-legal services were provided to law firm clients in connection with, and concurrent to, the provision of legal services by the lawyer or law firm. The provision of such services afforded benefits to clients, including making available a greater range of services from one source and maintaining technical expertise in various fields within a law firm. However, the provision of both legal and ancillary non-legal services raises ethical concerns, including conflicts of interest, confusion on the part of clients and possible loss (or inapplicability) of the attorney-client privilege, which may not have been addressed adequately by the other Model Rules of Professional Conduct.

[2] Eventually, law firms began to form affiliates, largely staffed by non-lawyers, to provide ancillary non-legal services to both clients and customers who were not clients for legal services. In addition to exacerbating the ethical problems of conflicts of interest, confusion and threats to confidentiality, the large-scale movement of law firms

into ancillary non-legal businesses raised serious professionalism concerns, including compromising lawyers' independent judgment, the loss of the bar's right to self-regulation and the provision of legal services by entities controlled by non-lawyers.

[3] Rule 5.7 addresses both the ethical and professionalism concerns implicated by the provision of ancillary non-legal services by lawyers and law firms. It preserves the ability of lawyers to provide additional services to their clients and maintain within the law firm a broad range of technical expertise. However, Rule 5.7 restricts the ability of law firms to provide ancillary non-legal services through affiliates to non-client customers and clients alike, the rendition of which raises serious ethical and professionalism concerns.

1992 Deletion: The 1991 version of Rule 5.7 was deleted from the ABA Model Rules in its entirety at the ABA's 1992 Annual Meeting, just one year after its adoption. The report urging deletion of the rule was jointly submitted by the Illinois State Bar Association, the ABA Standing Committee on Lawyers Title Guaranty Funds, and six ABA sections. The House of Delegates voted 190-183 to delete the rule. Rule 5.7 was the first rule ever to be deleted from the Model Rules. From August 1992 (when the original version of Rule 5.7 was deleted) until February 1994 (when a new version was adopted), the Model Rules did not contain any version of Rule 5.7.

1994 Version: In 1994, by a margin of 237-183, the ABA House of Delegates adopted a new and radically different version of Rule 5.7. The new version was the work of a Special Committee on Ancillary Business Services that was appointed by the Chair of the House of Delegates after the ABA voted in 1992 to delete the original version of Rule 5.7. The Special Committee recommended that the ABA adopt the 1994 version of Rule 5.7. The House of Delegates did so, and the 1994 version stayed in effect until 2002. Here are excerpts from the Special Committee's Report in support of the 1994 version of Rule 5.7:

*Excerpt from Report of the Special House of Delegates Committee on Ancillary Business in Support of the 1994 Version of Rule 5.7**

[T]he Committee is satisfied that law-related services are being provided wherever lawyers practice, that law-related services are often provided by separate entities, and that there has been no reported disciplinary infraction or malpractice claim resulting from the provision of law-related services. . . . Several respondents expressed concern about potential confusion on the part of recipients of law-related services regarding the nature of their relationship with the lawyer, although no instances of actual confusion were reported to the Committee. Responses also indicated a profusion of law-related services, some traditional in the jurisdiction, and others of more recent origin. These include not only the provision of trust services, title insurance, accounting and escrow services, but also the furnishing of insurance investigation, psychological counseling, lobbying, arbitration and mediation, registered corporate agent representation, and environmental consulting services. The Committee believes that the list of law-related services is not only long, but growing longer.

The Committee concluded that law-related services should not be prohibited. Instead, the Committee proposes adoption of a rule that specifically treats lawyers' dealings with recipients of law-related services. The proposed rule supplements existing Rules that apply to such relationships. . . .

* Committee Reports do not represent official policy of the ABA. They are for information only, and the opinions are those of the author of the report.

> Examples of law-related services are provided in the Comment to the proposed Rule, but these are by no means exhaustive. The Committee found that the types of law-related services are virtually unlimited, and that new types continue to be developed. Accordingly, the definition is intended to encompass a wide range of services whether or not the services are of a type currently being provided. . . .
>
> Even when the recipient of law-related services is not a client of the lawyer, the law of principal and agent affords the recipient significant protections against disclosure or use of confidence, conflicts of interest, and self-dealing. The Committee notes, in this context, that it found no justification for affording recipients of law-related services through separate entities greater protection than that to which they would otherwise be entitled solely because lawyers control the separate entity.

2002 Amendments: In its May 2001 report to the ABA House of Delegates, the ABA Ethics 2000 Commission proposed to amend the Comment, but not the text, of Rule 5.7. Before the House of Delegates acted on the proposal, however, the Commission revised its proposal to broaden the text of Rule 5.7(a)(2) so that it would apply to law-related services provided directly by a lawyer or the lawyer's law firm. In 2002, the ABA House of Delegates adopted without change a revised ABA Ethics 2000 Commission proposal to amend Rule 5.7 and its Comment. The amendments deleted references to a "separate" entity in the 1994 version of Rule 5.7(a)(2), inserted the phrase "and whether the law-related services are performed through a law firm or a separate entity" in Comment 2, and added the second sentence of Comment 3.

Selected State Variations

Arkansas retains the 1994 version of Rule 5.7(a)(2), which applies if law-related services are provided by a "separate" entity controlled by the lawyer and if the lawyer fails to take reasonable measures to assure that a person obtaining the law-related services knows that the services "of the separate entity" are not legal services.

California has no equivalent provision in its Rules of Professional Conduct.

Connecticut omits ABA Model Rule 5.7.

Georgia adopts the pre-2002 version of ABA Model Rule 5.7 and its Comment essentially verbatim.

Illinois has not adopted Rule 5.7.

New York: New York incorporates the substance of Model Rule 5.7 in a longer version of the rule that, among other things, gives lawyers a duty to ensure that nonlawyers at an affiliated entity who are providing nonlegal services do not give legal advice or compromise client confidential information. The New York rule also creates a presumption when nonlegal services are "distinct" from legal services provided by the law firm, or when a separate entity affiliated with the law firm is providing nonlegal services. The presumption in either situation is as follows:

> It will be presumed that the person receiving nonlegal services believes the services to be the subject of a client-lawyer relationship unless the lawyer or law firm has advised the person receiving the services in writing that the services are not legal services and that the protection of a client-lawyer relationship does not exist with respect to the nonlegal services, or if the interest of the lawyer or law firm in the entity providing nonlegal services is de minimis.

Ohio: Rule 5.7(a) generally tracks ABA Model Rule 5.7(a), with minor changes, and Ohio Rule 5.7(e) is nearly the same as ABA Model Rule 5.7(b), but Ohio Rules

5.7(b), (c), and (d) differ significantly from the ABA Model Rule. They provide as follows:

> (b) A lawyer who controls or owns an interest in a business that provides a law-related service shall not require any customer of that business to agree to legal representation by the lawyer as a condition of the engagement of that business. A lawyer who controls or owns an interest in a business that provides law-related services shall disclose the interest to a customer of that business, and the fact that the customer may obtain legal services elsewhere, before performing legal services for the customer.
>
> (c) A lawyer who controls or owns an interest in a business that provides a law-related service shall not require the lawyer's client to agree to use that business as a condition of the engagement for legal services. A lawyer who controls or owns an interest in a business that provides a law-related service shall disclose the interest to the client, and the fact that the client may obtain the law-related services elsewhere, before providing the law-related services to the client.
>
> (d) Limitations or obligations imposed by this rule on a lawyer shall apply to all lawyers in that lawyer's firm and every lawyer in a firm that controls or owns an interest in a business that provides a law-related service.

Oklahoma has adopted ABA Model Rule 5.7 verbatim.

Oregon omits ABA Model Rule 5.7.

Pennsylvania adopted a version of Rule 5.7 in 1996, becoming the first state to do so. The Pennsylvania rule, which differs significantly from ABA Model Rule 5.7, provides:

> *Rule 5.7 Responsibilities Regarding Nonlegal Services*
>
> (a) A lawyer who provides nonlegal services to a recipient that are not distinct from legal services provided to that recipient is subject to the Rules of Professional Conduct with respect to the provision of both legal and nonlegal services.
>
> (b) A lawyer who provides nonlegal services to a recipient that are distinct from any legal services provided to the recipient is subject to the Rules of Professional Conduct with respect to the nonlegal services if the lawyer knows or reasonably should know that the recipient might believe that the recipient is receiving the protection of a client-lawyer relationship.
>
> (c) A lawyer who is an owner, controlling party, employee, agent, or is otherwise affiliated with an entity providing nonlegal services to a recipient is subject to the Rules of Professional Conduct with respect to the nonlegal services if the lawyer knows or reasonably should know that the recipient might believe that the recipient is receiving the protection of a client-lawyer relationship.
>
> (d) Paragraph (b) or (c) does not apply if the lawyer makes reasonable efforts to avoid any misunderstanding by the recipient receiving nonlegal services. Those efforts must include advising the recipient that the services are not legal services and that the protection of a client-lawyer relationship does not exist with respect to the provision of nonlegal services to the recipient.
>
> (e) The term "nonlegal services" denotes services that might reasonably be performed in conjunction with and in substance are related to the provision of legal services, and that are not prohibited as unauthorized practice of law when provided by a nonlawyer.

Texas omits Rule 5.7.

Virginia omits Rule 5.7.

Wisconsin omits ABA Model Rule 5.7. (Wisconsin SCR 20:5.7 governs lawyers practicing in limited liability organizations. A Wisconsin Committee Comment to that rule says expressly that "Model Rule 5.7, concerning law-related services, is not part of these rules.")

Related Materials

ABA Formal Ethics Opinions: See ABA Formal Ethics Ops. 97-407 (1997) and 01-423 n.18 (2001).

Ancillary Businesses: Many law firms own, operate, or otherwise affiliate with ancillary non-legal businesses. A 2003 survey by the law firm consulting company Hildebrandt International entitled Beyond Legal Practice: Organizing and Managing Ancillary Businesses indicates that law firms offer more than 70 separate lines of law-related businesses. The most common ancillary businesses at that time, according to the Hildebrandt survey, were (a) lobbying or government relations services; (b) financial counseling and planning; (c) client asset management through registered investment companies; (d) human resources or benefits consulting or training; (e) international trade or finance services; and (f) educational, environmental, or health care consulting. The survey is available for purchase at *www.Hildebrandt.com.*

Professionalism Report: The ABA's Stanley Commission Report on Professionalism, 112 F.R.D. 243 (1986), called the trend toward law firm involvement in nonlegal services "disturbing" and urged the ABA to "initiate a study to see what, if any, controls or prohibitions should be imposed." The ultimate result of the study was ABA Model Rule 5.7.

Restatement of the Law Governing Lawyers: The Restatement has no provision comparable to ABA Model Rule 5.7.

ARTICLE 6. PUBLIC SERVICE

Rule 6.1 Voluntary Pro Bono Publico Service

Every lawyer has a professional responsibility to provide legal services to those unable to pay. A lawyer should aspire to render at least (50) hours of pro bono publico legal services per year. In fulfilling this responsibility, the lawyer should:

(a) provide a substantial majority of the (50) hours of legal services without fee or expectation of fee to:

(1) persons of limited means or

(2) charitable, religious, civic, community, governmental and educational organizations in matters that are designed primarily to address the needs of persons of limited means; and

(b) provide any additional services through:

(1) delivery of legal services at no fee or substantially reduced fee to individuals, groups or organizations seeking to secure or protect civil rights, civil liberties or public rights, or charitable, religious, civic, community, governmental and educational organizations in

matters in furtherance of their organizational purposes, where the payment of standard legal fees would significantly deplete the organization's economic resources or would be otherwise inappropriate;

(2) delivery of legal services at a substantially reduced fee to persons of limited means; or

(3) participation in activities for improving the law, the legal system or the legal profession.

In addition, a lawyer should voluntarily contribute financial support to organizations that provide legal services to persons of limited means.

COMMENT

[1] Every lawyer, regardless of professional prominence or professional work load, has a responsibility to provide legal services to those unable to pay, and personal involvement in the problems of the disadvantaged can be one of the most rewarding experiences in the life of a lawyer. The American Bar Association urges all lawyers to provide a minimum of 50 hours of pro bono services annually. States, however, may decide to choose a higher or lower number of hours of annual service (which may be expressed as a percentage of a lawyer's professional time) depending upon local needs and local conditions. It is recognized that in some years a lawyer may render greater or fewer hours than the annual standard specified, but during the course of his or her legal career, each lawyer should render on average per year, the number of hours set forth in this Rule. Services can be performed in civil matters or in criminal or quasi-criminal matters for which there is no government obligation to provide funds for legal representation, such as post-conviction death penalty appeal cases.

[2] Paragraphs (a)(1) and (2) recognize the critical need for legal services that exists among persons of limited means by providing that a substantial majority of the legal services rendered annually to the disadvantaged be furnished without fee or expectation of fee. Legal services under these paragraphs consist of a full range of activities, including individual and class representation, the provision of legal advice, legislative lobbying, administrative rule making and the provision of free training or mentoring to those who represent persons of limited means. The variety of these activities should facilitate participation by government lawyers, even when restrictions exist on their engaging in the outside practice of law.

[3] Persons eligible for legal services under paragraphs (a)(1) and (2) are those who qualify for participation in programs funded by the Legal Services Corporation and those whose incomes and financial resources are slightly above the guidelines utilized by such programs but, nevertheless, cannot afford counsel. Legal services can be rendered to individuals or to organizations such as homeless shelters, battered women's centers and food pantries that serve those of limited means. The term "governmental organizations" includes, but is not limited to, public protection programs and sections of governmental or public sector agencies.

[4] Because service must be provided without fee or expectation of fee, the intent of the lawyer to render free legal services is essential for the work performed to fall within the meaning of paragraphs (a)(1) and (2). Accordingly, services

rendered cannot be considered pro bono if an anticipated fee is uncollected, but the award of statutory attorneys' fees in a case originally accepted as pro bono would not disqualify such services from inclusion under this section. Lawyers who do receive fees in such cases are encouraged to contribute an appropriate portion of such fees to organizations or projects that benefit persons of limited means.

[5] While it is possible for a lawyer to fulfill the annual responsibility to perform pro bono services exclusively through activities described in paragraphs (a)(1) and (2), to the extent that any hours of service remained unfulfilled, the remaining commitment can be met in a variety of ways as set forth in paragraph (b). Constitutional, statutory or regulatory restrictions may prohibit or impede government and public sector lawyers and judges from performing the pro bono services outlined in paragraphs (a)(1) and (2). Accordingly, where those restrictions apply, government and public sector lawyers and judges may fulfill their pro bono responsibility by performing services outlined in paragraph (b).

[6] Paragraph (b)(1) includes the provision of certain types of legal services to those whose incomes and financial resources place them above limited means. It also permits the pro bono lawyer to accept a substantially reduced fee for services. Examples of the types of issues that may be addressed under this paragraph include First Amendment claims, Title VII claims and environmental protection claims. Additionally, a wide range of organizations may be represented, including social service, medical research, cultural and religious groups.

[7] Paragraph (b)(2) covers instances in which lawyers agree to and receive a modest fee for furnishing legal services to persons of limited means. Participation in judicare programs and acceptance of court appointments in which the fee is substantially below a lawyer's usual rate are encouraged under this section.

[8] Paragraph (b)(3) recognizes the value of lawyers engaging in activities that improve the law, the legal system or the legal profession. Serving on bar association committees, serving on boards of pro bono or legal services programs, taking part in Law Day activities, acting as a continuing legal education instructor, a mediator or an arbitrator and engaging in legislative lobbying to improve the law, the legal system or the profession are a few examples of the many activities that fall within this paragraph.

[9] Because the provision of pro bono services is a professional responsibility, it is the individual ethical commitment of each lawyer. Nevertheless, there may be times when it is not feasible for a lawyer to engage in pro bono services. At such times a lawyer may discharge the pro bono responsibility by providing financial support to organizations providing free legal services to persons of limited means. Such financial support should be reasonably equivalent to the value of the hours of service that would have otherwise been provided. In addition, at times it may be more feasible to satisfy the pro bono responsibility collectively, as by a firm's aggregate pro bono activities.

[10] Because the efforts of individual lawyers are not enough to meet the need for free legal services that exists among persons of limited means, the government and the profession have instituted additional programs to provide those services. Every lawyer should financially support such programs, in addition to either providing direct pro bono services or making financial contributions when pro bono service is not feasible.

[11] Law firms should act reasonably to enable and encourage all lawyers in the firm to provide the pro bono legal services called for by this Rule.

[12] The responsibility set forth in this Rule is not intended to be enforced through disciplinary process.

Canon and Code Antecedents

ABA Canons of Professional Ethics: No comparable Canon.

ABA Model Code of Professional Responsibility: No comparable Disciplinary Rule.

Cross-References in Other Rules

Rule 6.2, Comment 1: "All lawyers have a responsibility to assist in providing pro bono publico service. See Rule 6.1."

Legislative History of Model Rule 6.1

1980 Discussion Draft of Rule 6.1 (then Rule 8.1) provided as follows: "A lawyer shall render unpaid public interest legal services. . . . A lawyer shall make an annual report concerning such service to appropriate regulatory authority."

1981 and ***1982 Drafts*** were the same as adopted in 1983, except that neither draft contained the final clause, "by financial support for organizations that provide legal services to persons of limited means."

1983 Rule: The version of Rule 6.1 originally adopted by the ABA in 1983 (which remained in effect until its amendment in 1993) provided as follows:

> A lawyer should render public interest legal service. A lawyer may discharge this responsibility by providing professional services at no fee or a reduced fee to persons of limited means or to public service or charitable groups or organizations, by service in activities for improving the law, the legal system or the legal profession, and by financial support for organizations that provide legal services to persons of limited means.

1993 Amendment: In 1993, the ABA amended Rule 6.1 substantially and rewrote its Comment entirely. As amended in 1993, the rule was substantially longer and more detailed than the 1983 rule, but was identical to the version of the rule in force since 2002, except that the opening sentence ("Every lawyer has a professional responsibility to provide legal services to those unable to pay.") and Comment 11 were not added until 2002. The 1993 amendment was highly controversial and passed by the close vote of 228-215.

The principal sponsor and author of the amended rule was the ABA's Standing Committee on Lawyers' Public Service Responsibility (SCLPSR). SCLPSR attempted to develop a joint proposal with the ABA's Standing Committee on Ethics and Professional Responsibility, which usually drafts proposed amendments to the Model Rules, but the joint effort failed because the Standing Committee on Ethics and Professional Responsibility (1) opposed setting a specific target number of 50 hours of pro bono service per year (preferring a word like "substantial" instead of a number); (2) opposed urging lawyers to allocate a substantial majority of their pro bono hours to serving the poor (out of concern that pro bono work for civil rights, the environment, and other important areas would diminish); and (3) favored adding a "buy-out" provision allowing lawyers to substitute financial support for personal service.

We reprint below excerpts from the Committee Report issued by SCLPSR and its five co-sponsors in support of the 1993 amendment to Rule 6.1:

*Excerpts from ABA Committee Report Supporting 1993 Amendment to Rule 6.1**

THE CURRENT CRISIS IN THE DELIVERY OF LEGAL SERVICES TO THE POOR

[B]ecause the legal problems of the economically disadvantaged often involve areas of basic need such as minimum levels of income and entitlements, shelter, utilities and child support, their inability to obtain legal services can have dire consequences. For example, the failure of a poor person to have effective legal counsel in an eviction proceeding may well result in homelessness; the failure to have legal counsel present at a public aid hearing may result in the denial of essential food or medical benefits.

The inability of the poor to obtain needed legal services has been well documented: since 1983, when Rule 6.1 was adopted, at least one national and 13 statewide studies assessing the legal needs of the poor have been conducted. Of those studies reporting unmet legal need, there has been a consistent finding that only about 15%-20% of the legal needs of the poor are being addressed. The legal need studies also confirmed that unmet need exists in critical areas such as public benefits, utilities, shelter, medical benefits and family matters. . . .

The Committee firmly believes that the private bar alone cannot be expected to fill the gap for service that exists among the poor. Rather, the federal government, through adequate funding of the Legal Services Corporation (LSC), should bear the major responsibility for addressing the problem. . . .

The Association . . . must again turn to members of the private bar and call upon them to help ease the crisis that exists in the provision of legal services to the poor. The Committee believes that one effective means of doing this is by revising Model Rule 6.1 to reflect a new emphasis on service to the disadvantaged. . . .

. . . To address the crisis in the delivery of legal services to the poor, the proposed revision provides that a substantial majority of the annual hours of pro bono legal services should be rendered at no cost to persons of limited means or to organizations in matters which are designed primarily to address the needs of persons of limited means. The Committee purposely chose the words "substantial majority" to make clear that a simple majority of the hours would not suffice. While the Committee recognizes the value and importance of other types of pro bono activity, it strongly believes that due to the enormity of the unmet need for legal services that exists among the disadvantaged, the provision of legal services to that group must be given priority over all other types of pro bono service. . . .

In addition to voluntarily rendering pro bono service, the revised Rule 6.1 calls upon every lawyer to voluntarily make financial contributions to organizations

* Committee Reports do not represent official policy of the ABA. They are for information only, and the opinions are those of the authors of the report.

providing legal services to persons of limited means. In those cases in which a lawyer determines that it is not feasible to render legal services and makes a financial contribution instead, he or she is expected to make an additional contribution pursuant to the last sentence of the new Rule. . . .

It is the Committee's intent that the ethical responsibilities set forth in Rule 6.1 apply to all lawyers and not just those currently engaged in the practice of law. . . .

Although neither the Rule nor the Comment explicitly so states, it should be self evident that every lawyer is expected to provide the same quality of legal services to pro bono clients as he or she would provide to paying clients. . . . Therefore, to the extent that an attorney is unfamiliar with a given area of the law, he or she is expected to seek advice or training in that area before advising a client, either for a fee or on a pro bono basis. Many pro bono programs provide free training on a wide range of topics to assist their volunteer attorneys in attaining competency to handle the cases referred to them. The Committee strongly endorses the provision of these training events and urges pro bono attorneys to take advantage of them whenever possible.

[T]he Comment to the revised Rule explicitly states that the pro bono responsibility is not intended to be enforced through the disciplinary process. Thus as drafted, revised Rule 6.1 does not mandate pro bono. Although the Committee recognizes that since 1988, mandatory pro bono proposals have been considered in many states and remain under active consideration in several of them, it nevertheless believes that it is not practical nor feasible at this time to address the issue of mandatory pro bono on a national level. Rather, the Committee views the question of mandatory pro bono as an issue that needs to be examined by state and local bar associations.

2002 Amendments: At its February 2002 Mid-Year Meeting, the ABA House of Delegates adopted with only minor changes the ABA Ethics 2000 Commission proposal to amend Rule 6.1 and its Comment. The amendments added the first sentence of the rule and a new Comment 11. (Comment 11 was not in the Ethics 2000 Commission's proposal but rather was added by the House of Delegates.)

Selected State Variations

Editors' Note. No state yet requires lawyers to perform pro bono work, and no state is actively considering mandatory pro bono. Some states, however, require lawyers to report their pro bono hours, and other states encourage lawyers to do so. When we went to press in September 2011, a state-by-state chart of pro bono reporting rules and policies found at *http://apps.americanbar.org/legalservices/probono/reporting.html* indicated that 7 states have mandatory pro bono reporting (Florida, Hawaii, Illinois, Maryland, Mississippi, Nevada, and New Mexico); 8 states have formally rejected mandatory pro bono reporting (Colorado, Indiana, Massachusetts, Minnesota, New York, Pennsylvania, Tennessee, and Utah); 11 states encourage voluntary pro bono reporting (Arizona, Georgia, Kentucky, Louisiana, Missouri, Montana, New Mexico, Oregon, Texas, Utah, and Washington); and 2 states were actively considering voluntary pro bono reporting (Michigan and Vermont).

Alabama: See the Alabama entry following Rule 6.5.

Arizona: Rule 6.1 contains the following key provisions:

(a) A lawyer should voluntarily render public interest legal service. A lawyer may discharge this responsibility by rendering a minimum of fifty hours of service per calendar year. . . .

(c) A law firm or other group of lawyers may satisfy their responsibility under this Rule, if they desire, collectively. For example, the designation of one or more lawyers to work on pro bono publico matters may be attributed to other lawyers within the firm or group who support the representation. . . .

(d) The efforts of individual lawyers are not enough to meet the needs of the poor. The profession and government have instituted programs to provide direct delivery of legal services to the poor. The direct support of such programs is an alternative expression of support to provide law in the public interest, and a lawyer is encouraged to provide financial support for organizations that provide legal services to persons of limited means or to the Arizona Bar Foundation for the direct delivery of legal services to the poor.

California: California has no rule of professional conduct comparable to ABA Model Rule 6.1, but California Business and Professions Code §6068(h) makes it the duty of a lawyer "[n]ever to reject, for any consideration personal to himself or herself, the cause of the defenseless or the oppressed." In addition, the California State Bar's Board of Governors has adopted a Pro Bono Resolution that echoes the substance of ABA Model Rule 6.1. It provides as follows:

(3) Urges all law schools to promote and encourage the participation of law students in pro bono activities, including requiring any law firm wishing to recruit on campus to provide a written statement of its policy, if any, concerning the involvement of its attorneys in public service and pro bono activities. . . .

Colorado: Colorado adds the following paragraph at the end of the rule:

Where constitutional, statutory or regulatory restrictions prohibit government and public sector lawyers or judges from performing the pro bono services outlined in paragraphs (a)(1) and (2), those individuals should fulfill their pro bono responsibility by performing services or participating in activities outlined in paragraph (b).

In 1999, the Colorado Supreme Court rejected a recommendation by the state's Judicial Advisory Council to institute mandatory pro bono reporting. The court said that mandatory reporting was a step toward mandatory pro bono, and "[s]ince we are unwilling to arrive at that destination, we are also unwilling to take the first step." However, the Colorado Supreme Court has adopted a detailed "recommended Model Pro Bono Policy" for law firms, which is reprinted in the Colorado Rules of Professional Conduct immediately after Rule 6.1. Among other things, the Model Pro Bono Policy urges firms to include "a statement that the firm will value at least 50 hours of such pro bono service per year by each Colorado licensed attorney in the firm, for all purposes of attorney evaluation, advancement, and compensation in the firm as the firm values compensated client representation." In addition, the Colorado Supreme Court will annually recognize Colorado law firms that "voluntarily advise the Court . . . that their attorneys, on average, during the previous calendar year, performed 50 hours of pro bono legal service, primarily for persons of limited means or organizations serving persons of limited means. . . ."

Connecticut, Georgia, Indiana, Kansas, Michigan, Missouri, Pennsylvania, and ***South Carolina*** have retained the 1983 version of ABA Model Rule 6.1, which provides as follows:

A lawyer should render public interest service. A lawyer may discharge this responsibility by providing professional services at no fee or a reduced fee to persons of limited means or to public service or charitable groups or organizations, by service in activities for improving the law, the legal system or the legal profession, and by financial support for organizations that provide legal services to persons of limited means.

District of Columbia: D.C. Rule 6.1 provides as follows:

> A lawyer should participate in serving those persons, or groups of persons, who are unable to pay all or a portion of reasonable attorneys' fees or who are otherwise unable to obtain counsel. A lawyer may discharge this responsibility by providing professional services at no fee, or at a substantially reduced fee, to persons and groups who are unable to afford or obtain counsel, or by active participation in the work of organizations that provide legal services to them. When personal representation is not feasible, a lawyer may discharge this responsibility by providing financial support for organizations that provide legal representation to those unable to obtain counsel.

Florida: In 1993, in a divided opinion, the Florida Supreme Court adopted an elaborate pro bono rule requiring lawyers to report their pro bono hours. See 630 So. 2d 501 (Fla. 1993). The Florida Bar subsequently sought to eliminate mandatory reporting, but the Florida Supreme Court refused to do so at 696 So. 2d 734 (1997). In *Schwarz v. Kogan,* 132 F.3d 1387 (11th Cir. 1998), the court upheld Florida's mandatory reporting provisions against a federal constitutional challenge. The full rule provides as follows:

> *4-6.1 Pro Bono Public Service*
>
> (a) *Professional Responsibility.* Each member of The Florida Bar in good standing, as part of that member's professional responsibility, should (1) render pro bono legal services to the poor or (2) participate, to the extent possible, in other pro bono service activities that directly relate to the legal needs of the poor. This professional responsibility does not apply to members of the judiciary or their staffs or to government lawyers who are prohibited from performing legal services by constitutional, statutory, rule, or regulatory prohibitions. Neither does this professional responsibility apply to those members of The Bar who are retired, inactive, or suspended, or who have been placed on the inactive list for incapacity not related to discipline.
>
> (b) *Discharge of the Professional Responsibility to Provide Pro Bono Legal Service to the Poor.* The professional responsibility to provide pro bono legal services as established under this rule is aspirational rather than mandatory in nature. The failure to fulfill one's professional responsibility under this rule will not subject a lawyer to discipline. The professional responsibility to provide pro bono legal service to the poor may be discharged by:
>
> (1) annually providing at least 20 hours of pro bono legal service to the poor; or
>
> (2) making an annual contribution of at least $350 to a legal aid organization.
>
> (c) *Collective Discharge of the Professional Responsibility to Provide Pro Bono Legal Service to the Poor.* Each member of the bar should strive to individually satisfy the member's professional responsibility to provide pro bono legal service to the poor. Collective satisfaction of this professional responsibility is permitted by law firms only under a collective satisfaction plan that has been filed previously with the circuit pro bono committee and only when providing pro bono legal service to the poor:
>
> (1) in a major case or matter involving a substantial expenditure of time and resources; or
>
> (2) through a full-time community or public service staff; or
>
> (3) in any other manner that has been approved by the circuit pro bono committee in the circuit in which the firm practices.

> (d) *Reporting Requirement.* Each member of the bar shall annually report whether the member has satisfied the member's professional responsibility to provide pro bono legal services to the poor. Each member shall report this information through a simplified reporting form that is made a part of the member's annual dues statement . . . . The failure to report this information shall constitute a disciplinary offense under these rules. . . .

Florida also adds a lengthy Rule 6.5 (Voluntary Pro Bono Plan). Rule 6.5(c)(2) instructs every judicial circuit to "(a) prepare in written form a circuit pro bono plan after evaluating the needs of the circuit and making a determination of present available pro bono services; (b) implement the plan and monitor its results; [and] (c) submit an annual report to The Florida Bar standing committee. . . ." Rule 6.5(d) provides as follows:

> The following are suggested pro bono service opportunities that should be included in each circuit plan:
>
> (1) representation of clients through case referral;
>
> (2) interviewing of prospective clients;
>
> (3) participation in pro se clinics and other clinics in which lawyers provide advice and counsel;
>
> (4) acting as co-counsel on cases or matters with legal assistance providers and other pro bono lawyers;
>
> (5) providing consultation services to legal assistance providers for case reviews and evaluations;
>
> (6) participation in policy advocacy;
>
> (7) providing training to the staff of legal assistance providers and other volunteer pro bono attorneys;
>
> (8) making presentations to groups of poor persons regarding their rights and obligations under the law;
>
> (9) providing legal research;
>
> (10) providing guardian ad litem services;
>
> (11) providing assistance in the formation and operation of legal entities for groups of poor persons; and
>
> (12) serving as a mediator or arbitrator at no fee to the client-eligible party.

Georgia: Rule 6.1 tracks the pre-2002 version of ABA Model Rule 6.1, but Georgia adds the following: "No reporting rules or requirements may be imposed without specific permission of the Supreme Court granted through amendments to these Rules. There is no disciplinary penalty for a violation of this Rule."

Illinois: Illinois omits Rule 6.1. Comment 6B of the Preamble explains the omission as follows:

> The absence from the Illinois Rules of a counterpart to ABA Model Rule 6.1 regarding *pro bono* and public service should not be interpreted as limiting the responsibility of lawyers to render uncompensated service in the public interest. Rather, the rationale is that this responsibility is not appropriate for disciplinary rules because it is not possible to articulate an appropriate disciplinary standard regarding *pro bono* and public service.

However, Illinois encourages *pro bono* obligations through court rules. The Preamble's Comment 6A refers to Illinois Supreme Court Rule 756(f), which provides as follows:

> (f) *Disclosure of Voluntary Pro Bono Service.* As part of registering under this rule, each lawyer shall report the approximate amount of his or her pro bono legal service and the amount of qualified monetary contributions made during the preceding 12 months. . . .

Rule 756(f) then defines the term "*Pro bono* legal service," stating explicitly that legal services for which payment "was expected, but is uncollectible, do not qualify as *pro bono* legal service." The rule also sets out the precise contents of the form for reporting such service on the annual registration statement. Information provided pursuant to Rule 756(f) is considered "confidential," but the information may be reported "in the aggregate." Rule 756(g) instructs the Bar's Administrator to "remove from the master roll" any attorney who has failed to provide the information on voluntary pro bono service required by Rule 756(f). A person whose name is not on the master roll and who practices law in Illinois "is engaged in the unauthorized practice of law and may also be held in contempt of the court."

Finally, Rule 756(j) permits retired and inactive attorneys, as well as in-house attorneys who have a more limited registration status, to provide pro bono legal services under certain circumstances that are described in the Rule.

Kentucky: Rule 6.1, entitled "Donated Legal Services," encourages lawyers to render voluntary public interest legal service and permits lawyers to report donated legal services on the Bar's annual dues statement. "Lawyers rendering a minimum of fifty (50) hours of donated legal service shall receive a recognition award for such service from the Kentucky Bar Association."

Maryland adds that a lawyer "in part-time practice" should aspire to render at least "a pro rata number of hours." Maryland also makes an exception for lawyers who are "prohibited by law" from rendering certain types of pro bono legal services. Maryland allows a substantial majority of pro bono services to be rendered to "individuals, groups, or organizations seeking to secure or protect civil rights, civil liberties, or public rights. . . ." Maryland Rule 6.1 concludes: "This Rule is aspirational, not mandatory. Noncompliance with this Rule shall not be grounds for disciplinary action or other sanctions."

Massachusetts: Rule 6.1 states that a lawyer "should provide annually at least 25 hours of pro bono publico legal services for the benefit of persons of limited means." Alternatively, the lawyer should "contribute from $250 to 1 percent of the lawyer's annual taxable, professional income to one or more organizations that provide or support legal services to persons of limited means."

Michigan essentially retains the 1983 version of ABA Model Rule 6.1.

New Jersey: Rule 6.1 tracks the original (1983) version of ABA Model Rule 6.1 except that the first sentence reads: "Every lawyer has a professional responsibility to render public interest legal service."

New York: Rule 6.1 provides as follows:

> Lawyers are strongly encouraged to provide pro bono legal services to benefit poor persons.
>
> (a) Every lawyer should aspire to: (1) provide at least 20 hours of pro bono legal services each year to poor persons; and (2) contribute financially to organizations that provide legal services to poor persons.
>
> (b) Pro bono legal services that meet this goal are: (1) professional services rendered in civil matters, and in those criminal matters for which the government is not obliged to provide funds for legal representation, to persons who are financially unable to compensate counsel; (2) activities related to improving the administration of justice by simplifying the legal process for, or increasing the availability and quality of legal services to, poor persons; and (3) professional services to charitable, religious, civic and educational organizations in matters designed predominantly to address the needs of poor persons.

(c) Appropriate organizations for financial contributions are: (1) organizations primarily engaged in the provision of legal services to the poor; and (2) organizations substantially engaged in the provision of legal services to the poor, provided that the donated funds are to be used for the provision of such legal services.

(d) This Rule is not intended to be enforced through the disciplinary process, and the failure to fulfill the aspirational goals contained herein should be without legal consequence.

North Carolina omits Rule 6.1, but Paragraph 6 of North Carolina's Preamble states that "all lawyers should devote professional time and resources and use civic influence to ensure equal access to our system of justice for all those who because of economic or social barriers cannot afford or secure adequate legal counsel," and Paragraph 7 of the Preamble contains language almost identical to the 1983 version of ABA Model Rule 6.1.

Ohio omits ABA Model Rule 6.1. The Supreme Court of Ohio explains that it "deferred consideration of Model Rule 6.1 in light of recommendations contained in the final report of the Supreme Court Task Force on Pro Se & Indigent Representation and recommendations from the Ohio Legal Assistance Foundation." (The Task Force on Pro Se & Indigent Representation, which was appointed by the Supreme Court of Ohio in 2004, recommended in its April 2006 final report that Ohio attorneys be required to report their pro bono activities. The report is available at *www.sconet.state.oh.us/publications/prose/report_april06.pdf.*)

Texas omits Rule 6.1, but Paragraph 6 of the Texas Preamble addresses pro bono services by stating, among other things: "The provision of free legal services to those unable to pay reasonable fees is a moral obligation of each lawyer as well as the profession generally."

Virginia: Rule 6.1 says that a lawyer "should render at least 2 percent per year of the lawyer's professional time to pro bono publico legal services." The Rule also defines pro bono services and allows a law firm or group of lawyers to satisfy their responsibility under the Rule collectively. Further, "direct financial support of programs that provide direct delivery of legal services to meet the need described" in the Rule "is an alternative method for fulfilling a lawyer's responsibility."

Related Materials

AALS Commission on Pro Bono and Public Service Opportunities: In 1999, the Association of American Law Schools (AALS) issued a report entitled "Learning to Serve" (*see www.aals.org/probono/report.html*), which then–AALS President Deborah Rhode identified as "the first systematic effort by the Association of American Law Schools to address the role of pro bono and public service in legal education." The report recommended that law schools "make available to all law students at least once during their law school careers a well-supervised law-related pro bono opportunity and either require participation or find ways to attract the great majority of students to volunteer." The report also urged law schools to adopt a policy (a) stating an annual pro bono expectation for all faculty members, (b) going beyond teaching and institutional service, (c) extending institutional support similar to research support, (d) granting autonomy, and (e) requiring annual reporting. For details on faculty pro bono, see *www.abanet.org/legalservices/probono/lawschools/pb_faculty.html.*

ABA Formal Ethics Opinions: No formal ethics opinions have construed Rule 6.1, but ABA Formal Ethics Op. 96-399 (1996) mentioned Rule 6.1.

ABA Model Guidelines for the Utilization of Paralegal Services: The ABA has approved Model Guidelines for the Utilization of Paralegal Services. Guideline 10 provides: "A lawyer who employs a paralegal should facilitate the paralegal's participation in appropriate continuing education and pro bono publico activities." The Model Guidelines are at *http://apps.americanbar.org/legalservices/paralegals/downloads/modelguidelines.pdf.*

ABA Pro Bono Disclosure Requirements for Law School Recruiters: In 2006, the ABA adopted a resolution urging law schools (a) to "require legal employers that recruit on campus to disclose, and to make available to the schools' students and alumni, specific information regarding the employer's pro bono policies, practices and activities," and (b) to adopt an August 2006 document entitled "Pro Bono Disclosure Requirements for Law School Recruiters" that requires on-campus recruiters to disclose information such as "(a) stated goals regarding the number of pro bono hours to be contributed by the employer each year; (b) the number of actual pro bono hours contributed by the employer in the prior calendar year; (c) the average number of pro bono hours contributed by junior associates, midlevel associates, senior associates, and partners at the firm in the prior calendar year; [and] (d) whether and to what extent pro bono hours are counted as billable hours (if attorneys are expected to meet billable hours targets). . . ." The resolution and supporting report are available at *www.abanet.org/leadership/2006/annual/dailyjournal/hundredtwentyoneb.doc.*

ABA Resolution on Encouraging Pro Bono Work: In 2006, the ABA adopted a resolution urging law firms and corporate legal departments to adopt policies and procedures designed to increase the willingness of lawyers to perform pro bono work. The resolution is available at *www.abanet.org/leadership/2006/annual/dailyjournal/hundredtwentyonea.doc.* An accompanying report recommended various specific procedures, including:

> **Count pro bono hours as billable hours.** It is essential that pro bono hours be counted as billable hours and that they also count, like hours spent on client work, toward annual billable hours targets, requirements or expectations. The failure to treat pro bono hours as billable hours sends a signal that the firm does not truly value and support this work.
>
> **Consider attorneys' commitment to pro bono activity as a favorable factor in advancement and compensation decisions.** If a pro bono culture is to flourish, the attorneys who engage in pro bono work need to know that their efforts will be viewed favorably by the firm when the time comes to make advancement and compensation decisions.
>
> **Set annual goals regarding the number of hours contributed through firm pro bono programs and the number of attorneys who participate.** By setting goals, firms can continually monitor participation while demonstrating their commitment to pro bono and public service to their lawyers, clients and prospective recruits.

ABA Standards for Approval of Law Schools: The ABA has adopted Standards for the Approval of Law Schools, as well as formal interpretations of the Standards, to determine whether law schools merit ABA accreditation. The Standards are available in full at *www.abanet.org/legaled/standards/standards.html.*Some of the Standards relate to pro bono work. For example, Standard 302(b)(2) requires every law school to offer "substantial opportunities for . . . student participation in pro bono activities." Interpretation 302-10 states as follows:

> *Interpretation 302-10.* Each law school is encouraged to be creative in developing substantial opportunities for student participation in pro bono activities. Pro bono opportunities should at a minimum involve the rendering of meaningful law-related service to persons of limited means or to organizations that serve such persons; however volunteer programs that involve meaningful services that are not law-related also may be included within the law school's overall program. . . .

ABA Standards for Programs Providing Civil Pro Bono Legal Services to Persons of Limited Means: In 1996, the ABA approved Standards for Programs Providing Civil Pro Bono Legal Services to Persons of Limited Means. The Standards cover such things as fundraising (Standard 1.1-4), conflicts of interest (Standard 1.1-7), communication with clients (Standard 3.4-4), training of volunteers (Standard 3.5-3), and case acceptance policy (Standard 4.1). The complete Standards are available online at *http://www.americanbar.org/groups/probono_public_service/policy/standards.html.*

ABA Standing Committee on Pro Bono and Public Service: The ABA Standing Committee on Pro Bono and Public Service is the lead ABA committee for developing and promoting pro bono policies and initiatives. The Pro Bono Committee's mission includes "fostering the development of pro bono programs and activities by law firms, bar associations, corporate legal departments, law schools, government attorney offices and others; analyzing the scope and function of pro bono programs; and proposing and reviewing legislation that affects lawyers' ability to provide pro bono legal services." For example, the Pro Bono Committee took the lead in drafting the 1993 amendments to ABA Model Rule 6.1. For more information about the Pro Bono Committee and its activities, visit *http://www.americanbar.org/groups/probono_public_service.html.*

Federal Statutes: Certain federal statutes or other regulations may preclude federal government lawyers from doing any pro bono work adverse to any federal agency or department. As Comment 5 to Rule 6.1 notes, "Constitutional, statutory or regulatory restrictions may prohibit or impede government and public sector lawyers and judges from performing the pro bono services outlined in paragraphs (a)(1) and (2)." For example, 18 U.S.C. §205 makes it a criminal offense for a federal government lawyer, "other than in the proper discharge of his official duties," to act as an attorney for anyone "before any department, agency, court, court-martial, officer, or civil, military, or naval commission in connection with any covered matter in which the United States is a party or has a direct and substantial interest. . . ."

Law School Pro Bono Requirements: More than 30 law schools require law students to complete a specified amount of pro bono work as a condition of graduation. Columbia Law School, for example, requires all students to perform 40 hours of uncompensated public interest service between the end of the first year and graduation. Students who do not complete the 40 hours cannot graduate. Harvard Law School also requires 40 hours of pro bono work before graduation. For a Directory of Law School Public Interest and Pro Bono Programs maintained by the ABA Standing Committee on Pro Bono and Public Service, visit *http://apps.americanbar.org/legalservices/probono/lawschools/pb_programs_chart.html#graduation_requirement.*

Legal Services Corporation's "Justice Gap" Study: In 2007, the Legal Services Corporation re-issued a report (originally issued in 2005) entitled "Documenting the Justice Gap in America: The Current Unmet Civil Legal Needs of Low-Income

Americans." The report concluded that at least 80 percent of the civil legal needs of low-income Americans are not being met and that programs funded by Legal Services Corporation turn away half of their potential clients (about one million cases per year) because the programs lack sufficient resources. The full "Justice Gap" study is available online at *www.lsc.gov/JusticeGap.pdf.*

Model Rules of Professional Conduct for Federal Lawyers adds a new paragraph to Rule 6.1 providing that government lawyers "should provide pro bono legal services consistent with applicable law." In addition, Rule 5.1(d) provides that a supervisory government lawyer "should encourage subordinate lawyers to participate in pro bono publico service activities and the activities of bar associations and law reform organizations." However, the Comment by the Federal Lawyers to Rule 6.1 explains that "18 U.S.C. §205 and §209 and other laws . . . may regulate a Government lawyer's ability to provide legal services on a pro bono basis outside the scope of the Government lawyer's official duties."

Restatement of the Law Governing Lawyers: The Restatement has no provision comparable to ABA Model Rule 6.1.

Rule 6.2 Accepting Appointments

A lawyer shall not seek to avoid appointment by a tribunal to represent a person except for good cause, such as:

(a) representing the client is likely to result in violation of the Rules of Professional Conduct or other law;

(b) representing the client is likely to result in an unreasonable financial burden on the lawyer; or

(c) the client or the cause is so repugnant to the lawyer as to be likely to impair the client-lawyer relationship or the lawyer's ability to represent the client.

COMMENT

[1] A lawyer ordinarily is not obliged to accept a client whose character or cause the lawyer regards as repugnant. The lawyer's freedom to select clients is, however, qualified. All lawyers have a responsibility to assist in providing pro bono publico service. See Rule 6.1. An individual lawyer fulfills this responsibility by accepting a fair share of unpopular matters or indigent or unpopular clients. A lawyer may also be subject to appointment by a court to serve unpopular clients or persons unable to afford legal services.

Appointed Counsel

[2] For good cause a lawyer may seek to decline an appointment to represent a person who cannot afford to retain counsel or whose cause is unpopular. Good cause exists if the lawyer could not handle the matter competently, see Rule 1.1, or if undertaking the representation would result in an improper conflict of interest, for example,

when the client or the cause is so repugnant to the lawyer as to be likely to impair the client-lawyer relationship or the lawyer's ability to represent the client. A lawyer may also seek to decline an appointment if acceptance would be unreasonably burdensome, for example, when it would impose a financial sacrifice so great as to be unjust.

[3] An appointed lawyer has the same obligations to the client as retained counsel, including the obligations of loyalty and confidentiality, and is subject to the same limitations on the client-lawyer relationship, such as the obligation to refrain from assisting the client in violation of the Rules.

Canon and Code Antecedents

ABA Canons of Professional Ethics: Canon 4 provided as follows:

4. *When Counsel for an Indigent Prisoner*

A lawyer assigned as counsel for an indigent prisoner ought not to ask to be excused for any trivial reason, and should always exert his best efforts in his behalf.

ABA Model Code of Professional Responsibility: No comparable Disciplinary Rule.

Cross-References in Other Rules

Rule 1.1, Comment 4: "A lawyer may accept representation where the requisite level of competence can be achieved by reasonable preparation. This applies as well to a lawyer who is appointed as counsel for an unrepresented person. See also Rule 6.2."

Rule 1.16, Comment 3: "When a lawyer has been appointed to represent a client, withdrawal ordinarily requires approval of the appointing authority. See also Rule 6.2."

Legislative History of Model Rule 6.2

1980 Discussion Draft and ***1981 Draft*** were substantially the same as adopted, with only minor changes in phrasing.

1982 Draft was the same as adopted *except* that it completely omitted subparagraph (c).

1983 Rule: As originally adopted in 1983, Rule 6.2 was the same as the 2002 version.

2002 Amendments: The ABA Ethics 2000 Commission did not propose any changes to the text or Comment of Rule 6.2.

Selected State Variations

California has no comparable provision in its Rules of Professional Conduct.

Georgia shortens ABA Model Rule 6.2 to a single sentence: "For good cause a lawyer may seek to avoid appointment by a tribunal to represent a person."

New York: omits Rule 6.2.

North Carolina omits Rule 6.2.

Ohio substitutes the word "court" for "tribunal" in the first line of the rule to reflect the Ohio Supreme Court's view that "the inherent authority to make appointments is limited to courts and does not extend to other bodies" included within the definition of "tribunal." Ohio also omits ABA Model Rule 6.2(c) because "the substance . . . is addressed in Rule 1.1, which mandates that a lawyer shall provide competent representation to a client."

Related Materials

ABA Formal Ethics Opinions: See ABA Formal Ethics Op. 06-441 n.16 (2006).

In Forma Pauperis Status: 28 U.S.C. §1915 governs in forma pauperis status for prisoners who file civil suits in federal court. The language most relevant to ABA Model Rule 6.2 is found in §1915(e)(1), which provides: "The court may *request* an attorney to represent any person unable to afford counsel." (Emphasis added.) In *Mallard v. United States District Court,* 490 U.S. 296 (1989), the Supreme Court held 5-4 that the word "request" does not give federal courts the power to compel lawyers to represent indigent prisoners. However, the *Mallard* Court declined to rule on whether federal statutes that permit courts to "assign" or "appoint" counsel, such as 18 U.S.C. §3006A and 42 U.S.C. §2000e-5(f)(1), empower courts to compel unwilling attorneys to represent indigents. The court also did not reach the question whether federal courts have "inherent authority to require lawyers to serve" because this issue had not been raised below. Justice Brennan's majority opinion concluded by saying:

> We do not mean to question, let alone denigrate, lawyers' ethical obligation to assist those who are too poor to afford counsel, or to suggest that requests made pursuant to [§1915] may be lightly declined because they give rise to no ethical claim. On the contrary, in a time when the need for legal services among the poor is growing and public funding for such services has not kept pace, lawyers' ethical obligation to volunteer their time and skills pro bono publico is manifest. . . .

Restatement of the Law Governing Lawyers: See Restatement §§9 and 13 in our chapter on the Restatement later in this volume.

Rule 6.3 Membership in Legal Services Organization

A lawyer may serve as a director, officer or member of a legal services organization, apart from the law firm in which the lawyer practices, notwithstanding that the organization serves persons having interests adverse to a client of the lawyer. The lawyer shall not knowingly participate in a decision or action of the organization:

(a) if participating in the decision or action would be incompatible with the lawyer's obligations to a client under Rule 1.7; or

(b) where the decision or action could have a material adverse effect on the representation of a client of the organization whose interests are adverse to a client of the lawyer.

COMMENT

[1] Lawyers should be encouraged to support and participate in legal service organizations. A lawyer who is an officer or a member of such an organization does not thereby have a client-lawyer relationship with persons served by the organization. However, there is potential conflict between the interests of such persons and the interests of the lawyer's clients. If the possibility of such conflict disqualified a lawyer from serving on the board of a legal services organization, the profession's involvement in such organizations would be severely curtailed.

[2] It may be necessary in appropriate cases to reassure a client of the organization that the representation will not be affected by conflicting loyalties of a member of the board. Established, written policies in this respect can enhance the credibility of such assurances.

Canon and Code Antecedents

ABA Canons of Professional Ethics: No comparable Canon.

ABA Model Code of Professional Responsibility: No comparable Disciplinary Rule.

Cross-References in Other Rules

None.

Legislative History of Model Rule 6.3

1980 Discussion Draft (then Rule 8.2(c)) provided as follows:

> (c) A lawyer may serve as a director, member or officer of an organization involved in reform of the law or its administration notwithstanding the fact that the reform may affect interests of a client of the lawyer if:
>
> (1) when the interests of the client could be affected, the fact is disclosed in the course of deliberations on the matter, but the identity of the client need not be disclosed;
>
> (2) when the client could be adversely affected, the lawyer complies with Rule 1.8 with respect to the client; and
>
> (3) the lawyer takes no part in any decision that could result in a direct material benefit or detriment to the client.

1981 Draft was similar to the adopted version of Rule 6.3, except that it contained an additional requirement that "the organization complies with Rule 5.4 concerning the professional independence of its legal staff."

1982 Draft was adopted.

1983 Rule: As originally adopted in 1983, Rule 6.3 was the same as the 2002 version.

2002 Amendments: The ABA Ethics 2000 Commission did not propose any changes to the text or Comment of Rule 6.3.

Selected State Variations

California has no equivalent provision in its Rules of Professional Conduct.

Georgia adds that there is "no disciplinary penalty for a violation of this Rule."

Illinois: Rule 6.3 applies to a "not-for-profit" legal services organization.

Michigan: Rule 6.3 adds extensive rules governing lawyer participation in "not-for-profit referral service[s] that recommend legal services to the public."

New Jersey: Rule 6.3(a) requires that the organization comply with Rule 5.4 "concerning the professional independence of its legal staff," and Rule 6.3(b) includes adverse effect on the interest of a client "or class of clients of the organization or upon the independence of professional judgment of a lawyer representing such a client."

New York: Rule 6.3(a) extends the restriction to any conflict that would arise "under Rule 1.7 through Rule 1.13."

Ohio omits ABA Model Rule 6.3 because the Supreme Court of Ohio believes the substance of Rule 6.3 is addressed by other rules governing conflicts of interest, including Rule 1.7(a).

Texas: Rule 1.13 (entitled "Conflicts: Public Interest Activities") is similar to ABA Model Rule 6.3, but the Texas rule also governs a lawyer's activities in a "civic, charitable or law reform organization." Texas Rule1.13 omits the clause "notwithstanding that the organization serves persons having interests adverse to a client of the lawyer."

Related Materials

ABA Formal Ethics Opinions: No formal ethics opinions have construed Rule 6.3.

Restatement of the Law Governing Lawyers: See Restatement §135 in our chapter on the Restatement later in this volume.

Rule 6.4 Law Reform Activities Affecting Client Interests

A lawyer may serve as a director, officer or member of an organization involved in reform of the law or its administration notwithstanding that the reform may affect the interests of a client of the lawyer. When the lawyer knows that the interests of a client may be materially benefitted by a decision in which the lawyer participates, the lawyer shall disclose that fact but need not identify the client.

COMMENT

[1] Lawyers involved in organizations seeking law reform generally do not have a client-lawyer relationship with the organization. Otherwise, it might follow that a lawyer could not be involved in a bar association law reform program that might indirectly affect a client. See also Rule 1.2(b). For example, a lawyer specializing in antitrust litigation might be regarded as disqualified from participating in drafting revisions of rules governing that subject. In determining the nature and scope of participation in such activities, a lawyer should be mindful of obligations to clients under other Rules, particularly Rule 1.7. A lawyer is professionally obligated to protect the integrity of the program by making an appropriate disclosure within the organization when the lawyer knows a private client might be materially benefitted.

Canon and Code Antecedents

ABA Canons of Professional Ethics: No comparable Canon.

ABA Model Code of Professional Responsibility: No comparable Disciplinary Rule.

Cross-References in Other Rules

None.

Legislative History of Model Rule 6.4

1980 Discussion Draft (then Rule 8.2(a) and (b)) provided as follows:

Conflict of Interest in Pro Bono Publico Service

(a) A lawyer engaged in service pro bono publico shall avoid improper conflicts of interest therein.

(b) A lawyer may serve as a director, officer, or member of an organization providing legal services to persons of limited means notwithstanding that such services are provided to persons having interests adverse to a client of the lawyer if:

(1) the organization complies with Rule 7.5 [now Rule 5.4(c)] concerning the professional independence of its legal staff;

(2) when the interests of a client of the lawyer could be affected, the lawyer takes no part in any decision by the organization that could have a material adverse effect on the interest of a client of the organization or upon the independence of professional judgment of a lawyer representing such a client; and

(3) the lawyer otherwise complies with Rule 1.8 with respect to the lawyer's client.

1981 Draft provided as follows:

A lawyer may serve as a director, officer or member of an organization involved in reform of the law or its administration notwithstanding the fact that the reform may affect the interests of a client of the lawyer if the lawyer takes no part in any decision that could have a direct material effect on the client.

1982 Draft was adopted.

1983 Rule: As originally adopted in 1983, Rule 6.4 was the same as the 2002 version.

2002 Amendments: The ABA Ethics 2000 Commission did not propose any changes to the text or Comment of Rule 6.4.

Selected State Variations

California has no comparable provision.

District of Columbia: Rule 6.4 adds the following paragraph (a): "A lawyer should assist in improving the administration of justice. A lawyer may discharge this requirement by rendering services in activities for improving the law, the legal system, or the legal profession."

Florida replaces "materially benefited" with "materially affected" in the second sentence of Rule 6.4.

Georgia adds that "[t]here is no disciplinary penalty for a violation of this Rule."

New Hampshire: New Hampshire substitutes the word "affected" for the word "benefitted" in the second sentence of Rule 6.4. A special New Hampshire Comment explains the reasoning: "Since situations may arise in which law reform activities may materially impinge on a client's interest in an adverse, as well as beneficial manner, the change was made to reflect that possibility."

New York: Rule 6.4 adds a third sentence stating: "In determining the nature and scope of participation in such activities, a lawyer should be mindful of obligations to clients under other Rules, particularly Rule 1.7."

Ohio omits ABA Model Rule 6.4 because the Supreme Court of Ohio believes that the "substance of Model Rule 6.4 is addressed by other provisions of the Ohio Rules of Professional Conduct that address conflicts of interest."

Related Materials

ABA Formal Ethics Opinions: No formal ethics opinions have construed Rule 6.4.

Model Rules of Professional Conduct for Federal Lawyers: Rule 6.4 adds a sentence providing that a federal lawyer "shall not knowingly participate in a decision or action of the organization if participating in the decision would be incompatible with the Federal lawyer's obligations to the client under Rule 1.7."

Restatement of the Law Governing Lawyers: The Restatement has no comparable provision.

Rule 6.5 Nonprofit and Court-Annexed Limited Legal Services Programs

(a) A lawyer who, under the auspices of a program sponsored by a nonprofit organization or court, provides short-term limited legal services to a client without expectation by either the lawyer or the client that the lawyer will provide continuing representation in the matter:

(1) is subject to Rules 1.7 and 1.9(a) only if the lawyer knows that the representation of the client involves a conflict of interest; and

(2) is subject to Rule 1.10 only if the lawyer knows that another lawyer associated with the lawyer in a law firm is disqualified by Rule 1.7 or 1.9(a) with respect to the matter.

(b) Except as provided in paragraph (a)(2), Rule 1.10 is inapplicable to a representation governed by this Rule.

COMMENT

[1] Legal services organizations, courts and various nonprofit organizations have established programs through which lawyers provide short-term limited legal services—such as advice or the completion of legal forms—that will assist persons to address their legal problems without further representation by a lawyer. In these programs, such as legal advice hotlines, advice-only clinics or pro se counseling programs, a client-lawyer relationship is established, but there is no expectation that the lawyer's representation of the client will continue beyond the limited consultation. Such programs are normally operated under circumstances in which it is not feasible for a lawyer to systematically screen for conflicts of interest as is generally required before undertaking a representation. See, e.g., Rules 1.7, 1.9 and 1.10.

[2] A lawyer who provides short-term limited legal services pursuant to this Rule must secure the client's informed consent to the limited scope of the representation. See Rule 1.2(c). If a short-term limited representation would not be reasonable under the circumstances, the lawyer may offer advice to the client but must also advise the client of the need for further assistance of counsel. Except as provided in this Rule, the Rules of Professional Conduct, including Rules 1.6 and 1.9(c), are applicable to the limited representation.

[3] Because a lawyer who is representing a client in the circumstances addressed by this Rule ordinarily is not able to check systematically for conflicts of interest, paragraph (a) requires compliance with Rules 1.7 or 1.9(a) only if the lawyer knows that the representation presents a conflict of interest for the lawyer, and with Rule 1.10 only if the lawyer knows that another lawyer in the lawyer's firm is disqualified by Rules 1.7 or 1.9(a) in the matter.

[4] Because the limited nature of the services significantly reduces the risk of conflicts of interest with other matters being handled by the lawyer's firm, paragraph (b) provides that Rule 1.10 is inapplicable to a representation governed by this Rule except as provided by paragraph (a)(2). Paragraph (a)(2) requires the participating lawyer to comply with Rule 1.10 when the lawyer knows that the lawyer's firm is disqualified by Rule 1.7 or 1.9(a). By virtue of paragraph (b), however, a lawyer's participation in a short-term limited legal services program will not preclude the lawyer's firm from undertaking or continuing the representation of a client with interests adverse to a client being represented under the program's auspices. Nor will the personal disqualification of a lawyer participating in the program be imputed to other lawyers participating in the program.

[5] If, after commencing a short-term limited representation in accordance with this Rule, a lawyer undertakes to represent the client in the matter on an ongoing basis, Rules 1.7, 1.9(a) and 1.10 become applicable.

Cross-References in Other Rules

Rule 1.16, Comment 1: "Ordinarily, a representation in a matter is completed when the agreed-upon assistance has been concluded. See Rules 1.2(c) and 6.5. See also Rule 1.3, Comment [4]."

Canon and Code Antecedents

ABA Canons of Professional Ethics: No comparable Canon.

ABA Model Code of Professional Responsibility: No comparable Disciplinary Rule.

Legislative History of Model Rule 6.5

2002 Amendments: Rule 6.5 was added to the Model Rules in February 2002. The new rule and its Comment were based on a proposal by the ABA Ethics 2000 Commission, which the ABA House of Delegates adopted without change. The Reporter's Explanation that accompanied the Ethics 2000 Commission proposal provided, in relevant part, as follows:

*Model Rule 6.5—Reporter's Explanation of Changes**

Rule 6.5 is a new Rule in response to the Commission's concern that a strict application of the conflict-of-interest rules may be deterring lawyers from serving as volunteers in programs in which clients are provided short-term limited legal services under the auspices of a nonprofit organization or a court-annexed program. The paradigm is the legal-advice hotline or pro se clinic, the purpose of which is to provide short-term limited legal assistance to persons of limited means who otherwise would go unrepresented.

Paragraph (a) limits Rule 6.5 to situations in which lawyers provide clients short-term limited legal services under the auspices of a program sponsored by a nonprofit organization or court. The Commission believes that the proposed relaxation of the conflict rules does not pose a significant risk to clients when the lawyer is working in a program sponsored by a nonprofit organization or a court and will eliminate an impediment to lawyer participation in such programs. See Comment [1].

Paragraph (a)(1) provides that the lawyer is subject to the requirements of Rules 1.7 and 1.9(a) only if the lawyer knows that the representation involves a conflict of interest. The purpose is to make it unnecessary for the lawyer to do a comprehensive conflicts check in a practice setting in which it normally is not feasible to do so. See Comment [3]. In cases in which the lawyer knows of a conflict of interest, however, compliance with Rules 1.7 and 1.9(a) is required.

Paragraph (a)(2) provides that a lawyer participating in a short-term legal services program must comply with Rule 1.10 if the lawyer knows that a lawyer with whom the lawyer is associated in a firm would be disqualified from handling the matter by Rules 1.7 or 1.9(a). By otherwise exempting a representation governed by this Rule

* Committee Reports do not represent official policy of the ABA. They are for information only, and the opinions are those of the authors of the report.

from Rule 1.10, however, paragraph (b) protects lawyers associated with the participating lawyer from a vicarious disqualification that might otherwise be required. Thus, as explained in Comment [4], a lawyer's participation in a short-term limited legal services program will not preclude the lawyer's firm from undertaking or continuing the representation of a client with interests adverse to a client being represented under the program's auspices. Nor will a personal disqualification of a lawyer participating in the program be imputed to other lawyers participating in the program. Given the limited nature of the representation provided in nonprofit short-term limited legal services programs, the Commission thinks that the protections afforded clients by Rule 1.10 are not necessary except in the circumstances specified in paragraph (a)(2).

The remainder of the Reporter's Explanation of Changes tracks each paragraph of the Comment to Rule 6.5. To view the full Reporter's Explanation, visit *www.abanet.org/cpr/e2k-rule65rem.html.*

Selected State Variations

Alabama: Rule 6.5 is based on Model Rule 6.5, but Alabama also has a Rule 6.6, which has no Model Rule equivalent. Rule 6.6 states that any inactive member of the Alabama State Bar may render pro bono services by paying special membership dues and becoming a special member of the Alabama State Bar for the year in which the pro bono services are rendered.

California has adopted Rule 1-650 that is substantially similar to Model Rule 6.5, but Rule 1-650(A) also refers to programs sponsored by a "government agency, bar association, [or] law school," and California adds a new Rule 1-650(C) that states as follows: "The personal disqualification of a lawyer participating in the program will not be imputed to other lawyers participating in the program."

Connecticut adds the following paragraph that is identical to Comment 2 to ABA Rule 6.5:

> (b) A lawyer who provides short-term limited legal services pursuant to this Rule must secure the client's informed consent to the limited scope of the representation. See Rule 1.2 (c). If a short-term limited representation would not be reasonable under the circumstances, the lawyer may offer advice to the client but must also advise the client of the need for further assistance of counsel. Except as provided in this Rule, the Rules of Professional Conduct, including Rules 1.6 and 1.9(c), are applicable to the limited representation.

New Hampshire: Rule 6.5(a) applies only to a "one time consultation with a client" instead of the ABA's version "short-term limited legal services to a client." Also, echoing ABA Comment 2 to Rule 6.5, New Hampshire's Rule 6.5(c) provides that "Rules 1.6 and 1.9(c) are applicable to a representation governed by this Rule." Finally, a special New Hampshire Comment states as follows:

> Should a lawyer participating in a one-time consultation under this Rule later discover that the lawyer's firm was representing or later undertook the representation of an adverse client, the prior participation of the attorney will not preclude the lawyer's firm from continuing or undertaking representation of such adverse client. But the participating lawyer will be disqualified and must be screened from any involvement with the firm's adverse client. See ABA Comment [4].

New York: Rule 6.5(a) covers programs sponsored by government agencies and bar associations. The Rule also specifies that a conflict arises only if a lawyer "has actual knowledge [of the conflict] at the time of commencement of representation." New York also adds Rule 6.5(c)-(e), which provides as follows:

> (c) Short-term limited legal services are services providing legal advice or representation free of charge as part of a program described in paragraph (a) with no expectation that the assistance will continue beyond what is necessary to complete an initial consultation, representation or court appearance.
>
> (d) The lawyer providing short-term limited legal services must secure the client's informed consent to the limited scope of the representation, and such representation shall be subject to the provisions of Rule 1.6.
>
> (e) This Rule shall not apply where the court before which the matter is pending determines that a conflict of interest exists or, if during the course of the representation, the lawyer providing the services becomes aware of the existence of a conflict of interest precluding continued representation.

Wisconsin: Rule 6.5(a) also applies to a program sponsored by "a bar association" or "an accredited law school."

Related Materials

ABA Formal Ethics Opinions: No formal ethics opinions have construed Rule 6.5.

Restatement of the Law Governing Lawyers: See Restatement §§121 and 123 in our chapter on the Restatement later in this volume.

ARTICLE 7. INFORMATION ABOUT LEGAL SERVICES

Rule 7.1 Communications Concerning a Lawyer's Services

7.2

5.5 ct. 21

A lawyer shall not make a false or misleading communication about the lawyer or the lawyer's services. A communication is false or misleading if it contains a material misrepresentation of fact or law, or omits a fact necessary to make the statement considered as a whole not materially misleading.

togstad v. vesely, otto, miller & keefe
S.O.L Ran
In re peters – S/H claim

COMMENT

[1] This Rule governs all communications about a lawyer's services, including advertising permitted by Rule 7.2. Whatever means are used to make known a lawyer's services, statements about them must be truthful.

[2] Truthful statements that are misleading are also prohibited by this Rule. A truthful statement is misleading if it omits a fact necessary to make the lawyer's communication considered as a whole not materially misleading. A truthful statement is also misleading if there is a substantial likelihood that it will lead a reasonable

person to formulate a specific conclusion about the lawyer or the lawyer's services for which there is no reasonable factual foundation.

[3] An advertisement that truthfully reports a lawyer's achievements on behalf of clients or former clients may be misleading if presented so as to lead a reasonable person to form an unjustified expectation that the same results could be obtained for other clients in similar matters without reference to the specific factual and legal circumstances of each client's case. Similarly, an unsubstantiated comparison of the lawyer's services or fees with the services or fees of other lawyers may be misleading if presented with such specificity as would lead a reasonable person to conclude that the comparison can be substantiated. The inclusion of an appropriate disclaimer or qualifying language may preclude a finding that a statement is likely to create unjustified expectations or otherwise mislead a prospective client.

[4] See also Rule 8.4(e) for the prohibition against stating or implying an ability to influence improperly a government agency or official or to achieve results by means that violate the Rules of Professional Conduct or other law.

Canon and Code Antecedents

ABA Canons of Professional Ethics: Canons 27 and 43 provided as follows:

27. *Advertising, Direct or Indirect*

It is unprofessional to solicit professional employment by circulars, advertisements, through touters or by personal communications or interviews not warranted by personal relations. Indirect advertisements for professional employment such as furnishing or inspiring newspaper comments, or procuring his photograph to be published in connection with causes in which the lawyer has been or is engaged or concerning the manner of their conduct, the magnitude of the interest involved, the importance of the lawyer's position, and all other like self-laudation, offend the traditions and lower the tone of our profession and are reprehensible; but the customary use of simple professional cards is not improper.

Publication in reputable law lists in a manner consistent with the standards of conduct imposed by these canons of brief biographical and informative data is permissible. Such data must not be misleading and may include only a statement of the lawyer's name and the names of his professional associates; addresses, telephone numbers, cable addresses; branches of the profession practiced; date and place of birth and admission to the bar; schools attended; with dates of graduation, degrees and other educational distinctions; public or quasi-public offices; posts of honor; legal authorships; legal teaching positions; memberships and offices in bar associations and committees thereof, in legal and scientific societies and legal fraternities; foreign language ability; the fact of listings in other reputable law lists; the names and addresses of references; and, with their written consent, the names of clients regularly represented. A certificate of compliance with the Rules and Standards issued by the Standing Committee on Law Lists may be treated as evidence that such list is reputable.

It is not improper for a lawyer who is admitted to practice as a proctor in admiralty to use that designation on his letterhead or shingle or for a lawyer who has complied with the statutory requirements of admission to practice before the patent office, to so use the designation "patent attorney" or "patent lawyer" or "trademark attorney" or "trademark lawyer" or any combination of those terms.

43. Approved Law Lists

> It shall be improper for a lawyer to permit his name to be published in a law list the conduct, management or contents of which are calculated or likely to deceive or injure the public or the profession, or to lower the dignity or standing of the profession.

ABA Model Code of Professional Responsibility: Compare DR 2-101 and DR 9-101(C) (reprinted later in this volume).

Cross-References in Other Rules

Rule 5.5, Comment 21: "Whether and how lawyers may communicate the availability of their services to prospective clients in this jurisdiction is governed by **Rules 7.1** to 7.5."

Rule 5.7, Comment 10: "The promotion of the law-related services must also in all respects comply with **Rules 7.1** through 7.3, dealing with advertising and solicitation."

Rule 7.2(a): "Subject to the requirements of **Rules 7.1** and 7.3, a lawyer may advertise services through written, recorded or electronic communication, including public media."

Rule 7.3, Comment 3: The "potential for informal review is itself likely to help guard against statements and claims that might constitute false and misleading communications, in violation of **Rule 7.1**."

Rule 7.3, Comment 5: "[A]ny solicitation which contains information which is false or misleading within the meaning of **Rule 7.1** . . . is prohibited."

Rule 7.3, Comment 8: "Lawyers who participate in a legal service plan must reasonably assure that the plan sponsors are in compliance with **Rules 7.1**, 7.2 and 7.3(b). See 8.4(a)."

Rule 7.4, Comment 1: Communications claiming specialization "are subject to the 'false and misleading' standard applied in **Rule 7.1** to communications concerning a lawyer's services."

Rule 7.5(a): "A lawyer shall not use a firm name, letterhead or other professional designation that violates **Rule 7.1**. A trade name may be used by a lawyer in private practice if it does not imply a connection with a government agency or with a public or charitable legal services organization and is not otherwise in violation of **Rule 7.1**."

Legislative History of Model Rule 7.1

1980 Discussion Draft of Rule 7.1 (then Rule 9.1) was substantially the same as adopted, except that the first sentence prohibited a lawyer from making any "false, fraudulent, or misleading statement. . . ."

1981 and ***1982 Drafts*** were the same as adopted.

1983 Rule: From 1983 until its amendment in 2002, Rule 7.1 provided as follows:

> A lawyer shall not make a false or misleading communication about the lawyer or the lawyer's services. A communication is false or misleading if it:

(a) contains a material misrepresentation of fact or law, or omits a fact necessary to make the statement considered as a whole not materially misleading;

(b) is likely to create an unjustified expectation about results the lawyer can achieve, or states or implies that the lawyer can achieve results by means that violate the Rules of Professional Conduct or other law; or

(c) compares the lawyer's services with other lawyers' services, unless the comparison can be factually substantiated.

2002 Amendments: In 2002, the ABA House of Delegates adopted with only minor changes the ABA Ethics 2000 Commission proposal to amend Rule 7.1 and its Comment. The amendments deleted paragraphs (b) and (c) from the former rule, deleted language in Comment 1 relating to "unjustified expectations," and added Comments 2, 3, and 4 to address subjects previously covered in the language deleted from the text and Comment of Rule 7.1.

Selected State Variations

California: Rule 1-400 provides, in pertinent part, as follows:

(A) For purposes of this rule, "communication" means any message or offer made by or on behalf of a member concerning the availability for professional employment of a member or a law firm directed to any former, present, or prospective client, including but not limited to the following:

(1) Any use of firm name, trade name, fictitious name, or other professional designation of such member or law firm; or

(2) Any stationery, letterhead, business card, sign, brochure, or other comparable written material describing such member, law firm, or lawyers; or

(3) Any advertisement (regardless of medium) of such member or law firm directed to the general public or any substantial portion thereof; or

(4) Any unsolicited correspondence from a member or law firm directed to any person or entity. . . .

(C) A communication or a solicitation (as defined herein) shall not:

(1) Contain any untrue statement; or

(2) Contain any matter, or present or arrange any matter in a manner or format which is false, deceptive, or which tends to confuse, deceive, or mislead the public; or

(3) Omit to state any fact necessary to make the statements made, in the light of circumstances under which they are made, not misleading to the public; or

(4) Fail to indicate clearly, expressly, or by context, that it is a communication or solicitation, as the case may be; or

(5) Be transmitted in any manner which involves intrusion, coercion, duress, compulsion, intimidation, threats, or vexatious or harassing conduct. . . .

(E) The Board of Governors of the State Bar shall formulate and adopt standards as to communications which will be presumed to violate this rule 1-400. The standards shall only be used as presumptions affecting the burden of proof in disciplinary proceedings involving alleged violations of these rules. . . . Such standards . . . shall be effective and binding on all members.

The Standards adopted by the State Bar's Board of Governors pursuant to rule 1-400(E) are long and detailed. For example, Standards 1 and 2 provide that the following forms of communication "are presumed to be in violation of rule 1-400":

(1) A "communication" which contains guarantees, warranties, or predictions regarding the result of the representation.

(2) A "communication" which contains testimonials about or endorsements of a member unless such communication also contains an express disclaimer such as "this testimonial or endorsement does not constitute a guarantee, warranty, or prediction regarding the outcome of your legal matter."

See also Business & Professions Code §§6157-6159.2 (generally prohibiting "any false, misleading, or deceptive statement" in a lawyer advertisement; imposing detailed restrictions on advertisements containing dramatizations, impersonations, and spokespersons; and prohibiting various specific claims and techniques); California Labor Code §139.45 ("the Industrial Medical Council and the administrative director shall take particular care to preclude any advertisements with respect to industrial injuries or illnesses that are false or mislead the public with respect to workers' compensation. In promulgating rules with respect to advertising, the State Bar . . . shall also take particular care to achieve the same goal"); and California Labor Code §5432 (requiring every advertisement soliciting workers' compensation clients to state conspicuously: "Making a false or fraudulent workers' compensation claim is a felony subject to up to 5 years in prison or a fine of up to $50,000 or double the value of the fraud, whichever is greater, or by both imprisonment and fine").

Colorado: Colorado retains the pre-2002 version of ABA Model Rule 7.1(a) and adds the following paragraphs:

(b) No lawyer shall, directly or indirectly, pay all or a part of the cost of communications concerning a lawyer's services by a lawyer not in the same firm unless the communication discloses the name and address of the non-advertising lawyer, the relationship between the advertising lawyer and the non-advertising lawyer, and whether the advertising lawyer may refer any case received through the advertisement to the non-advertising lawyer.

(c) Unsolicited communications concerning a lawyer's services mailed to prospective clients shall be sent only by regular U.S. mail, not by registered mail or other forms of restricted delivery, and shall not resemble legal pleadings or other legal documents.

(d) Any communication that states or implies the client does not have to pay a fee if there is no recovery shall also disclose that the client may be liable for costs. This provision does not apply to communications that only state that contingent or percentage fee arrangements are available, or that only state the initial consultation is free.

District of Columbia: Rule 7.1(a) adds that a communication is false or misleading if it "[c]ontains an assertion about the lawyer or the lawyer's services that cannot be substantiated."

Florida: Florida's lawyer advertising rules are more comprehensive and detailed than the ABA Model Rules of Professional Conduct or those in any other American jurisdiction. They are often revised and defy easy summary or comparison with the ABA rules. (Indeed, in July 2011, just before this book went to press, the Florida Bar submitted to the Florida Supreme Court substantial proposed revisions to the advertising rules.) The rules address in depth the content of advertisements, electronic and computer advertising, referral services, and filing requirements. Some of the more noteworthy Florida advertising and solicitation provisions appear in Selected State Variations under other rules in Article 7.

Georgia generally tracks the pre-2002 version of ABA Model Rule 7.1, but adds special subparagraphs requiring that all advertisements mentioning contingent fees or stating "no fee unless you win or collect" or any similar phrase must also conspicuously present a disclaimer stating: "Court costs and other additional expenses of legal action usually must be paid by the client. Contingent fees are not permitted in all types of cases."

Indiana: Effective January 1, 2011, Comment 2 to Rule 7.1 identifies ten types of statements that are presumptively misleading, such as a statement that "appeals primarily to a lay person's fear, greed, or desire for revenge" or "contains a dramatization or re-creation of events unless the advertising clearly and conspicuously discloses that a dramatization or re-creation is being presented."

Iowa has many rules on lawyer advertising. Its version of Rule 7.1 adds the following:

> (b) A lawyer shall not communicate with the public using statements that are unverifiable. In addition, advertising permitted under these rules shall not rely on emotional appeal or contain any statement or claim relating to the quality of the lawyer's legal services.

Louisiana: Rule 7.1(a) identifies a non-exclusive list of advertising methods that lawyers may use. Among other variations, Rule 7.1(c) explicitly exempts from the rules any advertising that is not "motivated by pecuniary gain."

Mississippi: Rule 7.5(a) requires that a copy or recording of any lawyer advertisement to be published must be submitted to the Office of the General Counsel of the Mississippi Bar "prior to its first dissemination" unless exempted under an extensive list in Rule 7.5(b). If a lawyer submits a proposed advertisement 45 days before its dissemination, the lawyer may request an "advisory opinion." If the Office of the General Counsel does not respond within 45 days, the advertisement will be "deemed approved," but if the Office of General Counsel determines within the 45-day period that there is "reasonable doubt" that the advertisement complies with the rules, it may extend the 45-day period.

Missouri: Rule 7.1 adds that a communication is false or misleading if it:

> (b) is likely to create an unjustified expectation about results the lawyer can achieve;
>
> (c) proclaims results obtained on behalf of clients, such as the amount of a damage award or the lawyer's record in obtaining favorable verdicts or settlements, without stating that past results afford no guarantee of future results and that every case is different and must be judged on its own merits;
>
> (d) states or implies that the lawyer can achieve results by means that violate the Rules of Professional Conduct or other law;
>
> (e) compares the quality of a lawyer's or a law firm's services with other lawyers' services, unless the comparison can be factually substantiated;
>
> (f) advertises for a specific type of case concerning which the lawyer has neither experience nor competence;
>
> (g) indicates an area of practice in which the lawyer routinely refers matters to other lawyers, without conspicuous identification of such fact;
>
> (h) contains any paid testimonial about or endorsement of the lawyer, without conspicuous identification of the fact that payment has been made for the testimonial or endorsement;
>
> (i) contains any simulated portrayal of a lawyer, client, victim, scene, or event without conspicuous identification of the fact that it is a simulation. . . .

(j) provides an office address for an office staffed only part-time or by appointment only, without conspicuous identification of such fact; or

(k) states that legal services are available on a contingent or no-recovery-no-fee basis without stating conspicuously that the client may be responsible for costs or expenses, if that is the case.

The presumptions that statements are misleading contained in Rule 4-7.1(c), (g), (h), and (k) shall not apply to a not-for-profit organization funded in whole or in part by the Legal Services Corporation . . . or to pro bono services provided free of charge by a not-for-profit organization, a court-annexed program, a bar association, or an accredited law school.

Nevada: Among many other variations, Rule 7.1(d) adds that a communication is false or misleading if it "contains a testimonial or endorsement which violates any portion of this Rule."

In addition, Rule 1.4(c) requires every lawyer or law firm to "have available" a "Lawyer's Biographical Data Form" that must "be provided upon request of the State Bar or a client or prospective client. . . ." Rule 1.4(c) also specifies information that must be included in the form and included with every written advertisement, and it specifies other detailed information that must be provided to a client or prospective client upon request (such as a "good faith estimate of the number of jury trials tried to a verdict by the lawyer to the present date, identifying the court or courts"). These requirements are also reinforced in Rule 1.18(g) (relating to prospective clients).

New Jersey: Rule 7.1 prohibits a lawyer from making a false or misleading communication about the lawyer, the lawyer's services, or "any matter in which the lawyer has or seeks professional involvement." A communication is false or misleading under New Jersey Rule 7.1(a) if (among other things) it "(2) is likely to create an unjustified expectation about results the lawyer can achieve," or "(3) compares the lawyer's services with other lawyers' services, unless (i) the name of the comparing organization is stated, (ii) the basis for the comparison can be substantiated, and (iii) the communication includes the following disclaimer in a readily discernable manner: 'No aspect of this advertisement has been approved by the Supreme Court of New Jersey'" or "(4) relates to legal fees other than" a specified list of permitted statements, including "the fee for an initial consultation," "fees for specifically described legal services, provided there is a reasonable disclosure of all relevant variables and considerations so that the statement would not be misunderstood or deceptive," and "specified hourly rates, provided the statement makes clear that the total charge will vary according to the number of hours devoted to the matter, and in relation to the varying hourly rates charged for the services of different individuals who may be assigned to the matter. . . ." Rule 7.1(b) makes it "unethical" for a lawyer to use an advertisement "known to have been disapproved by the Committee on Attorney Advertising, or one substantially the same as the one disapproved, until or unless modified or reversed by the Advertising Committee. . . ."

New York: New York adds the following definitions to Rule 1.0 (terminology):

(a) "Advertisement" means any public or private communication made by or on behalf of a lawyer or law firm about that lawyer or law firm's services, the primary purpose of which is for the retention of the lawyer or law firm. It does not include communications to existing clients or other lawyers.

(c) "Computer-accessed communication" means any communication made by or on behalf of a lawyer or law firm that is disseminated through the use of a computer or related electronic device, including, but not limited to, web sites, weblogs, search engines, electronic mail, banner advertisements, pop-up and pop-under advertisements, chat rooms, list servers, instant messaging, or other internet presences, and any attachments or links related thereto.

Rule 7.1 varies considerably from the Model Rule and contains many unique prohibitions, requirements, and comments. For example, Rule 7.1(b) lists numerous items (*e.g.*, "legal and nonlegal education," "foreign language fluency," "fees for initial consultation," and "bona fide professional ratings") that may be included in an advertisement. Rule 7.1(e)-(f) mandates various disclosures and disclaimers.

Effective April 15, 2011, Rule 7.1(c) was amended to remove or revise several advertising provisions restrictions that were held to be unconstitutional in *Alexander v. Cahill*, 598 F.3d 79 (2d Cir. 2010), including restrictions on endorsements by current clients, a ban on the portrayal of a judge, and a ban on the use of a "nickname, moniker, motto or trade name that implies an ability to obtain results in a matter." Other restrictions remain intact, however, including mandatory disclosures when using actors or depicting fictionalized events.

North Carolina retains the subparagraphs that were deleted from the pre-2002 version of ABA Model Rule 7.1. North Carolina also adds a Rule 7.1(b) providing that a "dramatization depicting a fictional situation is misleading unless it . . . contains a conspicuous written or oral statement at the beginning and end of the communication, explaining that the communication contains a dramatization and does not depict actual events or real persons."

Ohio: Rule 7.1 also prohibits a lawyer from making or using a "nonverifiable" communication about the lawyer or the lawyer's services.

Oregon: Rule 7.1(a) contains a list of 12 specific items that may not appear in advertisements or may only appear under particular circumstances. Actors may be used if the communication "clearly and conspicuously discloses" that status.

Pennsylvania: Rule 7.1 tracks ABA Model Rule 7.1 verbatim—but Pennsylvania Rule 7.2 contains numerous restrictions designed to prevent false or misleading communications. For example, Rule 7.2 prohibits endorsements by any celebrity or public figure; prohibits lawyers from stating or implying that they are associated together in a law firm if that is not the case; prohibits any portrayal of a client by a non-client; and prohibits the use of "pictures, or persons, which are not actual or authentic, without a disclosure that such depiction is a dramatization." An unusual Rule 7.2(k) provides that "[i]f a lawyer or law firm advertises for a particular type of case that the lawyer or law firm ordinarily does not handle from intake through trial, that fact must be disclosed. A lawyer or law firm shall not advertise as a pretext to refer cases obtained from advertising to other lawyers."

Virginia has divided the substance of ABA Model Rule 7.1 into two separate rules. Rule 7.1 applies to all "public communication," defined as "all communication other than 'in-person' communication," while Rule 7.2 applies only to "advertising." Rule 7.1 generally tracks the pre-2002 version of ABA Model Rule 7.1, but adds that a communication is improper if it "states or implies that the outcome of a particular legal matter was not or will not be related to its facts or merits." Rule 7.2 governs various specific types and styles of lawyer advertising. For example, Rule 7.2(a) provides that an advertisement violates Rule 7.1 if it "(1) contains an endorsement by a celebrity or public figure who is not a client of the firm without disclosure (i) of the fact that the speaker is not a client of the lawyer or the firm, and

(ii) whether the speaker is being paid for the appearance or endorsement," or "(2) contains a portrayal of a client by a non-client without disclosure that the depiction is a dramatization," or:

> (3) advertises specific or cumulative case results, without a disclaimer that (i) puts the case results in a context that is not misleading; (ii) states that case results depend upon a variety of factors unique to each case; and (iii) further states that case results do not guarantee or predict a similar result in any future case undertaken by the lawyer. The disclaimer shall precede the communication of the case results. . . .

Related Materials

ABA Aspirational Goals for Lawyer Advertising: In 1988, the ABA's House of Delegates endorsed a series of nonbinding "aspirational" goals written by the ABA's Commission on Advertising. These Aspirational Goals are intended to permit lawyers to advertise "effectively yet with dignity." They are available in full online at *http://www.americanbar.org/groups/professional_responsibility/resources/professionalism/professionalism_ethics_in_lawyer_advertising/abaaspirationalgoals.html.* Here are some significant excerpts:*

> *Preamble*
>
> [E]mpirical evidence suggests that undignified advertising can detract from the public's confidence in the legal profession and respect for the justice system.
>
> Under present case law, the matter of dignity is widely believed to be so subjective as to be beyond the scope of constitutionally permitted regulation. Nevertheless, it seems entirely proper for the organized bar to suggest non-binding aspirational goals urging lawyers who wish to advertise to do so in a dignified manner. . . .
>
> *Aspirational Goals*
>
> 6. Lawyers should consider that the use of inappropriately dramatic music, unseemly slogans, hawkish spokespersons, premium offers, slapstick routines or outlandish settings in advertising does not instill confidence in the lawyer or the legal profession and undermines the serious purpose of legal services and the judicial system. . . .
>
> 9. Lawyers should design their advertising to attract legal matters which they are competent to handle.
>
> 10. Lawyers should be concerned with making legal services more affordable to the public. Lawyer advertising may be designed to build up client bases so that efficiencies of scale may be achieved that will translate into more affordable legal services.

* Copyright © 1983, 1989-2011 by the American Bar Association. All rights reserved. Reprinted with permission of the American Bar Association. Copies of these rules are available from ABA Member Service, Order Fulfillment, 750 North Lake Shore Drive, Chicago, Illinois 60611.

ABA Best Practice Guidelines for Legal Information Web Site Providers: In 2003, the ABA adopted a set of Best Practice Guidelines for Legal Information Web Site Providers. The goal of the Guidelines is "to promote the development of quality legal web sites and to provide guidance to legal web site developers." The Guidelines are available online at *http://meetings.abanet.org/webupload/commupload/EP024500/relatedresources/best_practice_presentation.pdf.*

ABA Commission on Ethics 20/20: In 2009, the ABA created the ABA Commission on Ethics 20/20, which is comprehensively reviewing the ABA Model Rules of Professional Conduct and other lawyer regulatory sources in light of globalization and changes in technology. In 2010, the ABA House of Delegates approved a resolution stating: "Resolved, that the American Bar Association examine any efforts to publish national, state, territorial, and local rankings of law firms and law schools." ABA President Carolyn Lamm then asked the Commission on Ethics 20/20 to examine the issue of lawyer and law firm ratings and rankings. (A special committee of the ABA Section of Legal Education and Admissions to the Bar was created to study law school rankings, which are a separate subject.) The Ethics 20/20 Commission, in turn, formed a Working Group on Lawyer and Law Firm Ratings and Rankings and asked former ABA President Roberta Cooper Ramo and Donald B. Hilliker to co-chair it.

In August 2011, the Commission finalized its Informational Report. The Report identified various issues associated with rankings and ratings, but concluded that "no change is currently required to the black letter text of or Comment to Model Rule 7.1." However, the Commission recommended that the ABA Standing Committee on Ethics and Professional Responsibility draft a Formal Opinion that discusses related issues, including (i) the extent to which lawyers can respond to requests for information from rankings and ratings providers in a manner that is consistent with lawyers' duty to protect confidential information and (ii) the extent to which lawyers can communicate to the public the results of various rankings and ratings while ensuring that those communications are truthful and not misleading. A copy of the Informational Report, as well as more information about the Ethics 20/20 Commission, is available on the website of the Commission on Ethics 20/20 at *www.americanbar.org/Ethics2020.*

ABA Commission on Responsibility in Client Development (formerly the ABA Commission on Advertising) and ABA Standing Committee on Professionalism: In 1977, the year that the United States Supreme Court extended First Amendment protection to lawyer advertising, the ABA appointed a Commission on Advertising. In 1994, the Commission on Advertising held public hearings to explore whether advertising by lawyers was contributing to a perceived decline in the public's opinion of lawyers, and whether advertising by lawyers was helping a significant number of people, especially the poor, to locate lawyers. In 1995, the Commission issued a final report entitled Lawyer Advertising at the Crossroads (ISBN No. 1-57073-142-X). The Executive Summary of the report included the following observations:

> While many find some forms of advertising offensive, regulations which violate the right of lawyers to communicate their services do nothing more than create stop-gap measures that forestall true solutions. . . .
>
> Public opinion research recurrently shows that the principal factors contributing to a decline in the public image of lawyers involve perceptions of honesty, caring and value. Those who dislike lawyers believe they are dishonest, selfish and too expensive. While the legal profession strongly believes that advertising contributes to the decline

of the profession's image, the public rarely mentions advertising as a factor. Dominant influences in forming opinions about lawyers are personal contacts, media reports and fictional representations on television, in movies and in books.

Research specifically on lawyer advertising indicates the public considers it a source of information, but tends to find it objectionable when it becomes increasingly invasive. Therefore, people tend to object to television commercials, billboards, and direct mail more so than ads in the Yellow Pages and in newspapers. . . .

[I]t is clear that advertising is a major factor in the delivery of legal services, especially to the poor. While 70 to 80 percent of those who have used a lawyer found the lawyer through some form of personal referral, an increasing number of people find their lawyers through impersonal methods such as lawyer referral services, prepaid services and group legal plans and advertising. Advertising, including the use of the Yellow Pages, is consistently the most frequently used of the impersonal methods of finding a lawyer. . . .

In 1999, to reflect its expanding mission, the Commission on Advertising changed its name to the Commission on Responsibility in Client Development. In 2002, however, the ABA "sunset" the Commission because its work duplicated the work of the ABA Standing Committee on Professionalism. Questions on lawyer advertising should now be directed to the ABA Standing Committee on Professionalism. For more information, visit *http://www.americanbar.org/groups/professional_responsibility/resources/professionalism/professionalism_ethics_in_lawyer_advertising.html.*

ABA Formal Ethics Opinions: See ABA Formal Ethics Ops. 87-355 (1987), 90-357 (1990), 93-379 (1993), 94-388 (1994), 95-391 (1995), 03-430 (2003), 08-451 (2008), and 10-457 (2010).

IRS Regulations: In the regulations governing practice before the Internal Revenue Service, 31 C.F.R. §10.30(a)(1) provides that a lawyer admitted to practice before the IRS "may not, with respect to any Internal Revenue Service matter, in any way use or participate in the use of any form of public communication or private solicitation containing a false, fraudulent, or coercive statement or claim; or a misleading or deceptive statement or claim."

Lanham Act: False advertising by a lawyer may violate §1125(a)(1)(B) of the Lanham Act, 15 U.S.C. §1125(a)(1)(B), which imposes potential civil liability on any person who "uses in commerce any . . . false or misleading description of fact, or false or misleading representation of fact, which . . . in commercial advertising or promotion, misrepresents the nature, characteristics, qualities, or geographic origin of his or her . . . services, or commercial activities. . . ." In *Haymond v. Lundy*, 2001 WL 15956 (E.D. Pa. 2001), the court held that advertising by a lawyer, if false or misleading, would be actionable under §1125(a) of the Lanham Act.

National Federation of Paralegal Associations: The National Federation of Paralegal Associations, Inc. (NFPA) is an organization comprised of paralegal associations and individual paralegals throughout the United States and Canada. In 1993, the NFPA adopted a Model Code of Ethics and Professional Responsibility to "delineate the principles for ethics and conduct to which every paralegal should aspire." The Code, last updated in 2006, contains the following language related to ABA Model Rule 7.1:

Rule 1.7 A Paralegal's Title Shall be Fully Disclosed

EC-1.7(a) A paralegal's title shall clearly indicate the individual's status and shall be disclosed in all business and professional communications to avoid misunderstandings and misconceptions about the paralegal's role and responsibilities.

EC-1.7(b) A paralegal's title shall be included if the paralegal's name appears on business cards, letterhead, brochures, directories, and advertisements.

EC-1.7(c) A paralegal shall not use letterhead, business cards or other promotional materials to create a fraudulent impression of his/her status or ability to practice in the jurisdiction in which the paralegal practices.

The full NFPA Model Code of Ethics and Professional Responsibility and other ethics resources regarding paralegals are available at *www.paralegals.org* (click on the top menu on "Positions & Issues," then on "Ethics," then on "Model Code of Ethics and Professional Responsibility and Guidelines for Enforcement").

Restatement of the Law Governing Lawyers: The Restatement has no provision comparable to ABA Model Rule 7.1.

Rule 7.2 Advertising

(a) Subject to the requirements of Rules 7.1 and 7.3, a lawyer may advertise services through written, recorded or electronic communication, including public media.

(b) A lawyer shall not give anything of value to a person for recommending the lawyer's services except that a lawyer may

(1) pay the reasonable costs of advertisements or communications permitted by this Rule;

(2) pay the usual charges of a legal services plan or a not-for-profit or qualified lawyer referral service. A qualified lawyer referral service is a lawyer referral service that has been approved by an appropriate regulatory authority;

(3) pay for a law practice in accordance with Rule 1.17; and

(4) refer clients to another lawyer or a nonlawyer professional pursuant to an agreement not otherwise prohibited under these Rules that provides for the other person to refer clients or customers to the lawyer, if

(i) the reciprocal referral agreement is not exclusive, and

(ii) the client is informed of the existence and nature of the agreement.

(c) Any communication made pursuant to this rule shall include the name and office address of at least one lawyer or law firm responsible for its content.

COMMENT

[1] To assist the public in obtaining legal services, lawyers should be allowed to make known their services not only through reputation but also through organized information campaigns in the form of advertising. Advertising involves an active quest for clients, contrary to the tradition that a lawyer should not seek clientele. However, the public's need to know about legal services can be fulfilled in part through advertising. This need is particularly acute in the case of persons of

moderate means who have not made extensive use of legal services. The interest in expanding public information about legal services ought to prevail over considerations of tradition. Nevertheless, advertising by lawyers entails the risk of practices that are misleading or overreaching.

[2] This Rule permits public dissemination of information concerning a lawyer's name or firm name, address and telephone number; the kinds of services the lawyer will undertake; the basis on which the lawyer's fees are determined, including prices for specific services and payment and credit arrangements; a lawyer's foreign language ability; names of references and, with their consent, names of clients regularly represented; and other information that might invite the attention of those seeking legal assistance.

[3] Questions of effectiveness and taste in advertising are matters of speculation and subjective judgment. Some jurisdictions have had extensive prohibitions against television advertising, against advertising going beyond specified facts about a lawyer, or against "undignified" advertising. Television is now one of the most powerful media for getting information to the public, particularly persons of low and moderate income; prohibiting television advertising, therefore, would impede the flow of information about legal services to many sectors of the public. Limiting the information that may be advertised has a similar effect and assumes that the bar can accurately forecast the kind of information that the public would regard as relevant. Similarly, electronic media, such as the Internet, can be an important source of information about legal services, and lawful communication by electronic mail is permitted by this Rule. But see Rule 7.3(a) for the prohibition against the solicitation of a prospective client through a real-time electronic exchange that is not initiated by the prospective client.

[4] Neither this Rule nor Rule 7.3 prohibits communications authorized by law, such as notice to members of a class in class action litigation.

Paying Others to Recommend a Lawyer

[5] Lawyers are not permitted to pay others for channeling professional work. Paragraph (b)(1), however, allows a lawyer to pay for advertising and communications permitted by this Rule, including the costs of print directory listings, on-line directory listings, newspaper ads, television and radio airtime, domain-name registrations, sponsorship fees, banner ads, and group advertising. A lawyer may compensate employees, agents and vendors who are engaged to provide marketing or client development services, such as publicists, public-relations personnel, business-development staff and website designers. See Rule 5.3 for the duties of lawyers and law firms with respect to the conduct of nonlawyers who prepare marketing materials for them.

[6] A lawyer may pay the usual charges of a legal service plan or a not-for-profit or qualified lawyer referral service. A legal service plan is a prepaid or group legal service plan or a similar delivery system that assists prospective clients to secure legal representation. A lawyer referral service, on the other hand, is any organization that holds itself out to the public as a lawyer referral service. Such referral services are understood by laypersons to be consumer-oriented organizations that provide unbiased referrals to lawyers with appropriate experience in the subject matter of the

representation and afford other client protections, such as complaint procedures or malpractice insurance requirements. Consequently, this Rule only permits a lawyer to pay the usual charges of a not-for-profit or qualified lawyer referral service. A qualified lawyer referral service is one that is approved by an appropriate regulatory authority as affording adequate protections for prospective clients. See, e.g., the American Bar Association's Model Supreme Court Rules Governing Lawyer Referral Services and Model Lawyer Referral and Information Service Quality Assurance Act (requiring that organizations that are identified as lawyer referral services (i) permit the participation of all lawyers who are licensed and eligible to practice in the jurisdiction and who meet reasonable objective eligibility requirements as may be established by the referral service for the protection of prospective clients; (ii) require each participating lawyer to carry reasonably adequate malpractice insurance; (iii) act reasonably to assess client satisfaction and address client complaints; and (iv) do not refer prospective clients to lawyers who own, operate or are employed by the referral service).

[7] A lawyer who accepts assignments or referrals from a legal service plan or referrals from a lawyer referral service must act reasonably to assure that the activities of the plan or service are compatible with the lawyer's professional obligations. See Rule 5.3. Legal service plans and lawyer referral services may communicate with prospective clients, but such communication must be in conformity with these Rules. Thus, advertising must not be false or misleading, as would be the case if the communications of a group advertising program or a group legal services plan would mislead prospective clients to think that it was a lawyer referral service sponsored by a state agency or bar association. Nor could the lawyer allow in-person, telephonic, or real-time contacts that would violate Rule 7.3.

[8] A lawyer also may agree to refer clients to another lawyer or a nonlawyer professional, in return for the undertaking of that person to refer clients or customers to the lawyer. Such reciprocal referral arrangements must not interfere with the lawyer's professional judgment as to making referrals or as to providing substantive legal services. See Rules 2.1 and 5.4(c). Except as provided in Rule 1.5(e), a lawyer who receives referrals from a lawyer or nonlawyer professional must not pay anything solely for the referral, but the lawyer does not violate paragraph (b) of this Rule by agreeing to refer clients to the other lawyer or nonlawyer professional, so long as the reciprocal referral agreement is not exclusive and the client is informed of the referral agreement. Conflicts of interest created by such agreements are governed by Rule 1.7. Reciprocal referral agreements should not be of indefinite duration and should be reviewed periodically to determine whether they comply with these Rules. This Rule does not restrict referrals or divisions of revenues or net income among lawyers within firms comprised of multiple entities.

Canon and Code Antecedents

ABA Canons of Professional Ethics: Canons 40 and 46 provided as follows:

40. Newspapers

A lawyer may with propriety write articles for publications in which he gives information upon the law; but he should not accept employment from such publications to advise inquirers in respect to their individual rights.

46. Notice to Local Lawyers

A lawyer available to act as an associate of other lawyers in a particular branch of the law or legal service may send to local lawyers only and publish in his local legal journal, a brief and dignified announcement of his availability to serve other lawyers in connection therewith. The announcement should be in a form which does not constitute a statement or representation of special experience or expertness.

ABA Model Code of Professional Responsibility: Compare DR 2-101(B), DR 2-101(D), DR 2-101(I), DR 2-103(B), and DR 2-103(D) (reprinted later in this volume).

Cross-References in Other Rules

Rule 5.5, Comment 21: "Whether and how lawyers may communicate the availability of their services to prospective clients in this jurisdiction is governed by **Rules 7.1 to 7.5.**"

Rule 5.7, Comment 10: "The promotion of the law-related services must also in all respects comply with **Rules 7.1 through 7.3**, dealing with advertising and solicitation."

Rule 7.1, Comment 1: "This Rule governs all communications about a lawyer's services, including advertising permitted by **Rule 7.2.**"

Rule 7.3, Comment 2: "This potential for abuse inherent in direct in-person, live telephone or real-time electronic solicitation of prospective clients justifies its prohibition, particularly since lawyer advertising and written and recorded communication permitted under **Rule 7.2** offer alternative means of conveying necessary information to those who may be in need of legal services."

Rule 7.3, Comment 3: "The contents of advertisements and communications permitted under **Rule 7.2** can be permanently recorded so that they cannot be disputed and may be shared with others who know the lawyer."

Rule 7.3, Comment 5: "[I]f after sending a letter or other communication to a client as permitted by **Rule 7.2** the lawyer receives no response, any further effort to communicate with the prospective client may violate the provisions of Rule 7.3(b)."

Rule 7.3, Comment 6: Rule 7.3 does not prohibit lawyers from communicating with representatives of organizations or groups regarding group or prepaid legal service plans because such communications "are functionally similar to and serve the same purpose as advertising permitted under **Rule 7.2.**"

Rule 7.3, Comment 8: "Lawyers who participate in a legal service plan must reasonably assure that the plan sponsors are in compliance with **Rules** 7.1, **7.2** and 7.3(b). See 8.4(a)."

Legislative History of Model Rule 7.2

1980 Discussion Draft (then Rule 9.2) provided as follows:

(b) A copy or record of an advertisement in its entirety shall be kept for one year after its dissemination.

(c) A lawyer shall not give anything of value to a person for recommending the lawyer's services, except that a lawyer may pay the reasonable cost of advertising permitted by this rule.

1981 and *1982 Drafts* were substantially the same as adopted, except that subparagraph (a) permitted any "written communication not involving personal contact."

1983 Rule: As originally adopted in 1983, Rule 7.2 provided as follows:

> (a) Subject to the requirements of Rule 7.1, a lawyer may advertise services through public media, such as a telephone directory, legal directory, newspaper or other periodical, outdoor, radio or television, or through written communications not involving solicitation as defined in Rule 7.3.
>
> (b) A copy or recording of an advertisement or written communication shall be kept for two years after its last dissemination along with a record of when and where it was used.
>
> (c) A lawyer shall not give anything of value to a person for recommending the lawyer's services, except that a lawyer may pay the reasonable cost of advertising or written communication permitted by this rule, and may pay the usual charges of a not-for-profit lawyer referral service or other legal service organization.
>
> (d) Any communication made pursuant to this rule shall include the name of at least one lawyer responsible for its content.

1989 Amendments: In 1989, the ABA House of Delegates made minor amendments to Rule 7.2(a) and (c), but did not amend the Comment in any way.

1990 Amendment: At its 1990 Mid-Year Meeting, the ABA House of Delegates added subparagraph 7.2(b)(3) to reflect the addition of Rule 1.17 (Sale of Law Practice).

2002 Amendments: In 2002, the ABA House of Delegates adopted with minor changes the ABA Ethics 2000 Commission proposal to amend Rule 7.2 and its Comment. The amendments simplified Rule 7.2(a), deleted former Rule 7.2(b), added the last sentence of current Rule 7.2(b)(2), expanded Comment 3, deleted former Comment 5, revised current Comment 5, and added Comments 6 and 7.

In addition, the ABA added Rule 7.2(b)(4) based on a proposal by the ABA Standing Committee on Ethics and Professional Responsibility. (The ABA simultaneously added a new sentence to the Comment to Rule 7.5—see the Legislative History following that rule.) We reprint the following excerpts from the Report that the Standing Committee submitted in support of its proposal to add Rule 7.2(b)(4):

*ABA Committee Report in Support of August 2002 Amendment**

> In July 2000 the House of Delegates adopted Resolution 10F relating to the issue of multi-disciplinary practice. By that resolution, the Standing Committee on Ethics and Professional Responsibility was directed to review the Model Rules of Professional Conduct . . . and to recommend any changes the Committee believed necessary "to assure that there are safeguards in the [Model Rules of Professional Conduct] relating to strategic alliances and other contractual relationships with non-legal professional services providers consistent with the statement of principles in [Resolution 10F]."
>
> The Committee reviewed the Model Rules and Resolution 10F as directed by the House of Delegates. It considered the "strategic alliance" or "contractual relationship" arrangements identified in Resolution 10F to be arrangements by professional services providers and lawyers to steer business to each other on a systematic and regular basis.

*Committee Reports do not represent official policy of the ABA. They are for information only, and the opinions are those of the authors of the report.

Such arrangements may range from a simple understanding generally to refer business to each other to an agreement that includes sharing space, computer systems, and the like to reduce costs by obtaining economies of scale or other efficiencies.

The Committee took into account the "core values" of the profession as described in paragraph 1 of Resolution 10F: the duty of loyalty, the duty to exercise independent professional judgment for the benefit of the client, the duty to protect client confidences, and the traditional prohibitions against sharing legal fees with nonlawyers and against ownership and control of the practice of law by nonlawyers. . . .

[W]hen lawyers enter into cross-referral agreements with other lawyers and nonlawyer professionals, clients need to be informed of those agreements in order to decide whether to accept the lawyer's suggestions to use the other professionals' services. A per se prohibition against exclusive referral arrangements also is required, to ensure that a lawyer is free to exercise independent professional judgment when counseling clients to consult with other professionals. Each of these concepts is therefore embodied in the Committee's proposed changes to the black-letter of Rule 7.2(b).

The . . . Comment to Rule 7.2(b) should be amplified to address lawyers' participation in referral arrangements in the context of related Model Rules. For example, the independent professional judgment required of a lawyer who is making referrals to other professionals is set out in Rules 2.1 and 5.4(c), which are therefore included in the Comment. Similarly, the Comment notes that actual payment by a lawyer to a referring nonlawyer professional for the referral itself is prohibited, except in the narrow lawyer-to-lawyer referral situation that is permitted under Rule 1.5(e)'s exception to the prohibition against fee-sharing. Finally, reference is made in the Comment to Rule 1.7 ("Conflict of Interest"), to remind lawyers that they must not allow their contractual relationships for reciprocal referrals, which might be considered "related business interests," to adversely affect the representation of their clients.

The Committee believes that these proposed amendments to Model Rule 7.2 and its Comment, addressing reciprocal referral agreements between lawyers and other lawyers or nonlawyer professionals, and its amendment to Model Rule 7.5's Comment, will provide necessary and helpful safeguards to the ethical practice of law, . . . and therefore urges their adoption.

Selected State Variations

Arizona: Rule 7.2(b)(2) explicitly permits a lawyer to pay a not-for-profit or qualified lawyer referral service "a fee calculated as a percentage of legal fees earned by the lawyer to whom the service or organization has referred a matter, provided that any such percentage fee shall not exceed ten percent, and shall be used only to help defray the reasonable operating expenses of the service or organization and to fund public service activities, including the delivery of pro bono legal services. The fees paid by a client referred by such service shall not exceed the total charges that the client would have paid had no such service been involved." Arizona omits Rule 7.2(b)(4) (governing reciprocal referral agreements), but adds Rule 7.2(d) (setting forth detailed requirements for all advertisements containing information about legal fees). Arizona also adds Rule 7.2(e), which provides:

(e) . . . If a law firm advertises on electronic media and a person appears purporting to be a lawyer, such person shall in fact be a lawyer employed full-time at the advertising law firm. If a law firm advertises a particular legal service on electronic media, and a lawyer appears as the person purporting to render the service, the lawyer appearing shall be the lawyer who will actually perform the service advertised unless the advertisement discloses that the service may be performed by other lawyers in the firm.

Finally, Arizona adds Rule 7.2(f), which requires that certain information be presented to potential clients in a manner that is "clear and conspicuous."

Arkansas permits actors to be used in advertisements so long as they are identified by name and relationship to the advertising lawyer. Dramatizations are forbidden. Clients and former clients "shall not be used in any manner whatsoever in advertisements."

California: Rule 1-320 provides, in pertinent part, as follows:

> (A) Neither a member nor a law firm shall directly or indirectly share legal fees with a person who is not a lawyer, except that . . .
>
> (4) A member may pay a prescribed registration, referral, or participation fee to a lawyer referral service established, sponsored, and operated in accordance with the State Bar of California's Minimum Standards for a Lawyer Referral Service in California.
>
> (B) A member shall not compensate, give, or promise anything of value to any person or entity for the purpose of recommending or securing employment of the member or the member's law firm by a client, or as a reward for having made a recommendation resulting in employment of the member or the member's law firm by a client. A member's offering of or giving a gift or gratuity to any person or entity having made a recommendation resulting in the employment of the member or the member's law firm shall not of itself violate this rule, provided that the gift or gratuity was not offered or given in consideration of any promise, agreement, or understanding that such a gift or gratuity would be forthcoming or that referrals would be made or encouraged in the future.
>
> (C) A member shall not compensate, give, or promise anything of value to any representative of the press, radio, television, or other communication medium in anticipation of or in return for publicity of the member, the law firm, or any other member as such in a news item, but the incidental provision of food or beverage shall not of itself violate this rule.

Rule 1-400(F) provides:

> (D) A member shall retain for two years a true and correct copy or recording of any communication made by written or electronic media. Upon written request, the member shall make any such copy or recording available to the State Bar, and, if requested, shall provide to the State Bar evidence to support any factual or objective claim contained in the communication.

The Standards adopted by the State Bar pursuant to Rule 1-400 provide that a communication is "presumed to be in violation of rule 1-400" if it "implies that the member or law firm is participating in a lawyer referral service which has been certified by the State Bar of California or as having satisfied the Minimum Standards for Lawyer Referral Services in California, when that is not the case." Rule 1-600(B) provides that the State Bar's Board of Governors "shall formulate and adopt Minimum Standards for Lawyer Referral Services, which . . . shall be binding on members." Those standards are found after California Business & Professions Code §6155, which governs lawyer referral services.

Also relevant to ABA Model Rule 7.2 are Business & Professions Code §6129 (prohibiting lawyers from purchasing claims) and §§6157.1-6159.2 (governing lawyer advertising, especially in the electronic media).

Connecticut adds many paragraphs with no counterpart in ABA Model Rule 7.2 but omits ABA Model Rule 7.2(b)(4) (regarding reciprocal referral agreements).

District of Columbia omits ABA Model Rule 7.2, but D.C. Rule 7.1(c) provides that a lawyer "shall not knowingly assist an organization that furnishes or pays for legal services to others to promote the use of the lawyer's services . . . as a private practitioner, if the promotional activity involves the use of coercion, duress, compulsion, intimidation, threats, or vexatious or harassing conduct."

Florida: Rule 4-7.1(e), (g) expressly exempts from the advertising rules any communications to other lawyers as well as to existing or former clients. Rule 4-7.4(b)(2) provides that "[e]very written communication disseminated by a lawyer referral service shall be accompanied by a written statement detailing the background, training, and experience of each lawyer to whom the recipient may be referred." Rule 4-7.10 sets forth elaborate requirements for lawyer referral services. In addition, Chapter 8 of the Rules Regulating the Florida Bar sets forth extensive requirements for the operation of lawyer referral services by local bar associations, and no local bar association may operate a referral service absent express approval from the state bar.

Georgia moves Rule 7.2(b) and its Comment to Georgia Rule 7.3(c), and modifies and expands the exceptions in ABA Model Rule 7.2(c) regarding lawyer referral services.

Indiana: Effective January 1, 2011, Rule 7.2(b) defines "advertising" as "any manner of public communication partly or entirely intended or expected to promote the purchase or use of the professional services of a lawyer, law firm, or any employee of either involving the practice of law or law-related services." Comment 2 identifies 20 different permissible subjects for advertising, such as the lawyer's "date and place of birth," "names and addresses of bank references," and "whether credit cards . . . are accepted."

Iowa: Rule 7.2 does not govern communications between lawyers, but prohibits any "visual display" on television unless the same display would be "allowed in print"; prohibits "background sound" in electronic media; and expressly permits lawyers to communicate 14 items to the public provided if it is done "in a dignified style." Rule 7.2 also imposes extensive limitations on advertising fee information; and requires any communication advising the institution of litigation to "disclose that the filing of a claim or suit solely to coerce a settlement or to harass another could be illegal and could render the person so filing liable for malicious prosecution or abuse of process." In addition, borrowing from the ABA Model Code of Professional Responsibility, Iowa has a detailed rule (Rule 7.7) called "Recommendation of Professional Employment" and another (Rule 7.8) on "Suggestion of Need of Legal Services."

Louisiana: Some portions of Rule 7.2(c) were struck down as unconstitutional in *Public Citizen, Inc. v. Louisiana Attorney Disciplinary Board*, 632 F.3d 212 (5th Cir. 2011). Rule 7.2(c) nevertheless contains many other detailed restrictions that survived the constitutional challenge, including provisions related to how long a lawyer must honor an advertised fee and a provision concerning the use of dual language advertisements. Finally, subject to some exceptions in Rule 7.8, Rule 7.7 requires lawyers to file their advertising with the Louisiana State Bar Association, which is charged with ensuring that advertising complies with the advertising rules.

Maine: Maine Rule 7.2-A offers a variety of aspirational goals for lawyer advertising, including that lawyers use "dignified" advertisements and avoid "crass" marketing that "undermines the serious purpose of legal services and the judicial system."

Maryland: Among other variations, Maryland adds Rule 7.2(e), which provides that "[a]n advertisement or communication indicating that no fee will be charged in the absence of a recovery shall also disclose whether the client will be liable for any expenses," and Rule 7.2(f), which requires lawyers, including those participating in an advertising group or lawyer referral service, to be "personally responsible for compliance with the provisions of Rules 7.1, 7.2, 7.3, 7.4, and 7.5."

Massachusetts: Rule 7.2(a) adds that lawyers may advertise in "an electronic or computer accessed directory." Comment 3A provides, in part, as follows:

> The advertising and solicitation rules can generally be applied to computer-accessed or other similar types of communications by analogizing the communication to its hard-copy form. Thus, because it is not a communication directed to a specific recipient, a web site or home page would generally be considered advertising subject to this rule, rather than solicitation subject to Rule 7.3. . . .

Michigan: Rule 6.3(b) permits a lawyer to "participate in and pay the usual charges of a not-for-profit lawyer referral service that recommends legal services to the public" only if the referral service meets detailed requirements, including that the service:

> (3) is open to all lawyers licensed and eligible to practice in this state who maintain an office within the geographical area served, and who:
>
> (i) meet reasonable and objective requirements of experience . . . ;
>
> (ii) pay reasonable registration and membership fees not to exceed an amount established by the State Bar to encourage widespread lawyer participation; and
>
> (iii) maintain a policy of errors and omissions insurance, or provide proof of financial responsibility, in an amount at least equal to the minimum established by the State Bar.
>
> (4) ensures that the combined fees and expenses charged a prospective client by a qualified service and a lawyer to whom the client is referred not exceed the total charges the client would have incurred had no referral service been involved. . . .

Under Rule 6.3(d), the State Bar or "any aggrieved person" may seek an injunction against violations of Rule 6.3(b), and if the injunction is granted, the petitioner shall be entitled to reasonable costs and attorney fees.

Missouri: Rule 7.2(a) adds permission to advertise "through direct mail advertising distributed generally to persons not known to need legal services of the kind provided by the lawyer in a particular matter." Missouri omits ABA Model Rule 7.2(b)(4). Rule 7.2(d) provides that a lawyer may not "pay all or a part of the cost of an advertisement in the public media unless such advertisement discloses the name and address of the financing lawyer, the relationship between the advertising lawyer and the financing lawyer, and whether the advertising lawyer is likely to refer cases received through the advertisement to the financing lawyer." In addition, Rules 7.2(f) and (g) require all advertisements (except targeted letters and emails and advertisements limited to specified basic information such as name, address, and fields of practice) to state the following: "The choice of a lawyer is an important decision and should not be based solely upon advertisements." Rule 7.2(h) governs advertisements that use more than one language, and Rule 7.2(i) explains that the Rule does not apply to "services provided by a not-for-profit organization funded in whole or in part by the Legal Services Corporation . . . or to pro bono services provided free of charge by a not-for-profit organization, a court-annexed program, a bar association, or an accredited law school." The Rule also does not apply to "law firms or lawyers who promote, support or publicize through advertising that substantially and predominantly features any of the following: legal services corporation; community or other non-profit organization; recognized community events or celebrations; institutions; entities; or individuals other than themselves."

Nevada: Rule 7.2(b) provides, in part, as follows:

> If a person appears as a lawyer in an advertisement for legal services . . . such person must be a member of the State Bar of Nevada . . . and must be the lawyer who will actually perform the service advertised or a lawyer associated with the law firm that is advertising. If a person appears in an advertisement as an employee of a lawyer or law firm, such person must be an actual employee of the lawyer or law firm whose services are advertised unless the advertisement discloses that such person is an actor. If an actor appears in any other role not prohibited by these Rules, the advertisement must disclose that such person is an actor.

Among other variations, Nevada Rule 7.2A requires lawyers to file all advertisements with the State Bar "within 15 days of first dissemination. . . ." Rule 7.2B(a) commands the State Bar to create "Standing Lawyer Advertising Advisory Committees . . . to review filings submitted under Rule 7.2A and to respond to written requests from an advertising lawyer or law firm voluntarily seeking an advance opinion regarding that lawyer's compliance with the advertising rules." Rule 7.2B(c) permits a lawyer or law firm to "file a written request with the state bar seeking an advance opinion on whether a proposed advertisement complies with these Rules."

New Hampshire: Rule 7.2(b)(2) permits payment only to "an organization that is recognized by the Internal Revenue Service as exempt from taxation pursuant to Section 501(c)(3) of the Internal Revenue Code." New Hampshire omits ABA Model Rule 7.2(b)(4) (governing reciprocal referral agreements).

New Jersey: Rule 7.3(c) adds that a lawyer in private practice "shall not knowingly assist an organization that furnishes or pays for legal services to others to promote the use of the lawyer's services" if the organization's promotional activity (1) uses false or misleading statements or claims, or (2) uses "coercion, duress, compulsion, intimidation, threats, unwarranted promises of benefits, over-reaching, or vexatious or harassing conduct." New Jersey regulates lawyer referral services in a lengthy Rule 7.3(e). New Jersey omits ABA Model Rule 7.2(b)(4) (governing reciprocal referral agreements).

To regulate broadcast advertising, New Jersey Rule 7.2(a) incorporates the following language taken verbatim from the New Jersey Supreme Court's opinion in *Felmeister & Isaacs*, 518 A.2d 188, 208 (1986):

> . . . All advertisements shall be predominantly informational. No drawings, animations, dramatizations, music, or lyrics shall be used in connection with televised advertising. No advertisement shall rely in any way on techniques to obtain attention that depend upon absurdity and that demonstrate a clear and intentional lack of relevance to the selection of counsel; included in this category are all advertisements that contain any extreme portrayal of counsel exhibiting characteristics clearly unrelated to legal competence.

New York: Rule 7.2(a) is substantially similar to DR 2-103(B) of the old Model Code, but it adds an exception that permits lawyers to refer clients to a nonlegal professional pursuant to a contractual agreement under New York Rule 5.8, which has no Model Rule equivalent. Rule 5.8 provides that a lawyer or law firm "may enter into and maintain a contractual relationship with a nonlegal professional or nonlegal professional service firm for the purpose of offering to the public, on a systematic and continuing basis, legal services performed by the lawyer or law firm as well as other nonlegal professional services, notwithstanding the provisions of Rule 1.7(a)," when certain requirements are satisfied.

New York Rule 7.2(b) is substantially similar to DR 2-103(D) of the old Model Code. Notably, rather than adopting ABA Model Rule 7.6 (prohibiting pay-to-play arrangements), New York has added two new Comments to Rule 7.2 explaining the pay-to-play prohibition as a logical consequence of Rule 7.2(b)—see the New York entry in the Selected State Variations following Rule 7.6 below.

North Carolina omits ABA Model Rule 7.2(b)(4) and adds an unusual Rule 7.2(d) that permits a lawyer to participate in a lawyer referral service only if the lawyer and the referral service satisfy seven specific conditions.

Ohio: Rule 7.2(b) deletes the ABA reference to a "qualified lawyer referral service" and substitutes a reference to the Ohio Supreme Court Rules governing lawyer referral services. Ohio also deletes ABA Model Rule 7.2(b)(4), thus effectively prohibiting reciprocal referral agreements between two lawyers or between a lawyer and a nonlawyer professional. Ohio adds Rule 7.2(d), which prohibits a lawyer from soliciting employment if the lawyer does not intend to participate in the matter but instead will refer the matter to other counsel.

Pennsylvania: Rule 7.2 differs significantly from ABA Model Rule 7.2. For example, Pennsylvania omits ABA Model Rule 7.2(b)(4) (governing reciprocal referral agreements). Pennsylvania Rule 7.2(j) provides that a lawyer shall not pay "any part of the costs of an advertisement by a lawyer not in the same firm" unless the advertisement discloses the name and principal office address of each lawyer paying for the advertisement and, "if any lawyer or law firm will receive referrals from the advertisement, the circumstances under which referrals will be made and the basis and criteria on which the referral system operates."

Pennsylvania also adds Rule 7.7, which forbids lawyers to accept referrals from a "lawyer referral service" (a defined term) "if the service engaged in communication with the public or direct contact with prospective clients in a manner that would violate the Rules of Professional Conduct if the communication or contact were made by the lawyer."

Rhode Island: Among other variations, Rhode Island has adopted Rule 7.2(f), which provides as follows:

> (f) Any lawyer or law firm who advertises that his or her practice includes or concentrates in particular fields of law and then refers the majority of cases in those fields of law or of that type to another lawyer, law firm or group of lawyers shall clearly state the following disclaimer:
>
> (1) "Most cases of this type are not handled by this firm, but are referred to other attorneys," or if applicable:
>
> (2) "While this firm maintains joint responsibility, most cases of this type are referred to other attorneys for principal responsibility."

Tennessee: In the rules effective January 1, 2011, Tennessee adds Rule 7.6 (Intermediary Organizations), which provides that a lawyer shall not seek or accept a referral of a client or compensation for representing a client from an "intermediary organization" (a defined term) if the lawyer "knows or reasonably should know that: (1) the organization: (i) is owned or controlled by the lawyer, a law firm with which the lawyer is associated, or a lawyer with whom the lawyer is associated in a firm; or (ii) is engaged in the unauthorized practice of law; or (iii) engages in marketing activities that are false or misleading or are otherwise prohibited by the Board of Professional Responsibility; or (iv) has not registered with the Board of Professional Responsibility and complied with all requirements imposed by the Board." In addition, Supreme Court Rule 44, entitled "Regulation of Lawyer Intermediary Organizations," sets forth the requirements that lawyer intermediary organizations must meet in order to do business in Tennessee under Rule 7.6.

Texas: Rule 7.02 forbids "false or misleading communication about the qualifications or the services of any lawyer or firm." In addition, Texas has adopted guidelines for advertising on the Internet, including a requirement that "homepages" be submitted for review.

Virginia: Rule 7.2(d) requires targeted written or e-mail communications to display the statement "ADVERTISING MATERIAL" on the first page in a specified type size. Registered mail and other forms of restricted delivery are forbidden. Lawyers who advertise or solicit by e-mail must tell recipients how to "notify the sender that they wish not to receive such communications in the future." But Rule 7.2(d) does not apply to any communication that is "directed to be sent by a court or tribunal, or otherwise required by law."

Wisconsin: Rule 7.2(b)(4) permits referrals pursuant to a nonexclusive reciprocal referral agreement between a lawyer and another lawyer or nonlawyer professional if "(ii) the client gives informed consent; (iii) there is no interference with the lawyer's independence of professional judgment or with the client-lawyer relationship; and (iv) information relating to representation of a client is protected. . . . "

Related Materials

ABA Commission on Ethics 20/20: In 2009, the ABA created the Commission on Ethics 20/20, which is comprehensively reviewing the ABA Model Rules of Professional Conduct and other lawyer regulatory sources in light of globalization and changes in technology. In September 2011, the Commission circulated for public comment revised proposals for amending several Comments to Rule 7.2, including the following proposal to amend Comment 5, which is headed "Paying Others to Recommend a Lawyer":

> [5] Lawyers are not permitted to pay others for channeling professional work recommending the lawyer's services. A communication contains a recommendation if it endorses or vouches for a lawyer's credentials, abilities, competence, character, or other professional qualities. Paragraph (b)(1), however, allows a lawyer to pay for advertising and communications permitted by this Rule, including the costs of print directory listings, on-line directory listings, newspaper ads, television and radio airtime, domain-name registrations, sponsorship fees, banner ads, Internet-based pop-up advertisements, and group advertising. A lawyer may compensate employees, agents and vendors who are engaged to provide marketing or client development services, such as publicists, public-relations personnel, business-development staff and website designers. Moreover, a lawyer may pay others for generating client leads, such as Internet-based client leads, as long as the lead generator does not

recommend the lawyer, any payment to the lead generator is consistent with Rules 1.5(e) (division of fees) and 5.4 (professional independence of the lawyer), and the lead generator's communications to potential clients are consistent with Rule 7.1 (communications concerning a lawyer's services). To comply with Rule 7.1, the lawyer must ensure that the lead generator discloses that the lawyer has paid a fee in exchange for the lead and that the lead generator does not state or imply that it has analyzed the potential client's legal problems when determining which lawyer should receive the referral. See also Rule 5.3 for the duties of lawyers and law firms with respect to the conduct of nonlawyers. who prepare marketing materials for them.

The Commission may present these proposals (or revised versions of them) to the ABA House of Delegates at its August 2012 Annual Meeting. For updates on the Ethics 20/20 Commission's work, visit *www.americanbar.org/Ethics2020.*

ABA Formal Ethics Opinions: See ABA Formal Ethics Ops. 84-351 (1984), 87-355 (1987), 93-374 (1993), and 94-388 (1994).

ABA Model Supreme Court Rules Governing Lawyer Referral and Information Services: In 1993, the ABA House of Delegates voted to adopt Model Supreme Court Rules Governing Lawyer Referral and Information Services (LRIS), as well as model legislation to implement the rules. (Because many referral services are run by nonlawyers, referral services cannot be regulated solely through rules governing lawyers. Since courts do not possess inherent jurisdiction over nonlawyers, legislation is typically needed to govern nonlawyers.)

The Model Supreme Court Rules Governing Lawyer Referral and Information Services are summarized in ABA Model Rule 7.2, Comment 6. The Model Supreme Court Rules reflect concern over sham referral services operated by lawyers who refer cases only to themselves or their partners. The Model Supreme Court Rules are available online at *http://apps.americanbar.org/legalservices/lris/modelrules.html.*

Criminal Statutes: Some states make it a crime for a nonlawyer to accept anything of value for referring a matter to a lawyer. For example, California Labor Code §3215 makes it a crime for anyone to receive money or any non-monetary thing "as compensation or inducement for referring clients. . . ." Similarly, New York Judiciary Law §479 makes it a crime for any person to "make it a business" to solicit business for an attorney.

Pay-to-Play: The term "pay-to-play" refers to an informal system in which law firms allegedly are not eligible to be retained to perform government legal work unless the lawyers have made or solicited campaign contributions to the government officials who retain (or influence the selection of) outside counsel. In 1997, the ABA adopted a resolution condemning so-called pay-to-play practices and directing the ABA President to appoint a Task Force to study and report on the pay-to-play issue. In 1998, the ABA received a report from the Task Force and passed a resolution directing the ABA's Standing Committee on Ethics and Professional Responsibility to draft a new Model Rule 7.6 to govern pay-to-play. The ABA House of Delegates rejected the Standing Committee's proposed rule in 1999 but approved an identical proposal in 2000.

Restatement of the Law Governing Lawyers: The Restatement has no provision comparable to ABA Model Rule 7.2.

Rule 7.3 Direct Contact with Prospective Clients

(a) A lawyer shall not by in-person, live telephone or real-time electronic contact solicit professional employment from a prospective client when a significant motive for the lawyer's doing so is the lawyer's pecuniary gain, unless the person contacted:

(1) is a lawyer; or

(2) has a family, close personal, or prior professional relationship with the lawyer.

(b) A lawyer shall not solicit professional employment from a prospective client by written, recorded or electronic communication or by in-person, telephone or real-time electronic contact even when not otherwise prohibited by paragraph (a), if:

(1) the prospective client has made known to the lawyer a desire not to be solicited by the lawyer; or

(2) the solicitation involves coercion, duress or harassment.

(c) Every written, recorded or electronic communication from a lawyer soliciting professional employment from a prospective client known to be in need of legal services in a particular matter shall include the words "Advertising Material" on the outside envelope, if any, and at the beginning and ending of any recorded or electronic communication, unless the recipient of the communication is a person specified in paragraphs (a)(1) or (a)(2).

(d) Notwithstanding the prohibitions in paragraph (a), a lawyer may participate with a prepaid or group legal service plan operated by an organization not owned or directed by the lawyer that uses in-person or telephone contact to solicit memberships or subscriptions for the plan from persons who are not known to need legal services in a particular matter covered by the plan.

COMMENT

[1] There is a potential for abuse inherent in direct in-person, live telephone or real-time electronic contact by a lawyer with a prospective client known to need legal services. These forms of contact between a lawyer and a prospective client subject the layperson to the private importuning of the trained advocate in a direct interpersonal encounter. The prospective client, who may already feel overwhelmed by the circumstances giving rise to the need for legal services, may find it difficult fully to evaluate all available alternatives with reasoned judgment and appropriate self-interest in the face of the lawyer's presence and insistence upon being retained immediately. The situation is fraught with the possibility of undue influence, intimidation, and over-reaching.

[2] This potential for abuse inherent in direct in-person, live telephone or real-time electronic solicitation of prospective clients justifies its prohibition, particularly since lawyer advertising and written and recorded communication permitted

under Rule 7.2 offer alternative means of conveying necessary information to those who may be in need of legal services. Advertising and written and recorded communications which may be mailed or autodialed make it possible for a prospective client to be informed about the need for legal services, and about the qualifications of available lawyers and law firms, without subjecting the prospective client to direct in-person, telephone or real-time electronic persuasion that may overwhelm the client's judgment.

[3] The use of general advertising and written, recorded or electronic communications to transmit information from lawyer to prospective client, rather than direct in-person, live telephone or real-time electronic contact, will help to assure that the information flows cleanly as well as freely. The contents of advertisements and communications permitted under Rule 7.2 can be permanently recorded so that they cannot be disputed and may be shared with others who know the lawyer. This potential for informal review is itself likely to help guard against statements and claims that might constitute false and misleading communications, in violation of Rule 7.1. The contents of direct in-person, live telephone or real-time electronic conversations between a lawyer and a prospective client can be disputed and may not be subject to third-party scrutiny. Consequently, they are much more likely to approach (and occasionally cross) the dividing line between accurate representations and those that are false and misleading.

[4] There is far less likelihood that a lawyer would engage in abusive practices against an individual who is a former client, or with whom the lawyer has a close personal or family relationship, or in situations in which the lawyer is motivated by considerations other than the lawyer's pecuniary gain. Nor is there a serious potential for abuse when the person contacted is a lawyer. Consequently, the general prohibition in Rule 7.3(a) and the requirements of Rule 7.3(c) are not applicable in those situations. Also, paragraph (a) is not intended to prohibit a lawyer from participating in constitutionally protected activities of public or charitable legal-service organizations or bona fide political, social, civic, fraternal, employee or trade organizations whose purposes include providing or recommending legal services to its members or beneficiaries.

[5] But even permitted forms of solicitation can be abused. Thus, any solicitation which contains information which is false or misleading within the meaning of Rule 7.1, which involves coercion, duress or harassment within the meaning of Rule 7.3(b)(2), or which involves contact with a prospective client who has made known to the lawyer a desire not to be solicited by the lawyer within the meaning of Rule 7.3(b)(1) is prohibited. Moreover, if after sending a letter or other communication to a client as permitted by Rule 7.2 the lawyer receives no response, any further effort to communicate with the prospective client may violate the provisions of Rule 7.3(b).

[6] This Rule is not intended to prohibit a lawyer from contacting representatives of organizations or groups that may be interested in establishing a group or prepaid legal plan for their members, insureds, beneficiaries or other third parties for the purpose of informing such entities of the availability of and details concerning the plan or arrangement which the lawyer or lawyer's firm is willing to offer. This form of communication is not directed to a prospective client. Rather, it is usually addressed to an individual acting in a fiduciary capacity seeking a supplier of legal services for others who may, if they choose, become prospective clients of

the lawyer. Under these circumstances, the activity which the lawyer undertakes in communicating with such representatives and the type of information transmitted to the individual are functionally similar to and serve the same purpose as advertising permitted under Rule 7.2.

[7] The requirement in Rule 7.3(c) that certain communications be marked "Advertising Material" does not apply to communications sent in response to requests of potential clients or their spokespersons or sponsors. General announcements by lawyers, including changes in personnel or office location, do not constitute communications soliciting professional employment from a client known to be in need of legal services within the meaning of this Rule.

[8] Paragraph (d) of this Rule permits a lawyer to participate with an organization which uses personal contact to solicit members for its group or prepaid legal service plan, provided that the personal contact is not undertaken by any lawyer who would be a provider of legal services through the plan. The organization must not be owned by or directed (whether as manager or otherwise) by any lawyer or law firm that participates in the plan. For example, paragraph (d) would not permit a lawyer to create an organization controlled directly or indirectly by the lawyer and use the organization for the in-person or telephone solicitation of legal employment of the lawyer through memberships in the plan or otherwise. The communication permitted by these organizations also must not be directed to a person known to need legal services in a particular matter, but is to be designed to inform potential plan members generally of another means of affordable legal services. Lawyers who participate in a legal service plan must reasonably assure that the plan sponsors are in compliance with Rules 7.1, 7.2 and 7.3(b). See Rule 8.4(a).

Canon and Code Antecedents

ABA Canons of Professional Ethics: Canon 28 provided as follows:

28. Stirring Up Litigation, Directly or Through Agents

It is unprofessional for a lawyer to volunteer advice to bring a lawsuit, except in rare cases where ties of blood, relationship or trust make it his duty to do so. Stirring up strife and litigation is not only unprofessional, but it is indictable at common law. It is disreputable to hunt up defects in titles or other causes of action and inform thereof in order to be employed to bring suit or collect judgment, or to breed litigation by seeking out those with claims for personal injuries or those having any other grounds of action in order to secure them as clients, or to employ agents or runners for like purposes, or to pay or reward, directly or indirectly, those who bring or influence the bringing of such cases to his office, or to remunerate policemen, court or prison officials, physicians, hospital *attachés* or others who may succeed, under the guise of giving disinterested friendly advice, in influencing the criminal, the sick and the injured, the ignorant or others, to seek his professional services. A duty to the public and to the profession devolves upon every member of the Bar having knowledge of such practices upon the part of any practitioner immediately to inform thereof, to the end that the offender may be disbarred.

ABA Model Code of Professional Responsibility: Compare DR 2-104(A) (reprinted later in this volume).

Cross-References in Other Rules

Rule 5.5, Comment 21: "Whether and how lawyers may communicate the availability of their services to prospective clients in this jurisdiction is governed by **Rules 7.1 to 7.5**."

Rule 5.7, Comment 10: "The promotion of the law-related services must also in all respects comply with **Rules** 7.1 through **7.3**, dealing with advertising and solicitation."

Rule 7.2(a): "Subject to the requirements of **Rules** 7.1 and **7.3**, a lawyer may advertise services through written, recorded or electronic communication, including public media."

Rule 7.2, Comment 3: "[S]ee **Rule 7.3(a)** for the prohibition against the solicitation of a prospective client through a real-time electronic exchange that is not initiated by the prospective client."

Rule 7.2, Comment 4: "Neither this Rule nor **Rule 7.3** prohibits communications authorized by law, such as notice to members of a class in class action litigation."

Rule 7.2, Comment 7: A lawyer accepting assignments or referrals from a legal service plan or referrals from a lawyer referral service is not permitted to "allow in-person, telephonic, or real-time contacts that would violate **Rule 7.3**."

Legislative History of Model Rule 7.3

1980 Discussion Draft (then Rule 9.3) provided as follows:

Solicitation

(a) A lawyer shall not initiate contact with a prospective client if:

(1) the lawyer reasonably should know that the physical, emotional, or mental state of the person solicited is such that the person could not exercise reasonable judgment in employing a lawyer;

(2) the person solicited has made known a desire not to receive communications from the lawyer; or

(3) the solicitation involves coercion, duress, or harassment.

(b) subject to the requirements of paragraph (a), a lawyer may initiate contact with a prospective client in the following circumstances:

(1) if the prospective client is a close friend or relative of the lawyer;

(2) by a letter concerning a specific event or transaction if the letter is followed up only upon positive response from the addressee;

(3) under the auspices of a public or charitable legal services organization or a bona fide political, social, civic, fraternal, employee, or trade organization whose purposes include but are not limited to providing or recommending legal services.

(c) A lawyer shall not give another person anything of value to initiate contact with a prospective client on behalf of the lawyer.

1981 and ***1982 Drafts*** both provided as follows:

Personal Contact with Prospective Clients

(a) A lawyer may initiate personal contact with a prospective client for the purpose of obtaining professional employment only in the following circumstances and subject to the requirements of paragraph (b):

(1) if the prospective client is a close friend, relative, former client or one whom the lawyer reasonably believes to be a client;

(2) under the auspices of a public or charitable legal services organization; or

(3) under the auspices of a bona fide political, social, civic, fraternal, employee or trade organization whose purposes include but are not limited to providing or recommending legal services, if the legal services are related to the principal purposes of the organization.

(b) A lawyer shall not contact, or send a written communication to, a prospective client for the purpose of obtaining professional employment if:

(1) the lawyer knows or reasonably should know that the physical, emotional or mental state of the person is such that the person could not exercise reasonable judgment in employing a lawyer;

(2) the person has made known to the lawyer a desire not to receive communications from the lawyer; or

(3) the communication involves coercion, duress or harassment.

1983 Rule: As originally adopted in 1983, Rule 7.3 provided as follows:

A lawyer may not solicit professional employment from a prospective client with whom the lawyer has no family or prior professional relationship by mail, in-person or otherwise, when a significant motive for the lawyer's doing so is the lawyer's pecuniary gain. The term "solicit" includes contact in person, by telephone or telegraph, by letter or other writing or by other communications directed to a specific recipient, but does not include letters addressed or advertising circulars distributed generally to persons not known to need legal services of the kind provided by the lawyer in a particular matter but who are so situated that they might in general find such services useful.

1989 Amendments: In 1989, the ABA House of Delegates substantially amended Rule 7.3 and its Comment. The 1989 version of Rule 7.3 provided as follows:

(a) A lawyer shall not by in-person or live telephone contact solicit professional employment from a prospective client with whom the lawyer has no family or prior professional relationship when a significant motive for the lawyer's doing so is the lawyer's pecuniary gain.

(b) A lawyer shall not solicit professional employment from a prospective client by written or recorded communication or by in-person or telephone contact even when not otherwise prohibited by paragraph (a), if:

(1) [Same as 2002 version of Rule 7.3(b)(1).]

(2) [Same as 2002 version of Rule 7.3(b)(2).]

(c) Every written or recorded communication from a lawyer soliciting professional employment from a prospective client known to be in need of legal services in a particular matter, and with whom the lawyer has no family or prior professional relationship, shall include the words "Advertising Material" on the outside envelope, if any, and at the beginning and ending of any recorded or electronic communication.

(d) [Same as 2002 version of Rule 7.3(d).]

The 1989 amendments also deleted the following paragraphs from the Comment to Rule 7.3:

These dangers [of false and misleading representations] attend direct solicitation whether in-person or by mail. Direct mail solicitation cannot be effectively regulated by means less drastic than outright prohibition. One proposed safeguard is to require that the designation "Advertising" be stamped on any envelope containing a solicitation letter. This would do nothing to assure the accuracy and reliability of the contents. Another suggestion is that solicitation letters be filed with a state regulatory agency. This would be ineffective as a practical matter. State lawyer discipline agencies struggle for resources to investigate specific complaints, much less for those necessary to screen lawyers' mail solicitation material. Even if they could examine such materials, agency staff members are unlikely to know anything about the lawyer or about the prospective client's underlying problem. Without such knowledge they cannot determine whether the lawyer's representations are misleading. In any event, such review would be after the fact, potentially too late to avert the undesirable consequences of disseminating false and misleading material.

General mailings not speaking to a specific matter do not pose the same danger of abuse as targeted mailings, and therefore are not prohibited by this Rule. The representations made in such mailings are necessarily general rather than tailored, less importuning than informative. They are addressed to recipients unlikely to be specially vulnerable at the time, hence who are likely to be more skeptical about unsubstantiated claims. General mailings not addressed to recipients involved in a specific legal matter or incident, therefore, more closely resemble permissible advertising rather than prohibited solicitation.

The amendments to Rules 7.2 and 7.3 were explained by the ABA's Standing Committee on Ethics and Professional Responsibility as follows:

*ABA Committee Report Explaining 1989 Amendments to Rule 7.3**

The Supreme Court of the United States, in Shapero v. Kentucky Bar Association, 486 U.S. 466 (1988), ruled that the First Amendment does not allow states to impose blanket bans on targeted mail solicitation by lawyers of prospective clients. Held unconstitutional was a Kentucky Supreme Court rule identical to Model Rule 7.3. The principal purpose of the amendments proposed here is to bring the Model Rules into compliance with the *Shapero* decision. . . .

2002 Amendments: In 2002, the ABA House of Delegates adopted with only minor changes the ABA Ethics 2000 Commission proposal to amend Rule 7.3 and its Comment. The main changes were to add express prohibitions on "real-time electronic" contact in Rules 7.3(a) and (b) and in Comments 1, 2, and 3, and to amend Comment 4 by adding the second sentence ("Nor is there . . .") and the last sentence ("Also, paragraph (a) is not intended . . .").

Selected State Variations

Arizona adds a subparagraph (b)(3) prohibiting solicitation relating to a personal injury or wrongful death within 30 days after the occurrence, and Arizona adds detailed requirements regarding targeted mail.

California: Rule 1-400 provides, in pertinent part, as follows:

(B) For purposes of this rule, a "solicitation" means any communication:

(1) Concerning the availability for professional employment of a member or a law firm in which a significant motive is pecuniary gain; and

(2) Which is . . . .

* Committee Reports do not represent official policy of the ABA. They are for information only, and the opinions are those of the authors of the report.

(b) delivered in person or by telephone, or

(c) directed by any means to a person known to the sender to be represented by counsel in a matter which is a subject of the communication.

(C) A solicitation shall not be made by or on behalf of a member or law firm to a prospective client with whom the member or law firm has no family or prior professional relationship, unless the solicitation is protected from abridgment by the Constitution of the United States or by the Constitution of the State of California. A solicitation to a former or present client in the discharge of a member's or law firm's professional duties is not prohibited. . . .

In addition, California Business & Professions Code §6152(a)(1) provides, in part, that it is unlawful for any person "to act as a runner or capper for any attorneys or to solicit any business for any attorneys in and about the state prisons, county jails, city jails, city prisons, or other places of detention of persons, city receiving hospitals, city and county receiving hospitals, county hospitals, superior courts, or in any public institution or in any public place or upon any public street or highway or in and about private hospitals, sanitariums or in and about any private institution or upon private property of any character whatsoever. . . ."

Colorado: Rule 7.3(c) imposes a waiting period of 30 days after an event causing personal injury or death before a lawyer may solicit professional employment in connection with the event unless the lawyer has "a family or prior professional relationship with the prospective client." The rule also prohibits solicitation if the sending lawyer "knows or reasonably should know" that the recipient is represented by a lawyer in the matter, and requires the sending lawyer to say whether that lawyer will "actually handle the case or matter" or if it "will be referred to another lawyer or firm." Rule 7.3(d) prohibits the envelope from revealing "the nature of the prospective client's legal problem."

Connecticut: Rule 7.3 differs significantly from ABA Model Rule 7.3. For example, Rule 7.3(a)(4) does not prohibit personal, live telephone, or real-time electronic contact with a prospective client that is "a business organization, a notfor-profit organization or governmental body and the lawyer seeks to provide services related to the organization." Rule 7.3(b)(b) forbids a lawyer to "contact, or send, a written or electronic communication to, a prospective client" if:

(1) The lawyer knows or reasonably should know that the physical, emotional or mental state of the person makes it unlikely that the person would exercise reasonable judgment in employing a lawyer; . . .

(3) The communication involves coercion, duress, fraud, overreaching, harassment, intimidation or undue influence; [or]

(4) The written communication concerns a specific matter and the lawyer knows or reasonably should know that the person to whom the communication is directed is represented by a lawyer in the matter. . . .

Connecticut Rule 7.3(b)(5) prohibits written solicitation in personal injury or wrongful death matters for 40 days after an accident or disaster. Rule 7.3(c) requires every written communication used by a lawyer "for the purpose of obtaining professional employment from a prospective client known to be in need of legal services in a particular matter" to say "Advertising Material" on the envelope and first page "in red ink." Rule 7.3(d) requires the first sentence of a written communication about a specific matter to say: "If you have already retained a lawyer for this matter, please disregard this letter."

District of Columbia omits Rule 7.3, but D.C. Rule 7.1(b) generally permits in-person solicitation by providing as follows:

> (1) A lawyer shall not seek by in-person contact, employment (or employment of a partner or associate) by a nonlawyer who has not sought the lawyer's advice regarding employment of a lawyer, if:
>
> (A) The solicitation involves use of a statement or claim that is false or misleading . . . ;
>
> (B) The solicitation involves the use of coercion, duress or harassment; or
>
> (C) The potential client is apparently in a physical or mental condition which would make it unlikely that the potential client could exercise reasonable, considered judgment as to the selection of a lawyer.
>
> (2) A lawyer shall not give anything of value to a person (other than the lawyer's partner or employee) for recommending the lawyer's services through in-person contact.

D.C. also has adopted an unusual Rule 7.1(e) that provides, in part, as follows:

> Any lawyer . . . who solicits . . . any person incarcerated at the District of Columbia Jail . . . for the purpose of representing that person for a fee paid by or on behalf of that person . . . in any then-pending criminal case in which that person is represented, must provide timely and adequate notice to the person's then-current lawyer prior to accepting any fee from or on behalf of the incarcerated person.

Florida: Rule 4-7.4(a) defines the term "solicit" to include (among other things) contact by fax. Rule 4-7.4(b)(1), which is essentially the rule upheld in *Florida Bar v. Went for It, Inc.*, 515 U.S. 618 (1995), prohibits a lawyer from soliciting prospective clients in writing if:

> (A) the written communication concerns an action for personal injury or wrongful death or otherwise relates to an accident or disaster involving the person to whom the communication is addressed or a relative of that person, unless the accident or disaster occurred more than 30 days prior to the mailing of the communication;
>
> (B) the written communication concerns a specific matter and the lawyer knows or reasonably should know that the person to whom the communication is directed is represented by a lawyer in the matter. . . .

Rule 4-7.4(b)(2) imposes stringent, detailed requirements on all written communications to prospective clients, including that the first sentence of every written communication prompted by a specific occurrence must be: "If you have already retained a lawyer for this matter, please disregard this letter."

Florida Rule 4-7.6, entitled "Computer-Accessed Communications," provides that all websites controlled or sponsored by a lawyer or law firm and that contain information concerning the lawyer's or law firm's services "shall disclose all jurisdictions in which the lawyer or members of the law firm are licensed to practice law." A lawyer shall not send an "unsolicited electronic mail communication directly or indirectly to a prospective client for the purpose of obtaining professional employment" unless it complies with a host of requirements, including that the subject line of the communication must begin with "LEGAL ADVERTISEMENT."

Georgia: Rule 7.3(a)(3) prohibits a written communication relating to an accident or disaster involving the person to whom the communication is sent for 30 days after the accident or disaster. Georgia omits ABA Model Rule 7.3(c), but adds Rule 7.3(e), which provides that a lawyer "shall not accept employment when the lawyer knows or it is obvious that the person who seeks to employ the lawyer does so as a result of conduct by any person or organization prohibited under" these rules. Georgia's rule also adds detailed provisions regarding a lawyer's participation in referral services.

Kentucky: An elaborate Rule 7.60 (Kentucky Disaster Response Plan) addresses problems that occur when lawyers and nonlawyers who are not subject to disciplinary jurisdiction in Kentucky "engage in the provision of legal services, legal advice, and outright solicitation of persons and their families affected by a disastrous event." The policy of Rule 7.60 is to "[m]onitor the conduct of all attorneys, both members and non-members of the Kentucky Bar Association, and thereby deter violations of the rules of ethical conduct. . . ."

Kentucky has also enacted a criminal statute, Ky. Rev. Stat. §21A.300, providing that for 30 days after "the filing of a criminal or civil action, or claim for damages, or a traffic citation, injury, accident, or disaster," an attorney "shall not directly solicit . . . a victim of the accident or disaster, or a relative of the victim, for the purpose of obtaining professional employment," and "shall not knowingly accept a referral from an attorney referral service" if the referral service has violated that prohibition. Ky. Rev. Stat. §21A.310 makes violation of the 30-day blackout law a Class A misdemeanor, and may subject an attorney to professional discipline in addition to any criminal penalty. Kentucky Supreme Court Rule 3.130 provides:

> If a lawyer illegally or unethically solicited a client for which compensation is paid or payable, all fees arising from such transaction shall be deemed waived and forfeited and shall be returned to the client. A civil action for recovery of such fees may be brought in a court of competent jurisdiction.

Louisiana deletes Rule 7.3 and addresses solicitation in Rule 7.4. Among other variations, Rule 7.4(b)(1)(A) contains a provision that prohibits any solicitation (including letters) that concern "an action for personal injury or wrongful death . . . unless the accident or disaster occurred more than thirty days prior to the mailing of the communication." Rule 7.4(b)(2) also requires lawyers to include a variety of information in letters to potential clients.

Maine: The restrictions on in-person solicitation apply only to "non-commercial" clients. Moreover, the Rule provides that a variety of factors are relevant when determining the permissibility of a solicitation, including "the prospective client's sophistication regarding legal matters; the physical, emotional state of the prospective non-commercial client; and the circumstances in which the solicitation is made. . . ."

Massachusetts: Rule 7.3(b)(1) prohibits solicitation if "the lawyer knows or reasonably should know that the physical, mental, or emotional state of the prospective client is such that there is a substantial potential that the person cannot exercise reasonable judgment in employing a lawyer," unless the solicitation is "not for a fee." Rule 7.3(d) prohibits solicitation in person "or by personal communication by telephone, electronic device, or otherwise," but Rule 7.3(e) exempts: (1) communications with "members of the bar of any state or jurisdiction"; (2)(A) "grandparents of the lawyer or the lawyer's spouse, (B) descendants of the grandparents of the lawyer or the lawyer's spouse, or (C) the spouse of any of the foregoing persons"; (3) "prospective clients with whom the lawyer had a prior attorney-client relationship"; (4)(i) "non-profit and governmental entities" regarding their activities, and (ii) "persons engaged in trade or commerce" in connection with their trade or commerce.

Mississippi: Rule 7.2(a) defines an "advertisement" as "an active quest for clients involving a public or non-public communication." Rule 7.5(a) requires a lawyer to submit a "copy or recording of any advertisement" to the Office of the General Counsel of the Mississippi Bar (OGCMB) "prior to its first dissemination," but Rule 7.5(b) exempts 13 categories of advertisements from the filing requirement, such as telephone directory advertisements, business cards, web pages, and "scholarly writings." Under Rule 7.5(d), a lawyer may request an "advisory opinion concerning the compliance of a contemplated advertisement or communication with these Rules in advance of disseminating the advertisement or communication," provided the advertisement is submitted at least 45 days in advance. The OGCMB must "render its advisory opinion within forty-five days of receipt of a request unless the OGCMB determines that there is reasonable doubt that the advertisement or communication is in compliance with the Rules and that further examination is warranted but such evaluation cannot be completed within the forty-five day time period. . . ." In that event, "the OGCMB shall complete its review as promptly as the circumstances reasonably allow. If the OGCMB does not send any correspondence or notice to the lawyer within forty-five days, the advertisement or communication will be deemed approved." Under Rule 7.5(d)(2), a "finding by the OGCMB of either compliance or non-compliance shall not be binding in disciplinary proceedings, but may be offered as evidence."

Missouri: Rule 7.3(a) provides that a lawyer may not "initiate" in-person, telephone, or real-time electronic solicitation of legal business "under any circumstance, other than with an existing or former client, lawyer, close friend or relative." Regarding written communications to "others," Rules 7.3(b) and (c) provide as follows:

> (b)(3) each written solicitation must include the following:
>
> "Disregard this solicitation if you have already engaged a lawyer in connection with the legal matter referred to in this solicitation. You may wish to consult your lawyer or another lawyer instead of me (us). The exact nature of your legal situation will depend on many facts not known to me (us) at this time. You should understand that the advice and information in this solicitation is general and that your own situation may vary. This statement is required by rule of the Supreme Court of Missouri." . . .
>
> (8) if a lawyer knows that a lawyer other than the lawyer whose name or signature appears on the solicitation will actually handle the case or matter or that the case or matter will be referred to another lawyer or law firm, any written solicitation concerning a specific matter shall include a statement so advising the potential client; and
>
> (9) a lawyer shall not send a written solicitation regarding a specific matter if the lawyer knows or reasonably should know that the person to whom the solicitation is directed is represented by a lawyer in the matter.
>
> (c) A lawyer shall not send, nor knowingly permit to be sent . . . a written solicitation to any prospective client . . . if: . . .
>
> (4) the written solicitation concerns an action for personal injury or wrongful death or otherwise relates to an accident or disaster involving the person solicited or a relative of that person if the accident or disaster occurred less than 30 days prior to the solicitation . . . ; or
>
> (5) the written solicitation vilifies, denounces or disparages any other potential party.

Montana: Rule 7.3(b)(4) prohibits a lawyer from contacting a prospective client if "the lawyer reasonably should know that the person is already represented by another lawyer."

Nevada: Rule 7.3(d) provides, in part: "Written communication directed to a specific prospective client who may need legal services due to a particular transaction or occurrence is prohibited in Nevada within 45 days of the transaction or occurrence giving rise to the communication."

New Hampshire: Rule 7.3(a) does not use the words "solicit" or "pecuniary gain" but provides that a lawyer "shall not initiate, by in-person, live voice, recorded or other real-time means, contact with a prospective client for the purpose of obtaining professional employment," unless the person contacted fits the exemptions in ABA Model Rule 7.3(a)(1)-(2) or:

> (3) is an employee, agent, or representative of a business, non-profit or governmental organization not known to be in need of legal services in a particular matter, and the lawyer seeks to provide services on behalf of the organization; or
>
> (4) is an individual who regularly requires legal services in a commercial context and is not known to be in need of legal services in a particular matter.

New Hampshire Rule 7.3(d)(iii) exempts contact with "those the lawyer is permitted under applicable law to seek to join in litigation in the nature of a class action, if success in asserting rights or defenses of the litigation is dependent upon the joinder of others."

New Jersey omits Rule 7.3(c) and Rule 7.3(d). In addition, to control solicitation after mass disasters, New Jersey adds Rule 7.3(b)(4), which provides that a lawyer shall not contact, or send a written communication to, a prospective client for the purpose of obtaining professional employment if "the communication involves unsolicited direct contact with a prospective client within thirty days after a specific mass-disaster event, when such contact concerns potential compensation arising from the event." To prevent out-of-state attorneys from improperly soliciting New Jersey victims and their families after mass disasters, the Court's Clerk has issued a statement saying that it "has jurisdiction over out-of-state attorneys who make such solicitations to prospective claimants in New Jersey."

Regarding events other than mass disasters, New Jersey adds Rule 7.3(b)(5)(iii), which generally permits targeted mail if (among other things) it contains an additional notice that "the recipient may, if the letter is inaccurate or misleading, report same to the Committee on Attorney Advertising, Hughes Justice Complex, P.O. Box 037, Trenton, New Jersey 08625."

New York: Rule 7.3(b) defines "solicitation" to mean "any advertisement initiated by or on behalf of a lawyer or law firm that is directed to, or targeted at, a specific recipient or group of recipients, or their family members or legal representatives, the primary purpose of which is the retention of the lawyer or law firm, and a significant motive for which is pecuniary gain. It does not include a proposal or other writing prepared and delivered in response to a specific request of a prospective client."

Rule 7.3(a) provides as follows: "A lawyer shall not engage in solicitation . . . by in-person or telephone contact, or by real-time or interactive computer-accessed communication unless the recipient is a close friend, relative, former client or existing client. . . ." Solicitation by any means is forbidden if (among other things) "the lawyer intends or expects, but does not disclose, that the legal services necessary to handle the matter competently will be performed primarily by another lawyer who is not affiliated with the soliciting lawyer as a partner, associate or of counsel." Rule 7.3(c) imposes detailed filing requirements for most solicitations, including "a transcript of the audio portion of any radio or television solicitation" and "if the solicitation is in a language other than English, an accurate English-language translation."

Rule 7.3(e) restricts solicitation in personal injury and wrongful death cases as follows: "No solicitation relating to a specific incident involving potential claims for personal injury or wrongful death shall be disseminated before the 30th day after the date of the incident, unless a filing must be made within 30 days of the incident as a legal prerequisite to the particular claim, in which case no unsolicited communication shall be made before the 15th day after the date of the incident." New York addresses a similar issue in Rule 4.5, which has no Model Rule equivalent. That Rule restricts defense lawyers from engaging in unsolicited communications with prospective claimants in personal injury or wrongful death cases during the same time period described in Rule 7.3(e), unless the communication is with the claimant's counsel.

Rule 7.3(i) provides that New York's solicitation rules apply to lawyers from out of state who solicit clients in New York.

Also, under 22 NYCRR §130-1.1a, an attorney filing an "initiating pleading" must certify that "(i) the matter was not obtained through illegal conduct, or that if it was, the attorney or other persons responsible for the illegal conduct are not participating in the matter or sharing in any fee earned therefrom" and "(ii) the matter was not obtained in violation of [the rules of professional conduct]."

North Carolina: Rule 7.3(d)(1) defines the phrase "prepaid or group legal services plan," and Rule 7.3(d)(2) sets forth detailed conditions that a lawyer must satisfy before participating in such a plan.

Ohio: Rule 7.3(c) requires targeted direct mail solicitation to: "(1) Disclose accurately and fully the manner in which the lawyer or law firm became aware of the identity and specific legal need of the addressee" and "(2) Disclaim or refrain from expressing any predetermined evaluation of the merits of the addressee's case." Rule 7.3(d) provides that before soliciting professional employment from a defendant in a civil action, a lawyer "shall verify that the party has been served with notice of the action filed against that party." Service shall be verified by "consulting the docket of the court in which the action was filed. . . ."

Ohio Rule 7.3(e) provides that if a communication solicits professional employment in a potential claim for personal injury or wrongful death within 30 days of an accident or disaster, the communication must include a lengthy text headed "Understanding Your Rights," which provides, in relevant part, as follows:

> 2. *You do not have to sign anything*—You may not want to give an interview or recorded statement without first consulting with an attorney, because the statement can be used against you. If you may be at fault or have been charged with a traffic or other offense, it may be advisable to consult an attorney right away. However, if you have insurance, your insurance policy probably requires you to cooperate with your insurance company and to provide a statement to the company. If you fail to cooperate with your insurance company, it may void your coverage.
>
> 3. *Your interests versus interests of insurance company*—Your interests and those of the other person's insurance company are in conflict. Your interests may also be in conflict with your own insurance company. Even if you are not sure who is at fault, you should contact your own insurance company and advise the company of the incident to protect your insurance coverage. . . .

> 8. *Check a lawyer's qualifications*—Before hiring any lawyer, you have the right to know the lawyer's background, training, and experience in dealing with cases similar to yours.
>
> 9. *How much will it cost?*—In deciding whether to hire a particular lawyer, you should discuss, and the lawyer's written fee agreement should reflect:
>
> a. How is the lawyer to be paid? If you already have a settlement offer, how will that affect a contingent fee arrangement?
>
> b. How are the expenses involved in your case, such as telephone calls, deposition costs, and fees for expert witnesses, to be paid? Will these costs be advanced by the lawyer or charged to you as they are incurred? Since you are obligated to pay all expenses even if you lose your case, how will payment be arranged?
>
> c. Who will handle your case? If the case goes to trial, who will be the trial attorney?

Furthermore, a footnote to "Understanding Your Rights" says, in part: "THE SUPREME COURT OF OHIO . . . NEITHER PROMOTES NOR PROHIBITS THE DIRECT SOLICITATION OF PERSONAL INJURY VICTIMS."

Pennsylvania omits Rules 7.3(c) and (d).

Rhode Island: Rule 7.3(a)(3) permits "in-person, live telephone or real-time electronic contact" solicitation for profit if the prospective client is "a business organization, a not-for-profit organization, or governmental body and the lawyer seeks to provide services related to the organization."

South Carolina: Effective August 22, 2011, Rule 7.3(d) provides:

> (2) Each solicitation must include the following statements:
>
> (A) "You may wish to consult your lawyer or another lawyer instead of me (us). You may obtain information about other lawyers by consulting directories, seeking the advice of other, or calling the South Carolina Bar Lawyer Referral Service at 799-7100 in Columbia or toll free at 1-800-868-2284. If you have already engaged a lawyer in connection with the legal matter referred to in this communication, you should direct any questions you have to that lawyer" and
>
> (B) "The exact nature of your legal situation will depend on many facts not known to me (us) at this time. You should understand that the advice and information in this communication is general and that your own situation may vary."

Where the solicitation is written, the above statements must be in a type no smaller than that used in the body of the communication.

> (3) Each solicitation must include the following statement:
>
> "ANY COMPLAINTS ABOUT THIS COMMUNICATION OR THE REPRESENTATIONS OF ANY LAWYER MAY BE DIRECTED TO THE COMMISSION ON LAWYER CONDUCT, 1015 SUMTER STREET, SUITE 305, COLUMBIA, SOUTH CAROLINA 29201 TELEPHONE NUMBER 803-734-2037." Where the solicitation is written, this statement must be printed in capital letters and in a size no smaller than that used in the body of the communication.

See more discussion of South Carolina Rule 418 in Selected State Variations under Rule 8.5.

Texas: Rule 7.06 provides that a lawyer "shall not accept or continue employment when the lawyer knows or reasonably should know that the person who seeks the lawyer's services does so as a result of conduct prohibited by these Rules." In addition, under §38.12 of the Texas Penal Code it is a crime if a lawyer, "with intent to obtain an economic benefit . . . (2) solicits employment, either in person or by telephone, for himself or for another." Section 38.01(11) of the Texas Penal Code defines the phrase "solicit employment" as follows:

> (11) "Solicit employment" means to communicate in person or by telephone with a prospective client or a member of the prospective client's family concerning professional employment . . . arising out of a particular occurrence or event, or series of occurrences or events, or concerning an existing problem of the prospective client . . . for the purpose of providing professional services to the prospective client, when neither the person receiving the communication nor anyone acting on that person's behalf has requested the communication. The term does not include a communication initiated by a family member of the person receiving a communication. . . .

Virginia: Rule 7.3 prohibits "in-person" communications to a "non-lawyer" if the communication "has a substantial potential for or involves the use of coercion, duress, compulsion, intimidation, threats, unwarranted promises of benefits, over-persuasion, overreaching, or vexatious or harassing conduct, taking into account the sophistication regarding legal matters, the physical, emotional or mental state of the person to whom the communication is directed and the circumstances in which the communication is made." Rule 7.3(c) prohibits a lawyer from assisting a "nonprofit organization" that engages in such communications, or in communications on the lawyer's behalf that are "false, fraudulent, misleading, or deceptive," and Rule 7.3(f) provides that in no event may a lawyer "initiate" in-person solicitation "for compensation in a personal injury or wrongful death claim of a prospective client with whom the lawyer has no family or prior professional relationship."

Wisconsin: Rule 7.3(b)(1) adds that solicitation is prohibited if "(1) the lawyer knows or reasonably should know that the physical, emotional or mental state of the person makes it unlikely that the person would exercise reasonable judgment in employing a lawyer." Rule 7.3(e) (e) provides that ordinarily a lawyer "shall not draft legal documents, such as wills, trust instruments or contracts, which require or imply that the lawyer's services be used in relation to that document."

Related Materials

ABA Commission on Ethics 20/20: In 2009, the ABA created the Commission on Ethics 20/20, which is comprehensively reviewing the ABA Model Rules of Professional Conduct and other lawyer regulatory sources in light of globalization and changes in technology. In September 2011, the Commission circulated for public comment a proposal to amend Rule 7.3 and its Comment by substituting the phrase "potential client" for the phrase "prospective client" in numerous places to make clear that Rule 7.3 applies to all possible future clients, not just those who fit the definition of "prospective client" in Rule 1.18(a). The Commission also proposed relatively minor amendments to several Comments. For example, the revised draft proposal deletes the word "autodialed" from the Comment because the Commission's research revealed that autodialing (also called "robo-calling") is now unlawful in many situations. The revised proposal instead reminds lawyers that "other law" often governs solicitation. *See, e.g.,* 47 U.S.C. 227(b) (Telephone Consumer Protection Act). Finally, the Commission proposed adding the following new Comment [1] to Rule 7.3 to define the key term "solicitation":

[1] A solicitation is a targeted communication initiated by the lawyer that is directed to a specific potential client and that offers to provide, or can reasonably be understood as offering to provide, legal services. In contrast, a lawyer's communication typically does not constitute a solicitation if it is directed to the general public, such as through a billboard, an Internet banner advertisement, a website or a television commercial, or if it is in response to a request for information or is automatically generated in response to Internet searches.

The Commission may present these proposals (or revised versions of them) to the ABA House of Delegates at its August 2012 Annual Meeting. For updates on the Ethics 20/20 Commission's work, visit *www.americanbar.org/Ethics2020.*

ABA Formal Ethics Opinions: See ABA Formal Ethics Ops. 88-356 (1988), 99-414 (1999), 04-432 n.7 (2004), and 07-445 (2007).

American Prepaid Legal Services Institute: In certain circumstances, ABA Model Rule 7.3(d) permits lawyers to participate with "a prepaid or group legal service plan operated by an organization not owned or directed by the lawyer that uses in-person or telephone contact to solicit memberships or subscriptions for the plan . . .". For more information about prepaid legal services, visit the website maintained by the American Prepaid Legal Services Institute (API) at *www.aplsi.org.* The API is a professional trade organization representing the legal services plan industry. It is affiliated with the American Bar Association and is headquartered in Chicago, Illinois.

Aviation Disaster Family Assistance Act: In 1996, amidst allegations that lawyers had improperly solicited relatives of the victims of the crashes of ValueJet Flight 109 in the Florida Everglades and TWA Flight 800 off Long Island, Congress passed the Aviation Disaster Family Assistance Act, 49 U.S.C. §1136(g)(2). As amended in 2000, that statute restricts solicitation of air crash victims and their relatives as follows:

> *Unsolicited communications.* In the event of an accident involving an air carrier . . . no unsolicited communication concerning a potential action for personal injury or wrongful death may be made by an attorney (including any associate, agent, employee, or other representative of an attorney) or any potential party to the litigation to an individual injured in the accident, or to a relative of an individual involved in the accident, before the 45th day following the date of the accident.

IRS Regulations: In the regulations governing practice before the Internal Revenue Service, 31 C.F.R. §10.30(a)(2) provides:

> A practitioner may not make, directly or indirectly, an uninvited written or oral solicitation of employment in matters related to the Internal Revenue Service if the solicitation violates Federal or State law or other applicable rule, *e.g.*, attorneys are precluded from making a solicitation that is prohibited by conduct rules applicable to all attorneys in their State(s) of licensure. Any lawful solicitation made by or on behalf of a practitioner eligible to practice before the Internal Revenue Service must, nevertheless, clearly identify the solicitation as such and, if applicable, identify the source of the information used in choosing the recipient.

In addition, 31 C.F.R. §10.30(d) provides that a practitioner may not "assist, or accept assistance from, any person or entity who, to the knowledge of the practitioner, obtains clients or otherwise practices in a manner forbidden under this section."

"Jail Mail": In 1996, to make it more difficult for private criminal defense attorneys to send targeted mail to potential clients who had recently been arrested (so-called "jail mail"), California amended Government Code §6254(f)(3) to require any person requesting an arrestee's address to declare under penalty of perjury that the information "shall not be used directly or indirectly to sell a product or service. . . ." In *Los Angeles Police Dep't v. United Reporting Publishing Corp.*, 528 U.S. 32 (1999), the United States Supreme Court held that this statute was not *facially* invalid, but left open the possibility that it might be invalid as applied. The Court therefore remanded for further proceedings. (No decision on the merits is reported on remand.)

Prepaid and Group Legal Services Plans: ABA Model Rule 7.3(d) refers to but does not define a "prepaid or group legal services plan." A helpful definition is found in North Carolina Rule 7.3(d)(1), which provides as follows:

> (1) *Definition.* A prepaid legal services plan or a group legal services plan ("a plan") is any arrangement by which a person, firm, or corporation, not otherwise authorized to engage in the practice of law, in exchange for any valuable consideration, offers to provide or arranges the provision of legal services that are paid for in advance of the need for the service ("covered services"). In addition to covered services, a plan may provide specified legal services at fees that are less than what a non-member of the plan would normally pay. The legal services offered by a plan must be provided by a licensed lawyer who is not an employee, director or owner of the plan. A plan does not include the sale of an identified, limited legal service, such as drafting a will, for a fixed, one-time fee.

According to the American Prepaid Legal Services Institute (APLSI):

> Almost every legal plan provides legal advice and consultation by telephone as a basic service and may also include brief office consultations, review of simple legal documents, preparation of a simple will, and short letters written or phone calls made by a lawyer. Other plans offer more comprehensive coverage for trials, marital problems, bankruptcy, real estate matters and the like. In addition to the member, most plans include or offer coverage for his or her spouse and dependent children.

For more information about prepaid and group legal services plans, see *www.aplsi.org* (click on "Legal Plans").

Restatement of the Law Governing Lawyers: The Restatement has no provision comparable to ABA Model Rule 7.3.

Rule 7.4 Communication of Fields of Practice and Specialization

(a) A lawyer may communicate the fact that the lawyer does or does not practice in particular fields of law.

(b) A lawyer admitted to engage in patent practice before the United States Patent and Trademark Office may use the designation "Patent Attorney" or a substantially similar designation.

(c) A lawyer engaged in Admiralty practice may use the designation "Admiralty," "Proctor in Admiralty" or a substantially similar designation.

(d) A lawyer shall not state or imply that a lawyer is certified as a specialist in a particular field of law, unless:

(1) the lawyer has been certified as a specialist by an organization that has been approved by an appropriate state authority or that has been accredited by the American Bar Association; and

(2) the name of the certifying organization is clearly identified in the communication.

COMMENT

[1] Paragraph (a) of this Rule permits a lawyer to indicate areas of practice in communications about the lawyer's services. If a lawyer practices only in certain fields, or will not accept matters except in a specified field or fields, the lawyer is permitted to so indicate. A lawyer is generally permitted to state that the lawyer "specialist," practices a "specialty," or "specializes in" particular fields, but such communications are subject to the "false and misleading" standard applied in Rule 7.1 to communications concerning a lawyer's services.

[2] Paragraph (b) recognizes the long-established policy of the Patent and Trademark Office for the designation of lawyers practicing before the Office. Paragraph (c) recognizes that designation of Admiralty practice has a long historical tradition associated with maritime commerce and the federal courts.

[3] Paragraph (d) permits a lawyer to state that the lawyer is certified as a specialist in a field of law if such certification is granted by an organization approved by an appropriate state authority or accredited by the American Bar Association or another organization, such as a state bar association, that has been approved by the state authority to accredit organizations that certify lawyers as specialists. Certification signifies that an objective entity has recognized an advanced degree of knowledge and experience in the specialty area greater than is suggested by general licensure to practice law. Certifying organizations may be expected to apply standards of experience, knowledge and proficiency to insure that a lawyer's recognition as a specialist is meaningful and reliable. In order to insure that consumers can obtain access to useful information about an organization granting certification, the name of the certifying organization must be included in any communication regarding the certification.

Canon and Code Antecedents

ABA Canons of Professional Ethics: Canons 45 and 46 provided as follows:

45. Specialists

The canons of the American Bar Association apply to all branches of the legal profession; specialists in particular branches are not to be considered as exempt from the application of these principles.

46. Notice to Local Lawyers

A lawyer available to act as an associate of other lawyers in a particular branch of the law or legal service may send to local lawyers only and publish in his local legal journal, a brief and dignified announcement of his availability to serve other lawyers in connection therewith. The announcement should be in a form which does not constitute a statement or representation of special experience or expertness.

ABA Model Code of Professional Responsibility: Compare DR 2-105(A) (reprinted later in this volume).

Cross-References in Other Rules

Rule 5.5, Comment 21: "Whether and how lawyers may communicate the availability of their services to prospective clients in this jurisdiction is governed by **Rules 7.1** to **7.5**."

Legislative History of Model Rule 7.4

1979 Unofficial Pre-Circulation Draft (then Rule 9.3) provided, in pertinent part, as follows:

> (a) A lawyer whose practice is limited to specified types of legal matters may communicate that fact except as otherwise provided by regulations governing specialization. A lawyer may indicate that he or she is a specialist only as permitted by paragraphs (b) and (c) and as follows: [Insert applicable provisions on designation of specialization.]

The remainder of the 1979 Draft was substantially the same as adopted.

1980 Discussion Draft was substantially the same as adopted.

1981 and ***1982 Drafts*** were the same as adopted.

1983 Rule: As originally adopted in 1983, Rule 7.4 provided as follows:

> A lawyer may communicate the fact that the lawyer does or does not practice in particular fields of law. A lawyer shall not state or imply that the lawyer is a specialist except as follows:
>
> (a) [Same as 2002 version of Rule 7.4(a)(1).]
>
> (b) [Same as 2002 version of Rule 7.4(a)(2).]
>
> (c) (Provisions on designation of specialization of the particular state)

1989 Amendments: In 1989, the ABA House of Delegates substantially amended the Comment (but not the text) to Rule 7.4. The changes were explained in the following report:

*ABA Committee Report Explaining 1989 Amendment to Rule 7.4**

> Rule 7.4 prohibits a lawyer from stating or implying that he or she is a "specialist," with certain limited exceptions. The Rule further provides for designation of specialty in accordance with the rules of the particular jurisdiction. Rule 7.4(c). This rule operates only to prohibit factually inaccurate or misleading information. . . .
>
> As presently written, however, the Comment to Rule 7.4 *also* prohibits statements that the lawyer's practice is "limited to" or "concentrated in" certain fields, under the theory that these terms also connote formal recognition of the lawyer as a "specialist." . . . The use of the words "limited to" or "concentrated in" in denoting areas of practice do not clearly imply *formal* recognition as a "specialist" and simply do not pose sufficient danger of misleading to warrant a proscription of their use. . . .
>
> Therefore, the Comment to Rule 7.4 should not prohibit statements that a lawyer's practice is "limited to" or "concentrated in" a particular field.

1992 Amendments: In 1992, the ABA House of Delegates substantially amended Rule 7.4 and its Comment to conform the rule to the holding of *Peel v. Attorney*

* Committee Reports do not represent official policy of the ABA. They are for information only, and the opinions are those of the authors of the report.

Registration and Disciplinary Commission, 496 U.S. 91 (1990). The amendments are explained in the following committee report:

*ABA Committee Report Explaining 1992 Amendment to Rule 7.4**

Background

> The findings in a recent survey conducted by the ABA Young Lawyers Division . . . revealed that 64 percent of all lawyers in private practice spend at least 50 percent of their time in one substantive field of law. Further, this phenomenon is not limited to large firms. Fifty five percent of sole practitioners responding to the survey were found to spend half or more of their time in just one field. . . .

The Peel Decision

In 1990 the legal specialization issue was addressed again by the Supreme Court in *Peel v. Attorney Registration and Disciplinary Commission.* . . .

The *Peel* decision invalidated the broad prohibition of ABA Model Rule 7.4 on lawyers' communications about their specialties, holding that states may not categorically ban a truthful communication by a lawyer that he or she is certified as a specialist by a bona fide private certifying organization. . . .

> The proposed amendment of Model Rule 7.4 would bring the ABA Model Rules of Professional Conduct into compliance with the *Peel* decision. . . . Amending Model Rule 7.4 as we have proposed will help to insure protection of the users of legal services while authorizing legitimate, truthful advertising claims of lawyer specialists.

1994 Amendments: In 1994, the ABA House of Delegates amended Rule 7.4 by adding a single new sentence to the text of the existing rule (and an identical sentence to the end of the Comment) to bring Rule 7.4 into line with the ABA's new system for accrediting organizations that certify lawyers as specialists. (The ABA Standing Committee on Specialization began approving such organizations in 1993.) In essence, the amendment made it unnecessary for lawyers in states without certifying procedures to use a disclaimer when claiming certification by an organization accredited by the American Bar Association.

Below are excerpts from the joint report and recommendation submitted by the two co-sponsors in support of the amendment.

*ABA Committee Report Explaining 1994 Amendment to Rule 7.4**

> The purpose of this recommendation is to harmonize Model Rule 7.4 with the Association's newly enacted procedure for accrediting organizations that certify specialists in particular areas of the law. . . .
>
> In August, 1993 the Standing Committee on Specialization reported to the House that six specialty certification programs . . . had met the Standards. The Standing Committee on Specialization therefore recommended that those programs be accredited, which recommendation was approved by the House.
>
> However, under the 1992 amendments, a lawyer who is certified by one of those accredited programs, and who practices in a State that has not yet adopted a procedure for approving certifying organizations, would have to add, to any communication

* Committee Reports do not represent official policy of the ABA. They are for information only, and the opinions are those of the authors of the report.

setting forth his or her certification, a statement to the effect that there is no procedure in that particular jurisdiction for approving certifying organizations. Many lawyers believe that such a disclaimer would dilute the positive fact of certification; therefore, those lawyers would end up refraining from publicizing their certification rather than adding the required statement, even though the certifying organization had been fully accredited by the ABA. As a consequence, the value of the ABA accreditation would be considerably diminished.

The Standing Committee on Specialization and the Standing Committee on Ethics and Professional Responsibility believe that Rule 7.4 should now be further amended to permit any accreditations authorized by the House to have their intended effect and be given recognition in those states which have not yet created a mechanism for approving organizations that grant certification.

2002 Amendments: At its February 2002 Mid-Year Meeting, the ABA House of Delegates adopted without change the ABA Ethics 2000 Commission proposal to amend Rule 7.4 and its Comment. The amendments substituted Rule 7.4(d) in place of several longer subparagraphs covering essentially the same ground in greater detail, including an alternative paragraph for jurisdictions lacking any procedures for certifying specialties or for approving organizations that grant specialty certifications. Comments 1, 2, and 3 were amended, and Comments 4 and 5 were deleted.

Selected State Variations

Editors' Note. For a state-by-state chart of rules governing lawyer specialty certification, see the ABA Standing Committee on Specialization's website at *http://www.americanbar.org/groups/professional_responsibility/committees_commissions/specialization.html.*

Arizona: The equivalent to Rule 7.4(d) permits lawyers to state or imply that they are specialists only if they are "certified by the Arizona Board of Legal Specialization" or by a "national entity" that the Board has recognized as having standards substantially the same as the Board's standards.

California has no rule comparable to ABA Model Rule 7.4 in the California Rules of Professional Conduct, but California has developed an extensive program of specialty certification. To be eligible for certification, an attorney must be a member of the California State Bar in good standing and must (1) have spent at least 25 percent of his or her occupational time during the previous five years working in the area of law in which certification is sought, (2) pass a written exam tailored to the particular specialty field, (3) demonstrate a high level of experience in the specialty field by meeting specific task and experience requirements, (4) complete at least 45 hours of continuing legal education in the specialty field, and (5) be favorably evaluated by other attorneys and judges familiar with the attorney's work. California offers specialty certification in eight areas of practice, including Appellate Law, Bankruptcy Law (both Personal and Small Business), Criminal Law, Estate Planning, Trust and Probate Law, Family Law, Immigration and Nationality Law, Taxation Law, and Workers' Compensation Law. Each field has its own particular requirements. For more information, including links to the Rules Governing the State Bar of California Program for Certifying Legal Specialists (most recently amended effective November 1, 2003) and the requirements for each specialty field, visit the California State Bar's website at *www.calbar.org* and enter "Legal Specialization" in the site's search box.

Connecticut: Rule 7.4A(d) describes in some detail 27 different fields of law in which lawyers may be certified as specialists. Rule 7.4B concerns the appointment, powers, and duties of a Legal Specialization Screening Committee that evaluates certifying entities, and Rule 7.4C concerns applications for approval as a certifying entity.

District of Columbia omits ABA Model Rule 7.4.

Florida: Rule 4-7.2(c)(6) divides the rules regulating claims and disclaimers for specialty certification into three categories, depending on whether a lawyer is certified as a specialist by (A) the Florida Bar, (B) another state bar, or (C) an entity not connected with any state bar.

Georgia tracks the first sentence of ABA Model Rule 7.4 verbatim, but eliminates the rest of the ABA rule and instead states the following: "A lawyer who is a specialist in a particular field of law by experience, specialized training or education, or is certified by a recognized and bona fide professional entity, may communicate such specialty or certification so long as the statement is not false or misleading."

Illinois: Rule 7.4(c) requires that if a lawyer's advertisement uses the terms "certified," "specialist," or "expert," then the terms (1) must be "truthful and verifiable and may not be misleading," and (2) must state that "the Supreme Court of Illinois does not recognize certifications of specialties in the practice of law and that the certificate, award or recognition is not a requirement to practice law in Illinois."

Iowa: Rule 7.4 contains a list of 71 distinct fields of practice that a lawyer may identify or describe in communications.

Louisiana addresses this issue in Rule 7.2(c)(5) and specifies that lawyers generally cannot state or imply that they are specialists or experts unless they fit within certain narrow exceptions identified in the rule.

Massachusetts: Rule 7.4(a) permits lawyers to hold themselves out as "specialists" if the holding out does not include a false or misleading communication. The rule defines "holding out" to include "(1) a statement that the lawyer concentrates in, specializes in, is certified in, has expertise in, or limits practice to a particular service, field, or area of law, (2) directory listings, including electronic, computer-accessed or other similar types of directory listings, by particular service, field, or area of law, and (3) any other association of the lawyer's name with a particular service, field, or area of law." Comment 3A to Rule 7.2 provides, in part, as follows:

> Depending upon the topic or purpose of the newsgroup, bulletin board, or chat group, the posting might also constitute an association of the lawyer or law firm's name with a particular service, field, or area of law amounting to a claim of specialization under Rule 7.4 and would therefore be subject to the restrictions of that rule.

Michigan: Rule 7.4 stops after the first sentence of ABA Model Rule 7.4.

Missouri: Rule 7.4 provides that a lawyer other than an admiralty or patent attorney shall not state or imply that the lawyer is a specialist "unless the communication contains a disclaimer that neither the Supreme Court of Missouri nor The Missouri Bar reviews or approves certifying organizations or specialist designations."

Nevada: Rule 7.4(d)(2)(iii) requires that any lawyer claiming to be a specialist "shall carry a minimum of $500,000 in professional liability insurance, with the exception of lawyers who practice exclusively in public law." Nevada also adds a Rule 7.4A to establish procedures for the State Bar Board of Governors to approve organizations that certify lawyers as specialists.

New Jersey: Rule 7.4(d) permits a lawyer to communicate that the lawyer has been certified as a specialist only if the lawyer states (among other things) that "the certification has been granted by the Supreme Court of New Jersey or by an organization that has been approved by the American Bar Association." If the certification has been granted by an organization that has not been approved, or has been denied approval, by either the Supreme Court of New Jersey or the American Bar Association, "the absence or denial of such approval shall be clearly identified in each such communication by the lawyer."

New York: Rule 7.4(c)(1) provides that a lawyer who is "certified as a specialist in a particular area of law or law practice by a private organization approved for that purpose by the American Bar Association" may advertise the certification only if the lawyer identifies the certifying organization and "prominently" makes the following disclaimer: "The [name of the private certifying organization] is not affiliated with any governmental authority. Certification is not a requirement for the practice of law in the State of New York and does not necessarily indicate greater competence than other attorneys experienced in this field of law." If the lawyer is certified as a specialist by an "authority having jurisdiction over specialization under the laws of another state" (rather than by an ABA-approved private organization), Rule 7.4(c)(2) requires a slightly different disclaimer.

North Carolina relegates the substance of ABA Model Rule 7.4(b) (regarding patent and trademark practice) to a Comment and deletes Rule 7.4(c) (regarding admiralty practice).

Ohio: Rule 7.4(a) expressly adds that a lawyer may state that the lawyer "limits his or her practice to or concentrates in particular fields of law." Rule 7.4(c) provides that a lawyer engaged in "trademark practice" may use the designation "Trademarks," "Trademark Attorney," or a substantially similar designation. "Ohio's equivalent to ABA Model Rule 7.4(d)(1) applies if the lawyer has been certified as a specialist by an organization approved by the Supreme Court Commission on Certification of Attorneys as Specialists."

Pennsylvania: Rule 7.4 permits lawyers to advertise that they are certified by organizations approved by the Supreme Court. The Supreme Court may approve an organization upon recommendation of the State Bar Association if the court finds that advertising certification by the organization "will provide meaningful information, which is not false, misleading or deceptive, for use of the public in selecting or retaining a lawyer." Certification must be available to all lawyers "who meet objective and consistently applied standards relevant to practice in the area of law to which the certification relates."

Texas: Rule 7.04(b)(2) permits lawyers to advertise that they have been certified as specialists by the Texas Board of Legal Specialization or by an organization that has been:

> accredited by the Texas Board of Legal Specialization as a bona fide organization that admits to membership or grants certification only on the basis of objective, exacting, publicly available standards (including high standards of individual character, conduct, and reputation) that are reasonably relevant to the special training or special competence that is implied and that are in excess of the level of training and competence generally required for admission to the Bar. . . .

Virginia: Rule 7.4(d) permits a lawyer to communicate that the lawyer has been certified as a specialist by a particular organization if the communication "clearly states that there is no procedure in the Commonwealth of Virginia for approving certifying organizations."

Related Materials

ABA Formal Ethics Opinions: See ABA Formal Ethics Op. 90-357 n.8 (1990).

ABA Standards for Accreditation of Specialty Certification Programs for Lawyers: In 1992, the ABA amended Rule 7.4 to allow lawyers to advertise that they were "certified" by private organizations as specialists. In 1993, the ABA adopted Standards for Accreditation of Specialty Certification Programs for Lawyers. The ABA Standards are strict—accredited certifying organizations must be made up primarily of lawyers and must only certify lawyers who (1) have been involved in the specialty area for at least the past three years; (2) devote at least 25 percent of their practice to the specialty area; (3) have passed a written examination of "suitable length and complexity"; (4) have been favorably recommended by five or more lawyers or judges knowledgeable in the specialty area; and (5) have taken at least 36 hours of CLE in the specialty area during the three years before applying for specialty certification. The Standards for Accreditation of Specialty Certification Programs are available at *http://www.americanbar.org/groups/professional_responsibility/committees_commissions/specialization/resources/resources_for_programs/accreditation_standards.html.*

Since 1993, the ABA has accredited more than ten specialty certification programs offered by seven private organizations. Those organizations are: the American Board of Certification (Business Bankruptcy, Consumer Bankruptcy, Creditors Rights); the American Board of Professional Liability Attorneys (Accounting Professional Liability, Legal Professional Liability, Medical Professional Liability); the National Association of Counsel for Children (Juvenile Law-Child Welfare); the National Association of Estate Planners & Councils Estate Law Specialist Board, Inc. (Estate Planning Law); the National Board of Trial Advocacy (Civil Trial Advocacy, Criminal Trial Advocacy, Family Law Trial Advocacy, Social Security Disability Law); the National College for DUI Defense, Inc. (DUI Defense Law); and the National Elder Law Foundation (Elder Law).

The Standing Committee on Specialization continues to help private groups develop new certification programs that meet the ABA Standards. For an up-to-date list of certification programs accredited by the ABA and by various state authorities (including a state-by-state chart of available certifications), visit the Standing Committee's website at *http://www.americanbar.org/groups/professional_responsibility/committees_commissions/specialization.html.*

ABA Standing Committee on Specialization: The ABA maintains a Standing Committee on Specialization. The Standing Committee (a) publishes a quarterly newsletter, "Certification Link," that reports legal specialization news from around the country; (b) holds an annual National Roundtable on Lawyer Specialty Certification; (c) assists certifying organizations in developing additional certification programs; and (d) maintains a state-by-state summary of specialty advertising regulations on its website. For more information, visit *http://www.americanbar.org/groups/professional_responsibility/committees_commissions/specialization.html.*

Paralegal Certification: Since 1976, the National Association of Legal Assistants (NALA) has administered a certifying examination for paralegals. Passing the exam entitles a paralegal to the designation "Certified Legal Assistant" (CLA) or "Certified Paralegal" (CP). The NALA may revoke the CLA or CP designation for a variety of reasons, including "[v]iolation of the NALA Code of Ethics and Professional Responsibility."

Paralegals who hold the CLA credential are eligible to take four-hour specialty certification examinations in more than a dozen areas of law, including Alternative Dispute Resolution, Bankruptcy, Contracts, Civil Litigation, Corporations/Business Law, Criminal Law and Procedure, Discovery, Intellectual Property, Estate Planning and Probate, and Real Estate. Those who pass a specialty certification exam earn the designation "APC" (standing for "Advanced Paralegal Certification") and a specialty (*e.g.*, "APC-Civil Litigation" or "APC-Bankruptcy"). Since 1976, more than 15,000 people have become Certified Legal Assistants. For more information, check the NALA's website at *www.nala.org* (click "Certification" at top of screen).

Restatement of the Law Governing Lawyers: The Restatement has no provision comparable to ABA Model Rule 7.4.

Rule 7.5 Firm Names and Letterheads

(a) A lawyer shall not use a firm name, letterhead or other professional designation that violates Rule 7.1. A trade name may be used by a lawyer in private practice if it does not imply a connection with a government agency or with a public or charitable legal services organization and is not otherwise in violation of Rule 7.1.

(b) A law firm with offices in more than one jurisdiction may use the same name or other professional designation in each jurisdiction, but identification of the lawyers in an office of the firm shall indicate the jurisdictional limitations on those not licensed to practice in the jurisdiction where the office is located.

(c) The name of a lawyer holding a public office shall not be used in the name of a law firm, or in communications on its behalf, during any substantial period in which the lawyer is not actively and regularly practicing with the firm.

(d) Lawyers may state or imply that they practice in a partnership or other organization only when that is the fact.

COMMENT

[1] A firm may be designated by the names of all or some of its members, by the names of deceased members where there has been a continuing succession in the firm's identity or by a trade name such as the "ABC Legal Clinic." A lawyer or law firm may also be designated by a distinctive website address or comparable professional designation. Although the United States Supreme Court has held that legislation may prohibit the use of trade names in professional practice, use of such names in law practice is acceptable so long as it is not misleading. If a private firm

uses a trade name that includes a geographical name such as "Springfield Legal Clinic," an express disclaimer that it is a public legal aid agency may be required to avoid a misleading implication. It may be observed that any firm name including the name of a deceased partner is, strictly speaking, a trade name. The use of such names to designate law firms has proven a useful means of identification. However, it is misleading to use the name of a lawyer not associated with the firm or a predecessor of the firm, or the name of a nonlawyer.

[2] With regard to paragraph (d), lawyers sharing office facilities, but who are not in fact associated with each other in a law firm, may not denominate themselves as, for example, "Smith and Jones," for that title suggests that they are practicing law together in a firm.

Canon and Code Antecedents

ABA Canons of Professional Ethics: Canon 33 provided as follows:

33. Partnerships-Names

Partnerships among lawyers for the practice of their profession are very common and are not to be condemned. In the formation of partnerships and the use of partnership names care should be taken not to violate any law, custom, or rule of court locally applicable. Where partnerships are formed between lawyers who are not all admitted to practice in the courts of the state, care should be taken to avoid any misleading name or representation which would create a false impression as to the professional position or privileges of the member not locally admitted. In the formation of partnerships for the practice of law, no person should be admitted or held out as a practitioner or member who is not a member of the legal profession duly authorized to practice, and amenable to professional discipline. In the selection and use of a firm name, no false, misleading, assumed or trade name should be used. The continued use of the name of a deceased or former partner, when permissible by local custom, is not unethical, but care should be taken that no imposition or deception is practiced through this use. When a member of the firm, on becoming a judge, is precluded from practicing law, his name should not be continued in the firm name.

Partnerships between lawyers and members of other professions or nonprofessional persons should not be formed or permitted where any part of the partnership's employment consists of the practice of law.

ABA Model Code of Professional Responsibility: Compare DR 2-102(A), DR 2-102(B), DR 2-102(C), and DR 2-102(D) (reprinted later in this volume).

Cross-References in Other Rules

Rule 5.5, Comment 21: "Whether and how lawyers may communicate the availability of their services to prospective clients in this jurisdiction is governed by **Rules 7.1 to 7.5.**"

Legislative History of Model Rule 7.5

1980 Discussion Draft (then Rule 9.5) did not include the clause in subparagraph (b) requiring lawyers to indicate their jurisdictional limitations, and did not contain subparagraph (d).

1981 Draft was generally the same as adopted, except that Rule 7.5(d) provided: "Lawyers shall not hold themselves out as practicing in a law firm unless the association is in fact a firm."

1982 Draft was adopted.

1983 Rule: As originally adopted in 1983, Rules 7.5(a), (c), and (d) were identical to the 2002 version, and Rule 7.5(b) was nearly identical to the 2002 version but did not contain the phrase "or other professional designation."

2002 Amendments: In 2002, the ABA House of Delegates adopted without change the ABA Ethics 2000 Commission proposal to amend Rule 7.5 and its Comment. The amendments added "or other professional designation" to Rule 7.5(b), added the second sentence (regarding web addresses) to Comment 1, and made minor changes to Comment 2.

In addition, in 2002, the House of Delegates approved a proposal by the ABA Standing Committee on Ethics and Professional Responsibility to add the final clause ("or the name of a nonlawyer") to Comment 1 of Rule 7.5. The Report submitted by the Standing Committee in support of this proposal (and a companion proposal to amend Rule 7.2) noted that the Standing Committee had consulted with the New York State Bar Association, which recommended amending Rule 7.5 to address "its concern that law firms engaged in offering certain services jointly with other nonlawyer professionals not create confusion by adding names of nonlawyer professionals to their law firm names." The Standing Committee agreed with this recommendation, and therefore recommended adding the final clause of Comment 1 to Model Rule 7.5. The House of Delegates approved the recommendation.

Selected State Variations

Alaska adds the following paragraph (e): "The term 'of counsel' shall be used only to refer to a lawyer who has a close continuing relationship with the firm."

Arizona deletes the qualification in the second sentence of subparagraph (a) beginning, "if it does not imply a connection with a government agency. . . ."

California: Compare Standards 6 through 9 following Rule 1-400. In addition, §16952 of the California Corporations Law, entitled "Requirements for Name," provides that the name of a registered limited liability partnership must contain the words "Registered Limited Liability Partnership" or "Limited Liability Partnership" or one of the abbreviations "L.L.P.," "LLP," "R.L.L.P.," or "RLLP" as the last words or letters of its name.

Florida: Rule 4-7.9(b) permits a lawyer to practice under a trade name if the name is "not deceptive" and "does not imply that the firm is something other than a private law firm." The same rule permits a lawyer to use the term "legal clinic" or "legal services" in conjunction with the lawyer's own name "if the lawyer's practice is devoted to providing routine legal services for fees that are lower than the prevailing rate in the community for those services."

Under Rule 4-7.9(c) a lawyer may not advertise under a trade or fictitious name "unless the same name is the law firm name that appears on the lawyer's letterhead, business cards, office sign, and fee contracts, and appears with the lawyer's signature on pleadings and other legal documents." The Comment to Rule 4-7.9 notes that a lawyer may not advertise under "a nonsense name designed to obtain an advantageous position for the lawyer in alphabetical directory listings unless the lawyer actually practices under that nonsense name."

Georgia adds Rule 7.5(e)(1), which permits a lawyer in private practice to use a trade name if it "includes the name of at least one of the lawyers practicing under said name. A law firm name consisting solely of the name or names of deceased or retired members of the firm does not have to include the name of an active member of the firm."

Iowa: Rule 7.5 provides in paragraph (f) that a "lawyer who is engaged both in the practice of law and in another profession or business shall not so indicate on the lawyer's letterhead, office sign, or professional card, and shall not be identified as a lawyer in any publication in connection with the lawyer's other profession or business."

Massachusetts adds to ABA Comment 2 that the term "associates" implies practice in either a partnership or sole proprietorship form and "may not be used by a group in which the individual members disclaim the joint or vicarious responsibility inherent in such forms of business in the absence of an effective disclaimer of such responsibility."

Nevada: Rule 7.5(b) provides that a law firm with offices in more than one jurisdiction "that has registered with the State Bar of Nevada under Rule 7.5A" may use the same name in each jurisdiction. Rule 7.5A(a) provides: "All law firms having an office in Nevada and in one or more other jurisdictions shall register with the State Bar of Nevada and shall pay an annual fee of $500 for such registration." The remainder of the rule sets out lengthy, detailed disclosure requirements such as: "(1) The names and addresses of all lawyers employed by the firm, the jurisdictions in which each lawyer is licensed, and verification that each lawyer is in good standing in the jurisdictions in which each lawyer is licensed; (2) Any pending disciplinary action or investigation against a lawyer employed by the firm;" and (5) a certification that:

> (i) The firm will maintain a permanent office in Nevada with a resident member of the firm who is also an active member in good standing of the State Bar of Nevada at all times the firm is practicing in Nevada . . . [and]
>
> (ii) The firm agrees to disclose in writing to its Nevada clients whether all of its lawyers are licensed to practice in Nevada and, if any of its lawyers are not so licensed, to disclose what legal work will be performed by lawyers not admitted to practice in this state. Upon request of the State Bar of Nevada, the firm shall provide documentation evidencing its compliance with these disclosure requirements. . . .

New Jersey: Rule 7.5(b) permits a law firm with offices in more than one jurisdiction to use the same name in each jurisdiction, but all advertisements, letterheads or "anywhere else that the firm name is used," must indicate the jurisdictional limitations on those not licensed to practice in New Jersey. If a firm name includes the name of any lawyer not licensed in New Jersey, then any advertisement, letterhead or other communication containing the firm name "must include the name of at least one licensed New Jersey attorney who is responsible for the firm's New Jersey practice or the local office thereof. . . ." Rule 7.5(d) permits lawyers to state or imply that they practice in a partnership "only if the persons designated in the firm name and the principal members of the firm share in the responsibility and liability for the firm's performance of legal services." Rule 7.5(e) provides as follows:

> (e) A law firm name may include additional identifying language such as "& Associates" only when such language is accurate and descriptive of the firm. Any firm name including additional identifying language such as "Legal Services" or other similar phrases shall inform all prospective clients in the retainer agreement or other writing that the law firm is not affiliated or associated with a public, quasi-public or charitable organization. However, no firm shall use the phrase "legal aid" in its name or in any additional identifying language.

However, in *In the Matter of the Decision on CAA 47-2007,* 2009 WL 468292 (N.J. 2009), the New Jersey Supreme Court ordered its Committee on Attorney Advertising to consider and make recommendations on "any additional information, or change in format, that this Court should allow in respect of law firm names, including specifically any additional or changed language that the Committee recommends for insertion into the present *RPC* 7.5," and "to consider (among other things) "whether special rules should be established for attorney practices that include the performance of activities that may be performed by non-attorneys." When we went to press in September 2011, the Committee had submitted its recommendations to the New Jersey Supreme Court, and the Supreme Court had released proposed amendments for comment. The proposed amendments are available online at *http://www.judiciary.state.nj.us/notices/2011/n110408a.pdf.*

New York sets forth detailed regulations in Rule 7.5(a) regarding "internet web sites, professional cards, professional announcements, office signs, letterheads or similar professional notices or devices." Rule 7.5(b), which is based on DR 2-102(B) of the old ABA Model Code, provides as follows:

> A lawyer in private practice shall not practice under a trade name, a name that is misleading as to the identity of the lawyer or lawyers practicing under such name, or a firm name containing names other than those of one or more of the lawyers in the firm, except that . . . a firm may use as, or continue to include in its name, the name or names of one or more deceased or retired members of the firm or of a predecessor firm in a continuing line of succession. . . . A lawyer or law firm may not include the name of a nonlawyer in its firm name. . . .

New York adds Rule 7.5(e)-(f), which addresses domain names and firm names as follows:

> (e) A lawyer or law firm may utilize a domain name for an internet web site that does not include the name of the lawyer or law firm provided:
>
> (1) all pages of the web site clearly and conspicuously include the actual name of the lawyer or law firm;
>
> (2) the lawyer or law firm in no way attempts to engage in the practice of law using the domain name;
>
> (3) the domain name does not imply an ability to obtain results in a matter; and
>
> (4) the domain name does not otherwise violate these Rules.
>
> (f) A lawyer or law firm may utilize a telephone number which contains a domain name, nickname, moniker or motto that does not otherwise violate a disciplinary rule.

North Carolina: Rule 7.5(a) adds the following: "Every trade name used by a law firm shall be registered with the North Carolina State Bar for a determination of whether the name is misleading." Rule 7.5(d) ends with the words "whether or not the lawyer is precluded from practicing law."

Ohio: Rule 7.5(a) expressly provides that a lawyer in private practice "shall not practice under a trade name," and generally permits a law firm to "use as, or continue to include in, its name the name or names of one or more deceased or retired members of the firm or of a predecessor firm in a continuing line of succession." Rule 7.5(b) provides that a law firm with offices in more than one jurisdiction that lists attorneys associated with the firm "shall indicate the jurisdictional limitations on those not licensed to practice in Ohio."

Oregon: Rule 7.5(d) forbids a lawyer to "permit his or her name to remain in the name of a law firm or to be used by the firm during the time the lawyer is not actively and regularly practicing law as a member of the firm" and forbids members of the firm to use the lawyer's name. The rule does not apply for absences of one year or less during which the lawyer is not actively practicing law if the lawyer plans to return to the firm. The rule also does not apply to the names of "retiring, deceased, or retired members of the firm or a predecessor law firm in a continuing line of succession."

Virginia: The first sentence of Rule 7.5(a) permits a lawyer or law firm to use "a professional card, professional announcement, card, office sign, letterheads, telephone directory listing, law list, legal directory listing, website, or a similar professional notice or device unless it includes a statement or claim that is false, fraudulent, misleading, or deceptive." Rule 7.5(b) prohibits lawyers licensed in different jurisdictions from forming or continuing a law firm "unless all enumerations of the members and associates of the firm on its letterhead and in other permissible listings make clear the jurisdictional limitations of those members and associates of the firm not licensed to practice in all listed jurisdictions; however, the same firm name may be used in each jurisdiction."

Related Materials

ABA Formal Ethics Opinions: See ABA Formal Ethics Op. 84-351 (1984), 88-356 (1988), 90-357 (1990), 94-388 (1994), 95-391 (1995), 01-423 (2001), 03-430 (2003), and 08-451 (2008).

Partnership Law: ABA Model Rule 7.5(d) provides that lawyers may state or imply that they practice in a partnership "only when that is the fact." In the Revised Uniform Partnership Act, §202(a) (Formation of Partnership) provides that "the association of two or more persons to carry on as co-owners a business for profit forms a partnership, whether or not the persons intend to form a partnership." Section 202(c)(3) elaborates on this general rule by stating: "A person who receives a share of the profits of a business is presumed to be a partner in the business, unless [among other exceptions] the profits were received in payment . . . (ii) for services as an independent contractor or of wages or other compensation to an employee."

Restatement of the Law Governing Lawyers: The Restatement has no provision comparable to ABA Model Rule 7.5.

Rule 7.6 Political Contributions to Obtain Government Legal Engagements or Appointments by Judges

A lawyer or law firm shall not accept a government legal engagement or an appointment by a judge if the lawyer or law firm makes a

political contribution or solicits political contributions for the purpose of obtaining or being considered for that type of legal engagement or appointment.

COMMENT

[1] Lawyers have a right to participate fully in the political process, which includes making and soliciting political contributions to candidates for judicial and other public office. Nevertheless, when lawyers make or solicit political contributions in order to obtain an engagement for legal work awarded by a government agency, or to obtain appointment by a judge, the public may legitimately question whether the lawyers engaged to perform the work are selected on the basis of competence and merit. In such a circumstance, the integrity of the profession is undermined.

[2] The term "political contribution" denotes any gift, subscription, loan, advance or deposit of anything of value made directly or indirectly to a candidate, incumbent, political party or campaign committee to influence or provide financial support for election to or retention in judicial or other government office. Political contributions in initiative and referendum elections are not included. For purposes of this Rule, the term "political contribution" does not include uncompensated services.

[3] Subject to the exceptions below, (i) the term "government legal engagement" denotes any engagement to provide legal services that a public official has the direct or indirect power to award; and (ii) the term "appointment by a judge" denotes an appointment to a position such as referee, commissioner, special master, receiver, guardian or other similar position that is made by a judge. Those terms do not, however, include (a) substantially uncompensated services; (b) engagements or appointments made on the basis of experience, expertise, professional qualifications and cost following a request for proposal or other process that is free from influence based upon political contributions; and (c) engagements or appointments made on a rotational basis from a list compiled without regard to political contributions.

[4] The term "lawyer or law firm" includes a political action committee or other entity owned or controlled by a lawyer or law firm.

[5] Political contributions are for the purpose of obtaining or being considered for a government legal engagement or appointment by a judge if, but for the desire to be considered for the legal engagement or appointment, the lawyer or law firm would not have made or solicited the contributions. The purpose may be determined by an examination of the circumstances in which the contributions occur. For example, one or more contributions that in the aggregate are substantial in relation to other contributions by lawyers or law firms, made for the benefit of an official in a position to influence award of a government legal engagement, and followed by an award of the legal engagement to the contributing or soliciting lawyer or the lawyer's firm would support an inference that the purpose of the contributions was to obtain the engagement, absent other factors that weigh against existence of the proscribed purpose. Those factors may include among others that the contribution or solicitation was made to further a political, social, or economic interest or because of an existing personal, family, or professional relationship with a candidate.

[6] If a lawyer makes or solicits a political contribution under circumstances that constitute bribery or another crime, Rule 8.4(b) is implicated.

Canon and Code Antecedents

ABA Canons of Professional Ethics: No comparable Canon.

ABA Model Code of Professional Responsibility: No comparable Disciplinary Rule.

Cross-References in Other Rules

None.

Legislative History of Model Rule 7.6

1983 Rule: As originally adopted in 1983, the ABA Model Rules did not contain Rule 7.6 or any close equivalent.

1997 Proposal and Resolution: At the ABA's August 1997 Annual Meeting, the Association of the Bar of the City of New York proposed that the ABA adopt a detailed and highly restrictive "pay-to-play" rule. As described in a later ABA report:

> The practice commonly known as "pay-to-play" . . . is a system whereby lawyers and law firms are considered for or awarded either government legal engagements or appointments by a judge only upon their making or soliciting contributions for the political campaigns of officials who are in a position to "steer" such business their way. . . .

The heart of the 1997 proposal provided as follows:

3. Prohibitions on Certain Government Finance Engagements

> (a) No lawyer shall undertake a Government Finance Engagement awarded by an Official of an Issuer within two years after making either a Political Contribution or a Political Solicitation; provided, however, that this Rule shall not prohibit a lawyer from undertaking a Government Finance Engagement with a particular Official of an Issuer if:
>
> (i) (A) the only Political Contribution made by the lawyer to that Official of an Issuer within the previous two years was (I) for a position for which the lawyer was entitled to vote and (II) not in excess of $250 for each stage of the electoral campaign (i.e., primary and general election) and (B) the lawyer did not make any political contribution in excess of $1,000 to any political party or committee of the State or of any political subdivision, agency or instrumentality thereof; or
>
> (ii) the only Political Solicitation made by the lawyer on behalf of that Official of an Issuer or any political party or committee of the State or of any political subdivision, agency or instrumentality thereof, was for Political Contributions made within the previous two years for an Official of an Issuer for whom the lawyer was entitled to vote, no Political Contribution solicited was in excess of $100 to the Official of an Issuer for each complete electoral campaign (primary and general election combined), and the aggregate of all Political Contributions solicited in any such campaign within the previous two years did not exceed $2,500. . . .

> (b) Notwithstanding subsection (a), any lawyer who is personally involved in the undertaking of Government Finance Engagements who solicits Political Contributions in any amount at the request of an Official of an Issuer or one of the Official's subordinates, is prohibited from undertaking a Government Finance Engagement awarded by that Official of an Issuer for a period of two years. . . .
>
> (c) To the extent that a lawyer is prohibited from undertaking a Government Finance Engagement by operation of this Rule, the law firm employing such lawyer (whether or not that lawyer is admitted to practice in New York) shall also be prohibited from undertaking a Government Finance Engagement. . . .
>
> (d) If a law firm or a political action committee controlled by a law firm itself makes a Political Contribution or a Political Solicitation that would operate to prohibit a lawyer from undertaking certain Government Finance Engagements, the law firm is likewise prohibited from undertaking such Government Finance Engagements for the same two year period that would be applicable to a lawyer prohibited through operation of the Rule.

The ABA House of Delegates did not approve the New York City Bar's proposal. Instead, the House of Delegates approved a resolution (a) condemning pay-to-play practices wherever they existed, and (b) calling for the creation of a Task Force that would study the problems created by a pay-to-play system, develop appropriate professional standards or rules on the subject, and report to the House of Delegates within a year.

The next month, in keeping with this resolution, the ABA President appointed a Task Force on Lawyer's Political Contributions. The twelve-member Task Force was chaired by John W. Martin, Jr., Vice-President and General Counsel of Ford Motor Company, and included such distinguished members as former CIA and FBI Director William H. Webster, former United States Senator Howard H. Baker Jr., and SEC General Counsel Harvey J. Goldschmid. The Task Force collected and reviewed empirical data and media reporting on pay-to-play practices and considered possible ways to discourage or prevent such practices.

1998 Resolution: Shortly before the ABA's 1998 Annual Meeting, the ABA Task Force on Lawyer's Political Contributions issued a report unanimously condemning pay-to-play practices, urging the ABA to adopt a new Model Rule making pay-to-play practices unethical, and recommending broader disclosure of campaign contributions. However, the Task Force was sharply divided as to whether a new Model Rule alone would be sufficient, and what the new Model Rule should say. Six of the 12 Task Force members favored a strict rule that would

> (a) disqualify both lawyers who made political contributions and their law firms,
>
> (b) require lawyers to publicly disclose their political contributions, and
>
> (c) require lawyers facing disciplinary charges to show that their political contributions were not made to obtain government legal work.

Five other Task Force members believed that requiring lawyers to disclose their contributions and to prove that the contributions were not made to obtain government work would be ineffective and would have an undue chilling effect on the First Amendment rights of lawyers to take part in the political process. In the face of this split, the House of Delegates did not adopt a new Model Rule but adopted the following resolution:

> RESOLVED, That the American Bar Association urges the following actions be taken to address any conduct by lawyers making or soliciting campaign contributions

to public officials for the purpose of being considered or retained for government legal engagements.

(1) All state, territorial and local bar associations should unequivocally condemn any arrangement under which the selection or consideration of lawyers to be retained for government legal engagements depends, in whole or in part, on whether the lawyer has made or solicited campaign contributions.

(2) State, territorial and local government entities should create, establish and maintain full and effective systems for the reporting and disclosure of campaign contributions to candidates for elective public office so that the public may have reasonable notice of contributions made by lawyers or law firms, and where they have not, bar and disciplinary authorities should adopt rules that require disclosure of campaign contributions by lawyers and law firms to government officials in a position to influence the award of legal engagements to the contributor.

(3) Merit procurement processes should be adopted for the selection of lawyers performing legal services for government agencies as a means of ensuring that no political contribution or solicitation has influenced the selection.

(4) The Standing Committee on Ethics and Professional Responsibility is directed to report to the House of Delegates by its 1999 Annual Meeting a proposed Model Rule that declares that a lawyer or law firm shall not make a political contribution or solicitation for the purpose of obtaining or being considered for a legal engagement. . . .

Regarding paragraph (4) of the resolution, a motion was made to give the Standing Committee "discretion" to address the problem of pay-to-play either by amending the comment to an existing rule, by issuing a formal ethics opinion, or by proposing a new model rule. That motion failed by a vote of 158-151.

1999 Proposal: At the ABA's August 1999 Annual Meeting, the ABA Standing Committee on Ethics and Professional Responsibility proposed a new Rule 7.6, but the ABA House of Delegates voted 164 to 146 to reject the proposed rule. We reprint below substantial excerpts from the report submitted by the ABA Standing Committee on Ethics and Professional Responsibility in support of the proposal that the House of Delegates rejected.

*ABA Committee Report Submitted in Support of Rejected Rule 7.6**

[A]lthough lawyers and their political contributions are an important component of the pay-to-play system, lawyers are not the most important players in such a system. The primary actor in any pay-to-play situation is the public official who . . . may be acting in dereliction of official duties. For this reason, the rules of professional conduct governing lawyer behavior should not be relied upon as the primary method of preventing the practice of pay-to-play. Rather, consistent and diligent enforcement of statutory provisions governing fair campaign finance practices and the conduct of public officials is the most fundamental method of addressing the problem of pay-to-play. The fundamental harm done by a pay-to-play system is the harm that befalls the public when a government official, motivated by campaign contributions, chooses lawyers or law firms that may not be the best qualified to perform legal services on the public's behalf. Thus it is the integrity of a basic governmental process, and not just the integrity of the legal profession, that is undermined when such action by a public official is tolerated.

* Committee Reports do not represent official policy of the ABA. They are for information only, and the opinions are those of the authors of the report.

[A] second method of protecting against the evils of a pay-to-play system exists, and it also lies outside the scope of rules governing lawyer conduct: the use of uniform procurement or acquisition procedures for the placement of legal services engagements by government entities and the granting of appointments by judges. The Association has strongly supported . . . fundamental principles of competition in public acquisitions. . . .

The Standing Committee therefore notes emphatically that where there is aggressive enforcement of prohibitions against pay-to-play conduct by public officials, and where there is reliance on uniform procurement codes and procedures in the placement of legal engagements and in appointments by judges, the need to focus on lawyer conduct will be diminished. . . .

Background for Developing a Model Rule

. . . In carrying out its charge, the Task Force expanded the scope of its investigation in two important ways. Initial concerns had focused on the existence of the phenomenon in the area of municipal finance engagements. The Task Force's review revealed at least some evidence that the practice occurs in a wider range of practice areas. Early proposals for a Model Rule limited in application to lawyers engaged in municipal finance work were therefore put aside and the Task Force focused on developing a Rule of wider application.

The Task Force also discovered that a similar system was sometimes in evidence as well in the context of appointments of lawyers made by judges following the making or soliciting of substantial contributions to the judges' election campaigns.

Development of The Proposed Rule

The Committee . . . develop[ed] two possible "trial" rules addressing lawyers' roles in the pay-to-play system. One was . . . prohibiting political contributions when the purpose of such contributions was the obtaining of legal business. Because the Committee questioned the wisdom of basing the restriction solely on a lawyer's purpose for making political contributions, and recognized the difficulty of proving "purpose," it developed a second rule . . . prohibiting lawyers from accepting legal engagements where the awarding of the engagements was based upon lawyer's political contributions. Each draft rule was accompanied by extensive commentary that was intended, among other things, to establish criteria whereby a contributing lawyer's "purpose" could be proven.

. . . The following summary . . . explains the Committee's ultimate decision to advance the proposed Model Rule presented here, which represents a combination of its two initial alternative proposals with refinements.

Constitutional Issues

. . . The Committee undertook a review of recent First Amendment jurisprudence treating legislatively-enacted campaign contribution limits. It found, not surprisingly, that limitations on the making and solicitation of political contributions must be predicated on the need to protect a valid state interest; that they must be narrowly drawn; and that their language must be sufficiently clear as to provide fair notice of when and how they operate, thereby satisfying the requirements of due process. . . .

ENACTED OR PROPOSED REGULATIONS

The Committee examined numerous regulations that have been either adopted or proposed in different forums to regulate lawyers' contributions to political campaigns in connection with "pay-to-play" type problems. They ranged from federal criminal statutes (18 U.S.C. Sec. 201) relating to the most egregious violations (bribery or the giving of illegal gratuities) to a considerably more narrowly-drawn Association of the Bar of the City of New York proposal which, like Municipal Securities Rulemaking Board Rule GS-37, applicable to municipal finance professionals, would prohibit a lawyer or law firm from undertaking a municipal finance engagement within a certain period of time after having made a contribution in excess of a de minimis amount to a public official capable of influencing the public finance engagement.

[I]n some circumstances, the Model Rules of Professional Conduct already apply to lawyers' participation in pay-to-play. For example, the prophylactic effect of criminal statutes potentially applicable to pay-to-play participation by lawyers already has a parallel in the Model Rules of Professional Conduct: a lawyer whose style of participation in pay-to-play is so egregious as to result in conviction of bribery or a similar serious crime would also violate Model Rule 8.4 ("Misconduct"). Model Rule 7.2(c), which prohibits a lawyer from giving anything of value to another for recommending the lawyer for employment, may in some pay-to-play circumstances also be applicable. . . .

The House has, however, adopted the Task Force's position that the Association should adopt more stringent restrictions on pay-to-play than these Model Rules would afford. The Rule submitted herewith accords with that position.

ENFORCEMENT ISSUES

. . . A common and understandable concern of the bar counsel was the number of elements that would need to be proven in order to find that a lawyer's conduct in making political contributions constituted a violation of either draft rule. In this regard, bar counsel comment echoed that of other commentators, both proponents and opponents of either draft rule.

The successful enforcement of each of the draft proposals was considered to depend on the ability of disciplinary counsel to prove an element of purpose, whether it were the purpose of the lawyer making the contribution, or the purpose of the official or judge in giving the engagement or appointment to reward the lawyer's contribution. . . .

The lawyer's purpose in making or soliciting political contributions was deemed by many commentators to be the most significant test in determining if a Rule violation exists. Hence, it has been retained in the submitted Rule along with carefully crafted standards in the Comments designed to explain how "purpose" will be identified.

Disciplinary counsel . . . also appeared generally unpersuaded that pay-to-play exists as a significant problem. Hence self-enforcement of this Rule to stem pay-to-play practices by lawyers and law firms is an even more important consideration than it is in enforcement of certain other Model Rules.

2000 Amendment: In 2000, the House of Delegates voted 266-157 to adopt the very same version of Rule 7.6 and its Comment that the delegates had rejected in 1999. In 2000, however, the proposed rule was sponsored not only by the ABA Standing Committee on Ethics and Professional Responsibility (which had been the sole sponsor in 1999), but also by the ABA Section of Business Law, the ABA Section of State and Local Government Law, and the Association of the Bar of the City of New York. (The New York City Bar had sponsored the original proposal to add a pay-to-play rule back in 1997.) The report submitted in support of the new rule was nearly identical to the report submitted in 1999, but it began with the following passages explaining the 1999 proposal and why it failed:

*ABA Committee Report Submitted in Support of Rule 7.6 as Adopted**

> . . . At the 1999 Annual Meeting, the House of Delegates, by a vote of 164 to 146, rejected the Standing Committee's proposal.
>
> The Sponsors believe that the very important issue of pay-to-play should be reconsidered by the House. The [1999] vote was taken very late in the session after a substantial number of delegates had departed (only 310 of the 530 members of the House were present and voting) and without adequate opportunity for balanced debate (only one "pro" speaker, other than the moving sponsor, was recognized before a tired House called the question). Accordingly, the Sponsors resubmit the proposed Model Rule 7.6 governing lawyers' political contributions to the House of Delegates at the 2000 Midwinter Meeting.

2002 Amendments: The ABA Ethics 2000 Commission did not propose any changes to Rule 7.6 or its Comment.

Selected State Variations

Arizona, California, the District of Columbia, Illinois, Michigan, New Jersey, Ohio, Pennsylvania, Texas, and ***Virginia*** (among others) have no rule equivalent to ABA Model Rule 7.6.

New York omits Rule 7.6. However, Comment 5 to New York Rule 7.2 provides as follows:

> Campaign contributions by lawyers to government officials or candidates for public office who are, or may be, in a position to influence the award of a legal engagement may threaten governmental integrity by subjecting the recipient to a conflict of interest. Correspondingly, when a lawyer makes a significant contribution to a public official or an election campaign for a candidate for public office and is later engaged by the official to perform legal services for the official's agency, it may appear that the official has been improperly influenced in selecting the lawyer, whether or not this is so. This appearance of influence reflects poorly on the integrity of the legal profession and government as a whole. For these reasons, just as the Code prohibits a lawyer from compensating or giving anything of value to a person or organization to recommend or obtain employment by a client, the Code prohibits a lawyer from making or soliciting a political contribution to any candidate for government office, government official, political campaign committee or political party, if a disinterested person would conclude that the contribution is being made or solicited for the purpose of obtaining or being considered eligible to obtain a government legal engagement. This would be true even in the absence of an understanding between the lawyer and any government official or candidate that special consideration will be given in return for the political contribution or solicitation.

* Committee Reports do not represent official policy of the ABA. They are for information only, and the opinions are those of the authors of the report.

> [J]ust as the Code prohibits a lawyer from compensating or giving anything of value to a person or organization to recommend or obtain employment by a client, the Code prohibits a lawyer from making or soliciting a political contribution to any candidate for government office, government official, political campaign committee or political party, if a disinterested person would conclude that the contribution is being made or solicited for the purpose of obtaining or being considered eligible to obtain a government legal engagement. This would be true even in the absence of an understanding between the lawyer and any government official or candidate that special consideration will be given in return for the political contribution or solicitation.

Comment 6 complements Comment 5 by setting forth seven factors to consider in determining "whether a disinterested person would conclude that a contribution to a candidate for government office, government official, political campaign committee or political party is or has been made for the purpose of obtaining or being considered eligible to obtain a government legal engagement. . . ." For example, the factors include "(a) whether legal work awarded to the contributor or solicitor, if any, was awarded pursuant to a process that was insulated from political influence, such as a 'Request for Proposal' process" and "(c) whether the contributor or any law firm with which the lawyer is associated has sought or plans to seek government legal work from the official or candidate." (The Comments have been adopted only by the New York State Bar Association, not by the courts, but Comments 5 and 6 have special status. In an extraordinary press release in March of 2000 explaining why the courts were rejecting a proposed pay-to-play Disciplinary Rule, the courts expressly endorsed the language of old Ethical Considerations 2-37 and 2-38, and these ECs have been incorporated verbatim into Comments 5 and 6 to Rule 7.2.)

Ohio omits ABA Model Rule 7.6, explaining as follows: "The substance of Model Rule 7.6 is addressed by provisions of the Ohio Ethics Law . . . and other criminal prohibitions relative to bribery and attempts to influence the conduct of elected officials. A lawyer or law firm that violates these statutory prohibitions would be in violation of other provisions of the Ohio Rules of Professional Conduct, such as Rule 8.4."

Related Materials

Municipal Securities Rulemaking Board Rule G-37: This rule, entitled "Political Contributions and Prohibitions on Municipal Securities Business," was cited in the 1999 and 2000 ABA Committee Reports submitted in support of Rule 7.6. In essence, Rule G-37 prohibits brokers and dealers from engaging in municipal securities business with any issuer of municipal securities for two years after contributing in excess of $250 to such an issuer. Rule G-37 is available online at *www.msrb.org/Rules-and-Interpretations/MSRB-Rules/General/Rule-G-37.aspx.* (In 2006, the SEC approved amendments to the definition of "solicitation" in Rule G-37. See *http://sec.gov/rules/sro/msrb/2006/34-53960.pdf.*)

Restatement of the Law Governing Lawyers: The Restatement has no provision comparable to ABA Model Rule 7.6.

ARTICLE 8. MAINTAINING THE INTEGRITY OF THE PROFESSION

Rule 8.1 Bar Admission and Disciplinary Matters

An applicant for admission to the bar, or a lawyer in connection with a bar admission application or in connection with a disciplinary matter, shall not:

(a) knowingly make a false statement of material fact; or

(b) fail to disclose a fact necessary to correct a misapprehension known by the person to have arisen in the matter, or knowingly fail to respond to a lawful demand for information from an admissions or disciplinary authority, except that this rule does not require disclosure of information otherwise protected by Rule 1.6.

COMMENT

[1] The duty imposed by this Rule extends to persons seeking admission to the bar as well as to lawyers. Hence, if a person makes a material false statement in connection with an application for admission, it may be the basis for subsequent disciplinary action if the person is admitted, and in any event may be relevant in a subsequent admission application. The duty imposed by this Rule applies to a lawyer's own admission or discipline as well as that of others. Thus, it is a separate professional offense for a lawyer to knowingly make a misrepresentation or omission in connection with a disciplinary investigation of the lawyer's own conduct. Paragraph (b) of this Rule also requires correction of any prior misstatement in the matter that the applicant or lawyer may have made and affirmative clarification of any misunderstanding on the part of the admissions or disciplinary authority of which the person involved becomes aware.

[2] This Rule is subject to the provisions of the Fifth Amendment of the United States Constitution and corresponding provisions of state constitutions. A person relying on such a provision in response to a question, however, should do so openly and not use the right of nondisclosure as a justification for failure to comply with this Rule.

[3] A lawyer representing an applicant for admission to the bar, or representing a lawyer who is the subject of a disciplinary inquiry or proceeding, is governed by the rules applicable to the client-lawyer relationship, including Rule 1.6 and, in some cases, Rule 3.3.

Canon and Code Antecedents

ABA Canons of Professional Ethics: Canon 29 provided in pertinent part:

29. Upholding the Honor of the Profession

. . . The lawyer should aid in guarding the Bar against the admission to the profession of candidates unfit or unqualified because deficient in either moral character or education. He should strive at all times to uphold the honor and to maintain the dignity of the profession and to improve not only the law but the administration of justice.

ABA Model Code of Professional Responsibility: Compare DR 1-101(A), DR 1-101(B), and DR 1-102(A)(5) (reprinted later in this volume).

Cross-References in Other Rules

Rule 1.6, Comment 13: Some Rules require "disclosure of information relating to a client's representation to accomplish the purposes specified in paragraphs (b)(1) through (b)(6)," only if such disclosure would be permitted by paragraph (b). See **Rules** 1.2(d), 4.1(b), **8.1** and 8.3.

Rule 1.8, Comment 5: It is prohibited to partake in the "disadvantageous use of client information unless the client gives informed consent, except as permitted or required by these Rules. See **Rules** 1.2(d), 1.6, 1.9(c), 3.3, 4.1(b), **8.1** and 8.3."

Legislative History of Model Rule 8.1

1980 Discussion Draft of Rule 8.1 was substantially the same as adopted, except that subparagraph (a) prohibited a lawyer from making "a knowing misrepresentation of fact," and subparagraph (b) did not include the clause beginning "or knowingly fail to respond. . . ."

1981 and ***1982 Drafts*** were substantially the same as adopted.

1983 Rule: As originally adopted in 1983, the text of Rule 8.1 was identical to the 2002 version of Rule 8.1.

2002 Amendments: At its February 2002 Mid-Year Meeting, the ABA House of Delegates adopted without change the ABA Ethics 2000 Commission proposal to amend Comments 1 and 3 to Rule 8.1 in relatively minor ways. (The Ethics 2000 Commission did not propose any changes to the text of Rule 8.1.)

Selected State Variations

California: Rule 1-200 provides as follows:

> (A) A member shall not knowingly make a false statement regarding a material fact or knowingly fail to disclose a material fact in connection with an application for admission to the State Bar.
>
> (B) A member shall not further an application for admission to the State Bar of a person whom the member knows to be unqualified in respect to character, education, or other relevant attributes.
>
> (C) This rule shall not prevent a member from serving as counsel of record for an applicant for admission to practice in proceedings related to such admission.

Colorado: Rule 8.1(a) also applies to "readmission" and "reinstatement."

Georgia has adopted a Rule 9.3, entitled "Cooperation with Disciplinary Authority," which provides as follows: "During the investigation of a grievance filed under these Rules, the lawyer complained against shall respond to disciplinary authorities in accordance with State Bar Rules." Comment 2 to this provision states: "Nothing in this Rule prohibits a lawyer from responding by making a Fifth Amendment objection, if appropriate. However, disciplinary proceedings are civil in nature and the use of a Fifth Amendment objection will give rise to a presumption against the lawyer."

Michigan adds the following new language to its version of ABA Model Rule 8.1:

> (b) An applicant for admission to the bar
> (1) shall not engage in the unauthorized practice of law (this does not apply to activities permitted under MCR 8.120), and
> (2) has a continuing obligation, until the date of admission, to inform the standing committee on character and fitness, in writing, if any answers in the applicant's affidavit of personal history change or cease to be true.

New York: Rule 8.1(a) provides as follows:

> (a) A lawyer shall be subject to discipline if, in connection with the lawyer's own application for admission to the bar previously filed in this state or in any other jurisdiction, or in connection with the application of another person for admission to the bar, the lawyer knowingly:
> (1) has made or failed to correct a false statement of material fact; or
> (2) has failed to disclose a material fact requested in connection with a lawful demand for information from an admissions authority.

Ohio: Rule 8.1(a) deletes the opening phrase "[a]n applicant for admission to the bar." According to the Ohio Supreme Court's note, Rule 8.1(b) clarifies the "unwieldy" language of the ABA Model Rule but does not lower the standard of candor expected of a lawyer in bar admission or disciplinary matters.

Virginia: Rule 8.1 adds language to cover certifications required to be filed as a condition of maintaining or renewing a law license. Virginia also moves the second clause of Rule 8.1(b) to a separate subparagraph (c), and adds Rule 8.1(d), which makes it a separate violation to "obstruct a lawful investigation by an admissions or disciplinary authority."

Related Materials

ABA Formal Ethics Opinions: No ABA formal ethics opinion has discussed ABA Model Rule 8.1.

ABA Model Federal Rules of Disciplinary Enforcement: To provide guidance for federal courts to operate independent disciplinary systems, in 1978 the ABA approved the Model Federal Rules of Disciplinary Enforcement. These rules, which were amended in 1991 and have been adopted by a number of federal district courts, can be found at *www.americanbar.org/content/dam/aba/migrated/cpr/discipline/mfrde.pdf*. Separate federal rules of disciplinary enforcement are needed because in *Theard v. United States*, 354 U.S. 278 (1957), the Supreme Court held that a state court disbarment was entitled to "high respect" but was "not conclusively binding on the federal courts." Consequently "disbarment by federal courts does not automatically flow from disbarment by state courts."

ABA Model Rules for Judicial Disciplinary Enforcement: In 1994, to assist jurisdictions in reviewing the procedures of their judicial discipline systems and in drafting fair and efficient procedures for enforcing the Code of Judicial Conduct, the ABA developed Model Rules for Judicial Disciplinary Enforcement. These replaced the ABA Standards Relating to Judicial Discipline and Disability Retirement, which had been adopted in 1979. The history and summary of these rules, with links to the full text of each rule and the official ABA commentary, are available online at *http://www.americanbar.org/groups/professional_responsibility/model_rules_judicial_disciplinary_enforcement/contents.html.*

ABA Model Rules for Lawyer Disciplinary Enforcement: The ABA Model Rules for Lawyer Disciplinary Enforcement provide a blueprint for the structure, procedures, and standards of a comprehensive system of lawyer regulation. Rule 1, entitled "Comprehensive Lawyer Regulatory System," provides that such a system should include, at a minimum: (a) a discipline and disability system, (b) a client protection fund, (c) mandatory arbitration of fee disputes, (d) voluntary arbitration of lawyer malpractice claims and other disputes, (e) mediation, (f) lawyer practice assistance, and (g) lawyer substance abuse counseling.

The Model Rules for Lawyer Disciplinary Enforcement have a long history. In the late 1960s, the ABA appointed a Special Committee on Evaluation of Disciplinary Enforcement, commonly known as the "Clark Committee" after its Chair, recently retired Supreme Court Justice Tom Clark. The Clark Committee conducted the first nationwide examination of lawyer disciplinary procedures in the United States. In 1970, the Clark Committee published a report that warned of a "scandalous situation" in professional discipline and called for "the immediate attention of the profession." The ABA responded by creating a Standing Committee on Professional Discipline in 1973 and by developing the ABA Standards for Lawyer Discipline, which the ABA approved in 1979. In 1985, the ABA amended these Standards and renamed them the ABA Model Rules for Lawyer Disciplinary Enforcement.

In 1987, the National Organization of Bar Counsel (NOBC) urged a new nationwide study to evaluate the developments in professional discipline since 1970. In 1989, the ABA adopted a revised set of Model Rules for Lawyer Disciplinary Enforcement, and the ABA appointed the Commission on Evaluation of Disciplinary Enforcement, commonly called the "McKay Commission." In February 1992, the ABA House of Delegates adopted most of the McKay Commission's recommendations. The Model Rules for Lawyer Disciplinary Enforcement were approved by the ABA House of Delegates in 1993 and have been amended three times, most recently in 2002. The rules are available online at *http://www.americanbar.org/groups/professional_responsibility/resources/lawyer_ethics_regulation/model_rules_for_lawyer_disciplinary_enforcement.html.* For more information on the history of lawyer disciplinary enforcement, see the law review article by Mary Devlin entitled "The Development of Lawyer Disciplinary Procedures in the United States," available online at *http://www.americanbar.org/content/dam/aba/migrated/cpr/pubs/devlin.authcheckdam.pdf.*

ABA Standards for Lawyer Discipline and Disability Proceedings: In 1979, the ABA published Standards for Lawyer Discipline and Disability Proceedings. Standard 7.1 states that the discipline imposed should depend upon the facts and circumstances of the case, should be fashioned in light of the purpose of lawyer discipline, and may take into account aggravating or mitigating circumstances. (In 1994, the Discipline and Disability Standards were replaced by the ABA Model Rules for Judicial Disciplinary Enforcement—see entry above.)

ABA Standing Committee on Professional Discipline: The ABA is not a disciplinary agency and has no authority to investigate or act upon complaints filed against lawyers or judges, but in 1973 the ABA created a Standing Committee on Professional Discipline. The Standing Committee's mission is to assist the judiciary and the Bar in every jurisdiction in developing, coordinating, and strengthening disciplinary enforcement. For example, when invited by a jurisdiction's highest court, the Standing Committee sends an experienced team to consult regarding the structure, operation, practice, and procedures of the jurisdiction's disciplinary system. Since 1980, the Standing Committee has reviewed the disciplinary systems in more than 40 jurisdictions (five of them twice). After a review, the Standing Committee files a confidential report with the jurisdiction's highest court, which determines whether to make the report public. For more information, visit *http://www.americanbar.org/groups/professional_responsibility/committees_commissions/standing_committee_on_professional_discipline.html.*

ABA Survey on Lawyer Discipline Systems: Since 1999, the ABA Standing Committee on Professional Discipline and the ABA Center for Professional Responsibility have annually conducted a comprehensive survey of lawyer discipline in more than 50 lawyer disciplinary agencies around the United States. The survey includes eight separate charts showing data on such things as Lawyer Population and Agency Caseload Volume, Sanctions Imposed, and Reinstatement and Readmission Statistics. The 2009 annual survey is available online at *http://www.americanbar.org/content/dam/aba/migrated/cpr/discipline/2009sold.pdf-2011-03-15.*

Association of Professional Responsibility Lawyers (APRL): The Association of Professional Responsibility Lawyers (APRL) is an independent national organization of lawyers concentrating in the fields of professional responsibility and legal ethics. The organization includes law professors, bar association counsel, counsel for respondents in disciplinary hearings, expert witnesses, legal malpractice litigators, disciplinary counsel, and in-house law firm ethics counsel. APRL provides a national clearinghouse of information regarding recent developments and emerging issues in the areas of admission to practice law, professional ethics, disciplinary standards and procedures, and professional liability. For more information, including a nationwide directory of APRL members, visit *www.aprl.net.*

Character and Fitness: Nearly every state requires bar applicants to demonstrate good moral character and fitness. In New York, for example, 22 N.Y.C.R.R. §602.1(b) provides: "Every completed application shall be referred for investigation of the applicant's character and fitness to a committee on character and fitness. . . ." In Illinois, §2 of the Illinois Attorney Act provides that no person shall be entitled to receive a law license "until he shall have obtained a certificate of his good moral character from a circuit court."

About 33 states have adopted written standards for character and fitness. A good example of these rules is Rule IV of the Texas Board of Law Examiners, which provides, in pertinent part, as follows:

> *Good Moral Character and Fitness Requirement*
>
> (b) Good moral character is a functional assessment of character and fitness of a prospective lawyer. The purpose of requiring an Applicant to possess present good moral character is to exclude from the practice of law those persons possessing character traits that are likely to result in injury to future clients, in the obstruction of the administration of justice, or in a violation of the Texas Disciplinary Rules of Professional Conduct. These character traits usually involve either dishonesty or lack

of trustworthiness in carrying out responsibilities. There may be other character traits that are relevant in the admission process, but such traits must have a rational connection with the Applicant's present fitness or capacity to practice law and accordingly must relate to the legitimate interests of Texas in protecting prospective clients and in safeguarding the system of justice within Texas.

(c) Fitness, as used in these Rules, is the assessment of mental and emotional health as it affects the competence of a prospective lawyer. The purpose of requiring an Applicant to possess this fitness is to exclude from the practice of law any person having a mental or emotional illness or condition which would be likely to prevent the person from carrying out duties to clients, courts or the profession. A person may be of good moral character, but may be incapacitated from proper discharge of his or her duties as a lawyer by such illness or condition. The fitness required is a present fitness, and prior mental or emotional illness or conditions are relevant only so far as they indicate the existence of a present lack of fitness. . . .

Under Rule IV(e)(2) of the Texas Board of Law Examiners, an individual who has been disciplined in another jurisdiction is "deemed not to have present good moral character and fitness and is therefore ineligible to file an Application for Admission to the Texas Bar during the period of such discipline. . . ." But Rule IV(e)(3) allows such a person to file an Application for Admission if:

(A) The procedure followed in the disciplining jurisdiction was so lacking in notice or opportunity to be heard as to constitute a deprivation of due process.

(B) There was such an infirmity of proof establishing the misconduct in the other jurisdiction as to give rise to the clear conviction that the Board, consistent with its duty, should not accept as final the conclusion on the evidence reached in the disciplining jurisdiction.

(C) The deeming of lack of present good moral character and fitness by the Board during the period required under the provisions of section (e) would result in grave injustice.

(D) The misconduct for which the individual was disciplined does not constitute professional misconduct in Texas.

(4) If the Board determines that one or more of the foregoing defenses has been established, it shall render such orders as it deems necessary and appropriate.

Rule IV(f) of the Texas Board of Law Examiners provides that an individual who applies for admission to practice law in Texas after completing a period of professional discipline must prove, by a preponderance of the evidence:

(1) that the best interest of the public and the profession, as well as the ends of justice, would be served by his or her admission to practice law;

(2) that (s)he is of present good moral character and fitness; and

(3) that during the five years immediately preceding the present action, (s)he has been living a life of exemplary conduct.

Finally, Rule IV(g) provides that if an applicant receives a negative determination of character and fitness based on a felony conviction, felony probation, professional misconduct, or resignation in lieu of disciplinary action, the applicant is not eligible to petition for redetermination for three years.

Model Rules of Professional Conduct for Federal Lawyers: Rule 8.1 also applies to an "applicant for admission to a bar or employment as a lawyer with a Federal Agency, [and] a Federal lawyer seeking the right to practice before a Federal Agency. . . ."

National Lawyer Regulatory Data Bank: In 1968, the ABA established a National Lawyer Regulatory Data Bank, the only national repository of information concerning public disciplinary sanctions imposed against lawyers throughout the United States. Today the Data Bank operates under the aegis of the ABA Standing Committee on Professional Discipline. The courts of all states and the District of Columbia, as well as many federal courts and some federal agencies, now voluntarily provide disciplinary information to the Data Bank. The Data Bank is particularly useful to bar admissions agencies evaluating applications from out-of-state lawyers and to disciplinary agencies considering reciprocal discipline on lawyers who have been disbarred or suspended elsewhere. For more information, visit *http://www.americanbar.org/groups/professional_responsibility/services/databank.html.*

National Organization of Bar Counsel (NOBC): The National Organization of Bar Counsel (NOBC) is a nonprofit organization of legal professionals whose members enforce ethics rules that regulate the professional conduct of lawyers in the United States, Canada, and Australia. Among its purposes are (1) protecting the public and the courts against unethical conduct; (2) protecting attorneys against unfounded complaints; (3) initiating joint, coordinated action to promote solutions to nationwide problems relating to the legal profession; and (4) providing mutual assistance in gathering evidence and testimony at the request of fellow bar counsel. For more information, visit the NOBC's website at *www.nobc.org.*

Restatement of the Law Governing Lawyers: See Restatement §2 in our chapter on the Restatement later in this volume.

Rule 8.2 Judicial and Legal Officials

(a) A lawyer shall not make a statement that the lawyer knows to be false or with reckless disregard as to its truth or falsity concerning the qualifications or integrity of a judge, adjudicatory officer or public legal officer, or of a candidate for election or appointment to judicial or legal office.

(b) A lawyer who is a candidate for judicial office shall comply with the applicable provisions of the Code of Judicial Conduct.

COMMENT

[1] Assessments by lawyers are relied on in evaluating the professional or personal fitness of persons being considered for election or appointment to judicial office and to public legal offices, such as attorney general, prosecuting attorney and public defender. Expressing honest and candid opinions on such matters contributes to improving the administration of justice. Conversely, false statements by a lawyer can unfairly undermine public confidence in the administration of justice.

[2] When a lawyer seeks judicial office, the lawyer should be bound by applicable limitations on political activity.

[3] To maintain the fair and independent administration of justice, lawyers are encouraged to continue traditional efforts to defend judges and courts unjustly criticized.

Canon and Code Antecedents

ABA Canons of Professional Ethics: Canons 1 and 2 provided as follows:

1. The Duty of the Lawyer to the Courts

It is the duty of the lawyer to maintain towards the Courts a respectful attitude, not for the sake of the temporary incumbent of the judicial office, but for the maintenance of its supreme importance. Judges, not being wholly free to defend themselves, are peculiarly entitled to receive the support of the Bar against unjust criticism and clamor. Whenever there is proper ground for serious complaint of a judicial officer, it is the right and duty of the lawyer to submit his grievances to the proper authorities. In such cases, but not otherwise, such charges should be encouraged and the person making them should be protected.

2. The Selection of Judges

It is the duty of the Bar to endeavor to prevent political considerations from outweighing judicial fitness in the selections of Judges. It should protest earnestly and actively against the appointment or election of those who are unsuitable for the Bench; and it should strive to have elevated thereto only those willing to forego other employments, whether of a business, political or other character, which may embarrass their free and fair consideration of questions before them for decision. The aspiration of lawyers for judicial position should be governed by an impartial estimate of their ability to add honor to the office and not by a desire for the distinction the position may bring to themselves.

ABA Model Code of Professional Responsibility: Compare DR 8-102(A), DR 8-102(B), and DR 8-103 (reprinted later in this volume).

Cross-References in Other Rules

None.

Legislative History of Model Rule 8.2

1980 Discussion Draft (then Rule 10.2): Subparagraph (a) provided: "A lawyer who is a candidate for judicial office shall comply with the applicable provisions of the code of judicial conduct." Subparagraph (b) was the same as adopted.

1981 and ***1982 Drafts*** were substantially the same as adopted.

1983 Rule: As originally adopted in 1983, the text of Rule 8.2 was identical to the 2002 version of Rule 8.2.

2002 Amendments: The ABA Ethics 2000 Commission did not propose any changes to the text or Comment of Rule 8.2.

Selected State Variations

California: The California Rules of Professional Conduct have no comparable provision, but California Business & Professions Code §6068(b) provides that it is the duty of an attorney to "maintain the respect due to the courts of justice and judicial officers."

District of Columbia omits ABA Model Rule 8.2.

Florida: Rule 8.2(a) also applies to statements about a mediator, arbitrator, juror or member of the venire.

Georgia omits ABA Model Rule 8.2(a) but adopts Rule 8.2(b) verbatim.

Maryland: Rule 8.2(b)(2) provides that a lawyer who is a candidate for judicial office "with respect to a case, controversy or issue that is likely to come before the court, shall not make a commitment, pledge, or promise that is inconsistent with the impartial performance of the adjudicative duties of the office."

New Jersey: Rule 8.2(b) provides that a lawyer who "has been confirmed for judicial office" shall comply with the applicable provisions of the Code of Judicial Conduct. The rule does not apply to lawyers who are only candidates for judicial office.

New York: Rule 8.2 provides as follows: "(a) A lawyer shall not knowingly make a false statement of fact concerning the qualifications, conduct or integrity of a judge or other adjudicatory officer or of a candidate for election or appointment to judicial office. (b) A lawyer who is a candidate for judicial office shall comply with the applicable provisions of Part 100 of the Rules of the Chief Administrator of the Courts."

Ohio: Rule 8.2(a) omits the ABA reference to an "adjudicatory officer or public legal officer."

Pennsylvania: Rule 8.2 replaces all of ABA Model Rule 8.2(a) with language taken verbatim from DR 8-102(A) and (B) and 8-103(A) of the ABA Model Code of Professional Responsibility.

Virginia: Rule 8.2 provides, in its entirety, as follows: "A lawyer shall not make a statement that the lawyer knows to be false or with reckless disregard as to its truth or falsity concerning the qualifications or integrity of a judge or other judicial officer."

Related Materials

ABA Formal Ethics Opinions: No ABA formal ethics opinions have discussed ABA Model Rule 8.2.

ABA Model Code of Judicial Conduct: Rule 8.2(b) requires candidates for judicial office to "comply with the applicable provisions of the code of judicial conduct." The applicable provisions vary from state to state, but in the ABA Model Code of Judicial Conduct as amended in February 2007, which is reprinted later in this book, the applicable provisions governing judicial candidates are found in Canon 4. (In the ABA's 1990 Code of Judicial Conduct, the applicable provisions were found in Canon 5.)

Restatement of the Law Governing Lawyers: See Restatement §114 in our chapter on the Restatement later in this volume.

Rule 8.3 Reporting Professional Misconduct

Kelly v. Hunton & Williams retaliation

(a) A lawyer who knows that another lawyer has committed a violation of the Rules of Professional Conduct that raises a substantial question

as to that lawyer's honesty, trustworthiness or fitness as a lawyer in other respects, shall inform the appropriate professional authority.

(b) A lawyer who knows that a judge has committed a violation of applicable rules of judicial conduct that raises a substantial question as to the judge's fitness for office shall inform the appropriate authority.

(c) This Rule does not require disclosure of information otherwise protected by Rule 1.6 or information gained by a lawyer or judge while participating in an approved lawyers assistance program.

COMMENT

[1] Self-regulation of the legal profession requires that members of the profession initiate a disciplinary investigation when they know of a violation of the Rules of Professional Conduct. Lawyers have a similar obligation with respect to judicial misconduct. An apparently isolated violation may indicate a pattern of misconduct that only a disciplinary investigation can uncover. Reporting a violation is especially important where the victim is unlikely to discover the offense.

[2] A report about misconduct is not required where it would involve violation of Rule 1.6. However, a lawyer should encourage a client to consent to disclosure where prosecution would not substantially prejudice the client's interests. 1.6, 1.0

[3] If a lawyer were obliged to report every violation of the Rules, the failure to report any violation would itself be a professional offense. Such a requirement existed in many jurisdictions but proved to be unenforceable. This Rule limits the reporting obligation to those offenses that a self-regulating profession must vigorously endeavor to prevent. A measure of judgment is, therefore, required in complying with the provisions of this Rule. The term "substantial" refers to the seriousness of the possible offense and not the quantum of evidence of which the lawyer is aware. A report should be made to the bar disciplinary agency unless some other agency, such as a peer review agency, is more appropriate in the circumstances. Similar considerations apply to the reporting of judicial misconduct.

[4] The duty to report professional misconduct does not apply to a lawyer retained to represent a lawyer whose professional conduct is in question. Such a situation is governed by the Rules applicable to the client-lawyer relationship. Similar to 1.13

[5] Information about a lawyer's or judge's misconduct or fitness may be received by a lawyer in the course of that lawyer's participation in an approved lawyers or judges assistance program. In that circumstance, providing for an exception to the reporting requirements of paragraphs (a) and (b) of this Rule encourages lawyers and judges to seek treatment through such a program. Conversely, without such an exception, lawyers and judges may hesitate to seek assistance from these programs, which may then result in additional harm to their professional careers and additional injury to the welfare of clients and the public. These Rules do not otherwise address the confidentiality of information received by a lawyer or judge participating in an approved lawyers assistance program; such an obligation, however, may be imposed by the rules of the program or other law.

Canon and Code Antecedents

ABA Canons of Professional Ethics: Canon 29 provided as follows:

29. Upholding the Honor of the Profession

Lawyers should expose without fear or favor before the proper tribunals corrupt or dishonest conduct in the profession, and should accept without hesitation employment against a member of the Bar who has wronged his client. The counsel upon the trial of a cause in which perjury has been committed owe it to the profession and to the public to bring the matter to the knowledge of the prosecuting authorities. The lawyer should aid in guarding the Bar against the admission to the profession of candidates unfit or unqualified because deficient in either moral character or education. He should strive at all times to uphold the honor and to maintain the dignity of the profession and to improve not only the law but the administration of justice.

ABA Model Code of Professional Responsibility: Compare DR 1-103(A) (reprinted later in this volume).

Cross-References in Other Rules

Rule 1.6, Comment 15: Some Rules require "disclosure of information relating to a client's representation to accomplish the purposes specified in paragraphs (b)(1) through (b)(6)," only if such disclosure would be permitted by paragraph (b). See **Rules** 1.2(d), 4.1(b), 8.1 and **8.3**.

Rule 1.8, Comment 5: It is prohibited to partake in the "disadvantageous use of client information unless the client gives informed consent, except as permitted or required by these Rules. See **Rules** 1.2(d), 1.6, 1.9(c), 3.3, 4.1(b), 8.1 and **8.3**."

Legislative History of Model Rule 8.3

1980 Discussion Draft (then Rule 10.3) provided:

A lawyer having information indicating that another lawyer has committed a substantial violation of the Rules of Professional Conduct shall report the information to the appropriate disciplinary authority.

1981 Draft was substantially the same as adopted, except that it did not include any equivalent to Rule 8.3(b).

1982 Draft was adopted.

1983 Rule: As originally adopted in 1983, Rules 8.3(a) and (b) were identical to the 2002 version of those rules, except that the word "knows" in the 2002 version was originally "having knowledge" in both paragraphs. The 1983 version of Rule 8.3(c) provided simply: "This rule does not require the disclosure of information otherwise protected by Rule 1.6."

1991 Amendments: At its August 1991 Annual Meeting, the ABA House of Delegates added the clause beginning "or information gained . . ." to Rule 8.3(c). The following excerpts from the Report of the ABA Standing Committee on Ethics and Professional Responsibility explain the rationale and scope of the amendments:

*16. ABA Committee Report Explaining 1991 Amendments to Rule 8.3**

The serious concerns that have arisen recently as a result of "lawyer impairment" have led to the creation of special programs throughout the nation to assist lawyers and judges who face alcohol or drug addiction or other serious problems which threaten to affect or have already affected the performance of their professional responsibilities.

. . . The Committee believes that it is in the interest of the legal profession and the public that the ABA Model Rules be amended to provide for the confidentiality of information that is furnished by the impaired lawyer or judge.

Under the amendment to Model Rule 8.3, the protection of information obtained in the circumstances of a lawyer's or judge's participation in an assistance program is similar to the protection ordinarily provided by the attorney-client privilege. Where the attorney-client privilege would not apply because the information relates to the intention to commit a crime, for example where a lawyer indicates the intention to continue to convert client funds to his or her own use, such information may be disclosed to the appropriate authority, permitting the recipient of the information to comply with the obligation imposed upon him or her by paragraphs (a) or (b). In such situations concerns other than the recovery of the impaired lawyer or judge necessarily outweigh the impaired lawyer's or judge's right to confidentiality. . . . Although the Committee recognizes that disclosure of such information by one member of the profession to the detriment of a professional colleague is painful and difficult, it considers such a situation indistinguishable from other situations in which important public policy considerations require disclosure of confidential information. To extend the confidentiality protection to a lawyer's or judge's intention to commit a crime likely to result in significant harm to others, moreover, would lend support to claims that the profession is unable or unwilling to live up to its obligation to regulate itself in the public interest.

2002 Amendments: At its February 2002 Mid-Year Meeting, the ABA House of Delegates adopted without change the ABA Ethics 2000 Commission proposal to amend Rule 8.3 and its Comment. The main changes were to modify Rule 8.3(c) by substituting the phrase "while participating in an approved lawyers assistance program" for the phrase "while serving as a member of an approved lawyers assistance program to the extent that such information would be confidential if it were communicated subject to the attorney-client privilege," and to rewrite much of Comment 5.

Selected State Variations

Alaska exempts a lawyer from making a report under Rule 8.3(a) or (b) if "the lawyer reasonably believes that the misconduct has been or will otherwise be reported."

Arizona: Rule 8.3(c) retains language similar to the pre-2002 version of the ABA Model Rule, protecting information gained while serving in a lawyer assistance program that "would be confidential if it related to the representation of a client" and if confidentiality has not otherwise been waived.

Arkansas: Rule 8.3(d) generally exempts lawyers working with the Arkansas Lawyer Assistance Program from mandatory reporting obligations "unless it appears

* Committee Reports do not represent official policy of the ABA. They are for information only, and the opinions are those of the authors of the report.

. . . that the attorney in question, after entry into the ALAP, is failing to desist from said violation, or is failing to cooperate with a program of assistance to which said attorney has agreed, or is engaged in the sale of a controlled substance or theft of property constituting a felony under Arkansas law, or the equivalent thereof if the offense is not within the State's jurisdiction."

California: The California Rules of Professional Conduct have no comparable provision.

Connecticut adds the following sentence to Rule 8.3(a): "A lawyer may not condition settlement of a civil dispute involving allegations of improprieties on the part of a lawyer on an agreement that the subject misconduct not be reported to the appropriate disciplinary authority." Rule 8.3(c) tracks the pre-2002 version of ABA Model Rule 8.3(c), but Connecticut's version also refers to Connecticut General Statutes §51-81d(f), which governs crisis intervention assistance to attorneys.

District of Columbia: Rule 8.3(c) omits the phrase "or information gained by a lawyer or judge while participating in an approved lawyers assistance program." The phrase is unnecessary because D.C. Rule 1.6(i) provides as follows:

> [A] lawyer who serves as a member of the D.C. Bar Lawyer Counseling Committee, or as a trained intervenor for that committee, shall be deemed to have a lawyer-client relationship with respect to any lawyer-counselee being counseled under programs conducted by or on behalf of the committee. Information obtained from another lawyer being counseled under the auspices of the committee . . . shall be treated as a confidence or secret within the terms of paragraph (b) [of Rule 1.6]. Such information may be disclosed only to the extent permitted by this rule.

D.C. Rule 1.6(j) contains parallel language regarding information that a lawyer receives in connection with service on the D.C. Bar Practice Management Service Committee (formerly known as the Lawyer Practice Assistance Committee).

Florida: Rule 8.3 ends by providing that "if a lawyer's participation in an approved lawyers assistance program is part of a disciplinary sanction this limitation shall not be applicable and a report about the lawyer who is participating as part of a disciplinary sanction shall be made to the appropriate disciplinary agency." Florida also adds Rule 8.3(d), which provides as follows:

> *Limited Exception for LOMAS Counsel.* A lawyer employed by or acting on behalf of the Law Office Management Assistance Service (LOMAS) shall not have an obligation to disclose knowledge of the conduct of another member . . . if the lawyer employed by or acting on behalf of LOMAS acquired the knowledge while engaged in a LOMAS review of the other lawyer's practice. *Provided further,* however, that if the LOMAS review is conducted as a part of a disciplinary sanction this limitation shall not be applicable and a report shall be made to the appropriate disciplinary agency.

Georgia changes "shall" to "should" in Rule 8.3(a) and (b), and replaces ABA Model Rule 8.3(c) by stating: "There is no disciplinary penalty for a violation of this Rule." Georgia also adds a special self-reporting provision, Rule 9.1, which requires members of the Georgia Bar to notify the State Bar of Georgia of (a) all other jurisdictions in which they are admitted to practice law and the dates of admission; and (b) "the conviction of any felony or of a misdemeanor involving moral turpitude where the underlying conduct relates to the lawyer's fitness to practice law, within sixty days of conviction." Finally, Georgia adds a special Rule 9.2, regarding agreements not to report, which provides as follows:

> In connection with the settlement of a controversy or suit involving misuse of funds held in a fiduciary capacity, a lawyer shall not enter into an agreement that the person bringing the claim will be prohibited or restricted from filing a disciplinary complaint, or will be required to request the dismissal of a pending disciplinary complaint concerning that conduct.

Georgia's Comment to Rule 9.2 provides as follows:

> [1] The disciplinary system provides protection to the general public from those lawyers who are not morally fit to practice law. One problem in the past has been the lawyer who settles the civil claim/disciplinary complaint with the injured party on the basis that the injured party not bring a disciplinary complaint or request the dismissal of a pending disciplinary complaint. The lawyer is then free to injure other members of the general public.
>
> [2] To prevent such abuses in settlements, this rule prohibits a lawyer from settling any controversy or suit involving misuse of funds on any basis which prevents the person bringing the claim from pursuing a disciplinary complaint.

Illinois: Rule 8.3(a) deletes the reference to "honesty, trustworthiness or fitness as a lawyer" and simply imposes a duty to report when "another lawyer has committed a violation of Rule 8.4(b) or 8.4(c). . . ." Moreover, Rule 8.3(c) excludes from the reporting obligation any information that is "protected by the attorney-client privilege." This provision is narrower than the Model Rule's exception, which applies to all information protected by Rule 1.6. Illinois also adds Rule 8.3(d), which requires lawyers to report to the Illinois Disciplinary Commission any discipline that has been imposed on them by a body other than the Illinois Commission.

Kansas: Rule 8.3(c) adds that lawyers are "not required to disclose information" learned through participation in a variety of self-help organizations, such as Alcoholics Anonymous.

Also, Rule 223 of the Kansas Rules Relating to Discipline of Attorneys, entitled "Immunity," provides as follows: "Complaints, reports, or testimony in the course of disciplinary proceedings under these Rules shall be deemed to be made in the course of judicial proceedings. All participants shall be entitled to judicial immunity and all rights, privileges and immunities afforded public officials and other participants in actions filed in the courts of this state."

Massachusetts: The Comment to Rule 8.3 provides as follows:

> [3] While a measure of judgment is required in complying with the provisions of the Rule, a lawyer must report misconduct that, if proven and without regard to mitigation, would likely result in an order of suspension or disbarment, including misconduct that would constitute a "serious crime." . . . Section 12(3) of Rule 4:01 provides that a serious crime is "any felony, and . . . any lesser crime a necessary element of which . . . includes interference with the administration of justice, false swearing, misrepresentation, fraud, willful failure to file income tax returns, deceit, bribery, extortion, misappropriation, theft, or an attempt or a conspiracy, or solicitation of another, to commit [such a crime]." In addition to conviction of a felony, misappropriation of client funds or perjury before a tribunal are common examples of reportable conduct. . . .
>
> [3A] In most situations, a lawyer may defer making a report under this Rule until the matter has been concluded, but the report should be made as soon as practicable thereafter. An immediate report is ethically compelled, however, when a client or third person will likely be injured by a delay in reporting, such as where the lawyer has knowledge that another lawyer has embezzled client or fiduciary funds and delay may impair the ability to recover the funds.

Michigan adds the word "significant" before "violation" in Rules 8.3(a) and (b). The duty to report is suspended if the lawyer gained the information "while serving as an employee or volunteer of the substance abuse counseling program of the State Bar of Michigan, to the extent that the information would be protected under Rule 1.6 from disclosure if it were a communication between lawyer and client." Rule 8.3(c)(2).

New Jersey cuts off Rule 8.3(c) after "Rule 1.6" and adds Rule 8.3(d), which provides as follows:

> Paragraph (a) of this Rule shall not apply to knowledge obtained as a result of participation in a Lawyers Assistance Program established by the Supreme Court and administered by the New Jersey State Bar Association, except as follows:
>
> (i) if the effect of discovered ethics infractions on the practice of an impaired attorney is irremediable or poses a substantial and imminent threat to the interests of clients, then attorney volunteers, peer counselors, or program staff have a duty to disclose the infractions to the disciplinary authorities, and attorney volunteers have the obligation to apply immediately for the appointment of a conservator, who also has the obligation to report ethics infractions to disciplinary authorities; and
>
> (ii) attorney volunteers or peer counselors assisting the impaired attorney in conjunction with his or her practice have the same responsibility as any other lawyer to deal candidly with clients, but that responsibility does not include the duty to disclose voluntarily, without inquiry by the client, information of past violations or present violations that did not or do not pose a serious danger to clients.

New York: Rule 8.3(b) provides as follows: "A lawyer who possesses knowledge or evidence concerning another lawyer or a judge shall not fail to respond to a lawful demand for information from a tribunal or other authority empowered to investigate or act upon such conduct."

North Carolina: Rule 8.3(c) provides only that Rule 8.3 "does not require disclosure of information otherwise protected by Rule 1.6," omitting the ABA reference to a lawyers' assistance program, but North Carolina accomplishes the same result by providing in Rule 1.6(c) that the duty of confidentiality under Rule 1.6 "encompasses information received by a lawyer then acting as an agent of a lawyers' or judges' assistance program . . . regarding another lawyer or judge seeking assistance or to whom assistance is being offered." (Rule 1.6 also defines the term "client" to include lawyers seeking assistance from approved lawyers' or judges' assistance programs.)

North Carolina also adds a Rule 8.3(d), which provides that a lawyer who has been disciplined in any state or federal court for violating that court's Rules of Professional Conduct must "inform the . . . State Bar of such action in writing no later than 30 days after entry of the order of discipline." Finally, North Carolina Rule 1.15-2(o), entitled "Duty to Report Misappropriation," provides that a lawyer who "discovers or reasonably believes that entrusted property has been misappropriated or misapplied shall promptly inform the North Carolina State Bar."

Ohio: Rule 8.3 provides as follows:

> (a) A lawyer who possesses unprivileged knowledge of a violation of the Ohio Rules of Professional Conduct that raises a question as to any lawyer's honesty, trustworthiness, or fitness as a lawyer in other respects, shall inform a disciplinary authority empowered to investigate or act upon such a violation.
>
> (b) A lawyer who possesses unprivileged knowledge that a judge has committed a violation of the Ohio Rules of Professional Conduct or applicable rules of judicial conduct shall inform the appropriate authority.

> (c) Any information obtained by a member of a committee . . . of a bar association . . . designed to assist lawyers with substance abuse or mental health problems . . . shall be privileged for all purposes under this rule.

South Carolina: Rule 8.3(a) requires that a "lawyer who is arrested for or has been charged by way of indictment, information or complaint with a serious crime shall inform the Commission on Lawyer Conduct in writing within fifteen days of being arrested or being charged by way of indictment, information or complaint."

Texas alters Rule 8.3(c) as follows:

> (c) A lawyer having knowledge or suspecting that another lawyer or judge whose conduct the lawyer is required to report pursuant to paragraphs (a) or (b) of this Rule is impaired by chemical dependency on alcohol or drugs or by mental illness may report that person to an approved peer assistance program rather than to an appropriate disciplinary authority. If a lawyer elects that option, the lawyer's report to the approved peer assistance program shall disclose any disciplinary violations that the reporting lawyer would otherwise have to disclose to the authorities referred to in paragraphs (a) and (b).

Texas also adds a Rule 8.3(d), which makes clear that Rule 8.3 does not require disclosure of knowledge or information otherwise protected as confidential information by Texas Rule 1.05 (the Texas equivalent to ABA Model Rule 1.6) or by "any statutory or regulatory provisions applicable to the counseling activities of the approved peer assistance program."

Virginia: Rule 8.3(b) replaces the phrase "who knows" with the phrase "having reliable information." Virginia Rule 8.3(c) provides that if a lawyer serving as a third-party neutral receives "reliable information" in that capacity about another lawyer's misconduct that would otherwise have to be reported, the lawyer/neutral "shall attempt to obtain the parties' written agreement to waive confidentiality and permit disclosure of such information to the appropriate professional authority." Rule 8.3(d)—equivalent to ABA Model Rule 8.3(c)—also exempts disclosure by a lawyer who is a "trained intervenor or volunteer" for an approved lawyers' assistance committee, or who is "cooperating in a particular assistance effort," when the information is obtained "for the purposes of fulfilling the recognized objectives of the program."

Virginia also adds Rule 8.3(e), which requires a lawyer to inform the Virginia State Bar if (1) the lawyer has been disciplined by a state or federal disciplinary authority, agency or court in any jurisdiction for violating that jurisdiction's rules of professional conduct, or (2) the lawyer has been convicted of a felony in any United States jurisdiction, or (3) the lawyer has been convicted of either "a crime involving theft, fraud, extortion, bribery or perjury," or "an attempt, solicitation or conspiracy to commit any of the foregoing offenses" in any United States jurisdiction.

Related Materials

ABA Commission on Lawyer Assistance Programs (CoLAP): The ABA Commission on Lawyer Assistance Programs educates the legal profession concerning alcoholism, chemical dependencies, stress, depression and other emotional health issues. The ABA originally formed a Commission on Impaired Attorneys in 1988 to assist state and local bar associations in establishing programs to help addicted lawyers and judges. In 1995, the ABA House of Delegates adopted the Commission's Model Lawyer Assistance Program, which is designed to assist state and local bar associations in developing and maintaining effective lawyer assistance programs and to identify lawyers, judges, and law students impaired by alcoholism, drugs, or mental health problems.

In 1996, the ABA changed the name of the Commission on Impaired Attorneys to the Commission on Lawyer Assistance Programs (CoLAP). CoLAP reviews lawyer assistance programs, makes recommendations for expanding and improving them, holds an annual National Workshop for Lawyer Assistance Programs, and circulates guidelines and policies. In 2002, after a Special Committee of the Association of American Law Schools (AALS) issued a disturbing report entitled "Substance Abuse in the Law Schools," CoLAP appointed a new Law School Outreach Committee in an effort to reach lawyers at the earliest possible stage. The Law School Outreach Committee seeks to develop the best strategy possible to encourage law schools to (1) develop close working relationships with local lawyers assistance programs, and (2) "have ongoing programs in place to educate law students and faculty about stress-related issues (depression, substance abuse, eating disorders, gambling addictions, etc.) and a procedure for identifying and assisting law students and faculty who may be affected by these issues."

For further information about CoLAP and its programs, visit CoLAP's website at *http://apps.americanbar.org/legalservices/colap/resourcelib.html.*

ABA Formal Ethics Opinions: See ABA Formal Ethics Ops. 92-363 (1992), 94-383 (1994), 03-429 (2003), 03-431 (2003), 04-433 (2004), 07-449 (2007), and 08-453 (2008).

Lawyer Assistance Programs: Since 1991, ABA Model Rule 8.3(c) has referred to information gained by a lawyer or judge while participating in "an approved lawyers assistance program." Lawyer assistance programs, or LAPs, are operated by the bar to help lawyers who have problems with alcoholism, drug addiction, mental health, or extreme stress. To assist lawyers and judges in the recovery process, LAPs use techniques such as intervention, peer counseling, and referral to 12-Step Programs. In 1980, lawyer assistance programs operated in only 26 states, but today lawyer assistance programs operate in every state. For a state-by-state directory of lawyer assistance programs, see the directory maintained by the ABA Commission on Lawyer Assistance Programs at *www.americanbar.org/groups/lawyer_assistance/resources/lap_programs_by_state.html.*

Oath of Office: All states require new attorneys to take an oath upon being admitted to the bar. In Illinois, for example, §4 of the Attorney Act requires every new attorney to take the following oath:

> I do solemnly swear (or affirm, as the case may be), that I will support the constitution of the United States and the constitution of the state of Illinois, and that I will faithfully discharge the duties of the office of attorney and counselor at law to the best of my ability.

Reporting Obligations by Courts and Nonlawyers: Certain judges and nonlawyers may be obligated to report lawyer misconduct. For example, California Business & Professions Code §6086.7 requires courts to notify the State Bar whenever an attorney is held in contempt or commits other specified wrongs, and California Insurance Code §1872.83 requires certain government officials to report lawyer fraud to lawyer disciplinary authorities.

Restatement of the Law Governing Lawyers: See Restatement §5(3) in our chapter on the Restatement later in this volume.

Rule 8.4 Misconduct

It is professional misconduct for a lawyer to:

(a) violate or attempt to violate the Rules of Professional Conduct, knowingly assist or induce another to do so, or do so through the acts of another;

(b) commit a criminal act that reflects adversely on the lawyer's honesty, trustworthiness or fitness as a lawyer in other respects;

(c) engage in conduct involving dishonesty, fraud, deceit or misrepresentation; 3.3, 4.1(a), 7.1 *In re Gatti*

(d) engage in conduct that is prejudicial to the administration of justice; 3.5

(e) state or imply an ability to influence improperly a government agency or official or to achieve results by means that violate the Rules of Professional Conduct or other law; or

(f) knowingly assist a judge or judicial officer in conduct that is a violation of applicable rules of judicial conduct or other law.

COMMENT

1.8(h)(1), (2) liability settlement

[1] Lawyers are subject to discipline when they violate or attempt to violate the Rules of Professional Conduct, knowingly assist or induce another to do so or do so through the acts of another, as when they request or instruct an agent to do so on the lawyer's behalf. Paragraph (a), however, does not prohibit a lawyer from advising a client concerning action the client is legally entitled to take.

[2] Many kinds of illegal conduct reflect adversely on fitness to practice law, such as offenses involving fraud and the offense of willful failure to file an income tax return. However, some kinds of offenses carry no such implication. Traditionally, the distinction was drawn in terms of offenses involving "moral turpitude." That concept can be construed to include offenses concerning some matters of personal morality, such as adultery and comparable offenses, that have no specific connection to fitness for the practice of law. Although a lawyer is personally answerable to the entire criminal law, a lawyer should be professionally answerable only for offenses that indicate lack of those characteristics relevant to law practice. Offenses involving violence, dishonesty, breach of trust, or serious interference with the administration of justice are in that category. A pattern of repeated offenses, even ones of minor significance when considered separately, can indicate indifference to legal obligation.

[3] A lawyer who, in the course of representing a client, knowingly manifests by words or conduct, bias or prejudice based upon race, sex, religion, national origin, disability, age, sexual orientation or socioeconomic status, violates paragraph (d) when such actions are prejudicial to the administration of justice. Legitimate advocacy respecting the foregoing factors does not violate paragraph (d). A trial judge's finding that peremptory challenges were exercised on a discriminatory basis does not alone establish a violation of this rule.

[4] A lawyer may refuse to comply with an obligation imposed by law upon a good faith belief that no valid obligation exists. The provisions of Rule 1.2(d) concerning a good faith challenge to the validity, scope, meaning or application of the law apply to challenges of legal regulation of the practice of law.

[5] Lawyers holding public office assume legal responsibilities going beyond those of other citizens. A lawyer's abuse of public office can suggest an inability to fulfill the professional role of lawyers. The same is true of abuse of positions of private trust such as trustee, executor, administrator, guardian, agent and officer, director or manager of a corporation or other organization.

Canon and Code Antecedents

ABA Canons of Professional Ethics: No comparable Canon.

ABA Model Code of Professional Responsibility: Compare DR 1-102(A) and DR 9-101(C) (reprinted later in this volume).

Cross-References in Other Rules

Preamble, 3: "[T]here are Rules that apply to lawyers who are not active in the practice of law or to practicing lawyers even when they are acting in a non-professional capacity. . . . See **Rule 8.4**."

Rule 3.3, Comment 3: "Regarding compliance with Rule 1.2(d), see the Comment to that Rule. See also the Comment to **Rule 8.4(b)**."

Rule 3.8, Comment 1: "Applicable law may require other measures by the prosecutor and knowing disregard of those obligations or a systematic abuse of prosecutorial discretion could constitute a violation of **Rule 8.4**."

Rule 4.1, Comment 1: "For dishonest conduct that does not amount to a false statement or for misrepresentations by a lawyer other than in the course of representing a client, see **Rule 8.4**."

Rule 4.2, Comment 4: "A lawyer may not make a communication prohibited by this Rule through the acts of another. See **Rule 8.4(a)**."

Rule 5.1, Comment 4: "Paragraph (c) expresses a general principle of personal responsibility for acts of another. See also **Rule 8.4(a)**."

Rule 5.1, Comment 7: "Apart from this Rule and **Rule 8.4(a)**, a lawyer does not have disciplinary liability for the conduct of a partner, associate or subordinate."

Rule 5.7, Comment 2: "[T]he conduct of a lawyer involved in the provision of law-related services is subject to those Rules that apply generally to lawyer conduct, regardless of whether the conduct involves the provision of legal services. See, e.g., **Rule 8.4**."

Rule 5.7, Comment 11: "When the full protections of all of the Rules of Professional Conduct do not apply to the provision of law-related services, principles of law external to the Rules, for example, the law of principal and agent, govern the legal duties owed to those receiving the services. . . . See also **Rule 8.4** (Misconduct)."

Rule 7.1, Comment 4: "See also **Rule 8.4(e)** for the prohibition against stating or implying an ability to influence improperly a government agency or official or to achieve results by means that violate the Rules of Professional Conduct or other law."

Rule 7.3, Comment 8: "Lawyers who participate in a legal service plan must reasonably assure that the plan sponsors are in compliance with Rules 7.1, 7.2 and 7.3(b). See **Rule 8.4(a)**."

Rule 7.6, Comment 6: "If a lawyer makes or solicits a political contribution under circumstances that constitute bribery or another crime, **Rule 8.4(b)** is implicated."

Legislative History of Model Rule 8.4

1980 Discussion Draft (then Rule 10.4) provided:

> It is professional misconduct for a lawyer to:
> (a) violate the Rules of Professional Conduct or knowingly aid another to do so;
> (b) commit a crime or other deliberately wrongful act that reflects adversely on the lawyer's honesty, trustworthiness, or fitness in other respects to practice law. . . .

1981 and ***1982 Drafts:*** Subparagraph (b) of both drafts provided that it was misconduct for a lawyer to "commit a criminal or *fraudulent* act that reflects adversely . . . ," and neither draft included subparagraphs (c) and (d) of the rule as adopted (relating to conduct involving "dishonesty, fraud, deceit or misrepresentation" and to conduct "prejudicial to the administration of justice").

1983 Rule: As originally adopted in 1983, Rules 8.4(a)-(d) and (f) were identical to the 2002 versions of those rules, but the original version of Rule 8.4(e) provided simply that a lawyer shall not "state or imply an ability to influence improperly a government agency or official."

1994 Proposals: Two competing "anti-discrimination" proposals, each in the form of a proposed new paragraph (g) to Rule 8.4, were on the agenda at the ABA's February 1994 Mid-Year Meeting. However, at the last minute both proposals were withdrawn, and the competing sponsors announced their intention to work together to develop a single proposal. The two proposals withdrawn in 1994 differed mainly in their scope. The narrower proposal was submitted by the ABA Standing Committee on Ethics and Professional Responsibility. It provided that it would be professional misconduct for a lawyer to:

> (g) knowingly manifest by words or conduct, in the course of representing a client, bias or prejudice based upon race, sex, religion, national origin, disability, age, sexual orientation or socio-economic status. This paragraph does not apply to a lawyer's confidential communications to a client or preclude legitimate advocacy with respect to the foregoing factors.

The Report submitted in support of the Standing Committee's 1994 proposal explained that the Committee's proposed amendment has three essential aspects:*

> The first is its limitation to situations in which the lawyer is representing a client in a legal matter. . . .
> The second aspect is the Rule's identification of particular types of bias or prejudice that are to be prohibited. . . . The proposed amendment establishes a standard of conduct broader than that mandated by statutory enactments; this standard enables

* Committee Reports do not represent official policy of the ABA. They are for information only, and the opinions are those of the authors of the report.

the profession to set an example of fairness and impartiality that is at the core of its commitment to the public interest. . . .

The third aspect of the rule comprises its exceptions. In order to avoid inquiry into a lawyer's confidential communications to a client, the rule excepts those communications from its ambit. The rule, as well, does not preclude legitimate advocacy by the lawyer with respect to the specified factors. An example of this would be when the national origin of a party is a factor in selecting a jury for a particular case. . . .

A broader proposal was submitted by the ABA Young Lawyers Division. It provided that it would be professional misconduct for a lawyer to:

(g) commit a discriminatory act prohibited by law or to harass a person on the basis of sex, race, age, creed, religion, color, national origin, disability, sexual orientation or marital status, where the act of discrimination or harassment is committed in connection with a lawyer's professional activities.

The Report submitted in support of the Young Lawyers Division's 1994 proposal explained the proposed language as follows:

The amendment is designed to regulate conduct in all manifestations of a lawyer's professional activities, and thereby avoid the inexplicable nuances of a rule which would allow reprehensible behavior to go unchecked merely because it is calculatedly inflicted outside the courtroom or after a case is concluded. . . . [T]he proposed rule will reach also to each situation where a lawyer is engaged in endeavors associated with professional activities.

The proposed amendment will apply to professional activities regardless of whether the lawyer is representing a client. Implicit therein is the notion that the administration of justice must be protected from offensive conduct committed by officers of the court in all instances where a lawyer is called upon by virtue of the distinction of being a member of our profession. To do otherwise makes a mockery of the concept of fair and impartial administration of justice for all, and enhances the perception that lawyers are somehow outside or above the law. . . .

The proposal must regulate a lawyer's conduct both inside and outside the courtroom because all lawyers represent the judicial system each time they act within their professional capacity. . . .

1995 Resolution: After the Young Lawyers Division and the Standing Committee on Ethics and Professional Responsibility withdrew their competing 1994 proposals to add a new paragraph 8.4(g), the Young Lawyers Division worked with the Standing Committee in an attempt to produce a unified proposal. That attempt failed, partly because of concerns that a rule prohibiting bias and prejudice could infringe First Amendment rights. The Young Lawyers Division therefore decided to recommend the following policy statement, which the House of Delegates approved:

RESOLVED, That the American Bar Association:

(a) condemns the manifestation by lawyers in the course of their professional activities, by words or conduct, of bias or prejudice against clients, opposing parties and their counsel, other litigants, witnesses, judges and court personnel, jurors and others, based upon race, sex, religion, national origin, disability, age, sexual orientation or socio-economic status, unless such words or conduct are otherwise permissible as legitimate advocacy on behalf of a client or a cause;

(b) opposes unlawful discrimination by lawyers in the management or operation of a law practice in hiring, promoting, discharging or otherwise determining the conditions of employment, or accepting or terminating representation of a client;

(c) condemns any conduct by lawyers that would threaten, harass, intimidate or denigrate any other person on the basis of the aforementioned categories and characteristics;

(d) discourages members from belonging to any organization that practices invidious discrimination on the basis of the aforementioned categories and characteristics;

(e) encourages affirmative steps such as continuing education, studies, and conferences to discourage the speech and conduct described above.

1998 Mid-Year Proposals: As in 1994 and 1995, proposals condemning bias and prejudice were withdrawn on the eve of the ABA meeting. A withdrawn proposal to amend the text of Rule 8.4, sponsored by the ABA's Criminal Justice Section, would have made it professional misconduct to:

(1) commit, in the course of representing a client, any verbal or physical discriminatory act, on account of race, ethnicity, or gender, if intended to abuse litigants, jurors, witnesses, court personnel, opposing counsel or other lawyers, or to gain a tactical advantage; or

(2) engage, in the course of representing a client, in any continuing course of verbal or physical discriminatory conduct, on account of race, ethnicity or gender, in dealings with litigants, jurors, witnesses, court personnel, opposing counsel or other lawyers, if such conduct constitutes harassment.

A competing withdrawn proposal, sponsored by the ABA's Standing Committee on Ethics and Professional Responsibility, would not have amended the text of Rule 8.4 but would have added the following new paragraph to the comment:

A lawyer who, in the course of representing a client, knowingly manifests by words or conduct, bias or prejudice based on race, sex, religion, national origin, disability, age, sexual orientation or socioeconomic status, violates paragraph (d) [of Rule 8.4] when such actions are prejudicial to the administration of justice. Legitimate advocacy respecting the foregoing factors does not violate paragraph (d).

1998 Amendment: After the 1998 Mid-Year Meeting proposals to amend the text of Rule 8.4 were withdrawn, the sponsors realized that the House of Delegates would not support an amendment to the text of Rule 8.4 but might support an amendment to the Comment. Eventually, the ABA's Standing Committee on Ethics and Professional Responsibility (later joined by the ABA Section on Criminal Justice and the ABA Commission on Minorities in the Profession) proposed adding a new paragraph 2 to the Comment to make clear that words and conduct manifesting bias or prejudice in the course of representing a client violate Rule 8.4(d) when such actions are prejudicial to the administration of justice. The proposal to amend the Comment passed by a voice vote. We reprint the following excerpts (with most citations omitted) from the report of the ABA Standing Committee on Ethics and Professional Responsibility in support of the amendment:

*Excerpts from ABA Report Explaining 1998 Amendment to Comment to Rule 8.4**

. . . For a lawyer to display bias or discrimination in the course of representing a client, whether in the courtroom or a conference room, discredits the fundamental principles that all people are equal before the law, and that controversies should be resolved according to their merits under the law. . . .

* Committee Reports do not represent official policy of the ABA. They are for information only, and the opinions are those of the authors of the report.

Formulation of a black-letter rule barring unacceptable conduct while preserving legitimate advocacy and First Amendment freedoms is a difficult task because manifestations of bias and prejudice may include protected speech and because race, gender and other factors are sometimes legitimate subjects of consideration and comment in the legal process. At the heart of the First Amendment is the right to free speech regarding matters relating to the functioning of government, including the judicial process. . . .

When a personal attack is made upon a judge, witness, or court official for the sole purpose of ridicule or harassment, however, such speech does not enjoy First Amendment protection. . . .

The . . . Comment to the existing model rule prohibiting conduct prejudicial to the administration of justice should be amended to make explicit that expressions of bias and prejudice are among the actions of a lawyer that can prejudice the administration of justice and subject a lawyer to disciplinary action.

. . . Three important issues are addressed in the proposed new Comment: (1) the context in which expressions of bias or prejudice will be subject to possible discipline; (2) the specific characteristics that must not be the basis for bias or prejudice; and (3) a guarantee that the rule is not intended and will be ineffective to diminish a lawyer's advocacy where a listed characteristic is at issue in a matter. This report addresses these three issues.

The amended Comment identifies as conduct subject to scrutiny that which occurs "in the course of representing a client." . . . Conduct and communications by a lawyer other than in the course of representing a client are not intended to be made subject to review under the revised Comment. . . .

We have included language in the Comment to address a concern of the criminal bar, namely whether a finding by a trial judge that a lawyer exercised a peremptory challenge in a discriminatory manner could be considered a per se violation of this Rule. We think that it should not. A trial court may find that a lawyer has exercised a peremptory challenge with impermissible, discriminatory intent if it disbelieves the lawyer's neutral explanation for striking the juror. See, Batson v. Kentucky, 476 U.S. 79, 98 (1986). Although . . . some reasons for striking a juror . . . are easily verifiable, neutral grounds for striking the juror, more subjective reasons such as body language, eye contact, or tone of voice are less subject to verification. . . .

The Comment, reasonably interpreted, is meant only to reach conduct of such a nature or frequency that it is prejudicial to the administration of justice. Single incidents that suggest or imply bias or prejudice, or expressions of so slight a nature that they do not give serious offense, are not necessarily prejudicial to the administration of justice and therefore violative of Rule 8.4(d). The determination of when this threshold is met is left to the disciplinary process, which will properly be informed by a variety of considerations that may differ from one situation or jurisdiction to another.

2002 Amendments: At its February 2002 Mid-Year Meeting, the ABA House of Delegates adopted with only minor changes the ABA Ethics 2000 Commission proposal to amend Rule 8.4 and its Comment. The only significant changes were to add the phrase "or achieve results by means that violate the Rules of Professional Conduct or other law" at the end of Rule 8.4(e), to add all of Comment 1, and to renumber all subsequent comments.

Selected State Variations

Alabama adds Rule 3.10, which provides that a lawyer "shall not present, participate in presenting, or threaten to present criminal charges solely to obtain an advantage in a civil matter."

Arizona adds Rule 8.4(g), which makes it professional misconduct for a lawyer to "file a notice of change of judge under Rule 10.2, Arizona Rules of Criminal Procedure, for an improper purpose, such as obtaining a trial delay. . . ."

California: Rule 2-400 provides, in part, as follows:

> (B) In the management or operation of a law practice, a member shall not unlawfully discriminate or knowingly permit unlawful discrimination on the basis of race, national origin, sex, sexual orientation, religion, age or disability in:
>
> (1) hiring, promoting, discharging or otherwise determining the conditions of employment of any person; or
>
> (2) accepting or terminating representation of any client.
>
> (C) No disciplinary investigation or proceeding may be initiated by the State Bar against a member under this rule unless and until a tribunal of competent jurisdiction, other than a disciplinary tribunal, shall have first adjudicated a complaint of alleged discrimination and found that unlawful conduct occurred. Upon such adjudication, the tribunal finding or verdict shall then be admissible evidence of the occurrence or non-occurrence of the alleged discrimination in any disciplinary proceeding initiated under this rule. In order for discipline to be imposed under this rule, however, the finding of unlawfulness must be upheld and final after appeal, the time for filing an appeal must have expired, or the appeal must have been dismissed.

In addition, California Business & Professions Code §125.6 (Discrimination in the Performance of Licensed Activity) subjects a lawyer to professional discipline if, because of a prospective client's "race, color, sex, religion, ancestry, disability, marital status, or national origin," the lawyer "refuses to perform the licensed activity" (i.e., the practice of law) or "makes any discrimination or restriction in the performance of the licensed activity."

Also, Business & Professions Code §490.5 permits the State to suspend a lawyer's license if the lawyer "is not in compliance with a child support order or judgment." Finally, Rule 290(a) of the Rules of Procedure of the California State Bar provides that (unless otherwise ordered by the Supreme Court) a member of the bar "shall be required to satisfactorily complete the State Bar Ethics School in all dispositions or decisions involving the imposition of discipline, unless the member previously completed the course within the prior two years."

Colorado: In addition to Rule 8.4(g), which forbids bias in various forms, Colorado adds Rule 4.5, which addresses threats of "criminal, administrative or disciplinary charges" to gain a civil case advantage. See Selected State Variations under Rule 4.4.

District of Columbia: Rule 8.4(d) prohibits conduct that "seriously interferes with" the administration of justice. Rule 8.4(e) omits the ABA phrase "or to achieve results by means that violate the Rules of Professional Conduct or other law." D.C. adds Rule 8.4(g), which makes it misconduct to "[s]eek or threaten to seek criminal charges or disciplinary charges solely to obtain an advantage in a civil matter."

In addition, D.C. adds Rule 9.1, which provides that a lawyer "shall not discriminate against any individual in conditions of employment because of the individual's race, color, religion, national origin, sex, age, marital status, sexual orientation, family responsibility, or physical handicap."

Florida expands Rule 8.4(d) to provide that a lawyer shall not:

> (d) engage in conduct in connection with the practice of law that is prejudicial to the administration of justice, including to knowingly, or through callous indifference, disparage, humiliate, or discriminate against litigants, jurors, witnesses, court

> personnel, or other lawyers on any basis, including, but not limited to, on account of race, ethnicity, gender, religion, national origin, disability, marital status, sexual orientation, age, socioeconomic status, employment, or physical characteristic.

Florida also adds Rule 8.4(g), which provides that a lawyer shall not "fail to respond, in writing, to any official inquiry by bar counsel or a disciplinary agency . . . when bar counsel or the agency is conducting an investigation into the lawyer's conduct."

In addition, Florida adds Rule 8.4(h) that makes it professional misconduct for a lawyer to "willfully refuse, as determined by a court of competent jurisdiction, to timely pay a child support obligation." The Comment explains that subparagraph (h) was added to make the treatment of lawyers who fail to pay child support consistent with the treatment of other professionals in Florida who fail to pay child support. Those other professionals are governed by §61.13015 of the Florida Statutes, which provides for the suspension or denial of a professional license due to delinquent child support payments after all other available remedies for the collection of child support have been exhausted.

Florida also adds Rule 4-8.4(i), which relates to sexual conduct with a client and provides that a lawyer shall not engage in sexual conduct with a client "or a representative of a client." See the Selected Variations following Rule 1.8 for more detail.

Finally, the Florida Supreme Court has promulgated Rule 3-4.7, which provides:

> Violation of the oath taken by an attorney to support the constitutions of the United States and the State of Florida is ground for disciplinary action. Membership in, alliance with, or support of any organization, group, or party advocating or dedicated to the overthrow of the government by violence or by any means in violation of the Constitution of the United States or constitution of this state shall be a violation of the oath.

Georgia deletes ABA Model Rule 8.4(b) in favor of two subparagraphs making it a violation to be "convicted of a felony" or to be "convicted of a misdemeanor involving moral turpitude where the underlying conduct relates to the lawyer's fitness to practice law." Rule 8.4(a)(4)—Georgia's equivalent to ABA Model Rule 8.4(c)—makes it improper to engage in "professional" conduct involving dishonesty, fraud, deceit or misrepresentation. Georgia adds a Rule 8.4(a)(5) that makes it improper for a lawyer to "fail to pay any final judgment or rule absolute rendered against such lawyer for money collected by him or her as a lawyer within ten (10) days after the time appointed in the order or judgment." Rule 8.4(d) provides that Rule 8.4(a)(1) "does not apply to Part Six of the Georgia Rules of Professional Conduct" (which covers pro bono work, court appointments, legal service organizations, and law reform organizations). Georgia deletes ABA Model Rules 8.4(d), (e), and (f).

For Georgia attorneys seeking guidance on their ethical conduct, Georgia Supreme Court Rule 4-401 authorizes the Georgia State Bar's Office of General Counsel to "render Informal Advisory Opinions concerning the Office of the General Counsel's interpretation of the Rules of Professional Conduct or any of the grounds for disciplinary action as applied to a given state of facts." However, the rule cautions that an Informal Advisory Opinion is merely "the personal opinion of the issuing attorney of the Office of the General Counsel and is neither a defense to any complaint nor binding on the State Disciplinary Board, the Supreme Court of Georgia, or the State Bar of Georgia." Rule 4-403 describes the procedures by which the Supreme Court of Georgia issues Formal Advisory Opinions and describes the weight to be given to Formal Advisory Opinions in various circumstances.

Illinois expands Rule 8.4(f) and adds paragraphs (g)-(k), some of which are taken directly from the old ABA Model Code of Professional Responsibility. They provide that it is professional misconduct for a lawyer to:

> (f) . . . give or lend anything of value to a judge, official, or employee of a tribunal, except those gifts or loans that a judge or a member of the judge's family may receive under Rule 65(C)(4) of the Illinois Code of Judicial Conduct. Permissible campaign contributions to a judge or candidate for judicial office may be made only by check, draft, or other instrument payable to or to the order of an entity that the lawyer reasonably believes to be a political committee supporting such judge or candidate. Provision of volunteer services by a lawyer to a political committee shall not be deemed to violate this paragraph.
>
> (g) present, participate in presenting, or threaten to present criminal or professional disciplinary charges to obtain an advantage in a civil matter.
>
> (h) enter into an agreement with a client or former client limiting or purporting to limit the right of the client or former client to file or pursue any complaint before the Illinois Attorney Registration and Disciplinary Commission.
>
> (i) avoid in bad faith the repayment of an education loan guaranteed by the Illinois Student Assistance Commission or other governmental entity. The lawful discharge of an education loan in a bankruptcy proceeding shall not constitute bad faith under this paragraph, but the discharge shall not preclude a review of the lawyer's conduct to determine if it constitutes bad faith.
>
> (j) violate a federal, state or local statute or ordinance that prohibits discrimination based on race, sex, religion, national origin, disability, age, sexual orientation or socioeconomic status by conduct that reflects adversely on the lawyer's fitness as a lawyer. Whether a discriminatory act reflects adversely on a lawyer's fitness as a lawyer shall be determined after consideration of all the circumstances, including: the seriousness of the act; whether the lawyer knew that the act was prohibited by statute or ordinance; whether the act was part of a pattern of prohibited conduct; and whether the act was committed in connection with the lawyer's professional activities. No charge of professional misconduct may be brought pursuant to this paragraph until a court or administrative agency of competent jurisdiction has found that the lawyer has engaged in an unlawful discriminatory act, and the finding of the court or administrative agency has become final and enforceable and any right of judicial review has been exhausted.
>
> (k) if the lawyer holds public office:
>
> > (1) use that office to obtain, or attempt to obtain, a special advantage in a legislative matter for a client under circumstances where the lawyer knows or reasonably should know that such action is not in the public interest;
> >
> > (2) use that office to influence, or attempt to influence, a tribunal to act in favor of a client; or
> >
> > (3) represent any client, including a municipal corporation or other public body, in the promotion or defeat of legislative or other proposals pending before the public body of which such lawyer is a member or by which such lawyer is employed.

Iowa: Rule 8.4(g) forbids lawyers to "engage in sexual harassment or other unlawful discrimination in the practice of law or knowingly permit staff or agents subject to the lawyer's direction and control to do so."

Louisiana: Among other variations, Louisiana adds a Rule 8.4(g), which makes it professional misconduct for a lawyer to "[t]hreaten to present criminal or disciplinary charges solely to obtain an advantage in a civil matter."

Maryland: Rule 8.4(e) provides that a lawyer may not "manifest by words or conduct" various kinds of bias or prejudice when such action is prejudicial to the administration of justice.

Massachusetts: Rule 8.4(h) forbids a lawyer to "engage in any other conduct that adversely reflects on his or her fitness to practice law." Comment 5 states that such conduct is subject to discipline even if it "does not constitute a criminal, dishonest, or fraudulent or other act specifically described in the other paragraphs of this rule."

Michigan: Rule 6.5, entitled "Professional Conduct," provides as follows:

> (a) A lawyer shall treat with courtesy and respect all persons involved in the legal process. A lawyer shall take particular care to avoid treating such a person discourteously or disrespectfully because of the person's race, gender, or other protected personal characteristic. To the extent possible, a lawyer shall require subordinate lawyers and nonlawyer assistants to provide such courteous and respectful treatment.
>
> (b) A lawyer serving as an adjudicative officer shall, without regard to a person's race, gender, or other protected personal characteristic, treat every person fairly, with courtesy and respect. To the extent possible, the lawyer shall require staff and others who are subject to the adjudicative officer's direction and control to provide such fair, courteous, and respectful treatment to persons who have contact with the adjudicative tribunal.

In addition, the Michigan Court Rules include the following Rule 9.104:

> (A) The following acts or omissions by an attorney, individually or in concert with another person, are misconduct and grounds for discipline, whether or not occurring in the course of an attorney-client relationship:
>
> (1) conduct prejudicial to the proper administration of justice;
>
> (2) conduct that exposes the legal profession or the courts to obloquy, contempt, censure, or reproach;
>
> (3) conduct that is contrary to justice, ethics, honesty, or good morals;
>
> (4) conduct that violates the standards or rules of professional responsibility adopted by the Supreme Court;
>
> (5) conduct that violates a criminal law of a state or of the United States;
>
> (6) knowing misrepresentation of any facts or circumstances surrounding a request for investigation or complaint;
>
> (7) failure to answer a request for investigation or complaint in conformity with MCR 9.113 and 9.115(D);
>
> (8) contempt of the board or a hearing panel; or
>
> (9) violation of an order of discipline.
>
> (B) Proof of an adjudication of misconduct in a disciplinary proceeding by another state or a United States court is conclusive proof of misconduct in a disciplinary proceeding in Michigan. The only issues to be addressed in the Michigan proceeding are whether the respondent was afforded due process of law in the course of the original proceedings and whether imposition of identical discipline in Michigan would be clearly inappropriate.

Minnesota adds Rule 8.4(g)-(h), which prohibits various kinds of harassment and discrimination.

Missouri: Rule 8.4(g) forbids a lawyer to "manifest by words or conduct, in representing a client, bias or prejudice based upon race, sex, religion, national origin, disability, age, or sexual orientation." However, the rule "does not preclude legitimate advocacy when race, sex, religion, national origin, disability, age, sexual orientation, or other similar factors, are issues."

New Jersey: Rule 8.4(g) makes it professional misconduct for a lawyer to "engage, in a professional capacity, in conduct involving discrimination (except employment discrimination unless resulting in a final agency or judicial determination) because of race, color, religion, age, sex, sexual orientation, national origin, language, marital status, socio-economic status, or handicap, where the conduct is intended or likely to cause harm." The Supreme Court's comment states that the rule

> would, for example, cover activities in the court house, such as a lawyer's treatment of court support staff, as well as conduct more directly related to litigation; activities related to practice outside of the court house, whether or not related to litigation, such as treatment of other attorneys and their staff; bar association and similar activities; and activities in the lawyer's office and firm. Except to the extent that they are closely related to the foregoing, purely private activities are not intended to be covered by this rule amendment, although they may possibly constitute a violation of some other ethical rule. Nor is employment discrimination in hiring, firing, promotion, or partnership status intended to be covered unless it has resulted in either an agency or judicial determination of discriminatory conduct.

New Mexico creates a Rule 3.0 (Rule 16-300), which specifies as follows:

> In the course of any judicial or quasi-judicial proceeding before a tribunal, a lawyer shall refrain from intentionally manifesting, by words or conduct, bias or prejudice based on race, gender, religion, national origin, disability, age or sexual orientation against the judge, court personnel, parties, witnesses, counsel or others. This rule does not preclude legitimate advocacy when race, gender, religion, national origin, disability, age or sexual orientation is material to the issues in the proceeding.

New York adds Rule 8.4(g) and (h), which provides that a lawyer or law firm shall not:

> (g) unlawfully discriminate in the practice of law, including in hiring, promoting or otherwise determining conditions of employment on the basis of age, race, creed, color, national origin, sex, disability, marital status or sexual orientation. Where there is a tribunal with jurisdiction to hear a complaint, if timely brought, other than a Departmental Disciplinary Committee, a complaint based on unlawful discrimination shall be brought before such tribunal in the first instance. A certified copy of a determination by such a tribunal, which has become final and enforceable and as to which the right to judicial or appellate review has been exhausted, finding that the lawyer has engaged in an unlawful discriminatory practice shall constitute prima facie evidence of professional misconduct in a disciplinary proceeding; or
>
> (h) engage in any other conduct that adversely reflects on the lawyer's fitness as a lawyer.

North Carolina: Rule 8.4(e) omits the clause "or to achieve results by means that violate the Rules of Professional Conduct or other law," and a Rule 8.4(g) makes it professional misconduct for a lawyer to "intentionally prejudice or damage his or her client during the course of the professional relationship, except as may be required by Rule 3.3." North Carolina also adds a Rule 6.6, which prohibits lawyers who hold "public office" from abusing their public positions.

Ohio adds Rule 8.4(g)-(h), which makes it professional misconduct for a lawyer to:

(g) engage, in a professional capacity, in conduct involving discrimination prohibited by law because of race, color, religion, age, gender, sexual orientation, national origin, marital status, or disability;

(h) engage in any other conduct that adversely reflects on the lawyer's fitness to practice law.

Ohio also adds an unusual Comment 2A, which provides that Rule 8.4(c) "does not prohibit a lawyer from supervising or advising about lawful covert activity in the investigation of criminal activity or violations of constitutional or civil rights when authorized by law."

Oregon: Rule 8.4(b) is the result of a decision of the Oregon Supreme Court, *In re Gatti,* 8 P.3d 966 (Or. 2000). It provides that, notwithstanding Rules 8.4(a)(1), (3), and (4) and Rule 3.3(a)(1), "it shall not be professional misconduct for a lawyer to advise clients or others about or to supervise lawful covert activity in the investigation of violations of civil or criminal law or constitutional rights," provided the lawyer's conduct otherwise complies with the Rules of Professional Conduct. "Covert activity" is defined in Rule 8.4(b) to mean "an effort to obtain information on unlawful activity through the use of misrepresentations or other subterfuge." The rule permits covert activity to "be commenced by a lawyer or involve the lawyer as an advisor or supervisor only when the lawyer in good faith believes there is a reasonable possibility that unlawful activity has taken place, is taking place, or will take place in the foreseeable future."

Rhode Island adds Rule 9.1, which establishes an ethics advisory panel to be appointed by the Supreme Court and provides that "[a]ny lawyer who acts in accordance with an opinion given by the panel shall be conclusively presumed to have abided by the Rules of Professional Conduct."

Texas: Rule 5.08, entitled "Prohibited Discriminatory Activities," provides as follows:

(a) A lawyer shall not willfully, in connection with an adjudicatory proceeding, except as provided in paragraph (b), manifest, by words or conduct, bias or prejudice based on race, color, national origin, religion, disability, age, sex, or sexual orientation towards any person involved in that proceeding in any capacity.

(b) Paragraph (a) does not apply to a lawyer's decision whether to represent a particular person in connection with an adjudicatory proceeding, nor to the process of jury selection, nor to communications protected as "confidential information" under these Rules. See Rule 1.05(a), (b). It also does not preclude advocacy in connection with an adjudicatory proceeding involving any of the factors set out in paragraph (a) if that advocacy:

(i) is necessary in order to address any substantive or procedural issues raised by the proceeding; and

(ii) is conducted in conformity with applicable rulings and orders of a tribunal and applicable rules of practice and procedure.

Texas Rule 8.04(a)(9) forbids a lawyer to "engage in conduct that constitutes barratry as defined by the laws of this state." Rule 8.04(a)(2) forbids a lawyer to "commit a serious crime or commit any other criminal act that reflects adversely on the lawyer's honesty, trustworthiness or fitness as a lawyer in other respects." Rule 8.04(b) defines "serious crime" to include "barratry; any felony involving moral turpitude; any misdemeanor involving theft, embezzlement, or fraudulent or reckless misappropriation of money or other property; or any attempt, conspiracy, or solicitation of another to commit any of the foregoing crimes."

Virginia: Rule 8.4(b) applies to a criminal "or deliberately wrongful act," and Rule 8.4(c) applies to conduct involving dishonesty, fraud, deceit or misrepresentation "which reflects adversely on the lawyer's fitness to practice law." Virginia omits Rule 8.4(d) (which forbids "conduct that is prejudicial to the administration of justice"), and retains the pre-2002 version of ABA Model Rule 8.4(e), which made it professional misconduct for a lawyer to "state or imply an ability to influence improperly or upon irrelevant grounds any tribunal, legislative body or public official," without any reference to "means that violate the Rules of Professional Conduct or other law."

Wisconsin: Among other variations, Wisconsin omits paragraph (d) and adds several additional paragraphs, including one relating to harassment.

Related Materials

ABA Formal Ethics Opinions: See ABA Formal Ethics Ops. 92-362 (1992), 92-363 (1992), 94-383 (1994), 94-387 (1994) (dissent only), 95-391 (1995), 95-394 (1995), 01-422 (2001), 04-433 (2004), 06-439 nn.2 & 19 (2006), 06-442 n.10 (2006), 07-446 (2007), 07-449 (2007), 08-451 (2008), and 10-457 (2010).

ABA Model Rule for Minimum Continuing Legal Education (MCLE): In 1987, the ABA House of Delegates approved a Model Rule for Minimum Continuing Legal Education (MCLE). The Comment to §2 of the ABA Model MCLE Rule, which relates to ABA Model Rule 8.4 and Comment 3 to Rule 8.4, provides as follows:

> Regulatory systems should require that lawyers . . . complete programs related to the promotion of racial and ethnic diversity in the legal profession, the promotion of full and equal participation in the profession of women and persons with disabilities, and the elimination of all forms of bias in the profession. Lawyers who practice in states and territories that do not require mandatory continuing legal education are encouraged to complete such programs as part of their continuing legal education.

For MCLE details, see *http://www.americanbar.org/publications_cle/mandatory_cle.html.*

ABA Model Rules for Lawyer Disciplinary Enforcement: In 1989, the ABA adopted Model Rules for Lawyer Disciplinary Enforcement, which set forth model procedures for state disciplinary agencies to follow. The ABA amended these rules in 1993, 1999, and 2002. Rule 19 provides for immediate interim suspension of a lawyer who is found guilty of a serious crime. Rule 25 provides that a lawyer who is disbarred may not apply for reinstatement for five years and must pass the bar examination as a condition of reinstatement. (In 2002, the ABA rejected a proposal to prohibit applications for reinstatement for at least eight years after disbarment.) The full set of Rules is available at *http://www.americanbar.org/groups/professional_responsibility/resources/lawyer_ethics_regulation/model_rules_for_lawyer_disciplinary_enforcement.html.*

ABA Resolution Against Bias and Prejudice: In 1995, after various ABA committees could not agree on a new Model Rule prohibiting bias and prejudice, the House of Delegates passed a resolution recommended by the ABA Young Lawyers Division to condemn bias and prejudice by lawyers in their professional activities and to encourage affirmative steps to reduce bias and prejudice among lawyers. The full resolution is set out in the Legislative History following Rule 8.4 under the heading "1995 Resolution."

ABA Resolution on Increasing Diversity in the Legal Profession: In 2006, the ABA approved a resolution urging all state and territorial bar associations to take four steps to increase diversity in the legal profession: (1) collaborate with the state or territory's bar examiner to "ensure that the bar examination does not result in a disparate impact on bar passage rates of minority candidates"; (2) "collaborate with accredited law schools to combat high rates of minority student attrition and to ensure that admission policies do not result in a disparate impact on acceptance rates of minority applicants"; (3) "collaborate with colleges and universities to develop and support prelaw programs that will increase minority applications to law schools and will increase the readiness of minority applicants for law school"; and (4) "collaborate with elementary and secondary schools to develop and support programs that will increase minority applications to college and will increase the readiness of minority applicants for college." The text of the resolution (No. 113) and a background report are available online at *www.abanet.org/leadership/2006/annual/onehundredthirteen.doc.*

ABA Standards for Approval of Law Schools: In 1921 the ABA began promulgating Standards for Approval of Law Schools. Today, a majority of the states rely upon the ABA to determine whether a law school satisfies the state's legal education requirement for admission to the bar. The Standards have been amended periodically. In 2006, the ABA amended Standards 211 through 213, which address discrimination by law schools and thus relate to ABA Model Rule 8.4(d) and Comment 3 to Rule 8.4. The amended Standards provide:

Standard 211. Non-discrimination and Equality of Opportunity.

(a) A law school shall foster and maintain equality of opportunity in legal education, including employment of faculty and staff, without discrimination or segregation on the basis of race, color, religion, national origin, gender, sexual orientation, age or disability.

(b) A law school shall not use admission policies or take other action to preclude admission of applicants or retention of students on the basis of race, color, religion, national origin, gender, sexual orientation, age or disability.

(c) This Standard does not prevent a law school from having a religious affiliation or purpose and adopting and applying policies of admission of students and employment of faculty and staff that directly relate to this affiliation or purpose so long as (i) notice of these policies has been given to applicants, students, faculty, and staff before their affiliation with the law school, and (ii) the religious affiliation, purpose, or policies do not contravene any other Standard, including Standard 405(b) concerning academic freedom. These policies may provide a preference for persons adhering to the religious affiliation or purpose of the law school, but shall not be applied to use admission policies or take other action to preclude admission of applicants or retention of students on the basis of race, color, religion, national origin, gender, sexual orientation, age or disability. This Standard permits religious affiliation or purpose policies as to admission, retention, and employment only to the extent that these policies are protected by the United States Constitution. It is administered as though the First Amendment of the United States Constitution governs its application.

(d) Non-discrimination and equality of opportunity in legal education includes equal opportunity to obtain employment. A law school shall communicate to every employer to whom it furnishes assistance and facilities for interviewing and other placement functions the school's firm expectation that the employer will observe the principles of non-discrimination and equality of opportunity on the basis of race, color, religion, national origin, gender, sexual orientation, age and disability in regard to hiring, promotion, retention and conditions of employment.

Standard 212. Equal Opportunity and Diversity.

(a) Consistent with sound legal education policy and the Standards, a law school shall demonstrate by concrete action a commitment to providing full opportunities for the study of law and entry into the profession by members of underrepresented groups, particularly racial and ethnic minorities, and a commitment to having a student body that is diverse with respect to gender, race, and ethnicity.

(b) Consistent with sound educational policy and the Standards, a law school shall demonstrate by concrete action a commitment to having a faculty and staff that are diverse with respect to gender, race and ethnicity.

Standard 213. Reasonable Accommodation for Qualified Individuals with Disabilities.

Assuring equality of opportunity for qualified individuals with disabilities, as required by Standard 211, may require a law school to provide such students, faculty and staff with reasonable accommodations.

More information on the ABA Standards for Approval of Law Schools can be found at *http://www.americanbar.org/groups/legal_education/resources/standards.html.*

ABA Standards for Imposing Lawyer Sanctions:

5.1. Failure to Maintain Personal Integrity

5.11. Disbarment is generally appropriate when:

(a) a lawyer engages in serious criminal conduct a necessary element of which includes intentional interference with the administration of justice, false swearing, misrepresentation, fraud, extortion, misappropriation, or theft; or the sale, distribution or importation of controlled substances; or the intentional killing of another; or an attempt or conspiracy or solicitation of another to commit any of these offenses; or

(b) a lawyer engages in any other intentional conduct involving dishonesty, fraud, deceit, or misrepresentation that seriously adversely reflects on the lawyer's fitness to practice.

5.12. Suspension is generally appropriate when a lawyer knowingly engages in criminal conduct which does not contain the elements listed in Standard 5.11 and that seriously adversely reflects on the lawyer's fitness to practice.

5.13. Reprimand is generally appropriate when a lawyer knowingly engages in any other conduct that involves dishonesty, fraud, deceit, or misrepresentation and that adversely reflects on the lawyer's fitness to practice law.

5.14. Admonition is generally appropriate when a lawyer engages in any other conduct that reflects adversely on the lawyer's fitness to practice law.

5.2. Failure to Maintain the Public Trust

5.21. Disbarment is generally appropriate when a lawyer in an official or governmental position knowingly misuses the position with the intent to obtain a significant benefit or advantage for himself or another, or with the intent to cause serious or potentially serious injury to a party or to the integrity of the legal process.

5.22. Suspension is generally appropriate when a lawyer in an official or governmental position knowingly fails to follow proper procedures or rules and causes injury or potential injury to a party or to the integrity of the legal process.

8.0. Prior Discipline Orders

8.1. Disbarment is generally appropriate when a lawyer:

(a) intentionally or knowingly violates the terms of a prior disciplinary order and such violation causes injury or potential injury to a client, the public, the legal system, or the profession; or

(b) has been suspended for the same or similar misconduct, and intentionally or knowingly engages in further similar acts of misconduct that cause injury or potential injury to a client, the public, the legal system, or the profession.

8.2. Suspension is generally appropriate when a lawyer has been reprimanded for the same or similar misconduct and engages in further similar acts of misconduct that cause injury or potential injury to a client, the public, the legal system, or the profession.

The ABA Standards for Imposing Lawyer Sanctions, are available online at *www.americanbar.org/content/dam/aba/migrated/cpr/regulation/standards_sanctions.pdf.*

ABA Study of Women of Color in Law Firms: In 2006, with help from the University of Chicago's National Opinion Research Center, the ABA released a study entitled "Visible Invisibility: Women of Color in Law Firms." The 141-page study, which has many tables and charts, explores the experiences of women of color who formerly worked in law firms of at least 25 attorneys. It attempts to answers such critical questions as: "What attracts women of color to the legal profession? Do their work experiences surpass or fall short of expectations? How do legal employers hinder or increase job satisfaction? Why do women attorneys of color change practice areas and organizations, or leave the profession at an alarming rate?" The study concludes that discrimination is causing growing numbers of minority women to leave large law firms. The full study is available for purchase online. The Executive Summary is available online without charge.

Discipline: Professional discipline for engaging in misconduct of the kinds described in ABA Model Rule 8.4 (and sometimes for other types of misconduct) can take many varieties. For example, Illinois Supreme Court Rule 770 provides as follows:

Rule 770. Types of Discipline

Conduct of attorneys which violates the Rules of Professional Conduct . . . or which tends to defeat the administration of justice or to bring the courts or the legal profession into disrepute shall be grounds for discipline by the court. Discipline may be:

(a) disbarment;

(b) disbarment on consent;

(c) suspension for a specified period and until further order of court;

(d) suspension for a specified period of time;

(e) suspension until further order of the court;

(f) suspension for a specified period of time or until further order of the court with probation;

(g) censure; or

(h) reprimand by the court, the Review Board or a hearing panel.

Discrimination Statutes: Comment 3 to Rule 8.4 discusses bias or prejudice that is "prejudicial to the administration of justice," but some state ethics rules, such as New York's Rule 8.4(g) and California's Rule 2-400(B), prohibit bias and discrimination only to the extent that the conduct would violate federal or state laws prohibiting discrimination. Under federal law, three major statutes prohibit discrimination in employment: Title VII of the Civil Rights Act of 1964, 42 U.S.C §§2000 *et seq.*; the Americans with Disabilities Act, 42 U.S.C. §§12101 *et seq.*; and the Age Discrimination in Employment Act, 29 U.S.C. §§621 *et seq.* Most states have parallel laws, and some state and local laws reach further than the federal statutes, prohibiting employment discrimination based on such factors as sexual orientation, color, and marital status in addition to the federal criteria.

Federal Rules of Appellate Procedure: Fed. R. App. P. 46(c) gives a federal court of appeals power to discipline any attorney who practices before it for "conduct unbecoming a member of the bar or for failure to comply with any court rule."

IRS Regulations: In the regulations governing practice before the Internal Revenue Service, 31 C.F.R. §10.50(a) authorizes the Secretary of the Treasury to "censure, suspend or disbar" any practitioner from practice before the IRS who is shown to be "incompetent or disreputable, fails to comply with any regulation in this part, or with intent to defraud, willfully and knowingly misleads or threatens a client or prospective client."

Section 10.51 defines "incompetence and disreputable conduct" to encompass a long list of misdeeds, including conviction of any crime under federal revenue laws; conviction of any offense involving "dishonesty, or breach of trust"; knowingly giving false or misleading information to "any tribunal authorized to pass upon Federal tax matters, in connection with any matter pending or likely to be pending before them . . ."; misappropriating client funds; "[c]ontemptuous conduct in connection with practice before the Internal Revenue Service, including the use of abusive language, making false accusations and statements, knowing them to be false, or circulating or publishing malicious or libelous matter" or "[g]iving a false opinion, knowingly, recklessly, or through gross incompetence, including an opinion which is intentionally or recklessly misleading, or engaging in a pattern of providing incompetent opinions on questions arising under the Federal tax laws."

Misconduct: Many states define "misconduct" in a statute or court rule. In Washington, D.C., for example, Rule XI §2(b) of the Rules Governing the District of Columbia Bar provides: "Acts or omissions by an attorney . . . which violate the attorney's oath of office or the rules or code of professional conduct currently in effect in the District of Columbia shall constitute misconduct and shall be grounds for discipline, whether or not the act or omission occurred in the course of an attorney-client relationship."

Readmission: When a lawyer is suspended or disbarred, readmission generally is not automatic. An example of a state readmission rule is Florida Supreme Court Rule 2-13.1 (Disbarred or Resigned Pending Disciplinary Proceedings). As amended effective December 16, 2010, Rule 2-13.1 provides as follows:

> A person who has been disbarred from the practice of law, or who has resigned pending disciplinary proceedings . . . based on conduct that occurred in Florida for the disbarment or resignation, will not be eligible to apply for readmission for a period of 5 years from the date of disbarment, or 3 years from the date of resignation . . . or longer period set for readmission by the Supreme Court of Florida. If the person's disbarment or disciplinary resignation is based on conduct that occurred in a foreign jurisdiction, then the person will not be eligible to apply for admission or readmission to The Florida Bar until the person is readmitted in the foreign jurisdiction in which the conduct that resulted in discipline occurred. . . .

Restatement of the Law Governing Lawyers: See Restatement §§1, 5, and 113 in our chapter on the Restatement later in this volume.

Securities and Exchange Commission Rules: The Securities and Exchange Commission (the SEC or the Commission) has power to discipline attorneys who appear or practice before the SEC. The main regulatory provision for imposing discipline is Rule 102(e), 17 C.F.R. §201.102(e) (formerly numbered Rule 2(e)), which provides as follows:

> (e) *Suspension and disbarment.*
>
> (1) *Generally.* The Commission may censure a person or deny, temporarily or permanently, the privilege of appearing or practicing before it in any way to any person who is found by the Commission after notice and opportunity for hearing in the matter:
>
> (i) Not to possess the requisite qualifications to represent others; or
>
> (ii) To be lacking in character or integrity or to have engaged in unethical or improper professional conduct; or
>
> (iii) To have willfully violated, or willfully aided and abetted the violation of any provision of the Federal securities laws or the rules and regulations thereunder. . . .

In addition, in 2003 the SEC adopted a new regulation, 17 C.F.R. §205.6, which is part of the Standards of Professional Conduct for Attorneys that the SEC promulgated to implement §307 of the Sarbanes-Oxley Act of 2002, 15 U.S.C. §7245. Section 205.6 provides as follows:

> *§205.6. Sanctions and Discipline.*
>
> (a) A violation of this part by any attorney appearing and practicing before the Commission in the representation of an issuer shall subject such attorney to the civil penalties and remedies for a violation of the federal securities laws available to the Commission in an action brought by the Commission thereunder.
>
> (b) An attorney appearing and practicing before the Commission who violates any provision of this part is subject to the disciplinary authority of the Commission, regardless of whether the attorney may also be subject to discipline for the same conduct in a jurisdiction where the attorney is admitted or practices. An administrative disciplinary proceeding initiated by the Commission for violation of this part may result in an attorney being censured, or being temporarily or permanently denied the privilege of appearing or practicing before the Commission.
>
> (c) An attorney who complies in good faith with the provisions of this part shall not be subject to discipline or otherwise liable under inconsistent standards imposed by any state or other United States jurisdiction where the attorney is admitted or practices.
>
> (d) An attorney practicing outside the United States shall not be required to comply with the requirements of this part to the extent that such compliance is prohibited by applicable foreign law.

Statutes of Limitations: Some states have adopted statutes of limitations for disciplinary matters. For example, in 1995, the Florida Supreme Court adopted the following statute of limitations provision:

> *Rule 3-7.16. Limitation on Time to Bring Complaint*
>
> (a) *Time for Inquiries, Complaints and Reopened Cases.* Inquiries raised or complaints presented by or to The Florida Bar under these rules shall be commenced within 6 years from the time the matter giving rise to the inquiry or complaint is discovered or, with due diligence, should have been discovered. . . .

(b) *Exception for Theft or Conviction of a Felony Criminal Offense.* There shall be no limit on the time in which to present or bring a matter alleging theft or conviction of a felony criminal offense by a member of The Florida Bar.

(c) *Tolling Based on Fraud, Concealment or Misrepresentation.* In matters covered by this rule where it can be shown that fraud, concealment, or intentional misrepresentation of fact prevented the discovery of the matter giving rise to the inquiry or complaint, the limitation of time in which to bring an inquiry or complaint within this rule shall be tolled. . . .

Rule 8.5 Disciplinary Authority; Choice of Law

(a) Disciplinary Authority. A lawyer admitted to practice in this jurisdiction is subject to the disciplinary authority of this jurisdiction, regardless of where the lawyer's conduct occurs. A lawyer not admitted in this jurisdiction is also subject to the disciplinary authority of this jurisdiction if the lawyer provides or offers to provide any legal services in this jurisdiction. A lawyer may be subject to the disciplinary authority of both this jurisdiction and another jurisdiction for the same conduct.

(b) Choice of Law. In any exercise of the disciplinary authority of this jurisdiction, the rules of professional conduct to be applied shall be as follows:

(1) for conduct in connection with a matter pending before a tribunal, the rules of the jurisdiction in which the tribunal sits, unless the rules of the tribunal provide otherwise; and

(2) for any other conduct, the rules of the jurisdiction in which the lawyer's conduct occurred, or, if the predominant effect of the conduct is in a different jurisdiction, the rules of that jurisdiction shall be applied to the conduct. A lawyer shall not be subject to discipline if the lawyer's conduct conforms to the rules of a jurisdiction in which the lawyer reasonably believes the predominant effect of the lawyer's conduct will occur.

COMMENT

Disciplinary Authority

[1] It is longstanding law that the conduct of a lawyer admitted to practice in this jurisdiction is subject to the disciplinary authority of this jurisdiction. Extension of the disciplinary authority of this jurisdiction to other lawyers who provide or offer to provide legal services in this jurisdiction is for the protection of the citizens of this jurisdiction. Reciprocal enforcement of a jurisdiction's disciplinary findings and sanctions will further advance the purposes of this Rule. See Rules 6 and 22, ABA Model Rules for Lawyer Disciplinary Enforcement. A lawyer who is subject to the disciplinary authority of this jurisdiction under Rule 8.5(a) appoints an official to be designated by this Court to receive service of process in this jurisdiction. The

fact that the lawyer is subject to the disciplinary authority of this jurisdiction may be a factor in determining whether personal jurisdiction may be asserted over the lawyer for civil matters.

Choice of Law

[2] A lawyer may be potentially subject to more than one set of rules of professional conduct which impose different obligations. The lawyer may be licensed to practice in more than one jurisdiction with differing rules, or may be admitted to practice before a particular court with rules that differ from those of the jurisdiction or jurisdictions in which the lawyer is licensed to practice. Additionally, the lawyer's conduct may involve significant contacts with more than one jurisdiction.

[3] Paragraph (b) seeks to resolve such potential conflicts. Its premise is that minimizing conflicts between rules, as well as uncertainty about which rules are applicable, is in the best interest of both clients and the profession (as well as the bodies having authority to regulate the profession). Accordingly, it takes the approach of (i) providing that any particular conduct of a lawyer shall be subject to only one set of rules of professional conduct, (ii) making the determination of which set of rules applies to particular conduct as straightforward as possible, consistent with recognition of appropriate regulatory interests of relevant jurisdictions, and (iii) providing protection from discipline for lawyers who act reasonably in the face of uncertainty.

[4] Paragraph (b)(1) provides that as to a lawyer's conduct relating to a proceeding pending before a tribunal, the lawyer shall be subject only to the rules of the jurisdiction in which the tribunal sits unless the rules of the tribunal including its choice of law rule, provide otherwise. As to all other conduct, including conduct in anticipation of a proceeding not yet pending before a tribunal, paragraph (b)(2) provides that a lawyer shall be subject to the rules of the jurisdiction in which the lawyer's conduct occurred, or, if the predominant effect of the conduct is in another jurisdiction, the rules of that jurisdiction shall be applied to the conduct. In the case of conduct in anticipation of a proceeding that is likely to be before a tribunal, the predominant effect of such conduct could be where the conduct occurred, where the tribunal sits or in another jurisdiction.

[5] When a lawyer's conduct involves significant contacts with more than one jurisdiction, it may not be clear whether the predominant effect of the lawyer's conduct will occur in a jurisdiction other than the one in which the conduct occurred. So long as the lawyer's conduct conforms to the rules of a jurisdiction in which the lawyer reasonably believes the predominant effect will occur, the lawyer shall not be subject to discipline under this Rule.

[6] If two admitting jurisdictions were to proceed against a lawyer for the same conduct, they should, applying this rule, identify the same governing ethics rules. They should take all appropriate steps to see that they do apply the same rule to the same conduct, and in all events should avoid proceeding against a lawyer on the basis of two inconsistent rules.

[7] The choice of law provision applies to lawyers engaged in transnational practice, unless international law, treaties or other agreements between competent regulatory authorities in the affected jurisdictions provide otherwise.

Canon and Code Antecedents

ABA Canons of Professional Ethics: No comparable Canon.

ABA Model Code of Professional Responsibility: No comparable Disciplinary Rule.

Cross-References in Other Rules

Rule 5.5, Comment 19: "A lawyer who practices law in this jurisdiction pursuant to paragraph (c) or (d) or otherwise is subject to the disciplinary authority of this jurisdiction. See **Rule 8.5(a)**."

Legislative History of Model Rule 8.5

1980 Discussion Draft had no comparable provision.

1981 Draft was substantially the same as the 1982 draft (see next entry).

1982 Draft was adopted.

1983 Rule: As originally adopted in 1983, Rule 8.5 consisted of a single sentence: "A lawyer admitted to practice in this jurisdiction is subject to the disciplinary authority of this jurisdiction although engaged in practice elsewhere."

1993 Amendment: At its August 1993 Annual Meeting, the ABA House of Delegates voted to amend Rule 8.5 by (i) rephrasing the first sentence of paragraph (a) (which had been the only sentence in the entire rule), (ii) adding a second sentence to paragraph (a), and (iii) adding an entirely new paragraph (b). The purpose of the new paragraph (b) was to provide guidelines for deciding which jurisdiction's disciplinary rules apply to lawyers who are licensed (either generally or pro hac vice) to practice in more than one jurisdiction. The amendment also included a wholesale revision of the Comment, replacing the three existing paragraphs with six completely new paragraphs, five of which explained the new choice of law rules contained in paragraph (b). The text of the Rule 8.5 as amended in 1993 thus provided as follows:

> (a) *Disciplinary Authority.* [First sentence was same as 2002 version of Rule 8.5(a). Second sentence of 2002 version had not yet been added.] A lawyer may be subject to the disciplinary authority of both this jurisdiction and another jurisdiction where the lawyer is admitted for the same conduct.
>
> (b) *Choice of Law.* In any exercise of the disciplinary authority of this jurisdiction, the rules of professional conduct to be applied shall be as follows:
>
> (1) for conduct in connection with a proceeding in a court before which a lawyer has been admitted to practice (either generally or for purposes of that proceeding), the rules to be applied shall be the rules of the jurisdiction in which the court sits, unless the rules of the court provide otherwise; and
>
> (2) for any other conduct,
>
> (i) if the lawyer is licensed to practice only in this jurisdiction, the rules to be applied shall be the rules of this jurisdiction, and
>
> (ii) if the lawyer is licensed to practice in this and another jurisdiction, the rules to be applied shall be the rules of the admitting jurisdiction in which the lawyer principally practices; provided, however, that if particular conduct clearly

has its predominant effect in another jurisdiction in which the lawyer is licensed to practice, the rules of that jurisdiction shall be applied to that conduct.

The 1993 amendment was proposed by the ABA's Standing Committee on Ethics and Professional Responsibility. We reprint here excerpts from the committee report submitted in support of the amendment (with most citations omitted):

*ABA Committee Report Explaining 1993 Amendment to Rule 8.5**

The objective of this proposed change in Rule 8.5 is to bring some measure of certainty and clarity to the frequently encountered, and often difficult, decisions a lawyer must make when encountering a situation in which the lawyer is potentially subject to differing ethical requirements of more than one jurisdiction. It is generally the case that such decisions cannot await an authoritative ruling or advisory opinion from an independent source.

The most compelling circumstance of a lawyer caught between conflicting ethical obligations in all likelihood is that where a lawyer has become aware of a client's fraud committed in the course of the lawyer's representation, and the rule of one jurisdiction with authority over the lawyer would require disclosure of the fraud and that of another jurisdiction with authority would forbid it. But this is by no means the only circumstance in which the problem arises. . . .

[E]xisting authority as to choice of law in the area of ethics rules is unclear and inconsistent. Some authorities suggest that particular conduct should be subject to only one set of rules, while others suggest that more than one set of rules can apply simultaneously to the same conduct. Widely differing approaches to how to identify the applicable rules have been taken. . . .

The proposed amendment to Rule 8.5 seeks to provide clear answers to these problems in nearly all cases. In litigation, the ethical rules of the tribunal, and only those rules, would apply. In other matters, the multiply admitted lawyer would be subject only to the rules of the jurisdiction where he or she principally practices, except when the particular conduct clearly has its predominant effect in another admitting jurisdiction. . . .

[I]t might be argued that, because of the exception for particular conduct that clearly has its predominant effect in another jurisdiction, the proposal falls short of achieving perfect clarity and certainty. This is indeed true, and there may be instances in which it is difficult to define the "particular conduct" and to decide whether it has its "predominant effect" in one jurisdiction or another. However, to provide for no exception would allow substantial conduct to occur in a second admitting jurisdiction without being subject to that jurisdiction's rules. . . .

2002 Amendments: At its August 2002 Annual Meeting, by voice vote, the ABA House of Delegates approved significant amendments to ABA Model Rule 8.5. The main changes were (i) to add the second sentence of Rule 8.5(a) (regarding a lawyer not admitted in the jurisdiction), (ii) to delete the phrase "where the lawyer is admitted" in the last sentence of Rule 8.5(a), and (iii) to replace the pre-2002 version of Rules 8.5(b)(1) and (2) (see "1993 Amendment" above).

The Comment was extensively amended as well in 2002, and Comment 5 was added. Most of the amendments were proposed by the ABA Commission on Multijurisdictional Practice, which was formed in July 2000 to study issues pertaining to the practice of law by lawyers in jurisdictions where they are not admitted

* Committee Reports do not represent official policy of the ABA. They are for information only, and the opinions are those of the authors of the report.

to practice, either permanently or pro hac vice. However, the last two sentences of Comment 1 (regarding service of process and personal jurisdiction) were added based on negotiations between the MJP Commission and lawyers from the Ohio State Bar Association. The Ohio lawyers wanted to ensure that lawyers who harmed clients in states where they were not admitted would be amenable to disciplinary and civil jurisdiction in those states.

The Final Reports of the ABA Commission on Multijurisdictional Practice regarding Rule 8.5 and related issues are available online at the MJP Commission's website at *http://www.americanbar.org/groups/professional_responsibility/committees_commissions/commission_on_multijurisditional_practice.html* (look for "Final Reports, as adopted August 12, 2002"). We excerpt here (with footnotes omitted) the portions of Report 201C that relate directly to the 2002 Amendments to Rule 8.5:

*Excerpts from Final Report of the ABA Commission on Multijurisdictional Practice in Support of Amendments to Rule 8.5**

> It is important that state regulatory authorities acknowledge the increasing prevalence of cross-border law practice and respond appropriately. Allowances must be made for effectively regulating lawyers who practice law outside the states in which they are licensed. Sanctions must be available both against lawyers who do unauthorized work outside their home states and against those who violate rules of professional conduct when they engage in otherwise permissible multijurisdictional law practice.
>
> The Ethics 2000 Commission proposed amending Rule 8.5(a) (Disciplinary Authority) to make clear that a jurisdiction in which a lawyer engages in disciplinary misconduct may sanction the lawyer regardless of whether the lawyer is licensed to practice law in that jurisdiction. Most significantly, a sentence would be added to provide that: "A lawyer not admitted in this jurisdiction is also subject to the disciplinary authority of this jurisdiction if the lawyer provides or offers to provide any legal services in this jurisdiction." . . . As the Ethics 2000 Commission noted, "this is an appropriate Rule to adopt in the *Model Rules of Professional Conduct,* given that a jurisdiction in which a lawyer is not admitted may be the one most interested in disciplining the lawyer for improper conduct." As a further enhancement to this Rule, the MJP Commission recommends that the following statement be added to the end of Comment [1]: "Reciprocal enforcement of a jurisdiction's disciplinary findings and sanctions will further advance the purposes of this Rule. See Rules 6 and 22, *ABA Model Rules for Lawyer Disciplinary Enforcement.*"
>
> Additionally, the Ethics 2000 Commission proposed amending Rule 8.5(b) (Choice of Law) in two principal respects. First, a number of changes would clarify the choice of law rule applicable to lawyers participating in adjudications. It would provide that a lawyer who participates in a formal adjudication before any "tribunal"—and not only a "court"—is bound by the rules of professional conduct of the jurisdiction in which the tribunal sits or by the rules of the tribunal itself if they provide otherwise.
>
> Second, the Ethics 2000 Commission proposed changing the choice of law rule applicable to legal work outside the context of adjudications. . . . Under the proposed amendment, the applicable rules would be those of the jurisdiction in which the lawyer's conduct had its predominant effect or, where the conduct did not have its predominant effect in a single jurisdiction, the rules of the jurisdiction in which the conduct occurred. However, a lawyer who acts reasonably in the face of uncertainty about which jurisdiction's rules apply would not be subject to discipline.

* Committee Reports do not represent official policy of the ABA. They are for information only, and the opinions are those of the authors of the report.

Selected State Variations

California: Rule 1-100(D), headed "Geographic Scope of Rules," provides as follows:

> (1) As to members: These rules shall govern the activities of members in and outside this state, except as members lawfully practicing outside this state may be specifically required by a jurisdiction in which they are practicing to follow rules of professional conduct different from these rules.
>
> (2) As to lawyers from other jurisdictions who are not members: These rules shall also govern the activities of lawyers while engaged in the performance of lawyer functions in this state; but nothing contained in these rules shall be deemed to authorize the performance of such functions by such persons in this state except as otherwise permitted by law.

In addition, in 2004 California Supreme Court adopted Rules 964 and 965, which permit "Registered Legal Services Attorneys" and "Registered In-House Counsel" to practice law in California without being members of the California Bar. Each requires that qualifying attorneys "[a]bide by all of the laws and rules that govern members of the State Bar of California, including the Minimum Continuing Legal Education (MCLE) requirements." Rules 966 and 967, respectively entitled "Attorneys Practicing Law Temporarily in California as Part of Litigation" and "Non-Litigating Attorneys Temporarily in California to Provide Legal Services," each contain the following language:

> [*Conditions*] By practicing law in California pursuant to this rule, an attorney agrees that he or she is providing legal services in California subject to:
>
> (1) The jurisdiction of the State Bar of California;
>
> (2) The jurisdiction of the courts of this state to the same extent as is a member of the State Bar of California; and
>
> (3) The laws of the State of California relating to the practice of law, the State Bar of Professional Conduct, the rules and regulations of the State Bar of California, and these rules.

Substantial excerpts from Rules 964 through 967 are reprinted below in our chapter on California Materials following Rule 1-300 of the California Rules of Professional Conduct.

District of Columbia: Rule 8.5(a) omits the second sentence of ABA Model Rule 8.5(a) ("A lawyer not admitted in this jurisdiction is also subject to the disciplinary authority of this jurisdiction if the lawyer provides or offers to provide any legal services in this jurisdiction.") Rule 8.5(b)(2) provides as follows:

> (2) For any other conduct,
>
> (i) If the lawyer is licensed to practice only in this jurisdiction, the rules to be applied shall be the rules of this jurisdiction, and
>
> (ii) If the lawyer is licensed to practice in this and another jurisdiction, the rules to be applied shall be the rules of the admitting jurisdiction in which the lawyer principally practices; provided, however, that if particular conduct clearly has its predominant effect in another jurisdiction in which the lawyer is licensed to practice, the rules of that jurisdiction shall be applied to that conduct.

Florida: In Supreme Court Rule 3-4.6, Florida has adopted the language of Rule 8.5(b) except for the second sentence of paragraph (b)(2). In addition, Florida Rule 3-4.1 provides as follows:

> Every member of The Florida Bar and every attorney of another state or foreign country who provides or offers to provide any legal services in this state is within the jurisdiction and subject to the disciplinary authority of this court and its agencies under this rule and is charged with notice and held to know the provisions of this rule and the standards of ethical and professional conduct prescribed by this court. Jurisdiction over an attorney of another state who is not a member of The Florida Bar shall be limited to conduct as an attorney in relation to the business for which the attorney was permitted to practice in this state and the privilege in the future to practice law in the state of Florida.

When the Florida Supreme Court rejected a proposal to amend this rule in 1999, it said: "Out-of-state lawyers are not lawyers who are subject to the Rules Regulating the Florida Bar; rather, they are 'nonlawyers' subject to chapter 10 unlicensed practice of law charges if they . . . engage in improper solicitation or advertising in Florida." See Amendments to Rules Regulating the Florida Bar—Advertising Rules, 762 So. 2d 392, 393-395 (Fla. 1999).

Georgia: Rules 8.5(a) and (b) both use the phrase "Domestic and Foreign Lawyer" in place of the phrase "lawyer." Georgia defines those terms as follows:

> "Domestic Lawyer" denotes a person authorized to practice law by the duly constituted and authorized government body of any State or Territory of the United States or the District of Columbia but not authorized by the Supreme Court of Georgia or its rules to practice law in the State of Georgia.
>
> "Foreign Lawyer" denotes a person authorized to practice law by the duly constituted and authorized government body of any foreign nation but not authorized by the Supreme Court of Georgia or its Rules to practice law in the State of Georgia.

In addition, Georgia Rule 9.4 generally tracks Rules 6 and 22 of the ABA Model Rules of Lawyer Disciplinary Enforcement (reprinted below in the Related Materials for ABA Model Rule 8.5), which govern jurisdiction and reciprocal discipline.

Illinois: Illinois Supreme Court Rules 716 and 717 (summarized above in the Related Materials following ABA Model Rule 5.5) permit in-house and legal services lawyers to engage in limited law practice in Illinois. Rules 716 and 717 both provide that all lawyers licensed under the rules "shall be subject to the jurisdiction of the Court for disciplinary purposes to the same extent as all other lawyers licensed to practice law in this state."

Maryland: Rule 8.5(a) explicitly extends disciplinary jurisdiction to any lawyer who "holds himself or herself out as practicing law in this State," or who "has an obligation to supervise or control another lawyer practicing law in this State whose conduct constitutes a violation of these Rules."

Massachusetts: Rule 8.5(b)(2) refers to the "jurisdiction in which the lawyer's principal office is located" instead of where "the predominant effect of the conduct" occurred. The rule also adds several comments that clarify how the choice of law provisions are supposed to operate.

Nevada: Rule 8.5 consists of only one sentence: "A lawyer admitted to practice in this jurisdiction is subject to the disciplinary authority of this jurisdiction although engaged in practice elsewhere." Also relevant is Nevada Rule 7.2(a), which states as follows: "These Rules shall not apply to any advertisement broadcast or disseminated in another jurisdiction in which the advertising lawyer is admitted if such advertisement complies with the rules governing lawyer advertising in that jurisdiction and the advertisement is not intended primarily for broadcast or dissemination within the State of Nevada."

New Jersey deletes the last sentence of Rule 8.5(b) ("A lawyer shall not be subject to discipline. . . .").

New York: Rule 8.5 provides as follows:

> (a) A lawyer admitted to practice in this state is subject to the disciplinary authority of this state, regardless of where the lawyer's conduct occurs. A lawyer may be subject to the disciplinary authority of both this state and another jurisdiction where the lawyer is admitted for the same conduct.
>
> (b) In any exercise of the disciplinary authority of this state, the Rules of Professional Conduct to be applied shall be as follows:
>
> (1) For conduct in connection with a proceeding in a court before which a lawyer has been admitted to practice (either generally or for purposes of that proceeding), the rules to be applied shall be the rules of the jurisdiction in which the court sits, unless the rules of the court provide otherwise; and
>
> (2) For any other conduct:
>
> (i) If the lawyer is licensed to practice only in this state, the rules to be applied shall be the rules of this state, and
>
> (ii) If the lawyer is licensed to practice in this state and another jurisdiction, the rules to be applied shall be the rules of the admitting jurisdiction in which the lawyer principally practices; provided, however, that if particular conduct clearly has its predominant effect in another jurisdiction in which the lawyer is licensed to practice, the rules of that jurisdiction shall be applied to that conduct.

Oregon: Rule 8.6 designates certain entities authorized to issue advisory ethics opinions and provides that in any disciplinary matter, the tribunal "may consider any lawyer's good faith effort to comply with an opinion" in evaluating the lawyer's conduct or in mitigation of sanction.

South Carolina: S.C. Appellate Court Rule 418 requires any "unlicensed lawyer" (defined as "any person who is admitted to practice law in another jurisdiction but who is not admitted to practice law in South Carolina") to comply with South Carolina's lawyer advertising rules (Rules 7.1 through 7.5) if the unlicensed lawyer engages in any of six specified forms of advertising or solicitation.

Texas: Rule 8.05(b) provides as follows:

> (b) A lawyer admitted to practice in this state is also subject to the disciplinary authority of this state for:
>
> (1) an advertisement in the public media that does not comply with these rules and that is broadcast or disseminated in another jurisdiction, even if the advertisement complies with the rules governing lawyer advertisements in that jurisdiction, if the broadcast or dissemination of the advertisement is intended to be received by prospective clients in this state and is intended to secure employment to be performed in this state; and
>
> (2) a written solicitation communication that does not comply with these rules and that is mailed in another jurisdiction, even if the communication complies with the rules governing written solicitation communications by lawyers in that jurisdiction, if the communication is mailed to an addressee in this state or is intended to secure employment to be performed in this state.

Virginia rejects the "predominant effect" test used in Rule 8.5(b)(2), favoring instead the rules from the jurisdiction where the lawyer's conduct occurred. The Virginia rule also contains specific provisions regarding lawyers who hold themselves out as Virginia attorneys. Virginia also explicitly rejects Comments 2 through

7 of the Model Rule and adopts its own explanations for how to resolve conflicts between different choice of law rules.

Related Materials

ABA Commission on Ethics 20/20: In 2009, the ABA created the Commission on Ethics 20/20, which is comprehensively reviewing the ABA Model Rules of Professional Conduct and other regulatory sources in the context of globalization and changes in technology. With respect to Rule 8.5, the Commission is particularly interested in differing approaches to conflicts of interest, because a representation may create a conflict requiring client consent in one jurisdiction (in the U.S. or overseas) but not in another jurisdiction. Reflecting this interest, on January 18, 2011 the Commission released an Issues Paper discussing various problems with the current version of Rule 8.5, and the Commission has preliminarily discussed possible amendments to Rule 8.5.

When we went to press in September 2011, the Commission had not released (and had no immediate plans to release) any proposals to amend Rule 8.5. However, in September 2011 the Commission proposed for public comment a new Comment 23 to Rule 1.7 that would (according to the Commission's report) "provide more predictability to clients and their lawyers by permitting them to agree in advance to be bound by the conflict rules of a particular jurisdiction." We reprint the text of that proposed Comment in our entry entitled "ABA Commission on Ethics 20/20" in the Related Materials after Rule 1.7.

ABA Formal Ethics Opinions: See ABA Formal Ethics Ops. 91-360 (1991) and 01-423 n.21 (2001).

ABA Model Rules of Lawyer Disciplinary Enforcement: Comment 1 to ABA Model Rule 8.5 expressly mentions Rules 6 and 22 of the ABA Model Rules for Lawyer Disciplinary Enforcement. Those rules provide, in relevant part, as follows:

Rule 6. Jurisdiction

A. *Lawyers Admitted to Practice.* Any lawyer admitted to practice law in this jurisdiction, including any formerly admitted lawyer with respect to acts committed prior to resignation, suspension, disbarment, or transfer to inactive status . . . and any lawyer specially admitted by a court of this jurisdiction for a particular proceeding and any lawyer not admitted in this jurisdiction who practices law or renders or offers to render any legal services in this jurisdiction, is subject to the disciplinary jurisdiction of this court and the board.

Rule 22. Reciprocal Discipline and Reciprocal Disability Inactive Status

A. *Disciplinary Counsel Duty to Obtain Order of Discipline or Disability Inactive Status from Other Jurisdiction.* Upon being disciplined or transferred to disability inactive status in another jurisdiction, a lawyer admitted to practice in [this jurisdiction] shall promptly inform disciplinary counsel of the discipline or transfer. . . .

D. *Discipline to be Imposed.* . . . [T]his court shall impose the identical discipline or disability inactive status unless disciplinary counsel or the lawyer demonstrates, or this court finds that it clearly appears upon the face of the record from which the discipline is predicated, that:

(1) The procedure was so lacking in notice or opportunity to be heard as to constitute a deprivation of due process; or

(2) There was such infirmity of proof establishing the misconduct as to give rise to the clear conviction that the court could not, consistent with its duty, accept as final the conclusion on that subject; or

(3) The discipline imposed would result in grave injustice or be offensive to the public policy of the jurisdiction; or

(4) The reason for the original transfer to disability inactive status no longer exists.

If this court determines that any of those elements exists, this court shall enter such other order as it deems appropriate. The burden is on the party seeking different discipline in this jurisdiction to demonstrate that the imposition of the same discipline is not appropriate.

E. *Conclusiveness of Adjudication in Other Jurisdictions.* In all other aspects, a final adjudication in another jurisdiction that a lawyer, whether or not admitted in that jurisdiction, has been guilty of misconduct or should be transferred to disability inactive status shall establish conclusively the misconduct or the disability for purposes of a disciplinary or disability proceeding in this jurisdiction.

For more information concerning the ABA Model Rules of Disciplinary Enforcement, go to *http://www.americanbar.org/groups/professional_responsibility/resources/lawyer_ethics_regulation/model_rules_for_lawyer_disciplinary_enforcement.html.*

Federal Government Attorneys: In 1998, Congress passed 28 U.S.C. §530B, entitled "Ethical Standards for Attorneys for the Government" (commonly called the McDade Act), which provides, in pertinent part, as follows:

(a) An attorney for the Government shall be subject to State laws and rules, and local Federal court rules, governing attorneys in each State where such attorney engages in that attorney's duties, to the same extent and in the same manner as other attorneys in that State.

When the McDade Act became law, all federal government lawyers were for the first time formally required to comply with the rules of professional conduct of the states in which they practiced. The long and winding history leading up to §530B is recounted in the Related Materials following Rule 4.2 in the entry entitled "Department of Justice Rules."

Federal Rules of Appellate Procedure: Fed. R. App. P. 46(b)(1) provides that a federal court of appeals may suspend or disbar a member of the court's bar if the member "(A) has been suspended or disbarred from practice in any other court; or (B) is guilty of conduct unbecoming a member of the court's bar."

Jurisdiction Over Out-of-State Lawyers: A state's willingness to exercise jurisdiction over an unethical lawyer licensed only in other states may depend on whether the alleged misconduct in the non-licensing state is related to the practice of law. For example, Florida Supreme Court Rule 3-4.1 provides: "Every . . . attorney of another state or foreign country who provides or offers to provide any legal services in this state is within the jurisdiction and subject to the disciplinary authority of this court and its agencies. . . . Jurisdiction over an attorney of another state who is not a member of The Florida Bar shall be limited to conduct as an attorney in relation to the business for which the attorney was permitted to practice in this state. . . ." In South Carolina, S.C. Appellate Court Rule 418 requires any "unlicensed lawyer" (defined as "any person who is admitted to practice law in another jurisdiction but who is not admitted to practice law in South Carolina") to comply with South

Carolina's lawyer advertising rules (Rules 7.1 through 7.5) if the unlicensed lawyer engages in any of six specified forms of advertising or solicitation.

Model Rules of Professional Conduct for Federal Lawyers: Rule 8.5 provides:

> (a) A Federal lawyer shall comply with the rules of professional conduct applicable to the Federal Agency that employs the Government lawyer or the Federal Agency before which the Federal lawyer practices.
>
> (b) If the Federal Agency has not adopted or promulgated rules of professional conduct, the Federal lawyer shall comply with the rules of professional conduct of the state bars in which the Federal lawyer is admitted to practice.

The Comment to this rule states:

> While the Federal lawyer may remain subject to the governing authority of their licensing jurisdiction, the Federal lawyer is also subject to these Rules. However, when a Government lawyer is engaged in the conduct of Federal Agency legal functions, whether servicing the Federal Agency as a client or serving an individual client in the course of official duties, these Rules are regarded as superseding any conflicting rules applicable in the jurisdictions in which the Government lawyer may be licensed.

Restatement of the Law Governing Lawyers: See Restatement §§1 and 5 in our chapter on the Restatement later in this volume.

INDEX TO THE ABA MODEL RULES OF PROFESSIONAL CONDUCT

Editors' Note. This index was originally prepared by the American Bar Association following the February 2002 Amendments to the ABA Model Rules of Professional Conduct, and was updated by the ABA after the August 2003 amendments to Model Rules 1.6 and 1.13. The authors of this volume have further enhanced the ABA index by adding some additional terms. For example, the Comment to Rule 5.5 was amended in February 2007 to add a reference to the ABA Model Court Rule on Provision of Legal Services Following Determination of Major Disaster, and we have added new entries to the Index to reflect that amendment. For the 2009 edition, we added references to new provisions in Rule 3.8 that govern a prosecutor's duties upon discovering a wrongful conviction. Finally, for the 2010 edition, we added references to the new screening provisions in Rule 1.10. The index was up to date when we went to press in September 2011.

A

D

Restatement of the Law Governing Lawyers*

Editors' Introduction. The Restatement of the Law Governing Lawyers is published by the American Law Institute (ALI), an organization established in 1923 "to promote the clarification and simplification of the law and its better adaptation to social needs." The ALI drafts restatements of the law in many fields (*e.g.*, contracts, agency, and torts).

In 1986, realizing that the regulation of lawyers had become a specialized and highly developed field of law, the ALI began organizing the massive project of drafting a restatement of the law governing lawyers. The ALI appointed Professor Charles Wolfram as the Reporter, and named Professors John Leubsdorf, Thomas Morgan, and Linda Mullenix as Associate Reporters. From 1988 through 1997, the ALI annually published proposed drafts of various sections of the Restatement, accompanying each section with Comments, Illustrations, and a Reporter's Note. In 1998, the full membership of the ALI approved the entire draft Restatement and sent it on to the Reporters to make final changes (in consultation with the various groups within the ALI) to reflect amendments and discussions over the years.

In 2000, the ALI published the final version of the Restatement of the Law Governing Lawyers. With all of the Comments, Illustrations, and Reporter's Notes, it is over 1,000 pages. We reprint below only the black letter sections from the Restatement, without any of the Comments, Illustrations, or Reporter's Notes. Our version of the Restatement is based on the final version of the Restatement as published in 2000, which has not been amended in any way since then. The full Restatement of the Law Governing Lawyers (and a pocket part) can be ordered from the ALI's website at *www.ali.org* (click on "Publications Catalog").

In our Related Materials following each ABA Model Rule of Professional Conduct above, we have cross-referenced the Restatement sections most relevant to the ABA Model Rule at hand. However, some ABA Model Rules have no counterpart in the Restatement, and some Restatement sections have no counterpart in the ABA Model Rules.

*Copyright © 1988-2000 by the American Law Institute. Reprinted by permission. All rights reserved.

Contents

TOPIC 3. AUTHORITY TO MAKE DECISIONS

TOPIC 4. A LAWYER'S AUTHORITY TO ACT FOR A CLIENT

TOPIC 5. ENDING A CLIENT-LAWYER RELATIONSHIP

CHAPTER 3 CLIENT AND LAWYER: THE FINANCIAL AND PROPERTY RELATIONSHIP

TOPIC 1. LEGAL CONTROLS ON ATTORNEY FEES

TOPIC 2. A LAWYER'S CLAIM TO COMPENSATION

TOPIC 3. FEE-COLLECTION PROCEDURES

TOPIC 4. PROPERTY AND DOCUMENTS OF CLIENTS AND OTHERS

TOPIC 2. CONFLICTS OF INTEREST BETWEEN A LAWYER AND A CLIENT

TOPIC 3. CONFLICTS OF INTEREST AMONG CURRENT CLIENTS

TOPIC 4. CONFLICTS OF INTEREST WITH A FORMER CLIENT

TOPIC 5. CONFLICTS OF INTEREST DUE TO A LAWYER'S OBLIGATION TO A THIRD PERSON

CHAPTER 1 REGULATION OF THE LEGAL PROFESSION

TOPIC 1. REGULATION OF LAWYERS—IN GENERAL

§1. Regulation of Lawyers—In General

Upon admission to the bar of any jurisdiction, a person becomes a lawyer and is subject to applicable law governing such matters as professional discipline, procedure and evidence, civil remedies, and criminal sanctions.

TOPIC 2. PROCESS OF PROFESSIONAL REGULATION

Title A. Admission to Practice Law

§2. Admission to Practice Law

In order to become a lawyer and qualify to practice law in a jurisdiction of admission, a prospective lawyer must comply with requirements of the jurisdiction relating to such matters as education, other demonstration of competence such as success in a bar examination, and character.

Title B. Authorized and Unauthorized Practice

§3. Jurisdictional Scope of the Practice of Law by a Lawyer

A lawyer currently admitted to practice in a jurisdiction may provide legal services to a client:

(1) at any place within the admitting jurisdiction;

(2) before a tribunal or administrative agency of another jurisdiction or the federal government in compliance with requirements for temporary or regular admission to practice before that tribunal or agency; and

(3) at a place within a jurisdiction in which the lawyer is not admitted to the extent that the lawyer's activities arise out of or are otherwise reasonably related to the lawyer's practice under Subsection (1) or (2).

§4. Unauthorized Practice by a Nonlawyer

A person not admitted to practice as a lawyer (see §2) may not engage in the unauthorized practice of law, and a lawyer may not assist a person to do so.

Title C. Professional Discipline

§5. Professional Discipline

(1) A lawyer is subject to professional discipline for violating any provision of an applicable lawyer code.

(2) A lawyer is also subject to professional discipline under Subsection (1) for attempting to commit a violation, knowingly assisting or inducing another to do so, or knowingly doing so through the acts of another.

(3) A lawyer who knows of another lawyer's violation of applicable rules of professional conduct raising a substantial question of the lawyer's honesty or trustworthiness or the lawyer's fitness as a lawyer in some other respect must report that information to appropriate disciplinary authorities.

TOPIC 3. CIVIL JUDICIAL REMEDIES IN GENERAL

§6. Judicial Remedies Available to a Client or Nonclient for Lawyer Wrongs

For a lawyer's breach of a duty owed to the lawyer's client or to a nonclient, judicial remedies may be available through judgment or order

entered in accordance with the standards applicable to the remedy awarded, including standards concerning limitation of remedies. Judicial remedies include the following:

(1) awarding a sum of money as damages;

(2) providing injunctive relief, including requiring specific performance of a contract or enjoining its nonperformance;

(3) requiring restoration of a specific thing or awarding a sum of money to prevent unjust enrichment;

(4) ordering cancellation or reformation of a contract, deed, or similar instrument;

(5) declaring the rights of the parties, such as determining that an obligation claimed by the lawyer to be owed to the lawyer is not enforceable;

(6) punishing the lawyer for contempt;

(7) enforcing an arbitration award;

(8) disqualifying a lawyer from a representation;

(9) forfeiting a lawyer's fee (see §37);

(10) denying the admission of evidence wrongfully obtained;

(11) dismissing the claim or defense of a litigant represented by the lawyer;

(12) granting a new trial; and

(13) entering a procedural or other sanction.

§7. Judicial Remedies Available to a Lawyer for Client Wrongs

A lawyer may obtain a remedy based on a present or former client's breach of a duty to the lawyer if the remedy:

(1) is appropriate under applicable law governing the remedy; and

(2) does not put the lawyer in a position prohibited by an applicable lawyer code.

TOPIC 4. LAWYER CRIMINAL OFFENSES

§8. Lawyer Criminal Offenses

The traditional and appropriate activities of a lawyer in representing a client in accordance with the requirements of the applicable lawyer code are relevant factors for the tribunal in assessing the propriety of the lawyer's conduct under the criminal law. In other respects, a lawyer is guilty of an offense for an act committed in the course of representing a client to the same extent and on the same basis as would a nonlawyer acting similarly.

TOPIC 5. LAW-FIRM STRUCTURE AND OPERATION

Title A. Association of Lawyers in Law Organizations

§9. Law-Practice Organizations—In General

(1) A lawyer may practice as a solo practitioner, as an employee of another lawyer or law firm, or as a member of a law firm constituted as a partnership, professional corporation, or similar entity.

(2) A lawyer employed by an entity described in Subsection (1) is subject to applicable law governing the creation, operation, management, and dissolution of the entity.

(3) Absent an agreement with the firm providing a more permissive rule, a lawyer leaving a law firm may solicit firm clients:

(a) prior to leaving the firm:

(i) only with respect to firm clients on whose matters the lawyer is actively and substantially working; and

(ii) only after the lawyer has adequately and timely informed the firm of the lawyer's intent to contact firm clients for that purpose; and

(b) after ceasing employment in the firm, to the same extent as any other nonfirm lawyer.

Title B. Limitations on Nonlawyer Involvement in a Law Firm

§10. Limitations on Nonlawyer Involvement in a Law Firm

(1) A nonlawyer may not own any interest in a law firm, and a nonlawyer may not be empowered to or actually direct or control the professional activities of a lawyer in the firm.

(2) A lawyer may not form a partnership or other business enterprise with a nonlawyer if any of the activities of the enterprise consist of the practice of law.

(3) A lawyer or law firm may not share legal fees with a person not admitted to practice as a lawyer, except that:

(a) an agreement by a lawyer with the lawyer's firm or another lawyer in the firm may provide for payment, over a reasonable period of time after the lawyer's death, to the lawyer's estate or to one or more specified persons;

(b) a lawyer who undertakes to complete unfinished legal business of a deceased lawyer may pay to the estate of the deceased lawyer a portion of the total compensation that fairly represents services rendered by the deceased lawyer; and

(c) a lawyer or law firm may include nonlawyer employees in a compensation or retirement plan, even though the plan is based in whole or in part on a profit-sharing arrangement.

Title C. Supervision of Lawyers and Nonlawyers Within an Organization

§11. A Lawyer's Duty of Supervision

(1) A lawyer who is a partner in a law-firm partnership or a principal in a law firm organized as a corporation or similar entity is subject to professional discipline for failing to make reasonable efforts to ensure that the firm has in effect measures giving reasonable assurance that all lawyers in the firm conform to applicable lawyer-code requirements.

(2) A lawyer who has direct supervisory authority over another lawyer is subject to professional discipline for failing to make reasonable efforts to ensure that the other lawyer conforms to applicable lawyer-code requirements.

(3) A lawyer is subject to professional discipline for another lawyer's violation of the rules of professional conduct if:

(a) the lawyer orders or, with knowledge of the specific conduct, ratifies the conduct involved; or

(b) the lawyer is a partner or principal in the law firm, or has direct supervisory authority over the other lawyer, and knows of the conduct at a time when its consequences can be avoided or mitigated but fails to take reasonable remedial measures.

(4) With respect to a nonlawyer employee of a law firm, the lawyer is subject to professional discipline if either:

(a) the lawyer fails to make reasonable efforts to ensure:

(i) that the firm in which the lawyer practices has in effect measures giving reasonable assurance that the nonlawyer's conduct is compatible with the professional obligations of the lawyer; and

(ii) that conduct of a nonlawyer over whom the lawyer has direct supervisory authority is compatible with the professional obligations of the lawyer; or

(b) the nonlawyer's conduct would be a violation of the applicable lawyer code if engaged in by a lawyer, and

(i) the lawyer orders or, with knowledge of the specific conduct, ratifies the conduct; or

(ii) the lawyer is a partner or principal in the law firm, or has direct supervisory authority over the nonlawyer, and knows of the conduct at a time when its consequences can be avoided or mitigated but fails to take reasonable remedial measures.

§12. Duty of a Lawyer Subject to Supervision

(1) For purposes of professional discipline, a lawyer must conform to the requirements of an applicable lawyer code even if the lawyer acted at the direction of another lawyer or other person.

(2) For purposes of professional discipline, a lawyer under the direct supervisory authority of another lawyer does not violate an applicable lawyer code by acting in accordance with the supervisory lawyer's direction based on a reasonable resolution of an arguable question of professional duty.

Title D. Restrictions on the Right to Practice Law

§13. Restrictions on the Right to Practice Law

(1) A lawyer may not offer or enter into a law-firm agreement that restricts the right of the lawyer to practice law after terminating the relationship, except for a restriction incident to the lawyer's retirement from the practice of law.

(2) In settling a client claim, a lawyer may not offer or enter into an agreement that restricts the right of the lawyer to practice law, including the right to represent or take particular action on behalf of other clients.

CHAPTER 2 THE CLIENT-LAWYER RELATIONSHIP

TOPIC 1. CREATING A CLIENT-LAWYER RELATIONSHIP

§14. Formation of a Client-Lawyer Relationship

A relationship of client and lawyer arises when:

(1) a person manifests to a lawyer the person's intent that the lawyer provide legal services for the person; and either

(a) the lawyer manifests to the person consent to do so; or

(b) the lawyer fails to manifest lack of consent to do so, and the lawyer knows or reasonably should know that the person reasonably relies on the lawyer to provide the services; or

(2) a tribunal with power to do so appoints the lawyer to provide the services.

§15. A Lawyer's Duties to a Prospective Client

(1) When a person discusses with a lawyer the possibility of their forming a client-lawyer relationship for a matter and no such relationship ensues, the lawyer must:

(a) not subsequently use or disclose confidential information learned in the consultation, except to the extent permitted with respect to confidential information of a client or former client as stated in §§61–67;

(b) protect the person's property in the lawyer's custody as stated in §§44–46; and

(c) use reasonable care to the extent the lawyer provides the person legal services.

(2) A lawyer subject to Subsection (1) may not represent a client whose interests are materially adverse to those of a former prospective client in the same or a substantially related matter when the lawyer or another lawyer whose disqualification is imputed to the lawyer under §§123 and 124 has received from the prospective client confidential information that could be significantly harmful to the prospective client in the matter, except that such a representation is permissible if:

(a)(i) any personally prohibited lawyer takes reasonable steps to avoid exposure to confidential information other than information appropriate to determine whether to represent the prospective client, and (ii) such lawyer is screened as stated in §124(2)(b) and (c); or

(b) both the affected client and the prospective client give informed consent to the representation under the limitations and conditions provided in §122.

TOPIC 2. SUMMARY OF THE DUTIES UNDER A CLIENT-LAWYER RELATIONSHIP

§16. A Lawyer's Duties to a Client—In General

To the extent consistent with the lawyer's other legal duties and subject to the other provisions of this Restatement, a lawyer must, in matters within the scope of the representation:

(1) proceed in a manner reasonably calculated to advance a client's lawful objectives, as defined by the client after consultation;

(2) act with reasonable competence and diligence;

(3) comply with obligations concerning the client's confidences and property, avoid impermissible conflicting interests, deal honestly with the client, and not employ advantages arising from the client-lawyer relationship in a manner adverse to the client; and

(4) fulfill valid contractual obligations to the client.

§17. A Client's Duties to a Lawyer

Subject to the other provisions of this Restatement, in matters covered by the representation a client must:

(1) compensate a lawyer for services and expenses as stated in Chapter 3;

(2) indemnify the lawyer for liability to which the client has exposed the lawyer without the lawyer's fault; and

(3) fulfill any valid contractual obligations to the lawyer.

§18. Client-Lawyer Contracts

(1) A contract between a lawyer and client concerning the client-lawyer relationship, including a contract modifying an existing contract, may be enforced by either party if the contract meets other applicable requirements, except that:

(a) if the contract or modification is made beyond a reasonable time after the lawyer has begun to represent the client in the matter (see §38(1)), the client may avoid it unless the lawyer shows that the contract and the circumstances of its formation were fair and reasonable to the client; and

(b) if the contract is made after the lawyer has finished providing services, the client may avoid it if the client was not informed of facts needed to evaluate the appropriateness of the lawyer's compensation or other benefits conferred on the lawyer by the contract.

(2) A tribunal should construe a contract between client and lawyer as a reasonable person in the circumstances of the client would have construed it.

§19. Agreements Limiting Client or Lawyer Duties

(1) Subject to other requirements stated in this Restatement, a client and lawyer may agree to limit a duty that a lawyer would otherwise owe to the client if:

(a) the client is adequately informed and consents; and

(b) the terms of the limitation are reasonable in the circumstances.

(2) A lawyer may agree to waive a client's duty to pay or other duty owed to the lawyer.

TOPIC 3. AUTHORITY TO MAKE DECISIONS

§20. Lawyer's Duty to Inform and Consult with a Client

(1) A lawyer must keep a client reasonably informed about the matter and must consult with a client to a reasonable extent concerning decisions to be made by the lawyer under §§21–23.

(2) A lawyer must promptly comply with a client's reasonable requests for information.

(3) A lawyer must notify a client of decisions to be made by the client under §§21-23 and must explain a matter to the extent reasonably necessary to permit the client to make informed decisions regarding the representation.

§21. Allocating the Authority to Decide Between a Client and a Lawyer

As between client and lawyer:

(1) A client and lawyer may agree which of them will make specified decisions, subject to the requirements stated in §§18, 19, 22, 23, and other provisions of this Restatement. The agreement may be superseded by another valid agreement.

(2) A client may instruct a lawyer during the representation, subject to the requirements stated in §§22, 23, and other provisions of this Restatement.

(3) Subject to Subsections (1) and (2) a lawyer may take any lawful measure within the scope of representation that is reasonably calculated to advance a client's objectives as defined by the client, consulting with the client as required by §20.

(4) A client may ratify an act of a lawyer that was not previously authorized.

§22. Authority Reserved to a Client

(1) As between client and lawyer, subject to Subsection (2) and §23, the following and comparable decisions are reserved to the client except when the client has validly authorized the lawyer to make the particular decision: whether and on what terms to settle a claim; how a criminal defendant should plead; whether a criminal defendant should waive jury trial; whether a criminal defendant should testify; and whether to appeal in a civil proceeding or criminal prosecution.

(2) A client may not validly authorize a lawyer to make the decisions described in Subsection (1) when other law (such as criminal procedure rules governing pleas, jury-trial waiver, and defendant testimony) requires the client's personal participation or approval.

(3) Regardless of any contrary contract with a lawyer, a client may revoke a lawyer's authority to make the decisions described in Subsection (1).

§23. Authority Reserved to a Lawyer

As between client and lawyer, a lawyer retains authority that may not be overridden by a contract with or an instruction from the client:

(1) to refuse to perform, counsel, or assist future or ongoing acts in the representation that the lawyer reasonably believes to be unlawful;

(2) to make decisions or take actions in the representation that the lawyer reasonably believes to be required by law or an order of a tribunal.

§24. A Client with Diminished Capacity

(1) When a client's capacity to make adequately considered decisions in connection with the representation is diminished, whether because of minority, physical illness, mental disability, or other cause, the lawyer must, as far as reasonably possible, maintain a normal client-lawyer relationship with the client and act in the best interests of the client as stated in Subsection (2).

(2) A lawyer representing a client with diminished capacity as described in Subsection (1) and for whom no guardian or other representative is available to act, must, with respect to a matter within the scope of the representation, pursue the lawyer's reasonable view of the client's objectives or interests as the client would define them if able to make adequately considered decisions on the matter, even if the client expresses no wishes or gives contrary instructions.

(3) If a client with diminished capacity as described in Subsection (1) has a guardian or other person legally entitled to act for the client, the client's lawyer must treat that person as entitled to act with respect to the client's interests in the matter, unless:

(a) the lawyer represents the client in a matter against the interests of that person; or

(b) that person instructs the lawyer to act in a manner that the lawyer knows will violate the person's legal duties toward the client.

(4) A lawyer representing a client with diminished capacity as described in Subsection (1) may seek the appointment of a guardian or take other protective action within the scope of the representation when doing so is practical and will advance the client's objectives or interests, determined as stated in Subsection (2).

TOPIC 4. A LAWYER'S AUTHORITY TO ACT FOR A CLIENT

§25. Appearance Before a Tribunal

A lawyer who enters an appearance before a tribunal on behalf of a person is presumed to represent that person as a client. The presumption may be rebutted.

§26. A Lawyer's Actual Authority

A lawyer's act is considered to be that of a client in proceedings before a tribunal or in dealings with third persons when:

(1) the client has expressly or impliedly authorized the act;

(2) authority concerning the act is reserved to the lawyer as stated in §23; or

(3) the client ratifies the act.

§27. A Lawyer's Apparent Authority

A lawyer's act is considered to be that of the client in proceedings before a tribunal or in dealings with a third person if the tribunal or third person reasonably assumes that the lawyer is authorized to do the act on the basis of the client's (and not the lawyer's) manifestations of such authorization.

§28. A Lawyer's Knowledge; Notification to a Lawyer; and Statements of a Lawyer

(1) Information imparted to a lawyer during and relating to the representation of a client is attributed to the client for the purpose of determining the client's rights and liabilities in matters in which the lawyer represents the client, unless those rights or liabilities require proof of the client's personal knowledge or intentions or the lawyer's legal duties preclude disclosure of the information to the client.

(2) Unless applicable law otherwise provides, a third person may give notification to a client, in a matter in which the client is represented by a lawyer, by giving notification to the client's lawyer, unless the third person knows of circumstances reasonably indicating that the lawyer's authority to receive notification has been abrogated.

(3) A lawyer's unprivileged statement is admissible in evidence against a client as if it were the client's statement if either:

(a) the client authorized the lawyer to make a statement concerning the subject; or

(b) the statement concerns a matter within the scope of the representation and was made by the lawyer during it.

§29. A Lawyer's Act or Advice as Mitigating or Avoiding a Client's Responsibility

(1) When a client's intent or mental state is in issue, a tribunal may consider otherwise admissible evidence of a lawyer's advice to the client.

(2) In deciding whether to impose a sanction on a person or to relieve a person from a criminal or civil ruling, default, or judgment, a tribunal may consider otherwise admissible evidence to prove or disprove that the lawyer who represented the person did so inadequately or contrary to the client's instructions.

§30. A Lawyer's Liability to a Third Person for Conduct on Behalf of a Client

(1) For improper conduct while representing a client, a lawyer is subject to professional discipline as stated in §5, to civil liability as stated in Chapter 4, and to prosecution as provided in the criminal law (see §7).

(2) Unless at the time of contracting the lawyer or third person disclaimed such liability, a lawyer is subject to liability to third persons on contracts the lawyer entered into on behalf of a client if:

(a) the client's existence or identity was not disclosed to the third person; or

(b) the contract is between the lawyer and a third person who provides goods or services used by lawyers and who, as the lawyer knows or reasonably should know, relies on the lawyer's credit.

(3) A lawyer is subject to liability to a third person for damages for loss proximately caused by the lawyer's acting without authority from a client under §26 if:

(a) the lawyer tortiously misrepresents to the third person that the lawyer has authority to make a contract, conveyance, or affirmation on behalf of the client and the third person reasonably relies on the misrepresentation; or

(b) the lawyer purports to make a contract, conveyance, or affirmation on behalf of the client, unless the lawyer manifests that the lawyer does not warrant that the lawyer is authorized to act or the other party knows that the lawyer is not authorized to act.

TOPIC 5. ENDING A CLIENT-LAWYER RELATIONSHIP

§31. Termination of a Lawyer's Authority

(1) A lawyer must comply with applicable law requiring notice to or permission of a tribunal when terminating a representation and with an order of a tribunal requiring the representation to continue.

(2) Subject to Subsection (1) and §33, a lawyer's actual authority to represent a client ends when:

(a) the client discharges the lawyer;

(b) the client dies or, in the case of a corporation or similar organization, loses its capacity to function as such;

(c) the lawyer withdraws;

(d) the lawyer dies or becomes physically or mentally incapable of providing representation, is disbarred or suspended from practicing law, or is ordered by a tribunal to cease representing a client; or

(e) the representation ends as provided by contract or because the lawyer has completed the contemplated services.

(3) A lawyer's apparent authority to act for a client with respect to another person ends when the other person knows or should know of facts from which it can be reasonably inferred that the lawyer lacks actual authority, including knowledge of any event described in Subsection (2).

§32. Discharge by a Client and Withdrawal by a Lawyer

(1) Subject to Subsection (5), a client may discharge a lawyer at any time.

(2) Subject to Subsection (5), a lawyer may not represent a client or, where representation has commenced, must withdraw from the representation of a client if:

(a) the representation will result in the lawyer's violating rules of professional conduct or other law;

(b) the lawyer's physical or mental condition materially impairs the lawyer's ability to represent the client; or

(c) the client discharges the lawyer.

(3) Subject to Subsections (4) and (5), a lawyer may withdraw from representing a client if:

(a) withdrawal can be accomplished without material adverse effect on the interests of the client;

(b) the lawyer reasonably believes withdrawal is required in circumstances stated in Subsection (2);

(c) the client gives informed consent;

(d) the client persists in a course of action involving the lawyer's services that the lawyer reasonably believes is criminal, fraudulent, or in breach of the client's fiduciary duty;

(e) the lawyer reasonably believes the client has used or threatens to use the lawyer's services to perpetrate a crime or fraud;

(f) the client insists on taking action that the lawyer considers repugnant or imprudent;

(g) the client fails to fulfill a substantial financial or other obligation to the lawyer regarding the lawyer's services and the lawyer has given the client reasonable warning that the lawyer will withdraw unless the client fulfills the obligation;

(h) the representation has been rendered unreasonably difficult by the client or by the irreparable breakdown of the client-lawyer relationship; or

(i) other good cause for withdrawal exists.

(4) In the case of permissive withdrawal under Subsections (3)(f)-(i), a lawyer may not withdraw if the harm that withdrawal would cause significantly exceeds the harm to the lawyer or others in not withdrawing.

(5) Notwithstanding Subsections (1)-(4), a lawyer must comply with applicable law requiring notice to or permission of a tribunal when terminating a representation and with a valid order of a tribunal requiring the representation to continue.

§33. A Lawyer's Duties When a Representation Terminates

(1) In terminating a representation, a lawyer must take steps to the extent reasonably practicable to protect the client's interests, such as

giving notice to the client of the termination, allowing time for employment of other counsel, surrendering papers and property to which the client is entitled, and refunding any advance payment of fee the lawyer has not earned.

(2) Following termination of a representation, a lawyer must:

(a) observe obligations to a former client such as those dealing with client confidences (see Chapter 5), conflicts of interest (see Chapter 8), client property and documents (see §§44-46), and fee collection (see §41);

(b) take no action on behalf of a former client without new authorization and give reasonable notice, to those who might otherwise be misled, that the lawyer lacks authority to act for the client;

(c) take reasonable steps to convey to the former client any material communication the lawyer receives relating to the matter involved in the representation; and

(d) take no unfair advantage of a former client by abusing knowledge or trust acquired by means of the representation.

CHAPTER 3 CLIENT AND LAWYER: THE FINANCIAL AND PROPERTY RELATIONSHIP

TOPIC 1. LEGAL CONTROLS ON ATTORNEY FEES

§34. Reasonable and Lawful Fees

A lawyer may not charge a fee larger than is reasonable in the circumstances or that is prohibited by law.

§35. Contingent-Fee Arrangements

(1) A lawyer may contract with a client for a fee the size or payment of which is contingent on the outcome of a matter, unless the contract violates §34 or another provision of this Restatement or the size or payment of the fee is:

(a) contingent on success in prosecuting or defending a criminal proceeding; or

(b) contingent on a specified result in a divorce proceeding or a proceeding concerning custody of a child.

(2) Unless the contract construed in the circumstances indicates otherwise, when a lawyer has contracted for a contingent fee, the lawyer is entitled to receive the specified fee only when and to the extent the client receives payment.

§36. Forbidden Client-Lawyer Financial Arrangements

(1) A lawyer may not acquire a proprietary interest in the cause of action or subject matter of litigation that the lawyer is conducting for a client, except that the lawyer may:

(a) acquire a lien as provided by §43 to secure the lawyer's fee or expenses; and

(b) contract with a client for a contingent fee in a civil case except when prohibited as stated in §35.

(2) A lawyer may not make or guarantee a loan to a client in connection with pending or contemplated litigation that the lawyer is conducting for the client, except that the lawyer may make or guarantee a loan covering court costs and expenses of litigation, the repayment of which to the lawyer may be contingent on the outcome of the matter.

(3) A lawyer may not, before the lawyer ceases to represent a client, make an agreement giving the lawyer literary or media rights to a portrayal or account based in substantial part on information relating to the representation.

§37. Partial or Complete Forfeiture of a Lawyer's Compensation

A lawyer engaging in clear and serious violation of duty to a client may be required to forfeit some or all of the lawyer's compensation for the matter. Considerations relevant to the question of forfeiture include the gravity and timing of the violation, its willfulness, its effect on the value of the lawyer's work for the client, any other threatened or actual harm to the client, and the adequacy of other remedies.

TOPIC 2. A LAWYER'S CLAIM TO COMPENSATION

§38. Client-Lawyer Fee Contracts

(1) Before or within a reasonable time after beginning to represent a client in a matter, a lawyer must communicate to the client, in writing when applicable rules so provide, the basis or rate of the fee, unless the communication is unnecessary for the client because the lawyer has previously represented that client on the same basis or at the same rate.

(2) The validity and construction of a contract between a client and a lawyer concerning the lawyer's fees are governed by §18.

(3) Unless a contract construed in the circumstances indicates otherwise:

(a) a lawyer may not charge separately for the lawyer's general office and overhead expenses;

(b) payments that the law requires an opposing party or that party's lawyer to pay as attorney-fee awards or sanctions are credited to the client, not the client's lawyer, absent a contrary statute or court order; and

(c) when a lawyer requests and receives a fee payment that is not for services already rendered, that payment is to be credited against whatever fee the lawyer is entitled to collect.

§39. A Lawyer's Fee in the Absence of a Contract

If a client and lawyer have not made a valid contract providing for another measure of compensation, a client owes a lawyer who has performed legal services for the client the fair value of the lawyer's services.

§40. Fees on Termination

If a client-lawyer relationship ends before the lawyer has completed the services due for a matter and the lawyer's fee has not been forfeited under §37:

(1) a lawyer who has been discharged or withdraws may recover the lesser of the fair value of the lawyer's services as determined under §39 and the ratable proportion of the compensation provided by any otherwise enforceable contract between lawyer and client for the services performed; except that

(2) the tribunal may allow such a lawyer to recover the ratable proportion of the compensation provided by such a contract if:

(a) the discharge or withdrawal is not attributable to misconduct of the lawyer;

(b) the lawyer has performed severable services; and

(c) allowing contractual compensation would not burden the client's choice of counsel or the client's ability to replace counsel.

TOPIC 3. FEE-COLLECTION PROCEDURES

§41. Fee-Collection Methods

In seeking compensation claimed from a client or former client, a lawyer may not employ collection methods forbidden by law, use confidential information (as defined in Chapter 5) when not permitted under §65, or harass the client.

§42. Remedies and the Burden of Persuasion

(1) A fee dispute between a lawyer and a client may be adjudicated in any appropriate proceeding, including a suit by the lawyer to recover an

unpaid fee, a suit for a refund by a client, an arbitration to which both parties consent unless applicable law renders the lawyer's consent unnecessary, or in the court's discretion a proceeding ancillary to a pending suit in which the lawyer performed the services in question.

(2) In any such proceeding the lawyer has the burden of persuading the trier of fact, when relevant, of the existence and terms of any fee contract, the making of any disclosures to the client required to render a contract enforceable, and the extent and value of the lawyer's services.

§43. Lawyer Liens

(1) Except as provided in Subsection (2) or by statute or rule, a lawyer does not acquire a lien entitling the lawyer to retain the client's property in the lawyer's possession in order to secure payment of the lawyer's fees and disbursements. A lawyer may decline to deliver to a client or former client an original or copy of any document prepared by the lawyer or at the lawyer's expense if the client or former client has not paid all fees and disbursements due for the lawyer's work in preparing the document and nondelivery would not unreasonably harm the client or former client.

(2) Unless otherwise provided by statute or rule, client and lawyer may agree that the lawyer shall have a security interest in property of the client recovered for the client through the lawyer's efforts, as follows:

(a) the lawyer may contract in writing with the client for a lien on the proceeds of the representation to secure payment for the lawyer's services and disbursements in that matter;

(b) the lien becomes binding on a third party when the party has notice of the lien;

(c) the lien applies only to the amount of fees and disbursements claimed reasonably and in good faith for the lawyer's services performed in the representation; and

(d) the lawyer may not unreasonably impede the speedy and inexpensive resolution of any dispute concerning those fees and disbursements or the lien.

(3) A tribunal where an action is pending may in its discretion adjudicate any fee or other dispute concerning a lien asserted by a lawyer on property of a party to the action, provide for custody of the property, release all or part of the property to the client or lawyer, and grant such other relief as justice may require.

(4) With respect to property neither in the lawyer's possession nor recovered by the client through the lawyer's efforts, the lawyer may obtain a security interest on property of a client only as provided by other law and consistent with §§18 and 126. Acquisition of such a security interest is a business or financial transaction with a client within the meaning of §126.

TOPIC 4. PROPERTY AND DOCUMENTS OF CLIENTS AND OTHERS

§44. Safeguarding and Segregating Property

(1) A lawyer holding funds or other property of a client in connection with a representation, or such funds or other property in which a client claims an interest, must take reasonable steps to safeguard the funds or property. A similar obligation may be imposed by law on funds or other property so held and owned or claimed by a third person. In particular, the lawyer must hold such property separate from the lawyer's property, keep records of it, deposit funds in an account separate from the lawyer's own funds, identify tangible objects, and comply with related requirements imposed by regulatory authorities.

(2) Upon receiving funds or other property in a professional capacity and in which a client or third person owns or claims an interest, a lawyer must promptly notify the client or third person. The lawyer must promptly render a full accounting regarding such property upon request by the client or third person.

§45. Surrendering Possession of Property

(1) Except as provided in Subsection (2), a lawyer must promptly deliver, to the client or nonclient so entitled, funds or other property in the lawyer's possession belonging to a client or nonclient.

(2) A lawyer may retain possession of funds or other property of a client or non-client if:

(a) the client or non-client consents;

(b) the lawyer's client is entitled to the property, the lawyer appropriately possesses the property for purposes of the representation, and the client has not asked for delivery of the property;

(c) the lawyer has a valid lien on the property (see §43);

(d) there are substantial grounds for dispute as to the person entitled to the property; or

(e) delivering the property to the client or non-client would violate a court order or other legal obligation of the lawyer.

§46. Documents Relating to a Representation

(1) A lawyer must take reasonable steps to safeguard documents in the lawyer's possession relating to the representation of a client or former client.

(2) On request, a lawyer must allow a client or former client to inspect and copy any document possessed by the lawyer relating to the representation, unless substantial grounds exist to refuse.

(3) Unless a client or former client consents to non-delivery or substantial grounds exist for refusing to make delivery, a lawyer must deliver to the client or former client, at an appropriate time and in any event promptly after the representation ends, such originals and copies of other documents possessed by the lawyer relating to the representation as the client or former client reasonably needs.

(4) Notwithstanding Subsections (2) and (3), a lawyer may decline to deliver to a client or former client an original or copy of any document under circumstances permitted by §43(1).

TOPIC 5. FEE-SPLITTING WITH A LAWYER NOT IN THE SAME FIRM

§47. Fee-Splitting Between Lawyers Not in the Same Firm

A division of fees between lawyers who are not in the same firm may be made only if:

(1)(a) the division is in proportion to the services performed by each lawyer or (b) by agreement with the client, the lawyers assume joint responsibility for the representation;

(2) the client is informed of and does not object to the fact of division, the terms of the division, and the participation of the lawyers involved; and

(3) the total fee is reasonable (see §34).

CHAPTER 4 LAWYER CIVIL LIABILITY

TOPIC 1. LIABILITY FOR PROFESSIONAL NEGLIGENCE AND BREACH OF FIDUCIARY DUTY

§48. Professional Negligence — Elements and Defenses Generally

In addition to the other possible bases of civil liability described in §§49, 55, and 56, a lawyer is civilly liable for professional negligence to a person to whom the lawyer owes a duty of care within the meaning of §50 or §51, if the lawyer fails to exercise care within the meaning of §52 and if that failure is a legal cause of injury within the meaning of §53, unless the lawyer has a defense within the meaning of §54.

§49. Breach of Fiduciary Duty — Generally

In addition to the other possible bases of civil liability described in §§48, 55, and 56, a lawyer is civilly liable to a client if the lawyer breaches a fiduciary duty to the client set forth in §16(3) and if that failure is a legal

cause of injury within the meaning of §53, unless the lawyer has a defense within the meaning of §54.

§50. Duty of Care to a Client

For purposes of liability under §48, a lawyer owes a client the duty to exercise care within the meaning of §52 in pursuing the client's lawful objectives in matters covered by the representation.

§51. Duty of Care to Certain Nonclients

For purposes of liability under §48, a lawyer owes a duty to use care within the meaning of §52 in each of the following circumstances:

(1) to a prospective client, as stated in §15;

(2) to a nonclient when and to the extent that:

(a) the lawyer or (with the lawyer's acquiescence) the lawyer's client invites the nonclient to rely on the lawyer's opinion or provision of other legal services, and the nonclient so relies; and

(b) the nonclient is not, under applicable tort law, too remote from the lawyer to be entitled to protection;

(3) to a nonclient when and to the extent that:

(a) the lawyer knows that a client intends as one of the primary objectives of the representation that the lawyer's services benefit the nonclient;

(b) such a duty would not significantly impair the lawyer's performance of obligations to the client; and

(c) the absence of such a duty would make enforcement of those obligations to the client unlikely; and

(4) to a nonclient when and to the extent that:

(a) the lawyer's client is a trustee, guardian, executor, or fiduciary acting primarily to perform similar functions for the nonclient;

(b) the lawyer knows that appropriate action by the lawyer is necessary with respect to a matter within the scope of the representation to prevent or rectify the breach of a fiduciary duty owed by the client to the nonclient, where (i) the breach is a crime or fraud or (ii) the lawyer has assisted or is assisting the breach;

(c) the nonclient is not reasonably able to protect its rights; and

(d) such a duty would not significantly impair the performance of the lawyer's obligations to the client.

§52. The Standard of Care

(1) For purposes of liability under §§48 and 49, a lawyer who owes a duty of care must exercise the competence and diligence normally exercised by lawyers in similar circumstances.

(2) Proof of a violation of a rule or statute regulating the conduct of lawyers:

(a) does not give rise to an implied cause of action for professional negligence or breach of fiduciary duty;

(b) does not preclude other proof concerning the duty of care in Subsection (1) or the fiduciary duty; and

(c) may be considered by a trier of fact as an aid in understanding and applying the standard of Subsection (1) or §49 to the extent that (i) the rule or statute was designed for the protection of persons in the position of the claimant and (ii) proof of the content and construction of such a rule or statute is relevant to the claimant's claim.

§53. Causation and Damages

A lawyer is liable under §48 or §49 only if the lawyer's breach of a duty of care or breach of fiduciary duty was a legal cause of injury, as determined under generally applicable principles of causation and damages.

§54. Defenses; Prospective Liability Waiver; Settlement with a Client

(1) Except as otherwise provided in this Section, liability under §§48 and 49 is subject to the defenses available under generally applicable principles of law governing respectively actions for professional negligence and breach of fiduciary duty. A lawyer is not liable under §48 or §49 for any action or inaction the lawyer reasonably believed to be required by law, including a professional rule.

(2) An agreement prospectively limiting a lawyer's liability to a client for malpractice is unenforceable.

(3) The client or former client may rescind an agreement settling a claim by the client or former client against the person's lawyer if:

(a) the client or former client was subjected to improper pressure by the lawyer in reaching the settlement; or

(b)(i) the client or former client was not independently represented in negotiating the settlement, and (ii) the settlement was not fair and reasonable to the client or former client.

(4) For purposes of professional discipline, a lawyer may not:

(a) make an agreement prospectively limiting the lawyer's liability to a client for malpractice; or

(b) settle a claim for such liability with an unrepresented client or former client without first advising that person in writing that independent representation is appropriate in connection therewith.

TOPIC 2. OTHER CIVIL LIABILITY

§55. Civil Remedies of a Client Other Than for Malpractice

(1) A lawyer is subject to liability to a client for injury caused by breach of contract in the circumstances and to the extent provided by contract law.

(2) A client is entitled to restitutionary, injunctive, or declaratory remedies against a lawyer in the circumstances and to the extent provided by generally applicable law governing such remedies.

§56. Liability to a Client or Nonclient Under General Law

Except as provided in §57 and in addition to liability under §§48-55, a lawyer is subject to liability to a client or nonclient when a nonlawyer would be in similar circumstances.

§57. Nonclient Claims — Certain Defenses and Exceptions to Liability

(1) In addition to other absolute or conditional privileges, a lawyer is absolutely privileged to publish matter concerning a nonclient if:

(a) the publication occurs in communications preliminary to a reasonably anticipated proceeding before a tribunal or in the institution or during the course and as a part of such a proceeding;

(b) the lawyer participates as counsel in that proceeding; and

(c) the matter is published to a person who may be involved in the proceeding, and the publication has some relation to the proceeding.

(2) A lawyer representing a client in a civil proceeding or procuring the institution of criminal proceedings by a client is not liable to a nonclient for wrongful use of civil proceedings or for malicious prosecution if the lawyer has probable cause for acting, or if the lawyer acts primarily to help the client obtain a proper adjudication of the client's claim in that proceeding.

(3) A lawyer who advises or assists a client to make or break a contract, to enter or dissolve a legal relationship, or to enter or not enter a contractual relation, is not liable to a nonclient for interference with contract or with prospective contractual relations or with a legal relationship, if the lawyer acts to advance the client's objectives without using wrongful means.

TOPIC 3. VICARIOUS LIABILITY

§58. Vicarious Liability

(1) A law firm is subject to civil liability for injury legally caused to a person by any wrongful act or omission of any principal or employee of the

firm who was acting in the ordinary course of the firm's business or with actual or apparent authority.

(2) Each of the principals of a law firm organized as a general partnership without limited liability is liable jointly and severally with the firm.

(3) A principal of a law firm organized other than as a general partnership without limited liability as authorized by law is vicariously liable for the acts of another principal or employee of the firm to the extent provided by law.

CHAPTER 5 CONFIDENTIAL CLIENT INFORMATION

TOPIC 1. CONFIDENTIALITY RESPONSIBILITIES OF LAWYERS

Title A. Lawyer's Confidentiality Duties

§59. Definition of "Confidential Client Information"

Confidential client information consists of information relating to representation of a client, other than information that is generally known.

§60. A Lawyer's Duty to Safeguard Confidential Client Information

(1) Except as provided in §§61-67, during and after representation of a client:

(a) the lawyer may not use or disclose confidential client information as defined in §59 if there is a reasonable prospect that doing so will adversely affect a material interest of the client or if the client has instructed the lawyer not to use or disclose such information;

(b) the lawyer must take steps reasonable in the circumstances to protect confidential client information against impermissible use or disclosure by the lawyer's associates or agents that may adversely affect a material interest of the client or otherwise than as instructed by the client.

(2) Except as stated in §62, a lawyer who uses confidential information of a client for the lawyer's pecuniary gain other than in the practice of law must account to the client for any profits made.

Title B. Using or Disclosing Confidential Client Information

§61. Using or Disclosing Information to Advance Client Interests

A lawyer may use or disclose confidential client information when the lawyer reasonably believes that doing so will advance the interests of the client in the representation.

§62. Using or Disclosing Information with Client Consent

A lawyer may use or disclose confidential client information when the client consents after being adequately informed concerning the use or disclosure.

§63. Using or Disclosing Information When Required by Law

A lawyer may use or disclose confidential client information when required by law, after the lawyer takes reasonably appropriate steps to assert that the information is privileged or otherwise protected against disclosure.

§64. Using or Disclosing Information in a Lawyer's Self-Defense

A lawyer may use or disclose confidential client information when and to the extent that the lawyer reasonably believes necessary to defend the lawyer or the lawyer's associate or agent against a charge or threatened charge by any person that the lawyer or such associate or agent acted wrongfully in the course of representing a client.

§65. Using or Disclosing Information in a Compensation Dispute

A lawyer may use or disclose confidential client information when and to the extent that the lawyer reasonably believes necessary to permit the lawyer to resolve a dispute with the client concerning compensation or reimbursement that the lawyer reasonably claims the client owes the lawyer.

§66. Using or Disclosing Information to Prevent Death or Serious Bodily Harm

(1) A lawyer may use or disclose confidential client information when the lawyer reasonably believes that its use or disclosure is necessary to prevent reasonably certain death or serious bodily harm to a person.

(2) Before using or disclosing information under this Section, the lawyer must, if feasible, make a good-faith effort to persuade the client not to act. If the client or another person has already acted, the lawyer must, if feasible, advise the client to warn the victim or to take other action to prevent the harm and advise the client of the lawyer's ability to use or disclose information as provided in this Section and the consequences thereof.

(3) A lawyer who takes action or decides not to take action permitted under this Section is not, solely by reason of such action or inaction, subject

to professional discipline, liable for damages to the lawyer's client or any third person, or barred from recovery against a client or third person.

§67. Using or Disclosing Information to Prevent, Rectify, or Mitigate Substantial Financial Loss

(1) A lawyer may use or disclose confidential client information when the lawyer reasonably believes that its use or disclosure is necessary to prevent a crime or fraud, and:

(a) the crime or fraud threatens substantial financial loss;

(b) the loss has not yet occurred;

(c) the lawyer's client intends to commit the crime or fraud either personally or through a third person; and

(d) the client has employed or is employing the lawyer's services in the matter in which the crime or fraud is committed.

(2) If a crime or fraud described in Subsection (1) has already occurred, a lawyer may use or disclose confidential client information when the lawyer reasonably believes its use or disclosure is necessary to prevent, rectify, or mitigate the loss.

(3) Before using or disclosing information under this Section, the lawyer must, if feasible, make a good-faith effort to persuade the client not to act. If the client or another person has already acted, the lawyer must, if feasible, advise the client to warn the victim or to take other action to prevent, rectify, or mitigate the loss. The lawyer must, if feasible, also advise the client of the lawyer's ability to use or disclose information as provided in this Section and the consequences thereof.

(4) A lawyer who takes action or decides not to take action permitted under this Section is not, solely by reason of such action or inaction, subject to professional discipline, liable for damages to the lawyer's client or any third person, or barred from recovery against a client or third person.

TOPIC 2. THE ATTORNEY-CLIENT PRIVILEGE

Title A. The Scope of the Privilege

Swindler
death ≠ waiver

§68. Attorney-Client Privilege

Except as otherwise provided in this Restatement, the attorney-client privilege may be invoked as provided in §86 with respect to:

(1) a communication

(2) made between privileged persons

(3) in confidence

(4) for the purpose of obtaining or providing legal assistance for the client.

§69. Attorney-Client Privilege — "Communication"

A communication within the meaning of §68 is any expression through which a privileged person, as defined in §70, undertakes to convey information to another privileged person and any document or other record revealing such an expression.

§70. Attorney-Client Privilege — "Privileged Persons"

Privileged persons within the meaning of §68 are the client (including a prospective client), the client's lawyer, agents of either who facilitate communications between them, and agents of the lawyer who facilitate the representation.

§71. Attorney-Client Privilege — "In Confidence"

A communication is in confidence within the meaning of §68 if, at the time and in the circumstances of the communication, the communicating person reasonably believes that no one will learn the contents of the communication except a privileged person as defined in §70 or another person with whom communications are protected under a similar privilege.

§72. Attorney-Client Privilege — Legal Assistance as the Object of a Privileged Communication

A communication is made for the purpose of obtaining or providing legal assistance within the meaning of §68 if it is made to or to assist a person:

(1) who is a lawyer or who the client or prospective client reasonably believes to be a lawyer; and

(2) whom the client or prospective client consults for the purpose of obtaining legal assistance.

Title B. The Attorney-Client Privilege for Organizational and Multiple Clients

§73. The Privilege for an Organizational Client

When a client is a corporation, unincorporated association, partnership, trust, estate, sole proprietorship, or other for-profit or not-for-profit organization, the attorney-client privilege extends to a communication that:

(1) otherwise qualifies as privileged under §§68-72;

(2) is between an agent of the organization and a privileged person as defined in §70;

(3) concerns a legal matter of interest to the organization; and

(4) is disclosed only to:

(a) privileged persons as defined in §70; and

(b) other agents of the organization who reasonably need to know of the communication in order to act for the organization.

§74. The Privilege for a Governmental Client

Unless applicable law otherwise provides, the attorney-client privilege extends to a communication of a governmental organization as stated in §73 and of an individual employee or other agent of a governmental organization as a client with respect to his or her personal interest as stated in §§68-72.

§75. The Privilege of Co-Clients

(1) If two or more persons are jointly represented by the same lawyer in a matter, a communication of either co-client that otherwise qualifies as privileged under §§68-72 and relates to matters of common interest is privileged as against third persons, and any co-client may invoke the privilege, unless it has been waived by the client who made the communication.

(2) Unless the co-clients have agreed otherwise, a communication described in Subsection (1) is not privileged as between the co-clients in a subsequent adverse proceeding between them.

§76. The Privilege in Common-Interest Arrangements

(1) If two or more clients with a common interest in a litigated or nonlitigated matter are represented by separate lawyers and they agree to exchange information concerning the matter, a communication of any such client that otherwise qualifies as privileged under §§68-72 that relates to the matter is privileged as against third persons. Any such client may invoke the privilege, unless it has been waived by the client who made the communication.

(2) Unless the clients have agreed otherwise, a communication described in Subsection (1) is not privileged as between clients described in Subsection (1) in a subsequent adverse proceeding between them.

Title C. Duration of the Attorney-Client Privilege; Waivers and Exceptions

§77. Duration of the Privilege

Unless waived (see §§78-80) or subject to exception (see §§81-85), the attorney-client privilege may be invoked as provided in §86 at any time during or after termination of the relationship between client or prospective client and lawyer.

§78. Agreement, Disclaimer, or Failure to Object

The attorney-client privilege is waived if the client, the client's lawyer, or another authorized agent of the client:

(1) agrees to waive the privilege;

(2) disclaims protection of the privilege and

(a) another person reasonably relies on the disclaimer to that person's detriment; or

(b) reasons of judicial administration require that the client not be permitted to revoke the disclaimer; or

(3) in a proceeding before a tribunal, fails to object properly to an attempt by another person to give or exact testimony or other evidence of a privileged communication.

§79. Subsequent Disclosure

The attorney-client privilege is waived if the client, the client's lawyer, or another authorized agent of the client voluntarily discloses the communication in a non-privileged communication.

§80. Putting Assistance or a Communication in Issue

(1) The attorney-client privilege is waived for any relevant communication if the client asserts as to a material issue in a proceeding that:

(a) the client acted upon the advice of a lawyer or that the advice was otherwise relevant to the legal significance of the client's conduct; or

(b) a lawyer's assistance was ineffective, negligent, or otherwise wrongful.

(2) The attorney-client privilege is waived for a recorded communication if a witness:

(a) employs the communication to aid the witness while testifying; or

(b) employed the communication in preparing to testify, and the tribunal finds that disclosure is required in the interests of justice.

§81. Dispute Concerning a Decedent's Disposition of Property

The attorney-client privilege does not apply to a communication from or to a decedent relevant to an issue between parties who claim an interest

through the same deceased client, either by testate or intestate succession or by an inter vivos transaction.

§82. Client Crime or Fraud

The attorney-client privilege does not apply to a communication occurring when a client:

(a) consults a lawyer for the purpose, later accomplished, of obtaining assistance to engage in a crime or fraud or aiding a third person to do so, or

(b) regardless of the client's purpose at the time of consultation, uses the lawyer's advice or other services to engage in or assist a crime or fraud.

§83. Lawyer Self-Protection

The attorney-client privilege does not apply to a communication that is relevant and reasonably necessary for a lawyer to employ in a proceeding:

(1) to resolve a dispute with a client concerning compensation or reimbursement that the lawyer reasonably claims the client owes the lawyer; or

(2) to defend the lawyer or the lawyer's associate or agent against a charge by any person that the lawyer, associate, or agent acted wrongfully during the course of representing a client.

§84. Fiduciary-Lawyer Communications

In a proceeding in which a trustee of an express trust or similar fiduciary is charged with breach of fiduciary duties by a beneficiary, a communication otherwise within §68 is nonetheless not privileged if the communication:

(a) is relevant to the claimed breach; and

(b) was between the trustee and a lawyer (or other privileged person within the meaning of §70) who was retained to advise the trustee concerning the administration of the trust.

§85. Communications Involving a Fiduciary Within an Organization

In a proceeding involving a dispute between an organizational client and shareholders, members, or other constituents of the organization toward whom the directors, officers, or similar persons managing the organization bear fiduciary responsibilities, the attorney-client privilege of the organization may be withheld from a communication otherwise within §68 if the tribunal finds that:

(a) those managing the organization are charged with breach of their obligations toward the shareholders, members, or other constituents or toward the organization itself;

(b) the communication occurred prior to the assertion of the charges and relates directly to those charges; and

(c) the need of the requesting party to discover or introduce the communication is sufficiently compelling and the threat to confidentiality sufficiently confined to justify setting the privilege aside.

Title D. Invoking the Privilege and Its Exceptions

§86. Invoking the Privilege and Its Exceptions

(1) When an attempt is made to introduce in evidence or obtain discovery of a communication privileged under §68:

(a) A client, a personal representative of an incompetent or deceased client, or a person succeeding to the interest of a client may invoke or waive the privilege, either personally or through counsel or another authorized agent.

(b) A lawyer, an agent of the lawyer, or an agent of a client from whom a privileged communication is sought must invoke the privilege when doing so appears reasonably appropriate, unless the client:

(i) has waived the privilege; or

(ii) has authorized the lawyer or agent to waive it.

(c) Notwithstanding failure to invoke the privilege as specified in Subsections (1)(a) and (1)(b), the tribunal has discretion to invoke the privilege.

(2) A person invoking the privilege must ordinarily object contemporaneously to an attempt to disclose the communication and, if the objection is contested, demonstrate each element of the privilege under §68.

(3) A person invoking a waiver of or exception to the privilege (§§78-85) must assert it and, if the assertion is contested, demonstrate each element of the waiver or exception.

TOPIC 3. THE LAWYER WORK-PRODUCT IMMUNITY

Title A. The Scope of the Lawyer Work-Product Immunity

§87. Lawyer Work-Product Immunity

(1) Work product consists of tangible material or its intangible equivalent in unwritten or oral form, other than underlying facts, prepared by a lawyer for litigation then in progress or in reasonable anticipation of future litigation.

(2) Opinion work product consists of the opinions or mental impressions of a lawyer; all other work product is ordinary work product.

(3) Except for material which by applicable law is not so protected, work product is immune from discovery or other compelled disclosure to the extent stated in §§88 (ordinary work product) and 89 (opinion work product) when the immunity is invoked as described in §90.

§88. Ordinary Work Product

When work product protection is invoked as described in §90, ordinary work product (§87(2)) is immune from discovery or other compelled disclosure unless either an exception recognized in §§91-93 applies or the inquiring party:

(1) has a substantial need for the material in order to prepare for trial; and

(2) is unable without undue hardship to obtain the substantial equivalent of the material by other means.

§89. Opinion Work Product

When work product protection is invoked as described in §90, opinion work product (§87(2)) is immune from discovery or other compelled disclosure unless either the immunity is waived or an exception applies (§§91-93) or extraordinary circumstances justify disclosure.

Title B. Procedural Administration of the Lawyer Work-Product Immunity

§90. Invoking the Lawyer Work-Product Immunity and Its Exceptions

(1) Work-product immunity may be invoked by or for a person on whose behalf the work product was prepared.

(2) The person invoking work-product immunity must object and, if the objection is contested, demonstrate each element of the immunity.

(3) Once a claim of work product has been adequately supported, a person entitled to invoke a waiver or exception must assert it and, if the assertion is contested, demonstrate each element of the waiver or exception.

Title C. Waivers and Exceptions to the Work-Product Immunity

§91. Voluntary Acts

Work-product immunity is waived if the client, the client's lawyer, or another authorized agent of the client:

(1) agrees to waive the immunity;

(2) disclaims protection of the immunity and:

(a) another person reasonably relies on the disclaimer to that person's detriment; or

(b) reasons of judicial administration require that the client not be permitted to revoke the disclaimer; or

(3) in a proceeding before a tribunal, fails to object properly to an attempt by another person to give or exact testimony or other evidence of work product; or

(4) discloses the material to third persons in circumstances in which there is a significant likelihood that an adversary or potential adversary in anticipated litigation will obtain it.

§92. Use of Lawyer Work Product in Litigation

(1) Work-product immunity is waived for any relevant material if the client asserts as to a material issue in a proceeding that:

(a) the client acted upon the advice of a lawyer or that the advice was otherwise relevant to the legal significance of the client's conduct; or

(b) a lawyer's assistance was ineffective, negligent, or otherwise wrongful.

(2) The work-product immunity is waived for recorded material if a witness

(a) employs the material to aid the witness while testifying, or

(b) employed the material in preparing to testify, and the tribunal finds that disclosure is required in the interests of justice.

§93. Client Crime or Fraud

Work-product immunity does not apply to materials prepared when a client consults a lawyer for the purpose, later accomplished, of obtaining assistance to engage in a crime or fraud or to aid a third person to do so or uses the materials for such a purpose.

CHAPTER 6 REPRESENTING CLIENTS—IN GENERAL

TOPIC 1. LAWYER FUNCTIONS IN REPRESENTING CLIENTS—IN GENERAL

§94. Advising and Assisting a Client — In General

(1) A lawyer who counsels or assists a client to engage in conduct that violates the rights of a third person is subject to liability:

(a) to the third person to the extent stated in §§51 and 56-57; and

(b) to the client to the extent stated in §§ 50, 55, and 56.

(2) For purposes of professional discipline, a lawyer may not counsel or assist a client in conduct that the lawyer knows to be criminal or fraudulent or in violation of a court order with the intent of facilitating or encouraging the conduct, but the lawyer may counsel or assist a client in conduct when the lawyer reasonably believes:

(a) that the client's conduct constitutes a good-faith effort to determine the validity, scope, meaning, or application of a law or court order; or

(b) that the client can assert a nonfrivolous argument that the client's conduct will not constitute a crime or fraud or violate a court order.

(3) In counseling a client, a lawyer may address non-legal aspects of a proposed course of conduct, including moral, reputational, economic, social, political, and business aspects.

§95. An Evaluation Undertaken for a Third Person

(1) In furtherance of the objectives of a client in a representation, a lawyer may provide to a nonclient the results of the lawyer's investigation and analysis of facts or the lawyer's professional evaluation or opinion on the matter.

(2) When providing the information, evaluation, or opinion under Subsection (1) is reasonably likely to affect the client's interests materially and adversely, the lawyer must first obtain the client's consent after the client is adequately informed concerning important possible effects on the client's interests.

(3) In providing the information, evaluation, or opinion under Subsection (1), the lawyer must exercise care with respect to the nonclient to the extent stated in §51(2) and not make false statements prohibited under §98.

TOPIC 2. REPRESENTING ORGANIZATIONAL CLIENTS

§96. Representing an Organization as Client

(1) When a lawyer is employed or retained to represent an organization:

(a) the lawyer represents the interests of the organization as defined by its responsible agents acting pursuant to the organization's decision-making procedures; and

(b) subject to Subsection (2), the lawyer must follow instructions in the representation, as stated in §21(2), given by persons authorized so to act on behalf of the organization.

(2) If a lawyer representing an organization knows of circumstances indicating that a constituent of the organization has engaged in action or intends to act in a way that violates a legal obligation to the organization that will likely cause substantial injury to it, or that reasonably can be foreseen to be imputable to the organization and likely to result in substantial injury to it, the lawyer must proceed in what the lawyer reasonably believes to be the best interests of the organization.

(3) In the circumstances described in Subsection (2), the lawyer may, in circumstances warranting such steps, ask the constituent to reconsider the matter, recommend that a second legal opinion be sought, and seek review by appropriate supervisory authority within the organization, including referring the matter to the highest authority that can act in behalf of the organization.

§97. Representing a Governmental Client

A lawyer representing a governmental client must proceed in the representation as stated in §96, except that the lawyer:

(1) possesses such rights and responsibilities as may be defined by law to make decisions on behalf of the governmental client that are within the authority of a client under §§22 and 21(2);

(2) except as otherwise provided by law, must proceed as stated in §§96(2) and 96(3) with respect to an act of a constituent of the governmental client that violates a legal obligation that will likely cause substantial public or private injury or that reasonably can be foreseen to be imputable to and thus likely result in substantial injury to the client;

(3) if a prosecutor or similar lawyer determining whether to file criminal proceedings or take other steps in such proceedings, must do so only when based on probable cause and the lawyer's belief, formed after due investigation, that there are good factual and legal grounds to support the step taken; and

(4) must observe other applicable restrictions imposed by law on those similarly functioning for the governmental client.

TOPIC 3. LAWYER DEALINGS WITH A NONCLIENT

Title A. Dealings with a Nonclient—Generally

§98. Statements to a Nonclient

A lawyer communicating on behalf of a client with a nonclient may not:

(1) knowingly make a false statement of material fact or law to the nonclient;

(2) make other statements prohibited by law; or

(3) fail to make a disclosure of information required by law.

Title B. Contact with a Represented Nonclient

§99. A Represented Nonclient — The General Anti-Contact Rule

(1) A lawyer representing a client in a matter may not communicate about the subject of the representation with a nonclient whom the lawyer knows to be represented in the matter by another lawyer or with a representative of an organizational nonclient so represented as defined in §100, unless:

(a) the communication is with a public officer or agency to the extent stated in §101;

(b) the lawyer is a party and represents no other client in the matter;

(c) the communication is authorized by law;

(d) the communication reasonably responds to an emergency; or

(e) the other lawyer consents.

(2) Subsection (1) does not prohibit the lawyer from assisting the client in otherwise proper communication by the lawyer's client with a represented nonclient.

§100. Definition of a Represented Nonclient

Within the meaning of §99, a represented nonclient includes:

(1) a natural person represented by a lawyer; and:

(2) a current employee or other agent of an organization represented by a lawyer:

(a) if the employee or other agent supervises, directs, or regularly consults with the lawyer concerning the matter or if the agent has power to compromise or settle the matter;

(b) if the acts or omissions of the employee or other agent may be imputed to the organization for purposes of civil or criminal liability in the matter; or

(c) if a statement of the employee or other agent, under applicable rules of evidence, would have the effect of binding the organization with respect to proof of the matter.

§101. A Represented Governmental Agency or Officer

(1) Unless otherwise provided by law (see §99(1)(c)) and except as provided in Subsection (2), the prohibition stated in §99 against contact with a represented nonclient does not apply to communications with employees of a represented governmental agency or with a governmental officer being represented in the officer's official capacity.

(2) In negotiation or litigation by a lawyer of a specific claim of a client against a governmental agency or against a governmental officer in the

officer's official capacity, the prohibition stated in §99 applies, except that the lawyer may contact any officer of the government if permitted by the agency or with respect to an issue of general policy.

§102. Information of a Nonclient Known to Be Legally Protected

A lawyer communicating with a nonclient in a situation permitted under §99 may not seek to obtain information that the lawyer reasonably should know the nonclient may not reveal without violating a duty of confidentiality to another imposed by law.

Title C. Dealings with an Unrepresented Nonclient

§103. Dealings with an Unrepresented Nonclient

In the course of representing a client and dealing with a nonclient who is not represented by a lawyer:

(1) the lawyer may not mislead the nonclient, to the prejudice of the nonclient, concerning the identity and interests of the person the lawyer represents; and

(2) when the lawyer knows or reasonably should know that the unrepresented nonclient misunderstands the lawyer's role in the matter, the lawyer must make reasonable efforts to correct the misunderstanding when failure to do so would materially prejudice the nonclient.

TOPIC 4. LEGISLATIVE AND ADMINISTRATIVE MATTERS

§104. Representing a Client in Legislative and Administrative Matters

A lawyer representing a client before a legislature or administrative agency:

(1) must disclose that the appearance is in a representative capacity and not misrepresent the capacity in which the lawyer appears;

(2) must comply with applicable law and regulations governing such representations; and

(3) except as applicable law otherwise provides:

(a) in an adjudicative proceeding before a government agency or involving such an agency as a participant, has the legal rights and responsibilities of an advocate in a proceeding before a judicial tribunal; and

(b) in other types of proceedings and matters, has the legal rights and responsibilities applicable in the lawyer's dealings with a private person.

CHAPTER 7 REPRESENTING CLIENTS IN LITIGATION

TOPIC 1. ADVOCACY IN GENERAL

§105. Complying with Law and Tribunal Rulings

In representing a client in a matter before a tribunal, a lawyer must comply with applicable law, including rules of procedure and evidence and specific tribunal rulings.

§106. Dealing with Other Participants in Proceedings

In representing a client in a matter before a tribunal, a lawyer may not use means that have no substantial purpose other than to embarrass, delay, or burden a third person or use methods of obtaining evidence that are prohibited by law.

§107. Prohibited Forensic Tactics

In representing a client in a matter before a tribunal, a lawyer may not, in the presence of the trier of fact:

(1) state a personal opinion about the justness of a cause, the credibility of a witness, the culpability of a civil litigant, or the guilt or innocence of an accused, but the lawyer may argue any position or conclusion adequately supported by the lawyer's analysis of the evidence; or

(2) allude to any matter that the lawyer does not reasonably believe is relevant or that will not be supported by admissible evidence.

§108. An Advocate as a Witness

(1) Except as provided in Subsection (2), a lawyer may not represent a client in a contested hearing or trial of a matter in which:

(a) the lawyer is expected to testify for the lawyer's client; or

(b) the lawyer does not intend to testify but (i) the lawyer's testimony would be material to establishing a claim or defense of the client, and (ii) the client has not consented as stated in §122 to the lawyer's intention not to testify.

(2) A lawyer may represent a client when the lawyer will testify as stated in Subsection (1)(a) if:

(a) the lawyer's testimony relates to an issue that the lawyer reasonably believes will not be contested or to the nature and value of legal services rendered in the proceeding;

(b) deprivation of the lawyer's services as advocate would work a substantial hardship on the client; or

(c) consent has been given by

(i) opposing parties who would be adversely affected by the lawyer's testimony and,

(ii) if relevant, the lawyer's client, as stated in §122 with respect to any conflict of interest between lawyer and client (see §125) that the lawyer's testimony would create.

(3) A lawyer may not represent a client in a litigated matter pending before a tribunal when the lawyer or a lawyer in the lawyer's firm will give testimony materially adverse to the position of the lawyer's client or materially adverse to a former client of any such lawyer with respect to a matter substantially related to the earlier representation, unless the affected client has consented as stated in §122 with respect to any conflict of interest between lawyer and client (see §125) that the testimony would create.

(4) A tribunal should not permit a lawyer to call opposing trial counsel as a witness unless there is a compelling need for the lawyer's testimony.

§109. An Advocate's Public Comment on Pending Litigation

(1) In representing a client in a matter before a tribunal, a lawyer may not make a statement outside the proceeding that a reasonable person would expect to be disseminated by means of public communication when the lawyer knows or reasonably should know that the statement will have a substantial likelihood of materially prejudicing a juror or influencing or intimidating a prospective witness in the proceeding. However, a lawyer may in any event make a statement that is reasonably necessary to mitigate the impact on the lawyer's client of substantial, undue, and prejudicial publicity recently initiated by one other than the lawyer or the lawyer's client.

(2) A prosecutor must, except for statements necessary to inform the public of the nature and extent of the prosecutor's action and that serve a legitimate law-enforcement purpose, refrain from making extrajudicial comments that have a substantial likelihood of heightening public condemnation of the accused.

TOPIC 2. LIMITS ON ADVOCACY

§110. Frivolous Advocacy

(1) A lawyer may not bring or defend a proceeding or assert or controvert an issue therein, unless there is a basis for doing so that is not frivolous, which includes a good-faith argument for an extension, modification, or reversal of existing law.

(2) Notwithstanding Subsection (1), a lawyer for the defendant in a criminal proceeding or the respondent in a proceeding that could result in incarceration may so defend the proceeding as to require that the prosecutor establish every necessary element.

(3) A lawyer may not make a frivolous discovery request, fail to make a reasonably diligent effort to comply with a proper discovery request of another party, or intentionally fail otherwise to comply with applicable procedural requirements concerning discovery.

§111. Disclosure of Legal Authority

In representing a client in a matter before a tribunal, a lawyer may not knowingly:

(1) make a false statement of a material proposition of law to the tribunal; or

(2) fail to disclose to the tribunal legal authority in the controlling jurisdiction known to the lawyer to be directly adverse to the position asserted by the client and not disclosed by opposing counsel.

§112. Advocacy in Ex Parte and Other Proceedings

In representing a client in a matter before a tribunal, a lawyer applying for ex parte relief or appearing in another proceeding in which similar special requirements of candor apply must comply with the requirements of §110 and §§118-120 and further:

(1) must not present evidence the lawyer reasonably believes is false;

(2) must disclose all material and relevant facts known to the lawyer that will enable the tribunal to reach an informed decision; and

(3) must comply with any other applicable special requirements of candor imposed by law.

Florida Bar Opinion 95-4

TOPIC 3. ADVOCATES AND TRIBUNALS

§113. Improperly Influencing a Judicial Officer

(1) A lawyer may not knowingly communicate ex parte with a judicial officer before whom a proceeding is pending concerning the matter, except as authorized by law.

(2) A lawyer may not make a gift or loan prohibited by law to a judicial officer, attempt to influence the officer otherwise than by legally proper procedures, or state or imply an ability so to influence a judicial officer.

§114. A Lawyer's Statements Concerning a Judicial Officer

A lawyer may not knowingly or recklessly make publicly a false statement of fact concerning the qualifications or integrity of an incumbent of a judicial office or a candidate for election to such an office.

§115. Lawyer Contact with a Juror

A lawyer may not:

(1) except as allowed by law, communicate with or seek to influence a person known by the lawyer to be a member of a jury pool from which the jury will be drawn;

(2) except as allowed by law, communicate with or seek to influence a member of a jury; or

(3) communicate with a juror who has been excused from further service:

(a) when that would harass the juror or constitute an attempt to influence the juror's actions as a juror in future cases; or

(b) when otherwise prohibited by law.

TOPIC 4. ADVOCATES AND EVIDENCE

§116. Interviewing and Preparing a Prospective Witness

(1) A lawyer may interview a witness for the purpose of preparing the witness to testify.

(2) A lawyer may not unlawfully obstruct another party's access to a witness.

(3) A lawyer may not unlawfully induce or assist a prospective witness to evade or ignore process obliging the witness to appear to testify.

(4) A lawyer may not request a person to refrain from voluntarily giving relevant testimony or information to another party, unless:

(a) the person is the lawyer's client in the matter; or

(b)(i) the person is not the lawyer's client but is a relative or employee or other agent of the lawyer or the lawyer's client, and (ii) the lawyer reasonably believes compliance will not materially and adversely affect the person's interests.

§117. Compensating a Witness

A lawyer may not offer or pay to a witness any consideration:

(1) in excess of the reasonable expenses of the witness incurred and the reasonable value of the witness's time spent in providing

evidence, except that an expert witness may be offered and paid a noncontingent fee;

(2) contingent on the content of the witness's testimony or the outcome of the litigation; or

(3) otherwise prohibited by law.

§118. Falsifying or Destroying Evidence

(1) A lawyer may not falsify documentary or other evidence.

(2) A lawyer may not destroy or obstruct another party's access to documentary or other evidence when doing so would violate a court order or other legal requirements, or counsel or assist a client to do so.

§119. Physical Evidence of a Client Crime

With respect to physical evidence of a client crime, a lawyer:

(1) may, when reasonably necessary for purposes of the representation, take possession of the evidence and retain it for the time reasonably necessary to examine it and subject it to tests that do not alter or destroy material characteristics of the evidence; but

(2) following possession under Subsection (1), the lawyer must notify prosecuting authorities of the lawyer's possession of the evidence or turn the evidence over to them.

§120. False Testimony or Evidence

(1) A lawyer may not:

(a) knowingly counsel or assist a witness to testify falsely or otherwise to offer false evidence;

(b) knowingly make a false statement of fact to the tribunal;

(c) offer testimony or other evidence as to an issue of fact known by the lawyer to be false.

(2) If a lawyer has offered testimony or other evidence as to a material issue of fact and comes to know of its falsity, the lawyer must take reasonable remedial measures and may disclose confidential client information when necessary to take such a measure.

(3) A lawyer may refuse to offer testimony or other evidence that the lawyer reasonably believes is false, even if the lawyer does not know it to be false.

CHAPTER 8 CONFLICTS OF INTEREST

TOPIC 1. CONFLICTS OF INTEREST—IN GENERAL

§121. The Basic Prohibition of Conflicts of Interest

Unless all affected clients and other necessary persons consent to the representation under the limitations and conditions provided in §122, a lawyer may not represent a client if the representation would involve a conflict of interest. A conflict of interest is involved if there is a substantial risk that the lawyer's representation of the client would be materially and adversely affected by the lawyer's own interests or by the lawyer's duties to another current client, a former client, or a third person.

§122. Client Consent to a Conflict of Interest

(1) A lawyer may represent a client notwithstanding a conflict of interest prohibited by §121 if each affected client or former client gives informed consent to the lawyer's representation. Informed consent requires that the client or former client have reasonably adequate information about the material risks of such representation to that client or former client.

(2) Notwithstanding the informed consent of each affected client or former client, a lawyer may not represent a client if:

(a) the representation is prohibited by law;

(b) one client will assert a claim against the other in the same litigation; or

(c) in the circumstances, it is not reasonably likely that the lawyer will be able to provide adequate representation to one or more of the clients.

§123. Imputation of a Conflict of Interest to an Affiliated Lawyer

Unless all affected clients consent to the representation under the limitations and conditions provided in §122 or unless imputation hereunder is removed as provided in §124, the restrictions upon a lawyer imposed by §§125-135 also restrict other affiliated lawyers who:

(1) are associated with that lawyer in rendering legal services to others through a law partnership, professional corporation, sole proprietorship, or similar association;

(2) are employed with that lawyer by an organization to render legal services either to that organization or to others to advance the interests or objectives of the organization; or

(3) share office facilities without reasonably adequate measures to protect confidential client information so that it will not be available to other lawyers in the shared office.

§124. Removing Imputation

(1) Imputation specified in §123 does not restrict an affiliated lawyer when the affiliation between the affiliated lawyer and the personally prohibited lawyer that required the imputation has been terminated, and no material confidential information of the client, relevant to the matter, has been communicated by the personally prohibited lawyer to the affiliated lawyer or that lawyer's firm.

(2) Imputation specified in §123 does not restrict an affiliated lawyer with respect to a former-client conflict under §132, when there is no substantial risk that confidential information of the former client will be used with material adverse effect on the former client because:

(a) any confidential client information communicated to the personally prohibited lawyer is unlikely to be significant in the subsequent matter;

(b) the personally prohibited lawyer is subject to screening measures adequate to eliminate participation by that lawyer in the representation; and

(c) timely and adequate notice of the screening has been provided to all affected clients.

(3) Imputation specified in §123 does not restrict a lawyer affiliated with a former government lawyer with respect to a conflict under §133 if:

(a) the personally prohibited lawyer is subject to screening measures adequate to eliminate involvement by that lawyer in the representation; and

(b) timely and adequate notice of the screening has been provided to the appropriate government agency and to affected clients.

TOPIC 2. CONFLICTS OF INTEREST BETWEEN A LAWYER AND A CLIENT

§125. A Lawyer's Personal Interest Affecting the Representation of a Client

Unless the affected client consents to the representation under the limitations and conditions provided in §122, a lawyer may not represent a client if there is a substantial risk that the lawyer's representation of the client would be materially and adversely affected by the lawyer's financial or other personal interests.

§126. Business Transactions Between a Lawyer and a Client

A lawyer may not participate in a business or financial transaction with a client, except a standard commercial transaction in which the lawyer does not render legal services, unless:

(1) the client has adequate information about the terms of the transaction and the risks presented by the lawyer's involvement in it;

(2) the terms and circumstances of the transaction are fair and reasonable to the client; and

(3) the client consents to the lawyer's role in the transaction under the limitations and conditions provided in §122 after being encouraged, and given a reasonable opportunity, to seek independent legal advice concerning the transaction.

§127. A Client Gift to a Lawyer

(1) A lawyer may not prepare any instrument effecting any gift from a client to the lawyer, including a testamentary gift, unless the lawyer is a relative or other natural object of the client's generosity and the gift is not significantly disproportionate to those given other donees similarly related to the donor.

(2) A lawyer may not accept a gift from a client, including a testamentary gift, unless:

(a) the lawyer is a relative or other natural object of the client's generosity;

(b) the value conferred by the client and the benefit to the lawyer are insubstantial in amount; or

(c) the client, before making the gift, has received independent advice or has been encouraged, and given a reasonable opportunity, to seek such advice.

TOPIC 3. CONFLICTS OF INTEREST AMONG CURRENT CLIENTS

§128. Representing Clients with Conflicting Interests in Civil Litigation

Unless all affected clients consent to the representation under the limitations and conditions provided in §122, a lawyer in civil litigation may not:

(1) represent two or more clients in a matter if there is a substantial risk that the lawyer's representation of one client would be materially and adversely affected by the lawyer's duties to another client in the matter; or

(2) represent one client to assert or defend a claim against or brought by another client currently represented by the lawyer, even if the matters are not related.

§129. Conflicts of Interest in Criminal Litigation

Unless all affected clients consent to the representation under the limitations and conditions provided in §122, a lawyer in a criminal matter may not represent:

(1) two or more defendants or potential defendants in the same matter; or

(2) a single defendant, if the representation would involve a conflict of interest as defined in §121.

§130. Multiple Representation in a Nonlitigated Matter

Unless all affected clients consent to the representation under the limitations and conditions provided in §122, a lawyer may not represent two or more clients in a matter not involving litigation if there is a substantial risk that the lawyer's representation of one or more of the clients would be materially and adversely affected by the lawyer's duties to one or more of the other clients.

§131. Conflicts of Interest in Representing an Organization

Unless all affected clients consent to the representation under the limitations and conditions provided in §122, a lawyer may not represent both an organization and a director, officer, employee, shareholder, owner, partner, member, or other individual or organization associated with the organization if there is a substantial risk that the lawyer's representation of either would be materially and adversely affected by the lawyer's duties to the other.

TOPIC 4. CONFLICTS OF INTEREST WITH A FORMER CLIENT

§132. A Representation Adverse to the Interests of a Former Client

Unless both the affected present and former clients consent to the representation under the limitations and conditions provided in §122, a lawyer who has represented a client in a matter may not thereafter represent another client in the same or a substantially related matter in which the interests of the former client are materially adverse. The current matter is substantially related to the earlier matter if:

(1) the current matter involves the work the lawyer performed for the former client; or

(2) there is a substantial risk that representation of the present client will involve the use of information acquired in the course of representing the former client, unless that information has become generally known.

§133. A Former Government Lawyer or Officer

(1) A lawyer may not act on behalf of a client with respect to a matter in which the lawyer participated personally and substantially while

acting as a government lawyer or officer unless both the government and the client consent to the representation under the limitations and conditions provided in §122.

(2) A lawyer who acquires confidential information while acting as a government lawyer or officer may not:

(a) if the information concerns a person, represent a client whose interests are materially adverse to that person in a matter in which the information could be used to the material disadvantage of that person; or

(b) if the information concerns the governmental client or employer, represent another public or private client in circumstances described in §132(2).

TOPIC 5. CONFLICTS OF INTEREST DUE TO A LAWYER'S OBLIGATION TO A THIRD PERSON

§134. Compensation or Direction of a Lawyer by a Third Person

(1) A lawyer may not represent a client if someone other than the client will wholly or partly compensate the lawyer for the representation, unless the client consents under the limitations and conditions provided in §122 and knows of the circumstances and conditions of the payment.

(2) A lawyer's professional conduct on behalf of a client may be directed by someone other than the client if:

(a) the direction does not interfere with the lawyer's independence of professional judgment;

(b) the direction is reasonable in scope and character, such as by reflecting obligations borne by the person directing the lawyer; and

(c) the client consents to the direction under the limitations and conditions provided in §122.

§135. A Lawyer with a Fiduciary or Other Legal Obligation to a Nonclient

Unless the affected client consents to the representation under the limitations and conditions provided in §122, a lawyer may not represent a client in any matter with respect to which the lawyer has a fiduciary or other legal obligation to another if there is a substantial risk that the lawyer's representation of the client would be materially and adversely affected by the lawyer's obligation.

ABA Model Code of Professional Responsibility*

In effect from August 1969 until August 1983

Editors' Introduction. From 1908 to 1969, the ABA's formal position on matters of legal ethics was embodied in the ABA's Canons of Professional Ethics. In 1964, however, amidst growing dissatisfaction with the Canons, the ABA appointed a Special Committee on the Evaluation of Ethical Standards (the "Wright Committee") to study the Canons. The Wright Committee drafted a proposed Code of Professional Responsibility, which was ultimately approved by the ABA House of Delegates in August of 1969. By 1980, nearly every state had adopted a Code of Professional Responsibility modeled on the ABA Code. The Code of Professional Responsibility consists of a Preamble, a Preliminary Statement, nine Canons (which essentially divide the rules into chapters, much like the Article headings do in the ABA Model Rules of Professional Conduct), and a set of Definitions. Each Canon consists of non-binding "aspirational" Ethical Considerations (ECs) and binding "mandatory" Disciplinary Rules (DRs).

The ABA replaced the Model Code with the Model Rules of Professional Conduct in 1983. Since then, every U.S. jurisdiction has revised its ethical rules to conform, in some degree, to the ABA Model Rules. Today, no state uses the Model Code's format or numbering system. Many of the Model Rules, however, closely parallel their counterparts in the Model Code. After each Canon of the ABA Model Code of Professional Responsibility, we have included a table relating each Disciplinary Rule (DR) in the Model Code to comparable provisions in the latest version of the ABA Model Rules. (To find a Disciplinary Rule comparable to a Model Rule, see our "Canon and Code Antecedents" after each Model Rule.)

*Copyright © 1983 by the American Bar Association. All rights reserved. Reprinted with permission of the American Bar Association.

The Model Code was amended seven times during the 1970s, principally in response to Supreme Court opinions concerning advertising and group legal services. The version of the Model Code reprinted below is the 1980 version of the Code, which remained in effect until the ABA adopted the Model Rules of Professional Conduct in August 1983. Because the ABA has not amended the Model Code in more than three decades, and because no state still uses the Code format, we reprint only the Preamble, the Preliminary Statement, the Canons, the Disciplinary Rules, and the Definitions. We omit all footnotes (whose main purpose was to relate the Code to the old ABA Canons of Professional Ethics), and we omit all Ethical Considerations (which are lengthy and non-binding). The full ABA Model Code of Professional Responsibility is available at *http://www.americanbar.org/content/dam/aba/migrated/cpr/mrpc/mcpr.authcheckdam.pdf.*

Contents

PREAMBLE

The continued existence of a free and democratic society depends upon recognition of the concept that justice is based upon the rule of law grounded in respect for the dignity of the individual and his capacity through reason for enlightened self-government. Law so grounded makes justice possible, for only through such law does the dignity of the individual attain respect and protection. Without it, individual rights become subject to unrestrained power, respect for law is destroyed, and rational self-government is impossible.

Lawyers, as guardians of the law, play a vital role in the preservation of society. The fulfillment of this role requires an understanding by lawyers of their relationship with and function in our legal system. A consequent obligation of lawyers is to maintain the highest standards of ethical conduct.

In fulfilling his professional responsibilities, a lawyer necessarily assumes various roles that require the performance of many difficult tasks. Not every situation which he may encounter can be foreseen, but fundamental ethical principles are always present to guide him. Within the framework of these principles, a lawyer must with courage and foresight be able and ready to shape the body of the law to the ever-changing relationships of society.

The Model Code of Professional Responsibility points the way to the aspiring and provides standards by which to judge the transgressor. Each lawyer must find within his own conscience the touchstone against which to test the extent to which his actions should rise above minimum standards. But in the last analysis it is the desire for the respect and confidence of the members of his profession and of the society which he serves that should provide to a lawyer the incentive for the highest possible degree of ethical conduct. The possible loss of that respect and confidence is the ultimate sanction. So long as its practitioners are guided by these principles, the law will continue to be a noble profession. This is its greatness and its strength, which permit of no compromise.

PRELIMINARY STATEMENT

In furtherance of the principles stated in the Preamble, the American Bar Association has promulgated this Model Code of Professional Responsibility, consisting of three separate but interrelated parts: Canons, Ethical Considerations, and Disciplinary Rules. The Model Code is designed to be adopted by appropriate agencies both as an inspirational guide to the members of the profession and as a basis for disciplinary action when the conduct of a lawyer falls below the required minimum standards stated in the Disciplinary Rules.

Obviously the Canons, Ethical Considerations, and Disciplinary Rules cannot apply to non-lawyers; however, they do define the type of ethical conduct that the public has a right to expect not only of lawyers but also of their non-professional employees and associates in all matters pertaining to professional employment. A lawyer should ultimately be responsible for the conduct of his employees and associates in the course of the professional representation of the client.

The Canons are statements of axiomatic norms, expressing in general terms the standards of professional conduct expected of lawyers in their relationships with the public, with the legal system, and with the legal profession. They embody the general concepts from which the Ethical Considerations and the Disciplinary Rules are derived.

The Ethical Considerations are aspirational in character and represent the objectives toward which every member of the profession should strive. They constitute a body of principles upon which the lawyer can rely for guidance in many specific situations.

The Disciplinary Rules, unlike the Ethical Considerations, are mandatory in character. The Disciplinary Rules state the minimum level of conduct below which no lawyer can fall without being subject to disciplinary action. Within the framework of fair trial, the Disciplinary Rules should be uniformly applied to all lawyers, regardless of the nature of their professional activities. The Model Code makes no attempt to prescribe either disciplinary procedures or penalties for violation of a Disciplinary Rule, nor does it undertake to define standards for civil liability of lawyers for professional conduct. The severity of judgment against one found guilty of violating a Disciplinary Rule should be determined by the character of the offense and the attendant circumstances. An enforcing agency, in applying the Disciplinary Rules, may find interpretive guidance in the basic principles embodied in the Canons and in the objectives reflected in the Ethical Considerations.

CANON 1. A LAWYER SHOULD ASSIST IN MAINTAINING THE INTEGRITY AND COMPETENCE OF THE LEGAL PROFESSION

DR 1-101 Maintaining Integrity and Competence of the Legal Profession

(A) A lawyer is subject to discipline if he has made a materially false statement in, or if he has deliberately failed to disclose a material fact requested in connection with, his application for admission to the bar.

(B) A lawyer shall not further the application for admission to the bar of another person known by him to be unqualified in respect to character, education, or other relevant attribute.

DR 1-102 Misconduct

(A) A lawyer shall not:

(1) Violate a Disciplinary Rule.

(2) Circumvent a Disciplinary Rule through actions of another.

(3) Engage in illegal conduct involving moral turpitude.

(4) Engage in conduct involving dishonesty, fraud, deceit, or misrepresentation.

(5) Engage in conduct that is prejudicial to the administration of justice.

(6) Engage in any other conduct that adversely reflects on his fitness to practice law.

DR 1-103 Disclosure of Information to Authorities

(A) A lawyer possessing unprivileged knowledge of a violation of DR 1-102 shall report such knowledge to a tribunal or other authority empowered to investigate or act upon such violation.

(B) A lawyer possessing unprivileged knowledge or evidence concerning another lawyer or a judge shall reveal fully such knowledge or evidence upon proper request of a tribunal or other authority empowered to investigate or act upon the conduct of lawyers or judges.

Model Rules Comparison

Model Code	*ABA Model Rules*
DR 1-101	8.1(a)
DR 1-102(A)(1)	8.4(a)
DR 1-102(A)(2)	5.1(c), 5.3(b), 8.4(a)
DR 1-102(A)(3)	8.4(b), (f)
DR 1-102(A)(4)	3.3(a), 3.4(a) &(b), 4.1, 8.4(c)
DR 1-102(A)(5)	3.1 through 3.9, 8.1, 8.4(d) & (f)
DR 1-102(A)(6)	3.4(b), 8.4
DR 1-103(A)	5.1, 8.3
DR 1-103(B)	8.1(b)

CANON 2. A LAWYER SHOULD ASSIST THE LEGAL PROFESSION IN FULFILLING ITS DUTY TO MAKE LEGAL COUNSEL AVAILABLE

DR 2-101 Publicity

(A) lawyer shall not, on behalf of himself, his partner, associate or any other lawyer affiliated with him or his firm, use or participate in the use of any form of public communication containing a false, fraudulent, misleading, deceptive, self-laudatory or unfair statement or claim.

(B) In order to facilitate the process of informed selection of a lawyer by potential consumers of legal services, a lawyer may publish or broadcast, subject to DR 2-103, the following information in print media distributed or over television or radio broadcast in the geographic area or areas in which the lawyer resides or maintains offices or in which a significant part of the lawyer's clientele resides, provided that the information disclosed by the lawyer in such publication or broadcast complies with DR 2-101(A), and is presented in a dignified manner:

(1) Name, including name of law firm and names of professional associates; addresses and telephone numbers;

(2) One or more fields of law in which the lawyer or law firm practices, a statement that practice is limited to one or more fields of law, or a statement that the lawyer or law firm specializes in a particular field of law practice, to the extent authorized under DR 2-105;

(3) Date and place of birth;

(4) Date and place of admission to the bar of state and federal courts;

(5) Schools attended, with dates of graduation, degrees and other scholastic distinctions;

(6) Public or quasi-public offices;

(7) Military service;

(8) Legal authorships;

(9) Legal teaching positions;

(10) Memberships, offices, and committee assignments, in bar associations;

(11) Membership and offices in legal fraternities and legal societies;

(12) Technical and professional licenses;

(13) Memberships in scientific, technical and professional associations and societies;

(14) Foreign language ability;

(15) Names and addresses of bank references;

(16) With their written consent, names of clients regularly represented;

(17) Prepaid or group legal services programs in which the lawyer participates;

(18) Whether credit cards or other credit arrangements are accepted;

(19) Office and telephone answering service hours;

(20) Fee for an initial consultation;

(21) Availability upon request of a written schedule of fees and/or an estimate of the fee to be charged for specific services;

(22) Contingent fee rates subject to DR 2-106(C), provided that the statement discloses whether percentages are computed before or after deduction of costs;

(23) Range of fees for services, provided that the statement discloses that the specific fee within the range which will be charged will vary depending upon the particular matter to be handled for each client and the client is entitled without obligation to an estimate of the fee within the range likely to be charged, in print size equivalent to the largest print used in setting forth the fee information;

(24) Hourly rate, provided that the statement discloses that the total fee charged will depend upon the number of hours which must be devoted to the particular matter to be handled for each client and the client is entitled to without obligation an estimate of the fee likely to be charged, in print size at least equivalent to the largest print used in setting forth the fee information;

(25) Fixed fees for specific legal services, the description of which would not be misunderstood or be deceptive, provided that the statement discloses that the quoted fee will be available only to clients whose matters fall into the services described and that the client is entitled without obligation to a specific estimate of the fee likely to be charged in print size at least equivalent to the largest print used in setting forth the fee information.

(C) Any person desiring to expand the information authorized for disclosure in DR 2-101(B), or to provide for its dissemination through other forums may apply to [the agency having jurisdiction under state law]. Any such application shall be served upon [the agencies having jurisdiction under state law over the regulation of the legal profession and consumer matters] who shall be heard, together with the applicant, on the issue of whether the proposal is necessary in light of the existing provisions of the Code, accords with standards of accuracy, reliability and truthfulness, and would facilitate the process of informed selection of lawyers by potential consumers of legal services. The relief granted in response to any such application shall be promulgated as an amendment to DR 2-101(B), universally applicable to all lawyers.

(D) If the advertisement is communicated to the public over television or radio, it shall be prerecorded, approved for broadcast by the lawyer, and a recording of the actual transmission shall be retained by the lawyer.

(E) If a lawyer advertises a fee for a service, the lawyer must render that service for no more than the fee advertised.

(F) Unless otherwise specified in the advertisement if a lawyer publishes any fee information authorized under DR 2-101(B) in a publication that is published more frequently than one time per month, the lawyer shall be bound by any representation made therein for a period of not less than 30 days after such publication. If a lawyer publishes any fee information authorized under DR 2-101(B) in a publication that is published once a month or less frequently, he shall be bound by any representation made therein until the publication of the succeeding issue. If a lawyer publishes any fee information authorized under DR 2-101(B) in a publication which has no fixed date for publication of a succeeding issue, the lawyer shall be bound by any representation made therein for a reasonable period of time after publication but in no event less than one year.

(G) Unless otherwise specified, if a lawyer broadcasts any fee information authorized under DR 2-101(B), the lawyer shall be bound by any representation made therein for a period of not less than 30 days after such broadcast.

(H) This rule does not prohibit limited and dignified identification of a lawyer as a lawyer as well as by name:

(1) In political advertisements when his professional status is germane to the political campaign or to a political issue.

(2) In public notices when the name and profession of a lawyer are required or authorized by law or are reasonably pertinent for a purpose other than the attraction of potential clients.

(3) In routine reports and announcements of a bona fide business, civic, professional, or political organization in which he serves as a director or officer.

(4) In and on legal documents prepared by him.

(5) In and on legal textbooks, treatises, and other legal publications, and in dignified advertisements thereof.

(I) A lawyer shall not compensate or give any thing of value to representatives of the press, radio, television, or other communication medium in anticipation of or in return for professional publicity in a news item.

DR 2-102 Professional Notices, Letterheads and Offices

(A) A lawyer or law firm shall not use or participate in the use of professional cards, professional announcement cards, office signs, letterheads, or similar professional notices or devices, except that the following may be used if they are in dignified form:

(1) A professional card of a lawyer identifying him by name and as a lawyer, and giving his addresses, telephone numbers, the name of his law firm, and any information permitted under DR 2-105. A professional card of a law firm may also give the names of members and associates. Such cards may be used for identification.

(2) A brief professional announcement card stating new or changed associations or addresses, change of firm name, or similar matters pertaining to the professional offices of a lawyer or law firm, which may be mailed to lawyers, clients, former clients, personal friends, and relatives. It shall not state biographical data except to the extent reasonably necessary to identify the lawyer or to explain the change in his association, but it may state the immediate past position of the lawyer. It may give the names and dates of predecessor firms in a continuing line of succession. It shall not state the nature of the practice except as permitted under DR 2-105.

(3) A sign on or near the door of the office and in the building directory identifying the law office. The sign shall not state the nature of the practice, except as permitted under DR 2-105.

(4) A letterhead of a lawyer identifying him by name and as a lawyer, and giving his addresses, telephone numbers, the name of his law firm, associates and any information permitted under DR 2-105. A letterhead of a law firm may also give the names of members and associates, and names and dates relating to deceased and retired members. A lawyer may be designated "Of Counsel" on a letterhead if he has a continuing relationship with a lawyer or law firm, other than as a partner or associate. A lawyer or law firm may be designated as "General Counsel" or by similar professional reference on stationery of a client if he or the firm devotes a substantial amount of professional time in the representation of that client. The letterhead of a law firm may give the names and dates of predecessor firms in a continuing line of succession.

(B) A lawyer in private practice shall not practice under a trade name, a name that is misleading as to the identity of the lawyer or lawyers practicing under such name, or a firm name containing names other than those of one or more of the lawyers in the firm, except that the name of a professional corporation or professional association may contain "P.C." or "P.A." or similar symbols indicating the nature of the organization, and if otherwise lawful a firm may use as, or continue to include in, its name the name or names of one or more deceased or retired members of the firm or of a predecessor firm in a continuing line of succession. A lawyer who assumes a judicial, legislative, or public executive or administrative post or office shall not permit his name to remain in the name of a law firm or to be used in professional notices of the firm during any significant period in which he is not actively and regularly practicing law as a member of the firm, and during such period other members of the firm shall not use his name in the firm name or in professional notices of the firm.

(C) A lawyer shall not hold himself out as having a partnership with one or more other lawyers or professional corporations unless they are in fact partners.

(D) A partnership shall not be formed or continued between or among lawyers licensed in different jurisdictions unless all enumerations of the members and associates of the firm on its letterhead and in other permissible listings make clear the jurisdictional limitations on those members and associates of the firm not licensed to practice in all listed jurisdictions; however, the same firm name may be used in each jurisdiction.

(E) Nothing contained herein shall prohibit a lawyer from using or permitting the use of, in connection with his name, an earned degree or title derived therefrom indicating his training in the law.

DR 2-103 Recommendation of Professional Employment

(A) A lawyer shall not, except as authorized in DR 2-101(B), recommend employment as a private practitioner, of himself, his partner, or associate to a layperson who has not sought his advice regarding employment of a lawyer.

(B) A lawyer shall not compensate or give anything of value to a person or organization to recommend or secure his employment by a client, or as a reward for having made a recommendation resulting in his employment by a client, except that he may pay the usual and reasonable fees or dues charged by any of the organizations listed in DR 2-103(D).

(C) A lawyer shall not request a person or organization to recommend or promote the use of his services or those of his partner or associate, or any other lawyer affiliated with him or his firm, as a private practitioner, except as authorized in DR 2-101, and except that

(1) He may request referrals from a lawyer referral service operated, sponsored, or approved by a bar association and may pay its fees incident thereto.

(2) He may cooperate with the legal service activities of any of the offices or organizations enumerated in DR 2-103(D)(1) through (4) and may perform legal services for those to whom he was recommended by it to do such work if:

(a) The person to whom the recommendation is made is a member or beneficiary of such office or organization; and

(b) The lawyer remains free to exercise his independent professional judgment on behalf of his client.

(D) A lawyer or his partner or associate or any other lawyer affiliated with him or his firm may be recommended, employed or paid by, or may cooperate with, one of the following offices or organizations that promote the use of his services or those of his partner or associate or any other lawyer affiliated with him or his firm if there is no interference with the exercise of independent professional judgment in behalf of his client:

(1) A legal aid office or public defender office:

(a) Operated or sponsored by a duly accredited law school.

(b) Operated or sponsored by a bona fide nonprofit community organization.

(c) Operated or sponsored by a governmental agency.

(d) Operated, sponsored, or approved by a bar association.

(2) A military legal assistance office.

(3) A lawyer referral service operated, sponsored, or approved by a bar association.

(4) Any bona fide organization that recommends, furnishes or pays for legal services to its members or beneficiaries provided the following conditions are satisfied:

(a) Such organization, including any affiliate, is so organized and operated that no profit is derived by it from the rendition of legal services by lawyers, and that, if the organization is organized for profit, the legal services are not rendered by lawyers employed, directed, supervised or selected by it except in connection with matters where such organization bears ultimate liability of its member or beneficiary.

(b) Neither the lawyer, nor his partner, nor associate, nor any other lawyer affiliated with him or his firm, nor any non-lawyer, shall have initiated or promoted such organization for the primary purpose of providing financial or other benefit to such lawyer, partner, associate or affiliated lawyer.

(c) Such organization is not operated for the purpose of procuring legal work or financial benefit for any lawyer as a private practitioner outside of the legal services program of the organization.

(d) The member or beneficiary to whom the legal services are furnished, and not such organization, is recognized as the client of the lawyer in the matter.

(e) Any member or beneficiary who is entitled to have legal services furnished or paid for by the organization may, if such member or beneficiary so desires, select counsel other than that furnished, selected or approved by the organization for the particular matter involved; and the legal service plan of such organization provides appropriate relief for any member or beneficiary who asserts a claim that representation by counsel furnished, selected or approved would be unethical, improper or inadequate under the circumstances of the matter involved and the plan provides an appropriate procedure for seeking such relief.

(f) The lawyer does not know or have cause to know that such organization is in violation of applicable laws, rules of court and other legal requirements that govern its legal service operations.

(g) Such organization has filed with the appropriate disciplinary authority at least annually a report with respect to its legal service plan, if any, showing its terms, its schedule of benefits, its subscription charges, agreements with counsel, and financial results of its legal service activities or, if it has failed to do so, the lawyer does not know or have cause to know of such failure.

(E) A lawyer shall not accept employment when he knows or it is obvious that the person who seeks his services does so as a result of conduct prohibited under this Disciplinary Rule.

DR 2-104 Suggestion of Need of Legal Services

(A) A lawyer who has given in-person unsolicited advice to a layperson that he should obtain counsel or take legal action shall not accept employment resulting from that advice, except that:

(1) A lawyer may accept employment by a close friend, relative, former client (if the advice is germane to the former employment), or one whom the lawyer reasonably believes to be a client.

(2) A lawyer may accept employment that results from his participation in activities designed to educate laypersons to recognize legal problems, to make intelligent selection of counsel, or to utilize available legal services if such activities are conducted or sponsored by a qualified legal assistance organization.

(3) A lawyer who is recommended, furnished or paid by a qualified legal assistance organization enumerated in DR 2-103(D)(1) through (4) may represent a member or beneficiary thereof, to the extent and under the conditions prescribed therein.

(4) Without affecting his right to accept employment, a lawyer may speak publicly or write for publication on legal topics so long as he does not emphasize his own professional experience or reputation and does not undertake to give individual advice.

(5) If success in asserting rights or defenses of his client in litigation in the nature of a class action is dependent upon the joinder of others, a lawyer may accept, but shall not seek, employment from those contacted for the purpose of obtaining their joinder.

DR 2-105 Limitation of Practice

(A) A lawyer shall not hold himself out publicly as a specialist, as practicing in certain areas of law or as limiting his practice permitted under DR 2-101(B), except as follows:

(1) A lawyer admitted to practice before the United States Patent and Trademark Office may use the designation "Patents," "Patent Attorney," "Patent Lawyer," or "Registered Patent Attorney" or any combination of those terms, on his letterhead and office sign.

(2) A lawyer who publicly discloses fields of law in which the lawyer or the law firm practices or states that his practice is limited to one or more fields of law shall do so by using designations and definitions authorized and approved by [the agency having jurisdiction of the subject under state law].

(3) A lawyer who is certified as a specialist in a particular field of law or law practice by [the authority having jurisdiction under state law over the subject of specialization by lawyers] may hold himself out as such, but only in accordance with the rules prescribed by that authority.

DR 2-106 Fees for Legal Services

(A) A lawyer shall not enter into an agreement for, charge, or collect an illegal or clearly excessive fee.

(B) A fee is clearly excessive when, after a review of the facts, a lawyer of ordinary prudence would be left with a definite and firm conviction that the fee is in excess of a reasonable fee. Factors to be considered as guides in determining the reasonableness of a fee include the following:

(1) The time and labor required, the novelty and difficulty of the questions involved, and the skill requisite to perform the legal service properly.

(2) The likelihood, if apparent to the client, that the acceptance of the particular employment will preclude other employment by the lawyer.

(3) The fee customarily charged in the locality for similar legal services.

(4) The amount involved and the results obtained.

(5) The time limitations imposed by the client or by the circumstances.

(6) The nature and length of the professional relationship with the client.

(7) The experience, reputation, and ability of the lawyer or lawyers performing the services.

(8) Whether the fee is fixed or contingent.

(C) A lawyer shall not enter into an arrangement for, charge, or collect a contingent fee for representing a defendant in a criminal case.

DR 2-107 Division of Fees Among Lawyers

(A) A lawyer shall not divide a fee for legal services with another lawyer who is not a partner in or associate of his law firm or law office, unless:

(1) The client consents to employment of the other lawyer after a full disclosure that a division of fees will be made.

(2) The division is made in proportion to the services performed and responsibility assumed by each.

(3) The total fee of the lawyers does not clearly exceed reasonable compensation for all legal services they rendered the client.

(B) This Disciplinary Rule does not prohibit payment to a former partner or associate pursuant to a separation or retirement agreement.

DR 2-108 Agreements Restricting the Practice of a Lawyer

(A) A lawyer shall not be a party to or participate in a partnership or employment agreement with another lawyer that restricts the right of a lawyer to practice law after the termination of a relationship created by the agreement, except as a condition to payment of retirement benefits.

(B) In connection with the settlement of a controversy or suit, a lawyer shall not enter into an agreement that restricts his right to practice law.

DR 2-109 Acceptance of Employment

(A) A lawyer shall not accept employment on behalf of a person if he knows or it is obvious that such person wishes to:

(1) Bring a legal action, conduct a defense, or assert a position in litigation, or otherwise have steps taken for him, merely for the purpose of harassing or maliciously injuring any person.

(2) Present a claim or defense in litigation that is not warranted under existing law, unless it can be supported by good faith argument for an extension, modification, or reversal of existing law.

DR 2-110 Withdrawal from Employment

(A) *In general.*

(1) If permission for withdrawal from employment is required by the rules of a tribunal, a lawyer shall not withdraw from employment in a proceeding before that tribunal without its permission.

(2) In any event, a lawyer shall not withdraw from employment until he has taken reasonable steps to avoid foreseeable prejudice to the rights of his client, including giving due notice to his client, allowing time for employment of other counsel, delivering to the client all papers and property to which the client is entitled, and complying with applicable laws and rules.

(3) A lawyer who withdraws from employment shall refund promptly any part of a fee paid in advance that has not been earned.

(B) *Mandatory withdrawal.*

A lawyer representing a client before a tribunal, with its permission if required by its rules, shall withdraw from employment, and a lawyer representing a client in other matters shall withdraw from employment, if:

(1) He knows or it is obvious that his client is bringing the legal action, conducting the defense, or asserting a position in the litigation, or is otherwise having steps taken for him, merely for the purpose of harassing or maliciously injuring any person.

(2) He knows or it is obvious that his continued employment will result in violation of a Disciplinary Rule.

(3) His mental or physical condition renders it unreasonably difficult for him to carry out the employment effectively.

(4) He is discharged by his client.

(C) *Permissive withdrawal.*

If DR 2-110(B) is not applicable, a lawyer may not request permission to withdraw in matters pending before a tribunal, and may not withdraw in other matters, unless such request or such withdrawal is because:

(1) His client:

(a) Insists upon presenting a claim or defense that is not warranted under existing law and cannot be supported by good faith argument for an extension, modification, or reversal of existing law.

(b) Personally seeks to pursue an illegal course of conduct.

(c) Insists that the lawyer pursue a course of conduct that is illegal or that is prohibited under the Disciplinary Rules.

(d) By other conduct renders it unreasonably difficult for the lawyer to carry out his employment effectively.

(e) Insists, in a matter not pending before a tribunal, that the lawyer engage in conduct that is contrary to the judgment and advice of the lawyer but not prohibited under the Disciplinary Rules.

(f) Deliberately disregards an agreement or obligation to the lawyer as to expenses or fees.

(2) His continued employment is likely to result in a violation of a Disciplinary Rule.

(3) His inability to work with co-counsel indicates that the best interests of the client likely will be served by withdrawal.

(4) His mental or physical condition renders it difficult for him to carry out the employment effectively.

(5) His client knowingly and freely assents to termination of his employment.

(6) He believes in good faith, in a proceeding pending before a tribunal, that the tribunal will find the existence of other good cause for withdrawal.

Model Rules Comparison

Model Code	*ABA Model Rules*
DR 2-101(A)	7.1
DR 2-101(B)	7.1, 7.2(a)
DR 2-101(C)	No comparable Rule
DR 2-101(D)	No comparable Rule
DR 2-101(E)	7.1
DR 2-101(F)	7.1
DR 2-101(G)	7.1
DR 2-101(H)	7.2(a)
DR 2-101(I)	7.2(b)
DR 2-102(A)	7.2(a), 7.5
DR 2-102(B)	7.1, 7.5(a), (c)
DR 2-102(C)	7.5(d)
DR 2-102(D)	7.5(b)
DR 2-102(E)	7.1(a), 7.4
DR 2-103(A)	7.3
DR 2-103(B)	5.4(c), 7.2(b), 7.6

Model Code	*ABA Model Rules*
DR 2-103(C)	5.4(c), 7.2(b), 7.3
DR 2-103(D)	5.4(c), 7.2(b), 7.3
DR 2-103(E)	1.16(a), 8.4(a)
DR 2-104	1.16(a), 7.3
DR 2-105	7.4
DR 2-106(A)	1.5(a)
DR 2-106(B)	1.5(a)
DR 2-106(C)	1.5(d)
DR 2-107(A)	1.5(e)
DR 2-107(B)	5.4(a)
DR 2-108(A)	5.6(a)
DR 2-108(B)	5.6(b)
DR 2-109(A)	1.16(a), 3.1, 3.2
DR 2-110(A)	1.16(c), (d)
DR 2-110(B)	1.16(a), 3.1, 4.4(a)
DR 2-110(C)	1.16(b)

CANON 3. A LAWYER SHOULD ASSIST IN PREVENTING THE UNAUTHORIZED PRACTICE OF LAW

DR 3-101 Aiding Unauthorized Practice of Law

(A) A lawyer shall not aid a non-lawyer in the unauthorized practice of law.

(B) A lawyer shall not practice law in a jurisdiction where to do so would be in violation of regulations of the profession in that jurisdiction.

DR 3-102 Dividing Legal Fees with a Non-Lawyer

(A) A lawyer or law firm shall not share legal fees with a non-lawyer, except that:

(1) An agreement by a lawyer with his firm, partner, or associate may provide for the payment of money, over a reasonable period of time after his death, to his estate or to one or more specified persons.

(2) A lawyer who undertakes to complete unfinished legal business of a deceased lawyer may pay to the estate of the deceased lawyer that proportion of the total compensation which fairly represents the services rendered by the deceased lawyer.

(3) A lawyer or law firm may include non-lawyer employees in a compensation or retirement plan, even though the plan is based in whole or in part on a profit-sharing arrangement, providing such plan does not circumvent another Disciplinary Rule.

DR 3-103 Forming a Partnership with a Non-Lawyer

(A) A lawyer shall not form a partnership with a non-lawyer if any of the activities of the partnership consist of the practice of law.

Model Rules Comparison

Model Code	*ABA Model Rules*
DR 3-101(A)	5.5(a)
DR 3-101(B)	5.5(a)
DR 3-102	5.4(a)
DR 3-103	5.4(b)

CANON 4. A LAWYER SHOULD PRESERVE THE CONFIDENCES AND SECRETS OF A CLIENT

DR 4-101 Preservation of Confidences and Secrets of a Client

(A) "Confidence" refers to information protected by the attorney-client privilege under applicable law, and "secret" refers to other information gained in the professional relationship that the client has requested be held inviolate or the disclosure of which would be embarrassing or would be likely to be detrimental to the client.

(B) Except when permitted under DR 4-101(C), a lawyer shall not knowingly:

(1) Reveal a confidence or secret of his client.

(2) Use a confidence or secret of his client to the disadvantage of the client.

(3) Use a confidence or secret of his client for the advantage of himself or of a third person, unless the client consents after full disclosure.

(C) A lawyer may reveal:

(1) Confidences or secrets with the consent of the client or clients affected, but only after a full disclosure to them.

(2) Confidences or secrets when permitted under Disciplinary Rules or required by law or court order.

(3) The intention of his client to commit a crime and the information necessary to prevent the crime.

(4) Confidences or secrets necessary to establish or collect his fee or to defend himself or his employees or associates against an accusation of wrongful conduct.

(D) A lawyer shall exercise reasonable care to prevent his employees, associates, and others whose services are utilized by him from disclosing or using confidences or secrets of a client, except that a lawyer may reveal the information allowed by DR 4-101(C) through an employee.

Model Rules Comparison

Model Code	*ABA Model Rules*
DR 4-101(A)	1.6(a)
DR 4-101(B)	1.6(a), 1.8(b), 1.9(c), 1.18(b)
DR 4-101(C)	1.6(a), (b), 1.9(c), 1.13(c)
DR 4-101(D)	5.1(a), (b), 5.3(a), (b)

CANON 5. A LAWYER SHOULD EXERCISE INDEPENDENT PROFESSIONAL JUDGMENT ON BEHALF OF A CLIENT

DR 5-101 Refusing Employment When the Interests of the Lawyer May Impair His Independent Professional Judgment

(A) Except with the consent of his client after full disclosure, a lawyer shall not accept employment if the exercise of his professional judgment on behalf of his client will be or reasonably may be affected by his own financial, business, property, or personal interests.

(B) A lawyer shall not accept employment in contemplated or pending litigation if he knows or it is obvious that he or a lawyer in his firm ought to be called as a witness, except that he may undertake the employment and he or a lawyer in his firm may testify:

(1) If the testimony will relate solely to an uncontested matter.

(2) If the testimony will relate solely to a matter of formality and there is no reason to believe that substantial evidence will be offered in opposition to the testimony.

(3) If the testimony will relate solely to the nature and value of legal services rendered in the case by the lawyer or his firm to the client.

(4) As to any matter, if refusal would work a substantial hardship on the client because of the distinctive value of the lawyer or his firm as counsel in the particular case.

DR 5-102 Withdrawal as Counsel When the Lawyer Becomes a Witness

(A) If, after undertaking employment in contemplated or pending litigation, a lawyer learns or it is obvious that he or a lawyer in his firm ought to be called as a witness on behalf of his client, he shall withdraw from the conduct of the trial and his firm, if any, shall not continue representation in the trial, except that he may continue the representation and he or a lawyer in his firm may testify in the circumstances enumerated in DR 5-101(B)(1) through (4).

(B) If, after undertaking employment in contemplated or pending litigation, a lawyer learns or it is obvious that he or a lawyer in his firm may be called as a witness other than on behalf of his client, he may continue the representation until it is apparent that his testimony is or may be prejudicial to his client.

DR 5-103 Avoiding Acquisition of Interest in Litigation

(A) A lawyer shall not acquire a proprietary interest in the cause of action or subject matter of litigation he is conducting for a client, except that he may:

(1) Acquire a lien granted by law to secure his fee or expenses.

(2) Contract with a client for a reasonable contingent fee in a civil case.

(B) While representing a client in connection with contemplated or pending litigation, a lawyer shall not advance or guarantee financial assistance to his client, except that a lawyer may advance or guarantee the expenses of litigation, including court costs, expenses of investigation, expenses of medical examination, and costs of obtaining and presenting evidence, provided the client remains ultimately liable for such expenses.

DR 5-104 Limiting Business Relations with a Client

(A) A lawyer shall not enter into a business transaction with a client if they have differing interests therein and if the client expects the lawyer to exercise his professional judgment therein for the protection of the client, unless the client has consented after full disclosure.

(B) Prior to conclusion of all aspects of the matter giving rise to his employment, a lawyer shall not enter into any arrangement or understanding with a client or a prospective client by which he acquires an interest in publication rights with respect to the subject matter of his employment or proposed employment.

DR 5-105 Refusing to Accept or Continue Employment If the Interests of Another Client May Impair the Independent Professional Judgment of the Lawyer

(A) A lawyer shall decline proffered employment if the exercise of his independent professional judgment in behalf of a client will be or is likely to be adversely affected by the acceptance of the proffered employment, or if it would be likely to involve him in representing differing interests, except to the extent permitted under DR 5-105(C).

(B) A lawyer shall not continue multiple employment if the exercise of his independent professional judgment in behalf of a client will be or is likely to be adversely affected by his representation of another client, or if it would be likely to involve him in representing differing interests, except to the extent permitted under DR 5-105(C).

(C) In the situations covered by DR 5-105(A) and (B), a lawyer may represent multiple clients if it is obvious that he can adequately represent the interest of each and if each consents to the representation after full disclosure of the possible effect of such representation on the exercise of his independent professional judgment on behalf of each.

(D) If a lawyer is required to decline employment or to withdraw from employment under a Disciplinary Rule, no partner, or associate, or any other lawyer affiliated with him or his firm, may accept or continue such employment.

DR 5-106 Settling Similar Claims of Clients

(A) A lawyer who represents two or more clients shall not make or participate in the making of an aggregate settlement of the claims of or against his clients, unless each client has consented to the settlement after being advised of the existence and nature of all the claims involved in the proposed settlement, of the total amount of the settlement, and of the participation of each person in the settlement.

DR 5-107 Avoiding Influence by Others Than the Client

(A) Except with the consent of his client after full disclosure, a lawyer shall not:

(1) Accept compensation for his legal services from one other than his client.

(2) Accept from one other than his client any thing of value related to his representation of or his employment by his client.

(B) A lawyer shall not permit a person who recommends, employs, or pays him to render legal services for another to direct or regulate his professional judgment in rendering such legal services.

(C) A lawyer shall not practice with or in the form of a professional corporation or association authorized to practice law for a profit, if:

(1) A non-lawyer owns any interest therein, except that a fiduciary representative of the estate of a lawyer may hold the stock or interest of the lawyer for a reasonable time during administration;

(2) A non-lawyer is a corporate director or officer thereof; or

(3) A non-lawyer has the right to direct or control the professional judgment of a lawyer.

Model Rules Comparison

Model Code	*ABA Model Rules*	*Model Code*	*ABA Model Rules*
DR 5-101(A)	1.7, 1.8(a)-(j), 6.3, 6.4	DR 5-105(A)	1.7, 1.13(e)
DR 5-101(B)	1.7, 3.7	DR 5-105(B)	1.7, 1.13(e)
DR 5-102(A)	1.7, 3.7	DR 5-105(C)	1.7, 1.9, 1.13(e)
DR 5-102(B)	1.7, 3.7	DR 5-105(D)	1.10(a), 1.12(c), 1.18(c), (d), 6.5
DR 5-103(A)	1.5(c), 1.8(c), (i), 1.15(e)	DR 5-106	1.8(g)
DR 5-103(B)	1.8(e)	DR 5-107(A)	1.7, 1.8(f)
DR 5-104(A)	1.7, 1.8(a)	DR 5-107(B)	1.7, 1.8(f), 1.13(b), 2.1, 5.4(c)
DR 5-104(B)	1.8(d)	DR 5-107(C)	5.4(d)

CANON 6. A LAWYER SHOULD REPRESENT A CLIENT COMPETENTLY

DR 6-101 Failing to Act Competently

(A) A lawyer shall not:

(1) Handle a legal matter which he knows or should know that he is not competent to handle, without associating with him a lawyer who is competent to handle it.

(2) Handle a legal matter without preparation adequate in the circumstances.

(3) Neglect a legal matter entrusted to him.

DR 6-102 Limiting Liability to Client

(A) A lawyer shall not attempt to exonerate himself from or limit his liability to his client for his personal malpractice.

Model Rules Comparison

Model Code	*ABA Model Rules*
DR 6-101	1.1, 1.3, 1.4
DR 6-102	1.8(h)

CANON 7. A LAWYER SHOULD REPRESENT A CLIENT ZEALOUSLY WITHIN THE BOUNDS OF THE LAW

DR 7-101 Representing a Client Zealously

(A) A lawyer shall not intentionally:

(1) Fail to seek the lawful objectives of his client through reasonably available means permitted by law and the Disciplinary Rules, except as provided by DR 7-101(B). A lawyer does not violate this Disciplinary Rule, however, by acceding to reasonable requests of opposing counsel which do not prejudice the rights of his client, by being punctual in fulfilling all professional commitments, by avoiding offensive tactics, or by treating with courtesy and consideration all persons involved in the legal process.

(2) Fail to carry out a contract of employment entered into with a client for professional services, but he may withdraw as permitted under DR 2-110, DR 5-102, and DR 5-105.

(3) Prejudice or damage his client during the course of the professional relationship, except as required under DR 7-102(B).

(B) In his representation of a client, a lawyer may:

(1) Where permissible, exercise his professional judgment to waive or fail to assert a right or position of his client.

(2) Refuse to aid or participate in conduct that he believes to be unlawful, even though there is some support for an argument that the conduct is legal.

DR 7-102 Representing a Client Within the Bounds of the Law

(A) In his representation of a client, a lawyer shall not:

(1) File a suit, assert a position, conduct a defense, delay a trial, or take other action on behalf of his client when he knows or when it is obvious that such action would serve merely to harass or maliciously injure another.

(2) Knowingly advance a claim or defense that is unwarranted under existing law, except that he may advance such claim or defense if it can be supported by good faith argument for an extension, modification, or reversal of existing law.

(3) Conceal or knowingly fail to disclose that which he is required by law to reveal.

(4) Knowingly use perjured testimony or false evidence.

(5) Knowingly make a false statement of law or fact.

(6) Participate in the creation or preservation of evidence when he knows or it is obvious that the evidence is false.

(7) Counsel or assist his client in conduct that the lawyer knows to be illegal or fraudulent.

(8) Knowingly engage in other illegal conduct or conduct contrary to a Disciplinary Rule.

(B) A lawyer who receives information clearly establishing that:

(1) His client has, in the course of the representation, perpetrated a fraud upon a person or tribunal shall promptly call upon his client to rectify the same, and if his client refuses or is unable to do so, he shall reveal the fraud to the affected person or tribunal, except when the information is protected as a privileged communication.

(2) A person other than his client has perpetrated a fraud upon a tribunal shall promptly reveal the fraud to the tribunal.

DR 7-103 Performing the Duty of Public Prosecutor or Other Government Lawyer

(A) A public prosecutor or other government lawyer shall not institute or cause to be instituted criminal charges when he knows or it is obvious that the charges are not supported by probable cause.

(B) A public prosecutor or other government lawyer in criminal litigation shall make timely disclosure to counsel for the defendant, or to the defendant if he has no counsel, of the existence of evidence, known to the prosecutor or other government lawyer, that tends to negate the guilt of the accused, mitigate the degree of the offense, or reduce the punishment.

DR 7-104 Communicating with One of Adverse Interest

(A) During the course of his representation of a client a lawyer shall not:

(1) Communicate or cause another to communicate on the subject of the representation with a party he knows to be represented by a lawyer in that matter unless he has the prior consent of the lawyer representing such other party or is authorized by law to do so.

(2) Give advice to a person who is not represented by a lawyer, other than the advice to secure counsel, if the interests of such person are or have a reasonable possibility of being in conflict with the interests of his client.

DR 7-105 Threatening Criminal Prosecution

(A) A lawyer shall not present, participate in presenting, or threaten to present criminal charges solely to obtain an advantage in a civil matter.

DR 7-106 Trial Conduct

(A) A lawyer shall not disregard or advise his client to disregard a standing rule of a tribunal or a ruling of a tribunal made in the course of a proceeding, but he may take appropriate steps in good faith to test the validity of such rule or ruling.

(B) In presenting a matter to a tribunal, a lawyer shall disclose:

(1) Legal authority in the controlling jurisdiction known to him to be directly adverse to the position of his client and which is not disclosed by opposing counsel.

(2) Unless privileged or irrelevant, the identities of the clients he represents and of the persons who employed him.

(C) In appearing in his professional capacity before a tribunal, a lawyer shall not:

(1) State or allude to any matter that he has no reasonable basis to believe is relevant to the case or that will not be supported by admissible evidence.

(2) Ask any question that he has no reasonable basis to believe is relevant to the case and that is intended to degrade a witness or other person.

(3) Assert his personal knowledge of the facts in issue, except when testifying as a witness.

(4) Assert his personal opinion as to the justness of a cause, as to the credibility of a witness, as to the culpability of a civil litigant, or as to the guilt or innocence of an accused; but he may argue, on his analysis of the evidence, for any position or conclusion with respect to the matters stated herein.

(5) Fail to comply with known local customs of courtesy or practice of the bar or a particular tribunal without giving to opposing counsel timely notice of his intent not to comply.

(6) Engage in undignified or discourteous conduct which is degrading to a tribunal.

(7) Intentionally or habitually violate any established rule of procedure or of evidence.

DR 7-107 Trial Publicity

(A) A lawyer participating in or associated with the investigation of a criminal matter shall not make or participate in making an extrajudicial statement that a reasonable person would expect to be disseminated by means of public communication and that does more than state without elaboration:

(1) Information contained in a public record.

(2) That the investigation is in progress.

(3) The general scope of the investigation including a description of the offense and, if permitted by law, the identity of the victim.

(4) A request for assistance in apprehending a suspect or assistance in other matters and the information necessary thereto.

(5) A warning to the public of any dangers.

(B) A lawyer or law firm associated with the prosecution or defense of a criminal matter shall not, from the time of the filing of a complaint, information, or indictment, the issuance of an arrest warrant, or arrest until the commencement of the trial or disposition without trial, make or participate in making an extrajudicial statement that a reasonable person would expect to be disseminated by means of public communication and that relates to:

(1) The character, reputation, or prior criminal record (including arrests, indictments, or other charges of crime) of the accused.

(2) The possibility of a plea of guilty to the offense charged or to a lesser offense.

(3) The existence or contents of any confession, admission, or statement given by the accused or his refusal or failure to make a statement.

(4) The performance or results of any examinations or tests or the refusal or failure of the accused to submit to examinations or tests.

(5) The identity, testimony, or credibility of a prospective witness.

(6) Any opinion as to the guilt or innocence of the accused, the evidence, or the merits of the case.

(C) DR 7-107(B) does not preclude a lawyer during such period from announcing:

(1) The name, age, residence, occupation, and family status of the accused.

(2) If the accused has not been apprehended, any information necessary to aid in his apprehension or to warn the public of any dangers he may present.

(3) A request for assistance in obtaining evidence.

(4) The identity of the victim of the crime.

(5) The fact, time, and place of arrest, resistance, pursuit, and use of weapons.

(6) The identity of investigating and arresting officers or agencies and the length of the investigation.

(7) At the time of seizure, a description of the physical evidence seized, other than a confession, admission, or statement.

(8) The nature, substance, or text of the charge.

(9) Quotations from or references to public records of the court in the case.

(10) The scheduling or result of any step in the judicial proceedings.

(11) That the accused denies the charges made against him.

(D) During the selection of a jury or the trial of a criminal matter, a lawyer or law firm associated with the prosecution or defense of a criminal matter shall not make or participate in making an extrajudicial statement that a reasonable person would expect to be disseminated by means of public communication and that relates to the trial, parties, or issues in the trial or other matters that are reasonably likely to interfere with a fair trial, except that he may quote from or refer without comment to public records of the court in the case.

(E) After the completion of a trial or disposition without trial of a criminal matter and prior to the imposition of sentence, a lawyer or law firm associated with the prosecution or defense shall not make or participate in making an extrajudicial statement that a reasonable person would expect to be disseminated by public communication and that is reasonably likely to affect the imposition of sentence.

(F) The foregoing provisions of DR 7-107 also apply to professional disciplinary proceedings and juvenile disciplinary proceedings when pertinent and consistent with other law applicable to such proceedings.

(G) A lawyer or law firm associated with a civil action shall not during its investigation or litigation make or participate in making an extrajudicial statement, other than a quotation from or reference to public records, that a reasonable person would expect to be disseminated by means of public communication and that relates to:

(1) Evidence regarding the occurrence or transaction involved.

(2) The character, credibility, or criminal record of a party, witness, or prospective witness.

(3) The performance or results of any examinations or tests or the refusal or failure of a party to submit to such.

(4) His opinion as to the merits of the claims or defenses of a party, except as required by law or administrative rule.

(5) Any other matter reasonably likely to interfere with a fair trial of the action.

(H) During the pendency of an administrative proceeding, a lawyer or law firm associated therewith shall not make or participate in making a statement, other than a quotation from or reference to public records, that a reasonable person would expect to be disseminated by means of public communication if it is made outside the official course of the proceeding and relates to:

(1) Evidence regarding the occurrence or transaction involved.

(2) The character, credibility, or criminal record of a party, witness, or prospective witness.

(3) Physical evidence or the performance or results of any examinations or tests or the refusal or failure of a party to submit to such.

(4) His opinion as to the merits of the claims, defenses, or positions of an interested person.

(5) Any other matter reasonably likely to interfere with a fair hearing.

(I) The foregoing provisions of DR 7-107 do not preclude a lawyer from replying to charges of misconduct publicly made against him or from participating in the proceedings of legislative, administrative, or other investigative bodies.

(J) A lawyer shall exercise reasonable care to prevent his employees and associates from making an extrajudicial statement that he would be prohibited from making under DR 7-107.

DR 7-108 Communication with or Investigation of Jurors

(A) Before the trial of a case a lawyer connected therewith shall not communicate with or cause another to communicate with anyone he knows to be a member of the venire from which the jury will be selected for the trial of the case.

(B) During the trial of a case:

(1) A lawyer connected therewith shall not communicate with or cause another to communicate with any member of the jury.

(2) A lawyer who is not connected therewith shall not communicate with or cause another to communicate with a juror concerning the case.

(C) DR 7-108(A) and (B) do not prohibit a lawyer from communicating with veniremen or jurors in the course of official proceedings.

(D) After discharge of the jury from further consideration of a case with which the lawyer was connected, the lawyer shall not ask questions of or make comments to a member of that jury that are calculated merely to harass or embarrass the juror or to influence his actions in future jury service.

(E) A lawyer shall not conduct or cause, by financial support or otherwise, another to conduct a vexatious or harassing investigation of either a venireman or a juror.

(F) All restrictions imposed by DR 7-108 upon a lawyer also apply to communications with or investigations of members of a family of a venireman or a juror.

(G) A lawyer shall reveal promptly to the court improper conduct by a venireman or a juror, or by another toward a venireman or a juror or a member of his family, of which the lawyer has knowledge.

DR 7-109 Contact with Witnesses

(A) A lawyer shall not suppress any evidence that he or his client has a legal obligation to reveal or produce.

(B) A lawyer shall not advise or cause a person to secrete himself or to leave the jurisdiction of a tribunal for the purpose of making him unavailable as a witness therein.

(C) A lawyer shall not pay, offer to pay, or acquiesce in the payment of compensation to a witness contingent upon the content of his testimony or the outcome of the case. But a lawyer may advance, guarantee, or acquiesce in the payment of:

(1) Expenses reasonably incurred by a witness in attending or testifying.

(2) Reasonable compensation to a witness for his loss of time in attending or testifying.

(3) A reasonable fee for the professional services of an expert witness.

DR 7-110 Contact with Officials

(A) A lawyer shall not give or lend any thing of value to a judge, official, or employee of a tribunal except as permitted by Section C(4) of Canon 5 of the Code of Judicial Conduct, but a lawyer may make a contribution to the campaign fund of a candidate for judicial office in conformity with Section B(2) under Canon 7 of the Code of Judicial Conduct.

(B) In an adversary proceeding, a lawyer shall not communicate, or cause another to communicate, as to the merits of the cause with a judge or an official before whom the proceeding is pending, except:

(1) In the course of official proceedings in the cause.

(2) In writing if he promptly delivers a copy of the writing to opposing counsel or to the adverse party if he is not represented by a lawyer.

(3) Orally upon adequate notice to opposing counsel or to the adverse party if he is not represented by a lawyer.

(4) As otherwise authorized by law, or by Section A(4) under Canon 3 of the Code of Judicial Conduct.

Model Rules Comparison

Model Code	*ABA Model Rules*	*Model Code*	*ABA Model Rules*
DR 7-101(A)	1.2(a), (d), 1.3, 3.2, 3.5, 4.4	DR 7-106(C)	3.4(a), (c), (d), (e), 3.5, 4.4
DR 7-101(B)	1.2(a), (c), (d), 1.16(b)	DR 7-107(A)-(H)	3.6
DR 7-102(A)(1)	3.1, 3.2, 4.4	DR 7-107(I)	1.6(b), 3.9
DR 7-102(A)(2)	3.1	DR 7-107(J)	3.8(f), 5.1(a), (b), 5.3(a), (b)
DR 7-102(A)(3)	3.3(a), 3.4(a), 4.1	DR 7-108(A)	3.5(a), (b), 8.4(a)
DR 7-102(A)(4)	3.3(a), (b)	DR 7-108(B)	3.5(a), (b), 5.1(c), 5.3(a), (b), 8.4(a)
DR 7-102(A)(5)	3.3(a), 4.1	DR 7-108(C)	3.5(a), (b)
DR 7-102(A)(6)	1.2(d), 3.3(a), (b), 3.4(b)	DR 7-108(D)	3.5(c), 4.4
DR 7-102(A)(7)	1.2(d), 3.3(a), 4.1	DR 7-108(E)	3.5(b), 4.4, 5.1(c), 5.3(a), (b), 8.4(a)
DR 7-102(A)(8)	1.2(d), 8.4(a), (b)	DR 7-108(F)	4.4
DR 7-102(B)	1.6(b), 3.3(a), (b), 4.1(b)	DR 7-108(G)	3.3(b), (c)
DR 7-103(A)	3.8(a)	DR 7-109(A)	3.3(a), (b), 3.4(a)
DR 7-103(B)	3.8(d)	DR 7-109(B)	3.4(a), (f)
DR 7-104(A)(1)	4.2, 8.4(a)	DR 7-109(C)	3.4(b)
DR 7-104(A)(2)	3.4(f), 4.3	DR 7-110(A)	3.5(a), 8.4(f)
DR 7-105	No comparable Rule	DR 7-110(B)	3.5(a), (b), 8.4(a)
DR 7-106(A)	1.2(d), 3.4(c), (d)		
DR 7-106(B)	3.3(a), 3.9		

CANON 8. A LAWYER SHOULD ASSIST IN IMPROVING THE LEGAL SYSTEM

DR 8-101 Action as a Public Official

(A) A lawyer who holds public office shall not:

(1) Use his public position to obtain, or attempt to obtain, a special advantage in legislative matters for himself or for a client under

circumstances where he knows or it is obvious that such action is not in the public interest.

(2) Use his public position to influence, or attempt to influence, a tribunal to act in favor of himself or of a client.

(3) Accept any thing of value from any person when the lawyer knows or it is obvious that the offer is for the purpose of influencing his action as a public official.

DR 8-102 Statements Concerning Judges and Other Adjudicatory Officers

(A) A lawyer shall not knowingly make false statements of fact concerning the qualifications of a candidate for election or appointment to a judicial office.

(B) A lawyer shall not knowingly make false accusations against a judge or other adjudicatory officer.

DR 8-103 Lawyer Candidate for Judicial Office

(A) A lawyer who is a candidate for judicial office shall comply with the applicable provisions of Canon 7 of the Code of Judicial Conduct.

Model Rules Comparison

Model Code	*ABA Model Rules*
DR 8-101	1.11(d), 3.5(a), 8.4(b), (c), (e)
DR 8-102	8.2(a), 8.4(c), (d)
DR 8-103	8.2(b)

CANON 9. A LAWYER SHOULD AVOID EVEN THE APPEARANCE OF PROFESSIONAL IMPROPRIETY

DR 9-101 Avoiding Even the Appearance of Impropriety

(A) A lawyer shall not accept private employment in a matter upon the merits of which he has acted in a judicial capacity.

(B) A lawyer shall not accept private employment in a matter in which he had substantial responsibility while he was a public employee.

(C) A lawyer shall not state or imply that he is able to influence improperly or upon irrelevant grounds any tribunal, legislative body, or public official.

DR 9-102 Preserving Identity of Funds and Property of a Client

(A) All funds of clients paid to a lawyer or law firm, other than advances for costs and expenses, shall be deposited in one or more identifiable bank accounts maintained in the state in which the law office is situated and no funds belonging to the lawyer or law firm shall be deposited therein except as follows:

(1) Funds reasonably sufficient to pay bank charges may be deposited therein.

(2) Funds belonging in part to a client and in part presently or potentially to the lawyer or law firm must be deposited therein, but the portion belonging to the lawyer or law firm may be withdrawn when due unless the right of the lawyer or law firm to receive it is disputed by the client, in which event the disputed portion shall not be withdrawn until the dispute is finally resolved.

(B) A lawyer shall:

(1) Promptly notify a client of the receipt of his funds, securities, or other properties.

(2) Identify and label securities and properties of a client promptly upon receipt and place them in a safe deposit box or other place of safekeeping as soon as practicable.

(3) Maintain complete records of all funds, securities, and other properties of a client coming into the possession of the lawyer and render appropriate accounts to his client regarding them.

(4) Promptly pay or deliver to the client as requested by a client the funds, securities, or other properties in the possession of the lawyer which the client is entitled to receive.

Model Rules Comparison

Model Code	*ABA Model Rules*
DR 9-101(A)	1.12(a), (b)
DR 9-101(B)	1.11(a), 1.12(a), (b)
DR 9-101(C)	1.2(d), 7.1, 8.4(e)
DR 9-102	1.4(a), 1.15

DEFINITIONS*

As used in the Disciplinary Rules of the Model Code of Professional Responsibility:

(1) "Differing interests" include every interest that will adversely affect either the judgment or the loyalty of a lawyer to a client, whether it be a conflicting, inconsistent, diverse, or other interest.

*"Confidence" and "secret" are defined in DR 4-101(A).

(2) "Law firm" includes a professional legal corporation.

(3) "Person" includes a corporation, an association, a trust, a partnership, and any other organization or legal entity.

(4) "Professional legal corporation" means a corporation, or an association treated as a corporation, authorized by law to practice law for profit.

(5) "State" includes the District of Columbia, Puerto Rico, and other federal territories and possessions.

(6) "Tribunal" includes all courts and all other adjudicatory bodies.

(7) "A Bar association" includes a bar association of specialists as referred to in DR 2-105(A)(1) or (3).

(8) "Qualified legal assistance organization" means an office or organization of one of the four types listed in DR 2-103(D)(1)-(4), inclusive, that meets all the requirements thereof.

Model Rules Comparison

Model Code	*ABA Model Rules*
Definitions	Rule 1.0 (Terminology)

Federal Materials

Federal Provisions on Conflicts, Confidentiality, and Crimes

Editors' Introduction. This chapter reprints a number of federal statutes and regulations that govern lawyers. Many of the provisions also govern nonlawyers, including lawyers' clients. These federal statutes and regulations amplify, reinforce, and sometimes supersede the obligations imposed by state rules of professional conduct. For example, lawyers who work for the federal government (or who have previously worked for the federal government) are governed not only by state rules of professional conduct on conflicts and confidentiality equivalent to ABA Model Rules 1.6, 1.9 and 1.11, but also by stringent federal statutes such as 18 U.S.C. §207. Lawyers who appear and practice before the federal Securities and Exchange Commission in the representation of securities issuers are governed by rules found at 17 C.F.R. Part 205.

Since our last edition went to press in October 2010, the statutes and regulations reprinted below have not been amended.

Contents

SELECTED PROVISIONS FROM 18 U.S.C.

SELECTED PROVISIONS FROM 28 U.S.C.

SELECTED PROVISIONS FROM 28 C.F.R. PART 77

SELECTED PROVISIONS FROM 28 C.F.R. PART 50

SELECTED PROVISIONS FROM 15 U.S.C

Editors' Note. Title 15 of the United States Code is entitled "Commerce and Trade." On July 30, 2002, in the wake of the massive corporate scandals at Enron, WorldCom, and other companies, President George W. Bush signed into law the Sarbanes-Oxley Act of 2002. Section 307 of that law (later codified at 15 U.S.C. §7245) commanded the Securities and Exchange Commission (the "SEC" or the "Commission") to adopt rules to govern the responsibilities of attorneys who appear and practice before the SEC in the representation of issuers (*i.e.*, companies that issue stock). We reprint §307 below, followed by the regulations that the SEC adopted in 2003 pursuant to the mandate of §307. For additional background information about §307 of the Sarbanes-Oxley Act, see the Special Section at the back of the 2004 edition of this book.

§7245 Rules of Professional Responsibility for Attorneys

Not later than 180 days after the date of enactment of this Act, the Commission shall issue rules, in the public interest and for the protection of investors, setting forth minimum standards of professional conduct for attorneys appearing and practicing before the Commission in any way in the representation of issuers, including a rule—

(1) requiring an attorney to report evidence of a material violation of securities law or breach of fiduciary duty or similar violation by the company or any agent thereof, to the chief legal counsel or the chief executive officer of the company (or the equivalent thereof); and

(2) if the counsel or officer does not appropriately respond to the evidence (adopting, as necessary, appropriate remedial measures or sanctions with respect to the violation), requiring the attorney to report the evidence to the audit committee of the board of directors of the issuer or to another committee of the board of directors comprised solely of directors not employed directly or indirectly by the issuer, or to the board of directors.

SELECTED PROVISIONS FROM 17 C.F.R. PART 205

Editors' Note. The regulations that follow were promulgated pursuant to the mandate of Congress contained in §307 of the Sarbanes-Oxley Act of 2002, 15 U.S.C. §7245 (reprinted above), and took effect on August 5, 2003. For background information about the regulations and proposed regulations, see the Special Section at the back of the 2004 edition of this book.

STANDARDS OF PROFESSIONAL CONDUCT FOR ATTORNEYS APPEARING AND PRACTICING BEFORE THE COMMISSION IN THE REPRESENTATION OF AN ISSUER

§205.1 Purpose and Scope

This part sets forth minimum standards of professional conduct for attorneys appearing and practicing before the Commission in the representation of an issuer. These standards supplement applicable standards of any jurisdiction where an attorney is admitted or practices and are not intended

to limit the ability of any jurisdiction to impose additional obligations on an attorney not inconsistent with the application of this part. Where the standards of a state or other United States jurisdiction where an attorney is admitted or practices conflict with this part, this part shall govern.

§205.2 Definitions

For purposes of this part, the following definitions apply:

(a) *Appearing and practicing* before the Commission:

(1) Means:

(i) Transacting any business with the Commission, including communications in any form;

(ii) Representing an issuer in a Commission administrative proceeding or in connection with any Commission investigation, inquiry, information request, or subpoena;

(iii) Providing advice in respect of the United States securities laws or the Commission's rules or regulations thereunder regarding any document that the attorney has notice will be filed with or submitted to, or incorporated into any document that will be filed with or submitted to, the Commission, including the provision of such advice in the context of preparing, or participating in the preparation of, any such document; or

(iv) Advising an issuer as to whether information or a statement, opinion, or other writing is required under the United States securities laws or the Commission's rules or regulations thereunder to be filed with or submitted to, or incorporated into any document that will be filed with or submitted to, the Commission; but

(2) Does not include an attorney who:

(i) Conducts the activities in paragraphs (a)(1)(i) through (a)(1)(iv) of this section other than in the context of providing legal services to an issuer with whom the attorney has an attorney-client relationship; or

(ii) Is a non-appearing foreign attorney.

(b) *Appropriate response* means a response to an attorney regarding reported evidence of a material violation as a result of which the attorney reasonably believes:

(1) That no material violation, as defined in paragraph (i) of this section, has occurred, is ongoing, or is about to occur;

(2) That the issuer has, as necessary, adopted appropriate remedial measures, including appropriate steps or sanctions to stop any material violations that are ongoing, to prevent any material violation that has yet to occur, and to remedy or otherwise appropriately address any material violation that has already occurred and to minimize the likelihood of its recurrence; or

(3) That the issuer, with the consent of the issuer's board of directors, a committee thereof to whom a report could be made pursuant to §205.3(b)(3), or a qualified legal compliance committee, has retained or directed an attorney to review the reported evidence of a material violation and either:

(i) Has substantially implemented any remedial recommendations made by such attorney after a reasonable investigation and evaluation of the reported evidence; or

(ii) Has been advised that such attorney may, consistent with his or her professional obligations, assert a colorable defense on behalf of the issuer (or the issuer's officer, director, employee, or agent, as the case may be) in any investigation or judicial or administrative proceeding relating to the reported evidence of a material violation.

(c) *Attorney* means any person who is admitted, licensed, or otherwise qualified to practice law in any *jurisdiction*, domestic or foreign, or who holds himself or herself out as admitted, licensed, or otherwise qualified to practice law.

(d) *Breach of fiduciary duty* refers to any breach of fiduciary or similar duty to the issuer recognized under an applicable Federal or State statute or at common law, including but not limited to misfeasance, nonfeasance, abdication of duty, abuse of trust, and approval of unlawful transactions.

(e) *Evidence of a material violation* means credible evidence, based upon which it *would* be unreasonable, *under* the circumstances, for a prudent and competent attorney not to conclude that it is reasonably likely that a material violation has occurred, is ongoing, or is about to occur. . . .

(f) *Foreign government issuer* . . .

(g) *In the representation of an issuer* means providing legal services as an *attorney* for an issuer, regardless of whether the attorney is employed or retained by the issuer.

(h) *Issuer* . . . does not include a foreign government issuer. For purposes of paragraphs (a) and (g) of this section, the term "issuer" includes any person controlled by an issuer, where an attorney provides legal services to such person on behalf of, or at the behest, or for the benefit of the issuer, regardless of whether the attorney is employed or retained by the issuer.

(i) *Material violation* means a material violation of an applicable United States federal or state securities law, a *material* breach of fiduciary duty arising under United States federal or state law, or a similar material violation of any United States federal or state law.

(j) *Non-appearing foreign attorney* . . .

(k) *Qualified legal compliance committee* . . .

(l) *Reasonable* or *reasonably* denotes, with respect to the actions of an attorney, conduct that would not be unreasonable for a prudent and competent attorney.

(m) *Reasonably believes* means that an attorney believes the matter in question and that the circumstances are such that the belief is not unreasonable.

(n) *Report* means to make known to directly, either in person, by telephone, by e-mail, electronically, or in writing.

§205.3 Issuer as Client

(a) *Representing an issuer.* An attorney appearing and practicing before the Commission in the representation of an issuer owes his or her professional and ethical duties to the issuer as an organization. That the attorney may work with and advise the issuer's officers, directors, or employees in the course of representing the issuer does not make such individuals the attorney's clients.

(b) *Duty to report evidence of a material violation.*

(1) If an attorney, appearing and practicing before the Commission in the representation of an issuer, becomes aware of evidence of a material violation by the issuer or by any officer, director, employee, or agent of the issuer, the attorney shall report such evidence to the issuer's chief legal officer (or the equivalent thereof) or to both the issuer's chief legal officer and its chief executive officer (or the equivalents thereof) forthwith. By communicating such information to the issuer's officers or directors, an attorney does not reveal client confidences or secrets or privileged or otherwise protected information related to the attorney's representation of an issuer.

(2) The chief legal officer (or the equivalent thereof) shall cause such inquiry into the evidence of a material violation as he or she reasonably believes is appropriate to determine whether the material violation described in the report has occurred, is ongoing, or is about to occur. If the chief legal officer (or the equivalent thereof) determines no material violation has occurred, is ongoing, or is about to occur, he or she shall notify the reporting attorney and advise the reporting attorney of the basis for such determination. Unless the chief legal officer (or the equivalent thereof) reasonably believes that no material violation has occurred, is ongoing, or is about to occur, he or she shall take all reasonable steps to cause the issuer to adopt an appropriate response, and shall advise the reporting attorney thereof. . . .

(3) Unless an attorney who has made a report under paragraph (b)(1) of this section reasonably believes that the chief legal officer or the chief executive officer of the issuer (or the equivalent thereof) has provided an appropriate response within a reasonable time, the attorney shall report the evidence of a material violation to:

(i) The audit committee of the issuer's board of directors;

(ii) Another committee of the issuer's board of directors consisting solely of directors who are not employed, directly or indirectly, by the issuer . . . ; or

(iii) The issuer's board of directors (if the issuer's board of directors has no committee consisting solely of directors who are not employed, directly or indirectly, by the issuer . . .).

(4) If an attorney reasonably believes that it would be futile to report evidence of a material violation to the issuer's chief legal officer and chief executive officer (or the equivalents thereof) under paragraph (b)(1) of this section, the attorney may report such evidence as provided under paragraph (b)(3) of this section.

(5) An attorney retained or directed by an issuer to investigate evidence of a material violation reported under paragraph (b)(1), (b)(3), or (b)(4) of this section shall be deemed to be appearing and practicing before the Commission. Directing or retaining an attorney to investigate reported evidence of a material violation does not relieve an officer or director of the issuer to whom such evidence has been reported under paragraph (b)(1), (b)(3), or (b)(4) of this section from a duty to respond to the reporting attorney.

(6) An attorney shall not have any obligation to report evidence of a material violation under this paragraph (b) if:

(i) The attorney was retained or directed by the issuer's chief legal officer (or the equivalent thereof) to investigate such evidence of a material violation and:

(A) The attorney reports the results of such investigation to the chief legal officer (or the equivalent thereof); and

(B) Except where the attorney and the chief legal officer (or the equivalent thereof) each reasonably believes that no material violation has occurred, is ongoing, or is about to occur, the chief legal officer (or the equivalent thereof) reports the results of the investigation to the issuer's board of directors, a committee thereof to whom a report could be made pursuant to paragraph (b)(3) of this section, or a qualified legal compliance committee; or

(ii) The attorney was retained or directed by the chief legal officer (or the equivalent thereof) to assert, consistent with his or her professional obligations, a colorable defense on behalf of the issuer (or the issuer's officer, director, employee, or agent, as the case may be) in any investigation or judicial or administrative proceeding relating to such evidence of a material violation, and the chief legal officer (or the equivalent thereof) provides reasonable and timely reports on the progress and outcome of such proceeding to the issuer's board of directors, a committee thereof to whom a report could be made pursuant to paragraph (b)(3) of this section, or a qualified legal compliance committee. . . .

(8) An attorney who receives what he or she reasonably believes is an appropriate and timely response to a report he or she has made pursuant to paragraph (b)(1), (b)(3), or (b)(4) of this section need do nothing more under this section with respect to his or her report.

(9) An attorney who does not reasonably believe that the issuer has made an appropriate response within a reasonable time to the report or reports made pursuant to paragraph (b)(1), (b)(3), or (b)(4) of this section shall explain his or her reasons therefor to the chief legal officer (or the equivalent thereof), the chief executive officer (or the equivalent thereof), and directors to whom the attorney reported the evidence of a material violation pursuant to paragraph (b)(1), (b)(3), or (b)(4) of this section.

(10) An attorney formerly employed or retained by an issuer who has reported evidence of a material violation under this part and reasonably believes that he or she has been discharged for so doing may notify the issuer's board of directors or any committee thereof that he or she believes that he or she has been discharged for reporting evidence of a material violation under this section. . . .

(d) *Issuer confidences.*

(1) Any report under this section (or the contemporaneous record thereof) or any response thereto (or the contemporaneous record thereof) may be used by an attorney in connection with any investigation, proceeding, or litigation in which the attorney's compliance with this part is in issue.

(2) An attorney appearing and practicing before the Commission in the representation of an issuer may reveal to the Commission, without the issuer's consent, confidential information related to the representation to the extent the attorney reasonably believes necessary:

(i) To prevent the issuer from committing a material violation that is likely to cause substantial injury to the financial interest or property of the issuer or investors;

(ii) To prevent the issuer, in a Commission investigation or administrative proceeding from committing perjury, proscribed in 18 U.S.C. 1621; suborning perjury, proscribed in 18 U.S.C. 1622; or committing any act proscribed in 18 U.S.C. 1001 that is likely to perpetrate a fraud upon the Commission; or

(iii) To rectify the consequences of a material violation by the issuer that caused, or may cause, substantial injury to the financial interest or property of the issuer or investors in the furtherance of which the attorney's services were used.

§205.4 Responsibilities of Supervisory Attorneys

(a) An attorney supervising or directing another attorney who is appearing and practicing before the Commission in the representation of an issuer is a supervisory attorney. An issuer's chief legal officer (or the equivalent thereof) is a supervisory attorney under this section.

(b) A supervisory attorney shall make reasonable efforts to ensure that a subordinate attorney, as defined in §205.5(a), that he or she supervises or directs conforms to this part. To the extent a subordinate attorney appears and practices before the Commission in the representation of an issuer, that subordinate attorney's supervisory attorneys also appear and practice before the Commission.

(c) A supervisory attorney is responsible for complying with the reporting requirements in §205.3 when a subordinate attorney has reported to the supervisory attorney evidence of a material violation. . . .

§205.5 Responsibilities of a Subordinate Attorney

(a) An attorney who appears and practices before the Commission in the representation of an issuer on a matter under the supervision or direction of another attorney (other than under the direct supervision or direction of the issuer's chief legal officer (or the equivalent thereof)) is a subordinate attorney.

(b) A subordinate attorney shall comply with this part notwithstanding that the subordinate attorney acted at the direction of or under the supervision of another person.

(c) A subordinate attorney complies with §205.3 if the subordinate attorney reports to his or her supervising attorney under §205.3(b) evidence of a material violation of which the subordinate attorney has become aware in appearing and practicing before the Commission.

(d) A subordinate attorney may take the steps permitted or required by §205.3(b) or (c) if the subordinate attorney reasonably believes that a supervisory attorney to whom he or she has reported evidence of a material violation under §205.3(b) has failed to comply with §205.3.

§205.6 Sanctions and Discipline

(a) A violation of this part by any attorney appearing and practicing before the Commission in the representation of an issuer shall subject such attorney to the civil penalties and remedies for a violation of the federal securities laws available to the Commission in an action brought by the Commission thereunder.

(b) An attorney appearing and practicing before the Commission who violates any provision of this part is subject to the disciplinary authority of the Commission, regardless of whether the attorney may also be subject to discipline for the same conduct in a jurisdiction where the attorney is admitted or practices. An administrative disciplinary proceeding initiated by the

Commission for violation of this part may result in an attorney being censured, or being temporarily or permanently denied the privilege of appearing or practicing before the Commission.

(c) An attorney who complies in good faith with the provisions of this part shall not be subject to discipline or otherwise liable under inconsistent standards imposed by any state or other United States jurisdiction where the attorney is admitted or practices.

(d) An attorney practicing outside the United States shall not be required to comply with the requirements of this part to the extent that such compliance is prohibited by applicable foreign law.

§205.7 No Private Right of Action

(a) Nothing in this part is intended to, or does, create a private right of action against any attorney, law firm, or issuer based upon compliance or noncompliance with its provisions.

(b) Authority to enforce compliance with this part is vested exclusively in the Commission.

SELECTED PROVISIONS FROM 18 U.S.C.

> **Editors' Note.** Title 18 of the United States Code is entitled "Crimes and Criminal Procedure." A violation of any of the provisions reprinted below from Title 18 is a crime.

§201. Bribery of Public Official and Witnesses . . .

(c) Whoever—. . .

(2) directly or indirectly, gives, offers or promises anything of value to any person, for or because of the testimony under oath or affirmation given or to be given by such person as a witness upon a trial, hearing, or other proceeding, before any court, any committee of either House or both Houses of Congress, or any agency, commission, or officer authorized by the laws of the United States to hear evidence or take testimony, or for or because of such person's absence therefrom;

(3) directly or indirectly, demands, seeks, receives, accepts, or agrees to receive or accept anything of value personally for or because of the testimony under oath or affirmation given or to be given by such person as a witness upon any such trial, hearing, or other proceeding, or for or because of such person's absence therefrom; shall be fined under this title or imprisoned for not more than two years, or both.

(d) Paragraphs (3) and (4) of subsection (b) and paragraphs (2) and (3) of subsection (c) shall not be construed to prohibit the payment or receipt of witness fees provided by law, or the payment, by the party upon whose behalf a witness is called and receipt by a witness, of the reasonable cost of travel and subsistence incurred and the reasonable value of time lost in attendance at any such trial, hearing, or proceeding, or in the case of expert witnesses, a reasonable fee for time spent in the preparation of such opinion, and in appearing and testifying.

§202. Definitions

(b) For the purposes of sections 205 and 207 of this title, the term "official responsibility" means the direct administrative or operating authority, whether intermediate or final, and either exercisable alone or with others, and either personally or through subordinates, to approve, disapprove, or otherwise direct Government action. . . .

§207. Restrictions on Former Officers, Employees, and Elected Officials of the Executive and Legislative Branches

(a) Restrictions on all officers and employees of the executive branch and certain other agencies.—

(1) *Permanent restrictions on representation on particular matters.*—Any person who is an officer or employee (including any special Government employee) of the executive branch of the United States (including any independent agency of the United States), or of the District of Columbia, and who, after the termination of his or her service or employment with the United States or the District of Columbia, knowingly makes, with the intent to influence, any communication to or appearance before any officer or employee of any department, agency, court, or court-martial of the United States or the District of Columbia, on behalf of any other person (except the United States or the District of Columbia) in connection with a particular matter—

(A) in which the United States or the District of Columbia is a party or has a direct and substantial interest,

(B) in which the person participated personally and substantially as such officer or employee, and

(C) which involved a specific party or specific parties at the time of such participation, shall be punished as provided in section 216 of this title.

(2) *Two-year restrictions concerning particular matters under official responsibility.*—Any person subject to the restrictions contained in

paragraph (1) who, within 2 years after the termination of his or her service or employment with the United States or the District of Columbia, knowingly makes, with the intent to influence, any communication to or appearance before any officer or employee of any department, agency, court, or court-martial of the United States or the District of Columbia, on behalf of any other person (except the United States or the District of Columbia), in connection with a particular matter—

(A) in which the United States or the District of Columbia is a party or has a direct and substantial interest,

(B) which such person knows or reasonably should know was actually pending under his or her official responsibility as such officer or employee within a period of 1 year before the termination of his or her service or employment with the United States or the District of Columbia, and

(C) which involved a specific party or specific parties at the time it was so pending, shall be punished as provided in section 216 of this title.

(3) *Clarification of restrictions.*— The restrictions contained in paragraphs (1) and (2) shall apply—

(A) in the case of an officer or employee of the executive branch of the United States (including any independent agency), only with respect to communications to or appearances before any officer or employee of any department, agency, court, or court-martial of the United States on behalf of any other person (except the United States), and only with respect to a matter in which the United States is a party or has a direct and substantial interest. . . .

Editors' Note. Violations of these provisions carry sentences of up to five years if willful, one year if not willful. Further, the Attorney General is authorized to seek civil penalties and injunctive relief. *See* 18 U.S.C. §216. The remainder of §207, which is lengthy and detailed, imposes restrictions on various categories of former government officers and employees, including (among others) trade negotiators and treaty negotiators; certain "senior personnel" and "very senior personnel" of the executive branch and independent agencies; and former Members of Congress and their "personal staff," "committee staff," and "leadership staff."

§1503. Influencing or Injuring Officer or Juror Generally

(a) Whoever corruptly, or by threats or force, or by any threatening letter or communication, endeavors to influence, intimidate, or impede any grand or petit juror, or officer in or of any court of the United States, or officer who may be serving at any examination or other proceeding before

any United States magistrate judge or other committing magistrate, in the discharge of his duty, or injures any such grand or petit juror in his person or property on account of any verdict or indictment assented to by him, or on account of his being or having been such juror, or injures any such officer, magistrate judge, or other committing magistrate in his person or property on account of the performance of his official duties, or corruptly or by threats or force, or by any threatening letter or communication, influences, obstructs, or impedes, or endeavors to influence, obstruct, or impede, the due administration of justice, shall be punished as provided in subsection (b). If the offense under this section occurs in connection with a trial of a criminal case, and the act in violation of this section involves the threat of physical force or physical force, the maximum term of imprisonment which may be imposed for the offense shall be the higher of that otherwise provided by law or the maximum term that could have been imposed for any offense charged in such case.

(b) The punishment for an offense under this section is—

(1) in the case of a killing, the punishment provided in sections 1111 and 1112;

(2) in the case of an attempted killing, or a case in which the offense was committed against a petit juror and in which a class A or B felony was charged, imprisonment for not more than 20 years, a fine under this title, or both; and

(3) in any other case, imprisonment for not more than 10 years, a fine under this title, or both.

§1505. Obstruction of Proceedings Before Departments, Agencies, and Committees

Whoever, with intent to avoid, evade, prevent, or obstruct compliance, in whole or in part, with any civil investigative demand duly and properly made under the Antitrust Civil Process Act, willfully withholds, misrepresents, removes from any place, conceals, covers up, destroys, mutilates, alters, or by other means falsifies any documentary material, answers to written interrogatories, or oral testimony, which is the subject of such demand; or attempts to do so or solicits another to do so; or

Whoever corruptly, or by threats or force, or by any threatening letter or communication influences, obstructs, or impedes or endeavors to influence, obstruct, or impede the due and proper administration of the law under which any pending proceeding is being had before any department or agency of the United States, or the due and proper exercise of the power of inquiry under which any inquiry or investigation is being had by either House, or any committee of either House or any joint committee of the Congress—

Shall be fined under this title, imprisoned not more than 5 years or, if the offense involves international or domestic terrorism (as defined in section 2331), imprisoned not more than 8 years, or both.

§1510. Obstruction of Criminal Investigations

(a) Whoever willfully endeavors by means of bribery to obstruct, delay, or prevent the communication of information relating to a violation of any criminal statute of the United States by any person to a criminal investigator shall be fined under this title, or imprisoned not more than five years, or both . . . .

§1512. Tampering with a Witness, Victim, or an Informant . . .

> **Editors' Note.** Section 1512(c) was added by the Sarbanes-Oxley Act of 2002, Pub. L. No. 107-204, which was signed into law by President Bush on July 30, 2002.

(b) Whoever knowingly uses intimidation, threatens, or corruptly persuades another person, or attempts to do so, or engages in misleading conduct toward another person, with intent to—

(1) influence, delay, or prevent the testimony of any person in an official proceeding;

(2) cause or induce any person to—

(A) withhold testimony, or withhold a record, document, or other object, from an official proceeding;

(B) alter, destroy, mutilate, or conceal an object with intent to impair the object's integrity or availability for use in an official proceeding;

(C) evade legal process summoning that person to appear as a witness, or to produce a record, document, or other object, in an official proceeding; or

(D) be absent from an official proceeding to which such person has been summoned by legal process; or

(3) hinder, delay, or prevent the communication to a law enforcement officer or judge of the United States of information relating to the commission or possible commission of a Federal offense or a violation of conditions of probation, parole, or release pending judicial proceedings; shall be fined under this title or imprisoned not more than 20 years, or both.

(c) Whoever corruptly—

(1) alters, destroys, mutilates, or conceals a record, document, or other object, or attempts to do so, with the intent to impair the object's integrity or availability for use in an official proceeding; or

(2) otherwise obstructs, influences, or impedes any official proceeding, or attempts to do so, shall be fined under this title or imprisoned not more than 20 years, or both.

(d) Whoever intentionally harasses another person and thereby hinders, delays, prevents, or dissuades any person from—

(1) attending or testifying in an official proceeding;

(2) reporting to a law enforcement officer or judge of the United States the commission or possible commission of a Federal offense or a violation of conditions of probation, supervised release, parole, or release pending judicial proceedings;

(3) arresting or seeking the arrest of another person in connection with a Federal offense; or

(4) causing a criminal prosecution, or a parole or probation revocation proceeding, to be sought or instituted, or assisting in such prosecution or proceeding; or attempts to do so, shall be fined under this title or imprisoned not more than 3 years, or both.

(e) In a prosecution for an offense under this section, it is an affirmative defense, as to which the defendant has the burden of proof by a preponderance of the evidence, that the conduct consisted solely of lawful conduct and that the defendant's sole intention was to encourage, induce, or cause the other person to testify truthfully.

(f) For the purposes of this section—

(1) an official proceeding need not be pending or about to be instituted at the time of the offense; and

(2) the testimony, or the record, document, or other object need not be admissible in evidence or free of a claim of privilege . . . .

(j) If the offense under this section occurs in connection with a trial of a criminal case, the maximum term of imprisonment which may be imposed for the offense shall be the higher of that otherwise provided by law or the maximum term that could have been imposed for any offense charged in such case.

(k) Whoever conspires to commit any offense under this section shall be subject to the same penalties as those prescribed or the offense the commission of which was the object of the conspiracy.

§1513. Retaliating Against a Witness, Victim, or an Informant . . .

Editors' Note. Section 1513(e) was added by the Sarbanes-Oxley Act of 2002, Pub. L. 107-204, which was signed into law by President Bush on July 30, 2002.

(e) Whoever knowingly, with the intent to retaliate, takes any action harmful to any person, including interference with the lawful employment or livelihood of any person, for providing to a law enforcement officer any truthful information relating to the commission or possible commission of any Federal offense, shall be fined under this title or imprisoned not more than 10 years, or both.

§1515. Definitions for Certain Provisions; General Provisions

(a) As used in sections 1512 and 1513 of this title and in this section . . .

(1) the term "official proceeding" means—

(A) a proceeding before a judge or court of the United States . . . ;

(B) a proceeding before the Congress;

(C) a proceeding before a Federal Government agency which is authorized by law; or

(D) a proceeding involving the business of insurance whose activities affect interstate commerce before any insurance regulatory official or agency . . . ;

(2) the term "physical force" means physical action against another, and includes confinement;

(3) the term "misleading conduct" means—

(A) knowingly making a false statement;

(B) intentionally omitting information from a statement and thereby causing a portion of such statement to be misleading, or intentionally concealing a material fact, and thereby creating a false impression by such statement;

(C) with intent to mislead, knowingly submitting or inviting reliance on a writing or recording that is false, forged, altered, or otherwise lacking in authenticity;

(D) with intent to mislead, knowingly submitting or inviting reliance on a sample, specimen, map, photograph, boundary mark, or other object that is misleading in a material respect; or

(E) knowingly using a trick, scheme, or device with intent to mislead; . . . and

(6) the term "corruptly persuades" does not include conduct which would be misleading conduct but for a lack of a state of mind.

(b) As used in section 1505, the term "corruptly" means acting with an improper purpose, personally or by influencing another, including making a false or misleading statement, or withholding, concealing, altering, or destroying a document or other information.

(c) This chapter does not prohibit or punish the providing of lawful, bona fide, legal representation services in connection with or anticipation of an official proceeding.

§1519. Destruction, Alteration, or Falsification of Records in Federal Investigations and Bankruptcy

Editors' Note. Section 1519 was added by the Sarbanes-Oxley Act of 2002, Pub. L. No. 107-204, which was signed into law by President Bush on July 30, 2002.

Whoever knowingly alters, destroys, mutilates, conceals, covers up, falsifies, or makes a false entry in any record, document, or tangible object with the intent to impede, obstruct, or influence the investigation or proper administration of any matter within the jurisdiction of any department or agency of the United States or any case filed under title 11, or in relation to or contemplation of any such matter or case, shall be fined under this title, imprisoned not more than 20 years, or both.

§1621. Perjury Generally

Whoever—

(1) having taken an oath before a competent tribunal, officer, or person, in any case in which a law of the United States authorizes an oath to be administered, that he will testify, declare, depose, or certify truly, or that any written testimony, declaration, deposition, or certificate by him subscribed, is true, willfully and contrary to such oath states or subscribes any material matter which he does not believe to be true; or

(2) in any declaration, certificate, verification, or statement under penalty of perjury as permitted under section 1746 of title 28, United States Code, willfully subscribes as true any material matter which he does not believe to be true;

is guilty of perjury and shall, except as otherwise expressly provided by law, be fined under this title or imprisoned not more than five years, or both. This section is applicable whether the statement or subscription is made within or without the United States.

Editors' Note. 28 U.S.C. §1746, which is mentioned in 18 U.S.C. §1621, provides, in essence, that whenever federal law permits or requires a person to support any matter with an affidavit or other sworn declaration, then "such matter may, with like force and effect, be supported . . . by the unsworn declaration . . . in writing of such person which is subscribed by him, as true under penalty of perjury . . . in substantially the following form: . . . 'I declare . . . under penalty of perjury under the laws of the United States of America that the foregoing is true and correct.' "

§1622. Subornation of Perjury

Whoever procures another to commit any perjury is guilty of subornation of perjury, and shall be fined under this title or imprisoned not more than five years, or both.

§1905. Disclosure of Confidential Information Generally

Whoever, being an officer or employee of the United States or of any department or agency thereof, . . . publishes, divulges, discloses, or makes known in any manner or to any extent not authorized by law any information coming to him in the course of his employment or official duties or by reason of any examination or investigation made by, or return, report or record made to or filed with, such department or agency or officer or employee thereof, which information concerns or relates to the trade secrets, processes, operations, style of work, or apparatus, or to the identity, confidential statistical data, amount or source of any income, profits, losses, or expenditures of any person, firm, partnership, corporation, or association; or permits any income return or copy thereof or any book containing any abstract or particulars thereof to be seen or examined by any person except as provided by law; shall be fined under this title, or imprisoned not more than one year, or both; and shall be removed from office or employment.

§3500. Demands for Production of Statements and Reports of Witnesses ["Jencks Act"]

(a) In any criminal prosecution brought by the United States, no statement or report in the possession of the United States which was made by a Government witness or prospective Government witness (other than the defendant) shall be the subject of subpoena, discovery, or inspection until said witness has testified on direct examination in the trial of the case.

(b) After a witness called by the United States has testified on direct examination, the court shall, on motion of the defendant, order the United States to produce any statement (as hereinafter defined) of the witness in the possession of the United States which relates to the subject matter as to which the witness has testified. If the entire contents of any such statement relate to the subject matter of the testimony of the witness, the court shall order it to be delivered directly to the defendant for his examination and use.

(c) If the United States claims that any statement ordered to be produced under this section contains matter which does not relate to the

subject matter of the testimony of the witness, the court shall order the United States to deliver such statement for the inspection of the court in camera. Upon such delivery the court shall excise the portions of such statement which do not relate to the subject matter of the testimony of the witness. With such material excised, the court shall then direct delivery of such statement to the defendant for his use . . . .

(d) If the United States elects not to comply with an order of the court under subsection (b) or (c) hereof to deliver to the defendant any such statement, or such portion thereof as the court may direct, the court shall strike from the record the testimony of the witness, and the trial shall proceed unless the court in its discretion shall determine that the interests of justice require that a mistrial be declared.

(e) The term "statement", as used in subsections (b), (c), and (d) of this section in relation to any witness called by the United States, means —

(1) a written statement made by said witness and signed or otherwise adopted or approved by him;

(2) a stenographic, mechanical, electrical, or other recording, or a transcription thereof, which is a substantially verbatim recital of an oral statement made by said witness and recorded contemporaneously with the making of such oral statement; or

(3) a statement, however taken or recorded, or a transcription thereof, if any, made by said witness to a grand jury.

SELECTED PROVISIONS FROM 28 U.S.C.

Editors' Note. The section reprinted here, 28 U.S.C. §530B, resolved a disagreement between courts and the U.S. Department of Justice over whether the so-called no-contact rule applied to lawyers working for the federal government. (The no-contact rule, which is set forth in Rule 4.2 of the ABA Model Rules of Professional Conduct, generally prohibits a lawyer who represents a client from communicating about the subject of the representation with a person the lawyer knows to be represented by counsel in the matter.) For more information about the history of 28 U.S.C. §530B, see the entry entitled "Department of Justice Rules" in the Related Materials following ABA Model Rule 4.2 above.

§530B. Ethical Standards for Attorneys for the Government

(a) An attorney for the Government shall be subject to State laws and rules, and local Federal court rules, governing attorneys in each State where such attorney engages in that attorney's duties, to the same extent and in the same manner as other attorneys in that State.

(b) The Attorney General shall make and amend rules of the Department of Justice to assure compliance with this section.

(c) As used in this section, the term "attorney for the Government" includes any attorney described in section 77.2(a) of part 77 of title 28 of the Code of Federal Regulations and also includes any independent counsel, or employee of such a counsel, appointed under chapter 40.

SELECTED PROVISIONS FROM 28 C.F.R. PART 77

Editors' Note. The Department of Justice has issued the following regulations implementing 28 U.S.C. §530B.

§77.1. Purpose and Authority

(a) The Department of Justice is committed to ensuring that its attorneys perform their duties in accordance with the highest ethical standards. The purpose of this part is to implement 28 U.S.C. 530B and to provide guidance to attorneys concerning the requirements imposed on Department attorneys by 28 U.S.C. 530B.

(b) Section 530B requires Department attorneys to comply with state and local federal court rules of professional responsibility, but should not be construed in any way to alter federal substantive, procedural, or evidentiary law or to interfere with the Attorney General's authority to send Department attorneys into any court in the United States.

(c) Section 530B imposes on Department attorneys the same rules of professional responsibility that apply to non-Department attorneys, but should not be construed to impose greater burdens on Department attorneys than those on non-Department attorneys or to alter rules of professional responsibility that expressly exempt government attorneys from their application.

(d) The regulations set forth in this part seek to provide guidance to Department attorneys in determining the rules with which such attorneys should comply.

§77.2. Definitions

As used in this part, the following terms shall have the following meanings, unless the context indicates otherwise: . . .

(b) The term *case* means any proceeding over which a state or federal court has jurisdiction, including criminal prosecutions and civil actions. This term also includes grand jury investigations and related proceedings (such as motions to quash grand jury subpoenas and motions to compel

testimony), applications for search warrants, and applications for electronic surveillance.

(c) The phrase *civil law enforcement investigation* means an investigation of possible civil violations of, or claims under, federal law that may form the basis for a civil law enforcement proceeding.

(d) The phrase *civil law enforcement proceeding* means a civil action or proceeding before any court or other tribunal brought by the Department of Justice under the authority of the United States to enforce federal laws or regulations, and includes proceedings related to the enforcement of an administrative subpoena or summons or civil investigative demand.

(e) The terms *conduct* and *activity* mean any act performed by a Department attorney that implicates a rule governing attorneys, as that term is defined in paragraph (h) of this section. . . .

(g) The term *person* means any individual or organization.

(h) The phrase *state laws and rules and local federal court rules governing attorneys* means rules enacted or adopted by any State or Territory of the United States or the District of Columbia or by any federal court, that prescribe ethical conduct for attorneys and that would subject an attorney, whether or not a Department attorney, to professional discipline, such as a code of professional responsibility. The phrase does not include:

(1) Any statute, rule, or regulation which does not govern ethical conduct, such as rules of procedure, evidence, or substantive law, whether or not such rule is included in a code of professional responsibility for attorneys;

(2) Any statute, rule, or regulation that purports to govern the conduct of any class of persons other than attorneys, such as rules that govern the conduct of all litigants and judges, as well as attorneys; or

(3) A statute, rule, or regulation requiring licensure or membership in a particular state bar.

(i) The phrase *state of licensure* means the District of Columbia or any State or Territory where a Department attorney is duly licensed and authorized to practice as an attorney. . . .

(j)(1) The phrase *where such attorney engages in that attorney's duties* identifies which rules of ethical conduct a Department attorney should comply with, and means, with respect to particular conduct:

(i) If there is a case pending, the rules of ethical conduct adopted by the local federal court or state court before which the case is pending; or

(ii) If there is no case pending, the rules of ethical conduct that would be applied by the attorney's state of licensure.

(2) A Department attorney does not "engage[] in that attorney's duties" in any states in which the attorney's conduct is not substantial

and continuous, such as a jurisdiction in which an attorney takes a deposition (related to a case pending in another court) or directs a contact to be made by an investigative agent, or responds to an inquiry by an investigative agent. Nor does the phrase include any jurisdiction that would not ordinarily apply its rules of ethical conduct to particular conduct or activity by the attorney.

(k) The phrase *to the same extent and in the same manner as other attorneys* means that Department attorneys shall only be subject to laws and rules of ethical conduct governing attorneys in the same manner as such rules apply to non-Department attorneys. The phrase does not, however, purport to eliminate or otherwise alter state or federal laws and rules and federal court rules that expressly exclude some or all government attorneys from particular limitations or prohibitions.

§77.3. Application of 28 U.S.C. 530B

In all criminal investigations and prosecutions, in all civil investigations and litigation (affirmative and defensive), and in all civil law enforcement investigations and proceedings, attorneys for the government shall conform their conduct and activities to the state rules and laws, and federal local court rules, governing attorneys in each State where such attorney engages in that attorney's duties, to the same extent and in the same manner as other attorneys in that State, as these terms are defined in §77.2 of this part.

§77.4. Guidance

(a) *Rules of the court before which a case is pending.* A government attorney shall, in all cases, comply with the rules of ethical conduct of the court before which a particular case is pending.

(b) *Inconsistent rules where there is a pending case.*

(1) If the rule of the attorney's state of licensure would prohibit an action that is permissible under the rules of the court before which a case is pending, the attorney should consider:

(i) Whether the attorney's state of licensure would apply the rule of the court before which the case is pending, rather than the rule of the state of licensure;

(ii) Whether the local federal court rule preempts contrary state rules; and

(iii) Whether application of traditional choice-of-law principles directs the attorney to comply with a particular rule.

(2) In the process of considering the factors described in paragraph (b)(1) of this section, the attorney is encouraged to consult with a

supervisor or Professional Responsibility Officer to determine the best course of conduct.

(c) *Choice of rules where there is no pending case.*

(1) Where no case is pending, the attorney should generally comply with the ethical rules of the attorney's state of licensure, unless application of traditional choice-of-law principles directs the attorney to comply with the ethical rule of another jurisdiction or court, such as the ethical rule adopted by the court in which the case is likely to be brought.

(2) In the process of considering the factors described in paragraph (c)(1) of this section, the attorney is encouraged to consult with a supervisor or Professional Responsibility Officer to determine the best course of conduct.

(d) *Rules that impose an irreconcilable conflict.* If, after consideration of traditional choice-of-law principles, the attorney concludes that multiple rules may apply to particular conduct and that such rules impose irreconcilable obligations on the attorney, the attorney should consult with a supervisor or Professional Responsibility Officer to determine the best course of conduct.

(e) *Supervisory attorneys.* Each attorney, including supervisory attorneys, must assess his or her ethical obligations with respect to particular conduct. Department attorneys shall not direct any attorney to engage in conduct that violates section 530B. A supervisor or other Department attorney who, in good faith, gives advice or guidance to another Department attorney about the other attorney's ethical obligations should not be deemed to violate these rules.

(f) *Investigative Agents.* A Department attorney shall not direct an investigative agent acting under the attorney's supervision to engage in conduct under circumstances that would violate the attorney's obligations under section 530B. A Department attorney who in good faith provides legal advice or guidance upon request to an investigative agent should not be deemed to violate these rules.

§77.5. No Private Remedies

The principles set forth herein, and internal office procedures adopted pursuant hereto, are intended solely for the guidance of attorneys for the government. They are not intended to, do not, and may not be relied upon to create a right or benefit, substantive or procedural, enforceable at law by a party to litigation with the United States, including criminal defendants, targets or subjects of criminal investigations, witnesses in criminal or civil cases (including civil law enforcement proceedings), or plaintiffs or defendants in civil investigations or litigation; or any other person, whether or not a party to litigation with the United States, or their counsel; and shall not be a basis for dismissing criminal or civil charges or proceedings or for excluding relevant evidence in any judicial or administrative proceeding. Nor are any limitations placed on otherwise lawful litigative prerogatives of the Department of Justice as a result of this part.

SELECTED PROVISIONS FROM 28 C.F.R. PART 50

Editors' Note. Employees of the U.S. Department of Justice (including lawyers) must abide by various guidelines set out in 28 C.F.R. Part 50. We reprint here 28 C.F.R. §50.2, which establishes guidelines regarding extrajudicial statements and the release of information to the press.

§50.2 Release of Information by Personnel of the Department of Justice Relating to Criminal and Civil Proceedings

(a) *General.*

(1) The availability to news media of information in criminal and civil cases is a matter which has become increasingly a subject of concern in the administration of justice. The purpose of this statement is to formulate specific guidelines for the release of such information by personnel of the Department of Justice.

(2) While the release of information for the purpose of influencing a trial is, of course, always improper, there are valid reasons for making available to the public information about the administration of the law. The task of striking a fair balance between the protection of individuals accused of crime or involved in civil proceedings with the Government and public understandings of the problems of controlling crime and administering government depends largely on the exercise of sound judgment by those responsible for administering the law and by representatives of the press and other media.

(3) Inasmuch as the Department of Justice has generally fulfilled its responsibilities with awareness and understanding of the competing needs in this area, this statement, to a considerable extent, reflects and formalizes the standards to which representatives of the Department have adhered in the past. Nonetheless, it will be helpful in ensuring uniformity of practice to set forth the following guidelines for all personnel of the Department of Justice.

(4) Because of the difficulty and importance of the questions they raise, it is felt that some portions of the matters covered by this statement, such as the authorization to make available Federal conviction records and a description of items seized at the time of arrest, should be the subject of continuing review and consideration by the Department on the basis of experience and suggestions from those within and outside the Department.

(b) *Guidelines to criminal actions.*

(1) These guidelines shall apply to the release of information to news media from the time a person is the subject of a criminal investigation until any proceeding resulting from such an investigation has been terminated by trial or otherwise.

(2) At no time shall personnel of the Department of Justice furnish any statement or information for the purpose of influencing the outcome of a defendant's trial, nor shall personnel of the Department furnish any statement or information, which could reasonably be expected to be disseminated by means of public communication, if such a statement or information may reasonably be expected to influence the outcome of a pending or future trial.

(3) Personnel of the Department of Justice, subject to specific limitations imposed by law or court rule or order, may make public the following information:

(i) The defendant's name, age, residence, employment, marital status, and similar background information.

(ii) The substance or text of the charge, such as a complaint, indictment, or information.

(iii) The identity of the investigating and/or arresting agency and the length or scope of an investigation.

(iv) The circumstances immediately surrounding an arrest, including the time and place of arrest, resistance, pursuit, possession and use of weapons, and a description of physical items seized at the time of arrest.

Disclosures should include only incontrovertible, factual matters, and should not include subjective observations. In addition, where background information or information relating to the circumstances of an arrest or investigation would be highly prejudicial or where the release thereof would serve no law enforcement function, such information should not be made public.

(4) Personnel of the Department shall not disseminate any information concerning a defendant's prior criminal record.

(5) Because of the particular danger of prejudice resulting from statements in the period approaching and during trial, they ought strenuously to be avoided during that period. Any such statement or release shall be made only on the infrequent occasion when circumstances absolutely demand a disclosure of information and shall include only information which is clearly not prejudicial.

(6) The release of certain types of information generally tends to create dangers of prejudice without serving a significant law enforcement function. Therefore, personnel of the Department should refrain from making available the following:

(i) Observations about a defendant's character.

(ii) Statements, admissions, confessions, or alibis attributable to a defendant, or the refusal or failure of the accused to make a statement

(iii) Reference to investigative procedures such as fingerprints, polygraph examinations, ballistic tests, or laboratory tests, or to the refusal by the defendant to submit to such tests or examinations.

(iv) Statements concerning the identity, testimony, or credibility of prospective witnesses.

(v) Statements concerning evidence or argument in the case, whether or not it is anticipated that such evidence or argument will be used at trial.

(vi) Any opinion as to the accused's guilt, or the possibility of a plea of guilty to the offense charged, or the possibility of a plea to a lesser offense.

(7) Personnel of the Department of Justice should take no action to encourage or assist news media in photographing or televising a defendant or accused person being held or transported in Federal custody. Departmental representatives should not make available photographs of a defendant unless a law enforcement function is served thereby.

(8) This statement of policy is not intended to restrict the release of information concerning a defendant who is a fugitive from justice.

(9) Since the purpose of this statement is to set forth generally applicable guidelines, there will, of course, be situations in which it will limit the release of information which would not be prejudicial under the particular circumstances. If a representative of the Department believes that in the interest of the fair administration of justice and the law enforcement process information beyond these guidelines should be released, in a particular case, he shall request the permission of the Attorney General or the Deputy Attorney General to do so.

(c) *Guidelines to civil actions.* Personnel of the Department of Justice associated with a civil action shall not during its investigation or litigation make or participate in making an extrajudicial statement, other than a quotation from or reference to public records, which a reasonable person would expect to be disseminated by means of public communication if there is a reasonable likelihood that such dissemination will interfere with a fair trial and which relates to:

(1) Evidence regarding the occurrence or transaction involved.

(2) The character, credibility, or criminal records of a party, witness, or prospective witness.

(3) The performance or results of any examinations or tests or the refusal or failure of a party to submit to such.

(4) An opinion as to the merits of the claims or defenses of a party, except as required by law or administrative rule.

(5) Any other matter reasonably likely to interfere with a fair trial of the action.

Attorney-Client Privilege and Work Product Provisions

Editors' Introduction. The ethical obligation of confidentiality addressed in Rule 1.6 of the ABA Model Rules of Professional Conduct is closely related to the evidentiary rules governing the attorney-client privilege and the procedural rules protecting attorney work product. The materials in this chapter show how the attorney-client privilege and the work product doctrine are codified in the Federal Rules of Evidence and the Federal Rules of Civil Procedure.

Additional privilege and work product provisions are found in this book in the Restatement (Third) of the Law Governing Lawyers (see the attorney-client privilege and work product provisions in §§59-93). Those editions of the book that contain the California or New York materials (or both) have privilege and work product provisions from those states in their respective chapters.

Rule 26 of the Federal Rules of Civil Procedure was last amended effective December 1, 2010. Specifically, amendments to Rule 26(b)(4)(B) and (C) provide heightened protection against discovery of communications between experts and counsel. Amended Rule 26(b)(4)(B) protects "drafts of any report or disclosure required under Rule 26(a)(2), regardless of the form in which the draft is recorded." Amended Rule 26(b)(4)(C) protects "communications between the party's attorney and any witness required to provide a report under Rule 26(a)(2)(B)" unless the communications: (i) relate to the expert's compensation; or (ii) "identify facts or data that the party's attorney provided and that the expert considered in forming the opinions to be expressed"; or (iii) "identify assumptions that the party's attorney provided and that the expert relied on in forming the opinions to be expressed."

For updates on future rule amendments, and for a wealth of information about recent and proposed amendments to the Federal Rules of Civil Procedure, the Federal Rules of Evidence, and other federal court rules that may affect privilege or work product, visit the official website of the United States Courts at *www.uscourts.gov* or call John Rabiej, Chief of the Rules Committee Support Office, at (202) 502-1820.

Contents

FEDERAL RULES OF EVIDENCE

Rule 501. General Rule

Except as otherwise required by the Constitution of the United States or provided by Act of Congress or in rules prescribed by the Supreme Court pursuant to statutory authority, the privilege of a witness, person, government, State, or political subdivision thereof shall be governed by the principles of the common law as they may be interpreted by the courts of the United States in the light of reason and experience. However, in civil actions and proceedings, with respect to an element of a claim or defense as to which State law supplies the rule of decision, the privilege of a witness, person, government, State, or political subdivision thereof shall be determined in accordance with State law.

Rule 502. Attorney-Client Privilege and Work Product; Limitations on Waiver

The following provisions apply, in the circumstances set out, to disclosure of a communication or information covered by the attorney-client privilege or work-product protection.

(a) *Disclosure made in a federal proceeding or to a federal office or agency; scope of a waiver.* — When the disclosure is made in a federal proceeding or to a federal office or agency and waives the attorney-client privilege or work-product protection, the waiver extends to an undisclosed communication or information in a federal or state proceeding only if:

(1) the waiver is intentional;

(2) the disclosed and undisclosed communications or information concern the same subject matter; and

(3) they ought in fairness to be considered together.

(b) *Inadvertent disclosure.* — When made in a federal proceeding or to a federal office or agency, the disclosure does not operate as a waiver in a federal or state proceeding if:

(1) the disclosure is inadvertent;

(2) the holder of the privilege or protection took reasonable steps to prevent disclosure; and

(3) the holder promptly took reasonable steps to rectify the error, including (if applicable) following Fed. R. Civ. P. 26(b)(5)(B).

(c) *Disclosure made in a state proceeding.* — When the disclosure is made in a state proceeding and is not the subject of a state-court order concerning waiver, the disclosure does not operate as a waiver in a federal proceeding if the disclosure:

(1) would not be a waiver under this rule if it had been made in a federal proceeding; or

(2) is not a waiver under the law of the state where the disclosure occurred.

(d) *Controlling effect of a court order.* — A federal court may order that the privilege or protection is not waived by disclosure connected with the litigation pending before the court — in which event the disclosure is also not a waiver in any other federal or state proceeding.

(e) *Controlling effect of a party agreement.* — An agreement on the effect of disclosure in a federal proceeding is binding only on the parties to the agreement, unless it is incorporated into a court order.

(f) *Controlling effect of this rule.* — Notwithstanding Rules 101 and 1101, this rule applies to state proceedings and to federal court-annexed and federal court-mandated arbitration proceedings, in the circumstances set out in the rule. And notwithstanding Rule 501, this rule applies even if state law provides the rule of decision.

(g) *Definitions.* — In this rule:

(1) "attorney-client privilege" means the protection that applicable law provides for confidential attorney-client communications; and

(2) "work-product protection" means the protection that applicable law provides for tangible material (or its intangible equivalent) prepared in anticipation of litigation or for trial.

Proposed Rule 503. Lawyer-Client Privilege (not enacted)

Editors' Note. When the Supreme Court transmitted the proposed Federal Rules of Evidence to Congress in 1973, the proposals contained 13 separate rules on privileges, ranging from Rule 501 through Rule 513. The proposed privilege rules were extremely controversial, however. Congress substantially altered proposed Rule 501, and completely rejected proposed Rules 502 through 513. We reprint Rule 503 here because, despite its rejection, it is an accurate general statement of the law governing the attorney-client privilege in many jurisdictions and has been adopted nearly verbatim in the evidence codes of some states (*see, e.g.*, Rule 503 of the Texas Rules of Criminal Evidence). To indicate that it did not become law, we reprint it in ordinary type rather than in bold.

(a) *Definitions.* As used in this rule:

(1) A "client" is a person, public officer, or corporation, association, or other organization or entity, either public or private, who is rendered professional legal services by a lawyer, or who consults a lawyer with a view to obtaining professional legal services from him.

(2) A "lawyer" is a person authorized, or reasonably believed by the client to be authorized, to practice law in any state or nation.

(3) A "representative of the lawyer" is one employed to assist the lawyer in the rendition of professional legal services.

(4) A communication is "confidential" if not intended to be disclosed to third persons other than those to whom disclosure is in furtherance of the rendition of professional legal services to the client or those reasonably necessary for the transmission of the communication.

(b) *General rule of privilege.* A client has a privilege to refuse to disclose and to prevent any other person from disclosing confidential communications made for the purpose of facilitating the rendition of professional legal services to the client, (1) between himself or his representative and his lawyer or his lawyer's representative, or (2) between his lawyer and the lawyer's representative, or (3) by him or his lawyer to a lawyer representing another in a matter of common interest, or (4) between representatives of the client or between the client and a representative of the client, or (5) between lawyers representing the client.

(c) *Who may claim the privilege?* The privilege may be claimed by the client, his guardian or conservator, the personal representative of a deceased client, or the successor, trustee, or similar representative of a corporation, association, or other organization, whether or not in existence. The person who was the lawyer at the time of the communication may claim the privilege but only on behalf of the client. His authority to do so is presumed in the absence of evidence to the contrary.

(d) *Exceptions.* There is no privilege under this rule:

(1) *Furtherance of crime or fraud.* If the services of the lawyer were sought or obtained to enable or aid anyone to commit or plan to commit what the client knew or reasonably should have known to be a crime or fraud; or

(2) *Claimants through same deceased client.* As to a communication relevant to an issue between parties who claim through the same deceased

client, regardless of whether the claims are by testate or intestate succession or by inter vivos transaction; or

(3) *Breach of duty by lawyer or client.* As to a communication relevant to an issue of breach of duty by the lawyer to his client or by the client to his lawyer; or

(4) *Document attested by lawyer.* As to a communication relevant to an issue concerning an attested document to which the lawyer is an attesting witness; or

(5) *Joint clients.* As to a communication relevant to a matter of common interest between two or more clients if the communication was made by any of them to a lawyer retained or consulted in common, when offered in an action between any of the clients.

FEDERAL RULES OF CIVIL PROCEDURE

Editors' Note. In federal courts, the work product doctrine is codified in Rules 26(b)(3)-(4) of the Federal Rules of Civil Procedure. These provisions were added to the rules in 1970 to resolve confusion and disagreement over the scope of the judicially created work product doctrine stemming from *Hickman v. Taylor,* 329 U.S. 495 (1947). Rule 26(b)(3) governs work product generally, including the mental opinions and impressions of lawyers, and Rule 26(b)(4) governs work product relating to experts. Rule 26(b)(5) was added in 1993 to enable parties to assess the applicability of privilege and work product protection to items withheld during discovery.

The Federal Rules of Criminal Procedure, in Rules 16(a)(2) and (b)(2) (which are not reprinted in this book), contain a form of work product protection, but the criminal work product protection is subject to many exceptions. For example, Rule 26.2 requires lawyers in criminal cases to turn over upon request any relevant statement made by a witness who has completed a direct examination at trial.

In addition, the Federal Rules, as interpreted by cases such as *Zubulake v. UBS Warburg LLC,* 229 F.R.D 422 (S.D.N.Y. 2004) and 220 F.R.D. 212 (S.D.N.Y. 2003), impose significant duties on lawyers with regard to a client's electronically stored information (ESI). See especially Rules 26(a)(1)(A)(ii); 26(b)(2)(B); 26(f)(3); and 37(f).

Rule 26. Duty to Disclose; General Provisions Governing Discovery . . .

(b) Discovery Scope and Limits . . .

(3) *Trial Preparation: Materials.*

(A) *Documents and Tangible Things.* Ordinarily, a party may not discover documents and tangible things that are prepared in anticipation of litigation or for trial by or for another party or its representative

(including the other party's attorney, consultant, surety, indemnitor, insurer, or agent). But, subject to Rule 26(b)(4), those materials may be discovered if:

(i) they are otherwise discoverable under Rule 26(b)(1); and

(ii) the party shows that it has substantial need for the materials to prepare its case and cannot, without undue hardship, obtain their substantial equivalent by other means.

(B) ***Protection Against Disclosure.*** **If the court orders discovery of those materials, it must protect against disclosure of the mental impressions, conclusions, opinions, or legal theories of a party's attorney or other representative concerning the litigation.**

(C) ***Previous Statement.*** **Any party or other person may, on request and without the required showing, obtain the person's own previous statement about the action or its subject matter. If the request is refused, the person may move for a court order, and Rule 37(a)(5) applies to the award of expenses. A previous statement is either:**

(i) a written statement that the person has signed or otherwise adopted or approved; or

(ii) a contemporaneous stenographic, mechanical, electrical, or other recording — or a transcription of it — that recites substantially verbatim the person's oral statement.

(4) ***Trial Preparation: Experts.***

(A) ***Expert Who May Testify.*** **A party may depose any person who has been identified as an expert whose opinions may be presented at trial. If Rule 26(a)(2)(B) requires a report from the expert, the deposition may be conducted only after the report is provided.**

(B) ***Trial-Preparation Protection for Draft Reports or Disclosures.*** **Rule 26(b)(3)(A) and (B) protect drafts of any report or disclosure required under Rule 26(a)(2), regardless of the form in which the draft is recorded.**

(C) ***Trial-Preparation Protection for Communications Between a Party's Attorney and Expert Witnesses.*** **Rule 26(b)(3)(A) and (B) protect communications between the party's attorney and any witness required to provide a report under Rule 26(a)(2)(B) regardless of the form of the communications, except to the extent that the communications:**

(i) relate to compensation for the expert's study or testimony;

(ii) identify facts or data that the party's attorney provided and that the expert considered in forming the opinions to be expressed; or

(iii) identify assumptions that the party's attorney provided and that the expert relied on in forming the opinions to be expressed.

(D) ***Expert Employed Only for Trial Preparation.*** **Ordinarily, a party may not, by interrogatories or deposition, discover facts known or opinions held by an expert who has been retained or specially employed by another party in anticipation of litigation or to prepare for trial and**

who is not expected to be called as a witness at trial. But a party may do so only:

(i) as provided in Rule 35(b); or

(ii) on showing exceptional circumstances under which it is impracticable for the party to obtain facts or opinions on the same subject by other means.

(E) *Payment.* Unless manifest injustice would result, the court must require that the party seeking discovery:

(i) pay the expert a reasonable fee for time spent in responding to discovery under Rule 26(b)(4)(A) or (B); and

(ii) for discovery under (B), also pay the other party a fair portion of the fees and expenses it reasonably incurred in obtaining the expert's facts and opinions.

(5) *Claiming Privilege or Protecting Trial-Preparation Materials.*

(A) *Information Withheld.* When a party withholds information otherwise discoverable by claiming that the information is privileged or subject to protection as trial-preparation material, the party must:

(i) expressly make the claim; and

(ii) describe the nature of the documents, communications, or tangible things not produced or disclosed — and do so in a manner that, without revealing information itself privileged or protected, will enable other parties to assess the claim.

(B) *Information Produced.* If information produced in discovery is subject to a claim of privilege or of protection as trial-preparation material, the party making the claim may notify any party that received the information of the claim and the basis for it. After being notified, a party must promptly return, sequester, or destroy the specified information and any copies it has; must not use or disclose the information until the claim is resolved; must take reasonable steps to retrieve the information if the party disclosed it before being notified; and may promptly present the information to the court under seal for a determination of the claim. The producing party must preserve the information until the claim is resolved.

Judicial Conduct Materials

ABA Model Code of Judicial Conduct*

As amended through August 2008

Editors' Introduction. The ABA House of Delegates approved extensive revisions to the ABA Code of Judicial Conduct at its February 2007 meeting. The major changes in the 2007 Code are discussed below, following discussion of the evolution of ABA judicial conduct codes from 1924-2006. (In addition, on November 1, 1993, in an unusual press release, seven Justices of the Supreme Court issued an announcement, entitled "Statement of Recusal Policy." The Statement is closely related to the recusal and disqualification provisions of Rule 2.11 of the Code of Judicial Conduct, but it primarily construes 28 U.S.C. §455. We therefore reprint the Statement following 28 U.S.C. §455 in our chapter entitled "Statutes on Disqualification and Discipline of Federal Judges.")

Historical background: The first three ABA codes. The ABA first adopted a code of judicial conduct, originally called the Canons of Judicial Ethics, in 1924. (The original spur for judicial canons came from Judge Kennesaw Mountain Landis, a federal judge who was appointed as the first Commissioner of Baseball after the infamous "Black Sox" scandal of 1919. Despite demands that he resign his federal judgeship after he began serving as Commissioner, he refused to step down. The ABA promptly began drafting Canons of Judicial Ethics.) With occasional amendments, the Canons of Judicial Ethics served the profession well for nearly 50 years and were adopted by most states.

In 1969, however, the ABA created a Special Committee on Standards of Judicial Conduct, chaired by California Supreme Court Justice Roger Traynor, "to draw up modern standards and to replace the Canons of Judicial Ethics."

* Copyright © 1990, 1997, 1999, 2003 by the American Bar Association. All rights reserved. Reprinted with permission.

In August 1972, the ABA House of Delegates formally adopted the ABA Model Code of Judicial Conduct to replace the Canons. The ABA made minor changes in 1982 and 1984. The 1972 ABA Model Code of Judicial Conduct proved widely influential. Nearly all states (plus the District of Columbia) eventually adopted codes of judicial conduct closely modeled on the 1972 ABA Code.

In August 1990, the ABA revised the Model Code of Judicial Conduct. Although the 1990 Code (as it came to be called) is like the 1972 Code in many regards, it also contains many differences, affecting such issues as judicial membership in exclusionary clubs and judicial responsibility to prohibit race and sex discrimination and other kinds of bias in the courtroom. For a legislative history of the 1990 Code, see L. Milord, The Development of the ABA Judicial Code (1992).

The problem of political contributions. At the ABA's 1997 Annual Meeting, the House of Delegates voted to amend the 1990 Judicial Code for the first time since its adoption. The amendment substantially changed the Commentary to (but not the text of) Canon 5C(2), a provision that governed the solicitation and acceptance of campaign contributions by judges and judicial candidates who are "subject to public election" (as distinct from appointed judges). The amendment to the Commentary addressed widespread concern about "the appearance of impropriety that may arise when parties whose interests may come before a judge or the lawyers who represent such parties have made contributions to the election campaigns of judicial candidates."

Shortly before the ABA's 1998 Annual Meeting, the ABA's elite Task Force on Lawyers' Political Contributions (which was appointed in 1997 to study so-called "pay-to-play" issues) issued a report recommending various amendments to the Code of Judicial Conduct intended "to protect the integrity and independence of judges and candidates for judicial office." The Task Force noted that judges in 42 states were then required to stand for election in some fashion and that their need to raise campaign funds created an appearance of impropriety. The Task Force therefore recommended amendments to Canon 5 of the Code of Judicial Conduct that would (a) require judicial candidates and/or their campaign committees to publicly disclose all campaign contributions from lawyers; (b) limit the amount of money a judicial candidate may accept from any one lawyer, law firm, political action committee, or political party; (c) require judges, upon motion, to recuse themselves from hearing any case in which a litigant or lawyer has contributed more than a specified amount to the judge's campaign; (d) prohibit judges from appointing a lawyer as a guardian, executor, special master, or other paid position if the lawyer, the lawyer's firm, or any employee of the firm has contributed more than a specified limit to the judge's campaign; and (e) require unopposed judicial candidates and judicial candidates who have campaign funds remaining after an election to return the surplus funds to contributors pro rata and/or give the funds to an entity to be determined by the jurisdiction.

In 1999, the ABA adopted a definition of the word "aggregate" in computing the value of a person's or entity's contributions and new provisions in Canons 3 and 5 as part of the Association's continuing efforts to address "concern about the relationship between lawyers making political contributions and the award of engagements to perform legal services in a variety of contexts." (These provisions survive in somewhat different language in Rules 2.11 and 4.4 of the 2007 Code.)

First Amendment concerns. In June 2002, in a 5-4 opinion by Justice Scalia, the Supreme Court held that a Minnesota rule limiting judicial campaign speech violated the First Amendment. *Republican Party of Minnesota v. White,* 536 U.S. 765 (2002). The Minnesota state rule, which had been derived from the 1972 ABA Code of Judicial Conduct, prohibited a judicial candidate to "announce his or her views on disputed legal or political issues." Lower federal courts and the Minnesota Supreme Court had interpreted this language to encompass only those disputed issues likely to come before the candidate if elected and not to forbid general discussion of case law and judicial philosophy. (Another Minnesota provision, not before the Court, prohibited judicial candidates from making "pledges or promises of conduct in office." This prohibition also appeared in Canon 5A(3)(d)(i) of the ABA Code.) Justices O'Connor and Kennedy concurred in the Court's opinion and also wrote separate opinions. Justices Stevens, Souter, Ginsburg, and Breyer dissented in opinions by Justices Stevens and Ginsburg.

At the ABA's August 2003 Annual Meeting, the House of Delegates amended the Code of Judicial Conduct to bring it into conformity with *White.* The amendments added a definition of "impartiality" and "impartial." They also prohibited judges, with respect to cases, controversies or issues that are likely to come before the court, from making "pledges, promises or commitments that are inconsistent with the impartial performance of the adjudicative duties of the office;" required a judge to disqualify himself or herself if, while either serving as a judge or running for judicial office, the judge has made a public statement that "commits, or appears to commit," the judge with respect to either "(i) an issue in the proceeding; or (ii) the controversy in the proceeding;" and deleted a subparagraph that had prohibited judicial candidates from making statements that committed or appeared to commit them on issues that were likely to come before their courts.

Also at the ABA's 2003 Annual Meeting, the House of Delegates adopted a series of recommendations by the ABA Commission on the 21st Century Judiciary that set forth "principles" intended to preserve judicial independence, accountability and efficiency. The principles affirm that the ABA prefers merit selection rather than elections to select state court judges. Under the system of judicial selection that the ABA Commission recommended to the states, governors would appoint judges from a pool of aspirants reviewed and approved by a neutral commission. Judges would be appointed to serve a single lengthy term, and they would not be subject to reselection. The Commission also developed alternative recommendations for states in which judges are elected or subject to reselection. Specifically, the Commission recommended nonpartisan elections for judges, both initially and for reselection. Where elections remained partisan, however, the Commission recommended that election campaigns should be funded with public financing.

The 2007 Code of Judicial Conduct. As the historical account above shows, the ABA has twice before amended the Code of Judicial Conduct comprehensively since its original promulgation in 1924—once in 1970, and again in 1990. In September 2003, ABA President Dennis W. Archer, Jr., appointed a Joint Commission to Evaluate the Model Code of Judicial Conduct. The Commission's charge was to review the Code of Judicial Conduct and to recommend revisions. The Chair of the Commission was attorney Mark I. Harrison of Phoenix, and its Reporters were Professor Charles G. Geyh of Indiana University School of Law and attorney W. William Hodes of Indianapolis, formerly a professor at Indiana University School of Law.

The Commission held hearings in 2004, 2005, and 2006 and made extensive recommendations for revision. The House of Delegates adopted the revisions in February 2007. Aside from the substantive changes, summarized below, the Commission recommended that the Code follow the same format as the Model Rules of Professional Conduct — i.e., with numbered rules and comments. For more information about the Commission's work, including various drafts, testimony at hearings, and reports, visit its website at *http://www.americanbar.org/groups/professional_responsibility/publications/model_code_of_judicial_conduct.html.* The site also contains tables comparing the new Code with the 1990 Code, the Reporters' notes, and other legislative history. For a critique of the Code from the American Judicature Society, which submitted many suggestions (not all adopted), see Cynthia Gray, The 2007 ABA Model Code: Taking Judicial Ethics to the Next Level, 90 Judicature 284 (May-June 2007). It can also be found at *www.ajs.org/ethics/pdfs/Judicaturemodelcodearticle.pdf.*

In August 2010, the ABA amended the Code mainly to revise the section marked APPLICATION. It also amended Comment [2] to Rule 2.10. These changes are shown in legislative format.

Following are some significant new and carryover provisions in the 2007 ABA Model Code of Judicial Conduct:

- The "appearance of impropriety" standard as an independent basis for discipline appears in Rule 1.2. The Commission's final draft deleted this standard as an independent basis for discipline, but the Conference of Chief Justices objected and the Commission agreed to reinstate it.
- In Rule 1.3, the new Code forbids judges to "abuse the prestige of judicial office to advance the personal or economic interests of the judge or others," whereas the 1990 Code said a judge "shall not lend the prestige of office" to such interests.
- Rule 2.2 cmt. 4, which is new, allows judges "to make reasonable accommodations to ensure pro se litigants the opportunity to have their matters fairly heard." Rule 2.2 itself requires that judges perform all duties "fairly and impartially."
- Rule 2.3(B) adds "or engage in harassment" to the prohibition against a judge manifesting bias based on a list of categories and adds "gender, ethnicity, marital status, and political affiliation" to that list. Rule 2.3(C), which states that judges "shall require lawyers . . . to refrain from manifesting bias or prejudice," also adds "harassment" and adds the same categories to the list.
- Rule 2.6(B) continues to permit judges to "encourage parties . . . and their lawyers to settle" but directs that the judge "not act in a manner that coerces any party into settlement." New commentary identifies six factors a judge may consider in deciding the judge's "settlement practice" and raises the possibility that in some instances participation in settlement talks may lead to disqualification.

- Rule 2.8 cmt. 3, which is new, permits a judge, if not legally prohibited, to "meet with jurors who choose to remain after trial but should be careful not to discuss the merits of the case."
- Rule 2.9(A)(2) continues to permit a judge to consult with an independent expert but the rule now requires "advance notice to the parties" and "a reasonable opportunity to object and respond to the notice and to the advice received."
- Rule 2.9(B) is new and requires notification to the parties if a judge "inadvertently receives an unauthorized ex parte communication bearing upon the substance of a matter." The Reporter explains that this rule responds to the risk of such things as a misdirected fax.
- For some specialized courts, Rule 2.9 cmt. 4 contains a new exception to the prohibition against ex parte contacts as follows:

> A judge may initiate, permit, or consider ex parte communications expressly authorized by law, such as when serving on therapeutic or problem-solving courts, mental health courts, or drug courts. In this capacity, judges may assume a more interactive role with parties, treatment providers, probation officers, social workers, and others.

- Rule 2.9 cmt. 6, which is new, makes it clear that the prohibition against independently investigating the facts extends to doing so by electronic research.
- Rule 2.9 cmt. 7 is new and allows a judge to "consult ethics advisory committees, outside counsel, or legal experts concerning the judge's compliance with this Code."
- Rule 2.10(E) is new. It permits a judge "to respond directly or through a third party to allegations in the media or elsewhere concerning the judge's conduct in a matter." This new authority is subject to Rule 2.10(A), which is present in the 1990 Code and which forbids public comment "that might reasonably be expected to affect the outcome or impair the fairness of a matter pending or impending in any court. . . . "
- Disqualification based on the interests of family members in Rule 2.11 now extends to a "domestic partner," which the Terminology now defines as "a person with whom another person maintains a household and an intimate relationship, other than a person to whom he or she is legally married."
- Comment 2 to Rule 2.11, on disqualification, is new. It provides that "a judge's obligation not to hear or decide matters in which disqualification is required applies regardless of whether a motion to disqualify is filed."
- Rule 2.14 newly provides that a judge who has "a reasonable belief" that a judge's or lawyer's performance "is impaired" by mental or physical illness or alcohol or substance abuse must "take appropriate action, which may include a confidential referral to a lawyer or judicial assistance program."
- Rule 3.2(B), which is new, allows a judge to make a voluntary appearance at a public hearing convened by an executive or legislative body "in connection with matters about which the judge acquired knowledge or expertise in the course of the judge's judicial duties."
- The prior Code prohibited a judge from belonging to an organization that discriminated based on race, sex, religion, or national origin. Rule 3.6 adds gender, ethnicity, and sexual orientation to the list. Comment 3 now requires a

judge to "resign immediately" from any such organization, whereas previously judges were allowed to remain members for a year during which time they could work to change the rules of the organization. As before, there are exceptions for organizations identified in cmts. [2], [4], and [5] of the rule, including religious organizations, and for "national or state military service."

- A new set of rules (Rules 3.7(A)(3-5)) permits judges to solicit members for an organization even though membership dues help support the organization; to appear, speak, and be honored at fundraising events of an organization; and to make recommendations to a grant-making organization, *but in each case* only if the particular organization is "concerned with the law, the legal system, or the administration of justice." Also, Rule 3.7(A)(4) allows a judge to be featured and receive an award at events sponsored by educational, charitable, and like organizations that are not "concerned with" the law, but only if the event is not a fundraiser. (The Rule 3.7 authority is subordinate to Rule 3.1, which, among other things, forbids conduct "that would appear to a reasonable person to undermine the judge's independence, integrity, or impartiality.")
- Rule 3.7 cmt. 4 continues to allow a judge's name to appear on fundraising and membership solicitation letters of organizations identified in Rule 3.7. The judge's title or office may also be listed "if comparable designations" are used for others.
- Rule 3.14, which is new, addresses expenses to travel to and at seminars. It permits a judge to "accept reimbursement of necessary and reasonable expenses for travel, food, lodging, and other incidental expenses" associated with participation in "extrajudicial activities permitted by this Code." The rule also permits reimbursement of these expenses "when appropriate to the occasion, by the judge's spouse, domestic partner, or guest." The fact of reimbursement for expenses at these events must be made known "within 30 days following the conclusion of the event or program." Posting on the court's website is required "when technically feasible." Comment 3 to Rule 3.14 lists eight separate factors a judge should consider "when deciding whether to accept reimbursement or a fee waiver for attendance at a particular activity." These factors bear on whether or not reimbursement would "appear to a reasonable person to undermine the judge's independence, integrity, or impartiality."
- Rule 4.1, whose subject is political activity of judges and judicial candidates (via election or appointment), is mostly unchanged except for three additional prohibitions in paragraphs (A)(6, 7, 10). Most notable, though, are new cmts. 11-15, which describe what judges and non-judge candidates may ethically say and not say consistent with the ABA's reading of *Republican Party of Minnesota v. White.*

To monitor the progress of the adoption of the Code nationwide, go to the interactive map at *http://www.americanbar.org/groups/professional_responsibility/resources/judicial_ethics_regulation/mcjc.html.*

Code of Conduct for U.S. Judge. The Committee on Codes of Conduct of the Judicial Conference of the United States adopts ethical rules for all federal judges, including magistrate judges and bankruptcy judges, but excluding the justices of the Supreme Court. The latest version of this code, which is based on but different from, the ABA Code, was effective July 1, 2009, and can be found at the following website or by Googling "Code of Conduct for U.S. Judges": *www.uscourts.gov/library/codeOfConduct/Revised_ Code_Effective_July-01-09.pdf.* In addition, the Judicial Conference has adopted rules governing a judge's attendance at privately funded educational programs, which critics have called "judicial junkets." These can be found at *www.uscourts.gov/uscourts/RulesAndPolicies/SeminarDisclosure/judbrappc906c.pdf.*

A committee of the U.S. Judicial Conference will answer questions from judges about the application of the Code to proposed conduct. Many of these answers are published and they can be found at *www.uscourts.gov/uscourts/RulesAndPolicies/conduct/Vol02B-Ch02-OGC-Post2USCOURTS-PublAdvisoryOps.pdf.*

Caperton v. A.T. Massey Coal Co., 129 S. Ct. 2252 (2009). On June 8, 2009, the Supreme Court issued its opinion in this much-watched case. The question before the Court was whether, on the facts of the case, the plaintiff's due process rights were violated. The plaintiff had won a $50 million judgment in the state trial court. While the defendant's appeal to the West Virginia Supreme Court of Appeals was pending, its chief executive officer contributed $3 million to the campaign effort of a candidate for the state high court, amounting to 60 percent of the candidate's campaign funds. That candidate was elected, and he then cast a deciding vote that overturned the plaintiff's victory. The Court held, 5-4, in a decision by Justice Kennedy, that the Due Process Clause was violated on these facts. The decision rested on the Due Process Clause, not an ethical rule. The Supreme Court has no power to enforce a state's ethical rules. During 2011, ABA committees were reviewing the Code of Judicial Conduct to determine what if any amendments might be appropriate in light of the *Caperton* decision. At the 2011 ABA Annual Meeting, the House of Delegates adopted the following roslution:

RESOLVED, That the American Bar Association urges states to establish clearly articulated procedures for:

A. Judicial disqualification determinations; and

B. Prompt review by another judge or tribunal, or as otherwise provided by law or rule of court, of denials of requests to disqualify a judge.

FURTHER RESOLVED, That the American Bar Association urges states in which judges are subject to elections of any kind to adopt:

A. Disclosure requirements for litigants and lawyers who have provided, directly or indirectly, campaign support in an election involving a judge before whom they are appearing.

B. Guidelines for judges concerning disclosure and disqualification obligations regarding campaign contributions.

FURTHER RESOLVED, That the Standing Committee on Ethics and Professional Responsibility and the Standing Committee on Professional

Discipline should proceed on an expedited basis to consider what amendments, if any, should be made to the ABA Model Code of Judicial Conduct or to the ABA Model Rules of Professional Conduct to provide necessary additional guidance to the states on disclosure requirements and standards for judicial disqualification.

Contents

ABA MODEL CODE OF JUDICIAL CONDUCT (2007)

ABA MODEL CODE OF JUDICIAL CONDUCT

February 2007

PREAMBLE

[1] An independent, fair and impartial judiciary is indispensable to our system of justice. The United States legal system is based upon the principle that an independent, impartial, and competent judiciary, composed of men and women of integrity, will interpret and apply the law that governs our society. Thus, the judiciary plays a central role in preserving the principles of justice and the rule of law. Inherent in all the Rules contained in this Code are the precepts that judges,

individually and collectively, must respect and honor the judicial office as a public trust and strive to maintain and enhance confidence in the legal system.

[2] Judges should maintain the dignity of judicial office at all times, and avoid both impropriety and the appearance of impropriety in their professional and personal lives. They should aspire at all times to conduct that ensures the greatest possible public confidence in their independence, impartiality, integrity, and competence.

[3] The Model Code of Judicial Conduct establishes standards for the ethical conduct of judges and judicial candidates. It is not intended as an exhaustive guide for the conduct of judges and judicial candidates, who are governed in their judicial and personal conduct by general ethical standards as well as by the Code. The Code is intended, however, to provide guidance and assist judges in maintaining the highest standards of judicial and personal conduct, and to provide a basis for regulating their conduct through disciplinary agencies.

SCOPE

[1] The Model Code of Judicial Conduct consists of four Canons, numbered Rules under each Canon, and Comments that generally follow and explain each Rule. Scope and Terminology sections provide additional guidance in interpreting and applying the Code. An Application section establishes when the various Rules apply to a judge or judicial candidate.

[2] The Canons state overarching principles of judicial ethics that all judges must observe. Although a judge may be disciplined only for violating a Rule, the Canons provide important guidance in interpreting the Rules. Where a Rule contains a permissive term, such as "may" or "should," the conduct being addressed is committed to the personal and professional discretion of the judge or candidate in question, and no disciplinary action should be taken for action or inaction within the bounds of such discretion.

[3] The Comments that accompany the Rules serve two functions. First, they provide guidance regarding the purpose, meaning, and proper application of the Rules. They contain explanatory material and, in some instances, provide examples of permitted or prohibited conduct. Comments neither add to nor subtract from the binding obligations set forth in the Rules. Therefore, when a Comment contains the term "must," it does not mean that the Comment itself is binding or enforceable; it signifies that the Rule in question, properly understood, is obligatory as to the conduct at issue.

[4] Second, the Comments identify aspirational goals for judges. To implement fully the principles of this Code as articulated in the Canons, judges should strive to exceed the standards of conduct established by the Rules, holding themselves to the highest ethical standards and seeking to achieve those aspirational goals, thereby enhancing the dignity of the judicial office.

[5] The Rules of the Model Code of Judicial Conduct are rules of reason that should be applied consistent with constitutional requirements, statutes, other court rules, and decisional law, and with due regard for all relevant circumstances. The Rules should not be interpreted to impinge upon the essential independence of judges in making judicial decisions.

[6] Although the black letter of the Rules is binding and enforceable, it is not contemplated that every transgression will result in the imposition of discipline. Whether discipline should be imposed should be determined through a reasonable and reasoned application of the Rules, and should depend upon factors such as the seriousness of the transgression, the facts and circumstances that existed at the time of the transgression, the extent of any pattern of improper activity, whether there have been previous violations, and the effect of the improper activity upon the judicial system or others.

[7] The Code is not designed or intended as a basis for civil or criminal liability. Neither is it intended to be the basis for litigants to seek collateral remedies against each other or to obtain tactical advantages in proceedings before a court.

TERMINOLOGY

The first time any term listed below is used in a Rule in its defined sense, it is followed by an asterisk (*).

"Aggregate," in relation to contributions for a candidate, means not only contributions in cash or in kind made directly to a candidate's campaign committee, but also all contributions made indirectly with the understanding that they will be used to support the election of a candidate or to oppose the election of the candidate's opponent. See Rules 2.11 and 4.4.

"Appropriate authority" means the authority having responsibility for initiation of disciplinary process in connection with the violation to be reported. See Rules 2.14 and 2.15.

"Contribution" means both financial and in-kind contributions, such as goods, professional or volunteer services, advertising, and other types of assistance, which, if obtained by the recipient otherwise, would require a financial expenditure. See Rules 2.11, 2.13, 3.7, 4.1, and 4.4.

"De minimis," in the context of interests pertaining to disqualification of a judge, means an insignificant interest that could not raise a reasonable question regarding the judge's impartiality. See Rule 2.11.

"Domestic partner" means a person with whom another person maintains a household and an intimate relationship, other than a person to whom he or she is legally married. See Rules 2.11, 2.13, 3.13, and 3.14.

"Economic interest" means ownership of more than a de minimis legal or equitable interest. Except for situations in which the judge participates in the management of such a legal or equitable interest, or the interest could be substantially affected by the outcome of a proceeding before a judge, it does not include:

(1) an interest in the individual holdings within a mutual or common investment fund;

(2) an interest in securities held by an educational, religious, charitable, fraternal, or civic organization in which the judge or the judge's spouse, domestic partner, parent, or child serves as a director, an officer, an advisor, or other participant;

(3) a deposit in a financial institution or deposits or proprietary interests the judge may maintain as a member of a mutual savings association or credit union, or similar proprietary interests; or

(4) an interest in the issuer of government securities held by the judge.

See Rules 1.3 and 2.11.

"Fiduciary" includes relationships such as executor, administrator, trustee, or guardian. See Rules 2.11, 3.2, and 3.8.

"Impartial," "impartiality," and **"impartially"** mean absence of bias or prejudice in favor of, or against, particular parties or classes of parties, as well as maintenance of an open mind in considering issues that may come before a judge. See Canons 1, 2, and 4, and Rules 1.2, 2.2, 2.10, 2.11, 2.13, 3.1, 3.12, 3.13, 4.1, and 4.2.

"Impending matter" is a matter that is imminent or expected to occur in the near future. See Rules 2.9, 2.10, 3.13, and 4.1.

"Impropriety" includes conduct that violates the law, court rules, or provisions of this Code, and conduct that undermines a judge's independence, integrity, or impartiality. See Canon 1 and Rule 1.2.

"Independence" means a judge's freedom from influence or controls other than those established by law. See Canons 1 and 4, and Rules 1.2, 3.1, 3.12, 3.13, and 4.2.

"Integrity" means probity, fairness, honesty, uprightness, and soundness of character. See Canon 1 and Rule 1.2.

"Judicial candidate" means any person, including a sitting judge, who is seeking selection for or retention in judicial office by election or appointment. A person becomes a candidate for judicial office as soon as he or she makes a public announcement of candidacy, declares or files as a candidate with the election or appointment authority, authorizes or, where permitted, engages in solicitation or acceptance of contributions or support, or is nominated for election or appointment to office. See Rules 2.11, 4.1, 4.2, and 4.4.

"Knowingly," "knowledge," "known," and **"knows"** mean actual knowledge of the fact in question. A person's knowledge may be inferred from circumstances. See Rules 2.11, 2.13, 2.15, 2.16, 3.6, and 4.1.

"Law" encompasses court rules as well as statutes, constitutional provisions, and decisional law. See Rules 1.1, 2.1, 2.2, 2.6, 2.7, 2.9, 3.1, 3.4, 3.9, 3.12, 3.13, 3.14, 3.15, 4.1, 4.2, 4.4, and 4.5.

"Member of the candidate's family" means a spouse, domestic partner, child, grandchild, parent, grandparent, or other relative or person with whom the candidate maintains a close familial relationship.

"Member of the judge's family" means a spouse, domestic partner, child, grandchild, parent, grandparent, or other relative or person with whom the judge maintains a close familial relationship. See Rules 3.7, 3.8, 3.10, and 3.11.

"Member of a judge's family residing in the judge's household" means any relative of a judge by blood or marriage, or a person treated by a judge as a member of the judge's family, who resides in the judge's household. See Rules 2.11 and 3.13.

"Nonpublic information" means information that is not available to the public. Nonpublic information may include, but is not limited to, information that is sealed by statute or court order or impounded or communicated in camera, and information offered in grand jury proceedings, presentencing reports, dependency cases, or psychiatric reports. See Rule 3.5.

"Pending matter" is a matter that has commenced. A matter continues to be pending through any appellate process until final disposition. See Rules 2.9, 2.10, 3.13, and 4.1.

"Personally solicit" means a direct request made by a judge or a judicial candidate for financial support or in-kind services, whether made by letter, telephone, or any other means of communication. See Rule 4.1.

"Political organization" means a political party or other group sponsored by or affiliated with a political party or candidate, the principal purpose of which is to further the election or appointment of candidates for political office. For purposes of this Code, the term does not include a judicial candidate's campaign committee created as authorized by Rule 4.4. See Rules 4.1 and 4.2.

"Public election" includes primary and general elections, partisan elections, nonpartisan elections, and retention elections. See Rules 4.2 and 4.4.

"Third degree of relationship" includes the following persons: great-grandparent, grandparent, parent, uncle, aunt, brother, sister, child, grandchild, great-grandchild, nephew, and niece. See Rule 2.11.

APPLICATION

The Application section establishes when the various Rules apply to a judge or judicial candidate.

I. Applicability of This Code

(A) The provisions of the Code apply to all full-time judges. Parts II through V of this section identify those provisions that apply to the four distinct categories of part-time judges only while they are serving as judges, and provisions that do not apply to part-time judges at any time. All other Rules are therefore applicable to part-time judges at all times. The four categories of judicial service in other than a full-time capacity are necessarily defined

in general terms because of the widely varying forms of judicial service. Canon 4 applies to judicial candidates.

(B) A judge, within the meaning of this Code, is anyone who is authorized to perform judicial functions, including an officer such as a justice of the peace, magistrate, court commissioner, special master, referee, or member of the administrative law judiciary.[1]

COMMENT

[1] The Rules in this Code have been formulated to address the ethical obligations of any person who serves a judicial function, and are premised upon the supposition that a uniform system of ethical principles should apply to all those authorized to perform judicial functions.

[2] The determination of which category and, accordingly, which specific Rules apply to an individual judicial officer, depends upon the facts of the particular judicial service.

[3] In recent years many jurisdictions have created what are often called "problem solving" courts, in which judges are authorized by court rules to act in nontraditional ways. For example, judges presiding in drug courts and monitoring the progress of participants in those courts' programs may be authorized, and even encouraged, to communicate directly with social workers, probation officers, and others outside the context of their usual judicial role as independent decision makers on issues of fact and law. When local rules specifically authorize conduct not otherwise permitted under these Rules, they take precedence over the provisions set forth in the Code. Nevertheless, judges serving on "problem solving" courts shall comply with this Code except to the extent local rules provide and permit otherwise.

II. Retired Judge Subject to Recall

A retired judge subject to recall for service, who by law is not permitted to practice law, is not required to comply:

(A) with Rule 3.9 (Service as Arbitrator or Mediator), except while serving as a judge.; or

(B) at any time with Rule 3.8 (Appointments to Fiduciary Positions).

1. Each jurisdiction should consider the characteristics of particular positions within the administrative law judiciary in adopting, adapting, applying, and enforcing the Code for the administrative law judiciary. *See, e.g.,* Model Code of Judicial Conduct for Federal Administrative Law Judges (1989) and Model Code of Judicial Conduct for State Administrative Law Judges (1995). Both Model Codes are endorsed by the ABA National Conference of Administrative Law Judiciary.

COMMENT

[1] For the purposes of this section, as long as a retired judge is subject to being recalled for service, the judge is considered to "perform judicial functions."“

III. Continuing Part-Time Judge

A judge who serves repeatedly on a part-time basis by election or under a continuing appointment, including a retired judge subject to recall who is permitted to practice law ("continuing part-time judge"),

(A) is not required to comply:

(1) with Rule s 2.10(A), and 2.10(B) (Judicial Statements on Pending and Impending Cases), and 4.1 (Political and Campaign Activities of Judges and Judicial Candidates in General) (A)(1) through (7), except while serving as a judge; or

(2) at any time with Rules 3.4 (Appointments to Governmental Positions), 3.8 (A) (Appointments to Fiduciary Positions), 3.9 (Service as Arbitrator or Mediator), 3.10 (Practice of Law), and 3.11(B) (Financial, Business, or Remunerative Activities) 3.14 (Reimbursement of Expenses and Waivers of Fees or Charges), 3.15 (Reporting Requirements), 4.1 (Political and Campaign Activities of Judges and Judicial Candidates in General), 4.2 (Political and Campaign Activities of Judicial Candidates in Public Elections), 4.3 (Activities of Candidates for Appointive Judicial Office), 4.4 (Campaign Committees), and 4.5 (Activities of Judges Who Become Candidates for Nonjudicial Office); and

(B) shall not practice law in the court on which the judge serves, or in any court subject to the appellate jurisdiction of the court on which the judge serves, and shall not act as a lawyer in a proceeding in which the judge has served as a judge or in any other proceeding related thereto.

COMMENT

[1] When a person who has been a continuing part-time judge is no longer a continuing part-time judge, including a retired judge no longer subject to recall, that person may act as a lawyer in a proceeding in which he or she has served as a judge, or in any other proceeding related thereto only with the informed consent of all parties, and pursuant to any applicable Model Rules of Professional Conduct. An adopting jurisdiction should substitute a reference to its applicable rule.

IV. Periodic Part-Time Judge

A periodic part-time judge who serves or expects to serve repeatedly on a part-time basis, but under a separate appointment for each limited period of service or for each matter,

(A) is not required to comply:

(1) with Rule 2.10 (Judicial Statements on Pending and Impending Cases), and 4.1 (Political and Campaign Activities of Judges and Judicial Candidates in General) (A)(1) through (7), except while serving as a judge; or

(2) at any time with Rules 3.4 (Appointments to Governmental Positions), 3.7 (Participation in Educational, Religious, Charitable, Fraternal, or Civic Organizations and Activities), 3.8(A) (Appointments to Fiduciary Positions), 3.9 (Service as Arbitrator or Mediator), 3.10 (Practice of Law), and 3.11(B) (Financial, Business, or Remunerative Activities), 3.13 (Acceptance and Reporting of Gifts, Loans, Bequests, Benefits, or Other Things of Value), 3.15 (Reporting Requirements), 4.1 (Political and Campaign Activities of Judges and Judicial Candidates in General), and 4.5 (Activities of Judges Who Become Candidates for Nonjudicial Office); and

(B) shall not practice law in the court on which the judge serves, or in any court subject to the appellate jurisdiction of the court on which the judge serves, and shall not act as a lawyer in a proceeding in which the judge has served as a judge or in any other proceeding related thereto.

V. Pro Tempore Part-Time Judge

A pro tempore part-time judge who serves or expects to serve once or only sporadically on a part-time basis under a separate appointment for each period of service or for each case heard is not required to comply:

(A) except while serving as a judge, with Rules 1.2 (Promoting Confidence in the Judiciary), 2.4 (External Influences on Judicial Conduct), 2.10 (Judicial Statements on Pending and Impending Cases), or 3.2 (Appearances before Governmental Bodies and Consultation with Government Officials); and 4.1 (Political and Campaign Activities of Judges and Judicial Candidates in General) (A)(1) through (7); or

(B) at any time with Rules 3.4 (Appointments to Governmental Positions), 3.6 (Affiliation with Discriminatory Organizations), 3.7 (Participation in Educational, Religious, Charitable, Fraternal, or Civic Organizations and Activities), 3.8(A) (Appointments to Fiduciary Positions), 3.9 (Service as Arbitrator or Mediator), 3.10 (Practice of Law), and 3.11(B) (Financial, Business, or Remunerative Activities),

3.13 (Acceptance and Reporting of Gifts, Loans, Bequests, Benefits, or Other Things of Value), 3.15 (Reporting Requirements), 4.1 (Political and Campaign Activities of Judges and Judicial Candidates in General), and 4.5 (Activities of Judges Who Become Candidates for Nonjudicial Office).

VI. Time for Compliance

A person to whom this Code becomes applicable shall comply immediately with its provisions, except that those judges to whom Rules 3.8 (Appointments to Fiduciary Positions) and 3.11 (Financial, Business, or Remunerative Activities) apply shall comply with those Rules as soon as reasonably possible, but in no event later than one year after the Code becomes applicable to the judge.

COMMENT

[1] If serving as a fiduciary when selected as judge, a new judge may, notwithstanding the prohibitions in Rule 3.8, continue to serve as fiduciary, but only for that period of time necessary to avoid serious adverse consequences to the beneficiaries of the fiduciary relationship and in no event longer than one year. Similarly, if engaged at the time of judicial selection in a business activity, a new judge may, notwithstanding the prohibitions in Rule 3.11, continue in that activity for a reasonable period but in no event longer than one year.

CANON 1. A JUDGE SHALL UPHOLD AND PROMOTE THE INDEPENDENCE, INTEGRITY, AND IMPARTIALITY OF THE JUDICIARY, AND SHALL AVOID IMPROPRIETY AND THE APPEARANCE OF IMPROPRIETY.

RULE 1.1 *Compliance with the Law*

A judge shall comply with the law,* including the Code of Judicial Conduct.

RULE 1.2 *Promoting Confidence in the Judiciary*

A judge shall act at all times in a manner that promotes public confidence in the independence,* integrity,* and impartiality* of the judiciary, and shall avoid impropriety and the appearance of impropriety.

COMMENT

[1] Public confidence in the judiciary is eroded by improper conduct and conduct that creates the appearance of impropriety. This principle applies to both the professional and personal conduct of a judge.

[2] A judge should expect to be the subject of public scrutiny that might be viewed as burdensome if applied to other citizens, and must accept the restrictions imposed by the Code.

[3] Conduct that compromises or appears to compromise the independence, integrity, and impartiality of a judge undermines public confidence in the judiciary. Because it is not practicable to list all such conduct, the Rule is necessarily cast in general terms.

[4] Judges should participate in activities that promote ethical conduct among judges and lawyers, support professionalism within the judiciary and the legal profession, and promote access to justice for all.

[5] Actual improprieties include violations of law, court rules or provisions of this Code. The test for appearance of impropriety is whether the conduct would create in reasonable minds a perception that the judge violated this Code or engaged in other conduct that reflects adversely on the judge's honesty, impartiality, temperament, or fitness to serve as a judge.

[6] A judge should initiate and participate in community outreach activities for the purpose of promoting public understanding of and confidence in the administration of justice. In conducting such activities, the judge must act in a manner consistent with this Code.

RULE 1.3 *Avoiding Abuse of the Prestige of Judicial Office*

A judge shall not abuse the prestige of judicial office to advance the personal or economic interests* of the judge or others, or allow others to do so.

COMMENT

[1] It is improper for a judge to use or attempt to use his or her position to gain personal advantage or deferential treatment of any kind. For example, it would be improper for a judge to allude to his or her judicial status to gain favorable treatment in encounters with traffic officials. Similarly, a judge must not use judicial letterhead to gain an advantage in conducting his or her personal business.

[2] A judge may provide a reference or recommendation for an individual based upon the judge's personal knowledge. The judge may use official letterhead if the judge indicates that the reference is personal and if there is no likelihood that the use of the letterhead would reasonably be perceived as an attempt to exert pressure by reason of the judicial office.

[3] Judges may participate in the process of judicial selection by cooperating with appointing authorities and screening committees, and by responding to

inquiries from such entities concerning the professional qualifications of a person being considered for judicial office.

[4] Special considerations arise when judges write or contribute to publications of for-profit entities, whether related or unrelated to the law. A judge should not permit anyone associated with the publication of such materials to exploit the judge's office in a manner that violates this Rule or other applicable law. In contracts for publication of a judge's writing, the judge should retain sufficient control over the advertising to avoid such exploitation.

CANON 2. A JUDGE SHALL PERFORM THE DUTIES OF JUDICIAL OFFICE IMPARTIALLY, COMPETENTLY, AND DILIGENTLY.

RULE 2.1 *Giving Precedence to the Duties of Judicial Office*

The duties of judicial office, as prescribed by law,* shall take precedence over all of a judge's personal and extrajudicial activities.

COMMENT

[1] To ensure that judges are available to fulfill their judicial duties, judges must conduct their personal and extrajudicial activities to minimize the risk of conflicts that would result in frequent disqualification. See Canon 3.

[2] Although it is not a duty of judicial office unless prescribed by law, judges are encouraged to participate in activities that promote public understanding of and confidence in the justice system.

RULE 2.2 *Impartiality and Fairness*

A judge shall uphold and apply the law,* and shall perform all duties of judicial office fairly and impartially.*

COMMENT

[1] To ensure impartiality and fairness to all parties, a judge must be objective and open-minded.

[2] Although each judge comes to the bench with a unique background and personal philosophy, a judge must interpret and apply the law without regard to whether the judge approves or disapproves of the law in question.

[3] When applying and interpreting the law, a judge sometimes may make good-faith errors of fact or law. Errors of this kind do not violate this Rule.

[4] It is not a violation of this Rule for a judge to make reasonable accommodations to ensure pro se litigants the opportunity to have their matters fairly heard.

RULE 2.3 *Bias, Prejudice, and Harassment*

(A) A judge shall perform the duties of judicial office, including administrative duties, without bias or prejudice.

(B) A judge shall not, in the performance of judicial duties, by words or conduct manifest bias or prejudice, or engage in harassment, including but not limited to bias, prejudice, or harassment based upon race, sex, gender, religion, national origin, ethnicity, disability, age, sexual orientation, marital status, socioeconomic status, or political affiliation, and shall not permit court staff, court officials, or others subject to the judge's direction and control to do so.

(C) A judge shall require lawyers in proceedings before the court to refrain from manifesting bias or prejudice, or engaging in harassment, based upon attributes including but not limited to race, sex, gender, religion, national origin, ethnicity, disability, age, sexual orientation, marital status, socioeconomic status, or political affiliation, against parties, witnesses, lawyers, or others.

(D) The restrictions of paragraphs (B) and (C) do not preclude judges or lawyers from making legitimate reference to the listed factors, or similar factors, when they are relevant to an issue in a proceeding.

COMMENT

[1] A judge who manifests bias or prejudice in a proceeding impairs the fairness of the proceeding and brings the judiciary into disrepute.

[2] Examples of manifestations of bias or prejudice include but are not limited to epithets; slurs; demeaning nicknames; negative stereotyping; attempted humor based upon stereotypes; threatening, intimidating, or hostile acts; suggestions of connections between race, ethnicity, or nationality and crime; and irrelevant references to personal characteristics. Even facial expressions and body language can convey to parties and lawyers in the proceeding, jurors, the media, and others an appearance of bias or prejudice. A judge must avoid conduct that may reasonably be perceived as prejudiced or biased.

[3] Harassment, as referred to in paragraphs (B) and (C), is verbal or physical conduct that denigrates or shows hostility or aversion toward a person on bases such as race, sex, gender, religion, national origin, ethnicity, disability, age, sexual orientation, marital status, socioeconomic status, or political affiliation.

[4] Sexual harassment includes but is not limited to sexual advances, requests for sexual favors, and other verbal or physical conduct of a sexual nature that is unwelcome.

RULE 2.4 *External Influences on Judicial Conduct*

(A) A judge shall not be swayed by public clamor or fear of criticism.

(B) A judge shall not permit family, social, political, financial, or other interests or relationships to influence the judge's judicial conduct or judgment.

(C) A judge shall not convey or permit others to convey the impression that any person or organization is in a position to influence the judge.

COMMENT

[1] An independent judiciary requires that judges decide cases according to the law and facts, without regard to whether particular laws or litigants are popular or unpopular with the public, the media, government officials, or the judge's friends or family. Confidence in the judiciary is eroded if judicial decision making is perceived to be subject to inappropriate outside influences.

RULE 2.5 *Competence, Diligence, and Cooperation*

(A) A judge shall perform judicial and administrative duties, competently and diligently.

(B) A judge shall cooperate with other judges and court officials in the administration of court business.

COMMENT

[1] Competence in the performance of judicial duties requires the legal knowledge, skill, thoroughness, and preparation reasonably necessary to perform a judge's responsibilities of judicial office.

[2] A judge should seek the necessary docket time, court staff, expertise, and resources to discharge all adjudicative and administrative responsibilities.

[3] Prompt disposition of the court's business requires a judge to devote adequate time to judicial duties, to be punctual in attending court and expeditious in determining matters under submission, and to take reasonable measures to ensure that court officials, litigants, and their lawyers cooperate with the judge to that end.

[4] In disposing of matters promptly and efficiently, a judge must demonstrate due regard for the rights of parties to be heard and to have issues resolved without unnecessary cost or delay. A judge should monitor and supervise cases in ways that reduce or eliminate dilatory practices, avoidable delays, and unnecessary costs.

RULE 2.6 *Ensuring the Right to Be Heard*

(A) A judge shall accord to every person who has a legal interest in a proceeding, or that person's lawyer, the right to be heard according to law.*

(B) A judge may encourage parties to a proceeding and their lawyers to settle matters in dispute but shall not act in a manner that coerces any party into settlement.

COMMENT

[1] The right to be heard is an essential component of a fair and impartial system of justice. Substantive rights of litigants can be protected only if procedures protecting the right to be heard are observed.

[2] The judge plays an important role in overseeing the settlement of disputes, but should be careful that efforts to further settlement do not undermine any party's right to be heard according to law. The judge should keep in mind the effect that the judge's participation in settlement discussions may have, not only on the judge's own views of the case, but also on the perceptions of the lawyers and the parties if the case remains with the judge after settlement efforts are unsuccessful. Among the factors that a judge should consider when deciding upon an appropriate settlement practice for a case are (1) whether the parties have requested or voluntarily consented to a certain level of participation by the judge in settlement discussions, (2) whether the parties and their counsel are relatively sophisticated in legal matters, (3) whether the case will be tried by the judge or a jury, (4) whether the parties participate with their counsel in settlement discussions, (5) whether any parties are unrepresented by counsel, and (6) whether the matter is civil or criminal.

[3] Judges must be mindful of the effect settlement discussions can have, not only on their objectivity and impartiality, but also on the appearance of their objectivity and impartiality. Despite a judge's best efforts, there may be instances when information obtained during settlement discussions could influence a judge's decision making during trial, and, in such instances, the judge should consider whether disqualification may be appropriate. See Rule 2.11(A)(1).

RULE 2.7 *Responsibility to Decide*

A judge shall hear and decide matters assigned to the judge, except when disqualification is required by Rule 2.11 or other law.*

COMMENT

[1] Judges must be available to decide the matters that come before the court. Although there are times when disqualification is necessary to protect the rights of litigants and preserve public confidence in the independence, integrity, and

impartiality of the judiciary, judges must be available to decide matters that come before the courts. Unwarranted disqualification may bring public disfavor to the court and to the judge personally. The dignity of the court, the judge's respect for fulfillment of judicial duties, and a proper concern for the burdens that may be imposed upon the judge's colleagues require that a judge not use disqualification to avoid cases that present difficult, controversial, or unpopular issues.

RULE 2.8 *Decorum, Demeanor, and Communication with Jurors*

(A) A judge shall require order and decorum in proceedings before the court.

(B) A judge shall be patient, dignified, and courteous to litigants, jurors, witnesses, lawyers, court staff, court officials, and others with whom the judge deals in an official capacity, and shall require similar conduct of lawyers, court staff, court officials, and others subject to the judge's direction and control.

(C) A judge shall not commend or criticize jurors for their verdict other than in a court order or opinion in a proceeding.

COMMENT

[1] The duty to hear all proceedings with patience and courtesy is not inconsistent with the duty imposed in Rule 2.5 to dispose promptly of the business of the court. Judges can be efficient and businesslike while being patient and deliberate.

[2] Commending or criticizing jurors for their verdict may imply a judicial expectation in future cases and may impair a juror's ability to be fair and impartial in a subsequent case.

[3] A judge who is not otherwise prohibited by law from doing so may meet with jurors who choose to remain after trial but should be careful not to discuss the merits of the case.

RULE 2.9 *Ex Parte Communications*

(A) A judge shall not initiate, permit, or consider ex parte communications, or consider other communications made to the judge outside the presence of the parties or their lawyers, concerning a pending* or impending matter,* except as follows:

(1) When circumstances require it, ex parte communication for scheduling, administrative, or emergency purposes, which does not address substantive matters, is permitted, provided:

(a) the judge reasonably believes that no party will gain a procedural, substantive, or tactical advantage as a result of the ex parte communication; and

(b) the judge makes provision promptly to notify all other parties of the substance of the ex parte communication, and gives the parties an opportunity to respond.

(2) A judge may obtain the written advice of a disinterested expert on the law applicable to a proceeding before the judge, if the judge gives advance notice to the parties of the person to be consulted and the subject matter of the advice to be solicited, and affords the parties a reasonable opportunity to object and respond to the notice and to the advice received.

(3) A judge may consult with court staff and court officials whose functions are to aid the judge in carrying out the judge's adjudicative responsibilities, or with other judges, provided the judge makes reasonable efforts to avoid receiving factual information that is not part of the record, and does not abrogate the responsibility personally to decide the matter.

(4) A judge may, with the consent of the parties, confer separately with the parties and their lawyers in an effort to settle matters pending before the judge.

(5) A judge may initiate, permit, or consider any ex parte communication when expressly authorized by law* to do so.

(B) If a judge inadvertently receives an unauthorized ex parte communication bearing upon the substance of a matter, the judge shall make provision promptly to notify the parties of the substance of the communication and provide the parties with an opportunity to respond.

(C) A judge shall not investigate facts in a matter independently, and shall consider only the evidence presented and any facts that may properly be judicially noticed.

(D) A judge shall make reasonable efforts, including providing appropriate supervision, to ensure that this Rule is not violated by court staff, court officials, and others subject to the judge's direction and control.

COMMENT

[1] To the extent reasonably possible, all parties or their lawyers shall be included in communications with a judge.

[2] Whenever the presence of a party or notice to a party is required by this Rule, it is the party's lawyer, or if the party is unrepresented, the party, who is to be present or to whom notice is to be given.

[3] The proscription against communications concerning a proceeding includes communications with lawyers, law teachers, and other persons who are not participants in the proceeding, except to the limited extent permitted by this Rule.

[4] A judge may initiate, permit, or consider ex parte communications expressly authorized by law, such as when serving on therapeutic or problem-solving courts, mental health courts, or drug courts. In this capacity, judges may assume a

more interactive role with parties, treatment providers, probation officers, social workers, and others.

[5] A judge may consult with other judges on pending matters, but must avoid ex parte discussions of a case with judges who have previously been disqualified from hearing the matter, and with judges who have appellate jurisdiction over the matter.

[6] The prohibition against a judge investigating the facts in a matter extends to information available in all mediums, including electronic.

[7] A judge may consult ethics advisory committees, outside counsel, or legal experts concerning the judge's compliance with this Code. Such consultations are not subject to the restrictions of paragraph (A)(2).

RULE 2.10 *Judicial Statements on Pending and Impending Cases*

(A) A judge shall not make any public statement that might reasonably be expected to affect the outcome or impair the fairness of a matter pending* or impending* in any court, or make any nonpublic statement that might substantially interfere with a fair trial or hearing.

(B) A judge shall not, in connection with cases, controversies, or issues that are likely to come before the court, make pledges, promises, or commitments that are inconsistent with the impartial* performance of the adjudicative duties of judicial office.

(C) A judge shall require court staff, court officials, and others subject to the judge's direction and control to refrain from making statements that the judge would be prohibited from making by paragraphs (A) and (B).

(D) Notwithstanding the restrictions in paragraph (A), a judge may make public statements in the course of official duties, may explain court procedures, and may comment on any proceeding in which the judge is a litigant in a personal capacity.

(E) Subject to the requirements of paragraph (A), a judge may respond directly or through a third party to allegations in the media or elsewhere concerning the judge's conduct in a matter.

COMMENT

[1] This Rule's restrictions on judicial speech are essential to the maintenance of the independence, integrity, and impartiality of the judiciary.

[2] This Rule does not prohibit a judge from commenting on proceedings in which the judge is a litigant in a personal capacity, **or represents a client as permitted by these Rules.** In cases in which the judge is a litigant in an official capacity, such as a writ of mandamus, the judge must not comment publicly.

[3] Depending upon the circumstances, the judge should consider whether it may be preferable for a third party, rather than the judge, to respond or issue statements in connection with allegations concerning the judge's conduct in a matter.

RULE 2.11 *Disqualification*

(A) A judge shall disqualify himself or herself in any proceeding in which the judge's impartiality* might reasonably be questioned, including but not limited to the following circumstances:

(1) The judge has a personal bias or prejudice concerning a party or a party's lawyer, or personal knowledge* of facts that are in dispute in the proceeding.

(2) The judge knows* that the judge, the judge's spouse or domestic partner,* or a person within the third degree of relationship* to either of them, or the spouse or domestic partner of such a person is:

(a) a party to the proceeding, or an officer, director, general partner, managing member, or trustee of a party;

(b) acting as a lawyer in the proceeding;

(c) a person who has more than a de minimis* interest that could be substantially affected by the proceeding; or

(d) likely to be a material witness in the proceeding.

(3) The judge knows that he or she, individually or as a fiduciary,* or the judge's spouse, domestic partner, parent, or child, or any other member of the judge's family residing in the judge's household,* has an economic interest* in the subject matter in controversy or in a party to the proceeding.

(4) The judge knows or learns by means of a timely motion that a party, a party's lawyer, or the law firm of a party's lawyer has within the previous [insert number] year[s] made aggregate* contributions* to the judge's campaign in an amount that [is greater than $[insert amount] for an individual or $[insert amount] for an entity] [is reasonable and appropriate for an individual or an entity].

(5) The judge, while a judge or a judicial candidate,* has made a public statement, other than in a court proceeding, judicial decision, or opinion, that commits or appears to commit the judge to reach a particular result or rule in a particular way in the proceeding or controversy.

(6) The judge:

(a) served as a lawyer in the matter in controversy, or was associated with a lawyer who participated substantially as a lawyer in the matter during such association;

(b) served in governmental employment, and in such capacity participated personally and substantially as a lawyer or public official concerning the proceeding, or has publicly expressed in such capacity an opinion concerning the merits of the particular matter in controversy;

(c) was a material witness concerning the matter; or

(d) previously presided as a judge over the matter in another court.

(B) A judge shall keep informed about the judge's personal and fiduciary economic interests, and make a reasonable effort to keep informed about the personal economic interests of the judge's spouse or domestic partner and minor children residing in the judge's household.

(C) A judge subject to disqualification under this Rule, other than for bias or prejudice under paragraph (A)(1), may disclose on the record the basis of the judge's disqualification and may ask the parties and their lawyers to consider, outside the presence of the judge and court personnel, whether to waive disqualification. If, following the disclosure, the parties and lawyers agree, without participation by the judge or court personnel, that the judge should not be disqualified, the judge may participate in the proceeding. The agreement shall be incorporated into the record of the proceeding.

COMMENT

[1] Under this Rule, a judge is disqualified whenever the judge's impartiality might reasonably be questioned, regardless of whether any of the specific provisions of paragraphs (A)(1) through (6) apply. In many jurisdictions, the term "recusal" is used interchangeably with the term "disqualification."

[2] A judge's obligation not to hear or decide matters in which disqualification is required applies regardless of whether a motion to disqualify is filed.

[3] The rule of necessity may override the rule of disqualification. For example, a judge might be required to participate in judicial review of a judicial salary statute, or might be the only judge available in a matter requiring immediate judicial action, such as a hearing on probable cause or a temporary restraining order. In matters that require immediate action, the judge must disclose on the record the basis for possible disqualification and make reasonable efforts to transfer the matter to another judge as soon as practicable.

[4] The fact that a lawyer in a proceeding is affiliated with a law firm with which a relative of the judge is affiliated does not itself disqualify the judge. If, however, the judge's impartiality might reasonably be questioned under paragraph (A), or the relative is known by the judge to have an interest in the law firm that could be substantially affected by the proceeding under paragraph (A)(2)(c), the judge's disqualification is required.

[5] A judge should disclose on the record information that the judge believes the parties or their lawyers might reasonably consider relevant to a possible motion for disqualification, even if the judge believes there is no basis for disqualification.

[6] "Economic interest," as set forth in the Terminology section, means ownership of more than a de minimis legal or equitable interest. Except for situations in which a judge participates in the management of such a legal or equitable interest, or the interest could be substantially affected by the outcome of a proceeding before a judge, it does not include:

(1) an interest in the individual holdings within a mutual or common investment fund;

(2) an interest in securities held by an educational, religious, charitable, fraternal, or civic organization in which the judge or the judge's spouse, domestic partner, parent, or child serves as a director, officer, advisor, or other participant;

(3) a deposit in a financial institution or deposits or proprietary interests the judge may maintain as a member of a mutual savings association or credit union, or similar proprietary interests; or

(4) an interest in the issuer of government securities held by the judge.

RULE 2.12 *Supervisory Duties*

(A) A judge shall require court staff, court officials, and others subject to the judge's direction and control to act in a manner consistent with the judge's obligations under this Code.

(B) A judge with supervisory authority for the performance of other judges shall take reasonable measures to ensure that those judges properly discharge their judicial responsibilities, including the prompt disposition of matters before them.

COMMENT

[1] A judge is responsible for his or her own conduct and for the conduct of others, such as staff, when those persons are acting at the judge's direction or control. A judge may not direct court personnel to engage in conduct on the judge's behalf or as the judge's representative when such conduct would violate the Code if undertaken by the judge.

[2] Public confidence in the judicial system depends upon timely justice. To promote the efficient administration of justice, a judge with supervisory authority must take the steps needed to ensure that judges under his or her supervision administer their workloads promptly.

RULE 2.13 *Administrative Appointments*

(A) In making administrative appointments, a judge:

(1) shall exercise the power of appointment impartially* and on the basis of merit; and

(2) shall avoid nepotism, favoritism, and unnecessary appointments.

(B) A judge shall not appoint a lawyer to a position if the judge either knows* that the lawyer, or the lawyer's spouse or domestic partner,* has contributed more than $[insert amount] within the prior [insert number] year[s] to the judge's election campaign, or learns of such a contribution* by means of a timely motion by a party or other person properly interested in the matter, unless:

(1) the position is substantially uncompensated;

(2) the lawyer has been selected in rotation from a list of qualified and available lawyers compiled without regard to their having made political contributions; or

(3) the judge or another presiding or administrative judge affirmatively finds that no other lawyer is willing, competent, and able to accept the position.

(C) A judge shall not approve compensation of appointees beyond the fair value of services rendered.

COMMENT

[1] Appointees of a judge include assigned counsel, officials such as referees, commissioners, special masters, receivers, and guardians, and personnel such as clerks, secretaries, and bailiffs. Consent by the parties to an appointment or an award of compensation does not relieve the judge of the obligation prescribed by paragraph (A).

[2] Unless otherwise defined by law, nepotism is the appointment or hiring of any relative within the third degree of relationship of either the judge or the judge's spouse or domestic partner, or the spouse or domestic partner of such relative.

[3] The rule against making administrative appointments of lawyers who have contributed in excess of a specified dollar amount to a judge's election campaign includes an exception for positions that are substantially uncompensated, such as those for which the lawyer's compensation is limited to reimbursement for out-of-pocket expenses.

RULE 2.14 *Disability and Impairment*

A judge having a reasonable belief that the performance of a lawyer or another judge is impaired by drugs or alcohol, or by a mental, emotional, or physical condition, shall take appropriate action, which may include a confidential referral to a lawyer or judicial assistance program.

COMMENT

[1] "Appropriate action" means action intended and reasonably likely to help the judge or lawyer in question address the problem and prevent harm to the justice system. Depending upon the circumstances, appropriate action may include but is not limited to speaking directly to the impaired person, notifying an individual with supervisory responsibility over the impaired person, or making a referral to an assistance program.

[2] Taking or initiating corrective action by way of referral to an assistance program may satisfy a judge's responsibility under this Rule. Assistance programs have many approaches for offering help to impaired judges and lawyers, such

as intervention, counseling, or referral to appropriate health care professionals. Depending upon the gravity of the conduct that has come to the judge's attention, however, the judge may be required to take other action, such as reporting the impaired judge or lawyer to the appropriate authority, agency, or body. See Rule 2.15.

RULE 2.15 *Responding to Judicial and Lawyer Misconduct*

(A) A judge having knowledge* that another judge has committed a violation of this Code that raises a substantial question regarding the judge's honesty, trustworthiness, or fitness as a judge in other respects shall inform the appropriate authority.*

(B) A judge having knowledge that a lawyer has committed a violation of the Rules of Professional Conduct that raises a substantial question regarding the lawyer's honesty, trustworthiness, or fitness as a lawyer in other respects shall inform the appropriate authority.

(C) A judge who receives information indicating a substantial likelihood that another judge has committed a violation of this Code shall take appropriate action.

(D) A judge who receives information indicating a substantial likelihood that a lawyer has committed a violation of the Rules of Professional Conduct shall take appropriate action.

COMMENT

[1] Taking action to address known misconduct is a judge's obligation. Paragraphs (A) and (B) impose an obligation on the judge to report to the appropriate disciplinary authority the known misconduct of another judge or a lawyer that raises a substantial question regarding the honesty, trustworthiness, or fitness of that judge or lawyer. Ignoring or denying known misconduct among one's judicial colleagues or members of the legal profession undermines a judge's responsibility to participate in efforts to ensure public respect for the justice system. This Rule limits the reporting obligation to those offenses that an independent judiciary must vigorously endeavor to prevent.

[2] A judge who does not have actual knowledge that another judge or a lawyer may have committed misconduct, but receives information indicating a substantial likelihood of such misconduct, is required to take appropriate action under paragraphs (C) and (D). Appropriate action may include, but is not limited to, communicating directly with the judge who may have violated this Code, communicating with a supervising judge, or reporting the suspected violation to the appropriate authority or other agency or body. Similarly, actions to be taken in response to information indicating that a lawyer has committed a violation of the Rules of Professional Conduct may include but are not limited to communicating directly with the lawyer who may have committed the violation, or reporting the suspected violation to the appropriate authority or other agency or body.

RULE 2.16 *Cooperation with Disciplinary Authorities*

(A) A judge shall cooperate and be candid and honest with judicial and lawyer disciplinary agencies.

(B) A judge shall not retaliate, directly or indirectly, against a person known* or suspected to have assisted or cooperated with an investigation of a judge or a lawyer.

COMMENT

[1] Cooperation with investigations and proceedings of judicial and lawyer discipline agencies, as required in paragraph (A), instills confidence in judges' commitment to the integrity of the judicial system and the protection of the public.

CANON 3. A JUDGE SHALL CONDUCT THE JUDGE'S PERSONAL AND EXTRAJUDICIAL ACTIVITIES TO MINIMIZE THE RISK OF CONFLICT WITH THE OBLIGATIONS OF JUDICIAL OFFICE.

RULE 3.1 *Extrajudicial Activities in General*

A judge may engage in extrajudicial activities, except as prohibited by law* or this Code. However, when engaging in extrajudicial activities, a judge shall not:

(A) participate in activities that will interfere with the proper performance of the judge's judicial duties;

(B) participate in activities that will lead to frequent disqualification of the judge;

(C) participate in activities that would appear to a reasonable person to undermine the judge's independence,* integrity,* or impartiality;*

(D) engage in conduct that would appear to a reasonable person to be coercive; or

(E) make use of court premises, staff, stationery, equipment, or other resources, except for incidental use for activities that concern the law, the legal system, or the administration of justice, or unless such additional use is permitted by law.

COMMENT

[1] To the extent that time permits, and judicial independence and impartiality are not compromised, judges are encouraged to engage in appropriate

extrajudicial activities. Judges are uniquely qualified to engage in extrajudicial activities that concern the law, the legal system, and the administration of justice, such as by speaking, writing, teaching, or participating in scholarly research projects. In addition, judges are permitted and encouraged to engage in educational, religious, charitable, fraternal or civic extrajudicial activities not conducted for profit, even when the activities do not involve the law. See Rule 3.7.

[2] Participation in both law-related and other extrajudicial activities helps integrate judges into their communities, and furthers public understanding of and respect for courts and the judicial system.

[3] Discriminatory actions and expressions of bias or prejudice by a judge, even outside the judge's official or judicial actions, are likely to appear to a reasonable person to call into question the judge's integrity and impartiality. Examples include jokes or other remarks that demean individuals based upon their race, sex, gender, religion, national origin, ethnicity, disability, age, sexual orientation, or socioeconomic status. For the same reason, a judge's extrajudicial activities must not be conducted in connection or affiliation with an organization that practices invidious discrimination. See Rule 3.6.

[4] While engaged in permitted extrajudicial activities, judges must not coerce others or take action that would reasonably be perceived as coercive. For example, depending upon the circumstances, a judge's solicitation of contributions or memberships for an organization, even as permitted by Rule 3.7(A), might create the risk that the person solicited would feel obligated to respond favorably, or would do so to curry favor with the judge.

RULE 3.2 *Appearances before Governmental Bodies and Consultation with Government Officials*

A judge shall not appear voluntarily at a public hearing before, or otherwise consult with, an executive or a legislative body or official, except:

(A) in connection with matters concerning the law, the legal system, or the administration of justice;

(B) in connection with matters about which the judge acquired knowledge or expertise in the course of the judge's judicial duties; or

(C) when the judge is acting pro se in a matter involving the judge's legal or economic interests, or when the judge is acting in a fiduciary* capacity.

COMMENT

[1] Judges possess special expertise in matters of law, the legal system, and the administration of justice, and may properly share that expertise with governmental bodies and executive or legislative branch officials.

[2] In appearing before governmental bodies or consulting with government officials, judges must be mindful that they remain subject to other provisions of this Code, such as Rule 1.3, prohibiting judges from using the prestige of office to

advance their own or others' interests, Rule 2.10, governing public comment on pending and impending matters, and Rule 3.1(C), prohibiting judges from engaging in extrajudicial activities that would appear to a reasonable person to undermine the judge's independence, integrity, or impartiality.

[3] In general, it would be an unnecessary and unfair burden to prohibit judges from appearing before governmental bodies or consulting with government officials on matters that are likely to affect them as private citizens, such as zoning proposals affecting their real property. In engaging in such activities, however, judges must not refer to their judicial positions, and must otherwise exercise caution to avoid using the prestige of judicial office.

RULE 3.3 *Testifying as a Character Witness*

A judge shall not testify as a character witness in a judicial, administrative, or other adjudicatory proceeding or otherwise vouch for the character of a person in a legal proceeding, except when duly summoned.

COMMENT

[1] A judge who, without being subpoenaed, testifies as a character witness abuses the prestige of judicial office to advance the interests of another. See Rule 1.3. Except in unusual circumstances where the demands of justice require, a judge should discourage a party from requiring the judge to testify as a character witness.

RULE 3.4 *Appointments to Governmental Positions*

A judge shall not accept appointment to a governmental committee, board, commission, or other governmental position, unless it is one that concerns the law, the legal system, or the administration of justice.

COMMENT

[1] Rule 3.4 implicitly acknowledges the value of judges accepting appointments to entities that concern the law, the legal system, or the administration of justice. Even in such instances, however, a judge should assess the appropriateness of accepting an appointment, paying particular attention to the subject matter of the appointment and the availability and allocation of judicial resources, including the judge's time commitments, and giving due regard to the requirements of the independence and impartiality of the judiciary.

[2] A judge may represent his or her country, state, or locality on ceremonial occasions or in connection with historical, educational, or cultural activities. Such representation does not constitute acceptance of a government position.

RULE 3.5 *Use of Nonpublic Information*

A judge shall not intentionally disclose or use nonpublic information* acquired in a judicial capacity for any purpose unrelated to the judge's judicial duties.

COMMENT

[1] In the course of performing judicial duties, a judge may acquire information of commercial or other value that is unavailable to the public. The judge must not reveal or use such information for personal gain or for any purpose unrelated to his or her judicial duties.

[2] This rule is not intended, however, to affect a judge's ability to act on information as necessary to protect the health or safety of the judge or a member of a judge's family, court personnel, or other judicial officers if consistent with other provisions of this Code.

RULE 3.6 *Affiliation with Discriminatory Organizations*

(A) A judge shall not hold membership in any organization that practices invidious discrimination on the basis of race, sex, gender, religion, national origin, ethnicity, or sexual orientation.

(B) A judge shall not use the benefits or facilities of an organization if the judge knows* or should know that the organization practices invidious discrimination on one or more of the bases identified in paragraph (A). A judge's attendance at an event in a facility of an organization that the judge is not permitted to join is not a violation of this Rule when the judge's attendance is an isolated event that could not reasonably be perceived as an endorsement of the organization's practices.

COMMENT

[1] A judge's public manifestation of approval of invidious discrimination on any basis gives rise to the appearance of impropriety and diminishes public confidence in the integrity and impartiality of the judiciary. A judge's membership in an organization that practices invidious discrimination creates the perception that the judge's impartiality is impaired.

[2] An organization is generally said to discriminate invidiously if it arbitrarily excludes from membership on the basis of race, sex, gender, religion, national origin, ethnicity, or sexual orientation persons who would otherwise be eligible for admission. Whether an organization practices invidious discrimination is a complex question to which judges should be attentive. The answer cannot be determined from a mere examination of an organization's current membership rolls,

but rather, depends upon how the organization selects members, as well as other relevant factors, such as whether the organization is dedicated to the preservation of religious, ethnic, or cultural values of legitimate common interest to its members, or whether it is an intimate, purely private organization whose membership limitations could not constitutionally be prohibited.

[3] When a judge learns that an organization to which the judge belongs engages in invidious discrimination, the judge must resign immediately from the organization.

[4] A judge's membership in a religious organization as a lawful exercise of the freedom of religion is not a violation of this Rule.

[5] This Rule does not apply to national or state military service.

RULE 3.7 *Participation in Educational, Religious, Charitable, Fraternal, or Civic Organizations and Activities*

(A) Subject to the requirements of Rule 3.1, a judge may participate in activities sponsored by organizations or governmental entities concerned with the law, the legal system, or the administration of justice, and those sponsored by or on behalf of educational, religious, charitable, fraternal, or civic organizations not conducted for profit, including but not limited to the following activities:

(1) assisting such an organization or entity in planning related to fund-raising, and participating in the management and investment of the organization's or entity's funds;

(2) soliciting* contributions* for such an organization or entity, but only from members of the judge's family,* or from judges over whom the judge does not exercise supervisory or appellate authority;

(3) soliciting membership for such an organization or entity, even though the membership dues or fees generated may be used to support the objectives of the organization or entity, but only if the organization or entity is concerned with the law, the legal system, or the administration of justice;

(4) appearing or speaking at, receiving an award or other recognition at, being featured on the program of, and permitting his or her title to be used in connection with an event of such an organization or entity, but if the event serves a fund-raising purpose, the judge may participate only if the event concerns the law, the legal system, or the administration of justice;

(5) making recommendations to such a public or private fund-granting organization or entity in connection with its programs and activities, but only if the organization or entity is concerned with the law, the legal system, or the administration of justice; and

(6) serving as an officer, director, trustee, or nonlegal advisor of such an organization or entity, unless it is likely that the organization or entity:

(a) will be engaged in proceedings that would ordinarily come before the judge; or

(b) will frequently be engaged in adversary proceedings in the court of which the judge is a member, or in any court subject to the appellate jurisdiction of the court of which the judge is a member.

(B) A judge may encourage lawyers to provide pro bono publico legal services.

COMMENT

[1] The activities permitted by paragraph (A) generally include those sponsored by or undertaken on behalf of public or private not-for-profit educational institutions, and other not-for-profit organizations, including law-related, charitable, and other organizations.

[2] Even for law-related organizations, a judge should consider whether the membership and purposes of the organization, or the nature of the judge's participation in or association with the organization, would conflict with the judge's obligation to refrain from activities that reflect adversely upon a judge's independence, integrity, and impartiality.

[3] Mere attendance at an event, whether or not the event serves a fund-raising purpose, does not constitute a violation of paragraph 4(A). It is also generally permissible for a judge to serve as an usher or a food server or preparer, or to perform similar functions, at fund-raising events sponsored by educational, religious, charitable, fraternal, or civic organizations. Such activities are not solicitation and do not present an element of coercion or abuse the prestige of judicial office.

[4] Identification of a judge's position in educational, religious, charitable, fraternal, or civic organizations on letterhead used for fund-raising or membership solicitation does not violate this Rule. The letterhead may list the judge's title or judicial office if comparable designations are used for other persons.

[5] In addition to appointing lawyers to serve as counsel for indigent parties in individual cases, a judge may promote broader access to justice by encouraging lawyers to participate in pro bono publico legal services, if in doing so the judge does not employ coercion, or abuse the prestige of judicial office. Such encouragement may take many forms, including providing lists of available programs, training lawyers to do pro bono publico legal work, and participating in events recognizing lawyers who have done pro bono publico work.

RULE 3.8 *Appointments to Fiduciary Positions*

(A) A judge shall not accept appointment to serve in a fiduciary* position, such as executor, administrator, trustee, guardian, attorney in fact, or other personal representative, except for the estate, trust, or person of a member of the judge's family,* and then only if such service will not interfere with the proper performance of judicial duties.

(B) A judge shall not serve in a fiduciary position if the judge as fiduciary will likely be engaged in proceedings that would ordinarily come before the judge, or if the estate, trust, or ward becomes involved in adversary proceedings in the court on which the judge serves, or one under its appellate jurisdiction.

(C) A judge acting in a fiduciary capacity shall be subject to the same restrictions on engaging in financial activities that apply to a judge personally.

(D) If a person who is serving in a fiduciary position becomes a judge, he or she must comply with this Rule as soon as reasonably practicable, but in no event later than [one year] after becoming a judge.

COMMENT

[1] A judge should recognize that other restrictions imposed by this Code may conflict with a judge's obligations as a fiduciary; in such circumstances, a judge should resign as fiduciary. For example, serving as a fiduciary might require frequent disqualification of a judge under Rule 2.11 because a judge is deemed to have an economic interest in shares of stock held by a trust if the amount of stock held is more than de minimis.

RULE 3.9 *Service as Arbitrator or Mediator*

A judge shall not act as an arbitrator or a mediator or perform other judicial functions apart from the judge's official duties unless expressly authorized by law.*

COMMENT

[1] This Rule does not prohibit a judge from participating in arbitration, mediation, or settlement conferences performed as part of assigned judicial duties. Rendering dispute resolution services apart from those duties, whether or not for economic gain, is prohibited unless it is expressly authorized by law.

RULE 3.10 *Practice of Law*

A judge shall not practice law. A judge may act pro se and may, without compensation, give legal advice to and draft or review documents for a member of the judge's family,* but is prohibited from serving as the family member's lawyer in any forum.

COMMENT

[1] A judge may act pro se in all legal matters, including matters involving litigation and matters involving appearances before or other dealings with governmental bodies. A judge must not use the prestige of office to advance the judge's personal or family interests. See Rule 1.3.

RULE 3.11 *Financial, Business, or Remunerative Activities*

(A) A judge may hold and manage investments of the judge and members of the judge's family.*

(B) A judge shall not serve as an officer, director, manager, general partner, advisor, or employee of any business entity except that a judge may manage or participate in:

(1) a business closely held by the judge or members of the judge's family; or

(2) a business entity primarily engaged in investment of the financial resources of the judge or members of the judge's family.

(C) A judge shall not engage in financial activities permitted under paragraphs (A) and (B) if they will:

(1) interfere with the proper performance of judicial duties;

(2) lead to frequent disqualification of the judge;

(3) involve the judge in frequent transactions or continuing business relationships with lawyers or other persons likely to come before the court on which the judge serves; or

(4) result in violation of other provisions of this Code.

COMMENT

[1] Judges are generally permitted to engage in financial activities, including managing real estate and other investments for themselves or for members of their families. Participation in these activities, like participation in other extrajudicial activities, is subject to the requirements of this Code. For example, it would be improper for a judge to spend so much time on business activities that it interferes with the performance of judicial duties. See Rule 2.1. Similarly, it would be improper for a judge to use his or her official title or appear in judicial robes in business advertising, or to conduct his or her business or financial affairs in such a way that disqualification is frequently required. See Rules 1.3 and 2.11.

[2] As soon as practicable without serious financial detriment, the judge must divest himself or herself of investments and other financial interests that might require frequent disqualification or otherwise violate this Rule.

RULE 3.12 *Compensation for Extrajudicial Activities*

A judge may accept reasonable compensation for extrajudicial activities permitted by this Code or other law* unless such acceptance would

appear to a reasonable person to undermine the judge's independence,* integrity,* or impartiality.*

COMMENT

[1] A judge is permitted to accept honoraria, stipends, fees, wages, salaries, royalties, or other compensation for speaking, teaching, writing, and other extrajudicial activities, provided the compensation is reasonable and commensurate with the task performed. The judge should be mindful, however, that judicial duties must take precedence over other activities. See Rule 2.1.

[2] Compensation derived from extrajudicial activities may be subject to public reporting. See Rule 3.15.

RULE 3.13 *Acceptance and Reporting of Gifts, Loans, Bequests, Benefits, or Other Things of Value*

(A) A judge shall not accept any gifts, loans, bequests, benefits, or other things of value, if acceptance is prohibited by law* or would appear to a reasonable person to undermine the judge's independence,* integrity,* or impartiality.*

(B) Unless otherwise prohibited by law, or by paragraph (A), a judge may accept the following without publicly reporting such acceptance:

(1) items with little intrinsic value, such as plaques, certificates, trophies, and greeting cards;

(2) gifts, loans, bequests, benefits, or other things of value from friends, relatives, or other persons, including lawyers, whose appearance or interest in a proceeding pending* or impending* before the judge would in any event require disqualification of the judge under Rule 2.11;

(3) ordinary social hospitality;

(4) commercial or financial opportunities and benefits, including special pricing and discounts, and loans from lending institutions in their regular course of business, if the same opportunities and benefits or loans are made available on the same terms to similarly situated persons who are not judges;

(5) rewards and prizes given to competitors or participants in random drawings, contests, or other events that are open to persons who are not judges;

(6) scholarships, fellowships, and similar benefits or awards, if they are available to similarly situated persons who are not judges, based upon the same terms and criteria;

(7) books, magazines, journals, audiovisual materials, and other resource materials supplied by publishers on a complimentary basis for official use; or

(8) gifts, awards, or benefits associated with the business, profession, or other separate activity of a spouse, a domestic partner,* or other family member of a judge residing in the judge's household,* but that incidentally benefit the judge.

(C) Unless otherwise prohibited by law or by paragraph (A), a judge may accept the following items, and must report such acceptance to the extent required by Rule 3.15:

(1) gifts incident to a public testimonial;

(2) invitations to the judge and the judge's spouse, domestic partner, or guest to attend without charge:

(a) an event associated with a bar-related function or other activity relating to the law, the legal system, or the administration of justice; or

(b) an event associated with any of the judge's educational, religious, charitable, fraternal or civic activities permitted by this Code, if the same invitation is offered to nonjudges who are engaged in similar ways in the activity as is the judge; and

(3) gifts, loans, bequests, benefits, or other things of value, if the source is a party or other person, including a lawyer, who has come or is likely to come before the judge, or whose interests have come or are likely to come before the judge.

COMMENT

[1] Whenever a judge accepts a gift or other thing of value without paying fair market value, there is a risk that the benefit might be viewed as intended to influence the judge's decision in a case. Rule 3.13 imposes restrictions upon the acceptance of such benefits, according to the magnitude of the risk. Paragraph (B) identifies circumstances in which the risk that the acceptance would appear to undermine the judge's independence, integrity, or impartiality is low, and explicitly provides that such items need not be publicly reported. As the value of the benefit or the likelihood that the source of the benefit will appear before the judge increases, the judge is either prohibited under paragraph (A) from accepting the gift, or required under paragraph (C) to publicly report it.

[2] Gift-giving between friends and relatives is a common occurrence, and ordinarily does not create an appearance of impropriety or cause reasonable persons to believe that the judge's independence, integrity, or impartiality has been compromised. In addition, when the appearance of friends or relatives in a case would require the judge's disqualification under Rule 2.11, there would be no opportunity for a gift to influence the judge's decision making. Paragraph (B)(2) places no restrictions upon the ability of a judge to accept gifts or other things of value from friends or relatives under these circumstances, and does not require public reporting.

[3] Businesses and financial institutions frequently make available special pricing, discounts, and other benefits, either in connection with a temporary promotion

or for preferred customers, based upon longevity of the relationship, volume of business transacted, and other factors. A judge may freely accept such benefits if they are available to the general public, or if the judge qualifies for the special price or discount according to the same criteria as are applied to persons who are not judges. As an example, loans provided at generally prevailing interest rates are not gifts, but a judge could not accept a loan from a financial institution at below-market interest rates unless the same rate was being made available to the general public for a certain period of time or only to borrowers with specified qualifications that the judge also possesses.

[4] Rule 3.13 applies only to acceptance of gifts or other things of value by a judge. Nonetheless, if a gift or other benefit is given to the judge's spouse, domestic partner, or member of the judge's family residing in the judge's household, it may be viewed as an attempt to evade Rule 3.13 and influence the judge indirectly. Where the gift or benefit is being made primarily to such other persons, and the judge is merely an incidental beneficiary, this concern is reduced. A judge should, however, remind family and household members of the restrictions imposed upon judges, and urge them to take these restrictions into account when making decisions about accepting such gifts or benefits.

[5] Rule 3.13 does not apply to contributions to a judge's campaign for judicial office. Such contributions are governed by other Rules of this Code, including Rules 4.3 and 4.4.

RULE 3.14 *Reimbursement of Expenses and Waivers of Fees or Charges*

(A) Unless otherwise prohibited by Rules 3.1 and 3.13(A) or other law,* a judge may accept reimbursement of necessary and reasonable expenses for travel, food, lodging, or other incidental expenses, or a waiver or partial waiver of fees or charges for registration, tuition, and similar items, from sources other than the judge's employing entity, if the expenses or charges are associated with the judge's participation in extrajudicial activities permitted by this Code.

(B) Reimbursement of expenses for necessary travel, food, lodging, or other incidental expenses shall be limited to the actual costs reasonably incurred by the judge and, when appropriate to the occasion, by the judge's spouse, domestic partner,* or guest.

(C) A judge who accepts reimbursement of expenses or waivers or partial waivers of fees or charges on behalf of the judge or the judge's spouse, domestic partner, or guest shall publicly report such acceptance as required by Rule 3.15.

COMMENT

[1] Educational, civic, religious, fraternal, and charitable organizations often sponsor meetings, seminars, symposia, dinners, awards ceremonies, and similar events. Judges are encouraged to attend educational programs, as both teachers

and participants, in law-related and academic disciplines, in furtherance of their duty to remain competent in the law. Participation in a variety of other extrajudicial activity is also permitted and encouraged by this Code.

[2] Not infrequently, sponsoring organizations invite certain judges to attend seminars or other events on a fee-waived or partial-fee-waived basis, and sometimes include reimbursement for necessary travel, food, lodging, or other incidental expenses. A judge's decision whether to accept reimbursement of expenses or a waiver or partial waiver of fees or charges in connection with these or other extrajudicial activities must be based upon an assessment of all the circumstances. The judge must undertake a reasonable inquiry to obtain the information necessary to make an informed judgment about whether acceptance would be consistent with the requirements of this Code.

[3] A judge must assure himself or herself that acceptance of reimbursement or fee waivers would not appear to a reasonable person to undermine the judge's independence, integrity, or impartiality. The factors that a judge should consider when deciding whether to accept reimbursement or a fee waiver for attendance at a particular activity include:

(a) whether the sponsor is an accredited educational institution or bar association rather than a trade association or a for-profit entity;

(b) whether the funding comes largely from numerous contributors rather than from a single entity and is earmarked for programs with specific content;

(c) whether the content is related or unrelated to the subject matter of litigation pending or impending before the judge, or to matters that are likely to come before the judge;

(d) whether the activity is primarily educational rather than recreational, and whether the costs of the event are reasonable and comparable to those associated with similar events sponsored by the judiciary, bar associations, or similar groups;

(e) whether information concerning the activity and its funding sources is available upon inquiry;

(f) whether the sponsor or source of funding is generally associated with particular parties or interests currently appearing or likely to appear in the judge's court, thus possibly requiring disqualification of the judge under Rule 2.11;

(g) whether differing viewpoints are presented; and

(h) whether a broad range of judicial and nonjudicial participants are invited, whether a large number of participants are invited, and whether the program is designed specifically for judges.

RULE 3.15 *Reporting Requirements*

(A) A judge shall publicly report the amount or value of:

(1) compensation received for extrajudicial activities as permitted by Rule 3.12;

(2) gifts and other things of value as permitted by Rule 3.13(C), unless the value of such items, alone or in the aggregate with other items received from the same source in the same calendar year, does not exceed $[insert amount]; and

(3) reimbursement of expenses and waiver of fees or charges permitted by Rule 3.14(A), unless the amount of reimbursement or waiver, alone or in the aggregate with other reimbursements or waivers received from the same source in the same calendar year, does not exceed $[insert amount].

(B) When public reporting is required by paragraph (A), a judge shall report the date, place, and nature of the activity for which the judge received any compensation; the description of any gift, loan, bequest, benefit, or other thing of value accepted; and the source of reimbursement of expenses or waiver or partial waiver of fees or charges.

(C) The public report required by paragraph (A) shall be made at least annually, except that for reimbursement of expenses and waiver or partial waiver of fees or charges, the report shall be made within thirty days following the conclusion of the event or program.

(D) Reports made in compliance with this Rule shall be filed as public documents in the office of the clerk of the court on which the judge serves or other office designated by law,* and, when technically feasible, posted by the court or office personnel on the court's website.

CANON 4. A JUDGE OR CANDIDATE FOR JUDICIAL OFFICE SHALL NOT ENGAGE IN POLITICAL OR CAMPAIGN ACTIVITY THAT IS INCONSISTENT WITH THE INDEPENDENCE, INTEGRITY, OR IMPARTIALITY OF THE JUDICIARY.

RULE 4.1 *Political and Campaign Activities of Judges and Judicial Candidates in General*

(A) Except as permitted by law,* or by Rules 4.2, 4.3, and 4.4, a judge or a judicial candidate* shall not:

(1) act as a leader in, or hold an office in, a political organization;*

(2) make speeches on behalf of a political organization;

(3) publicly endorse or oppose a candidate for any public office;

(4) solicit funds for, pay an assessment to, or make a contribution* to a political organization or a candidate for public office;

(5) attend or purchase tickets for dinners or other events sponsored by a political organization or a candidate for public office;

(6) publicly identify himself or herself as a candidate of a political organization;

(7) seek, accept, or use endorsements from a political organization;

(8) personally solicit* or accept campaign contributions other than through a campaign committee authorized by Rule 4.4;

(9) use or permit the use of campaign contributions for the private benefit of the judge, the candidate, or others;

(10) use court staff, facilities, or other court resources in a campaign for judicial office;

(11) knowingly,* or with reckless disregard for the truth, make any false or misleading statement;

(12) make any statement that would reasonably be expected to affect the outcome or impair the fairness of a matter pending* or impending* in any court; or

(13) in connection with cases, controversies, or issues that are likely to come before the court, make pledges, promises, or commitments that are inconsistent with the impartial* performance of the adjudicative duties of judicial office.

(B) A judge or judicial candidate shall take reasonable measures to ensure that other persons do not undertake, on behalf of the judge or judicial candidate, any activities prohibited under paragraph (A).

COMMENT

General Considerations

[1] Even when subject to public election, a judge plays a role different from that of a legislator or executive branch official. Rather than making decisions based upon the expressed views or preferences of the electorate, a judge makes decisions based upon the law and the facts of every case. Therefore, in furtherance of this interest, judges and judicial candidates must, to the greatest extent possible, be free and appear to be free from political influence and political pressure. This Canon imposes narrowly tailored restrictions upon the political and campaign activities of all judges and judicial candidates, taking into account the various methods of selecting judges.

[2] When a person becomes a judicial candidate, this Canon becomes applicable to his or her conduct.

Participation in Political Activities

[3] Public confidence in the independence and impartiality of the judiciary is eroded if judges or judicial candidates are perceived to be subject to political influence. Although judges and judicial candidates may register to vote as members of a political party, they are prohibited by paragraph (A)(1) from assuming leadership roles in political organizations.

[4] Paragraphs (A)(2) and (A)(3) prohibit judges and judicial candidates from making speeches on behalf of political organizations or publicly endorsing or

opposing candidates for public office, respectively, to prevent them from abusing the prestige of judicial office to advance the interests of others. See Rule 1.3. These Rules do not prohibit candidates from campaigning on their own behalf, or from endorsing or opposing candidates for the same judicial office for which they are running. See Rules 4.2(B)(2) and 4.2(B)(3).

[5] Although members of the families of judges and judicial candidates are free to engage in their own political activity, including running for public office, there is no "family exception" to the prohibition in paragraph (A)(3) against a judge or candidate publicly endorsing candidates for public office. A judge or judicial candidate must not become involved in, or publicly associated with, a family member's political activity or campaign for public office. To avoid public misunderstanding, judges and judicial candidates should take, and should urge members of their families to take, reasonable steps to avoid any implication that they endorse any family member's candidacy or other political activity.

[6] Judges and judicial candidates retain the right to participate in the political process as voters in both primary and general elections. For purposes of this Canon, participation in a caucus-type election procedure does not constitute public support for or endorsement of a political organization or candidate, and is not prohibited by paragraphs (A)(2) or (A)(3).

Statements and Comments Made during a Campaign for Judicial Office

[7] Judicial candidates must be scrupulously fair and accurate in all statements made by them and by their campaign committees. Paragraph (A)(11) obligates candidates and their committees to refrain from making statements that are false or misleading, or that omit facts necessary to make the communication considered as a whole not materially misleading.

[8] Judicial candidates are sometimes the subject of false, misleading, or unfair allegations made by opposing candidates, third parties, or the media. For example, false or misleading statements might be made regarding the identity, present position, experience, qualifications, or judicial rulings of a candidate. In other situations, false or misleading allegations may be made that bear upon a candidate's integrity or fitness for judicial office. As long as the candidate does not violate paragraphs (A)(11), (A)(12), or (A)(13), the candidate may make a factually accurate public response. In addition, when an independent third party has made unwarranted attacks on a candidate's opponent, the candidate may disavow the attacks, and request the third party to cease and desist.

[9] Subject to paragraph (A)(12), a judicial candidate is permitted to respond directly to false, misleading, or unfair allegations made against him or her during a campaign, although it is preferable for someone else to respond if the allegations relate to a pending case.

[10] Paragraph (A)(12) prohibits judicial candidates from making comments that might impair the fairness of pending or impending judicial proceedings. This provision does not restrict arguments or statements to the court or jury by a lawyer who is a judicial candidate, or rulings, statements, or instructions by a judge that may appropriately affect the outcome of a matter.

Pledges, Promises, or Commitments Inconsistent With Impartial Performance of the Adjudicative Duties of Judicial Office

[11] The role of a judge is different from that of a legislator or executive branch official, even when the judge is subject to public election. Campaigns for judicial office must be conducted differently from campaigns for other offices. The narrowly drafted restrictions upon political and campaign activities of judicial candidates provided in Canon 4 allow candidates to conduct campaigns that provide voters with sufficient information to permit them to distinguish between candidates and make informed electoral choices.

[12] Paragraph (A)(13) makes applicable to both judges and judicial candidates the prohibition that applies to judges in Rule 2.10(B), relating to pledges, promises, or commitments that are inconsistent with the impartial performance of the adjudicative duties of judicial office.

[13] The making of a pledge, promise, or commitment is not dependent upon, or limited to, the use of any specific words or phrases; instead, the totality of the statement must be examined to determine if a reasonable person would believe that the candidate for judicial office has specifically undertaken to reach a particular result. Pledges, promises, or commitments must be contrasted with statements or announcements of personal views on legal, political, or other issues, which are not prohibited. When making such statements, a judge should acknowledge the overarching judicial obligation to apply and uphold the law, without regard to his or her personal views.

[14] A judicial candidate may make campaign promises related to judicial organization, administration, and court management, such as a promise to dispose of a backlog of cases, start court sessions on time, or avoid favoritism in appointments and hiring. A candidate may also pledge to take action outside the courtroom, such as working toward an improved jury selection system, or advocating for more funds to improve the physical plant and amenities of the courthouse.

[15] Judicial candidates may receive questionnaires or requests for interviews from the media and from issue advocacy or other community organizations that seek to learn their views on disputed or controversial legal or political issues. Paragraph (A)(13) does not specifically address judicial responses to such inquiries. Depending upon the wording and format of such questionnaires, candidates' responses might be viewed as pledges, promises, or commitments to perform the adjudicative duties of office other than in an impartial way. To avoid violating paragraph (A)(13), therefore, candidates who respond to media and other inquiries should also give assurances that they will keep an open mind and will carry out their adjudicative duties faithfully and impartially if elected. Candidates who do not respond may state their reasons for not responding, such as the danger that answering might be perceived by a reasonable person as undermining a successful candidate's independence or impartiality, or that it might lead to frequent disqualification. See Rule 2.11.

RULE 4.2 *Political and Campaign Activities of Judicial Candidates in Public Elections*

(A) A judicial candidate* in a partisan, nonpartisan, or retention public election* shall:

(1) act at all times in a manner consistent with the independence,* integrity,* and impartiality* of the judiciary;

(2) comply with all applicable election, election campaign, and election campaign fund-raising laws and regulations of this jurisdiction;

(3) review and approve the content of all campaign statements and materials produced by the candidate or his or her campaign committee, as authorized by Rule 4.4, before their dissemination; and

(4) take reasonable measures to ensure that other persons do not undertake on behalf of the candidate activities, other than those described in Rule 4.4, that the candidate is prohibited from doing by Rule 4.1.

(B) A candidate for elective judicial office may, unless prohibited by law,* and not earlier than [insert amount of time] before the first applicable primary election, caucus, or general or retention election:

(1) establish a campaign committee pursuant to the provisions of Rule 4.4;

(2) speak on behalf of his or her candidacy through any medium, including but not limited to advertisements, websites, or other campaign literature;

(3) publicly endorse or oppose candidates for the same judicial office for which he or she is running;

(4) attend or purchase tickets for dinners or other events sponsored by a political organization* or a candidate for public office;

(5) seek, accept, or use endorsements from any person or organization other than a partisan political organization; and

(6) contribute to a political organization or candidate for public office, but not more than $[insert amount] to any one organization or candidate.

(C) A judicial candidate in a partisan public election may, unless prohibited by law, and not earlier than [insert amount of time] before the first applicable primary election, caucus, or general election:

(1) identify himself or herself as a candidate of a political organization; and

(2) seek, accept, and use endorsements of a political organization.

COMMENT

[1] Paragraphs (B) and (C) permit judicial candidates in public elections to engage in some political and campaign activities otherwise prohibited by Rule 4.1. Candidates may not engage in these activities earlier than [insert amount of time] before the first applicable electoral event, such as a caucus or a primary election.

[2] Despite paragraphs (B) and (C), judicial candidates for public election remain subject to many of the provisions of Rule 4.1. For example, a candidate

continues to be prohibited from soliciting funds for a political organization, knowingly making false or misleading statements during a campaign, or making certain promises, pledges, or commitments related to future adjudicative duties. See Rule 4.1(A), paragraphs (4), (11), and (13).

[3] In partisan public elections for judicial office, a candidate may be nominated by, affiliated with, or otherwise publicly identified or associated with a political organization, including a political party. This relationship may be maintained throughout the period of the public campaign, and may include use of political party or similar designations on campaign literature and on the ballot.

[4] In nonpartisan public elections or retention elections, paragraph (B)(5) prohibits a candidate from seeking, accepting, or using nominations or endorsements from a partisan political organization.

[5] Judicial candidates are permitted to attend or purchase tickets for dinners and other events sponsored by political organizations.

[6] For purposes of paragraph (B)(3), candidates are considered to be running for the same judicial office if they are competing for a single judgeship or if several judgeships on the same court are to be filled as a result of the election. In endorsing or opposing another candidate for a position on the same court, a judicial candidate must abide by the same rules governing campaign conduct and speech as apply to the candidate's own campaign.

[7] Although judicial candidates in nonpartisan public elections are prohibited from running on a ticket or slate associated with a political organization, they may group themselves into slates or other alliances to conduct their campaigns more effectively. Candidates who have grouped themselves together are considered to be running for the same judicial office if they satisfy the conditions described in Comment [6].

RULE 4.3 *Activities of Candidates for Appointive Judicial Office*

A candidate for appointment to judicial office may:

(A) communicate with the appointing or confirming authority, including any selection, screening, or nominating commission or similar agency; and

(B) seek endorsements for the appointment from any person or organization other than a partisan political organization.

COMMENT

[1] When seeking support or endorsement, or when communicating directly with an appointing or confirming authority, a candidate for appointive judicial office must not make any pledges, promises, or commitments that are inconsistent with the impartial performance of the adjudicative duties of the office. See Rule 4.1(A)(13).

RULE 4.4 *Campaign Committees*

(A) A judicial candidate* subject to public election* may establish a campaign committee to manage and conduct a campaign for the candidate, subject to the provisions of this Code. The candidate is responsible for ensuring that his or her campaign committee complies with applicable provisions of this Code and other applicable law.*

(B) A judicial candidate subject to public election shall direct his or her campaign committee:

(1) to solicit and accept only such campaign contributions* as are reasonable, in any event not to exceed, in the aggregate,* $[insert amount] from any individual or $[insert amount] from any entity or organization;

(2) not to solicit or accept contributions for a candidate's current campaign more than [insert amount of time] before the applicable primary election, caucus, or general or retention election, nor more than [insert number] days after the last election in which the candidate participated; and

(3) to comply with all applicable statutory requirements for disclosure and divestiture of campaign contributions, and to file with [name of appropriate regulatory authority] a report stating the name, address, occupation, and employer of each person who has made campaign contributions to the committee in an aggregate value exceeding $[insert amount]. The report must be filed within [insert number] days following an election, or within such other period as is provided by law.

COMMENT

[1] Judicial candidates are prohibited from personally soliciting campaign contributions or personally accepting campaign contributions. See Rule 4.1(A)(8). This Rule recognizes that in many jurisdictions, judicial candidates must raise campaign funds to support their candidacies, and permits candidates, other than candidates for appointive judicial office, to establish campaign committees to solicit and accept reasonable financial contributions or in-kind contributions.

[2] Campaign committees may solicit and accept campaign contributions, manage the expenditure of campaign funds, and generally conduct campaigns. Candidates are responsible for compliance with the requirements of election law and other applicable law, and for the activities of their campaign committees.

[3] At the start of a campaign, the candidate must instruct the campaign committee to solicit or accept only such contributions as are reasonable in amount, appropriate under the circumstances, and in conformity with applicable law. Although lawyers and others who might appear before a successful candidate for judicial office are permitted to make campaign contributions, the candidate should instruct his or her campaign committee to be especially cautious in connection with

such contributions, so they do not create grounds for disqualification if the candidate is elected to judicial office. See Rule 2.11.

RULE 4.5 *Activities of Judges Who Become Candidates for Nonjudicial Office*

(A) Upon becoming a candidate for a nonjudicial elective office, a judge shall resign from judicial office, unless permitted by law* to continue to hold judicial office.

(B) Upon becoming a candidate for a nonjudicial appointive office, a judge is not required to resign from judicial office, provided that the judge complies with the other provisions of this Code.

COMMENT

[1] In campaigns for nonjudicial elective public office, candidates may make pledges, promises, or commitments related to positions they would take and ways they would act if elected to office. Although appropriate in nonjudicial campaigns, this manner of campaigning is inconsistent with the role of a judge, who must remain fair and impartial to all who come before him or her. The potential for misuse of the judicial office, and the political promises that the judge would be compelled to make in the course of campaigning for nonjudicial elective office, together dictate that a judge who wishes to run for such an office must resign upon becoming a candidate.

[2] The "resign to run" rule set forth in paragraph (A) ensures that a judge cannot use the judicial office to promote his or her candidacy, and prevents post-campaign retaliation from the judge in the event the judge is defeated in the election. When a judge is seeking appointive nonjudicial office, however, the dangers are not sufficient to warrant imposing the "resign to run" rule.

Statutes on Disqualification and Discipline of Federal Judges

Editors' Introduction. This chapter reprints statutes governing the disqualification of federal judges for bias or prejudice or other reasons, and summarizes statutes governing discipline of federal judges who engage in improper conduct.

Regarding disqualification, the grounds on which federal judges may be disqualified are set forth in two federal statutes, 28 U.S.C. §§144 and 455, which we reprint below. (Section 144 is rarely the basis for a decision in view of the greater detail and modern language in §455, which is based on provisions in the 1990 ABA Model Code of Judicial Conduct.) Immediately following §455, we reprint an unusual press release entitled "Statement of Recusal Policy" in which seven Justices of the United States Supreme Court explained how they intend to interpret and apply §455 in certain situations. For a fascinating study of the application of §455 to Justices of the United States Supreme Court, see the Special Section at the end of the 2005 edition of this book, entitled "Should Justice Scalia Have Recused Himself in Vice President Cheney's Appeal to the Supreme Court?"

Regarding discipline, federal judges appointed under Article III of the Constitution enjoy life tenure and can be removed from office only through impeachment proceedings in Congress. This principle is established by Article III, §1 of the United States Constitution, which provides as follows:

> The judicial Power of the United States, shall be vested in one supreme Court, and in such inferior Courts as the Congress may from time to time ordain and establish. The Judges, both of the supreme and inferior Courts, shall hold their Offices during good Behaviour, and shall, at stated Times, receive for their Services, a Compensation, which shall not be diminished during their Continuance in Office.

However, federal judges who engage in conduct 'prejudicial to the effective and expeditious administration of the business of the courts' (*see* 28 U.S.C. §351) may be disciplined by sanctions short of removal from office, such as public or private censure or an order that no new cases be assigned to a judge for a limited time. Provisions for discipline short of removal were formerly contained in 28 U.S.C. §372(c), but in 2002 Congress moved the substance of

§372(c), with minor amendments, to a series of sections designated 28 U.S.C. §§351 through 364. These statutes, which we do not reprint, permit anyone to file a complaint against a federal judge (but not a Justice of the Supreme Court) and also permit the chief judge of the circuit to invoke the discipline procedures without need for a complaint. There are provisions for investigation by a special committee and, where warranted, a due process hearing to determine if the alleged conduct merits discipline. Hearings are conducted before circuit and district judges in the circuit (called the Judicial Council). Review by the Judicial Conference of the United States in Washington (also composed of federal judges) is contemplated. Where the underlying conduct warrants impeachment, the Judicial Conference is instructed to inform Congress.

Resignation and retirement of judges is governed by 28 U.S.C. §§371 through 377, which we also do not reprint. Nor do we reprint the Code of Conduct for United States Judges, which is generally based on the 1990 ABA Model Code of Judicial Conduct but differs from it in some significant ways. A committee of the Judicial Conference of the United States is reviewing the Code of Conduct for United States Judges in light of the new Model Code of Judicial Conduct adopted by the ABA in February 2007, set out elsewhere in this volume.

In September 2006, a committee appointed by former Chief Justice Rehnquist and chaired by Justice Breyer issued a lengthy report on the disciplinary system for federal judges and recommended changes to improve its accuracy and fairness. The report is at *www.fjc.gov/public/pdf.nsf/lookup/breyer06.pdf/$file/breyer06.pdf.* Since the last edition of this book went to press in October 2009, Congress has not amended any of the statutes reprinted below. (Indeed, §144 has not been amended since 1949, and §455 has not been amended since 1990.)

On March 11, 2008, the Judicial Conference of the United States approved a binding, nationwide set of rules for handling conduct and disability complaints against federal judges. The new rules, which took effect on April 10, 2008, respond to the recommendations of the Breyer committee. The rules cover such topics as complaint initiation and review, venue, confidentiality and publication, remedies, the conduct of investigations, and the rights and roles of participants in the process. Judicial councils in each circuit retain the power to adopt local rules regarding procedural details of the complaint-handling process, provided that those rules do not contradict the new uniform rules. The new rules are available online at *www.uscourts.gov/uscourts/News/2008/docs/jud_conduct_and_disability_308_app_B_rev.pdf.*

Contents

SELECTED STATUTES ON JUDICIAL DISQUALIFICATION

§144. Bias or Prejudice of Judges

Whenever a party to any proceeding in a district court makes and files a timely and sufficient affidavit that the judge before whom the matter is pending has a personal bias or prejudice either against him or in favor of any adverse party, such judge shall proceed no further therein, but another judge shall be assigned to hear such proceeding.

The affidavit shall state the facts and the reasons for the belief that bias or prejudice exists, and shall be filed not less than ten days before the beginning of the term at which the proceeding is to be heard, or good cause shall be shown for failure to file it within such time. A party may file only one such affidavit in any case. It shall be accompanied by a certificate of counsel of record stating that it is made in good faith.

§455. Disqualification of Justice, Judge, or Magistrate

(a) Any justice, judge, or magistrate of the United States shall disqualify himself in any proceeding in which his impartiality might reasonably be questioned.

(b) He shall also disqualify himself in the following circumstances:

(1) Where he has a personal bias or prejudice concerning a party, or personal knowledge of disputed evidentiary facts concerning the proceeding;

(2) Where in private practice he served as lawyer in the matter in controversy, or a lawyer with whom he previously practiced law served during such association as a lawyer concerning the matter, or the judge or such lawyer has been a material witness concerning it;

(3) Where he has served in governmental employment and in such capacity participated as counsel, adviser or material witness concerning the proceeding or expressed an opinion concerning the merits of the particular case in controversy;

(4) He knows that he, individually or as a fiduciary, or his spouse or minor child residing in his household, has a financial interest in the subject matter in controversy or in a party to the proceeding, or any other interest that could be substantially affected by the outcome of the proceeding;

(5) He or his spouse, or a person within the third degree of relationship to either of them, or the spouse of such a person:

(i) Is a party to the proceeding, or an officer, director, or trustee of a party;

(ii) Is acting as a lawyer in the proceeding;

(iii) Is known by the judge to have an interest that could be substantially affected by the outcome of the proceeding;

(iv) Is to the judge's knowledge likely to be a material witness in the proceeding.

(c) A judge should inform himself about his personal and fiduciary financial interests, and make a reasonable effort to inform himself about the personal financial interests of his spouse and minor children residing in his household.

(d) For the purposes of this section the following words or phrases shall have the meaning indicated:

(1) "Proceeding" includes pretrial, trial, appellate review, or other stages of litigation;

(2) the degree of relationship is calculated according to the civil law system;

(3) "fiduciary" includes such relationships as executor, administrator, trustee, and guardian;

(4) "financial interest" means ownership of a legal or equitable interest, however small, or a relationship as director, adviser, or other active participant in the affairs of a party, except that:

(i) Ownership in a mutual or common investment fund that holds securities is not a 'financial interest' in such securities unless the judge participates in the management of the fund;

(ii) An office in an educational, religious, charitable, fraternal, or civic organization is not a 'financial interest' in securities held by the organization;

(iii) The proprietary interest of a policyholder in a mutual insurance company, of a depositor in a mutual savings association, or a similar proprietary interest, is a 'financial interest' in the organization only if the outcome of the proceeding could substantially affect the value of the interest;

(iv) Ownership of governmental securities is a "financial interest" in the issuer only if the outcome of the proceeding could substantially affect the value of the securities.

(e) No justice, judge, or magistrate shall accept from the parties to the proceeding a waiver of any ground for disqualification enumerated in subsection (b). Where the ground for disqualification arises only under subsection (a), waiver may be accepted provided it is preceded by a full disclosure on the record of the basis for disqualification.

(f) Notwithstanding the preceding provisions of this section, if any justice, judge, magistrate, or bankruptcy judge to whom a matter has been assigned would be disqualified, after substantial judicial time has been devoted to the matter, because of the appearance or discovery, after the matter was assigned to him or her, that he or she individually or as a fiduciary, or his or her spouse or minor child residing in his or her household, has a financial interest in a party (other than an interest that could be substantially

affected by the outcome), disqualification is not required if the justice, judge, magistrate, bankruptcy judge, spouse or minor child, as the case may be, divests himself or herself of the interest that provides the grounds for the disqualification.

Editors' Note. The Department of Justice has adopted the following regulation in 28 C.F.R. for procedures to follow before a Department lawyer seeks recusal of a federal judge.

§50.19. Procedures to Be Followed by Government Attorneys Prior to Filing Recusal or Disqualification Motions

The determination to seek for any reason the disqualification or recusal of a justice, judge, or magistrate is a most significant and sensitive decision. This is particularly true for government attorneys, who should be guided by uniform procedures in obtaining the requisite authorization for such a motion. This statement is designed to establish a uniform procedure.

(a) No motion to recuse or disqualify a justice, judge, or magistrate (see, e.g., 28 U.S.C. 144, 455) shall be made or supported by any Department of Justice attorney, U.S. Attorney (including Assistant U.S. Attorneys) or agency counsel conducting litigation pursuant to agreement with or authority delegated by the Attorney General, without the prior written approval of the Assistant Attorney General having ultimate supervisory power over the action in which recusal or disqualification is being considered.

(b) Prior to seeking such approval, Justice Department lawyer(s) handling the litigation shall timely seek the recommendations of the U.S. Attorney for the district in which the matter is pending, and the views of the client agencies, if any. Similarly, if agency attorneys are primarily handling any such suit, they shall seek the recommendations of the U.S. Attorney and provide them to the Department of Justice with the request for approval. In actions where the United States Attorneys are primarily handling the litigation in question, they shall seek the recommendation of the client agencies, if any, for submission to the Assistant Attorney General.

(c) In the event that the conduct and pace of the litigation does not allow sufficient time to seek the prior written approval by the Assistant Attorney General, prior oral authorization shall be sought and a written record fully reflecting that authorization shall be subsequently prepared and submitted to the Assistant Attorney General.

(d) Assistant Attorneys General may delegate the authority to approve or deny requests made pursuant to this section, but only to Deputy Assistant Attorneys General or an equivalent position.

(e) This policy statement does not create or enlarge any legal obligations upon the Department of Justice in civil or criminal litigation, and it is not intended to create any private rights enforceable by private parties in litigation with the United States.

Editors' Note. On November 1, 1993, in an unusual press release, seven Justices of the Supreme Court issued the following announcement, entitled "Statement of Recusal Policy." The Statement was signed by Chief Justice Rehnquist and Justices Stevens, Scalia, Thomas, O'Connor, Kennedy, and Ginsburg. However, Justices Blackmun and Souter did not sign.

STATEMENT OF RECUSAL POLICY

We have spouses, children or other relatives within the degree of relationship covered by 28 U.S.C. §455 who are or may become practicing attorneys. In connection with a case four Terms ago, the Chief Justice announced his policy (with which we are all in accord) regarding recusal when a covered relative is "an associate in the law firm representing one of the parties before this Court" but has "not participated in the case before the Court or at previous stages of the litigation." [The letter concluded that recusal was not required.] We think it desirable to set forth what our recusal policy will be in additional situations—specifically, when the covered lawyer has participated in the case at an earlier stage of the litigation, or when the covered lawyer is a *partner* in a firm appearing before us. Determining and announcing our policy in advance will make it evident that future decisions to recuse or not to recuse are unaffected by irrelevant circumstances of the particular case, and will provide needed guidance to our relatives and the firms to which they belong.

The provision of the recusal statute that deals specifically with a relative's involvement as a lawyer in the case requires recusal only when the covered relative "[i]s acting as a lawyer in the proceeding." §455(b)(5)(ii). It is well established that this provision requires personal participation in the representation, and not just membership in the representing firm, see, e.g., Potashnick v. Port City Constr. Co., 609 F.2d 1101, 1113 (CA5), cert. denied, 449 U.S. 820 (1980). It is also apparent, from use of the present tense, that current participation as a lawyer, and not merely past involvement in earlier stages of the litigation, is required.

A relative's partnership status, or participation in earlier stages of the litigation, is relevant, therefore, only under one of two less specific provisions of §455, which require recusal when the judge knows that the relative has "an interest that could be substantially affected by the outcome of the proceeding," §455(b)(5)(iii), or when for any reason the judge's "impartiality might reasonably be questioned," §455(a). We think that a relative's partnership in the firm appearing before us, or his or her previous work as a lawyer on a case that later comes before us, does not *automatically* trigger these provisions. If that were the intent of the law, the per se "lawyer-related recusal" requirement of §455(b)(5)(ii) would have expressed it. Per se recusal for a relative's membership in the partnership appearing here, or for a relative's work on the case below, would render the limitation of §455(b)(5)(ii) to *personal* work, and to *present* representation, meaningless.

We do not think it would serve the public interest to go beyond the requirements of the statute, and to recuse ourselves, out of an excess of caution, whenever a relative is a partner in the firm before us or acted as a lawyer at an earlier stage. Even one unnecessary recusal impairs the functioning of the Court. Given the size and number of today's national law firms, and the frequent appearance before us of many of them in a single case, recusal might become a common occurrence, and opportunities would be multiplied for "strategizing" recusals, that is, selecting law firms with an eye to producing the recusal of particular Justices. In this Court, where the absence of one Justice cannot be made up by another, needless recusal deprives litigants of the nine Justices to which they are entitled, produces the possibility of an even division on the merits of the case, and has a distorting effect upon the certiorari process, requiring the petitioner to obtain (under our current practice) four votes out of eight instead of four out of nine.

Absent some special factor, therefore, we will not recuse ourselves by reason of a relative's participation as a lawyer in earlier stages of the case. One such special factor, perhaps the most common, would be the relative's functioning as lead counsel below, so that the litigation is in effect "his" or "her" case and its outcome even at a later stage might reasonably be thought capable of substantially enhancing or damaging his or her professional reputation. We shall recuse ourselves whenever, to our knowledge, a relative has been lead counsel below.

Another special factor, of course, would be the fact that the amount of the relative's compensation could be substantially affected by the outcome here. That would require our recusal even if the relative had not worked on the case, but was merely a partner in the firm that shared the profits. It seems to us that in virtually every case before us with retained counsel there exists a genuine possibility that success or failure will affect the amount of the fee, and hence a genuine possibility that the outcome will have a substantial effect upon each partner's compensation. Since it is impractical to assure ourselves of the absence of such consequences in each individual case, we shall recuse ourselves from all cases in which appearances on behalf of parties are made by firms in which our relatives are partners, unless we have received from the firm written assurance that income from Supreme Court litigation is, on a permanent basis, excluded from our relatives' partnership shares.